Ships
of the
Royal Navy

Ships
of the
Royal
Navy

J. J. Colledge

**The Complete Record of all Fighting Ships
of the Royal Navy
From the Fifteenth Century to the Present**

Foreword by David Brown

NAVAL INSTITUTE PRESS

Published and distributed in the United States of America
by the Naval Institute Press, Annapolis, Maryland 21402.

This edition is authorized for sale only in
the United States, its territories and possessions.

Library of Congress Catalog Card No 87-72201

ISBN 0-87021-652-X

Publishing History
Ships of the Royal Navy was first published in 1969 in two volumes.
This edition presents the content of the original Volume I,
totally revised and expanded.

Printed from lasermasters co-ordinated by
Scriptmate, London NW3

Printed and Bound in Great Britain

CONTENTS

FOREWORD

When they appeared, nearly twenty years ago, Mr James Colledge's historical indices, the two volumes of *Ships of the Royal Navy*, immediately became a standard work of reference, indispensable to researchers and enthusiasts alike. Amateurs and professionals appreciated the almost unique combination of simplicity and completeness which, in effect, eliminated a basic level of research.

The one disadvantage of the first edition of *Ships of the Royal Navy* was that it soon became a collector's item, to be found by the fortunate and/or in specialist second-hand booksellers, at several times its original publication price. The appearance of this long-overdue edition will be welcomed by those who were disappointed the first time around—the feelings of owners of the first edition may, in some cases, be mixed, for it is now superseded.

Since the original text of Volume 1—'Major ships'—went to press in 1968 there have been many changes in the List of the Navy. Nearly 100 ships' names have been resurrected (and *Ships of the Royal Navy* has been at the collective elbow of the Ships' Names Committee as an invaluable source) and some have lived out the full span of their new careers during the two decades. While these additions would justify a revised edition, they are, in practice, almost a minor aspect.

It was inevitable, in collating data on 13,000 ships, that there would be a number of errors and omissions, as well as blanks which the author could not fill. In the years which have passed, Mr Colledge has steadily worked to correct the errors, supplement the data and eliminate the lacunae. In this he has been assisted by members of the World Ship Society, who have already seen, in a special column in their magazine, *Warship Supplement*, the first published form of the amendments. A further significant contribution has also been made by Mr David Lyons, another indefatigably helpful researcher, well known to users of the National Maritime Museum's documentary collection of naval records.

But the work as a whole remains that of J.J. Colledge, who has now improved on excellence. The Navy Historical Library's two battered, broken and annotated copies of the original will now go into honourable retirement to join other 'first editions'—I suspect that many others will be similarly retired.

David Brown
Naval Historical Library
1987

INTRODUCTION

The scope of the book:
This 'ABC' of the ships of the Royal Navy is the result of many years' research in the Admiralty Library and elsewhere, and it is hoped that most of the ships which have served at any time in the British or Commonwealth navies are included. Ships noted as 'Indian' include those of the Hon. East India Company, which developed into the Bombay Marine and later into the Royal Indian Marine. The term 'Australian' is used in the text to cover ships of the various State navies of Australia before the formation of the Royal Australian Navy. Names of ships captured from the French or Spanish are printed in an English form with their English counterparts where convenient, the definite article being omitted except in the few cases when it is known to have been used in the Royal Navy and 'UNITE' for example will have to be read as 'Unite' and 'IMMORTALITE' as 'Immortalite'. Mercantile names are printed in italics.
For the sake of brevity, details of the engines of steam ships have had to be omitted, as also have most of the changes in armament. For modern ships, only a tonnage is given since other details are readily available in current reference books.
Trawlers, tugs etc and auxiliaries are not listed other than as a continuation of a ship-name.

Tonnage:
Up to the year 1873, the tonnage is the builder's measurement (bm), a capacity measurement arrived at from, perhaps, the 15th century, by calculating the number of *tuns* (casks) of wine that the ship could carry.
After 1873 displacement tonnage is used, changed in 1926 to standard displacement.

Dimensions:
Length and beam are given, the former being that of the gun-deck for sailing vessels, which closely approximated to the length between perpendiculars used for the steam ships.

Armament:
Until the latter half of the 19th century, guns in the main were smooth-bore muzzle-loaders firing round iron shot, the 'size' of the gun listed being actually the weight of the shot. After this, rifled guns were introduced which later brought about the change in the shape of the projectile fired. Breech-loaders were used for a short time in the 1850s, being permanently introduced in the 1880s. Carronades (abbreviated to 'carr.' in the text) took their name from Carron in Scotland where they were first manufactured in 1777; these were short-barrelled short-range weapons which had a devastating effect in close action. During the Napoleonic wars, ships of the line and frigates mounted up to twelve of these, 24- or 32-pounders, which were not included in the gun rating of the ship; eg, a 32-gun frigate mounting 44 weapons. Some of the smaller vessels were often armed almost entirely with carronades. In the text, sailing ship

armament is given (when known) only when it differed from the establishment tables.

Building materials:
Shortage of oak during the Napoleonic wars resulted in trials with various softwoods, some 50 frigates and sloops being thus built; they were useless after a few years, as were five frigates so built in 1757. Teak was used for all ships built at Bombay, and pencil cedar for the sloops and schooners built in Bermuda; these were all very durable vessels.

Iron shipbuilding, with a few exceptions, started with the floating batteries of 1855, and iron used in conjunction with surplus timber resulted in composite construction for most of the corvettes and sloops from 1867 to 1889. Steel was used from 1877.

Building yards:
The first Royal dockyard was founded in 1520 at Woolwich (arguably at Portsmouth), though naval ships had been built there before this. Enlarged in 1701, it was closed in October 1869.

Henry VIII also founded the dockyard at Deptford which eventually became more important than its near neighbour until the close of the French wars, when it was little used; it was practically derelict by 1818 and finally closed in 1833 with WORCESTER still on stocks. It reopened in 1843 and finally closed in March 1869.

Portsmouth DY was founded in 1540, though the harbour had been used as a base since 1512 when it superseded Southampton Water. It had a period of decline during the reign of Elizabeth I when Chatham yard was started.

The dockyard at Chatham dates from 1588 and the Medway then became the main fleet base, the chief enemy threat at that time coming from the Spanish Netherlands. Chatham remained pre-eminent until the advent of the 'Dreadnought' type battleship, whose draught rendered the entrance to the yard rather hazardous. It was enlarged in 1662 and again in 1864-83 and closed in 1984.

A royal dockyard was started at Harwich in 1650 which lasted until 1714. The site was reopened in 1742 as a private yard under various owners until about 1827.

The next to be founded was at Sheerness in 1667. This, however, was little used after 1674 and was closed in 1686. Reopened two years later and enlarged 1815-26, it finally closed in March 1960.

Plymouth dockyard was opened in 1691 though the area had long been a naval base. Known as Devonport DY from 1824, it was enlarged in 1844. Milford dockyard started on the site of Jacobs' private yard in 1794 and moved to Pembroke Dock in 1814. It was closed in 1926.

The remaining two royal yards at home, Haulbowline (transferred to the Irish government in 1921) and Rosyth, were not building yards. It will be noticed that most of the private yards were located originally in three main areas adjacent to the royal dockyards - the Thames/Medway group, the Solent/Isle of Wight group and those near Plymouth. There were others on the west and east coasts and one of these, Yarmouth, needs some comment: although the east coast port has been known as Great Yarmouth since the 15th century, this name rarely occurs as such in Admiralty lists; a close study of local records in the Isle of Wight has failed to find any trace of naval building at the Wight Yarmouth, so it seems that all Yarmouth-built vessels must have originated at the east coast port. Little need be said about the steamship builders; most of their names would be familiar to the reader. It might be pointed out, however, that only one firm who contracted for the sailing navy still existed in recent times—that of J.S. White of Cowes, who moved there in 1804 and built for the Royal Navy until 1966.

Early ship types:
Many of those in early lists of the navy are not easily described, since few details of them exist. As far as can be ascertained the *ballinger* (or *balinger*), for instance, seems to have been a moderate-sized oared vessel and the *barge* a larger ship of the same type but fitted with sails. The 16th century *brigantine*

seems to have been an alternative name for the galley. The *busse* was a stoutly-built fishing type vessel with three square-rigged masts, though by the 18th century it had two masts only. The *cog* was a merchant type, probably with one square-rigged mast, while the Elizabethan *frigate* remains an enigma. The English *galleasse* was a low flush-decked vessel fitted with a ram and sometimes with oars, while the *galley* was a very similar craft with three masts and lateen sails; some of these oared galleys were often used as tugs for getting large ships out of harbours. The *hoy* was a coastal store carrier with one square-rigged mast, jib and gaff sails. The *pinnace* in Tudor times was probably a small fast-sailing vessel equipped with oars, while the *row-barge* was similar but fitted with a ram. The Stuart *yacht*, of Dutch origin, was cutter-rigged with a square topsail.

The establishment of guns

In 1677

		42pdr	32pdr	18pdr	12pdr	6pdr	3pdr
1st Rate	100	26	–	28	–	44	–
2nd Rate	90	–	26	26	–	36	2
3rd Rate	70	–	26	–	26	14	4

Ships built after 1716

		32pdr	24pdr	18pdr	12pdr	9pdr	6pdr	4pdr
1st Rate	100	28	28	–	28	–	16	–
2nd Rate	90	26	–	26	–	26	12	–
2nd Rate	80	26	–	–	26	–	30	–
3rd Rate	70	–	26	–	26	–	18	–
3rd Rate	60	–	24	–	–	26	10	–
4th Rate	50	–	–	26	–	22	6	–
5th Rate	40	–	–	–	20	–	20	–
5th Rate	30	–	–	–	–	8	20	2
6th Rate	20	–	–	–	–	–	20	–

Ships built after 1740

		42pdr	32pdr	24pdr	18pdr	12pdr	9pdr	6pdr
1st Rate	100	28	–	28	–	28	–	16
2nd Rate	90	–	26	–	26	26	–	12
3rd Rate	80	–	26	–	26	–	24	4
3rd Rate	64	–	26	–	26	–	12	–
4th Rate	58	–	–	24	–	24	–	10
4th Rate	50	–	–	22	–	22	–	6
5th Rate	44	–	–	–	20	–	20	4
6th Rate	20	–	–	–	–	–	20	–

SHIPS OF THE ROYAL NAVY

Ships built after 1757

		42pdr	32pdr	24pdr	18pdr	12pdr	9pdr	6pdr	4pdr	3pdr
1st Rate	100	28	–	28	–	28	–	16	–	–
2nd Rate	90	–	28	–	30	30	2	–	–	–
3rd Rate	80	–	26	–	–	26	–	28		
Large	74	–	28	30	–	–	16	–	–	–
Small	74	–	28	–	28	–	18	–	–	–
3rd Rate	70	–	28	–	28	–	14	–	–	–
3rd Rate	64	–	–	26	–	26	–	12	–	–
4th Rate	60	–	–	26	–	26	–	8	–	–
4th Rate	50	–	–	–	22	22	–	6	–	–
5th Rate	44	–	–	–	20	–	22	2	–	–
5th Rate	36	–	–	–	–	26	–	10	–	–
5th Rate	32	–	–	–	–	26	–	6	–	–
6th Rate	28	–	–	–	–	–	24	–	–	4
6th Rate	24	–	–	–	–	–	22	–	–	2
6th Rate	20	–	–	–	–	–	20	–	–	–
Sloop	14	–	–	–	–	–	–	14	–	–
Sloop	12	–	–	–	–	–	–	–	12	–
Sloop	10	–	–	–	–	–	–	–	10	–
Sloop	8	–	–	–	–	–	–	–	–	8

After 1792

		42pdr	32pdr	24pdr	18pdr	12pdr	9pdr	6pdr	4pdr	3pdr
1st Rate	110	–	30	30	32	18	–	–	–	–
1st Rate	100	28	–	28	–	44	–	–	–	–
		–	30	28	30	12	–	–	–	–
		30	28	–	–	42	–	–	–	–
2nd Rate	98	–	28	–	28	42	–	–	–	–
		–	28	–	60	10	–	–	–	–
2nd Rate	90	–	26	–	26	38	–	–	–	–
3rd Rate	80	–	30	32	–	–	–	18	–	–
Large	74	–	28	30	–	–	16	–	–	–
Common	74	–	28	–	28	–	18	–	–	–
5th Rate	40	–	–	–	28	–	12	–	–	–
5th Rate	38	–	–	–	28	2	8	–	–	–
5th Rate	36	–	–	–	26	2	8	–	–	–
Large	32	–	–	–	26	–	–	6	–	–
Common	32	–	–	–	–	26	–	6	–	–
Sloop	18	–	–	–	–	–	–	18	–	–
Sloop	16	–	–	–	–	–	–	16	–	–

(other ships as 1757)

Details of the ship 'classes' mentioned in the text:

'Cherokee' class brig-sloops, average 236bm, 90 x 25 ft, 8-18pdr carr., 2-6pdr. 115 laid down between 1807 and 1830.

'Cruiser' class brig-sloops, average 384bm, 100½ x 30½ ft, 16-32pdr carr., 2-6pdr. 110 laid down 1797-1826.

'A' class submarines, 1,120 tons, 280 x 22 ft, 1-4in, 1-20mm, 10-TT. 46 ordered 1943-44.

'Acacia' class sloops, 1,200 tons, 250 x 33 ft, 2-12pdr, 2-3pdr. 36 ordered 1915.

'Albacore' class sloops wood S. gunboats, average 232bm, 106 x 22ft, 1-68pdr, 1 -32pdr, 2-20pdr. 98 ordered 1855.

'Algerine' class minesweepers, average 860 tons, 212½ x 35½ ft, 1 -4in, 8-20mm. 115 laid down 1941-44 including 12 RCN and 9 on lendlease.

'Anchusa' class sloops, 1,290 tons, 250 x 35 ft, 2-4in, 2-12pdr. 33 ordered 1917.

'Ant' class iron S. gunboats, 254 tons, 85 x 26 ft, 1-10in. 20 laid down 1870-73.

'Arabis' class sloops, 1,250 tons, 255 x 33½ ft, 2-4in (or 4.7in), 2-3 pdr. 36 ordered 1915.

'Ascot' class paddle minesweepers, 810 tons (8 vessels 820), 235 x 29ft, 2-12pdr. 32 ordered 1915 or 1917.

'Aubrietia' class sloops, as 'Arabis' class but mercantile profile. 6 ordered 1916.

Diesel 'Bangor' class minesweepers, 590 tons, 153½ x 28 ft, 1-3in. 14 laid down 1939-41 including 10 RCN.

TE 'Bangor' class minesweepers, 672 tons, 171½ x 28½ ft, 1-3in. 73 laid down 1940-41 including 36 RCN and 7 RIN.

Turbine 'Bangor' class minesweepers, 656 tons, 162 x 28½ ft, 1-3 in. 26 laid down 1939-41 including 6 RIN.

'Bathurst' class minesweepers, 650 tons, 162 x 31 ft, 1-4in, (1-3in. in some), 1-20mm. 63 laid down 1940-42 including 43 RAN and 7 RIN.

'Bay' class frigates, 1,580 tons, 286 x 38½ ft, 4-4in, 4-40mm, 4-20mm. 26 laid down 1944 as 'Loch' class and altered on stocks.

'Britomart' class wood S. gunboats, average 268bm, 330 tons, 120 x 22 ft, 2-68pdr. 20 laid down 1859-61.

'C' class destroyers, 1,710 tons, 339½ x 36 ft, 4-4.5in, 4-40mm, 8-TT. 32 ordered 1942 plus 8 (only two named) ordered 1943 redesigned as 'Weapon' class.

'Castle' class corvettes, 1,010 tons, 225 x 36½ ft, 1-4in, 10-20mm. 96 ordered 1943-44 including 12 RCN.

DE (diesel-electric) 'Captain' class frigates, 1,085 tons, 289(oa) x 35 ft, 3-3in, 2-40mm, 10-20mm. 34 ordered 1942-43 on lend-lease, 32 handed over.

TE (turbo-electric) 'Captain' class frigates, 1,300 tons, 300 x 37 ft, 3-3in, 2-40mm, 8-20mm. 46 handed over on lend-lease 1943.

'Catherine' class minesweepers, 890 tons, 215 x 32 ft, 1-3in, 6-20mm. 22 handed over on lend-lease 1943-44 and 12 retained by the USN

'Cheerful' class wood S. gunboats, 212bm, 100 x 22 ft, 2-32pdr. 20 ordered 1855.

'Clown' class wood S. gunboats, 233bm, 110 x 22 ft, 1-68pdr, 1-32pdr. 12 ordered 1855.

'Colony' class frigates, 1,318 tons, 285½ x 37½ ft, 3-3in, 4-40mm, 4-20mm. 21 transferred on lend-lease 1943-44.

'Dapper' class wood S. gunboats, 232bm, 284 tons, 106 x 22 ft, 1-68pdr, 2-24pdr. 20 ordered 1854.

'Flower' class corvettes, average 925 tons, 190 x 33 ft, 1-4in. 222 laid down 1939-41 including 70 RCN and four seized French vessels. Modified 'Flower' class corvettes, average 980 tons, 193 x 33 ft, 1-4in, 6-20mm. 57 laid down 1942-44 including 36 RCN, 7 on lend-lease and 8 transferred to the USN.

'Fly' class river gunboats, 98 tons, 120 x 20 ft, 1-4 in, 1-12pdr. 1-3 pdr. 16 laid down 1916.

Early 'Hunt' class minesweepers, 750 tons, 220 x 28 ft, 2-12pdr. 20 ordered 1916. Later 'Hunt' class minesweepers, 800 tons, 220 x 28½ ft, 1-4in, 1-12 pdr (most originally had 1-6pdr only). 119 ordered 1917-18.

'Hunt' class destroyers type I, 907 tons, 264 x 29 ft, 4-4in, 2-20mm (designed for 6-4in, 2-TT and ATHERSTONE completed thus). 20 laid down 1939.

'Hunt' class destroyers type II, 1,050 tons, 264 x 31½ ft, 6-4in, 2-20 mm. 36 laid down 1939-40 including BLENCATHRA, BROCKLESBY and LIDDESDALE of

1,000 tons, 4-4in.

'Hunt' class destroyers type III, 1,087 tons, 264 x 31½ ft, 4-4in, 2-20 mm, 2-TT. 28 laid down 1940-41. (All 'Hunt' class rated as frigates from 1947.)

'Leander' class frigates, 2,350 tons, 360 x 41 to 43 ft, 2-4.5in, 2-40mm or 4-GWS. 25 laid down 1959-67.

'M' class destroyers, average 1,025 tons, 265 x 26½ ft (Thornycroft design 265 x 27½ ft and Yarrow design 260 x 26 ft), 4-TT. 110 laid down 1913-16.

'Philomel' class wood S. gunvessels, 428bm, 570 tons, 145 x 25½ ft, 1-68pdr, 2-24pdr, 2-20pdr. 27 laid down 1859-61.

'R' class destroyers, average 1,065 tons, 265 x 26½ ft, 3-4in, 4-TT.44 laid down 1915-16.

Modified 'R' class destroyers, average 1,085 tons and as 'R' class. 11 laid down 1916.

'River' class frigates, average 1,375 tons, 283 x 36 ft, 2-4in. 10-20mm. 167 ordered 1941-42 including 78 RCN and 22 RAN and two transferred to the USN.

'S' class destroyers, average 1,075 tons, 265 x 26½ ft (Thornycroft design 1,087 tons, 267 x 27 ft and Yarrow design 930 tons, 260 x 26 ft), 3-4in, 6-TT (reduced to 4). 69 laid down 1917-18.

'S' class submarines, 640 tons, 187 x 23½ ft (1931 boats), 670 tons, 193 x 24 ft (1934 boats), 715 tons, 202½ x 24 ft (others), 1-3in or 1-4in, 6 or 7-TT. 66 laid down 1931-44. (Note: all war-programme boats were ordered with 'P' numbers and received names in 1.43; this number is given in the text only if the vessel had been launched without a name.)

'T' class submarines, 1,090 tons, 265 x 26½ ft, 1-4in, 10 to 11-TT. 58 laid down 1937-44 (see note after 'S' class).

'24' class minesweeping sloops, 1,320 tons, 267½ x 35 ft, 2-4in (not mounted in all). 24 ordered 1917.

'U' class submarines, 540 tons, 180 x 16 ft, 1-3in, 4-TT. 49 laid down 1937-42 (see note after 'S' class).

'V' class submarines, 545 tons, 200 x 16 ft, 1-3 in, 4-TT. 34 ordered 1942-43 (see note after 'S' class).

'V/W' class destroyers, average 1,300 tons, 300 x 29 ft, 4-4in, 4-TT (6-TT by 1922). ('W' boats all built with 6-TT.) 51 laid down 1916-17.

Modified 'W' class destroyers, average 1,325 tons, 4-4.7in, 6-TT. 56 ordered 1918.

Acknowledgments

Grateful thanks are due to the staff of the Admiralty Library, to Mr. H. Langley and Mr. D. Brown of the Naval Historical Branch, Ministry of Defence and to the following members of the World Ship Society: M. Crowdy (founder), J. Meirat for assistance with French ships, P. Silverstone and F. Dittmar (American navy), G. Osbon, G. Ransome, R. Coleman, I. Buxton, D. Hepper, and H.T. Lenton, and to Mr. D. Lyon of the National Maritime Museum.

References

Admiralty Progress Books and Navy Lists, Admiralty Library. World Ship Society records.
British Warship Names (Manning & Walker).
Repertoire des Navires de Guerre Francais (Musees de la Marine, Paris).
The Naval Service of Canada (Tucker).
Royal Australian Navy (Gill).
The Naval History of Great Britain (James).

Abbreviations Used:

A/A	anti-aircraft
ABS	armed boarding steamer
ABV	armed boarding vessel
A/C	aircraft
AMC	armed merchant cruiser
BDV	boom defence vessel
BU	broken up; break up
carr.	carronades
compos.	composite
DY	dockyard
MG	machine gun
M/L	minelayer
mm	millimetre
M/S	minesweeper
OBV	ocean boarding vessel
pdr	pounder
RAN	Royal Australian Navy
RCN	(Royal) Canadian Navy
RIM	Royal Indian Marine
RIN	(Royal) Indian Navy
RNZN	Royal) New Zealand Navy
RPN	(Royal) Pakistan Navy
requis.	requisitioned
S	screw
SAN	South African Navy
S/M	submarine
Stmr	steamer
SY	shipyard
TRV	torpedo recovery vessel
TT	torpedo tubes
USN	United States Navy
YC	yard craft

NOTE ON REBUILDS

From researches made by Mr. Hepper and Mr. Lyon it seems that many of the ships listed in Admiralty lists as 'rebuilds' in the early 18th Century should count as new ships, though using frames and timbers of ships of the same names of an earlier date. Examples are:

ANTELOPE (1702) BU at Woolwich 2.1738, new ship launched at Woolwich DY 1741.
BEDFORD (1698) BU 11.1736, new ship launched at Portsmouth DY 1741.
BOYNE (1692) BU 11.1733, new ship launched at Deptford 28.5.1739.
CANTERBURY (1693) BU 4.1741, new ship launched Plymouth DY 2.2.1744
CORNWALL (1692) BU 3.1722, new ship launched Deptford DY 17.10.1726.
CUMBERLAND (1710) BU 10.1732, new ship launched Woolwich DY 11.7.1739.
DARTMOUTH (1798) BU 9.1736, new ship launched Woolwich DY 22.4.1741.
ELIZABETH (1706) BU 1732, new ship launched Chatham DY 29.11.1737.
FALKLAND (1690) BU 3.1742, new ship launched Bursledon 17.3.1744.
GREENWICH (1666) BU 7.1724, new ship launched Chatham DY 15.2.1730.
HUMBER (1693) BU 11.1723, new ship launched Portsmouth DY 4.10.1726.
KINGSTON (1697) BU 11.1736, new ship launched Plymouth DY 8.10.1740.
LANCASTER (1694) BU 5.1719, new ship launched Portsmouth DY 1.9.1722.
LION (1709) BU 11.1735, new ship launched Deptford DY 25.4.1738.
MONMOUTH (1666) BU 7.1739, new ship launched Deptford DY 10.9.1742.
NAMUR (1697) BU 7.1723, new ship launched Deptford DY 13.9.1729.
NASSAU (1706) BU 6.1736, new ship launched Chatham DY 25.9.1740.
NEPTUNE (1683) BU 9.1724, new ship launched Woolwich DY 15.10.1730.
NEWARK (1695) BU 5.1741, new ship launched Chatham DY 27.8.1747.

NORFOLK (1693) BU 2.1717, new ship launched Plymouth DY 21.9.1728.
NOTTINGHAM (1703) BU 4.1739, new ship launched Sheerness DY 17.8.1745.
OXFORD (1694) BU 7.1723, new ship launched Portsmouth DY 10.7.1727.
PEARL (1700) BU 1722, new ship launched Deptford DY 1726.
PRINCE FREDERICK (EXPEDITION 1679) BU 6.1736, new ship launched Deptford DY 18.3.1740.
PRINCESS MARY (MARY 1704) BU 1.1736, new ship launched 3.10.1742.
RAMILLIES (KATHERINE 1664) BU 8.1741, new ship launched Portsmouth DY 8.2.1749.
RANELAGH (1697) BU 9.1723, new ship launched as PRINCESS CAROLINE 15.3.1740.
ROYAL OAK (1674) BU 5.1737, new ship launched Plymouth DY 29.8.1741.
RUPERT (1666) BU 11.1736, new ship launched Sheerness DY 27.10.1740.
RUSSELL (1692) BU 9.1726, new ship launched Deptford DY 8.9.1735.
ST ALBANS (1706) BU 9.1734, new ship launched Plymouth DY 30.8.1737.
ST GEORGE (1701) BU 11.1726, new ship launched Portsmouth DY 3.4.1740.
SALISBURY (1698) As PRESTON BU 2.1739, new ship launched 18.9.1742.
SEVERN (1695) BU 6.1734, new ship launched Plymouth DY 28.3.1739.
SUFFOLK (1680) BU 1.1736, new ship launched Woolwich DY 5.3.1739.
SWIFTSURE (1673) As REVENGE BU 6.1740, new ship launched Deptford DY 25.5.1742.
TRIUMPH (1698) As PRINCE BU 12.1730, new ship launched Chatham DY 8.8.1750.
WARSPITE (1666) As EDINBURGH BU 1741, new ship launched Chatham DY 31.5.1744.
WINDSOR (1695) BU 10.1742, new ship launched Woolwich DY 26.2.1745.
WOOLWICH (1675) BU 8.1736, new ship launched Deptford DY 6.2.1741.

'A' class submarines. 165 tons (1st 4), 180 (others), 100 x 11½ ft (1st 4), 94 x 12 ft. (others), 2-TT.

A.1 (ordered as H.6) Vickers 9.7.1902. Sunk 8.1911 as a target.

A.2 Vickers 16.4.1903. Wrecked 1.1920 while on sale list; wreck sold 22.10.25 J.H. Pounds, Portsmouth.

A.3 Vickers 9.3.1903. Sunk 17.5.12. as a target.

A.4 Vickers 9.6.1903. Sold 16.1.20. J.H. Lee, Bembridge.

A.5 Vickers 3.3.1904. BU 1920.

A.6 Vickers 3.3.1904. Sold 16.1.20 J.H. Lee, Bembridge.

A.7 Vickers 23.1.1905. Lost 16.1.14 in Whitesand Bay by diving in to mud.

A.8 Vickers 23.1.1905. Sold 8.10.20 Philip, Dartmouth.

A.9 Vickers 8.2.1905. BU 1920.

A.10 Vickers 8.2.1905. Sold 1.4.19 Ardrossan DD Co.

A.11 Vickers 8.3.1905. BU 5.20 at Portsmouth.

A.12 Vickers 8.3.1905. Sold 16.1.20 J.H. Lee, Bembridge.

A.13 Vickers 18.4.1905. BU 1920.

ABBOTSHAM Inshore Minesweeper, 'Ham' class. Blackmore, Bideford 16.12.1955. Sold Pounds, Portsmouth 16.7.67.

ABDIEL (ex-ITHURIEL renamed 1915) Destroyer minelayer 1,687 tons, 325 x 32 ft, 3-4 in, 70 mines. Cammell Laird 12.10.1915. Sold 7.36 Rees, Llanelly.

ABDIEL Minelayer 2,650 tons, 410 x 39 ft, 6-4 in, 160 mines. White 23.4.1940. Sunk 9.9.43 by mine off Taranto.

ABDIEL Minelayer 1,200 tons, 244½ x 38½ ft. Thornycroft 27.1.1967.

ABEILLE Cutter 14. French, captured 2.5.1796 by DRYAD off the Lizard. Listed until 1798.

ABEILLE French tugs in WW.II.

ABELARD Trawler requis. 1914-16.

ABELARD Submarine 1945 'A' class. Portsmouth DY. Cancelled 1945.

ABELIA Corvette, 'Flower' class. Harland & Wolff 28.11.1940. Sold 1947, renamed *Kraft*.

ABERCROMBIE 3rd Rate 74, 1,871 tons. French D'HAUTPOUL captured 17.4.1809 by a squadron in the W.Indies. Sold 30.4.1817 to Mr Freake.

ABERCROMBIE (ex-GENERAL ABERCROMBIE renamed 20.6.1915, ex-M.1 19.6.15. ex-ADMIRAL FARRAGUT 31.5.15, ex-FARRAGUT) monitor 6,150 tons, 320 x 90 ft, 2-14 in, 2-6 in. Harland & Wolff 15.4.15. Sold 7.27 Ward, Inverkeithing.

ABERCROMBIE Monitor 7,850 tons, 365 x 90 ft, 2-15 in, 8-4 in. Vickers Armstrong, Tyne 31.3.1942, Arrived 24.12.54 Ward, Barrow to BU.

ABERDARE Minesweeper later 'Hunt' class. Ailsa, Troon 29.4.1918. Sold 13.3.47.

ABERDEEN Trawler requis. 1914-19.

ABERDEEN Sloop 990 tons, 250 x 36 ft, 4-4in. Devonport DY 22.1.1936. Sold 16.12.48; arrived 18.1.49 Ward, Hayle to BU.

ABERFORD Seaward defence boat,'Ford' class. Yarrow 22.9.1952. Nigerian naval NYATI 1966.

ABERFOYLE Tender 210 tons, 100 x 19 ft. Purchased 4.11.1920. For disposal 1947. (see DOLPHIN 1938)

ABERGAVENNY (ex-E.Indiaman purchased 1795) 4th Rate 54, 1182bm, 160 x 41 ft. Sold 1807.

ABIGAIL Fireship 4, 143bm. Purchased 1666. Expended 25.7.1666.

ABIGAIL Cutter 3. Captured 12.12.1812 from the Danes by HAMADRYAD. Sold 1814.

ABIGAIL. Salvage vessel requis. 1941-43.

ABINGDON Minesweeper later 'Hunt' class. Ailsa 11.6.1918. Bombed 5.4.42 by Italian aircraft at Malta and beached; BU there in 1950.

ABOUKIR 3rd Rate 74, 1,870bm, 186 x 48 ft. French AQUILON captured 1.8.1798 at the Nile. BU 3.1802 at Plymouth.

ABOUKIR 3rd Rate 74, 1,703bm, 172½

x 47 ft. Brindley, Frindsbury 18.11.1807. Harbour service 6.1824; sold 16.8.1838 to J. Lachlan.

ABOUKIR 2nd Rate 90, 3,080bm, 204 x 60 ft. Devonport DY 4.4.1848. Undocked 1.1.1858 as screw ship 3,091bm. Sold 23.11.1877 in Jamaica.

ABOUKIR Armoured cruiser 12,000 tons, 440 x 69½ ft, 2-9.2in, 12-6in. Fairfield 16.5.1900. Sunk 22.9.14 by 'U.9' in the North Sea.

ABRAHAM Flyboat 4, 202bm. Purchased 1665. Sold 1666.

ABRAMS OFFERING Fireship 63bm. Purchased 1694. Expended 12.9.1694 at Dunkirk.

L'ABONDANCE Storeship 24, 524bm, 182½ x 29½ ft, 24-9pdr, 4-4pdr. French, captured 1781. Sold 29.4.1784.

ABUNDANCE Storeship 24,673bm, 140 x 32½ ft. Adams, Bucklers Hard 30.9.1799 and purchased 1799. Sold 22.5.1823.

ABUNDANCE (see ALFRED of 1855)

ABYSSINIA Turret ship (Indian) 2,900 tons, 225 x 42 ft, 4-10in MLR. Dudgeon, Poplar 19.2.1870. Sold 1. 1903.

ACACIA Sloop, 'Acacia' class. Swan Hunter 15.4.1915. Sold 9.22 Dornom Bros.

ACACIA. Drifter requis. 1914-15; Trawler 1940-47.

ACANTHUS Corvette, 'Flower' class. Ailsa 26.5.1941. Lent Norwegian navy 10.41 to 1946. Sold 1946, renamed *Colin Frye.*

ACASTA 5th rate 40, 1,142bm, 154 x 41 ft. Wells, Rotherhithe 14.3.1797. BU 1.1.1821.

ACASTA Wood S. frigate, 3,202bm, 280 x 50 ft. Deptford DY laid down 16.4.1861 cancelled 12.12.1863.

ACASTA Destroyer 996 tons, 260 x 27 ft, 3-4 in, 2-TT. J. Brown 10.9.1912. Sold 9.5.21 Ward, Hayle.

ACASTA Destroyer 1,350 tons, 311 x 32½ ft, 4-4.7 in, 8-TT. J. Brown 8.8.1929. Sunk 8.6.40 by German battlecruisers west of Narvik.

ACASTA Submarine 1945 'A' class. Portsmouth DY. Cancelled 1945. ACE Submarine 1945 'A' class. Devonport DY 14.3.1945 (not completed).

Arrived 6.50 Smith & Houston, Port Glasgow to BU.

ACERTIF Brig-sloop 18. Danish, captured 8.1808 by DAPHNE in the Baltic. Sold 1809.

ACHATES 13-gun ship, 100bm, 6-9pdr, 2-4pdr, 5 small. Deptford 11.10.1573.

Hulked 1590. Sold 1605.

ACHATES Brig-sloop 10, 'Cherokee' class, 238bm. Brent, Rotherhithe 1.2.1808. Wrecked 7.2.1810 at Guadeloupe, W. Indies.

ACHATES Brig-sloop 16, 327bm, 95½ x 28½ ft. French Le MILAN captured 3.10.1809. Sold 11.6.1818 Mr Ledger.

ACHATES Destroyer 982 tons, 260 x 27 ft, 3-4 in, 2-TT. J. Brown 14.11.1912. Sold 9.5.21 Ward, Rainham.

ACHATES Destroyer 1,350 tons, 311 x 32½ ft, 4-4.7 in, 8-TT. J. Brown 4.10.1929. Sunk 31.12.42 by German ADMIRAL HIPPER in the Barents Sea.

ACHATES Submarine 1945 'A' class. Devonport DY 20.9.1945 (not completed). Sunk 6.50 as a target, off Gibraltar.

ACHERON Bomb 8, 388bm, 108 x 29 ft. Purchased 10.1803. Captured 3.2.1805 by the French in the Mediterranean and burnt.

ACHERON Wood pad. sloop, 722bm, 150 x 33 ft, 2-9pdr. Sheerness DY 23.8.1838. Sold 24.9.1855 at Sydney NSW.

ACHERON Wood S.sloop, 675bm, 162 x 30 ft. Deptford DY laid down 14.10.1861, cancelled 12.12.1863.

ACHERON Torpedo boat (Australian) 16 tons, 78 x 10 ft, 1-TT. Built in 1879. Sold in 12.1902.

ACHERON (see NORTHUMBERLAND of 1866).

ACHERON Destroyer 773 tons, 245 x 26 ft, 2-4 in, 2-12pdr, 2-TT. Thornycroft 27.6.1911. Sold 9.5.21 Ward, resold 20.6.23 J.J. King to BU.

ACHERON Destroyer 1,350 tons, 311 x 32 ft, 4-4.7 in, 8-TT. Thornycroft 18.3.1930. Sunk 17.12.40 by mine in the Channel.

ACHERON Submarine 1945 'A' class. Chatham DY 25.3.1947. BU Newport 2.72.

ACHILLE Sloop 8. French, captured 1744. Captured 14.11.1745 by the Spanish off Jamaica.

ACHILLES Schooner 8. Purchased 1747. Captured 1748 by the Spanish.

ACHILLES 4th Rate 60, 1234bm, 154 x 42½ ft. Barnard, Harwich 16.7.1757. Hulked 1780. Sold 1.6.1784.

ACHILLE Storeship 14, 420bm, 97 x 31 ft. Purchased 1780. Sold 8.1.1784.

ACHILLE 3rd Rate 78, 1,801bm, 178 x 48 ft. French, captured 1.6.1794 at the battle of '1st of June'. BU 2.1796 at Plymouth.

ACHILLE 3rd Rate 74, 1,981bm, 184 x

50½ ft. Cleverley, Gravesend 16.4.1798. Sold 11.1865 Castle & Beech.

ACHILLES Iron S.ship 9,820 tons, 380 x 58 ft, 20-100pdr (rearmed 14-9 in, 2-7 in MLR). Chatham DY 23.12.1863. Base ship HIBERNIA 1902; EGMONT 3.04; EGREMONT 6.16; PEMBROKE 6.19; sold 26.1.23 Granton S.Bkg.Co.

ACHILLES Armoured cruiser 13,550 tons, 480 x 73½ ft, 6-9.2 in, 4-7.5 in, 24-3pdr. Armstrong 17.6.1905. Sold 9.5.21 Ward, BU Swansea & Briton Ferry 1923.

ACHILLES Cruiser 7,030 tons, 530 x 55 ft, 8-6 in, 8-4 in. Cammell Laird 1.9.1932. RIN DELHI 5.7.48.

ACHILLES Frigate 'Leander' class, Yarrow 21.11.1968.

ACONITE Corvette, 'Flower' class. Ailsa, Troon 31.3.1941. Free-French ACONIT 7.41 to 30.4.47. Sold 7.47, renamed *Terje II*.

ACORN 22-gun ship hired 1649-54.

ACORN Sloop 18, 430bm, 110 x 30 ft. Croker, Bideford 30.10.1807. BU 5.1819.

ACORN Sloop 18, 455bm, 112 x 30½ ft. Chatham DY 16.11.1826. Wrecked 14.4.1828 off Halifax NS.

ACORN Sloop 18,480bm, 114 x 31 ft. Portsmouth DY. Cancelled 6.1831.

ACORN Brig 12, 485bm, 105 x 33½ ft, 12-32pdr. Devonport DY 15.11.1838. Coal hulk 1861. Sold 15.2.1869 at Yokohama.

ACORN Compos. S.sloop 970 tons, 167 x 32 ft, 8-5 in. Milford Haven SB Co 6.9.1884. Sold 15.12.1899 Harris, Bristol BU 1904.

ACORN Destroyer 760 tons, 246 x 25 ft, 2-4 in, 2-12pdr, 2-TT. J. Brown 1.7.1910. Sold 29.11.21 Marple & Gillott, Saltash.

ACTAEON 6th Rate 28 (fir-built), 595bm, 118 x 34 ft. Chatham DY 30.9.1757. Sold 9.9.1766 as unserviceable.

ACTAEON 6th Rate 28, 594bm, 120½ x 33½ ft. Woolwich DY 18.4.1775. Grounded 29.6.1776 at Charlestown and burnt.

ACTAEON 5th Rate 44, 887bm, 140 x 38 ft. Randall, Rotherhithe 29.1.1778. Harbour service 7.1795. Sold 30.4.1802.

ACTEON Big-sloop 16, 335bm. French, captured 3.10.1805 by EGYPTIENNE off Rochefort. BU 10.1816.

ACTAEON 6th Rate 26, 620bm, 121½ x 34½ ft. Portsmouth DY 31.1.1831. Survey ship 1856; lent Cork Harbour

Board 2.1870 as a hulk. Sold 2.1889 J. Read, Portsmouth.

ACTAEON (see VERNON of 1832, ARIADNE of 1859 and DIDO of 1869).

ACTAEON Sloop 1,350 tons, 283 x 38½ ft, 6-4 in, 4-40mm. Thornycroft 25.7.1945. W.German HIPPER 9.12.58.

ACTEON (see ACTAEON)

ACTIF (see ACTIVE)

ACTIVE 6th Rate 28, 594bm, 118½ x 34 ft. Stanton, Deptford 11.1.1758. Captured 1.9.1778 by the French off San Domingo.

ACTIVE Brig-sloop 14, 109bm, 76 x 20 ft. Purchased 1776. Captured 1780 by Americans off New York.

ACTIVE Cutter 12 in service 1779. Captured 18.8.1779 by the French cutter Le MUTIN in the Channel.

ACTIVE 5th Rate 32, 697bm, 126 x 36 ft. Raymond, Northam 30.8.1780. Wrecked 7.1796 in the St Lawrence.

ACTIVE Brig-sloop 14 in service in 1782.

ACTIF Gun-brig 10, 165bm, 10-4pdr. French, captured 16.3.1794 by IPHIGENIA in the W.Indies. Foundered 26.11.1794 off Bermuda.

ACTIVE 5th Rate 38, 1,058bm, 150 x 41 ft. Chatham DY 14.12.1799. Harbour service 2.1826; renamed ARGO 15.11.1833. BU 10.1860 at Plymouth.

ACTIVE 5th Rate 36, 1,627bm, 160 x 49 ft. Chatham DY 19.7.1845 (originally ordered at Pembroke). Renamed TYNE training ship 30.7.1867; renamed DURHAM 18.11.1867. Sold 12.5.1908, BU at Bo'ness.

ACTIVE Iron S.corvette 3,080 tons, 270 x 42 ft, 18-64pdr. Blackwall 13.3.1869. Sold 10.7.1906.

ACTIVE Scout cruiser 3,360 tons, 385 x 41½ ft, 10-4in. Pembroke Dock 14.3.1911. Sold 21.4.20.

ACTIVE Destroyer 1,350 tons, 311 x 32 ft, 4-4.7 in, 8-TT. Hawthorn Leslie 9.7.1929. Sold 20.5.47; BU at Troon.

ACTIVE Frigate 2,750 tons, Vosper/Thornycroft 23.11.1972.

ACTIVE 3 cutters hired between 1794 & 1814. Tug requis. 1915-18. Trawler and 3 Drifters requis. in WW.I.

ACTIVITY (ex-*Empire Activity*, ex-*Telemachus* converted) Escort carrier 11,800 tons, 475 x 66½ ft, 2-4in, 15-A/C. Caledon 30.5.1942. Sold 4.46, renamed *Breconshire*.

ACUTE (Gunboat No.6) Gunvessel 12, 159bm, 75 x 22 ft. Randall, Rotherhithe 4.1797. Sold 10.1802.

ACUTE Gun-brig 12, 178bm, 80 x 22½

ft. Rowe, Newcastle 21.7.1804. Harbour service 5.1813 then to coastguard service to 1831.

ACUTE (ex-ALERT renamed 12.1941) Minesweeper, 'Algerine' class. Harland & Wolff 14.4.1942. Destroyed 1964 as target.

ACUTE Patrol Boat (RAN), 100 tons. Evans Deakin 26.8.1967; handed over to Indonesia 6.5.83.

ADAM & EVE Storeship 20. Dutch, captured 1652. Sold 1657.

ADAM & EVE Hoy 6, 72bm. Dutch, captured 1665. Sunk 1673 as a foundation at Sheerness.

ADAMANT 4th Rate 50, 1,060bm, 146½ x 41 ft. Baker, Liverpool 24.1.1780. Harbour service 7.1809. BU 6.1814.

ADAMANT Depot ship 935 tons, 190 x 32½ ft. Cammell Laird 12.7.1911. Sold 21.9.32 Rees, Llanelly.

ADAMANT II (see LILY of 1915).

ADAMANT Depot ship 12,700 tons, 620 x 70½ ft, 8-4.5 in. Harland & Wolff 30.11.1940. Arrived Inverkeithing 11.9.70 to BU.

ADAMANT Drifter requis. 1938-41.

ADDA (see FIDGET of 1905).

ADDER Galley 8 purchased 1782, sold 5.1787.

ADDER (Gunboat No 17) Gunvessel 12, 159bm, 75 x 22 ft. Barnard, Deptford 22.4.1797. BU 2.1805.

ADDER Gun-brig 12, 180bm, 85 x 22 ft. Ayles, Topsham 9.11.1805. Captured 9.12.1806 by the French while aground on the French coast.

ADDER Gun-brig 12, 182bm, 85 x 22 ft. Davy, Topsham 28.6.1813. Coastguard 1.1826. Wrecked 1832, near Newhaven.

ADDER (see SEAGULL of 1814).

ADDER (ex-GPO vessel *Crocodile*) Wood pad. packet 240bm, 117 x 21 ft. Transferred 5.1837. Sold 13.5.1870 Wilson Maclay.

ADDER (ex-War Dept *Burgoyne*) Tender 125 tons, 95 x 17½ ft. Transferred 7.1905. Renamed ATTENTIVE II 7.19; sold 31.1.23 Carriden S.Bkg.Co.

ADDER Tug requis. 1918-19.

ADELAIDE (ex-slaver *Delta Josephine* purchased 1827) Tender 95bm, 67 x 19 ft. Sold 1833 at Rio de Janeiro.

ADELAIDE (ex-slaver purchased 5.1848) 140bm. Wrecked 9.10.1850 on Banana Island, W. Africa.

ADELAIDE (see FIDGET of 1905)

ADELAIDE Light cruiser (RAN) 5,440 tons, 430 x 50 ft, 9-6in, 3-4in. Cockatoo DY 27.7.1918. Sold 1.49 to BU at Port Kembla.

ADELAIDE Frigate (RAN) 2,100 tons. Todd, Seattle 21.6.1978.

ADELAIDE Tug 1891-1907.

ADEPT Submarine 1945 'A' class. Chatham DY. Cancelled 23.10.1945 (not laid down).

ADEPT Tug 1941-42; Tug 1947-59.

ADMIRABLE Submarine 1945 'A' class. Vickers Armstrong, Tyne. Cancelled 1945.

ADMIRABLE Drifter requis. 1914-17.

ADMIRAL DEVRIES 3rd Rate 68, 1,360bm, 157 x 44½ ft. Dutch, captured 11.10.1797 at Camperdown. Harbour service 1800. Sold 2.1806 in Jamaica.

ADMIRAL FARRAGUT Monitor (see ABERCROMBIE).

ADMIRALTY Yacht, 115bm, 69 x 20 ft. Woolwich DY 21.5.1814. Renamed PLYMOUTH 7. 1830; harbour service 'YC.1' 1866. Sold 10.5.1870 Lethbridge & Drew.

ADMIRALTY Yacht, 136bm, 69 x 21½ ft. Portsmouth DY 28.2.1831, renamed FANNY (qv).

ADONIS Schooner 10, 111bm, 68 x 20 ft. Bermuda 1806. Sold 1.9.1814.

ADROIT Patrol Boat (RAN), 100 tons. Evans Deakin 3.2.1968.

ADUR Frigate, 'River' class. Vickers, Montreal 22.8.1942. To RCN as NADUR 1942; to USN as ASHEVILLE 11.42.

ADVANCE Patrol Boat (RAN) 100 tons, Walker 16.8.1967.

ADVANTAGE 18-gun ship, 144/182bm, 6-9pdr, 8-6pdr, 4-2pdr. Built 1590. Burnt 1613.

ADVANTAGE 26-gun ship. Dutch, captured 1652. Sold 1655.

ADVANTAGIA Galley 100bm. Woolwich 1601; sold 1629.

ADVENTURE Galley 26, 343bm, 4-18pdr, 11-9pdr, 11 small. Built 1594 at Deptford. BU 1645.

ADVENTURE 32-gun ship, 438bm, 116 x 28 ft. Woolwich DY 1646. Re-built Chatham 1691 as 4th Rate 44, 117 x 29 ft. Captured 1.3.1709 by the French off Martinique, W. Indies.

ADVENTURE PRIZE Hoy 25bm, 38 x 12½ ft. French, captured 1693. Made a pitch boat 1695. Sold 1698.

ADVENTURE GALLEY in service 1696 to 1699.

ADVENTURE 5th Rate 40, 530bm, 118 x 32 ft. Sheerness DY 16.6.1709. Re-built Portsmouth 1726 as 598bm. BU 6.1741 at Deptford.

ADVENTURE 4th Rate 683bm, 124 x 36 ft. Blaydes, Hull 1.10.1741; 32-gun

5th Rate 1758. Sold 20.3.1770.

ADVENTURE Cutter 12, 61 bm, 48 x 18 ft. Purchased 2.1763. Sold 5.4.1768.

ADVENTURE (ex-RAYLEIGH renamed 25.12.1771, ex-*Marquis of Rockingham*) Discovery vessel 336bm, 99 x 28 ft, 10-4pdr. Purchased 11.1771. Made a fireship 1780. Sold 7.5.1783.

ADVENTURE 5th Rate 44, 896bm, 140½ x 38½ ft. Perry, Blackwall 19.7.1784. Troopship 7.1789; harbour service 6.1801. BU 9. 1816 at Sheerness.

ADVENTURE (see AID of 1809)

ADVENTURE (see RESOLUTE of 1855)

ADVENTURE Torpedo Ram, 2,640 tons. Ordered Chatham DY 6.3.1885 and cancelled 12.8.1885.

ADVENTURE River gunboat 85 tons, 75 x 12 ft. Yarrow 1891. Re-erected on Lake Nyasa 1893; transferred to the BCA Govt. 1896. Sold 1921.

ADVENTURE Scout cruiser 2,670 tons, 374 x 38 ft, 10-12pdr. Armstrong 8.9.1904. Sold 3.3.20 Ward, Morecambe.

ADVENTURE Minelayer 6,740 tons, 500 x 59 ft, 4-4.7in, 280 mines. Devonport DY 18.6.1924. Repair ship 3.44. Sold 10.7.47, BU Ward, Briton Ferry.

ADVENTURE 2 hired ships 1654; Tug 1900 ren. TYRIAN 1904; Trawler 1915-19.

ADVERSARY Submarine 1945 'A' class. Vickers Armstrong, Tyne. Cancelled 1945.

ADVICE Pinnace 9, 50bm, 4-6pdr, 2-4pdr, 3 small. Woolwich DY 1586. Sold 1617.

ADVICE 48-gun ship, 516bm, 118½ x 31 ft. Pett, Woodbridge 1650. Rebuilt Woolwich 1698 as 550bm. Captured 27.6.1711 by the French.

ADVICE PRIZE Sloop. French, captured 1693. Sold 1695.

ADVICE PRIZE 6th Rate 18, 200bm, 82 x 24½ ft. French, captured 19.6.1704. Sold 10.4.1712.

ADVICE 4th Rate 50, 714bm, 131 x 35½ ft. Deptford DY 8.7.1712. Renamed MILFORD 23.5.1744. Sold 11.5.1749.

ADVICE 4th Rate 50, 983bm, 140 x 40 ft. Rowcliffe, Southampton 26.2.1745. BU 10.1756 at Portsmouth.

ADVICE Cutter 10, 95bm, 56 x 21 ft, 10-3pdr. Purchased 1779. Wrecked 1.6.1793 in the Bay of Honduras.

ADVICE Cutter 4, 47bm, 45½ x 16 ft, 4-3pdr. Itchen Ferry 1796. Last listed 8.1799.

ADVICE Advice boat, 180bm. Randall, Rotherhithe 30.12.1800. Sold 1805.

ADVICE (ex-GPO vessel *Vixen*) Wood pad. packet, 197bm, 108 x 20 ft. Transferred 4.1837. Sold 12.5.1870 J.J. Stark.

ADVICE Tug 1899-1950; Tug 1958-85.

ADVISER Pink 8 in service 1654. Captured 1655 by a privateer.

AE.1 and AE.2 (see under 'E' class submarines)

AENEAS Submarine 1945 'A' class. Cammell Laird 9.10.1945. BU Dunston 12.74.

AEOLUS 5th Rate 32, 704bm, 125½ x 36 ft. West, Deptford 29.11.1758. Harbour service 5.1796; renamed GUERNSEY 1800. BU 5.1801.

AEOLUS 5th Rate 32, 910bm, 144 x 37½ ft. Barnard, Deptford 28.2.1801. BU 10.1817 at Deptford.

AEOLUS 5th Rate 46, 1,078bm, 152 x 40 ft. Deptford DY 17.6.1825. Harbour service 1855. BU 3.1886 Castle, Thames.

AEOLUS 2nd class cruiser 3,600 tons, 300 x 44 ft, 2-6in, 6-4.7in, 8-6 pdr. Devonport DY 13.11.1891. Sold 26.5.1914 Ward, Preston.

AETNA Fireship 8, 283bm, 91 x 26 ft. Freame, Hull 19.3.1691. Captured 18.4.1697 by the French.

AETNA (ex-*Mermaid*) Fireship 8, 183bm, 82 x 23 ft. Purchased 14.9.1739.Sold 23.10.1746.

ETNA (ex-*Charlotte*) Fireship 8, 316bm, 98½ x 27 ft. Purchased 10.11.1756. Made a sloop 12.1756. Sold 15.2.1763.

ETNA (ex-*Borryan*) Fireship 8, 294bm, 94½ x 27 ft. Purchased 1.1771. Renamed SCORPION sloop 10.8.1771. Sold 27.12.1780 in N. America.

AETNA Bomb 8, 300bm, 92 x 27½ ft. Randall, Rotherhithe 20.6.1776. BU 5.1784.

ETNA 6th Rate 20, 564bm, 119½ x 33 ft. French ETNA captured 13.11.1796 by MELAMPUS and CHILDERS on the coast of France. Renamed CORMORANT 1797. Wrecked 20.5.1800 on the coast of Egypt.

AETNA (ex-*Success*) Bomb 8, 368bm,. Purchased 10.1803. Sold 11.1.1816.

AETNA Bomb 6, 375bm, 106 x 28½ ft. Chatham DY 14.4.1824. Survey vessel 1826. Sold 20.2.1846 Bristol Seamen's Friendly Society.

AETNA Wood S. floating battery, 1,469bm, 172½ x 44 ft, 14-68pdr.

Scott Russell, Millwall. Laid down 9.10.1854, caught fire and launched herself 3.5.1855; BU on river bank.

AETNA Wood S. floating battery, 1,588 bm, 186 x 44 ft, 16-68pdr. Chatham DY 5.4.1856. Harbour service 1866. Burnt out at Sheerness 1873 and BU 1874.

AFFLECK (ex-USS OSWALD) Frigate, TE 'Captain' class. Bethlehem, Hingham 30.6.1943. Badly damaged 27.12.44; nominally returned to the USN 1.9.45. Sold 4.10.47 to Portuguese owners as a hulk.

AFFRAY Submarine 1945 'A' class. Cammell Laird 20.4.1945. Foundered 17.4.51 in the Channel.

AFRICA 46-gun ship in service 1694 to 1696.

AFRICA 3rd Rate 64, 1,354bm, 158 x 44½ ft. Perry, Blackwall 1.8.1761. Sold 15.7.1774.

AFRICA 3rd Rate 64, 1,415bm, 160 x 46 ft. Barnard, Deptford 11.4.1781. Harbour service 9.1798. BU 5.1814 at Portsmouth.

AFRICA (see EURYALUS of 1803)

AFRICA Wood s. Sloop, 669bm, 160 x 30 ft. Devonport DY 29.3.1862. Sold 13.8.1862 to the Emperor of China, renamed CHINA.

AFRICA (see GOOD HOPE)

AFRICA Battleship 16,350 tons, 439 x 78 ft, 4-12in, 4-9.2in, 10-6in, 12-12pdr. Chatham DY 20.5.1905. Sold 30.6.20 Ellis, Newcastle.

AFRICA A/C carrier 36,800 tons, 720 x 112 ft, 16-4.5in, 58-40mm, 100-A/C. Fairfield, ordered 8.1943, cancelled 10.45.

AFRICA Hired cutter 1803-04.

AFRICAINE 5th rate 38, 1,085bm, 154 x 40 ft. French, captured 19.2. 1801 by PHOEBE in the Mediterranean. BU 9.1816.

AFRICAINE 5th Rate 46, 1,173bm, 159 x 41 ft. Chatham DY 20.12.1827. Sold 9.5.1867 to Trinity House as a hulk. BU 1903.

AFRIDI Destroyer 872 tons, 250 x 25 ft, 3-12pdr, 2-TT. Armstrong 8.5.1907. Sold 9.12.19 F. Wilkinson.

AFRIDI Destroyer 1,870 tons, 355½ x 36½ ft, 8-4.7in, 4-TT. Vickers Armstrong, Tyne 8.6.1937. Sunk 3.5.40 by air attack off Namsos, Norway.

AFRIKANDER Base ships. (see TICKLER of 1879, GRIPER of 1879)

AGAMEMNON 3rd Rate 64, 1,384bm, 160 x 45 ft. Adams, Bucklers Hard 10.4.1781. Wrecked 16.6.1809 in the River Plate.

AGAMEMNON S. 2nd Rate 91, 3,102bm, 230 x 55½ ft, 36-8in, 54-32 pdr. Woolwich DY 22.5.1852. Sold 12.5.1870 W.H.Moore.

AGAMEMNON Battleship 8,510 tons, 280 x 66 ft, 4-12.5in. MLR, 2-6in. Chatham DY 17.9.1879. BU 1.1903 in Germany.

AGAMEMNON Battleship 16,500 tons, 435 x 79½ ft, 4-12in, 10-9.2in, 24-12pdr. Fairfield 23.6.1906. Target ship 9.20. Sold 24.1.27 Cashmore, Newport.

AGAMEMNON II Trawler. Requis. WW.I.

AGAMEMNON Minelayer 7,593 tons. Requis. WW.II.

AGASSIZ Corvette, 'Flower' class (RCN). Burrard DD Co. 15.8.1940. Sold 1946 Irving & Brunswick Motors, Moncton.

AGATE Submarine 1945 'A' class. Cammell Laird. Cancelled 1945.

AGATE Two trawlers. Requis. WW.I, WW.II.

AGGRESSOR Gun-brig 14, 179bm, 85 x 22 ft. Perry, Blackwall 1.4.1801. Sold 23.11.1815.

AGGRESSOR Submarine 1945 'A' class. Cammell Laird. Cancelled 1945.

AGILE Submarine 1945 'A' class. Cammell Laird. Cancelled 1945.

AGILE Trawler WW.I and Tug built 1958.

L'AGLAIA Sloop 18. French privateer captured 18.4.1782 by AEOLUS. Sold 5.6.1783.

AGINCOURT (ex-E. Indiaman Earl Talbot purchased on stocks) 3rd Rate 64, 1,440bm, 161 x 46 ft. Perry, Blackwall 23.7.1796. Became a prison ship and renamed BRISTOL 6.1.1812. Sold 15.12.1814.

AGINCOURT 3rd Rate 74, 1,747bm, 176 x 48½ ft. Plymouth DY 19.3.1817. Harbour service 3.1848; renamed VIGO 4.1865. Sold 10.1884 Castle, Thames.

AGINCOURT (ex-CAPTAIN renamed 1861) Iron S.ship, 6,621 bm, 10,600 tons, 400 x 59½ ft, 17-9in. MLR. Laird 27.3.1865. Harbour service BOSCAWEN III 3.1904; GANGES II 21.6.06; coal hulk 'C.109' 9.08. Arrived 21.10.60 Ward, Grays to BU.

AGINCOURT Battleship 27,500 tons. Portsmouth DY. Ordered 1914, cancelled 26.8.14.

AGINCOURT (ex-Turkish SULTAN OSMAN I seized 8.1914, ex-Brazilian RIO de JANEIRO) 27,500 tons, 632 x 89 ft, 14-12in, 20-6in. Armstrong 22.1.1913. Sold 19.12.22 Rosyth

S.Bkg. Co.,

AGINCOURT Destroyer 2,400 tons, 355 x 40 ft, 5-4.5in, 8-TT. Hawthorn Leslie 29.1.1945. BU 10.74 Sunderland.

AID 18-gun ship, 300 bm, 8-9pdr, 2-6pdr, 4-4pdr, 4 small. Deptford 6.10.1562. Rebuilt 1580. BU 1599.

AID Transport 10, 314bm, 105½ x 26 ft, 10-12pdr carr. Brindley, Lynn 4.4.1809. Survey ship 3.1817; renamed ADVENTURE 24.5.1821. Sold 19.3.1853.

AIGLE 5th Rate 38, 1,003bm, 147½ x 39 ft. French, captured 14.9.1782 off the Delaware. Wrecked 18.7.1798 off Cape Farina, Spain.

AIGLE 5th Rate 36, 990bm, 150 x 39 ft. Adams, Bucklers Hard 23.9. 1801. Coal hulk 1853; sunk in shallow water during torpedo experiments at Sheerness and sold 24.11.1870 to BU.

AIMABLE 5th Rate 32, 782bm, 133½ x 36½ ft. French, captured 19.4. 1782. BU 5.1814.

AIMWELL Gunvessel 12, 148bm, 75 x 21 ft. Perry, Blackwall 12.5.1794. BU 11.1811 at Sheerness.

AIMWELL Lend-lease tug WW.I.

AINTHORPE Coastal M/S ordered 9.9.1950 Thornycroft, cancelled 1953.

AIRE Frigate, 'River' class. Fleming & Ferguson 22.4.1943. Renamed TAMAR 3.46; reverted to AIRE 12.46. Wrecked 20.12.46 on Bombay Reef.

AIREDALE Destroyer, 'Hunt' class type III. J. Brown 12.8.1941. Sunk 15.6.42 by German aircraft north of Sollum.

AIREDALE Tug 1961-.

AISNE Destroyer 2,380 tons, 355 x 40 ft, 5-4.5in, 8-TT. Vickers Armstrong, Tyne 12.5.1945. Arrived Inverkeithing 26.6.70 to BU.

AISNE Trawler requis. WW.I.

AITAPE Patrol Boat (RAN) 100 tons. Walker 6.7.1967. To Papua/New Guinea in 9.75.

AJAX 3rd Rate 74, 1,615bm, 168 x 47½ ft, Portsmouth DY 23.12.1767. Sold 10.2.1785.

AJAX 3rd Rate 74, 1,953bm, 183 x 49½ ft, Randall, Rotherhithe 3.3.1798. Burnt 11.2.1807 by accident off Tenedos.

AJAX 3rd Rate 74, 1,761bm, 176 x 48½ ft, Perry, Blackwall 2.5.1809. Undocked 1846 as screw ship. BU 1864.

AJAX (see VANGUARD of 1835)

AJAX Battleship 8,660 tons, 280 x 66 ft, 4-12.5in.MLR, 2-6in. Pembroke Dock 10.3.1880. Sold 3.1904 Castle,

Thames.

AJAX Battleship 23,000 tons, 555 x 89 ft, 10-13.5in, 12-4in. Scotts 21.3.1912. Sold 11.26 Alloa S. Bkg Co, Rosyth & Charlestown to BU.

AJAX Cruiser 6,985 tons, 522 x 55½ ft, 8-6in, 8-4in. Vickers Armstrong Barrow 1.3.1934. Arrived 13.11.49 Cashmore, Newport to BU.

AJAX Frigate, 'Leander' class. Cammell Laird 16.8.1962.

AJAX Tug and drifter in WW.I.

AJDAHA Wood pad. frigate (Indian), 1,440bm. Fletcher, Limehouse 1846. Sold 4.1863.

AKBAR 3rd Rate 74. Laid down 4.4.1807 at Prince of Wales Island, Malabar and cancelled 12.10.1809.

AKBAR (see CORNWALLIS of 1801)

AKBAR (see HERO of 1816)

AKBAR Wood pad. frigate (Indian), 1,143bm. Napier, Glasgow 1841. Sold 2.1859.

AKBAR (see TEMERAIRE of 1876)

AKBAR Minesweeper, 'Catherine' class. Gen. Eng., Alameda 12.12.1942 for the RN but retained by the USN.

AKERS Fireship,85bm. Purchased 4.1794. Sold 16.12.1801.

ALAART (see under ALERT)

ALACRITY Brig-sloop 18, 'Cruizer' class. Rowe, Newcastle 13.11.1806. Captured 26.5.1811 by the French ABEILLE off Corsica.

ALACRITY Brig-sloop 10, 'Cherokee' class. Deptford DY 29.12.1818. Sold 28.8.1835.

ALACRITY Wood S. sloop, 675bm, 180½ x 28½ ft. Mare, Blackwall 20.3.1856. Sold 7.10.1864 Castle, Thames.

ALACRITY (ex-*Ethel*) 85bm, 1-12pdr. Purchased 4.11.1872. Sold 1882 at Sydney NSW.

ALACRITY Despatch vessel 1,700 tons, 250 x 32½ ft, 4-5in, 4-6pdr. Palmer 28.2.1885. Sold 9.1913 at Hong Kong.

ALACRITY (see SURPRISE of 1885)

ALACRITY Sloop 1,350 tons, 283 x 38 ft, 6-4in. Denny 1.9.1944. Arrived 15.9.56 Arnott Young, Dalmuir to BU.

ALACRITY Frigate 2,750 tons. Yarrow 18.9.1974.

ALACRITY Yacht in WW.I.

ALADDIN Submarine 1945 'A' class. Cammell Laird, cancelled 1945.

ALAMEIN Destroyer 2,400 tons, 355 x 40 ft, 5-4.5in, 8-40mm, 10-TT. Hawthorn Leslie 28.5.1945. Arrived

1.12.64 Hughes Bolckow, Blyth to BU.

ALARIC 5th Rate 36, 1,020bm. Name chosen in 1811 for IRIS but not used.

ALARIC Submarine 1945 'A' class. Cammell Laird 20.2.1946. BU Inverkeithing 7.71.

ALARM 5th Rate 32, 683bm, 125 x 35½ ft. Barnard, Harwich 19.9.1758. BU 9.1812 at Portsmouth.

ALARM Cutter 4, 81bm, 53 x 19½ ft. Purchased 2.1763. Sold 23.10.1780.

ALARM Galley purchased 6.1777 in N. America. Lost 1.8.1778 at Rhode Island.

ALARM 6th Rate 24, 635bm, 122 x 34 ft. Dutch captured 28.8.1799 in the Texel. Renamed HELDER 4.1800, HELDIN 24.4.1800, sold 3.1802.

ALARM 6th Rate 28, 652bm, 125 x 34½ ft. Pembroke Dock. Laid down 1.1832, cancelled 10.1832.

ALARM 6th Rate 28, 910bm, 131 x 40½ ft. Sheerness DY 22.4.1845. Coal hulk 1860. Sold 7.7.1904.

ALARM Torpedo gunboat 810 tons, 230 x 27 ft, 2-4.7in, 4-3pdr. Sheerness DY 13.9.1892. Sold 9.4.1907 Thames S. Bkg Co.

ALARM Destroyer 780 tons, 246 x 25 ft, 2-4in, 2-12pdr, 2-TT. J.Brown 29.8.1910. Sold 9.5.21 Ward, Hayle.

ALARM Minesweeper, 'Algerine' class.. Harland & Wolff 5.2.1942. Badly damaged by mine 1.43 and sold at Bone 12.43 to BU.

ALARM M/S tug. Requis. WW.II.

ALAUNIA II (see MARSHAL NEY)

ALBACORE Sloop 16, 320bm, 97 x 27 ft, 16-6pdr. American privateer ROYAL LOUIS captured 1781 by NYMPHE and AMPHION. Sold 29.4.1784.

ALBACORE Sloop 16, 361bm, 105 x 28 ft. Randall, Rotherhithe 4.1793. Sold 1802.

ALBACORE Sloop 18, 370bm, 106½ x 28 ft. Hillhouse, Bristol 10.5.1804. Sold 14.12.1815.

ALBACORE Schooner, 37bm, 44 x 15 ft. Bermuda 1828. Sold 1832.

ALBACORE Wood S. gunboat 'Albacore' class. White 3.4.1856. Tank vessel 1874; hulk 1882. BU 6.1885 at Bermuda.

ALBACORE Composite S. gunboat 560 tons, 135 x 26 ft, 2-5in, 2-4in. Laird 13.1.1883. Sold 18.5.1906.

ALBACORE Destroyer 440 tons, 215 x 21 ft, 3-12pdr, 2-TT. Palmer 19.9.1906 and purchased 3.1909.

Sold 1.8.1919 T.R. Sales.

ALBACORE Minesweeper, 'Algerine' class. Harland & Wolff 2.4.1942. Arrived 9.9.63 Smith & Houston, Port Glasgow to BU.

ALBAN Schooner 10, 111bm. Bermuda 1806. In Danish hands 25.5.10 to 11.5.11. Wrecked 18.12.1812 off Aldeburgh.

ALBAN Schooner 14, 253bm, 94½ x 24½ ft. American WILLIAM BAYARD captured 12.3.1813 by WARSPITE. BU 18.2.1822.

ALBAN Wood pad. vessel (ex-brig-sloop), 294bm, 110 x 25 ft, 4-18pdr, 2-18pdr carr. Deptford DY 27.12.1826. Rebuilt as 405bm. BU 5.1860.

ALBAN Wood S. gunvessel, 'Philomel' class. Deptford DY laid down 1.10.1860, cancelled 12.12.1863.

ALBANAISE Brig-sloop 14, 238bm. French, captured 3.6.1800 by PHOENIX off Cape Feno. Handed over 23.11.1800 to the Spanish at Malaga by mutineers and returned to French navy.

ALBANY Sloop 14, 270bm, 91 x 26 ft. Darby, Gosport 23.3.1745. Captured 7.7.1746 by the French off N. America.

ALBANY (see TAVISTOCK of 1744)

ALBANY (ex-American *Rittenhouse*) Purchased 1776. BU 1780.

ALBATROSS Brig-sloop 16, 366bm, 96 x 30 ft. Ross, Rochester 30.12.1795. Sold 1807 in the East Indies.

ALBATROSS Survey schooner 64bm. Purchased 1826. Sold 30.8.1833 Mr Ledger.

ALBATROSS Brig 16, 484bm, 105 x 33 ft, 16-32pdr. Portsmouth DY 28.3.1842. BU 19.5.1860.

ALBATROSS Wood S.sloop 695bm, 185 x 28½ ft, 2-68pdr, 2-32pdr. Chatham DY laid down 1862, cancelled 12.12.1863.

ALBATROSS Compos.S.sloop 940 tons, 160 x 31 ft, 2-7in, 2-64pdr. Chatham DY 27.8.1873. BU 2.1889 at Chatham.

ALBATROSS Destroyer 430 tons, 228 x 21 ft, 1-12pdr, 5-6pdr, 2-TT. Thornycroft, Chiswick 19.7.1898. Sold 7.6.20 J.W. Houston.

ALBATROSS Seaplane carrier (RAN) 4,800 tons, 422 x 61 ft, 4-4.7in.9-A/C. Cockatoo DY 21.2.1928. To RN 1938; repair ship 1942. Sold 19.8.46 renamed *Pride of Torquay*.

ALBATROSS Four vessels hired during 1914-15.

ALBEMARLE Ship in service 1664.

ALBEMARLE Fireship 6,164bm. Purchased 1667. Expended 1667.

ALBEMARLE 2nd Rate 90, 1,376bm, 162 x 44½ ft. Betts, Harwich 1680. Renamed UNION 29.12.1709; rebuilt 1726 as 1578bm. BU 11.1749 at Chatham.

ALBEMARLE 6th Rate 28, 543bm, 125 x 32 ft. French MENAGERE captured 18.12.1779. Sold 1.6.1784.

ALBEMARLE Battleship 14,000 tons, 405 x 75½ ft, 4-12in, 12-6in. Chatham DY 5.3.1901. Sold 19.11.19 Cohen, Swansea.

ALBERNI Corvette (RCN), 'Flower' class. Yarrow, Esquimalt 22.8.1940. Sunk 21.8.44 by mine in the Channel.

ALBERT Iron pad. troopship, 459bm, 134 x 37 ft, 3 guns. Laird 9.1840. Wrecked 13.7.1843; salved and transferred 1.3.1845 to the Gambia government.

ALBERT Gunvessel (Australian) 350 tons, 115 x 25 ft, 1-8 in, 1-6 in, 2-9pdr. Armstrong Mitchell 1883. Sold circa 1896.

ALBERTA Wood pad. yacht, 370bm, 391 tons, 160 x 22½ ft. Pembroke Dock 3.10.1863. BU 1912 at Portsmouth.

ALBION 3rd Rate 74, 1,662bm, 168 x 46 ft. Deptford DY 16.5.1763. Floating battery 1794. Wrecked 26.4.1797 in the Swin.

ALBION Armed ship 22, 393bm, 103 x 30 ft. Hired 1793 to 9.94 and purchased 1798. Sold 1803 at Sheerness.

ALBION 3rd Rate 74, 1,743bm, 175 x 48½ ft. Perry, Blackwall 17.6.1802. Harbour service 7.31. BU 6.1836 at Deptford.

ALBION 2nd Rate 90, 3,111bm, 204 x 60 ft, 8-8in, 4-68pdr, 78-32pdr. Plymouth DY 6.9.1842. Undocked 21.5.1861 as screw ship 3,117bm. BU 1884.

ALBION Battleship 12,950 tons, 390 x 74 ft, 4-12 in, 12-6in. Thames Iron Works 21.6.1898. Sold 11.12.19 Ward, Morecambe.

ALBION A/C carrier 22,000 tons, 650 x 90 ft, 32-40mm, 50-A/C. Swan Hunter 6.5.1947; commando carrier 8.62. Sold 9.7.73, resold 11.73, BU Faslane.

ALBION Cutter hired 1803-12, two vessels requis. WW.I.

ALBRIGHTON Destroyer, 'Hunt' class type III. J. Brown 11.10.1941. Sold 11.57 W. German navy, renamed RAULE 9.4.59.

ALBUERA Destroyer 2,380 tons, 355 x 40 ft, 5-4.5 in, 8-40mm, 10-TT. Vickers Armstrong, Tyne 28.8.1945. Not completed; used as target. BU 11.50 Ward, Inverkeithing.

ALBURY Minesweeper, later 'Hunt' class. Ailsa 21.11.1918. Sold 13.3.47 Dohmen & Habets, Liege.

ALCASTON Coastal minesweeper, 'Ton' class. Thornycroft 5.1.1953. Renamed SNIPE (RAN) 30.5.61.

ALCESTE 5th Rate 32, 932bm, 145 x 39 ft. French captured 29.8.1793 at Toulon and transferred to the Sardinians. Recaptured by the French 1794 and again captured 18.6.1799 by a squadron in the Mediterranean. Sold 5.1802.

ALCESTE 5th Rate 38, 1,101bm, 152½ x 40 ft. French MINERVE captured 25.9.1806 by a squadron off Rochefort. Wrecked 18.2.1817 in the China Sea.

ALCESTIS Submarine 1945 'A' class. Cammell Laird. Cancelled 1945.

ALCIDE 3rd Rate 64, 1,375bm, 159 x 45 ft. French captured 6.6.1755. Sold 27.5.1772.

ALCIDE 3rd Rate 74, 1,625bm, 168 x 47 ft. Deptford DY 30.7.1779. BU 4.1817.

ALCIDE Submarine 1945 'A' class. Vickers Armstrong, Barrow, 12.4.1945. Sold Draper & Sons 18.6.74, BU at Hull.

ALCMENE 5th Rate 32, 731bm, 131 x 35½ ft. French captured 21.10.1779 in the W. Indies. Sold 17.8.1784.

ALCMENE 5th Rate 32, 803bm, 135 x 36½ ft. Graham, Harwich 8.11.1794. Wrecked 29.4.1809 off Nantes.

ALCMENE (see JEWEL of 1809).

ALDBOROUGH Ketch 10, 100bm. Johnson, Aldborough 6.5.1691. Accidentally blown up 17.8.1696.

ALDBOROUGH 6th Rate 20, 288bm, 94 x 27 ft. Johnson, Blackwall 6.3.1706. Rebuilt 1727 as 374bm. BU 3.1743 Deptford.

ALDBOROUGH 6th Rate 24,506bm, 112 x 32 ft. Okill, Liverpool 16.3.1743. Sold 28.11.1749 at Deptford.

ALDBOROUGH 6th Rate 20, 440bm, 108 x 30½ ft. Perry, Blackwall 15.5.1756. BU 9.1777.

ALDBOROUGH (see LEAMINGTON)

ALDENHAM Destroyer, 'Hunt' class type III. Cammell Laird 27.8.1941. Sunk 14.12.44 by mine in the Adriatic.

ALDERNEY Bomb 8, 263bm, 90½ x 26 ft. Woolwich DY 29.3.1735. Hulked

2.1741 in Jamaica.

ALDERNEY (ex-SQUIRREL renamed 11.2.1742) 6th Rate 24, 504bm, 112 x 32 ft. Reed, Hull 18.3.1743. Sold 26.6.1749.

ALDERNEY Sloop 12, 235bm, 88½ x 25 ft. Snook, Saltash 5.2.1757. Sold 1.5.1783.

ALDERNEY Submarine 1945 'A' class. Vickers Armstrong, Barrow 25.6.1945. BU 8.72 at Cairnryan.

ALDINGTON (ex-PITTINGTON) Coastal M/S. Camper & Nicholson 15.9.1955. Sold Ghana 1964, renamed EJURA.

ALECTO Fireship 12, 432bm, 109 x 30 ft. King, Dover 26.5.1781. Sold 1802.

ALECTO Wood pad. sloop, 796bm, 164 x 32½ ft. Chatham DY 7.9.1839. BU 11.1865 Castle, Thames.

ALECTO Compos. pad. vessel 620 tons, 2 guns. Westwood Bailey, Poplar 18.4.1882. Sold 12.10.1899 at Sierra Leone.

ALECTO Depot ship 935 tons, 190 x 32½ ft. Laird 29.8.1911. Sold 7.7.1949; BU at Llanelly.

ALERT Cutter 8 in service 1753-54.

ALERT Cutter 10, 133bm, 69 x 26 ft. Ladd, Dover 24.6.1777. Became a sloop 10.77. Captured 17.7.1778 by the French in the Channel.

ALERT Cutter 10, 202bm, 78 x 25 ft. Dover 1778. Captured 10.1780 by the French in the Bay of Biscay.

ALERT Brig-sloop 14, 205bm, 78½ x 25 ft. King, Dover 1.10.1779. Sold 2.10.1792 at Deptford.

ALERT Schooner 4, 88bm. Purchased 1790. BU 1799.

ALERTE Brig-sloop 14, 248bm, 80 x 24 ft. French, captured 8.1793 at Toulon. Retaken 18.12.1793 and burnt at Toulon.

ALERT Sloop 16, 365bm, 105 x 28 ft. Randall, Rotherhithe 8.10.1793. Captured 5.1794 by the French UNITE off the coast of Ireland.

ALERT Brig-sloop 8 (Indian), 85bm. Bombay DY 1795.

ALERT (ex-collier *Oxford*) 393bm, 105 x 29 ft, 16-18pdr carr. Purchased 5.1804. Captured 13.8.1812 by the American ESSEX off N.

America. ALAART Sloop 16, 306bm, 94½ x 27½ ft, 16-24pdr carr. Danish, captured 1807. Retaken 10.8.1809 by the Danes off the coast of Denmark (Was to have been renamed CASSANDRA.)

ALERT Brig-sloop, 'Cruizer' class, 388bm. Pitcher, Northfleet

14.7.1813. Sold 11.1832 Cristall, Rotherhithe.

ALERT Packet brig 8, 358bm, 95 x 30 ft, 8-18pdr. Bottomley, Rotherhithe 24.9.1835. BU 5.1851.

ALERT Brig 8. Ex-slaver captured 1848 by BONETTA. Sold 1850.

ALERT Wood S. sloop, 751bm, 160 x 32 ft, 17-32pdr. Pembroke Dock 20.5.1856. Survey ship 8.78. Given to American research society 1884.

ALERT Sloop 960 tons, 180 x 32 ft, 6-4in, 4-3pdr. Sheerness DY 28.12.1894. Lent Basra civil authorities 1906; sold 12.1.26 at Basra as pilot vessel. BU 10.49.

ALERT (see ACUTE of 1942)

ALERT (see DUNDRUM BAY)

ALERT (see LOYAL GOVERNOR)

ALERT 3 cutters hired 1796-1814; 3 vessels requis. WW.II.

ALEXANDER Fireship 12,150bm. Captured 1688. Accidentally burnt 11.6.1689.

ALEXANDER 3rd Rate 74, 1,621bm, 169 x 47 ft. Deptford DY 8.10.1778. Hulk 1805. BU 11.1819. (Was in French hands 11.94 to 6.95.)

ALEXANDER Storeship in service 1788 to 1790.

ALEXANDER Schooner 6,125bm, Purchased 1796. Sold 1802.

ALEXANDRE 2nd Rate 80, 2,231bm. French, captured 6.2.1806 by the fleet off San Domingo. Harbour service 1811. Sold 16.5.1822.

ALEXANDER Transport (NZ government). Purchased 11.1864. Wrecked 8.8.1865 near Taranaki, NZ.

ALEXANDER Icebreaker 6,000 tons. Russian ALEXANDR NEVSKI seized 1917. Returned 1919 to the Russian government.

ALEXANDER Discovery vessel 1818-1819.

ALEXANDRA (ex-SUPERB renamed 4.3.1874) Battleship 9,490 tons, 325 x 64 ft, 2-11in. MLR, 10-10in. MLR, 6-64pdr. Chatham DY 7.4.1875. Sold 6.10.1908 Garnham.

ALEXANDRA S. yacht 2,050 tons, 275 x 40 ft, 2-7pdr. Inglis 30.5.1907. Sold 5.25, renamed *Prince Olaf*.

ALEXANDRA four vessels hired 1914/18.

ALEXANDRIA 5th Rate 38, 902bm, 144½ x 38 ft. French REGENEREE captured 2.9.1801 by the fleet at Alexandria. BU 4.1804.

ALEXANDRIA Tender in service 1802 to 1803.

ALEXANDRIA 5th Rate 32 (fir-built),

662bm, 127 x 34 ft. Portsmouth DY 18.2.1806. BU 7.1818.

ALEXANDRIA Frigate (RCN), 'River' class. Montreal, ordered 1943, cancelled 12.43.

ALFRED A. ship 20, 440bm. American, captured 9.3.1778. Sold 1782.

ALFRED 3rd Rate 74, 1,638bm, 169 x 47 ft. Chatham DY 22.10.1778. BU 5.1814.

ALFRED (see ASIA of 1811)

ALFRED Iron S. storeship, 617bm, 170 x 27½ ft. Purchased 6.1.1855. Renamed ABUNDANCE 2.1855; sold 1856.

ALFRED Brig hired 1793.

ALFRISTON Coastal M/S 'Ton' class. Thornycroft 29.4.1953. Renamed WARSASH 5.54; ALFRISTON 1958; KILMOREY 1961-75.

ALGERINE Cutter 10, 197bm. King, Upnor 3.3.1810. Wrecked 20.5.1813 in the W. Indies.

ALGERINE Cutter 14, (see TIGRESS of 1808).

ALGERINE Brig-sloop 10, 'Cherokee' class. Deptford DY 10.6.1823. Foundered 9.1.1826 in the Mediterranean.

ALGERINE Brig-sloop 10, 'Cherokee' class. Chatham DY 1.8.1829. Sold 30.4.1844 J. Ledger.

ALGERINE Wood S. gunvessel, 299bm, 126 x 23 ft, 1 - 10in.MLR. Pitcher, Northfleet 24.2.1857. Sold 2.4.1872 at Hong Kong; became mercantile *Algerine* and BU 1894.

ALGERINE Compos. S. gunvessel 835 tons, 157 x 29½ ft, 2-5in, 2-64pdr. Harland & Wolf 6.11.1880. Sold 10.5.1892.

ALGERINE Sloop 1,050 tons, 185 x 33 ft, 6-4in, 4-3pdr. Devonport DY 6.6.1895. Sold 11.4.1919 as salvage vessel.

ALGERINE Minesweeper, 'Algerine' class. Harland & Wolf 22.12.1941. Sunk 15.11.42 by Italian S/M AS-CIANGHI off Bougie.

ALGIERS 5th Rate 32, 344bm, Captured 1671. Wrecked 1673.

ALGIERS 1st Rate 110, 3,099bm. Pembroke Dock, ordered 1833, cancelled 1848.

ALGIERS Screw 2nd Rate 90, 3,340bm, 219 x 60 ft. Devonport DY 26.1.1854. Sold 26.2.1870 Cooper Scott.

ALGIERS (see ANSON of 1860)

ALGIERS (see TRIUMPH of 1870)

ALGOMA Corvette (RCN), 'Flower' class. Port Arthur SY 17.12.1940. Sold Venezuelan navy 1946, renamed CONSTITUCION.

ALGONQUIN (see VALENTINE of 1943)

ALGONQUIN Escort (RCN) 3,551 tons. Davie SB 23.4.1971.

ALICE Minesweeper, 'Catherine' class. Gen. Eng., Alameda 12.12.1942 for the RN but retained by the USN.

ALICE Tug 1916-25; Yacht 1941-46; Tug built 1961.

ALICE & FRANCIS Fireship 6, 266bm, Purchased 1672. Expended 28.5.1672.

ALISMA Corvette, 'Flower' class. Harland & Wolff 17.12.1940. Sold 1947, became mercantile *Laconia*.

ALKMAAR 4th Rate 54, 1,041bm, 142½ x 41 ft. Dutch, captured 11.10.1797 at Camperdown. Sold 30.11.1815.

ALLEGIANCE Sloop 14. American KING GEORGE captured 1779. Captured 6.8.1782 by the French.

ALLEPIN Fireship 6, 233bm. Purchased 1666. Foundered 1667.

ALLIANCE Storeship 20, 697bm, 130½ x 35 ft. Dutch ALLIANTE captured 22.8.1795 off the coast of Norway. Sold 5.1802.

ALLIANCE Submarine 1945 'A' class. Vickers Armstrong, Barrow 28.7.1945. Museum ship, Gosport from 6.81.

ALLIANCE Tug 1910-41; Tug requis. 1941-42.

ALLIGATOR Sloop 14, 300bm, 96½ x 26½ ft. Fisher, Liverpool 11.11.1780. Captured 26.6.1782 by the French La FEE.

ALLIGATOR 6th Rate 28, 599bm, 121 x 34 ft. Jacobs, Sandgate 18.4.1787. Sold 21.7.1814.

ALLIGATOR 6th Rate 28, 500bm, 114 x 32 ft. Cochin 29.3.1821. Harbour service 1846. Sold 30.10.1865 at Hong Kong.

ALLIGATOR Wood S. corvette 1,857bm, 225 x 43 ft. Woolwich DY laid down 1.11.1860, cancelled 12.12.1863.

ALLIGATOR Tug 1896-1919; 2 Tugs WW.II.

ALLINGTON CASTLE (ex-ALINGTON CASTLE renamed 6.1944, ex- AMARYLLIS renamed 5.43) Corvette, 'Castle' class. Fleming & Ferguson 29.2.1944. Arrived 20.12.58 Young, Sunderland to BU.

ALNWICK CASTLE Corvette, 'Castle' class. G. Brown 23.5.1944. Arrived 12.58 King, Gateshead to BU.

ALONZO Sloop 16, 384bm, 102 x 30 ft, 14-24pdr can., 2-18pdr. Purchased 1.1801. Harbour service 1817. Scuttled 2.1842 outside Leith harbour.

ALPHEA Schooner 10, 112bm, 68 x 20 ft, 8-18pdr carr., 2-6pdr. Bermuda 1806. Sunk 10.9.1813 in action with French privateer RENARD.

ALPHEUS 5th Rate 36 (pine-built), 949bm, 143½ x 38½ ft. Wallis, Thames 6.4.1814. Sold 10.9.1817 Mr Bailey.

ALRESFORD Minesweeper, later 'Hunt' class. Ailsa 17.1.1919. Sold 13.3.47 Dohmen & Habets, Liege.

ALTHAM Inshore M/S 'Ham' class. Camper & Nicholson 2.12.1952. Malaysian naval SRI JOHORE 1.4.59.

ALTON (see ARBROATH)

ALTON CASTLE Corvette, 'Castle' class. Fleming & Ferguson. Cancelled 12.1943.

ALVERTON Coastal M/S, 'Ton' class. Camper & Nicholson 18.11.1952. Renamed THAMES 8.6.54; ALVERTON 2.62. Sold Eire 11.70, renamed BANBA.

ALVINGTON Frigate (RCN), 'River' class. Vickers, Montreal 15.4.1944. Renamed ROYAL MOUNT 6.44. BU 11.47.

ALYSSUM Sloop, 'Arabis' class. Earle 5.11.1915. Sunk 18.3.17 by mine SW of Ireland.

ALYSSUM Corvette, 'Flower' class. G. Brown 3.3.1941. Renamed ALYSSE 8.41 on loan to the Free-French; sunk 8.2.42 by 'U.654' in the western Atlantic.

AMARANTHE Brig-sloop 14, 290bm, 86 x 28 ft. French AMARANTE captured 31.12.1796 by DIAMOND off Alderney. Wrecked 25.10.1799 off the coast of Florida.

AMARANTHE 6th Rate 28, 498bm, 112½ x 31½ ft. Dutch VENUS captured 28.8.1799 in the Texel. BU 3.1804 at Deptford.

AMARANTHE Brig-sloop 18, 'Cruizer' class, 386bm. Dudman, Deptford 20.11.1804. Sold 12.10.1815.

AMARANTHUS Corvette, 'Flower' class. Fleming & Ferguson 17.10.1940. Sold 1946.

AMARYLLIS Sloop, 'Arabis' class. Earle 9.12.1915. Sold 30.1.23 Fryer, Sunderland.

AMARYLLIS (see ALLINGTON CASTLE)

AMAZON 6th Rate 26, 471bm, 115 x 31 ft. French PANTHERE captured 1745. Sold 10.1763.

AMAZON 5th Rate 32, 687bm, 126 x 35 ft. Wells, Rotherhithe 24.5.1773. BU 6.1794 at Plymouth.

AMAZON 5th Rate 36, 934bm, 143 x 38 ft. Wells, Rotherhithe 4.7.1795. Wrecked 14.1.1797 on Ile de Bas, French coast.

AMAZON 5th Rate 38, 1,038bm, 150 x 39½ ft. Woolwich DY 18.5.1799. BU 5.1817 at Plymouth.

AMAZON 5th Rate 46, 1,078bm, 151 x 40½ ft. Deptford DY 15.8.1821. 24-gun 6th Rate 12.1844. Sold 9.1863 Lethbridge.

AMAZON Wood S. sloop, 1,040bm, 187 x 36 ft, 2-6in, 2-64pdr. Pembroke Dock 23.5.1865. Sunk 10.7.1866 in collision in the Channel.

AMAZON Destroyer 970 tons, 280 x 26½ ft, 2-4in, 2-TT. Thornycroft 29.7.1908. Sold 22.10.1919 Ward, Preston.

AMAZON Destroyer 1,330 tons, 312 x 31½ ft, 4-4.7 in, 1-3 in, 6-TT. Thornycroft 27.1.1926. Arrived 6.10.48 Troon to BU.

AMAZON Frigate 2,750 tons Vosper/Thornycroft 26.4.1971.

AMBERLEY CASTLE Corvette, 'Castle' class. Austin, Sunderland 27.11.1943. Became weather ship *Weather Adviser* 9.60.

AMBERWITCH Troopship (Indian) 1,010 tons, 175½ x 27 ft. Laird 1862. Sold circa 1890.

AMBLESIDE (see BEAUFORT of 1919).

AMBOYNA Brig-sloop 10, 180bm. Dutch HAERLEM captured 1796. BU 1802.

AMBROSE A. merchant cruiser 6,600 tons, 388 x 47½ ft. Hired and commissioned 10.12.1914. Purchased 20.10.15 and converted to depot ship; renamed COCHRANE 1.6.38. Sold 8.46 to BU. Arrived 13.11.46 Ward, Inverkeithing.

AMBUSCADE 5th Rate 40, 740bm, 132½ x 36 ft. French EMBUSCADE captured 21.4.1746. Sold 9.2.1762.

AMBUSCADE 5th Rate 32 684bm, 126½ x 35 ft. Adams, Deptford 17.9.1773. Captured 14.12.1798 by the French BAYONNAISE; recaptured 28.5.1803 as EMBUSCADE. BU 6.1810 at Deptford.

AMBUSCADE 5th Rate 40, 906bm, 143 x 37½ ft. French EMBUSCADE captured 12.10.1798 off the Donegal coast. Renamed SEINE 16.1.1804. BU 8.1813.

AMBUSCADE 5th Rate 38, 1,085bm, 152½ x 40 ft. French POMONE captured 29.11.1811 by ACTIVE & ALCESTE. BU 11.1812 at Woolwich.

AMBUSCADE 5th Rate 36, 1,284bm, 159 x 42 ft. Woolwich DY laid down

15.4.1830, renamed AMPHION 31.3.31 and launched 1846 as screw frigate.

AMBUSCADE Destroyer 935 tons, 266 x 27 ft, 3-4 in, 2-TT. J. Brown 25.1.1913. Sold 6.9.21 Petersen & Albeck.

AMBUSCADE Destroyer 1,170 tons, 307 x 31 ft, 4-4.7 in, 6-TT. Yarrow 15.1.1926. Sold 23.11.46, BU at Troon.

AMBUSCADE Frigate 2,750 tons. Yarrow 18.1.1973.

AMBUSH Gunboat 2. Purchased 1815 in the W. Indies. Sold 1815.

AMBUSH Submarine 1945 'A' class, Vickers Armstrong, Barrow 24.9.1945. Arrived Inverkeithing 5.7.71 to BU.

AMEER (ex-USS ALAZON BAY) Escort carrier laid down 1942 and retained by the USN as LISCOMBE BAY.

AMEER (ex-USS BAFFINS) Escort carrier 11,420 tons, 468½ x 69½ ft, 2-4 in, 16-40mm, 24-A/C, Seattle, Tacoma 18.10.1942. Returned to the USN 17.1.46 and sold as mercantile *Robin Kirk*.

AMELIA 5th Rate 38, 1,059bm, 151½ x 39½ ft. French PROSERPINE captured 13.6.1796 by DRYAD off Cape Clear. BU 12.1816.

AMELIA Wood S. gunboat, 'Albacore' class. White 19.5.1856. BU 10.1865 at Pembroke Dock.

AMELIA (see ARGUS of 1851).

AMELIA (ex-HAWK renamed 1888) 416 tons, 146 x 23 ft, 1-40pdr. Coastguard gunboat. Renamed COLLEEN 1905; COLLEEN OLD 1916; EMERALD 1918; CUCKOO 1918. Sold 10.8.22 Cove & Distinn.

AMELIA Minesweeper, 'Catherine' class. Gen. Eng., Alameda 9.1.1943 for the RN but retained by the USN.

AMERICA A. merchant in service 1650 to 1654.

AMERICA 5th Rate 44, 862bm, 139 x 37½ ft. Portsmouth, New England 4.5.1749. Renamed BOSTON 13.4.1756. Sold 13.9.1757.

AMERICA 4th Rate 60, 1,248bm, 154 x 43 ft. Wells Stanton, Thames 21.5.1757. BU 7.1771.

AMERICA 3rd Rate 64, 1,370bm, 158 x 45 ft. Deptford DY 5.8.1777. Stranded 1800, salved and became a prison ship; lent Transport Board 1804. BU 1807.

AMERICA 3rd Rate 74, 1,884bm, 182½ x 48½ ft. French AMERIQUE captured 1.6.1794 off Ushant at the battle of the 'First of June'. Renamed

IMPETUEUX 1795. BU 12.1813.

AMERICA 3rd Rate 74, 1,758bm, 176 x 48½ ft. Perry, Blackwall 21.4.1810. 4th Rate 3.27; target 3.64. BU 10.1867.

AMERSHAM (see COLLINSON).

AMERTON Coastal M/S, 'Ton' class. Camper & Nicholson 2.1953. Renamed MERSEY 1954; AMERTON 10.59. BU Bo'ness 8.71.

AMETHYST 5th Rate 36, 1,029bm, 150 x 39 ft. French PERLE captured 29.8.1793 at Toulon. Wrecked 29.12.1795 near Alderney.

AMETHYST 5th Rate 36, 1,046bm, 150 x 39 ft. Deptford DY 22.4.1799. Wrecked 16.2.1811 in Plymouth Sound; wreck BU 4.1811.

AMETHYST 6th Rate 26, 923bm, 131 x 41 ft. Plymouth DY 7.12.1844. Sold 16.10.1869 for use as cable vessel.

AMETHYST Wood S. corvette 1,970 tons, 220 x 37 ft, 14-64pdr. Devonport DY 10.4.1873. Sold 11.1887 G. Pethwick.

AMETHYST 3rd class cruiser 3,000 tons, 360 x 40 ft, 12-4 in, 8-3pdr. Armstrong 5.11.1903. Sold 1.10.20 Towers, Milford Haven.

AMETHYST Sloop 1,350 tons, 283 x 38½ ft, 6-4 in, 12-20mm. Stephen 7.5.1943. Arrived 19.1.57 Demmelweek & Redding, Plymouth to BU.

AMETHYST (see WAVENEY).

AMETHYST 2 vessels requis. WW.I; Trawler 1935-40.

AMFITRITE (see under AMPHITRITE)

AMHERST Corvette, 'Flower' class (RCN). St John DD 4.12.1940. To Venezuelan navy 1946 as FEDERACION.

AMITY 36-gun ship, 375bm. Purchased 1650. Sold 1667.

AMITY Fireship 6, 252bm. Purchased 1673. Sunk 1673 as a foundation at Sheerness.

AMITY Fireship 10, 100bm, 67½ x 19 ft. Purchased 4.1794. Sold circa 1800.

AMITIE Schooner 14. French, captured 1804. Expended 3.10.1804 as fireship at Boulogne.

AMITY Minesweeper, 'Catherine' class. Gen. Eng., Alameda 10.2.1943 for the RN but retained by the USN; renamed DEFENSE.

AMOKURA (see SPARROW of 1889).

AMPHION 5th Rate 32, 680bm, 126 x 35 ft. Chatham DY 21.12.1780. Blown up 22.9.1796 in the Hamoaze.

AMPHION 5th Rate 32, 914bm, 144 x 37½ ft. Betts, Mistleythorn

19.3.1798. Sunk 11.1820 as break-water at Woolwich; wreck sold 9.1823 Joiliffe & Banks.

AMPHION (ex-AMBUSCADE renamed 31.3.1831) Wood S. frigate, 1,474bm, 177 x 43½ ft. Woolwich DY 14.1.1846. Sold 12.10.1863 Williams. (see AMBUSCADE)

AMPHION 2nd class cruiser 4,300 tons, 300 x 46 ft, 10-6 in. Pembroke Dock 13.10.1883. Sold 15.5.1906 King, Garston.

AMPHION Scout cruiser 3,440 tons, 385 x 41½ ft, 10-4 in. Pembroke Dock 4.12.1911. Sunk 6.8.1914 by mine in the North Sea.

AMPHION Cruiser, 6,908 tons, 530 x 57 ft, 8-6 in, 8-4 in. Portsmouth DY 26.7.1934. Renamed PERTH (RAN) 6.39. Sunk 1.3.42 by torpedoes in the Sunda Straits action.

AMPHION (ex-ANCHORITE) Submarine 1945 'A' class. Vickers Armstrong, Barrow 31.8.1944. Arrived Inverkeithing 6.7.71 to BU.

AMPHION (see ANCHORITE of 1945).

AMPHITRITE 6th Rate 24, 513bm, 114 x 32 ft. Deptford DY 28.5.1778. Wrecked 30.1.1794 in the Mediterranean.

AMPHITRITE (see POMONA of 1778).

AMPHITRITE 5th Rate 40, 1,183bm, 151 x 41½ ft. Dutch, captured 30.8.1799 in the Texel. Renamed IMPERIEUSE 1801. BU 4.1805.

AMFITRITE 5th Rate 38, 1,036bm, 150 x 40 ft. Spanish, captured 25.11.1804 by DONEGAL off Cadiz. Renamed BLANCHE 3.12.1805. Wrecked 4.3.1807 off Ushant.

AMPHITRITE 5th Rate, 1,064bm, 150 x 49 ft, Bombay DY 14.4.1816. Lent 14.7.1862 to contractors at Plymouth. BU 1.1875 at Devonport.

AMPHITRITE 1st class cruiser 11,000 tons, 435 x 69 ft, 16-6 in, 14-12pdr. Vickers Maxim, Barrow 5.1.1898. Minelayer 1917 (4-6 in, 1-12pdr, 354 mines). Sold 12.4.1920 Ward, Milford Haven.

AMPHITRITE. Ship 328bm. Hired 1793-94.

AMSTERDAM 5th Rate 32, 849bm, 140½ x 37½ ft. Dutch PROSERPINE captured 4.5.1804 at Surinam. Sold 9.8.1815.

ANACONDA Brig-sloop 18, 387bm, 102½ x 29 ft, 18-9pdr. American privateer captured 11.7.1814 in Chesapeake Bay. Sold 5.7.1815 in Jamaica.

ANACONDA S.S.V. (RAN) 316 tons 5.1945. Transferred Army 12.45.

ANACREON Big-sloop 16, 151bm, 76 x 21½ ft. French, captured 7.1799. Sold 1802.

ANACREON Sloop 16 in service from 8.1804 to 6.1805.

ANACREON Sloop 16, 427bm, 110 x 29½ ft Laid down by Sutton, Ringmore 7.1809, frames to Plymouth DY 8.1810, launched 1.5.1813. Foundered 28.2.1814 in the Channel.

ANACREON Schooner built 1815. Transferred to Customs 1816.

ANCHORITE (see AMPHION of 1944)

ANCHORITE (ex-AMPHION) Submarine 1945 'A' class Vickers Armstrong, Barrow 22.1.1946. Arrived Troon 24.8.70 to BU.

ANCHORITE Mooring vessel 1916-44.

ANCHUSA Sloop, 'Anchusa' class. Armstrong 21.4.1917. Sunk 16.7.18 by 'U.54' off the north coast of Ireland.

ANCHUSA Corvette, 'Flower' class. Harland & Wolff 15.1.1941. Sold 1946, renamed *Silverlord*.

ANDREW Carrack captured 24.8.1417, foundered 15.8.1420.

ANDREW (see ST ANDREW of 1622)

ANDREW Submarine 1945 'A' class. Vickers Armstrong, Barrow 6.4.1946. Arrived Davies & Cann, Plymouth 4.5.77 to BU.

ANDROMACHE 5th Rate 32, 683bm, 126 x 35 ft. Barnard, Deptford 17.11.1781. BU 9.1811.

ANDROMACHE (see PRINCESS CHARLOTTE of 1799)

ANDROMACHE 6th Rate 28, 709bm, 130 x 35 ft. Pembroke Dock 27.8.1832. Powder hulk 1854. BU completed 3.1875 at Devonport.

ANDROMACHE 2nd class cruiser 3,400 tons, 300 x 44 ft, 2-6in, 6-4.7in. Chatham DY 14.8.1890. Minelayer 9.1909. Arrived 8.20 Castle Plymouth to BU.

ANDROMACHE Submarine 1945 'A' class. Vickers Armstrong, Barrow. Cancelled 1945.

ANDROMEDA 6th Rate 28, 609bm, 121 x 36 ft. Fabian, E. Cowes 18.11.1777. Lost in a hurricane 10.1780 off Martinique, W. Indies.

ANDROMEDA 5th Rate 32, 721bm, 129 x 35½ ft. Sutton, Liverpool 21.4.1784. Harbour service in 1808. BU 1811.

ANDROMEDA 6th Rate 24, 812bm, 130 x 37½ ft. 22-32pdr carr., 2-12pdr. American HANNIBAL captured 31.1.1812. Sold 18.4.1816.

ANDROMEDA (see NIMROD of 1828)

ANDROMEDA 5th Rate 46, 1,215bm,

159 x 42 ft. Bombay DY 6.1.1829. Sold 24.12.1863 Barnett & Wake.

ANDROMEDA 1st class cruiser 11,000 tons, 435 x 69 ft, 16-6in, 14-12 pdr. Pembroke Dock 30.4.1897. Renamed POWERFUL II, training ship 23.9.1913; IMPREGNABLE II 11.19; DEFIANCE 20.1.31. Arrived 14.8.56 at Burgt, Belgium to BU.

ANDROMEDA Sloop, 'Anchusa' class. Swan Hunter launched 6.1917 as ANDROMEDE (French navy).

ANDROMEDA Frigate, 'Leander' class. Portsmouth DY 24.5.1967.

ANDROMEDA Two hired vessels 1941-45.

ANEMONE Sloop, 'Acacia' class. Swan Hunter 30.6.1915. Sold 6.9.22 Marple & Gillott.

ANEMONE Corvette, 'Flower' class. Blyth 22.4.1940. Sold 1949, renamed *Pelikan*.

ANGEL Bomb 6, 132bm, 60 x 21 ft. Purchased 1694. Sold 1697.

ANGELICA Schooner 4 (Canadian lakes). Detroit 1771. Wrecked 12.1783.

ANGLER Wood S. gunboat, 'Cheerful' class. Devonport DY 8.3.1856. BU 1.1869 at Haslar.

ANGLER Destroyer 335 tons, 210 x 19½ ft, 1-12pdr, 5-6pdr, 2-TT. Thornycroft, Chiswick 2.2.1897. Sold 20.5.1920 Ward, Milford Haven.

ANGLESEA 4th Rate 44, 620bm, 125 x 33 ft. Plymouth DY 1694 (the first ship built at Plymouth DY). Rebuilt Chatham 1725 as 5th rate 601 bm. Sunk 1742 as breakwater at Sheerness.

ANGLESEA 5th Rate 44, 711bm, 126 x 36 ft. Blaydes, Hull 3.11.1742. Captured 28.3.1745 by the French APOLLON.

ANGLESEA 5th Rate 44, 714bm, 126 x 36½ ft. Gorrill & Parks, Liverpool. 3.12.1746. Storeship 1759. Sunk 8.1764 as breakwater in Mounts Cove.

ANGLESEY Patrol boat 925 tons. Hall Russell 18.10.1978.

ANGUILLA (ex-HALLOWELL) Frigate, 'Colony' class. Walsh Kaiser, Providence R.I. 14.7.1943. Returned to the USN 5.46.

ANN & CHRISTOPHER Fireship 6, 266bm, Purchased 1672. Sold 1686.

ANN & JUDITH Fireship 6, 264bm. Purchased 1672. Lost in action 1672.

ANNA Storeship 8, 400bm. Hired 1739, purch. 1741. Scuttled 28.8.41 off Juan Fernandez Is. as unserviceable.

ANNA Schooner tender 12, 106bm, 73 x 19 ft, 12-12pdr carr. Purchased 1805. BU 1809.

ANNA TERESA Gunvessel ex-barge purchased 6.1797.

ANNAN Frigate, 'River' class. Vickers, Montreal 12.9.1942. Transferred 11.42 to the USN as NATCHEZ.

ANNAN Frigate, 'River' class. Hall Russell 29.12.1943. Lent RCN 13.6.44 to 21.6.45; sold Danish navy 27.11.45 as NIELS EBBESEN.

ANNAPOLIS (ex-USS MACKENZIE) Destroyer 1,060 tons, 309 x 30½ ft, 3-4in, 1-3in, 6-TT. Commissioned in RCN 2.10.1940. Training ship 1944. BU 1945 Boston Iron & Metal Co.

ANNAPOLIS Frigate (RCN), 2,335 tons. Halifax SY 27.4.1963.

ANNE Ballinger, 120bm. Southampton 1416. Sold 26.6.1424.

ANNE GALLANT Ship 140/160bm. Built 1512. Wrecked 1518.

ANNE GALLANT Galley 50, 300/450bm. Last listed in 1559.

ANNE ROYAL (see ARK ROYAL of 1587)

ANNE (see BRIDGEWATER of 1654)

ANNE Yacht, 100bm. Woolwich DY 1661. Sold 1686.

ANNE 3rd Rate 70, 1,051bm, 151 x 40 ft, 26-32pdr, 26-12pdr, 14-6 pdr, 4-3pdr. Chatham DY 1678. Burnt 6.7.1690 at the battle of Beachy Head.

ANNE Fireship purchased 1702.

ANNE GALLEY Fireship 8, 302bm, 98 x 26½ ft. Purchased 22.6.1739. Expended 11.2.1744 at Toulon.

ANNE A. Ship 14, 345bm, 104 x 28½ ft. Purchased 1798. Sold 1802.

ANNE Seaplane carrier 4,083 gross, 367 x 48 ft, 1-12pdr, 2-A/C. German mercantile *Aenne Rickmers* seized 1914 and renamed 5.8.15. Became fleet collier 29.1.18 and sold 1919.

ANNE Brig. 10, 120bm. Hired 1804-09; Seaplane carrier 1915-20. Yacht 1940-46.

ANSON 4th Rate 60, 1,197bm, 150 x 43 ft. Ewer, Bursledon 10.10.1747. Sold 25.6.1773.

ANSON Cutter 6, 95bm, 51 x 22 ft. Purchased 2.1763. Sold 15.7.1774.

ANSON 3rd Rate 64, 1,369bm, 159½ x 45 ft. Plymouth DY 4.9.1781. 44-gun ship 1794. Wrecked 29.12.1807 in Mounts Bay.

ANSON 3rd Rate 74, 1,742bm, 175½ x 48½ ft. Steemson, Paul near Hull 11.5.1812. Harbour service 1.1831; convict ship in Tasmania 1844. BU

1851 at Hobart.

ANSON Screw ship 91, 3,336bm, 245 x 55½ ft. Woolwich DY 15.9.1860. Renamed ALGIERS 11.1.1883. BU 4.1904 by Castle.

ANSON Battleship 10,600 tons, 330 x 68½ ft, 4-13.5in, 6-6in, 12-6 pdr. Pembroke Dock 17.2.1886. Sold 13.7.1909 Clarkson, BU at Upnor.

ANSON Battlecruiser, sister to HOOD. Armstrong ordered 4.1916, cancelled 10.18.

ANSON (see DUKE of YORK)

ANSON (ex-JELLICOE renamed 2.1940) Battleship 35,000 tons, 700 x 103 ft, 10-14in, 16-5.25in. Swan Hunter 24.2.40. Arrived 17.12.57 at Faslane to BU.

ANSWER Galleon 21, 200bm, 5-9pdr, 8-6pdr, 2-4pdr, 6 small. Built 1590. Rebuilt Chatham DY 5.1604. Sold 1629.

ANSWER Submarine 1945 'A' class. Vickers Armstrong, Barrow. Cancelled 1945.

ANT Schooner 8, 86bm, 61 x 19 ft. French, captured 6.1797. Sold 23.3.1815.

ANT Cutter tender 4, 107bm, 71 x 21 ft. Woolwich DY 1815. To dockyard service 1817, later becoming R. Victoria Yard craft No 1. Sold 12.1.1869 Mr Hapgood.

ANT Wood S. gunboat, 'Cheerful' class. Devonport DY 22.3.1856. BU 2.1869 at Haslar.

ANT Gunboat, (NZ) ex-merchant purchased 1862. Sold 1864.

ANT Iron S. gunboat, 'Ant' class. Laird 14.8.1873. Boom defence 1917; target 1921. BU 6.26 Granton S. Bkg Co.

ANT Tender purchased 5.1913. 545 gross, 164½ x 33 ft. Murdoch & Murray 23.7.13. Sold 12.6.24 G. Nichol; renamed *Rangitoto*.

ANT 2 cutters hired 1803, 1808; 2 Trawlers 1915-19.

ANTAEUS Submarine 1945 'A' class. Vickers Armstrong, Barrow. Cancelled 1945.

ANTAGONIST Submarine 1945 'A' class. Vickers Armstrong, Barrow. Cancelled 1945.

ANTARES Minesweeper, 'Algerine' class. Redfern, Canada 15.8.1942, on lend-lease. Returned USN 1.47.

ANTARES Two trawlers WW.I.

ANTELOPE Galleon 38/44, 384bm, 4-9pdr, 13-6pdr, 8-4pdr, 13 small. Built 1546. Rebuilt 1577 and again in 1618 as 512bm. Burnt 1649 by Parliamentarians.

ANTELOPE 50-gun ship 828bm, Woolwich DY 1651. Wrecked 30.9.1652 off Jutland.

ANTELOPE (see PRESTON of 1653)

ANTELOPE 4th Rate 54, 684bm, 131½ x 34½ ft. Taylor, Rotherhithe 3.1703. Rebuilt Woolwich DY 1741 as 858bm, 134 x 38½ ft. Sold 30.10.1783.

ANTELOPE Sloop 14. Lost 30.7.1784 in a hurricane off Jamaica.

ANTELOPE Brig 14 (Indian), 199bm. Bombay DY 1793. Sold after 1830.

ANTELOPE 4th Rate 50, 1,107bm, 150 x 41 ft. Sheerness DY 10.11.1802. Troopship 1818; harbour service 1.1824. BU 7.1845.

ANTELOPE Schooner 14, 172bm. ex-*Firefly* ex-Spanish prize Purchased 1808. BU 1814.

ANTELOPE Iron pad. sloop, 650bm, 1,010 tons, 170 x 28 ft, 3 guns. Mare, Blackwall 25.7.1846. Sold 20.9.1883 at Malta.

ANTELOPE Torpedo gunboat 810 tons, 230 x 27 ft, 2-4.7in, 4-3pdr, 5-TT. Devonport DY 12.7.1893. Harbour service 1910. Sold 27.5.19 T.R. Sales.

ANTELOPE Destroyer 1,350 tons, 312 x 32 ft, 4-4.7in, 8-TT. Hawthorn Leslie 27.7.1929. Sold 1.46; BU by Hughes Bolckow, Blyth.

ANTELOPE Frigate 2,750 tons Vosper/Thornycroft 16.3.1972. Lost in Falklands operations 24.5.82.

ANTHONY Ship built 1417.

ANTHONY Ship in service 1588 to 1599.

ANTHONY BONAVENTURE 36-gun ship, 450bm. In service 1649. Captured 30.11.1652 by the Dutch.

ANTHONY Destroyer 1,350 tons, 312 x 32 ft, 4-4.7in, 8-TT. Scotts 24.4.1929. Sold 18.8.47; BU 5.48 at Troon.

ANTIGONISH Frigate (RCN). 'River' class. Yarrow, Esquimalt 10.2.44. Sold 10.46.

ANTIGUA Brig-sloop 14, 157bm, 71½ x 23½ ft. Ex-privateer purchased 4.6.1757. Sold 13.8.1763 in the W. Indies.

ANTIGUA Sloop 14 from 8.1779. Sold 12.1.1782.

ANTIGUA Prison ship 856bm, 145 x 37 ft. French privateer EGYPTIENNE captured 25.3.1804. BU 1816.

ANTIGUA Frigate, 'Colony' class. Walsh Kaiser 26.7.1943. Returned 5.46 USN.

ANTRIM Armoured cruiser 10,850 tons, 450 x 68½ ft, 4-7.5in, 6-6in, 2-12pdr. J. Brown 8.10.1903. Sold 19.12.22

Hughes Bolckow, arrived Blyth 3.23 to BU.

ANTRIM GM destroyer, 5,600 tons, 505 x 54 ft. Fairfield 19.10.1967. Handed over to Chile 25.6.84, renamed AL-MIRANTE COCHRANE.

ANZAC Destroyer leader 1,666 tons, 325 x 32 ft, 4-4in, 4-TT. Denny 11.1.1917. To RAN 21.3.19. Sold 8.8.35 Abrahams & Wilson, Redfern NSW to dismantle; hull scuttled 7.5.36.

ANZAC Submarine 1945 A class. Vickers Armstrong, Barrow. Cancelled 1945.

ANZAC Destroyer (RAN) 2,325 tons, 355 x 41 ft, 4-4.5in, 12-40mm, 8-TT. Williamstown DY 20.8.1948. Sold 24.11.75, BU Hong Kong.

ANZAC Trawler 1916 to 1919.

ANZIO (see LST.3003)

APELLES Brig-sloop 14, 251bm, 92 x 25½ ft. Woolwich DY 10.8.1808. Sold 15.2.1816.

APHIS River gunboat 645 tons, 230 x 36 ft, 2-6in, 1-3in. Ailsa 15.9.1915. Sold 1947 at Singapore.

APHRODITE Submarine 1945 'A' class, Vickers Armstrong, Barrow. Cancelled 1945.

APOLLO Storeship 20, 744bm, 127½ x 36½ ft, 16-9pdr, 4-6pdr. French, captured 3.5.1747. Wrecked 12.4.1749 off Madras.

APOLLO (see GLORY of 1763)

APOLLO 5th Rate 38, 984bm, 146 x 39 ft. Perry, Blackwall 18.3.1794. Wrecked 7.1.1799 on Haak Sand, Dutch coast.

APOLLO 5th Rate 36, 956bm, 145 x 38½ ft. Dudman, Deptford 16.8.1 799. Wrecked 2.4.1804 coast of Portugal.

APOLLO 5th Rate 38, 1,086bm, 154½ x 40 ft. Parsons, Bursledon 27.6.1805. Harbour service then troopship 4. 1846. BU 9.1856.

APOLLO 2nd class cruiser 3,400 tons, 300 x 44 ft, 2-6in, 6-4.7in, 8-6 pdr. Chatham DY 10.2.1891. Minelayer 8.1909. Arrived 8.20 Castle, Plymouth to BU.

APOLLO Cruiser 7,105 tons, 555 x 57 ft, 8-6in, 8-4in. Devonport DY 9.10.1934. To RAN as HOBART 14.10.38. Left Sydney 3.3.62 to BU in Japan.

APOLLO Minelayer 2,650 tons, 410 x 39 ft, 4-4.7in, 8-40mm, 100 mines. Hawthorn Leslie 5.4.1943. Arrived 11.62 Hughes Bolckow, Blyth to BU.

APOLLO Frigate 'Leander' class. Yarrow 15.10.1970.

APPLEBY CASTLE Corvette, 'Castle' class. Austin, Sunderland, Cancelled 12.1943.

APPLEDORE Minesweeper, later 'Hunt' class. Ailsa 15.8.1919. Sold 16.10.20, renamed *Kamlavati.*

APPLETON Coastal M/S, 'Ton' class. Goole SB 4.9.1952. Sold 24.9.72, BU at Neath 11.72.

APPROACH Submarine 1945 'A' class. Vickers Armstrong, Barrow. Cancelled 1945.

AQUARIUS Water tanker (RFA) 3,660 tons, 268 x 38 ft. Ex-*Hampstead* purchased 1902. Completed as depot ship 6.07. Sold 14.5.20 mercantile.

AQUILON 6th Rate 28, 599bm, 118½ x 34 ft. Inwood, Rotherhithe 24.5.1758. Sold 29.11.1776.

AQUILON 5th Rate 32, 724bm, 129 x 36 ft. Young & Woolcombe, Thames 23.11.1786. BU 9.1815.

ARAB Sloop 16, 424bm, 107 x 30 ft. French JEAN BART captured 29.3.1795 by CERBERUS and SANTA MARGARITA in the Channel. Wrecked 10.6.1796 on the Penmarcks.

ARAB Schooner 8, 86bm, 61 x 19 ft. French ARABE captured 6.1797. Renamed ANT 1798. Sold 23.3.1815.

ARAB 6th Rate 22, 505bm, 110 x 33 ft. French Le BRAVE captured 24.4.1798 by PHOENIX off Cape Clear. Sold 20.9.1810.

ARAB Brig-sloop 18, 'Cruizer' class 390bm. Pelham, Frindsbury 22.8.1812. Wrecked 18.12.1823 off Belmullet, Ireland.

ARAB Brig-sloop 16, 481bm, 105 x 33½ ft, 4-32pdr, 12-32pdr. carr. Chatham DY 31.3.1847. Became coastguard watch vessel No 18 24.5.1863. BU completed 1.6.1879 at Chatham.

ARAB Compos. S. sloop 720 tons, 150 x 28 ft, 1-7in.ML, 2-64pdr. Napier, Glasgow 13.10.1874. Rated gunvessel 1876. Sold 1889.

ARAB Destroyer 470 tons, 218 x 20 ft, 1-12pdr, 5-6pdr, 2-TT. Thomson 9.2.1901. Sold 23.7.19 Fryer, Sunderland.

ARABIS Sloop, 'Arabis' class. Henderson 6.11.1915. Sunk 10.2.16 by German TBs off the Dogger Bank.

ARABIS Corvette, 'Flower' class. Harland & Wolff 14.2.1940. Lent USN as SAUCY 30.4.42; returned to RN 1945 and renamed SNAPDRAGON. Sold 1946, renamed *Katina.*

ARABIS Corvette, modified 'Flower' class. G. Brown 28.10.1943.

Arrived 8.51 Ward, Grays to BU. AR-

ACHNE Brig-sloop 18, 'Cruizer' class 386bm. Hills, Sandwich 18.2.1809. Sold 1.1837 Ledger.

ARACHNE Sloop 18, 602bm, 115 x 35½ ft, 18-32pdr. Devonport DY 30.3.1847. BU completed 12.2.1866 by Marshall, Plymouth.

ARARAT Minesweeper Bathurst class (RAN). Evans Deakin 20.2.1943. Sold 6.1.61, BU Japan.

ARAXES 5th Rate 36 (red pine-built), 1,070bm, 150½ x 40 ft. Pitcher Northfleet 13.9.1813. Sold 10.9.1817 Mr Manlove.

ARBITER (ex-USS ST SIMON) Escort carrier 11,420 tons, 468½ x 69½ ft, 2-4in, 16-40mm, 24-A/C. Seattle Tacoma 9.9.1943. Returned to the USN 3.3.46 and sold as *Caracero.*

ARBROATH (ex-ALTON) Minesweeper, later 'Hunt' class. Ailsa. Cancelled 1918.

ARBUTUS Sloop, 'Anchusa' class. Armstrong 8.9.1917. Sunk 16.12.17 by 'UB. 65' in St Georges Channel.

ARBUTUS Corvette, 'Flower' class. G.Brown 5.6.40. Sunk 9.2.42 by 'U.136' in the Atlantic.

ARBUTUS Corvette, modified 'Flower' class. G. Brown 26.1.1944. BU 6.51 by Clayton & Davie, Dunston.

ARCADIAN Submarine 1945 'A' class. Vickers Armstrong, Barrow. Cancelled 1945.

ARC-EN-CIEL 4th Rate 50, 1,077bm, 146 x 41 ft. French, captured 1756. Sold 6.9.1759.

ARCHER Gun-brig 12, 179bm, 80 x 22½ ft. Perry, Blackwall 2.4.1801. Sold 14.12.1815.

ARCHER Wood S. sloop, 973bm, 186 x 34 ft, 2-68pdr, 12-32pdr. Deptford DY 27.3.1849. Arrived 15.3.1866 Castle, Charlton to BU.

ARCHER Torpedo cruiser 1,770 tons, 225 x 36 ft, 6-6in, 5-TT. Thomson 23.12.1885. Sold 4.4.1905 Forrester, Swansea.

ARCHER Destroyer 775 tons, 240 x 25½ ft, 2-4 in, 2-12pdr, 2-TT. Yarrow 21.10.1911. Sold 9.5.21 Ward, Rainham.

ARCHER Escort carrier 9,000 tons, 469 x 66 ft, 3-4in, 15-A/C. Sun SB, Chester, Pa. 14.12.1939 and to RN on lend-lease 17.11.41. To MWT 1945 as *Empire Lagan;* returned USN 8.1.46 and sold as *Anna Salen.*

ARCHER Patrol boat (RAN) 100 tons. Walker 2.12.1967. Sold Indonesia 10.74.

ARCHER Patrol boat. Watercraft 25.6.1985.

ARCTURUS Minesweeper, 'Algerine' class. Redfern, Toronto 31.8.1942 (on lend-lease). Returned USN 1946 and sold Greek navy as PYRPOLITIS.

ARCTURUS Trawler 1915 to 1919.

ARDENT 3rd Rate 64, 1,376bm, 160 x 45 ft. Blaydes, Hull 13.8.1764. Captured 17.8.1779 by the French off Plymouth; recaptured 4.1782 and renamed TIGER. Sold 6.1784.

ARDENT 3rd Rate 64, 1,387bm, 160½ x 45 ft. Stares & Parsons, Bursledon 21.12.1782. Caught fire and blew up 4.1794 off Corsica.

ARDENT (ex-Indiaman *Princess Royal*) 3rd Rate 64, 1,422bm, 161 x 46 ft. Pitcher; Northfleet 9.4.1796. Harbour service 1812. BU 3.1824 at Bermuda.

ARDENT (see RATTLER of 1843)

ARDENT Wood pad. sloop 801bm, 165 x 33 ft, 5-32pdr. Chatham DY 12.2.1841. Arrived 2.3.1865 Castle, Charlton to BU.

ARDENT Destroyer 280 tons, 202 x 19 ft, 1-12pdr, 5-6pdr, 2-TT. Thornycroft, Chiswick 16.10.1894. Sold 10.10.1911.

ARDENT Destroyer 981 tons, 260 x 27 ft, 3-4in, 2-TT. Denny 8.9.1913. Sunk 1.6.16 at the battle of Jutland.

ARDENT Destroyer 1,350 tons, 311 x 32½ ft, 4-4.7in, 8-TT. Scotts 26.6.1929. Sunk 8.6.40 by German battlecruisers off Narvik.

ARDENT Submarine 1945 'A' class. Vickers Armstrong, Barrow. Cancelled 1945.

ARDENT Frigate 2,750 tons. Yarrow 9.5.1975. Lost 21.5.82 in Falklands operations.

ARDENT Patrol boat (RAN) 100 tons. Walker 27.4.1968.

ARDENT Two hired vessels WW.I.

ARD PATRICK M/S sloop '24' class. Swan Hunter 6.6.1918. Sold 12.8.20 Moise Mazza; resold 1.12.21 Stanlee, Dover.

ARDROSSAN Minesweeper, 'Bangor' (turbine) class. Blyth 22.7.1941. Sold 1.1.48, arrived 29.8.48 Thornaby-on-Tees to BU.

ARETHUSA 5th Rate 32, 700bm, 132 x 34½ ft. French ARETHUSE captured 18.5.1759. Wrecked 19.3.1779 off Ushant.

ARETHUSA 5th Rate 38, 948bm, 141 x 39 ft. Hilhouse, Bristol 10.4.1781. BU 5.1814 at Sheerness.

ARETHUSE 5th Rate 38, 1,064bm, 152 x 39½ ft. French captured 29.8.1 793 at Toulon. Renamed UNDAUNTED

1795. Wrecked 27.8.1796 on Morant Keys, W. Indies.

ARETHUSA 5th Rate 46, 1,085bm, 151 x 40½ ft. Pembroke Dock 29.7.1817. Harbour service 6.1836; renamed BACCHUS 12.3.1844. BU 8.1883 Castle, Thames.

ARETHUSA 4th Rate 50, 2,132bm, 3,832 tons, 180 x 53 ft, 10-8in, 40-32pdr. Pembroke Dock 20.6.1849. Undocked 9.8.1861 as screw frigate; training ship 1874. BU 1934 Castle, Thames.

ARETHUSA 2nd class cruiser 4,300 tons, 300 x 46 ft, 10-6in. Napier 23.12.1882. Sold 4.4.1905 Garnham.

ARETHUSA Light cruiser 3,500 tons, 410 x 39 ft, 2-6in, 6-4in. Chatham DY 25.10.1913. Wrecked 11.2.16 near Harwich after being damaged by mine.

ARETHUSA Cruiser 5,220 tons, 500 x 51 ft, 6-6in, 4-4in. Chatham DY 6.3.1934. Arrived 9.5.50 Cashmore, Newport to BU.

ARETHUSA Frigate, 'Leander' class. White 5.11.1963.

ARETHUSA Store carrier 480 tons. Requis. 1915-20.

ARGO 6th Rate 28, 601 bm, 118½ x 34 ft. Bird, Rotherhithe 20.7.1758. BU completed 8.11.1776 at Portsmouth.

ARGO Schooner 10. Purchased 6.1780. Sold in 4.1783.

ARGO 5th Rate 44, 892bm, 141 x 38 ft. Baker, Howden Dock 7.6.1781. Sold 11.1.1816.

ARGO (see ACTIVE of 1799)

ARGO (see ESPIEGLE of 1880)

ARGON (see ARGUS of 1904)

ARGON Trawler. Requis. 1915-19.

ARGONAUT 3rd Rate 64, 1,452bm, 166 x 45 ft. French JASON captured 19.4.1782 in the W. Indies. Harbour service 1797. BU 2.1831 at Chatham.

ARGONAUT 1st class cruiser 11,000 tons, 435 x 69 ft, 16-6in, 14-12 pdr. Fairfield 24.1.1898. Sold 18.5.1920 Ward, Milford; arrived 4.9.21.

ARGONAUT Cruiser 5,450 tons, 506 x 51½ ft, 10-5.25in. Cammell Laird 6.9.1941. Sold 16.11.55, BU Cashmore, Newport.

ARGONAUT Frigate, 'Leander' class. Hawthorn Leslie 8.2.1966.

ARGOSY Submarine 1945 'A' class. Vickers Armstrong, Barrow. Cancelled 1945.

ARGUS Sloop 10, 326bm, 103 x 27 ft. French privateer captured 1799. BU4.1811.

ARGUS Brig-sloop 18, 'Cruizer' class,

387bm,. Hill, Sandwich 11.9.1813. Sold 11.7.1827 Mr Freake; sale cancelled; sold 26.3.1828 Ledger.

ARGUS 5th Rate 36. Sheerness DY. Ordered 1812 and cancelled 1812.

ARGUS Sloop 18, 480bm, 114 x 31 ft. Portsmouth DY-laid down 3.1831, cancelled 6.1831.

ARGUS Wood pad. sloop, 981bm, 190 x 33 ft. Portsmouth DY 15.12.1849. BU 10.1881.

ARGUS Coastguard vessel 318bm, 357 tons, 136 x 22 ft, 2-32pdr. Green Blackwall 1851. Renamed AMELIA 16.4.1872 and FANNY 4.1889. Hulked 1899; BDV 1902. Sold 1907 to BU.

ARGUS (see IMOGENE of 1864)

ARGUS Coastguard vessel 380 tons, 130 x 23 ft, 2-6pdr. Bow McLachlan 6.12.1904. Renamed ARGON 1918. Sold 2.20.

ARGUS (ex-*Conte Rosso* purchased and renamed 8.1916) Aircraft carrier 14,450 tons, 535 x 68 ft, 4-4in, 20-A/C. Beardmore 2.12.1917. Harbour service 12.44. Sold 5.12.46, BU by Ward, Inverkeithing.

ARGUS Aux A/C Carrier, ex-*Contender Bezant* (11,445/81) purchased 1984.

ARGUS Two hired vessels 1794.

ARGYLL (see BONAVENTURE of 1711)

ARGYLL Armoured cruiser 10,850 tons, 450 x 68½ ft, 4-7.5in, 6-6in, 2-12pdr. Scotts 3.3.1904. Wrecked 28.10.1915 on Bell Rock.

ARGYLL Frigate 3,000 tons. Yarrow. Ordered 15.7.1986.

ARIADNE 6th Rate 20, 430bm, 108 x 30 ft. Chatham DY 27.12.1776. Rebuilt at Northam 1792 as 6th Rate 24. Sold 7.8.1814.

ARIADNE Advice boat, 187bm. Purchased 5.1805. Renamed DOVE 21.5.05, FLIGHT 1806. Foundered 9.1806.

ARIADNE 6th Rate 20, 511bm, 121½ x 31 ft. Pembroke Dock 10.2.1816. Coal hulk 1837. Sold 23.7.1842.

ARIADNE Wood pad. sloop (Indian), 432bm, 139 x 26 ft. Laird 12.1839. Foundered 23.6.1842. off Chusan.

ARIADNE Wood S. frigate, 3,214bm, 4,583 tons, 280 x 51 ft, 24-10in, 2-68pdr. Deptford DY 4.6.1859. Harbour service 1884; renamed ACTAEON 6.6.1905. Sold 11.12.22.

ARIADNE 1st class cruiser 11,000 tons, 435 x 69 ft, 16-6in, 14-12pdr. Thomson 22.4.1898. Minelayer 3.1917, 4-6in, 1-4in, 400 mines. Sunk 26.7.17 by 'UC.65' off Beachy Head.

ARIADNE Minelayer 2,650 tons, 4-4in, 4-40mm, 160 mines. Stephens 16.2.1943. BU Dalmuir and Troon 6.65.

ARIADNE Frigate Leander class. Yarrow 10.9.1971.

ARIADNE II Trawler requis. 1914-19.

ARIEL 6th Rate 20, 429bm, 108 x 30 ft. Perry, Blackwall 7.7.1777. Captured 10.9.1779 by the French AMAZONE and lent to the Americans until 1781. Lost 1793.

ARIEL Sloop 16,314bm, 98 x 27½ ft. Baker, Liverpool 18.10.1781. Sold 8.1802.

ARIEL Sloop 18, 367bm, 106 x 28 ft. Palmer, Yarmouth 19.4.1806. Sold 12.7.1816 at Deptford.

ARIEL Brig 14 (Indian), 160bm. Bombay DY 1809. Foundered 12.3.1820.

ARIEL Brig-sloop 10 ('Cherokee' class) Deptford DY 28.7.1820. Completed 9.1827 as packet brig. Wrecked 8.12.1828 on Sable Island.

ARIEL (ex-GPO vessel *Arrow* transferred 1.2.1837) Wood pad. packet, 149bm, 108 x 17½ ft. Sold 17.5.1850 T. Marston.

ARIEL Wood S. sloop, 486bm, 139 x 28 ft, 9-32pdr. Pembroke Dock 11.7.1854. Sold 23.5.1865 Shaw & Thompson.

ARIEL 2nd class gunboat 436 tons, 125 x 22 ft, 2-64pdr MLR, 2-20 pdr. Chatham DY 11.2.1873. Coastguard 26.11.1877. Sold 8.1889.

ARIEL Destroyer 310 tons, 210 x 19½ ft, 1-12pdr, 5-6pdr, 2-TT. Thornycroft, Chiswick 5.3.1897. Wrecked 19.4.1907 on Ricasoli breakwater, Malta while testing harbour defences.

ARIEL Destroyer 763 tons, 250 x 26½ ft, 2-4in, 2-12pdr, 2-TT. Thornycroft, Woolston 26.9.1911. Sunk 2.8.18 by mine in the North Sea.

ARIEL II Trawler 1914-19; Cable ship 1940-46.

ARIES Minesweeper, 'Algerine' class, Toronto 19.9.1942 on lend-lease. Returned USN 1946 and sold Greek navy as ARMATOLOS.

ARIES Three hired vessels 1914-19.

ARK ROYAL (ex-ARK RALEIGH) Galleon 55, 694bm, 4-60pdr, 4-30 pdr, 12-18pdr, 12-9pdr, 6-6pdr, 17 small. Deptford 1587. Renamed ANNE ROYAL and rebuilt Woolwich 1608. Wrecked 4.1636 in Tilbury Hope and BU.

ARK ROYAL (ex-mercantile purchased 5.1914) Seaplane carrier 7,080 tons, 352½ x 51 ft, 4-12pdr, 4-A/C. Blyth SB 5.9.1914. Depot ship 1923; renamed PEGASUS 21.12.34; catapult ship 4.41; accommodation ship 1944. Sold 18.10.46 as *Anita I*; BU 1950.

ARK ROYAL A/C carrier 22,000 tons, 685 x 94 ft, 16-4.5in, 72-A/C. Cammell Laird 13.4.1937. Sunk 14.11.41 by 'U.81' off Gibraltar.

ARK ROYAL (ex-IRRESISTIBLE) A/C carrier 36,800 tons, 720 x 113 ft, 16-4.5in, 58-40mm, 100-A/C. Cammell Laird 3.5.50. BU Cairnryan 9.80.

ARK ROYAL A/S Cruiser 16,256 tons. Swan Hunter 2.6.1981.

ARLINGHAM Inshore M/S, 'Ham' class. Camper & Nicholson 1.4.1953. TRV 4.67. Sold in 1977.

ARMADA 3rd Rate 74, 1,749bm, 176 x 48½ ft. Blackburn, Turnchapel 22.3.1810. Sold 27.5.1863 Marshall, Plymouth.

ARMADA Destroyer 2,325 tons, 355 x 40 ft, 4-4.5in, 1-4in, 8-TT. Hawthorn Leslie 9.12.1943. Arrived 18.12.65 Ward, Inverkeithing.

ARMERIA Corvette, 'Flower' class. Harland & Wolff 16.1.1941. Sold 1947, renamed *Deppie*.

ARMIDALE Minesweeper, 'Bathurst' class (RAN). Morts Dock, Sydney 23.1.1942. Sunk 21.12.42 by Japanese A/C off Timor.

ARMIDE 5th Rate 38, 1,104bm, 152 x 40 ft. French, captured by a squadron off Rochefort 26.9.1806. BU 11.1815.

ARMS OF HOLLAND 34-gun ship. Dutch, captured 1652. Blown up by accident 1656 in the W. Indies.

ARMS OF HORN Hulk, 516bm. Dutch, 4th rate captured 1673. Sunk 1694 as a foundation at Sheerness.

ARMS OF ROTTERDAM 3rd Rate 60, 987bm. Dutch, captured 1673. Hulked 1675. BU 1703.

ARMS OF TERVER 4th Rate 52, 523bm. Dutch, captured 1673. Given away 1674.

ARNO (ex-Portuguese LIZ purchased 3.1915) Destroyer 600 tons, 230 x 22 ft, 4-14pdr, 3-TT. Ansaldo, Genoa 1915. Sunk 23.8.18 in collision with destroyer HOPE off the Dardanelles.

ARNPRIOR (see COURIER of 1943)

ARNPRIOR (ex-RISING CASTLE) Corvette, 'Castle' class. Harland & Wolff 8.2.1944. Sold 5.9.46 Uruguay as MONTEVIDEO.

ARO (ex-*Albertville* purchased 10.1914) Depot ship 3,794 gross, 352 x 44 ft. Transport 14.8.18. Sold 1.20 W.R. Davis.

ARRAS Sloop 644 tons, 246 x 31 ft, 2-5.5in. French, seized 7.1940 at Portsmouth. Free-French accommodation ship 5.41; oil hulk 1943; returned French navy 1946.

ARRAS Trawler (RCN) 1918-57.

ARROGANT 3rd Rate 60, 928bm. French, captured 10.3.1705. Foundered 5.1.1709 on passage to Port Mahon.

ARROGANT 3rd Rate 74, 1,644bm, 168 x 47½ ft. Barnard, Harwich 22.1.1761. Sheer hulk circa 1801. BU 1810 at Bombay.

ARROGANTE Gunvessel 14, 258bm, 92 x 26 ft. French, captured 19.4.1798 by JASON off Brest. Renamed INSOLENT 31.8.1798. Sold 11.6.1818 J.Cristall.

ARROGANT (ex-*Adasier* purchased 7.8.1810) Store hulk, 1,439bm. Sold 1842.

ARROGANT Wood S. frigate, 1,872bm, 200 x 46 ft, 12-8in, 2-68pdr, 32-32pdr. Portsmouth DY 5.4.1848. Sold 3.1867 Castle & Beech.

ARROGANT 2nd class cruiser 5,750 tons, 320 x 57½ ft, 4-6in, 6-4.7in (rearmed 1902: 10-6in, 9-12pdr). Devonport DY 26.5.1896. Depot ship 6.1911. Sold 11.10.23 Hughes Bolckow, Blyth.

ARROGANT A/C Carrier 18,300 tons, 650 x 90 ft, 32-40mm, 50-A/C. Swan Hunter, cancelled 1945.

ARROW Sloop 20, 386bm, 128½ x 30 ft, 28-32pdr carr. Hobbs, Redbridge 1796 and purchased. Captured 4.2.1805 by two French frigates off Gibraltar.

ARROW Cutter 14, 152bm, 91 x 19 ft. Deptford DY 7.9.1805. Used as breakwater from 5.1814. BU 5.1828.

ARROW Cutter 10, 157bm, 64 x 25 ft. Portsmouth DY 14.3.1823. BU 1.1852.

ARROW Wood S. despatch vessel, 477bm, 160 x 25½ ft, 2-98pdr. Mare, Blackwall 26.6.1854. Sold 19.5.1862 Marshall, Plymouth.

ARROW Iron S. gunboat, 'Ant' class. Rennie, Greenwich 22.4.1871. Sold 1.3.1922 W.H. Webber.

ARROW Destroyer 1,350 tons, 311 x 32½ ft, 4-4.7in, 8-TT. Vickers Armstrong, Barrow 22.8.1929. Damaged beyond repair 4.8.43 in Algiers harbour by explosion of ammunition ship *Fort la Montee*; stripped 1944 and BU in 5.49.

ARROW Patrol Boat (RAN) 100 tons. Walker 17.2.1968. Wrecked 25.12.74 at Darwin.

ARROW Frigate 2,750 tons. Yarrow 5.2.1974.

ARROWHEAD Corvette, 'Flower' class. Marine Industries, Canada 8.8.1940. Lent RCN until 6.45. Sold 5.47, renamed *Southern Larkspur*.

ARTEMIS Submarine 1945 'A' class. Scotts 26.8.1946. Sold Pounds, Portsmouth 12.12.71.

ARTFUL Submarine 1945 'A' class. Scotts 22.5.1947. Sold 16.6.72, BU Cairnryan.

ARTIFEX (ex-AMC AURANIA renamed 11.1942) 19,000 tons, 520 x 65 ft, 20-20mm. Completed conversion 7.44. Sold 28.12.60 to Italian shipbreakers.

ARTIGO Ship, 14Obm. French FERRONIERE, captured 1543. Sold 1547.

ARTOIS 5th Rate 40, 1,152bm, 158½ x 40½ ft. French, captured 1.7.1780. Sold 2.2.1786.

ARTOIS 5th Rate 38, 984bm, 146 x 39 ft. Wells, Rotherhithe 3.1.1794. Wrecked 31.7.1797 near Rochelle.

ARUN Destroyer 550 tons, 225 x 23½ ft, 1-12pdr, 5-6pdr, 2-TT, altered to 4-12pdr, 2-TT in 1907. Laird 29.4.1903. Sold 30.6.20 Ward, Hayle.

ARUN Minesweeper 857 tons. Richards 20.8.1985.

ARUNDEL 5th Rate 32, 378bm, 109 x 28 ft. Ellis, Shoreham 13.9.1695. Sold by order dated 11.6.1713.

ARUNDEL 6th Rate 24, 509bm, 112 x 32½ ft. Chitty & Vernon, Chichester 23.11.1746. Sold 9.7.1765.

ARUNDEL (see WARSPITE of 1758)

ARUNDEL (see MEDWAY of 1755)

ARUNTA Destroyer (RAN) 1,927 tons 355½ x 36½ ft, 6-4.7in, 2-4in, 4-TT. Cockatoo DY 30.11.1940. Foundered 13.2.69 on passage to Taiwan to BU.

ARVE PRINCEN (see HEIR APPARENT).

ARVIDA Corvette, 'Flower' class (RCN). Morton, Quebec 21.9.1940. Sold circa 1946, renamed *La Ceiba*.

ASBESTOS Corvette, modified 'Flower' class (RCN). Morton 22.11.1943. BU 3.49.

ASCENSION (ex-HARGOOD) Frigate, 'Colony' class. Walsh Kaiser 6.8.1943. Returned to the USN 31.5.46.

ASCOT Pad. minesweeper, 'Ascot' class. Ailsa 26.1.1916. Sunk 10.11.18 by 'UB.67' off the Farn Islands.

ASGARD Submarine 1945 'A' class. Scotts. Cancelled 1945.

ASHANTI Destroyer 1,870 tons, 355½ x 36½ ft, 8-4.7 in, 4-TT. Denny

5.11.1937. Sold 12.4.49, BU at Troon.

ASHANTI Frigate 2,300 tons, 348 x 42½ ft, 2-4.5 in, 2-40mm, 6-TT. Yarrow 9.3.1959.

ASHBURTON Minesweeper, later 'Hunt' class. Ailsa, cancelled 1919.

ASHELDHAM Inshore M/S 'Ham' class. Philip 30.9.1952. Malaysian SRI PERLIS 1.4.59.

ASHTON Coastal M/S, 'Ton' class. White's SY, Itchen 5.9.1956. Sold 24.6.77 to BU Middlesbrough.

ASIA Hulk, 420bm. Purchased 11.12.1694. Foundered 7.4.1701 in the Bay of Bulls, Newfoundland.

ASIA 3rd Rate 64, 1,364bm, 158 x 44½ ft. Portsmouth DY 3.3.1764. BU 8.1804.

ASIA 3rd Rate 74, 1,763bm, 176 x 48 ft. Brindley, Frindsbury 2.12.1811. Renamed ALFRED 1819; reduced to 50 guns 8.1828. BU 5.1865 at Portsmouth.

ASIA 2nd Rate 84, 2,289bm, 197 x 52 ft. Bombay DY 19.1.1824. Guardship 1858. Sold 7.4.1908 Merveille, Dunkirk.

ASP (Gunboat No. 5) Gunvessel 12, 160bm, 75 x 22 ft. Randall, Rotherhithe 10.4.1797. Sold 1803.

ASP Sloop 16, 333bm, 99 x 28½ ft. French SERPENT captured 17.7.1808 by ACASTA. Sold 16.3.1814.

ASP Cutter purchased 1826, sold 2.1829.

ASP (ex-GPO vessel Fury transferred 1837) Wood pad. packet, 112bm, 90 x 16 ft. BU 7.1881 at Chatham.

ASPERITY Submarine 1945 'A' class. Vickers Armstrong, Tyne. Cancelled 1945.

ASPHODEL Sloop, 'Arabis' class. Henderson 21.12.1915. Sold 16.6.20 Danish navy as FYLLA.

ASPHODEL Corvette, 'Flower' class. G.Brown 25.5.1940. Sunk 9.3.44 by 'U.575' off NW Spain.

ASSAIL Patrol boat (RAN) 100 tons. Evans Deakin 18.11.1967. To Indonesia 1986.

ASSAM Minesweeper (RIN) 'Bathurst' class. Garden Reach, Calcutta. Cancelled 3.1945.

ASSAM (see BUGLOSS).

ASSAULT (Gunboat No. 4) Gunvessel, 159bm, 75 x 22 ft. Randall, Rotherhithe 10.4.1797. Became dockyard lighter 1817. Sold 6.6.1827.

ASSAYE Pad. frigate (Indian) 1,800bm. Bombay DY 15.3.1854. Sold 1863 as sailing vessel. Wrecked 1865 coast of Ireland.

ASSAYE Torpedo gunboat (RIM) 735 tons, 230 x 27 ft. 2-4.7 in, 4-3pdr, 5-TT. Armstrong 11.2.1890. Sold 5.1904.

ASSIDUOUS Schooner 94bm, ex-pirate JACKAL, captured 1823, sold 5.5.25

ASSINIBOINE (see KEMPENFELT).

ASSINIBOINE Frigate (RCN) 2,263 tons, 4-3 in, 2-40mm. Marine Industries 12.2.1954.

ASSISTANCE 50-gun ship, 521bm, 121 x 31 ft. Deptford 1650. Rebuilt 1699 as 607bm; rebuilt Limehouse 1712 as 710bm; rebuilt Woolwich 1725 as 750bm. Sunk 14.2.1746 as breakwater at Sheerness.

ASSISTANCE 4th Rate 50, 1,063bm, 144 x 41½ ft. Ledger, River Medway 22.12.1747. Sold 11.8.1773.

ASSISTANCE Transport, 94bm, 59 x 19 ft. Plymouth 1771. Sold 1802.

ASSISTANCE 4th Rate 50, 1,045bm, 146 x 41 ft. Baker, Liverpool 12.3.1781. Wrecked 29.3.1802 near Dunkirk.

ASSISTANCE (see ROYAL OAK of 1769).

ASSISTANCE (ex-Baboo) Discovery vessel, 420bm, 117 x 28½ ft. Purchased 3.1850. Abandoned in the Arctic 1854.

ASSISTANCE S.storeship, 1,793bm, 283 x 36 ft. Purchased 16.1.1855. Laird 5.4.1855. Wrecked 7.6.1860 near Hong Kong and wreck sold 30.7.1860.

ASSISTANCE Iron S.storeship 2,515 tons, 250 x 38 ft, 2 guns. Green, Blackwall 26.9.1874. Sold 1897.

ASSISTANCE Repair ship 9,600 tons, 436 x 53 ft, 10-3pdr.Purchased 19.9.1900. Raylton Dixon 22.12.1900. Handed over to Messrs. Ward in part payment for Majestic (CALEDONIA) and arrived 11.3.37 Pembroke Dock to BU.

ASSISTANCE Repair ship 7,100 tons, 416 x 57 ft, 1-5 in, 10-40mm. Maryland DD, Baltimore 20.6.1944 on lend-lease. Returned USN 15.8.46.

ASSISTANT Transport 4, 110bm, 63 x 20 ft, 4-3pdr. Purchased 4.1791. Sold 12.10.1802.

ASSOCIATION 2nd Rate 90, 1,459bm, 165 x 45½ ft. Portsmouth DY 1697. Wrecked 22.10.1707 off Scilly.

ASSURANCE (see HOPE of 1559).

ASSURANCE 42-gun ship, 456bm, 106½ x 29 ft. Deptford 1646. Sold 1698.

ASSURANCE 3rd Rate 70, 1,102bm,

146 x 42 ft. French ASSURE captured 12.10.1702. BU 4.1712 at Chatham.

ASSURANCE 5th Rate 44, 823bm, 133 x 38 ft. Heather, Bursledon 26.9.1747. Wrecked 24.4.1753 on the Needles.

ASSURANCE 5th Rate 44, 898bm, 140½ x 38 ft. Randall, Rotherhithe 20.4.1780. Troopship 7.1796; harbour service 3.1799. BU 3.1815.

ASSURANCE Wood S.gunvessel 681 bm, 181½ x 28½ ft. Green, Blackwall 13.3.1856. Sold 8.3.1870 Marshall, Plymouth.

ASSURANCE Submarine 1945 'A' class. Scotts. Cancelled 1945.

ASSURANCE Two tugs 1899-1923 and 1940-41.

ASTARTE Submarine 1945 'A' class. Scotts. Cancelled 1945.

ASTER Sloop, 'Acacia' class. Earle 1.5.1915. Sunk 4.7.17 by mine off Malta.

ASTER Corvette, 'Flower' class. Harland & Wolff 12.2.1941. Sold 29.5.46, BU McLellan, Bo'ness.

ASTER Hired yacht 1914 to 1916.

ASTRAEA Storeship, circa 500bm. Spanish, captured 25.3.1739. Burnt 17.1.1743 by accident at Piscatagua.

ASTRAEA 5th Rate 32, 703bm, 126 x 36 ft. Fabian, E. Cowes 24.7.1781, Wrecked 23.3.1808 off Anegada, W.Indies.

ASTRAEA 5th Rate 36, 956bm, 145 x 38½ ft. Guillaum, Northam 5.1810. Harbour service 8.1823. BU 4.1851.

ASTREE 5th Rate 38, 1,085bm, 152½ x 40 ft. French, captured 6.12.1810 at the reduction of Mauritius. Renamed POMONE 26.10.1811. BU 6.1816.

ASTREA Wood S.frigate, 2,478bm, 240 x 48 ft. Devonport DY. Laid down 21.10.1861, cancelled 12.12.1863.

ASTRAEA 2nd class cruiser 4,360 tons, 320 x 49 ft, 2-6 in, 8-4.7 in, 8-6pdr. Devonport DY 17.3.1893. Sold 1.7.20 Castle: resold and BU in Germany.

ASTUTE Submarine 1945 'A' class. Vickers Armstrong, Barrow, 31.1.1945. Sold Clayton & Davie 2.9.70, BU Dunston.

ATALANTA Sloop 14, 300bm, 96½ x 26½ ft. Sheerness DY 12.8.1775. On sale list 13.3.1797; renamed HELENA 1801. Sold 8.1802.

ATALANTA Brig-sloop 16, 310bm, 98 x 27½ ft. French, captured 10.1.1797 by PHOEBE off Scilly. Wrecked 12.2.1807 off Isle de Rhe.

ATALANTE Sloop 18, 416bm, 100 x 30 ft. Bermuda 8.1808. Wrecked 10.11.1813 off Halifax.

ATALANTA Schooner 12, 225bm. American SIRO captured 13.1.1814. Recaptured by Americans 1814.

ATALANTA Tender. Deptford DY 1816. Transferred to Customs service 1817.

ATALANTA Wood pad. sloop (Indian), 620bm, 6 guns. Built on the Thames 1836. BU circa 1850.

ATALANTA Brig 16, 549bm, 110 x 35 ft, 16-32pdr. Pembroke Dock 9.10.1847. BU completed at Devonport 12.12.1868.

ATALANTE S.storeship, 295bm. Purchased 7. 1860. Renamed MANILLA 19.7.1861; exchanged 28.2.70 for barque *Ingeberg* (renamed MANILLA).

ATALANTA (see JUNO of 1844).

ATALANTA 6 hired vessels, between 1915 and 1945.

ATHABASKAN (see IROQUOIS).

ATHABASKAN Destroyer (RCN) 1,927 tons, 355½ x 36½ ft, 6-4.7 in, 2-4 in. Vickers Armstrong, Tyne 18.11.41. Sunk 29.4.44 in action with German TBs off the French Channel coast.

ATHABASKAN Destroyer (RCN) 1,927 tons, 355½ x 36- ft, 8-4 in, 4-40mm, 4-TT. Halifax SY 14.5.46. BU 7.69 in Italy.

ATHABASKAN Escort (RCN) 3,551 tons. Davie 27.11.70.

ATHELENEY Minesweeper, later 'Hunt' class. Clyde SB Co. Cancelled 1918.

ATHELING (ex-USS MISSION BAY) Escort carrier 11,420 tons, 468½ x 69½ ft, 2-4 in, 16-40mm, 24-A/C. Kaiser, Vancouver, USA 26.5.1943. Retained by the USN as MISSION BAY.

ATHELING (ex-USS ANGUILLA BAY) Escort carrier (as No.1) Kaiser, Vancouver 12.8.43. Retained by the USN as CORREGIDOR.

ATHELING (ex-USS GLACIER) Escort carrier (as No.1) Seattle, Tacoma 7.9.42; on lend-lease to the RN 28.10.43. Returned to the USN 13.12.46 and sold as *Roma*.

ATHENIENNE Gun-brig 14, 202bm. French, captured 8.6.1796 by ALBACORE off Barbados. Sold 1802.

ATHENIENNE 3rd Rate 64, 1,404bm, 164 x 44½ ft. French, ex-Maltese, captured 4.9.1800 at Malta. Wrecked 20.10.1806 off Sicily.

ATHERSTONE Pad. minesweeper, 'Ascot' class. Ailsa 4.4.1916. Sold 12.8.27, renamed *Queen of Kent*.

(QUEEN OF KENT WW.II).

ATHERSTONE Destroyer, 'Hunt' class type I. Cammell Laird 12.12.1939. Sold 23.11.57; BU Smith & Houston, Port Glasgow.

ATHERSTONE Minesweeper 615 tons. Vosper/Thornycroft 1.3.1986.

ATHOLL 6th Rate 28, 503bm, 114 x 32 ft, 20-32pdr carr., 6-18pdr carr., 2-9pdr. Woolwich DY 23.11.1820. Troopship 7.1832. BU 4.1863 at Devonport.

ATHOLL Corvette (RCN), modified 'Flower' class. Morton, 5.5.1943. BU 10.52 Steel Co of Canada.

ATLANTIS Submarine 1945 'A' class. Vickers Armstrong, Barrow. Cancelled 1945.

ATLAS 2nd Rate 90, 1,950bm, 178 x 50 ft. Chatham DY 13.2.1782. 3rd Rate 1802; harbour service 1814. BU 5.1821.

ATLAS Screw 2nd Rate 91, 3,318bm, 5,260 tons, 245 x 55½ ft, 34-8 in, 1-68pdr, 56-32pdr. Chatham DY 21.7.1860. Not completed; lent 11.1884 Metropolitan Asylum Board. BU 1904.

ATLAS Three tugs between 1895 and 1958.

ATTACK Gunvessel 12, 147bm, 75 x 21 ft. Brindley, Frindsbury 1794. Sold 9.1802.

ATTACK Gun-brig, 181 bm, 80 x 22½ ft. Adams, Chapel 9.8.1804. Captured 16.8.1812 by the Danes in the Cattegat.

ATTACK Destroyer 785 tons, 240 x 25½ ft, 2-4 in, 2-12pdr, 2-TT. Yarrow 21.12.1911. Sunk 30.12.17 by 'UC.34' off Alexandria.

ATTACK Patrol boat (RAN) 100 tons. Evans Deakin 8.4.1967.

ATTACKER Escort carrier 11,420 tons, 468½ x 69½ ft, 2-4 in, 8-40mm, 18-A/C. Western Pipe & Steel Co, 27.9.1941. On lend-lease 4.42; returned 5.1.46 to USN. Sold 1952 as Castel Forte.

ATTACKER (see LST.3010).

ATTACKER Training boat 34 tons. Fairey Marine, Cowes 1983.

ATTENTIVE Gun-brig 12, 178bm, 80 x 23 ft. Bools & Co, Bridport 18.9.1804. BU 8.1812 at Deptford.

ATTENTIVE Prison ship, 359bm, 96 x 28½ ft. American brig MAGNET captured 1812. BU in 1.1817 at Portsmouth.

ATTENTIVE Scout cruiser 2,670 tons, 374 x 38 ft, 10-12pdr. Armstrong 24.11.1904. Sold 12.4.20 Ward, Preston.

ATTENTIVE II (see ADDER of 1905).

AUBRIETIA (Q.13) Sloop, 'Aubrietia' class. Blyth SB 17.6.1916. Sold 25.10.22 R.H. Partridge.

AUBRIETIA Corvette, 'Flower' class. G.Brown 5.9.1940. Sold 29.7.46, renamed Arnfinn Bergen.

AUCKLAND Wood pad. frigate (Indian), 946bm, 6-8in MLR. Bombay DY 9.1.1840. Harbour service 1863. Sold circa 1874.

AUCKLAND (ex-HERON renamed 1937) Sloop 1,200 tons, 276 x 37½ ft, 8-4 in. Denny 30.6.1938. Sunk 24.6.41 by Italian A/C off Tobruk.

AUCKLAND Trawler. Requis. 1914-19.

AUDACIOUS 3rd Rate 74, 1,624bm, 168 x 47 ft. Randall, Rotherhithe 23.7.1785. BU 8.1815.

AUDACIEUX Sloop 14, 408bm, 114½ x 28½ ft. French, captured 1797. Last listed 1801.

AUDACIOUS (see JAMES WATT).

AUDACIOUS Battleship 6,010 tons, 280 x 54 ft, 10-9 in MLR, 4-64pdr MLR. Napier 27.2.1869. Depot ship 1902; renamed FISGARD 4.04; training ship 1.1.06; renamed IMPERIEUSE repair ship 1914. Sold 12.3.27 Ward, BU at Inverkeithing.

AUDACIOUS Battleship 23,000 tons, 555 x 89 ft, 10-13.5 in, 12-4 in. Cammell Laird 14.9.1912. Sunk 27.10.14 by mine off Tory Island.

AUDACIOUS (see EAGLE of 1946).

AUDACITY (ex-Empire Audacity) Escort carrier 11,000 tons, 435 x56 ft, 1-4 in, 6-20mm, 6-A/C. German Hannover captured 2.1940, completed as carrier 9.41. Sunk 21.12.41 by 'U.751' in the Atlantic.

AUGUSTE 4th Rate 60, 932bm, 141½ x 39 ft. French, captured 1705. Wrecked 10.11.1716 on Island of Anholt.

AUGUSTA 4th Rate 60, 1,068bm, 144 x 41½ ft. Deptford DY 1.7.1736. BU completed 6.7.1765 at Portsmouth.

AUGUSTA (see CHARLOTTE of 1677).

AUGUSTA 3rd Rate 64, 1,381bm, 159 x 44½ ft. Stanton & Wells, Rotherhithe 24.10.1763. Burnt by American gunfire 23.10.1777 at Mud Island, USA.

AUGUSTA Yacht, 184bm, 80½ x 23 ft. Deptford DY 1771. Renamed PRINCESS AUGUSTA 23.7.1773, sold 13.8.1818.

AUGUSTA Gunboat, ex-barge purchased 9.1795. In service in 1801.

AUGUSTA 3rd Rate 74. Portsmouth DY laid down 1806, cancelled 1809.

AUGUSTA Schooner ex-*Policy* purchased 1.1819, sold 24.4.1823.

AUGUSTA Schooner 2, 114bm (Indian). Bombay DY 1853. In service in 1866.

AUGUSTA Minesweeper, 'Catherine' class. Gen.Eng., Alameda 19.4.1943 for the RN but retained by the USN as DEVASTATOR.

AUGUSTINE Storeship 26, 360bm. Dutch, captured 1653. Sunk 1655 as a foundation at Harwich.

AUGUSTUS Gunvessel 1. In commission 1798. Wrecked 7.7.1801 in Plymouth Sound.

AURICULA Sloop, 'Anchusa' class. Armstrong 4.10.1917. Sold 1.2.23 J.Hornby.

AURICULA Corvette, 'Flower' class. G.Brown 14.11.1940. Mined 5.5.42 in Courier Bay, Madagascar and foundered on the next day.

AURICULA Trials vessel 1,200 tons. Ferguson 22.11.1979.

AURIGA Submarine 1945 'A' class. Vickers Armstrong, Barrow 29.3.1945. Sold Cashmore 14.11.74. BU at Newport.

AUROCHS Submarine 1945 'A' class. Vickers Armstrong, Barrow 28.7.1945. Arrived 7.2.67 at Troon to BU.

AURORA 5th Rate 36, 946bm, 144 x 38½ ft. French ABENAKISE captured by UNICORN 23.1.1757. BU 4.1763.

AURORA 5th Rate 32, 679bm, 125 x 35 ft. Chatham DY 13.1.1766. Burnt out 1770 on passage Cape to E.Indies.

AURORA 6th Rate 28, 596bm, 121 x 35 ft. Perry, Blackwall 7.6.1777. Sold 3.11.1814.

AURORE 5th Rate 32, 860bm. French, captured 29.8.1793 at Toulon. Prison ship 1799 to circa 1803.

AURORA Sloop 14 (Indian), 247bm. Bombay DY 1809. Captured by the French 9.1810 off Mauritius.

AURORA 5th Rate 38, 1,083bm, 152 x 40½ ft. French CLORINDE captured 26.2.1814 by DRYAD and EUROTUS in the Atlantic. BU 5.1851.

AURORA Wood S.frigate, 2,558bm, 227 x 50 ft, 1-110pdr, 8-8 in, 4-70pdr, 8-40pdr, 18-32pdr. Pembroke Dock 22.6.1861. BU 12.81.

AURORA Armoured cruiser 5,600 tons, 300 x 56 ft, 2-9.2 in, 10-6 in. Pembroke Dock 28.10.1887. Sold 2.10.1907 Payton, Milford Haven.

AURORA Light cruiser 3,500 tons, 410 x 39 ft, 2-6 in, 6-4 in. Devonport DY 30.9.1913. Commissioned in RCN 1.11.20. Sold 8.27 A.A. Lasseque, Sorel.

AURORA Cruiser 5,270 tons, 480 x 51 ft, 6-6 in, 8-4 in. Portsmouth DY 20.8.1936. Sold 19.5.48 Chinese navy as CHUNG KING; Communist TCHOUNG KING 1949.

AURORA Frigate, 'Leander' class. J.Brown 28.11.1962.

AURORA Drifter requis. 1915-19 and 1940-41.

AUSONIA A.merchant cruiser 19,000 tons, 520 x 65 ft, 8-6 in, 2-3 in. Hired 9.1939. Completed as repair ship 5.44. BU in Spain 9.65.

AUSTERE Submarine 1945 'A' class. Vickers Armstrong, Tyne. Cancelled 1945.

AUSTRALIA Armoured cruiser 5,600 tons, 300 x 56 ft, 2-9.2 in, 10-6 in. Fairfield 25.11.1886. Sold 4.4.1905 King, Troon.

AUSTRALIA Battlecruiser (RAN) 18,800 tons, 555 x 80 ft, 8-12 in, 14-4 in. J.Brown 25.10.1911. Sunk 12.4.24 as target off Sydney NSW.

AUSTRALIA Cruiser (RAN) 9,870 tons, 590 x 68½ ft, 8-8 in, 4-4 in. J.Brown 17.3.1927. Sold 25.1.55, BU 7.55 Ward, Barrow.

AUSTRALIA Trawler. Requis. 1915-19.

AUTUMN Sloop 16, 335bm, Purchased 1801. Renamed STROMBOLO bomb vessel 15.2.1811. Sold 9.2.1815.

AVELEY Inshore M/S, 'Ley' class. White, Cowes 16.2.1953. Sold 1983, renamed 'Woolwich'.

AVENGER (see LUCIFER of 1778).

AVENGER Sloop 16, 330bm. French VENGEUR captured 17.3.1794 at Martinique. Sold 9.9.1802.

AVENGER Sloop 208bm ex-*Elizabeth* purchased 8.1803, foundered off Heligoland 5.12.1803.

AVENGER (ex-collier *Thames*) Sloop 18, 390bm. Purchased 5.1804. Wrecked 8.10.1812 off St Johns, Newfoundland.

AVENGER Pad. frigate, 1,444bm, 210 x 39 ft. Devonport DY 5.8.1845. Wrecked 20.12.1847 north coast of Africa.

AVENGER (ex-mercantile *Rio Hudson*) Escort carrier 8,200 tons 468½ x 66 ft, 2-4 in, 40-40mm, 15-A/C. Sun SB Co,Chester, USA on lend-lease 27.11.1940. Sunk 15.11.42 by 'U.155' west of Gibraltar.

AVENGER (see LST.3011).

AVENGER A.merchant cruiser 15,000 tons. Requis. 1915-17.

AVENGER Frigate 2,750 tons. Yarrow 20.11.1975.

AVERNUS Torpedo boat (Australian) 16 tons, 1-TT. Built 1879, sold 12.1902.

AVON Brig-sloop 18, 'Cruiser' class. Symons, Falmouth 31.1.1805. Sunk 27.8.1814 in action with American Wasp in the Channel.

AVON (ex-GPO vessel *Thetis*) Wood pad. packet, 360bm, 144 x 23 ft, 3 guns. Transferred 1837. Sold 19.1.1863 Marshall, Plymouth.

AVON Pad. gunboat (New Zealand), 40bm, 60 ft, 1-12pdr. Purchased 1862. Sold 12.1863 as coal hulk; later became *Clyde*.

AVON Compos. S.gunvessel, 467bm, 603 tons, 155 x 25 ft, 1-7 in, 1-64pdr, 2-20pdr. Portsmouth DY 2.10.1867. Sold 26.4.1890 to BU at Charlton.

AVON Destroyer 355 tons, 210 x 21½ ft, 1-12pdr, 5-6pdr, 2-TT. Vickers 10.10.1896. Sold 1.7.20 Castle, Plymouth.

AVON Frigate, 'River' class. Hill 19.6.1943. Handed over to Portuguese navy 5.49 as NUNO TRISTAO.

AVON Trawler. Requis. 1914-19 and 1940-41.

AVON VALE Destroyer, 'Hunt' class type II. J.Brown 23.10.1940. Greek AEGEAN 3.44 to 5.44. Arrived 15.5.58 Young, Sunderland to BU.

AWAKE Submarine 1945 'A' class. Vickers Armstrong, Tyne. Cancelled 1945.

AWARE Patrol boat (RAN) 100 tons. Evans Deakin 7.10.1967.

AWE Frigate, 'River' class. Fleming & Ferguson 28.12.1943. Handed over to Portuguese navy 5.49 as DIOGO GOMES.

AXFORD Seaward defence boat, 'Ford' class. Simons 3. 1953. To Nigeria 9.9.66 as KADUNA.

AYDON CASTLE Corvette, 'Castle' class. Kingston SY. Cancelled 12.1943.

AYLMER (ex-USS HARMON) Frigate, TE 'Captain' class. Bethelehem, Hingham 10.7.1943 on lend-lease. Returned to the USN 5.11.45.

AZALEA Sloop, 'Acacia' class. Barclay Curle 10.9.1915. Sold 1.2.23 J.Hornby & Sons.

AZALEA Corvette, 'Flower' class. Cook Welton & Gemmell 8.7.1940. Sold 5.4.46, renamed *Norte*.

AZOV Schooner gunboat, 94bm, 64 x 18½ ft, 2 guns. Messrs. German, Malta 14.7.1855. Harbour service 1859. Sold 9.6.1899 at Malta.

AZOV (see MUTINE of 1880).

AZTEC Submarine 1945 'A' class. Vickers Armstrong, Tyne. Cancelled 1945.

'B' class submarines. 280 tons, 135 x 13½ ft, 2-TT (1-12pdr gun added to five boats in 1917 when converted to surface patrol vessels).

B.1 (ordered as A.14) Vickers 25.10.1904. Sold 25.8.21 A.J. Anderson; resold 2.5.22 J. Smith, Poole.

B.2 Vickers 31.10.1905. Sunk 4.10.12 in collision with *Amerika* in the Dover Straits.

B.3 Vickers 31.10.1905. Sold 20.12.19 J. Jackson.

B.4 Vickers 14.11.1905. Sold 1.4.19 Ardrossan DD Co.

B.5 Vickers 14.11.1905. Sold 25.8.21 A.J.Andersen; resold 1.3.22 J. Smith, Poole.

B.6 Vickers 30.11.1905. Completed 8.17 as surface patrol boat S.6. Sold 1919 Messrs Francotosti, Malta.

B.7 Vickers 30.11.1905. Completed 8.17 as surface patrol boat S.7. Sold 31.10.19 at Malta.

B.8 Vickers 23.1.1906. Completed 8.17 as surface patrol boat S.8. Sold 1919.

B.9 Vickers 24.1.1906. Completed 8.17 as surface patrol boat S.9. Sold 1919 Messrs. Francotosti, Malta.

B.10 Vickers 23.3.1906. Sunk 9.8.16 by air attack while under repair at Venice.

B.11 Vickers 21.2.1906. Completed 8.17 as surface patrol boat S.11. Sold 1919 Messrs Francotosti, Malta.

BABET 6th Rate 20, 511bm, 119 x 31 ft. French, captured 23.4.1794 off Ile Bas. Foundered 1801 in the W. Indies.

BACCHANTE 6th Rate 20, 642bm, 131 x 33 ft. French, captured 25.6.1803 by ENDYMION in the Atlantic. Sold 27.7.1809.

BACCHANTE 5th Rate 38, 1,077bm, 154 x 39½ ft. Deptford DY 16.3.1811. Harbour service 2.1837; BU completed 20.2.1858 at Deptford.

BACCHANTE Wood S. frigate, 2,064bm, 188 x 50½ ft, 28-8in, 22-32 pdr. Portsmouth DY ordered 1849 and cancelled 1851.

BACCHANTE Wood S. frigate, 2,667bm, 235 x 50 ft, 30-8in, 1-68pdr, 20-32pdr. Portsmouth DY 30.7.1859. BU 1869 at Portsmouth.

BACCHANTE Iron S. corvette,

2,679bm, 4,130 tons, 280 x 45½ ft, 14-7in, 2-64pdr. Portsmouth DY 19.10.1876. Sold 1897 Cohen.

BACCHANTE 1st class cruiser, 12,000 tons, 454 x 69½ ft, 2-9.2in, 12-6in, 13-12pdr. J. Brown 21.2.1901. Sold 1.7.20 S. Castle, Plymouth.

BACCHANTE II Yacht. Requis. 1915-16.

BACCHANTE Frigate, 'Leander' class. Vickers Armstrong, Tyne 29.2.1968. To RNZN 1.10.82, renamed WELLINGTON.

BACCHUS Cutter 10, 111bm, 68 x 20 ft. Bermuda 1806. Captured 1808 by the French in the W. Indies.

BACCHUS Sloop 12, 141 bm. Dutch, captured 1807. BU 1812.

BACCHUS Brig-sloop 18, 384bm, 'Cruizer' class. Chatham DY 17.4.1813. Towed to Harwich 13.8.1829 to be used as a breakwater.

BACCHUS (see ARETHUSA of 1817).

BACCHUS Three store carriers 1915-38, 1936-62 and 1962-81.

BADDECK Corvette (RCN), 'Flower' class. Davie SB 20.11.1940. Sold 1946 renamed *Efthalia*.

BADGER Sloop 14, 274bm, 91½ x 26½ ft. Janvrin, Bursledon 5.8.1745. Lost 1762.

BADGER (ex-*Pitt*) Brig 14, 138bm. Purchased 6.1776; condemned 1777.

BADGER Brig. Purchased 1777. Sold in Jamaica 1784.

BADGER Gunvessel 3, 59bm, 61 x 14½ ft, 2-32pdr carr., 1-24pdr. Dutch hoy purchased 4.1794. Sold 1802.

BADGER Brig-sloop 10, 240bm, 'Cherokee' class. Brindley, Frindsbury 23.7.1808. Mooring vessel 1835. Beached at the Cape 22.3.1860 and BU 1864.

BADGER (ex-RANGER renamed before launch) Wood S. gunboat, 216bm, 100 x 22 ft, 1-68pdr, 1-32pdr, 2-24pdr howitzers. Pitcher, Northfleet 23.9.1854. BU 6.1864 at Portsmouth.

BADGER Iron S. gunboat, 'Ant' class. Chatham DY 13.3.1872. Sold 6.10.1908 Loveridge, Hartlepool.

BADGER Destroyer 799 tons, 240 x 26 ft, 2-4in, 2-12pdr, 2-TT. Denny 11.7.1911. Sold 9.5.21 Ward, Hayle.

BADMINTON Minesweeper, later 'Hunt' class. Ardrossan DD 18.3.1918. Sold 19.5.28 Ward, Inverkeithing.

BADMINTON (see ILSTON).

BADSWORTH Destroyer, 'Hunt' class type II. Cammell Laird 17.3.1941.

Renamed ARENDAL 16.11.44 on loan to R. Norwegian navy; sold 1945 R. Norwegian navy.

BAGSHOT Minesweeper, later 'Hunt' class. Ardrossan DD 23.5.1918. Depot ship MEDWAY II 1.4.45; reverted to BAGSHOT 28.2.46. Sold 1947 Greek shipbreakers; sunk 1.9.51 by mine off Corfu while in tow.

BAHAMA 3rd Rate 74, 1,772bm, 175½ x 48 ft. Spanish, captured at Trafalgar 21.10.1805. Prison ship in 1809. BU 12.1814 at Chatham.

BAHAMAS (ex-HOTHAM renamed 1943) Frigate, 'Colony' class. Walsh Kaiser, 17.8.1943 on lend-lease. Returned 11.6.46 to the USN.

BALA Minesweeper, later 'Hunt' class. Clyde SB Co. Cancelled 1918.

BALEINE 6th Rate 20, 702bm, 150 x 32 ft. French, captured 10.1760 at Pondicherry. Sold 23.6.1767.

BALFOUR Trawler. Requis. 1914-18.

BALFOUR (ex-USS McANN) Frigate, TE 'Captain' class. Bethlehem, Hingham 10.7.1943 on lend-lease. Returned 10.45 to the USN.

BALIKPAPAN landing craft (RAN) 310 tons. Walker 8.1971.

BALLAHOU Gunvessel in service in 1800.

BALLAHOU Schooner 4, 78bm, 56 x 18 ft. Bermuda 1804. Captured 29.4.1814 by the American privateer PERRY off the N. American coast.

BALLARAT Minesweeper, 'Bathurst' class. Melbourne Harbour Trust, Williamstown 10.12.1940. Sold 10.7.47 to Hong Kong Sh. Co., renamed *Carmencita*.

BALLINDERRY Frigate, 'River' class. Blyth SB 7.12.1942. Handed over 7.7.61 Ward, Barrow to BU.

BALM Corvette, 'Flower' class. Alex Hall, ordered 30.7.1942, cancelled 12.11.42.

BALMAIN Frigate, (RAN), 'River' class. Sydney, ordered 12.1942, cancelled 12.6.44.

BALSAM (ex-CHELMER renamed 5.1941) Corvette, 'Flower' class. G. Brown 30.5.1942. Arrived 20.4.47 Cashmore, Newport to BU.

BALTIC Cutter 14. Russian APITH captured 24.6.1808 by SALSETTE off Norgen Is. Sold 1810.

BALTIMORE 5th Rate 28. Deptford 1695. Fate unknown.

BALTIMORE Sloop 14, 251bm, 89 x 25 ft. West, Deptford 30.12.1742. Converted to bomb vessel 1758. Sold 12.1762.

BALUCHI (see Indian TB.01 of 1888)

BALUCHI (see PC.55).

BALUCHISTAN (ex-GREENOCK renamed 1941) Minesweeper (RIN), turbine 'Bangor' class. Blyth SB 11.5.1942. To RPN 1948.

BAMBOROUGH CASTLE Corvette, 'Castle' class. J. Lewis 11.1.1944. Arrived 22.5.59 Rees. Llanelly to BU.

BANBURY Pad minesweeper 820 tons, 250 x 29 ft, 1-3in, 1-12pdr. Ailsa 19.12.1917. Sold 14.9.23 Hayes, Pembroke Dock.

BANCHORY Minesweeper, later 'Hunt' class. Ayrshire Co., Irvine 5.1918. Sold 18.5.22 B. Zammitt, Malta.

BANDOLIER Patrol boat (RAN) 100 tons. Walker 2.10.1968. Sold Indonesia 16.11.73, renamed SIBARU.

BANFF Corvette (RCN), 'Flower' class. Burrard 18.7.1940; renamed WETASKIWIN 1941. Sold 1946 Venezuelan navy as VICTORIA.

BANFF Minesweeper, turbine 'Bangor' class. Ailsa, laid down 20.7.1940, renamed HYTHE 6.41 and launched 4.9.41.

BANFF (ex-USS SARANAC) Coastguard cutter 1,546 tons, 1-5in, 2-3in. Transferred on lend-lease 30.4.1941. Returned USN 27.2.46, renamed SEBEC.

BANGOR Minesweeper, diesel 'Bangor' class. Harland & Wolff, Govan 23.5.1940. Lent R. Norwegian navy 1946; renamed GLOMMA.

BANKS Fishery Protection vessel (RAN) 250 tons. Walker 15.12.1959.

BANN 6th Rate 20, 466bm, 116 x 30 ft. King, Upnor 8.6.1814. Sold 8.1.1829 H. Cropman.

BANN Iron pad. gunboat, 267bm, 140 x 20 ft, 2-8in. Scott Russell 5.7.1856. Sold 18.2.1873 Moss Isaacs to BU.

BANN Tank vessel 1886-1908.

BANN Frigate, 'River' class. Hill 29.12.1942. To RIN as TIR 3.12.45. Training ship, 1-4in, 1-40mm in 1948.

BANSHEE Pad. packet, 670bm, 189 x 27 ft. Rotherhithe 13.10.1847. BU 1864.

BANSHEE Destroyer 330 tons, 210 x 19½ ft, 1-12pdr, 5-6pdr, 2-TT. Laird 17.11.1894. Sold 10.4.1912 Ward, Briton Ferry.

BANTERER (ex-BANTER renamed 1805) 6th Rate 22, 532bm, 118½ x 31½ ft. Temple, S. Shields 24.2.1807. Wrecked 4.12.1808 in the St Lawrence.

BANTERER Sloop 16, 250bm, 92 x 25½ ft. Woolwich DY 2.6.1810. Sold 6.3.1817 Gordon & Co.

BANTERER Wood S. gunboat, 'Albacore' class. Pitcher, Northfleet 29.9.1855. Sold 30.12.1872 at Hong Kong.

BANTERER Compos. gunboat 465 tons, 125 x 23½ ft, 2-64pdr MLR, 2-20pdr BL. Barrow SB 2.11.1880. Sold 14.5.1907 Harris, Bristol.

BANTERER (see PLUCKY of 1870).

BANTRY (see SWINDON).

BANTUM Fireship 6, 276bm. Purchased 1672. Lost 1672.

BARBADOES Fireship 8, 223bm. Purchased 1666. Sunk 1667 to block the Medway.

BARBADOES Sloop 14, 130bm, 80 x 21½ ft. Purchased 25.11.1757. Sold 15.3.1763.

BARBADOES Brig-sloop 14. Purchased in the W. Indies 1778. Foundered 4.10.1780 in a hurricane, W. Indies.

BARBADOES Sloop 14, 270bm. American RHODES captured 15.2.1782 W. Indies. Sold 2.12.1784.

BARBADOES 6th Rate 28, 755bm, 140 x 36½ ft, 10-24pdr. carr., 24-9pdr, 2-6pdr. French privateer Le BRAVE captured 5.1803 presented 1804 by the inhabitants of Barbados. Wrecked 28.9.1812 on Sable Is.

BARBADOES Brig-sloop 16, 308bm, 102 x 26 ft. American HERALD captured 1813. Became powder hulk in Jamaica to 1817.

BARBADOES 6th Rate 24, 460bm, 115½ x 30 ft. Davy, Topsham. Launched 8.3.1814 as HIND.

BARBADOS Two trawlers. Requis. between 1914 and 1919.

BARBADOS (ex-HALSTED renamed 1943) Frigate, 'Colony' class. Walsh Kaiser 27.8.1943 on lend-lease. Returned 13.4.46 to USN.

BARBARA Schooner 14. Purchased 1796. In service 1801.

BARBARA Schooner 10, 112bm, 68 x 20 ft. Bermuda 1806. Sold 9.2.1815. (In French hands as privateer PERATY 17.9.07 to 17.7.08.)

BARBETTE 6th Rate 22, 604bm. French privateer VAILLANTE captured 25.6.1805. BU 5.1811.

BARBETTE Two boom defence vessels 1937-41 and 1943-65.

BARBETTE Patrol boat (RAN) 100 tons. Walker 10.4.1968. Sold Indonesia 1985.

BARBUDA Sloop 16 in service in 1780. Lost 2.1782 at the surrender of Demerara.

BARCOO Frigate (RAN), 'River' class. Cockatoo DY 26.8.1943. Sold 27.1.72 to BU in Taiwan.

BARFLEUR 2nd Rate 90, 1,476bm, 163 x 46½ ft. Deptford DY 10.8.1697. Rebuilt Deptford 1716 as 1,565bm, 80 guns; hulked 1764. BU 7.1783.

BARFLEUR 2nd Rate 98, 1,947bm, 178 x 50½ ft. Chatham DY 30.7.1768. BU 9.1819 at Chatham.

BARFLEUR (see BRITANNIA of 1762).

BARFLEUR Battleship 10,500 tons, 360 x 70 ft, 4-10in, 10-4.7in, 2-9pdr. Chatham DY 10.8.1892. Sold 12.7.1910 C. Ewen, Glasgow, resold and BU by Hughes Bolckow.

BARFLEUR Destroyer 2,325 tons, 355 x 40 ft, 4-4.5in, 8-TT. Swan Hunter 1.11.1943. Arrived 29.9.66 Dalmuir to BU.

BARHAM 3rd Rate 74, 1,761 bm, 176 x 48½ ft. Perry, Wells & Green, Blackwall 8.7.1811. Reduced to 50 guns 12.1826. BU 9.1840.

BARHAM Wood S. frigate, 3,027bm, 250 x 52 ft, 30-8in, 1-68pdr, 20-32pdr. Portsmouth DY, ordered 1860 and cancelled.

BARHAM 3rd class cruiser 1,830 tons, 280 x 35 ft, 6-4.7in, 4-3pdr. Portsmouth DY 11.9.1889. Sold 19.2.1914 Ward, Preston.

BARHAM Battleship 27,500 tons, 600 x 90½ ft, 8-15in, 14-6in, 2-3in. J. Brown 31.12.1919. Sunk 25.11.41 by 'U.331' in the Mediterranean.

BARK OF BULLEN Ship 80bm, captured from French in 7.1522. Listed to 1525.

BARK OF MURLESSE Ship 60bm, captured from French in 7.1522. Listed to 1530.

BARLE Trawler. Requis. 1915-19.

BARLE Frigate, 'River' class. Vickers, Montreal 26.9.1942 on lend-lease. Returned 27.2.46 to the USN.

BARNARD CASTLE (see EMPIRE SHELTER).

BARNSTAPLE Minesweeper, later 'Hunt' class. Ardrossan DD 20.3.1919. Sold 1.12.21, renamed *Lady Cynthia*. BU 1957.

BARNWELL CASTLE Corvette, 'Castle' class. Kingston SB, Canada. Cancelled 12.1943.

BARRACOUTA Sloop 14, 197bm, 75 x 26 ft. Ex-cutter purchased 6.1782. Sold 19.1.1792.

BARRACOUTA Schooner 4, 78bm, 56 x 18 ft. Bermuda 1804. Wrecked 2.10.1805 on the coast of Cuba.

BARRACOUTA Brig-sloop, 'Cruizer'

class 385bm. Bailey, Ipswich 6.7.1807. Sold 23.3.1815.

BARRACOUTA Brig-sloop 10, 'Cherokee' class 235bm. Woolwich DY 13.5.1820. Commissioned as packet brig 5.1829; sold 21.1.1836.

BARRACOUTA Wood pad. sloop, 1,053bm, 6 guns. Pembroke Dock 31.3.1851. BU 12.1881 at Chatham.

BARRACOUTA 3rd class cruiser 1,580 tons, 220 x 35 ft, 6-4.7in, 4-3 pdr. Sheerness DY 16.5.1889. Sold 4.4.1905 McLellan, resold and BU at Bo'ness.

BARRIE Corvette (RCN), 'Flower' class. Collingwood SY 23.11.1940. Sold 1946 Argentine navy as GASESTADO.

BARRINGTON Destroyer leader 1,750 tons, 318 x 32 ft. Cammell Laird Ordered 4.1918, cancelled 26.11.18.

BARROSA 5th Rate 36, 947bm, 145 x 38½ ft. Deptford DY 21.10.1812. Harbour service 1823. Sold 27.5.1841.

BARROSA Wood S. corvette, 1,700bm, 225 x 41 ft, 16-8in, 1-7in, 4-40pdr. Woolwich DY 10.3.1860. BU 1.1877 at Chatham.

BARROSA 3rd class cruiser 1,580 tons, 220 x 35 ft, 6-4.7in, 4-3pdr. Portsmouth DY 16.4.1889. Sold 11.7.1905.

BARROSA Destroyer 2,380 tons, 355 x 40 ft, 5-4.5in, 10-TT. J. Brown 17.1.1945. Sold 2.8.78. BU at Blyth 12.78.

BARWON Frigate (RAN), 'River' class. Cockatoo DY 3.8.1944. Sold 1.62 Sleigh Bros to BU in Japan; left Sydney 17.8.62.

BASILISK Bomb 4, 163bm, 72 x 23 ft. Reading, Wapping 4.5.1695. BU 1729.

BASILISK Bomb 4, 270bm, 92 x 26 ft. Snelgrove, Limehouse 30.8.1740. Sold 14.8.1750.

BASILISK Bomb 8, 312bm, 92 x 28 ft. Wells, Deptford 10.2.1759. Captured 29.10.1762 by the French privateer AUDACIEUX.

BASILISK (see GRASSHOPPER of 1777).

BASILISK Gun-brig 12, 186bm, 80 x 23 ft. Randall, Rotherhithe 2.4.1801. Sold 14.12.1815.

BASILISK Cutter 6, 161bm, 67½ x 24 ft, 6-6pdr. Chatham DY 7.5.1822. Sold 1.1846.

BASILISK Wood pad. sloop, 1,031bm, 185 x 34 ft. Woolwich DY 22.8.1848. BU 1882 at Chatham.

BASILISK Sloop 1,170 tons, 195 x 28 ft, 8-5in. Sheerness DY 6.4.1889. Be-

47

came coal hulk C.7 and sold 1905 as *Maggie Grech.*

BASILISK Destroyer 976 tons, 265 x 28 ft, 1-4in, 3-12pdr, 2-TT. White 9.2.1910. Sold 1.11.21 Fryer, Sunderland.

BASILISK Destroyer 1,360 tons, 312 x 32½ ft, 4-4.7in, 8-TT. J. Brown 6.8.1930. Sunk 1.6.40 by air attack off Dunkirk.

BASING 22-gun ship, 255bm. Shish, Walderswick 1654. Renamed GUERNSEY 1660; made a fireship 1688. BU 1693.

BASING 6th Rate 18, 121bm. Purchased 1693. Captured 5.2.1694 by the French.

BASS Survey vessel (RAN), 250 tons. Walker 28.3.1960.

BASSINGHAM Inshore M/S, 'Ham' class. Vosper, Portsmouth 24.6.1952. Sold 1966 Pounds, Portsmouth.

BASTION (ex-LCT.4040 renamed 1956) Tank landing craft 657 tons, 225 x 39 ft, 4-20mm. Sold Zambia 15.9.66.

BAT Destroyer 360 tons, 215 x 21 ft, 1-12pdr, 5-6pdr, 2-TT. Palmer, Jarrow 7.10.1896. Sold 30.8.1919 Hayes, Porthcawl.

BATAAN (ex-KURNAI renamed 1944) Destroyer (RAN) 1,927 tons, 355½ x 36½ ft, 6-4.7in, 2-4in, 4-TT. Cockatoo DY 15.1.1944. Sold 1958 T. Carr & Co, Sydney, resold to BU in Japan 1962.

BATAVIA 4th Rate 56, 1,048bm. Dutch, captured 30.8.1799 in the Texel. Floating battery 7.1801; harbour service 9.1817. BU 3.1823.

BATH (ex-USS HOPEWELL) Destroyer 1,060 tons, 309 x 30½ ft, 3-4 in, 1-3in, 6-TT. Commissioned in the RN 10.1940. Lent to the R. Norwegian navy 1.1.41. Sunk 19.8.41 by 'U.201' SW of Ireland.

BATHGATE Minesweeper, later 'Hunt' class. Clyde SB Co. Cancelled 1918.

BATHURST Brig 10, 170bm. Purchased 7.1821 at Port Jackson. Survey vessel 1822; coastguard service 2. 1824. Sold Castle 11.4.1858 to BU.

BATHURST Minesweeper, 'Bathurst' class. Cockatoo DY 1.8.1940. On loan to RAN. Sold 21.6.48 at Sydney to BU.

BATMAN Iron S. gunboat (Australian) 388 tons, 1-6in, 2-3pdr. Simons Renfrew 1883. Listed in 1895.

BATTLE Minesweeper, later 'Hunt' class. Dundee SB Co. Cancelled 10.1919, launched incomplete and sold 3.22 Ward, Inverkeithing.

BATTLEAXE Trawler 1916-20, renamed DEE.

BATTLEAXE Landing ship, dock, 4,270 tons, 454 x 72 ft, 1-3in, 20-light. Newport News 21.5.1943 on lend-lease. Renamed EASTWAY 8.43. Returned USN 5.47.

BATTLEAXE Destroyer 1,980 tons, 341½ x 38 ft, 6-4in, 6-40mm, 10-TT. Yarrow 12.6.1945. Arrived 20.10.64 Hughes Bolckow, Blyth to BU.

BATTLEAXE Frigate 3,500 tons. Yarrow 18.5.1977.

BATTLEFORD Corvette (RCN), 'Flower' class. Collingwood SY 15.4.1941. Sold 1946 Venezuelan navy as LIBERTAD.

BATTLER (ex-*Mormacmail* (ii))Escort carrier 11,420 tons, 468½ x 69½ ft, 2-4in, 8-40mm, 18-A/C. Ingalls 4.4.1942 on lend-lease. Returned 12.2.46 to the USN.

BATTLER (see LST 3015).

BAYFIELD Minesweeper, TE 'Bangor' class. N. Vancouver SR 26.5. 1941. Sold 1.1.48, BU by King, Gateshead.

BAYNTUN Frigate, DE 'Captain' class. Boston Navy Yd 27.6.1942 on lend-lease. Returned 22.8.45 to the USN.

BAYONET Patrol boat (RAN) 100 tons. Walker 6.11.1968.

BAZELY Frigate, DE 'Captain' class. Boston Navy Yd 27.6.1942. To RN 18.2.43 on lend-lease. Returned 8.45 to USN.

BEACHAMPTON Coastal M/S, 'Ton' class. Goole SB 29.6.1953.

BEACHY HEAD Repair ship 8,580 tons, 425 x 57 ft, 16-20mm. Burrard, Vancouver 27.9. 1944. On loan Dutch navy 1946-49 as VULKAAN. To RCN 1954 as CAPE SCOTT. Sold 1977.

BEACON (ex-*Duff*) Fireship, 150bm. Purchased 6.1804. Sold 3.11.1808.

BEACON (see METEOR of 1823).

BEACON Mortar vessel, 117bm, 65 x 21 ft, 1-13in. mortar. Wigram, Blackwall 21.4.1855. Renamed MV.16 19.10.1855. Made a DY lighter 5.1862.

BEACON Wood S. gunboat, 'Albacore' class. Laird 11.2.1856. BU 8.1864.

BEACON Compos. S. gunvessel, 465bm, 603 tons, 155 x 25 ft, 1-7in MLR, 1-64pdr MLR, 2-20pdr. Chatham DY 17.8.1867. Sold 12.1888.

BEACON HILL Frigate (RCN), 'River' class. Yarrow, Esquimalt 6.11.1943. Sold 1968.

BEAGLE Brig-sloop, 'Cruizer' class, firbuilt 383bm. Perry, Wells & Green, Blackwall 8.8.1804. Sold 21.7.1814.

BEAGLE Brig-sloop 10, 'Cherokee' class. Woolwich DY 11.5.1820. Survey ship 1825; Customs watch vessel 1846; renamed WV.7 in 5.1863. Sold 13.5.1870 Murray & Trainer.

BEAGLE Wood S. gunvessel, 477bm, 160 x 25½ ft, 2-68pdr ML. Mare, Blackwall 20.7.1854. Sold 1863 at Hong Kong; became Japanese KANKO 1865. BU 1889.

BEAGLE Schooner 1, 120bm, 80 x 18 ft, 1-12pdr. Cuthbert, Sydney NSW 5.12.1872. Sold 1883 at Sydney.

BEAGLE Sloop 1,170 tons, 195 x 28 ft, 8-5in. Portsmouth DY 28.2. 1889. Sold 11.7.1905.

BEAGLE Destroyer 950 tons, 269 x 27 ft, 1-4in, 3-12pdr, 2-TT. J. Brown 16.10.1909. Sold 1.11.21 Fryer, Sunderland.

BEAGLE Destroyer 1,360 tons, 312 x 32½ ft, 4-4.7in, 8-TT. J.Brown 26.9.1930. Sold 15.1.46; arrived 6.46 Rosyth to BU.

BEAGLE Tug 1963, renamed BASSET 1967.

BEAGLE Survey ship 1,050 tons. Brooke Marine 7.9.1967.

BEAR 40-gun ship, 398bm. Prize, rebuilt 1580. Last listed in 1665.

BEAR 36-gun ship captured 1664. Sold 1665.

BEATRICE Survey schooner (Australian). Purchased 1868. Sold 1880.

BEATTY (see HOWE of 1940).

BEAUFORT (ex-minesweeper AMBLESIDE renamed 1918). Survey ship 800 tons, 1-3pdr. Ailsa 21.2.1919. Sold 30.6.38 Cashmore resold 27.7.39 Rees, Llanelly.

BEAUFORT Destroyer, 'Hunt' class type II. Cammell Laird 15.4.1941. To Norwegian navy 1952, renamed HAUGESUND 30.9.54.

BEAUHARNOIS Corvette (RCN), modified Flower class. Morton 11.5.1944. Sold 1946, renamed *Colon.*

BEAULIEU 5th Rate 40, 1,020bm, 147½ x 39½ft, 28-18pdr, 12-9pdr. Adams, Bucklers Hard 4.5.1791 (built on speculation & purchased 6.1790). BU 8.1806.

BEAULIEU Minesweeper, TE 'Bangor' class. Hong Kong and Whampoa laid down 22.7.1941, renamed LANTAU 9.41; captured on stocks by the Japanese and launched 2.43 as Minesweeper No 101.

BEAULIEU Tug requis. 1914-19. Tender built 1963.

BEAULY FIRTH (ex-EMPIRE SARAWAK renamed 1944). Repair ship 8,650 tons, 439 x 62ft, 12-20mm. Readhead, S.Shields 24.8.1944. Sold 1948, renamed *Stanfirth.*

BEAUMARIS (see BOLTON of 1918).

BEAUMARIS Minesweeper, turbine 'Bangor' class. Ailsa 31.10.1940. Sold 1.1.1948; BU Ward, Milford Haven.

BEAUMONT Sloop 16. American, captured 5.1780 at Charlestown. Sold in 4.1783.

BEAVER Ketch 6 (Royalist) captured by Parliament 1656. BU 1658.

BEAVER Sloop 18, 338bm, 95 x 28½ft, 18-6pdr. French privateer TRUDAINE captured 4.1757. Sold 22.1.1761.

BEAVER Sloop 14, 285bm, 96½ x 26ft. Inwood, Rotherhithe 3.2.1761. Sold 17.7.1783.

BEAVER PRIZE Sloop 18, 263bm, 88 x 27ft. American privateer OLIVER CROMWELL captured 18.5.1778 by BEAVER. Wrecked 11.10.1780 at St Lucia, W. Indies. (Was CONVERT until 1778).

BEAVER Sloop 14, 269bm, 94 x 25½ft. Graham, Harwich 29.9.1795. Sold 21.12.1808.

BEAVER Brig-sloop 10, 'Cherokee' class 236bm. Bailey, Ipswich 16.2.1809. Sold 24.6.1829 J. Cristall.

BEAVER (ex-GPO vessel *Salamander*) Wood pad. packet, 114bm, 102 x 16ft. Transferred 1837. Made a dockyard lighter 1845.

BEAVER Wood S. gunboat, 'Albacore' class. Wigram, Northam 28.11.1855. BU 1864 at Portsmouth.

BEAVER (ex-War Dept vessel *Victor*) Tender 125 tons, 95 x 17½ft. Transferred 1905. Sold 7.7.1911 Laidler, Sunderland.

BEAVER Destroyer 810 tons, 240 x 26ft, 2-4in. 2-12pdr, 2-TT. Denny 6.10.1911. Sold 9.5.21 Ward, Hayle, resold J.J.King 6.23 to BU.

BEAVER Frigate 4,200 tons. Yarrow 8.5.1982.

BEAVER. Tug 1914-23; 3 vessels requis. WW.II.

BECCLES Minesweeper, later 'Hunt' class. Dundee SB Co. Cancelled 1918.

BECKFORD Seaward defence boat, 'Ford' class. Simons 3.1953. Renamed DEE 1965. Sold Pounds, Portsmoutn in 1.83.

BECKWITH Schooner (Canadian lakes). Kingston Ont. 8.7.1816. Sold circa 1837.

BEDALE Destroyer, 'Hunt' class type II. Hawthorn Leslie 23.7.1941. Lent

Polish navy 4.42 as SLAZAK; reverted to BEDALE 11.46. To Indian Navy as GODAVERI 27.4.53. Sold 4.59.

BEDFORD GALLEY 5th Rate 34, 372bm, 103 x 29ft. Built in New England 1697 and purchased 1697. Rebuilt Portsmouth 1709 as 410bm; made a fireship 1716. Sunk 3.5.1725 as a foundation at Sheerness.

BEDFORD 3rd Rate 70, 1,073 bm, 151 x 40ft. Woolwich DY 12.9.1698. Rebuilt Portsmouth 1741 as 1,230bm, 64 guns; hulked 11.1767. Sold 1787.

BEDFORD 3rd Rate 74, 1,606bm, 168½ x 47ft. Woolwich DY 27.10.1775. Prison ship 1801. BU 10.1817.

BEDFORD Armoured cruiser 9,800 tons, 440 x 66ft, 14-6in, 9-12pdr. Fairfield 31.8.1901. Wrecked 21.8.10 in the Korea Sea.

BEDHAM Inshore M/S, 'Ham' class. Bolson, Poole 29.7.1953. To Malaysian Navy 1959, renamed LANKA SUKA.

BEDOUIN Trawler. Requis. 1914-15.

BEDOUIN Destroyer 1,870 tons, 355½ x 36½ft, 8-4. 7in, 4-TT. Denny 21.12.1937. Sunk 15.6.42 by Italian A/C torpedo in the Mediterranean.

BEE Wood S. and pad. vessel, 42bm, 60 x 12½ft. Chatham DY 28.2.1842. BU 1874.

BEE River gunboat 645 tons, 230 x 36ft, 2-6in, 1-3in. Ailsa 8.12.1915. Sold 22.3.39 at Shanghai to BU.

BEE River gunboat 585 tons. White, Cowes, ordered 1939, cancelled 3.40

BEE Tender 213 tons. Holmes 5.6.1969.

BEESTON CASTLE Corvette, 'Castle' class. Kingston SB cancelled 12.1943.

BEGONIA Sloop, 'Acacia' class. Barclay Curle 26.8.1915. Sunk 2.10.18 in collision with 'U.151' off Casablanca while serving as decoy ship 'Q.10'.

BEGONIA II Drifter. Requis. 1915-19.

BEGONIA Corvette, 'Flower' class. Cook, Welton and Gemmell 18.9.1940. On loan to the USN as IMPULSE 16.3.42 to 1945. Sold 22.7.46, renamed *Beganlock*.

BEGUM (ex-USS NATOMA BAY) Escort carrier 7,800 tons. Kaiser, Vancouver USA 20.7.1943. Retained by the USN as NATOMA BAY.

BEGUM (ex-*Balinas*) Escort carrier 11,400 tons, 468½ x 69½ft. Seattle,Tacoma 11.11.42; to RN 2.8.43 on lend-lease. Returned 4.1.46 USN; sold as *Raki*.

BELEM Schooner 4, 88bm. Spanish, captured 27.6.1806 at Montevideo.

Retaken by the Spanish 12.8.1806 at Buenos Aires.

BELETTE 6th Rate 24, 580bm, 120 x 32 ft. French, captured 29.8.1793 at Toulon. Burnt 20.10.1796 at Agaccio, unserviceable.

BELETTE Sloop 18, 346bm, 104½ x 27½ft. French BELLIQUEUSE captured 2.1798. Sold 14.9.1801.

BELETTE Brig-sloop 18, 'Cruizer' class. 384bm. King, Dover 21.3.1806. Wrecked 24.11.1812 in the Kattegat.

BELETTE Brig-sloop 18, 'Cruizer' class, 386bm Larking, Lynn 18.6.1814. Sold 26.3.1828 Adam Gordon.

BELFAST Cruiser, 10,000 tons, 579 x 63 ft, 12-6in, 12-4in. Harland and Wolff 17.3.1938. Museum ship 21.10.71 on Thames.

BELFORT Sloop 644 tons, 246 x 31ft, 1-3in. French, seized 3.7.1940 at Plymouth. Free-French depot ship 9.40-44; returned to French navy 1946.

BELISARIUS 6th Rate 24, 514bm, 164 x 27½ft. American, captured 7.8.1781 by MEDEA. Sold 2.12.1783.

BELLECHASSE Minesweeper (RCN), TE 'Bangor' class. Burrard, Vancouver 20.10.1941. Sold 1946.

BELLE ISLE 3rd Rate 64, 1,494bm, 168½ x 45ft. French E.Indiaman *Bertin* captured 1761. Harbour service 12.1784. Sold 3.2.1819.

BELLEISLE 3rd Rate 74, 1,889bm 184 x 49ft. French FORMIDABLE captured 23.6.1795 at Belle Isle. BU 8.1814.

BELLEISLE 3rd Rate 74, 1,709bm, 174 x 48ft. Pembroke Dock 26.4.1819. Reduced to 20-gun troopship 1841; harbour service 5.1854. BU completed 12.10.1872 at Chatham.

BELLEISLE (ex-Turkish PEIKI SHEREEF purchased 1878) Coast defence ship 4,870 tons, 245 x 52ft, 4-12in MLR, 6-6pdr. Samuda, Poplar 12.2.1876. Wrecked as target 4.9.1903; wreck sold 12.4.04 to BU. in Germany.

BELLEISLE Destroyer 2,380 tons, 355 x 40ft, 5-4.5in, 10-TT. Fairfield 7.2.1946 (not completed). Arrived 4.46 Arnott Young to BU at Troon.

BELLE POULE 5th Rate 36, 902bm, 140 x 38ft. French, captured 17.7.1780 by NONSUCH off the mouth of the Loire. Sold 14.9.1801.

BELLE POULE 5th Rate 38, 1,077bm, 151½ x 40ft. French, captured 13.3.1806 by a squadron in the S. Atlantic. Troopship 1814; prison ship 1815. Sold 11.6.1818.

BELLEROPHON 3rd Rate 74, 1,643bm, 168 x 47ft. Graves, Frindsbury 6.10.1786. Prison ship 10.1815; renamed CAPTIVITY 5.10.1824. Sold 21.1.1836.

BELLEROPHON (see WATERLOO of 1818)

BELLEROPHON Battleship, 4,270bm, 7,551 tons, 300 x 56ft, 10-9in MLR, 5-7in MLR. Chatham DY 26.5.1865. Training ship INDUS III 3.1904. Sold 12.12.22 McLellan, Bo'ness.

BELLEROPHON Battleship, 18,600 tons, 490 x 82½ft, 10-12in, 16-4in. Portsmouth DY 27.7.1907. Sold 8.11.21 Slough TC; towed to Germany 14.9.22 to BU.

BELLEROPHON (see TIGER of 1945)

BELLEROPHON (see TIGER ordered 3.42)

BELLEVILLE Corvette (RCN), modified 'Flower' class. Kingston SB 17.6.1944. Sold 1948 Dominican navy as JUAN BAUTISTA CAMBIASO.

BELLIQUEUX 3rd Rate 64, 1,372bm, 158 x 45ft. French, captured 2.11.1758 by ANTELOPE in the Bristol Channel. BU 9.1772.

BELLIQUEUX 3rd Rate 64, 1,379bm, 160 x 48½ft. Perry, Blackwall 5.6.1780. Prison ship 2.1814. BU 3.1816 at Chatham.

BELLONA 6th Rate 30, 541bm, 112 x 33½ft, 24-9pdr, 6-4pdr. French privateer BELLONE captured 2.2.1747 by NOTTINGHAM in the Channel. Sold 2.2.1749.

BELLONA 3rd Rate 74, 1,615bm, 168 x 47ft. Chatham DY 19.2.1760. BU 9.1814 at Chatham.

BELLONA Gunvessel 3, 86bm, 62 x 18ft. Purchased 3.1794. Made a mud boat 1799. BU 8.1805 at Woolwich.

BELLONA 6th Rate 28, 648bm, 132 x 34ft. French BELLONE captured 9.7.1806 by POWERFUL off Ceylon. Renamed BLANCHE 1809. BU 1814.

BELLONA (see INDUS of 1812)

BELLONA 3rd class cruiser 1,830 tons, 280 x 35ft, 6-4.7in, 4-3pdr. Hawthorn 29.8.1890. Sold 10.7.1906.

BELLONA Scout cruiser 3,350 tons, 385 x 41ft, 6-4in. Pembroke Dock 20.3.1909. Sold 9.5.21 Ward, Lelant.

BELLONA Trawler and Drifter requis. in WWI.

BELLONA Cruiser 5,770 tons, 485 x 50½ft, 8-5.25in, 6-4in. Fairfield 29.9.1942. Arrived 5.2.59 Ward, Briton Ferry to BU. (Was on loan to RNZN 1948-56.)

BELLWORT Corvette, 'Flower' class. G. Brown 11.8.1941 To Irish govt. 1947 as CLIONA.

BELMONT Trawler. Requis. 1915-19.

BELMONT (ex-USS SATTERLEE) Destroyer 1,190 tons, 311 x 31ft, 3-4in, 1-3in, 6-TT. Commissioned in the RN 8.10.1940. Sunk 31.1.42 by 'U.82' off Halifax NS.

BELTON Coastal M/S, 'Ton' class. Doig, Grimsby 3.10.1955. Sold 28.10.74, BU in Spain.

BELVIDERA 5th Rate 36, 946bm, 145 x 38½ft. Deptford DY 23.12.1809. Harbour service 10.1846. Sold 10.7.1906 J.B. Garnham.

BELVIDERA Wood S.frigate, 3,027bm, 250 x 52ft. Chatham DY. Laid down 30.4.1860, cancelled 16.12.1864.

BELVOIR Minesweeper, early 'Hunt' class. Ailsa 8.3.1917. Sold 7.22 Stanlee, Dover.

BELVOIR Destroyer, 'Hunt' class type III. Cammell Laird 18.11.1941. Arrived 21.10.57 McLellan, Bo'ness to BU.

BELZEBUB Bomb 8, 334bm, 102½ x 27½ft. Taylor, Bideford 30.7.1813. BU completed 23.9.1820.

BELZEBUB Bomb 8, 372bm, 105 x 29ft, 10-24pdr carr., 2-6pdr, 1-13in mortar, 1-10in mortar. Plymouth DY. Ordered 1821, cancelled 1832..

BELZEBUB (see FIREBRAND of 1842).

BENALLA Minesweeper (RAN), 'Bathurst' class. Williamstown DY 19.12.1942. Sold 20.2.58 to BU in Japan.

BENARES Sloop 14 (Indian), 230bm. Bombay DY 1807. Sold 1836.

BENARES Trawler (RIN) cancelled 1945.

BENBOW 3rd Rate 72, 1,773bm, 176½ x 49ft. Brent, Rotherhithe 3.2.1813. Harbour service 2.1848; coal hulk 8.1859; sold 23.11.1892, BU 1895 Castle, Woolwich.

BENBOW Battleship 10,600 tons, 330 x 68½ft, 2-16.25in, 10-6in, 15-small. Thames Iron Works 15.6.1885. Sold 13.7.1909 Ward, Morecambe.

BENBOW Battleship 25,000 tons, 580 x 89½ft, 10-13.5in, 12-6in. Beardmore 12.11.1913. Sold 3.31 Metal Industries, Rosyth.

BENDIGO Minesweeper, 'Bathurst' class. Cockatoo DY 1.3.1941. Sold 5.5.47, renamed *Cheung Hing*.

BENDIGO Patrol vessel (RAN), 211 tons. North Queensland Eng. Co., Cairns. 9.4.1983.

BEND OR M/S sloop, '24' class. Barclay Curle 24.9.1918. Sold 12.8.20 Moise Mazza, Malta; resold 8.22 C.A. Beard.

BENGAL Name chosen 1812 for ex-Danish FIJEN 74; name not used.

BENGAL Two trawlers. Requis. 1915-19.

BENGAL Minesweeper (RIN), 'Bathurst' class. Cockatoo DY 28.5.1942. Sold 1960.

BENJAMIN Fireship 6, 130bm. Purchased 1673. Captured 1673 by the Dutch.

BENJAMIN AND ANN Gunvessel 3, 72bm, 59½ x 16½ft. Purchased 1794. Fate unknown.

BEN LOMOND (see LST. 3013)

BEN NEVIS (see LST. 3012)

BENTINCK Iron pad. vessel (Indian). Rennie 28.7.1832. For sale in 1855.

BENTINCK Frigate, DE 'Captain' class. Mare Island 22.8.1942 for the RN but retained by the USN as BRENNAN.

BENTINCK Frigate, TE 'Captain' class. Bethlehem, Hingham 3.2.1943 on lend-lease. Returned 5.1.46 to the USN.

BENTLEY Frigate, TE 'Captain' class. Bethlehem, Hingham 17.7.1943 on lend-lease. Returned 5.11.45 to the USN.

BERBERIS Sloop, 'Arabis' class. Henderson 3.2.1916. Sold 30.1.23 Stuart Gen. Trading Co.

BERBICE Schooner 121bm. Purchased 1780, condemned 12.9.1788.

BERBICE Schooner 8, 120bm, 73 x 20½ft, 2-12pdr. carr., 6-3pdr. Ex-prize, purchased 1793. Wrecked 11.1796 at Dominica.

BERBICE Schooner 4, 78bm. Purchased 1804. Foundered 1806 near Demerara.

BERE CASTLE Corvette, 'Castle' class. G. Brown. Cancelled 12.1943.

BERENICE Pad. sloop (Indian), 630bm, 170 x 29ft, 1-68pdr, 2-32pdr. Napier, Glasgow 1836. Burnt 31.10.1866 by accident in the Persian Gulf.

BERESFORD (see PRINCE REGENT of 1812).

BERGAMOT Sloop, 'Anchusa' class. Armstrong 5.5.1917. Sunk 13.8.17 by 'U.84' in the Atlantic.

BERGAMOT Corvette, 'Flower' class. Harland and Wolff 15.2.1941. Sold 5.46, renamed Syros.

BERGERE Sloop 18. 442bm. French, captured 17.4.1806 by SIRIUS in the Mediterranean. BU 10.1811.

BERKELEY Destroyer, 'Hunt' class type I. Cammell Laird 29.1.1940. Sunk 19.8.42 by HMS ALBRIGHTON after bomb damage off Dieppe.

BERKELEY Minehunter 615 tons. Vosper Thornycroft 3.12.1986.

BERKELEY CASTLE 48-gun ship captured 25.10.1695 by the French.

BERKELEY CASTLE Corvette, 'Castle' class. Barclay Curle 19.8.1943. Arrived 29.2.56, Grays to BU.

BERMUDA Brig-sloop 14, 170bm, 80 x 24ft, 14-12pdr. carr. Purchased 1795 while building in Bermuda. Foundered 9.1796 in the Gulf of Florida.

BERMUDA Sloop 18, 399bm, 100 x 30ft. Bermuda 1805. Wrecked 22.4.1808 in the Bahamas.

BERMUDA Brig-sloop 10, 'Cherokee' class, 237bm. Pelham, Frindsbury 20.12.1808. Wrecked 24.11.1816 in the Gulf of Mexico.

BERMUDA Yacht, 43bm, ex-pilot boat presented 1813. BU 9.1841 in Bermuda.

BERMUDA Schooner, purchased 1819. Foundered 3.1821 between Halifax and Bermuda.

BERMUDA Schooner 3, 180bm, 80 x 23ft. Outerbridge and Hollis, Bermuda 3.1848. Wrecked 24.2.1855 on Turks Is, W. Indies.

BERMUDA Trawler requis. 1914-19.

BERMUDA Cruiser 8,000 tons, 538 x 62ft, 12-6in, 8-4in. J. Brown 11.9.1941. Arrived 26.8.65 Ward, Briton Ferry to BU.

BERRY Frigate, DE 'Captain' class. Boston Navy Yd 23.11.1942 on lend-lease. Returned 15.2.46 to the USN.

BERRY HEAD Repair ship 8,580 tons, 439 x 60ft, 16-20mm. Burrard, Vancouver 21.10.1944.

BERWICK 3rd Rate 70, 1,041bm, 151 x 40ft. Chatham DY 1679. Rebuilt 1700 as 1,090bm; hulked 10.1715. BU 1742.

BERWICK 3rd Rate 70, 1,147bm, 151 x 42ft. Deptford DY 23.7.1723. Hulked 5.1743. BU 6.1783.

BERWICK 3rd Rate 70, 1,280bm, 154 x 44ft. Deptford 1743. BU 9.1760 at Chatham.

BERWICK 3rd Rate 74, 1,623bm, 168½ x 47ft. Portsmouth DY 18.4.1775. Captured 7.3.1795 by three French frigates in the Mediterranean; recaptured 21.10.1805 at Trafalgar and wrecked off San Lucar.

BERWICK Storeship 22, 512bm, 110 x 33ft. Purchased 11.1781. Renamed SIRIUS 10.1786 and made a 6th rate. Wrecked 15.3.1790 on Norfolk Island.

BERWICK (see SAN JUAN of 1805).

BERWICK 3rd Rate 74, 1,761 bm, 176 x

48ft. Perry, Blackwall 11.9.1809. BU 3.1821.

BERWICK 1st class cruiser 9,800 tons, 440 x 66ft, 14-6in, 9-12pdr. Beardmore 20.9.1902. Sold 1.7.20; towed to Hamburg 28.8.22 to BU.

BERWICK Cruiser 9,750 tons, 590 x 68ft, 8-8in, 8-4in. Fairfield 30.3.1926. Sold 15.6.48, arrived 12.7.48 Hughes Bolckow, Blyth to BU.

BERWICK Frigate 2,144 tons, 360 x 41 ft, 2-4.5in, 1-40mm. Harland and Wolff 15.12.1959. Sunk in 8.86 as a target, N. Atlantic.

BESCHERMER 4th Rate 56, 1,052bm. Dutch, captured 30.8.1799 in the Texel. Made a floating battery 7.1801; lent E India Dk Co. 4.11.1806 to 8.38. Sold 9.1838 J. Cristall.

BETANO Landing craft (RAN) 310 tons. Walker 5.12.1972.

BETONY Corvette, modified 'Flower' class. Alex Hall 22.4.1943. Lent RIN 24.8.45 as SIND; reverted to BETONY (RN) 17.5.46; sold Siamese navy 1947, renamed PRASAE. Wrecked 1.51.

BETTY 5th Rate 36, 372bm, 103 x 28½ft. Purchased 1695. In French hands 14.8.1695 to 1696. Sold 1702.

BEVERLEY (ex-USS BRANCH) Destroyer 1,190 tons, 311 x 31 ft, 1-4in, 1-3in, 4-20mm. Commissioned in the RN 8.10.1940. Sunk 11.4.43 by 'U.188' south of Greenland after collision with SS *Cairnrona* on 9.4.43.

BEVINGTON Coastal M/S, 'Ton' class. White, Southampton 1.7.1953. Sold 1967 Argentine navy, renamed TIERRA del FUEGO.

BEZAN Yacht 4, 35bm, Presented by the Dutch 1661. BU 1687.

BHAMO Pad. gunboat (RIM) 255 tons, 163 x 30ft, 2-MG. Kidderpore DY 1896. Sold circa 1922.

BICESTER Minesweeper, early 'Hunt' class. Ailsa 8.6.1917. Sold 18.1.23 Alloa, arrived Charlestown 22.3.23 to BU.

BICESTER Destroyer, 'Hunt' class type II. Hawthorn Leslie 5.9.1941. Arrived 22.8.56 Ward, Grays to BU.

BICESTER Minehunter 615 tons. Vosper/Thornycroft 4.6.1985.

BICKERTON (ex-USS EISELE) Frigate, TE 'Captain' class. Bethlehem, Hingham 26.7.1943 on lend-lease. Sunk 22.8.44 by HMS VIGILANT after torpedo damage by 'U.354' in the Barents Sea.

BICKINGTON Coastal M/S, 'Ton' class. White, Southampton 3.1953.

Renamed CURZON. 1954-60.

BIDDEFORD 6th Rate 24, 256bm, 93 x 25ft. Barrett, Harwich 25.10.1695. Wrecked 12.11.1699 on Point Baque.

BIDDEFORD 6th Rate 20, 282bm, 94 x 26½ ft. Deptford DY 14.3.1711. Rebuilt Chatham 1727 as 371bm. Foundered 18.3.1736 off Flamborough Head.

BIDEFORD 6th Rate 24, 433bm, 106 x 31 ft. Barnard, Ipswich 15.4.1740. BU completed 19.8.1754 at Portsmouth.

BIDEFORD 6th Rate 20, 403bm, 105 x 29½ ft. Deptford DY 2.3.1756. Wrecked 30.12.1761 on Flamborough Head.

BIDEFORD Minesweeper, later 'Hunt' class. Ardrossan DD. Cancelled 1918.

BIDEFORD Sloop 1,105 tons, 250 x 34 ft, 2-4in. Devonport DY 1.4.1931. Sold 14.7.49; BU Howells, Milford Haven.

BIENFAISANT 3rd Rate 64, 1,360bm, 159 x 44½ ft. French, captured 25.7.1758 at Louisburg. BU 11.1814.

BIGBURY BAY (ex-LOCH CARLOWAY renamed 1944) Frigate, 'Bay' class. Hall Russell 16.11.1944. Sold 11.5.59 Portuguese navy as PACHECO PEREIRA.

BIHAR Minesweeper (RIN), TE 'Bangor' class. Garden Reach, Calcutta 7.7.1942. Sold circa 1949.

BILDESTON Coastal M/S, 'Ton' class. Doig, Grimsby 9.6.1952.

BILSTHORPE Coastal Minesweeper ordered Thornycroft 9.9.1950 and cancelled.

BIRD Survey sloop. Purchased 4.1764. BU 3.1775 at Deptford.

BIRDHAM Inshore M/S 'Ham' class. Taylor 19.8.1955. Sold Sutton & Smith 1980.

BIRKENHEAD (ex-VULCAN renamed 1843) Iron pad. frigate, 1400bm, 210 x 37½ ft. Laird 30.12.1845. Troopship 1848. Wrecked 26.2.1852 in Algoa Bay, S. Africa.

BIRKENHEAD (ex-Greek ANTINANARKOS CONDOUROTIS purchased 1914) Light cruiser 5,235 tons, 430 x 50 ft, 10-5.5 in, 1-3 in. Cammell Laird 18.1.1915. Sold 26.10.21 Cashmore, Newport.

BIRMINGHAM 2nd class cruiser 5,440 tons, 430 x 50 ft, 9-6 in, 1-3in. Armstrong 7.5.1913. Sold 2.31 Pembroke Dock to BU.

BIRMINGHAM Cruiser 9,100 tons, 558 x 62 ft, 12-6 in, 8-4in. Devonport DY 1.9.1936. Arrived 7.9.60 Ward, Inverkeithing to BU.

BIRMINGHAM Destroyer 3,150 tons. Cammell Laird 30.7.1973.

BISHAM Inshore M/S, 'Ham' class. Bolson, Poole 6.3.1954. Burnt by accident 29.9.56 at Haslar; wreck sold 8.8.57.

BITER (Gunboat No. 10) Gunvessel 12, 169bm, 75 x 22 ft, Wells, Rotherhithe 13.4.1797. Sold 5.1802.

BITER Gun-brig 12, 177bm, 80 x 22½ ft. Wallis, Blackwall 27.7.1804. Wrecked 10.11.1805 near Calais.

BITER Wood screw gunvessel, 301 bm, 130 x 22 ft. Chatham DY. Ordered 26.3.1846, cancelled 22.5.1849.

BITER Wood S.gunboat, 'Dapper' class. Pitcher, Northfleet 5.5.1855. Made a coal hulk 24.1.1865, later renamed 'C. 16'; sold 3.1904 Castle, Woolwich.

BITER (ex-War Dept. vessel *Sir William Reid*) Tender 110 tons, 80 x 17 ft. Transferred 1905. Sold 5.23 Dover S. Bkg. Co.

BITER (ex-*Rio Parana* converted) Escort carrier 8,200 tons, 468½ x66 ft, 3-4 in, 15-20mm, 15-A/C. Sun SB Co, Chester, USA 18.12.1940. Lend-lease to the RN 1.4.42. Transferred French navy 9.4.45 as DIXMUDE.

BITER Patrol boat 43 tons. Watercroft 17.10.1985.

BITTERN Sloop 18, 422bm, 110 x 30 ft. Adams, Bucklers Hard 7.4.1796. Sold 30.8.1833 Tibbett & Spence.

BITTERN Brig 12, 484bm, 105 x 34 ft. Portsmouth DY 18.4.1840. Sold 20.2.1860 at Hong Kong.

BITTERN Wood S. sloop, 669bm, 160 x 30 ft. Devonport DY. Laid down 17.12.1861, cancelled 16.12.1864.

BITTERN Wood S.gunvessel, 663bm, 805 tons, 170 x 29 ft, 1-7 in ML, 2-40pdr. Pembroke Dock 20.9.1869. Sold 11.1887 to BU.

BITTERN Destroyer 360 tons, 210½ x 21½ ft, 1-12pdr, 5-6pdr, 2-TT. N.C & A (Vickers) 1.2.1897. Sunk 4.4.1918 in collision with SS *Kenilworth* in the Channel.

BITTERN Trawler. Requis. 1914-19.

BITTERN (see ENCHANTRESS of 1934).

BITTERN Sloop 1,190 tons, 266 x 37 ft, 6-4 in. White, Cowes 14.7.1937. Sunk 30.4.40 by air attack off Namsos

BITTERSWEET Corvette, 'Flower' class. Marine Industries, Canada 12.9.1940. Lent RCN until 22.6.45. Arrived 25.8.49 Charlestown to BU.

BLACK BULL 36-gun ship, 480bm.

Dutch WAPEN van EDAW captured 1665. Recaptured 1666.

BLACKBURN (ex-BURNHAM renamed 1918) Minesweeper, later 'Hunt' class. Bow McLachlan 8.1918. Sold 17.10.22 Fryer, Sunderland.

BLACKBURN A/C transport 990 tons, 160 x 30 ft, 1-12pdr. Blyth DD 25.3.1944. RNVR drillship 1950. Sold Pounds, Portsmouth 16.7.68.

BLACK DOG Galliot, 69bm. Dutch, captured 1665. Sunk 1673 as a foundation at Sheerness.

BLACK EAGLE (see FIREBRAND of 1831).

BLACKFLY River gunboat, 'Fly' class. Yarrow in sections 1916 and launched 22.3.17 at Abadan. Sunk 26.5.23 in collision with a bridge at Baghdad while on loan to Air Ministry.

BLACKMORE Destroyer, 'Hunt' class type II. Stephen 2.12.1941. Lent Danish navy 1952, renamed ESBERN SNARE. BU 1966 in Sweden.

BLACKMORE KETCH 12-gun ship, 90bm, Chatham DY 1656. Sold 1667.

BLACKMORE LADY 18-gun ship (Royalist), 180bm. Captured 1648 by Parliamentarians. Sold 1650 at Lisbon.

BLACKMOREVALE Minesweeper, early 'Hunt' class. Ardrossan DD 23.3.1917. Sunk 1.5.18 by mine off Montrose.

BLACKPOOL Minesweeper, diesel 'Bangor' class. Harland & Wolff, Govan 4.7.1940. Sold 1946.

BLACKPOOL Frigate 2,144 tons, 360 x 41 ft, 2-4.5 in, 2-40mm. Thornycroft 14.2.1957. Lent RNZN 7.6.66. Sold 11.5.78 to BU.

BLACK POSTHORSE Galliot, 100bm. Dutch, captured 1665. Given away 1670.

BLACK PRINCE 10-gun ship (Royalist). Purchased 3.1650. Burnt 4.11.1650 by Parliamentarians.

BLACK PRINCE 3rd Rate 74, 1,751bm, 176 x 48½ ft. Woolwich DY 30.3.1816. Prison ship in 1848. BU completed 10.2.1855 Portsmouth.

BLACK PRINCE (ex-INVINCIBLE renamed 1859) Armoured frigate, 6,109bm, 9,210 tons, 380 x 58½ ft, 10-110pdr, 4-70pdr, 26-68pdr. (later 4-8 in, 22-7 in). Napier 27.2.1861. Training ship 1899; renamed EMERALD 3.04; IMPREGNABLE III 6.10. Sold 21.2.23.

BLACK PRINCE Armoured cruiser 13,550 tons, 480 x 73 ft, 6-9.2 in, 10-6 in, 22-3pdr. Thames Iron Works

8.11.1904. Sunk 31.5.16 at Jutland.

BLACK PRINCE Cruiser 5,770 tons, 485 x 50½ ft, 8-5.25in, 24 small. Harland & Wolff 27.8.1942. Lent RNZN 1948. BU 8.62 in Japan.

BLACK RAVEN 38-gun ship captured 1653. Sold 1654.

BLACK SNAKE SSV (RAN) 80 tons. Savage, Williamstown 12.1944. To N. Borneo in 11.45.

BLACK SPREAD-EAGLE 44-gun ship, 367bm. Dutch GROENINGEN captured 1665. Lost in action 1666.

BLACK SWAN Sloop 1,250 tons, 383 x 37½ ft, 6-4 in. Yarrow 7.7.1939. Arrived 13.9.56 Troon to BU.

BLACKWALL 4th Rate 48, 678bm, 131½ x 34 ft. Johnson, Blackwall 1696. Captured 20.10.1705 by the French PROTEE; recaptured 15.3.08 and BU.

BLACKWATER Destroyer 550 tons, 225 x 23 ft, 1-12pdr, 5-6pdr (4-12pdr 1907), 2-TT. Laird 25.7.1903. Sunk 6.4.09 in collision with SS *Hero* off Dungeness.

BLACKWATER Minesweeper 757 tons. Richards 29.8.1984.

BLACKWOOD Frigate, DE 'Captain' class. Mare Island 1942 for the RN but retained by the USN as AUSTIN.

BLACKWOOD Frigate, DE 'Captain' class. Boston Navy Yd 23.11.1942 on lend-lease. Sunk 15.6.44 by 'U.764' in the Channel.

BLACKWOOD Frigate 1,180 tons, 300 x 33 ft, 3-40mm. Thornycroft 4.10.1955. BU at Troon in 11.76.

BLADE (ex-torpedo boat Z.5 renamed 5.1943) S/M tender 263 tons, 195 x 19½ ft, 2-3 in. Dutch, commissioned in the RN 1.3.1942. Arrived 10.45 Troon to BU.

BLAIRMORE Minesweeper (RCN), TE 'Bangor' class. Port Arthur SY 14.5.1942. Sold 3.4.46; repurchased. Sold 29.3.58 Turkish navy as BEKOZ.

BLAKE 3rd Rate 74, 1,701bm, 172 x 48 ft, Deptford DY 23.8.1808. Prison ship 1.1814. Sold 17.10.1816.

BLAKE (see BOMBAY of 1808).

BLAKE Screw 2nd Rate 91, 3,716bm, 252 x 57 ft. Pembroke Dock. Ordered 1860, cancelled 1863.

BLAKE 1st class cruiser 9,000 tons, 375 x 65 ft, 2-9.2in, 10-6 in, 16-3pdr. Chatham DY 23.11.1889. Depot ship 8.1908. Sold 9.6.22 Rees, Llanelly.

BLAKE (see TIGER ordered 3.42).

BLAKE (ex-TIGER renamed 2.45, ex-BLAKE renamed 12.44) Cruiser

9,550 tons, 538 x 64 ft, 4-6 in, 6-3 in. Fairfield 20.12.45. Suspended 1946-54; completed 18.3.61. Sold 25.8.82, BU at Cairnryan.

BLAKENEY (see BURSLEM).

BLANCHE 5th Rate 36. French, captured 21.12.1779. Foundered 11.10.1780 in a hurricane in the W. Indies.

BLANCHE 5th Rate 32, 722bm, 129 x 39½ ft. Calhoun, Burlesdon 10.7.1786. Wrecked 28.9.1799 in the Texel.

BLANCHE 5th Rate 36, 951bm, 145 x 38 ft. Dudman, Deptford 2.10.1800. Captured 19.7.1805 and burnt by the French in the W. Indies.

BLANCHE (see AMFITRITE).

BLANCHE (see BELLONA of 1806).

BLANCHE 5th Rate 46, 1,074bm, 150 x 40½ ft. Chatham DY 26.5.1819. Harbour service 1852. BU 10.1865 at Cowes.

BLANCHE Wood S.sloop 1,268bm, 1,760 tons, 212 x 36 ft, 2-7 in, 4-64pdr. Chatham DY 17.8.1867. Sold 9.1886 Castle to BU.

BLANCHE 3rd class cruiser 1,580 tons, 220 x 35 ft, 6-4.7 in, 4-3pdr. Pembroke Dock 6.9.1889. Sold 11.7.1905 Ward, Preston.

BLANCHE Scout cruiser 3,360 tons, 385 x 41½ ft, 10-4 in. Pembroke Dock 25.11.1909. Sold 27.7.21 Fryer, Sunderland.

BLANCHE Destroyer 1,360 tons, 312 x 32½ ft, 4-4.7 in, 8-TT. Hawthorn Leslie 29.5.1930. Sunk 13.11.39 by mine in the Thames estuary.

BLANCHE Trawler. Requis. 1915-19.

BLANDFORD 6th Rate 20, 276bm, 94 x 26 ft. Woolwich DY 29.10.1711. Foundered 28.3.1719 in the Bay of Biscay.

BLANDFORD 6th Rate 20, 375bm, 106 x 28½ ft. Deptford 1719. Sold 28.10.1742.

BLANDFORD 6th Rate 24, 455bm, 109 x 31 ft. West, Deptford 2.10.1741. Sold 12.1763. (Was seized by the French 13.8.1755 off Brest in retaliation for the seizure by the British of French ships in Canada in time of peace; later released.)

BLANKNEY Destroyer, 'Hunt' class type II. J. Brown 19.12.1940. Arrived 3.59 Hughes Bolckow, Blyth to BU.

BLAST Bomb 4. Johnson, Blackwall 1695. Made a pitch boat 1720. BU 1724.

BLAST Bomb 8, 271bm, 91 x 26½ ft. West, Deptford 28.8.1740. Captured 19.10.1745 by the Spanish in the W.

Indies.

BLAST Bomb 8, 303bm, 91½ x 28 ft. Bird, Northam 27.2.1759. BU 10.1771 at Woolwich.

BLAST (see DRUID of 1776).

BLAXTON Coastal M/S, 'Ton' class. Thornycroft 21.6.1955. To Eire 11.70, renamed FOLA.

BLAZE Fireship 8, 260bm. Snelgrove, Rotherhithe 5.3.1691. Expended 22.5.1692 at Cherbourg.

BLAZE Fireship 8, 253bm. Purchased 1694. Captured 5.5.1697 by the French off the Scilly Isles.

BLAZE (ex-America) Fireship 8, 181bm, 80 x 23½ ft. Purchased 7.9.1739. BU 4.1742 at Woolwich.

BLAZE Fireship 10. Purchased 1745. In service 1750.

BLAZE Fireship 10. Purchased 22.7.1756. Sold 28.2.1759 at Bombay.

BLAZE Minesweeper, 'Catherine' class. Gen. Eng., Alameda 7.5.1943 for the RN but retained by the USN as GLADIATOR.

BLAZER (Gunboat No. 12) Gunvessel 12, 159bm, 75 x 22 ft. Dudman, Deptford 14.4.1797. Sold 1.1803.

BLAZER Gun-brig 12, 180bm, 80 x 23 ft. Pitcher, Northfleet 3.5.1804. Sold 15.12.1814.

BLAZER Wood pad. sloop, 527bm, 145 x 28½ ft. Chatham DY 5.1834. Survey ship 1.1843. BU 1853 at Portsmouth.

BLAZER Mortar vessel, 117bm, 66 x 20 ft, 1-13 in mortar. Mare, Blackwall 5.5. 1855. Renamed 'MV.3' 19.10.1855; transferred to Thames Conservancy Board 10.1867.

BLAZER Wood S.gunboat, 'Albacore' class. Laird 23.2.1856. Became dredger YC.29 in 6.1868. Sold 4.5.1877 at Gibraltar.

BLAZER Iron S.gunboat, 'Ant' class. Portsmouth DY 7.12.1870. Tender 1904; gunboat 8.14. Sold 19.8.19 W. Loveridge.

BLAZER Patrol boat 43 tons. Watercraft 1985.

BLEAN Destroyer, 'Hunt' class type III. Hawthorn Leslie 15.1.1942. Sunk 11.12.42 by 'U.443' west of Oran.

BLEASDALE Destroyer, 'Hunt' class type III. Vickers Armstrong, Tyne 23.7.1941. Arrived 14.9.56 Hughes Bolckow, Blyth to BU.

BLENCATHRA Destroyer, 'Hunt' class 1,000 tons, 4-4 in, Cammell Laird 6.8.1940. Arrived 2.1.57 Ward, Barrow to BU.

BLENHEIM (see DUCHESS of 1679).

BLENHEIM 2nd Rate 90, 1,827bm, 176 x 49 ft. Woolwich DY 5.7.1761. Made a 3rd rate 1800. Wrecked 1807 on Rodriguez Is. Indian Ocean.

BLENHEIM Name chosen for ex-Danish CHRISTIAN VII but not used.

BLENHEIM 3rd Rate 74, 1,747bm, 176 x 48½ ft. Deptford DY 31.5.1813. Harbour service 1831; converted to screw 3.1847, 1,822bm, 181 x 48½ ft. BU 1865.

BLENHEIM 1st class cruiser 9,000 tons, 375 x 65 ft, 2-9.2 in, 10-6 in, 16-3pdr. Thames Iron Works 5.7.1890. Depot ship 1907. Sold 13.7.26 Ward, Pembroke Dock.

BLENHEIM (ex-Achilles) Depot ship 13,893 tons, 507 x 63 ft, 4-4 in, 16 small. Purchased 1940. Arrived 16.3.48 Ward, Barrow to BU.

BLESSING Fireship 4, 173bm. Purchased 1666. Lost 1666 in action.

BLESSING Fireship 4, 109bm. Purchased 1673. Expended 1673.

BLESSING 'Machine' (fireship), 18bm. Purchased 1694. Sold 1696.

BLICKLING Minesweeper, later 'Hunt' class. Dundee SB Co. Cancelled 1918.

BLIGH (ex-USS LIDDLE) Frigate, TE 'Captain' class. Bethlehem, Hingham 31.7.1943 on lend-lease. Returned 11.45 USN.

BLOEMFONTEIN (ex-ROSAMUND renamed 1947) Minesweeper (SAN), 'Algerine' class. Training ship 1961. Sold 16.3.66 at the Cape.

BLONDE 5th Rate 32, 704bm, 132 x 34½ ft. French, captured 28.2.1760 by AEOLUS in the Irish Sea. Wrecked 21.1.1782 on Nantucket Shoal.

BLONDE 5th Rate 32, 678bm, 126 x 35 ft. Betts, Mistleythorn 1783. (Fate unknown, may have been cancelled or renamed.)

BLONDE 5th Rate 32, 682bm, 126½ x 35 ft. Calhoun, Burlesdon 22.1.1787. Troopship 6.1798. Sold 6.1805.

BLONDE 6th Rate 28, 580bm. French, captured 27.11.1793 by LATONA and PHAETON off Ushant. Sold 1794.

BLONDE (see HEBE of 1782).

BLONDE (see ISTER).

BLONDE 5th Rate 46, 1,103bm, 155 x 40½ ft, 16-32pdr. carr., 28-18pdr, 2-9pdr. Deptford DY 12.1.1819. Harbour service 11.1850; renamed CALYPSO 9.3.1870. Sold 28.2.1895.

BLONDE Wood S.frigate 36, 2,478bm, 240 x 48 ft. Woolwich DY. Laid down 10.9.1860, cancelled 12.12.1863.

BLONDE (see SHAH of 1873).

BLONDE 3rd class cruiser 1,580 tons, 220 x 35 ft, 6-4.7 in, 4-3pdr. Pembroke Dock 22.10.1889. Sold 11.7.1905, BU at Bo'ness.

BLONDE Scout cruiser 3,350 tons, 385 x 41½ ft, 10-4 in. Pembroke Dock 22.7.1910. Sold 6.5.20 T.C. Pas. BU in Holland.

BLOODHOUND Gun-brig 12, 186bm, 80 x 23 ft. Randall, Rotherhithe 2.4.1801. Sold 18.9.1816.

BLOODHOUND Iron pad. vessel 378bm, 147 x 23 ft. Napier 9.1.1845. BU 1866.

BLOODHOUND Iron S.gunboat, 'Ant' class. Armstrong Mitchell, 22.4.1871. Tender 1905; BDV 1917. Sold 28.6.21 F.Bevis.

BLOODHOUND Motor torpedo boat, 35 tons, 68 x 19 ft, 1-TT. Vosper, Portsmouth 1937. Wrecked 1.43 at Bincleaves.

BLOODHOUND, see LONDON.

BLOOM Tender 14. Purchased 1795. Captured 24.2.1797 by the French off Holyhead.

BLOSSOM Sloop 18, 427bm, 108½ x 30 ft. Guillaum, Northam 10.12.1806. Survey ship 1825; hulk 1.1833. BU 8.1848.

BLOSSOM (ex-CAREFUL renamed 1855) Wood S.gunboat, 'Cheerful' class. Laird 21.4.1856. BU 11.1864 at Haslar.

BLOSSOM. Vessel hired 1692; Tank vessel 1901-61; 3 Drifters WW.I.

BLOXHAM (ex-BRIXHAM renamed 1918) Minesweeper, later 'Hunt' class. Ayrshire Co 11.9.1919. Sold incomplete 23.10.23 Lithgow, Port Glasgow.

BLUEBELL Sloop, 'Acacia' class. Scott 24.7.1915. Sold 26.5.30 Cashmore, Newport.

BLUEBELL Five hired vessels in WW.I.

BLUEBELL Corvette, 'Flower' class. Fleming & Ferguson 24.4.1940. Sunk by 'U.711' in the Barents Sea 17.2.45.

BLUETHROAT Minelayer (RCN) 785 tons. G.T.Davie 15.9.1955.

BLYTH Minesweeper, TE 'Bangor' class. Blyth SB 2.9.1940. Sold 25.5.48 renamed *Radbourne*. BU 11.52.

BOADICEA 5th Rate 38, 1,052bm, 148½ x 40½ ft. Adams, Bucklers Hard 12.4.1797. Harbour service 1854. BU 5.1858.

BOADICEA Wood S.frigate 51, 3,353bm, 270 x 52½ ft. Chatham DY. Ordered 1861, cancelled 1863.

BOADICEA Iron S.corvette 4,140 tons, 280 x 45 ft, 14-7in MLR, 2-64pdr. Portsmouth DY 16.10.1875. Sold 6.1.1905 Ward, Preston.

BOADICEA Scout cruiser 3,300 tons, 385 x 41 ft, 6-4 in. Pembroke Dock 14.5.1908. Harbour service 1.21 (was to have been renamed POMONE). Sold 13.7.26 Alloa, Rosyth.

BOADICEA Yacht. Requis. 1915-19 and 1943-45.

BOADICEA Destroyer 1,360 tons, 312 x 32½ ft, 4-4.7in, 8-TT. Hawthorn Leslie 23.9.1930. Sunk 13.6.44 by air attack off Portland.

BODENHAM Inshore M/S, 'Ham' class. Brooke, Lowestoft 21.8.1952. Handed over to Saudi-Arabia 4.3.68.

BODIAM CASTLE Corvette, 'Castle' class. Coilingwood SY. Cancelled 12.1943.

BOGAM Frigate (RAN), 'River' class. Newcastle, NSW. Cancelled 12.6.1944.

BOLD Gunvessel 14, 179bm, 80 x 23 ft, 2-32pdr carr., 10-18pdr carr., 2-8 in howitzers. Perry & Wells, Blackwall 16.4.1801. BU 4.1811.

BOLD Gun-brig 12, 182bm, 84½ x 22 ft. Tyson & Blake, Bursledon 26.6.1812. Wrecked 27.9.1813 on Prince Edward Is.

BOLD (see MANLY of 1804).

BOLD Rescue tug 1942-46.

BOLEBROKE Destroyer, 'Hunt' class type III. Swan Hunter 5.11.1941. Lent Greek navy as PINDOS 5.42 to 12.11.59. BU in Greece 1960.

BOLTON Yacht 6, 42bm, 53 x 14½ ft. Portsmouth DY 19.7.1709. BU 1817 at Portsmouth.

BOLTON Gun-brig 12. In service 1775. Captured 5.4.1776 by Americans.

BOLTON (ex-BEAUMARIS renamed 1918) Minesweeper, later 'Hunt' class. Cancelled 1918.

BOLTON CASTLE Corvette, Castle class. Collingwood SY. Cancelled 12.1943.

BOMBARD Patrol boat (RAN) 100 tons. Walker 6.7.1968. Sold Indonesia 9.83.

BOMBAY 24 gun ship, 363bm, 90 x 30 ft. (Indian) Bombay DY 1739. Burnt 29.7.1789 by accident at Bombay.

BOMBAY Storeship in service in 1790.

BOMBAY 5th Rate 38 (Indian), 672bm, 130 x 35 ft. Bombay DY 1793. Purchased by the RN 1805, armed 14-24pdr carr., 24-18pdr, 2-9pdr. Renamed CEYLON 1.7.1808. Sold 4.7.1857.

BOMBAY 3rd Rate 74, 1,701bm, 174 x 48 ft. Deptford DY 28.3.1808. Renamed BLAKE 28.4.1819; harbour service 1828. BU 12.1855 at Portsmouth.

BOMBAY 2nd Rate 84, 2,279bm, 196 x 52 ft. Bombay DY 17.2.1828. Completed 5.1861 as screw ship 81, 2,782bm. Burnt 14.12.1864 by accident off Montevideo.

BOMBAY Trawler. Requis. 1915-19 and 1939-40.

BOMBAY Minesweeper (RIN), 'Bathhurst' class. Morts Dock, Sydney 6.12.1941. Sold 1960.

BOMBAY CASTLE 3rd Rate 74, 1,628bm, 168 x 47 ft. Perry, Blackwall 14.6.1782. Wrecked 21.12.1796 off the Tagus. (Was to have been renamed BOMBAY 1.1780.)

BONAVENTURE Warship built 1489. Gone by 1509.

BONAVENTURE (also EDWARD BONAVENTURE) Ship, 160bm. Built 1551. Wrecked 11.1556 near Aberdeen.

BONAVENTURE (also ELIZABETH BONAVENTURE) 47-gun ship, 300/550bm, 2-6opdr, 2-34pdr, 11-18pdr, 14-9pdr, 18 small. Purchased 1567. In service in 1599.

BONAVENTURE 32-gun ship 410/500bm. Deptford 1621. Lost 1653 in action.

BONAVENTURE (see PRESIDENT of 1650). BU 1711.

BONAVENTURE Three hired ships 1620-96.

BONAVENTURE 4th Rate 50, 703bm, 130 x 35 ft. Chatham DY 1711. Renamed ARGYLL 2.1.1715. Rebuilt 1722 as 763bm. Sunk 23.11.1748 as breakwater at Harwich.

BONAVENTURE 2nd class cruiser 4,360 tons, 320 x 49½ ft, 2-6 in, 8-4.7 in, 8-6pdr. Devonport DY 2.12.1 892. Depot ship 1910. Sold 12.4.20 Forth S.Bkg Co, arrived Bo'ness 10.20 to BU.

BONAVENTURE Cruiser 5,450 tons, 485 x 50½ ft, 10-5.25 in. Scotts 19.4.1939. Sunk 31.3.41 by Italian S/M AMBRA off Crete.

BONAVENTURE Depot ship 9,166 tons, 457 x 63 ft, 2-4 in, 12-20mm. Greenock DY Co. 27.10.1942 and converted by Scotts. Sold 1948.

BONAVENTURE (see POWERFUL of 1945).

BONAVOLIA Galley, 180bm, ex-ELLYNOR renamed 1584. Sold 1600.

(Presented by France in 10.1562).

BONETTA Sloop 4, 57bm. Woolwich 1673. Sold 1687.

BONETTA Sloop 4, 66bm. Deptford 1699. Sold 10.4.1712.

BONETTA Sloop in service 1718. Sold 28.8.1719.

BONETTA Sloop 3, 66bm, 56 x 17 ft. Deptford DY 18.4.1721. Sold 12.1731.

BONETTA Sloop 14, 201bm, 81 x 24 ft. Woolwich DY 24.8.1732. Foundered 20.10.1744 off Jamaica.

BONETTA Sloop 10, 227bm, 86½ x 24½ ft. Bird, Rotherhithe 4.2.1756. Sold 1.11.1776.

BONETTA Sloop 14, 307bm, 97 x 27 ft. Perry, Blackwall 29.4.1779. BU 10.1797. (In French hands 19.10.81 to 4.1.82.)

BONETTA (ex-Roebuck) Sloop 18, 272bm. Purchased 11.1781. Renamed SWAN 2.3.1782. Capsized 4.8.1782 off Waterford.

BONETTA Brig-sloop 18, 384bm, 103 x 27 ft, French, captured 1797. Wrecked 25.10.1801 on coast of Cuba.

BONETTA Sloop 18, 208bm, 86 x 24 ft. Purchased 1803. Sold 20.9.1810.

BONETTA Brigantine 3, 319bm, 91 x 29½ ft, 3-32pdr. Sheerness DY 5.4.1836. BU completed 23.4.1861 at Deptford.

BONETTA Iron S.gunboat, 'Ant' class. Rennie 20.5.1871. Sold 12.1.1909 as salvage vessel Disperser. Lost 4.40.

BONETTA Destroyer 440 tons, 215 x 21 ft, 3-12pdr, 2-TT. Palmer (on speculation) 14.1.1907 and accepted 3.09. Sold 7.6.20 Ward, Hayle; BU at Briton Ferry.

BONITA DY cutter 78bm, purchased 8.1864, sold 11.87.

BONITO Iron S.gunboat (Australian) 120 tons, 1-64pdr MLR. Built 1884.

BONNE CITOYENNE 6th Rate 20, 511bm, 120 x 31 ft, 18-32pdr carr., 2-9pdr. French, captured 10.3.1796 by PHAETON off Cape Finisterre. Sold 3.2.1819 J. Cristall.

BOOMERANG (see WHITING of 1889).

BOOTLE (ex-BUCKIE renamed 1918) Minesweeper, later 'Hunt' class. Bow McLachlan 11.6.1918. Sold 21.2.23 Alloa S.Bkg Co. Arrived Charlestown 18.4.23 to BU.

BOOTLE Minesweeper, turbine 'Bangor' class. Ailsa 23.10.1941. Sold 1.1.48; arrived 6.49 Charlestown to BU.

BORAGE Corvette, 'Flower' class. G.

Brown 22.11.1941. Irish MACHA 1947.

BORDER Destroyer, 'Hunt' class type III. Swan Hunter 3.2.1942. Lent Greek navy as ADRIAS 5.42; CTL 22.10.43 by mine in the Mediterranean. BU 11.45 King, Gateshead.

BORDER CITIES Minesweeper, (RCN), 'Algerine' class. Port Arthur 3.5.1943. Sold 1947.

BOREAS 6th Rate 28 (fir-built), 587bm, 118 x 34 ft. Woolwich DY 29.7.1757. Sold 29.6.1770 as useless.

BOREAS 6th Rate 28, 626bm, 125 x 34 ft. Blaydes & Hodgson, Hull 23.8.1774. Slop ship 1797. Sold 5.1802.

BOREAS 6th Rate 22, 533bm, 119 x 31½ ft. Stone, Yarmouth 19.4.1806. Wrecked 7.12.1807 on Guernsey.

BOREAS Name chosen for ex-Danish HARFRUEN; not used.

BOREAS Trawler. Requis. 1914-19, renamed CUCKOO 1940.

BOREAS Destroyer 1,360 tons, 312 x 32½ ft, 4-4.7in, 8-TT. Palmer, Hebburn 18.7.1930. Lent Greek navy as SALAMIS 4.44 to 9.51. Sold 23.11.51; arrived Rosyth 15.4.52 to BU.

BOREHAM Inshore M/S,'Ham' class. Brooke 21.10.1952. Malaysian JERONG 5.3.66.

BORER Gunvessel 14, 148bm, 75 x 21 ft, 2-32pdr carr., 12-18pdr carr. Randall, Rotherhithe 17.5.1794. Sold 1810 at Heligoland.

BORER Gun-brig 12, 184bm, 85 x 22 ft. Tyson & Blake, Bursledon 27.7.1812. Brig-sloop 14in 1813. Sold 12.10.1815.

BOSCAWEN Cutter 4, 48bm, 43 x 17 ft. Purchased 2.1763. Sold 4.5.1773.

BOSCAWEN 2nd Rate 80, 2,048bm, 187½ x 51 ft. Woolwich DY. Laid down 1811; cancelled.

BOSCAWEN 3rd Rate 70, 2,212bm, 180 x 54 ft. Woolwich DY 3.4.1844 (18 years on slip). Renamed WELLESLEY training ship 21.3.1874. Damaged by fire 3.1914 in the Tyne and BU at Blyth.

BOSCAWEN Training ships. (see TRAFALGAR of 1841, MINOTAUR of 1863 and AGINCOURT of 1865.)

BOSSINGTON (ex-EMBLETON renamed 1955) Coastal M/S, 'Ton' class. Thornycroft 2.12.1955.

BOSTON 5th Rate 32. Built in America 1692 and presented by the citizens of Boston 1694. Captured 4.1.1695 by the French in the Atlantic.

BOSTON 6th Rate 24, 561bm, 119 x 33 ft. Hallowell, Boston 3.5.1748. BU 2.1752.

BOSTON (see AMERICA of 1749).

BOSTON 5th Rate 32, 676bm, 127½ x 34½ ft. Inwood, Rotherhithe 11.5.1762. BU 5.1811.

BOSTON Schooner 6 (Canadian lakes). Navy Island 1764. Burnt 1768.

BOSTON Minesweeper, turbine 'Bangor' class. Ailsa 30.12.1940. Sold 1.1.48; BU at Charlestown.

BOTHA (ex-Chilian ALMIRANTE WILLIAMS) Destroyer leader 1,742 tons, 320 x 32½ ft, 6-4 in, 3-TT. White, Cowes 2.12.1914, purchased 8.14. Resold Chile 5.20 as ALMIRANTE WILLIAMS.

BOTTISHAM Inshore M/S, 'Ham' class. Ailsa 16.2.1953. Transferred Air Ministry 11.1.66 as No 5001. Sold Gomba Marina Ltd in 11.73.

BOUCLIER Destroyer 610 tons, 245½ x 26 ft, 2-3.9 in, 2-TT. French torpedo boat seized 3.7.40 at Plymouth. Dutch crew 9.40; Free-French crew 2.41; training ship 1941; returned 1946 to the French navy.

BOULOGNE 5th Rate 32, 657bm, 133½ x 33½ ft. French E.Indiaman *Boullongne* captured 3.1762 by VENUS. Storeship 1776. Hulked 7.1784 as part of a wharf at Halifax NS.

BOULSTON Coastal M/S, 'Ton' class. Richards, Lowestoft 5.10.1952. Renamed WARSASH 1961. Sold H.K.Vickers 28.10.74, BU at Hayle.

BOUNCER (Gunboat No.8) Gunvessel 12, 160bm, 75 x 22 ft. Wells, Rotherhithe 4.1797. Sold 4.1802.

BOUNCER Gun-brig 12, 177bm, 80 x 22½ ft. Rowe, Newcastle 11.8.1804. Stranded 2.1805 near Dieppe and captured by the French. Became French L'ECUREUIL to 1814.

BOUNCER Wood S.gunboat, 'Albacore' class. Mare, Blackwall 23.2.1856. Sold 1.2.1871 at Hong Kong.

BOUNCER Steel S.gunboat 265 tons, 87½ x 26 ft, 1-10 in MLR. Pembroke Dock 15.3.1881. Sold 4.4.1905.

BOUNCER (ex-War Dept vessel *Sir Richard Fletcher*) Tender 100 tons, 77 x 15½ ft. Transferred 1905. Sold 14.5.20. F.Bevis.

BOUNTIFUL Storeship 46, 778bm, 143½ x 34½ ft. Purchased 5.2.1782. Sold 1784 at Bombay.

BOUNTY (ex-*Bethia*) A.Ship 4, 215bm, 85 x 24½ ft, 4-4pdr. Purchased 23.5.1787. Taken by mutineers 28.4.1789 at Otaheite; burnt 1791.

BOURBONNAISE 5th Rate 38, 1,078bm, 151½ x 40 ft. French CAROLINE captured 16.9.1809 at

Ile Bourbon (Reunion) by a squadron. BU 4.1817.

BOURDELAIS 6th Rate 24, 625bm. French privateer captured 11.10.1799 off the Irish coast. BU in 8.1804.

BOWEN Minesweeper (RAN), 'Bathurst' class. Walker, Maryborough 28.7.1942. Sold 18.5.56 to BU.

BOWES CASTLE Corvette, 'Castle' class. Kingston SY. Cancelled 12.1943.

BOWMANVILLE (see COQUETTE of 1943).

BOWMANVILLE (ex-NUNNEY CASTLE renamed 1943) Corvette (RCN), 'Castle class. Pickersgill 26.1.1944. Sold 5.9.46, renamed *Yuan Pei*.

BOXER (Gunboat No 9) Gunvessel 12, 161bm, 75½ x 22 ft. Wells, Rotherhithe 11.4.1797. Sold 7.1809.

BOXER Gun-brig 12, 182bm, 84½ x 22 ft. Hobbs, Redbridge 25.7.1812. Captured 5.9.1813 by the American ENTERPRISE off Portland, Maine.

BOXER (ex-GPO vessel *Ivanhoe*) Pad. packet, 159bm, 101 x 19 ft. Transferred 1.4.1837. Sold circa 27.5.1841 to BU.

BOXER Wood screw gunvessel, 301bm, 130 x 22 ft. Chatham DY. Laid down 5.1846, cancelled 6.1847.

BOXER Wood S.gunboat, 'Dapper' class. Pitcher, Northfleet 7.4.1855. BU 10.1865 at Malta.

BOXER Compos. S gunvessel, 465bm, 605 tons, 155 x 25 ft, 1-7 in ML, 1-64pdr ML, 2-20pdr. Deptford DY 25.1.1868. Sold 6.1887 to BU.

BOXER Destroyer 280 tons, 201½ x 19 ft, 1-12pdr, 5-6pdr, 2-TT. Thornycroft, Chiswick 28.11.1894. Sunk 8.2.1918 in collision with SS *St Patrick* in the Channel.

BOXER Tank landing ship 3,620 tons, 390 x 49 ft, 8-20mm. Harland & Wolff 12.12.1942. Fighter-direction ship 1944; radar training 1947. Sold 1.12.58 Ward, Barrow.

BOXER Frigate 4,200 tons. Yarrow 17.6.1981.

BOYNE 2nd Rate 80, 1,160bm, 157 x 41½ ft. Deptford DY 21.5.1692. Rebuilt Blackwall 1708 as 1,301bm and Deptford 1739 as 1,390bm; prison ship 1750. BU completed 3.1763 at Portsmouth.

BOYNE 3rd Rate 70, 1,426bm, 162 x 44½ ft. Plymouth DY 31.5.1766. BU 5.1783.

BOYNE 2nd Rate 98, 2,010bm, 182 x 50 ft. Woolwich DY 27.6.1790. Burnt 1.5.1795 by accident at Spithead.

BOYNE 2nd Rate 98, 2,155bm, 186 x 52 ft. Portsmouth DY 3.7.1810. Renamed EXCELLENT 1.12.1834 gunnery ship; renamed QUEEN CHARLOTTE 22.11.1859. BU completed 25.6.1861 Portsmouth.

BOYNE Destroyer 545 tons, 222 x 23½ ft, 1-12pdr, 5-6pdr (1907: 4-12pdr), 2-TT. Hawthorn 12.9.1904. Sold 30.8.19 Hayes, Porthcawl.

BRAAK Brig-sloop 14, 255bm. Dutch, seized 20.8.1795 by FORTUNE at Falmouth. Capsized 23.5.1798 in the Delaware.

BRAAK 6th Rate 24, 613bm, 116½ x 34½ ft. Dutch MINERVA captured 28.8.1799 in the Texel. Sold 1802.

BRAAVE (see under BRAVE).

BRADFIELD Minesweeper, later 'Hunt' class. Ayrshire Co 14.5.1919. Sold 10.20, renamed *Champavati*.

BRADFORD 24-gun ship, 294bm. Chatham DY 1658. Renamed SUCCESS 1660. Wrecked 1680.

BRADFORD Trawler 1915.

BRADFORD (ex-USS McLANAHAN) Destroyer 1,190 tons, 311 x 31 ft, 3-4in, 1-3in, 6-TT. Commissioned in the RN 8.10.1940. Arrived 8.46 at Troon to BU.

BRAID Frigate, 'River' class. Simons 30.11.1943. To French navy 21.1.44 as L'AVENTURE.

BRAITHWAITE (ex-USS STRAUB) Frigate, TE 'Captain' class. Bethlehem, Hingham 31.7.1943 on lend-lease. Returned 17.12.45 to the USN.

BRAKEL 4th Rate 54, 1,010bm. Dutch, seized 4.3.1796 at Plymouth. Troopship 6.1799. Sold 29.9.1814.

BRAMBER CASTLE Corvette, 'Castle' class. Collingwood SY. Cancelled 12.1943.

BRAMBLE 14-gun ship, 125bm. Ostend privateer captured 1656. Fireship 1665. Expended 6.1667 against the Dutch in the Medway.

BRAMBLE Schooner 10, 150bm, 79 x 22 ft. Bermuda 1808. Sold 14.12.1815.

BRAMBLE Cutter 10, 161bm, 71 x 23½ ft. Plymouth DY 8.4.1822. Survey vessel 4.1842: lent Colonial Dept 31.5.1853 as diving-bell vessel at Sydney. Sold 23.12.1876 as lightship.

BRAMBLE Wood S.gunboat, 'Britomart' class. Haslar. Laid down 1861, cancelled 12.12.1863.

BRAMBLE 1st class gunboat 715 tons, 165 x 29 ft, 6-4in. Harland & Wolff 11.12.1886. Renamed COCKATRICE 6.1896; sold 3.4.1906 at Chatham.

BRAMBLE 1st class gunboat 710 tons, 180 x 33 ft, 2-4 in, 4-12pdr. Potter, Liverpool 26.11.1898. Sold 26.1.20 at Bombay.

BRAMBLE Drifter. Requis. 1915-19.

BRAMBLE Minesweeper 875 tons, 230 x 33½ ft, 2-4 in. Devonport DY 12.7.1938. Sunk 31.12.42 by German destroyers in the Barents Sea.

BRAMBLE Minesweeper, 'Algerine' class. Lobnitz 26.1.1945. Arrived 8.61 King, Gateshead to BU.

BRAMHAM Destroyer, 'Hunt' class type II. Stephen 29.1.1942. Lent Greek navy as THEMISTOKLIS 3.43 to 12.11.59. BU 1960 in Greece.

BRAMPTON Corvette (RCN), modified 'Flower' class. Morton. Cancelled 12.1943.

BRANDON Corvette, (RCN) 'Flower' class. Davie SB 29.4.1941. Sold 1946.

BRANLEBAS Destroyer 610 tons, 245½ x 26 ft, 2-3.9 in, 2-TT. French torpedo boat seized 3.7.40 at Portsmouth. Free-French crew 10.40; foundered 14.12.40 in a gale in the Channel.

BRANTFORD Corvette (RCN), 'Flower' class. Midland SY 6.9.1941. Sold 1945, renamed *Olympic Arrow*.

BRANTINGHAM Inshore M/S, 'Ham' class. Ailsa 4.12.1953. Malaysian TEMASEK 1959.

BRAVE Ship hired 1588.

BRAVE Xebec 154bm, 76 x 22½ ft. Captured 1747. Sold 1748.

BRAAVE 5th Rate 40, 883bm. Dutch, captured 17.8.1796 at Saldanha Bay. Harbour service 1811. Sold 20.7.1825.

BRAVE 3rd Rate 74, 1,890bm. French, captured 6.2.1806 at San Domingo. Foundered 12.4.1806 on passage Jamaica to UK.

BRAVE 3rd Rate 80, 2,249bm, 194½ x 51½ ft, 32-32pdr, 18-32pdr carr., 30-18pdr, 4-12pdr. French FORMIDABLE captured 4.11.1805 in an action off the coast of Spain. Prison ship 1.1808; powder hulk 10.1814. Sold 4.1816 to BU at Plymouth.

BRAVE Wood S. gunboat, 'Albacore' class. Laird 11.2.1856. BU 3.1869 at Portsmouth.

BRAVE Minesweeper, 'Algerine' class. Blyth DD 4.2.1943. RNVR drillship SATELLITE 9.51. Arrived 25.11.58 Clayton & Davie to BU.

BRAVE Name originally chosen for A/C carrier WARRIOR launched 20.5.1944.

BRAVE Frigate 4,200 tons. Yarrow 19.11.1983.

BRAVO Floating battery 16, 360bm, 96 x 31 ft, 16-18pdr. Woolwich DY 31.5.1794. Deleted 1803.

BRAYFORD Seaward defence boat, 'Ford' class. Inglis 19.2.1954. To SAN 1955 as GELDERLAND.

BRAZEN Cutter 14, 123bm, 58 x 22 ft. Purchased 6.1781. Sold 10.1799.

BRAZEN Sloop 18, 420bm, 110 x 29 ft. Portsmouth DY. Ordered 6.11.1794, cancelled 1799.

BRAZEN Sloop 18, 363bm, 105 x 28 ft. French privateer L'INVINCIBLE GENERAL BUONAPARTE captured 4.1799 by BOADICEA. Wrecked 26.1.1800 near Brighton.

BRAZEN 6th rate 26, 422bm, 110 x 29½ ft. Portsmouth DY 26.5.1808. Floating chapel 1827. BU 7.1848.

BRAZEN Wood S. gunboat, 'Albacore' class. Laird 8.3.1856. BU 8.1864.

BRAZEN Destroyer 390 tons, 218 x 20 ft, 7-12pdr, 5-6pdr, 2-TT. Thomson 3.7.1896. Sold 4.11.1919 J.H.Lee.

BRAZEN Destroyer 1,360 tons, 312 x 32½ ft, 4-4.7in, 8-TT. Palmer 25.7.1930. Sunk 20.7.40 by air attack off Dover.

BRAZEN Frigate 3,500 tons. Yarrow 4.3.1980.

BREAM Schooner 4, 80bm, 56 x 18 ft, 4-12pdr carr. Bermuda 5.1807. Sold circa 1816.

BREARLEY Inshore M/S 'Ley' class. White, Cowes 16.6.1953. Sold Pounds 13.5.71. Became yacht.

BRECON Destroyer 1,175 tons, 276 x 33 ft, 6 4in, 3-TT. Thornycroft 27.6.1942. Arrived 17.9.62 Shipbreaking Ind., Faslane to BU.

BRECON Minehunter 615 tons. Vosper-Thornycroft 21.6.1978.

BRECONSHIRE Store carrier 8,952 tons, 482 x 56 ft. Taikoo DY 1939 and purchased. Sunk 27.3.42 by air attack at Malta. Wreck BU 1954 in Italy.

BREDAH (see NANTWICH of 1654)

BREDAH 3rd Rate 70, 1,055bm, 151½ x 40 ft, 26-32pdr, 26-12pdr,4-3pdr, 14 light. Betts, Harwich 1679. Blown up 12.10.1690 by accident at Cork.

BREDAH 3rd Rate 70, 1,094bm, 151 x 40½ ft. Woolwich DY 23.4.1692. BU completed 7.10.1730 at Portsmouth.

BREDAH (see PRINCE of ORANGE)

BRENCHLEY Inshore M/S, 'Ley' class. Saunders Roe, Anglesea 19.7.1954. Sold 11.1.66.

BRERETON Coastal M/S, 'Ton' class. Richards, Lowestoft 14.5.1953. Renamed ST DAVID 1954; BRERETON

11.61.

BREVDRAGEREN Brig-sloop 12, 182bm, 83 x 23 ft, 10-18pdr carr., 2-6pdr. Danish, captured 7.9.1807 at Copenhagen. Prison ship 7.1818; army depot 1820. Sold 13.10.1825 J. Cristall (was to have been renamed COCKATRICE 1812).

BRIAR (ex-Royalist PETER) 16-gun ship, 252bm. Captured 1651. Fireship 1666; given away 1667.

BRIDGEWATER 58-gun ship, 743bm. Deptford DY 1654. Renamed ANNE 1660. Blown up 2.12.1673 at Sheerness.

BRIDGEWATER 5th Rate 32, 411bm, 110½ x 29 ft. Sheerness DY 1698. Fireship 1.1727; rebuilt 1729 as a 6th Rate. BU 4.1738.

BRIDGEWATER 6th Rate 24, 436bm, 106 x 30½ ft. Pearson, Lynn 11.12.1740. Wrecked 18.9.1743 off Newfoundland.

BRIDGEWATER 6th Rate 24, 500bm, 112 x 30 ft. Rowcliffe, Southampton 13.10.1744. Run ashore 28.4.1758 at Cuddalore and burnt to avoid capture by the French.

BRIDGEWATER Sloop 1,045 tons, 250 x 34 ft, 2-4in. Hawthorn Leslie 14.9.1928. Sold 25.5.47 Howells, Gelleswick Bay to BU.

BRIDGNORTH CASTLE Corvette, 'Castle' class. Collingwood SY. Cancelled 12.1943.

BRIDLINGTON (see GOOLE of 1919).

BRIDLINGTON Minesweeper, diesel 'Bangor' class. Denny 29.2.1940. Transferred Air Ministry 1946. BU 2.60 at Plymouth.

BRIDPORT Minesweeper, diesel 'Bangor' class. Denny 29.2.1940. Transferred Air Ministry 1946. BU 5.59 at Plymouth.

BRIGANDINE Ship 406bm Dover 1545. Captured by the French in 10.1562.

BRIGANTINE Ship 90bm. Built 1583. Listed 1588.

BRIGHAM Inshore M/S, 'Ham' class. Berthon Bt Co 17.1.1953. Sold Pounds 10.12.68; became a yacht.

BRIGHTON Tender 14. Purchased 1795. Captured 24.2.1797 by the French off Holyhead.

BRIGHTON Two vessels requis. in WW.I.

BRIGHTON (ex-USS COWELL) Destroyer 1,060 tons, 309 x 30½ ft, 3-4in, 1-3in, 6-TT. Commissioned in the RN 23.9.1940. Target ship 11.42; lent Russian navy as ZHARKI 16.7.44 to 28.2.49. Sold 5.4.49, BU by McLellan, Bo'ness.

BRIGHTON Frigate 2,144 tons, 360 x 41 ft, 2-4.5in, 1-40mm. Yarrow 30.10.1959.

BRILLIANT-PRIZE Sloop 6, 60bm. Captured 1696. Sold 1698.

BRILLIANT Sloop in service in 1729.

BRILLIANT 5th Rate 36, 718bm, 128½ x 36 ft. Plymouth DY 27.10.1757. Sold 1.11.1776.

BRILLIANT 6th Rate 28, 600bm, 120½ x 34 ft. Adams, Bucklers Hard 13.7.1779. BU 11.1811 at Portsmouth.

BRILLIANT (see ORONTES of 1813).

BRILLIANT 5th Rate 36, 954bm, 146 x 38½ ft. Lungley, Deptford 28.12.1814. Reduced to 22 guns 1843; RNR training ship 1859; renamed BRITON 8.11.1889. Sold 12.5.1908. Forth S. Bkg Co, Bo'ness.

BRILLIANT 2nd class cruiser 3,600 tons, 300 x 44 ft, 2-6in, 6-4.7in, 8-6pdr. Sheerness DY 24.6.1891. Sunk 23.4.1918 as blockship at Ostend.

BRILLIANT Hired vessel 1915.

BRILLIANT Destroyer 1,360 tons, 312 x 32½ ft, 4-4.7in, 8-TT. Swan Hunter 9.10.1930. Sold 18.8.47, BU at Troon.

BRILLIANT Frigate 3,500 tons. Yarrow 15.12.1978.

BRINKLEY Inshore M/S, 'Ley' class. Saunders Roe 14.9.1954. Sold 10.1.66.

BRINTON Coastal M/S, 'Ton' class. Cook, Welton & Gemmell 8.8.1952.

BRISBANE Light cruiser (RAN), 5,400 tons, 430 x 50 ft, 8-6in, 1-3in. Cockatoo DY 30.9.1915. Sold 16.6.36, BU Ward, Briton Ferry.

BRISBANE GM destroyer (RAN), 3,370 tons, 420 x 47ft, 2-5in, 6-TT, 2-GWS. Defoe, Bay City, USA 5.5.1966.

BRISEIS Brig-sloop 10, 'Cherokee' class 238bm. King, Upnor 19.5.1808. Wrecked 5.11.1816 off Cuba.

BRISEIS Brig-sloop 6, 'Cherokee' class 230bm. Deptford DY 3.7.1829. Completed as packet brig. Wrecked 1.1838 on passage Falmouth to Halifax.

BRISK Sloop 16, 340bm, 101 x 28 ft. Jacobs, Sandgate 6.5.1784. Sold 5.1805.

BRISK Sloop 18, 371bm, 106 x 28 ft. Dartmouth 4.1805. Sold 15.2.1816.

BRISK Brig-sloop 10, 'Cherokee' class 237bm. Chatham DY 10.2.1819. Sold 7.11.1843 J. Levy, Rochester.

BRISK Wood S. sloop 1,087bm, 190½ x 35 ft, 2-68pdr, 12-32pdr. Woolwich DY 2.6.1851. Sold 31.1.1870 mercantile.

BRISK Torpedo cruiser 1,770 tons, 225 x 36 ft, 6-6in, 8-3pdr, 1-TT. Thomson 8.4.1886. Sold 15.5.1906 Ward, Preston.

BRISK Destroyer 780 tons, 246 x 25 ft, 2-4in, 2-12pdr, 2-TT. J. Brown 20.9.1910. Sold 11.21 J. Distin, Devonport.

BRISSENDEN Destroyer 1,175 tons, 276 x 33 ft, 6-4in, 3-TT. Thornycroft 15.9.1942. Arrived 3.3.65 Arnott Young, Dalmuir to BU.

BRISTOL 48-gun ship 532bm, 24-18pdr, 6-9pdr, 8-6pdr, 10-small. Portsmouth DY 1653. Rebuilt Deptford 1693 as 670bm; captured 12.4.1709 by the French; recaptured and sunk 25.4.1709 in the Channel.

BRISTOL 4th Rate 54, 703bm, 130 x 35 ft. Plymouth DY 8.5.1711. Rebuilt Woolwich 1746 as 1,021 bm, 50 guns. BU 10.1768 at Plymouth.

BRISTOL 4th Rate 50, 1,049bm, 146 x 41 ft. Sheerness DY 25.10.1775. Prison ship 1794. BU 6.1810.

BRISTOL (see AGINCOURT of 1796).

BRISTOL Wood S. frigate 3,027bm, 4,020 tons, 250 x 52 ft. Woolwich DY 12.2.1861. Sold 7.1883. Castle to BU.

BRISTOL 2nd class cruiser 4,820 tons, 430 x 47 ft, 2-6in, 10-4in. J. Brown 23.2.1910. Sold 9.5.21 Ward, Hayle.

BRISTOL Destroyer 6,100 tons. Swan Hunter 30.6.1969.

BRITANNIA 1st Rate 100, 1,708bm, 167½ x 48½ ft. Chatham DY 1682. Taken to pieces 1715 and frames used for next ship.

BRITANNIA 1st Rate 100, 1,894bm, 174½ x 50 ft. Woolwich DY 3.10.1719. Harbour service 1745; BU completed 9.1749 at Chatham.

BRITANNIA 1st Rate 100, 2,116bm, 178 x 52 ft. Portsmouth DY 19.10.1762 (11 years on stocks). Renamed PRINCESS ROYAL 6.1.1812; ST GEORGE 18.1.1812; BARFLEUR 2.6.1819. BU 2.1825.

BRITANNIA Storeship 20, 535bm, 115 x 32 ft. Purchased 1781. Wrecked 4.1782 on Kentish Knock.

BRITANNIA 1st Rate 120, 2,616bm, 205 x 55 ft., 2-68pdr, 64-32pdr, 18-32pdr carr., 34-24pdr, 4-18pdr. Plymouth DY 20.10.1820.Training ship 1.1.1859. BU completed 20.11.1869 at Devonport.

BRITANNIA (see PRINCE of WALES of 1860).

BRITANNIA Battleship 16,350 tons, 425 x 78 ft, 4-12in, 4-9.2in, 10-6in, 14-12pdr. Portsmouth DY 10.12.1904.

Sunk 9.11.18 by 'UB.50' off Cape Trafalgar.

BRITANNIA Two Drifters requis. 1915-19.

BRITANNIA R. Yacht 3,990 tons, 380 x 55 ft, 2-3pdr. J. Brown 16.4.1953.

BRITOMART (see GLOMMEN).

BRITOMART Brig-sloop 10, 'Cherokee' class 238bm. Dudman, Deptford 28.7.1808. Sold 3.2.1819 G. Bailey.

BRITOMART Brig-sloop 10, 'Cherokee' class 237bm. Portsmouth DY 24.8.1820. Sold 1843 at Singapore.

BRITOMART Brig 8, 329bm, 93 x 29 ft, 8-18pdr. Pembroke Dock 12.6.1847. Coastguard 21.10.1857. Renamed WV.25 in 5.1863. BU completed 25.7.1874 at Chatham.

BRITOMART Wood S. gunboat, 'Britomart' class. Smith, Newcastle 7.5.1860. Sold 12.1.1892 Castle; resold S. Williams, Dagenham as mooring hulk. BU 6.1946.

BRITOMART 1st class gunboat 710 tons, 180 x 33 ft, 2-4in, 4-12pdr. Potter, Liverpool 28.3.1899. Sold 6.10.1920 at Bombay; renamed *Sakuntala*.

BRITOMART Minesweeper 875 tons, 230 x 33½ ft, 2-4in. Devonport DY 23.8.1938. Sunk 27.8.44 in error by allied aircraft off Normandy.

BRITON 5th Rate 38, 1,080bm, 150 x 40½ ft. Chatham DY 11.4.1812. Convict ship 1841; target 2.1860. BU 9.1860 at Portsmouth.

BRITON Wood S. frigate 51, 3,027bm, 250 x 52 ft. Portsmouth DY. Ordered 1860, cancelled 1863.

BRITON Wood S. corvette 1,331bm, 1,860 tons, 220 x 36 ft, Sheerness DY 6.11.1869. Sold 1887 at Bombay.

BRITON (see BRILLIANT of 1814).

BRITON (see CALYPSO of 1883).

BRITON Trawler and Drifter requis. WW.I.

BRIXHAM Storeship 1915.

BRIXHAM (see BLOXHAM of 1919).

BRIXHAM Minesweeper, turbine 'Bangor' class. Blyth SB 21.11.1941. Sold 7.7.48, BU Clayton & Davie.

BROADLEY Inshore M/S, 'Ley' class. Blackmore, Bideford 24. 11.1953. Burnt 29.9.56 by accident at Haslar; wreck sold 8.8.57.

BROADSWORD Destroyer 1,980 tons, 341½ x 38 ft, 6-4in, 6-40mm, 10-TT. Yarrow 4.2.1946. Arrived Inverkeithing 10.68 to BU.

BROADSWORD Frigate 3,500 tons. Yarrow 12.5.1976.

BROADWATER (ex-USS MASON) Destroyer 1,190 tons, 311 x 31 ft, 3-4in, 1-3in, 6-TT. Commissioned in the RN 8.10.1940. Sunk 18.10.41 by 'U.101' south of Ireland.

BROADWAY (ex-USS HUNT) Destroyer 1,190 tons, 311 x 31 ft, 1-4in, 1-3in, 4-20mm, 3-TT. Commissioned in the RN 8.10.1940. Sold 18.2.47; arrived 3.48 Charlestown to BU.

BROCK Schooner 2 (Canadian lakes), 141bm, 69½ x 22 ft. Kingston, Ont. 4.1817. Sold 1837.

BROCKLESBY Destroyer, 'Hunt' class, 1,000 tons, 4-4in. Cammell Laird 30.9.1940. Arrived Faslane 28.10.68 to BU.

BROCKLESBY Minehunter 615 tons. Vosper-Thornycroft 12.1.1982.

BROCKVILLE Minesweeper (RCN), diesel 'Bangor' class. Marine Ind. 20.6.1941. RCMP ship *Macleod* 1950; BROCKVILLE (RCN) 1951. BU 1961.

BROADERSCHAP 4th Rate 50, 1,063bm, 140 x 41½ ft. Dutch, captured 28.8.1799 in the Texel. Floating battery 1803. BU 10.1805.

BROKE Cutter. Hired 1814.

BROKE (ex-Chilian ALMIRANTE GONI purchased 8.1914) Destroyer leader 1,704 tons, 331½ x 32½ ft, 2-4.7in, 2-4in, 4-TT. White 25.5.14. Resold Chile 5.20, renamed ALMIRANTE URIBE.

BROKE (ex-ROOKE renamed 13.4.1921) Destroyer leader, 1,750 tons, 318 x 32 ft, 5-4.7in, 1-3in, 6-TT. Thornycroft 16.9.20. Foundered in tow 9.11.42 after damage 8.11.42 by shore batteries at Algiers.

BRONINGTON Coastal M/S, 'Ton' class. Cook, Welton & Gemmell 19.3.1953. Renamed HUMBER; renamed BRONINGTON 1959.

BROOM (see VERVAIN).

BROOME Minesweeper, 'Bathurst' class. Evans Deakin 6. 10.1941. Sold 8.46 Turkish navy as ALANYA.

BROOMLEY inshore M/S, 'Ley' class. Harris, Appledore 14.4.1953. Renamed WATCHFUL 10.1.59. Sold 27.11.67, BU at Rotterdam.

BROTHERS Gunvessel 2. Purchased 10.1795. Sold 1.1802.

BROUGH CASTLE Corvette, 'Castle' class. Collingwood SY. Cancelled 12.1943.

BRUCE Trawler. Requis. 1917-19.

BRUCE Destroyer leader 1,800 tons, 320 x 32 ft, 5-4.7in, 1-3in, 6-TT. Cammell Laird 26.2.1918. Sunk 22.11.39 as a torpedo target off the Isle of Wight.

BRUIZER (Gunboat No. 11) Gunvessel 12, 160bm, 75 x 22 ft, 2-24pdr, 10-18pdr carr. Wells, Rotherhithe 11.4.1797. Sold 1.1802.

BRUIZER Gun-brig 12, 180bm, 80 x 23 ft, 10-18pdr carr., 2-12pdr. Pitcher, Northfleet 28.4.1804. Sold 24.2.1815.

BRUIZER (ex-*Robert Stephenson* purchased on stocks) Iron S. provision vessel 580bm, 183 x 25 ft. Stockton on Tees 8.12.1854. Sold 12.1.1857 C. Colman.

BRUIZER Wood S. gunboat, 'Britomart' class. Haslar 23.4.1867. BU 5.1886.

BRUIZER Destroyer 280 tons, 201½ x 19 ft, 1-12pdr, 5-6pdr, 2-TT. Thornycroft, Chiswick 27.2.1895. Sold 26.5.1914 Cashmore, Newport.

BRUISER Tank landing ship 3,620 tons, 390 x 49 ft, 8-20mm. Harland & Wolff 24.10.1942. Sold 1946.

BRUISER (see LST.3025).

BRUNE 5th Rate 32, 694bm, 131 x 34½ ft, 26-12pdr, 6-6pdr. French, captured 30.1.1761 by VENUS & JUNO. Sold 2.10.1792.

BRUNE 5th Rate 38, 1,090bm, 154 x 40½ ft. French THETIS captured 10.11.1808 by AMETHYST. Troopship 1810. Sold 16.8.1838 Mr Levy.

BRUNE Iron pad. gunboat 267bm, 140 x 20 ft, 2-Sin ML. Scott Russell, Millwall 30.8.1856. Sold 19.5.1863 at Lagos.

BRUNEI Landing craft (RAN) 310 tons. Walker 10.1971.

BRUNSWICK Schooner (Canadian lakes). Oswego 1765. Condemned 1778.

BRUNSWICK 3rd Rate 74, 1,836bm, 176 x 48½ ft. Deptford DY 30.4.1790. Harbour service 6.1812. BU 8.1826 at Sheerness.

BRUNSWICK Screw 3rd Rate 80, 2,492bm. Pembroke Dock 1.6.1855 (ex-3rd Rate, 8 years on stocks). Sold 3.1867 Marshall.

BRUTUS Trawler. Requis. 1914-19.

BRUTUS Minesweeper, 'Catherine' class. Gen. Eng. Alemeda 21.5.1943 for the RN but retained by the USN as IMPECCABLE.

BRYANSFORD Seaward defence boat, 'Ford' class. Inglis 3.1953. Sold Nigeria 5.68, renamed IBADAN.

BRYONY Sloop, 'Anchusa' class. Armstrong 27.10.1917. Arrived 3.4.1938 Cashmore, Newport to BU.

BRYONY Corvette, 'Flower' class. Harland & Wolff 15.3.1941. Sold Norwegian government 1948; renamed POLARFRONT II.

BUCCANEER Patrol Boat (RAN) 100 tons. Evans Deakin 14.9.1968.

BUCEPHALUS 5th Rate 32, 976bm, 150 x 38 ft. Rowe, Newcastle 3.11.1808. Troopship 5.1814; harbour service 6.1822. BU 9.1834.

BUCEPHALUS Wood S. frigate 51, 3,353bm, 270 x 52½ ft. Portsmouth DY. Ordered 1861, cancelled 1863.

BUCHAN NESS Repair ship 8,580 tons, 425 x 57 ft, 16-20mm. W. Coast SB, Vancouver 10.2.1945. Sold 25.9.59, BU Faslane.

BUCK Dogger 6. Dutch, captured 1672. Sold 1674.

BUCKIE (see BOOTLE of 1918).

BUCKINGHAM (see REVENGE of 1699).

BUCKINGHAM 3rd Rate 70, 1,128bm, 151 x 41½ ft. Deptford 13.4.1731. BU 1745.

BUCKINGHAM 3rd Rate 70, 1,436bm, 160 x 45½ ft. Deptford DY 13.4.1751. Renamed GRAMPUS storeship 19.4.1777; lost 11.1778.

BUCKINGHAM (see EAGLE of 1774).

BUCKINGHAM Two trawlers. Requis. 1918-19; 1939-45.

BUCKINGHAM (see ROYAL MOUNT).

BUCKLESHAM Inshore M/S, 'Ham' class. Ardrossan DD 8.8.1952. Sold Pounds 1981.

BUCTOUCHE Corvette (RCN), 'Flower' class. Davie SB 20.11.1940. Sold 1946 Int. Iron & Metal Co.

BUDDLEIA (see GIFFARD).

BUDE Minesweeper, TE 'Bangor' class. Lobnitz 4.9.1940. Sold 1946.

BUFFALO (see CAPTAIN of 1743).

BUFFALO (ex-*Fremantle* purchased on stocks) Storeship 12, 468bm, 100 x 31 ft. Dudman, Deptford 3.11.1797. Hulked 1814. Sold 30.4.1817.

BUFFALO (ex-E. Indiaman *Hindostan*) Storeship 16, 589bm, 120 x 34 ft. Purchased 1.11.1813. Timber carrier 1831. Wrecked 28.7.1841 in Mercury Bay, New Zealand.

BUFFALO (ex-*Baron von Humboldt*) Iron S. storeship, 440bm, 137 x-ft. Transferred from Treasury Dept 5.9.1855 and renamed 26.11.1856. Sold 11.1888.

BUFFALO (ex-*Earl de Gray & Ripon*) Iron S. storeship 335 tons, 150 x 21½ ft. Transferred from War Dept 1.10.1891. Sold 1903.

BUFFALO Minesweeper, 'Catherine' class. Gen. Eng, Alameda 22.6.1943 for the RN but retained by the USN as ARDENT.

BUFFALO Mooring vessel 1916-41.

Trawler 1915-19.

BUGLOSS Corvette, modified 'Flower' class. Crown 21.6.1943. Renamed ASSAM (RIN) 19.2.45.

BULL 26-gun ship 343bm. Built 1546. May have been rebuilt as ADVENTURE 1594.

BULL Fireship 4, 121bm. Dutch, captured 1666. Sold 1674.

BULLDOG Sloop 16, 317bm, 98 x 27 ft. Ladd, Dover 10.11.1782. Made a bomb 1798; powder hulk 1801; BU completed 12.1829 at Portsmouth. (Was in French hands 27.2.1801 to 16.9.1801.)

BULLDOG Gunvessel 4, 58bm, 64 x 14 ft. Dutch hoy purchased 3.1794. Sold 1794.

BULLDOG Wood pad. sloop, 1,124bm, 190 x 36 ft. Chatham DY 2.10.1845. Stranded 23.10.1865 and destroyed while attacking rebel steamer in Haiti.

BULLDOG 3rd class gunboat, 'Ant' class. Campbell, Johnston, Woolwich 17.9.1872. Sold 16.7.1906.

BULLDOG Destroyer 952 tons, 269 x 28 ft. 1-4in, 3-12pdr, 2-TT. J. Brown 13.11.1909. Sold 21.9.20 Ward, Rainham.

BULLDOG Destroyer 1,360 tons, 312 x 32½ ft, 4-4.7in, 8-TT. Swan Hunter 6.12.1930. Sold 15.1.46; arrived 3.46 Rosyth to BU.

BULLDOG Survey vessel, 950 tons. Brooke Marine 12.7.1967.

BULLDOG Trawler requis. 1917-19.

BULLEN Frigate, TE 'Captain' class. Bethlehem, Hingham 17.8.1943 on lend-lease. Sunk 6.12.44 by 'U.775' off NW Scotland.

BULLFINCH Wood S. gunboat, 'Albacore' class. Laird 25.2.1856. BU 8.1864.

BULLFINCH Wood S. gunvessel, 664bm, 805 tons, 170 x 29 ft, 1-7in ML, 2-40pdr. Sheerness DY 13.2.1868. Sold 6.1885.

BULLFINCH Destroyer 370 tons, 210 x 20½ ft, 1-12pdr, 5-6pdr, 2-TT. Earle 10.2.1898. Sold 10.6.1919 Young, Sunderland.

BULLFINCH Cable ship 1,950 tons. 1940-80

BULLFROG Schooner 4 (Canadian Lakes) 96bm. Purchased 17.8.1838, sold 1841.

BULLFROG Wood S. gunboat, 'Albacore' class. Pitcher, Northfleet 6.10.1855. BU 6.1875 at Sheerness.

BULLFROG Compos. S. gunboat 465 tons, 125 x 23½ ft, 2-64pdr MLR,

2-20pdr. Pembroke Dock 3.2.1881. Harbour service 1905; renamed EGMONT 3.23; ST ANGELO 1.7.33. Sold 1933.

BULLFROG Salvage vessel 1915-23. Cable ship 1944-47.

BULRUSH (see MIMICO).

BULWARK 3rd Rate 74, 1,620bm, 169 x 47 ft. Portsmouth DY. Ordered 11.6.1778 and cancelled 4.3.1783.

BULWARK (ex-SCIPIO renamed 1806) 3rd Rate 74, 1,940bm, 183 x 49 ft. Portsmouth DY 23.4.1807. BU 9.1826 at Portsmouth.

BULWARK Screw 2nd Rate 81, 3,716bm, 252 x 58 ft. Chatham DY Laid down 8.3.1859, suspended 7.3.1861, cancelled and BU 3.1873.

BULWARK (see HOWE of 1860).

BULWARK Battleship 15,000 tons, 400 x 75 ft, 4-12in, 12-6in, 18-12pdr. Devonport DY 18.10.1899. Blown up 26.11.14 by accident in the Medway.

BULWARK A/C carrier 22,000 tons, 650 x 90 ft, 32-40mm, 50-A/C. Harland & Wolff 22.6.1948. Completed as commando carrier 19.1.60, 16-helicopters. Arrived Cairnryan 17.4.84 to BU.

BUNA Landing craft (RAN) 310 tons. Walker 1972.

BUNBURY Minesweeper (RAN), 'Bathurst' class. Evans, Deakin Brisbane 16.5.1942. Sold 6.1.61 to BU in Japan.

BUNBURY Patrol boat (RAN) 211 tons. N. Queensland Eng. Co. 3.11.1984.

BUNDABERG Minesweeper (RAN), 'Bathurst' class. Evans, Deakin 1.12.1941. Left Sydney 20.2.62 to BU in Japan.

BURCHETT Sloop 6. Purchased 6.1708. Captured 6.2.1709 by the French.

BURDEKIN Frigate (RAN), 'River' class. Walker, Maryborough 30.6. 1943. Sold 9.61 to BU in Japan.

BURDOCK Corvette, 'Flower' class. Crown 14.12.1940. BU 6.47 Ward, Hayle.

BURFORD 3rd Rate 70, 1,051bm, 152½ x 40½ ft. Woolwich DY 1679. Rebuilt Deptford 1699 as 1,113bm. Wrecked 14.2.1719 on the coast of Italy.

BURFORD 3rd Rate 70, 1,147bm, 151 x 42 ft. Deptford DY 19.7.1722. BU 1752.

BURFORD 3rd Rate 70, 1,424bm, 162 x 44½ ft. Chatham DY 1757. Sold 31.3.1785.

BURGES Frigate, DE 'Captain' class. Mare Island 1942 for the RN but retained by the USN as EDGAR G. CHASE.

BURGES Frigate, DE 'Captain' class. Boston N. Yard 26.1.43 on lendlease. Returned 7.2.46 to the USN.

BURGHEAD BAY (ex-LOCH HARPORT renamed 1944) Frigate, 'Bay' class. Hill 3.3.1945. To Portuguese navy 11.5.59 as ALVARES CABRAL.

BURLEY Inshore M/S, 'Ley' class. Dorset Yt Co, Poole 6.1.1954. Renamed SQUIRREL 11.59. Sold 27.11.67, BU at Rotterdam..

BURLINGTON 4th Rate 48, 680bm, 131½ x 34½ ft. Johnson, Blackwall 1695. BU 8.1733 at Sheerness.

BURLINGTON (see PRINCESS CHARLOTTE of 1814).

BURLINGTON Minesweeper (RCN), TE 'Bangor' class. Dufferin, Toronto 23.11.1940. Sold 1946 T. Harris.

BURLINGTON Mine destructor 1940, renamed FAIRFAX.

BURNASTON Coastal M/S, 'Ton' class. Fleetlands, Gosport 18.12.1952. Sold 29.3.71, BU at Newhaven.

BURNET Corvette, modified 'Flower' class. Ferguson 31.5.1943. Renamed GONDWANA (RIN) 15.5.45 on loan; renamed BURNET 17.5.46. Sold Siamese navy 15.5.47 as BANGPAKONG.

BURNHAM (see BLACKBURN).

BURNHAM (ex-USS AULICK) Destroyer 1,190 tons, 311 x 31 ft, 1-4in, 1-3in, 4-20mm, 3-TT. Commissioned in the RN 8.10.1940. Target ship 1943. Sold 4.3.47; arrived 12.48 Hayes, Pembroke Dk.

BURNIE Minesweeper, 'Bathurst' class. Morts Dock, Sydney 25.10.1940. Sold Dutch navy 1946 as CERAM.

BURSLEM (ex-BLAKENEY renamed 1918) Minesweeper, later 'Hunt' class. Ayrshire Co. 4.1918. Sold 19.5.28 Ward, Inverkeithing.

BURTON (see EXMOOR).

BURWELL (ex-USS LAUB) Destroyer 1,190 tons, 311 x 31 ft, 1-4in, 1-3in, 4-20,nm, 3-TT. Commissioned in the RN 8.10.1940. Target ship 1943. Sold 4.3.47; BU Ward, Milford Haven.

BURY Minesweeper, later 'Hunt' class. Eltringham 17.5.1919. Sold 20.1.23 J. Smith.

BUSS Fireship 4, 80bm. Captured 1672. Sold 1684.

BUSTARD (ex-revenue cutter ROYAL GEORGE renamed 1806) Brig sloop 16, 270bm, 83 x 27 ft. Sold 12.10.1815.

BUSTARD Brig-sloop 10, 'Cherokee'

class, 327bm. Chatham DY 12.12.1818. Sold 24.6.1829 T. Surflen.

BUSTARD Wood S. gunboat, 'Albacore' class. Pitcher, Northfleet 20.10.1855. Sold 18.11.1869 at Hong Kong.

BUSTARD Iron S. gunboat, 'Ant' class. Napier 7.1.1871. Reported sold Ward 11.17 but listed to 1921.

BUSTLER Brig-sloop 16, 209bm, 76 x 25½ft, 16-6pdr. Purchased 1780. Sold 25.8.1788.

BUSTLER Gun-brig 12, 180bm, 84 x 22 ft, 10-18pdr carr., 2-12pdr.Ayles, Topsham 12.8.1805. Stranded 26.12.1808 near Cape Gris-nez and captured by the French.

BUSTLER Three tugs between 1855 and 1973. Tug 1981.

BUSY Cutter 10, 190bm, 75 x 26 ft, 10-4pdr. Farley, Folkestone 6.1778 and purchased. Sold 7.6.1792.

BUSY Brig-sloop 18, 337bm, 96 x 29 ft. Graham, Harwich 20.11.1797. Foundered 1807 on the Halifax Station.

BUSY Tug 1941-47.

BUTTERCUP Sloop, 'Arabis' class. Barclay Curle 24.10.1915. Sold 5.2.20 Hughes & Co as salvage vessel.

BUTTERCUP Corvette, 'Flower' class. Harland & Wolff 10.4.1941. Lent R. Norwegian navy 24.4.42. Sold 1946.

BUTTERFLY River gunboat, 'Fly' class. Yarrow 1915 and re-erected on the Tigris 11.15. Sold 1.3.23 locally.

BUTTINGTON Coastal M/S, 'Ton' class. Fleetlands, Gosport 11.6.1953. Renamed VENTURER then BUTTINGTON then THAMES 2.62. Sold 12.5.70, BU Newhaven.

BUTTRESS (ex-LCT 4099 renamed 1956) Tank landing craft 657 tons, 225 x 39 ft, 4-20mm. Sold 5.66 French navy as L.9061.

BUXTON (ex-USS EDWARDS) Destroyer 1,190 tons, 311 x 31 ft, 1-4in, 1-3in, 4-20mm, 3-TT. Commissioned in the RN 8.10.1940. Lent RCN 1942; training ship (RCN) 10.43. BU 1945 locally.

BUZZARD (see HAWK of 1806).

BUZZARD Brigantine 3 ex-sloop, 'Cherokee' class, 231bm. Portsmouth DY 23.3.1834. Sold 7.11.1843 Greenwood & Clark.

BUZZARD Wood pad. sloop 980bm, 185 x 34 ft. Pembroke Dock 24.3.1849. BU 1883.

BUZZARD Compos. S. sloop 1,140 tons, 195 x 28 ft, 8-5in. Sheerness DY 10.5.1887. Drill ship 1904; renamed PRESIDENT 1.4.11. Sold 6.9.21 C.A. Beard. Resold Dutch shipbreakers.

BUZZARD Trawler requis. 1914-20 and Boom trawler 1940.

BYARD Frigate, DE 'Captain' class. Mare Island 1942 for the RN, but retained by the USN as EDWARD C. DALY.

BYARD Frigate, TE 'Captain' class. Bethlehem, Hingham 6.3.1943 on lend-lease. Returned 1.46 to the USN.

BYRON Frigate, TE 'Captain' class. Bethlehem, Hingham 14.8.1943 on lend-lease. Returned 11.45 to the USN.

'C' class submarines. 280 tons, 135 x 13½ft, 2-TT.

C.1 Vickers 10.7.1906. Sold 22.10.20 Stanlee; resold 14.11.21 Young, Sunderland.

C.2 Vickers 10.7.06. Sold 8.10.20 Maden & McKee.

C.3 Vickers 3.10.06. Expended 23.4.18 at Zeebrugge.

C.4 Vickers 18.10.06. Sold 28.2.22 Hampshire Metal Co.

C.5 Vickers 20.8.06. Sold 31.10.19 at Malta.

C.6 Vickers 20.8.06. Sold 20.11.19 J.A. Walker.

C.7 Vickers 15.2.07. Sold 20.12.19 J. Jackson.

C.8 Vickers 15.2.07. Sold 22.10.20 Stanlee; resold 14.11.21 T. Young.

C.9 Vickers 3.4.07. Sold 7.22 Stanlee, Dover.

C.10 Vickers 15.4.07. Sold 7.22 Stanlee, Dover.

C.11 Vickers 27.5.07. Sunk 14.7.09 in collision with SS *Eddystone*off Cromer.

C.12 Vickers 9.9.07. Sold 2.2.20 J.H. Lee.

C.13 Vickers 9.11.07. Sold 2.2.20 J.H. Lee.

C.14 Vickers 7.12.07. Sold 5.12.21 C.A. Beard, Upnor.

C.15 Vickers 21.1.08. Sold 28.2.22 Hampshire Metal Co.

C.16 Vickers 19.3.08. Sold 12.8.22 C.A. Beard, Upnor.

C.17 Chatham DY 13.8.08. Sold 20.11.19 J.A. Walker.

C.18 Chatham DY 10.10.08. Sold 26.5.21 B. Fryer.

C.19 Chatham DY 20.3.09. Sold 2.2.20 J.H. Lee.

C.20 Chatham DY 27.11.09. Sold

26.5.21 B. Fryer.

C.21 Vickers 26.9.08. Sold 5.12.21 C.A. Beard, Upnor.

C.22 Vickers 10.10.08. Sold 2.2.20 J.H. Lee.

C.23 Vickers 26.11.08. Sold 5.12.21 C.A. Beard, Upnor.

C.24 Vickers 26.11.08. Sold 26.5.21 B. Fryer.

C.25 Vickers 10.3.09. Sold 5.12.21 C.A. Beard, Upnor.

C.26 Vickers 20.3.09. Sunk 4.4.18 in Helsingfors Bay to avoid capture; raised 1954 and BU.

C.27 Vickers 22.4.09. Lost with C.26; raised 1954 and BU.

C.28 Vickers 22.4.09. Sold 25.8.21 Fryer, Sunderland.

C.29 Vickers 19.6.09. Sunk 29.8.15 by mine, North Sea.

C.30 Vickers 19.7.09. Sold 25.8.21 Fryer, Sunderland.

C.31 Vickers 2.9.09. Sunk 4.1.15 off the Belgian coast by unknown cause.

C.32 Vickers 29.9.09. Stranded 24.10.17 and destroyed in the Gulf of Riga.

C.33 Chatham DY 10.5.10. Sunk 4.8.15 in the North Sea by unknown cause.

C.34 Chatham DY 8.6.10. Sunk 21.7.17 by 'U.52' off the north coast of Ireland.

C.35 Vickers 2.11.09. Lost with C.26; raised 1954 and BU.

C.36 Vickers 30.11.09. Sold 25.6.19 at Hong Kong.

C.37 Vickers 1.1.10. Sold 26.6.19 at Hong Kong.

C.38 Vickers 10.2.10. Sold 25.6.19 at Hong Kong.

CC.1 (ex-Chilian IQUIQUE purchased 4.8.1914) Submarine (RCN) 313 tons, 144½ x 15 ft, 5-TT. Seattle 3.6.1913. Discarded 1925.

CC.2 (ex-Chilian ANTOFAGASTA purchased 4.8.1914) Submarine (RCN) 310 tons, 157½ x 15 ft, 3-TT. Seattle 31.12.13. Discarded 1925.

CH.14 (ex-H.14) see 'H' Class submarines.

CH.15 (exH.15) see 'H' class submarines.

CABOT Brig-sloop 14, 189bm, 74 x 24 ft, 14-4pdr. American captured 26.3.1777 by MILFORD off Nova Scotia and purchased 6.1777. Sold 25.6.1783.

CACHALOT Submarine minelayer 1,520 tons, 271½ x 25½ ft, 1-4in, 6-TT, 50mines. Scotts 2.12.1937. Rammed and sunk 8.41 by the Italian TB PAPA off Cyrenaica.

CACHALOT Submarine 1,605 tons, 241 x 26½ ft, 8-TT. Scotts 11.12.1957. Sold 12.11.79, BU at Blyth.

CACHALOT Whaler 1915-33.

CADDISFLY River gunboat, 'Fly' class. Yarrow 1915. Sold 17.2.23 Anglo-Persian Oil Co.

CADIZ Fireship 320bm, Purchased 1688. Expended 19.5.1692 at Barfleur.

CADIZ Destroyer 2,315 tons, 355 x 40 ft, 4-4.5in, 8-TT. Fairfield 18.9.1944. To Pakistan navy 1.2.57 as KAIBAR.

CADMUS Brig-sloop 10, 'Cherokee' class, 237bm. Dudman, Deptford 26.2.1808. Coastguard watch vessel 2.1835; renamed WV.24 on 25.5.1863. Sold 12.3.1864 W. Lethbridge.

CADMUS (see DESPATCH of 1851).

CADMUS Wood s. corvette 1,466bm, 200 x 40½ ft. Chatham DY 20.5.1856. BU 9.1879 at Devenport.

CADMUS Sloop 1,070 tons, 185 x 33 ft, 6-4in, 4-3pdr. Sheerness DY 29.4.1903. Sold 1.9.21 at Hong Kong.

CADMUS Minesweeper, 'Algerine' class. Harland & Wolff 27.5.1942. Sold 1.50 Belgian navy as GEORGES LECONTE.

CAERLEON Minesweeper, lated 'Hunt' class. Bow McLachlan 12.1918. Sold 4.22 Stanlee, Dover.

CAESAR 3rd Rate 74, 1,621bm, 169 x 47 ft. Plymouth DY. Ordered 31.7.1777 and cancelled 4.3.1783.

CAESAR 3rd Rate 80, 1,992bm, 181 x 50½ ft. Plymouth DY 16.11.1793. Army depot 2.1814. BU 2.1821.

CESAR Brig-sloop 16, 320bm. French, captured 15.7.1806 by boats of a squadron in Verdun Roads. Wrecked 3.1807 off the Gironde.

CAESAR Screw 2nd Rate 90, 2,767bm, 207 x 56 ft. Pembroke Dock 7.8.1853. Sold 19.4.1870 C.J. Mare.

CAESAR Battleship 14,900 tons, 390 x 75 ft, 4-12in, 12-6in, 16-12pdr. Portsmouth DY 2.9.1896. Sold 8.11.1921 Slough TC; left 7.22 to BU in Germany.

CAESAR (ex-RANGER renamed 11.1942) Destroyer, 'C' class. J.Brown 14.2.1944. Arrived 6.1.67 Hughes Bolckow, Blyth to BU.

CAESAR Ship hired 1642-43; Trawler 1914-19.

CAICOS (ex-HANNAM renamed 1943) Frigate 'Colony' class. Walsh Kaiser 6.9.1943 on lend-lease. Returned 1.46 to the USN.

ÇA IRA 3rd Rate 80, 2,210bm. French,

captured off Genoa 14.3.1795. Burnt 11.4.1796 by accident in San Fiorenzo Bay.

CAIRNS Minesweeper, 'Bathurst' class. Walker, Maryborough 7.10.1941. Sold Dutch navy 1946 as AMBON.

CAIRO Light cruiser 4,190 tons, 425 x 43½ ft, 5-6in, 2-3in. Cammell Laird 19.11.1918. A/A ship 1939. Sunk 12.8.42 by Italian S/M AXUM off Bizerta.

CAIRO Trawler. Requis. 1914-19.

CAISTER CASTLE Corvette, 'Castle' class. Lewis 22.5.1944. Arrived 3.56 Troon to BU.

CAISTER CASTLE Drifter. Requis. 1915-19.

CALABASH Fireship 262bm, Captured from the Algerines 1680. Sold 1684.

CALCUTTA (ex-E. Indiaman *Warley*) 4th Rate 54, 1,176bm, 157 x 41 ft, 26-32pdr, 28-18pdr, 2-9pdr. Purchased 1795. Transport 24 guns 1804; captured 26.9.1805 by French off Scilly Isles. Destroyed 12.4.1809 in action with British ships.

CALCUTTA 2nd Rate 84, 2,299bm, 197 x 52½ ft. Bombay DY 14.3.1831. Gunnery ship 1865. Sold 12.5.1908 Castle.

CALCUTTA (see HERCULES of 1868)

CALCUTTA (see HANDY of 1884)

CALCUTTA Light cruiser 4,190 tons, 425 x 43½ ft, 5-6in, 2-3in. Vickers 9.7.1918. A/A ship 1939. Sunk 1.6.41 by air attack off Crete.

CALCUTTA Trawler (RIN). 1943-47.

CALDECOT CASTLE Corvette, 'Castle' class. G. Brown. Cancelled 12.1943.

CALDER Frigate, DE 'Captain' class. Mare Island 1942 for the RN but retained bt the USN as GILMORE.

CALDER Frigate, DE 'Captain' class. Mare Island for the RN but retained 1943 by the USN as FINNEGAN.

CALDER Frigate, TE 'Captain' class. Bethlehem, Hingham 27.2.1943 on lend-lease. Returned 10.45 to the USN.

CALDWELL Sloop 2 (Canadian Lakes) Lake Niagara 1774. Made a sheer hulk 1790.

CALDWELL (ex-USS HALE) Destroyer 1,090 tons, 309 x 30½ ft, 3-4in, 1-3in, 6-TT. Commissioned in the RN 9.9.1940. Sold 20.3.45, BU Granton.

CALEDON Sloop 16, circa 220bm. French HENRI captured 1808. Sold 11.1811.

CALEDON Light cruiser 4,120 tons, 425 x 43 ft, 5-6in, 2-3in. Cammell Laird 25.11.1916. A/A ship 12.43. Sold

22.1.48; arrived 14.2.48 Dover Industries, Dover, to BU.

CALEDONIA Brig 3 (Canadian lakes) 1-32pdr carr. 2-24pdr. Amherstburg, Lake Erie 1807. Captured 9.10.1812 by Americans on Lakes Erie; burnt 13.10.1812 by British forces.

CALEDONIA 1st Rate 120, 2,616bm, 205 x 54 ft. Plymouth.DY 25.6.1808. Hospital ship DREADNOUGHT 21.6.1856. BU 1875.

CALEDONIA 2nd Rate 91,3,715bm, 252 x 57 ft, altered 6.1861 to ironclad, 4,125bm, 6,832 tons, 273 x 58 ft, 24-7inML. Woolwich DY 24.10.1862. Sold 30.9.1886., BU by Castle, Charlton.

CALEDONIA (see IMPREGNABLE of 1810)

CALEDONIA (ex-*Majestic* handed over by Messrs Ward in exchange for a number of obsolete waterships 8.10.1936). Training ship, 56,621 tons. Commissioned 23.4.37. Burnt 29.9.39 by accident at Rosyth; wreck sold 3.48; BU 10.42. Fifth of Forth and Inverkeithing 7.83.

CALEDONIA Three hired vessels W.W.I.

CALENDULA Corvette, 'Flower' class. Harland & Wolff 3.1940. Lent to the USN 12.3.42 to 1945 as USS READY. Sold 22.7.46, renamed Villa Cisneros.

CALGARY Corvette (RCN), 'Flower' Class. Marine Ind. 23.8.41. Sold 1946 Victory Transport & Salvage Co.

CALGARY Destroyer (RCN) 1985

CALLIOPE Brig-sloop 10, 'Cherokee' class, 237bm. Dudman, Deptford 28.7.1808. BU completed 13.8.1829 at Portsmouth.

CALLIOPE 6th Rate 28, 717bm, 130 x 35½ ft. Sheerness DY 5.10.1837. Floating chapel 1860; factory 1865. BU completed 1.11.1883 at Devonport.

CALLIOPE S. corvette 2,770 tons, 235 x 44½ ft, 4-6in, 12-5in. Portsmouth DY 24.7.1884. RNVR drillship 29.10.1907; renamed HELICON 6.15; reverted to CALLIOPE 10.31. Sold 4.10.51, BU Hughes Bolckow, Blyth.

CALLIOPE Light cruiser 3,750 tons, 420 x 41½ ft, 2-6in, 8-4in. Chatham DY 17.1.1914. Sold 28.8.31 Ward, Inverkeithing.

CALLIOPE (see FALMOUTH of 1932).

CALLIOPE Trawler. Requis. 1914-16.

CALPE Sloop 14, 209 bm, 75½ x 26½ ft. Spanish SAN JOSEF captured 27.10.1800 at Malaga. Sold 1802.

CALPE Destroyer, 'Hunt' class type II.

Swan Hunter 28.4.1941. Danish ROLF KRAKE 1952. Sold 10.66 to BU in Sweden.

CALSHOT CASTLE Corvette, 'Castle class. Inglis. Cancelled 12.1943.

CALTON Coastal M/S, 'Ton' class. Wivenhoe SY 24.10.1953. Sold C.H. Rugg 17.6.68, BU in Belgium.

CALYPSO Sloop 16, 342bm, 102 x 28 ft. Graves, Deptford 27.9.1783. Run down and sunk 8.1803 by a merchantman in the Atlantic.

CALYPSO Sloop 18, 'Cruizer' class, 382bm. Dudman, Deptford 2.2.1805. BU 3.1821.

CALYPSO Brig-sloop 10, 'Cherokee' class, 239bm. Deptford DY. Ordered 1824, renamed HYAENA 1826, cncelled 1828.

CALYPSO (ex-HYAENA renamed 1826) Brig-sloop 10, 'Cherokee' class, 233bm. Chatham DY 19.8.1826. Completed as a yacht 2 guns for the governor of Malta and name removed from Navy list. Returned RN circa 1830 as packet brig. Foundered 1.2.1833 after collision with an iceberg in N. Atlantic.

CALYPSO Brig-sloop 10, 'Cherokee' class, 235bm. Woolwich DY. Laid down 1829, renamed HYAENA 1830 cancelled 1831.

CALYPSO 6th Rate 20, 731bm, 120 x 37½ ft. Chatham DY 5.1845. BU completed 29.1.1.1866 Castle & Beech, Charlton.

CALYPSO (see BLONDE of 1819).

CALYPSO S. corvette, 2,770 tons 235 x 44½ ft, 4-6in, 12-5in. Chatham DY 7.6.1883. Training ship (Newfoundland Govt) 2.9.1902; renamed BRITON 15.2.16. Sold 7.4.22 as store hulk.

CALYPSO Light cruiser 4,120 tons, 425 x 43 ft, 5-6in, 2-3in. Hawthorn Leslie 24.1.1917. Sunk 12.6l.40 by Italian S/M BAGNOLINI south of Crete.

CALYPSO Trawler requis. 1918-19.

CAM Frigate, 'River' class. G. Brown 31.7.1943. Sold 22.6.45; BU by Young, Sunderland in 7.45.

CAMBERFORD Seaward Defence boat, 'Ford' class. Vosper, Portsmouth 2.1953. Sold 5.7.67 at Singapore.

CAMBERLEY Minesweeper, later 'Hunt' class. Bow McLachlan 28.12.1918. Sold 7.23 C.A. Beard.

CAMBRIA (see DERG).

CAMBRIA Two vessels requis. WW.I, one in WW.II.

CAMBRIAN 5th Rate 40, 1,160bm, 154 x 41½ ft. Parsons, Bursledon 13.2.1797. Wrecked 3.1.1828 in the Mediterranean.

CAMBRIAN 5th Rate 36, 1,622bm, 160 x 49 ft, Pembroke Dock 5.7.1841. Hulk 1872; floating factory 1880. Sold 12.1.1892 J. Read.

CAMBRIAN 2nd class cruiser 4,360 tons, 320 x 49½ ft, 2-6in, 8-4.7in. Pembroke Dock 30.1.1893. Renamed HARLECH base ship 2.3.16; VIVID 9.21; sold 21.2.23 Young, Sunderland.

CAMBRIAN light cruiser 3,750 tons, 420x 41½ ft, 4-6in, 1-4in, 2-3in. Pembroke Dock 3.3.1916. Sold 28.7.34 Metal Industries Rosyth.

CAMBRIAN (ex-SPITFIRE renamed 1942) Destroyer, 'C' class Scotts 10.12.1943. Sold Ward, arrived Briton Ferry 3.9.71 to BU.

CAMBRIAN Trawler requis. 1914-19. Cable ship 1941-45.

CAMBRIDGE 3rd Rate 70, 881bm, 26-34pdr, 26-12pdr, 16-pdr, 2-3pdr. Deptford DY 1666. Wrecked 19.2.1694 off Gibraltar.

CAMBRIDGE 3rd Rate 80, 1,194bm, 156 x 42 ft. Deptford DY 21.2.1695. Rebuilt Woolwich 1715 as 1,286bm. BU completed 12.2.1750 at Chatham.

CAMBRIDGE 3rd Rate 80, 1,615bm, 166 x 47 ft. Deptford DY 21.10.1755. Harbour service 1793. BU 7.1808 at Plymouth.

CAMBRIDGE 3rd Rate 80, 2,139bm, 187 x 52 ft. Deptford DY 23.6.1815. Gunnery ship 8.1856. BU completed 22.3.1869 at Devenport.

CAMRIDGE (see WINDSOR CASTLE of 1858).

CAMBRIDGE Minesweeper. Requis. 1914-19.

CAMEL Fireship 6, 130bm. Captured 1667. Expended 1667.

CAMEL (ex-Yorkshire) Storeship 26, 516bm, 113 x 31½ ft. Purchased 1776. Sold 27.8.1784.

CAMEL (see MEDIATOR of 1782).

CAMEL Storeship, 109bm, 64½ x 20½ ft. Purchased 1798. Sold 22.4.1831.

CAMEL (ex-E.Indiaman *Severn*) Storeship 16, 558bm, 115½ x 34 ft. Purchased 1813. Sold 21.4.1831.

CAMEL Mortar vessel 117bm, 65 x 21 ft, 1-13in mortar. Wigram, Blackwall 21.4.1855. Renamed MV.14 on 19.10.1855. Made a crane lighter 1871, renamed YC.6.

CAMEL Wood S.gunboat, 'Albacore' class. Green, Blackwall 3.5.1856. BU 6.1864.

CAMEL Two DY tugs 1866-1913 and 1914-62.

CAMELEON (see under CHAMELEON).

CAMELLIA Sloop, 'Acacia' class. Bow McLachlan 25.9.1915. Sold 15.1.23.

CAMELLIA Corvete, 'Flower' class. Harland & Wolff 4.5.1940. Sold 9.8.46, renamed *Hetty W.Vinke*.

CAMELLIA Drifter. Requis. 1915-19.

CAMERON (ex-USS WELLES) Destroyer 1,190 tons, 311 x 31 ft, 3-4in, 1-3in, 6-TT. Commissioned in the RN 9.9.1940. Bombed 15.12.40 by German aircraft and capsized in dock at Portsmouth; refloated 23.2.41 and used for shock trails; left Portsmouth 11.44 to BU at Falmouth.

CAMILLA 6th Rate 20, 433bm, 108 x 30 ft. Chatham DY 20.4.1776. Harbour service in 1814. Sold 13.4.1831.

CAMILLA Sloop 16, 549bm, 110 x 35 ft, 16-32pdr. Pembroke Dock 8.9.1847. Foundered 3.1861 on the China Station.

CAMPANIA A/C carrier 18,000 tons, 601 x 65 ft, 6-4.7in, 1-3, 10- A/C. Purchased 27.11.1914; conversion completed 4.16; Sunk 5.11.18 in collison with ROYAL OAK and GLORIOUS in the Forth.

CAMPANIA Escort carrier 12,450 tons, 510x 70 ft, 2-4in, 16, 16-20mm, 15-A/C. Harland & Wolff 17.6.1943. Arrived 11.11.55 Hughes Bolckow, Blyth to BU.

CAMPANIA Trawler and Drifter requis. WW.I.

CAMPANULA Sloop, 'Arabis' class. Barclay Curle 25.12.1915. Sold 6.9.22 Cove & Distinn.

CAMPANULA Corvette, 'Flower' class. Fleming & Ferguson 23.5.1940. Arrived 21.8.47 Clayton & Davie, Dunston to BU.

CAMPANULA Drifter requis. 1915-19.

CAMPASPE Frigate (RAN), 'River' class. Sydney. Ordered 12.1942, cancelled 12.6.44.

CAMPBELL Schooner 4. Purchased 1796 in the W.Indies. Sold 1803.

CAMPBELL Destroyer leader, 1,800 tons, 320 x 32 ft, 5-4.7 in, 1-4in, 6-TT. Cammell Laird 21.9.1918. Sold 18.2.47; arrived 6.48 Metal Industries, Rosyth to BU.

CAMPBELTOWN (ex-USS BUCHANAN) Destroyer 1,090 tons, 309 x 30½ ft, 3-4in, 1-3in, 6-TT. Commissioned in the RN 9.9.1940. Was to have been lent Dutch navy 1.41 as MIDDLEBURG but not taken over; lent Polish navy 3.41 to 9.41. Expended 28.3.42 at St. Nazaire.

CAMPELTOWN Frigate 4,200 tons. Cammell Laird LD. 4.12.1985

CAMPERDOWN 3rd Rate 64, 1,559bm, 167½ x 46½ ft. Dutch. JUPITER captured 11.10.1797 at Camperdown. Harbour service 1798. Sold 10.9.1817.

CAMPERDOWN (See TRAFALGAR of 1820).

CAMPERDOWN Battleship 10,600 tons, 330 x 68½ ft, 4-13.5in, 6-6in, 12-6pdr. Portsmouth DY 24.11.1885. Hulk 10.1908. Sold 11.7.11 Cohen, Swansea.

CAMPERDOWN Destroyer 2,315 tons, 355 x 40 ft, 4-4.5in, 8-TT. Fairfield 8.2.1944. Sold 9.9.70, BU at Faslane.

CAMPERDOWN Cutter hired 1798-1804, Drifter 1915-19.

CAMPHAAN Brig-sloop 16. Dutch, captured 22.8.1799 at Surinam. Sold in 4,1802 to BU.

CAMPION Corvette, 'Flower' class. Crown 26.4.1941. Arrived 20.4.47 Cashmore, Newport to BU.

CAMROSE Corvette (RCN), 'Flower' class, Marine Industries 16.11.1940. BU 6.47 at Hamilton Ont.

CANADA 3rd Rate 74, 1,605bm 170 x 47 ft. Woolwich DY 17.9.1765. Prison ship 3.1810. BU 11.1834 at Chatham.

CANADA 1st Rate 112, 2,152bm, 191½ x 51 ft, 36-32pdr, 76-24pdr. Kingston Ont. Laid down circa 1814, cancelled 1832 and BU on stocks.

CANADA S.corvette 2,380 tons, 225 x 44½ ft, 10-6in. Portsmouth DY 26.8.1881. Sold 10.5.1897 Cohen, Blackwall.

CANADA (ex-Chilian ALMIRANTE LATORRE purchased 9.9.1914) Battleship 28,000 tons, 625 x 92½ ft, 10-14in, 14-6in. Armstrong 27.11.1913. Resold Chile 5.20 as ALMIRANTE LATORRE. BU 1959 in Japan.

CANADA Trawler requis. 1915-19.

CANBERRA Cruiser (RAN) 9,850 tons 590 x 68 ft, 8-8in, 8-4in. J. Brown 31.5.1927. Sunk 9.8.42 after torpedo damage at the Savo Island battle, Pacific.

CANBERRA Frigate (RAN) 2700 tons. Todd, Seattle 1.12.1978

CANCEAUX A.ship 20, 226bm, 80½ x 24½ ft. Purchased 2.1764 at Quebec. Survey ship 1766. Sold 1783 at Quebec.

CANDYTUFT Sloop, 'Anchusa' class. Armstrong 19.5.1917. Sunk 18.11.17 by 'U.39' off Bougie.

CANDYTUFT Corvette, 'Flower' class.

Grangemouth DY Co. 8.7.1940. Lent USN 4.3.42 to 1945 as TENACITY. Sold 9.7.46.

CANDYTUFT (see LONGBRANCH).

CANNING (EX GOLCONDA) Troopship (RIM) 2,246 tons, 370 x 36 ft. Inglis 15.11.1882.

CANNING (see LAWRENCE).

CANOPUS 3rd Rate 80, 2,257bm, 194 x 52½ ft, 32-32pdr, 6-32pdr carr.,36-18pdr, 6-9pdr. French FRANKLIN captured 1.8.1798 at the Nile. Harbour service 1863. Sold 10.1887 and BU.

CANOPUS Battleship 12,950 tons, 390 x 74 ft, 4-12in, 12-6in, 12-12pdr. Portsmouth DY 13.10.1897. Sold 18.2.1920 Stanlee, Dover.

CANSO Schooner 12, 225bm, 93 x 24 ft. American LOTTERY captured 8.2.1813 in Chesapeake Bay. Sold 30.5.1816.

CANSO Minesweeper, TE 'Bangor' class. N. Vancouver SR Co. 9.6.1941. Sold. 1.1.48; BU Young, Sunderland.

CANTERBURY Storeship 8, 367bm, 96 x 29ft. Purchased 7.9.1692. Foundered 26.11.1703 near Bristol; raised and sold.

CANTERBURY 4th Rate 60, 903bm, 145 x 38 ft. Snelgrove, Deptford 18.12.1693. Rebuilt Portsmouth 1722 as 963bm. Rebuilt Plymouth 1744 as 1,117bm, 58 guns; harbour service 1761. BU.7.1770 at Plymouth.

CANTERBURY Light cruiser 3,750 tons, 420 x 41½ ft, 4-6in, 1-4in, 2-3in. J. Brown 21.12.1915. Sold 27.7.34 Metal Industries Rosyth.

CANTERBURY Frigate (RNZN) Leander class. Yarrow 6.5.1970

CANTERBURY CASTLE Corvette, 'Castle' class. Midland SY. Cancelled 12.1943.

CAP de la MADELEINE Frigate (RCN), 'River' class. Morton, Quebec 13.5.1944. For disposal in 1965.

CAPE BRETON Frigate (RCN), 'River' class. Morton, Quebec 24.11.1942. Sold 13.12.47; hull sunk 1948 as a breakwater.

CAPE BRETON (see FLAMBOROUGH HEAD).

CAPE SCOTT (see BEACHY MEAD).

CAPE WRATH Repair ship 8,775 tons, 439 x 62 ft. West Coast SB, Vancouver 24.8.1945. Sold 1951, renamed *Marine Fortune.*

CAPEL Frigate, DE 'Captain' class. Philadelphia N.Yd. 1942 for the RN but retained by the USN as ANDRES.

CAPEL Frigate, DE 'Captain' class. Boston N.Yd. 22.4.1943 on lendlease. Sunk 26.12.44 by 'U.486' off Cherbourg.

CAPELIN Schooner 4, 78bm, 56 x 18 ft, 4-12pdr carr. Bermuda 1804. In service in 1806.

CAPELIN Cutter 8. Wrecked 30.6.1808 off Brest. (This may be the vessel launched 1804, above.)

CAPETOWN Light cruiser 4,190 tons, 425 x 43½ ft, 5-6in, 2-3in. Cammell Laird 28.6.1919; completed 2.22 at Pembroke Dock. Sold 5.4.46; arrived 2.6.46 Ward, Preston to BU.

CAPETOWN Trawler and Drifter requis. WW.I.

CAPILANO Frigate (RCN), 'River' class. Yarrow, Vancouver 8.4.1944. Sold 17.11.47, renamed *Irving Frances M,* lost 1953.

CAPRICE (ex-SWALLOW renamed 11.1942) Destroyer 'C' class. Yarrow 16.9.43. Sold 22.6.79, BU at Queenborough.

CAPRICE Drifter requis. 1940, renamed Capricorn 1943-46.

La CAPRICIEUSE S/M Escort 630 tons, 256 x 28 ft, 2-3.9in French sloop seized 3.7.1940 at Portsmouth. Returned 1945 to the French navy.

CAPTAIN 3rd Rate 70, 1,041bm, 149½ x 40½ ft, 26-34pdr, 26-12pdr, 18 small. Woolwich DY 1678. Rebuilt 1708 as 1,075bm; rebuilt 1722 as 1,131bm; hulked 2.1739. BU.5.1762 Portsmouth.

CAPTAIN 3rd Rate 70, 1,230bm, 151 x 43½ ft. Woolwich DY 14.4.1743. Reduced 1760 to 64 guns; renamed BUFFALO 7.2.177 storeship. BU 10.1783.

CAPTAIN 3rd Rate 74, 1,639bm, 170 x 47 ft. Batson, Limehouse 26.11.1787. Harbour service 12.1809. Burnt 22.3.1813 by accident at Plymouth; BU 7.1813.

CAPTAIN (see CARNATIC of 1783).

CAPTAIN (see ROYAL SOVEREIGN of 1786).

CAPTAIN (see AGINCOURT of 1865).

CAPTAIN Iron S. turret ship, 4,272bm, 6.950 tons, 320 x 53 ft. 4-12in ML,2-7inML. Laird 29.31.1869. Capsized 7.9.1870 in a storm off Cape Finisterre.

CAPTAIN Trawler requis. 1917-19.

CAPTIVITY (see MONMOUTH of 1772).

CAPTIVITY (see BELLEROPHON of 1786).

CARADOC Iron pad. gunboat 676bm,

193 x 37 ft, 2-pdr. Ditchburn & Mare, Blackwall 3.7.1847. Sold 12.5.1870 E. Bates.

CARADOC Light cruiser 4,120 tons, 425 x 43 ft, 5-6in, 2-3in. Scotts 23.12.1916. Base ship 4.44 Arrived 3.46 Ward, Briton Ferry to BU.

CARAQUET Minesweeper, TE 'Bangor' class. N.Vancouver SR Co. 2.6.1941. Sold 29.6.46 Portuguese navy as AL-MIRANTE LACERDA.

CARCASS Bomb 8, 143bm, 66½ x 23ft. Taylor, Cuckolds Point 16.4.1695. Sold 8.1713.

CARCASS Bomb 14, 274bm, 92 x 26 ft. Taylor, Rotherhithe 27.9.1740. Sold 2.3.1748.

CARCASS Bomb 8, 309bm, 92 x 28 ft. Stanton, Rotherhithe 27.1.1759. Sold 5.8.1784.

CARCASS Two tugs. requis in W.W.I.

CARDIFF 34-gun ship, 300bm. Dutch FORTUNE captured 1652. Sold 1658 in Jamaica.

CARDIFF Light cruiser 4,190 tons, 425 x43½ ft, 5-6in, 2-3in. Fairfield 12.4.1917. Sold 23.1.46, BU at Troon.

CARDIFF Destroyer 3150 tons. Vickers 22.2.1974.

CARDIGAN BAY (ex-LOCH LAX-FORD renamed 1944) Frigate, 'Bay' class. Robb 28.12.1944. Arrived 5.3.62 Troon to BU.

CARDINGHAM Inshore M/S, 'Ham' class. Herd & Mackenzie, Buckie 24.6.1952. Sold 4.67 at Hong Kong to BU.

CAREFUL (See BLOSSOM of 1856).

CAREFUL Rescue tug. 1945-73. Tug 1982.

CAREW CASTLE Corvette, 'Castle' class. Midland SY. Cancelled 12.1943.

CAREW CASTLE Trawler. Requis. 1915-17.

CARHAMPTON Coastal M/S, 'Ton' class. Wivenhoe SY 21.7.1955. Sold H.K. Vickers 22.6.70 to BU.

CARISBROOKE CASTLE Corvette, 'Castle' class. Caledon 31.7.1943. Arrived 14.6.58 Faslane to BU.

CARLISLE 4th Rate 60, 912bm, 145 x38 ft. Snelgrove, Deptford 11.2.1693. Wrecked 28.1.1696 on the Shipwash.

CARLISLE 4th Rate 48, 709bm. Plymouth DY 1698. Blown up 19.9.1700 by accident in the Downs.

CARLISLE Light cruiser 4,190 tons, 425 x 43½ ft, 5-6in, 2-3in. Fairfield 9.7.1918. A/A ship 1939; damaged beyond repair 9.10.43 by air attack in the Mediterranean; base ship

3.44. Last listed as hulk at Alexandria in 1948.

CARLOTTA Brig-sloop 14, 204bm, 90½ x 23 ft. Captured 1810. BU 5.1815.

CARLPLACE Frigate (RCN), 'River' class. Davie, Lauzon 6.7.1944. Sold 1946 Dominican navy as PRESIDENTE TRUJILLO.

CARMEN 5th Rate 32, 908bm, 147 x 37½ ft. Spanish, captured 6.4.1800 by LEVIATHAN and EMERALD off Cadiz. Sold 2.1802.

CARNARVON Armoured cruiser 10,850 tons, 450 x 68 ft, 4-7.5in, 6-6in, 2-12pdr, 22-3pdr. Beardmore 7.10.1903. Sold 8.11.21 Slough TC; BU in Germany.

CARNARVON BAY (ex-LOCH MADDY renamed 1944) Frigate, 'Bay' class. Robb 15.3.1945. Arrived 28.8.59 at Spezia to BU.

CARNATIC 3rd Rate 74, 1,720bm, 172 x 48 ft. Deptford 21.1.1783. Renamed CAPTAIN 14.7.1815. BU 9.1825.

CARNATIC 3rd Rate 72, 1,790bm, 177 x 49 ft. Portsmouth DY 21.10.1823 (never commissioned). Coal hulk 1.1860; powder hulk 1886; lent War Dept 8.1886 to 10.1891. Sold 19.2.1914, BU in Germany.

CARNATIC (ex-NEWHAVEN renamed 10.1941) Minesweeper (RIN), turbine 'Bangor' class. Hamilton 9.7.42.

CARNATION Brig-Sloop 18, 'Cruiser' class 383 bm. Taylor, Bideford 3.10.1807. Captured 3.10.1808 by the French PALINURE off Martinique; burnt 2.1809 to avoid recapture at Martinique.

CARNATION Brig-sloop, 'Cruiser' class 385bm. Durkin, Southampton 29.7.1813. Breakwater 8.1826; sold 21.1.1836.

CARNATION Wood S.gunboat, 'Albacore' class. Pitcher, Northfleet 20.10.1855. BU 1863 at Sheerness.

CARNATION Sloop, 'Acacia' class. Greenock & Grangemouth 6.9.1915. Sold 14.1.22 Stanlee, Dover.

CARNATION Corvette, 'Flower' class. Grangemouth DY Co. 3.9.1940. Lent Dutch navy as FRISO 1943 to 18.2.45. Sold 31.3.48, renamed *Southern Laurel.*

CAROLINA (see PEREGRINE GALLEY).

CAROLINA A.ship in service in 1780. Sold 29.4.1784.

CAROLINE Gunvessel 3, 101bm, 64 x 19½ ft. Ex-barge purchased 4.1794. Sold 3.1802.

CAROLINE 5th Rate 36, 924 bm, 142½ x 38 ft. Randall, Rotherhithe

17.6.1795. BU 9.1815.

CAROLINE Gun-brig 14, 158bm, 12-12pdr carr., 2-6pdr. French AF-FRONTEUR captured 18.5.1803 by DORIS off Ushant. BU 1806.

CAROLINE Schooner. French, captured 1809. Listed to 1814.

CAROLINE Wood S.gunboat. 'Albacore' class. Green, Blackwall 9.5.1856. BU in 2.1862 at Portsmouth.

CAROLINE Sailing gunboat (NZ). Purchased 1859. Sold 1863.

CAROLINE Compos. S.corvette 1,420 tons, 200 x 38 ft, 14-5in. Sheerness DY 25.11.1882. Harbour service 1897; renamed GANGES 4.1908 training ship; renamed POWERFUL III in 9.13, IMPREGNABLE IV in 11.19. Sold 31.8.29.

CAROLINE Light cruiser 3,750 tons, 420 x 41½ ft, 2-6in, 8-4in. Cammell Laird 29.9.1914. RNVR drillship 1.4.24.

CAROLINE Trawler 1940-41.

CARRICK (ex-*City of Adelaide*, ex-hospital hulk) RNVR drill ship 860 tons, 176½ x 33½ ft. Purchased 27.3.1923, commissioned 5.25. Accommodation ship 10.40. Given away 1947 as club ship.

CARRICK II (ex-training ship *Indefatigable*, ex-PHAETON renamed 1941) 4,300 tons. Arrived 20.1.47 Ward, Preston to BU.

CARRERE 5th Rate 38, 1,013bm, 151 x 39½ ft, 12-32pdr carr., 22-18 pdr, 4-9pdr. French, captured 3.8.1801 by POMONE off Elba. Sold 1.9.1814.

CARRIER (ex-*Frisk*) Cutter 10, 54bm, 4-12pdr carr., 6-3pdr. Purchased 1805. Wrecked 5.2.1809 on the coast of France.

CARRON 6th Rate 20, 460bm, 116 x 30 ft, 18-32pdr carr., 2-9pdr. Adams, Bucklers Hard 9.11.1813. Wrecked 6.7.1820 near Puri, India.

CARRON Wood pad. vessel, 294bm, 110 x 25 ft (ex-brig-sloop 'Cherokee' class converted on stocks). Deptford DY 9.1.1827. Lent as coal hulk 1846; breakwater 1848; left navy list 6.1877. BU 1.1885 at Devonport.

CARRON Mortar vessel, 160bm. Wigram, Blackwall 28.4.1855. Renamed MV.17 on 19.10.1855; hulked 7.1866. BU 11.1884 at Devonport.

CARRON (ex-STRENUOUS renamed 11.1942) Destroyer, 'C' class. Scotts 28.3.44. Arrived 4.4.67 Ward. Inverkeithing to BU.

CARRON Minehunter 757 tons. Richards 23.9.1983.

CARRON Tug 1867-85. Tug 1888-1904. Hired vessel 1914-19.

CARRONADE Destroyer 1,980 tons, 341½ x38 ft. 6-4in, 6-40mm. 10-TT. Scotts 4.1946 (not completed). Arrived 5.4.46 at Troon to BU

CARSTAIRS (ex-CAWSAND renamed 1918) Minesweeper, later 'Hunt' class. Bow McLachlan 18.4.1919. Renamed DRYAD 4.1.24; CARSTAIRS 15.8.24. Sold 26.4.35 Ward, Grays.

CARYSFORT 6th Rate 28, 586bm, 118½ x 34 ft. Sheerness DY 23.8.1766. Sold 28.4.1813.

CARYSFORT 6th Rate 26, 911bm, 130 x 40 ft. Pembroke Dock 12.8.1836. Sold 22.11.1861 Ritherdon & Thompson.

CARYSFORT S.corvette 2,380 tons, 225 x 44½ ft, 2-7inMLR, 12-64 pdr. Elder 26.9.1878. Sold 15.12.1899 King, Garston.

CARYSFORT Light cruiser 3,750 tons, 420 x 41½ ft, 2-6in, 8-4in. Pembroke Dock 14.11.1914. Arrived 10.31 McLellan, Bo'ness to BU.

CARYSFORT Destroyer, 'C' class. White 25.7.1944. Sold Cashmore 23.10.70, BU Newport.

CARYSFORT II Trawler. requis. 1915-19.

CASHEL Minesweeper, later 'Hunt' class. Bow McLachlan. Cancelled 1918.

CASSANDRA 5th Rate 36, 897bm. Ordered Sheerness 16.1.1782, cancelled 2.4.1782.

CASSANDRA Cutter 10, 111bm, 68 x 20 ft, 8-18pdr carr., 2-6pdr. Bermuda 1806. Foundered 13.5.1807 off Bordeaux.

CASSANDRA Light cruiser 4,120 tons, 425 x 43 ft, 5-6in, 2-3in. Vickers 25.11.1916. Sunk 5.12.18 by mine in the Baltic.

CASSANDRA (ex-TOURMALINE renamed 11.1942) Destroyer, 'C' class. Yarrow 29.11.43. Arrived 28.4.67 Ward, Inverkeithing.

CASSANDRA II Trawler requis. 1915-19.

CASSIUS Diving-bell vessel, ex-American schooner purchased 7.9.1847. Last listed 1852.

CASTILIAN Brig-sloop 18, 'Cruizer' class, 387bm. Hill, Sandwich 29.5.1809. BU 10.1829.

CASTLE Fireship 8, 329bm. Purchased 1672. Sold 1683.

CASTLEMAIN Minesweeper (RAN), 'Bathurst' class. Williamstown DY 7.8.1941. Museum ship at Williamstown from 6.74.

CASTLEREAGH Survey schooner 93bm. Purchased 3.4.1846. Sold circa 1848.

CASTLETON (ex-USS AARON WARD) Destroyer 1,090 tons, 309 x 30½ ft, 1-4in, 1-3in, 4-20mm, 3-TT. Commissioned in the RN 9.9.1940. Sold 4.3.47; arrived 9.48 McLellan, Bo'ness.

CASTLETON Coastal M/S, 'Ton' class. White, Southampton 26.8.1957. To S.African navy 1958 as JOHANNESBERG.

CASTOR 5th Rate 36. Dutch, captured 23.5.1781 by FLORA. Captured 20.6.1781 by the French FRIPONNE off Cadiz.

CASTOR 5th Rate 32, 681bm, 126 x 35 ft. Graham, Harwich 26.5.1785. Sold 22.7.1819. (In French hands 9.5.94 to 29.5.94.)

CASTOR 5th Rate 26, 1,293bm, 1,808 tons, 159 x 43 ft, 36-32pdr. Chatham DY 2.5.1832. Training ship 1.1860. Sold 25.8.1902 at Sheerness.

CASTOR Light cruiser 3,750 tons, 420 x 41½ ft, 4-6in, 2-3in. Cammell Laird 28.7.1915. Sold 30.7.36; arrived 8.36 Rosyth to BU.

CASTOR Trawler and Tug requis. WW.I.

CAT Pink 8, in service in 1654. Captured 1656 by 'Dunkirkers'.

CAT Fireship 4, 224bm. Captured 1666. Sold 1668.

CATERHAM Minesweeper, later 'Hunt' class. Bow MacLachlan 6.3.1919. Sold 26.4.35 Cashmore, Newport.

CATHERINE Fireship 95bm, 58½ x 20ft. Purchased 4.1794. Sold 12.1801.

CATHERINE Minesweeper, 'Catherine' class. Associated SB, Seattle 7.9.1942 on lend-lease. Returned 1946 USN and sold Turkish navy as ERDEMLI.

CATHERINE Drifter requis. 1939-42.

CATHERINE (see also under Katherine).

CATON 3rd Rate 64, 1,407bm, 166 x 44ft. French, captured 19.4.1782 in the Mona Passage. Harbour service in 1798. Sold 9.2.1815.

CATO 4th Rate 50, 1,062bm, 146½ x 41 ft. Cleveley, Gravesend 29.5.1782. Foundered 1783 on passage to the E. Indies.

CATO Minesweeper, 'Catherine' class. Assoc. SB, Seattle 7.9.1942. To RN 28.7.43 on lend-lease. Sunk 6.7.44 by human torpedo off Normandy.

CATO Store carrier requis, 1914-15.

CATTERICK Destroyer, 'Hunt' class type III Vickers Armstrong, Barrow 22.11.1941. Lent Greek navy 5.46 as HASTINGS. Sold at Athens 7.63 to BU.

CATTISTOCK Minesweeper, early 'Hunt' class. Clyde SB 21.2.1917. Sold 22.2.23 Alloa S.Bkg Co; arrived Charlestown 4.23 to BU.

CATTISTOCK Destroyer, 'Hunt' class, type I. Yarrow 22.2.1940. BU 7.57 Cashmore, Newport.

CATTISTOCK Minehunter 615 tons Vosper-Thornycroft 22.1.1980

CAUNTON Coastal M/S, 'Ton' class. Montrose SY 20.2.1953. Sold 15.4.70 to BU Newhaven.

CAUVERY Sloop (RIN) 1,350 tons, 283 x 38½ ft, 6-4in, 12-20mm. Yarrow 15.6.1943. Renamed KAVERI 1968, sold 1979.

CAVALIER Destroyer, 'C' class. White 7.4.1944. Sold 10.77 for conversion to museum ship.

CAVAN (ex-CLOVELLY renamed 1918) Minesweeper, later 'Hunt' class. Bow McLachlan. Cancelled 1918.

CAVENDISH (see VINDICTIVE of 1918).

CAVENDISH (ex-SIBYL renamed 11.1942) Destroyer, 'C' class. J.Brown 12.4.1944. Arrived Blyth 17.8.67 to BU.

CAWSAND (see CARSTAIRS).

CAWSAND BAY (ex-LOCH ROAN renamed 1944) Frigate, 'Bay' class. Blyth DD 26.2.1945, completed by Hughes Bolckow, Blyth. Arrived 5.9.59 at Genoa to BU.

CAYMAN (ex-HARLAND) Frigate, 'Colony' class. Walsh Kaiser 22.8.1943 on lend-lease. Returned 22.4.46 to the USN.

CAYUGA Destroyer (RCN) 1,927 tons, 355½ x 36½ ft, 8-4in. Halifax SY 28.7.1945. Arrived 14.10.64 at Faslane to BU.

CC.1 and CC.2 (see 'C' class submarines).

CEANOTHUS Sloop, 'Anchusa' class. Armstrong 2.6.1917. To RIN 9.21 as ELPHINSTONE. Wrecked 29.1.25 Nicobar Islands.

CEANOTHUS (see FOREST HILL).

CEDARWOOD Survey vessel (RCN) 566 tons. Transferred from govt. dept 4.10.1948. For disposal 10.56.

CELANDINE Sloop, 'Arabis' class. Barclay Curle 19.2.1916. Sold 15.1.23 Unity S.Bkg Co.

CELANDINE Corvette, 'Flower' class. Grangemouth DY Co.28.12.1940. Arrived 10.48 at Portaferry to BU.

CELANDINE II Drifter requis. 1915-19.

CELEBES 5th Rate 36, Dutch PALLAS captured 26.7.1806 by GREYHOUND in the E.Indies. Gone by 1809.

CELERITY (see PIQUE of 1942).

CELT Destroyer, 'C' class. White. Redesigned, renamed SWORD 9.43 as 1,980 tons, 341½ x 38 ft, 6-4in and laid down 17.9.1945. Cancelled 5.10.45.

CENSEUR 3rd Rate 74, 1,820bm. French, captured 14.3.1795 by the fleet off Genoa. Recaptured 7.10.1795 by the French fleet off Cape St Vincent.

CENSOR Gun-brig 12, 186bm, 80 x 23ft, 2-32pdr carr., 10-18pdr carr. Randall, Rotherhithe 2.4.1801. Sold 11.1.1816.

CENTAUR 6th Rate 24, 504bm, 112 x 32 ft. Blaydes, Hull 11.6.1746. Sold 30.1.1761.

CENTAUR 3rd Rate 74, 1,739bm, 175½ x 47½ ft, 28-32pdr, 30-18pdr, 16-9pdr. French CENTAURE captured 18.8.1759 at Lagos. Foundered 21.9.1782 off the Newfoundland Banks.

CENTAUR 3rd Rate 74, 1,842bm, 176 x 49 ft. Woolwich DY 14.3.1797. BU 11.1819 at Plymouth.

CENTAUR Wood pad. frigate 1,269bm, 200 x 37½ ft. Portsmouth DY 6.10.1845. BU 9.1864 at Plymouth.

CENTAUR (see ROYAL ARTHUR).

CENTAUR Light cruiser 3,750 tons, 420 x 42 ft, 5-6in, 2-3in. Armstrong 6.1.1916. Sold 2.34 King, Troon, arrived 6.3.34.

CENTAUR Destroyer, 'C' class. White. Ordered 2.1942, redesigned as 1,980 tons and renamed TOMAHAWK 9.43; launched 15.8.46 as SCORPION.

CENTAUR A/C carrier 22,000 tons, 650 x 90 ft, 20-40mm, 50-A/C. Harland & Wolff 22.4.1947. Sold 19.7.72, arrived Cairnryan 6.9.72.

CENTURION 34-gun ship, 531bm. Pett, Ratcliffe 1650. Wrecked 25.12.1689 off Plymouth.

CENTURION 4th Rate 48, 614bm, 126 x 33 ft. Deptford 1691. BU 1728.

CENTURION 4th Rate 60, 1,005bm, 144 x 40 ft. Portsmouth DY 6.1.1732. BU 12.1769 at Chatham.

CENTURION 4th Rate 50, 1,044bm, 146 x 40½ ft. Barnard, Harwich 22.5.1774. Harbour service 1809. Sunk 21.2.1824 at moorings at Halifax, raised and BU 1825.

CENTURION (see CLARENCE of 1812).

CENTURION 3rd Rate 80, 2,580bm, 190

x57 ft. Pembroke Dock 2.5.1844. Undocked 12.11.1855 as screw ship 2,590bm. Sold 19.4.1870 Lethbridge.

CENTURION Battleship 10,500 tons, 360 x 70 ft, 4-10ins, 10-4.7in, 8-6pdr. Portsmouth DY 3.8.1892. Sold 12.7.1910 Ward, Morecambe.

CENTURION Battleship 23,000 tons, 555 x 89 ft, 10-13.5in, 12-4in. Devonport DY 18.11.1911. Converted to target ship at Chatham 1926; rated as escort ship 1940. Sunk 9.6.44 as breakwater at Arromanches.

CENTURION Cruiser, circa 9,000 tons, projected 1945, cancelled 3.46.

CENTURION Trawler requis. 1915-19.

CEPHALUS Brig-sloop 18, 'Cruizer' class. 382bm. Custance, Yarmouth 10.1.1807. BU completed 17.3.1830.

CERBERE (see CERBERUS).

CERBERUS 6th Rate 28, 593bm, 119 x 34 ft. Fenn, Cowes 5.9.1758. Abandoned and burnt 7.8.1778 at Rhode Island.

CERBERUS 5th Rate 32, 701bm, 126 x 35½ ft. Randall, Rotherthithe 15.7.1779. Wrecked 1783 near Bermuda.

CERBERUS 5th Rate 32, 796bm, 135 x 36 ft. Adams, Bucklers Hard 9.1794. Sold 29.9.1814.

CERBERUS Gun-brig 10, 138bm, 79½ x 20 ft, 10-18pdr carr. French, captured 29.7.1800 by VIPER at Mauritius. Wrecked 19.2.1804 on Berry Head, Torbay.

CERBERUS 5th Rate 46, 1,079bm, 152 x 40½ ft, Plymouth DY 30.3.1827. BU completed 10.1.1866 by Marshall, Plymouth.

CERBERUS Turret ship (Australian) 2,107bm, 3,344 tons, 225 x 45 ft, 4-10in ML. Palmer, Jarrow 2.12.1868. Harbour service in 1900; renamed PLATYPUS II, depot ship 1918. Sold 23.4.24 Melbourne Salvage Co; hull sunk 7.26 as breakwater.

CERBERUS (see PROTECTOR of 1884).

CERBERUS Tug requis. 1914-18. Trawler requis. 1915

CERES Sloop 18, 361bm, 108½ x 27½ ft. Woolwich DY 25.3.1777. Renamed RAVEN 4.7.1782; captured 15.12.1782 by the French in the West Indies.

CERES 5th Rate 32, 692bm, 129½ x 35½ ft. Fearon & Webb, Liverpool 19.9.1781. Slop ship 1804. BU 3.1830.

CERES Light cruiser 4,190 tons, 425 x 43½ ft, 5-6in, 2-3in. J.Brown 24.3.1917. Sold 5.4.46; arrived

12.7.46 Hughes Bolckow, Blyth to BU.

CERF Gun-brig 12, 172bm, 74 x 22 ft. French, captured 30.11.1803 at San Domingo. Sold 27.8.1806.

CERF (see CYANE).

CESAR (see CAESAR).

CESSNOCK Minesweeper, 'Bathurst' class. Cockatoo DY 17.10.1941. Sold 23.4.47 to Chinese shipbreakers.

CESSNOCK Patrol boat (RAN) 211 tons. N. Queensland Eng. Co 15.1.1983.

CEYLON (ex-BOMBAY renamed 1.7.1808) 5th Rate 38, 672bm, 130 x 35 ft, 14-24pdr carr., 24-18pdr, 2-9pdr. Troopship 1813; sold 4.7.1857 at Malta. (Was captured three times by the French, finally being recaptured 6.12.1810 at Mauritius.)

CEYLON Cruiser 8,800 tons, 538 x 62 ft, 9-6in, 8-4in. Stephen 30.7.1942. Sold Peruvian navy 12.59, renamed CORONEL BOLOGNESI 2.60.

CEYLON Tug and Yacht requis. WW.I.

CH.14 and CH.15 (see submarines H.14 and H.15).

CHAILEY Inshore M/S, 'Ley' class. Saunders Roe, Anglesea 11.11.1954. Sold 4.6.69, BU Canvey Island

CHALEUR Schooner 12, 117bm, 67 x 20 ft. Purchased 1764 in N. America. Sold 6.12.1768. (The first schooner in the RN.)

CHALEUR Coastal M/S (RCN) 370 tons, Port Arthur SY 5.1952. Transferred French navy 9.10.54 as DIEPPOISE.

CHALEUR Coastal M/S (RCN) 390 tons, 140 x 28 ft, 1-40mm. Marine Industries 11.5.1957.

CHALLENGER Brig-sloop 16 (pitch pine-built) 285bm, 96 x 25 ft. Wallis, Blackwall 30.7.1806. Captured 12.3.1811 by a French frigate off Mauritius.

CHALLENGER Brig-sloop 18, 'Cruizer' class, 387bm. Hobbs & Hillyer, Redbridge 15.5.1813. 10 guns 1816; mooring vessel 1820. store hulk 1820. Sold 3.1824 at Trincomalee.

CHALLENGER 6th Rate 28, 603bm, 125½ x 33 ft. Portsmouth DY 14.11.1826. Wrecked 19.5.1835 on the West coast of Chile.

CHALLENGER Corvette 18, 810bm 134 x 37½ ft. Chatham DY. Ordered 1845, cancelled 1848.

CHALLENGER Wood S. corvette 1,462bm, 2,306 tons, 200 x 40½ ft. 20-8in, 2-68pdr. Woolwich DY 13.2.1858. Survey ship 4 guns 1872; hulk 1880. Sold 6.1.1921 J.B. Garn-

ham.

CHALLENGER 2nd class cruiser 5,917 tons, 355 x 56 ft, 11-6in, 9-12pdr. Chatham DY 27.5.1902. Sold 31.5.20 Ward, Preston.

CHALLENGER Survey ship 1,140 tons, 200 x 36 ft. Chatham DY 1.6.1931. Arrived 12.1.54 Dover Industries Ltd., Dover to BU.

CHALLENGER Diving Vessel 6400 tons. Scotts, Greenock 19.5.1981.

CHAMBLY Corvette, (RCN) 'Flower' class. Vickers, Montreal 29.7.1940. Sold 1946, renamed Sonjia Vinke BU 1952.

CHAMELEON Sloop 14, 307bm, 97 x 27 ft. Randall, Rotherhithe 26.3.1777. Foundered 11.10.1780 in the W. Indies in a hurricane.

CHAMELEON ex-Hawke Brig-sloop 16, 267bm, 78 x 29 ft. Purchased 1780. Sold 1.5.1783.

CAMELEON Brig-sloop 16 (fir-built) 314bm, 95 x 28 ft. Randall, Rotherhithe 14.10.1795. BU 4.1811.

CAMELEON Brig-sloop 10, 'Cherokee' class, 240bm. Bombay DY 16.1.1816. BU 4.1849.

CAMELEON Wood S.sloop 952bm, 1,365 tons, 182 x 33 ft. Deptford DY 23.2.1860. Sold 1883.

CAMELEON Destroyer 747 tons, 246 x 26 ft, 2-4in, 2-13pdr, 2-TT. Fairfield 2.6.1910. Sold 15.11.21 Distin, Devonport.

CHAMELEON Minesweeper, 'Algerine' class. Harland & Wolff 6.5.1944. Arrived 3.4.66 at Silloth to BU.

CHAMOIS Destroyer 360 tons, 215 x 20½ ft, 1-12pdr, 5-6pdr, 2-TT. Palmer 3.11.1896. Foundered 26.9.1904 in the Gulf of Patras, Greece, after her screw had pierced her bottom.

CHAMOIS Minesweeper, 'Catherine' class. Assoc. SB, Seattle 26.10.1942; to RN on lend-lease 22.10.43; Returned 10.12.46 to the USN. BU Southampton 9.50.

CHAMPION 6th Rate 24, 519bm, 114½ x 32 ft. Barnard, Ipswich 17.5.1779. Harbour service 1810. Sold 28.8.1816.

CHAMPION Sloop 18, 456bm, 110 x 31 ft. Portsmouth DY 31.5.1824. Harbour service 1859. BU 10.1867 at Portsmouth after being wrecked as a target.

CHAMPION S. corvette 2,380 tons, 225 x 44½ ft, 2-7in ML, 12-64pdr. Elder 1.7.1878. Harbour service 1904; renamed CHAMPION (OLD) 1915. Sold 23.6.19 Hughes Bolckow, Blyth.

CHAMPION Light cruiser 3,750 tons,

420 x 41½ ft, 2-6in, 8-4in. Hawthorn Leslie 29.5.1915. Sold 28.7.34 Metal Industries Rosyth.

CHAMPION (see CHEQUERS)

CHAMPION Two cutters hired 1803. Two Drifters 1915-19.

CHAMPLAIN Brig (Canadian lakes) 111bm. Lake Champlain 1819. Sold circa 1832.

CHAMPLAIN (see TORBAY of 1919).

CHANCE Sloop 18, 395bm, 99 x 27 ft: Spanish GALGO captured 15.11.1799 by CRESCENT off Puerto Rico. Foundered 9.10.1800 in the W. Indies.

CHANCE Minesweeper, 'Catherine' class. Assoc. SB, Seattle 27.11.1942 and to the RN on lend-lease 13.11.43. Returned 1946 to the USN and sold 3.47 to Turkish navy as EDREMIT.

CHANCE Schooner hired 1815, Drifter 1914-16.

CHANTICLEER Brig-sloop 10, 'Cherokee' class, 237bm. List, Cowes 26.7.1808. Survey ship 4,1828; customs watch vessel 2.1830; renamed WV.5 on 25.5.1863. BU 6.1871 at Sheerness.

CHANTICLEER Wood S.sloop 950bm, 185 x 33 ft. Portsmouth DY 9.2.1861. Sold 23.1.1875 Castle.

CHANTICLEER Sloop 1,350 tons, 283 x 38½ ft, 6-4in, 12-20mm. Denny 24.9.1942. Damaged beyond repair 18.11.43 by 'U.238' west of Portugal and used as base ship; renamed LUSITANIA 31.12.43. BU 1945.

CHANTICLEER Trawler requis, 1914-19.

CHAPLET Destroyer, 'C' class. Thornycroft 18.7.1944. Arrived 6.11.65 Hughes Bolckow, Blyth to BU.

CHARGER Gun-brig 179bm, 80 x 22½ ft, 1-8in mortar, 10-18pdr carr., 2-18pdr. Dudman, Deptford 17.4.1801. Sold 9.6.1814.

CHARGER (see COURIER of 1830).

CHARGER Wood S.gunboat, 'Albacore' class. Pitcher, Northfleet 13.11.1855. Buoy boat 6.1866; later renamed YC.3. Sold 7.1887, renamed 'Rescue'. BU 1921.

CHARGER Destroyer 290 tons, 190 x 18½ ft, 1-12pdr, 5-6pdr, 2-TT. Yarrow, Poplar 15.5.1894. Sold 14.5.1912, Ward; BU at Silvertown.

CHARGER (ex-*Rio de la Plata* converted on stocks) Escort carrier 8,200 tons, 450 x 69½ ft. Sun SB, Chester, Pa 1.3.1941 for the RN but retained by the USN as USS CHARGER.

CHARGER Escort carrier 11,420 tons,

468½ x 69½ ft, 2-4in, 16-40mm, 24-A/C. Seattle, Tacoma. Launched 16.7.1942 as RAVAGER.

CHARGER (see LST.3026).

CHARGER Patrol boat 43 tons. Watercraft 1985.

CHARITY Fireship. French CHARITE captured 1650. Expended 1652.

CHARITY 36-gun ship, 453bm. Captured 1653. Captured 3.6.1665 by the Dutch. (Also known as GREAT CHARITY in 1656.)

LITTLE CHARITY 28-gun ship. Captured 1653. Sold 1656.

CHARITY Sloop (Canadian lakes) Lake Niagara 1770. Lost 1777 on lake Niagara.

CHARITY Destroyer, 'C' class Thornycroft 30.11.1944. To Pakistan navy 16.12.58 as SHAH JEHAN.

CHARITY Two drifters requis. W.W.I.

CHARLES Pinnace 16, 70/110bm, 8-6pdr, 2-2pdr, 6-small. Woolwich 1586. Sold 1616.

CHARLES Pinnace 16, 80/140bm. Built 1620. Last listed 1627.

CHARLES 44-gun ship, 607bm. Woolwich 1632. Renamed LIBERTY 1649. Wrecked 1650.

CHARLES 38-gun ship (Royalist) 500bm. Captured 25.4.1649. Renamed GUINEA 1649. Sold 1667.

CHARLES R.Yacht 6,38bm Woolwich DY 1662. Transferred 1668 to the Ordnance Office.

CHARLES V 4th Rate 52, 600bm. Dutch CAROLUS V captured 1665. Burnt 12.6.1667 by the Dutch at Chatham.

CHARLES Fireship 6, 209bm. Purchased 1666. Sold 1667.

CHARLES 1st Rate 96, 1,129bm, 163 x 42½ ft, 26-60pdr, 28-18pdr, 26-9pdr, 16-3pdr. Deptford DY 3.3.1668. Renamed ST GEORGE 1687. BU 1774. (see ST GEORGE)

CHARLES R. yacht 8, 120bm Rotherhithe 1675. Wrecked 1678 on the Dutch coast.

CHARLES GALLEY 5th Rate 32, 546bm, 131 x 28½ ft, 28-9pdt, 4-3pdr. Woolwich DY 1676. Rebuilt 1693 as 548bm. rebuilt Deptford 1710 as 537bm. renamed TORRINGTON 7.1729 and rebuilt as 594bm; hulk 1740. Sold 12.7.1744.

CHARLES Fireship 6, Purchased 1688. Expended 5.7.1695 at St. Malo.

CHARLES & HENRY Fireship 6, 120bm. Purchased 1688. Wrecked 29.11.1689 near Plymouth.

CHARLESTOWN 6th Rate 28, 514bm,

114 x 32 ft. American BOSTON captured 12.5.1780 at Charlestown. Sold 24.4.1783.

CHARLESTOWN (ex-USS ABBOTT) Destroyer 1,060, 309 x 30½ ft, 3-4in, 1-3in, 6-TT. Commissioned in the RN 23.9.1940. Sold 4.3.47, BU Young, Sunderland.

CHARLOCK Corvette, modified 'Flower' class Ferguson 16.11.1943. Renamed MAHRATTA (RIN) 6.2.46. Stranded 1947.

CHARLOTTE R.yacht 8, 143bm, Woolwich DY 1677. Rebuilt and renamed AUGUSTA 28.7.1761, 155bm. BU 1771.

CHARLOTTE Cutter 4, 70bm, 46½ x 20 ft. Purchased 2.1763. Sold 14.11.1770.

CHARLOTTE Schooner 8, 8-6pdr. Purchased 1798. Captured 1799 by the French; recaptured as VENGEUR 22.11.1799 and BU.

CHARLOTTE Schooner 6, 6-3pdr. Purchased 1800. Wrecked 28.3.1801 on the Isle of Ash.

CHARLOTTETOWN Corvette (RCN), 'Flower' class. Kingston SY 10.9.1941. Sunk 11.9.42 by 'U.517' in the Gulf of St. Lawrence.

CHARLOTTETOWN Frigate (RCN), 'River' class G.T. Davie 16.9.1943. Sold 1947 and hull sunk as breakwater 1948.

CHARON 5th Rate 44, 891bm, 140 x 38 ft. Barnard, Harwich 8.10.1778. Burnt 10.10.1781 at Yorktown.

CHARON 5th Rate 44, 889bm, 140 x 38 ft. Hillhouse, Bristol 17.5.1783. Harbour service 1795; troopship 2.1800. BU 12.1805.

CHARON (ex-GPO vessel *Crusader*) Wood pad. packet 125bm. Transferred 1.4.1837. Sold Trinity House 18.7.1849.

CHARON Wood S. gunboat, 'Albacore' class. Pitcher, Northfleet 9.2.1856. BU 10.1865 by Marshall, Plymouth.

CHARON Whaler 1915-19, Tug renamed ALLIGATOR 1947-59.

CHARWELL (see CHERWELL)

CHARYBDIS Brig-sloop 18, 'Cruizer' class, 385bm. Richards, Hythe 28.8.1809. Sold 3.2.1819 Pittman.

CHARYBDIS Brig-sloop 10, 'Cherokee' class, 232bm. Portsmouth DY 27.2.1831. Sold 7.11.1843 Beatson, Rotherhithe.

CHARYBDIS Wood S. corvette 1,506bm, 2,187 tons, 200 x 40½ ft, 20-8in, 1-68pdr. Chatham DY 1.6.1859. Lent Canadian govt 10.1880 to 8.1882 as training ship.

Sold 1884 at Halifax.

CHARYBDIS 2nd class cruiser 4,360 tons, 320 x 49½ ft, 2-6in, 8-4.7in, 8-6pdr. Sheerness DY 15.6.1893. Converted 3.1918 to cargo carrier; returned to RN 12.1919. Sold 27.1.22 at Bermuda; resold 10.23 and BU in Holland.

CHARYBDIS Cruiser 5,450 tons, 485 x 50½ ft, 8-4.5in, 8-20mm. Cammell Laird 17.9.1940. Sunk 23.10.43 by German MTBs in the Channel.

CHARYBDIS Frigate, 'Leander' class Harland & Wolff 28.2.1968.

CHASER Sloop 18, 320bm, 99 x 28 ft. Purchased 1.1.1781 in the E. Indies. Captured 25.2.1782 by the French in the Bay of Bengal; recaptured 3.1783. Sold 26.8.1784.

CHASER (ex-USS BRETON, ex-*Mormacgulf* converted on stocks) Escort carrier 11,420 tons, 468½ x 69½ ft, 2-4in, 8-40mm, 18-A/C. Ingalls 19.6.1942 on lend-lease. Returned 12.5.46 to the USN; sold as *Aagtekerk*.

CHASER (see LST 3029)

CHASER Patrol boat 34 tons. Fairey Marine 1983.

CHASSEUR Iron S. floating factory 543bm. Purchased 28.5.1855. Sold 25.5.1901 Ward, Preston.

CHATHAM Galliot, 91bm. Dutch, captured 1666. Given away 1667.

CHATHAM Sloop 4, 50bm. Chatham DY 1673. Wrecked 1677.

CHATHAM DOUBLE Sloop 4,50bm (built with double hull). Chatham DY 1673. Sold 1683.

CHATHAM 4th Rate, 696bm, 126 x 34½ ft. Chatham DY 20.4.1691. Rebuilt Deptford 1721 as 756bm; breakwater at Sheerness 5.1749. Raised and BU 1762.

CHATHAM HULK Sheer hulk, 714bm, 153 x 32 ft. Chatham DY 9.10.1694. BU 10.1813 at Chatham.

CHATHAM PRIZE 6th Rate 8, 65bm, 53 x 17 ft. French, captured 3.1703 by CHATHAM. Sold 8.1.1707.

CHATHAM Yacht 14, 60bm, 58 x 16 ft. Chatham DY 18.7.1716. Sold 28.3.1742.

CHATHAM Yacht 6, 74bm, 59 x 18 ft, 6-2pdr. Chatham DY 1.10.1741. Rebuilt Chatham 1793 as 93bm; rebuilt Chatham 1842 as 104bm. BU completed 9.3.1867 at Chatham.

CHATHAM 4th Rate 50, 1,052bm, 147 x 40½ft. Portsmouth DY 25.4.1758. Harbour service 3.1793; powder hulk 12.1805; renamed TILBURY 29.6.1810. BY 5.1814 at Chatham.

CHATHAM Survey brig 4, 133bm, 80 x 22 ft, 4-3pdr. King, Dover 1788 and purchased 12.2.1788. Sold 1830 in Jamaica.

CHATHAM Schooner 4, 93bm. Purchased 1790 at Halifax. Sold 1794 in Canada.

CHATHAM Transport 317bm, 109 x 26 ft. Brindley, Findsbury 22.6.1811. Sunk 9.1825 as a breakwater.

CHATHAM 3rd Rate 74, 1,860bm, 178 x 49 ft. French ROYAL

HOLLANDAIS captured on stocks at Flushing 17.8.1809; frames taken to Woolwich DY and launched 14.2.1812. Sold 10.9.1817 J. Cristall.

CHATHAM Sheer Hulk, 1,691bm, 146 x 46½ft. Chatham DY 2.4.1813. BU completed 5.8.1876 at Chatham.

CHATHAM Iron pad, gunboat (Indian), 375bm. Laird 1935. In service in 1850.

CHATHAM 2nd class cruiser 5,400 tons, 430 x 50 ft, 8-6in. Chatham DY 9.11.1911. Lent New Zealand 1920. Sold 13.7.26 Ward, Pembroke Dock.

CHATHAM Frigate 4200 tons Swan Hunter ordered 29.1.1985

CHATHAM Hired Sloop 1793.

CHAUDIERE (see HERO of 1936)

CHAUDIERE Frigate (RCN) 2,366 tons, 4-3in. Halifax SY 13.11.1957.

CHAWTON Coastal M/S, 'Ton' classs. Fleetlands, Gosport 24.9.1957. Sold Tees Marine Services 7.77.

CHEAM Minesweeper, later 'Hunt' class. Eltringham 2.7.1919. Sold 18.3.22 Coaster Construction Co.

CHEBOGUE Frigate (RCN), 'River' class. Yarrow, Esquimalt 16.8.1943. Foundered 11.10.44 off Swansea after being torpedoed by U-boat; raised and BU 2.48 at Milford Haven.

CHEDABUCTO Minesweeper (RCN), TE 'Bangor' class. Burrard 14.4.1941. Beached 6.2.44 after collision with SS *Lord Kelvin* in the St Lawrence.

CHEDISTON Coastal M/S, 'Ton' class, Montrose SY 1953. Renamed MONTROSE then CHEDISTON 1958 then CURLEW (RAN) 8.62.

CHEERFUL Cutter 12, 111bm, 68 x 20 ft, 8-18 pdr carr., 4-6pdr. Johnson, Dover 11.1806. Sold 31.7.1816.

CHEERFUL Wood S. gunboat, 'Cheerful' class. Deptford DY 6.10.1855. BU completed 16.1.1869 at Haslar.

CHEERFUL Destroyer 370 tons, 210 x 21 ft, 1-12pdr, 5-6pdr, 2-TT. Hawthorn 14.7.1897. Sunk 30.6.1917 by

mine off the Shetlands.

CHEERFUL Minesweeper, 'Algerine' class. Harland & Wolff 21.5.1944. BU 9.63 Lacmots, Queenborough.

CHEERLY Gun-brig 12, 178bm, 80 x 22½ ft, 10-18pdr carr., 2-9pdr. Boole, Bridport 10.1804. Sold 9.2.1815.

CHEERLY Rescue tug 1944 - 46.

CHELMER Destroyer 560 tons, 222 x 23½ ft, 1-12pdr, 5-6pdr (changed 1907 to 4-12pdr), 2-TT. Thornycroft, Chiswick 8.12.1904. sold 30.6.20 Ward, Hayle.

CHELMER (see BALSAM)

CHELMER Frigate, 'River' class. G.Brown 27.3.1943. Arrived 8.57 at Charlestown to BU.

CHELMSFORD Pad. Minesweeper, 'Ascot' Class. Ailsa 14.6.1916. sold 25.11.27 Hughes Bolckow, Blyth.

CHELSEA (ex-USS CROWNINSHIELD) Destroyer 1,090 tons, 309 x 30½ ft, 1-4in, 1-3in, 4-20mm, 3-TT. Commissioned in the RN 9.9.1940. Lent RCN 11.42 to 12.43; lent Russian navy 16.7.44 to 24.6.49 as DERZKY. Sold 12.7.49, BU by McLellan, Bo'ness

CHELSHAM Inshore M/S, 'Ham' class. Jones, Buckie 9.7.1952. Transferred RAF 13.12.1965, renamed No.5000. Returned and Sold 1977.

CHELTENHAM Pad. minesweeper, 'Ascot' class. Ardrossan DY Co 12.4.1916. Sold 7.10.27 Cashmore, Newport.

CHEPSTOW Pad. minesweeper, 'Ascot' class. Aryshire Co.29.2.1916. Sold 25.11.27 Hughes Bolckow, Blyth.

CHEPSTOW CASTLE Corvette, 'Castle' class. Collingwood SY. Cancelled 12.1943.

CHEQUERS (ex-CHAMPION renamed 1943) Destroyer, 'C' class. Scotts 30.10.1944. arrived 23.7.66 Cashmore , Newport to BU.

CHERITON 20-gun ship, 232bm. Deptford 1656. Renamed SPEEDWELL 1660. Wrecked 29.6.1676 on Novaia Zemlia .

CHERITON Coastal M/S, 'Ton' class. White, Southampton. Launched 5.9.1956 as ASHTON.

CHEROKEE (ex-*Codrington*) A.Ship 6, 177bm, 76 x 8½ ft. Purchased 9.1774. Renamed DESPATCH transport 4.1777. Sold 27.2.1783.

CHEROKEE Brig-sloop 10, 'Cherokee' class, 237bm. Perry, Wells & Green, Blackwall 24.2.1808. Sold 26.3.1828 J.Cristall.

CHEROKEE Wood pad. vessel (ex-brig) (Canadian) 750bm, 170 x 31 ft.

Kingston, Ont. 22.9.1842. Sold 30.10.1851.

CHEROKEE Wood S. gunboat, 'Albacore' class, Green, Blackwall 30.4.1856. BU 3.1869 at Portsmouth.

CHERUB Sloop 18, 424bm, 108½ x 29½ ft. King. Dover 27.12.1806. Sold 13.1.1820.

CHERUB Wood S. gunboat, 'Britomart' class. Haslar, 29.3.1865. Sold Castle 5.5.1890 to BU.

CHERUB Tank vessel. 1901-41.

CHARWELL Sloop 16, 346bm. 102 x 29 ft. French AURORE captured 18.1.1801. by THAMES, Sold 28.4.1813.

CHARWELL (see MOIRA)

CHARWELL Storeship (Canadian lakes), 439bm, 108 x 30 ft. Kingston Ont. In service in 1816. Renamed No.98 in 1832.

CHARWELL Destroyer 545 tons, 225 x 23½ ft, 1-12pdr, 5-6pdr (rearmed 1907 4-12pdr), 2-TT. Palmer 25.7.1903. Sold 23.6.19 Ward, Rainham.

CHERWELL. Trawler 1920-1946.

CHESAPEAKE 5th Rate 38, 1,135 bm, 151 x 41 ft. American Captured 1.6.1813 by SHANNON in Boston Bay. Sold 18.8.1819 J.Holmes.

CHESAPEAKE 5th Rate 36, 1,622bm, 160 x 49 ft. Chatham DY. Ordered 1834, cancelled 1851.

CHESAPEAKE Wood S. frigate 51, 2,377bm, 212 x 50 ft. Chatham DY 27.9.1855. Sold 1867 Castle & Beech.

CHESTER 4th Rate 48, 663bm, 125 x 34½ ft. Woolwich DY 21.3.1691. Captured 10.10.1707 by the French. HESTER 4th Rate 50, 704bm, 130 x 35 ft. Chatham DY 18.10.1708. Harbour service 8.1743. BU 2.1750.

CHESTER 4th Rate 50, 977bm, 140 x 40½ ft. Wells & Bronsdon, Deptford 18.2.1743. Sold 28.7.1767.

CHESTER (Ordered as Greek LAMBROS KATSONIS 1914) Light cruiser 5,185 tons, 430 x 50 ft, 10-5.5in, 1-3in. Cammell Laird 8.12.1915. Sold 9.11.21 Rees, Llanelly.

CHESTER Tank vessel 1891-1925. Trawler and Tug WW.1

CHESTER CASTLE Corvette, 'Castle' class, Collingwood SY. Cancelled 12.1943.

CHESTERFIELD 5th Rate 44, 719bm, 128 x 36½ ft. Quallet, Rotherhithe 31.10.1745. Foundered 21.7.1726 near the Bahamas.

CHESTERFIELD (ex-USS WELBORN C.WOOD) Destroyer 1,190 tons 311 x 31 ft, 1-4in, 1-3in, 4-20mm, 3-TT. Commissioned in the RN 1940 Sold 4.3.47, BU Clayton & Davie, Dunston.

CHESTERFIELD Store carrier. Requis. 1914-18.

CHESTNUT Ketch 8, 81bm. Portsmouth 1656. Wrecked 1665.

CHESTNUT Drifter WW.I. Trawler 1940.

CHEVIOT Destroyer, 'C' class. Stephen 2.5.1944. Arrived 22.10.62. Ward. Inverkeithing to BU.

CHEVREUIL M/S sloop 647 tons, 256 x 28 ft. 2-3.9in. French. Seized 3.7.1940 at Plymouth. Free-French crew 1940. Returned 1944 to the French navy.

CHEVRON Destroyer, 'C' class. Stephen 23.2.1944. Sold Ward 18.10.69. BU Inverkeithing.

CHICHESTER 2nd Rate 80, 1,210bm, 157½ x 42 ft. Chatham DY 6.3.1695. Rebuilt Woolwich 1706. BU completed 3.9.1749 at Plymouth.

CHICHESTER 3rd Rate 70, 1,401bm, 160 x 45 ft, Portsmouth DY 4.6.1753. BU 10.1803.

CHICHESTER 5th Rate 44, 901bm, 140 x 38½ ft. Taylor, Itchenor. 10.3.1785. Storeship 1799; lent W. India DK Co 3.1810 as training ship. BU 6.1815.

CHICHESTER Storeship 26, 777bm. French VAR captured 15.2.1809 by BELLE POULE off Valona. Wrecked 2.5.1811 off Madras.

CHICHESTER 4th Rate 52, 1,468bm, 172 x 44 ft. Woolwich DY 12.7.1843. Laid up at Chatham 1843; lent as training ship 1866. Sold 5.1889 Castle.

CHICHESTER Frigate 2,170 tons, 330 x 40 ft, 2-4.5in, 2-40mm. Fairfield 21.4.1955. Arrived Queenborough 17.3.81 to BU.

CHICHESTER Tug. Requis. 1914-19.

CHICOUTIMI Corvette (RCN), 'Flower' class. Vickers, Montreal 16.10.1940. BU 6.46.by Steel Co of Canada.

CHIDDINGFOLD Destroyer, 'Hunt' class type II. Scotts 10.3.1941. Renamed GANGA (Indian navy) 18.6.54 on loan. Sold Indian navy 4.59.

CHIDDINGFOLD Minehunter 615 tons. Vosper-Thornycroft. 6.10.1983.

CHIFFONNE Destroyer, 'C' class. Scotts 26.2.1945. Arrived 20.3.61 Young, Sunderland to BU.

CHIEFTAIN Trawler. Requis. 1915-19.

LA CHIEFTAIN 5th Rate 36, 945bm, 145 x 38 ft, 12-32pdr car., 26-12pdr, 4-9pdr. French, captured 19.8.1801 by SYBILLE at the Seychelles Sold 1.9.1814.

CHIGNECTO Minesweeper (RCN), TE, 'Bangor' class. N. Vancouver SR Co 12.12.1940. Sold Circa 1949.

CHIGNECTO Coastal M/S (RCN) 390 Tons, 140 x 28 ft, 1-40mm. Marine Ind 14.6.1952. Transferred French Navy 7.4.54 as La BAYONNAISE.

CHIGNECTO Coastal M/S (RCN), same dimensions etc. G.T. Davie 17.11.1956.

CHILCOMPTON Coastal M/S, 'Ton' class. Herd & Mackenzie. 23.10.1953. Sold Pounds 26.11.71.

CHILDERS Brig-Sloop 14, 202bm, 80 x 25 ft. Menetone, river Thames 7.9.1778. BU 1811. at Chatham.

CHILDERS Brig-sloop 18, 'Cruizer' class, 384bm. Portsmouth DY 8.7.1812. BU 3.1822.

CHILDERS Brig-sloop 16, 'Cruizer' class, 385bm. Chatham DY 23.8.1827. Sold 19.8.1865 Holloway Bros.

CHILDERS Torpedo boat (Australian) 65 tons, 113 x 12½ ft, 2-Hotchkiss. Thornycroft, Chiswick 16.8.1883. Sold 5.8.1918 and hulked.

CHILDERS Destroyer, 'C' class. Denny 27.2.1945. Arrived 22.9.63 at Spezia to BU.

CHILDERS Whaler 1915-19.

CHILDS PLAY 6th Rate 24, 373bm, 103 x 29½ ft. French, captured 1706. Foundered 30.8.1707 off St Kitts, W. Indies.

CHILLINGHAM Inshore M/S, 'Ham' class. McLean, Renfrew 19.12.1952. Sold 3.8.69 Societe Maseline, Channel Is.

CHILLIWACK (Corvette (RCN), 'Flower' class. Burrard 14.9.1940. Sold 1946.

CHILTON Coastal M/S, 'Ton' class. Cook Welton & Gemmell 15.7.1957. To S. African navy 1958, renamed EAST LONDON.

CHIPPEWAY Schooner 2 (Canadian lakes) Maumee 1812. Captured 10.9.1813 by Americans on Lake Erie; burnt 12.1813.

CHITTAGONG (see KATHIAWAR)

CHITTAGONG Trawler (RIN) in WW.II.

CHIVALROUS Destroyer, 'C' class. Denny 22.6.1945. To Pakistan navy 29.6.54 as TAIMUR.

CHOLMONDELY Cutter, 79bm. Pur-chased 2.1763. Sold 20.8.1771.

CHRIST Ship 300bm purchased 1512. Captured by Turks in 1515.

CHRISTCHURCH CASTLE Corvette, 'Castle' class. Midland SY. Cancelled 12.1943.

CHRISTIAN VII 3rd Rate 80, 2,131bm. Danish, captured 7.9.1807 at Copenhagen. Harbour service 1814. BU 3.1838 at Chatham. (Was to have been renamed BLENHEIM in 1812).

CHRISTOPHER Cog, a King's ship in 1338.

CHRISTOPHER Hulk listed 1410 to 1412.

CHRISTOPHER SPAYNE Galley 600bm. Spanish captured 29.6.1417, given away 8.1418.

CHRISTOPHER Carrack 600bm. Genoese PINELLI captured 24.8.1417, sold 5.1423.

CHRISTOPHER 53-gun ship, 400bm. Purchased 1545. Sold 1556.

CHRISTOPHER Pinnace 15bm. Dating from 1577. Burnt 1578.

CHRISTOPHER Destroyer 938 tons, 267½ x 27ft, 3-4in, 2-TT. Hawthorn Leslie 29.8.1912. Sold 9.5.21 Ward; resold 10.23 King, Garston.

CHRISTOPHER Trawler requis. 1915-17.

CHRYSANTHEMUM Sloop, 'Anchusa' class. Armstrong 10.11.1917. RNVR drill ship 1939.

CHRYSANTHEMUM Corvette, 'Flower' class. Harland & Wolff 11.4.1941. Lent Free-French 1942 to 5.47 as COMMANDANT DROGOU. Sold 7.8.47 renamed *Terje 10*.

CHRYSANTHEMUM Drifter requis. 1915-19.

CHUBB Schooner 4, 80bm, 56 x 18 ft, 4-12pdr carr. Bermuda 5.1807. Cap-sized 14.8.1812 on the Halifax Station.

CHUBB Schooner (Canadian lakes), 110bm, 10-18pdr carr., 1-6pdr. American EAGLE captured 9.1813 on Lake Champlain. Sold 1822.

CHUB Wood S. gunboat, 'Cheerful' class. Sheerness DY 15.10.1855. BU completed 29.1.1869 at Haslar.

CHUB. Tank vessel 1897-1932. Tug re-quis. 1914-19.

CHURCH 20-gun ship, 194bm. Cap-tured 1653. Sold 1660.

CHURCHILL (ex-USS HERNDON) De-stroyer 1,190 tons, 311 x 31 ft, 1-4in, 1-3in, 4-20mm, 3-TT. Commissioned in the RN 9.9.1940. Lent Russian navy 16.7.44 as DEIATELNYI. Sunk 16.1.45 by 'U.956' in the Arctic.

CHURCHILL Nuclear submarine 3,500 tons. Vickers Armstrong, Barrow 20.12.1968.

CICALA River gunboat 645 tons, 230 x 36 ft, 2-12pdr. Barclay Curle 10.12.1915. Sunk 21.12.41 by Japanese aircraft at Hong Kong.

CICALA Tender 213 tons. Holmes 22.6.1970.

CICERO M/S sloop, '24' class. Swan Hunter 26.7.1918. Sold 1.12.21 Stanlee, Dover.

CICERO (ex-EMPIRE ARQUEBUS renamed 1.1945) Infantry landing ship 11,650 tons, 396 x 60 ft, 1-4in, 1-12pdr, 12-20mm. Consolidated Steel Corp, Wilmington 16.11.43 on lend-lease. To MWT 9.45 as *Empire Arquebus*; returned 1946 to the USN. Sold 11.46 as *Al Sudan*.

CICERO Trawler requis. 1914-19.

CIRCASSIAN (ex-*Swan*) Wood pad. tender 74bm. Purchased 8.1854 at Constantinople. Sold 28.7.1856.

CIRCASSIAN (see ENTERPRISE of 1864)

CIRCASSIAN (see ENTERPRISE of 1863)

CIRCE 6th Rate 28, 598bm, 121 x 34 ft. Ladd, Dover 30.9.1785. Wrecked 16.11.1803 near Yarmouth.

CIRCE 5th Rate 32, 670bn, 127 x 34 ft. Plymouth DY 17.11.1804. Sold 20.8.1814.

CIRCE 5th Rate 46, 1,079bm, 152 x 40½ ft. Plymouth DY 22.9.1827. Harbour service 1866; renamed IMPREGNABLE IV 1916. Sold 7.22 S. Castle, Plymouth.

CIRCE Torpedo gunboat 810 tons, 230 x 27 ft, 2-4.7in, 4-3pdr, 3-TT. Sheerness DY 14.6.1892. Sold 30.7.1920 H. Auten & Co.

CIRCE Minesweeper, 'Algerine' class. Harland & Wolff 27.6.1942. RNVR drill ship 1956. BU 1967 at Dalmuir.

CIRCE Hired minesweeper 1939. Renamed MEDEA (RAN) 1942-46.

CITADEL (ex-LCT 4038 renamed 1956) Tank landing craft 657 tons, 225 x 39 ft. Sold Pounds 4.6.70 to BU.

CLACTON Minesweeper, turbine 'Bangor' class. Blyth SB 18.12.1941. Sunk 31.12.43 by mine off Corsica.

CLACTON Minesweeper requis 1914-16.

CLARA 5th Rate 38, 958bm. 144½ x 39 ft, 12-32pdr carr., 26-12pdr, 2-9pdr. Spanish, captured 5.10.1804 in the Atlantic. Harbour service 1811. Sold 11.1815.

CLARBESTON Coastal M/S, 'Ton'

class. Richards IW 18.2.1954. Sold H. K. Vickers 22.6.70.

CLARE (ex-USS ABEL P. UPSHUR) Destroyer 1,190 tons, 311 x 31 ft, 1-4in, 1-3in, 4-20mm, 3-TT. Commissioned in the RN 9.9.1940. Sold 25.8.45; arrived 18.2.47 at Troon to BU.

CLARE CASTLE Corvette, 'Castle' class. Collingwood SY. Cancelled 12.1943.

CLARENCE 3rd Rate 74, 1,749bm, 176 x 48 ft. Blackburn, Turnchapel 11.4.1812. Renamed CENTURION 1826. BU 10.1828.

CLARENCE (ex-GOLIATH renamed 1826) 2nd Rate 84, 2,288bm, 196½ x 52 ft. Pembroke Dock 25.7.1827. Training ship 1872. Burnt 17.1.1884 by accident in the Mersey.

CLARENCE (see ROYAL WILLIAM of 1833)

CLARKIA Corvette, 'Flower' class. Harland & Wolff 7.3.1940. Sold 30.7.47, BU by Ward, Hayle.

CLAUDIA Cutter 10, 110bm, 68 x 20 ft. Wrecked 20.1.1809 on the coast of Norway.

CLAVERHOUSE (see MACKAY of 1918)

CLAVERHOUSE (see M.23)

CLAVERING CASTLE Corvette, 'Castle' class. Collingwood SY. Cancelled 12.1943.

CLAYMORE Landing ship-dock, 4,270 tons, 454 x 72 ft, 1-3in, 16-20mm. Newport News 19.7.1943. Renamed HIGHWAY 8.43; returned to USN 4.46.

CLAYMORE Destroyer, 1,980 tons, 341½ x 38 ft, 6-4in, 6-40mm, 10-TT. Scotts, ordered 3.1945, cancelled 10.45.

CLAYMORE Yacht 1917-19. Boom Vessel (RNZN) 1943-53.

CLAYOQUOT (ex-ESPERANZA renamed 1940) Minesweeper (RCN), TE 'Bangor' class P. Rupert DD 3.10.40. Sunk 24.12.44 by 'U.806' off Halifax.

CLEMATIS Sloop, 'Acacia' class. Greenock & Grangemouth 29.7.1915. Sold 5.2.31 Young, Sunderland.

CLEMATIS Corvette, 'Flower' class. Hill 22.4.1940. Arrived 9.49 at Gateshead to BU.

CLEOPATRA 5th Rate 32, 689bm, 126½ x 35 ft. Hilhouse, Bristol 26.11.1779. BU completed 21.9.1814 at Deptford. (In French hands 17.2.05 to 23.2.05.)

CLEOPATRA 6th Rate 26, 918bm, 130 x 40½ ft, 24-32pdr, 2-12pdr. Pembroke Dock 28.4.1835. BU 2.1862 by

Castle & Beech.

CLEOPATRA Pad. sloop (Indian). Pitcher, Northfleet 1839. Foundered 14.4.1847 in the Indian Ocean.

CLEOPATRA S. corvette 2,380 tons, 225 x 44½ ft, 2-7in, 12-64pdr. Elder 1.8.1878. Harbour service 1905; renamed DEFIANCE III 1.22. Sold 7.31 S Castle, Millbay.

CLEOPATRA Light cruiser 3,750 tons, 420 x 41½ ft, 2-6in, 8-4in. Devonport DY 14.1.1915. Sold 26.6.31 Hughes Bolckow, Blyth.

CLEOPATRA Cruiser 5,450 tons, 485 x 50½ ft, 10-5.25 in. Hawthorn Leslie 27.3.1940. Arrived 12.12.58 Cashmore, Newport to BU.

CLEOPATRA Frigate, 'Leander' class. Devonport DY 25.3.1964.

CLEOPATRA Trawler requis. 1914-19.

CLEVELAND R. yacht 8, 107bm. Portsmouth DY 1671. Sold 1716.

CLEVELAND Destroyer, 'Hunt' class type I. Yarrow 24.4.1940. Stranded 28.6.57 near Swansea on passage to Rees Llanelly to BU; wreck stripped and blown up 14.12.59.

CLEVELAND Two vessels hired 1803 and 1809.

CLIFTON Minesweeper, later 'Hunt' class. Bow McLachlan. Cancelled 1918.

CLIFTON Transport hired 1854; Trawler WW.I; Trawler WW.II; Tug (RCN) 1944.

CLINKER (Gunboat No. 14) Gunvessel 12, 159bm, 75 x 22 ft, 2-24pdr, 10-18pdr carr. Dudman, Deptford 28.4.1797. Sold 10.1802.

CLINKER Gun-brig 14, 180bm, 85 x 22 ft. Pitcher, Northfleet 30.6.1804. Foundered 12.1806 off Havre.

CLINKER Gun-brig 12, 183bm, 84 x 22½ ft. 10-18pdr carr., 2-6pdr. Davy, Topsham 15.7.1813. Coastguard 11.1831; renamed WV.12 in 5.1863. Sold 24.1.1867.

CLINKER Wood S. gunboat, 'Dapper' class. Pitcher, Northfleet 2.4.1855. Sold 6.6.1871 Castle.

CLINKER (see WAVE of 1856)

CLINKER Tank vessel. 1901-48.

CLINTON 5th Rate 32,736bm, 134 x 35 ft. French ESPERANCE captured 30.9.1780 by PEARL. Sold 5.7.1784.

CLINTON Minesweeper, 'Algerine' class. Redfern, Toronto 5.10.1942, on lend-lease. Returned 1.47 to the USN.

CLIO Brig-sloop 18, 'Cruiser' class, 389bm. Betts, Mistleythorn 10.1.1807. BU 3.1845 at Portsmouth.

CLIO Wood S. corvette 1,472bm, 2,306 tons, 200 x 40 ft. Sheerness DY 28.8.1858. Training ship 1876. Sold 3.10.1919, BU at Bangor.

CLIO Sloop 1,070 tons, 185 x 33 ft, 6-4in, 4-3pdr. Sheerness DY 14.3.1903. Sold 12.11.20 at Bombay.

CLITHEROE CASTLE Corvette, 'Castle' class. Collingwood SY. Cancelled 12.1943.

CLIVE Sloop 18 (Indian) 387bm. Bombay DY 1826. Sold 7.1862.

CLIVE Troopship (RIM) 3,570 tons, 300 x 45½ ft. Laird 15.11.1882.

CLIVE Sloop (RIN) 2,100 tons, 240 x 38½ ft, 4-3pdr. Beardmore 10.12.1919. Sold circa 1946.

CLONMEL (ex-STRANRAER renamed 1918) Minesweeper, later 'Hunt' class. Simons 14.5.1918. Sold 7.22 S.D. Harrison.

CLORINDE 5th Rate 38, 1,161bm, 161 x 41 ft, 18-32pdr carr., 28-18 pdr, 2-12pdr. French, captured 30.11.1803 at San Domingo. Sold 6.3.1817 Mr Freake.

CLOVELLY (see CAVAN)

CLOVER Corvette, 'Flower' class. Fleming & Ferguson 30.1.1941. Sold 17.5.47, renamed *Cloverlock.*

CLOVER Tug 1876-82; Tank vessel 1895-1910.

CLOVE TREE 4th Rate 62, 700bm, Dutch NAGELBOOM captured 1665. Recaptured 6.1666 by the Dutch.

CLOWN Wood S. gunboat, 'Clown' class. Miller, Liverpool 20.5.1856 Coal lighter 1867, later renamed YC.1 then YC.6 and lost in 1871.

CLUN CASTLE Corvette, 'Castle' class. Midland SY. Cancelled 12.1943.

CLYDE 5th Rate 38 (fir-built), 1,002bm, 146 x 39 ft. Chatham DY 26.3.1796. Rebuilt Woolwich, re-launched 28.2.1806. Sold 8.1814.

CLYDE (ex-cutter *Atalanta*) Tender 4. Purchased 1805. Sold 1826 at Milford.

CLYDE 5th Rate 46, 1,081bm, 1,447 tons, 152 x 40 ft. Woolwich DY 9.10.1828. RNR drill ship 8.1870. Sold 5.7.1904.

CLYDE Wood S. gunboat (Indian) 300bm, 125 x 23 ft, 3 guns. Bombay DY 3.5.1859. Survey vessel 1872. Sold circa 1875.

CLYDE Paddle vessel (Newfoundland Govt) 440, 154½ x 25 ft, 1 gun. Inglis 1900. Wrecked 19.12.51 off Williamsport NF.

CLYDE (ex-WILD SWAN renamed 1.5.1904) Base ship 1,130 tons. 170 x

36 ft. Renamed COLUMBINE 7.13 (was to have been ROMULUS). Sold 4.5.20 Forth S. Bkg Co.

CLYDE Submarine 1,850 tons, 325 x 28 ft, 1-4in, 8-TT. Vickers Armstrong, Barrow 15.3.1934. Sold 30.7.46 Joubert Ltd, Durban to BU.

CLYDE (see CRICHTON)

CLYDE Trawler and Drifter in WW.I.

CLYDEBANK (see ORISSA)

COATICOOK Frigate (RCN), 'River' class. Davie SB 25.11.1943. Sold 13.12.47 Wagner, Stein & Greene and wrecked on coast of British Columbia while in tow; wreck blown up 2.62.

COBALT Corvette (RCN), 'Flower' class. Pt Arthur SY 17.8.1940. Sold 1946, renamed *Johanna W. Vinke.*

COBHAM Inshore M/S, 'Ham' class. Fairlie Yt Slip 14.5.1953. Sold in 5.66.

COBOURG Corvette (RCN), modified 'Flower' class. Midland SY 14.7.1943. Sold 1947, renamed *Camca.*

COBRA Destroyer 400 tons, 223 x 20½ ft, 1-12pdr, 5-6pdr, 2-TT. Armstrong 28.6.1899 (built on speculation, purchased 8.5.1900). Wrecked 19.9.01 near Cromer.

COCHIN Schooner, 54bm, 53½ x 15½ ft. Cochin 23.4.1820. Tank vessel 1840. Sold 4.1850 at Trincomalee.

COCHIN Wood S. gunboat, 'Albacore' class. Green, Blackwall 8.4.1856. BU in 3.1863 at Sheerness.

COCHIN Tug 1919-46; Trawler (RIN) renamed Kolaba 1943.

COCHRANE Armoured cruiser 13,550 tons, 480 x 73½ ft, 6-9.2in, 4-7.5in, 24-3pdr. Fairfield 28.5.1905. Stranded 14.11.18 in the Mersey; wreck BU.

COCHRANE (see AMBROSE)

COCKADE Destroyer, 'C' class. Yarrow 7.3.1944. Arrived 7.64 Cashmore, Newport to BU.

COCKADE Trawler ANSON renamed 1941-44.

COCKATRICE Cutter 14, 181bm, 70 x 26 ft. King, Dover 3.7.1781. Sold 9.1802.

COCKATRICE Name chosen in 1812 for BREVDRAGEREN; not used.

COCKATRICE Schooner 6, 182bm, 80 x 23½ ft. Pembroke Dock 14.5.1832. Sold 9.1858 at Callao.

COCKATRICE Wood S. gunboat, 'Britomart' class. Smith, Newcastle 26.5.1860. Renamed YC.10, luggage lighter 1882. Sold 1885.

COCKATRICE (see NIGER of 1880)

COCKATRICE (see BRAMBLE of 1886)

COCKATRICE (ex-War Dept vessel *Sir W. Harness*) Tender, 110 tons, 80 x 18 ft. Transferred 11.1906. Sold 10.10 at Bermuda.

COCKATRICE Destroyer 951 tons, 267½ x 27 ft, 3-4in, 2-TT. Hawthorn Leslie 8.11.1912. Sold 9.5.21 Ward, Hayle.

COCKATRICE Minesweeper, 'Algerine' class. Fleming & Ferguson 27.10.1942. Arrived 29.8.63 Ward, Inverkeithing to BU.

COCKBURN (ex-steam vessel *Braganza*) Schooner. Purchased 5.1822 at Rio. Foundered 1.4.1823 near Simonstown.

COCKBURN (Canadian lakes) Schooner 1, 70bm. Dating from 1827. Sold 1837.

COCKBURN (see DRURY)

COCKCHAFER Schooner tender 5, 104bm, 69½ x 19 ft, 1-12pdr. 4-12pdr carr. American SPENCER captured 1812. Sold 1815.

COCKCHAFER Wood S. gunboat, 'Albacore' class. Pitcher, Northfleet 24.11.1855. Sold 1872 at Shanghai.

COCKCHAFER Compos. S. Gunboat 465 tons. 125 x 23½ ft, 2-64pdr ML, 2-20pdr. Pembroke Dock 19.2.1881. Sold 6.12.1905.

COCKCHAFER River gunboat 645 tons, 230 x 36 ft, 2-6ins, 2-12pdr. Barclay Curle 17.12.1915. Hulk 1947; sold 1949 at Singapore.

COCKCHAFER Tender 213 tons. Holmes 22.1.1973

CODRINGTON Destroyer leader 1,540 tons, 332 x 34ft, 5-4.7in, 8-TT. Swan Hunter 7.8.1929. Sunk 27.7.40 by air attack at Dover.

COLAC Minesweeper (RAN), 'Bathurst' class. Morts Dk, Sydney 13.8.1941. Oil tank cleaning vessel 1962.

COLCHESTER 24-gun ship, 287bm. Edgar, Yarmouth 1654. Sunk 1666 in action.

COLCHESTER Ketch 8, 72bm. Colchester 1664. Captured 1667 by the French in the W.Indies.

COLCHESTER 4th Rate 48, 696bm, 131½ x 34 ft. Johnson, Blackwall 1694. Foundered 16.1.1704 in Whitesand Bay.

COLCHESTER 4th Rate 54, 682bm, 130½ x 34½ ft. Deptford DY 1707. Rebuilt Chatham 1721 as 756bm. BU 1742.

COLCHESTER 4th Rate 50, 976bm, 140 x 40 ft. Barnard, Harwich 1744. Wrecked 21.9.1744 off the Kentish Knock.

COLCHESTER 4th Rate 50, 978bm, 140½ x 40 ft. Carter, Southampton 20.9.1746. BU 2.1773 at Portsmouth.

COLCHESTER Wreck dispersal vessel. Requis. 1941-46.

COLCHESTER CASTLE Corvette, 'Castle' class. Midland SY. Cancelled 12.1943.

COLIBRI Sloop 16, 365bm, 99 x 29½ ft. French, captured 16.1.1809 by MELAMPUS in the W. Indies. Wrecked 22.8.1813 at Port Royal, Jamaica.

COLIBRI Brig-sloop (fir-built). Laid down 1.1814 at Chatham DY; frames taken down and sent to Halifax NS and re-laid there. Sold on stocks 5.1815 at Halifax.

COLLEEN (see AMELIA of 1888)

COLLEEN (see ROYALIST of 1883)

COLLINGWOOD 3rd Rate 80, 2,589bm, 190 x 57 ft, 4-68pdr, 72-32 pdr, 4-18pdr, Pembroke Dock 17.8.1841. Undocked 13.7.1861 at Sheerness as screw ship. Sold 3.1867 Castle.

COLLINGWOOD Battleship 9,150 tons, 325 x 68 ft, 4-12in, 6-6in. Pembroke Dock 22.11.1882. Sold 11.5.1909 Hughes, Bolckow, Dunston.

COLLINGWOOD Battleship 19,250 tons, 500 x 84 ft, 10-12in, 20-4in. Devonport DY 7.11.1908. Sold 12.12.22 Cashmore, arrived 3.3.23 at Newport to BU.

COLLINGWOOD Corvette (RCN), 'Flower' class. Collingwood SY 27.7.1940. BU 7.50 by Steel Co of Canada, Hamilton, Ont.

COLLINGWOOD Trawler requis. 1917-19 and 1940.

COLLINSON (ex-AMERSHAM renamed 1919) Survey ship 800 tons. Ailsa 30.4.1919. Sold 25.10.22 McLellan, Bo'ness.

COLNE Destroyer 560 tons, 222 x 23½ ft, 1-12pdr, 5-6pdr (4-12pdr from 1907), 2-TT. Thornycroft, Chiswick 21.2.1905. Sold 4.11.19 J.H. Lee, Dover.

COLNE Trawler 1920-46.

COLOMBE Sloop 16, 403bm, 108 x 29ft, 14-32pdr carr., 2-6pdr. French, captured 18.6.1803 by DRAGON off Ushant. BU 1811.

COLOMBO Light cruiser 4,190 tons, 425 x 43½ ft, 5-6in. Fairfield 18.12.1918. A/A ship 1943, 6-4in. Sold 22.1.48; arrived 1.5.48 Cashmore, Newport to BU.

COLOSSUS 3rd Rate 74, 1,703bm, 172 x 48 ft. Cleveley, Gravesend 4.4.1787. Wrecked 10.12.1798 on the Scilly Isles.

COLOSSUS 3rd Rate 74, 1,889bm, 180 x 49 ft. Deptford DY 23.4.1803. BU 8.2.1826.

COLOSSUS 3rd Rate 80, 2,590bm, 190 X 57 ft, 14-8in, 66-32pdr. Pembroke Dock 1.6.1848. Undocked 11.6.1864 as screw ship. Sold 3.1867 Castle & Beech.

COLOSSUS Battleship 9,150 tons, 325 x 68 ft, 4-12in, 5-6in. Portsmouth DY 21.3.1882. Sold 6.10.1908 Ward, Briton Ferry.

COLOSSUS Battleship 20,000 tons, 510 x 86 ft, 10-12in 20-4in. Scotts 9.4.1910. Sold 7.28 Alloa S. Bkg Co, Rosyth.; arrived 5.9.28

COLOSSUS A/C Carrier 13,190 tons, 630 x 80 ft, 19-40mm, 48 -A/C. Vickers Armstrong, Tyne 30.9.1943. Sold French navy 6.8.46 as AR-ROMANCHES.

COLTSFOOT Corvette, 'Flower' class. Alex Hall 12.5.1941. Sold 1947, renamed *Alexandra*.

COLUMBIA Sloop 18, 294bm, 94½ x 26 ft, 16-18pdr carr., 2-6pdr. American privateer CURLEW captured 1813 by ACASTA off Cape Sable. Sold 13.1.1820.

COLUMBIA Wood pad. packet (ex-brig-sloop 'Cherokee' class), 356bm, 130 x 25 ft. Woolwich DY 1.7.1829. Survey vessel 1842; coal hulk 1857. Sold 29.10.1859 at Halifax NS.

COLUMBIA (ex-USS HARADEN) Destroyer 1,060 tons, 209 x 30½ ft, 3-4in, 1-3in, 6-TT. Commissioned in the RCN 24.9.1940. Storeship 9.44. Sold 7.8.45 in Canada.

COLUMBIA Frigate (RCN) 2,366 tons, 4-3in. Burrard DD 1.11.1957.

COLUMBIA Trawler requis. 1914-18.

COLUMBINE (see CYANE)

COLUMBINE Brig-sloop 18, 'Cruizer' class, 386bm. Adams, Bucklers Hard 16.7.1806. Wrecked 25.1.1824 on Sapienza Is.

COLUMBINE Sloop 18, 492bm, 105 x 33½ ft. Portsmouth DY 1.12.1826. 12-gun brig 1849: coal hulk 4.1854. Sold 12.1.1892 Castle.

COLUMBINE Wood S.sloop 669bm, 913 tons, 160 x 30ft. Deptford DY 2.4.1862. BU 6.1875 at Chatham.

COLUMBINE (ex-*Hiarta*) Tender 270 tons, 125½ x 25 ft. Purchased 2.1897. Sold 10.7.1907.

COLUMBINE (see CLYDE)

COLUMBINE Corvette, 'Flower' class. Hill 13.8.1940. Sold 9.8.46, renamed *Lief Welding*.

COLUMBINE Two drifters bore the name as nominal base ships from 1919.

COLWYN Minesweeper, later 'Hunt' class. Bow McLachlan. Renamed CREDITON 1918 and cancelled.

COMBATANT 6th Rate 20, 417bm, 109 x 29½ ft. Betts, Mistleythorn 3.11.1804. Sold 17.10.1816.

COMBATANT Minesweeper, 'Catherine' class. Assoc. SB, Seattle 27.11.1942. To RN 13.11.43 on lend-lease. Returned 15.12.46 to the USN. Sold Greek navy 1947.

La COMBATTANTE (see HALDON)

COMBUSTION Fireship 8. Purchased 1782. Sold 26.8.1784 Mr. White; withdrawn from sale; sold 29.11.1784 Mr Maxwell.

COMET Bomb 4, 145bm, 66 x 23 ft. Blackwall 1695. Captured 10.10.1706 by the French.

COMET Bomb 14, 275bm, 92 x 26 ft. Taylor, Rotherhithe 29.3.1742. Sold 11.5.1749.

COMET Galley 8 in service in 1756.

COMET Brig-sloop 10 (Indian) 115bm. Bombay DY 1758.

COMET Sloop 10. Purchased 1777. Sold 15.9.1778.

COMET (SEE DILIGENCE of 1756)

COMET Fireship 14, 424bm, 109 x 30 ft. Game, Wivenhoe 11.11.1783. Expended 7.7.1800 in Dunkirk Roads.

COMET Sloop 18, 427bm, 109 x 30 ft. Taylor, Bideford 25.4.1807. Sold 12.10.1815.

COMET Wood Paddle vessel 238bm, 115 x 21 ft, 3 guns. Deptford DY 23.5.1822. (Not in navy list until 1831 - was the first steam vessel built by the RN.) BU at Portsmouth 1868.

COMET Sloop 18, 462bm, 113½ x 31 ft. Pembroke Dock 11.8.1828. Renamed COMUS 31.10.1832. BU completed 10.5.1862 at Chatham.

COMET (see THUNDERER of 1931)

COMET 3rd Class gunboat, 'Ant' class. Portsmouth DY 8.12.1870. Sold 12.5.1908, BU in Holland.

COMET Paddle vessel (Indian) 144bm, 2 guns. Built 1880. In service in 1890.

COMET Destroyer 747 tons, 246 x 26 ft, 2-4in, 2-12pdr, 2-TT. Fairfield 23.6.1910. Sunk 6.8.18 by Austrian S/M in the Mediterranean.

COMET Destroyer 1,375 tons, 326 x 33 ft, 4-4.7in, 8-TT. Portsmouth DY 30.9.1931. Renamed RESTIGOUCHE (RCN) 15.6.38. On sale list 1945.

COMET Destroyer, 'C' class. Yarrow 22.6.1944. Arrived 23.10.62 at Troon to BU.

COMET Tug 1915 and Trawler 1939.

COMFREY Corvette, 'Flower' class. Collingwood SY. Transferred to the USN while building; completed 21.11.1942 as USS ACTION.

COMMANDANT d'ESTIENNE d'ORVES (see LOTUS)

COMMANDANT DETROYAT (see CO-RIANDER)

COMMANDANT DOMINE M/S sloop 630 tons, 256 x 28 ft, 2-3.9in. French, seized 3.7.1940 at Falmouth. Free-French 8.40; returned to the French navy 1944.

COMMANDANT DROGOU (see CHRYSANTHEMUM).

COMMANDANT DUBOC M/S sloop 630 tons, 256 x 28 ft, 2-3.9in. French; seized 3.7.1940 at Plymouth. Free-French 7.40; returned to the French navy 1944.

COMMERCE DE MARSEILLE 1st Rate 120, 2,747bm, 212 x 55 ft. French, captured 29.8.1793 at Toulon. Sold 1802.

COMMONWEALTH Battleship 16,350 tons, 425 x 78 ft, 4-12in, 4-9.2in, 10-6in, 12-12pdr. Fairfield 13.5.1903. Sold 18.11.21; BU in Germany.

COMOX Coastal M/S (RCN), 370 tons, 140 x 28 ft, 1-40mm. Victoria Mcy Co 24.4.1952. Sold Turkish navy 1958.

COMUS 6th Rate 22, 522bm, 118 x 31½ ft. Custance, Yarmouth 28.8.1806. Wrecked 4.11.1816 Newfoundland.

COMUS (see COMET of 1828)

COMUS S. corvette 2,380 tons, 225 x 44½ ft, 4-6in, 8-64pdr. Elder 3.4.1878. Sold 17.5.1904.

COMUS Light cruiser 3,750 tons, 420 x 41½ ft, 2-6in, 8-4in. Swan Hunter 16.12.1914. Sold 28.7.34 Ward, Barrow.

COMUS Destroyer, 'C' class. Thornycroft 14.3.1945. Arrived 12.11.58 Cashmore, Newport to BU.

CONCEPTION 5th Rate, 375bm, 98 x 29½ ft. Captured 1690. Condemned 1694. Wrecked in New England.

CONCEPTION Hulk at Jamaica, purchased 1782. Sold 1783.

CONCORD 24-gun ship. Dutch, captured 1649. Hulk 1655; sold 8.1659.

CONCORD Sloop, 172bm, 77x22½ ft. French, captured 3.1697. Fate unknown.

CONCORDE 5th Rate 36, 889bm, 143 x 38 ft. French, captured 15.2 1783 by MAGNIFICENT Sold 21.1.1811.

CONCORD Light cruiser 3,750 tons, 420 x 42 ft, 5-6in, 2-3in. Armstrong. 1.4.1916. Arrived 16.9.35 Metal Industries, Rosyth to BU.

CONCORD (see CORSO of 1945)

CONCORD Trawler and Drifter WW.I.

CONCORDE (see CONCORD)

CONDAMINE Frigate (RAN), 'River' class. Newcastle DY NSW 4.11.1944. BU 12.61 in Japan.

CONDOR Compos. S. gunvessel 780 tons, 157 x 29½ ft, 1-7in, 2-64pdr. Devonport DY 28.12.1876. Sold 8.1889 G. Cohen.

CONDOR Sloop 980 tons, 180 x 33½ ft, 6-4in, 4-3dpr. Sheerness DY 17.12.1898. Foundered 3.12.1901 off Cape Flattery.

CONDOR Trawler and Drifter WW.I.

CONFEDERATE 5th Rate 32, 959bm, 159½ x 36½ ft. American

CONFEDERACY captured 14.4.1781 off the Delaware. BU 31.1782.

CONFIANCE 6th Rate 24. French, captured 1797. IN service in 1801.

CONFIANCE 6th Rate 22, 490bm, 22-18pdr carr., 2-6pdr. French, captured 4.6.1808 by LOIRE at Mudros. Sold 22.12.1810.

CONFIANCE (see MINERVE of 1795)

CONFIANCE Schooner 2 (Canadian lakes). Captured 5.10.1813 by Americans on Lake Erie.

CONFIANCE Brig-sloop, 18, 'Cruizer' class, 392bm. Ross, Rochester 30.8.1813. Wrecked 21.4.1822 at Crookhaven.

CONFIANCE 5th Rate 36, 831bm, 4-32pdr carr., 7-24pdr carr., 26-24pdr. Ile aux Noirs, Lake Champlain 25.8.1814. Captured 11.9.1814 by Americans on Lake Champlain.

CONFIANCE 5th Rate 32 (Canadian lakes) Built on Lake Erie in 1818. Fate unknown.

CONFIANCE Schooner 2 (Candian lakes) 95bm, 67½ x 18 ft. 2-24pdr. Lake Erie 1824. In service 1831.

CONFIANCE Wood pad. vessel (ex-brig sloop 'Cherokee' class) Woolwich DY 28.3.1827. Tug 1842. BU in 6.1873 Devonport.

CONFIANCE Tug 1865-1947; Tug 1955-84.

CONFLAGRATION (ex-Loyal Oak) Fireship 8. Purchased 1781. Wrecked 1781 in N. America.

CONFLAGRATION Fireship 14, 426bm, 108½ x 29½ ft. Pelham, Shoreham 28.10.1783. Destroyed 18.12.1793 to avoid capture by the French at Toulon.

CONFLAGRATION Drifter 1919-20.

CONFLICT Gun-brig 12, 180bm, 80 x 23 ft. Dudman, Deptford 17.4.1801. Wrecked 24.10.1804 on the French coast.

CONFLICT Gun-brig 12, 182bm, 84 x 22 ft, 10-18pdr carr., 2-12pdr. Davy, Topsham 14.5.1805. Foundered 9.11.1810 in the Bay of Biscay.

CONFLICT Gun-brig 12, 181bm, 84 x 22 ft, 10-18pdr carr. 2-6pdr. Good, Bridport 26.9.1812. Hulk 1832. Sold 30.12.1840 at Sierra Leone.

CONFLICT Wood S. sloop 1,038bm, 185 x 34½ ft, Pembroke Dock 5.8.1846. Rebuilt Blackwall 1848. Sold 1863.

CONFLICT Schooner 1, 120bm, 80 x 19 ft, 1-12pdr Cuthbert, Sydney NSW 11.2.1873. Sold 1882 at Sydney.

CONFLICT Destroyer 350 tons, 205½ x 20 ft, 1-12pdr, 5-6pdr, 2-TT. White 13.12.1894. Sold 20.5.1920 Ward, Milford.

CONFOUNDER Gun-brig 12, 183bm, 84 x 22 ft, 10-18pdr carr., 212pdr. Adams, Southampton 4.1805. Sold 6.6.1814.

CONFOUNDER Wood S. gunboat, 'Albacore' class. Green, Blackwall 21.5.1856. BU 10.1864.

CONGO Pad. survey schooner 83bm, 70 x 16 ft, 1-12pdr. Deptford DY 11.1.1816. Built for survey of the Congo; never used under steam, engine removed 1816. Sold 15.3.1826 at Rye.

CONGO Trawler requis. 1915-19.

CONISTON Coastal M/S, 'Ton' class. Thornycroft 9.7.1952. Sold 28.1.70, BU, Newhaven.

CONISTON Trawler requis. 1939-40.

CONN Frigate, TE 'Captain' class. Bethlehem, Hingham 21.8.1943 on lend-lease, Returned 26.11.45 to the USN.

CONQUERANT 3rd Rate 74, 1,681bm, 181½ x 46 ft. French, captured 2.8.1798 at the Nile. Harbour service 1799. BU 3.1802.

CONQUERANTE Patrol vessel 374 tons, 218 x 26 ft, 2-3.9in. French, seized 3.7.1940 at Falmouth. Foundered 14.4.41 near Falmouth.

CONQUERANT M/S tug 1940 French tug in RN. 1940-45

CONQUEROR Fireship 8, 308bm, 94 x 28 ft. French, captured 1745 by LOWESTOFFE in the Mediterranean. Sold 2.3.1748.

CONQUEROR 3rd Rate 70, 1,432bm, 160 x 45 ft. Barnard, Harwich 24.5.1758. Wrecked 26.10.1760 off

Plymouth.

CONQUEROR 3rd Rate 74, 1,606bm, 169 x 47 ft. Plymouth DY 10.10.1773. BU 11.1794.

CONQUEROR 3rd Rate 74, 1,854bm, 176 x 49 ft. Graham, Harwich 23.11.1801. BU 7.1822 at Chatham.

CONQUEROR Screw 1st Rate 101, 3,225bm, 240 x 55 ft. Devonport DY 2.5.1855. Wrecked 29.12.1861 on Rum Cay, W. Indies.

CONQUEROR (see WATERLOO of 1833)

CONQUEROR Battleship 6,200 tons, 270 x 58 ft. 2-12in, 4-6in. Chatham DY 8.9.1881. Sold 9.4.1907 Castle.

CONQUEROR Battleship 22,500 tons, 545 x 8½ ft, 10-13.5in, 14-4in. Beardmore. 1.5.1911. Sold 19.12.22 Upnor S. Bkg Co.

CONQUEROR Battleship 40,000 tons, 740 x 105 ft, 9-16in, 16-5.25in. J. Brown. Laid down 16.8.1939, suspended 10.39, cancelled 1940.

CONQUEROR Nuclear S/M 3500 tons. Cammell Laird 28.8.1969

CONQUEROR Tug in WW.I; Yacht in WW.II.

CONQUEST Gunvessel 12, 147bm, 75 x 21 ft, 10-18pdr carr., 2-12pdr. Brindley, Frindsbury 7.1794. Sold 30.4.1817.

CONQUEST S. corvette 2,380 tons, 225 x 44½ ft, 2-7in, 12-64pdr. Elder 28.10.1878. Sold 16.3.1899 King, Garston.

CONQUEST Light cruiser 3,750 tons, 420 x 41½ ft, 2-6in, 8-4in. Chatham DY 20.1.1915. Sold 29.8.30 Metal Industries, Rosyth.

CONQUESTADOR 4th Rate 60, 1,278bm, 156 x 43½ ft. Spanish, captured 12.8.1762 at Havana. Harbour service 10.1775. BU 1782. at Chatham.

CONQUESTADOR 3rd Rate 74, 1,1773bm, 176½ x 48½ ft. Guillaume, Northam 1.8.1810. 4th Rate 1831; powder hulk 1860. Sold 10.5.1897 H. Scawn, Plymouth.

CONRAD (see DANAE of 1918)

CONSORT Destroyer, 'C' class Stephen 19.10.1944. Arrived 15.3.61 at Swansea to BU by Prince of Wales DD Co.

CONSORT Trawler requis. 1915-19.

CONSTANCE 6th Rate 22, 535bm, 121½ x 31 ft. French, captured 9.3.1797 by ST FIORENZO and NYMPHE off Brest. Retaken by the French 12.10.1806 off the coast of France.

CONSTANCE 5th Rate 36, 1,622bm, 160 x 49 ft. Portsmouth DY. Laid down circa 1833, cancelled 1844.

CONSTANCE Schooner 3 (Indian), 182bm. Bombay DY 1838. Sold 1877 Rangoon Port authorities.

CONSTANCE 4th Rate 50, 2,132bm, 180 x 53 ft, 10-8in, 40-32pdr. Pembroke Dock 12.3.1846. Undocked 15.4.1862 as screw frigate 2,176 bm. Sold 1875 Castle.

CONSTANCE S. corvette 2,590 tons, 225 x 44½ ft, 2-7in, 12-64pdr. Chatham DY 9.6.1880. Sold 15.12.1899 King, Garston.

CONSTANCE Light cruiser 3,750 tons, 420 x 41½ ft, 4-6in, 2-3in Cammell Laird 12.9.1915. Sold 8.6.36 Arnott Young, Dalmuir.

CONSTANCE Destroyer, 'C' class. Vickers Armstrong, Tyne 22.8.1944. Arrived 8.3.56 Ward, Inverkeithing to BU.

CONSTANCE Two cutters hired 1799; Trawler W.W.I. Yacht W.W.I.

CONSTANT Gun-brig 12, 180bm, 80 x 22½ ft, 10-18pdr carr., 2-6pdr. Dudman, Deptford 20.4.1801. Sold 15.2.1816.

CONSTANT JOHN Fireship 6, 180bm. Purchased 1666. Sunk 6.1667 as blockship in the Medway.

CONSTANT REFORMATION 42-gun ship, 752bm. Deptford 1619 Captured 1648 by Royalists and lost 30.9.1651 at sea.

CONSTANT WARWICK 42-gun ship, 379bm. Ex-privateer purchased 20.1.1649. Rebuilt 1666. Captured 12.7.1691 by the French.

CONSTITUTION Schooner. Purchased 24.8.1835. Not listed in 1837.

CONSTITUTION cutters hired 1790 and 1804.

CONTENT 3rd Rate 70, 1,130bm, French, captured 7.1695 by CARLISLE Hulk 7.1703 and later sold Lisbon.

CONTENT Storeship, 100bm. Ex-hoy purchased 5.1708. Sold 15.12.1715.

CONTENT Gunvessel 12, 159bm. Lynn 1797. Wrecked 28.8.1799 on the Dutch coast. (There is some doubt about this vessel; may be a hired brig.)

CONTEST (Gunboat No. 16) Gunvessel 14, 159bm, 75 x 22 ft, 4-24pdr, 10-18pdr carr. Barnard, Deptford 11.4.1797. BU 10.1799.

CONTEST Gun-brig 5, 2-32pdr carr., 3-24pdr. Dutch HELL-HOUND captured 1799. BU 8.1803 at Sheerness.

CONTEST Schooner 14, 14-24pdr carr.

Purchased 1799. BU 1799.

CONTEST Gun-brig 12, 178bm, 80 x 23 ft, 10-18pdr carr., 2-12pdr. Courtney, Chester 6.1804. Foundered 12.1809 in the Atlantic.

CONTEST Gun-brig 12, 180bm, 84 x 22 ft, 10-18pdr carr., 2-6pdr. Good, Bridport 24.10.1812. Wrecked 14.4.1828 in N. America.

CONTEST Brig 12, 459bm, 109 x 32 ft. White, Cowes 11.4.1846. BU completed 9.9.1868 at Portsmouth.

CONTEST Compos. S. Gunboat 455 tons, 125 x 23½ ft, 2-64pdr MLR, 2-20pdr. Doxford 29.8.1874. BU 1889 Devonport.

CONTEST Destroyer 330 tons, 210 x 19½ ft, 1-12pdr, 5-6pdr, 2-TT. Laird 1.12.1894. Sold 11.7.1911 Ward, Preston.

CONTEST Destroyer 957 tons, 3-4in, 2-TT. Hawthorn Leslie 7.1.1913. Sunk 18.9.17 by U-boat SW of Ushant.

CONTEST Destroyer, 'C' class. White 16.12.1944. Arrived 2.2.60 Ward, Grays to BU.

CONVERT 30-gun ship, 324bm. French, captured 1652. Sold 1661.

CONVERT (see INCONSTANT OF 1778)

CONVERT 5th Rate 36, 930bm. French INCONSTANTE captured 29.10.1793 by PENELOPE and IPHIGENIA off San Domingo. Wrecked 8.3.1794 on Grand Cayman, W. Indies.

CONVERT 20-gun hired 1652.

CONVERTINE (see DESTINY of 1616)

CONVERTINE 40-gun ship, 500bm. Royalist, captured 1651. Captured 6.1666 by the Dutch. (May be same ship as above.)

CONVOLVULUS Sloop, 'Anchusa' class. Barclay Curle 19.5.1917. Sold 1922 Stanlee, Dover.

CONVOLVULUS Corvette, 'Flower' class. Hill, 21.9.1940. Sold 21.8.47; BU Cashmore, Newport.

CONVULSION Mortar vessel 5, 77bm, 60 x 17ft. Brent, Rotherhithe 31.8.1804. Sold 27.8.1806.

CONWAY 6th Rate 20, 451bm, 108 x 30½ ft. Pelham, Frindsbury 10.3.1814. Sold 13.10.1825 E. Cohen.

CONWAY 6th Rate 26, 652bm, 125½ x 34½ ft, 26-32pdr, 2-9pdr. Chatham DY 2.2.1832. Training ship 2.1859; renamed WINCHESTER 28.8.1861. BU 6.1871 at Sheerness.

CONWAY (see WINCHESTER of 1822)

CONWAY (see NILE of 1839)

CONWAY Trawler requis. 1915 and 1940.

COOK Sorvey vessel (RAN) 1976 tons. Williamstown DY 27.8.1977

COOK (see PEGWELL BAY)

COOKE (ex-USS DEMPSEY) Frigate, DE 'Captain' class. Boston Navy Yd 22.4.1943 on lend-lease. Returned 8.3.46 to USN.

COOTAMUNDRA Minesweeper (RAN), 'Bathurst' class. Poole & Steel, Sydney 3.12.1942. Sold in 1962.

COOTE Sloop 18 (Indian), 420bm. Bombay DY 1827. Stranded 1.12.1846 near Calicut.

COPPERCLIFF (see FELICITY OF 1944)

COPPERCLIFF (ex-HEVER CASTLE renamed 1943) Corvette, 'Castle' class (RCN). Blyth DD 24.2.1944. Sold 1946.

COQUETTE 6th Rate 28. French, captured 2.3.1783. In service in 1785.

COQUETTE (ex-*Queen Mab*) 6th Rate 20, 484bm, 113 x 31 ft, 18-32 pdr carr., 8-12pdr carr., 1-12pdr, 2-6pdr. Temple, S. Shields 24.4.1807 (purchased on stocks). Sold 30.4.1817.

COQUETTE Corvette 18, 731bm, 120 x 37½ ft, 18-32pdr. Chatham DY. Ordered 1835, cancelled 1851.

COQUETTE Wood S. gunvessel, 677bm, 181½ x 28½ ft, 1-110pdr, 1-68pdr, 2-20pdr. Green, Blackwall 25.10.1955. BU 1868 at Cowes

COQUETTE Compos. S. gunboat, 295bm, 430 tons, 125 x 23 ft, 2-64 pdr, 2-20pdr. Pembroke Dock 5.4.1871. Sold 8.1889.

COQUETTE Destroyer 355 tons, 210 x 19½ ft, 1-12pdr, 5-6pdr, 2-TT. Thornycroft, Chiswick 25.11.1897. Sunk 7.3.1916 by mine off the east coast.

COQUETTE (ex-BOWMANVILLE renamed 6.1943). Minesweeper, 'Algerine' class. Redfern, Toronto 24.11.43. Arrived 26.5.58 Charlestown to BU.

COQUILLE 5th Rate 36, 916bm. French, captured 12.10.1798 off the coast of Donegal. Burnt 14.12.1798 by accident at Plymouth.

CORAL SNAKE SSV(RAN) 80 tons. Building at Melbourne, cancelled in 8.1945.

CORDELIA Brig-sloop 10, 'Cherokee' class, 239bm. King, Upnor 26.7.1808. Sold 12.12.1833.

CORDELIA Wood S.sloop 579bm, 151 x 29 ft, 11-32pdr. Pembroke Dock 3.7.1856. Sold 12.5.1870 Marshall, Plymouth.

CORDELIA S. corvette 2,380 tons, 225 x 44½ ft, 10-6in, Portsmouth DY 25.10.1881. Sold 5.7.1904.

CORDELIA Light cruiser 3,750 tons, 420 x 41½ ft, 2-6, 8-4in. Pembroke Dock 23.2.1914. Sold 31.7.23 Cashmore, Newport.

CORDELIA Drifter W.W.I; Yacht W.W.I.

La CORDELIERE Destroyer 610 tons, 245 x 26 ft, 2-3.9in, 2-TT. French ssized 3.7.1940 at Portsmouth; commissioned in the RN 6.7.40. Returned 1945 to the French navy.

COREOPSIS Sloop, 'Anchusa' class. Barclay Curle 15.9.1917. Sold 6.9.22 Ward, Preston; arrived Preston 5.5.24.

COREOPSIS Corvette, 'Flower' class. Inglis 19.6.1940. Lent Greek navy 10.11.43 to 7.52 as KREZIS. Arrived 22.7.52 Young Sunderland to BU.

COREOPSIS Drifter requis. 1914 and 1939.

CORFE CASTLE Corvette, 'Castle' class. Canada. Cancelled 12.1943.

CORIANDER (ex-IRIS renamed 26.10.1940) Corvette, 'Flower' class. Hall Russell 9.6.41. Lent Free-French 1941 to 5.47 as COMMANDANT DETROYAT. Arrived Troon 2.48 to BU.

CORMORANT Fireship 16, 408bm, 101 x 31 ft. French MARCHAULT captured 4.1757. Sold 23.12.1762.

CORMORANT Sloop 14, 304bm, 97 x 27 ft. Barnard, Ipswich 21.5.1776. Captured 24.8.1781 by the French off Charlestown.

CORMORANT Brig-sloop 12, 198bm, 90 x 22 ft, 12-4pdr. American RATTLESNAKE captured 1781 by ASSURANCE. Renamed RATTLESNAKE 8.1783. Sold 10.10.1786.

CORMORANT Sloop 18, 427bm, 108 x 30 ft. Randall, Rotherhithe 2.1.1794. Blown up 24.12.1796 by accident at Port-au-Prince, Haiti.

CORMORANT 6th Rate 20, 564bm, 119 x 33 ft. French ETNA captured 13.11.1796 by MELAMPUS on the coast of France. Wrecked 20.5.1800 on the coast of Egypt.

CORMORANT (ex-Blenheim) Sloop 16, 328bm, 110 x 27 ft. Purchased 6.1804. Sold 4.12.1817.

CORMORANT Wood pad. Sloop, 1,057bm, 170 x 36 ft. Sheerness DY 29.3.1842. BU. in 8.1853.

CORMORANT Wood S. gunvessel, 675bm, 181 x 28 ft, 1-110pdr, 1-68pdr, 2-20pdr. Fletcher, Limehouse 23.2.1856. Sunk 28.6.1859

in action with Peiho forts, China.

CORMORANT Wood S. sloop, 695bm, 186 x 28½ ft, 2-68pdr, 2-32pdr. Wigram, Blackwall 9.2.1860. Sold 1870 at Hong Kong.

CORMORANT Compos. S. sloop 1,130 tons, 170 x 36 ft, 2-7in, 4-64pdr. Chatham DY 12.9.1877. Harbour service 11.1889; renamed ROOKE 7.1946. BU 1949 at Malaga, Spain.

CORMORANT Patrol boat Transferred from RAF 29.8.1985.

CORMORANT Two Trawlers and a Drifter requis, WW.I.

CORNEL Corvette, 'Flower' class. Collingwood SY. Laid down 6.1.1942; transferred to the USN 1942 as ALACRITY.

CORNELIA 5th Rate 32, 909bm, 142½ x 38 ft. Temple, S. Shields 26.7.1808. BU 6.1814.

CORNELIAN 12-gun ship, 100bm. Royalist CORNELIUS captured 1655. Last listed 1660.

CORNELIAN Trawler requis. 1917-19; Trawler 1935-45.

CORNET CASTLE Corvette, 'Castle' class. Collingwood SY. Cancelled 12.1943.

CORNFLOWER Sloop, 'Arabis' class. Barclay Curle 30.3.1916. RNVR drill ship 1935; sold 1940 at Hong Kong, renamed Tai Hing; repurchased 9.40, renamed CORNFLOWER. Sunk 15.12.41 by air attack at Hong Kong.

CORNFLOWER (see LYSANDER of 1943)

CORNWALL 2nd Rate 80, 1,186bm, 156½ x 41½ ft. Winter, Southampton 23.4.1692. Rebuilt Rotherhithe 1706 as 1,241bm; rebuilt Deptford 1726 as 1,350bm. BU completed 16.7.1761 at Chatham.

CORNWALL 3rd Rate 74, 1,634bm, 168½ x 47½ ft. Wells, Deptford 19.5.1761. Damaged 19.5.1780 in action with the French in the W. Indies and burnt 30.6.1780 at St Lucia as unserviceable.

CORNWALL Name chosen for HEIR APPARENT captured 1807, but not used.

CORNWALL 3rd Rate 74, 1,751bm, 176 x 48 ft. Barnard, Deptford 16.1.1812. Reduced to 50 guns 1831; renamed WELLESLEY 18.6.1869. as training ship. BU completed 18.1.1875 at Sheerness.

CORNWALL (see WELLESLEY of 1815)

CORNWALL Armoured cruiser 9,800 tons, 440 x 66 ft, 14-6in, 9-12pdr. Pembroke Dock 29.10.1902. Sold

7.7.20 Ward, Briton Ferry.

CORNWALL Cruiser 9,750 tons, 590 x 68 ft, 8-8in, 6-4in. Devonport DY 11.3.1926. Sunk 5.4.42 by Japanese aircraft in the Indian Ocean.

CORNWALL Frigate 4,200 tons. Yarrow 14.10.1985.

CORNWALLIS Galley 5, 1-24pdr, 4-4pdr. Purchased 1777 in N. America. Sold 1782.

CORNWALLIS Storeship 14, 443bm, 100 x 30 ft. Purchased 3.1781. Foundered 9,1782 in the Atlantic.

CORNWALLIS (ex-E. Indiaman *Marquis Cornwallis*) 4th Rate 54, 1,388bm, 166½ x 43½ ft. Purchased 1801. Renamed AKBAR 13.8.1806, troopship; harbour service 9.1824. Sold 1862.

CORNWALLIS 3rd Rate 74, 1,809bm, 177 x 48 ft. Bombay DY 12.5.1813. Undocked 8.2.1855 as screw ship, 60 guns; made a jetty at Sheerness 1865; renamed WILDFIRE base ship 1916. BU 1957 at Sheerness.

CORNWALLIS Battleship 14,000 tons, 405 x 75½ ft, 4-12in, 12-6in, 12-12pdr. Thames Iron Works 13.7.1901. Sunk 9.1.17 by 'U.32' SE of Malta.

CORNWALLIS (see LYCHNIS)

COROMANDEL (ex-E. Indiaman *Winterton* purchased on stocks) 4th Rate 56, 1,340bm, 169 x 42½ ft. Perry, Blackwall 9.5.1795. Storeship 1800; harbour service 10.1807. Sold 24.7.1813 at Jamaica.

COROMANDEL (see MALABAR of 1804)

COROMANDEL (ex-*Tartar*) Wood pad. despatch vessel, 303bm, 172 x 24 ft. Purchased 8.1.1855. Sold 17.8.1866 at Hong Kong; became Japanese NARUTO and BU 1876.

COROMANDEL Wood S. frigate (Indian) 1,026bm, 4 guns, River Thames 1856. In service in 1870.

CORONATION 2nd Rate 90, 1,346bm, 160½ x 45 ft, 26-34pdr, 26-18pdr, 26-6pdr, 12-3pdr. Portsmouth DY 1685. Wrecked 3.9.1691 on Rame Head.

CORONATION Tank Vessel 1937-62; Dredger 1940-47.

EL CORSO Brig-sloop 14, 234bm, 90½ x 24½ ft. Spanish, captured 2.12.1796 by SOUTHAMPTON in the Mediterranean. Harbour service 3.1803. Sold 1.9.1814.

CORSO Destroyer, 'C' class. Thornycroft 14.7.1945. Renamed CONCORD 6.46. Arrived 22.10.62 Inverkeithing to BU.

CORUNNA Destroyer 2,400 tons, 355 x 40 ft, 5-4.5in, 10-TT. Swan Hunter 29.5.1945. Sold 8.8.74; arrived Sunderland 23.11.74 to BU.

COSBY (ex-REEVES renamed 1943) Frigate, TE 'Captain' class. Bethlehem, Hingham 30.10.1943 on lend-lease. Returned 3.46 to the USN.

COSSACK (ex-PANDOUR renamed 1806) 6th Rate 22, 546bm, 118 x 32 ft. Temple, S. Shields 24.12.1806. BU 6.1816.

COSSACK Steam gunvessel, 483bm, 150 x 26 ft. Portsmouth DY. Laid down 1846, cancelled 1849.

COSSACK (ex-Russian WITJAS seized 5.4.1854) Wood S. corvette, 1,296bm, 195 x 39 ft, 20-8in. Pitcher, Northfleet 15.5.1854. Sold 19.5.1875 Castle.

COSSACK Torpedo cruiser 1,630 tons, 225 x 36 ft, 6-6in, 8-3pdr, 3-TT. Thomson 3.6.1886. Sold 4.4.1905 G. Graham.

COSSACK Destroyer 885 tons, 270 x 26 ft, 3-12pdr, 2-TT. Cammell Laird 16.2.1907. Sold 12.12.19 Ward, Preston.

COSSACK Destroyer 1,870 tons, 355½ x 36½ ft, 8-4.7in, 4-TT. Vickers Armstrong, Tyne 8.6.1937. Sunk 27.10.41 west of Gibraltar four days after being torpedoed by U-boat ('U.563' or 'U.1997').

COSSACK Destroyer, 'C' class. Vickers Armstrong. Tyne 10.5.1944. Arrived 1.3.61 to Troon to BU.

COTSWOLD Minesweeper, early 'HUNT' class. Bow McLachlan 28.11.1916. Sold 18.1.23 Alloa S. Bkg Co, Charlestown.

COTSWOLD Destroyer, 'Hunt' class type I. Yarrow 18.7.1940. Breakwater 1955. Arrived 11.9.57 Ward, Grays to BU.

COTTESMORE Minesweeper, early 'Hunt' class. Bow McLachlan 9.2.1917. Sold 18.1.23 Alloa, Charlestown.

COTTESMORE Destroyer, 'Hunt' class type I. Yarrow 5.9.1940. Sold 17.9.50 Egyptian navy.

COTTESMORE Minehunter 615 tons. Yarrow 9.2.1982.

COTTON Frigate, TE 'Captain' class. Bethlehem, Hingham 21.8.1943 on lend-lease. Returned 11.45 to the USN.

COUCY Depot ship 644 tons, 246 x 31 ft. French patrol vessel seized 3.7.1940 at Plymouth. Returned 1944 to the French navy.

COUNTERGUARD (ex-LCT 4043 renamed 1956) Tank landing craft. Sold Malaysian navy 1965 as SRI LANGKAWI.

COUNTESS OF HOPETOUN Torpedo boat (Australian) 93 tons, 130 x 13½ ft, 3-3pdr, 3-TT. Yarrow, Poplar 1891. Sold 4.1924 J. Hill, Melbourne.

COURAGEOUS 1st class cruiser 18,600 tons, 735 x 81 ft, 4-15in, 18-4in, 2-3in. Armstrong 5.2.1916. Completed as A/C carrier 5.28, 22,500 tons st., 16-4.7in, 48-A/C. Sunk 17.9.39 by 'U.29' in the Atlantic

COURAGEOUS Nuclear s/m 3500 tons. Vickers 7.3.1970.

COURAGEUX 3rd Rate 74, 1,721bm, 172 x 48 ft, 28-32pdr, 28-18pdr, 18-9pdr. French, captured 13.8.1761. Wrecked 18.12.1796 near Gibraltar.

COURAGEUX 5th Rate 32, 932bm, 145 x 39 ft. French COURAGEUSE captured 18.6.1799 by a squadron in the Mediterranean. In service in 1803.

COURAGEUX 3rd Rate 74, 1,772bm, 181 x 47 ft. Deptford DY 26.3.1800. Harbour service 2.1814. BU 10.1832.

COURBET Depot ship, 22,200 tons, 541 x 88½ ft. French battleship, seized 3.7.1940 at Portsmouth. Free-French to 1941. Sunk 9.6.44 as breakwater at Arromanches.

COUREUSE Schooner 12. French, captured 25.3.1795 by POMONE off the French coast. Sold 13.4.1799.

COUREUR Schooner 8, 138bm, 69 x 23 ft, 8-4pdr. French COUREUR captured 17.6.1778 by ALERT in the Channel. Captured 21.6.1780 by two American privateers off Newfoundland.

COUREUR Sloop 20, 355bm, 111 x 27½ ft. French privateer COUREUR captured 23.2.1798. Sold 14.9.1801.

COURIER (see QUEEN MAB)

COURIER (ex-*George IV*) Wood pad. packet, 733bm, 155½ x 32½ ft. Purchased 20.8.1830. Renamed HERMES 1831; renamed CHARGER 1835, coal hulk. BU 6.1854.

COURIER (ex-ARNPRIOR renamed 6.1943) Minesweeper, 'Algerine' class. Redfern, Toronto 22.12.1943. Arrived 25.3.59 Rees, Llanelly to BU.

COURIER Two cutters hired 1798 and 1804.

COURSER (Gunboat No. 20) Gunvessel 12, 168bm, 76 x 22½ ft. Hill, Limehouse 25.4.1797. Sold Customs Board in 8.1803.

COURSER Trawler requis. 1965-19 and 1940-46.

COURTENAY Minesweeper (RCN). TE 'Bangor' class. P. Rupert DD

2.8.1941. Sold 3.4.46 Union SS Co, Vancouver.

COVENTRY 28-gun ship, 191bm. Spanish SAN MIGUEL captured 1658. Captured 1666 by the French.

COVENTRY 4th Rate 48, 670bm. Deptford 1695. Captured 24.7.1704 by the French off the Scillies; recaptured and BU 1709.

COVENTRY 6th Rate 28, 599bm, 118½ x 34 ft. Adams, Beaulieu 20.5.1757. Captured 10.1.1783 by the French in the Bay of Bengal.

COVENTRY (ex-CORSAIR renamed 1916) Light cruiser 4,190 tons, 425 x 43½ ft, 5-6in, 2-3in. Swan Hunter 6.7.1917. A/A ship 1937. Sunk 14.9.42 by air attack in the Mediterranean.

COVENTRY Frigate. Vickers Armstrong, Tyne. Launched 17.8.1962 as PENELOPE, 'Leander' class.

COVENTRY Destroyer 3150 tons. Cammell Laird 21.6.1974. Lost 26.5.82 in Falklands operations.

COVENTRY Frigate 4200 tons. Swan Hunter 8.4.1986.

COWDRAY Destroyer, 'Hunt' class type II. Scotts 12.5.1941. Arrived 3.9.59 King, Gateshead to BU. (Bore the name ADMIRAL HASTINGS 3.44 to 8.44 for loan to Greek navy; not taken over.)

COWES CASTLE Corvette, 'Castle' class. Collingwood SY. Cancelled 12.1943.

COWICHAN Minesweeper (RCN), TE 'Bangor' class. N. Vancouver SR Co 9.8.1940. Sold 1946 mercantile; retained name.

COWICHAN Coastal M/S (RCN) Davie SB 12.11.1951. Transferred French navy 7.4.54 as La MALOUINE.

COWICHAN Coastal M/S (RCN) Yarrow, Esquimalt 26.2.1957.

COWLING CASTLE Corvette, 'Castle' class. Midland SY. Cancelled 12.1943.

COWPER Wood pad. vessel, 342bm, 178 x 27 ft. Purchased 20.10.1860 at Hong Kong. Sold 1861 at Hong Kong, renamed *Fei Seen.*

COWRA Minesweeper (RAN), 'Bathurst' class. Poole & Steel 27.5.1943. Sold 6.1.61; left 21.5.62 for Japan to BU.

COWSLIP Sloop, 'Anchusa' class. Barclay Curle 19.10.1917. Sunk 18.4.18 by 'UB.105' off Cape Spartel.

COWSLIP Corvette, 'Flower' class. Harland & Wolff 28.5.1941. Sold 7.48 mercantile. BU 4.49 at Troon.

CRACCHER Ballinger, 56bm. Built

1416. Last listed 1420.

CRACCHER Destroyer, 'C' class. White 23.6.1945. Renamed CRISPIN 6.46. Sold 18.3.58 Pakistan navy as JAHANGIR.

CRACHE-FEU Gunvessel 3, 144bm, 79½ x 20 ft. French, captured 9.5.1795 by a squadron on the French coast. BU 1797.

CRACKER (Gunboat No. 13) Gunvessel 12, 160bm, 75 x 22 ft, 2-24pdr, 10-18pdr carr. Dudman, Deptford 25.4.1797. Sold 12.1802.

CRACKER Gun-brig 12, 180bm, 80 x 23 ft, 10-18pdr carr., 2-6pdr. Pitcher, Northfleet 30.6.1804. Sold 23.11.1815.

CRACKER Cutter tender, 54bm. White, Cowes 1826 and purchased. Sold 11.1842.

CRACKER Schooner. Deptford DY. Ordered 1846, cancelled 1850.

CRACKER Wood S. gunboat, 'Dapper' class. Pitcher, Northfleet 2.4.1855. BU 4.1864.

CRACKER Compos. S. gunboat 465bm, 605 tons, 155 x 25 ft, 1-7in, 1-64pdr, 2-20pdr. Portsmouth DY 27.11.1867. BU 1889 at Portsmouth.

CRACKER DY tug. 1899-1956.

CRADLEY Inshore M/S. 'Ley' class. Saunders Roe 24.2.1955. Renamed ISIS 1963. Sold Pounds in 4.82.

CRAFTY Schooner 12, 146bm. French, captured 1804. Captured 9.3.1807 by three privateers off Gibraltar.

CRAIGIE Minesweeper, later 'Hunt' class. Clyde SB Co 5.1918. Sold 18.5.22 B. Zammitt, Malta.

CRANE 24-gun ship, 6-9bm, 6-9pdr, 7-6pdr, 6-4pdr, 5 small. Built 1590. Sold 1629.

CRANE Galley 1. Purchased 1777 in N. America. Sold 20.8.1783 at New York.

CRANE Schooner 4, 80bm, 56 x 18½ ft, 4-12pdr carr. Custance, Yarmouth 26.4.1806. Wrecked 26.10.1808 on West Hoe.

CRANE Brig-sloop 18, 'Cruizer' class, 385bm. Brindley, Frindsbury 29.7.1809. Foundered 30.9.1814 in the W. Indies.

CRANE Packet brig 6, 359bm, 96 x 31 ft, 6-18pdr. Woolwich DY 28.5.1839. Sold 11.1.1862 Marshall, Plymouth.

CRANE Destroyer 360 tons, 215 x 21 ft, 1-12pdr, 5-6pdr, 2-TT. Palmer 17.12.1896. Sold 10.6.1919 Ward, New Holland.

CRANE Sloop 1,350 tons, 283 x 38 ft, 6-4in, 12-20mm. Denny 10.11.1942.

BU 1965 at Queenborough.

CRANEFLY River gunboat, 'Fly' class. Yarrow 8.1915 and re-erected 12.15 on the Tigris. Sold 1.3.23 locally.

CRANEFLY Trawler requis. 1939-46.

CRANHAM Inshore M/S, 'Ham' class. White, Cowes 24.11.1953. Sold Pounds 9.6.66.

CRANSTOUN Frigate, TE 'Captain' class. Bethlehem, Hingham 28.8.1943 on lend-lease. Returned 12.45 to the USN.

CRASH (Gunboat No. 15) Gunvessel 12, 2-32pdr carr., 2-24pdr carr., 8-18pdr carr. Barnard, Deptford 5.4.1797. Sold 9.1802. (Was in Dutch hands 26.8.98 to 11.8.99.)

CRASH (see SCOURGE of 1794)

CRAUFURD Monitor (see GENERAL CRAUFURD).

CREDITON Minesweeper, later 'Hunt' class. Bow McLachlan. Laid down 1918, renamed COLWYN 1918 and cancelled.

CREOLE 5th Rate 38, 1,070bm. French, captured 1.7.1803 in the W. Indies. Foundered 2.1804 near Jamaica.

CREOLE 5th Rate 36, 944bm. Ordered Tanner, Dartmouth 17.3.1803, cancelled 2.6.09.

CREOLE 5th Rate 36, 949bm, 145 x 38½ ft. Plymouth DY 1.5.1813. BU 8.1833 at Deptford.

CREOLE 6th Rate 26, 911bm, 131 x 40½ ft, 24-32pdr, 2-12pdr. Plymouth DY 1.10.1845. BU 3.1875 at Devonport.

CREOLE Submarine 893 tons, 241 x 21 ft. French, towed to Swansea 70 per cent complete in 6.1940 and seized 3.7.40. Laid up at Swansea to 1946, then returned to French navy for completion.

CREOLE Destoyer, 'C' class. White 22.11.1945. Sold Pakistan navy 20.6.58. as ALAMGIR.

CREOLE Tank vessel 1902-48. Yacht requis. 1940-46.

CRESCENT 14-gun ship 167bm. Purchased 1643. Captured 1648 by Royalists and wrecked 1649.

CRESCENT Fireship 6, 234bm, 85 x 25 ft. French, captured 1692 by DOVER. Sold 1698.

CRESCENT 5th Rate 32, 731bm, 130½ x 36 ft. French privateer ROSTAN captured 10.1758 by TORBAY. Sold 13.6.1777.

CRESCENT 6th Rate 28, 611bm, 121 x 34 ft. Hillhouse, Bristol 3.1779. Captured 19.6.1781 by the French off Cadiz.

CRESCENT 5th Rate 36, 888bm, 137 x 38½ ft. Calhoun & Newland, Bursledon 28.10.1784. Wrecked 6.12.1808 on the coast of Jutland.

CRESCENT 5th Rate 38, 1,084bm, 154½ x 40ft. Woolwich DY 11.12. 1810. Harbour service 1.1840. Sold 1854.

CRESCENT Wood pad. tender 90bm, 80 x 16 ft. Purchased 21.7.1854 at Constantinople. Sold 7.7.1855.

CRESCENT 1st class cruiser 7,700 tons, 360 x 61 ft, 1-9.2in, 12-6in, 12-6pdr. Portsmouth DY 30.3.1892. Sold 22.9.1921 Cohen, BU in Germany.

CRESCENT (see GLORY of 1899)

CRESCENT Destroyer 1,375 tons, 326 x 33 ft, 4-4.7in, 1-3in, 8-TT. Vickers Armstrong, Barrow 29.9.1931. Renamed FRASER (RCN) 17.2.37. Sunk 25.6.40 in collision with CALCUTTA in the Gironde.

CRESCENT Destroyer, 'C' class.J. Brown 20.7.1944. To RCN 9.45 on loan; sold RCN 1951. BU in Taiwan in 5.71.

CRESCENT Trawler and Drifter requis. WW.I.

CRESSY 3rd Rate 74, 1,763bm, 176 x 48½ ft. Brindley, Frindsbury 7.3.1810. BU 12.1832.

CRESSY Screw 3rd Rate 80, 2,539bm, 198 x 55 ft, 14-8in, 66-32pdr. Chatham DY 21.7.1853. Sold 1867 Castle & Beech.

CRESSY Armoured cruiser 12,000 tons, 440 x 69½ ft, 2-9in, 12-6in, 13-12pdr. Fairfield 4.12.1899. Sunk 22.9.1914 by 'U.9' in the North Sea.

CRESSY (see UNICORN of 1824)

CRETAN Brig-sloop 16, 344bm, 95½ x 29 ft, 14-pdr carr., 2-6pdr. French, ex-Italian NETTUNO captured 1.6.1808 by UNITE off Zara. Sold 29.9.1814.

CRETAN Destroyer, 'C' class. Scotts 6.8.1945. Renamed CROMWELL 6.46; sold 7.46 Norwegian navy as BERGEN.

CRICCIETH CASTLE Corvette, 'Castle' class. Morton, Canada. Cancelled 12.1943.

CRICHTON Coastal M/S, 'Ton' class. Doig, Grimsby 17.5.1953. Renamed CLYDE then ST DAVID. CRICHTON 1974.

CRICKET Coastal destroyer 234 tons, 175 x 17½ ft, 2-12pdr, 3-TT. White 23.1.1906. Rated torpedo boat, renamed TB.1. 1906. Sold 7.10.20 Fowey Coaling & Ship Co.

CRICKET River gunboat 645 tons, 230 x 36 ft, 2-6in, 1-3in. Barclay Curle 17.12.1915. Minesweeper 1939; gunboat 1940. Damaged by mine 6.41 off Mersa Matruh and BU 1942 at Alexandria.

CRICKET Tender 213 tons. Holmes 30.8.1969

CRISPIN (see CRACCHER)

CROCODILE 6th Rate 24, 519bm, 114 x 32 ft. Portsmouth DY 25.4.1781 Lost 1784 off Start Point.

CROCODILE 6th Rate 22, 540bm, 119 x 31½ ft. Temple, S. Shields 19.4.1806. BU 10.1816.

CROCODILE 6th Rate 28, 500bm, 114 x 32 ft, 20-32pdr carr, 6-18 pdr, 2-6pdr. Chatham DY 28.10.1825. Harbour service 8.1850. Sold 22.11.1861 Castle.

CROCODILE Iron S. troopship 4,173bm, 6,211 tons, 360 x 49 ft, 3-4pdr. Wigram, Blackwall 7.1.1867. Sold 11.5.1894, BU.

CROCODILE Two DY tugs 1896-1924 and 1940-47.

CROCUS Sloop 14, 256bm, 92 x 25½ ft. Plymouth DY 10.6.1808. Sold 31.8.1815.

CROCUS Wood S. gunboat, 'Albacore' class. Green, Blackwall 4.6.1856. BU 7.1864.

CROCUS Sloop, 'Arabis' class. Lobnitz 24.12.1915. Sold 7.30 at Bombay.

CROCUS Corvette, 'Flower' class. Inglis 26.6.1940. Sold 22.7.46, renamed *Annlock*.

CROCUS DY tug 1897-1920.

CROFTON Coastal M/S, 'Ton' class. Thornycroft 3.1958. SOLENT 5.69-75.

CROMARTY Minesweeper turbine 'Bangor' class. Blyth DD 24.2.1941. Sunk 23.10.43 by mine in the central Mediterranean.

CROMER Wood S. gunboat, 'Britomart' class. Haslar, Portsmouth 20.8.1867. Sold 24.8.1886 to BU.

CROMER Minesweeper, TE 'Bangor' class. Lobnitz 7.10.1940. Sunk 9.11.42 by mine in the Mediterranean.

CROMER CASTLE Corvette, 'Castle' class. Midland SY. Cancelled 12. 1943.

CROMWELL (see CRETAN)

CROOME Minesweeper, early 'Hunt' class. Clyde SB Co 22.5.1917. Sold 7.22 Stanlee, Dover.

CROOME Destroyer, 'Hunt' class type 11.Stephen 30.1.1941. Arrived 13.8.57 Ward, Briton Ferry to BU.

CROSSBOW Destroyer 1,980 tons, 341½ x 38 ft, 6-4in, 10-TT. Thornycroft 20.12.1945. Sold Ward 14.12.71, BU at Briton Ferry.

CROW 36-gun ship. French, captured 1652. Sold 1656.

CROWN (see TAUNTON of 1654)

CROWN MALAGO Flyboat 6, 197bm. Spanish, captured 1664. Given away 1667.

CROWN PRIZE 6th Rate 26, 223bm. French, captured 1691. Wrecked 9.2.1692 near Dartmouth.

CROWN 5th Rate 44, 842bm, 134 x 38 ft. Taylor, Rotherhithe 13.7.1747. Storeship 7.1757. Sold 17.7.1770.

CROWN 3rd Rate, 1,405bm, 160½ x 45 ft. Perry, Blackwall 15.3.1782. Prison ship 5.1798; powder hulk 1802. BU 3.1816.

CROWN Gunvessel, 73bm, 58 x 17 ft. Purchased 3.1794. Sold 10.3.1800.

CROWN Wood S. gunboat, 'Britomart' class. Haslar, Portsmouth. Laid down 1861, cancelled 12.12.1863.

CROWN Destroyer, 'C' class. Scotts 19.12.1945. Sold Norwegian navy 7.46 as OSLO.

CROXTON Pad. Minesweeper, 'Ascot' class. Ayrshire Co 7.4.1916. Sold 3.22 Ward, Inverkeithing.

CROZIER (ex-VERWOOD renamed 1919, ex-VENTNOR) Survey ship, 800 tons, 220 x 28½ ft, 1-3pdr. Simons 1.7.1919. To SAN 1921; renamed PROTEA 11.10.22. Sold 10.33.

CROZIERS Destroyer, 'C' class. Yarrow 19.9.1944. Sold Norwegian navy 10.10.46, renamed TRONDHEIM

CRUELLE Cutter 8. French, captured 1.6.1800 by MERMAID off Toulon. Sold 1801.

CRUISER (see KINGFISHER of 1879)

CRUISER 6th Rate 24, 280bm. French De MERIC captured 5.5.1705 by TRYTON. Wrecked 15.12.1708 in the Azores.

CRUISER (ex-*Unity*) Sloop 14, 123bm. Purchased 7.6.1709. Sold 1712.

CRUISER Sloop 8. Captured 1721. Foundered 1724.

CRUISER Sloop 8, 100bm, 26 x 20 ft. Deptford 24.10.1721.BU 7.1732.

CRUISER Sloop 14, 200bm, 87½ x 23 ft. Deptford DY 6.9.1732. Sold 22.1.1744.

CRUISER Sloop 8, 141bm, 75½ x 20½ ft. Deptford DY 31.8.1752. Burnt 2.10.1776 off S. Carolina.

CRUISER Cutter 14, 199bm, 73½ x 26 ft, 14-4pdr. Purchased 5.1780. Lost 1792 on passage to Gibraltar.

CRUISER Brig-sloop 18, 'Cruiser' class (name-ship), 384bm. Teague, Ipswich

20.12.1797. Sold 3.2.1819 Mr Cockshot.

CRUISER Brig-sloop 18, 'Cruiser' class, 385bm (last of the class). Chatham DY 19.1.1828.Sold 3.1849 at Bombay.

CRUISER Wood S. Sloop 752bm, 960 tons, 160 x 32 ft, 17-32pdr. Deptford DY 19.6.1852. Listed as CRUISER from 1857; renamed LARK, sailing training ship 5.1893. Sold 1912 at Malta.

CRUSADER Destroyer 1,045 tons, 280 x 26 ft, 2-4in, 2-TT. White 20.3.1909.Sold 30.6.20 Ward, Preston.

CRUSADER Destroyer 1,375 tons, 318 x 33 ft, 4-4.7in, 8-TT. Portsmouth DY 30.9.1931. Renamed OTTAWA (RCN) 15.6.38. Sunk 14.9.42 by 'U.91' in the Gulf of St Lawrence.

CRUSADER Destroyer, 'C' class. J. Brown 4.10.1944. To RCN 11.45.Sold 1964 to BU.

CRYSTAL Destroyer, 'C' class. Yarrow 12.2.1945. Sold 10.10.46 Norwegian navy as STAVANGER.

CRYSTAL Trials vessel 3040 tons. Devonport DY 22.3.1971

CRYSTAL Trawler requis. 1917-19.

CUBA 5th Rate 32, Spanish POMONA captured 23.8.1806 by ARETHUSA off Havana.Sold 3.4.1817.

CUBA Schooner tender, 67bm. Ex-slaver captured 6.1857 by ARAB.BU 3.1866 in Jamaica.

CUBITT Frigate, TE 'Captain' class. Bethlehem, Hingham 11.9.1943 on lend-lease, Returned 1946 to the USN.

CUCKMERE Frigate, 'River' class. Vickers, Montreal 24.10.1942 on lend-lease, Returned 6.11.46 to the USN.

CUCKOO Schooner 4, 78bm, 56 x 18½ ft, 4-12pdr carr. Lovewell, Yarmouth 12.4.1806. Wrecked 4.4.1810 in the Texel.

CUCKOO (ex-GPO vessel *Cinderella*) Wood pad. packet, 234bm, 120½ x 20 ft. Transferred 1837. Sold 1864.

CUCKOO Iron S. gunboat, 'Ant' class. Laird 14.8.1873. Renamed VIVID, base ship 1912; VIVID (OLD) 1920; YC.37 in 1923. Sold 1958.

CUCKOO (see AMELIA of 1888)

CUFFLEY inshore M/S launched 1955 as WINTRINGHAM

CULLIN SOUND Repair ship 10,000 tons, 431 x 56 ft, 12-20mm. Gray, Hartlepool 2.11.1944. Sold 1948, renamed *James Clunies*

CULGOA (ex-MACQUARIE renamed 3.1943) Frigate (RAN), 'River' class.

Williamstown DY 22.9.45. Hulk in 1966. Sold 27.1.72, BU in Taiwan.

CULGOA (see MACQUARIE)

CULLODEN (see PRINCE HENRY)

CULLODEN 3rd Rate 74, 1,487bm, 161½ x 46½ ft. Deptford DY 9.9.1747. Sold 29.6.1770.

CULLODEN Storeship hoy 2, 35bm, 43 x 16 ft. Cleveland, Plymouth 12.1749. Sold 16.12.1765.

CULLODEN 3rd Rate 74, 1,659bm, 170 x 47 ft. Deptford 18.5.1776. Wrecked 23.1.1781 on Long Island.

CULLODEN 3rd Rate 74, 1,683bm, 170 x 48 ft. Randall, Rotherhithe 16.6.1783. BU 2.1813.

CULVER (ex-USS MENDOTA) Coast-guard cutter 1,546 tons, 1-5in, 2-3in. Transferred on lend-lease 30.4.1941. Sunk 31.1.42 by 'U.105' in the N. Atlantic.

CULVERIN Destroyer 1,980 tons, 341½ x 38 ft, 6-4in, 10-TT. Thornycroft 3.1946. Arrived 3.46 Ward, Grays to BU (Not completed.)

CUMBERLAND 3rd Rate 80, 1,219bm, 156 x 42 ft. Wyatt, Bursledon 12.11.1695. Captured 10.10.1707 by the French. Sold Spanish navy as PRINCIPE De ASTURIAS.

CUMBERLAND 3rd Rate 80, 1,308bm, 156 x 44 ft. Deptford DY 1710. Re-built Woolwich DY 1739 as 66 guns, 1,401bm. Foundered 2.11.1760 while at anchor at Goa.

CUMBERLAND (ex-*Alex Robert*) Fire-ship 8, 181bm, 79 x 23 ft. Purchased 29.6.1739. BU completed 31.3.1742 at Sheerness.

CUMBERLAND Fireship 8, in service in 1745.

CUMBERLAND 3rd Rate 74, 1,647bm, 169 x 46 ft. Deptford DY 29.3.1774. BU 1805 at Portsmouth.

CUMBERLAND Schooner, 30bm. Pur-chased 1803 at Port Jackson. Sold 1810. (In French hands 1804-09.)

CUMBERLAND 3rd Rate 74, 1,718bm, 174½ x 48 ft. Pitcher Northfleet 19.8.1807. Convict ship 3.1830; re-named FORTITUDE 15.11.1833. On sale list 2.1870. Sold Castle.

CUMBERLAND 3rd Rate 70, 2,214bm, 180 x 54 ft, 6-8in, 64-32pdr. Chat-ham DY 21.10.1842. Training ship 1870. Burnt 17.2.1889 on the Clyde; wreck BU in Rosneath Bay 1889.

CUMBERLAND Armoured cruiser 9,800 tons, 440 x 66 ft, 14-6in, 9-12pdr. London & Glasgow Co 16.12.1902. Sold 9.5.21 Ward, Briton Ferry; arrived 28.3.23 to BU.

CUMBERLAND Cruiser 9,750 tons, 590

x 68½ ft, 8-8in, 6-4in. Vickers Arm-strong, Barrow 16.3.1926. Arrived 3.11.59 Cashmore, Newport to BU

CUMBERLAND Frigate 4200 tons. Swan Hunter 21.6.1986.

CUPAR (ex-ROSSLARE renamed 1918) Minesweeper, later 'Hunt' class. McMillan Dumbarton 27.3.1918. Sunk 5.5.19 by mine off the Tyne.

CUPID Sloop 14, 290bm, 92½ x 27 ft. Purchased 1777. Foundered 28.12.1778 off the coast of New-foundland.

CUPID Cutter 12, 181bm. Purchased 1781. Sold 1782 Unsuitable.

CUPID Mortar vessel, 102bm, 60 x 20 ft. Laird 13.11.1855. (Also known as Mortar Float No 103.) Became yard craft YC.3 in 8.1865; gone by 1870.

CURACOA 5th Rate 36, 956bm, 145 x 38½ ft. Kidwell, Itchenor 23.9.1809. Reduced to 24 guns at Chatham 6.1831. BU 3.1849.

CURACOA Wood S. frigate, 1,570bm, 192 x 43 ft, 1-10in, 30-32pdr. Pem-broke Dock 13.4.1854. BU completed 17.7.1869.

CURACOA S. corvette 2,380 tons, 225 x 44½ ft, 2-7in, 12-6pdr. Elder, Glas-gow 18.4.1878. Sold 17.5.1904 King, Garston.

CURACOA Light cruiser 4,190 tons, 425 x 43½ ft, 5-6in, 2-3in. Pembroke Dock 5.5.1917. A/A ship 1939. Sunk 2.10.42 in collision with SS 'Queen Mary' north of Ireland.

CURIEUX Brig-sloop 18, 315bm, 97 x 28½ ft, 10-18pdr carr., 8-6pdr. French, captured 4.2.1804 by boats of CENTAUR at Fort Royal, Mar-tinique. Wrecked 3.11.1809 in the W. Indies.

CURIEUX Brig-sloop 16, 317bm. French BEARNAIS captured 14.12.1809 by MELAMPUS. Sold 5.1814.

CURLEW Brig-sloop 16(fir-built), 314bm, 95 x 28 ft. Randall, Rotherhithe 16.7.1795. Foundered 31.12.1796 in the North Sea.

CURLEW (ex-*Leander*) Sloop 16, 350bm, 98½ x 29½ ft, 8-24pdr carr., 6-24pdr, 2-6pdr. Purchased 6.1803. Sold 25.6.1810.

CURLEW Brig-sloop 18, 'Cruizer' class, 386bm. Good, Bridport 27.5.1812. Sold 28.12.1822 at Bombay, renamed *Jenica*.

CURLEW Brig-sloop 10, 'Cherokee' class, 233bm. Woolwich DY 25.2.1830. BU 8.1849.

CURLEW Wood S. sloop, 486bm, 139 x 28 ft, 9-32pdr. Deptford DY

31.5.1854. Sold 29.8.1865 Marshall, Plymouth.

CURLEW Wood S. gunvesssel, 665bm, 805 tons, 170 x 29 ft, 1-7in, 2-40pdr. Deptford DY 20.8.1868. Sold 7.11.1882.

CURLEW Torpedo sloop 950 tons, 195 x 28 ft, 1-6in, 3-5in, 5-TT, Devonport DY 23.10.1885. Sold 10.7.1906.

CURLEW Light cruiser 4.190 tons, 425 x 43½ ft, 5-6in, 2-3in. Vickers 5.7.1917. A/A ship 1938. Sunk 26.5.40 by air attack in Ofot Fiord, Norway.

CURLEW (see CHEDISTON)

CURLEW Trawler requis. 1917-19.

CURRAGH Mineswepper, later 'Hunt' class. Eltringham. Cancelled 1918.

CURZON Frigate, TE 'Captain' class. Bethlehem, Hingham 18.9.1943 on lend-lease. Returned 1946 to the USN.

CURZON (see BICKINGTON)

CUTLASS (see NORTHWAY)

CUTLASS Destroyer 1,980 tons, 341½ x 38 ft, 6-4in, 10-TT. Yarrow 20.3.1946 (not completed). Cancelled 1.46; arrived 20.3.46 at Troom to BU.

CUTLASS Patrol boat 102 tons. Dunston 6.10.1975

CUTTER Ketch 2, 46bm. Portsmouth 1673. Wrecked 1673.

CUTTLE Schooner 4, 78bm, 56 x 18 ft, 4-12pdr carr. Bermuda 5.1807. Foundered 1814 on the Halifax Station.

CUXTON Coastal M/S, 'Ton' class. Camper & Nicholson 9.11.1953.

CYANE Sloop 18, 423bm, 110 x 29½ ft. Wilson, Frindsbury 9.4.1796. Captured 12.5.1805 by the French in the W. Indies; recaptured 5.10.1805 off Tobago and renamed CERF. Sold 12.1.1809.

CYANE (ex-COLUMBINE renamed 1805) 6th Rate 22, 540bm, 118½ x 31½ ft. Bass, Topsham 14.10.1806. Captured 20.2.1815 by the American CONSTITUTION in the Atlantic.

CYBELE Mine Destructor 3,980 tons. Scotts 16.11.1943 BU 10.46 at Troon.

CYCLAMEN Sloop, 'Arabis' class. Lobnitz 22.2.1916. Sold 2.7.32 Metal Industries, Charlestown.

CYCLAMEN Corvette, 'Flower' class. Lewis 20.6.1940. Sold 1947, renamed 'Southern Briar'.

CYCLAMEN Drifter requis. 1915-19.

CYCLOPS 6th Rate 28, 603bm, 120 x 34 ft. Menetone, Limehouse 31.7.1779. Troopship 3.1800. Sold 1.9.1814.

CYCLOPS Wood pad. frigate, 1,195bm,

190 x 37½ ft, 2-98pdr, 4-68 pdr. Pembroke Dock 10.7.1839. Sold 26.1.1864 Castle.

CYCLOPS Coast defence turrent ship 3,480 tons, 225 x 45 ft, 4-10in. Green, Blackwall 18.7.1871. Sold 7.7.1903.

CYCLOPS (ex-Indrabarah) Repair ship 11,300 tons, 460 x 55 ft, 10-3 pdr. Laing, Sunderland 27.10.1905. Arrived 29.6.47 Cashmore, Newport to BU.

CYDNUS 5th Rate 38 (red pine-built), 1,080bm, 150 x 40½ ft. Wigram, Wells & Green, Blackwall 17.4.1813. BU 2.1816 at Portsmouth.

CYGNET Pink 3, 30bm, 1-2pdr, 2-1½pdr. Built 1585. Condemned 1603.

CYGNET 10-gun ship, 233bm. Dunkirk privateer (captured?) purchased 1643. Sold 1654.

CYGNET Sloop 8, 58bm. Chatham DY 1657. Sold 1664.

CYGNET Survey vessel. Purchased 9.1684. Foundered 1687 off Madagascar.

CYGNET Fireship 8, 100bm. Purchased 1688. Captured 20.9.1693 by the French.

CYGNET Sloop 18, 386bm, 111 x 28½ ft, 18-6pdr. French GUIRLANDE captured 7.1758. Sold 1768 in S. Carolina.

CYGNET Sloop 14, 301bm, 97 x 27 ft. Portsmouth DY 24.1.1776. Sold 8.1802.

CYGNET Sloop 16, 365 bm, 106 x 28ft. Palmer, Yarmouth 6.9.1804. Wrecked 7.3.1815 in the Courantine river, Guiana.

CYGNET Brig-sloop 10, 'Cherokee' class, 237bm. Portsmouth DY 11.5.1819. Sold 6.8.1835.

CYGNET Brig 8, 359bm, 95 x 30½ ft, 8-18pdr. Woolwich DY 6.4.1840. Renamed WV.30, coastguard 5.1863. BU completed 3.1.1877 at Portsmouth.

CYGNET Wood S. gunvessel, 428bm, 145 x 25½ ft, 1-68pdr, 4-24pdr howitzers. Wigram, Northam 6.6.1860. BU 8.1868 at Portsmouth.

CYGNET Compos. S. gunboat 455 tons, 125 x 23½ ft, 2-64pdr MLR, 2-20pdr. Doxford 30.5.1874. BU 1889.

CYGNET Destroyer 355 tons, 210 x 19½ ft, 1-12pdr, 5-6pdr, 2-TT. Thornycroft, Chiswick 8.1.1898. Sold 29.4.1920 Ward, Rainham.

CYGNET Destroyer 1,375 tons, 318 x 33 ft, 4-4.7in, 8-TT. Vickers Armstrong, Barrow 29.9.1931. Renamed ST

LAURENT (RCN) 17.2.37. Sold 1947.

CYGNET Sloop 1,350 tons, 283 x 38½ ft, 6-4in, 12-20mm. Cammell Laird 28.7.1942. arrived 16.3.56 Rosyth to BU.

CYGNET Two Trawlers requis. WW.I.

CYNTHIA Sloop 18, 410bm, 113 x 29 ft. Wells, Deptford 23.2.1796. BU 10.1809 at Chatham.

CYNTHIA Sloop 16 listed 1810 to 1815.

CYNTHIA Packet brig 6, 232bm, 87 x 25 ft. Purchased 1826. Wrecked 6.6.1827 at Barbados.

CYNTHIA Wood S. sloop, 669bm, 160 x 30 ft. Devonport DY. Laid down 2.12.1861, cancelled 12.12.1863.

CYNTHIA Destroyer 355 tons, 210 x 19½ ft, 1-12pdr, 5-6pdr, 2-TT. Thornycroft, Chiswick 3.9.1898. Sold 29.4.1920 Ward, Rainham.

CYNTHIA Minesweeper, 'Catherine' class. Assoc. SB, Seattle 25.1.1943. To the RN 7.12.43 on lend-lease. Returned 20.1.47 to the USN.

CYRENE 6th Rate 20, 457bm, 115½ x 30 ft. Chapman, Bideford 4.6.1814. Sold 4.1828 at Bombay.

CYRUS Transport 10, 461bm, 111 x 30½ ft. Purchased 1771. Lost 22.4.1786 at Barbados.

CYRUS 6th Rate 20, 464bm, 116 x 30 ft. Courtney, Chester 26.8.1813. Sold 23.5.1823 Bennet & Son.

CYRUS Mine destructor 3980 tons Scotts 12.10.1943. Wrecked 5.12.44 in Seine Bay.

CZAREVITCH Troopship (RIM) 1,990 tons, 185 x 32 ft. Sunderland 1866. Sold circa 1895.

'D' class submarines. 550 tons, 150 x 22½ ft. 1-12pdr, 3-TT.

D.1 Vickers 16.5.1908. Sunk 23.10.18. as a target.

D.2 Vickers 25.5.10. Sunk 25.11.14 by German patrol craft off Wester Eems.

D.3 Vickers 17.10.10. Sunk 15.3.18 by accident by a French airship in the Channel.

D.4 Vickers 27.5.11. Sold 17.12.21. H.Pounds, Portsmouth.

D.5 Vickers 28.8.11. Sunk 3.11.14. by mine. North Sea.

D.6 Vickers 23.10.11 Sunk 28.6.18. by 'UB.73' off the north coast of Ireland.

D.7 Chatham DY 14.1.11. Sold 19.12.21 H.Pounds.

D.8 Chatham DY 23.9.11. Sold 19.12.21. H.Pounds.

D.9 Chatham DY. Launched 9.11.12. as E.1.

D.10 Chatham DY. Launched 23.11.12 as E.2

DACRES (ex-USS DUFFY) Frigate, DE 'Captain' Class. Boston N.Yd 19.5.1943 on lend-lease. Returned 1.46 to the USN.

DAEDALUS 5th Rate 32, 703bm, 126 x 38ft. Fisher Liverpool 20.5.1780. Lent Trinity House 10.1803 to 1806 as Hulk. BU. 7.1811 at Sheerness.

DAEDALUS 5th Rate 38, 1,094bm, 153 x 40 ft. French, ex-Venetian CORONA captured 13.3.1811 at Lissa. Wrecked 2.7.1813 off Ceylon.

DAEDALUS 5th Rate 46, 1,083bm, 1,447 tons, 152 x 40½ ft Sheerness DY (ex-Deptford DY) 2.5.1826. Reduced to 20 guns 1843; RNR drill ship 1862. Sold 14.9.1911 J.B.Garnham.

DAEDALUS (see THUNDERBOLT of 1856)

DAEDALUS Light Crusier 4,765 tons, 445 x 46½ ft, 6-6in, 2-3in. Armstrong. Ordered 3.1918, cancelled 11.18.

DAFFODIL Sloop, 'Acacia' class. Scotts 17.8.1915. Sold 22.2.35 Cashmore, Newport.

DAFFODIL Corvette, 'Flower' class Lewis 3.9.1940. renamed DIANELLA 26.10.40. Arrived 24.6.47 at Portaferry to BU.

DAFFODIL. Two Drifters and a Ferry WW.1. Ferry WW.II

DAGGER (see OCEANWAY)

DAGGER Destroyer 1,980 tons, 341½ x 38 ft, 6-4in, 10-TT. Yarrow. Laid down 7.3.1945, cancelled 10.45.

DAHLIA Sloop, 'Acacia' class. Barclay Curle 21.3.1915. RNVR drill ship 1923. Sold 2.7.32 Metal Industries, Charlestown.

DAHLIA Corvette, Flower' class Lewis 31.10.1940. Arrived 20.10.48 Howells, Gelleswick Bay to BU.

DAHLIA Trawler. Requis. 1915-18.

DAINTY (ex-REPENTANCE renamed 1589) Discovery Ship. Captured 1594 by the Spanish.

DAINTY Pink 4, in service 1645.

DAINTY Destroyer 1,375 tons, 318 x 33 ft, 4-4.7in, 1-3in, 8-TT. Fairfield

3.5.1932. Sunk 24.2.41 by air attack off Tobruk.

DAINTY Destroyer 2,610 tons, 366 x 43 ft, 6-4.5in, 10-TT. White 16.8.1950. Sold 1.1.71, BU at Cairnryan.

DAINTY Rescue tug. 1918-22.

DAISY Pink 4, 4-6pdr, In service in 1599.

DAISY Wood S. gunboat, 'Cheerful' class. Westbrook, Blackwall 20.3.1856. BU 1.1869 at Haslar.

DAISY Survey vessel 510 tons, 125 x 22½ ft. Duthie, Torry 1911 and purchased on stocks 14.2.11. Sold 3.20 Newfoundland Government.

DAISY 5 Drifters WW.I. 3 Drifters WW.II.

DAKINS Frigate, TE 'Captain' class. Bethlehem, Hingham 18.9.1943 on lend-lease. Returned 1946 to the USN. BU 1.47 in Holland.

DALHOUSIE Troopship (Indian), 1.060 bm. Built 1858. In service in 1875.

DALHOUSIE Troopship (RIM) 1,960 tons, 239 x 36ft, 6-6pdr. Caird 5.6.1886.

DALRYMPLE (see LUCE BAY)

DALSWINTON Coastal M/S, 'Ton' class. White, Southampton 24.9.1953. Renamed MONTROSE 1962. Sold Pounds 11.11.72.

DAME DE GRACE Gunvessel 4, 87bm. French, Captured 18.3.1799 on the Coast of Syria. Retaken and Sunk by the French 8.5.1799.

DAMERHAM Inshore M/S, 'Ham' class. Brooke Marine 15.6.1953. Sold 27.9.66 at Singapore.

DAMPIER (see HERNE BAY)

DANAE 5th Rate 38, 941bm, 147½ x 38ft. French, captured 28.3.1759 by SOUTHAMPTON and MELAMPE. BU Completed 14.6.1771 at Chatham.

DANAE 5th Rate 32, 689bm, 129½ x 35 ft. French, Captured when stranded and abandoned near St Malo, 13.5.1779. Sold 10.1797.

DANAE 6th Rate 20, 508bm, 119 x 31 ft, 20-32pdr carr., 12-12pdr carr., 2-6pdr. French VAILLANTE captured 7.8.1798 by INDEFATIGABLE in the Bay of Biscay. Taken into Brest by her mutinous crew 14.3.1800 and handed over to the French 17.3.1800.

DANAE S Corvette, 1.287bm, 1.760 tons, 212 x36ft, 2-7in, 4-6pdr. Portsmouth DY 21.5.1867. Lent War Dept 1886 as a hulk. Sold 15.5.1906.

DANAE Light cruiser 4,650 tons, 445 x 46½ ft, 6-6in, 2-3in. Armstrong

26.1.1918. Lent Polish navy 4.10.44 to 28.9.46 as CONRAD. Sold 22.1.48, arrived 27.3.48 Ward, Barrow to BU.

DANAE (ex-VIMIERA renamed 3.1945) Destroyer 2,610 tons, 366 x 43 ft, 6-4.5in, 6-40mm, 10-TT. Cammell Laird. Cancelled 1.46.

DANAE Frigate, 'Leander' class. Devonport DY 21.10.1965.

DANGEREUSE Gunvessel 6. French, captured 18.3.1799 on the Coast of Syria. Sold 1800.

DANIEL Fireship 6, 160bm. Purchased 1666. Sold 1667.

DANNEMARK 3rd Rate 74, 1,836bm. Danish, captured 7.9.1807 at Copenhagen. Sold 14.12.1815. (was to have been renamed MARATHON)

DANUBE Wood Pad. Vessel, 110bm. Purchased 8.1854 at Constantinople. sold 23.7.1856.

DANUBE Wood S. gunboat, 'Britomart' class, Haslar, Portsmouth. Ordered 1861, cancelled 12.12.1863.

DANUBE Tug WW.I, 3 Tugs WW.II.

DAPHNE 6th Rate 20. 429bm, 108 x 30ft. Woolwich DY 21.3.1776. Sold 5.1802. (was in French hands 19.1.95 to 29.12.97.)

DAPHNE 6th Rate 24, 574bm 118 x 33½ft, 8-18pdr carr., 22-9pdr, 2-6pdr. Dutch SIRENE captured 17.8.1796. Renamed LAUREL. 16.2.1798, prison ship. Sold 7.6.1821 Holmes, Portsea to BU.

DAPHNE 6th Rate 22, 540bm, 118½ x 31½ ft. Davy, Topsham 2.7.1806. Sold 15.2.1816.

DAPHNE 6th Rate 28, 500bm, 114 x 32ft. Plymouth DY. Ordered 1820, cancelled 1832.

DAPHNE Corvette 18, 726bm, 120 x 38ft, 18-32pdr. Pembroke Dock 6.8.1838. Sold 7.10.1864 Castle.

DAPHNE Wood S, Sloop, 1,081bm, 1,574 tons, 187 x 36 ft. Pembroke Dock 23.10.1866. Sold 7.11.1882.

DAPHNE Sloop, 1,140 tons, 195 x 28 ft, 8-5in. Sheerness DY 29.5.1888. sold 2.1904

DAPHNE Sloop, 'Acacia' class. Barclay Curle 19.5.1915. Sold 15.1.23. Unity S.Bkg Co.

DAPHNE, DY. Tug 1968.

DAPPER Gun-brig 12, 185bm, 85 x 22½ ft, 10-18pdr carr., 2-12pdr. Adams, Chapel 12.1805. Sold 29.9.1814.

DAPPER Wood S. Gunboat, 'Dapper' class, Green, Blackwall 31.3.1855. Training hulk 1885; Cooking depot 1897 and renamed YC.37 in 1909. Sold 10.5.22 Mr Perry.

DAPPER Salvage ship. 1915 - 23 and 1940 - 46.

DARING Gun-brig 12, 178bm, 80 x 23 ft, 12-18pdr carr. Bailey, Ipswich 10.1804. Destroyed 7.2.1813 at Sierra Leone to avoid capture by the French.

DARING Sloop 319 bm. ordered Sheerness DY 14.5.1840 and cancelled 4.9.1843.

DARING Brig 12, 426bm, 104 x 31½ ft, 10-32pdr, 2-18pdr. Portsmouth DY 2.4.1844 (originally ordered at Sheerness) Sold 7.10.1864 Castle, Charlton.

DARING (see FLYING FISH of 1873)

DARING Compos. S. sloop 840 tons, 160 x 31½ ft, 2-7in, 2-64pdr. Wigram, Blackwall 4.2.1874. Sold 8.1889 J. Cohen.

DARING Destroyer 275 tons, 185 x 19 ft, 2-12pdr, 3-6pdr, 3-TT. Thornycroft, Chiswick 25.11.1893. Sold 10.4.1912.

DARING (see LANCE)

DARING Light cruiser 4,765 tons, 445 x 46½ ft, 6-6in, 2-3in. Armstrong. Ordered 3.1918, cancelled 11.18.

DARING Destroyer 1,375 tons, 318 x 33 ft, 4-4.7in 1-3in, 8-TT. Thornycroft 7.4.1932. Sunk 18.2.40 by 'U.23' off Duncansby Head.

DARING Destroyer 2.610 tons, 366 x 43 ft, 6-4.5in, 6-40mm, 10-TT. Swan Hunter 10.8.1949. Sold 26.5.71, arrived Blyth 15.6.71.

DARLASTON Coastal M/S, 'Ton' class. Cook, Welton & Gemmell 25.9.1953. To Malaysian navy 24.5.60 as MAHAMIRU.

DARSHAM Inshore M/S, 'Ham' class. Jones, Buckie 19.11.1952. Sold 1.4.66 at Singapore.

DART Sloop 28, 386bm, 129 x 30 ft, 28-32pdr carr. Hobbs, Redbridge 1796. BU 1809 in Barbados.

DART Lugger 8, French, ex-British privateer brig, captured 29.6.1803 by APOLLO in the Bay of Biscay. Sold 3.1808.

DART Cutter 10, 49bm, 47 x 16 ft. Deptford 1810. Foundered 12.1813.

DART Brigantine 3, 319bm, 90 x 29½ ft, 3-32pdr. Sheerness DY 1847. Renamed WV.26 on 25.5.1863. BU completed 9.1.1875 at Chatham.

DART Wood S. gunvessel, 'Philomel' class. Mare, Blackwall 10.3.1860. Renamed KANGAROO 1.4.1882. BU in 12.1884.

DART (ex-Colonial Office yacht *Cruiser*) Survey ship 470 tons, 133x 25 ft, 2 guns. Transferred 3.1882. Lent NSW government 1904 as training ship. Sold 9.5.12 at Sydney.

DART (see PC.73)

DART (see GODETIA)

DART Frigate, 'River' class. Blyth DD 10.10.1942. Sold 11.56, BU Cashmore, Newport.

DART Tug requis. 1941-45

DARTINGTON Coastal M/S, 'Ton' class. Philip 2.10.1956. Sold 12.2.70 at Hong Kong to BU.

DARTMOOR Minesweeper, early 'Hunt' class. Dunlop Bremner 30.3.1917. Sold 21.2.23 Alloa, Charlestown; arrived 22.4.23.

DARTMOUTH 22-gun ship, 260bm. Portsmouth 1655. Fireship 1688; 5th Rate 1689. Wrecked 9.10.1690 on the Isle of Mull.

DARTMOUTH Fireship 4, 127bm. Captured 1672. Sold 1674.

DARTHMOUTH 4th Rate 48, 614bm, 122 x 34 ft. Shish, Rotherhithe 24.7.1693. Captured 4.2.1695 by the French; recaptured 1702 and renamed VIGO. Wrecked 27.11.1703 on the Dutch coast.

DARTMOUTH 4th Rate 48, 681bm, 131½ x 34½ ft. Parker, Southampton 3.3.1698. Rebuilt Woolwich 1741 as 856bm. Sunk 8.10.1747 in action with the Spanish GLORIOSO.

DARTMOUTH 4th Rate 50, 853bm, 134 x 38½ ft. Plymouth DY. Ordered 10.1.1746, cancelled 20.3.1749.

DARTMOUTH 5th Rate 36, 952bm, 145 x 38½ ft. Cook (ex-Tanner), Dartmouth 28.8.1813. Harbour service 7.1831. BU completed 2.11.1854 at Deptford.

DARTMOUTH Wood S. frigate, 2,478bm, 240 x 48 ft. Woolwich DY. Laid down 6.11.1860, cancelled 16.12.1864.

DARTMOUTH 2nd class cruiser 5,250 tons, 430 x 48½ ft, 8-6in, 4-3 pdr. Vickers 14.12.1910. Sold 13.12.30. Metal Industries to BU.

DARTMOUTH Trawler requis. 1917-19.

DARWIN Destroyer (RAN) 3370 tons. Projected 1969 and cancelled

DARWIN Frigate (RAN) 2100 tons. Todd, Seattle 26.3.1982

DASHER Sloop 18, 402bm, 100 x 30 ft. Goodrich, Bermuda 1797. Convict hulk in 1832. BU 3.1838.

DASHER Wood pad. packet 260bm, 357 tons, 120 x 22 ft, 1-12pdr. Chatham DY 5.12.1837. Sold 23.3.1885 Castle to BU.

DASHER Destroyer 290 tons, 190 x 18½ ft, 1-12pdr, 5-6pdr, 2-TT. Yar-

row, Poplar 28.11.1894. Sold
14.5.1912 King & Sons.

DASHER (ex-*Rio de Janeiro*)Escort carrier 8,200 tons, 468½ x 66 ft, 3-4in, 15-20mm, 15-A/C. Sun SB Co 12.4.1941; to RN 2.7.42 on lend-lease. Lost 27.3.43 by petrol fire and explosion south of the Cumbraes.

DASHER Patrol boat 43. tons. Watercraft 1985.

DATE TREE 5th Rate. Captured 1678 from the Algerines. Foundered 1679.

DAUNTLESS Sloop 18, 426bm, 109 x 29½ ft. Blunt, Hull 11.1804. Captured 26.5.1807 by the French at Danzig.

DAUNTLESS Sloop 18, 423bm, 109 x 29½ ft. Deptford DY 20.12.1808. Sold 27.1.1825.

DAUNTLESS Wood S.frigate, 1,453bm, 210 x 40 ft, 4-10in, 2-68pdr, 18-32pdr. Portsmouth DY 5.1.1847. Lengthened 1850 to 219½ ft, 1,575bm. Sold 1.5.1885.

DAUNTLESS Light cruiser 4,650 tons, 445 x 46½ ft, 6-6in, 2-3in. Palmer 10.4.1918. BU 4.46 Ward, Inverkeithing.

DAUNTLESS Tug requis. 1915-18.

DAUPHIN ROYAL Schooner. Purchased 1796 in the W.Indies. Listed in 1801.

DAUPHIN Corvette (RCN), 'Flower' class. Vickers, Montreal 24.10.1940. Sold 1947, renamed *Cortes*.

DAVENHAM Inshore M/S, 'Ham' class. Weatherhead, Cockenzie 23.3.1953. Sold at Singapore 1.4.66.

DAVID 20-gun ship, 76bm. Scots navy, captured 1685. Sold 1685.

DAWLISH (see DERBY)

DAWSON Corvette (RCN), 'Flower' class. Victoria Mcy Co 8.2.1941. Foundered 22.3.46 at Hamilton, Ont.

DEALE Dogger 3. Dutch, captured 1672. Sold 1674.

DEALE Yacht 4, 28bm. Woolwich DY 1673. Sold 1686.

DEALE CASTLE 6th Rate 24, 240bm, 92 x 24 ft. Deptford 1697. Captured 3.7.1706 by the French off Dunkirk.

DEALE CASTLE 6th Rate 24, 272bm, 98 x 26½ ft. Burchett, Rotherhithe 9.9.1706. Rebuilt Sheerness 1727 as 375bm. Sold 14.8.1746.

DEALE CASTLE 6th Rate 24, 506bm, 112 x 32 ft. Golightly, Liverpool 2.12.1746. BU completed 30.7.1754 at Chatham.

DEALE CASTLE 6th Rate 20, 400bm, 107½ x 29 ft. Perry, Blackwall 20.1.1756. Foundered 11.10.1780 in a hurricane near Puerto Rico.

DEANE Frigate, TE 'Captain' class. Bethlehem, Hingham 25.9.1943 on lend-lease. Returned 3.46 to the USN.

DECADE 5th Rate 36, 915bm, 143½ x 38 ft. French, captured 24.8.1798 by MAGNANIME and NAIAD off Cape Finisterre. Sold 21.2.1811.

DECCAN Minesweeper (RIN), TE 'Bangor' class. Garden Reach 24.4.1944. Sold circa 1949, renamed *Kennery* pilot vessel.

DECIBEL (ex-*Bournemouth Belle*) Experimental tender 131 x 31½ ft. Bolson, Poole 21.11.1953. Sold 8.58 Mercantile.

DECOUVERTE Schooner 8, 165bm, 81½ x 21 ft, 8-12pdr carr. French, captured 30.11.1803 at San Domingo. Sold 1808.

DECOUVERTE (ex-schooner *Eclipse*) Gun-brig 12, 181bm, 80½ x 22½ ft, 10-12pdr carr., 2-6pdr. Purchased 1807. Sold 1816.

DECOY Cutter 10, 203bm. List, Fishbourne 22.3.1810. Captured 22.3.1814 by the French off Calais.

DECOY Wood S. Gunboat, 'Cheerful' class. Pembroke Dock 21.2.1856. BU completed 8.2.1869 at Haslar.

DECOY Compos. S. gunboat, 295bm, 430 tons, 125 x 22½ ft, 2-64pdr ML, 2-20pdr. Pembroke Dock 12.10.1871. Sold 10.1885.

DECOY Destroyer 275 tons, 185 x 19 ft, 1-12pdr, 3-6pdr, 3-TT. Thornycroft, Chiswick 2.8.1894. Sunk 13.8.1904 in collision with ARUN off the Wolf Rock.

DECOY Destroyer 1,375 tons, 318 x 33 ft, 4-4.7in, 1-3in, 8-TT. Thornycroft, Woolston 7.6.1932. Renamed KOOTENAY (RCN) 12.4.43. Sold 28.1.46.

DECOY Destroyer 2,610 tons, 366 x 43 ft, 6-4.5in, 6-40mm, 10-TT. Vickers Armstrong, Tyne. Ordered 1945, cancelled 1.46.

DECOY (ex-DRAGON renamed 6.46) Destroyer 2,610 tons, 366 x 43 ft, 6-4.5in, 6-40mm, 10-TT. Yarrow 29.3.49 Sold Peru in 12.69, renamed FERRE.

DEDAIGNEUSE 5th Rate 36, 987bm, 144 x 37½ ft, 12-24pdr carr., 26-12pdr, 4-6pdr. French, captured 28.1.1801 by three frigates off the coast of Portugal. Sold 21.5.1823.

DEE 6th Rate 20, 447bm, 108 x 30½ ft. Bailey, Ipswich 5.5.1814. Sold 22.7.1819 Pitman.

DEE Brig-Sloop 10, 'Cherokee' class.

Woolwich DY. Laid down 9.1824, renamed AFRICAN paddle vessel 5.1825 and launched 30.8.1825. BU 12.1862.

DEE Wood paddle vessel, 704bm, 167 x 30½ ft. Woolwich DY 5.4.1832. Troopship 1855; storeship 1868. BU 1871 Sheerness.

DEE Iron S. gunboat 363 tons, 110 x 34 ft, 3-64pdr. Palmer 4.4.1877. Sold 10.7.1902.

DEE Destroyer 545 tons, 225 x 23½ ft, 1-12pdr, 5-6pdr (rearmed 1907 with 4-12pdr), 2-TT. Palmer 10.9.1903. Sold 23.7.19 Ward, Briton Ferry.

DEE (see DROXFORD)

DEE (see BECKFORD)

DEE Trawler. 1920-46 (ex-BATTLEAXE)

DEEPWATER Diving tender 1,200 tons, 250 x 38 ft. German W. HOLTZAPFEL seized 8.1945. Arrived 13.9.60 at Northam to BU.

DEFENCE 10-gun ship 160bm. Purchased 1588. Listed to 1599.

DEFENCE 3rd Rate 74, 1,603bm, 168½ x 47 ft. Plymouth DY 31.3.1763. Wrecked 24.12.1811 on the coast of Jutland.

DEFENCE (ex-MARATHON renamed 1812) 3rd Rate 74, 1,754bm, 176 x 48½ ft. Chatham DY 25.4.1815. Convict ship 1849. Burnt by accident 14.7.1857; wreck BU 1.1858.

DEFENCE Iron S. ship, 3,270bm, 6,270 tons, 280 x 54 ft, 6-110pdr, 10-68pdr. Palmer 24.4.1861. Renamed INDUS 6.1898, training ship; hulk 1922. Arrived 16.8.35 at Cattedown, Plymouth to BU.

DEFENCE Armoured cruiser 14,600 tons, 490 x 74½ ft, 4-9.2in, 10-7.5in, 14-12pdr. Pembroke Dock 24.4.1907. Sunk 31.5.16 at Jutland.

DEFENCE Cruiser 9,550 tons, 538 x 64 ft, 4-6in, 6-3in. Scotts 2.9.1944. Renamed LION 8.10.57. Sold Ward 12.2.75, BU at Inverkeithing.

DEFENDER (Gunboat No 21) Gunvessel 12, 168bm, 76 x 22½ ft, 2-24 pdr, 10-18pdr carr. Hill, Limehouse 21.5.1797. Last listed 1802.

DEFENDER Gun-brig 14, 179bm, 80 x 22½ ft. Courtney, Chester 28.7.1804. Wrecked 14.12.1809 off Folkestone.

DEFENDER Lugger 8, 81bm, 8-12pdr carr. French privateer BONNE MARSEILLE captured 12.1809 by ROYALIST. Sold 1.9.1814.

DEFENDER Destroyer 762 tons, 240 x 25½ ft, 2-4in, 2-12pdr, 2-TT. Denny 30.8.1911. Sold 4.11.21 Rees, Llanelly.

DEFENDER Destroyer 1,375 tons, 318 x 33 ft, 4-4.7in, 1-3in, 8-TT. Vickers Armstrong, Barrow 7.4.1932. Sank in tow 11.7.41 after being bombed by Italian aircraft off Sidi Barani.

DEFENDER (ex-DOGSTAR renamed 6.46) Destroyer 2,610 tons, 366 x 43 ft, 6-4.5in, 6-40mm, 10-TT. Stephen 29.7.50. Sold White, St Davids, 10.5.72 to BU.

DEFIANCE Pinnace 8. In the fleet against the Armada in 1588; probably a hired vessel.

DEFIANCE Galleon 46, 500bm, 14-18pdr, 14-9pdr, 6-6pdr, 12 light guns. Built at Deptford 1590. Rebuilt Woolwich 1614 as 700bm, 34 guns. Sold 1650.

DEFIANCE 10-gun ship (Royalist). Captured 2.1652 from Parliamentarians and foundered 9.1652 off Anegada, W. Indies.

DEFIANCE 3rd Rate 66, 890bm. Johnson & Castle, Deptford 1666. Burnt 6.12.1668 by accident at Chatham.

DEFIANCE 3rd Rate 64, 898bm, 144 x 38 ft. Chatham DY 1675. Rebuilt Woolwich 1695; made a 4th Rate 1716; hulk 1743. BU 6.1749 at Chatham.

DEFIANCE Sloop in service 1671 to 1678.

DEFIANCE 4th Rate 69, 1,136 bm, 147½ x 42½ ft. West, Deptford 12.10.1744. Sold 10.4.1766.

DEFIANCE Sloop (Indian). Bombay DY 1766.

DEFIANCE 3rd Rate 64, 1,369bm, 159 x 44 ft. Woolwich DY 31.8.1772. Wrecked 18.2.1780 off the Savannah.

DEFIANCE 3rd Rate 74, 1,685bm, 169 x 47½ ft. Randall, Rotherhithe 10.12.1783. Prison ship 12.1813. BU 5.1817.

DEFIANCE Gunvessel 4, 71bm, 70 x 15 ft. Purchased 4.1794. Sold 10.1797.

DEFIANCE Screw 2nd Rate 81, 3,475bm, 5,270 tons, 255 x 56 ft, 1-110pdr, 34-8in, 4-70pdr, 10-40pdr, 32-32pdr. Pembroke Dock 27.3.1861. Torpedo school ship 26.11.1884. Sold 26.6.1931 S. Castle, Millbay, Plymouth.

For the various ships renamed DEFIANCE as torpedo school ships, see PERSEUS of 1861, SPARTAN of 1891, CLEOPATRA of 1878, INCONSTANT of 1868, ANDROMEDA of 1897 and VULCAN of 1889.

DEGO 3rd Rate 64. French, ex-Maltese ZACHARI captured 20.9.1800. Sold in 1802 at Malta.

DELAWARE 6th Rate 28, 563bm, 118 x

33 ft, 28-9pdr. American, captured 27.9.1777 by the British army in the Delaware and purchased 4.1778. Sold 14.4.1783.

DELFT 4-gun ship, 288bm. Dutch, captured 1665. Sold 1668.

DELFT 3rd Rate 64, 1,266bm, 157 x 43 ft. Dutch HERCULES captured 11.10.1797 at Camperdown. Powder hulk 8.1802. Sunk 9.1822 as a breakwater at Harwich.

DELHI (see EMPEROR of INDIA)

DELHI Light cruiser 4,650 tons, 445 x 46½ ft, 6-6in, 3-3in. Armstrong 23.8.1918. A/A ship 1942. Arrived 5.3.48 Cashmore, Newport to BU.

DELHI (see ACHILLES of 1932)

DELIGHT Discovery vessel, 120bm. Wrecked 1583.

DELIGHT Hoy 4, 84bm. Purchased 1686. Sold 1713 at Portsmouth.

DELIGHT 6th Rate 14, 163bm, 78 x 22 ft. Woolwich DY 18.10.1709. Sold 8.1.1712.

DELIGHT Sloop 14, 307bm, 97 x 27 ft. Graves, Limehouse 7.11.1778. Foundered 25.1.1781 in N. America.

DELIGHT Sloop 18, 336bm, 97½ x 28½ ft, 18-24pdr carr. French SANS PAREIL captured 20.1.1801 by MERCURY off Sardinia. Sold 4.1805.

DELIGHT Brig-Sloop 16, 300bm, 97 x 28 ft. Thorn, Fremington 6.1806. Captured 31.1.1808 by the French when stranded on the coast of Calabria.

DELIGHT Sloop 18, 340bm. French FRIEDLAND captured by STANDARD off Cape Blanco 26.3.1808. Sold 1.9.1814.

DELIGHT Brig-sloop 10, 'Cherokee' class, 237bm. Portsmouth DY 10.5.1819. Wrecked 23.2.1824 at Mauritius.

DELIGHT Brig-sloop 10, 'Cherokee' class, 231bm. Chatham DY 27.11.1829. Sold 30.4.1844.

DELIGHT Wood S. gunboat, Albacore' class. Wigram, Blackwall 15.3.1856. Sold 11.1867 at Halifax, renamed *M.A. Starr.*

DELIGHT Destroyer 1,375 tons, 318 x 33 ft, 4-4.7in, 1-3in, 8-TT. Fairfield 2.6.1932. Sunk 29.7.40 by air attack off Portland.

DELIGHT Destroyer 2,610 tons, 366 x 43 ft, 6-4.5in, 6-40mm, 10-TT. Vickers Armstrong, Tyne. Ordered 1945, cancelled 1.46.

DELIGHT (ex-DISDAIN renamed 6.1946) Destroyer 2,610 tons, 366 x 43 ft, 6-4.5in, 6-40mm, 10-TT. Fairfield 21.12.50. Sold Ward 12.9.70,

BU at Inverkeithing.

DELORAINE Minesweeper (RAN), 'Bathurst' class. Morts Dk 26.7.1941. Sold 8.8.56 to BU.

DELPHINEN Brig-sloop 16, 306bm, 97 x 27½ ft, 14-24dpr carr., 2-6pdr. Danish, captured 7.9.1807 at Copenhagen. Wrecked 4.8.1808 on the Dutch coast. (Was to have been renamed MONDOVI.)

DELPHINIUM Sloop, 'Arabis' class. Napier & Miller 23.12.1915. Sold 13.10.33 Rees, Llanelly.

DELPHINIUM Corvette, 'Flower' class. Robb 6.6.1940. Sold 2.49; BU Hayes, Pembroke Dock.

DEMERARA Schooner 6, 106bm. Purchased 1804. Captured 14.7.1804 by the French privateer GRAND-DECIDE in the W. Indies.

DEMERARA Brig-sloop 18, circa 220bm. French privateer COSMOPOLI captured 1806 and presented by the inhabitants of Demerara in 1808. Listed to 1813.

DEMIRHISAR Destroyer 1,360 tons, 312 x 33 ft, 4-4in, 8-TT. Turkish ship launched Denny 1941, commissioned in the RN 1.42 for passage out to Turkey. Returned Turkish navy 3.42.

DEMON destroyer 2,610 tons, 366 x 43 ft, 6-4.5in, 6-40mm, 10-TT. Swan Hunter. Ordered 3.1945, cancelled 1.46.

DENBIGH CASTLE Corvette, 'Castle' class. Lewis 5.8.1944. Damaged 13.2.45 by 'U.992' and grounded in Kola Inlet, N. Russia.

DENNIS Discovery vessel lost in the Arctic 1578.

DENNIS Storeship, 100bm, 57 x 20 ft. Plymouth DY 15.12.1743. Sold 30.8.1833.

DEPENDENCE Galley 7, 129bm, 1-24pdr, 6-4pdr. Purchased 12.1776 in N. America. Sold 1786.

DEPTFORD Sloop 4. Deptford 1652. Last listed 1659.

DEPTFORD Ketch 10, 89bm. Deptford 1665. Wrecked 26.8.1689 on the coast of Virginia.

DEPTFORD 4th Rate 50, 616bm, 125 x 33½ ft. Woolwich DY 1687. Rebuilt Woolwich DY 1700 as 667bm; rebuilt 1719 as 710bm. Sold per A.O. dated 3.5.1726.

DEPTFORD TRANSPORT Storeship hoy, 58bm, 53 x 16 ft. Deptford DY 3.1702. Sold .6.1713.

DEPTFORD 4th Rate 60, 951bm, 146 x 39 ft. Deptford DY 22.8.1732. 50 guns 1752. Sold 23.6.1767.

DEPTFORD Storeship 24, 678bm, 124 x

35½ ft, 4-12pdr, 16-9pdr, 4-6pdr. Deptford DY 29.4.1735. BU 5.1756.

DEPTFORD PRIZE Sloop, 147bm, 74 x 21½ ft. Spanish, captured off Ushant 23.5.1740. Sold 20.11.1744.

DEPTFORD Tender 12, 158bm, 64 x 21ft. Muddle, Gillingham 8.1781. Sold 17.2.1863.

DEPTFORD Transport, 198bm, 80½ x 24 ft. Batson, Limehouse 3.1784. Presented 24.8.1816 to Hibernian Marine Society.

DEPTFORD Transport brig 6. Woolcombe, River Thames 2.1788. Purchased 25.2.1788. Became mooring lighter and BU 6.1862 at Chatham.

DEPTFORD Sloop 990 tons, 250 x 36 ft, 2-4.7in, 1-3in. Chatham DY 5.2.1935. Sold 8.3.48; BU Ward, Milford Haven.

DERBY (ex-DAWLISH renamed 1918) Minesweeper, later 'Hunt' class, Clyde SB 9.8.1918. Sold 7.46 at Gibraltar; BU in Spain.

DERBY HAVEN (ex-LOCH ASSYNT renamed 1944) Depot ship 1,650 tons 286 x 38½ ft, 2-4in, 6-20mm. Swan Hunter 14.12.1944. To Persian navy 30.7.49 as BABR.

DERG Frigate, 'River' class. Robb 7.1.1943. renamed WESSEX 1951 AS RNVR drill ship then renamed CAMBRIA. Arrived 9.60 Cashmore, Newport to BU.

DERRINGTON Coastal M/S, 'Ton' class. Thonycroft 22.12.1953. Renamed KILLIECRANKIE 1955. to 1960. Sold in 2.71, BU Canvey Is.

DE RUYTER 3rd Rate 64, 1,264bm, 151 x 44 ft. Dutch, captured 30.8.1799 in the Texel. Harbour service 1800. Wrecked in a hurricane 3.9.1804 at Antigua.

DERVISH Destroyer 2,610 tons, 366 x 43 ft, 6-4.5in, 6-40mm, 10-TT. White Ordered 3.1945, cancelled 1.46.

DERVISH Trawler requis. 1940-40.

DERWENT Brig-sloop 16, 'Cruiser' class, 382bm. Blackburn, Turnchapel 23.5.1807. Sold 7.3.1817.

DERWENT Destroyer 555 tons, 222 x 23½ ft, 1-12pdr, 5-6pdr(4-12pdr 1907), 2-TT. Hawthorn 14.2.19903. Sunk 2.5.17 by mine off Le Havre.

DERWENT (see HUON)

DERWENT Destroyer, 'Hunt' class type III. Vickers Armstrong, Barrow 22.8.1941. Sold 11.46, BU Ward, Penryn in 2.47.

DERWENT Frigate (RAN) 2,144 tons, 360 x 41 ft, 2-4.5in Williamstown DY 17.4.1961.

DERWENT Trawler requis. 1917-199.

Trawler 1920-23.

DESFORD Seaward defence boat, 'Ford' class. Vosper 3.6.1954. To Ceylon navy 1955 as KOTIYA.

DESIRE Discovery vessel in service 1583 to 1593.

DESIRE Ketch 6, 63/84bm. Built 1616. Listed to 1628.

DESIRE Destroyer 2,610 tons, 366 x 46 ft, 6-4.5mm, 10-TT. Hawthorn Leslie. Ordered 3.1945, cancelled 1.46.

DESIRE Tug and Drifter requis. W.W.I.

DESIREE 5th Rate 36, 1,015bm, 149 x 39 ft, 10-32pdr carr., 26-18pdr, 4-9pdr. French, captured 8.7.1800 by DART in Dunkirk Roads. Sold 28.8.1832 to BU at Rotherhithe.

DESIREE Trawler requis. 1914-19 and 1939-41.

DESPATCH Brigantine 2, 77bm, 63½ x 17ft. Deptford 10.5.1691. Sold 10.4.1712.

DESPATCH Sloop 14, 269bm, 91 x 26 ft. Stow & Bartlett, Shoreham 30.12.1745. Sold 6.1763.

DISPATCH Sloop 14. Foundered 31.8.1772 in a hurricane in the W. Indies. (A sloop sold 27.10.1773 may be this vessel salved.)

DISPATCH Sloop 6. Captured 12.7.1776 by American privateer TYRANNICIDE. (May be a hired vessel.)

DESPATCH (see CHEROKEE OF 1774)

DISPATCH Sloop 16, 300bm, 90½ x 26½ ft. Deptford DY 10.2.1777. Capsized 8.12.1778 in the St Lawrence.

DISPATCH Schooner 8. Purchased in Jamaica 16.10.1780. Sold 11.1795.

DESPATCH (see ZEPHYR of 1779)

DISPATCH Sloop, French, captured 1790. Sold 7.8.1801.

DISPATCH Brig-sloop 16(fir-built), 365bm, 96 x 30½ ft. Nicholson, Chatham 19.12.1795. Sold 3.1796 to the Russian navy.

DISPATCH Tender 6 in service 1797 to 1801.

DISPATCH Sloop 14, 238bm, 90½ x 25ft, 16-18pdr carr., 2-6pdr. French privateer INDEFATIGABLE captured 4.1799 by ETHALION Sold 1801.

DISPATCH Brig-sloop 18, 'Cruiser' class, 382bm. Symons, Falmouth 26.5.1804. BU 9.1811.

DISPATCH Brig-sloop 18, 'Cruiser' class, 388 bm. King, Upnor 7.12.1812. Sold 5.1836.

DISPATCH (ex-*Cornwallis*) Brig storeship 6, 172bm, 77 x 23 ft. Transferred from Transport Office circa

1816. Hulk 1820; sheer hulk 1826. Wrecked 12.1846 at Bermuda and ordered to be BU; listed until 1865.

DESPATCH Brig 12, 483bm, 105 x 33½ ft, 12-32pdr. Chatham DY 25.11.1851. Renamed Watch Vessel No 24 (CADMUS) 25.5.1863 Sold 13.5.1901 at Sheerness.

DESPATCH Light cruiser 4,765 tons, 445 x 46½ ft, 6-6in, 2-4in. Fairfield 24.9.1919. Sold 5.4.46. BU at Troon.

DESPATCH Two tank vessels 1869-1905 and 1904, renamed DESPOT 1918-46.

DESPERANTE Schooner 8. In service 1799 to 1811.

DESPERATE Gun-brig 12, 179bm, 80 x 23ft, 12-18pdr. White, Broadstairs 2.1.1805. Mortar brig 1811. Sold 15.12.1814.

DESPERATE Wood S.sloop, 1,038bm, 192 x 34 ft. Pembroke Dock 23.4.1849. BU 8.1865 at Devonport.

DESPERATE Destroyer 340 tons, 210 x 19½ ft, 1-12pdr, 5-6pdr, 2-TT. Thornycroft 15.2.1896. Sold 20.5.1920 Ward, Milford Haven.

DESPERATE Light cruiser 4,765 tons, 445 x 46½ ft, 6-6in, 2-4in. Hawthorn Leslie. Ordered 3.1918, cancelled 11.18.

DESPERATE Destroyer 2,610 tons, 366 x 43 ft, 6-4in, 6-40mm, 10-TT.J.Brown. Ordered 3.1945, cancelled 1.46.

DESTINY 34-gun ship, 460/500bm. Woolwich 1616. Renamed CONVERTINE 1620. Captured 1648 by Royalists and sold 1650 at Lisbon.

DESTINY Two tugs 1942-46 and 1947-64.

DESTRUCTION Mortar vessel 5, 77bm, 60 x 17 ft, 1-10in mortar, 4-18pdr carr. Perry, Blackwall 3.9.1804. Sold 27.8.1806.

DETERMINEE 6th Rate 24, 545bm, 124½ x 31½ ft. French, captured 1799 by REVOLUTIONNAIRE. Wrecked 26.3.1803 on Jersey.

DETROIT Brig 6 (Canadian lakes), 6-6pdr. American army vessel *Adams* captured 16.7.1813 while stranded near Detroit. Recaptured 9.10.1813 on Lake Erie and burnt.

DETROIT Sloop 20 (Canadian lakes), 305bm. Amherstburgh, Lake Erie 8.1813. Captured 10.9.1813 by Americans on Lake Erie.

DEUX AMIS Schooner 14, 220bm. French privateer captured 12.1796 by POLYPHEMUS. Wrecked 23.5.1799 on the Isle of Wight.

DEVASTATION (ex-*Intrepid*) Bomb 8,

446bm, 104 x 31½ ft, 2-24pdr carr., 6-9pdr, 2 mortars. Purchased 10.1804. Sold 30.5.1816.

DEVASTATION Bomb 14,372bm, 105 x 29 ft. Plymouth DY. Laid down 1820, cancelled 1831.

DEVASTATION Wood pad. sloop 1,058bm, 180 x 36 ft. Woolwich DY 3.7.1841. BU 9.1866 Castle, Charlton.

DEVASTATION Turret ship, 4,406bm, 9,387 tons, 285 x 62 ft, 4-12in MLR. Portsmouth DY 12.7.1871. Sold 12.5.1908 Ward, Morecambe.

DEVERON Frigate, 'River' class. Smiths DK 12.10.1942. Renamed DHANUSH (RIN) 1945.

DEVERON Trawler requis. 1914-19.

DEVIZES CASTLE Corvette, 'Castle' class. Kingston SY. Cancelled 12.1943.

DEVONSHIRE 3rd Rate 80, 1,158bm, 154 x 41½ ft. Wyatt, Bursledon 5.4.1692. Rebuilt 1704 as 1,220bm. Blown up 10.10.1707 in action with the French off the Lizard.

DEVONSHIRE 3rd Rate 80, 1,305bm, 156 x 44 ft. Woolwich DY 12.12.1710. Hulked 10.1740. Sold 14.10.1760.

DEVONSHIRE 3rd Rate 74, 1,471bm, 161 x 46 ft. Woolwich DY 19.7.1745. BU 10.1772 at Portsmouth.

DEVONSHIRE Fireship, Purchased 1804. Expended 3.10.1804 at Boulogne.

DEVONSHIRE 3rd Rate 74, 1,742bm, 176 x 48½ ft. Barnard, Deptford 23.9.1812. Harbour service 11.1849. BU completed 5.6.1869 at Sheerness.

DEVONSHIRE Armoured cruiser 10,850 tons, 450 x 68½ ft, 4-7.5in, 6-6in, 2-12pdr, 22-3pdr. Chatham DY 30.4.1904. Sold 9.5.21 Ward, Barrow; BU 10.23.

DEVONSHIRE Cruiser 9,850 tons, 595 x 66 ft, 8-8in, 8-4in. Devonport DY 22.10.1927. Training ship 1947. Sold 16.6.54, BU Cashmore, Newport; arrived 14.12.54.

DEVONSHIRE GM destroyer 5,600 tons, 500 x 54 ft, 4-4.5in, 6-TT. Cammell Laird 10.6.1962. Sunk as target in the Channel 17.7.84.

DEXTEROUS Gun-brig 12, 180bm, 80 x 22½ ft, 2-18pdr, 10-18pdr carr. Adams, Eling 2.2.1805. Sold 17.10.1816.

DEXTROUS Wood S. frigate 51, 3,353bm, 720 x 52½ ft. Pembroke Dock. Ordered 1861, cancelled 1863.

DEXTEROUS Two tugs 1942-47 and 1956-81. Tug 1985.

DHYFFE CASTLE Corvette, 'Castle'

class. Collingwood SY. Cancelled 12.1943.

DIADEM 3rd Rate 64, 1,376bm, 160 x 44½ ft. Chatham DY 19.12.1782. Troopship 5.1798. BU 9.1832 at Plymouth.

DIADEM Sloop 14, 368bm, 102 x 29 ft. Purchased 1801. Renamed FALCON 1802. Sold 31.7.1816.

DIADEM Wood S. frigate, 2,483bm, 240 x 48 ft, 20-10in, 2-6pdr, 10-32pdr. Pembroke Dock 14.10.1856. Sold 23.1.1875 Castle, Charlton.

DIADEM 1st class cruiser 11,000 tons, 435 x 69 ft, 16-6in, 14-12pdr. Fairfield 21.10.1896. Sold 9.5.21 Ward Morecambe.

DIADEM Cruiser 5,770 tons, 485 x 50½ ft, 8-5.25in, 12-20mm. Hawthorn Leslie 26.8.1942. Sold 29.2.56 Pakistan navy renamed BABUR 5.7.57.

DIAMANTINA Frigate (RAN), 'River' class. Walker, Maryborough 6.4.1944. Survey ship 6.59.

DIAMOND 50-gun ship, 547bm, 127½ x 31½ ft. Deptford 15.3.1652. Captured 20.9.1693 by the French.

DIAMOND 5th Rate 50, 536bm, 117 x 32½ ft. Johnson, Blackwall 12.10.1708. Rebuilt Deptford 1722 as 595bm, 40 guns. Sold 18.12.1744.

DIAMOND 5th Rate 44, 697bm, 125 x 36 ft. Carter, Limehouse 30.10.1741. Sold 5.10.1756.

DIAMOND 5th Rate 32, 710bm, 130 x 35 ft. Blaydes & Hodgson, Hull 28.5.1774. Sold 30.12.1784.

DIAMOND 5th Rate 38, 984bm, 146 x 39 ft. Barnard, Deptford 17.3.1794. BU 6.1812 at Sheerness.

DIAMOND 5th Rate 38, 1,067bm, 150 x 40½ ft, Chatham DY 16.1.1816. Burnt 18.2.1827 by accident at Portsmouth; wreck BU 6.1827.

DIAMOND 6th Rate 28, 1,051bm, 140 x 42 ft, 2-8in, 26-32pdr. Sheerness DY 29.8.1848. Lent as training ship 4.1866 and renamed JOSEPH STRAKER 13.1.1868. Sold 9.1885 Castle.

DIAMOND Wood S.corvette, 1,405bm, 1,970 tons, 220 x 37 ft, 14-64 pdr. Sheerness DY 26.9.1874. Sold 8.1889.

DIAMOND 3rd class cruiser 3,000 tons, 360 x 40 ft, 12-4in, 8-3pdr. Laird 6.1.1904. Sold 9.5.21 Ward, Grays.

DIAMOND Destroyer 1,375 tons, 318 x 33 ft, 4-4.7in, 1-3in, 8-TT. Vickers Armstrong, Barrow 8.4.1932. Sunk 27.4.41 by air attack south of Morea.

DIAMOND Destroyer 2,610 tons, 366 x 43 ft, 6-4.5in, 6-40mm, 10-TT. J. Brown 14.6.1950. Sold Medway Sec-ondary Metals, BU Rainham, Kent 11.81.

DIAMOND Two Trawlers requis. WW.I.

DIAMOND SNAKE SSV (RAN) 80 tons, Savage, Williamstown 17.5.1945. To Army in 10.45

DIANA 5th Rate 32, 668bm, 124½ x 35 ft. Batson, Limehouse 30.8.1757. Sold 16.5.1793.

DIANA Schooner 6. Purchased 1775 in N. America. Abandoned and burnt 28.5.1775 at Boston.

DIANA 5th Rate 38, 984bm, 146 x 39 ft. Randall, Rotherhithe 3.3.1794. Sold 1815 to the Dutch navy.

DIANA Cutter 10, 150bm, 10-6pdr. Purchased 1807. Wrecked 5.1810 on Rodriguez Island, Indian Ocean.

DIANA 5th Rate 46, 1,083bm, 151½ x 40½ ft. Chatham DY 8.1.1822. Harbour service 1868. BU completed 9.2.1874 at Chatham.

DIANA Wood pad. vessel (Indian). Kidderpore DY 12.7.1823 and purchased 1824. Sold 1826 Burnese government. BU 1835 at Calcutta.

DIANA Wood pad. vessel (Indian) 133 bm, Currie Sulkie 10.1836. Sold 1846

DIANA 2nd class cruiser 5,600 tons, 350 x 54 ft, 5-6in 6-4.7in, 9-12 pdr. Fairfield 5.12.1895. Sold 1.7.1920 S.Castle, Plymouth.

DIANA Destroyer 1,375 tons, 318 x 33 ft, 4-4.7in, 1-3in, 8-TT. Hawthorn Leslie 16.6.1932. Renamed MARGAREE (RCN) 6.9.40; lost 22.10.40 in collision with *Port Fairy* in the N. Atlantic.

DIANA Destroyer 2,610 tons, 336 x 43 ft, 6-4.5in, 6-40mm, 10-TT. Hawthorn Leslie. Ordered 3.1945, cancelled 1.46.

DIANA (ex-DRUID renamed 6.46) Destroyer 2,610 tons, 366 x 43 ft, 6-4.5in, 6-40mm, 10-TT. Yarrow 8.5.52. Sold Peru 1.12.69, renamed PALACIOS.

DIANA Two Trawlers and a Yacht WW.I.

DIANELLA (see DAFFODIL)

DIANTHUS Sloop, 'Anchusa' class. Barclay Curle 1.12.1917. Sold 3.6.21 mercantile.

DIANTHUS Corvette, 'Flower' class. Robb 9.7.1940. Sold 5.47, renamed *Thorslep*.

DICTATOR 3rd Rate 64, 1,388bm, 159½ x 45 ft. Batson, Limehouse 6.1.1783. Troopship 6.1798; floating battery 5.1803. BU 6.1817.

DIDO 6th Rate 28, 595bm, 120½ x 34 ft. Stewart & Hall, Sandgate

27.11.1784. Harbour service 1804. Sold 3.4.1817.

DIDO Corvette 18, 734bm, 120 x 38 ft, 18-32pdr. Pembroke Dock 13.6.1836. Coal hulk 1860. Sold 3.3.1903.

DIDO Wood S. corvette, 1,857bm, 225 x 42 ft. Deptford DY. Laid down 14.1.1861, cancelled 12.12.1863.

DIDO Wood S. corvette, 1,277bm, 1,755 tons, 212 x 36 ft, 2-7in, 2-6pdr. Portsmouth DY 23.10.1869. Hulk 1886; renamed ACTAEON II 1906. Sold 17.7.22 J.B. Garnham.

DIDO 2nd class cruiser 5,600 tons, 350 x 54 ft, 5-6in, 6-4.7in, 9-12pdr. London & Glasgow Co 20.3.1896. Depot ship 1913. Sold 16.12.26 May & Butcher, Maldon.

DIDO Cruiser 5,450 tons, 492 x 51½ ft, 10-5.25in, Cammell Laird 18.7.1939. Arrived 16.7.58 Ward, Barrow to BU.

DIDO Frigate, 'Leander' class. Yarrow 22.12.1961. To RNZN 18.7.83, renamed SOUTHLAND.

DIDO Tug requis. 1941-45.

DIDON 5th Rate 38, 1,091bm. French, captured 10.8.1805 by PHOENIX off Cape Finisterre. BU 8.1811.

DIEPPE (see LST.3016)

DIGBY Minesweeper (RCN) diesel, 'Bangor' class. Davie SB 5.6.1942.

DIGBY A. merchant cruiser 3966 tons. Requis. 1914-19.

DILIGENCE (ex-INTELLIGENCE renamed 1692) Brigantine 2, 78bm, 64 x 17 ft. Deptford 23.3.1693. Sold 26.11.1708.

DILIGENCE 6th Rate 152bm. Purchased 23.5.1709. Sold 1712.

DILIGENCE Sloop 10, 236bm, 88½ x 24½ ft. Wells, Rotherhithe 29.7.1756. Renamed COMET fireship 27.8.1779. Sold 5.12.1780.

DILIGENCE (ex-SPENCER renamed 1795) Brig-sloop 18, 320bm, 95 x 28 ft. Parsons, Bursledon 24.11.1795. Wrecked 9.1800 on Honda Bank, Cuba.

DILIGENCE (ex-*Union*) Sloop 14, 361bm, 99 x 29 ft, 14-24pdr carr., 2-18pdr. Purchased 5.2.1801 Sold. 16.4.1812.

DILIGENCE (ex-*Thistle*) Lugger. Purchased 1812. Sold 15.12.1814.

DILIGENCE Transport, 317bm, 567 tons, 104 x 26 ft. Bailey, Ipswich 30.9.1814. Coal hulk 8.1861, later renamed C.72. Sold 5.7.1904 at Portsmouth.

DILIGENCE Wood S.sloop, 950bm, 185 x 33 ft. Chatham DY. Laid down 1862, cancelled 12.12.1863.

DILIGENCE (ex-*Tabaristan*) Depot ship 7,100 tons, 390 x 46 ft, 8-4in. Purchased 29.1.1913, completed 10.15 BU 11.26 Hughes Bolckow, Blyth.

DILIGENCE Repair ship 4,023 tons, 441½ x 57 ft. Bethlehem, Fairfield 8.7.1944 on lend-lease. Returned 1.46 to the USN.

DILIGENCE Repair ship *Stena Inspector*(5814/81) purchased 31.10.1983

DILIGENCE Tug 1906 renamed SECURITY 1914. Drifter 1915-19.

DILIGENT Sloop 10, 236bm, 10-3pdr. Purchased 1776 in N. America. Captured 7.5.1779 by the American PROVIDENCE off Newfoundland. Destroyed 15.8.1779 by the RN at Penobscot.

DILIGENTE 3rd Rate 68, 1,966bm, 176½ x 50 ft, 28-24pdr, 30-12pdr, 10-9pdr. Spanish, captured 16.1.1780 at Cape St Vincent. Sold 2.12.1784.

DILIGENT Schooner 8. In service 1781-90.

DILIGENT Schooner 8, 89bm. Purchased 1790.Sold 20.11.1794 to BU.

DILIGENT (see PORPOISE of 1798)

DILIGENTE Storeship 14. French, captured 1800 in the W. Indies. Sold 11.8.1814.

DILIGENT Brig-sloop 16, 317bm. French, captured 28.5.1806 by RENARD in the W.Indies. Renamed PRUDENTE 10.1806; renamed WOLF 1807. BU 6.1811.

DILIGENTE Lugger 2, 100bm. French, captured 6.1.1813.Sold 15.12.1814.

DILIGENT Tug 1898-1923. Tug 1947-71.

DILIGENTE (see under DILIGENT)

DILSTON Coastal M/S, 'Ton' class. Cook Welton & Gemmell 15.11.1954. Malaysian naval JERAI 1964.

DINGLEY Inshore M/S, 'Ley' class. White, Cowes 3.9.1952. Sold Pounds 16.7.67.

DIOMEDE 5th Rate 44, 891bm, 140 x 38 ft. Hilhouse, Bristol 18.10.1781. Wrecked 2.8.1795 near Trincomalee.

DIOMEDE (ex-FIRM renamed 1794) 4th Rate 50, 1,123bm, 151 x 41 ft. Deptford DY 17.1.1798. Sold 8.1815.

DIOMEDE Wood S.sloop 1268bm. Projected 12.1866 Cancelled 30.4.1867

DIOMEDE Light cruiser 4,765 tons, 445 x 46½ ft, 6-6in, 2-4in. Vickers 29.4.1919.Sold 5.4.46, BU by Arnott Young, Dalmuir.

DIOMEDE Frigate Leander class. Yarrow 15.4.1969

DIPPER Mining tender 120 tons, 60 x 16½ ft. German C.30 seized 1945, renamed 1948. Sold 1959.

DIRECTOR 3rd Rate 64, 1,388bm, 159 x 44½ ft. Cleveley, Gravesend 9.3.1784. Harbour service 4.1796. BU. 1.1801.

DIRECTOR Tug 1956-80.

DIRK Destroyer 1,980 tons, 341½ x 38 ft, 6-4in, 10-TT.Scotts. Not laid down. Cancelled 10.1945.

DIRK Trawler requis. 1917-18

DISDAIN Pinnace, 80bm. In service in 1585.

DISDAIN (see NIGER of 1945)

DISDAIN (see DELIGHT of 1950)

DISCOVERY Discovery vessel in service 1600-20.

DISCOVERY 20-gun ship, Purchased 1651. Burnt 25.5.1655 in Jamaica.

DISCOVERY Ketch 6, 75bm, 64 x 16 ft. Woolwich DY 9.5.1692. BU 1705 at Portsmouth.

DISCOVERY Discovery sloop. Lost 1719 in the Arctic.

DISCOVERY Storeship 6, 154bm, 74½ x 22½ ft. Purchased 4.1741. Sold 6.5.1750.

DISCOVERY (ex-*Diligence*) Discovery vessel 8, 299bm, 91½ x 27½ ft. Purchased 1775. DY transport 5.1781, BU Chatham 10.1797.

DISCOVERY Sloop 10, 337bm, 96 x 27 ft, 10-4pdr. Randall, Rotherhithe 1789 and purchased 11.1789. Bomb in 1799; convict ship 1818 BU 2.1834 at Deptford.

DISCOVERY Survey vessel (Indian) in service 1800.Sold 5.1828.

DISCOVERY Wood S. gunvessel, 425bm, 145 x 25 ft. Ordered 1861. cancelled 12.12.1863.

DISCOVERY (ex-*Bloodhound*) Wood S. storeship 1,247 tons, 160 x 29 ft. Purchased 5.12.1874. Sold 2.1902 D. Murray.

DISCOVERY Survey vessel, 480 tons. Dundee SB Co 1901.Sold 1905 Hudsons Bay Co; repurchased 1929 as training ship. Handed over 2.4.79 for preservation.

DISCOVERY II ABV. requis. 1939-45

DISPATCH (see DESPATCH)

DITTANY (ex-USS BEACON) Corvette, 'Flower' class. Collingwood SY 31.10.1942 on lend-lease. Returned 20.6.46 to the USN.Sold 1947 renamed *Olympic Cruiser*.

DITTISHAM Inshore M/S, 'Ham' class Fairlie Yt Slip 10.1953. For sale 1982.

DIVER Mining tender 120 tons, 60 x 16½ ft. German C.28 seized 1945, renamed 1948. DY tug 1960, Sold 1971 at Singapore.

DODMAN POINT Repair ship 8,580 tons, 439 x 62 ft. Burrard, Vancouver 14.4.1945. Arrived 16.4.63 at Spezia to BU.

DOGSTAR (see DEFENDER of 1950)

DOLPHIN Ketch 4. Royalist ANGEL captured 1648.Sold 1650.

DOLPHIN 30-gun ship. Captured 1652.Sold 1657.

DOLPHIN Ketch 4, 50bm. Condemned at Jamaica 1660.

DOLPHIN (see WEXFORD)

DOLPHIN Fireship 4, 143bm. Purchased 1666. Sunk 6.1667 as a blockship in the Medway.

DOLPHIN Sloop 2, 80bm. Deptford DY 1673.Lost 1673 in action.

DOLPHIN Fireship 8, 267bm, 93½ x 24½ ft. Chatham DY 29.3.1690. 5th Rate 1692; rebuilt Portsmouth 1711 as 424bm. BU 1730.

DOLPHIN 6th Rate 20, 428bm, 106 x 30½ ft. Deptford DY 4.1.1731. Fireship in 10.1746; renamed FIREBRAND 29.7.1755; renamed PENGUIN 6th Rate 1757. Captured 20.3.60 by the French.

DOLPHIN 6th Rate 24, 511bm, 113 x 32 ft. Woolwich DY 1.5.1751. Surveying 1764-70. BU 1.1777.

DOPLHINS PRIZE Sloop 12, 147bm. French privateer captured 8.1757.Sold 6.11.1760.

DOLPHIN 5th Rate 44, 880bm, 140 x 38 ft. Chatham DY 10.3.1781. Troopship 4, 1800. BU 7.1817.

DOLPHIN 6th Rate 24, Dutch DOLFIJN captured 15.9.1799 by WOLVERINE and ARROW at Vlie Island. Listed to 1801.

DOLPHIN Cutter 4, 93bm, 59 x 20 ft, 4-12pdr carr. Purchased 4.6.1801. Sold 1802.

DOLPHIN (see HINDOSTAN of 1804)

DOLPHIN Brigantine 3, 319bm, 91 x 29 ft, 3-32 pdr. Sheerness DY 14.6.1836. Customs watch vessel 2.1861. Sold 11.5.1894 to BU.

DOLPHIN Compos.S.sloop 925 tons, 157 x 32 ft, 2-6in, 2-5in. Raylton Dixon 9.12.1882. Sailing training ship 1899; hulk 1907; S/M depot ship 1912. Sold 13.3.25; foundered in tow 19.4.25, raised and beached. Accomodation school ship. BU 1977 Bo'ness.

DOLPHIN (see PANDORA of 1914)

DOLPHIN (ex-ABERFOYLE renamed 3.1938) S/M base tender 210 tons. For disposal 1947. (Doubt exists as to whether the name was ever painted up on ABERFOYLE.) (See ABER-

FOYLE)

DOLWEN Tender 502 tons, ex-'Hector Gull' purchased 1976

DOMETT (ex-USS EISNER) Frigate, DE 'Captain' class. Boston Navy Yd 19.5.1943 on lend-lease. Returned 8.3.46 to USN.

DOMINICA Schooner 6, 85bm. Purchased 1805. BU in 1.1808.

DOMINICA Gun-brig 14, 153bm. French privateer TAPE a L'OEIL captured 1807. Capsized 8.1809 off Tortola.

DOMINICA Schooner 10, 203bm, 89½ x 23 ft, 12-12pdr carr., 2-6pdr. French DUC de WAGRAM captured 1809. Captured 5.8.1813 by an American privateer off Charlestown; recaptured 22.5.1814. Wrecked 15.8.1815 off Bermuda.

DOMINICA (ex-HARMAN renamed 1943) Frigate, 'Colony' class. Walsh Kaiser 14.9.1943 on lend-lease. Returned 23.4.46 to USN.

DOMINION Battleship 16,500 tons, 439 x 78 ft, 4-12in, 4-9in, 10-6in, 12-12pdr. Vickers 25.8.1903. Sold 9.5.21 Ward; laid up at Belfast, arrived Preston 28.10.24 to BU.

DON Iron S. gunboat 363 tons, 110 x 34 ft, 3-6pdr. Palmer 14.4.1877. DY barge 1911. Sold 1914 at Malta.

DON Store carrier requis, 1914-15.

DONCASTER Pad. minesweeper, 'Ascot' class. Ayrshire Co 15.6.1916. Sold 3.22 Ward, Inverkeithing.

DONEGAL 3rd Rate 76, 1,901bm, 182 x 49½ ft. French HOCHE captured 12.10.1798 by a squadron off NW Ireland. BU 5.1845 at Portsmouth.

DONEGAL Screw 1st Rate 101, 3,245bm, 5,481 tons, 240 x 55 ft. Devonport DY 23.9.1858. Renamed VERNON 14.1.1886, torpedo school ship. Sold 18.5.1925. Pounds, Portsmouth.

DONEGAL Armoured cruiser 9,800 tons, 440 x 66 ft. 14-6in, 10-12pdr. Fairfield 4.9.1902. Sold 1.7.20 S. Castle, Plymouth; resold Granton S. Bkg Co.

DONOVAN M/S sloop, '24' class. Greenock & Grangemouth 27.4.1918. Sold 15.11.22 Ferguson Muir.

DONOVAN (see EMPIRE BATTLE-AXE)

DOON Destroyer 545 tons, 222 x 23½ ft, 1-12pdr, 5-6pdr (4-12pdr 1907), 2-TT. Hawthorn 8.11.1904. Sold 27.5.19 Ward, Rainham.

DOON Trawler requis. 1917-19. Trawler 1920-47.

DORDRECHT 3rd Rate 64, 1,440bm,

159½ x 45 ft. Dutch, captured 17.8.1796 at Saldanha Bay. Harbour service 1800. Sold 21.5.1823 to BU.

DORIS 5th Rate 36, 913bm, 142 x 38 ft. Cleveley, Gravesend 31.8.1795. Wrecked 21.1.1805 in Quiberon Bay.

DORIS 5th Rate 32, 885bm, 142 x 37 ft. Record, Appledore. Ordered 6.1.1806, cancelled 24.6.1806.

DORIS (ex-E. Indiaman *Pitt*) 5th Rate 36, 870bm, 137 x 38 ft. Purchased 9.1808. Sold 4.1829 at Valparaiso. (Launched 24.3.07 as SALSETTE, renamed PITT 3.10.07 and DORIS 3.4.08.)

DORIS Wood S. frigate, 2,483bm, 3,803 tons, 240 x 48 ft, 20-10in, 2-68pdr, 10-32pdr. Pembroke Dock 25.3.1857. Sold 1885.

DORIS 2nd class cruiser 5,600 tons, 350 x 54 ft, 5-6in, 6-4in, 9-12 pdr, N.C & A, Barrow (Vickers) 3.3.1896. Sold 20.2.1919 at Bombay.

DORKING Minesweeper, later 'Hunt' class. Dundee SB Co 26.9.1918. Arrived 27.5.28 Charlestown to BU.

DORNOCH Minesweeper, turbine 'Bangor' class. Ailsa 4.2.1942. Sold 1.1.48; BU by Stockholm Sh. Co.

DOROTHEA Discovery vessel. Hired 2.1818, purchased 3.1818. Sold 28.2.1819.

DORSET (ex-DUBLIN renamed 11.7.1753) Yacht 10, 164bm, 78 x 22 ft. Deptford DY 17.7.1753. Sold 23.3.1815.

DORSETSHIRE 3rd Rate 80, 1,176bm, 153½ x 42 ft. Winters, Southampton 8.12.1694. Rebuilt Portsmouth 1712 as 1,283bm. Sold 1749.

DORSETSHIRE 3rd Rate 70, 1,436bm, 162 x 45 ft. Portsmouth DY 13.12.1757. BU 3.1775.

DORSETSHIRE Cruiser 9,975 tons, 590 x 68½ ft, 8-8in, 4-4in. Portsmouth DY 29.1.1929. Sunk 5.4.42 by Japanese air attack in the Indian Ocean.

DOTTEREL Brig-sloop 18, 'Cruizer' class. Blake & Scott, Bursledon 6.10.1808. Hulked 4.1827. Sold 9.1848 at Bermuda.

DOTEREL (ex-GPO vessel *Escape*) Wood pad. packet, 237 bm, 119 x 21 ft. Transferred 1837. Sold 30.11.1850.

DOTEREL Wood S. gunboat, 'Britomart' class. Miller, Liverpool 5.7.1860. Sold 6.6.1871 Marshall, Plymouth.

DOTEREL Compos.S.sloop 1,130 tons, 170 x 36 ft, 2-7in, 4-64pdr. Chatham DY 2.3.1880. Blown up 26.4.1881 by accident off Punta Arenas.

DOTEREL Yacht requis. 1918 renamed DOTTER 1918-22.

DOUGLAS Destroyer leader 1,800 tons, 320 x 32 ft, 5-4.7in, 1-3in, 6-TT. Cammell Laird 8.6.1918. Sold 20.3.45, BU Ward, Inverkeithing.

DOVE Ketch 8, 84bm. Royalist FORTUNE captured by Parliamentarians 1644. Sunk 1650.

DOVE Ketch 4, 19bm. Deptford DY 1672. Sold 1683.

DOVE Dogger 8. Dutch, captured 1672. Wrecked 1674.

DOVE Schooner 4, 103bm, 4-12pdr carr. Purchased 5.1805. Captured 5.8.1805 by the French.

DOVE (see ARIADNE of 1805)

DOVE Packet brig 6. Purchased 1823. Sold 31.1.1829.

DOVE (see KANGAROO of 1852)

DOVE Wood S. gunboat, 'Albacore' class. Pitcher, Northfleet 24.11.1855. Sold 14.4.1873 at Shanghai.

DOVE Paddle gunboat 20 tons, 60 x 14 ft. Yarrow, Poplar in sections 1893; re-erected 30.5.93 in E. Africa. Transferred 1895 to BCA government.

DOVE Destroyer 370 tons, 210 x 20½ ft, 1-12pdr, 5-6pdr, 2-TT. Earle 21.3.1898. Sold 27.1.1920 Maden & McKee.

DOVER Pink. Royalist, captured 1649. Sold 1650.

DOVER 48-gun ship, 554bm, 119 x 32 ft. Castle, Shoreham 1654. Rebuilt Portsmouth 1695; rebuilt 1716 as 604bm. BU 1730.

DOVER Dogger 8. Dutch, captured 1672. Given away 1677.

DOVER PRIZE Hulk, captured 1689. Wrecked 1689.

DOVER PRIZE 5th Rate 32, 330bm, 105 x 27 ft. Captured 1693. Sold 1698.

DOVER 5th Rate 44, 693bm, 124½ x 36 ft. Bronsdon & Wells, Deptford 7.1.1740. Sold 6.10.1763.

DOVER 5th Rate 44, 905bm, 140 x 38½ ft. Parsons, Burlesdon 5.1786. Burnt 6.8.1806 by accident at Woolwich.

DOVER (see DUNCAN of 1804)

DOVER Troopship 38, 692bm, 132 x 35 ft. French BELLONE captured 11.3.1811 at Lissa. Harbour service 2.1825. Sold 21.1.1836.

DOVER Iron pad. packet, 224bm, 110½ x 21 ft. Laird 1840. Stationed in the Gambia from 1849. Sold 1866. (The 1st iron vessel in the RN.)

DOVER Trawler requis. 1914-19.

DOVER CASTLE Corvette, 'Castle' class. Inglis. Cancelled 12.1943.

DOVEY (ex-LAMBOURNE renamed 10.1942) Frigate, 'River' class. Fleming & Ferguson 14.10.1943. Arrived 2.11.55 Ward, Preston.

DOVEY Minehunter 757 tons. Richards 7.12.1983.

DOWNHAM Inshore M/S, 'Ham' class. White, Cowes 1.9.1955. TRV 1967. For sale 1982.

DOWNLEY Inshore m/s launched 1955 as WOLDINGHAM.

DRAGON Ship, 100bm. In service 1512 to 1514.

DRAGON 45-gun ship, 140bm. In service 1542 to 1552.

DRAGON (also RED DRAGON) Galleon, 900bm. Deptford 1593. Last mentioned 1613.

DRAGON 38-gun ship, 414bm, 120 x 28½ ft. Chatham DY 1647 (1st ship built at Chatham DY). Rebuilt Deptford 1690 as 479bm; rebuilt at Cuckolds Point 1707 as 719bm. Wrecked 15.3.1711 on Alderney.

DRAGON (see ORMONDE of 1711)

DRAGON 4th Rate 60, 1,067bm, 144 x 42 ft. Woolwich DY 11.9.1736. Sunk 7.1757 as a breakwater at Sheerness.

DRAGON 3rd Rate 74, 1,614bm, 168 x 47 ft. Deptford DY 4.3.1760. Harbour service 1781. Sold 1.6.1784.

DRAGON Cutter 10, 139bm, 61 x 24 ft, 10-4pdr. Purchased 5.1782. Sold 7.1785.

DRAGON 3rd Rate 74, 1,815bm, 178 x 49 ft. Wells, Rotherhithe 2.4.1798. Harbour service 9.1824; renamed FAME hulk 15.7.1842. BU 8.1850.

DRAGON Wood pad. frigate, 1,270bm, 200 x 37½ ft. Pembroke Dock 17.6.1845. Sold 7.10.1864 Castle, Charlton.

DRAGON Compos S. sloop 1,130 tons, 170 x 36 ft, 2-7in, 4-64pdr. Devonport DY 30.5.1878. Sold 24.9.1892.

DRAGON Destroyer 330 tons, 210 x 19½ ft, 1-12pdr, 5-6pdr, 2-TT. Laird 15.12.1894. Sold 9.7.1912 to BU.

DRAGON (see LOOKOUT)

DRAGON Light cruiser 4,650 tons, 445 x 46½ ft, 6-6in, 2-3in. Scotts 29.12.1917. Lent Polish navy 1.43. Sunk 8.7.44 as breakwater, Normandy beaches.

DRAGON (see DECOY of 1949)

DRAGON Tug requis. 1915, renamed DRAGE 1917-19.

DRAGONFLY Coastal destroyer 235 tons, 175 x 17½ ft, 2-12pdr, 3-TT. White 11.3.1906. Renamed TB.2 in 1906. Sold 7.10.20 Ward, Hayle.

DRAGONFLY River gunboat, 'Fly' class. Yarrow. Sections sent out 7.1915. Sold 16.2.23 at Basra.

DRAGONFLY River gunboat 585 tons, 2-4in, 1-3.7in. Thornycroft 8.12.1938. Sunk 14.2.42 by air attack off Singapore.

DRAKE 16-gun ship, 146bm. Deptford 1653. Sold 1691 in Jamaica.

DRAKE 6th Rate 24, 253bm, 93 x 25 ft. Fowler, Rotherhithe 26.9.1694. Wrecked 20.12.1694 on the coast of Ireland.

DRAKE Yacht 2, 60bm. Plymouth DY 1705. Rebuilt Plymouth 1727 as 68bm. Sold 16.10.1749.

DRAKE Sloop 14, 175bm, 84 x 22 ft. Woolwich DY 8.11.1705. Rebuilt 1729 as the following ship.

DRAKE Sloop 14, 207bm, 87 x 23 ft. Deptford DY 3.4.1729. BU 7.1740 at Deptford.

DRAKE Sloop 14 (Indian), 200bm, Bombay DY 1736. Made a bomb 1748. Sold 1755.

DRAKE Sloop 14, 206bm, 85 x 24ft. West, Wapping 2.1740. Wrecked 1742 in Gibraltar Bay; wreck sold 13.10.1748.

DRAKE Sloop 14, 249bm, 88 x 25 ft. Deptford 1743. Sold 1748.

DRAKE (ex-*Marquis of Granby*) Sloop, 462bm, 111 x 30½ ft, 12-6pdr. Renamed RESOLUTION discovery vessel 25.12.1771 (purchased 1770). Captured 9.6.1782 by the French SPHINX in the E. Indies.

DRAKE (ex-*Resolution*) Sloop 14, 275bm, 91 x 26 ft, 14-4pdr. Purchased 1777. Captured 24.4.1778 by the American RANGER off Belfast.

DRAKE Brig-sloop 14, 221bm, 79 x 26 ft. Ladd, Dover 5.1779. Condemned 7.1800 in Jamaica.

DRAKE Brig-sloop 14, 212bm, 80 x 24 ft. French privateer TIGRE captured 1799. Wrecked 9.1804 on Nevis, W. Indies.

DRAKE (ex-*Earl Mornington*) Sloop 16, 253bm, 104 x 24 ft. Purchased 1804. BU 8.1808.

DRAKE Brig-sloop 10, 'Cherokee' class, 235bm. Bailey, Ipswich 3.11.1808. Wrecked 22.6.1822 in Newfoundland.

DRAKE Mortar vessel, 109bm, 60 x 21 ft. Launched at Portsmouth 25.3.1834 as a DY lighter and converted at Portsmouth 10.1854. Renamed MV.1 on 19.10.1855; renamed SHEPPEY as DY lighter 7.7.1856. BU 1867.

DRAKE Wood S. gunboat, 'Clown' class. Pembroke Dock 8.3.1856. Sold 9.2.1869 at Hong Kong.

DRAKE (ex-YC.1 renamed 11.1870, ex-HART) Cutter, 80bm, 54 x 19 ft. BU completed 6.3.1875 at Chatham.

DRAKE (see SHELDRAKE of 1875)

DRAKE Armoured cruiser 14,100 tons, 529 x 71 ft, 2-9.2in, 16-6in, 14-12pdr. Pembroke Dock 5.3.1901. Sunk 2.10.17 by 'U.79', capsized in Rathlin Sound.

DRAKE (see MARSHAL NEY)

DRAKE 5 hired vessels between 1588 and 1805. Trawler and Drifter requis. WW.I.

DREADFUL Bomb 4, 147bm, 67 x 23½ft. Graves, Limehouse 6.5.1695. Burnt 5.7.1695 to avoid capture.

DREADFUL Tug 1917-20.

DREADNOUGHT 40-gun ship in service in 1553. (Existance doubtful.)

DREADNOUGHT 41-gun ship, 450bm, 2-60pdr, 4-18pdr, 11-9pdr, 10-6pdr, 12 small. Deptford 10.11.1573. Rebuilt 1592; rebuilt 1614 as 552bm. BU 1648.

DREADNOUGHT (see TORRINGTON of 1654)

DREADNOUGHT 4th Rate 60, 852bm, 142 x 36½ ft. Johnson, Blackwall 1691. Rebuilt Blackwall 1706 as 910bm; hulk 1740. BU 9.1748 at Portsmouth.

DREADNOUGHT 4th Rate 60, 1,093bm, 144 x 42 ft. Wells, Deptford 23.6.1742. Sold 17.8.1784.

DREADNOUGHT PRIZE Sloop, 109bm, 62 x 21 ft. Captured 1748 by DREADNOUGHT. Sold 1748.

DREADNOUGHT 2nd Rate 98, 2,110bm, 185 x 51 ft. Portsmouth DY 13.6.1801. Hospital ship 1827. BU completed 31.3.1857.

DREADNOUGHT (see CALEDONIA of 1808)

DREADNOUGHT (ex-FURY renamed 1.2.1875) Battleship, 10,820 tons, 320 x 64 ft, 4-12.5in, 6-QF. Pembroke Dock 8.3.1875. Hulk 1903. Sold 14.7.08 Ward; BU at Barrow (& Preston, from 2.09)

DREADNOUGHT Battleship 17,900 tons, 490 x 82 ft, 10-12in, 27-12pdr. Portsmouth DY 10.2.1906. Sold 9.5.21 Ward; arrived Inverkeithing 2.1.23 to BU.

DREADNOUGHT Nuclear submarine 3,000 tons, 266 x 32 ft, 6-TT. Vickers

Armstrong, Barrow 21.10.1960.

DRIVER Sloop 18.399bm, 105 x 30 ft. Goodrich, Bermuda 1797. Convict ship 1825. BU 7.1834.

DRIVER Wood pad. sloop, 1,058bm, 180 x 36 ft. Portsmouth DY 24.12.1940. Wrecked 8.1861 on Mariguana Island.

DRIVER Trawler 1910-20. Tug 1942-64.

DROCHTERLAND 4th Rate (hulk), 871bm, 135 x 38½ ft. Dutch UNIE captured 28.8.1799 in the Texel. Receiving ship 1800, BU 3.1815.

DROMEDARY (ex-*Duke of Cumberland*) Storeship 30, 754bm, 22-9pdr, 8-6pdr. Purchased 1777. Registered as 5th Rate 30 from 10.1779. BU 4.1783.

DROMEDARY (see JANUS of 1778)

DROMEDARY (see HOWE of 1805)

DROMEDARY Iron S. troopship, 657bm, Samuda, Poplar 16.1.1862. Sold 21.10.1869 J.P. Tate.

DROMEDARY (ex-*Briton*) Iron S. troopship, 1,122 tons. Purchased 4.11.1873. Sold 1885.

DROMEDARY DY craft 1870-94; Tug 1894-1923; Tug 1940-46.

DROXFORD Seaward defence boat, 'Ford' class. Pimblott, Northwich 28.1.1954. Renamed DEE 1955; DROXFORD 1965. For sale 1984.

DRUDGE Trials gunboat 890 tons, 125 x 35 ft, various guns for trial firing. Purchased 28.2.1901. Renamed EXCELLENT 21.11.16; renamed DRYAD 26.1.19; DRUDGE 1919. Sold 27.3.20 (Launched Elswick 15.6.87)

DRUDGE (see READY of 1872)

DRUID Sloop 10, 212bm, 87½ x 23½ ft. Barnard, Harwich 24.2.1761. Sunk 8,1773 as breakwater at Sheerness.

DRUID (ex-*Brilliant*) Sloop 16, 285bm, 97 x 25½ ft. Purchased 2.9.1776. Renamed BLAST fireship 16.9.1779. Sold 25.9.1783.

DRUID 5th Rate 32, 718bm, 129 x 35½ ft. Teast & Tombes, Bristol 16.6.1783. Troopship 4.1798. BU 10.1813.

DRUID 5th Rate 46, 1,170bm, 159 x 41 ft. Pembroke Dock 1.7.1825. Sold 4,1863 Marshall, Plymouth.

DRUID Wood S. corvette 1,322bm, 1,730 tons, 220 x 36 ft. Deptford DY 13.3.1869. Sold 10.11.1886 Castle. (The last ship built at Deptford DY.)

DRUID Destroyer 770 tons, 240 x 25½ ft, 2-4in, 2-12pdr, 2-TT. Denny 4.12.1911. Sold 9.5.21 Ward, Briton Ferry.

DRUID (see DIANA of 1952)

DRUMHELLER Corvette (RCN), 'Flower' class. Collingwood SY 5.7.1941. Sold 1946.

DRUMMONDVILLE Minesweeper (RCN), TE 'Bangor' class. Vickers, Montreal 21.5.1941. Sold 9.58, renamed *Fort Albany.*

DRURY Frigate, DE 'Captain' class. Philadelphia Navy Yd. Laid down 1.4.1942 for the RN but retained and launched as USS ENSTROM.

DRURY (ex-COCKBURN renamed 1942) Frigate, DE 'Captain' class. Philadelphia Navy Yd 24.7.42 on lend-lease. Returned 8.45 to USN.

DRYAD 5th Rate 36, 924bm, 143 x 38½ ft. Barnard, Deptford 4.6.1795. Harbour service 1832. BU 2.1860 at Portsmouth.

DRYAD Wood S. frigate 51, 3,027bm, 250 x 52 ft, 30-8in, 1-68pdr, 20-32pdr. Portsmouth DY. Laid down 2.1.1860, cancelled 16.12.1864.

DRYAD Wood S. sloop, 1,086bm, 1,574 tons, 187 x 36 ft, 9-64pdr. Devonport DY 25.9.1866. Sold 9.1885, BU 4.86.

DRYAD Torpedo gunboat 1,070 tons, 250 x 30½ ft, 2-4.7in, 4-6pdr 5-TT. Chatham DY 22.11.1893. Renamed HAMADRYAD 1.1918 harbour service. Sold 24.9.20 H.Auten.

DRYAD Light cruiser 4,765 tons, 445 x 46½ ft, 6-6in, 2-4in. Vickers. Ordered 3.1918, cancelled 11.18.

DRYAD Navigation school ships. (see DRUDGE, RATTLER of 1886 and CARSTAIRS.)

DUBBO Minesweeper (RAN), 'Bathurst' class. Morts Dk, Sydney 7.3.1942. Sold 20.2.58 to BU in Japan.

DUBBO patrol boat (RAN) 211 tons. Cairns 21.1.1984.

DUBFORD Seaward defence boat, 'Ford' class. White, Cowes 2.3.1953. To Nigerian navy 1968., renamed SAPELE.

DUBLIN Yacht 10, 148bm, 73 x 22 ft. Deptford DY 13.8.1709 BU 10.1752 Deptford.

DUBLIN (see DORSET)

DUBLIN 3rd Rate 74, 1,562bm, 165 x 47 ft. Deptford DY 6.5.1757. BU 13.5.1784 at Plymouth.

DUBLIN 3rd Rate 74, 1,772bm, 175 x 48½ ft. Brent, Rotherhithe 13.2.1812. Reduced to 50 guns in 12.1826; harbour service 1845. Sold 7.1885 Castle, Charlton.

DUBLIN 2nd class cruiser 5,400 tons, 430 x 50 ft, 8-6in. Beardmore 30.4.1912. Sold 7.26 King, Troon.

DUC'd'AQUITAINE 3rd Rate 64, 1,358bm, 159½ x 44½ ft. 24-24pdr, 26-12pdr, 14-9pdr. French E. Indiaman captured 30.5.1757 by EAGLE and MEDWAY. Foundered 1.1.1761 in the Bay of Bengal 'on an anchor'.

DUC de CHARTRES Ship-sloop 18, 426bm, 109 x 30½ ft, 18-6pdr. French privateer captured 1781 by CUMBERLAND in N. America. Sold 1.7.1784.

DUC d' ESTISSAC Sloop 18. French privateer captured 6.6.1781 by CERBERUS. Sold 30.10.1783.

DUC de La VAUGINON Cutter 12, 12-4pdr. French privateer DUC de La VAUGUYON captured 1779. Lost 12.1779.

DUCHESS 24gun-ship. French DUCHESSE captured 1652. Sold 1654.

DUCHESS 2nd Rate 90, 1,364bm, 163 x 45 ft, 26-34pdr, 26-18pdr, 26-6pdr, 12-3pdr. Deptford 1679. Renamed PRINCESS ANNE 31.12.1701; WINDSOR CASTLE 17.3.1702; BLENHEIM 18.12.1706. BU 8.1763.

DUCHESS Destroyer 1,375 tons, 318 x 33 ft, 4-4.7in, 1-3in, 8-TT. Hawthorn Leslie 19.7.1932. Sunk 12.12.39 in collision with BARHAM off W. Scotland.

DUCHESS Destroyer 2,610 tons, 366 x 43 ft, 6-4.5in, 6-40mm, 10-TT. Thornycroft 9.4.1951. Transferred RAN 8.5.64. BU in Japan 6.80.

DUCHESS M/S 1916-23. M/S (RNZN) 1940-47.

DUCHESS OF CUMBERLAND Sloop 16. Purchased 1781. Wrecked 1781 off Newfoundland.

DUCKWORTH Frigate, DE 'Captain' class. Mare Island, Laid down 15.4.1942 for the RN. Retained by the USN as BURDEN R. HASTINGS.

DUCKWORTH (ex-USS GARY) Frigate, TE 'Captain' class. Bethlehem Hingham 1.5.43 on lend-lease. Returned 17.12.45 to the USN.

DUDDON (see RIBBLE)

DUDLEY CASTLE Corvette, 'Castle' class. Inglis. Cancelled 12.1943.

DUE REPULSE (see REPULSE)

DUFF Frigate, DE 'Captain' class. Mare Island. Laid down 15.4.1942, launched as USS Le HARDY.

DUFF (ex-USS LAMONS) Frigate, Te 'Captain' class. Bethlehem, Hingham 22.5.43. Returned 1.11.46 to the USN. BU 1947 in Holland.

DUFFERIN Troopship (RIM) 7,457 tons, 437 x 53 ft, 8-4in, 8-3pdr. Vickers 14.8.1904. AMC 1914. Training

ship 1927. Hulk for sale 1955.

DUFTON Coastal M/S, 'Ton' class. Goole SB 13.11.1954. Sold Pounds, 6.77, BU Sittingbourne.

DUGUAY TROUIN Sloop 18, 252bm, 86 x 26 ft, 4-18pdr, 14-6pdr. French privateer captured 1780 by SURPRISE off the Dodman. Sold 30.10.1783.

DUKE 12-gun ship in service in 1652.

DUKE 2nd Rate 90, 1.346bm, 163 x 45 ft, 26-34pdr, 26-18pdr, 26-6pdr, 12-3pdr. Woolwich DY 1682. Rebuilt Chatham and renamed PRINCE GEORGE 31.12.1701. Lost 1758. (see PRINCE GEORGE)

DUKE (see VANGUARD of 1678)

DUKE Fireship 8, 199bm, 83 x 24 ft. Purchased 22.6.1739. Expended 16.6.1742 at St Tropez.

DUKE Fireship 8, 469bm, 107 x 32½ ft. French, captured 1745. Sold 9.2.1748.

DUKE Storeship 10. Foundered 1.1.1761 near Pondicherry.

DUKE 2nd Rate 90, 1,931bm, 177½ x 50 ft. Plymouth DY 18.10.1777. Harbour service 9.1799. BU 1843.

DUKE M/S requis. 1916-20.

DUKE OF EDINBURGH Armoured cruiser 13,550 tons, 480 x 73½ ft, 6-9.2in, 10-6in, 22-3pdr. Pembroke Dock 14.6.1904. Sold 12.4.20 Hughes Bolckow, Blyth.

DUKE OF KENT 1st Rate 170 (4-decker) 221 x 65½ Projected 1809 and cancelled

DUKE OF WELLINGTON (ex-WINDSOR CASTLE renamed 1.10.1852) Screw 1st Rate 131, 3,771bm, 6,071 tons, 240½ x 60 ft, 16-8in, 1-68 pdr, 114-32pdr. Pembroke Dock 14.9.1852. Harbour service 5.1863. Sold 12.4.1904 Castle, Charlton. (see WINDSOR CASTLE)

DUKE OF YORK Cutter 4, 54bm, 40½ x 18 ft. Purchased 2.1763. Sold 1.7.1766 at Sheerness.

DUKE OF YORK (ex-ANSON renamed 21.12.1938) Battleship 35,000 tons, 739½ x 103 ft, 10-14in, 16-5.25 in. J. Brown 28.2.40. BU 2.58 at Faslane.

DUKE OF YORK Four vessels hired between 1664 and 1910.

DUKE WILLIAM Cutter, 65bm. Purchased 2.1763. Lost 5.10.1768.

DULLISK COVE (ex-EMPIRE PERAK renamed 1944) Repair ship 8,402 tons, 425 x 56 ft. Short, Sunderland 4.9.1944. Sold 30.7.47, renamed Kafalonia.

DULVERTON Destroyer, 'Hunt' class. type II. Stephen 1.4.1941. Sunk

13.11.43 by German aircraft off Kos.

DULVERTON Minehunter 615 tons. Vosper-Thornycroft 3.11.1982

DUMBARTON 6th Rate 20, 191bm, Scottish, captured 1685. Condemned 6.6.1691 in Virginia.

DUMBARTON CASTLE 6th Rate 24. Scottish, transferred 29.11.1707. Captured 26.4.1708 by the French off Waterford.

DUMBARTON CASTLE Corvette, 'Flower' class. Caledon SB 28.9.1943. BU 3.61 at Gateshead.

DUMBARTON CASTLE Patrol vessel 1427 tons, Hall Russell 3.6.1981

DUMBLETON Coastal M/S, 'Ton' class. Harland & Wolff 8.11.1957. To S. African navy as PORT ELIZABETH 28.10.58.

DUNBAR 3rd Rate 64, 1,082bm. Deptford 1656. Renamed HENRY 1660. Burnt by accident 1682.

DUNBAR Minesweeper, turbine 'Bagnor' class. Blyth DD 5.6.1941. Sold 1.1.48; BU Pollock & Brown, Southampton.

DUNCAN (ex-Indiaman *Carron* purchased 1804) 5th Rate 38, 990bm, 130 x 35 ft. Bombay DY 1804. Renamed DOVER 1807. Wrecked 2.5.1811 off Madras.

DUNCAN 3rd Rate 74, 1,761bm, 176 x 48½ ft. Dudman, Deptford 2.12.1811. Harbour service 1826. BU 10.1863 at Chatham.

DUNCAN Screw 1st Rate 101, 3,727bm, 5,724 tons, 252 x 58 ft, 38-8in, 1-68pdr. 62-23pdr. Portsmouth DY 13.12.1859. Renamed PEMBROKE 1890 harbour service; renamed TENEDOS II 9.1905. Sold 11.10.10.

DUNCAN Battleship 14,000 tons, 405 x 75½ ft, 4-12in, 12-6in, 12-12 pdr. Thames Iron Works 21.3.1903. Sold 18.2.20 Stanlee, Dover.

DUNCAN Destroyer leader 1,400 tons, 318 x 33 ft, 4-4.7in 1-3in, 8-TT. Portsmouth DY 7.7.1932. Sold 9.45; arrived 11.45 Ward, Barrow, BU. in 2.49.

DUNCAN Frigate 1,180 tons, 300 x 33 ft, 2-40mm. Thornycroft 30.5.1957. Arrived Kingsnorth, Medway in 2.85 to BU.

DUNCANSBY HEAD Repair ship 9,000 tons, 416 x 57 ft. Barrard, Vancouver 17.11.1944. Sold 12.69, BU in Spain.

DUNDALK Minesweeper, later 'Hunt' class. Clyde SB Co 31.1.1919. Mined 16.10.40 and sank in tow 17.10.40 off Harwich.

DUNDALK Oiler (RCN) 1943-50

DUNDAS Corvette (RCN), 'Flower' class. Victoria Mcy 25.7.1941. Sold 23.10.45.

DUNDAS Frigate 1,180 tons, 300 x 33 ft, 3-40mm, 4-TT. White, Cowes 25.9.1953. BU at Troon 4.83.

DUNDEE Sloop 1,060 tons, 250 x 34 ft, 2-4in. Chatham DY 20.9.1932. Sunk 15.9.40 by 'U.48' in the Atlantic.

DUNDEE A. Boarding vessel and tug requis. in WW.I.

DUNDRUM BAY (ex-LOCH SCAMADALE) Frigate, 'Bay' class. Blyth DD 10.7.1945.Renamed ALERT 1945. Sold Ward 13.10.71, BU Inverkeithing.

DUNEDIN Light cruiser 4,650 tons, 445 x 46 ft, 6-6in, 2-3in. Armstrong 19.11.1918. Sunk 24.11.41 by 'U.124' north of Pernambuco.

DUNEDIN Drifter requis. 1915-19 and 1940-45.

DUNGENESS Repair ship 8,580 tons, 416 x 57 ft. W. Coast SB Vancouver 15.3.1945. Sold 9.47, renamed *Levuka*.

DUNGENESS Trawler requis. 1940-40

DUNIRA 5th Rate 38, 1,080bm, 153 x 40 ft. French ALCMENE captured 20.1.1814 by VENERABLE off Madeira. Renamed IMMORTALITE 1814. Sold 1.1837.

DUNKERTON Coastal M/S, 'Ton' class. Goole SB 8.3.1954. Renamed PRETORIA (SAN) 8.55.

DUNKIRK Ketch 2, 33bm. French, captured 1656. Sold 1660.

DUNKIRK (ex-WORCESTER renamed 1660) 4th Rate 48, 662bm, 141½ x 33½ ft. Rebuilt Blackwall 1704 as 906bm; rebuilt Portsmouth 1734 as 965bm, 60 guns. BU 3.1749 at Woolwich.

DUNKIRK PRIZE 6th Rate 24, 299bm. French privateer le HOCQUART captured 15.11.1705. Wrecked 25.10.1708 off Cape Francis, W. Indies.

DUNKIRK 4th Rate 60, 1,246bm, 153 x 43 ft. Woolwich DY 22.7.1754. Harbour service 9.1778. Sold 8.3.1792.

DUNKIRK Destroyer 2,380 tons, 355 x 40 ft, 5-4.5in, 10-TT.Stephen 27.8.1945. Arrived 22.11.65 at Faslane to BU.

DUNMORE Schooner 4 (Canadian lakes). Detroit 1772. In service in 1796.

DUNOON Minesweeper, later 'Hunt' class. Clyde SB 21.3.1919. Sunk 30.4.40 by mine in the North Sea.

DUNSTER CASTLE Corvette, 'Castle' class. Midland SY, Ontario. Cancelled 12.1943.

DUNVEGAN Corvette (RCN), 'Flower' class. Marine Ind 11.12.1940. Sold 1946 Venezuelan navy, renamed IN-DEPENDENCIA.

DUNVER (ex-VERDUN of CANADA renamed 1942) Corvette (RCN), 'River' class. Morton 10.11.1942. Sold 13.12.47; hull sunk 1949 as breakwater at Comox.

DUNWICH 6th Rate 24, 250bm, 94 x 24½ ft. Collins & Chatfield, Shoreham 15.10.1695. Sunk 15.10.1714. as breakwater at Plymouth.

DUQUESNE 3rd Rate 74, 1,901bm. French, captured 25.7.1803 by BEL-LEROPHON and VANGUARD off San Domingo. Stranded 1804 on Morant Key, W. Indies and BU 7.1805.

DURBAN Light cruiser 4,650 tons, 445 x 46 ft, 6-6in, 2-3in. Scotts 29.5.1919. Sunk 9.6.44 as breakwater, Normandy.

DURBAN Coastal M/S, 'Ton' class (SAN). Camper & Nicholson 12.6.1957.

DURHAM (see ACTIVE of 1845)

DURSLEY GALLEY 6th Rate 20. 371bm, 105 x 28½ ft. Deptford 13.2.1718. Sold 21.2.1744, became a privateer and captured 8.5.1746 by the French.

DURWESTON Coastal M/S, 'Ton' class. Dorset Yt Co 18.8.1955. Renamed KAKINADA (Indian navy) 1955.

DUTIFUL (see RELIANCE of 1944)

DUTIFUL Drifter requis. 1915-19.

DWARF Cutter 10, 203bm, 75 x 26 ft. Lowes, Sandgate 24.4.1810. Wrecked 3.3.1824 on Kingstown pier.

DWARF Cutter 2, 50bm, 52 x 15 ft. White, Cowes 1826. Dockyard service then coastguard. Sold 1862 Messrs Hood, Rye.

DWARF (ex-*Mermaid*) Iron screw vessel, 164bm, 130 x 16 ft. Purchased 22.6.1843. Sold 9.1853 J. Broughton. (The first screw vessel in the RN.)

DWARF Wood S. gunboat, 'Cheerful' class. Westbrook, Blackwall 8.4.1856. BU 1863 at Haslar.

DWARF Compos. S. gunvessel, 465bm, 584 tons, 155 x 25 ft, 1-7in, 1-64pdr, 2-20pdr. Woolwich DY 28.11.1867. BU 4.1886 at Devonport.

DWARF 1st class gunboat 710 tons, 180 x 33ft, 2-4in, 4-12pdr. London & Glasgow Co 15.11.1898. Sold 13.7.1926 Ward, Pembroke.

DWARF Tender 172 tons, 83½ x 19 ft. Philip, Dartmouth 20.8.1936. Sold 8.3.62 and hulked 1963 in the Gareloch.

'E' class submarines. 660 tons, 176 x 22½ ft, 1-12pdr, 4-TT (1st eight); 662 tons, 180 x 22½ ft, 1-12pdt, 5-TT (others, except minelayers, 3-TT, 20-mines).

E.1 (ex-D.9) Chatham DY 9.11.1912. Destroyed 8.4.18 at Helsingfors to avoid capture.

E.2 (ex-D.10) Chatham DY 23.11.12. Sold 7.3.21 B. Zammit, Malta.

E.3 Vickers 29.10.12. Sunk 18.10.14 by *U.27' in the North Sea.

E.4 Vickers 5.2.12. Sold 21.2.22 Upnor S. Bkg Co.

E.5 Vickers 17.5.12. Sunk 7.3.16 in the North Sea.

E.6 Vickers 12.11.12. Sunk 26.12.15 by mine in the north Sea.

A.E.1 (RAN) Vickers 22.5.13. Sunk 14.9.14 by unknown cause off the Bismarck Archipelago.

A.E.2 (RAN) Vickers 18.6.13. Scuttled 30.4.15 after damage by shore batteries, Sea of Marmora.

E.7 Chatham DY 2.10.13. Destroyed 5.9.15 by explosive charge of 'UB. 14' after being caught in S/M net, Dardanelles.

E.8 Chatham DY 30.10.13. Destroyed with E.1.

E.9 Vickers 29.11.13. Destroyed with E.1.

E.10 Vickers 29.11.13. Sunk 18.1.15 by unknown cause in the North Sea.

E.11 Vickers 23.4.14. Sold 7.3.21 B. Zammit, Malta.

E.12 Chatham DY 5.9.14. Sold 7.3.21 B. Zammit, Malta.

E.13 Chatham DY 22.9.14. Stranded 3.9.15 coast of Denmark and interned. Sold 14.12.21 Petersen & Albeck, Denmark, BU at Copenhagen.

E.14 Vickers 7.7.14. Sunk 27.1.18 by mine off Kum Kale, Dardanelles.

E.15 Vickers 23.4.14. Stranded 15.4.15 at Kephez Point and destroyed 18.4.15 by boats of MAJESTIC.

E.16 Vickers 23.9.14 Sunk 22.8.16 by mine in the North Sea.

E.17 Vickers 16.1.15. Wrecked 6.1.16 off the Texel.

E.18 Vickers 4.3.15. Sunk 1/2.6.16.

E.19 Vickers 13.5.15. Destroyed with E.1.

E.20 Vickers 12.6.15. Sunk 5.11.15 by 'UB.14' in the Sea of Marmora.

E.21 Vickers 24.7.15. Sold 14.12.21 Petersen & Albeck.

E.22 Vickers 27.8.15. Sunk 25.4.16 by 'UB.18' in the North Sea.

E.23 Vickers 28.9.15. Sold 6.9.22 Young, Sunderland.

E.24 (M/L) Vickers 9.12.15. Sunk 24.3.16 by mine in the North Sea.

E.25 (laid down for Turkish navy) Beardmore 23.8.15. Sold 14.12.21 Petersen & Albeck.

E.26 (laid down for Turkish navy) Beardmore 11.11.15. Sunk 6.7.16 in the North Sea.

E.27 Yarrow 9.6.17. Sold 6.9.22 Cashmore, Newport (was ordered 11.14, cancelled 4.15, restarted 8.15).

E.28 Yarrow. Ordered 11.14, cancelled 20.4.15.

E.29 Armstrong 1.6.15. Sold 21.2.22 Upnor S. Bkg Co.

E.30 Armstrong 29.6.15. Sunk 22.11.16 in the North Sea.

E.31 Scotts 23.8.15. Sold 6.9.22 Young, Sunderland.

E.32 White 16.8.16. Sold 6.9.22 Young Sunderland.

E.33 Thornycroft 18.4.16. Sold 6.9.22 Cashmore, Newport.

E.34 (M/L) Thornycroft 27.1.17. Sunk 20.7.18 by mine in the North Sea.

E.35 J. Brown 20.5.16. Sold 6.9.22 Ellis & Co.

E.36 J. Brown 16.9.16. Sunk 17.1.17 in the North Sea.

E.37 Fairfield 2.9.15. Sunk 1.12.16 in the North Sea.

E.38 Fairfield 13.6.16. Sold 6.9.22 Ellis & Co.

E.39 Palmer 18.5.16. Sold 13.10.21 S. Wales Salvage Co; foundered 9.22 in tow.

E.40 Palmer 9.11.16. Sold 14.12.21 Petersen & Albeck.

E.41 (M/L) Cammell Laird 28.7.15. Sold 6.9.22 Ellis & Co.

E.42 Cammell Laird 22.10.15. Sold 6.9.22 J. Smith.

E.43 Swan Hunter 1916. Sold 3.1.21 S. Wales Salvage Co; stranded and lost in tow at St Agnes, Cornwall.

E.44 Swan Hunter 21.2.16. Sold 13.10.21 S. Wales Salvage Co.

E.45 (M/L) Cammell Laird 25.1.16. Sold 6.9.22 Ellis & Co.

E.46 (M/L) Cammell Laird 4.4.16. Sold 6.9.22 Ellis & Co.

E.47 Fairfield 29.5.16. Sunk 20.8.17 in the North Sea.

E.48 Fairfield 2.8.16. Target 1920. Sold 7.28 Cashmore, Newport.

E.49 Swan Hunter 18.9.16 Sunk 12.3.17 by mine off the Shetlands.

E.50 J. Brown 13.11.16. Sunk 1.2.18 by mine in the North Sea.

E.51 (M/L)Scotts (ex-Yarrow transferred 3.15) 30.11.16. Sold 13.10.21 S. Wales Salvage Co.

E.52 Denny (ex-Yarrow transferred 3.15) 25.1.17. Sold 3.1.21 Brixham Marine & Eng. Co.

E.53 Beardmore 1916. Sold 6.9.22 Beard.

E.54 Beardmore 1916. Sold 14.12.21 Petersen & Albeck.

E.55 Denny 5.2.16. Sold 6.9.22 Ellis & Co.

E.56 Denny 19.6.16. Sold 9.6.23 Granton S. Bkg Co.

E.57 Vickers Laid down 5.16, launched 10.5.17 as L.1.

E.58 Vickers. Laid down 5.16, launched 6.7.17 as L.2.

EAGLE Careening hulk, 894bm. Ex-merchant purchased 1592. Sold 1683 at Chatham.

EAGLE SHALLOP Sloop 6. Built 1648. Listed to 1653.

EAGLE 12-gun ship, 150bm. French AIGLE captured 1650. Sold 1655.

EAGLE (see SELBY of 1654)

EAGLE Fireship 6, 50bm. Algerian, captured 1670. Expended 2.5.1671 in Bugia Bay.

EAGLE Fireship 6, Purchased 1672. Foundered 4.1673 on passage to St Helena.

EAGLE 3rd Rate 70, 1,053bm, 151½ x 40½ ft. Portsmouth DY 1679. Rebuilt Chatham 1699 as 1,099bm. Wrecked 22.10.1707 on the Scilly Isles.

EAGLE Advice boat 10, 153bm, 76 x 21 ft. Fugar, Arundel 1696. Wrecked 27.11.1703 on the Sussex coast.

EAGLE Fireship. Sunk 1745 as a breakwater.

EAGLE 4th Rate 58, 1,130bm, 147 x 42 ft. Barnard, Harwich 2.12.1745. Sold 9.6.1767.

EAGLE Sloop 14 (Indian) Bombay DY 1754. Fate unknown.

EAGLE 3rd Rate 64, 1,372bm, 160 x 44½ ft. Wells, Rotherhithe 2.5.1774. Harbour service 1790; renamed BUCKINGHAM 15.8.1800. BU 10.1812 at Chatham.

EAGLE Gunvessel 4, 71bm, 68 x 15ft. Dutch hoy purchased 4.1794. Sold 11.1804.

EAGLE Gun-brig 12, 158bm, 74 x 22 ft. French VENTEUX captured 1803.

Renamed ECLIPSE 26.8.1803. Sold 7.4.1807.

EAGLE 3rd Rate 74, 1,723bm, 174 x 48½ ft. Pitcher, Northfleet 27.2.1804. Reduced to 50 guns 4.1830; training ship 10.1860; renamed EAGLET 1918. Lost by fire 1926. Wreck sold 4.1.27 J. Hornby.

EAGLE Brig (Canadian lakes), 110bm. Built 1812. Captured 4.7.1812 by Americans; retaken 9.1813 and renamed CHUBB. Sold 1822.

EAGLE (ex-Chilian battleship ALMIRANTE COCHRANE converted on stocks)Aircraft carrier 22,790 tons, 625 x 94 ft, 9-6in, 4-4in, 21-A/C. Armstrong 8.6.1918. Sunk 11.8.42 by 'U.73' in the western Mediterranean.

EAGLE Aircraft carrier 36,800 tons, 720 x 112 ft, Vickers Armstrong, Tyne. Laid down 19.4.1944, cancelled 1945.

EAGLE (ex-AUDACIOUS renamed 21.1.46) Aircraft carrier 36,800 tons, 720 x 112 ft, 16-4.5in, 58-40mm, 100-A/C. Harland & Wolff 19.3.46. Arrived Cairnryan 19.10.78 to BU.

EAGLE Tug requis. 1914-19. Trawler 1914-16. M/S. 1916-20.

EAGLET Ketch 8, 54bm. Horsleydown 1655. Sold 1674.

EAGLET Ketch 10,95bm, 63 x 19 ft. Shish, Rotherhithe 7.4.1691. Captured 5.1693 by the French off Arran.

EAGLET (see EAGLE of 1804)

EAGLET (see SIR BEVIS)

EAGLET Paddle vessel hired 1855-57.

EARL Sloop, presented 2.1701 by the government of Jamaica and made a fireship. Sold 15.2.1705.

EARL of CHATHAM Gunvessel 12. Purchased 1792. Gone by 1800.

EARL OF DENBIGH Store hulk, 181bm, 73 x 24ft. Purchased in N.America for use at Antigua 6.4.1788. Lost 1797.

EARL OF DENBIGH (see PELICAN)

EARL OF EGMONT Schooner. purchased in 3.1767. Sold 11.8.1773.

EARL of NORTHAMPTON Survey Sloop. Sold 1774 in Jamaica. (Purchased 26.4.1769)

EARL of PETERBOROUGH (ex-M.8 renamed 1915) Monitor 5,900 tons, 320 x 87 ft, 2-12in, 2-6in, 2-12pdr. Harland & Wolff 26.8.1915. Sold 8.11.21 Slough TC; BU in Germany.

EARL ROBERTS Monitor (see ROBERTS)

EARNEST Gun-brig 12, 182bm, 80 x 23 ft, 10-18pdr, 2-18pdr carr. Menzies,

Leith 1.1805. Sold 2.5.1816.

EARNEST Wood S. gunboat, 'Albacore' class. Patterson, Bristol 29.3.1856. Sold 17.1.1885. Castle.

EARNEST Destroyer 355 tons, 210½ x 22ft, 1-12pdr, 5-6pdr, 2-TT. Laird 7.11.1896. Sold 1.7.1920 Castle, Plymouth.

EARNEST Rescue tug. 1943, renamed EARNER 1943-61.

EASTBOURNE Minesweeper, TE 'Bangor' class. Lobnitz 5.11.1940. Sold. 28.9.48; BU Clayton & Davie, Dunston.

EASTBOURNE Frigate 2,150 tons, 360 x 41 ft, 2-4.5in, 2-40mm. Vickers Armstrong, Tyne 29.12.1955. Sold J.A.White, arrived Inverkeithing 7.3.85.

EASTON Destroyer, 'Hunt' class type III. White 11.7.1942. Arrived 1.53 at Charlestown to BU.

EASTVIEW Frigate (RCN) 'River' class. Vickers, Montreal 17.11.1943. Sold 13.12.47. to BU; hull sunk 1948 as breakwater at Comox.

EASTWAY (see Battleaxe)

ECHO 6TH Rate 24, 539bm, 118 x 32½ ft, 24-9pdr. French, captured 5.1758 at Louisburg. Sold 5.6.1770.

ECHO Sloop 16. French HUSSARD captured 5.7.1780 by NONSUCH Wrecked 1791 in Plymouth Sound.

ECHO Sloop 16, 342bm, 101½ x 27½ ft Barton, Liverpool 8.10.1782. BU. 1797.

ECHO Sloop 16, 341bm, 96 x 29ft. King, Dover 9.1797. Sold 18.5.1809.

ECHO Brig-sloop 18, 'Cruizer' class, 388bm. Pelham, Frindsbury 1.7.1809 BU 5.1817.

ECHO Wood paddle vessel (ex-sloop 'Cherokee' class), 295bm, 112 x 25 ft, Woolwich DY 28.5.1827. Tug 1830. Sold 6.1885.

ECHO Destroyer 1,375 tons, 318 x 33 ft, 4-4.7in, 8-TT. Denny 16.2.1934. Lent Greek navy 5.4.44 to 4.56 as NAVARINON. BU 4.56 Clayton & Davie, Dunston.

ECHO Survey vessel 120 tons, 100 x 22 ft. White, Cowes 1.5.1957. Sold 1986

ECHO Whaler 1915-19. Trawler. Requis. 1915-19.

ECHUCA Minesweeper (RAN), 'Bathurst' class. Williamstown DY 17.1.1942. To RNZN 5.52. BU 4.67 Pacific Steel Co. Auckland.

ECLAIR 6th Rate 22, 444bm, French captured 9.6.1793 by LEDA in the Mediterranean. Powder hulk 4.1797. Sold 27.8.1806.

ECLAIR Gunvessel 3, 107bm, 60 x 20½ ft, 3-18pdr. French Captured 9.5.1795. by a squadron on the coast of France. Fitted as schooner 4.1796. Hulked 1802.

ECLAIR Schooner 12, 145bm, 12-12pdr carr. French. Captured 18.1.1801 by GARLAND at Guadeloupe. Renamed PICKLE 5.1809. Sold 11.6.1818.

ECLAIR Brig-Sloop 18, 'Cruizer' class, 387bm. Warren, Brightlingsea 8.7.1807. BU 3.1831.

ECLAIR (see INFERNAL of 1843)

ECLIPSE (Gunboat No.22) Gun-vessel 12, 169bm, 76 x 23 ft, 2-24pdr, 10-18pdr carr. Perry, Blackwall 29.3.1797. Sold 9.1802.

ECLIPSE (see EAGLE of 1803)

ECLIPSE Brig Sloop 18, 'Cruizer' class, 384bm, King, Dover 4.8.1807. Sold 31.8.1817.

ECLIPSE Brig-Sloop 10, 'Cherokee' class, 235bm, Plymouth DY 3.7.1819. Coastguard 12.1836; renamed WV.21 on 25.5.1863. Sold 10.11.1863. Castle, Charlton.

ECLIPSE Wood S. sloop, 700bm, 185 x 28½ ft, 2-68pdr, 2-32pdr. Scott Russell, Millwall 18.9.1860. BU 7.1867 at Sheerness.

ECLIPSE (ex-SAPPHO renamed 1867) Wood S. sloop, 1,276bm, 1,760 tons 212 x 36 ft, 2-7in, 4-64pdr, Sheerness DY 14.11.1867. Lent War Dept as hulk 1888 to 1892. Sale list 1921.

ECLIPSE 2nd class cruiser 5,600 tons, 350 x 53 ft, 5-6in, 6-4.7in (11-6in in 1904). Portsmouth DY 19.7.1894. Sold 8.1921 G.Cohen.

ECLIPSE Destroyer 1,375 tons, 318 x 33 ft, 4-4.7ins, 8-TT Denny 1.4.1934. Sunk 24.10.43 by mine in the Aegean.

EDDERTON Coastal M/S, 'Ton' class. Doig 1.11.1952. Renamed MYRMIDON survey vessel 4.64. Became Mayalasian PERANTAU in 3.69.

EDEN 6th Rate 24, 451bm, 108½ x 31 ft. Courtney, Chester 19.5.1814. BU 5.1833. (Was left submerged in the Hamoaze 11.1816 to 3.1817 to test effect of sea water on dry rot).

EDEN Destroyer 555 tons, 220 x 23 ft, 1-12pdr, 5-6pdr (3-12pdr 1907) 2-TT. Hawthorn 14.3.1903. Sunk 18.6.16 in collision with SS France in the Channel.

EDEN Trawler. 1920-47.

EDGAR 3rd Rate 70, 1,046bm, 154 x 40 ft. Bailey, Bristol 29.7.1668. Rebuilt Portsmouth 1700 as 1,119bm. Burnt 10.1711 by accident at Spithead.

EDGAR 4th Rate 60, 1,297 bm, 155 x

44 ft. Randall, Rotherhithe 16.11.1758. Sunk 8.1774 as breakwater at Sheerness.

EDGAR 3rd Rate 74, 1,644bm, 168 x 47 ft. Woolwich DY 30.6.1779. Convict hulk 12.1813; renamed RETRIBUTION 19.8.1814. BU 2.1835 at Deptford.

EDGAR 2nd Rate 80, 2,600bm. Chatham DY. Renamed HOOD 29.6.1848 and launched as screw ship, 3,308bm, 4.5.1859. (see HOOD)

EDGAR Screw 2nd rate 91, 3,094bm, 5,157 tons, 230 x 55½ ft, 8-10in, 36-8in, 2-68pdr, 34-32pdr. Woolwich DY 23.10.1858. Lent Customs as hulk 12.2.1870. Sold 12.4.1904 Castle Charlton.

EDGAR 1st class cruiser 7,350 tons, 360 x 60 ft, 2-9.2in, 10-6in, 12-6pdr. Devonport DY 24.11.1890. Sold 9.5.1921 Ward; arrived 3.4.23 at Morecambe to BU.

EDGAR A/C carrier 13,350 tons, 630 x 80 ft, Vickers Armstrong, Tyne 26.3.1944. Renamed PERSEUS 6.44 and completed as maintenance carrier. Arrived 6.5.58 Smith & Houston to BU, at Port Glasgow.

EDGAR Cruiser, circa 9,000 tons, projected 1945, cancelled 3.46.

EDGELEY Inshore M/S, 'Ley' class. Dorset Yt Co, Poole. Launched as WRENTHAM (qv)

EDINBURGH 5th Rate 32, 364bm, 99 x 29 ft. Scottish ROYAL WILLIAM transferred 5.8.1707. Sunk 10.8.1709 as a breakwater at Harwich.

EDINBURGH (see WARSPITE of 1666)

EDINBURGH 3rd Rate 74, 1,772bm, 176½ x 49 ft. Brent, Rotherhithe 26.1.1811. Undocked 31.12.1846 as screw ship. Sold 11.1865 Castle & Beech.

EDINBURGH (ex-MAJESTIC renamed 16.3.1882) Turret ship 9,420 tons, 325 x 68 ft, 4-12in, 5-6in, 4-6pdr. Pembroke Dock 18.3.1882. Sold 11.10.1910 Ward, Swansea, and Briton Ferry.

EDINBURGH Cruiser 10,000 tons, 579 x 63 ft, 12-6in, 12-4in. Swan Hunter 31.3.1938. Scuttled 2.5.42 in the Barents Sea after being torpedoed 30.4.42.

EDINBURGH Destroyer 3550 tons. Cammell Laird 14.4.1982

EDLINGHAM Inshore M/S, 'Ham' class. Weatherhead, Cockenzie 21.7.1955. Burnt 29.9.56 by accident in Haslar Creek; wreck sold 8.8.57.

EDMUNDSTON Corvette (RCN), 'Flower' class. Yarrow, Vancouver

22.2.1941. Sold 1946, renamed *Ampala*

EDWARD Ship in service in 1338.

EDWARD (see HENRY GRACE a DIEU)

EDWARD Ketch 6. Sunk 1667 as blockship.

EFFINGHAM Cruiser 9,750 tons, 565 x 58 ft, 7-7.5in, 4-3in, 6-12pdr. Portsmouth DY 8.6.1921. Wrecked 18.5.40 between Harstad and Bodo, Norway; wreck destroyed 21.5.40.

EGERIA 6th Rate 26, 424bm, 108½ x 30 ft. Boole, Bridport 31.10.1807. Harbour service 1825. BU 1865.

EGERIA Compos. S. sloop 940 tons, 160 x 31½ ft, 2-7in, 2-64pdr. Pembroke Dock 1.11.1873. Survey ship 10.1886. Sold 10.1911 Vancouver Navy League.

EGERIA Survey vessel 120 tons, 100 x 22 ft. Weatherhead, Cockenzie 13.9.1958. Lent Marine Socy in 12.86, renamed *Jonas Hartway.*

EGERIA Trawler requis. 1939-45.

EGGESFORD Destroyer, 'Hunt' class type III. White 12.9.1942. Sold 11.57 W. German navy, renamed BROMMY.

EGLANTINE Sloop, 'Anchusa' class. Barclay Curle 22.6.1917. Sold 1.12.21 Stanlee, Dover.

EGLANTINE Corvette, 'Flower' class. Harland & Wolff 11.6.1941. Lent R. Norwegian navy 29.8.41; sold 1946.

EGLINTON Paddle M/S, 'Ascot' class. Ayrshire Co 9.9.1916. Sold 7.22 King, Garston.

EGLINTON Destroyer, 'Hunt' class type I. Vickers Armstrong, Tyne 28.12.1939. Arrived 28.5.56 Hughes Bolckow, Blyth to BU.

EGMONT Schooner, 100bm, 62 x 20 ft. Purchased 3.1765. Lost 12.7.1776.

EGMONT 3rd Rate 74, 1,648bm, 169 x 47 ft. Deptford DY 29.8.1768. BU 11.1799 at Chatham.

EGMONT Schooner 10, 199bm, Purchased 1770. Captured 7.1779 by the American privateer WILD CAT off Newfoundland.

EGMONT 3rd Rate 74, 1,760bm, 178 x 49 ft. Pitcher, Northfleet 7.3.1810. Storeship 12.1862. Sold 2.1.1875 at Rio de Janeiro.

EGMONT Base ships (see ACHILLES of 1863, FIREFLY of 1877 and BULLFROG of 1881).

EGREMONT (see ACHILLES of 1863)

EGREMONT CASTLE Corvette, 'Castle' class. Kingston SY. Cancelled 12.1943.

EGRET Sloop 1,200 tons, 276 x 37½ ft, 8-4in. White 31.5.1938. Sunk 27.8.43 by air attack in the Bay of Biscay.

EGRET Store carrier and two Trawlers WW.I.

L'EGYPTIENNE 5th Rate 40, 1,430bm, 170 x 44 ft, 28-24pdr, 16-24 pdr carr., 4-9pdr. French, captured 2.9.1801 at Alexandria. Sold 30.4.1817 to BU.

EHKOLI Patrol boat (RCN), 84 x 20 ft, 1-MG. Victoria Boat & Repair Co 3.9.1941. Survey vessel 1951.

EIDEREN Sloop 18, 336bm. Danish, captured 7.9.1807 at Copenhagen. BU 6.1813 (was to have been renamed UTILE).

EKINS Frigate, TE 'Captain' class. Bethlehem, Higham 2.10.1943 on lend-lease. Badly damaged by mine 16.4.45; nominally returned USN 6.45; BU at Dordrecht, Holland in 1947.

ELEANOR Fireship, 193bm, 85½ x 24 ft. Purchased 22.6.1739. Sunk 5.1742 as breakwater at Sheerness.

ELECTRA Brig-sloop 16, 285bm, 93 x 26 ft. Betts, Mistleythorn 22.1.1806. Stranded 25.3.1808 on coast of Sicily; salved and sold 1808 at Malta.

ELECTRA Brig-sloop 16, 315bm, 94 x 28 ft. French ESPIEGLE captured 16.8.1808 by SYBILLE in the Atlantic. Sold 11.7.1816.

ELECTRA Sloop 18, 462bm, 113½ x 31 ft. Portsmouth DY 28.9.1837. Sold 17.2.1862 W. Foord.

ELECTRA Destroyer 385 tons, 218 x 20 ft, 1-12pdr, 5-6pdr, 2-TT. Thomson 14.7.1896. Sold 29.4.1920 Barking S. Bkg Co.

ELECTRA Destroyer 1,375 tons, 318 x 33 ft, 4-4.7in, 8-TT. Hawthorn Leslie 15.2.1934. Sunk 27.2.42 by the Japanese cruiser JINTSU in the Java Sea battle.

ELECTRA Trawler requis. 1915-19 and 1940-46.

ELEPHANT Storeship, 314bm, 102 x 26½ ft. Purchased 5.1705. Hulked 6.1709 at Port Mahon (Was a captured French ship).

ELEPHANT (ex-*Union*) Storeship 10, 382bm, 103 x 29 ft, 10-4pdr. Purchased 17.7.1776. Sold 2.12.1779 at Greenock.

ELEPHANT 3rd Rate 74, 1617bm, 168 x 47½ ft. Parsons, Bursledon 24.8.1786. Reduced to 58-gun 4th Rate 3.1818. BU 11.1830.

ELEPHANT (see MINOTAUR of 1863)

ELEPHANT (see HERMES of 1953)

ELEPHANT Tug. 1893-1920.

ELF (ex-*Rainbow*) Tender 180 tons, 115 x 18 ft. Purchased 1911. Sold 6.24 W.G. Keen.

ELF Tug 1896-1905. Trawler 1917-19. Tug 1947-60.

ELFIN Paddle yacht, 98bm (built of Spanish mahogany). Chatham DY 8.2.1849. On sale list 1901.

ELFIN (ex-War dept vessel *Dundas*) Tender 125 tons, 98 x 17½ ft. Transferred 1905. Sold 29.2.28 Ward, Pembroke Dock.

ELFIN Tender 222 tons, 102 x 26 ft. White 20.11.1933. Renamed NETTLE 28.8.41. On sale list 1957.

ELFREDA (ex-USS OVERSEER) Minesweeper, 'Catherine' class. Assoc. SB, Seattle 25.1.1943; on lend-lease from 22.12.43. Returned USN and sold Turkish navy 3.47 as CESMI.

ELGIN A. ship in service in 1814.

ELGIN (ex-TROON renamed 1918) Minesweeper, later 'Hunt' class. Simons 3.3.1919. Sold 20.3.45: BU King, Gateshead.

ELIAS 32-gun ship, 406bm. Captured 1653. Foundered 1664.

ELIAS Hulk, 350bm. Spanish ship captured 1656. Sold 1684.

ELIAS 34-gun ship, 301bm. Captured 1666. Sold 1667.

ELING Gunvessel 12, 149bm, 80½ x 22½ ft, 12-18pdr carr. Purchased 4.1798. BU 5.1814.

ELIZABETH (also GREAT ELIZABETH) (ex-*Salvator*) 900bm. Purchased 1514. Wrecked 1514.

ELIZABETH JONAS Galleon 56, 680bm, 3-60pdr, 6-32pdr, 8-18pdr, 9-9pdr, 9-6pdr, 21 small. Woolwich 3.7.1559. Rebuilt 1598 and renamed ELIZABETH. Sold 1618.

ELIZABETH BONAVENTURE Galleon 47, 600bm, 2-60pdr, 2-32pdr, 11-18pdr, 14-9pdr, 4-6pdr, 14 small. Built 1567. Rebuilt 1581. BU 1611.

ELIZABETH 16-gun vessel, 40bm. In service 1577-88.

ELIZABETH 3-gun ship, 474/643bm. Deptford 1647. Burnt 1667 in action with the Dutch in Virginia.

ELIZABETH Hoy (Royalist). Purchased 1648. Deserted 1649 to Parliament. Sold 1653.

ELIZABETH 3rd Rate 70, 1,073bm, 152 x 41 ft, 26-32pdr, 26-12pdr, 18 small. Castle, Deptford 1679. Rebuilt Portsmouth 1704 as 1,152bm. Captured 12.11.1704 by the French.

ELIZABETH 3rd Rate 70, 1,110bm, 150½ x 41 ft. Stacey, Woolwich

1.8.1706. Rebuilt Chatham 1737 as 1,224bm, 64 guns. BU completed 10.5.1766 at Portsmouth.

ELIZABETH 3rd Rate 74, 1,617bm, 168 x 47 ft. Portsmouth DY 17.10.1769. BU 8.1797 at Chatham.

ELIZABETH Gunvessel 3, 50bm. Purchased 7.1795. In service in 1801.

ELIZABETH Cutter 10, 110bm. Spanish, captured 3.4.1805 by BACCHANTE off Havana. Foundered 1807 in the W. Indies.

ELIZABETH Schooner 12, 141bm, 73 x 21½ fr. French, captured 1806. Capsized 10.1814.

ELIZABETH 3rd Rate 74, 1,724bm, 174 x 48½ ft. Perry, Blackwall 23.5.1807. BU 8.1820 at Chatham.

ELIZABETH Two vessels hired 1808. Tank vessel 1873-1921.

ELIZABETH & SARAH Fireship 6, 100bm. Purchased 1688. Sunk 1690 as foundation at Sheerness.

ELK Brig-sloop 18 (fir-built), 'Cruizer' class, 382bm. Barnard, Deptford 22.8.1804. BU 10.1812.

ELK Brig-sloop 18, 'Cruizer' class, 386bm. Hobbs & Hillyer, Redbridge 28.8.1813. Sold 21.1.1836.

ELK Brig-sloop 16, 482bm, 105 x 33½ ft, 4-32pdr, 12-32pdr carr. Chatham DY 27.9.1847. Renamed WV.13, coastguard 1863; renamed WV.28 on 25.5.1863. Sold 30.5.1893.

ELK Compos. S. gunvessel, 465bm, 603 tons, 155 x 25 ft, 1-7in, 1-64pdr, 2-20pdr. Portsmouth DY 10.1.1868. Tug 1890. Sold 1905 as a dredger.

ELK Three Trawlers WW.I. Yacht (RCN) 1940-45.

ELLINORE see BONAVOLIA.

ELLINOR (ex-S. yacht *Eberhard*) Survey ship, 593 gross, 180 (o/a) x 27 ft. Purchased 1901. Fate unknown.

ELPHINSTONE Sloop 18 (Indian), 387bm. Bombay DY 1824. Sold 7.1862.

ELPHINSTONE (ex-*Hindoo*) Troopship (RIM) 950 tons, 206 x 28 ft. Swan Hunter 14.11.1887 and purchased 1887. On sale list 1919.

ELPHINSTONE (see CEANOTHUS)

ELSENHAM Inshore M/S, 'Ham' class. Ailsa 25.5.1955. Sold Arabian Federation 9.10.67.

ELTHAM (ex-PORTSMOUTH?) 5th Rate 44, 678bm, 124 x 36 ft. Deptford 1736. BU 6.1763 at Plymouth.

ELVIN Sloop 18. Danish, captured 1807. Sold 3.11.1814. (Was to have been renamed HARLEQUIN.)

EMBLETON (see BOSSINGTON of

1955)

EMERALD 6th Rate 28, 571bm, 115½ x 34 ft, 24-pdr, 4-4pdr. French EMERAUDE captured 21.9.1757 by SOUTHAMPTON. BU 11.1761 at Portsmouth.

EMERALD 5th Rate 32, 681bm, 125 x 35½ ft. Blaydes, Hull 8.6.1762. BU 1793.

EMERALD 5th Rate 36, 934bm, 143 x 38½ ft. Pitcher, Northfleet 31.7.1795. BU 1.1836.

EMERALD Tender, 86bm, 58 x 19 ft. Purchased 1820. BU 12.1847.

EMERALD Wood S. frigate 51, 2,913bm (ex-4th Rate 60, 2,146bm), 237 x 52½ ft. 30-8in, 1-68pdr, 20-32pdr. Deptford DY 19.7.1856. Sold 2.12.1869 Castle, Charlton.

EMERALD Compos. S. corvette 2,120 tons, 220 x 40 ft, 12-6pdr. Pembroke Dock 18.8.1876. Powder hulk 1898. Sold 10.7.1906 Cox, Falmouth.

EMERALD (see BLACK PRINCE)

EMERALD (see AMELIA of 1888)

EMERALD Light cruiser 7,600 tons, 535 x 54½ ft, 7-6in, 2-4in. Armstrong 19.5.1920; completed at Chatham 14.1.26. Sold 23.7.48; BU at Troon.

EMERALD Three Trawlers requis. WW.I.

EMERSHAM Wood pad. vessel. Purchased 1830. Sold 1833.

EMILIA Brig. Ex-Brazilian slaver captured 1840 and purchased 29.12.1840. Fate unknown.

EMILIEN (see TRINCOMALE of 1801)

EMILY Schooner 2 (Indian), 90bm. Bombay DY 1855. Sold 7.1862.

EMILY Tug 1901-34; Tug 1934-42 : Drifter in WW.I.

EMPEROR Paddle yacht. Purchased 1856; commissioned 25.2.1857. Sold in 7.1858 and later became Japanese BANRYU.

EMPEROR (ex-USS NASSUK BAY) Escort carrier 7,800 tons. Oregon SB Co. Laid down 19.4.1943 for the RN; launched 6.10.43 as USS SOLOMONS.

EMPEROR (ex-USS PYBUS) Escort carrier 11,420 tons, 468½ x 69½ ft, 2-4in, 16-40mm, 24-A/C. Seattle Tacoma 7.10.42 and to RN 6.8.43 on lend-lease. Returned 12.2.46 USN.

EMPEROR Trawler. 1917-19.

EMPEROR of INDIA ex-DELHI renamed 10.1913) Battleship 25,000 tons, 580 x 89½ ft, 10-13.5in, 14-6in. Vickers 27.11.13. Target 1931. Sold 6.2.32 Metal Industries, Rosyth.

EMPEROR of INDIA Paddle vessel requis. 1916-20 and 1939-46.

EMPIRE ANVIL (ex-*Cape Argos*) Landing ship 11,650 tons, 396 x 60 ft, 1-4in, 1-12pdr, 12-20mm. Consolidated Steel Corp Wilmington 14.10.1943. Renamed ROCKSAND 11.44; returned to USN 6.46.

EMPIRE ARQUEBUS (ex-*Cape St. Vincent*) Landing ship (as EMPIRE ANVIL). C.S.C., Wilmington 16.11.43. Renamed CICERO 1.45; Empire Arquebus (MWT) 10.45; to Egyptian navy 11.46 as AL SUDAN.

EMPIRE BATTLEAXE (ex-*Cape Berkeley*) Landing ship (as EMPIRE ANVIL). C.S.C., Wilmington 12.7.43. Renamed DONOVAN 1945; *Empire Battleaxe* (MWT) 1946; returned 1947 USN.

EMPIRE BROADSWORD (ex-Cape Marshall) Landing ship (as EMPIRE ANVIL). C.S.C., Wilmington 16.8.43. Sunk 2.7.44 by mine off Normandy.

EMPIRE COMFORT (ex-YORK CASTLE renamed 1944) Rescue ship, ex'Castle' class corvette. Ferguson 20.9.1944. Sold 7.55.

EMPIRE CROSSBOW (ex-*Cape Washington*) Landing ship (as EMPIRE ANVIL). C.S.C., Wilmington 30.11.43. Renamed SAINFOIN 11.44; returned 9.46 to the USN.

EMPIRE CUTLASS (ex-*Cape Compass*) Landing ship (as EMPIRE ANVIL). C.S.C., Wilmington 29.7.43. Renamed SANSOVINO 1945; *Empire Cutlass* (MWT) 6.46; returned 1947 to the USN.

EMPIRE GAUNTLET (ex-*Cape Comorin*) Landing ship (as EMPIRE ANVIL). C.S.C., Wilmington 23.11.43. Renamed SEFTON 10.44; returned 9.46 to the USN.

EMPIRE HALBERD (ex-*Cape Gregory*) Landing ship (as EMPIRE ANVIL). C.S.C., Wilmington 24.7.43. Renamed SILVIO 12.44; *Empire Halberd* (MWT) 1946; returned 6.48 to the USN.

EMPIRE JAVELIN (ex-*Cape Lobos*) Landing ship (as EMPIRE ANVIL). C.S.C., Wilmington 25.10.43. Sunk 28.12.44 by U-boat in the Channel.

EMPIRE LANCE (ex-*Cape Pine*) Landing ship (as EMPIRE ANVIL). C.S.C., Wilmington 28.8.43. Renamed SIR HUGO 8.45; *Empire Lance* 1945; returned 1946 to the USN.

EMPIRE MACE (ex-*Cape St. Roque*) Landing ship (as EMPIRE ANVIL). C.S.C., Wilmington 8.9.43; Renamed GALTEEMORE 1.45; *Empire Mace* (MWT) 10.45; to Egyptian navy 1946 as MISR.

EMPIRE PEACEMAKER (ex-SCARBOROUGH CASTLE renamed 1944) Rescue ship; ex 'Castle' class corvette. Fleming & Ferguson 8.9.1944. Sold 7.55; BU in Belgium.

EMPIRE RAPIER (ex-*Cape Turner*) Landing ship (as EMPIRE ANVIL). C.S.C., Wilmington 21.9.43. *Empire Rapier* (MWT) 1945; returned 1946 to the USN. (Was to have been renamed SIR VISTO.)

EMPIRE REST (ex-RAYLEIGH CASTLE renamed 1944) Rescue ship, ex 'Castle' class corvette. Ferguson 19.6.44. Arrived 5.6.52 Ward, Briton Ferry to BU.

EMPIRE SHELTER (ex-BARNARD CASTLE renamed 1944) Rescue ship, ex-'Castle class corvette. G. Brown 5.10.44. BU in Belgium 1955.

EMPIRE SPEARHEAD (ex-*Cape Girardeau*) Landing ship (as EMPIRE ANVIL). C.S.C., Wilmington 7.11.43. Renamed ORMONDE 1945: *Empire Spearhead* (MWT) 1945; returned 8.47 to the USN.

EMPIRE (see REVENGE of 1859)

EMPRESS Tender 100 tons, 77 x 15½ ft. Transferred from War Dept 1906. Renamed HERON 25.11.06. Sold 20.9.23.

EMPRESS (ex-*Carnegie*) Escort carrier 11,420 tons, 468½ x 69½ ft, 2-4in, 16-40mm, 24-A/C. Seattle, Tacoma 30.12.1942 on lend-lease. Returned 4.2.46 to the USN.

EMPRESS Seaplane carrier. 1960 tons. Requis. 1914-19. Paddle vessel 1939-44.

EMPRESS MARY Storeship 16, 650bm, 123 x 34 ft. Purchased 17.4.1799. Sunk 1804 as breakwater at Harwich.

EMPRESS of INDIA (ex-RENOWN renamed 1890) Battleship, 14,150 tons, 380 x 75 ft, 4-13.5in, 10-6in, 16-6pdr. Pembroke Dock 7.5.1891. Sunk 41.11.1913 at target in Start Bay.

EMSWORTH Ketch 4, 40bm. Emsworth 1667. Sold 1683.

EMULOUS Brig-sloop 18, 'Cruizer' class, 384bm. Rowe, Newcastle 6.1806. Wrecked 7.8.1812 on Sable Island.

EMULOUS Sloop 14, 213bm. American NAUTILUS captured 6.7.1812 by SHANNON. Sold 8.1817.

EMULOUS Brig-sloop 10, 'Cherokee' class, 235bm. Plymouth DY 16.12.1819. Coastguard 1841. Sold 1864 M. Sargent.

EMULOUS Tug 1944-46. Tug 1947-58.

ENARD BAY (ex-LOCH BRACADALE renamed 1944) Frigate, 'Bay' class. Smith Dk 31.10.44. Arrived 15.11.57 at Faslane to BU.

ENCHANTRESS Sloop 14, 176bm, 80 x 23 ft, 14-6pdr. Purchased 1804. Harbour service 6.1813. Listed to 8.1818.

ENCHANTRESS Wood S. sloop, 992bm, 185 x 34½ ft. Pembroke Dock. Ordered 1847, cancelled 4.4.1851.

ENCHANTRESS Sloop, ex-slaver captured 10.8.1860. by BRISK. Wrecked 20.2.1861 in the Mozambique Channel. (Was to have been commissioned in the RN.)

ENCHANTRESS Wood pad. despatch vessel, 835bm, 1,000 tons, 220 x 28 ft, 2-20 pdr. Pembroke Dock 2.8.1862. Sold 1889, Read, Portsmouth to BU.

ENCHANTRESS (see HELICON of 1865)

ENCHANTRESS S. yacht 3,470 tons, 320 x 40 ft, 4-3pdr. Harland & Wolff 7.11.1903. Sold 24.6.35, BU at Blyth 7.35.

ENCHANTRESS (ex-BITTERN renamed 1934) Sloop 1,190 tons, 266 x 37 ft, 4-4.7in. J. Brown 21.12.34. Sold 1946. renamed *Lady Enchantress*.

ENCOUNTER Discovery vessel in service 1616.

ENCOUNTER Gun-brig 12, 185bm, 84½ x 22½ ft, 10-18pdr carr., 2-12pdr. Guillaume, Northam 16.5.1805. Wrecked 11.7.1812 off San Lucar, Spain

ENCOUNTER Wood S. corvette, 953bm, 190 x 33 ft. Pembroke Dock 24.9.1846. BU 5.1866 at Plymouth.

ENCOUNTER Wood S. corvette 1,970 tons, 220 x 37 ft, 14-64pdr. Sheerness DY 1.1.1873. Sold 10.1888.

ENCOUNTER 2nd class cruiser 5,880 tons, 355 x 56 ft, 11-6in, 9-12pdr. Devonport DY 18.6.1902. RAN 12.19; renamed PENGUIN depot ship 5.23. Hull scuttled 9.32 off Sydney.

ENCOUNTER Destroyer 1,375 tons, 318 x 33 ft, 4-4.7in, 8-TT. Hawthorn Leslie 29.3.1934. Sunk 1.3.42 by a Japanese squadron in the Java Sea.

ENDEAVOUR 36-gun ship. Purchased 1652. Sold 1656.

ENDEAVOUR Bomb 4, 60bm. Purchased 11.4.1694. Sold 1696.

ENDEAVOUR Fire vessel 18bm, 34 x 12 ft. Purchased 1694. Sold 1696.

ENDEAVOUR Storeship hoy, 18bm, 33 x 12 ft. Purchased 1694. Sold 20.7.1705.

ENDEAVOUR TRANSPORT Storeship, 211bm. Plymouth DY 1708. Sold 30.7.1713.

ENDEAVOUR Cutter, 55bm. Purchased 11.1763. Sold 24.12.1771.

ENDEAVOUR Sloop 14. Purchased 1763. Foundered 11.10.1780 near Jamaica in a hurricane.

ENDEAVOUR BARK (ex-*Earl of Pembroke*) Discovery ship 6, 366bm. 100 x 29 ft, 6-4pdr. Purchased 3.1768. Sold 7.3.1775.

ENDEAVOUR Schooner 10. Purchased 1775. Sold 1782.

ENDEAVOUR Survey ship 1,280 tons, 200 x 34 ft, 1-3pdr. Fairfield 30.3.1912. Depot ship 1940. Sold 30.9.46.

ENDEAVOUR (ex-*John Biscoe*, ex-PRETEXT) Antarctic support ship (RNZN) 1,058 tons, 172 x 34½ ft. Purchased and renamed 15.8.1956. Sold 1962.

ENDEAVOUR (ex-USS NAMAKUGON) Antarctic support ship (RNZN) 1,850 tons, 292(wl) x 48½ ft. Transferred 1962.

ENDEAVOUR Research ship (RCN) 1,560 tons, 215 x 38½ ft. Yarrow, Esquimalt 4.9.1964.

ENDEAVOUR Replenishment ship (RNZN) ordered 1987 in Korea.

ENDEAVOUR Trawler and Drifter requis. W.W.I.

ENDURANCE (ex-*Anita Dan*) Antarctic Support ship, 2,641 gross, 273½ x 46 ft. Purchased 1967, renamed 8.67.

ENDYMION (see HASTINGS OF 1740)

ENDYMION 5th Rate 44, 893bm, 140 x 38 ft, Graves, Limehouse 28.8.1779. Wrecked 20.8.1790 on Turks Is, W. Indies.

ENDYMION 4th Rate 50, 1,277bm, 159½ x 43 ft. Randall Rotherhithe 29.3.1797. Harbour service 1860. BU completed 18.8.1868 at Devonport.

ENDYMION Wood S.frigate, 2,486bm, 240 x 48 ft. Deptford DY 18.11.1865. Sold 1885 as hulk. BU 1905.

ENDYMION 1st class cruiser 7,350 tons, 360 x 60 ft, 2-9.2in, 10-6in, 12-6pdr. Earl 22.7.1891. Sold 16.3.1920 Evans, Cardiff.

ENDYMION Trawler requis. 1917-19.

ENGADINE A/C transport 10,700 tons, 464 x63 ft, 2-4in, 12-20mm, 40-A/C. Denny 26.5.1941. To MWT 6.7.45. Sold 1946, renamed *Clan Buchanan*.

ENGADINE Helicopter support ship 8,000 tons. Robb 16.9.1966.

ENGADINE Seaplane carrier 1676 tons, requis. 1914-19.

ENGAGEANTE 5th Rate 38, 931bm, 139½ ft. French, captured 23.4.1794 by CONCORDE in the Channel.

Harbour service 7.1794. BU 5.1811 at Plymouth.

ENGLAND 5th Rate 42, 400bm. Ex-merchant, hired 1692, purchased 19.8.1693. Sunk 1.2.1695 in action with the French off Cape Clear.

ENTERPRISE 6th Rate 24, 320bm. French ENTERPRISE captured in the Mediterranean 5.1705. Wrecked 12.10.1707 off Thornton.

ENTERPRISE 5th Rate 44, 531bm, 118 x 32 ft. Lock, Plymouth 24.4.1709. 'Great repair' at Chatham 1718 as 700bm; hulk 9.1745. Sold 3.4.1749.

ENTERPRISE (see LIVERPOOL of 1741)

ENTERPRISE (see NORWICH OF 1693)

ENTERPRISE Tender 10. Captured 14.5.1775 by Americans in the Richelieu River, N. America.

ENTERPRISE 6th Rate 28, 594bm, 120½ x 33½ ft. Deptford 1774. Harbour service 1799. BU 8.1807.

ENTERPRISE (see RESOURCE of 1778)

ENTERPRISE Wood pad. gunvessel (Indian). Gordon, Deptford 1824 and purchased. 470bm, 133 x 27 ft. In service in 1830.

ENTERPRISE Survey sloop, 471bm, 126 x 28½ft. Wigram, Blackwall 5.4.1848. Coal hulk 1860. Sold 15.9.1903.

ENTERPRISE Wood S. sloop, 669bm, 160 x 30 ft. Deptford DY. Laid down 1.5.1861, renamed CIRCASSIAN 22.7.1862, cancelled 12.12.1863.

ENTERPRISE (ex-CIRCASSIAN renamed 22.7.1862) Ironclad sloop (ex-wood S. sloop as preceding ship), 993bm, 1.530 tons, 180 x 36 ft, 2-11pdr, 2-100pdr. Deptford DY 9.2.1864. Sold 11.1886.

ENTERPRISE Light cruiser 7,600 tons, 535 x 54½ ft, 7-6in, 2-4in. J. Brown 23.12.1919. Sold 11.4.46, BU Cashmore, Newport.

ENTERPRISE Survey vessel 120 tons, 100 x 22ft. Blackmore, Bideford 30.9.1958. Sold 1986.

ENTERPRISE Tug 1899-renamed EMPRISE 1919-47. Two Drifters W.W.I.

ENTREPRENANTE Cutter, 123bm, 67 x 21½ ft. French, captured (1799?). BU 6.1812.

EPERVIER Brig-sloop 16, 254bm, 94 x 25 ft. French privateer captured 12.11.1797 by CERBERUS off coast of Ireland. Sold 7.9.1801. (Spelt EPERVOIR in some lists.)

EPERVIER Brig-sloop 16, 315bm, 95 x 28½ ft, 16-6pdr. French, captured 27.7.1803 by EGYPTIENNE in the Atlantic. BU 6.1811 at Chatham.

EPERVIER Brig-sloop 18, 'Cruizer' class, 388bm. Ross, Rochester 2.12.1812 Captured 29.4.1814 by the American PEACOCK off the east coast of the USA.

EPHIRA Brig-sloop 10, 'Cherokee' class, 237bm. King, Upnor 28.5.1808. Wrecked 26.12.11 near Cadiz.

EPHRAIM Fire vessel, 170bm. Purchased 1695. Expended 1.8 1695 at Dunkirk.

EPINAL Patrol vessel 644 tons, 246 x 31 ft, 2-5.5in. French, seized 3.7.1940 at Portsmouth. Laid up to 1943, then accommodation ship; returned 1945 to the French navy.

EPREUVE Sloop 14, 261bm, 92½ x 25½ x 25 ft. 14-6pdr. French, captured 1760 by NIGER. Foundered 3.1764 in the Atlantic.

EPSOM Paddle M/S, 'Ascot' class. G. Brown 4.5.1916. Sold 3.22 Ward, Inverkeithing.

EREBUS Rocket vessel, 424bm, 109 x 29½ ft. Owen Topsham 20.8.1807. 18-gun sloop 1808; fireship 1809; 24-gun 6th Rate 1810. Sold 22.7.1819 Mr Manlove.

EREBUS Bomb 14, 378bm, 106 x 29ft, 10-24pdr carr., 2-6pdr, 2-mortars. Pembroke Dock 7.6.1826. Screw Discovery vessel 1844. Abandoned 22.4.1848 in the Arctic. (Listed until 6.1854.)

EREBUS Iron S. floating battery, 1,854bm, 1,954 tons, 187 x 49 ft. 16-68pdr. Napier 19.4.1856. Sold 5.1884 to BU.

EREBUS (see INVINCIBLE of 1869)

EREBUS Monitor 8,000 tons, 380 x 88 ft, 2-15in, 8-4in, 2-3in. Harland & Wolff, Govan 19.6.1916. Arrived 29.1.47. Ward, Inverkeithing to BU.

ERICA Corvette, 'Flower' class. Harland & Wolff 18.6.1940. Sunk 9.2.43 by mine off Benghazi.

ERIDANUS (ex-LIFFEY renamed 1812) 5th Rate 36(red pine-built), 945bm, 143 x 38½ ft, 14-32pdr carr., 26-18pdr. Ross, Rochester 1.5.1813. Sold 29.1.1818 Mr Freake.

ERIDANUS Trawler requis. 1944-45.

ERIDGE Paddle M/S, 'Ascot' class, Clyde SB 23.2.1916. Sold 3.22 Ward, Inverkeithing.

ERIDGE Destroyer, 'Hunt' class type II. Swan Hunter 20.8.1940. Damaged 8.42 and made a base ship. Sold 10.46 at Alexandria.

ERIN (ex-Turkish RESHADIEH purchased 8.1914) Battleship 23,000 tons, 525 x 91½ ft, 10-13.5in. Vickers 3.9.1913. Sold 19.12.20 Cox & Danks, Queenborough; arrived 2.2.23.

ERIN Trawler and Drifter WW.I. Trawler and OBV WW.II.

ERNE 6th Rate 20, 457bm, 115½ x 30 ft, 18-32pdr carr., 2-9pdr. Newman, Dartmouth 18.12.1813. Wrecked 1.6.1819 on the Cape Verde Islands.

ERNE Wood S. gunboat, 'Albacore' class. Smith, N. Shields 18.2.1856. BU 1874 at Chatham.

ERNE Destroyer 550 tons, 225 x 23½ ft, 1-12pdr, 5-6pdr, 2-TT. Palmer 14.1.1903. Wrecked 6.2.15 on Rattray Head.

ERNE Sloop 1,250 tons, 283 x 37½ ft, 6-4in. Furness SB 5.8.1940. Drill ship WESSEX 4.6.52. Arrived Antwerp 27.10.65 to BU.

ERNE Trawler requis. 1915-18. Trawler 1920-22.

ERRANT Minesweeper. 'Catherine' class. Assoc. SB. Laid down 27.10.1942 for the RN but retained by the USN; launched 25.2.43 as USS SPEAR.

ERUPTION (ex-Unity) Fireship 4, 74bm, 65½ x 16½ ft. Purchased 5.1804. Sold 17.6.1807 Mr Freake.

ESCAPADE Destroyer 1,375 tons, 318 x 33 ft, 4-4in, 8-TT. Scotts 30.1.1934. Sold 26.11.46; arrived Newport 23.2.47 to BU.

ESCORT Sloop 14, 220bm, 86½ x 24½ ft. French privateer captured 1757. Sold 6.12.1768.

ESCORT Gun-brig 12, 184bm, 80 x 22½ ft, 10-18pdr carr., 2-6pdr. Perry, Blackwall 1.4.1801. Transferred to Customs 8.1815.

ESCORT Wood S. gunboat, 'Albacore' class. Patterson, Bristol 6.5.1856. BU 10.1865 at Pembroke Dock.

ESCORT Destroyer 1,375 tons, 318 x 33 ft, 4-4.7in, 8-TT. Scotts 29.3.1934. Torpedoed 8.7.40 by Italian S/M MARCONI north of Cyprus and foundered three days later.

ESCORT Tug 1873-87; Tug 1896-1922. Trawler WW.I.

ESK 6th Rate 20, 460bm, 115½ x 30 ft, 18-32pdr carr., 1-12pdr. 2-9pdr. Bailey, Ipswich 11.10.1813. Sold 8.1.1829.

ESK Wood S. Corvette, 1,169bm, 192 x 38½ ft, 20-8in, 1-68pdr. Scott Russell, Millwall 12.6.1854. BU 1870 at Portsmouth.

ESK Iron S. gunboat 363 tons, 110 x 34 ft, 3-64pdr. Palmer 28.4.1877. Sold 4.1903 at Hong Kong.

ESK (ex-Sir Francis Head) Tender 110 tons, 80 x 17 ft. Transferred from

War Dept 1905 and renamed 26.11.1906. Sold 6.20 W.P. Jobson.

ESK Destroyer 1,375 tons, 318 x 33 ft, 4-4.7in, 8-TT. Swan Hunter 19.3.1934. Sunk 31.8.40 by mine, NW of Texel.

ESKDALE Destroyer 'Hunt' class type III. Cammell Laird 16.3.1942. Sunk 14.4.43 by E-boat off the Lizard while on loan to the R. Norwegian navy.

ESKIMO Destroyer 1,870 tons, 355½ x 36½ ft, 8-4.7in, 4-TT. Vickers Armstrong. Tyne 3.9.1937. Sold 27.6.49; BU at Troon.

ESKIMO Frigate 2,300 tons, 350 x 42 ft, 2-4.5in, 2-40mm. White 20.3.1961.

ESKIMO AMC 3326 tons. Requis. 1914-15.

ESPERANCE Sloop, captured 1626. Given away 1632.

ESPERANCE Sloop 16, 345bm. French, captured 8.1.1795 by ARGONAUT off the Chesapeake. Sold 7.6.1798.

ESPERANZA (see CLAYOQUOT)

ESPIEGLE Brig-sloop 16. French, captured 30.11.1793 by NYMPHE and CIRCE off Ushant. Sold 2.1802.

ESPIEGLE Brig-sloop 14, 271bm, 92 x 26 ft. French, captured 16.3.1794 by IPHIGENIA in the W. Indies. Sold 1795.

ESPIEGLE (ex-*Wenbury*) Sloop 16, 305bm, 98 x 27 ft. Purchased 6.1804. BU 4.1811 at Plymouth.

ESPIEGLE Brig-sloop 18, 'Cruizer' class, 387bm. Bailey, Ipswich 10.8.1812. Sold 11.1832 T. Ward, Ratcliffe.

ESPIEGLE Brig 12, 443bm, 105 x 32 ft, 10-32pdr, 2-18pdr. Chatham DY 20.4.1844. Sold 22.11.1861 Castle & Beech.

ESPIEGLE Compos. S. sloop 1,130 tons, 170 x 36 ft, 2-7in, 4-64pdr. Devonport DY 3.8.1880. Boom vessel 1899; renamed ARGO 3.1904. Sold 25.8.21 W. Thorpe.

ESPIEGLE Sloop 1,070 tons, 185 x 33 ft, 6-4in, 4-3pdr. Sheerness DY 8.12.1900. Sold 7.9.23 at Bombay. (The last ship built with a figurehead.)

ESPIEGLE Minesweeper, 'Algerine' class. Harland & Wolff 12.8.1942. BU 1967 at Dalmuir.

ESPION Cutter 16. French, captured 24.1.1782. Sold 1784.

ESPION Sloop 16, 275bm. French privateer Le ROBERT captured 13.6.1793. Recaptured 22.7.1794 by the French. Recaptured 2.3.95, renamed SPY. Sold 7.9.1801.

ESPION 5th Rate 36, 986bm, 148 x 39 ft, 4-18pdr, 2-18pdr carr., 26-12pdr, 6-6pdr. French ATALANTE captured 7.5.1794 by SWIFTSURE off Cork. Wrecked 16.11.1799 on the Goodwins.

ESPION name chosen for LITTLE BELT, captured 1807 but not used.

ESPOIR Sloop sold 25.3.1784, origin unknown.

ESPOIR Brig-sloop 14, 251bm, 93 x 25 ft, 14-6pdr. French captured 11.9.1797 by THALIA in the Mediterranean. Sold 9.1804.

ESPOIR Brig-sloop 18, 'Cruizer' class, 385bm. King, Dover 22.9.1804. BU 4.1821.

ESPOIR Brig-sloop 10, 'Cherokee' class, 233bm. Chatham DY 9.5.1826. Sold 1857.

ESPOIR Wood S. gunvessel, 428bm, 145 x 25½ ft, 1-68pdr, 4-24pdr howitzers. Pembroke Dock 7.1.1860. Made a dredger 1869 and renamed YC.19. BU in Bermuda 6.1881.

ESPOIR Compos. S. gunvessel 465 tons, 125 x 23½ ft, 2-64pdr, 2-20pdr. Barrow SB (Vickers) 2.11.1880. Tug 1895. On sale list 1903.

ESPOIR Minesweeper, 'Catherine' class. Assoc. SB. Laid down 27.10.1942 for the RN but retained by the USN as TRIUMPH.

ESQUIMALT Minesweeper (RCN), diesel 'Bangor' class. Marine Ind. 31.8.1941. Sunk 16.4.45 by 'U.190' off Halifax.

ESSEX 60-gun ship, 652bm. Deptford 1653. Captured 6.1666 by the French in the 'Four Days' battle.

ESSEX 3rd Rate 70, 1,059bm, 150 x 40 ft. Johnson, Blackwall 1679. Rebuilt Rotherhithe 1700 as 1,090bm; rebuilt Woolwich 1740 as 1,226bm, 64 guns. Wrecked 21.11.1759 in action. Quiberon Bay.

ESSEX PRIZE Sloop 16, 152bm, 75 x 22½ ft. French, captured 16.7.1694. Sold 1.10.1702 at Deptford.

ESSEX 3rd Rate 64, 1,380bm, 158 x 45 ft. Wells & Stanton Rotherhithe 28.8.1760. Harbour service 1.1777. Sold 22.8.1799.

ESSEX 5th Rate 42, 867bm, 139 x 37½ ft. American, captured 28.3.1814 by PHOEBE off Valparaiso. Convict ship 10.1823. Sold 6.7.1837.

ESSEX Armoured cruiser 9,800 tons, 440 x 66 ft, 14-6in, 9-12pdr. Pembroke Dock 29.8.1901. Sold 8.11.21 Slough TC; BU in Germany.

ESSEX Two Trawlers requis. WW.I.

ESSINGTON Frigate, DE 'Captain'

class. Mare Island. Laid down 30.4.42 for the RN but retained by the USN as HAROLD C. THOMAS.

ESSINGTON Frigate, TE 'Captain' class. Bethelehem, Hingham 19.6.43 on lend-lease. Returned 10.45 to the USN.

ESSINGTON Coastal M/S, 'Ton' class. Camper & Nicholson 9.1954. Malaysian navy KINABALU 1964.

ESTHER Cutter 6, 101bm, 50 x 24 ft. Purchased 1763. Sold 12.6.1779 J. Linney.

ESTHER Survey vessel (ex-trawler purchased 2.1911) 510 tons, 125½ x 22½ ft. Duthie Torry 22.11.11. M/S 9.14. Sold 25.10.19.

ESTRIDGE (see under OSTRICH)

ETCHINGHAM Inshore M/S, 'Ham' class. Ailsa 9.12.1957. Sold 1967 at Hong Kong to BU.

ETHALION 5th Rate 38, 992bm, 146 x 36ft. Graham, Harwich 14.3.1797. Wrecked 25.12.1799 on the Penmarks.

ETHALION 5th Rate 36, 996bm, 152½ x 38 ft. Woolwich DY 29.7.1802. Harbour service 9.1823; lent 5.1835 to Harwich Corporation as breakwater. Listed until 6.1877.

ETHALION (see MARS of 1944)

ETNA (see AETNA)

L'ETOILE Training schooner 227 tons. French, seized 3.7.1940; at Falmouth. Handed over 9.40 to Free-French; laid up 1943; returned 1945 to the French navy.

ETRUSCO Storeship 24, 918bm, 137½ x 38½ ft. Purchased 1794. Foundered 15.8.1798 on passage from the W. Indies.

ETTRICK Destroyer 550 tons, 225 x 23½ ft, 1-12pdr, 5-6pdr (3-12pdr 1907), 2-TT. Palmer 28.2.1903. Sold 27.5.19 James Dredging Co.

ETTRICK (see TAMARISK)

ETTRICK Frigate 'River' class. Crown, 5.2.1943. Lent RCN 29.1.44 to 30.5.45. BU 6.53 Ward, Grays.

ETTRICK Trawler 1920-26. Tender 1969.

EUGENIE Sloop 16, 241bm, 85 x 26 ft, 16-6pdr. French privateer La NOUVELLE EUGENIE captured 1.5.1797. Sold 3.1.1803 to BU Blackheath.

EUGENIE (ex-Friends) Sloop 16, 273bm, 90½ x 26 ft, 14-18pdr carr.,2-9pdr. Purc hased 6.1804. Sold 22.12.1810.

EUPHRATES (ex-GREYHOUND renamed 7.12.1812) 5th Rate 36 (red pine-built), 943bm,143½ x 38½ ft,

14-32pdr carr., 26-18pdr. King, Upnor 8.11.1813. Sold 29.1.1818 W. Thomas.

EUPHRATES 5th Rate 46, 1,215bm, 159 x 42 ft. Portsmouth DY. Laid down with teak frames in Bombay. Cancelled 7.2.1831.

EUPHRATES Brig 10 (Indian), 255bm. Bombay DY 30.6.1828.

EUPHRATES Paddle gunboat, 179bm. Laird and re-erected 9.1834 on the Euphrates. Fate unknown.

EUPHRATES Wood S. frigate, 1,556bm, 210 x 40½ ft. Deptford DY. Laid down 1847, cancelled 1849.

EUPHRATES Iron S. troopship, 4,173bm, 6,211 tons, 360 x 49 ft, 3-4pdr. Laird 24.11.1866. Sold 23.11.1894 at Portsmouth.

EUPHRATES Light cruiser 7,600 tons, 535 x 54½ ft, 7-6in. Fairfield. Laid down 1918, cancelled 9.19.

EUPHROSYNE Fireship 14, 125bm. Purchased 1796. Sold 1802.

EUROPA Hulk, 406bm. Dutch ship captured 5.1673. Burnt 1675 by accident at Malta.

EUROPA 3rd Rate 64, 1,370bm, 159 x 41 ft. Adams, Lepe 21.4.1765. Renamed EUROPE 7.1778. BU 7.1814 at Plymouth.

EUROPA Gunboat commissioned 1782 at Gibraltar.

EUROPA 4th Rate 50, 1.050bm, 146 x 41 ft. Woolwich DY 19.4.1783. Troopship 1798. Sold 11.8.1814.

EUROPA 1st class cruiser 11,000 tons, 435 x 69 ft, 16-6in, 14-12pdr, 4-3pdr. J. Brown 20.3.1897. Sold 15.9.1920 C.F. Bletto, Malta; BU in Genoa.

EUROPA Transport hired 1854

EUROTAS 5th Rate 38, 1,084bm, 150 x 40 ft, 16-32pdr carr., 28-24pdr, 2-9pdr. Wigram & Green, Blackwall 17.4.1813. BU 8.1817.

EUROTAS 5th Rate 46, 1,170bm, 159 x 41 ft. Chatham DY 19.2.1829. Undocked 13.2.1856 as screw frigate, 1.102bm. Sold 1.11.1865 Castle & Beech.

EURUS 6th Rate 24, 547bm, 24-9pdr. French privateer DRAGON captured 1758. Wrecked 26.6.1760 in the St Lawrence.

EURUS 5th Rate 32, 703bm, 127 x 35 ft, 2-24pdr, 20-24pdr carr. Dutch ZEFIR seized in the river Forth 6.3.1796. Storeship 10.1803. BU 1834.

EURYALUS 5th Rate 36, 946bm, 145 x 38 ft. Adams, Bucklers Hard 6.6.1803. Prison ship 1826; renamed AFRICA 1859. Sold 16.8.1860 Mr Recano, Gibraltar.

EURYALUS Wood S. frigate, 2,371bm, 212 x 50 ft. Chatham DY 5.10.1853. Sold 3.1867 Castle & Beech.

EURYALUS Iron S. corvette 4,140 tons, 280 x 45½ ft, 16-7in. Chatham DY 31.1.1877. Sold 10.5.1897 Cohen, Blackwall.

EURYALUS Armoured cruiser 12,000 tons, 440 x 69½ ft, 2-9.2in, 12-6in, 14-12pdr. Vickers 20.5.1901. Minelayer 1918. Sold 1.7.20 S. Castle; BU in Germany.

EURYALUS Cruiser 5,450 tons, 485 x 50½ ft, 10-5.25in, 8-2pdr. Chatham DY 6.6.1939. Arrived 18.7.59 Hughes Bolckow, Blyth to BU.

EURYALUS Frigate 2,350 tons, 360 x 41 ft, 2-4.5in, 2-40mm. Scotts 6.6,1963.

EURYDICE 6th Rate 24, 521bm, 114½ x 32 ft. Portsmouth DY 26.3.1781. BU 3.1834.

EURYDICE 6th Rate 24, 908bm, 141 x 39 ft, 24-32pdr, 2-12pdr. Portsmouth DY 16.5.1843. Training ship 6.1861. Foundered 24.3.1878 off Isle of Wight; raised, BU 9.1878.

EUSTATIA 6th Rate 20, 514bm, 104 x 27½ ft. Dutch, captured 1781. Sold 1783 at Antigua (also SAINT EUSTATIUS)

EVENLODE (ex-USS DANVILLE) Frigate, 'River' class. Vickers, Montreal 9.11.1942 on lend-lease. Returned 5.3.46 to the USN.

EVERINGHAM Inshore M/S, 'Ham' class. Philip 4.3.1954. Sold in 1983.

EXCALIBUR Submarine 780 tons, 178 x 16ft, unarmed. Vickers Armstrong, Barrow 25.2.1955. Arrived Barrow 24.2.70 to BU.

EXCALIBUR Tug (ex-German) 1945-46.

EXCELLENT 3rd Rate 74, 1,645bm, 168 x 47 ft. Graham, Harwich 27.11.1787. 58-gun 4th Rate 6.1820; gunnery training ship 1830. BU 10.1835 at Deptford.

EXCELLENT (see BOYNE of 1810)

EXCELLENT (see QUEEN CHARLOTTE of 1810)

EXCELLENT Nominal base ship (see HANDY of 1884, DRUDGE of 1901)

EXCELLENT Drifter and Trawler WW1. Tug 1940.

EXE Destroyer 550 tons, 225 x 23½ ft, 1-12pdr, 5-6pdr (3-12pdr 1907), 2-TT. Palmer 27.4.1903. Sold 10.2.20 Ward, Rainham.

EXE Frigate, 'River' class. Fleming & Ferguson 19.3.1942. Arrived 20.9.56 Ward, Preston to BU.

EXE Trawler 1920-26.

EXERTION Gun-brig 12, 180bm, 84 x

22 ft, 10-18pdr carr., 2-12pdr. Preston, Yarmouth 2.5.1805. Grounded 8.7.1812 in the Elbe and destroyed to avoid capture by the French.

EXETER 3rd Rate 70, 1,030bm, 150 x 40 ft. Johnson, Blackwall 1680. Damaged by explosion 12.9.1691 and hulked. BU 1717 at Portsmouth.

EXETER 4th Rate 60, 949bm, 148 x 38 ft. Portsmouth DY 26.5.1697. Rebuilt Plymouth 1744 as 1,068bm, 58 guns. BU 11.1763 at Portsmouth.

EXETER 3rd Rate 64, 1,340 bm, 158½ x 41 ft. Henniker, Chatham 26.7.1763. Burnt 12.2.1784 at the Cape as unserviceable.

EXETER Cruiser 8,390 tons, 540 x 57 ft, 6-8in, 4-4in. Devonport DY 18.7.1929. Sunk 1.3.42 in action with Japanese squadron off Java.

EXETER Frigate 2,170 tons, 330 x 40 ft, 2-4.5in, 2-40mm. Fairfield. Ordered 1956 and cancelled.

EXETER Destroyer 3,150 tons, Swan Hunter 25.4.1978.

EXMOOR Destroyer, 'Hunt' class type I. Vickers Armstrong, Tyne 25.1.1940. Sunk 25.2.41 by E-boat torpedo off Lowestoft.

EXMOOR (ex-BURTON renamed 6.1941) Destroyer 'Hunt' class type II. Swan Hunter 12.3.41. To Danish navy 7.52 as VALDEMAR SEJR. Sold 10.66 to BU in Sweden.

EXMOUTH Screw 2nd Rate 90, 3,100bm, 4,382 tons, 204 x 60 ft. Devonport DY 12.7.1854. Lent 1877 Metropolitan Asylums Board as training ship. Sold 4.4.1905 Cohen, BU at Penarth.

EXMOUTH Battleship 14,000 tons, 405 x 75½ft, 4-12in, 12-6in, 12-12pdr. Laird 31.8.1901. Sold 15.1.20 Forth S. Bkg Co, Bo'ness. Hulk BU in Holland 1922.

EXMOUTH Training ship, 300 x 53 ft. Vickers 20.4.1905. Requisitioned as depot ship 1939-45. Renamed *Worcester* 1945.

EXMOUTH Destroyer leader 1,475 tons, 320 x 34 ft, 5-4.7in, 8-TT. Portsmouth DY 7.2.1934. Sunk 21.1.40 by 'U.22' off the Moray Firth.

EXMOUTH Frigate 1,180 tons, 300 x 33 ft, 2-40mm. White 16.11.1955. Arrived Swansea 9.2.79 to BU.

EXMOUTH store carrier and Trawler WW.1.

EXPEDITION 20-gun ship. French, captured 1618. Last listed 1652.

EXPEDITION 30-gun ship, 300bm. Bermondsey 1637. Sold 1667.

EXPEDITION 3rd Rate 70, 1,116bm, 152 x 41 ft. Portsmouth 1679. Rebuilt Chatham 1699 as 1,111bm; renamed PRINCE FREDERICK 2.1.1715. Rebuilt 1740 as 1,740bm, 64guns. Sold 1784.

EXPEDITION 5th Rate 44, 816bm, 133½ x 37½ ft. Okill, Liverpool 11.7.1747. BU 12.1764 at Plymouth.

EXPEDITION Cutter 14, 151bm, 67 x 24 ft Ladd, Dover 3.8.1778. Listed to 1801.

EXPEDITION 5th Rate 44, 910bm, 140½ x 38½ ft. Randall, Rotherhithe 29.10.1784. 26-gun troopship 4.1798. BU 2.1817.

EXPERIMENT Sloop (double hulled), built 1664. Lost 1687.

EXPERIMENT Sloop 4, Built 1667. Listed to 1682.

EXPERIMENT 5th Rate 32, 370bm, 105 x 27½ ft. Chatham DY 17.12.1689. Rebuilt 1727 at Plymouth as 374bm. BU 7.1738 at Portsmouth.

EXPERIMENT 6th Rate 24, 445bm, 107 x 31 ft. Bird, Rotherhithe 18.4.1740. Sold 15.3.1763.

EXPERIMENT Storeship, 342bm, 96 x 28 ft. Purchased 8.1765. Sold 6.12.1768.

EXPERIMENT Gunvessel. Woolwich 1772. Fate unknown.

EXPERIMENT 4th Rate 50, 923bm, 140 x 40 ft. Adams, Deptford 23.8.1774. Captured 24.9.1778 by the French SAGITTAIRE off the east coast of N. America.

EXPERIMENT Brig-sloop 14, 200bm, 80 x 23½ ft. Purchased 1781. Sold in Antigua 21.3.1785.

EXPERIMENT 5th Rate 44, 892bm, 140 x 38 ft. Fabian, E Cowes 27.11.1784. Storeship 1795; harbour serivce 1805. Sold 8.9.1836.

EXPERIMENT Lugger 10, 111bm, 73 x 19 ft, 10-12pdr carr. Parkins, Plymouth 5.1793. Captured 2.10 1796 by the Spanish in the Mediterranean.

EXPERIMENT Fireship, 85bm, 63 x 17½ ft. Purchased 4.1794. Sold 16.12.1801.

EXPERIMENT Gunvessel 2, 1-18pdr, 1-18pdr carr. Woolwich DY 5,1806. Gone by 1809.

EXPERIMENT Wood pad. sloop (Canadian lakes), 100bm, 97 x 14½ ft. Purchased 21.7.1838. Sold 1848.

EXPLOIT Minesweeper, 'Catherine' class. Assoc. SB. Laid down 28.11.1942 for the RN, retained by the USN as VIGILANCE.

EXPLORER Submarine 780 tons, 178 x 16 ft, unarmed. Vickers Armstrong, Barrow 5.3.1954. Sold 8.2.65 Ward, Barrow.

EXPLORER Examination service. 1940-46.

EXPLOSION (see SWAN of 1767)

EXPLOSION (ex-*Gloster*) Bomb 12, 323bm, 96½ x 27½ ft. Purchased 4.1797. Wrecked 10.9.1807 near Heligoland.

EXPRESS Advice boat 6, 77bm, 65½ x 16 ft. Portsmouth DY 1695. Sold 8.1.1712.

EXPRESS Schooner 6, 180bm, 88 x 21 ft. Randall, Rotherhithe 30.1.2.1800. Sold 5.1813 Walters, Rotherhithe.

EXPRESS (ex-American *Anna Marie*) advice boat, 92bm, 65 x 18½ ft. Purchased 1808. Fate unknown.

EXPRESS Schooner 12, 92bm, 64½ x 18 ft. Plymouth DY 5,1815. Sold 26.7.1827 at Malta.

EXPRESS Packet brig 6, 362bm, 95 x 30½ ft, 6-18pdr. Colson, Deptford 8.10.1835. Sold 11.1.1862 Marshall, Plymouth.

EXPRESS Compos.S. gunboat 455 tons, 125 x 23 ft, 2-64pdr, 2-20pdr. Doxford 16.7.1874. Sold 8.1889.

EXPRESS Destroyer 499 tons, 235 x 25½ ft, 1-12pdr, 5-6pdr, 2-TT. Laird 11.12.1897. Sold 17.3.1921 G. Clarkson, Whitby.

EXPRESS Destroyer 1,375 tons, 318 x 33 ft, 4-4.7in, 8-TT. Swan Hunter 29.5.1934. Renamed GATINEAU (RCN) 3.6.43; sale list 1947. Sold 1956 Mainewaring, Vancouver; hulk sunk as breakwater.

EXTRAVAGANT Fireship 10, 276bm, 95 x 25½ ft. French, captured 1692. Expended 19.5.1692 at the battle of Barfleur.

EYDEREN (spelling used in some lists for EIDEREN, qv)

EYEBRIGHT Corvette, 'Flower' class. Vickers, Montreal 22.7.1940. On loan to RCN until 17.6.45. Sold 17.5.47, renamed *Albert W. Vinke.*

'F' class submarines. 353 tons, 150 x 16 ft, 3-TT.

F.1 Chatham DY 31.3.1913. BU 1920 in Portsmouth DY.

F.2 White 7.7.1917. Sold 7.22 C. Welton, Portsmouth.

F.3 Thornycroft 9.2.1916. BU 1920 in Portsmouth DY.

F.4 - 8 Projected 1914 and cancelled.

FAGONS 22-gun ship, 262bm. Page,

Wivenhoe 1654. Renamed MIL-FORD 1660. Burnt 7.7.1673 by accident at Leghorn.

FAIRFAX 50-gun ship. 740bm. Deptford 1649. Burnt 1653 by accident at Chatham.

FAIRFAX 52-gun ship, 745bm. Chatham DY 1653. Wrecked 1682.

FAIRFAX Minesweeper 1941-45.

FAIRFIELD Minesweeper, later 'Hunt' class. Clyde SB 30.5.1919. Sold 3.3.20 S. American Tours, Buenos Aires.

FAIR RHODIAN Schooner. Purchased 1780. Listed 1781.

FAIR ROSAMOND (ex-slaver *Dos Amigos*). Purchased 22.2.1831. BU 20.11.1845.

FAIRY Sloop 14, 300bm, 97 x 29 ft. Sheerness DY 24.10.1778. Rebuilt Sheerness 1790 BU 7.1811 at Portsmouth.

FAIRY Brig-sloop, 'Cruiser' class, 386bm. Taylor, Bideford 11.6.1812. BU 1.1821 at Portsmouth.

FAIRY Brig-sloop 10, 'Cherokee' class, 233 bm. Chatham DY 25.4.1826. Survey vessel 1830. Wrecked 13.11.1840 on the Sussex coast.

FAIRY (ex-American *Marco Bazzaris*) Paddle vessel. Purchased 17.6.1834. Fate unknown.

FAIRY Iron S. yacht, 312bm, 145 x 21 ft. Ditchburn & Mare, Blackwall 3.1845. Sold 1.1868.

FAIRY Destroyer 380 tons, 227½ x 22 ft, 1-12pdr, 5-6pdr, 2-TT. Fairfield 29.5.1897. Foundered 31.5.1918 after ramming 'UC.75' in the North Sea.

FAIRY Minesweeper, 'Catherine' class. Assoc. SB, Seattle 5.4.1943 on lend-lease. Returned 13.12.46 to the USN.

FAIRY Tug requis. 1918-19.

FAIRY QUEEN Schooner 8, 55bm. Purchased 1781. Captured 19.11.1781 by the Spanish off the Orinoco.

FAITH Schooner (Canadian lakes). Detroit 1774. Wrecked 12.1783 on the lakes.

FAITHFUL Repair ship 14,250 tons, 416 x 57 ft, 1-5in, 10-40mm. Bethlehem, Fairfield 10.10.1944 for the RN but retained by the USN as DIONYSUS.

FAITHFUL Tank vessel 1903-48. Two Drifters WW.I. Tug 1957-83. Tug 1985.

FAL Frigate, 'River' class. Smiths Dk 9.11.1942. Renamed MAYU, Burmese navy 3.48.

FALCON Ballinger, dating from 1343. Sold 1352.

FALCON of the TOWER Ballinger, 80bm. Dating from 1420. Sold 1423.

FALCON ship in service 1461-85.

FALCON Pinnace, 83bm, '22 iron & 4 brass guns'. In service 1544-78.

FALCON in the FETTERLOCK Pinnace, 26bm, '8 iron & brass guns'. In service 1546. Sold 1549.

FALCON Ship, 180bm. In service in 1603.

FALCON 24-gun ship. Purchased 1646. Gone by 1659.

FALCON 6-gun vessel. Royalist, captured 1647. Last listed 1653.

FALCON FLYBOAT 28-gun ship, 200bm. Dutch, captured 1652. Sold 1658.

FALCON (also GOLDEN FALCON) 10-gun ship. Dutch, captured 1652; fireship 1653. Sold 1658.

FALCON 5th Rate 36, 349bm. Woolwich 1666. 42-gun 4th Rate 1668. Captured 1.5.1694 by the French in the Mediterranean.

FALCON 6th Rate 24, 240bm, 91½ x 24½ ft. Barrett, Shoreham 1694. Captured 10.6.1695 by three French ships off the Dodman; recaptured 1703 and BU.

FALCON 5th Rate 38. Ex-merchant converted 1694. Captured 3.1.1695. by the French.

FALCON 4th Rate 32, 412bm, 106 x 30 ft. Deptford 1704. Captured 29.12.1709 by the French Le SERIEUX in the Mediterranean.

FALCON Sloop 14, 272bm, 91½ x 26 ft. Barnard, Harwich 12.11.1744. Captured 12.8.1745 by the French off St Malo; recaptured 3.1746 and renamed FORTUNE. Sold 20.3.1770.

FALCON Sloop 14, 270bm, 91½ x 26 ft. Alexander, Rotherhithe 30.11.1745. 8-gun bomb 1758. Wrecked 19.4.1759 W. Indies.

FALCON Sloop 14, 302bm, 95 x 27 ft. Portsmouth DY 15.6.1771. Sunk 8.1778 as blockship, Narragansett Bay; salved, foundered 9.1779.

FALCON Brig-sloop 14, 201bm, 79 x 25 ft. Hills, Sandwich 23.9.1782. Fireship 6.1800; expended 7.7.1800 in Dunkirk Roads.

FALCON (see DIADEM of 1801)

FALCON Sloop 16. Danish, found abandoned at Danzig 14.4.1807. In service in 1808.

FALCON Brig-sloop 10, 'Cherokee' class, 237bm. Pembroke Dock 10.6.1820. Fitted with an engine 1833, taken out 1834. Sold 1838, renamed *Waterwitch*.

FALCON Wood S. sloop, 992bm, 185 x 34 ft. Pembroke Dock. Ordered 1847, cancelled 4.4.1851.

FALCON Wood S. sloop, 748bm, 160 x 31½ ft. 17-32pdr. Pembroke Dock 10.8.1854. Sold 27.9.1869 Marshall, Plymouth.

FALCON Compos.S. gunvessel 780 tons, 157 x 29½ ft, 1-7in, 2-64pdr. Laird 4.1.1877. Harbour service 1890. Sold 28.6.1920 E.W. Payne & Co.

FALCON Destroyer 375 tons, 220 x 21½ ft, 1-12pdr, 5-6pdr, 2-TT. Fairfield 29.12.1899. Sunk 1.4.1918 in collision with trawler JOHN FITZGERALD in the North Sea.

FALCON River gunboat 372 tons, 150 x 29 ft, 1-3.7in. howitzer, 2-6 pdr. Yarrow 18.5.1931. Handed over to Chinese navy 2.42 as LUNG HUAN.

FALCON Trawler requis. 1917-19; Tug 1941-45.

FALKLAND 4th Rate 48, 637bm, 128½ x 33ft. Built in New England 1690 and purchased 2.3.1696. Rebuilt Chatham 1702; rebuilt Bursledon 1744 as 974bm. Transferred 10.8.1768 to the Victualling Dept.

FALKLAND PRIZE 5th Rate 36, 732bm, 133½ x 35 ft. French La SEINE captured 24.8.1704 by DREADNOUGHT off the Azores. Wrecked 19.12.1705 in Sandwich Bay; salved and sold 11.3.1706.

FALKLAND Sloop 18 (Indian), 494bm. Bombay DY 11.1853. Sold 7.1862.

FALMOUTH 30-gun ship. Dutch ROTTERDAM captured 7.1652 in the Channel. Sold 1658.

FALMOUTH 4th Rate 58, 610bm, 124 x 33½ ft. Snelgrove, Deptford 25.6.1693. Captured 4.8.1704 by two French privateers in the Mediterranean.

FALMOUTH 4th Rate 50, 700bm, 130 x 35 ft. Woolwich DY 26.2.1708. Rebuilt Woolwich 1729 as 760bm. BU 1747 Woolwich.

FALMOUTH 4th Rate 50, 1,047bm, 144 x 41 ft. Woolwich DY 7.12.1752. Beached and abandoned 16.1.1765 at Batavia as unseaworthy after action at Manila.

FALMOUTH Schooner, 160bm, 70 x 23 ft. Topsham 1807. Dockyard service 1808; mortar vessel 5.1824; DY lighter YC.1 1846; YC.46 in 1870; reverted to FALMOUTH 11.1870. Sold 1883.

FALMOUTH 6th Rate 22, 455bm, 116 x 30 ft. Chapman, Bideford 8.1.1814. Sold 27.1.1825 T. Hutchinson.

FALMOUTH Wood S. sloop, 950bm, 185 x 33 ft. Deptford DY. Ordered 1860 and cancelled 1860.

FALMOUTH Wood S. corvette, 1,857bm, 225 x 43 ft. Chatham DY. Laid down 5.1.1861. Cancelled 12.12.1863.

FALMOUTH 2nd class cruiser 5,250 tons, 430 x 48½ ft, 8-6in. Beardmore 20.9.1910. Sunk 19.8.16 by 'U.63' in the North Sea.

FALMOUTH Sloop 1,060 tons, 250 x 34 ft, 2-4in. Devonport DY 19.4.32. Renamed CALLIOPE, drill ship 1.52. Arrived Hughes Bolckow, Blythe 30.4.68 to BU.

FALMOUTH Frigate 2,150 tons, 360 x 41 ft, 2-4.5in, 1-40mm. Swan Hunter 15.12.1959.

FALMOUTH Two trawlers requis. WW.I.

FAMA 5th Rate 36, 979bm, 145 x 39 ft. Spanish, captured 5.10.1804 by MEDEA and LIVELY off Cadiz. Sold 4.1812.

FAMA brig-sloop 18, 315bm. Danish, captured 8.1808 by boats of EDGAR off Nyborg. Wrecked 23.12.1808 in the Baltic.

FAME 20-gun ship (Irish Royalist). Purchased 1646. Captured by Parliament 1649; Blown up 1658.

FAME 30-gun ship, 208bm. French RENOMMEE captured 8.1655. Expended as fireship 6.1665.

FAME 6th Rate 24, 316bm, 106 x 26 ft. French, captured 7.1709. Re-taken by the French 21.9.1710 off Port Mahon.

FAME Sloop 14, 272bm, 14-3pdr. Purchased 1744 at Antigua. Foundered 7.1745 in the Atlantic.

FAME 3rd Rate 74, 1,565bm, 166 x 47 ft. Bird, Deptford 1.1.1759. Renamed GUILDFORD prison ship 1799. Sold 30.9.1814.

FAME 3rd Rate 74, 1,745bm, 176 x 48 ft. Deptford DY 8.10.1805. BU 9.1817 at Chatham.

FAME (see DRAGON of 1798)

FAME Wood S. sloop, 669bm, 162 x 30 ft. Deptford DY. Laid down 2.12.1861. Cancelled 12.12.1863.

FAME Destroyer 340 tons, 210½ x 19½ 1-12pdr, 5-TT. Thornycroft, Chiswick 15.4.1896. Sold 31.8.1921 at Hong Kong.

FAME Destroyer 1,350 tons, 318 x 33 ft, 4-4.7in, 8-TT. Vickers Armstrong, Barrow 28.6.1934. Handed over 2.49 to the Dominican navy as GENERALISSIMO.

FAME Drifter requis. WW.I.

FANCY Pinnace in the Armada action 1588, probably hired.

FANCY Gun-brig 12, 181bm, 85 x 22 ft, 10-18pdr carr., 2-12pdr. Preston, Yarmouth 7.1.1806. Foundered 24.12.1811 in the Baltic.

FANCY Wood S. gunboat, 'Dapper' class. Green, Blackwall 31.3.1855. Harbour service 1876. Sold 11.7.1905 at Portsmouth.

FANCY Minesweeper, 'Algerine' class. Blyth SB 5.4.1943 and completed by Hughes Bolckow. Sold. 9.8.51 Belgian navy as A.F. DUFOUR.

FANCY 3 cutters hired between 1808 and 1814. Trawler and Drifter WW.I.

FANDANGO Minesweeper 260 tons, 130 x 26 ft, 1-3pdr. Ex-War Dept tug built Lytham SB 1917 and transferred 1919. Sunk 3.7.19 by mine in the Dvina River.

FANDANGO Trawler. 1940-46.

FANFAN Ketch 4, 38bm, 58½ x 12 ft, 4-pdr. Deane, Harwich 1666. Made a DY pitch boat 1693.

FANNY Tender, 20bm, 34 x 11½ ft. Deptford DY 5.1827. BU 8.1835.

FANNY Cutter yacht, 136bm, 68½ x 22 ft, Portsmouth DY 28.2.1831. For disposal 1863.

FANNY Coastguard vessel, 153bm. Commissioned 12.1860. Sunk 31.10.1878 in collision with SS *Helvetia* off the Tuscar.

FANNY (see ARGUS of 1851)

FANNY (ex-yacht *Otter*) Coastguard vessel 155 tons. Purchased 1.1902. Sold 10.4.1912., renamed *Trefoil.*

FANTOME Brig-sloop 18, 385bm, 94 x 31 ft. French privateer captured 5.1810 by MELAMPUS. Wrecked 24.11.1814 in the St Lawrence.

FANTOME Brig-sloop 16, 483bm, 105 x 33½ ft, 4-32pdr, 12-32pdr carr. Chatham DY 30.5.1839. Sold 7.10.1864 Castle.

FANTOME Compos S. sloop 727bm, 940 tons, 160 x 31½ ft, 2-7in, 2-6pdr. Pembroke Dock 26.3.1873. Sold 2.89 Read, Portsmouth to BU.

FANTOME Sloop 1,070 tons, 185 x 33 ft, 6-4in, 4-3pdr. Sheerness DY 23.3.1901. Survey ship 1906. Sold 30.1.25 at Sydney NSW.

FANTOME Minesweeper, 'Algerine' class. Harland & Wolff 22.9.1942. Arrived 22.5.47 Ward, Milford Haven to BU.

FAREHAM Minesweeper later 'Hunt' class. Dunlop Bremner 7.6.1918. Sold 24.8.48, BU Ward, Hayle. (Was ST ANGELO II M/S base ship 1944-45)

FARNDALE Destroyer, 'Hunt' class type II. Swan Hunter 22.7.1940. Arrived 29.11.62 Hughes Bolckow, Blyth to BU.

FARNHAM CASTLE Corvette, 'Castle' class. Crown 25.4.1944. Arrived 31.10.60 Dorkin, Gateshead to BU.

FARRAGUT Monitor (see ABERCROMBIE).

FASTNET Scout cruiser. Launched 16.7.1904 as PATHFINDER.

FAULKNOR (ex-Chilian ALMIRANTE SIMPSON) Destroyer leader 1,694 tons, 331 x 32 ft, 4-4in, 4-TT. White 26.2.1914 and purchased 8.14. Resold Chile 5.20, renamed ALMIRANTE RIVEROS.

FAULKNOR (ex-*Po-On*) River gunboat 126 tons, 1-3pdr. Purchased at Hong Kong 10.1925. Sold 1928.

FAULKNOR Destroyer leader 1,457 tons, 332 x 34 ft, 5-4.7in, 8-TT. Yarrow 12.6.1934. Sold 22.1.46, BU Ward, Milford Haven.

FEVERSHAM 5th Rate 32, 372bm, 107 x 28 ft. Ellis, Shoreham 1.10.1696. Wrecked 7.10.1711 off Cape Breton.

FAVERSHAM 5th Rate 40, 561bm, 118 x 32 ft. Plymouth DY 22.7.1712. BU in 12.1730 at Portsmouth.

FAVERSHAM 5th Rate 44, 689bm, 124 x 36 ft. Perry, Blackwall 7.1.1741. Sold 13.4.1749.

FAVERSHAM Minesweeper, later 'Hunt' class. Dunlop Bremner 19.7.1918. Sold 25.11.27 Alloa S. Bkg Co; arrived Charlestown 21.1.28 to BU.

FAVORITE (see under FAVOURITE)

FAVOURITE Sloop 14, probably 206bm. Sheerness DY 1740. Fate unknown. (Existance doubtful.)

FAVOURITE Sloop 14, 313bm, 96½ x 27 ft. Sparrow, Shoreham 15.12.1757. Sold 21.10.1784.

FAVOURITE Sloop 16, 423bm, 108 x 30 ft, 12-12pdr carr., 16-pdr. Randall, Rotherhithe 1.2.1794. Captured 6.1.1806 by the French off Cape Verde; recaptured as FAVORITE 27.1.1807 by JASON on the coast of Guina and renamed GOREE. Prison ship in 1814. BU 1817 in Bermuda.

FAVORITE Survey cutter. Purchased 1805. Sold circa 1813.

FAVORITE Sloop 18, 427bm, 109 x 29½ ft, 16-32pdr, 6-18pdr carr., 2-6pdr. Bailey, Ipswich 13.9.1806. BU 2.1821.

FAVOURITE Sloop 18, 434bm, 110 x 31 ft. Portsmouth DY 21.4.1829. Coal hulk 8.1859. Sold 17.5.1905 at Devonport. (Listed as FAVORITE from

1836 to 1856; also bore the number 'C 3' and later 'C.77 while a coal hulk.)

FAVORITE Ironclad S. corvette, 2,094bm, 3,232 tons, 225 x 47 ft, 10-8in MLR. Deptford DY 5.7.1864. Sold 30.3.1886.

FAVORITE Two cutters hired 1803; Drifter 1915; Tug WW.II; Tug 1958.

FAWKNER Iron S. gunboat (Australian) 387 tons, 1-6in, 1-6pdr. Built 1887. Fate unknown.

FAWN Brig-sloop 16. French FAUNE captured 15.8.1805 by GOLIATH in the Channel. In service in 1806.

FAWN Sloop 18, 424bm, 180½ x 30 ft, 18-24pdr carr., 6-18pdr carr. Owen, Topsham 22.4.1807. Sold 20.8.1818.

FAWN (ex-slaver Caroline) Brigantine 6, 169bm, 75 x 23 ft. Purchased 27.5.1840 at Rio de Janeiro. Tank vessel 1842. Sold 5.1847 to the Natal Colonial Govt.

FAWN Wood S. sloop, 751bm, 1,045 tons, 160 x 32 ft, 17-32pdr. Deptford DY 30.9.1856. Survey ship 6.1876. Sold 1884.

FAWN Destroyer 380 tons, 215 x 20½ ft, 1-12pdr, 5-6pdr, 2-TT. Palmer 13.4.1897. Sold 23.7.1919 Ward, New Holland.

FAWN Survey ship. Brooke Marine 29.2.1968.

FAWN Trawler requis. 1918-19: Trawler and Drifter WW.II.

FEARLESS Gunvessel 12, 149bm, 75 x 21 ft. Cleveley, Gravesend 6.1794. Wrecked 2.1804 in Cawsand Bay.

FEARLESS Gun-brig 12, 180bm, 80½ x 22½ ft, 2-18pdr carr., 10-18 pdr. Graham, Harwich 18.12.1804. Wrecked 8.12.1812 near Cadiz.

FEARLESS (ex-GPO vessel Flamer) Wood pad. survey vessel, 165bm, 112½ x 18½ ft. Transferred 8.1837. BU 1875, at Chatham.

FEARLESS Torpedo cruiser 1,580 tons, 220 x 34 ft, 2-5in, 8-3pdr, 3-TT. Barrow SB (Vickers) 20.3.1886. Sold 11.7.1905 at Portsmouth.

FEARLESS Scout cruiser 3,440 tons, 385 x 41½ ft, 10-4in. Pembroke Dock 12.6.1912. Sold 8.11.21 Slough TC; BU in Germany.

FEARLESS Destroyer 1,375 tons, 318 x 33½ ft, 4-4.7in, 8-TT. Cammell Laird 12.5.1934. Sunk 23.7.41 by Italian A/C in the Mediterranean.

FEARLESS Assault ship 10,000 tons, 550 x 80 ft, 2-40mm, 16-GWS. Harland & Wolff 19.12.1963.

FEARLESS Drifter requis. 1914-19.

FELICIDADE (see under FELICITY)

FELICITY Sloop (Canadian lakes). Detroit 1773. Sold 1795.

FELICITE 5th Rate 36. French, captured 18.6.1809 by LATONA in the W. Indies. 16 guns by 1814. Sold 1818.

FELICIDADE Schooner. Brazilian slaver captured 27.2.1845 by WASP off Lagos. Foundered 5.4.1845.

FELICITY (ex-RCN COPPERCLIFF renamed 6.1943) Minesweeper, 'Algerine' class. Redfern, Toronto 19.1.44. Sold 1947, renamed Fairfree.

FELICITY Tug 1969

FELIX Schooner 14, 158bm, 80½ x 22 ft, 14-12pdr carr. French privateer captured 26.7.1803 by AMAZON. Wrecked 23.1.1807 near Santander.

FELIXSTOWE Minesweeper, TE 'Bangor' class. Lobnitz 15.1.1941. Sunk 18.12.43 by mine off Sardinia.

FELLOWSHIP 28-gun ship, 300bm. Royalist, captured 1643. Careening hulk 1651. Sold 1662.

FELMERSHAM Inshore M/S, 'Ham' clas. Camper & Nicholson 24.9.1953. Malaysian TODAK 5.3.66.

FENCER (ex-USS CROTON) Escort carrier 11,420 tons, 468½ x 69½ ft, 2-4in, 8-40mm, 18-A/C. Western Pipe & Steel Co 4.4.1942 on lend-lease. Returned 11.12.46 to the USN.

FENCER Patrol boat 34 tons. Fairey Marine 1983

FENELLA Wood S. gunboat, 'Clown' class. Pitcher, Northfleet 19.5.1856. Dredger 3.1867. BU 11.1878.

FENELLA Drifter requis. 1940-46.

FENNEL Corvette, 'Flower' class. Marine Industries, Sorel 20.8.1940. Lent RCN to 12.6.45. Sold 9.8.46, renamed William Kihl.

FENTON Coastal M/S, 'Ton' class. Camper & Nicholson 10.3.1955. BU at Newhaven 1968.

FERGUS (ex-FORT FRANCIS renamed 4.1943) Corvette (RCN), modified 'Flower' class. Collingwood SY 30.8.44. Sold 16.11.45, renamed Camco II.

FERMOY Minesweeper, later 'Hunt' class. Dundee SB 5.2.1919. Damaged beyond repair 30.4.41 by air attack at Malta and BU.

FERNIE Destroyer, 'Hunt' class type I.J. Brown 9.1.1940. Arrived 7.11.56 Smith & Houston, Port Glasgow to BU.

FEROZE Wood pad. frigate (Indian), 1,450bm, 240 x 44 ft. Bombay DY 18.5.1848. Yacht 1863.

FERRET Sloop 10, 128bm, 72 x 20 ft. Dummer, Blackwall 1704. Captured 25.2.1706 by the French off Dunkirk.

FERRET Sloop 10, 123bm, 65 x 21 ft. Deptford DY 2.4.1711. Captured 1.9.1718 by the Spanish in Cadiz Bay.

FERRET Sloop 6, 67bm, 55 x 17 ft. Woolwich DY 6.5.1721. Sold 18.11.1731.

FERRET Sloop 14, 255bm, 88½ x 25 ft. Bird, Rotherhithe 10.5.1743. Foundered 24.9.1757 in a hurricane off Louisburg.

FERRET Sloop 14, 300bm, 95½ x 27 ft. Stanton, Rotherhithe 6.12.1760. Foundered 8.1776 in a hurricane in the W. Indies.

FERRET Cutter 6, 83bm, 50 x 20 ft. Chatham DY 8.10.1763. Sold 18.6.1781.

FERRET Brig-sloop 12, 202bm, 79 x 25 ft. Hills, Sandwich 17.8.1784. Sold 16.12.1801.

FERRET Gunboat 4, 66bm, 64 x 15 ft. Ex-hoy purchased 4.1794. Sold 5.1802.

FERRET Schooner 6. Purchased 1799. Captured 1799 by the Spanish.

FERRET Brig-sloop 18, 'Cruizer' class, 387bm. Tanner, Dartmouth 4.1.1806. Wrecked 7.1.1813 near Leith.

FERRET (see NOVA SCOTIA)

FERRET Brig-sloop 10, 'Cherokee' class, 237bm. Portsmouth DY 12.10.1821. Sold 1.1837 H. Bailey.

FERRET Brig 8, 358bm, 95 x 30 ft, 8-18pdr. Devonport DY 1.6.1840. Wrecked 29.3.1869 off Dover pier.

FERRET Destroyer 325 tons, 194 x 19 ft, 1-12pdr, 3-6pdr, 2-TT. Laird 9.12.1893. Dismantled 1910 at Chatham and sunk 1911 as a target.

FERRET Destroyer 750 tons, 246 x 25½ ft, 2-4in, 2-12pdr, 2-TT. White 12.4.1911. Sold 9.5.21 Ward, Milford Haven.

FERRETER Gun-brig 12, 184bm, 80 x 23 ft. Perry, Blackwall 4.4.1801. Captured 31.5.1807 by the Dutch in the Ems.

FERVENT Gun-brig 12, 179bm, 80 x 23 ft, 2-18pdr, 10-18pdr carr. Adams, Bucklers Hard 15.12.1804. Made a mooring lighter at Portsmouth 8.1816. BU 1879.

FERVENT Wood S. frigate, 1,453bm, 210 x 40 ft. Woolwich DY. Ordered 1846, cancelled 1849.

FERVENT Wood S. gunboat, 'Albacore' class. Green, Blackwall 23.1.1856. BU 2.1879 at Devonport.

FERVENT Destroyer 310 tons, 200 x 19 ft, 1-12pdr, 5-6pdr, 2-TT. Hanna Donald, Paisley 28.3.1895. Sold 29.4.20 Ward, Rainham.

FEVERSHAM (see FAVERSHAM)

FIDELITY Decoy ship 2450 tons commissioned 24.9.1940 lost 30.12.42

FIDGET Wood S. gunboat, 'Cheerful' class Joyce, Greenhithe 7.4.1856. BU 1863 at Haslar.

FIDGET Iron S. gunboat, 'Ant' class. Chatham DY 13.3.1872. Hulked 1905.

FIDGET (ex-War Dept *Miner 18*) Tender, 70 x 15 ft. Transferred 1905. Renamed ADELAIDE 1907: ADDA 1915; ST ANGELO 12.33. Sold 6.37.

FIDGET Salvage vessel 1915-21. Drifter 1939-46. Tug 1947-71.

FIERCE (ex-*Desperate*) Schooner 16, 82bm, 59 x 19½ ft. Purchased 1806. BU 1813.

FIERCE Minesweeper, 'Algerine' class Lobnitz 11.9.1945. Arrived 2.8.59 Dorkin, Gateshead to BU.

FIFE GM destroyer 5,600 tons, 505 x 54 ft, 4-4.5in, 2-20mm, 10-GWS. Fairfield 9.7.1964.

FIFE NESS Repair ship 8,580 tons, 439 x 62 ft. Burrard, Vancouver 30.4.1945. To Air Ministry 1948 as ADASTRAL.

FIGHTER (see LST 3038)

FIJI Cruiser 8,000 tons, 538 x 62 ft, 12-6in, 8-4in. J. Brown 31.5.1939. Sunk 22.5.41 by air attack SW of Crete.

FILEY (see RUGBY)

FILEY Trawler 1914-20.

FINCH Brig 8 (Canadian lakes), 110bm, 1-18pdr, 6-18pdr carr., 1-6pdr. American GROWLER captured on Lake Champlain 9.1813. Recaptured 11.9.1814 by the Americans.

FINDHORN Frigate, 'River' class. Vickers, Montreal 5.12.1942 on lend-lease. Returned 20.3.46 to the USN.

FINISTERRE Destroyer 2,315 tons, 355 x 40 ft, 4-4in, 1-4in, 8-TT. Fairfield 22.6.1944. Arrived 12.6.67 Dalmuir to BU.

FINWHALE Submarine 1,605 tons, 241 x 26½ ft, 8-TT. Cammell Laird 21.7.1959.

FINWHALE Whaler 1915-20.

FIREBALL Minesweeper, 'Algerine' class. Lobnitz. Ordered 1943, cancelled 10.44.

FIREBRAND Fireship 8, 268bm, 92½ x 25½ ft. Haydon, Limehouse 31.3.1694. Wrecked 22.10.1707 on the Scillies.

FIREBRAND (ex-*Charming Jenny*) Fireship 8, 221bm, 87½ x 24½ ft. Purchased 14.9.1739. Sold 19.12.1743.

FIREBRAND (see DOLPHIN of 1731)

FIREBRAND (see PORPOISE of 1777)

FIREBRAND Fireship, 89bm, 60 x 19 ft. Purchased 5.1794. BU 6.1800.

FIREBRAND Fireship, 140bm, 80 x 20 ft. Ex-French prize purchased 1804. Wrecked 13.10.1804 near Dover.

FIREBRAND Wood paddle vessel, 494bm, 155 x 26½ ft, 1-18pdr. Curling & Co. Limehouse 11.7.1831. Rebuilt 1834 as 540bm, 168 x 26½ ft. Renamed BLACK EAGLE 1843. BU 3.1876 Portsmouth.

FIREBRAND (ex-BELZEBUB renamed 5.2.1842) Wood pad. frigate, 1,190bm, 190 x 37½ ft. Portsmouth DY 6.9.1842. Sold 7.10.1864 Castle, Charlton.

FIREBRAND Compos. S. Gunboat 455 tons, 125 x 23½ ft, 2-64pdr, 2-20pdr. Thomson 30.4.1877. Sold 1905, renamed *Hoi Tin*.

FIREBRAND (ex-War Dept vessel *Lord Heathfield*), Tender 125 tons, 95 x 17½ ft. Transferred 1906, renamed 26.11.06. Sold 10.2.20 Stanlee Dover.

FIREBRAND (see TORCH of 1894)

FIREDRAKE Bomb 12, 202bm, 86 x 27ft. Deptford 1688. Captured 12.11.1689 by the French.

FIREDRAKE Bomb 12, 279bm, 85 x 24ft. Deptford 6.1693. Foundered 12.10.1703.

FIREDRAKE Bomb 12, 283bm, 91½ x 26½ ft. Perry, Blackwall 26.2.1741. Sold 31.3.1763.

FIREDRAKE (ex-*Ann*Fire vessel. Purchased 1794. Sold 17.6.1807 Mr Freake to BU.

FIREDRAKE Destroyer 767 tons, 225 x 25½ ft, 2-4in, 2-12pdr, 2-TT. Yarrow 9.4.1912. Sold 10.10.21 J.Smith.

FIREDRAKE Destroyer 1,350 tons, 318 x 33 ft. 4-4.7in, 8-TT. Vickers Armstrong, Barrow 28.6.1934. Sunk 17.12.42 by 'U.211' in the Atlantic.

FIREFLY Galley 8 in service in 1781.

FIREFLY (ex-*John Gordon*) Storeship 6, 98bm, 6-12pdr carr. Purchased 1803. Gone by 1805.

FIREFLY (see FLYING FISH of 1803)

FIREFLY Cutter 8, 80bm. Captured 1807. Wrecked 1808 in the W. Indies.

FIREFLY Schooner 6. Bermuda 1828. Wrecked 27.2.1835 on the coast of British Honduras.

FIREFLY Wood pad. Survey vessel, 550bm, 155 x 28ft. Woolwich DY 29.9.1832. BU 1866 at Malta.

FIREFLY DY Tug 1868-1908

FIREFLY Compos. S. gunboat 455 tons, 125 x 23½ ft, 2-64pdr, 2-20 pdr. Thomson 28.6.1877. Boom defence 1904; renamed EGMONT base ship 3.4.14: FIREFLY 1.3.23. Sold 5.31.

FIREFLY Coastal destroyer 235 tons, 175 x 17½ ft, 2-12pdr, 3-TT. White 1.9.1906. Renamed TB.3 in 1906. Sold 7.10.20 Ward, Hayle.

FIREFLY River gunboat, 'Fly' class. Yarrow in sections 7.1915 and re-erected 11.15 on the Tigris. In Turkish hands 1.12.15 to 26.2.17. Sunk 6.24 by insurgents in the Euphrates.

FIREFLY Trawler requis 1939-45.

FIREQUEEN Iron pad. Vessel, 313bm, 164 x 20 ft. Purchased 24.7.1847. Sold 4.8.1883.

FIREQUEEN (ex-'Candace') Yacht 446 tons, 157 x 23½ ft. Purchased 1882. Sold 5.7.1920, renamed 'Firebird'.

FIRME 3rd Rate 70, 1,288bm, 156 x 43½ ft. French FERME captured 14.10.1702 at Vigo. Sold 12.11.1713, became Russian LEFERM.

FIRME 4th Rate 60, 1,297bm, 154½ x 43½ ft. Perry, Blackwall 15.1.1759. Harbour service 5.1784. Sold 10.11.1791.

FIRME (see DIOMEDE of 1798)

FIRM Floating battery 16, 397 bm, 96 x 31 ft, 16-18pdr Deptford DY 19.5.1794. Sold 1803.

FIRM Gun-brig 12, 181bm, 80 x 22½ ft, 10-18pdr carr., 2-12pdr. Brindley, Frindsbury 2.7.1804. Wrecked 28.6.1811 on the French coast.

FIRME 3rd Rate 74, 1,805bm. Spanish FERME captured 22.7.1805 at Cape Finisterre. Harbour service 1807. Sold 3.11.1814.

FIRM Mortar vessel, 117bm, 65 x 21ft, 1-13in mortar. Wigram Blackwall 1.3.1855. Renamed MV.11 on 19.10.1855. Sold 1858 at Malta.

FIRM Wood S. Gunboat, 'Albacore' class. Fletcher, Limehouse 22.3.1856. Sold 1872 in China.

FIRM Compos. S. gunboat 455 tons, 125 x 23½ ft, 2-64pdr, 2-20pdr. Earle 14.2.1877. Sold 14.5.1907 Cox, Falmouth.

FIRM Tug 1910-60.

FISGARD 5th Rate 44, 1,182bm, 160 x 41 ft, 8-32pdr carr., 28-18pdr, 10-9pdr. French RESISTANCE captured 9.3.1797 by SAN FIORENZO and NYMPHE off Brest. Sold 11.8.1814.

FISGARD 5th Rate 46, 1,068bm, 150 x

40½ft, 16-32pdr carr., 28-18pdr, 2-9pdr. Pembroke Dock 8.7.1819; not commissioned until 1843. BU completed 8.10.1879 at Chatham.

For ships renamed FISGARD as training ships, see AUDACIOUS of 1869, INVINCIBLE of 1869, HINDOSTAN of 1841, SULTAN of 1870, SPARTIATE of 1898, HERCULES of 1868 and TERRIBLE of 1895.

FISHGUARD (ex-USS TAHOE) Cutter 1,546 tons, 1-5in, 2-6pdr. Transferred 30.4.1941 on lend-lease. Returned 4.2.46 to USN.

FISKERTON Coastal M/S, 'Ton' class. Doig, Grimsby 12.4.1957. Sold 1971, BU Dartford 1976.

FITTLETON Coastal M/S, 'Ton' class. White, Southampton 5.2.1954. Renamed CURZON. 1961-75. Sold 20.9.77 to BU Sittingbourne.

FITZROY (ex-PINNER, ex-PORTREATH renamed 1919) Survey ship, ex-later 'Hunt' class minesweeper. Lobnitz 15.4.1919. M/S 1939. Sunk 27.5.42 by mine off Gt Yarmouth.

FITZROY Frigate, TE 'Captain' class. Bethlehem, Hingham 1.9.1943. Returned 1.46 to the USN.

FLAMBEAU (ex-*Good Intent*) Fireship. Purchased 1804. Sold 17.6.1807 J. Bailey.

FLAMBOROUGH 6th Rate 24, 252bm. Chatham DY 1697. Captured 10.10.1705 by the French JASON off Cape Spartel.

FLAMBOROUGH 6th Rate 24, 261bm, 94 x 25 ft. Woolwich DY 29.1.1707. Rebuilt Portsmouth 1727 as 377bm, 20 guns. Sold 10.1.1748.

FLAMBOROUGH 6th Rate 22, 435bm, 108½ x 30½ ft. Batson, Limehouse 14.5.1756. Sold 23.9.1772.

FLAMBOROUGH PRIZE Sloop 14, 115bm, 66 x 20½ ft, 14-4pdr. French privateer GENERAL LALLY captured 1757 by FLAMBOROUGH. Sold 15.3.1763.

FLAMBOROUGH HEAD Repair ship 8,580 tons, 439 x 62 ft, 16-20mm. Burrard, Vancouver 7.10.1944. To RCN 31.1.53 and renamed CAPE BRETON.

FLAME Fireship 8, 273bm, 92 x 25½ft Gressingham, Limehouse 6.3.1691. Foundered 22.8.1697 in the W. Indies.

FLAME Drifter 1918-21.

FLAMER (Gunboat No 24) Gunvessel 12, 168bm, 76 x 22½ ft, 2-24pdr, 10-18pdr carr. Perry, Blackwall 1.4.1797. Sold 4.1802.

FLAMER Gun-brig 12, 178bm, 80 x 22½ ft, 10-18pdr carr., 2-12pdr. Brindley, Frindsbury 8.5.1804. Harbour service 5.1815; coastguard 1841. Sold 16.9.1858 Castle, Charlton.

FLAMER Wood pad. vessel, 496bm, 155 x 26½ ft. Fletcher, Limehouse 11.8.1831. Wrecked 22.11.1850 W. Africa.

FLAMER Mortar vessel, 117bm, 65 x 21 ft, 1-13in mortar. Wigram, Blackwall 1.3.1855. Renamed MV.10 on 19.10.1856. Malta yard craft YC.5 by 1866. For disposal 1901.

FLAMER Wood S. gunboat, 'Albacore' class. Fletcher, Limehouse 10.4.1856. Harbour service 1868. Blown ashore in a typhoon 1874 at Hong Kong and wreck sold 1874.

FLAMER Store carrier 1891-1913. Tug 1915-48.

FLAMINGO Compos. S. gunvessel 780 tons, 157 x 29½ ft, 1-7in, 1-64pdr, 2-20pdr. Devonport DY 13.12.1876. Sold 25.5.1923 Plymouth Sanitary Authority after 30 years harbour service. BU 1931.

FLAMINGO Sloop 1,250 tons, 283 x 37½ ft, 6-4in. Yarrow 18.4.1939. Sold W. German navy, renamed GRAF SPEE 1.59.

FLASH (ex-*James*) Fire vessel, 62bm, 54 x 16 ft. Purchased 5.1804. Sold 17.6.1807 W. Bliss.

FLASH Drifter 1918-20, Whaler in WW.I.

FLAX Corvette, modified 'Flower' class. Kingston SY 15.6.1942. Lent USN from completion until 1945 as BRISK. Sold 1945, renamed *Ariana*.

FLECHE Brig-sloop 14, 227bm. French, captured 21.5.1794 by the Fleet at Bastia. Wrecked 12.11.1795 San Fiorenzo Bay.

FLECHE sloop 18, French privateer la CAROLINE captured 31.5.1798. Wrecked 24.5.1810 at mouth of the Elbe.

FLECHE Sloop 16, 280bm, 93 x 26½ ft. French, captured 5.9.1801 by VICTOR. Wrecked 24.5.1810 in mouth of the Elbe.

FLEETWOOD Ship (Royalist), 150bm. Captured by Parliamentarians 1655 and renamed WEXFORD.

FLEETWOOD (see FORD)

FLEETWOOD Sloop 990 tons, 250 x 36 ft, 4-4in. Devonport DY 24.3.1936. Arrived 10.10.59 Dorkin, Gateshead to BU.

FLEETWOOD Trawler requis. 1917-19.

FLEUR de la MER Schooner 8, 117bm, 72½ x 19½ft. Purchased 1808. Foundered 8.1.1811 in the Atlantic.

FLEUR de LYS (ex-French La DIEP-POISE seized 3.7.40 at Middles-brough) Corvette, 'Flower' class. Smiths Dk 21.6.1940. Sunk 14.10.41 by 'U.206' west of Gibraltar.

FLEWENDE FISCHE (see under FLYING FISH)

FLIGHT (see ARIADNE of 1805)

FLINDERS (ex-RADLEY renamed 1919) Survey ship, ex-'Hunt' class minesweeper 800 tons, 1-3pdr. Lob-nitz 27.8.1919. Accommodation ship 8.40. Sold 8.45, BU at Falmouth.

FLINDERS Survey ship (RAN) 720 tons, Williamstown DY 29.7.1972

FLINT Minesweeper, later 'Hunt' class. Eltringham. Cancelled 1918.

FLINT Trawler 1942-47. FLINT CAS-TLE Corvette, 'Castle' class. Robb 1.9.1943. Arrived 10.7.58 at Faslane to BU.

FLINTHAM Inshore M/S, 'Ham' class. Bolson 10.3.1955. Sold 1982.

FLIRT Ship in service in 1592.

FLIRT Brig-sloop 14, 209bm, 78 x 26 ft. King, Dover 4.3.1782. Sold 1.12.1795.

FLIRT Wood S. gunboat, 'Cheerful' class.Joyce, Greenhithe 7.6.1856. BU 4.1864 at Haslar.

FLIRT Gunboat (New Zealand). Pur-chased 1862. Sold 1864.

FLIRT Compos. S. gunvessel, 464bm, 603 tons, 155 x 25 ft, 1-7in, 1-64pdr, 2-20pdr. Devonport DY 20.12.1867. Sold 11.88 Cohen to BU.

FLIRT Destroyer 380 tons, 215 x 20½ ft, 1-12pdr, 5-6pdr, 2-TT. Palmer, Jarrow 15.5.1897. Sunk 27.10.1916 in action with German destroyer, Do-ver Straits.

FLOCKTON Coastal M/S, 'Ton' class. White, Southampton 3.6.1954. sold 28.7.69 to BU.

FLORA Sloop 313bm, Ordered Dept-ford by 1755 and cancelled.

FLORA 5th Rate 32, 698bm, 132 x 35 ft, 26-12pdr, 6-6pdr. French VESTALE captured 8.1.1761 by UNI-CORN. scuttled 7.8.1778 to avoid capture at Rhode Island; salved by Americans and became French pri-vateer FLORE 1784; recaptured 7.9.1798 by PHAETON and sold.

FLORA 5th Rate 36, 868bm, 137 x 38 ft. Deptford DY 6.5.1780. Wrecked 19.1.1809 on the Dutch coast.

FLORA 5th Rate 36, 1,634bm, 160 x 49 ft. Devonport DY 11.9.1844. Harbour service 1851. Sold 9.1.1891.

FLORA 2nd class cruiser 4,360 tons, 320 x 49½ ft, 2-6in, 8-4.7in, 8-6pdr.

Pembroke Dock 21.11.1893. Training ship INDUS II in 4.1915. Sold 12.12.22., BU at Dover.

FLORA (see GRIPER of 1879)

FLORA Drifter requis. 1914-19.

La FLORE Destroyer 610 tons, 245 x 26 ft, 2-39.in, 2-TT. French torpedo boat seized 3.7.1940 at Portsmouth. Returned to the French navy 1945.

FLORENTIA Wood S. sloop, 998bm, 185 x 34½ ft. Woolwich DY. Ordered 1847, cancelled 22.5.1849.

FLORENTINA 5th Rate 36, 902bm, 146½ x 37½ ft. Spanish, captured 7.4.1800 at Cadiz. Sold 1802.

FLORIDA Storeship, 299bm, 95 x 28 ft. Purchased 8.1764. BU completed 7.1772 at Deptford.

FLORIDA Storeship 14, 202bm, 68 x 19 ft. Purchased 1774 in the W. Indies. Sold 18.5.1778 at Pensacola.

FLORIDA 6th Rate 20, 539bm, 119½ x 32 ft, 18-32pdr carr., 2-9pdr. Ameri-can FROLIC captured 20.4.1814 by ORPHEUS. BU 5.1819 at Chatham.

FLORIDA Whaler (SAN) 1940-46.

FLORISTON coastal M/S, 'Ton' class. Richards IW 26.1.1955. Sold Pounds 27.5.68.

FLORIZEL (see LAFOREY)

FLORIZEL Minesweeper, 'Catherine' class. Assoc. SB, Seattle 20.5.1943 and on lend-lease from 14.4.44. Re-turned 12.46 to the USN and sold Greek navy.

FLOWER de LUCE Pinnace 30 tons. Dating from 1546. captured by the French 1562.

FLY Sloop 6. Built 1648. Last listed 1652.

FLY Dogger 6. Dutch, captured 1672. Wrecked 1673.

FLY Advice boat 6, 73bm, 62 x 16 ft. Portsmouth DY 1694. Wrecked 22.8.1695.

FLY Ketch 4, 70bm, 61½ x 20 ft. Ports-mouth DY 1696. Sold 10.4.1712.

FLY Sloop 12, 200bm, 87 x 23½ ft. Sheerness DY 15.9.1732. BU 2.1750 at Sheerness.

FLY Sloop 8, 140bm, 75 x 20½ ft. Portsmouth DY 9.4.1752. Sold 23.9.1772.

FLY Cutter, 78bm. Purchased 1.1763. Sold 29.10.1771.

FLY Sloop 14, 300bm, 96 x 26½ ft. Sheerness DY 1776. Founded 1802 off Newfoundland.

FLY Cutter 14. Puchased 1778. Cap-tured 1781 by the French.

FLY Sloop 16, 309bm, 89 x 27 ft. Deptford DY 1779. In service in 1782.

FLY Brig-sloop 14 (Indian), 176bm. Bombay DY 1793. Captured 1803 by the French in the Persian Gulf.

FLY Sloop 16, 369bm, 106 x 28 ft. Parsons, Bursledon 26.3.1804. Wrecked 5.1805 in the Gulf of Florida.

FLY Brig-sloop 16, 285bm, 93 x 26 ft. Boole, Bridport 24.10.1805. Wrecked 29.2.1812 on Anholt Island.

FLY Brig-sloop, 'Cruizer' class, 387bm. Bailey, Ipswich 16.2.1813. Sold 10.5.1828 at Bombay.

FLY Sloop 18, 485bm, 114½ x 32 ft. Pembroke Dock 25.8.1831. Coal hulk 1855. BU 1903. (Also bore the number C.2 then C.70 while a coal hulk.)

FLY Wood S. gunboat, 'Albacore' class. Fletcher, Limhouse 5.4.1856. BU 1862.

FLY Compos. S. Gunvessel, 464bm, 603 tons, 155 x 25 ft, 1-7in, 1-64 pdr, 2-20pdr. Devonport DY 20.12.1867. Sold 11.1887, Castle to BU.

FLY Minesweeper, 'Algerine' class. Lobnitz 1.6.1942. Sold 30.7.49 to Iran, renamed PALANG.

FLY Whaler (ex-German) 1914-19. Trawler WW.1.

FLYING FISH Cutter 12, 190bm, 75 x 25½ ft, 12-4pdr. Purchased 4.1778. 14-gun sloop 1781. Wrecked 3.12.1782 near Calais.

FLYING FISH Schooner 6, 80bm, 63 x 17 ft, 6-3pdr. French, captured 1793 by PROVIDENCE. Captured 16.6.1795 by two French privateers in the W. Indies; again captured as the privateer POISSON VOLANT 1797 by MAGICIENNE in the W. Indies. Gone by 1799.

FLYING FISH Schooner 12, 110bm. French POISSON VOLANT captured 30.6.1803 by a squadron off San Domingo. Renamed FIREFLY 1807. Foundered 17.11.1807 in the W. Indies.

FLYING FISH Schooner 4, 70bm, 55 x 18 ft, 4-12pdr carr. Bermuda 1804, Captured by her own prisoners (?) 1804. FLEWENDE FISCHE Brigsloop 18, 213bm, 77 x 26 ft. Danish FLYVENDFISKE captured 7.9.1807 at Copenhagen. Sold 13.6.1811. (Was to have been renamed VENTURE.)

FLYING FISH (ex-Lady Augusta) Schooner 1, 78bm, 62 x 17½ ft. Purchased 1817. Sold 31.1.1821 at Antigua.

FLYING FISH Brig 12, 445bm, 103 x 32½ ft, 10-32pdr, 2-18pdr. Pembroke Dock 3.4.1844. BU 8.1852 at Portsmouth.

FLYING FISH Wood S. despatch vessel, 871bm, 200 x 30½ ft, 2-68pdr, 4-32pdr. Pembroke Dock 20.12.1855. Arrived 8.1866 Castle, Charlton to BU.

FLYING FISH (ex-DARING renamed 14.1.1873) Compos. S. sloop 940 tons, 160 x 31½ ft, 2-7in, 2-64pdr. Chatham DY 8.11.1873. Completed as survey ship 4.1880. Sold 12.1888.

FLYING FISH Destroyer 380 tons, 215 x 20½ft, 1-12pdr, 5-6pdr, 2-TT. Palmer 4.3.1897. Sold 30.8.1919 T.R. Sales.

FLYING FISH (ex-RCN TILLSONBURG renamed 6.1943) Minesweeper, 'Algerine' class. Redfern. Toronto 16.2.44. Renamed VIJAYA, Ceylon navy 7.10.49.

FLYING FISH Tug requis. 1914-20.

FLYING FOX M/S sloop, '24' class. Swan Hunter 28.3.1918. RNVR Drillship 24.3.20. Sold 26.1.73, BU at Cardiff.

FLYING FOX Tug requis. 1914-18.

FLYING GREYHOUND 24-gun ship, 230bm. Captured 1665. Sold 1667.

FOAM Wood S. gunboat, 'Albacore' class. Wigram, Northam 8.5.1856. Sold 6.1867 to BU.

FOAM Compos. S. gunboat 430 tons, 125 x 23 ft, 2-64pdr, 2-20pdr. Pembroke Dock 29.8.1871. Sold 6.1887 to BU.

FOAM Destroyer 340 tons, 210 x 19½ ft, 1-12pdr, 5-6pdr, 2-TT. Thornycroft, Chiswick 8.10.1896. Sold 26.5.1914 at Chatham' BU in Norway.

FOAM Minesweeper, 'Catherine' class. Assoc. SB, Seattle 20.5.1943 and to the RN 28.4.44 on lend-lease. Returned 13.11.46 to the USN.

FOAM Yacht requis. 1918-19. Drifter 1918-21.

FOLEY Frigate, DE 'Captain' class, Mare Island. Laid down 30.4.1942 for the RN but retained by the USN as WILEMAN.

FOLEY (ex-USS GILLETTE) Frigate, DE 'Captain' class. Boston Navy Yd 19.5.43 on lend-lease. Returned 8.45 to the USN.

FOLKESTON Cog (Cinq Ports fleet). Listed in 1299.

FOLKESTON 4th Rate 44, 496bm, 116 x 31½ ft. Deptford DY 14.10.1703. BU 1727.

FOLKESTON 5th Rate 44, 698bm, 124½ x 36 ft. Bird, Rotherhithe 8.1.1741. Sold 1.8.1749.

FOLKESTONE Cutter 8, 84bm, Folkestone 13.10.1764. Captured

24.6.1778 by the French SURVEIL-LANTE in the Channel.

FOLKESTONE Sloop 1,045 tons, 250 x 34 ft, 2-4in. Swan Hunter 1.7.1930. Sold 22.5.47 Howells; BU at Milford, by Ward in 11.47.

FOLKESTONE M/S requis. 1914-20.

FORCE Gunvessel 12, 149bm, 75 x 21 ft. Pitcher, Northfleet 1794. Sold 11.1802.

FORCE Trawler requis. 1940-41.

FORD (ex-FLEETWOOD renamed 1918) Minesweeper, later 'Hunt' class. Dunlop Bremner 19.10.1918. Sold 10.28; resold 8.12.28, renamed *Forde*.

FORDHAM Inshore M/S, 'Ham' class. Jones, Buckie 7.8.1956. Sold Pounds 1981.

FORESIGHT 36-gun ship, 306bm, 14-9pdr, 8-6pdr, 3-4pdr, 11 small. Built 1570. BU 1604.

FORESIGHT 50-gun ship, 524bm, 121 x 32 ft. Deptford 1650. Wrecked 4.7.1698 in the W. Indies.

FORESIGHT Scout cruiser 2,850 tons, 360 x 39 ft, 10-12pdr, 8-3pdr. Fairfield 8.10.1904. Sold 3.3.20 Granton S. Bkg Co.

FORESIGHT Destroyer 1,350 tons, 318 x 33 ft, 4-4.7in, 8-TT. Cammell Laird 29.6.1934. Bombed 12.8.42 by Italian A/C central Mediterranean and sank next day.

FORESIGHT Drifter requis. 1914-19 and 1940-46.

FORESTER 22-gun ship. Lydney 1657. Blown up 1672.

FORESTER Hoy 7, 125bm, 66½ x 20½ ft. Portsmouth DY 2.11.1693. Wrecked 26.8.1752.

FORESTER Hoy 4, 112bm, 63½ x 20 ft. Ewer, Bursledon 1748. Transferred Coastguard 1828 as a hulk.

FORESTER Gunvessel 4, 172bm, 70 x 24 ft. Ex-hoy purchased 4.1794. In service in 1800.

FORESTER Brig-sloop 18, 'Cruizer' class, 385bm, King, Dover 3.8.1806. Harbour service 1816. Sold 8.3.1819.

FORESTER Brig 10. Deptford DY. Ordered 1824. Cancelled 1830 or contract transferred Chatham (see next vessel).

FORESTER Brig-sloop 10, 'Cherokee' class, 229bm. Chatham DY 28.8.1832 Sold 27.11.1843.

FORESTER Wood S. gunboat, 'Albacore' class. Green, Blackwall 22.1.1856. Renamed YC.7, yard craft 1868. Lost 1871 in a typhoon at Hong Kong.

FORESTER Compos. S. gunboat 455 tons, 125 x 23½ ft, 2-64pdr, 2-20pdr. Earle 26.2.1877. Coal hulk 1894. Sold 1904.

FORESTER Destroyer 760 tons, 246 x 25½ ft, 2-4in, 2-12pdr, 2-TT. White 1.6.1911. Sold 4.11.21 Rees, Llanelly.

FORESTER Destroyer 1,350 tons, 318 x 3 ft, 4-4.7in, 8-TT. White 28.6.1934. Sold 22.1.46; arrived 6.47 at Rosyth to BU.

FOREST HILL (see PROVIDENCE of 1943)

FOREST HILL (ex-CEANOTHUS renamed 9.43) Corvette (RCN), modified 'Flower' class. Ferguson 27.10.43. Sold 17.7.48.

FORFAR Minesweeper, later 'Hunt' class. Dundee SB Co 11.1918. Sold 3.22 Ward, Inverkeithing.

FORFAR AMC 16,400 tons. Requis 1939-40.

FORMIDABLE 2nd Rate 80, 2,002bm, 188 x 49½ ft, 30-32pdr, 32-24pdr, 18-9pdr. French, captured 20.11.1759. BU completed 24.1.1768 at Plymouth.

FORMIDABLE 2nd Rate 90, 1,945bm, 178 x 50 ft. Chatham DY 20.8.1777. Made a 3rd Rate 74 guns, 1813. BU 9.1813 at Chatham.

FORMIDABLE 2nd Rate 84, 2,289bm, 3,594 tons, 196 x 52½ ft. Chatham DY 19.5.1825 (from frames captured on stocks 18.4.1814 at Genoa). Lent as training ship 16.7.1869. Sold 10.7.1906.

FORMIDABLE Battleship 15,000 tons, 400 x 75 ft, 4-12in, 12-6in, 18-12pdr. Portsmouth DY 17.11.1898. Sunk 1.1.1915 by 'U.24' off Portland Bill.

FORMIDABLE A/C carrier 23,000 tons, 673 x 96 ft, 16-4.5in, 36-A/C. Harland & Wolff 17.8.1939. Arrived Faslane 12.5.53 to BU.

FORMIDABLE Drifter requis 1915-19.

FORRES (ex-FOWEY renamed 1918) minesweeper, later 'Hunt' class. Clyde SB Co 22.11.1918. Sold 26.4.35 Ward, Pembroke.

FORT ERIE (ex-La TUQUE renamed 3.1944) Frigate (RCN), 'River' class. G.T. Davie 27.5.44. Arrived 22.5.66 at Spezia to BU.

FORT FRANCIS (see FERGUS)

FORT FRANCIS Minesweeper (RCN), 'Algerine' class. Port Arthur SY 30.10.1943. Survey ship 1949.

FORT WILLIAM (see La MALBAIE)

FORT WILLIAM Minesweeper (RCN), TE 'Bangor' class. Port Arthur 30.12.1941. Sold 29.11.57 Turkish navy as BODRUM.

FORT YORK (ex-MINGAN renamed 8.1941) Minesweeper, TE 'Bangor' class. Dufferin, Toronto 24.8.41. sold 26.9.50 Portuguese navy as COMANDANTE ALMEIDA CARVALHO.

FORTE 4th Rate 50, 1,500bm, 170 x 43½ ft, 20-32pdr carr., 30-24pdr, 2-12pdr. French, captured 28.2.1799 by SYBILLE in the Bay of Bengal. Wrecked 6.1801 off Jeddah.

FORTE 5th Rate 40. Sheerness DY. Ordered 9.7.1801, cancelled, re-ordered as next ship.

FORTE 5th Rate 38, 1,155bm, 157½ x 40½ ft. Woolwich DY 21.5.1814. BU 10.1844.

FORTE screw Frigate 51, 2,364bm, 3,456 tons, 212 x 50 ft. Deptford DY 29.5.1858. Receiving ship 1880; coal hulk 1894. Burnt 23.11.1905 by accident at Sheerness.

FORTE (see PEMBROKE of 1812)

FORTE 2nd class cruiser 4,360 tons, 320 x 49½ ft, 2-6in, 8-4.7in, 8-6pdr. Chatham DY 9.12.1893. Sold 2.4.1914 Tydeman, Holland.

FORTE (see FURIOUS of 1896)

FORTH (see TIGRIS of 1813)

FORTH 4th Rate 50 (pitch pine-built), 1,251bm, 159 x 42 ft, 20-32pdr carr., 28-24pdr, 2-9pdr. Wigram & Green, Blackwall 14.6.1813. BU 10.1819.

FORTH 5th Rate 44, 1,215bm, 159 x 42 ft. Pembroke Dock 1.8.1833. Undocked 21.1.1856 as screw frigate, 1,228bm; renamed JUPITER coal hulk 12.1869. Sold Castle 4.8.1883 to BU.

FORTH 2nd class cruiser 4,050 tons, 300 x 46 ft, 2-8in, 10-6in, 3-6pdr. Pembroke Dock 23.10.1886. Sold 8.11.1921 Slough TC, BU in Germany. (Was to have been renamed HOWARD 12.20).

FORTH Depot ship 8,900 tons, 497 x 73 ft, 8-4.5in. J.Brown 11.8.1938. DEFIANCE 2.72-7.72 Sold 1985, BU Kingsnorth.

FORTH Tug requis 1914-19.

FORTITUDE 3rd Rate 74, 1,645bm, 168½ x 47 ft. Randall, Rotherhithe 22.3.1780. Prison ship 10.1795; powder hulk 5.1802. BU 3.1820.

FORTITUUD (see CUMBERLAND of 1807)

FORTITUDE Tug 1909-23. Drifter and Tug WW.I. Tug 1947-64.

FORTUNE Ship, 100bm, in service in 1512.

FORTUNE Ship in service in 1522.

FORTUNE Ship, 300bm. French FORTUNEE captured 1627. Last listed 1635.

FORTUNE Ship 12 (Royalist). Captured 1644 by Parliament and renamed ROBERT. Captured 1649 by Irish Royalists.

FORTUNE 10-gun ship, 84bm. Royalist, purchased 1644, captured 1644 by Parliament and renamed DOVE. Lost 1650.

FORTUNE Ship, captured 1651. Captured 1652 by the Dutch.

FORTUNE Fireship 10. Captured 1652. Last listed 1653.

FORTUNE 32-gun ship. French FORTUNEE captured 1653. Sold 1654.

FORTUNE Fireship 6, 392bm. Captured 1666. Expended 1666.

FORTUNE Flyboat 4, 180bm. Dutch, captured 1666. Sunk 1667 as blockship in the Thames.

FORTUNE Flyboat 8, 311bm. Dutch, captured 1672. Sold 1674.

FORTUNE PRIZE Fireship 8,262bm, 89 x 26 ft. French, captured 1693. Sold 24.5.1698.

FORTUNE Storeship, Purchased 1699. Wrecked 15.12.1700 on the coast of Cornwall.

FORTUNE Storeship, 192bm. Captured 1700. Listed 1702.

FORTUNE Storeship 24, 543bm, 126 x 31 ft, Deptford DY 31.5.1709. Sold 12.11.1713.

FORTUNE (see FALCON of 1744)

FORTUNE Sloop 18. In service in 1756. Made a fireship 1759. Sold 20.3.1770. (Was FALCON of 1744 (qv) recaptured.

FORTUNE Brig-sloop 10, 120bm, 70 x 24 ft. Purchased 1770. In service 1772.

FORTUNE Sloop 14, 300bm, 97 x 27 ft. Woolwich DY 28.7.1778. Captured 26.4.1780 by the French in the W. Indies.

FORTUNE Brig-sloop 14, 280bm, 85 x 29 ft, 14-4pdr. Stewart, Sandgate 8.1780 and purchased on stocks. Wrecked 15.6.1797 near Oporto.

FORTUNE Sloop 14, 120bm, 70 x 24 ft. American, captured 1779. Lost 1780.

FORTUNE Sloop 18. French, captured 11.8.1798 by SWIFTSURE off the Nile, Recaptured by the French 1799?

FORTUNE Destroyer 1,000 tons, 260 x 27 ft, 3-4in, 2-TT. Fairfield 17.5.1913. Sunk 31.5.16 at Jutland.

FORTUNE Destroyer 1,350 tons, 318 x 33 ft, 4-4.7in, 8-TT. J.Brown 29.8.1934. Renamed SASKATCHEWAN (RCN) 3.6.43. BU 1946.

FORTUNE Coastal M/S (RCN) 370 tons, 140 x 28 ft, 1-40mm. Victoria Mcy Co 14.4.1953. Sold 1966, renamed *Offshore.*

FORTUNEE 5th Rate 40, 948bm, 143½ x 38 ft. French, captured 22.12.1779. Convict ship 10.1785. BU (1800?).

FORTUNEE 5th Rate 36, 921bm, 14½ x 38 ft. Perry, Blackwall 17.11.1800. Sold 29.1.1818 Freake to BU.

FORWARD Gun-brig 12, 179bm, 80 x 22½ ft, 10-18pdr carr.,, 2-12pdr. Todd, Berwick 4.1.1805. Sold 14.12.1815.

FORWARD Wood S. gunboat, 'Albacore' class. Pitcher, Northfleet 8.12.1855. Sold 28.9.1869 Hill & Beedy, Esquimalt.

FORWARD Compos. S. gunboat 455 tons, 125 x 24 ft, 2-6pdr, 2-20 pdr. Barrow SB Co 29.1.1877. Coal hulk 1892.Sold 1904.

FORWARD Scout cruiser 2,850 tons, 360 x 39 ft, 10-12pdr, 8-3pdr. Cammell Laird 27.8.1904. Sold 27.7.21 Fryer.

FORWARD Two Trawlers, two Drifters WW.I.

FOSTER Frigate (RCN), 'River' class. G.T. Davie, Lauzon. Ordered 1943, cancelled 12.43.

FOTHERINGAY CASTLE Corvette, 'Castle' class. Morton. Cancelled 12.1943.

FOUDROYANT 2nd Rate 80, 1,978bm, 18½ x 50½ ft, 30-32pdr, 32-24pr, 18-9pdr. French, captured 28.2.1758 by MONMOUTH and SWIFTSURE BU 9.1787.

FOUDROYANT 2nd Rate 80, 2,062bm, 184 x 51½ ft. Plymouth DY 31.3.1798. Guardship 1820; training ship 1862. Sold 12.1.1892 J. Read; resold German S. Bkrs; resold J.R. Cobb as training ship.Wrecked 16.6.1897 near Blackpool.

FOUDROYANT (ex-TRINCOMALEE renamed 7.1897) Training ship. (The oldest RN ship afloat, still in service at Portsmouth.)

FOUDROYANT (see NEPTUNE of 1909)

FOUGUEUX 3rd Rate 64, 1,403bm, 160 x 44 ft, 26-32pdr, 28-18pdr, 10-12pdr. French, captured 14.10.1747 at Cape Finisterre. BU 5.1759.

FOUNTAIN 34-gun ship. Algerian, captured 1664. Lost 1672 in action.

FOWEY 5th Rate 32, 377bm, 108 x 28 ft. Burgess & Briggs, Shoreham 7.5.1696. Captured 1.8.1704 by the French off Scilly.

FOWEY 5th Rate 32, 414bm, 108 x 29½

ft. Chatham DY 10.3.1705. Captured 14.4.1709 by the French on the coast of Portugal.

FOWEY 5th Rate 44, 528bm, 118 x 32 ft. Portsmouth DY 7.12.1709. Renamed QUEENBOROUGH 5.11.1744. Sold 8.1746.

FOWEY 5th Rate 44, 709bm, 127 x 36 ft. Blaydes, Hull 14.8.1744. Wrecked 26.6.1748 in the Gulf of Florida.

FOWEY 6th Rate 24, 513bm, 113½ x 32 ft. Janvrin, Lepe 4.7.1749. Sunk 10.10.1781 in action with the French in the Chesapeake.

FOWEY Gunvessel 3. Ex-barge purchased 6.1795. Sold 1800.

(FOWY in navy lists 1813 is error for TOWEY, qv.)

FOWEY (see FORRES)

FOWEY Sloop 1,105 tons, 250 x 34 ft, 2-4in. Devonport DY 4.11.1930. Sold.10.46, renamed *Fowlock.*

FOWEY Frigate 2,150 tons. Cammell Laird. Renamed AJAX 1959 and launched 16.8.62 as 2,350 tons.

FOX 22-gun ship. French, captured 1650. Expended as fireship 1656 at Malaga.

FOX 14-gun ship, 203bm. Ostender ST ANTHONY captured 1658. Expended as fireship 1666.

FOX Fireship 8, 263bm, 93½ x 25 ft. Barrett, Shoreham 16.14.1690. Expended 19.5.1692 at La Hogue.

FOX Sloop 6, 68bm, 59 x 16 ft. Sheerness DY 1699. Wrecked 2.12.1699 on the west coast of Ireland.

FOX 6th Rate 24, 273bm, 93 x 26 ft. Captured 5.1705 by TRYTON. Wrecked 28.8.1706 in Holyhead Bay.

FOX (see NIGHTINGALE of 1702)

FOX 6th Rate 24, 440bm, 107 x 31 ft. Buxton, Rotherhithe 1.5.1740. Foundered 14.11.1745 off Dunbar.

FOX 6th Rate 24, 503bm, 112 x 32 ft. Horn & Ewer, Bursledon 26.4. 1746. Foundered 11.9.1751 in a hurricane off Jamaica.

FOX Ketch 8 (Indian). Bombay DY 1766. Listed in 1772.

FOX 6th Rate 28, 585bm, 120 x 34 ft. Calhoun, Northam 2.9.1773. Captured 7.6.1777 by the American HANCOCK; recaptured 8.7.1777 by FLORA; captured 17.9.1778 by the French JUNON.

FOX 5th Rate 32, 697bm, 126 x 35½ ft. Parsons, Bursledon 2.6.1780. BU 4.1816.

FOX Cutter 10, 104bm. Purchased 1794. Sunk 24.7.1797 in action with the Spanish at Santa Cruz.

FOX Schooner 14, 150bm. Ex-French prize purchased 1799. Wrecked 28.9.1799 in the Gulf of Mexico.

FOX 5th Rate 46, 1,080bm, 151 x 40½ ft. Portsmouth DY 17.8.1829. Undocked 18.3.1856 as screw frigate; completed 3.1862 as screw storeship. BU 3.1882 at Devonport.

FOX 2nd class cruiser 4,360 tons, 320 x 49½ ft, 2-6in, 8-4.7.in, 8-6pdr. Portsmouth DY 15.6.1893. Sold 14.7.1920 Cardiff Marine Stores.

FOX Survey vessel 950 tons. Brooke Marine 6.11.1967.

FOX Five cutters hired between 1793-1805.

FOXGLOVE Sloop, 'Acacia' class. Barclay Curle 30.3.1915. Harbour guardship 1941. Sold. 7.9.46, BU at Troon.

FOXHOUND Brig-sloop 18. 'Cruizer' class, 384bm. King, Dover 30.11.1806. Foundered 31.8.1809 in the Atlantic.

FOXHOUND Sloop 16, 348bm, 95 x 29 ft.French BASQUE captured 13.11.1809. Sold 15.2.1816.

FOXHOUND Brig-sloop 10, 'Cherokee' class, 231bm. Plymouth DY. Ordered 28.10.1826, cancelled 21.2.1831.

FOXHOUND Wood S. gunvessel, 681bm, 181½ x 28½ ft, 1-110pdr, 1-68pdr, 2-20pdr. Mare, Blackwall 16.8.1856. BU 8.1866 Castle.

FOXHOUND Compos. S. gunboat 455 tons, 125 x 23½ ft, 2-64pdr, 2-20pdr. Barrow SB Co 29.1.1877. Coastguard 1886; coal tug 1897 and renamed YC.20. Sold 1920 as hulk *Arabel*. BU 1975.

FOXHOUND Destroyer 953 tons, 274 x 27 ft, 1-4in, 3-12pdr, 2-TT. J. Brown 11.12.1909. Sold 1.11.21 Fryer, Sunderland.

FOXHOUND Destroyer 1,350 tons, 318 x 33 ft, 4-4.7in, 8-TT. J. Brown 12.10.1934. Renamed QU'APPELLE (RCN) 8.2.44. Sold 1948 to BU.

FOXHOUND Tug (ex-BOXER) renamed 22.10.1977

FOYLE Destroyer 550 tons, 225 x 33½ ft, 1-12pdr, 5-6pdr(4-12pdr in 1907), 2-TT. Laird 25.2.1903. Sunk 15.3.17 by mine in the Dover Straits.

FOYLE Trawler 1920-46.

FRANCHISE 5th Rate 36, 898bm. French, captured 28.5.1803 by a squadron in the Channel. BU 11.1815.

FRANCIS Discovery ship in 1578. Wrecked 1586.

FRANCIS Discovery ship captured 1595 by the Spanish.

FRANCIS 14-gun ship (Royalist), 85bm. Captured 1657 by Parliament. Renamed OLD FRANCIS 1666; fireship 1672. Sold 1674.

FRANCIS 6th Rate 16, 140bm, 16-6pdr. Deane, Harwich 1666. Wrecked 1.8.1684 in the W. Indies.

FRANCIS Fireship 4, 211bm. French, captured 1666. Sold 1667.

FRANCIS Gunvessel 5, 60bm, 55½ x 16 ft. Purchased 3.1794, Powder barge 1800. BU 5.1804.

FRNACIS Sloop (Canadian lakes). Detroit 1796. Fate unknown.

FRANKLIN (ex-S. yacht *Adele*) Training ship (RAN) 288 tons, 145 x 22½ ft. Purchased 1912. Sold 1924 and hired as ADELE 9.39.

FRANKLIN Survey ship 830 tons, 230 x 33½ ft. Ailsa 22.12.1937. BU 2.56 Clayton & Davie, Dunston.

FRASER (see CRESCENT of 1937)

FRASER Frigate (RCN) 2,265 tons, 2-3in, 2-40mm. Burrard 19.2.1953.

FRASER Trawler requis. 1916-17.

FRASERBURGH Minesweeper, TE 'Bangor' class. Lobnitz 12.5.1941. Sold 1.1.48; arrived 3.48 Thornaby on Tees to BU.

FREDERICKSTEIN 5th Rate 32, 680bm, 129½ x 34½ ft. Danish, captured 7.9.1807 at Copenhagen. BU 6.1813. (Was to have been renamed TERESA.)

FREDERICKSWAERN 5th Rate 36, 776bm, 130 x 37 ft. Danish FREDERICKSCOARN captured 16.8.1807 by COMUS in the Baltic. Sold 16.12.1814.

FREDERICK WILLIAM (ex-ROYAL FREDERICK renamed 18.1.1860) Screw 1st Rate 110, 3,241bm, 4,725 tons, 204 x 60 ft, 6-68pdr, 100-32pdr, 4-18pdr. Portsmouth DY 24.3.1860. Renamed WORCESTER training ship 19.10.1876. Sold 7.1948. Foundered 30.8.48 in the Thames; raised and BU 5.53 by Tennant & Horne, Grays.

FREDERICTON Corvette (RCN), 'Flower' class. Marine Industries 2.9.1941. Sold 16.11.45 renamed *Tra Los Montes*.

FREESIA Corvette, 'Flower' class. Harland & Wolff 10.1940. Sold 22.7.46, renamed *Freelock*.

FREESIA Trawler requis. 1914-19.

FREMANTLE Minesweeper (RAN), 'Bathurst' class. Evans, Deakin 18.8.1942. Sold 6.1.61; towed from Sydney 20.2.62 to BU in Japan.

FREMANTLE Patrol vessel (RAN) 200 tons. Brooke Marine 15.2.1979

FRERE Iron steam gunboat (Indian) 610 tons. Bombay DY 1857. Fate unknown.

FREYA 5th Rate 38, 1,022bm. Danish FREIJA captured 7.9.1807 at Copenhagen. Sold 11.1.1816. (Was to have been renamed HYPPOLITUS: listed as FREIJA in 1814.)

FREYA Trawler requis. 1940-45.

FRETTENHAM Inshore M/S, 'Ham' class. White 18.5.1954. Sold French navy 13.12.54.

FRIENDSHIP Fireship, 180bm. Purchased 1673. Sunk 1673 in action.

FRIENDSHIP Cutter, 60bm. Purchased 3.1.1763. Sold 29.10.1771.

FRIENDSHIP Fire vessel, 56bm, 51 x 17 ft. Purchased 4.1.1794. BU 9.1801.

FRIENDSHIP Gunvessel 2, ex-barge. Purchased 8.1795. Foundered 9.11.1801 off the Channel Islands.

FRIENDSHIP Minesweeper, 'Algerine' class. Toronto SY 24.10.1942 on lend-lease. Returned 1.47 to the USN.

FRIEZLAND Flyboat 8, 227bm. Dutch, captured 1665. Given to the Africa Co 1672.

FRITHAM Inshore M/S, 'Ham' class. Brooke Marine 24.9.1953. Sold 1980.

FRITILLARY Corvette, 'Flower' class. Harland & Wolff 22.7.1941. Sold 19.3.46, renamed *Andria*.

FROBISHER (see PARKER)

FROBISHER Cruiser 9,750 tons, 565 x 58 ft, 7-7.5in, 4-3in, 6-12pdr. Devonport DY 20.3.1920. Sold 26.3.49; arrived 5.49 Cashmore, Newport to BU.

FROG Dogger 6. Dutch, captured 1673. Sold 1674.

FROLIC Brig-sloop 18, 'Cruizer' class, 384bm. Boole, Bridport 9.12.1806. BU 11.1813.

FROLIC Brig-sloop 10,'Cherokee' class, 236bm. Pembroke Dock 10.6.1820. Sold 16.8.1838 Messrs Dowson.

FROLIC Sloop 16, 511bm, 105 x 34 ft, 16-32pdr carr. Portsmouth DY 23.8.1842. Sold 7.10.1864 Castle.

FROLIC Compos. S. gunvessel, 462bm, 610 tons, 155 x 25 ft, 1-7in, 1-6pdr, 2-20pdr. Chatham DY 29.2.1872. Drillship 1888; renamed WV.30 coastguard watch vessel 1893; WV. 41 in 1897. Sold 7.4.1908.

FROLIC Minesweeper. 'Catherine' class. Assoc. SB, Seattle 20.6.1943 on lend-lease. Returned 1947 to the USN and sold Turkish navy 3.47 as CANDARLI.

FROLIC Tug 1915-23.

FROME Minesweeper, later 'Hunt' class. Elthringham. Cancelled 1918.

FROME Frigate, 'River' class. Blyth SB 1.6.1943. To French navy 3.44 as L'ESCARMOUCHE.

FRONTENAC Transport (Canadian), 248 gross, 190 x 24 ft. Quebec 1930.

FRONTENAC Corvette (RCN), modified 'Flower' class. Kingston 2.6.1943. Sold 2.10.45.

FUBBS R.yacht 12, 148bm, 73½ x 21 ft. Greenwich DY 1682. Rebuilt Woolwich 1701 and Deptford 1724 as 157bm. BU 7.1781.

FUERTE 6th Rate 20. Spanish, captured 3.2.1807 at Montevideo. BU 1.1812 at Portsmouth.

FULMAR Paddle M/S. Ailsa, Troon. Cancelled 12.1918.

FULMAR Trawler requis. 1915-16.

FULMINANTE Cutter 8. French, captured 29.10.1798 by ESPOIR in the Mediterranean. Wrecked 24.3.1801 coast of Egypt.

FUNDY Coastal M/S (RCN), 'Ton' class. St John DD Co 4.1952. Sold 4.54 French navy as La DUNKERQUOISE.

FUNDY Coastal M/S (RCN), 'Ton' class, Davie, Lauzon 14.6.1956.

FUNDY Trawler (RCN) 1938-47.

FURIEUSE 5th Rate 38, 1,085bm, 158 x 39ft. French, captured 6.7.1809 by BONNE CITOYENNE in the Atlantic. BU 10.1816 at Deptford.

FURIOUS (Gunboat No.23) Gunvessel 12, 169bm, 76 x 23 ft, 2-24pdr, 10-18pdr carr. Perry, Blackwall 31.3.1797. Sold 10.1802.

FURIOUS Gun-brig 12, 179bm, 80 x 23 ft, 10-18pdr carr. 2-12pdr. Brindley, Lynn 21.7.1804. Sold 9.2.1815.

FURIOUS Wood pad. frigate 1,287bm, 210 x 36 ft, 2-110pdr, 4-40pdr, 10-32pdr. Portsmouth DY 26.8.1850. Coal hulk 3.1867. Sold 1884.

FURIOUS 2nd Class Cruiser 5,750 tons, 320 x 57½ ft, 4-6in, 6-4.7in, 9-12pdr. Devonport DY 3.12.1896. Renamed FORTE 6.1915, hulk. Sold 5.23 Cohen, Swansea.

FURIOUS 1st class cruiser 19,100 tons, 750 x 88ft, 1-18in (designed for 2-18in), 11-5.5.in. Armstrong 15.8.1916. Completed 3.18 as A/C carrier 10-5.5in, 10-A/C; rebuilt 1924,33-A/C. Sold 23.1.48, BU Dalmuir and Troon.

FURNACE Bomb 4, 144bm. Wells, Horsleydown 18.4.1695. BU 1725.

FURNACE Bomb 14, 273bm, 92 x 26½ ft. Quallet, Rotherhithe 25.10.1740.

Sold 31.3.1763.

FURNACE Fireship 8, 365bm, 100½ x 29 ft. Fisher, Liverpool, 6.12.1778. Sold 10.4.1783.

FURNACE (Gunboat No.25) Gunvessel 12, 170bm, 76 x 22 ft. Perry, Blackwall 10.4.1797. Sold 10.1802.

FURY Sloop 14, 306bm, 97 x 26½ ft. Lime & Mackenzie, Leith 18.3.1779. BU 4.1787.

FURY Gunboat 1 commissioned 1782 at Gibraltar.

FURY Sloop 16, 323bm, 100 x 27 ft. Portsmouth DY 2.3.1790. Bomb 16 in 1798. BU 6.1811.

FURY Gunvessel 4, 56bm, 58 x 14½ ft. Dutch hoy purchased 4.1794. Sold 5.1802.

FURY Bomb 8, 326bm, 102 x 27 ft, 8-2pdr carr., 2-6pdr, 1-mortar. Bridport. Ordered 30.3.1812, cancelled 3.12.1813.

FURY Bomb 8, 377bm, 109 x 28½ ft, 10-24pdr carr., 2-6pdr, 2-mortars. Ross, Rochester 4.4.1814. Arctic discovery 1824; bilged in ice 1.8.1825 in Regent Inlet.

FURY Wood pad. vessel, 166bm, 90 x 20 ft. Purchased 31.7.1834 in Bermuda. BU 8.1843 Bermuda.

FURY Wood pad. sloop. 1,124bm, 190 x 36 ft. Sheerness DY 31.12.1845. Sold 15.7.1864 Castle & Beech.

FURY Turret ship, 5,030bm, 10,460 tons, 320 x 62 ft. Pembroke Dock. Laid down 10.9.1870, redesigned and renamed DREADNOUGHT 1.2.1875. (See DREADNOUGHT)

FURY Destroyer 760 tons, 246 x 25 ft, 2-4in, 2-12pdr, 2-TT. Inglis, Glasgow 25.4.1911. Sold 4.11.21 Rees, Llanelly.

FURY Destroyer 1.350 tons, 318 x 33ft, 4-4.7in, 8-TT. White 10.9.1934. Damaged 21.6.44 by mine; arrived 18.9.44 Ward, Briton Ferry to BU.

FUZE Fire vessel, 55bm, 54½ x 16 ft. Purchased 10.1804. Sold 17.6.1807 T. Freake to BU.

FYEN 3rd Rate 74, 1,681bm. Danish FIJEN captured 7.9.1807 at Copenhagen. Prison ship 1809; sold 1.9.1814. (Was to have been renamed BENGAL; listed as FIJEN in 1814.)

FYLLA 6th Rate 22, 490bm. Danish captured 7.9.1807 at Copenhagen. Sold 30.6.1814. (Was to have been renamed LIFFEY.)

'G' class submarines. 700 tons, 185 x 22½ ft, 1-3in, 5-TT.

G.1 Chatham DY 14.8.1915. Sold 14.2.20 Fryer, Sunderland.

G.2 Chatham DY 23,12.15. Sold 16.1.20 Fyer, Sunderland.

G.3 Chatham DY 22.1.16. Sold 4.11.21 Young, Sunderland.

G.4 Chatham DY 23.10.15. Sold 27.6.28 Cashmore, Newport.

G.5 Chatham DY 23.11.15. Sold 25.10.22 Cashmore, Newport.

G.6 Armstrong 7.12.15. Sold 4.11.21 Young, Sunderland.

G.7 Armstrong 4.3.16. Sunk 1.11.18 in the North Sea.

G.8 Vickers 1.5.16. Sunk 14.1.18 in the North Sea.

G.9 Vickers 15.6.16. Sunk 16.9.17 in error by the British destroyer PETARD off the coast of Norway.

G.10 Vickers 11.1.16. Sold 20.1.23 J. Smith.

G.11 Vickers 22.2.16. Wrecked 22.11.18 off Hawick.

G.12 Vickers 24.3.16. Sold 14.2.20 J.G. Potts.

G.13 Vickers 18.7.16. Sold 20.1.23 J. Smith.

G.14 Scotts 17.5.17. Sold 11.3.21 Stanlee, Dover.

G.15 White. Ordered 30.9.14, cancelled 20.4.15.

G.13 Torpedo boat 180 tons, 162½ x 17 ft, 2-3in, 3-TT. Dutch, commissioned in the RN as S/M tender 10.1940. BU 2.43 Ward, Preston.

G.15 Torpedo boat (as G.13). Laid up 7.40; BU 2.43 Ward, Preston.

GABBARD Destroyer 2,315 tons, 355 x 40 ft, 4-4.5in, 1-4in, 12-40mm, 8-TT. Swan Hunter 16.3.1945. Renamed BADR (Pakistan navy) 3.1.57.

GABRIEL Ship 180bm. Purchased 1410, Given away 1413

GABRIEL Ship. Southampton 1416. Fate unknown.

GABRIEL HARFLEUR Ballinger 40bm, French St.GABRIEL captured 1415, Lost 1420.

GABRIEL ROYAL ship, 700bm. Purchased 1512. Listed to 1526.

GABRIEL Discovery vessel, 20bm. In service 1575.

GABRIEL (see ITHURIEL)

GABRIEL (ex-ABDIEL renamed 1915) Destroyer leader 1,655 tons, 325 x 32 ft, 4-4in, 4-TT. Cammell Laird 23.12.15. Sold 9.5.21 Ward, Lelant.

GABRIEL Minesweeper, 'Algerine' class. Lobnitz. Ordered 9.6.1943, cancelled 10.44.

GADDESDON Minesweeper, later 'Hunt' class. Eltringham 30.11.1917. Sold 4.11.22.

GADFLY Wood S.-gunboat, 'Cheerful' class. Laird 21.4.1856. BU 11.1864.

GADFLY Iron S.gunboat 265 tons, 87½ x 26 ft, 1-10in MLR. Pembroke Dock 5.5.1879. Coal lighter YC.230 on 18.5.00. Sold 1918 at the Cape.

GADFLY Coastal destroyer 215 tons, 166½ x 17½ ft, 2-12pdr, 3-TT. Thornycroft, Chiswick 24.6.1906. Renamed TB.6 in 1906. Sold 22.10.20 Stanlee, Dover.

GADFLY River gunboat, 'Fly' class. Yarrow 8.1915 in sections and re-erected 12.15 on the Tigris. To War Dept 1923.

GADFLY Trawler requis 1939-45.

GADWELL Paddle M/S Ailsa. Ordered 1918, cancelled 12.18.

GAEL Destroyer, circa 2,000 tons, 341½ x 39½ ft, 4-4.5in, 6-40mm, 10-TT. Yarrow. Ordered 24.7.1944, cancelled 12.12.45.

GAEL Yacht requis. 1917-19 and 1940.

GAIETE 6th Rate 20, 514bm, 120 x 31 ft. French, captured 20.8.1797 by ARETHUSA in the Atlantic. Sold 21.7.1808.

GAILLARDIA Sloop, 'Anchusa' class. Blyth DD 19.5.1917. Sunk 22.3.18 by mine in the Northern Barrage.

GAINSBOROUGH 40-gun ship, 550bm, 122 x 32 ft. Taylor, Plymouth 1653. Renamed SWALLOW 1660, 4th Rate. Wrecked 9.2.1692 on the coast of Ireland.

GAINSBOROUGH (ex-GORLESTON renamed 1918) Minesweeper, later 'Hunt' class. Eltringham 12.2.18. Sold 6.28 Alloa S.Bkg Co.

GALA Destroyer 570 tons, 222 x 23½ ft, 1-12pdr, 5-6ppdr, 2-TT. Yarrow, Poplar 7.1.1905. Sunk 27.4.08 in collision with ATTENTIVE off Harwich.

GALATEA 6th Rate 20, 429bm, 108 x 30 ft. Deptford DY 21.3.1776. BU 4.1783.

GALATEA 5th Rate 32, 808bm, 135 x 36½ ft. Parsons, Bursledon 17.5.1797. BU 5.1809.

GALATHEE Sloop 16, Dutch, captured 30.8.1799 in the Texel. Sold 15.10.1807 Cristall to BU Rotherhithe.

GALATEA 5th Rate 36, 947bm, 145 x 38½ ft. Deptford DY 31.8.1810. Coal hulk 8.1836. BU 1849 in Jamaica.

GALATEA Wood S.frigate, 3,227bm, 280 x 50 ft, 24-10in, 2-68pdr. Wool-wich DY 14.9.1859. BU. 6.1883 by Castle.

GALATEA Armoured cruiser 5,600 tons 300 x 56 ft, 2-9.2in, 10-6in, 10-3pdr. Napier 10.3.1887. Sold 4.4.1905.

GALATEA Light cruiser 3,500 tons, 410 x 39 ft, 2-6in, 6-4in. Beardmore 14.5.1914. Sold 25.10.21 Multilocular Co.

GALATEA Cruiser 5,220 tons, 480 x 51 ft, 6-6in, 8-4in. Scotts 9.8.1934. Sunk 14.12.41 by 'U.557' off Alexandria.

GALATEA Frigate, 'Leander' class. Swan Hunter 23.5.1963.

GALGO Sloop 12, 164bm, 78½ x 22 ft, 12-4dpr. Spanish, captured 4.1742 in the Channel. Sold 24.3.1743.

GALGO Sloop, 272bm, Buxton, Rotherhithe 17.2.1744. Renamed SWALLOW 31.1.1744 Wrecked 24.12.1744. W. Indies.

GALGO (ex-*Garland*) Sloop 16, 354bm, 102 x 28½ ft, 14-24pdr carr., 2-18pdr. Purchased 1801. Became a rock transport 1809. Sold 9.6.1814.

GALICIA 3rd Rate 70, Spanish, captured 25.3.1741 at Cartagena. Burnt 1741 as unseaworthy.

GALLANT (Gunboat No.29) Gunvessel, 169bm, 76 x 22 ft, 2-24pdr, 10-18pdr carr. Pitcher, Northfleet 4.1797. Sold 10.1802.

GALLANT Gun-brig 12, 180bm, 80½ x 22½ ft, 2-18pdr, 10-18pdr carr. Roxby, Wearmouth 20.9.1804. Sold 14.12.1815.

GALLANT Destroyer 1,335 tons, 312 x 33 ft, 4-4.7in, 8-TT. Stephen. 26.9.1935. Damaged 10.1.41 by mine and 5.4.42 by air attack at Malta; sunk 9.43 as blockship at Malta.

GALLANT Destroyer (as GAEL). Yarrow. Ordered 24.7.1944, cancelled 12.12.45.

GALLARITA Galley, 100bm. Limehouse 1602. Sold 1629.

GALLION Galleon, 570bm. Spanish JESU MARIA JOSEF captured 1656. Sunk 1670 as a foundation at Portsmouth.

GALLIOT Hoy 4, 49bm. Dutch, captured 1664. Sold 1667.

GALT Corvette (RCN), 'Flower' class. Collingwood SY 28.12.1940. Sold 1946.

GALTEEMORE M/S sloop '24' class. Osbourne Graham, Sunderland 1919. Cancelled 12.18 and sold incomplete.

GALTEEMORE Landing ship (see EMPIRE MACE).

GAMBIA Cruiser 8,000 tons, 538 x 62

ft, 12-6in, 8-4in. Swan Hunter 30.11.1940. Sold Ward 15.11.68, arrived Inverkeithing 6.12.68.

GAMSTON (see SOMERLEYTON)

GANANOQUE Minesweeper (RCN), TE 'Bangor' class. Dufferin, Toronto 23.4.1941. Laid up 1946. Sold 2.59 Marine Industries.

GANGA (ex-CHIDDINGFOLD renamed 18.6.1954) Destroyer (Indian navy), 'Hunt' class type II. Sold 4.59.

GANGES 3rd Rate 74, 1,679bm, 170 x 47½ ft. Randall, Rotherhithe 30.3.1782. Prison ship 10.1811; lent Transport Board 12.1814. BU 3.1816 at Plymouth.

GANGES 2nd Rate 84, 2,248bm, 3,594 tons, 196½ x 52 ft. Bombay DY 10.11.1821. Training ship 5.1865; renamed TENEDOS III 21.6.1906; INDUS V 13.8.10; IMPREGNABLE III 12.10.22. Sold 31.8.29 to BU.

GANGES Training ships (see MINOTAUR of 1863, AGINCOURT of 1865 and CAROLINE of 1882).

GANNET Brig-sloop 16, 289bm, 88½ x 28 ft, 14-18pdr, 2-6pdr. Purchased 1800. Sold 21.7.1814.

GANNET Brig-sloop 18, 'Cruizer' class, 386bm. Larking & Spong, Lynn 13.11.1814. Sold 16.8.1838 Mr Soames.

GANNET Wood S.sloop, 579bm, 151 x 29 ft, 11-32pdr. Pembroke Dock 29.12.1857. BU Devonport 2.1877.

GANNET Compos. S.sloop 1,130 tons, 170 x 36 ft, 2-7in, 4-6pdr. Sheerness DY 31.8.1878. Renamed PRESIDENT training ship 16.5.1903. Lent 10.13 as training ship *Mercury*. Arrived Chatham in tow 6.87 for preservation.

GANNET Iron S.gunboat (Australian) 346 tons, 1-6in. Built 1884. For sale 1895.

GANNET (see NYMPNHE of 1888)

GANNET (see TRENT of 1877)

GANNET River gunboat 310 tons, 177 x 29 ft, 2-3in. Yarrow 10.11.1927. Presented to Chinese navy 2.42 as YING SHAN.

GANYMEDE 6th Rate 26, 601bm, 127 x 33 ft, 22-32pdr carr., 10-18 pdr carr., 2-6pdr. French HEBE captured 5.1.1809 by LOIRE in the Atlantic. Convict ship 1819. Capsized 1838 and BU.

GANYMEDE Wood S.corvette, 1,857bm, 225 x 43 ft. Chatham DY. Ordered 1860, cancelled 12.12.1863.

GARDENIA Sloop, 'Anchusa' class. Barclay Curle 27.12.1917. Sold 15.1.23 Richardson Westgarth.

GARDENIA Corvette, 'Flower' class. Simons 10.4.1940. Sunk 9.11.42 in collision with trawler FLUELLEN off Oran.

GARDENIA Trawler requis. 1914-18.

GARDINER (ex-USS O'TOOLE) Frigate,DE 'Captain' class. Boston N.Yd 8.7.1943 on lend-lease. Returned 2.46 to the USN.

GARLAND (also GUARDLAND) Galleon 38/48, 530/700bm, 16-18pdr, 14-9pdr, 4-6pdr. 11 small.Built 1590. Sunk 1618 as a wharf at Chatham.

GARLAND Ship 34/40, 420/550bm. Deptford 1620. Captured 30.11.1652 by the Dutch.

GARLAND (see GRANTHAM of 1654)

GARLAND 5th Rate 44, 496bm, 115½ x 31 ft. Woolwich DY 5.1703. Wrecked 1709.

GARLAND Fireship in service in 1716. Sold 27.9.1744. (Was SCARBOROUGH of 1696)

GARLAND 6th Rate 24, 508bm, 113 x 32 ft. Sheerness DY 13.8.1748. Hulked 1768. Sold 2.12.1783.

GARLAND 6th Rate 20, French GUIRLANDE captured 18.8.1762. Sold 1783.

GARLAND (see SIBYL of 1779)

GARLAND Schooner tender 6. Purchased 1798. Gone by 1803.

GARLAND 6th Rate 22, 530bm, 124½ x 31½ ft. French privateer MARS captured 1.4.1800 by AMETHYST. Wrecked 11.1803 in the W. Indies.

GARLAND 6th Rate 22, 525bm, 118½ x 31½ ft, 22-32pdr carr., 8-18pdr carr., 2-6pdr. Chapman, Bideford 25.4.1807. Sold 9.5.1817 Mr Hill.

GARLAND Wood pad. packet, 295bm, 140 x 21 ft. Fletcher, Limehouse 26.2.1846. Sold 1855 Jenkins & Churhward, Dover.

GARLAND Wood S.gunboat 'Cheerful' class. Laird 7.5.1856. BU 6.1864.

GARLAND Destroyer 984 tons, 260 x 29 ft, 3-4in, 2-TT. Cammell Laird 23.4.1913. Sold 6.9.21 Petersen & Albeck.

GARLAND Destroyer 1,335 tons, 312 x 33 ft, 4-4.7in, 8-TT. Fairfield 21.10.1935. Lent Polish navy 1940-46. Sold Dutch navy 12.47 as MARNIX.

GARLIES (ex-USS FLEMING) Frigate, DE 'Captain' class. Boston N. Yd 19.5.1943 on lend-lease. Returned 8.45 to the USN.

GARNET Wood S.gunboat, 'Clown' class. Pitcher, Northfleet 31.5.1856. BU 5.1864.

GARNET Compos. S.corvette 2,120 tons, 220 x 40 ft, 12-64pdr. Chatham DY 30.6.1877. Sold 12.1904.

GARNET Minesweeper, 'Catherine' class. Assoc. SB, Seattle 20.6.1943 on lend-lease. Renamed JASPER 4.44. Returned 12.46 to the USN.

GARNET Trawler requis. 1917-19.

GARRY Destroyer 590 tons, 222 x 23½ ft, 1-12pdr, 5-6pdr (4-12pdr 1907), 2-TT. Yarrow, Poplar 21.3.1905. Sold 22.10.20 J.H. Lee.

GARRY Trawler 1916-47.

GARTH Minesweeper, early 'Hunt' class. Dunlop Bremner 9.5.1917. Sold 21.2.23 Alloa, Charlestown.

GARTH Destroyer, 'Hunt' class type I. J.Brown 14.2.1940. Arrived 25.8.58 Ward, Barrow to BU.

GASCOYNE Frigate (RAN) 'River' class. Morts Dk, Sydney 20.2.1943. Survey ship 6.59. Sold 27.1.72; left Sydney 6.7.72 to BU at Osaka.

GASPE Schooner, 102bm, 60 x 20 ft. Purchased 5.1764 in N. America. Burnt 9.6.1772 at Rhode Island.

GASPE Brig 6. In service 1774. Captured 11.1775 by Americans; recaptured 4.1776 and sold.

GASPE Coastal M/S (RCN), 'Ton' class. Davie SB, Lauzon 12.11.1951.

GASPE Trawler (RCN). 1938-47.

GATINEAU (see EXPRESS of 1934)

GATINEAU Frigate (RCN) 2,365 tons. Davie SB 3.6.1957.

GATWICK Paddle M/S, 'Ascot' class. Dundee SB 18.4.1916. Sold 3.22 Ward, Inverkeithing.

GAUNTLET Destroyer (as GAEL). Thornycroft. Ordered 8.1944, cancelled 12.12.45.

GAUNTLET Tug requis. 1917-19.

GAVINTON Coastal M/S, 'Ton' class. Doig, Grimsby 27.7.1953.

GAVOTTE Minesweeper 260 tons, 130 x 26 ft, 1-3pr. Ex-War Dept tug transferred 12.1917. Goole SB 3.18 Returned 1920 to War Dept.

GAVOTTE Trawler. 1940-46.

GAWLER Minesweeper, 'Bathurst' class. Broken Hill Co, Whyalla, 4.10.1941.Lent RAN 1942-46. Sold 8.46 Turkish navy as AYVALIK.

GAWLER Patrol boat (RAN) 211 tons, N. QUEENSLAND Co Cairns 9.7.1983

GAYUNDAH Gunvessel (Australia) 360 tons, 115 x 25 ft, 1-8in, 1-6in, 1-3pdr. Armstrong 1884. Sold 1921 mercantile.

GAZELLE Minesweeper, 'Catherine' class. Savannah Mcy 10.1.1943 on lend-lease. Returned 12.46 to th USN.

GAZELLE Tug 1903-24. M/S requis. 1914-20.

GEELONG Minesweeper (RAN), 'Bathurst' class. Melbourne Harbour Trust 22.4.1941. Sunk 18.10.44 in collision with SS *York* between New Guinea and Australia.

GEELONG Patrol boat (RAN) 211 tons, N. QUEENSLAND Co, 23.3.1984

GELYKHEID 3rd Rate 64, 1,305bm, 156 x 44 ft. Dutch, captured 11.10.1797 at Camperdown. Prison ship 1799.Sold 1.9.1814.

GENERAL ABERCROMBIE Monitor (see ABERCROMBIE).

GENERAL CRAUFURD (ex-CRAUFURD renamed 1915, ex-M.7) Monitor 5,900 tons, 320 x 87 ft, 2-12in, 2-6in, 2-12pdr. Harland & Wolf 8.7.1915. Sold 9.5.21 Ward, New Holland, arrived in 9.23.

GENERAL GRANT Monitor (see HAVELOCK).

GENERAL MONK A.ship 20. American privateer GENERAL WASHINGTON captured 9.1781 by CHATHAM. Recaptured 8.4.1782 by the American privateer HYDER ALI.

GENERAL PLATT Gunboat 280 tons, 2-3in. Italian PORTO CORSINI salved 1941 at Massawa. Sold 6.46 at Massawa.

GENERAL WOLFE (ex-SIR JAMES WOLFE renamed 1915, ex-WOLFE, ex-M.9) Monitor 5,900 tons, 320 x 87 ft, 2-12in, 2-6in, 2-12pdr. Palmer 9.9.15. Sold 9.5.21 Ward, Hayle; arrived in 12.23.

GENEREUX 3rd Rate 74, 1,962bm, 185½ x 49 ft. French, captured 18.2.1800 by a squadron in the Mediterranean. Prison ship 1805. BU 2.1816.

GENISTA Sloop, 'Arabis' class. Napier & Miller 22.2.1916. Sunk 23.10.16 by 'U.57' in the Atlantic.

GENISTA Corvette, 'Flower' class. Harland & Wolff 24.7.1941. To Air Ministry 1947, renamed *Weather Recorder*. BU 10.61 at Antwerp.

GENOA 3rd Rate 78, 1883bm, 181 x 47½ ft. French BRILLANT captured on stocks at Genoa 18.4.1814 and launched there. BU 1.1838.

GENTIAN Sloop, 'Arabis' class. Greenock & Grangemouth 23.12.1915. Sunk 16.7.19 by mine in the Gulf of Finland.

GENTIAN Corvette, 'Flower' class. Harland & Wolff 6.8.1940. BU 8.47

Chicks, Purfleet.

GENTILLE 5th Rate 40. French, captured 11.4.1795 by HANNIBAL in the Channel. Sold 9.1802 at Portsmouth.

GEORGE Ship. Built 1338 on the River Hamble.

GEORGE Carrack, 600bm. Genoese, captured 15.8.1416. Sold 10.8.1425.

GEORGE Ballinger, 120bm. Smallhithe 1420. Sold 8.1423.

GEORGE 28-gun ship, 80bm. Purchased 1546. Listed to 1557.

GEORGE Hoy, 50bm. Listed 1564 to 1585.

GEORGE Hoy, 100bm. Purchased 1588. Listed to 1603.

GEORGE Fireship. Listed in 1652.

GEORGE Dogger 8. Dutch, captured 1672. Sold 1674.

GEORGE Fireship 6, 393bm. Purchased 1672. Sunk 1674 as a foundation at Sheerness.

GEORGE Schooner 8 (Canadian lakes). Listed 1755. Captured 14.8.1756 by the French at Oswego.

GEORGE Tender. Listed 1774. Wrecked 26.12.1776 near Piscatagua, N. America.

GEORGE Sloop 6, 105bm, 6-4pdr. Captured 1796. Captured 3.1.1798 by two Spanish privateers in the W.Indies.

GEORGE Gunvessel 2, 61bm, 55 x 16½ ft. Purchased 3.1794. Sold 10.1798.

GEORGE Tug 1917-20.

GEORGEHAM Inshore M/S, 'Ham' class. Harris, Appledore 15.2.1957. Sold 27.11.67.

GEORGETOWN (ex-USS MADDOX) Destroyer 1,060 tons, 309 x 30½ ft, 1-4in, 1-3in, 4-20mm, 3-TT. Commissioned in the RN 23.9.1940. Lent RCN 9.42 to 12.43; lent Russian navy 10.8.44 to 9.52 as ZHOSTKY. Arrived 16.9.52 Ward, Inverkeithing to BU.

GEORGIANA Schooner 2 (Indian), 90bm. Bombay DY 1855. Listed in 1866.

GERALDTON Minesweeper. 'Bathurst' class. Poole & Steel, Sydney 16.8.1941. Lent RAN to 1946. Sold 8.46 Turkish navy as ANTALYA.

GERALDTON Patrol boat (RAN) N. Queensland Co 22.10.1983

GERANIUM Sloop, 'Arabis' class. Greenock & Grangemouth 8.11.1915. RAN 1920 dismantled 1932 at Sydney. Hull sunk 24.4.35 as target off Sydney.

GERANIUM Corvette, 'Flower' class.

Simons 23.4.1940. Sold 24.9.45 R. Norwegian navy as THETIS.

GERMAINE A.ship 20. Purchased 1779. Captured 1781 (by the French?).

GERMAINE Brig-sloop 16, 240bm, 88 x 26 ft. Purchased 1782. Sold 25.3.1784.

GERMOON PRIZE 6th Rate 10, 103bm. French, captured 1692. Sunk 4.7.1700 while careening at Porto Bello.

GERRANS BAY (ex-LOCH CARRON renamed 1944) Frigate, 'Bay' class. Smiths DK 14.3.1945. Renamed SURPRISE 1945, despatch vessel. Arrived 29.6.65 McLellan, Bo'ness to BU.

GEYSER Wood pad. sloop, 1,054bm, 180 x 36 ft. Pembroke Dock 6.4.1841. BU 1866.

GHURKA (see under GURKHA).

GIBRALTAR 6th Rate 20, 280bm, 94 x 26 ft. Deptford DY 18.10.1711. Rebuilt Deptford 1727 as 374bm. Sold 16.3.1748.

GIBRALTAR 6th Rate 20, 430bm, 108 x 30½ ft. Portsmouth DY 9.5.1754. BU completed 18.11.1773 at Portsmouth.

GIBRALTAR PRIZE Sloop 14, 117bm, 59 x 18½ ft, 14-4pdr. French privateer captured 2.1757 by GIBRALTAR. Sold 22.1.1761.

GIBRALTAR Brig, 14, 85bm, 63 x 21 ft. American, captured 1779. Captured 7.1781 by the Spanish off Gibraltar; recaptured 29.7.1800 as SALVADOR by ANSON.

GIBRALTAR 2nd Rate 80, 2,185bm, 179 x 53½ft ft. Spanish FENIX captured 16.3.1780. Powder hulk 12.1813; lazaretto 9.1824. BU 11.1836 at Pembroke Dock.

GIBRALTAR Screw 1st Rate 101, 3,716bm, 5,724 tons, 252 x 58 ft. Devonport DY 16.8.1860. 85 guns 1862: 1-110pdr, 36-8in, 4-70pdr, 12-40pdr, 32-32pdr. Lent as training ship 1872. Renamed GRAMPIAN 1889. Sold 1899.

GIBRALTAR 1st class cruiser 7,700 tons, 360 x 60 ft, 2-9.2in, 10-6in, 12-6pdr. Napier, Govan 27.4.1892. Depot ship 1914. Sold 9.23 Cashmore, Newport.

GIBRALTAR Aircraft carrier, circa 45,000 tons. Vickers Armstrong, Tyne. Ordered 15.9.1943, cancelled 10.45.

GIER Brig-sloop 14, 324bm, 91 x 29½ ft, 12-12pdr, 2-6pdr. Dutch, captured 12.9.1799 by WOLVERINE off the Texel. BU 9.1803.

GIFFARD (see TORONTO of 1943)

GIFFARD (ex-BUDDLEIA renamed 9.43) Corvette (RCN), modified 'Flower' class. Alex Hall 19.6.43. Sold 1946; BU 10.52. at Hamilton, Ont.

GIFFORD Seaward defence boat, 'Ford' class. Scarr, Hessle 30.6.1954. To Nigerian navy 1968.

GIFT 40-gun ship, 490bm. French DON de DIEU captured 1652. Renamed GIFT MAJOR 1658. Expended as fireship 1666.

GIFT (also GIFT MINOR) 16-gun ship, 128bm. Spanish BON JESUS captured 1658. Sold 1667.

GIFT Destroyer (as GAEL). Thornycroft. Ordered 8.1944, renamed GLOWWORM 9.45, cancelled 12.12.45.

GIFT (ex-GLOWWORM renamed 10.45, ex-GUINEVERE 9.45) Destroyer (as GAEL). Denny. Ordered 8.44, cancelled 12.12.45.

GILES Ketch 2,48bm. Purchased 1661. Sold 1667.

GILIA Sloop, 'Anchusa' class Barclay Curle 15.3.1918. Sold 15.1.23 Unity S. Bkg Co.

GILLIFLOWER Row-barge, 20bm. In service 1546-52.

GILLIFLOWER 32-gun ship. Royalist, purchased 1651; deserted to Parliament 1651. Sold 1667.

GIPSY Schooner 19. In service 1799 to 1804.

GIPSY Schooner 10, 121bm, 69 x 20 ft, 10-4pdr. Purchased 12.1804 in Jamaica. Sold 1808 in Jamaica.

GIPSY Schooner tender, 70bm, 53 x 18ft. Sheerness DY 27.10.1836. Sold 12.8.1892 W. Meehan.

GIPSY Destroyer 380 tons, 227 x 22 ft, 1-12pdr, 5-6pdr, 2-TT. Fairfield 9.3.1897. Sold 17.3.1921 Beard, Teignmouth. Hull used as pontoon at Dartmouth to 1937 or later.

GIPSY Destroyer 1,335 tons, 312 x 32 ft, 4-4.7in, 8-TT. Fairfield 7.11.1935. Sunk 21.11.39 by mine off Harwich.

GIRDLE NESS (ex-PENLEE POINT renamed 10.1944) Repair ship 8,580 tons, 425 x 57 ft, 16-20mm. Burrard, Vancouver 28.3.1945. Sold 10.7.70, BU Faslane.

GIRONDE Sloop 10, 239bm, 92 x 26 ft. French privateer captured by BOADICEA.9.1800. Sold 7.9.1801.

GLACE BAY (see LAUZON)

GLACE BAY (ex-LAUZON) Frigate (RCN), 'River' class GT Davie 26.4.1944. Sold 3.1.46 Chilian navy as ESMERALDA.

GLADIATOR 5th Rate 44, 882bm, 140 x 38 ft. Adams, Bucklers Hard 20.1.1783. BU 8.1817. (Harbour service, never at sea.)

GLADIATOR Wood pad. frigate, 1.190bm, 190 x 37½ ft, 2-110pdr, 4-10in. Woolwich DY 15.10.1844. BU 3.1879.

GLADIATOR 2nd class cruiser 5,750 tons, 320 x 57 ft, 4-6in, 6-4.7in, 9-12pdr. Portsmouth DY 18.12.1896. Sunk 25.4.1908 in collision with SS *St Paul* off the Isle of Wight; raised 10.08 and sold 5.8.09.

GLADIOLUS Sloop, 'Arabis' class. Connell, Scotstoun 25.10.1915. Sold 9.20 Portuguese navy as REPUBLICA.

GLADIOLUS Corvette. 'Flower' class. Smiths Dk 24.1.1940. Sunk 16.10.41 by 'U.568' in the N. Atlantic.

GLADSTONE Minesweeper (RAN), 'Bathurst' class. Walker, Maryborough 26.11.1942. Sold 16.6.56, renamed *Akuna.*

GLADSTONE Patrol Boat (RAN) 211 tons N. Queensland Co 28.7.1984

GLADSTONE Tug Requis 1916-18.

GLAISDALE Destroyer, 'Hunt' class type III. Cammell Laird 5.1.1942. Lent. R.Norwegian navy 1.6.42 and sold in Norway 1946.

GLAMORGAN GM destroyer 5,600 tons, 505 x 54 ft, 4-4.5in, 2-20mm, 10-GWS. Vickers Armstrong. Tyne 9.7.1964. Sold Chile 1986, renamed ALMIRANTE LATORRE

GLASGOW 6th Rate 20, 284bm, 92 x 26½ ft. Scots ROYAL MARY transferred 1.5.1707. Sold 20.8.1719.

GLASGOW 6th Rate 24, 504bm, 112 x 32 ft. Reed, Hull 22.5.1745. Sold 8.4.1756.

GLASGOW 6th Rate 20, 452bm, 109 x 30½ ft. Blaydes, Hull 31.8.1757. Burnt 19.6.1779 by accident in Montego Bay, Jamaica.

GLASGOW 4th Rate 50 (pitch pine-built), 1,260bm, 159 x 42 ft. Wigram & Green, Blackwall 21.2.1814. BU completed 29.1.1829 at Chatham.

GLASGOW Wood S.frigate, 3,027bm, 4,020 tons, 250 x 52 ft, 1-110 pdr, 26-8in, 4-70pdr. Portsmouth DY 28.3.1861. Sold 12. 1884.

GLASGOW 2nd class cruiser 4,800 tons, 430 x 47 ft, 2-6in, 10-4in. Fairfield 30.9.1909. Sold 29.4.27 Ward, Morecambe.

GLASGOW Cruiser 9,100 tons, 558 x 62 ft, 12-6in, 8-4in. Scotts 20.6.1936. Arrived 8.7.58 Hughes Bolckow, Blyth to BU.

GLASGOW Destroyer 3150 tons. Swan

Hunter 14.4.1976

GLASSERTON Inshore M/S, 'Ton' class. Doig, Grimsby 3.12.1953.

GLASSFORD Seaward defence boat, 'Ford' class. Dunston, Thorne 28.3.1955. Renamed NAUTILUS (SAN) 23.8.55.

GLATTON 4th Rate 56, 1,256bm, 164 x 42 ft, 28-32pdr carr., 28-18pdr. Ex-E.Indiaman purchased 1795. Water depot in 1814 Sunk 10.1830 as breakwater at Harwich.

GLATTON Wood S.floating Battery, 1,535bm, 172½ x 45 ft, 14-68pdr. Mare Blackwall 18.4.1855. BU 1864.

GLATTON Turret ship 4,910 tons, 245 x 54 ft, 2-12in,3-6pdr. Chatham DY 8.3.1871. Sold 7.7.1903, BU by King, Garston.

GLATTON (ex-Norwegian BJOERGVIN purchased 31.1.1915) Coast defence ship 5,700 tons, 310 (oa) x 74ft, 2-9.2in, 6-6in. Armstrong 8.8.14 Blown up 16.9.18 by accident in Dover harbour; raised and BU 1925.

GLEANER Survey ketch, 154bm. Hired 12.7.1808; purchased 1809. Made a DY lighter 8.1811. Lost 2.4.1814.

GLEANER (see GULNARE of 1833)

GLEANER Wood S.gunboat, 216bm, 100 x 22ft, 1-68pdr, 1-32pdr, 2-24pdr howitzers. Deptford DY 7.10.1854. Sold 4.1868 at Montevideo.

GLEANER Torpedo gunboat 735 tons, 230 x 27ft, 2-4.7in, 4-3pdr, 3-TT. Sheerness DY 9.1.1890. Sold 4.4.1905 G.Cohen.

GLEANER (ex-War Dept vessel *General Stothard*) Tender 160 tons, 90 x 19ft. Transferred 1906, renamed 26.11.06. Sold 2.11.21 M.S. Hilton.

GLEANER Survey vessel 835 tons, 230 x 33½ft (2-4in 1939). Gray, Hartlepool 10.6.1937. M/S 1939. Sold 20.4.50; BU 5.50 Ward, Preston.

GLEANER Survey launch 22tons, Emsworth SY 11.1983

GLENARM Frigate, 'River' class. Robb 8.3.1943. Renamed STRULE 1.2.44. To French navy 25.9,44 as CROIX de LORRAINE.

GLENELG (see WHYALLA).

GLENELG Minesweeper (RAN), 'Bathurst' class. Cockatoo DY 25.9.1942. Sold 2.5.57 to BU in Hong Kong.

GLENMORE (ex-TWEED renamed 1795) 5th Rate 36 (fir-built), 926bm, 142½ x 38 ft. Woolwich DY 24.3.1796. Sold 3.11.1814.

GLENMORE M/S requis. 1938-45

GLENTHAM Inshore M/S. 'Ham' class.

Ardrossan DY Co 29.4.1957. Sold 1.4.66 at Singapore.

GLOBE 24-gun ship, 250/330bm. Captured 1644. Sold 1648.

GLOIRE (see under GLORY)

GLOMMEN Brig-sloop 16, 303bm, 94½ x 27 ft, 16-24pdr carr., 2-6pdr. Danish, captured 7.9.1807 at Copenhagen. Wrecked 11.1809. at Barbados. (Was named BRITOMART 21.1.1808).

GLORIEUX 3rd Rate 74. French, captured 12.4.1782 off Dominica. Foundered 16.9.1782 in a gale off Newfoundland.

GLORIOSA Corvette, 'Flower' class. Harland & Wolff. Ordered 8.4.1940, cancelled 23.1.41.

GLORIOSO 3rd Rate 74. Spanish, captured off Lagos 8.10.1747. Sold 13.4.1749.

GLORIOUS 1st class cruiser 18,600 tons, 735 x 81 ft, 4-15 in, 18-4in, 2-3in. Harland & Wolff 20.4.1916. Completed 1.30 as A/C carrier. Sunk 8.6.40 by German battlecruisers off Narvik.

GLOIRE 5th Rate 44, 748bm, 131 x 36 ft. French, captured 3.5.1747 at Cape Finisterre. Sold 15.3.1763. (Also listed as GLORY)

GLORY 5th Rate 32, 679bm, 125 x 35 ft. Blaydes & Hodgson, Hull 24.10,1763. Renamed APOLLO 30.8.1774. BU 1.1786 at Woolwich.

GLORY Lugger 8, 114bm, 70 x 19 ft. French GLOIRE captured 1781. BU 3.1783 at Plymouth.

GLORY 2nd Rate 90, 1,944bm, 178 x 50 ft . Plymouth DY 5.7.1788. Prison ship 1809; powder hulk 1814. BU completed 30.7.1825 at Chatham.

GLOIRE 5th Rate 40, 876bm, 141 x 38 ft. French, captured 10.4.1795 by ASTREA in the Channel. Sold 24.3.1802.

GLOIRE 5th Rate 36, 1,153bm, 158 x 41 ft. French, captured 25.9.1809 by MARS and CENTAUR in the Channel. BU 9.1812 at Chatham.

GLOIRE (see PALMA of 1814).

GLORY Battleship 12,950 tons, 390 x 74 ft, 4-12in, 12-6in, 12-12 pdr. Laird 11.3.1899. Renamed CRESCENT, depot ship 1.5.1920. Sold 19.12.22 Granton S. Bkg Co.

GLORY IV (ex-Russian Cruiser AS-KOLD seized and renamed 3.8.1918) Depot ship 6,500 tons, 440 x 49 ft. Returned Russian navy 1920.

GLORY A/C carrier 13,190 tons, 630 x 80 ft, 19-40mm, 48-A/C. Harland & Wolff 27.11.1943. Arrived 8.61 Ward,

Inverkeithing to BU.

GLOUCESTER 54-gun ship, 755bm. Graves, Limehouse 1654. Wrecked 6.5.1682 off Yarmouth.

GLOUCESTER 4th Rate 60, 896bm, 145 x 37½ ft. Clements, Bristol 5.2.1695. Harbour service 1706. BU 10.1731.

GLOUCESTER 4th Rate 60, 923bm, 144 x 38½ ft. Burchett, Rotherhithe 25.7.1709. Captured 26.10.1709 by the French LYS off Cape Clear.

GLOUCESTER 4th Rate 50, 714bm, 130 x 35 ft. Deptford 4.10.1711. BU 20.1.1724 at Sheerness.

GLOUCESTER 4th Rate 50, 866bm, 134 x 38½ ft, Sheerness DY 22.3.1737. Damaged 7.1742 in a storm and burnt 16.81742 near the Landrones to avoid capture by the Spanish.

GLOUCESTER 4th Rate 50, 986bm, 141 x 40 ft. Whetstone & Greville, Rotherhithe 23.3.1745. Harbour service 1458. BU completed 13.2.1764 at Sheerness.

GLOUCESTER Brig 10 (Canadian Lakes), 165bm, 10-12pdr. Kingston Ont 5.1807. Captured 25.4.1813 by Americans at York, Lake Erie; destroyed 29.5.1813 by the British at Sackets Harbour.

GLOUCESTER 3rd Rate 74, 1,770bm, 177 x 49 ft. Pitcher, Northfleet 27.2.1812. 50-gun 4th Rate 1832; harbour service 1861. Sold 3.1884 Castle, Charlton.

GLOUCESTER 2nd class cruiser 4,800 tons, 430 x 47 ft, 2-6in, 10-4in. Beardmore 28.10.1909. Sold 9.5.21 Ward, Portishead & Briton Ferry.

GLOUCESTER Cruiser 9,400 tons, 558 x 62 ft, 12-6in, 8-4in. Devonport DY 19.10.1937. Sunk 22.5.41 by air attack SW of Crete.

GLOUCESTER (ex-PANTHER) Frigate 2,170 tins. Portsmouth DY. Ordered 1956 and cancelled.

GLOUCESTER Destroyer 3550 tons. Vosper-Thornycroft 2.11.1982

GLOWWORM Coastal destroyer 255 tons, 166½ x 17½ ft, 2-12pdr, 3-TT. Thornycroft, Chiswick 20.12.1906. Renamed TB.7 in 1906. Sold 9.5.21 Ward, Rainham.

GLOWWORM River gunboat 645 tons, 230 x 36 ft, 2-6in, 2-12pdr. Barclay Curle 5.2.1916. Sold 9.28 L. Gatt, Malta.

GLOWWORM Destroyer 1,345 tons, 4-4in, 10-TT. Thornycroft 22.7.1935. Sunk 8.4.40 by the German ADMIRAL HIPPER off Norway.

GLOWWORM (ex-GUINEVERE renamed 9.45) Destroyer (as GAEL). Denny. Renamed GIFT 10.45, cancelled 12.12.45.

GLOWWORM (ex-GIFT renamed 10.45) Destroyer (as GAEL). Thornycroft. Cancelled 12.12.45.

GLOXINIA Corvette, 'Flower' class. Harland & Wolff 27.7.1940. Arrived 15.7.47 Chicks, Purfleet to BU.

GLUCKSTADT Brig-Sloop 18, 338bm, 102 x 28 ft, 16-18pdr carr. 2-6pdr. Danish, Captured 7.9.1807 at Copenhagen. Sold 30.6.1814. (Was to have been renamed RAISON.)

GNAT Wood S. gunboat, 'Cheerful' class. Laird 10.5.1856. BU 8.1864.

GNAT Compos. S. gunvessel, 464bm, 155 x 25 ft, 1-7in, 1-64pdr, 2-20pdr, Pembroke Dock 26.11.1867. Wrecked 15.11.1868 on Balabac Island, China Sea.

GNAT Coastal destroyer 255 tons, 166½ x 17½ ft, 2-12pdr, 3-TT. Thornycroft, Chiswick 1.12.1906. Renamed TB.8 in 1906. Sold 9.5.21 Ward, Rainham.

GNAT River gunboat 645 tons, 230 x 36 ft, 2-6in, 2-12pdr. Lobnitz 3.12.1915. Torpedoed 21.10.41 by Italian S/M off Bardia and beached at Alexandria as an anti-aircraft platform. BU 1945.

GNAT Tender 213 tons. Holmes 25.11.1969.

GOATHLAND Destroyer, 'Hunt' class type III. Fairfield 3.2.1942. Damaged by mine 24.7.44 off Normandy; arrived 8.45 at Troon to BU

GODAVERI Sloop (RIN) 1,300 tons, 283 x 37½ ft, 6-4in. Thornycroft 21.1.1943. Renamed SIND (RPN) 1948. Sold circa 1958.

GODAVERI (see BEDALE)

GODERICH Minesweeper (RCN), 'Bangor' class. Dufferin, Toronto 15.5.1941. Laid up 1946. Sold 2.59 Marine Industries.

GODETIA Sloop, 'Arabis' class. Yarrow 8.1.1916. Handed over to Messes Ward 26.2.37 in part payment for *Majestic* (CALEDONIA). BU at Milford Haven.

GODETIA Corvette, 'Flower' class. Smiths DK 8.5.1940. Sunk 6.9.40 in collision with SS *Marsa* off Northern Ireland.

GODETIA (ex-DART renamed 1941) Corvette, 'Flower' class. Crown 24.9.41. Sold 22.5.47, BU Ward, Grays.

GOELAN Sloop 14. French GOELAND captured 4.1793 by PENELOPE in the W.Indies. Sold 16.10.1794.

GOELAN Brig-sloop 16, 334bm, 19½ x 28 ft. French GOELAND captured

13.10.1803 by PIQUE and PELICAN off San Domingo. BU 9.1810.

GOLD COAST (ex-HARVEY renamed 1943) Frigate. 'Colony' class. Walsh Kaiser 21.9.1943 on lend-lease. Renamed LABUAN 1943. Returned 5.46 to the USN.

GOLDEN FALCON (see FALCON)

GOLDEN FLEECE (ex-HUMBERSTONE renamed 6.1943) Minesweeper, 'Algerine' class. Redfern 29.2.44. Arrived 8.8.60 Rees, Llanelly to BU.

GOLDEN HIND (see PELICAN of 1577)

GOLDEN HORSE 4th Rate 46, 722bm, 126 x 37 ft. Algerian, captured 9.4.1681 by ADVENTURE. Sunk 1688 as a foundation at Chatham.

GOLDEN LION (see LION)

GOLDEN ROSE Fireship 6, 163bm, Algerian, captured 1681. Sold 1687.

GOLDFINCH Brig-sloop 10, 'Cherokee' class, 237bm. Warwick, Eling 8.8.1808. Sold 8.11.1838 R. Willis.

GOLDFINCH Wood S. gunboat, 'Albacore' class. Wigram, Blackwall 2.2.1856. BU 6.1869 at Pembroke Dock.

GOLDFINCH 1st class gunboat 805 tons, 165 x 31 ft, 6-4in, 2-3pdr. Sheerness DY 18.5.1889. Survey vessel 2.1902. Sold 14.5.07 to BU.

GOLDFINCH Destroyer 747 tons, 246 x 25 ft, 2-4in, 2-12pdr, 2-TT. Fairfield 12.7.1910. Wrecked 19.2.15 in the Orkneys; wreck sold 4.19.

GOLDFINCH Minelayer requis. 1940-44.

GOLIATH 3rd Rate 74, 1,604bm, 168 x 47 ft. Deptford DY 19.10.1781. 58-gun 4th Rate 1812. BU 6.1815.

GOLIATH (see CLARENCE of 1827)

GOLIATH 2nd Rate 80, 2,596bm, 190 x 57 ft. Chatham DY 25.7.1842. Undocked 30.11.1857 as screw ship; lent 1870 as training ship. Burnt 22.12.1875 by accident.

GOLIATH Battleship 12,950 tons, 390 x 74 ft, 4-12in, 12-12 pdr. Chatham DY 23.3.1898. Sunk 13.5.1915 by the Turkish TB MUAVENET off Cape Helles.

GOLIATH Two Tugs requis. WW.II.

GOMATI (see LAMERTON)

GONDWANA Minesweeper (RIN),'Bathurst' class. Garden Reach, Calcutta. Cancelled 2.1945.

GONDWANA (see BURNET)

GOODALL (ex-USS REYBOLD) Frigate, DE 'Captain' class. Boston N. Yd 8.7.1943 on lend-lease. Sunk

29.4.45 by U-boat in the Kola Inlet.

GOOD FORTUNE Dogger 6. Dutch, captured 1665. Sunk 7.1667 as blockship in the Medway.

GOOD HOPE 35-gun ship, 272bm, 101 x 24 ft. In service 1664. Captured 5.1665 by the French in the North Sea.

GOOD HOPE Flyboat 6, 180bm, 76 x 21 ft. Dutch, captured 1665. Sold 1667.

GOOD HOPE (ex-AFRICA renamed 2.10.1899) Armoured cruiser 14,100 tons, 500 x 71 ft, 2-9.2in, 16-6in, 12-12pdr. Fairfield 21.2.1901.Sunk 1.11.14 in action at Coronel.

GOOD HOPE (ex-LOCH BOISDALE renamed 1944) Frigate (SAN), 'Loch' class. Blyth DD.5.7.44.

GOOD HOPE Trawler and 3 Drifters requis. WW.1.

GOOD INTENT Gunvessel in service in 1792. Captured 1793 by the French.

GOOD INTENT Gunvessel. Purchased 8.1795. BU 12.1801.

GOODSON (ex-USS GEORGE) Frigate, DE 'Captain' class. Boston N. Yd 8.7.1943 on lend-lease. Torpedoed 25.6.44 off Cherbourg, damaged beyond repair; nominally returned 1.47 to the USN; BU 10.48 at Whitchurch.

GOOD WILL Cutter, 49bm. Purchased 1.1763. Listed to 1768.

GOODWIN 6th Rate 6, 74bm, 59 x 16 ft. French, captured 1691. Sunk 23.2.1695 by a French privateer off Dover.

GOODWIN A.boarding vessel requis. 1939-46.

GOODWOOD Paddle M/S, 'Ascot' class. Dundee SB 15.6.1916. Sold 7.22 Stanlee, Dover.

GOOLE (ex-BRIDLINGTON renamed 1918) Minesweeper, later 'Hunt' class. Ayrshire Co 12.8.1919; not completed. Completed 4.26 as RNVR drillship; renamed IRWELL 9.26. Arrived 27.11.62 Lacmotts Ltd, Liverpool to BU.

GORDON (ex-War Dept miner) Tender 125 tons, 95 x 17½ ft. Transferred 1907. Sold 1907.

GORE (ex-USS HERZOG) Frigate, DE 'Captain' class. Boston N.Yd 8.7.1943 on lend-lease. Returned 5.46 to the USN.

GOREE (see HAYLING of 1729)

GOREE Sloop captured from the French 2.1.1759 at Goree, Paid off 16.8.1763

GOREE Sloop 16, 217bm, 89 x 24½ ft,

12-12pdr carr., 4-6pdr. French, captured 1800. Sold 21.4.1806 T. Heather.

GOREE (see FAVOURITE of 1794)

GOREY CASTLE (see HEDINGHAM CASTLE)

GORGON 5th Rate 44, 911bm, 140 x 38½ ft. Perry, Blackwall 27.1.1785. Storehip 7.1793; floating battery 1805. BU 2.1817.

GORGON Wood pad. frigate (ex-5th Rate), 1,111bm, 178 x 37½ ftm 2-10in, 4-32pdr. Pembroke Dock 31.8.1837. Sold Castle 7.10.1864 to BU.

GORGON Turret ship 3,560 tons, 225 x 45 ft, 4-10in, 4-3pdr. Palmer 14.10.1871. Sold 12.5.1903.

GORGON (ex-Norwegian NIDAROS purchased 9.1.1915) Coast defence ship 5,700 tons 310 (oa) x 74ft. 2-9.2in, 4-6in. Armstrong 9.6.14 Sold 28.8.28 Ward, Pembroke Dock.

GORGON Minesweeper, 'Catherine' class. Savannah Mcy 24.1.1943. Returned 12.46 to the USN and sold Greek Navy.

GORLESTON (see GAINSBOROUGH)

GORLESTON (ex-USS ITASCA) Cutter 1,546 tons, 256 (oa) x 42 ft, 1-5in, 2-3in. Transferred 31.5.1941 on lend-lease. Returned 4.46 to the USN.

GOSHAWK Brig-sloop 16 (fir-built), 285bm, 96 x 26 ft. 14-24pdr carr., 2-6pdr. Wallis, Blackwall 17.7.1806. Wrecked 21.9.1813 in the Mediterranean.

GOSHAWK Brig-sloop 18 (fir-built). Frames made at Chatham DY 1814 and shipped to Halifax NS for completion on Canadian lakes. Found unsuitable and sold 5.1815 at Halifax.

GOSHAWK (see NERBUDDA)

GOSHAWK Wood S. gunboat, 'Albacore' class. Wigram, Blackwall 9.2.1856. BU 3.1869 at Devonport.

GOSHAWK Compos. S. gunboat 430 tons, 125 x 23 ft, 2-64pdr, 2-20pdr. Pembroke Dock 23.1.1872. Hulk 1902; sold circua 1906.

GOSHAWK Destroyer 760 tons, 240 x 25½ ft, 2-4in, 2-12pdr, 2-TT. Beardmore 18.10.1911. Sold 4.11.21 Rees, Llanelly.

GOSPORT 5th Rate 32, 376bm, 108 x 28 ft. Collins & Chatfield, Shoreham 3.9.1696. Captured 28.8.1706 by the French.

GOSPORT 5th Rate 44, 530bm, 118 x 32 ft., Woolwich DY 8.3.1707. BU 1735.

GOSPORT 5th Rate 44, 691bm, 124 x

36 ft. Snelgrove, Limehouse 20.2.1741. BU completed 16.6.1768 at Chatham.

GOSSAMER Tender, 48bm, 47 x 16 ft. Purchased 7.1821 on stocks at Gosport. Sold 22.11.1861 J Levy, Rochester.

GOSSAMER Torpedo gunboat 735 tons, 230 x 27 ft, 2-4.7in, 4-3pdr, 3-TT. Sheerness DY 9.1.1890. M/S 1908. Sold 20.3.20 Cornish Salvage Co, Ilfracombe.

GOSSAMER Minesweeper 835 tons, 230 x 33½ ft, 2-4in. Hamilton 5.10.1937. Sunk 24.6.42 by air attack, Kola Inlet.

GOSSAMER (see M.II of 1939)

GOULBURN Minesweeper, 'Bathurst' class. Cockatoo Dy 17.11.1940. Sold 16.3.47; resold, renamed Benita

GOULD (ex-USS LOVERING) Frigate, DE 'Captain' class. Boston N. Yd 4.6.1943. Sunk 1.3.44 by 'U.358' north of the Azores.

GOZO (see MALTA)

GOZO Minesweeper, 'Algerine' class. Redfern 27.1.1943 on lend-lease. Returned 1946 to the USN and sold Greek navy as POLEMISTIS.

GOZO Trawler requis. 1914-19.

GRACE Cutter, 101bm. Purchased 1.1763. BU 12.1772.

GRACE Gunvessel, 70bm 57 x 17 ft. Purchased 3.1794. Sold 10.1798.

GRACE DIEU Ship dating from 1390. Given away in 1400.

GRACE DIEU Ballinger Ratcliffe 1402. Given away 12.1409.

GRACE DIEU Ship, 400/600bm. Soper, Southampton 1418. Struck by lightning 7.1.1439 and burnt at Bursledon. (Was never at sea; ribs can still be seen at low water and salvage contemplated 1967.)

GRACE DIEU 100-gun ship, 600/1,000bm. Chatham 1488. Renamed REGENT 1489; lost 10.8.1512 in action with the French off the Isle of Wight.

GRACE OF GOD Discovery Vessel. Captured 1568 by the Spanish.

GRACIEUSE Schooner 14, 119bm, 72 x 21 ft. French Privateer captured 21.10.1804 by BLANCHE in the W.Indies. Listed to 1808.

GRAFTON 3rd Rate 70, 1,096bm, 150 x 40½ ft Woolwich DY 1679. Rebuilt Rotherhithe 1700 as 1,102bm; captured 1.5.1707 by the French off Beachy Head.

GRAFTON Fire Vessel, 18bm, 24 x 12 ft. Purchased 8.1694. Sold 17.2.1696.

GRAFTON 3rd Rate 70, 1,095bm, 151 x 40½ft. Swallow & Fowler, Limehouse 9.8.1709. Rebuilt Woolwich 1725 as 1,133bm. BU 1744.

GRAFTON 3rd Rate 70, 1,414bm, 160 x 45ft. Portsmouth DY 29.3.1750. Sold 25.8.1767.

GRAFTON 3rd Rate 74, 1,650bm, 168 x 47ft. Deptford DY 26.9.1771. Harbour Service 1.1792. BU 5.1816 at Portsmouth.

GRAFTON 1st Class cruiser 7,350 tons, 360 x 60 ft, 2-9.2in, 10-6in, 12-6pdr. Thames IW 30.1.1892. Sold 1.7.1920 S.Castle, Plymouth.

GRAFTON Destroyer 1,335 tons, 312 x 33ft, 4-4.7in, 8-TT. Thornycroft 18.9.1935. Sunk 29.5.40 by torpedo off Dunkirk.

GRAFTON Destroyer (as GAEL). White. Ordered 8.1944, cancelled 12.12.45.

GRAFTON Frigate 1,180 tons, 300 x 33 ft, 2-40mm. White 11.1.1957. Sold 7.12.71, BU at Inverkeithing.

GRAMONT Sloop 18, 325bm, 98 x 27½ ft, 18-6pdr. French Privateer COMTESSE de GRAMMONT captured 10.1757. Recaptured 12.7.1762 by the French at St Johns, NF.

GRAMPIAN (see GIBRALTAR of 1860)

GRAMPIAN Trawler Requis. 1939-46.

GRAMPUS Sloop 14, 160bm, 70 x 23 ft. Woolwich DY 21.10.1731. Foundered 10.1742 in the Channel.

GRAMPUS Sloop 14, 249bm (?) 87 x 25 ft. Perry, Blackwall 27.7.1743. Captured 30.9.1744 by the French in the Bay of Biscay.

GRAMPUS Sloop 14, 271bm, 92 x 26ft. Reed, Hull 3.11.1746. Renamed STROMBOLO, Fireship 1775. Hulk 1780 at New York.

GRAMPUS (see BUCKINGHAM of 1751)

GRAMPUS 4th Rate 50, 1,062bm, 148 x 40½ ft. Fisher, Liverpool 8.10.1782. BU 8.1794.

GRAMPUS (ex-E.Indiaman *Ceres*) 4th Rate 54, 1,165bm, 157 x 41 ft. Purchased 1795. Storeship 2.1797. Wrecked 19.1.1799 on Barking Shelf, near Woolwich.

GRAMPUS (ex-TIGER renamed 4.3.1802) 4th Rate 50, 1,114bm, 151 x 42ft. Portsmouth DY 20.3.1802. Harbour Service 7.1820. Sold 1832.

GRAMPUS (see TREMENDOUS)

GRAMPUS (see NAUTILUS of 1910)

GRAMPUS M/L submarine 1,520 tons, 27½ x 25½ ft, 1-4in, 6-TT, 50 mines. Chatham DY 25.2.1936. Sunk 24.6.40

by Italian TBs CIRCE and CLIO off Sicily.

GRAMPUS Submarine 1,605 tons, 241 x 26½ ft, 8-TT. Cammell Laird 30.5.1957.

GRANA 6th rate 28, 528bm, 118 x 32 ft. Spanish. Captured 25.2.1781. by CERBERUS off Cape Finisterre. Sold 9.1806.

GRANBY Minesweeper (RCN), diesel ' Bangor' class. Davie SB 9.6.1941 Diving Tender 1959. On sale list 10.66, Sold 1975.

GRANBY (see VICTORIAVILLE)

GRANDMERE Minesweeper (RCN), TE 'Bangor' class, Vickers, Montreal 21.8.1941. Sold 1947, Renamed *Elda.*

GRANDMISTRESS Ship, 450bm. Built 1545. Condemned 1552.

GRAND TURK 6th Rate 22, 366bm, 101 x 29 ft, 20-9pdr, 2-3pdr. French, Captured 26.5.1745. Sold 1.5.1749.

GRANICUS 5th Rate 36 (Yellow pine-built), 942bm, 144 x 38½ ft, 14-32pdr carr., 26-18pdr. Barton, Limehouse 25.10.1813. Sold 3.4.1817.

GRANTHAM 30-gun ship, 265bm, 98½ x 25½ ft. Furzer, Southampton 1654. Renamed GARLAND 1660. Fireship 1688, 5th Rate 1689. Sold 13.5.1698

GRANTHAM Slop ship, Purchased 10.1787. BU 6.1792.

GRAPH Submarine 760 tons, 213 x 20 ft, 5-TT. German U.570 captured 28.8.1941 by BURWELL and trawler NORTHERN CHIEF in the N.Atlantic; renamed 21.9.41. Ran aground 20.3.44. on Islay while in tow.

GRAPPLER (Gun-boat No.28) Gunvessel 12, 170bm, 76 x 22 ft, 2-24pdr, 10-18pdr carr. Pitcher, Northfleet 4.1797. Wrecked 31.12.1803 on Chansey Reef and burnt by the French.

GRAPPLER Iron pad. Vessel, 559bm, 165 x 26½ ft. Fairbairn, Poplar 30.12.1845. Sold 2.2.1850 P.Beech to BU.

GRAPPLER Mortar vessel. 161bm, 66 x 21 ft. 1-13in Mortor. Wigram, Blackwall 1.5.1855. Renamed MV.18 on 19.10.1855; hulked 7.1866. Sold 24.4.1896.

GRAPPLER Wood S.gunboat, 'Albacore' class Wigram, Blackwall 29.3.1856. Sold 6.1.1868 at Esquimalt as Merchant.

GRAPPLER Compos. S.gunboat 465 tons, 125 x 23½ ft, 2-64pdr, 2-20pdr. Barrow SB (Vickers) 5.10.1880. BDV 1904. Sold 14.5.07 King. Garston.

GRAPPLER Tug 1908-57,

GRASSHOPPER (ex-*London*) Sloop 14, 276bm, 94 x 27 ft. Purchased 29.12.1776. Renamed BASILISK fireship 27.8.1779. sold 4.1783 at Plymouth.

GRASSHOPPER Hoy. Muddle, Gillingham 1799.Sold 1812.

GRASSHOPPER Brig-sloop 18, 'Cruizer' class, 383bm. Richards, Hythe 29.9.1806. Captured 25.12.1811 by the French in the Texel.

GRASSHOPPER Brig-sloop 18, 'Cruizer' Class, 385bm, Portsmouth DY 17.5.1813. Sold 30.5.1832 T.Ward

GRASSHOPPER Wood S.gunboat, 'Albacore' class, Pitcher, Northfleet 8.12.1855. Sold 5.1871 at Newchang.

GRASSHOPPER Torpedo gunboat 550tons, 200 x 23 ft, 1-4i, 6-3pdr, 4-TT. Sheerness DY 30.8.1887. Sold 11.7.1905.

GRASSHOPPER Coastal destroyer 255 tons, 166½ x 17½ ft, 2-12odr , 3-TT. Thornycroft, Chiswick 18.3.1906. Renamed TB.9 in 1906. Sunk 26.7.16 in collision in the North Sea.

GRASSHOPPER Destroyer 923 tons, 274 x 28 ft, 1-4in, 3-12pdr, 2-TT. Fairfield 23.11.1909. Sold 1.11.21. Fryer, Sunderland.

GRASSHOPPER River gunboat 585 tons, 197 x 33 ft, 2-4in, 1-3.7in howitzer. Thornycroft 19.1.1939. Beached 14.2.42 after Japanese air attack near Singapore.

GRASS SNAKE SSV (RAN) 80 tons. Williamstown 1944. To N.Borneo in 12.45

GRAVELINES Destroyer 2,135 tons, 355 x 40 ft, 4-4.5in, 1-4in, 12-40mm, 8-TT. Cammell Laird. 30.11.1944. Arrived 22.3.61. at Rosyth to BU.

GRAYFLY River boat, 'Fly' class, Yarrow 8.1915 in sections. Transferred War Dept 1923.

GRAYS Minesweeper, later 'Hunt' class, Eltringahm. Cancelled 1918.

GREAT BARBARA Ship, 400bm, Purchased 1513 Listed to 1524.

GREAT BARK Ship, 200/400bm. Built 1512. Sold Circa 1531.

GREATFORD Seaward defence boat, 'Ford' class. White 29.1.1953. Sold 8.9.67, BU Singapore.

GREAT GALLEY Galleasse, 800bm. Greenwich 1515. rebuilt 1583 as GREAT BARK, 600bm. Last mentioned 1562.

GREAT HARRY (see HARRY GRACE a DIEU)

GREAT PINNACE, 80bm, Listed 1544-1545

GREAT ZABRA, Pinnace 50bm. Listed 1522 -1525

GRECIAN Schooner 10, 224bm. American Privateer captured 2.5.1814 by JASEUR. Sold 18.4.1822 J.Cristall to BU.

GRECIAN (ex-Revenue cutter DOLPHIN renamed 20.11.1821.) Cutter 10, 145bm, 69 x 23 ft. Sold 11.7.1827 Mr Freake.

GRECIAN Brig-sloop 16, 484bm, 105 x 33½ ft, 16-32pdr. Pembroke Dock 24.4.1838. BU completed 1.11.1865 Marshall.

GRECIAN Minesweeper, 'Catherine' class. Savannah Mcy 10.3.1943. on lend-lease. Returned 1947 to the USN. and sold 3.47 Turkish Navy as EDINCIK.

GREENFISH Storeship 2, 67bm, 61 x 16 ft. Purchased 1693. Sold 6.3.1705.

GREENFLY Coastal destroyer, 255 tons, 166½ x 17½ ft, 2-12pdr, 3-TT. Thornycroft 15.2.1907. Renamed TB.10 in 1906 Sunk 10.1.15 by mine in the North Sea.

GREENFLY River gunboat, 'Fly' class. Yarrow 9.1915.in sections. Sold 1.3.23 at Basra.

GREENFLY Trawler. 1939-45.

GREEN LINNET Gunvessel 6, 82bm. Purchased 1806. In 1810, gone by 1813.

GREENOCK (ex-PEGASUS renamed 1846) Iron S.Frigate, 1.413bm, 210 x 37½ ft, 6-8in, 4-32pdr. Scotts, Greenock 30.4.1849. Sold 8.1852. Australian Screw Shipping Co.

GREENOCK (see BALUCHISTAN)

GREENWICH 4th Rate 54, 659bm, 136 x 34 ft, 24-24pdr, 22-6pdr, 8-4pdr. Woolwich DY 1666. Rebuilt Portsmouth 1699; rebuilt Chatham 1730 as 756bm. Wrecked 20.10.1744 in Jamaica.

GREENWICH 4th Rate 50, 1,053bm, 144½ x 41½ ft. Janvrin, Lepe 19.3.1747. Captured 18.3.1757 by the French.

GREENWICH 6th Rate 26, 754bm, 145½ x 35 ft. E.Indiaman purchased 9.1777. Sold 10.4.1783.

GREENWICH Sloop 12 American captured 9.1778. Wrecked 22.5.1779 on coast of Carolina.

GREENWICH (see RODNEY of 1809).

GREENWICH (ex-Greek merchant converted on stocks) Depot ship 8,600 tons, 309 x 52 ft, 4-4in, 2-6pdr. Dobson, Tyne 5.7.1915; completed Swan Hunter. Sold 11.7.46, renamed *Hembury*.

GREETHAM Inshore M/S, 'Ham' class.

Herd & Mackenzie 19.4.1954. Sold 1962 Libyan Navy as ZUARA.

GRENADA Bomb 12, 279bm, 87 x 27 ft. Fowler, Rotherhithe 26.6.1693. Blown up 16.7.1694 at Havre de Grace.

GRENADA Bomb 4, 148bm, 64 x 23½ ft. Castle, Deptford 1695. BU 5.1718 at Woolwich. (Also listed as GRENADO.)

GRENADA Brig 10, 141bm, 71½ x 22 ft. French privateer HARMONIE captured 16.11.1803 and presented 1804 by the inhabitants of Grenada. Sold circa 1809.

GRENADA Sloop 16. French privateer JENA captured 6.1.1807 by CRUIZER in the North Sea. In 1810-1814.

GRENADE Destroyer 1,335 tons, 312 x 33 ft, 4-4.7in, 8-TT. Stephen 12.11.1935. Sunk 29.5.40 by air attack at Dunkirk.

GRENADE Destroyer 1,980 tons, 341½ x 38 ft, 6-4in, 6-40mm, 10-TT. Scotts. Ordered 4.1943, cancelled 1.45. (not laid down).

GRENADE Trawler requis. 1914-19. M/S requis. 1916-19.

GRENADO Bomb 12, 279bm, 91 x 26 ft. Barnard, Ipswich 22.6.1742. Sloop in 1750; sold 30.8.1763.

GRENVILLE (ex-*Sally*) Schooner 12, 69bm, 55 x 17 ft. Purchased 7.8.1763 in Newfoundland. Survey brig 1764. BU 3.1775.

GRENVILLE Fishery protection (Canadian govt) 497 tons, 155 x 31 ft. Polson, Toronto 1915.

GRENVILLE Destroyer leader 1,666 tons, 312 x 32 ft, 4-4in, 4-TT. Cammell Laird 17.6.1916. Sold 12.31 Rees, Llanelly.

GRENVILLE Destroyer leader 1,485 tons, 312 x 34½ ft, 5-4.7in, 8-TT. Yarrow 15.8.1935. Sunk 19.1.40 by mine in the North Sea.

GRENVILLE Destroyer 1,730 tons, 340 x 36 ft, 4-4.7in, 8-TT. Swan Hunter 12.10.1942. Frigate 2,240 tons, 2-4in, 2-3in 1954. BU 1983 at Rochester.

GRETNA Minesweeper, later 'Hunt' class. Eltringham 11.4.1918. Sold 3.10.28 Alloa, Rosyth.

GREYHOUND 45-gun ship, 160bm. Deptford 1545. Rebuilt 1558. Wrecked 1563 off Rye.

GREYHOUND Ship in service in 1585.

GREYHOUND 12-gun ship, 126bm. Woolwich 28.1.1636. Blown up 1656 in action with the Spanish.

GREYHOUND 20-gun ship, 145bm. Captured from Royalists 1657. Ex-

pended 1666 as fireship.

GREYHOUND 6th Rate 16, 180bm, 93 x 21½ ft, 16-6pdr. Portsmouth DY 1672, Sold 13.5.1698.

GREYHOUND Bomb 6, 94bm, 6-4pdr. Purchased 1694. Sold 3.5.1698.

GREYHOND 5th Rate 40, 494bm, 114 x 31½ ft. Hubbard, Ipswich 1703 Wrecked 26.8.1711 at Tynemouth.

GREYHOUND 6th Rate 20, 276bm, 94 x 26 ft. Woolwich DY 21.6.1712. Captured 1.9.1718 by the Spanish in St Jermyns Bay.

GREYHOUND 6th Rate 20, 371bm, 105 x 28½ ft. Stacey, Deptford 13.2.1719. BU completed 6.1741 at Deptford. (In Spanish hands 19.4.1722 to 1722.)

GREYHOUND 6th Rate 24, 450bm, 108 x 31 ft. Snelgrove, Limehouse 19.9.1741. Sold 5.4.1768.

GREYHOUND Cutter 15, 73bm, 52 x 18 ft. Purchased 2.1763. Hulk in 1776. Sold 23.10.1780 at Sheerness.

GREYHOUND 6th Rate 28, 617bm, 124 x 33 ft. Adams, Bucklers Hard 20.7.1773. Wrecked 1781 near Deal.

GREYHOUND Cutter 20, 148bm, 20-4pdr. Purchased 6.1780. Renamed VIPER 1781, 12 guns. Listed to 1803.

GREYHOUND 5th Rate 32, 682bm, 126 x 35 ft. Betts, Mistleythorn 11.12.1783, Wrecked 4.10.1808 in the Philippines.

GREYHOUND (see EUPHRATES of 1813).

GREYHOUND Wood S. sloop, 880bm, 1,260 tons, 173 x 33 ft. Pembroke Dock 15.6.1859. Harbour service 9.1869. Sold 3.4.1906.

GREYHOUND Destroyer 400 tons, 210 x 21 ft, 1-12pdr, 5-6pdr, 2-TT. Hawthorn 6.10.1900. Sold 10.6.19 Clarkson Whitby.

GREYHOUND Destroyer 1,335 tons, 312 x 33 ft, 4-4.7in, 8-TT. Vickers Armstrong, Barrow 15.8.1935. Sunk 22.5.41 by air attack south of Morea.

GREYHOUND Destroyer (as GAEL). White. Ordered 8.1944, cancelled 12.12.45.

GREYHOUND M/S requis. 1915-19.

GRIFFIN 12-gun ship, 121bm. Royalist, ex-French, captured 1665 by Parliament. Foundered 1664 off Jamaica.

GRIFFIN Fireship 8, 266bm, 95 x 25 ft. Rolfe & Castle, Rotherthithe 17.4.1690. Rebuilt Sheerness 1702. Sold 21.7.1737.

GRIFFIN 5th Rate 44. French GRIFFON captured 8.1712 off Finisterre. Restored to France 1713.

GRIFFON 6th Rate 28, 598bm, 118½ x 34 ft. Janvrin, Burlsedon 18.10.1758. Wrecked 14.10.1761 near Bermuda.

GRIFFIN Cutter 12, 186bm, 73 x 26ft, 12-4pdr. Purchased 3.1778. Sold 10.8.1786 at Chatham.

GRIFFON Brig-sloop 16, 368bm, 92 x 29 ft, 14-24pdr carr. 2-6pdr. French, captured 11.5.1808 by BACCHANTE in the W.Indies. Sold 11.3.1819 Hill & Co.

GRIFFON Brig-sloop 10, 'Cherokee' class. Deptford DY. Ordered 23.5.1820. cancelled 20.8.1828, transferred Chatham.

GRIFFON Brig-sloop 10, 'Cherokee' class. Chatham DY 11.9.1832. Harbour service 1854; coal hulk 1857. BU 2.1869 at Portsmouth. (Listed as GRIFFIN from 1858).

GRIFFON Wood S. gunvessel, 425bm, 145 x 25½ ft, 1-68pdr, 2-20pdr, 2-24pdr howitzers. Pitcher, Northfleet 25.2.1860. Stranded 10.1866 after collision with PANDORA off Little Popo, W.Africa.

GRIFFON Compos. S. gunvessel 780 tons, 157 x 29½ ft, 2-5in, 2-64pdr. Laird 16.12.1876. Sold 28.9.1891 Board of Trade as hulk *Richmond.*

GRIFFON Destroyer 355 tons, 210 x 20 ft, 1-12pdr, 5-6pdr, 2-TT. Laird 21.11.1896. Sold 1.7.1920 Castle, Plymouth.

GRIFFIN Destroyer 1,335 tons, 312 x 33 ft, 4-4.7in, 8-TT. Vickers Armstrong, Barrow 15.8.1935. Renamed OTTAWA (RCN) 20.3.43. Sold 1946.

GRIFFON (see under GRIFFIN)

GRILLE S. yacht 2,560 tons, 377 x 44 ft. German, seized 8.1945 in N.Germany. Sold 9.46 G.Arida.

GRILSE Torpedo boat (RCN) 225 tons, 207 x 18½ ft, 1-12pdr, 1-TT. Ex-yacht commissioned 1914. Sold 1919.

GRISLE (ex-USS BURRFISH) Submarine (RCN) 1,525 tons. Commissioned 11.5.1961. Returned USN 12.68.

GRILSE Trawler. Trawler 1943-46.

GRIMSBY Sloop 992 tons, 250 x 36 ft, 2-4.7in, 1-3in. Devonport DY 19.7.1933. Sunk 25.5.41 by Italian A/C off Tobruk.

GRIMSBY Trawler. requis. 1914-18.

GRINDALL (ex-USS SANDERS) Frigate, DE 'Captain' class. Boston N.Yd 4.6.1943. on lend-lease. Returned 8.45 to the USN.

GRINDER Tender (orgin unknown). Sold 22.8.1832.

GRINDER Steam sloop, 1,073bm. Sheerness DY. Ordered 3.11.1847.

Launched 1851 as MIRANDA.

GRINDER Wood S. gunboat,'Dapper' class. White 7.3.1855. BU 7.1864 at Haslar.

GRINDER Tug 1868 - 1919. Tug 1941. Tug 1958-79.

GRIPER (Gunboat No.27) Gunvessel, 170bm, 76 x 22 ft, 2-24pdr, 10-18pdr carr. Pitcher, Northfleet 10.4.1797. Sold 10.1802.

GRIPER Gun-brig 12, 182bm, 85 x 22 ft. Brindley, Lynn 24.9.1804. Wrecked 18.2.1807 near Ostend.

GRIPER Gun-brig 12, 182bm, 85 x 22 ft. Richards, Hythe 14.7.1813. Arctic discovery Sloop, 2 guns 1824; coastgaurd 1836; target 1856. BU completed 11.11.1868 at Portsmouth.

GRIPER Wood S.Gunboat, 'Albacore' class. Green, Blackwall 11.12.1855. BU 3.1.1869 at Devonport.

GRIPER Iron S.gunboat 265 tons, 87½ x 26 ft, 1 -10in MLR. Pembroke Dock 15.9.1879. (Was suspended 7.72 to 2.78). Harbour service 1905, renamed YC373; renamed FLORA 19.6.23 as base ship; renamed AFRIKANDER 1933. Sold circa 1937.

GRIPER Tug 1942-46. Tug 1958-79.

GROU Frigate(RCN), 'River' class. Vickers, Montreal 7.8.1943. Sold 13.12.47 to BU.

GROUPER Schooner 4, 78bm, 56 x 18 ft. 4-12pdr carr. Bermuda 1804. Wrecked 21.10.1811 at Guadeloupe, W.Indies.

GROVE Destroyer, 'Hunt' class type II. Swan Hunter 29.5.1941. Sunk 12.6.42 by 'U.77' north of Sollum.

GROWLER (Gunboat No.26) Gunvessel, 169bm, 76 x 22½ ft. 10-18pdr carr., 2-9pdr. Perry, Blackwall 10.4.1797. Captured 20.12.1797 by the French off Dungeness.

GROWLER Gun-brig 12, 178bm, 80 x 22½ ft. 10-18pdr carr., 2-12pdr. Adams, Bucklers Hard 10.8.1804. Sold 31.5.1815.

GROWLER (see LINNET of 1813)

GROWLER Wood pad. Sloop, 1,059bm, 180 x 36 ft. Chatham DY 20.7.1841. BU 1.1854

GROWLER Mortar vessel, 117bm, 65 x 21 ft, 1-13in mortar. Wigram, Blackwall 31.3.1855. Renamed MV.4 on 19.10.1855; completed 16.12.1863. as landing stage at Chatham.

GROWLER Wood S.gunboat, 'Albacore' class. Wigram, Blackwall 8.5.1856. BU 8.1864 at Malta.

GROWLER Compos. S.gunvessel, 464bm, 584 tons, 155 x 25 ft. 1-7in 1-64pdr, 2-20pdr. Laurie, Glasgow

1.12.1868. Sold 11.1887.

GROWLER Storeship. 1891-1921. Tug 1942, renamed CYCLONE 1964-82.

GUACHAPIN Brig-sloop 16, 176bm, Captured 1803. Wrecked 29.7.1811 in a hurricane at Antigua; salved and sold 1811 in Jamaica.

GUADELOUPE Sloop in service in 1762.

GUADELOUPE 6th Rate 28, 586bm, 119 x 33½ ft. Plymouth DY 5.12.1763. Sunk 10.10.1781 to avoid capture by the French in Virginia; salved and commissioned by the French. (Was ordered 9.1757 from Williams, Milford then transferred to Plymouth 6.1758.)

GUADELOUPE Sloop 16, 337bm, 99 x 28½ ft, 14-24pdr carr., 2-6pdr French NISUS captured 12.12.1809 at Guadeloupe. Sold 3.11.1814.

GUARDIAN 5th Rate 44, 901bm. 140 x 38½ ft. Batson, Limehouse 23.3.1784. Beached 8.2.1790 in Table Bay after collision with an iceberg: sold there 8.2.1791.

GUARDIAN Netlayer 2,860 tons, 310 x 53 ft. 2-4in Chatham DY. 1.9.1932. Arrived 12.62 at Troon to BU.

GUARDIAN Support Ship. *Seaforth Champion* purchased 12.19.1982. Sold Pounds 1987.

GUELDERLAND 3rd Rate 64, 1,342bm, 157 x 44½ft Dutch. Captured 30.8.1799 in the Texel, her crew having refused action, Harbour service. Sold 5.3.1817.Freake, to BU.

GUELDERLAND 5th Rate 36, 852bm, 135 x 38 ft. Dutch, Captured 19.5.1808. by VIRGINIE in the North Sea. Renamed HELDER 15.8.1809. Sunk 6.1817 as a breakwater.

GUELPH (ex-SEA CLIFF renamed 7.1943) Corvette (RCN), modified 'Flower' class. Collingwood SY 20.12.43. Sold 2.10.45.

GUEPE Sloop 14, 298bm, 101½ x 26ft. French Privateer captured 29.8.1800 in Vigo Bay. Renamed WASP 1801. Sold 17.5.1811.

GUERNSEY (see BASING)

GUERNSEY 4th Rate 48, 680bm, 132 x 34½ ft. Johnson, Blackwall 1696. Rebuilt Chatham 1740 as 863bm; hulk 4.1769. sold 1786.

GUERNSEY (see AEOLUS of 1758)

GUERNSEY Wood S.Sloop, 695bm, 185 x 28½ft. Pembroke Dock. Ordered 1861. Cancelled 12.12.1863.

GUERNSEY Destroyer (as GAEL) Denny. Ordered 8.1944, cancelled 28.12.45.

GUERNSEY Patrol Vessel. 925 tons. Hall Russell 17.2.1977

GUERRIERE 3rd Rate 74, French PEUPLE SOUVERAIN captured 2.7.1798 at the Nile. Sheer hulk 1800. BU in 8.1810 at Gibraltar.

GUERRIERE 5th Rate 38, 1,092bm, 16-32pdr carr, 30-18pdr, 2-9pdr French, captured 19.7.1806 by BLANCHE off the Faroes. Captured 19.8.1812 by the American CONSTITUTION in the Western Atlanic and burnt.

GUILDER de RUYTER 4th Rate 50, 684bm. Dutch GELDERSCHE RUITER captured 1665. Sold 1667.

GUILDFORD (see FAME of 1759)

GUILDFORD CASTLE (see HESPELER)

GUILLEMOT patrol vessel 580 tons, 243 x 26½ ft, 1-4in Denny. 6.7.1939. Sold 6.6.5, BU Ward, Grays.

GUILLEMOT Trawler Requis. 1914-19.

GUINEA (see CHARLES of 1648).

GUINEVERE Destroyer (as GAEL) Denny, Ordered 8.1944, renamed GLOWWORM 9.45. GIFT 10.45; cancelled 12.45.

GULL (see SWANSTON)

GULL Trawler, Requis. 1914-19. Tug 1941-45.

GULNARE Survey tender in service in 1827.

GULNARE Survey vessel, 146bm, Launched 18.5.1828. In service to 1842 (perhaps hired)

GULNARE Survey vessel, 270bm. In service 5.1844 to 1850 (perhaps hired)

GULNARE Wood pad. Gunvessel, 351bm. 120 x 23ft. 3-18pdr. Chatham DY 30.9.1833. Rebuilt 1838 as 371bm. and renamed GLEANER BU in 8.1849 at Deptford. (Built for the G.P.O. and transferred 29.6.37)

GULNARE Survey vessel (Canadian), 212bm. Quebec 1851. Listed in 1862.

GULNARE Survey cutter, 31bm. Purchased 24,5,1855. Sold 17.4.1863 at Glasgow.

GULNARE Survey vessel (Canadian) 500 tons, 110 x 20½ ft. Listed 1893 to 1936.

GULNARE Survey tender. Purchased 1939. Sold 10.49.

GHURKA (see Indian TB.7 of 1888)

GHURKA Destroyer 880 tons, 255 x 25½ ft. 3-12pdr (5-12pdr 1911). 2-TT. Hawthorn Leslie 29.4.1907. Sunk 8.2.17 by mine off Dungeness.

GURKHA (ex GHURKA renamed 1936) Destroyer 1,870 tons, 355½ x 36½ ft

8-4.4in, 4-TT. Fairfield 7.7.1937. Sunk 9.4.40 by air attack off Stavanger.

GURKHA (ex LARNE renamed 13.6.1940) Destroyer 1,920 tons, 354 x 37ft, 8-4in, 8-TT. Cammell Laird 8.7.40. Sunk by 'U.133' in the eastern Mediterranean.

GURKHA Frigate 2,300 tons. 350 x 42ft, 2-.5in, 2-40mm Thornycroft 10.7.1960. Sold Indonesia 1984, renamed WILHEMUS ZAKARIAS YOHANNA

GUYSBOROUGH Minesweeper, TE 'Bangor' class North Vancouver SR.Co. 21.7.1941. Sunk 17.3.45 by 'U878' off ushant while on loan to the RCN.

GYMPIE Minesweeper (RAN) 'Bathurst' class, Evans, Deakin, Brisbane 30.1.1942. Sold 6.1.61 to BU in Japan.

'(H)' or 'Holland' class submarines; all built by Vickers No.1, 75 tons, 63 x 11 ft, 1-TT; Nos 2-5 all 105 tons, 63½ x 12 ft, 1-TT.

(H).1 launched 2.10.1901. Sold 7.10.13; foundered on passage from Portsmouth. to BU Briton Ferry. Raised 9.82; became museum ship at Gosport.

(H).2 21.2.02. Sold 7.10.13 Pollock/Brown, Southampton.

(H).3 10.6.02. Sold 7.10.13 F. Rijsdijks.

(H).4 9.5.02. Foundered 3.9.12, raised and used as a target in 1914.

(H).5 21.5.02. Foundered 8.8.12 off the Nab in tow to ship-breakers.

(H).6 Improved 'Holland' type, launched 9.7.02 as A.1.

'H' class submarines, 364 tons, 150 x 16 ft, 4-TT (1st 20); 440 tons, 164½ x 16 ft, 4-TT (all others).

First 10 built Vickers, Montreal; 2nd 10 built Fore River, USA.

H.1 Completed 5.1915. Sold 7.3.21 B. Zammit, Malta.

H.2 Completed 5.15. Sold 7.3.21 B. Zammit. Malta.

H.3 Completed 3.6.15. Sunk 15.7.16 by mine off Cattaro.

H.4 Completed 3.6.15. Sold 30.11.21 Agius Bros, Malta.

H.5 Completed 21.6.15. Sunk 6.3.18 in collision in the Irish Sea.

H.6 Completed 10.6.15. Stranded 18.1.16 on the Dutch coast; interned and sold Dutch navy 1919 as 0.8.

H.7 Completed 20.6.15. Sold 30.11.21 Agius Bros, Malta.

H.8 Completed 15.6.15. Sold 29.11.21 J. Kelly, Arbroath.

H.9 Completed 24.6.15. Sold 30.11.21 Agius Bros, Malta.

H.10 Completed 27.6.15. Sunk 19.1.18 in the North Sea.

H.11 Completed 1915. Sold 1921 Stanlee, Dover.

H.12 Completed 1915. Sold 4.22 Stanlee, Dover.

H.13 Completed 3.7.17 for the Chilian navy as GUALCOLDA.

H.14 Completed 1918. To RCN 6.19 as CH.14; BU 1925.

H.15 Completed 14.9.18 To RCN 6.19 as CH.15; BU 1925.

H.16 Completed 3.7.17 for Chilian navy as TEGUALDA.

H.17 Completed 7.17 for Chilian navy as RUCUMILLA.

H.18 Completed 7.17 for Chilian navy as GUALE.

H.19 Completed 7.17 for Chilian navy as QUIDORA.

H.20 Completed 7.17 for Chilian navy as FRESIA.

H.21 Vickers 20.10.17. Sold 13.7.26 Cashmore, Newport.

H.22 Vickers 14.11.17. Sold 19.2.29, BU at Charlestown.

H.23 Vickers 29.1.18. Sold 4.5.34 Young, Sunderland.

H.24 Vickers 14.11.17. Sold 4.5.34 Young, Sunderland.

H.25 Vickers 27.4.18. Sold 19.2.29; BU Charlestown.

H.26 Vickers 15.11.17. Sold 21.4.28 Ward, Pembroke Dock.

H.27 Vickers 25.9.18. Sold 30.8.35 Cashmore, Newport.

H.28 Vickers 12.3.18. Sold 18.8.44; BU at Troon.

H.29 Vickers 8.6.18. Sold 7.10.27 Ward, Pembroke Dock.

H.30 Vickers 9.5.18. Sold 30.8.35 Cashmore, Newport.

H.31 Vickers 16.11.18. Sunk 24.12.41 in the Bay of Biscay.

H.32 Vickers 19.11.18. Sold 18.10.44; BU at Troon.

H.33 Cammell Laird 24.8.18. Sold 1944; BU at Troon.

H.34 Cammell Laird 5.11.18 Sold 1945; BU at Troon.

H.35 Cammell Laird. Cancelled 1919.

H.36 to H.40 (all as H.35)

H.41 Armstrong 1918 and damaged in collision 1919. Sold 12.3.20 Young,

Sunderland.

H.42 Armstong 5.11.18. Sunk 23.3.22 in collision with destroyer VERSATILE off Gibraltar.

H.43 Armstrong 3.2.19. Sold 1944; BU at Troom.

H.44 Armstrong 17.2.19. Sold 1944; BU at Troon.

H.45 Armstrong. Cancelled 1919.

H.46 Armstrong. Cancelled 1919.

H.47 Beardmore 19.11.18. Sunk 9.7.29 in collision with S/M L.12.

H.48 Beardmore 31.3.19. Sold 30.8.35 Rees, Llanelly.

H.49 Beardmore 15.7.19. Sunk 27.10.40 by German surface craft off the Dutch coast.

H.50 Beardmore 25.10.19. Sold 1945; BU at Troon.

H.51 Pembroke Dock 15.11.18. Sold 6.6.24 Keen, Bristol; resold 17.7.24 Davo S. Bkg Co.

H.52 Pembroke Dock 31.3.19. Sold 9.11.27 New Era Productions.

H.53 Pembroke Dock. Cancelled 1919.

HADDOCK Schooner 4, 78bm, 56 x 18 ft, 4-12pdr carr. Bermuda 1805. Captured 30.1.1809 by the French GÉNIE in the Channel.

HADLEIGH CASTLE Corvette, 'Castle' class. Smiths DK 21.6.1943. Arrived 1.59 Dorkin, Gateshead to BU.

HAERLEM Sloop 10. Captured 1778. Captured 7.1779 by an American privateer.

HAERLEM 3rd Rate 64, 1,324bm, 157 x 44½ft. Dutch HAARLEM captured 11.10.1797 at Camperdown. Harbour service 1.1811. Sold 2.5.1816.

HAIDA Destroyer (RCN) 1,927 tons, 355½ x 37½ ft, 6-4.7in, 2-4in, 4-TT. Vickers Armstrong, Tyne 25.8.1942. Presented to the City of Toronto 21.8.64 as a memorial.

HALBERD Destroyer 1,980 tons, 341½ x 38 ft, 6-4in, 6-40mm, 10-TT. Scotts. Ordered 4.1943, cancelled 1.45 (not laid down).

HALCYON Brig-sloop 16, 298bm, 91½ x 28 ft, 14-24pdr carr., 2-6pdr. French ALCION captured 8.7.1803 by NARCISSUS off Sardinia. BU 6.1812.

HALCYON Brig-sloop 18, 'Cruizer' class, 384bm. Larking, Lynn 16.5.1813. Wrecked 19.5.1814 in Jamaica.

HALCYON Brig-sloop 10, 'Cherokee' class. Woolwich DY (ex-Deptford DY). Ordered 2.11.1818, cancelled 21.2.1831.

HALCYON Torpedo gunboat 1,070

tons, 250 x 30½ ft, 2-4.7in, 4-6pdr, 5-TT. Devonport DY 6.4.1894. Sold 6.11.1919 J.H.Lee, BU at Dover.

HALCYON Minesweeper 815 tons, 230 x 33½ ft, 2-4in. J.Brown 20.12.1933. Sold 19.4.50; BU Ward, Milford Haven.

HALCYON Paddle M/s, 'Ascot' class. Dunlop Bremner 29.3.1916. Sold 14.12.21 Stanlee, Dover.

HALDON Destroyer, 'Hunt' class type III. Fairfield 27.4.1942. Lent Free-French 12.42 as La COMBAT-TANTE; sunk 23.2.45 by mine in the North Sea.

HALF MOON 30-gun ship, Captured 1653. Sold 1659.

HALF MOON 46-gun ship, 552bm, 114 x 33½ ft. Captured 1681. Sold 1686.

HALF MOON 32-gun ship, 214bm. Algerian, captured 1685. Fireship 1688, 8 guns. Expended 24.5.1692 at La Hogue.

HALF MOON Drifter requis. 1915-19.

HALIFAX Sloop 22. Oswego, Canada 1756. Captured 14.8.1756 by the French at the fall of Oswego.

HALIFAX Schooner 10, 83bm. Purchased 1768, wrecked 15.2.1775.

HALIFAX Sloop 18, 308bm, 18-6pdr. American RANGER captured 12.5.1780 at Charleston. Sold 13.10.1781.

HALIFAX Schooner. Purchased in N.America 6.1775. Sold 1780.

HALIFAX (see MARY of 1797)

HALIFAX Sloop 18, 378bm, 106½ x 28½ ft, 16-32pdr carr., 2-6pdr. Halifax NS 11.10.1806. BU 1.1814.

HALIFAX Corvette (RCN), 'Flower' class. Collingwood SY 4.10.1941. Sold 1946 as salvage vessel *Halifax*.

HALLADALE Frigate, 'River' class. Inglis 28.1.1944. Sold 1.4.49 Townsend Bros, as ferry *Halladale*.

HALLOWELL (see ANGUILLA)

HALLOWELL Frigate (RCN), 'River' class. Vickers, Montreal 28.3.1944. Sold 21.12.45, renamed *Sharon;* became Israeli MISNAK 1952.

HALSHAM Inshore M/S, 'Ham' class Jones, Buckie 9.1953. To Air Ministry 1966 as No 5002.

HALSTARR 5th Rate 32, 700bm. Dutch KENAU HASSELAAR captured 1.1.1807 by ARETHUSA at Curacoa. Listed to 1809.

HALSTED (see BARBADOS of 1943)

HALSTED (ex-USS REYNOLDS) Frigate, 'TE 'Captain' class. Bethlehem, Hingham 14.10.1943. Damaged

11.6.44 by Torpedoes and hulked. Nominally returned 1946 USN and sold 1.11.46 to BU in Holland.

HAMADRYAD 5th Rate 36, 890bm. Spanish NINFA captured 26.4.1797 by IRRESISTIBLE off Lisbon. Wrecked 24.12.1797 on coast of Portugal.

HAMADRYAD 5th Rate 36, 966bm. Spanish MATILDA captured 25.11.1804 by DONEGAL and MEDUSA off Cadiz. Sold 9.8.1815.

HAMADRYAD 5th Rate 46, 1,082bm, 152 x 40½ ft. Pembroke Dock 25.7.1823. Lent 3.1866 as seamen's hospital at Cardiff. Sold 11.7.1905.

HAMADRYAD (see DRYAD of 1893)

HAMBLEDON Minesweeper, early 'Hunt' class. Fleming & Ferguson 9.3.1917. Sold 7.22 Stanlee, Dover.

HAMBLEDON Destroyer, 'Hunt' class type I. Swan Hunter 12.12.1939. Arrived 9.57 Clayton & Davie, Tyne to BU.

HAMILTON (ex-USS KALK) Destroyer (RCN), 1,060 tons, 309 x 30½ ft, 1-4in, 1-3in, 4-20mm, 3-TT. Commissioned in the RCN 23.9.1940. Arrived 7.45 at Baltimore to BU.

HAMPSHIRE 46-gun ship, 490bm, 118 x 30 ft. Deptford 1653. Sunk 26.8.1697 in action with the French PELICAN in Hudsons Bay.

HAMPSHIRE 4th Rate 48, 690bm, 132 x 34½ ft. Taylor, Cuckolds Point Thames 3.3.1698. BU 1739 at Portsmouth.

HAMPSHIRE 4th Rate 50, 854bm, 134 x 38½ ft Barnard, Ipswich 13.11.1741. BU completed 22.12.1766 at Sheerness.

HAMPSHIRE Armoured cruiser 10,850 tons, 450 x 68½ ft, 4-7.5in, 6-16in, 2-12pdr. Armstrong 24.9.1903 Sunk 5.6.16 by mine off the Orkneys.

HAMPSHIRE GM destroyer 5,600 tons, 505 x 54 ft, 4-4.5in, 2-20mm, 10-GWS. J.Brown 16.3.1961. Arrived Ward, Briton Ferry 28.4.79. to BU.

HAMPSHIRE Trawler 1939. To French Navy 1939.

HAMPTON COURT 3rd Rate 70, 1,030bm, 150½ x 40 ft, Deptford DY 1678. Rebuilt Blackwall 1701 as 1,073bm. Captured 1.5.1707 by the French off Beachy Head. Went to Spanish Navy in 1712.

HAMPTON COURT 3rd Rate 70, 1,136bm, 151 x 42 ft, Taylor, Rotherhithe 19.8.1709. Rebuilt Depyford 1744 as 1,283, 64 guns. BU Completed 5.6.1774 at Plymouth.

HANDMAID Ship, 80/120bm. Deptford

1573. Hulked 1600.

HANDMAID. Tug 1941-70.

HANDY Wood S.Gunboat, 'Clown' Class. Pitcher, Northfleet 31.5.1856. Sold 5.1868 at Lagos, W.Africa.

HANDY (see NYMPHE of 1812)

HANDY Trials gunboat 508 tons, 115 x 37 ft, various guns. Armstrong 1883 and purchased 1884. Renamed EXCELLENT 5.1891; CALCUTTA 1.11.1916; SNAPPER 8.17 Sold 27.4.22. (Had been launched 30.12.82)

HANDY Destroyer 295 tons, 194 x 19 ft, 1-12pdr, 5-6pdr, 2-TT. Fairfield 9.3.1895. Sold at Hong Kong in 1916.

HANDY (ex-Brazilian JURUA purchased 9.1939) Destroyer 1,340 tons, 312 x 33 ft, 4-4.7in, 8-TT. Vickers Armstrong, Barrow, 29.9.39. Renamed HARVESTER 27.2.40 Sunk 11.3.43. by 'U.432' in the N.Atlantic.

HANDY. Tug 1915-20. Drifter requis.1915-19.

HANNAM (see CAICOS)

HANNIBAL 4th Rate 50, 1,054bm, 146 x 41 ft, Adams, Bucklers Hard 26.12.1779. Captured 21.1.1782. by the French HEROS off Sumatra.

HANNIBAL Sloop 14, 220bm, 94 x 25 ft, Purchased 1782. Foundered 1788.

HANNIBAL 3rd Rate 74, 1,619bm, 168 x 47 ft. Perry, Blackwall 15.4.1786. Captured 5.7.1801 by the French when aground at the battle of Algesiras.

HANNIBAL 3rd Rate 74, 1,749 bm, 176 x 48½ ft. Adams, Bucklers Hard 5.1810. Harbour Service 8.1825. BU 12.1833 at Pembroke Dock.

HANNIBAL 2nd Rate 90. Woolwich DY. Ordered 14.5.1840, Cancelled and re-ordered Woolwich as the following:

HANNIBAL Screw 2nd Rate 91, 3,136bm, 4,735 tons, 217 x 58 ft. 34-8in, 1-68 pdr, 56-32pdr. Deptford DY 31.1.1854. hulk 1874. Sold 12.4.1904 Castle.

HANNIBAL Battleship 14,900 tons, 390 x 75 ft, 4-12in, 12-6in, 18-12pdr. Pembroke Dock 28.4.1896. Sold 28.1.1920 M.Yates;. BU in Italy.

HANNIBAL Three hired vessel from 1652. to 1804.

HAPPY Sloop 14, 114bm. Woolwich DY 19.4.1711. Sold 28.8.1735.

HAPPY Sloop 8, 141bm. 76 x 20½ ft. Woolwich DY 22.7.1754. Wrecked 14.9.1766 off Gt Yarmouth.

HAPPY ENTRANCE 30-gun ship, 404/540bm. Deptford 8.11.1619.

Burnt in the Medway 28.9.1658.

HAPPY ENTRANCE Fireship in 1665. Expanded 1666.

HAPPY LADD Gunboat. Purchased 1855. Sold 8.1856 to the Turkish navy.

HAPPY RETURN (see WINSBY)

HAPPY RETURN Fire vessel, 846bm. Purchased 1695. Expended 1.8.1695 at Dunkirk.

HAPPY RETURN Discovery ship in 1720.

HAPPY RETURN Minesweeper, 'Algerine' class. Lobnitz. Ordered 1943. Cancelled 10.44.

HARDEREEN Flyboat 4, 138bm. Dutch, Captured 1665. Sold 1674.

HARDI Sloop 18. French Privateer Captured 1.4.1797 by HAZARD off the Skelligs, SW Ireland. Sold 1800.

HARDI 6th Rate 20, 425bm, 112 x 30 ft. French Le HARDI, Privateer captured 29.4.1800. Renamed ROSARIO 1800. Sold 1.1809.

HARDINGE Troopship (RIM) 6,520 tons, 423½ x 51 ft, 6-4.7in, 6-3pdr. Fairfield 11.8.1900. Sold circa 1930.

HARDROCK Frigate (RCN), 'River' Class. Montreal. Cancelled 12.1943.

HARDY (Gunboat No.30) Gunvessel 12, 170bm, 76 x 22 ft, 2-24pdr, 10-18pdr carr. Cleverly, Gravesend 10.4.1797. Sold 5.1802.

HARDY Gun-brig 12, 178bm. 80½ x 22½ ft, 2-18pdr, 10-18pdr carr. Roxby, Wearmouth 7.8.1804. Storeship 1818; hospital ship 11.1821. Sold 6.8.1835 Levy, Rochester.

HARDY Mortar vessel, 117bm. 65 x 21 ft, 1-13in mortor. Wigram, Blackwall 14.3.1855. Renamed MV.12 on 19.10.1855. Sold 21.4.1858. at Malta.

HARDY Wood S.Gunboat, 'Albacore' class. Hill, Bristol 1.3.1856. Sold 9.2.1869. at Hong Kong.

HARDY Destroyer 295 ton, 196 x 19 ft, 1-12pdr, 5-6pdr, 2-TT. Doxford 1895. Sold 11.7.1911 Garnham.

HARDY Destroyer 898 tons, 263 x 27 ft, 3-4in, 1-12pdr, 2-TT. Thornycroft 10.10.1912. Sold 9.5.21 Ward, Briton Ferry.

HARDY Destroyer Leader 1,505, tons, 326 x 34 ft, 5-4.7in, 8-TT Cammell Laird 7.4.1936. Beached 10.4.40 after damage at Narvik.

HARDY Destroyer 1,730 tons, 399½ x 36 ft, 4-4.7in, 2-40mm, 8-TT. J.Brown 18.3.1943. Sunk 30.1.44 by 'U.278' in the Barents Sea.

HARDY Frigate 1,180 tons, 300 x 33 ft, 3-40mm, 4-TT. Yarrow 25.11.1953.

Sunk in 7.83 as a target off Gibraltar.

HARE 10-Gun Vessel, 30bm. Dating from 1545. Rebuilt 1558 as 40bm. Sold 1573.

HARE Ketch (Royalist). Captured 1649; deserted to Parliament 1649. Wrecked 1655.

HARE Pink Listed 1653 to 1657.

HARE Fireship 6, 180bm. Captured 1665. Burnt 1666 by accident.

HARE Dogger 6. Dutch, Captured 1672. Sold 1674.

HARE Bomb listed in 1703.

HARE Sloop 10, 55bm, 53½ x 15½ ft. Captured 8.9.1709 by SPEEDWELL Sold 1712.

HARE Minesweeper, 'Algerine' class. Harland & Wolff 20.6.1944. Sold 1959 Nigerian navy as NIGERIA. BU 1962 at Faslane.

HAREBELL Sloop, 'Anchusa' class. Barclay Curle 10.5.1918. Arrived 2.39 at Dalmuir to BU.

HAREBELL Corvette, 'Flower' class. Harland & Wolff. Ordered 8.4.1940. Cancelled 23.1.41.

HARFRUEN 5th Rate 36, 1,030bm, Danish HANFRUE Captured 7.9.1807 at Copenhagen. Sold 29.9.1814. (was to have been renamed BOREAS).

HARGOOD Frigate, TE 'Captain' class. Bethlehem, Hingham 18.12.1943. on lend-lease. Returned 3.46 to the USN.

HARLAND (see CAYMAN)

HARLECH (see CAMBRIAN of 1893)

HARLEQUIN Sloop 16, 141bm, see PORTO

HARLEQUIN Schooner 14, Purchased 1796. Listed 1802.

HARLEQUIN Brig-sloop 18, 'Cruizer' Class, 385bm. Bailey, Ipswich. 15.7.1813. sold 4.9.1829 in Jamaica.

HARLEQUIN Gunboat. Purchased 1815 in the W.Indies. Listed 1816 as tender at Bermuda.

HARLEQUIN Brig-sloop 16, 433bm, 101½ x 32 ft, 14-32pdr, 2-9pdr. Pembroke Dock 18.3.1836. Coal hulk 1860. Sold 8.1889 Marshall, Plymouth.

HARLEQUIN Wood S.sloop, 950bm, 185 x 33 ft. Portsmouth DY. Laid down 13.2.1861, Cancelled 16.12.1864.

HARLEQUIN Ferry. 1908-42.

HARMAN Fireship. Presented 2.1702 by the government of Jamaica. Sunk 26.2.1705 at Port Royal, Jamaica.

HARMAN (see DOMINICA of 1943)
HARP pinnace 8, 20bm. Listed 1546-48.

HARP Ketch 10, 75bm. Dublin 1656. Sold 1671.

HARP KETCH 10, 96bm, 62½ x 19 ft. Frame, Scarborough 24.4.1691. Captured 6.1693 by the French.

HARPENDEN Paddle M/S, 'Ascot' class 820 tons. Ailsa 26.2.1918. Arrived 4.28 Charlestown to BU.

HARPHAM Inshore M/S, 'Ham' class. Jones, Buckie 14.9.1954. To Libyan navy 1962 as BRAK.

HARPY Sloop 18, 367bm, 103 x 28 ft. Fisher, Liverpool 8.5.1777. Fireship 10 guns, 8.1779. Sold 21.3.1783.

HARPY Brig-sloop 18, 316bm, 95 x 28 ft. King, Dover 2.1796. Sold 10.11.1817 Mr Kilsby.

HARPY Brig-sloop 10, 'Cherokee' class, 232bm. Chatham DY 16.7.1825. Sold 27.5.1841 Greenwood & Clarke.

HARPY Iron pad. gunboat, 344bm, 500 tons, 141 x 22½ ft. Ditchburn & Mare, Blackwall 4.3.1845. To War Dept 26.10.1892 as target. Sold circa 1909.

HARPY Destroyer 972 tons, 275 x 28 ft, 1-4in, 3-12pdr, 2-TT. White, 27.11.1909. Sold 1.11.21 Fryer, Sunderland.

HARRIER Brig-sloop 18 (fir-built) 'Cruizer' class, 383bm. Barnard, Deptford 22.8.1804. Foundered 3.1809 in the Indian Ocean.

HARRIER Brig-sloop 18, 'Cruizer' class, 386bm. Bailey, Ipswich 28.7.1813. Sold 8.1.1829 Tibbetts & Co.

HARRIER Sloop 18, 486bm, 114½ x 32 ft. Pembroke Dock 8.11.1831. BU 3.1840 at Portsmouth.

HARRIER Wood S. sloop, 895bm, 180 x 33½ ft. Pembroke Dock. Ordered 26.3.1846, cancelled 4.4.1851.

HARRIER Wood S.sloop, 747bm, 160 x 32 ft, 17-32pdr. Pembroke Dock 13.5.1845. BU completed 12.1866 at Portsmouth.

HARRIER Schooner 2, 190 tons, 92½ x 19 ft. Purchased 15.3.1881. Sold 4.1888 London Missionary Socy, Sydney NSW.

HARRIER Torpedo gunboat 1,070 tons, 250 x 30½ ft, 2-4.7in 4-6pdr, 5-TT. Devonport DY 20.2.1894. Sold 23.2.1920 at Haulbowline.

HARRIER Minesweeper 815 tons, 230 x 33½ ft, 2-4in. Thornycroft 17.4.1934. Sold 6.6.50; BU King, Gatehead.

HARRIOT Storeship 20, 407bm, 107 x 30 ft. Purchased 7.1781. Sold 17.3.1784 at Bombay.

HARROW Minesweeper, later 'Hunt' class. Eltringham 30.7.1918. Sold 1947 J. Dacoutos, Malta. BU at Genoa.

HART Galley, 56, 300bm. Built 1546. Rebuilt 1558. Listed to 1568.

HART 12-gun ship, 120bm. Royalist, captured 1643 by Parliament. Captured 1652 by the Dutch.

HART (or RED HART) Pink 6. Captured 1653. Sold 1654.

HART Pink 8, 55bm. Woolwich DY 1657. Sold 1683.

HART Dogger 8. Captured 1672. Captured 1673 by the Dutch.

HART Ketch 10, 96bm, 62½ x 19 ft. Rolfe & Castle, Rotherhithe 23.3.1691. Captured 5.1692 by two French privateers off St Ives.

HART Cutter. Deptford 1793. Sold 30.10.1817 J. Edgar.

HART Brig-sloop 16, 152bm, 78½ x 21 ft, 16-12pdr carr. French privateer EMPEREUR captured 6.1805 by EAGLE.Sold 1810 in Jamaica.

HART Compos, S.gunvessel, 464bm, 584 tons, 155 x 25 ft, 1-7in, 1-64pdr, 2-20pdr. Thomson, Glasgow 20.8.1868. Sold 12.1888.

HART Destroyer 295 tons, 185 x 19 ft, 1-12pdr, 5-6pdr, 2-TT. Fairfield 27.3.1895. Sold 1912 at Hong Kong.

HART (see RAPID of 1883)

HART Sloop 1,350 tons, 283 x 38 ft, 6.4in, 12-20mm. Stephen 7.7.1943. Sold 1958 W. German navy as SCHEER.

HART Patrol boat Transferred from RAF 29.8.1985

HARTLAND (ex-USS PONTCHARTRAIN) Cutter 1,546 tons, 256(oa) x 42 ft, 1-5in, 2-3in. Transferred 30.4.1941 to the RN on lend-lease. Sunk 8.11.42 by the French TYPHON and shore batteries at Oran.

HARTLAND POINT Repair ship 8,580 tons, 416 x 57 ft. Burrard 4.11.1944. Sold 2.7.74. BU 2.79 at Santander.

HARTLEPOOL (see KATHIAWAR)

HARVESTER M/S sloop, '24' class. Barclay Curle 2.11.1918.Sold 8.22 C.A.Beard.

HARVESTER (see HANDY of 1939)

HARVESTER Drifter requis. 1915-19.

HARVEY (see GOLD COAST)

HARWICH Hoy 5, 52bm. Deane, Harwich 1660. Sold 1680.

HARWICH 3rd Rate 70, 993bm, Deane, Harwich 12.4.1674. Wrecked 3.9.1691 off Plymouth.

HARWICH 4th Rate 48, 683bm, 132 x 34½ ft. Deptford 1695. Wrecked 5.10.1700 at Amoy, China.

HARWICH Storeship, 56bm. Butler, Harwich 10.8.1709. Sold 18.11.1714 W.Chamberlain.

HARWICH (see TIGER of 1742)

HARWICH (see KHYBER)

HASTINGS 5th Rate 32, 384bm, 109 x 28½ ft. Ellis, Shoreham 5.2.1695. Wrecked 1697 off Waterford.

HASTINGS 5th Rate 32, 381bm, 109 x 28 ft. Betts, Woodbridge, 17.5. 1698. Capsized 9.2.1707 off Yarmouth.

HASTINGS 5th Rate 44, 533bm, 118 x 32 ft. Portsmouth DY 2.10.1707. Hulk 2.1739. Sold 27.9.1744; became a privateer.

HASTINGS (ex-ENDYMION renamed 1739) 5th Rate 44, 682bm, 124 x 36 ft. Okill, Liverpool 7.3.1741. BU completed 19.9.1763 at Sheerness.

HASTINGS (ex-Indiaman) 3rd Rate 74, 1,763bm, 177 x 48½ ft. Purchased 22.6.1819 at Calcutta. Undocked Portsmouth 5.2.1855 as screw ship; coal hulk 1870. Sold 9.1885.

HASTINGS 5th Rate 32 (Indian), 566bm. Bombay DY 2.5.1821. BU 1855.

HASTINGS Sloop 1,045 tons, 250 x 34 ft, 2-4in. Devonport DY 10.4.1930.Sold 2.4.46; BU at Troom.

HASTINGS (see OTAGO)

HASTY (Gunboat No 33) Gunvessel 12, 170bm, 76 x 23 ft, 2-2pdr, 10-18pdr carr. Wilson, Frindsbury 6.1797. Sold 12.1802.

HASTY Gun-brig 12, 182bm, 84 x 23 ft, 10-18pdr carr., 2-6pdr. Hill, Sandwich 26.8.1812. Survey vessel 7.1819, made a mud-engine at Mauritius 1.1827 and in service in 1870.

HASTY Wood S.gunboat, 'Albacore' class. Pitcher, Northfleet 10.1.1856. Sold 11.1865 Castle, Charlton.

HASTY Destroyer 290 tons, 190 x 18½ ft, 1-12pdr, 5-6pdr, 2-TT. Yarrow, Poplar 16.6.1894. Sold 9.7.1912 Cox, Falmouth.

HASTY (see LINNET of 1906)

HASTY Destroyer 1,340 tons, 312 x 32 ft, 4-4.7in. 8-TT. Denny 5.5.1936. Sunk 16.6.42 by HMS HOTSPUR afer being torpedoed in the eastern Mediterrean.

HASTY Tug 1867-85.

HATHERLEIGH Destroyer, 'Hunt' class type III. Vickers Armstrong. Tyne 18.12.1941. On loan to Greek navy 7.42 to 12.11.59 as KANARIS. BU 1960 in Greece.

HAUGHTY (Gunboat No.31) Gunvessel 12, 168bm, 76 x 23 ft. Cleveley, Gravesend 4.1797. Sold 5.1802.

HAUGHTY Gun-brig 12, 178bm, 80 x 22½ ft. Dudman, Deptford 7.5.1804. Sold 11.1.1816.

HAUGHTY Wood S.gunboat, 'Albacore' class. Pitcher 9.2.1856. Sold 23.5.1867 at Hong Kong.

HAUGHTY Destroyer 295 tons, 196 x 19 ft, 1-12pdr, 5-6pdr, 2-TT. Doxford 18.9.1895. Sold 10.4.1912.

HAUGHTY (see LARK of 1913)

HAVANNAH 5th Rate 36, 949bm, 145 x 38½ ft. Wilson, Liverpool 26.3.1811. Lent 19.3.1860 as training ship. Sold 1905 to BU.

HAVANT Minesweeper, later 'Hunt' class. Eltringham 24.3.1919. Sold 8.22 Thornycroft for Siamese navy; renamed CHOW PRAYA.

HAVANT (ex-Brazilian JAVARY purchased 4.9.1939) Destroyer 1.340 tons, 312 x 33 ft, 4-4.7in, 8-TT. White 17.7.39. Bombed 1.6.40 off Dunkirk and sunk by HMS SALTASH.

HAVELOCK Paddle gunboat (Indian), 610bm. Bombay DY 1857. Fate unknown.

HAVELOCK (ex-M.2 renamed 20.6.1915, ex-GENERAL GRANT renamed 1.6.15) Monitor 6,1560 tons, 320 x 90 ft, 2-14in, 2-6in, 2-12 pdr. Harland & Wolff 29.4.15. Sold 20.6.27 Ward, Preston (originally sold Ward 9.5.21 but retained).

HAVELOCK (ex-Brazilian JUTAHY purchased 4.9.1939) White 16.10.39. Sold 31.10.46, BU Ward, Inverkeithing.

HAVERSHAM Inshore M/S; 'Ham' class. McLean, Renfrew 3.6.1954. For sale 1982.

HAVICK Sloop 16, 365bm, 102 x 26 ft. Dutch, captured 17.8.1796 at Saldanha Bay. Wrecked 9.11.1800 in St Aubins Bay, Jersey.

HAVOCK Gun-brig, 12, 184bm, 85 x 22½ ft. Stone, Yarmouth 25.7.1805. Light vessel 9.1821; watch vessel 3.1843. BU 7.1859.

HAVOCK Mortar vessel, 120bm, 65 x 21 ft, 1-13in mortar. Mare, Blackwall 14.3.1855. Renamed MV.5 on 19.10.1855. Became Customs watch vessel WV.27. BU 7.1874 at Chatham.

HAVOCK Wood S.gunboat, 'Albacore' class. Hill, Bristol 20.3.1856. Sold 31.3.1870 at Yokohama.

HAVOCK Destroyer 275 tons, 180 x 18½ ft, 1-12pdr, 3-6pdr, 3-TT. Yarrow, Poplar 12.8.1893. Sold 14.5.1912 at Chatham. (The 1st destroyer in the RN.)

HAVOCK (see LINNET of 1913)

HAVOCK Destroyer 1,340 tons, 312 x 32 ft, 4-4.7in, 8-TT. Denny 7.7.1936. Wrecked 6.4.42 near Kelibia, Tunisia.

HAWEA (see LOCH ECK)

HAWKE Discovery vessel, 100bm. Bristol 1593. Fate unknown.

HAWKE Ketch 8, 60bm. Woolwich DY 1655. Sold 1667.

HAWKE Fireship 8, 259bm, 94½ x 25 ft. Fream, Wapping 17.4.1690. Sunk 1712 as a foundation at Plymouth.

HAWKE Sloop 8, 103bm, 62 x 20 ft. Chatham DY 23.11.1721. Foundered 10.1739.

HAWK Sloop 10, 206bm, 85 x 24 ft. Greville, Limehouse 10.3.1741. BU 10.1747 at Deptford.

HAWK Sloop 10, 225bm, 89 x 24 ft. Batson, Limehouse 1.4.1756. Sold 13.8.1781. (In French hands 11.59 to 4.2.61.)

HAWK Sloop 10, 225bm, 89 x 24 ft. Barnard, Harwich 1761. (May be preceding vessel rebuilt.)

HAWK Schooner. In service 1775. Captured 4.4.1776 by Americans.

HAWK Sloop 16, 333bm, 100 x 28 ft. Deptford DY 24.7.1793. BU 5.1803.

HAWK Storeship 4, 68bm, 67 x 15 ft. Ex-hoy purchased 4.1794. Lost 1796.

HAWK Galley. In service 1795. Sold 12.2.1796 Mr Dormer.

HAWK Sloop 18, 320bm, 91 x 28 ft, 18-18pdr, 2-9pdr. French privateer ATALANTE captured 8.1803 by PLANTAGENET. Foundered 12.1804 in the Channel.

HAWK Brig-sloop 16, 311bm, 91 x 28 ft. French LUTIN captured 24.3.1806 by AGAMEMNON and CARYSFORT in the W.Indies. Renamed BUZZARD 8.1.1812. Sold 15.12.1814.

HAWK S.coastguard vessel, 372bm, 416 tons, 146 x 23 ft, 1-40pdr. White, Cowes 14.4.1869. Renamed AMELIA 1888. (see AMELIA)

HAWK (ex-OBERON renamed 5.5.1888, ex-*Lady Aline* purchased 1.88) Coastguard vessel 520 tons, 157 x 24 ft, 2-7pdr. Renamed UNDINE 1904. Sold 3.4.06 at Chatham.

HAWK (see SOMERLEYTON)

HAWK 3 cutters hired between 1782. & 1805. Trawler 1914-17.

HAWKE 3rd Rate 74, 1,754bm, 176 x 48½ ft. Woolwich DY 16.3.1820. Completed 5.1855 as screw ship. BU

1865.

HAWKE 1st class cruiser 7,350 tons, 360 x 60 ft, 2-9.2in, 10-6in, 12-6pdr. Chatham DY 11.3.1891. Sunk 15.10.1914 by 'U.9' in the North Sea.

HAWKE Cruiser 8,800 tons, 538 x 64 ft, 9-6in. Portsmouth DY. Suspended 1.1945, cancelled 1946.

HAWKESBURY Frigate (RAN), 'River' class. Morts Dk 24.7.1943. Sold 9.61 to BU; left Sydney 12.9.62 to BU in Japan.

HAWKESBURY Corvette (RCN), modified 'Flower' class. Morton, Quebec 16.11.1943. Sold (1946?), renamed *Campuchea*

HAWKINS Cruiser 9,750 tons, 565 x 58 ft, 7-7.5in, 4-3in, 6-12pdr. Chatham DY 1.10.1917. Sold 26.8.47, BU at Dalmuir.

HAWTHORN Pinnace, 20bm. Listed 1546 to 1548.

HAWTHORN Drifter and trawler in WW.I. Trawler 1935-47.

HAYDON Destroyer, 'Hunt' class type III. Vickers Armstrong, Tyne 2.4.1942. Arrived 18.5.58 Clayton & Davie, Dunston to BU.

HAYLING Storeship hoy 4, 114bm, 61 x 21 ft. Purchased 6.7.1705.

HAYLING Storeship hoy, 126bm. Portsmouth DY 1729. Renamed GOREE 1759, sloop 10-9pdr. BU 1763.

HAYLING Transport hoy 4, 132bm, 67 x 21½ ft. Adams, Bucklers Hard 1.4.1760. Foundered 1782 in the Channel.

HAYLING Trawler 1942-46.

HAZARD Sloop 14, 114bm, 63 x 21 ft. Woolwich 19.4.1711. Wrecked 12.10.1714 off Boston, New England.

HAZARD Sloop 14, 273bm, 93 x 26 ft. Buxton, Rotherhithe 11.12.1744. Sold 7.9.1749. (Was in the hands of the Young Pretender 24.11.45 to 4.46.)

HAZARD Sloop 8, 140bm, 77 x 20½ ft 8-3pdr. Portsmouth DY 3.10.1749. Sold 11.2.1783.

HAZARD PRIZE Sloop 8, 101bm, 62 x 20 ft, 8-4pdr. French privateer captured 10.9.1756. Sold 21.6.1759.

HAZARD Sloop 16, 423bm, 108 x 30 ft. Brindley, Frindsbury 3.3.1794. Sold 30.10.1817 Mr Spratley.

HAZARD Sloop 18, 431bm, 110½ x 31 ft. Portsmouth DY 21.4.1837. BU completed 12.2.1866 by White, Cowes.

HAZARD Torpedo gunboat 1,070 tons, 250 x 30½ ft, 2-4.7in, 4-6pdr, 5-TT. Pembroke Dock 17.2.1894. Sunk

28.1.1918 in collision in the Channel.

HAZARD Minesweeper 835 tons, 230 x 33½ft, 2-4in. Gray, Hartlepool 26.2.1937. Sold 22.4.49; BU Ward, Grays.

HAZARDOUS 4th Rate 54, 875bm, 137 x 38 ft. French HASARD captured 11.1703. Wrecked 11.1706 near Selsey Bill.

HAZLETON Coastal M/S, 'Ton' class. Cook Welton & Gemmell 6.2.1954. To S.African navy 1955 as KAAPSTAD.

HEART OF OAK Fire vessel 54bm. Purchased 1794. Sold in 12.1796

HEARTSEASE 36-gun ship. Captured 1652. Sold 1656.

HEARTSEASE (ex-PANSY renamed 1940) Corvette, 'Flower' class. Harland & Wolff 20.4.40. Lent USN 18.3.42 to 1945 as COURAGE. Sold 22.7.46, renamed *Roskva*.

HEARTY Gun-brig 12, 183bm, 85 x 22 ft, 10-18pdr carr., 2-12pdr. Bailey, Ipswich 12.4.1805. Sold 11.7.1816.

HEARTY Brig-sloop 10, 'Cherokee' class, 228bm. Chatham DY 22.10.1824. Packet brig 1.1827; burnt at sea 9.1827.

HEARTY (ex-*Indra* purchased 1885) Survey ship 1,300 tons, 212 x 30 ft, 4-3pdr. Thomson, Dundee 18.4.1885. Sold 6.11.1920 M.S. Hilton as salvage vessel.

HEARTY (ex-Brazilian JURUENA purchased 9.1939) Destroyer 1,340 tons, 312 x 33 ft, 4-4.7in, 8-TT. Thornycroft 3.8.39. Renamed HESPERUS 27.2.40. Sold 26.11.46, BU at Grangemouth.

HEARTY Tug 1855-76. Drifter requis, 1915-19.

HEATHER Sloop, 'Aubrietia' class. Greenock & Grangemouth 16.6.1916. Sold 16.2.32 Midland Iron & Hardware Co, Plymouth. (Served as decoy ship 'Q.16' to 1918).

HEATHER Corvette, 'Flower' class. Harland & Wolff 17.9.1940. Sold 22.5.47; BU Ward, Grays.

HEATHER Drifter and trawler requis. WW.I.

HEBE 5th Rate 38, 1,063bm, 150 x 40 ft. French, captured 9.1782 by RAINBOW off Ile Bas. Renamed BLONDE 24.12.1805. BU 6.1811.

HEBE 5th Rate 32 (fir-built), 658bm, 127 x 34 ft. Deptford DY 31.12.1804. Sold 28.4.1813.

HEBE 5th Rate 46, 1,078bm, 152 x 40 ft, 16-32pdr carr., 28-18pdr, 2-9pdr. Woolwich DY 14.12.1826. Receiving ship 1839, hulk 1861 BU completed 31.3.1873 at Chatham.

HEBE Torpedo gunboat 810 tons, 230 x 27 ft, 2-4.7in, 4-3pdr, 3-TT. Sheerness DY 15.6.1892. M/S 1909; depot ship 1910. Sold 22.10.19 Ward, Preston.

HEBE Minesweeper 835 tons, 230 x 33½ ft, 2-4in. Devonport DY 28.10.1936. Sunk 22.11.43 by mine off Bari.

HEBE Store carrier 1960 tons. 1962-

HEBRUS 5th Rate 36 (Yellow pine-built), 939bm, 143 x 38 ft, 14-32pdr carr., 28-12pdr, 2-9pdr, Barton, Limehouse 13.9.1813. Sold 3.4.1817 J. Cristall.

HECATE (Gunboat No.32) Gunvessel 12, 168bm, 76 x 22½ ft. Wilson, Frindsbury 2.5.1797. Sunk 1809 as breakwater at Harwich.

HECATE Brig-sloop 18, 'Cruizer' class, 385bm. King, Upnor 30.5.1809. Sold 30.10.1817 Mr Parker. (Resold Chilian navy?)

HECATE Wood pad. sloop, 817bm, 165 x 33 ft, 1-10in, 1-110pdr, 4-32pdr. Chatham DY 30.3.1839. Sold 1865, Castle to BU.

HECATE Iron S.turret ship 3,480 tons, 225 x 45 ft, 4-10in MLR. Dudgeon, Poplar 30.9.1871. Sold 12.5.1903.

HECATE Survey ship 2,800 tons, 235 x 49 ft. Blythswood 31.3.1965.

HECATE A-yacht. requis. 1914-19.

HECLA (ex-*Scipio*) Bomb 10, 300bm, 93 x 28 ft. Purchased 4.1797. BU 7.1813.

HECLA Bomb 10, 375bm, 105 x 29 ft, 10-24pdr carr., 2-6pdr, 1-13in mortar, 1-10in mortar. Barkworth & Hawkes, North Barton 22.7.1815. Arctic discovery 1819-27. Sold 13.4.1831.

HECLA Wood pad. sloop, 817bm, 165 x 33 ft, 2-84pdr, 4-32pdr. Chatham DY 14.1.1839. Sold 15.6.1863. Williams & Co.

HECLA (ex-*British Crown* purchased 1878) Depot ship 6,400 tons, 391½ x 39 ft, 5-64pdr, 1-40pdr. Harland & Wolff 7.3.1878. Rebuilt 1912 as 5,600 tons, 4-4in. Sold 13.7.26 Ward, Preston.

HECLA Depot ship 10,850 tons, 585 x 66 ft, 8-4.5in. J.Brown 14.3.1940. Sunk 12.11.42 by 'U.515' west of Gibraltar.

HECLA Repair ship 14,250 tons, 415 x 57 ft, 1-5in, 10-40mm. Bethlehem Fairfield 31.7.1944 for the RN but retained by the USN as XANTHUS.

HECLA Survey ship 2,800 tons, 235 x

49 ft. Blythswood 21.12.1964.

HECLA Trawler & two Drifters requis. WW.I.

HECTOR 22-gun ship, 200/266bm. Captured 1643. Sold 1656.

HECTOR 30-gun ship, 150bm. Captured 1653. Sold 1657.

HECTOR 22-gun ship, 111bm. Royalist? THREE KINGS captured 1657. Sunk 1665 in action with the Dutch.

HECTOR 5th Rate 44, 493bm, 116½ x 31 ft. Burchett, Rotherhithe 20.2.1703. Rebuilt Plymouth 1721 as 607bm. BU 1742.

HECTOR 5th Rate 44, 720bm, 126 x 36½ ft. Blaydes, Hull 24.10.1743. Sold 9.12.1762.

HECTOR Cutter. Purchased 2.1763. Sold 4.5.1773.

HECTOR 3rd Rate 74, 1,622bm, 169 x 47 ft. Adams, Deptford 27.5.1774. Prison ship circa 1808. BU 2.1816.

HECTOR 3rd Rate 74. French, captured 12.4.1782. Recaptured 5.9.1782 by the French.

HECTOR Iron S.ship, 4,089bm, 6,710 tons, 280 x 56½ ft, 2-8in, 16-7in. Napier 26.9.1862. Sold 11.7.1905 to BU.

HECTOR Balloon ship WW.I. AMC and Tug WW.II.

HEDINGHAM CASTLE (see ORANGEVILLE)

HEDINGHAM CASTLE (ex-GOREY CASTLE renamed 1943) Corvette, 'Castle' class. Crown, Sunderland 30.10.44. Arrived 4.58 at Granton to BU.

HEIR APPARENT 3rd Rate 74. Danish ARVEPRINDS FREDERICK Captured 7.9.1807 at Copenhagen. Sold 3.4.1817 Freake to BU. (Listed as ARVE PRINCEN from 1813; was to have been renamed CORNWALL.)

HELDER (see ALARM of 1799)

HELDER (see GUELDERLAND of 1808)

HELDERENBERG 5th Rate 30, 242bm. Dutch, captured from the Duke of Monmouth 1685. Sunk 17.11.1688 in collision off the Isle of Wight.

HELDIN 6th Rate 28, 636bm, 122 x 34 ft, 24-12pdr, 4-6pdr. Dutch, captured 28.8.1799 in the Texel. Sold 1802.

HELENA Sloop 14, 220bm, 76 x 26½ ft, 14-4pdr. Built 1778. Foundered 3.11.1796 off the Dutch coast. (In French hands 9.78 to 22.6.79.)

HELENA (see ATALANTA of 1775)

HELENA Sloop 18, 370bm, 106 x 28 ft. Preston, Yarmouth 26.4.1804. Sold 21.7.1814.

HELENA Brig-Sloop 10, 'Cherokee'

class, 231bm. Plymouth DY. Ordered 26.10.1826, cancelled 21.2.1831.

HELENA Brig-sloop 16, 549bm, 110 x 35 ft, 16-32pdr. Pembroke Dock 11.7.1843. Coal hulk 1861; Police hulk 11.1863; Church ship 12.1868; Police hulk 1883. Sold 6.1.1921 Garnham to BU.

HELENA Drifter. requis. 1915-19.

HELFORD Frigate, 'River' class. Hall Russell 6.2.1943. Arrived 29.6.56 at Troon to BU.

HELFORD Minehunter 890 tons. Richards 17.5.1984.

HELICON Brig-Sloop 10, 'Cherokee' class, 238bm. King, Upnor 5.8.1808. BU 7.1829 at Sheerness.

HELICON Wood pad. despatch vessel, 837bm, 1,000 tons, 220 x 28 ft. Portsmouth DY 31.1.1865. Renamed ENCHANTRESS 1.4.1888. Sold 11.7.1905 Laidler, Sunderland.

HELICON (see CALLIOPE of 1884)

HELIOTROPE Sloop, 'Acacia' class. Lobnitz 10.9.1915. Sold 7.1.35 Metal Industries, BU at Charlestown.

HELIOTROPE Corvette, 'Flower' class. Crown 5.6.1940. Lent USN 3.42 to 1945 as SURPRISE. Sold 18.7.46, renamed *Heliolock*.

HELMSDALE (see HUNTLEY)

HELMSDALE Frigate, 'River' class. Inglis 5.6.1943. Arrived 7.11.57 at Faslane to BU.

HELMSDALE Minehunter 757 tons. Richards 11.1.1985.

HELMSLEY CASTLE Corvette, 'Castle' class. Morton, Cancelled 12.1943.

HELVERSON 60-gun ship, 597bm. Dutch HILVERSUM captured 1665. Sunk 7.1667 as blockship in the Medway.

HEMLOCK Corvette, 'Flower' class. Harland & Wolff. Ordered 8.4.1940, cancelled 23.1.41.

HENRIETTA Pinnace 6, 68bm. Chatham 1626. Sold 1661.

HENRIETTA (see LANGPORT)

HENRIETTA Yacht 8, 104bm. Woolwich DY 1663. Sunk 11.8.1673 in action with the Dutch.

HENRIETTA Yacht 8, 153bm. Woolwich DY 1679. Sold 1721.

HENRIETTA MARIA 42-gun ship, 594/792bm. Deptford DY 1.1633. Renamed PARAGON 1650. Burnt at sea 13.7.1655.

HENRY GALLEY Galley, 80bm. Built 1512. Lost at sea 1513.

HENRY GRACE a DIEU Galleon 80, 1,500bm. Woolwich (Erith?) 18.6.1514. Rebuilt Portsmouth 1539 as 1,000bm; renamed EDWARD 1547. Burnt 27.8.1553 by accident.

HENRY OF HAMPTON Ship, 120bm. Purchased 1513. Hulked 1521.

HENRY (see DUNBAR)

HENRY PRIZE 6th Rate 24, 246bm, 86 x 25½ ft. French, captured 1690. Sold 1698.

HENRY Sloop 16. Purchased 1804. Listed 1805, not 1806.

HENRYVILLE Frigate (RCN), 'River' class. G.T.Davie, Lauzon. Cancelled 12.1943.

HEPATICA Corvette, 'Flower' class. Davie SB 6.7.1940. Lent RCN to 27.6.45. Arrived 1.1.48 Rees, Llanelly to BU.

HERALD 6th Rate 20, 422bm, 109 x 30 ft, 8-18pdr carr., 16-6pdr. Carver, Littlehampton 27.12.1806. BU 9.1817.

HERALD (see TERMAGANT of 1822)

HERALD Paddle river gunboat 82 tons, 90 x 18 ft, 4-3pdr. Yarrow, Poplar 1890. Sold 19.2.1903.

HERALD (see MERRY HAMPTON)

HERALD survey vessel 2,000 tons. Robb-Caledon 4.10.1973.

HERCULES 3rd Rate 74, 1,608bm, 166½ x 47 ft. Deptford DY 15.3.1759. Sold 17.8.1784.

L'HERCULE 3rd Rate 74, 1,876bm, 181 x 48½ ft. French, captured 21.4.1798 by MARS off Bec du Raz. BU 12.1810 at Portsmouth.

HERCULES 3rd Rate 74, 1,750bm, 176 x 48½ ft. Chatham DY 5.9.1815. Harbour service 1853. Sold 22.8.1865 at Hong Kong.

HERCULES Iron battleship, 5,234bm, 8,700 tons, 325 x 59 ft, 8-10in, 2-9in, 4-7in MLR. Chatham DY 10.2.1868. Coastguard and harbour service from 1881; barracks 1905; renamed CALCUTTA 1909. FISGARD II 4.15. Sold 7.32 Ward, Morecambe; hulk to Preston 1.12.32.

HERCULES Battleship 20,000 tons, 510 x 85 ft, 10-12in, 12-4in. Palmer 10.5.1910. Sold 8.11.21 Slough T.Co; BU in Germany 1922.

HERCULES A/C carrier 14,000 tons, 630 x 80 ft, 30-40mm, 34-A/C. Vickers Armstrong, Tyne 22.9.1945. Renamed VIKRANT (Indian navy) 4.3.61.

HERCULES Three hired vessels between 1588 & 1649. 3 trawlers WW.I., trawler WW.II.

HEREWARD (see LAVEROCK)

HEREWARD Destroyer 1,340 tons, 312 x 32 ft, 4-4.7in, 8-TT. Vickers Armstrong, Tyne 10.3.1936. Torpedoed 29.5.41 by Italian aircraft off Crete.

HERMES Brig-sloop 12, 210bm, 80 x 27 ft. Dutch MERCURIUS captured 12.5.1796 by SYLPH in the Texel. Foundered 1.1797.

HERMES A.ship 22, 331bm, 100 x 28 ft. Purchased 1798. Sold 6.1802.

HERMES (ex-*Majestic*) Sloop 16, 339bm, 107 x 27 ft, 14-24pdr, 2-6pdr. Purchased 7.1803. Sold 24.3.1810.

HERMES 6th Rate 20, 511bm, 120 x 31 ft, 18-32pdr carr., 2-9pdr. Portsmouth DY 22.7.1811. Grounded and burnt 15.9.1814 at Mobile, Mississippi.

HERMES (see COURIER of 1830)

HERMES Wood pad. sloop, 716bm, 150 x 33 ft. Portsmouth DY 26.6.1835. Rebuilt Chatham 1842 as 830bm. BU 1864.

HERMES (see MINOTAUR of 1816)

HERMES 2nd class cruiser 5,600 tons, 350 x 54 ft, 11-6in, 9-12pdr. Fairfield 7.4.1898. Fitted to carry seaplane in 1913. Sunk 31.10.14 by 'U.27' in the Dover Straits.

HERMES A/C carrier 10,950 tons, 548 x 70 ft, 10-6in, 4-4in, 20-A/C. Armstrong 11.9.1919. Sunk 9.4.42 by Japanese aircraft off Ceylon.

HERMES A/C Carrier 18,300 tons, 650 x 90 ft, 32-40mm, 45-A/C. Cammell Laird. Cancelled 10.1945.

HERMES (ex-ELEPHANT renamed 5.11.1945) A/C carrier 22,500 tons, 650 x 90 ft, 17-40mm, 20-A/C. Vickers Armstrong, Barrow 16.2.53. Sold India 11.86 and renamed VIRAAT.

HERMIONE 5th Rate 32, 716bm, 129 x 35 ft. Teast & Tombs, Bristol 9.9.1782. Handed over to the Spanish in the W.Indies 22.9.1797 by her mutinous crew. Recaptured 25.10.1799 and renamed RETALIATION: renamed RETRIBUTION 31.1.1800. BU 6.1805 at Deptford.

HERMIONE 2nd class cruiser 4,360 tons, 320 x 49½ ft, 2-6in, 8-4in, 8-6pdr. Devonport DY 7.11.1893. Sold 25.10.21 Multilocular S.Bkg Co. Resold 18.12.22; renamed *Warspite* training ship. Sold 9.40 Ward, Grays

HERMIONE Cruiser 5,450 tons, 485 x 50½ ft, 10-5.25in, Stephen 18.5.1939. Sunk 6.6.42 by 'U.205' in the eastern Mediterranean.

HERMIONE Frigate, 'Leander' class. Stephen 26.4.1967.

HERNE BAY (ex-LOCH EIL renamed 1944) Frigate, 'Bay' class. Smiths Dk 15.5.1945. Renamed DAMPIER, survey ship 9.46. Sold 13.9.68, BU in Belgium

HERO 3rd Rate 74, 1,574bm, 166 x 47 ft. Plymouth DY 28.3.1759. Prison ship 1793. Renamed ROCHESTER 15.8.1800. BU 7.1810 at Chatham.

HERO 3rd Rate 74, 1,730bm, 176 x 48 ft. Perry, Blackwall 18.8.1803. Wrecked 25.12.1811 in the Texel.

HERO 3rd Rate 74, 1,756bm, 176½ x 48½ ft. Deptford DY 21.9.1816. Renamed WELLINGTON 4.12.1816. Training ship AKBAR 10.5.1862. Sold 1908, Ward; arrived Morecombe 8.4.08 to BU.

HERO Screw 2nd Rate 91, 3,148bm, 234½ x 55½ ft, 1-110pdr, 34-8in, 4-7pdr, 10-40pdr, 30-32pdr (in 1862). Chatham DY 15.4.1858. Sold 20.6.1871 Castle, Charlton.

HERO Turret ship 6,200 tons, 270 x 58 ft, 2-12in, 4-6in, 7-6pdr. Chatham DY 27.10.1885. Target 11.1907 and sunk as such 18.2.08; raised and BU.

HERO Destroyer 1,340 tons, 312 x 32 ft, 4-4.7in, 8-TT. Vickers Armstrong Tyne 10.3.1936. Renamed CHAUDIERE (RCN) 15.11.43. Sold 1946.

HERO Two cutters hired 1805. 2 Trawlers & Drifter WW.1.

HEROINE 5th Rate 32, 779bm, 131 x 37 ft. Adams, Bucklers Hard 8.1783. Floating battery 1803. Sold 2.1806.

HEROINE (see VENUS of 1758).

HEROINE Packet brig 8, 359bm, 95 x 30½ ft, 8-18pdr. Woolwich DY 16.8.1841. Harbour service 1865. BU 12.1878 at Devonport.

HEROINE Compos. S. corvette 1,420 tons, 200 x 38 ft, 8-6in. Devonport DY 3.12.1881. Sold 28.8.1902. King, Bristol to BU.

HEROINE Tug requis. 1917-19. Trawler 1940-44.

HERON (ex-*Jason*) Sloop 16, 340bm. Purchased 6.1804. Renamed VOLCANO, bomb 1810. Sold 28.8.1816.

HERON (ex-RATTLESNAKE renamed 1812) Brig-sloop 18, (Cruizer class), 387bm. King, Upnor 22.10.1812. BU 3.1831.

HERON Brig 16, 482bm, 105 x 33½ ft, 4-32pdr, 12-32pdr carr. Chatham DY 27.9.1847. Foundered 9.5.1859 off W.Africa.

HERON Wood S. gunboat, 'Albacore' class Miller, Liverpool 5.7.1860. BU 1881 in Jamaica.

HERON River gunboat 85 tons, 100 x 20 ft, 2-6pdr. Yarrow 1897. Transferred govt of Nigeria 1.1899.

HERON (see EMPRESS of 1906).

HERON (see AUCKLAND).

HERON Trawler requis 1914-19.

HERRING Schooner 4, 78bm, 56 x 18 ft, 4-12pdr carr. Bermuda 1804. Foundered 1814 in N. America.

HERRING Wood S. gunboat, 'Albacore' class. Pitcher, Northfleet 10.1.1856. BU 8.1865 at Sheerness.

HERRING Trawler 1942-43.

HESPELER (see LYSANDER).

HESPELER (ex-GUILDFORD CASTLE renamed 1943) Corvette (RCN), 'Castle class. Robb 13.11.1943. Sold 1946, renamed *Chilcotin*.

HESPER Sloop 18, 424bm, 110 x 29½ ft. Tanner, Dartmouth 3.7.1809. Sold 8.7.1817.

HESPER (ex-*Hesperus*) Iron S. store-ship, 808bm. Transferred from Treasury Dept 24.5.1855. Sold 10.1868.

HESPER Tank vessel 1901-23.

HESPERUS (see HEARTY of 1939).

HESTOR Fireship 6, 101bm. Purchased 1673. Burnt 1673.

HESTOR Cutter listed 1763-67.

HEUREUX 6th Rate 22, 598bm, 127½ x 33 ft, 22-12pdr. French privateer captured 19.10.1799 by STAG in the Channel. Foundered 1806 in the Atlantic.

HEUREUX Sloop 16, 337bm. French LYNX captured 21.1.1807 by GALATEA off Caracas. Sold 1.9.1814.

HEVER CASTLE (see COPPERCLIFFE)

HEXHAM Transport 6. Purchased 1798. Listed 1801.

HEXHAM Paddle M/S, 'Ascot' class 820 tons. Clyde SB 15.12.1917. Sold 24.9.23 Hayes, Pembroke Dock.

HEXTON Coastal M/S, 'Ton' class. Cook, Welton & Gemmell 1954. Renamed LEDANG 10.63, Malaysian navy.

HEYTHROP Minesweeper, early 'Hunt' class. Fleming & Ferguson 4.6.1917. Sold 7.22 Stanlee, Dover.

HEYTHROP Destroyer, 'Hunt' class type II. Swan Hunter 30.10.1940. Sunk 20.3.42 by ERIDGE after being torpedoed by 'U.652' north of Sollum.

HIBERNIA (see PRINCE OF WALES of 1765)

HIBERNIA 1st Rate 110, 2,530bm, 203 x 54 ft. Plymouth DY 17.11.1804 (12 years on stocks). Base flagship at Malta 1855. Sold 14.10.1902.

HIBERNIA (see ACHILLES of 1863)

HIBERNIA Battleship 16,350 tons, 425 x 78 ft, 4-12in, 4-9.2in, 10-6in,

14-12pdr. Devonport DY 17.6.1905. Sold 8.11.21 Stanlee; resold and BU in Germany.

HIBERNIA Tug and Trawler requis. 1914-19.

HIBISCUS Sloop, 'Anchusa' class. Greenock & Grangemouth 17.11.1917. Sold 18.1.23 Metal Industries, Charlestown.

HIBISCUS Corvette, 'Flower' class. Harland & Wolff 6.4.1940. Lent USN 2.5.42 to 45 as SPRY. Sold 1946, renamed *Madonna*.

HICKLETON Coastal M/S, 'Ton' class. Thornycroft 26.1.1955. Sold 1967 Argentine navy, renamed NEUQUEN.

HIGHBURTON Coastal M/S, 'Ton' class. Thornycroft 2.6.1954. BU Middlesbrough 7.78.

HIGHFLYER Schooner 8, 144bm, 80 x 20 ft. American privateer captured 9.1.1813 by POICTIERS. Recaptured 8.9.1813 by the American PRESIDENT off Nantucket.

HIGHFLYER Tender 2, 81bm, 56 x 19 ft, 2-6pdr. Woolwich DY 11.6.1822. Sold 7.8.1833 Ledger, Rotherhithe.

HIGHFLYER Wood S.frigate, 1,153bm, 192 x 36½ ft, 1-10in, 20-8in Mare, Blackwall 13.8.1851. BU 5.1871 at Portsmouth.

HIGHFLYER 2nd class cruiser 5,600 tons, 350 x 54 ft, 11-6in, 9-12pdr. Fairfield 4.6.1898. Sold 10.6.1921 at Bombay.

HIGHLANDER Wood S.gunboat, 'Albacore' class. Hill, Bristol 4.1856. Renamed YC.51, dredger 1868. Sold 5.1884.

HIGHLANDER (ex-Brazilian JAGUARIBE purchased 4.9.1939) Destroyer 1,340 tons, 312 x 34 ft, 4-4.7in, 8-TT. Thornycroft 17.10.39. Sold 27.5.46; arrived 8.47 Rosyth to BU.

HIGHLANDER Trawler 1915-21.

HIGHWAY (ex-CLAYMORE renamed 8.1943) Dock landing ship 4,270 tons, 454 x 72 ft, 1-3in, 16-20mm. Newport News 19.7.43 on lendlease. Returned 4.46 to the USN.

HILDERSHAM Inshore M/S, 'Ham' class. Vosper, Gosport 5.2.1954. To Indian navy as BIMLIPATAN 1955.

HIMALAYA Iron S. troopship, 3, 553bm, 4,690 tons, 340 x 46ft. Mare Blackwall 24.5.1853 and purchased 7.1854. Renamed C.60 coal hulk 12.1895; sold 28.9.20 E.W. Payne. Sunk 1940 by air attack at Portland.

HIMALAYA AMC 6929 tons. Requis, 1914-22.

HINCHINBROOK Sloop 10, 271bm,

91½ x 26 ft. Janvrin, Bursledon 8.3.1744. Captured 10.11.1746 by the French.

HINCHINBROOK Sloop 12 in 1778. Captured 4.1778 by the Americans.

HINCHINBROOK Brig 14. American TARTAR captured 1777. Slop ship in 1782. Sold 21.3.1783.

HINCHINBROOK 6th Rate 28, 557bm, 115 x 33 ft. French ASTREE captured 1779. Foundered 19.1.1782 off Jamaica.

HIND 28-gun vessel, 80bm. Built 1545. Sold 1555.

HIND 18-gun ship, 140/200bm. Purchased 1643. Listed to 1651. (In Royalist hands 1648-9.)

HIND Ketch 8, 54bm. Page, Wivenhoe 1655. Wrecked 11.12.1668.

HIND Dogger 6. Dutch, captured 1672. Recaptured 1674 by the Dutch.

HIND Ketch 10,96bm. Snelgrove, Wapping 2.4.1691. Captured 7.1.1697 by the French in the North Sea.

HIND 6th Rate 12, 161bm, 78½ x 22½ ft. Purchased 8.6.1709. Stranded 16.9.1709 near Hurst castle. (was a French privateer)

HIND 6th Rate 16, 190bm, 78 x 23½ ft. Captured 21.9.1709 by MEDWAY. Bilged on her anchor 29.11.1711 in Dublin harbour and sank.

HIND 6th Rate 20, 282bm, 94 x 26 ft. Woolwich DY 31.10.1711. Wrecked 7.12.1721 on the Channel Islands.

HIND Sloop in 1741. Sold 6.10.1743.

HIND Sloop 14, 273bm, 91½ x 26 ft. Perry, Blakwall 19.4.1744. Foundered 1.9.1747 in N.America.

HIND 6th Rate 24, 510bm, 113 x 32½ ft. Chitty & Vernon Chichester 29.11.1749. Storeship 7.1783. Sold 8.1.1784.

HIND 6th Rate 28, 592bm, 121 x 35 ft. Clayton & Wilson, Sandgate 22.7.1785. BU 7.1811 at Deptford.

HIND Tender 10, ex-Revenue cutter, 161bm, 72 x 24 ft, 10-6pdr. Cowes 1790. Sold 22.2.1844 E.Smith.

HIND (ex-BARBADOES renamed 1813) 6th Rate 20, 460bm, 115½ x 30 ft. Davy, Topsham 8.3.1814. Sold 6.4.1829 at Bombay.

HIND Wood S.gunboat, 'Dapper' class. Thomson, Millwall 3.5.1855. BU 10.1872. at Devonport.

HIND Coastguard yawl, 131bm, 70 x 21 ft. White, Cowes 25.3.1880. Wrecked 27.11.1900 on the Shipwash.

HIND Destroyer 770 tons, 240 x 25½ ft, 2-4in, 2-12pdr, 2.TT.J. Brown 28.7.1911. Sold 9.5.21 Ward; BU

Preston 1924.

HIND Sloop 1,350 tons, 283 x 38 ft, 6-4in. Denny 30.9.1943. Arrived 10.12.58 Clayton & Davie, Dunston to BU.

HINDOSTAN (ex-E.Indiaman *Born*) 4th Rate 54 1,249bm, 160 x 42 ft. Purchased 1795. Storeship 1802. Burnt 2.4.1804 by accident in Rosas Bay, San Sebastian.

HINDOSTAN (ex-E.Indiaman *Admiral Rainer*) 4th Rate 50, 887bm, 158½ x 37 ft. Purchased 5.1804. Storeship 20 guns 1811; renamed DOLPHIN 22.9.1819; JUSTITIA 1830, convict ship. Sold 24.10.1855.

HINDOSTAN 2nd Rate 80, 2,029bm, 3,242 tons, 186 x 51 ft. Plymouth DY 2.8.1841. Training ship 1868. Renamed FISGARD III on 12.10.1905. HINDOSTAN 8.20. Sold 10.5.21 Garnham.

HINDUSTAN Battleship 16,350 tons, 425 x 78 ft, 4-12in, 4-9.2in, 10-6in. J.Brown 19.12.1903. Sold 9.5.21 Ward; laid up at Belfast arrived Preston 14.10.33 to BU.

HINDUSTAN Sloop (RIN) 1,190 tons, 280 x 35 ft, 2-4in. Swan Hunter 12.5.1930. Renamed KARSAZ (RPN) 1948. BU 1951.

HINKSFORD Seaward defence boat, 'Ford class Richards, Lowestoft 17.3.1955. To Nigerian navy 9.9.66 as BENIN.

HIPPOMENES Sloop 18, 407bm, 96 x 30 ft, 16-32pdr carr., 2-9pdr. Dutch, captured 20.9.1803 at Demerara. Sold 28.4.1813.

HIRA Gunboat (RIN) 331 tons, 170 X 22 ft, 2-3in. Iranian, captured 1941 by RIN forces. Returned Iran 1946.

HIRONDELLE Gun-brig 14, 210bm. French cutter captured 28.4.1804 by BITTERN in the Mediterranean. Wrecked 3.1808 near Tunis.

HIRONDELLE Store carrier WW.I. Store carrier WW.II.

HOBART Sloop 18, circa 400bm. French privateer La REVANCHE captured 21.10.1794 by RESISTANCE off Sunda. Sold 1803.

HOBART (see APOLLO of 1934)

HOBART GM destroyer (RAN) 3,370 tons, 420 x 47 ft, 2-5in, 1-GWS, 6-TT. Defoe SB, Bay City, USA 9.1.1964.

HOBART Trawler requis. 1915-19.

HODGESTON Coastal M/S 'Ton' class. Fleetlands SY 6.4.1954. Renamed NORTHUMBRIA 1955; VENTURER 1961-75.

HOGUE 3rd Rate 74, 1,750bm, 176 x

48½ ft. Deptford DY 3.10.1811. Completed as screw ship 1848, 1,846bm. BU 1965 at Devonport.

HOGUE Armoured cruiser 12,000 tons, 440 x 69½ ft, 2-9.2in, 12-6in. Vickers 13.8.1900. Sunk 22.9.14 by 'U.9' in the North Sea.

HOGUE Destroyer 2,315 tons, 355 x 40 ft, 4-4.5in, 1-4in, 12-40mm, 8-TT. Cammell Laird 21.4.1944. Sold 7.3.62 at Singapore to BU.

HOLCOMBE Destroyer, 'Hunt' class type III. Stephen 14.4.1942. Sunk 12.12.43 by 'U.593' off Bougie.

HOLDERNESSE Cutter 10. Origin unknown. Captured 1779 by the Spanish in the Channel.

HOLDERNESS Minesweeper, early 'Hunt' class. Henderson 9.11.1916. Sold 8.24 to BU. by Cashmore, Newport.

HOLDERNESS Destroyer, 'Hunt' class type I. Swan Hunter 8.2.1940. Arrived 20.11.56. Ward, Preston to BU.

HOLIGOST A 'King's ship' built 1300 at Sandwich.

HOLIGHOST Ship listed in 1400-1406

HOLIGOST 6-gun vessel. Spanish SANTA CLARA Captured 1413. Listed to 1452

HOLIGOST SPAYNE Ship captured from the Spanish 1.8.1419. Sold 15.6.1423.

HOLLESLEY BAY (ex-LOCH FANNICH renamed 1944) Frigate, 'Bay' class. Smiths Dk. Cancelled 1945.

HOLLY Schooner 10, 150bm, 79 x 22 ft. Bermuda 1809. Wrecked 29.1.1814 near San Sebastian.

HOLLY 3 Drifters WW.I. Trawler 1935-47

HOLLYHOCK Sloop, 'Acacia' class. Barclay Curle 1.5.1915. Sold 7.10.30 Ward, Pembroke Dock.

HOLLYHOCK Corvette, 'Flower' class. Crown 19.8.1940. Sunk 9.4.42 by Japanese A/C, east of Ceylon.

HOLMES 5th Rate 24, 220bm. Purchased 1671. Fireship 1677. Sold 1682.

HOLMES (see TOBAGO of 1943)

HOLMES Frigate, TE 'Captain' class. Bethlehem, Hingham 19.12.1943 on lend-lease. Returned 12.45 to the USN.

HOLM SOUND (ex-*Empire Labuan*) Repair ship 10,000 tons, 431 x 56 ft, 12-20mm. Gray, Hartlepool 5.9.1944. Sold 4.48, renamed Avisbay.

HOLSTEIN 3rd Rate 64, 1,395bm, 161 x 44½ ft, 24-24pdr, 38-24pdr carr., 2-12pdr. Danish, captured 2.4.1801 at Copenhagen. Renamed NASSAU 1805. Sold 3.11.1814.

HONESTY (ex-USS CAPRICE) Corvette, modified 'Flower' class. Kingston, Ont.28.9.1942 and to the RN 28.5.43 on lend-lease. Returned 5.1.46 to the USN. Sold 1946 as whaler.

HONEYSUCKLE Sloop, 'Acacia' class. Lobnitz 29.4.1915. Sold 6.9.22 Distin to BU.

HONEYSUCKLE Corvette, 'Flower' class. Ferguson 22.4.1940. BU. 11.50 Ward, Grays.

HONEYSUCKLE Stores drifter 1915-19.

HONG KONG Paddle tender. Purchased 1856. Sold circa 1858.

HONG KONG (see HOLMES).

HOOD (ex-EDGAR renamed 29.6.1848) Screw 2nd Rate 91, 3,308bm, 198 x 56 ft. Chatham DY 4.5.1859. Harbour service 1872. Sold 1888. (see EDGAR)

HOOD Battleship 14,150 tons, 380 x 75 ft, 4-13.5in, 10-6in, 10-6pdr. Chatham DY 30.7.1891. Sunk 4.11.14 as blockship, Portland harbour.

HOOD Battlecruiser 41,200 tons, 810 x 104 ft, 8-15in, 12-5in, 4-4in. J. Brown 22.8.1918. Sunk 24.5.41 in action with German BISMARCK south of Greenland.

HOPE Galleon 48, 403/500bm, 2-60pdr, 4-34pdr, 19pdr, 11-9pdr, 4-6pdr, 18 small. Deptford 1559. Rebuilt and renamed ASSURANCE 1604, 38 guns, 600bm. BU 1645.

HOPE Ship. French privateer ESPERANCE captured 1626. 'Released' 1630.

HOPE Storeship 26. Purchased 1652. Sold 1657.

HOPE 44-gun ship, 480bm. Dutch HOOP captured 1665. Wrecked 1666.

HOPE Hoy storeship 4, 46bm. Dutch, captured 1666. Recaptured 1672 by the Dutch.

HOPE PRIZE Fireship 2, 91bm. Dutch, captured 1672. Sold 1674.

HOPE 3rd Rate 70, 1,052bm, 152 x 40½ ft. Deptford DY 1678. Captured 16.4.1695 by the French off the Lizard.

HOPE Sloop 14. Listed from 1764. Captured 1779 by an American privateer.

HOPE Schooner. Purchased 3.1765. Condemned 14.1776 in N. America.

HOPE (ex-Amercan *Lady Washington*) Cutter 12, 156bm, 68 x 24½ ft, 12-4pdr. Purchased 4.1780. Sold 9.6.1785. (Was in French hands 16.8.81. to 21.8.81.)

HOPE Brig-sloop 14, 232bm, 91½ x 26½ ft. Purchased 1780. Wrecked 1781 off Savannah.

HOPE Gunvessel 3, 68bm, 57½ x 16½ ft, 1-32pdr carr., 2-18pdr. Ex-hoy purchased 3.1794. Listed to 1798.

HOPE Sloop 14, 220bm. Dutch STAR captured 18.8.1795 in Simons Bay. Sold 1807.

HOPE Brig-sloop 10, 'Cherokee' class, 237bm. Bailey, Ipswich 22.7.1808. Sold 3.2.1819 T.Pittman to BU.

HOPE Tender 10, 49bm, 47 x 16 ft. Deptford 1813. Made a tank vessel (YC.42) 7.1863. In service 1880.

HOPE Packet brig 3, 'Cherokee' class, 231bm. Plymouth DY 8.12.1824. Harbour service by 1854. BU 10.1882 Pembroke.

HOPE Destroyer 745 tons, 246 x 25 ft, 2-4in, 2-pdr, 2-TT. Swan Hunter 6.9.1910. Sold 2.20 at Malta.

HOPE 4 Vessels hired between 1795 & 1807. 5 Drifters WW.I.

HOPEWELL Pink 20. Purchased 1652. Sold 1657.

HOPEWELL Fireship 6, 242bm. Purchased 1672. Expended 1673.

HOPEWELL Fireship 8, 253bm, 94 x 25 ft. Ellis, Shoreham 15.4.1690. Burnt 3.6.1690 by accident in the Downs.

HOPEWELL Fireship 8, 157bm. Purchased 11.8.1690. Expended 19.5.1692 at La Hogue.

HOPEWELL Fire Vessel, 18bm. Purchased 7.1694. Sold 17.2.1696.

HORATIO 5th Rate 38, 1,090bm, 154½ x 39 ft. Parsons, Bursledon 23.4.1807. Completed 6.1850 as screw ship, 1,175bm. Sold 1865 Castle, Charlton.

HORATIO Trawler requis. 1914-19. Trawler 1940-43.

HORNBY (see MONTSERRAT)

HORNBY Tug requis. 1914-16.

HORNET Sloop 14, 272bm, 91 x 26½ ft. Chitty & Quallet, Chichester 3.8.1745. Sold 3.7.1770. (In French hands 12.46 to 10.47.)

HORNET Cutter 16, 98bm, 50 x 20 ft. Purchased 1.1763. Sold 13.3.1772.

HORNET Sloop 14, 305bm, 97 x 27 ft. Perry, Blackwall 19.3.1776. Sold 7.1791.

HORNET Sloop 16, 423bm, 108 x 30 ft. Stalkart, Rotherhithe 3.2.1794. Harbour service 1805. Sold 30.10.1817.

HORNET Gunvessel 4, 60bm, 63 x 14 ft. Purchased 3.1794. BU 7.1795.

HORNET Schooner 6, 181bm, 81 x 23½ ft. Chatham DY 24.8.1831; completed as brigantine. BU 7.1845 at Chatham.

HORNET Schooner ordered at Woolwich 12.8.1847, transferred Deptford and became the following ship:

HORNET Wood S.Sloop, 753bm, 160 x 32 ft, 17-32pdr. Deptford DY 13.4.1854. BU 1868 by White, Cowes.

HORNET Compos. S.gunvessel, 465bm, 603 tons, 155 x 25 ft, 1-7in, 1-64pdr, 2-20pdr. Penn, Stockton on Tees 10.3.1868. Sold 1889.

HORNET Destroyer 260 tons, 180 x 18½ ft, 1-12pdr, 3-6pdr, 3-TT. Yarrow, Poplar 23.12.1893. Sold 12.10.1909 Thames S.Bkg Co.

HORNET Destroyer 770 tons, 240 x 25½ ft, 2-4in, 2-12pdr, 2-TT. J. Brown 20.12.1911. Sold 9.5.21 Ward, Rainham.

HORNPIPE Minesweeper 260 tons, 130 x 26 ft, 1-3pdr. Ex-War Dept tug transferred 10.1917. Murdoch & Murry 25.7.17. Sold 1.5.20 Crichton Thomson.

HORNPIPE Trawler 1940-46.

HORSEMAN Flyboat 18, 191bm. Dutch, captured 1665. Sunk 7.1667 as blockship in the Thames.

HORSHAM Minesweeper (RAN), 'Bathurst' class. Williamstown DY 25.3.1942. Sold 8.8.56 to BU in Hong Kong.

HORSLEYDOWN Sloop 4. Horsleydown 1652. Sold 1654.

HORSLEYDOWN Sloop 4. Listed 1653. Sold 1656.

HOSTE Destroyer leader 1,666 tons, 325 x 32 ft, 4-4in, 4-TT. Cammell Laird 16.8.1916. Sunk 21.12.16 in collision with NEGRO in the North Sea.

HOSTE (see NYASALAND)

HOSTE (ex-MITCHELL) Frigate DE 'Captain' class. Boston N.Yd 24.9.1943 on lend-lease. Returned 22.2.45 to the USN.

HOSTILE Destroyer 1,340 tons, 312 x 32 ft, 4-4.7in, 8-TT. Scotts 24.1.1936. Sunk 23.8.40 by mine off Cape Bon.

HOTHAM (see BAHAMAS)

HOTHAM Frigate, TE 'Captain' class. Bethlehem, Hingham 22.12.1943 on lend-lease. Nominally returned 13.3.56 to the USN. BU 9.56.

HOTSPUR 5th Rate 36, 952bm, 145 x 38½ ft. Parsons, Warsash 13.10.1810. BU 1.1821.

HOTSPUR 5th Rate 46, 1,171bm, 159 x 41 ft. Pembroke Dock 9.10.1828. Chapel hulk 1859; renamed MONMOUTH 1968. Sold 1902.

HOTSPUR Armoured ram (turret ship) 4,331 tons, 235 x 50 ft, 1-12in, 2-64pdr. Napier, Govan 19.3.1870. Sold 2.8.1904.

HOTSPUR (see LANDRAIL of 1913).

HOTSPUR Destroyer 1,340 tons, 312 x 32 ft, 4-4.7in, 8-TT. Scotts. 23.3.1936. To Dominican Republic 23.11.48 as TRUJILLO.

HOTSPUR Tug 1918-20.

HOUGHTON Coastal M/S, 'Ton' class. Camper & Nicholson 22.11.1957. Sold 29.1.71, BU Plymouth

HOUND 36-gun ship. Captured 1652. Hulk 1656. BU 1660 in Jamaica.

HOUND 18-gun ship, 206bm. Captured 1656. Expended 1666 as fireship.

HOUND Sloop 4, 50bm. Chatham DY 1673. Sold 1686.

HOUND Fireship 8, 257bm, 94 x 25 ft. Graves, Limehouse 18.4.1690. Expended 22.5.1692 at Cherbourg.

HOUND Sloop 4, 83bm, 61 x 18 ft. Deptford DY 1700. Sold 29.7.1714.

HOUND Sloop 14, 200bm, 87½ x 23 ft. Deptford DY 6.9.1732. BU 6.1745 at Deptford.

HOUND Sloop 14, 267bm, 92 x 26 ft. Stow & Bartlett, Shoreham 22.5.1745. Sold 27.10.1773.

HOUND Sloop 14, 305bm, 97 x 27 ft. Adams & Barnard, Deptford 8.3.1776. BU 11.1784. (Was French LEVRETTE 1780-82.)

HOUND Sloop 16, 321bm, 100 x 26 ft. Deptford DY 31.3.1790. Captured 14.7.1794 by the French in the Atlantic.

HOUND Brig-sloop 16, 314bm, 95 x 28 ft. Hill, Sandwich 24.3.1796. Wrecked 26.9.1800 in the Shetlands.

HOUND (ex-*Monarch*) Sloop 16, 333bm, 103 x 27 ft, 12-24pdr carr., 4-18pdr. Purchased 2.1801. Bomb 1808. BU 11.1812.

HOUND Brig 8. Woolwich DY. Ordered 24.5.1839. Cancelled 6.44 and transferred to Deptford.

HOUND Brig 8, 358bm, 91 x 30½ ft, 8-18pdr. Deptford DY 23.5.1846. Breakwater 1872. Sold 11.1887 Castle, Charlton.

HOUND (see MASTIFF of 1856)

HOUND Minesweeper, 'Algerine' class. Lobnitz 29.7.1942. Arrived 1.9.62 at Troon to BU.

HOUSE de SWYTE 3rd Rate 70, 786bm. Dutch HUIS te SWIETEN captured 3.6.1665 sunk 3.1667 to block the Thames.

HOVERFLY River gunboat, 'Fly' class. Yarrow 4.1916 in sections. Sold 16.2.23 Basra Port Authority.

HOVERFLY Trawler requis. 1939-45.

HOVINGHAM Inshore M/S, 'Ham' class. Fairlie Yt Co 24.5.1956. Sold 27.9.66.

HOWE (ex-E. Indiaman *Kaikusroo*) Storeship 20, 1,048bm, 150 x 30 ft. Puchased 1805. Renamed DROME-DARY 6.8.1806. Convict ship 8.1819. Sold 8.1864 in Bermuda.

HOWE 1st Rate 120, 2,619bm, 205 x 56 ft. Chatham DY 28.3.1815. BU 2.1854 at Sheerness.

HOWE Screw 1st Rate 110, 4,245bm, 275 x 61 ft. Pembroke Dock 73.3.1860. Renamed BULWARK, harbour service 3.12.1885; IMPREG-NABLE 27.9.86. BULWARK 12.19. Sold 18.2.21 Garnham to BU.

HOWE Battleship 10,300 tons, 325 x 68 ft, 4-13.5in, 6-6in, 12-6pdr. Pem-broke Dock 28.4.1885. Sold 11.10.1910 Ward, Swansea; to Briton Ferry 1.12.

HOWE Battlecruiser 36,300 tons, 8-15in, 12-5.5in. Cammell Laird. Or-dered 4.1916, cancelled 10.18.

HOWE (ex-BEATTY renamed 2.1940) Battleship 35,000 tons, 700 x 103 ft, 10-14in, 16-5.25in. Fairfield 9.4.40. BU 1958 Ward Inverkeithing., ar-rived 4.6.58.

HOWETT (see PAPUA)

HOWITZER Destroyer 1,980 tons, 341½ x 38 ft, 6-4in, 6-40mm, 10-TT. Thornycroft. Laid down 26.2.1945, cancelled 10.45.

HUBBERSTON Coastal M/S, 'Ton' class. Camper & Nicholson 14.9.1954.

HUGHES Destroyer leader 1,750 tons, 329 x 32 ft, 5-4.7in, 1-3in, 6-TT. Cammell Laird. Ordered 4.1917, can-celled 1.19.

HUGH LINDSAY Wood pad. sloop (Indian), 441bm. Bombay DY 1829. Sold 1859.

HUGH ROSE Wood S.gunboat (Indian), 300bm, 125 x 23 ft, 1-68pdr, 2-24pdr. Bombay DY 18.9.1860. Listed to 1876.

La HULLOISE Frigate (RCN) 'River' class. Vickers,Montreal 29.10.1943. For disposal 1964.

HUMBER Fireship 8, 254bm. Built 1690. Fate unknown.

HUMBER 2nd Rate 80, 1,223bm, 156 x 42 ft. Frame, Hull 30.3.1693. Rebuilt Deptford 1708 as 1,294bm; rebuilt Portsmouth 1726 as 1,353bm. Re-named PRINCESS AMELIA 1727.

BU 6.1752 at Portsmouth.

HUMBER 5th Rate 44, 829bm, 134 x 38 ft. Smith, Bursledon 5.3.1748. Wrecked 16.9.1762 on Hazeboro Sand.

HUMBER Sloop 16. French, captured 1806. Listed 1808.

HUMBER Wood S.gunvessel, 'Philomel' class. Pembroke Dock. Laid down 8.2.1861, cancelled 12.12.1863.

HUMBER (ex-*Harar*) Iron S.storeship 1,640 tons, 246 x 29 ft. Earle, Hull 7.10.1876, purchased 28.5.1878. Sold 1907, renamed *Lucia Victoria*.

HUMBER (ex Brazilian JAVARY pur-chased 8.8.1914) River monitor 1,260 tons, 265 x 49 ft, 2-6in, 2-4.7in how-itzers. Vickers 17.6.13. Sold 17.9.20 F.Rijsdijks as crane ship.

HUMBER (see BRONINGTON)

HUMBER Minehunter 890 tons Rich-ards 17.5.1984

HUMBERSTONE (see GOLDEN FLEECE)

HUMBERSTONE (ex-NORHAM CAS-TLE renamed 1943, ex-TOTNES CASTLE) Corvette (RCN), 'Castle' class. Inglis 12.4.44. Sold 1946, re-named *Chang Chen*.

HUNTER Dogger, Captured 1646. Sold 1649.

HUNTER Fireship 10. French sloop CHASSEUR captured 1652. Burnt 31.7.1653 in action with the Dutch.

HUNTER 6-gun vessel, 50bm. Royalist, captured by Parliament 1656. Foun-dered 1661.

HUNTER 5th Rate 30, 260bm. Dutch, captured 1672. Listed to 1677.

HUNTER Sloop 4, 46bm. Portsmouth DY 1673. Sold 1683.

HUNTER Fireship 8, 277bm, 94 x 25 ft. Shish, Rotherhithe 29.4.1690. 6th Rate 24 guns 1710. Captured 20.9.1710 by the Spanish off Cape St. Mary.

HUNTER Fireship 10. Purchased 7.9.1739. Renamed VULCAN 1740. Hulked in Jamaica 10.43.

HUNTER Sloop 10, 238bm, 89 x 24½ ft. Wells & Stanton, Deptford 28.2.1756. Captured 23.11.1775 by an American privateer off Boston; re-captured by GREYHOUND. Sold 27.12.1780 at New York as unfit.

HUNTER Cutter 8, 72bm, 50 x 20 ft. Purchased 1.1763. Sold 1771.

HUNTER Sloop 16, 336bm, 103 x 26 ft, 16-24pdr. Pender, Bermuda 1796 (purchased on stocks). Wrecked 27.12.1797 on Hog Island, Virginia.

HUNTER Brig-sloop 18, 310bm, 91 x

28½ ft, 2-24pdr, 16-6pdr. Purchased 5.1801. BU 1809.

HUNTER Brig 10 (Canadian lakes), 180bm. Lake Erie 1812. Captured 10.9.1813 by Americans on Lake Erie.

HUNTER Wood S.gunboat, 'Clown' class. Pitcher, Northfleet 7.6.1856. Sale list 6.1869. Sold 1884.

HUNTER Destroyer 295 tons, 194 x 19 ft, 1-12pdr, 5-6pdr, 2-TT. Fairfield 28.12.1895. Sold 10.4.1912 Ward, Briton Ferry.

HUNTER Destroyer 1,340 tons, 312 x 32 ft, 4-4.7in 8-TT. Swan Hunter 25.2.1936. Damaged in action and lost in collision with HOTSPUR 10.4.40 at Narvik.

HUNTER (see TRAILER)

HUNTER (see LST.3042)

HUNTER Patrol boat 34 tons Fairey Marine 1983

HUNTER Trawler requis. 1914-19.

HUNTLEY (ex-HELMSDALE renamed 1918) Minesweeper, later 'Hunt' class. Eltringham 18.1.19. Sunk 31.1.41 by air attack in the eastern Mediterranean.

HUNTSVILLE (see PROMPT of 1944)

HUNTSVILLE (ex-WOOLVESEY CASTLE renamed 1943) Corvette (RCN), 'Castle' class. Ailsa 24.2.44. Sold 1946, renamed *Wellington Kent*.

HUON (ex-DERWENT renamed 1913) Destroyer (RAN) 700 tons, 1-4in, 3-12pdr, 3-TT. Cockatoo DY 19.12.14. Dismantled 1929 and sunk as target 9.4.30 off Jervis Bay.

HURON Schooner 2 (Canadian lakes), 2-24pdr, American OHIO captured 12.8.1814. Listed 1817.

HURON Schooner 2 (Canadian lakes), 66bm, 54 x 17½ ft, 2-24pdr. Kingston Ont 1817. (Above vessel rebuilt?)

HURON Destroyer (RCN) 1,927 tons, 355½ x 36½ ft, 6-4.7in, 2-4in, 4-TT. Vickers Armstrong, Tyne 25.6.1942. Arrived 20.8.65 at Spezia to BU.

HURON Destroyer (RCN) 3551 tons. Marine Industries 3.4.1971.

HURRICANE (ex-Brazilian JAPARUA purchased 9.1939) Destroyer 1,340 tons, 312 x 33 ft, 4-4.7in, 8-TT. Vickers Armstrong, Barrow 29.9.39. Sunk 24.12.43 by 'U.275' in the N.Atlantic.

HURRICANE Drifter 1919-1919. Tug requis. 1939-46.

HURSLEY Destroyer, 'Hunt' class type II. Swan Hunter 2.7.1941. Lent Greek navy 12.43 to 12.11.59 as KRITI. BU 1960.

HURST Paddle M/S, 'Ascot' class. Dunlop Bremner 6.5.1916. Sold 3.22 Ward, Inverkeithing.

HURST CASTLE Corvette, 'Castle' class. Caledon SB 23.2.1944. Sunk 1.9.44 by 'U.482'; NW of Ireland.

HURWORTH Destroyer, 'Hunt' class type II. Vickers Armstrong, Tyne 10.4.1941. Sunk 22.10.43 by mine east of Kalymnos, Dodecanese.

HURWORTH Minehunter 615 tons. Vosper Thornycroft 25.9.1984.

HUSSAR 6th Rate 28 (fir-built), 586bm, 118½ x 34 ft. Chatham DY 23.7.1757. Captured 5.1762 by the French when aground on the coast of Cuba.

HUSSAR 6th Rate 28, 627bm, 114 x 34 ft. Inwood, Rotherhithe 26.8.1763. Wrecked 1780 near New York.

HUSSAR Galley 1. American, captured 1780. Sold 1786.

HUSSAR 6th Rate 26, 586bm. American PROTECTOR captured 5.1780 by ROEBUCK. Sold 14.8.1783.

HUSSAR 6th Rate 28, 596bm, 120½ x 34 ft. Wilson, Sandgate 1.9.1784. Wrecked 27.12.1796 near Ile Bas, coast of France.

HUSSAR Sloop 14, 413bm, 105 x 30 ft. French privateer HUSSARD captured 10,1798 by AMERICA. Sold 1800.

HUSSAR 5th Rate 38, 1,043bm, 150½ x 39½ ft. Woolwich DY 1.10.1799. Wrecked 2.1804 in the Bay of Biscay.

HUSSAR 5th Rate 38, 1,077bm, 154 x 40 ft. Adams, Bucklers Hard 23.4.1807. Harbour service 9.1833; target 6.1861. Burnt 1861 at Shoeburyness by accident while in use as target.

HUSSAR Torpedo gunboat 1,070 tons, 250 x 30½ ft, 2-4.7in, 4-6pdr, 5-TT. Devonport DY 3.7.1894. Sold 12.1920; resold 13.7.21 L.Gatt, Malta to BU.

HUSSAR Minesweeper 815 tons, 230 x 33½ ft, 2-4in. Thornycroft. 27.8.1934. Sunk 27.8.44 in error by allied A/C off Normandy.

HYACINTH Sloop. French privateer HAYACINTHE captured 11.1692. Fate unknown.

HYACINTH 6th Rate 20, 424bm, 109 x 30 ft, 16-32pdr carr.,8-18pdr carr., 2-6pdr. Preston, Yarmouth 30.8.1806. BU 12.1820.

HYACINTH Sloop 18, 435bm, 110 x 31 ft. Plymouth DY 6.5.1829. Coal hulk 10.1860. BU completed 27.11.1871 at Portsmouth.

HYACINTH Compos. S.corvette 1,420 tons, 200 x 38 ft, 8-6in. Devonport DY 20.12.1881. Sold 25.8.1902, BU by King, Bristol.

HYANCITH 2nd class cruiser 5,600 tons, 350 x 54 ft, 11-6in, 9-12pdr. London & Glasgow Co. 27.10.1898. Sold 11.10.1923 Cohen, Swansea.

HYACINTH Corvette, 'Flower' class. Harland & Wolff 19.8.1940. Lent Greek navy 1943 as APOSTOLIS. BU 1962.

HYACNITH Drifter. 1914-20.

HYAENA 6th Rate 24, 522bm, 114½ x 32 ft. Fisher, Liverpool 2.3.1778. Sold.2.1802. (Captured 27.5.93 by the French CONCORDE in the W. Indies; recaptured 10.97 as the privateer HYENE and reverted to HYAENA.)

HYAENA (ex-*Hope*) 6th Rate 28, 519bm, 132 x 31 ft. Purchased 6.1804. Storeship 1813. Sold 18.4.1822 Cockshott.

HYAENA Brig-sloop 10, 'Cherokee' class. 233bm. Chatham DY. Laid down 3.1825. launched 19.8.1826 as CALYPSO.

HYAENA (ex-CALYPSO renamed 1826) Brig-sloop 10, 'Cherokee' class, 239bm. Deptford Dy. Cancelled 21.2.1831.

HYAENA Wood S.gunboat, 'Albacore' class. Mare, Blackwall 3.4.1856. Sold 8.3.1870. W.E. Joliffe as salvage vessel.

HYAENA Iron S.gunboat, 'Ant' class. Laird 30.8.1873. Sold 3.4.1906 at Chatham.

HYAENA Trawler requis. 1939-40.

HYDERABAD (ex-NETTLE renamed 23.4.1941) Corvette, 'Flower' class. A. Hall 23.9.41. Sold 1.1.48. BU 10.48 at Portaferry.

HYDERABAD Decoy ship 1917-20.

HYDRA 6th Rate 24, 454bm, 109½ 30½ ft. Adams & Barnard, Deptford 8.8.1778. Sold 1.5.1783.

HYDRA 5th Rate 38, 1,024bm, 148 x 39 ft. Cleveley, Gravesend 13.3.1797. Troopship 1812. Sold 13.1.1820.

HYDRA Wood pad. sloop, 818bm, 165 x 33 ft. Chatham DY 13.6.1838. Sold 13.5.1870 Castle, Charlton.

HYDRA Coast defence ship 3,480 tons, 225 x 45 ft, 4-10in MLR. Elder, Govan 28.12.1871. Sold 7.7.1903; BU at Genoa.

HYDRA Destroyer 700 tons, 240 x 25½ ft, 2-4in, 2-12pdr, 2-TT. J. Brown 19.2.1912. Sold 9.5.21 Ward, Portishead.

HYDRA Minesweeper, 'Algerine' class.

Lobnitz 29.9.1942. Damaged 10.11.44 by mine and not repaired; BU 11.45 by Ward, Grays.

HYDRA Survey ship 2,800 tons, 235 x 49 ft. Blythswood 14.7.1965. Handed over to Indonesia 18.4.80

HYDRA Trawler requis. 1915-19. Landing ship renamed KEREN 1941.

HYDRANGEA Sloop, 'Arabis' class. Connell, Greenock 2.3.1916. Sold 7.4.20 at Hong Kong.

HYDRANGEA Corvette, 'Flower' class. Ferguson 4.9.1940. Sold 1947, renamed *Hydralock.*

HYGEIA (see LEANDER of 1780)

HYPERION 5th Rate 32, 978bm, 144 x 39½ ft. Gibson, Hull 3.11.1807. BU 6.1833.

HYPERION Wood S.frigate, 3,202bm, 280 x 50 ft. Woolwich DY. Ordered 3.2.1861, cancelled 12.1863.

HYPERION Destroyer 1,340 tons, 312 x 32 ft, 4-4.7in, 8-TT. Swan Hunter 8.4.1936. Sunk 22.12.40 by HMS ILEX after being torpedoed by the Italian S/M SERPENTE in the Mediterranean.

HYTHE (ex-BANFF renamed 6.1941) Minesweeper, turbine 'Bangor' class. Ailsa 4.9.41. Sunk 11.10.43 by 'U.37' off Bougie.

HYTHE Minesweeper requis. 1914-15.

IBIS Sloop 1,250 tons, 283 x 37½ ft, 6-4in. Furness SB Co 28.11.1940. Sunk 10.11.42 by Italian A/C in the western Mediterranean.

IBIS (see SINGLETON)

IBIS 2 Trawlers WW.I. 2 Drifters WW.II

ICARUS Brig-sloop 10 'Cherokee' class, 234bm. Portsmouth DY 18.8.1814. Coastguard 1839. Sold 4.4.1861.

ICARUS Wood S.sloop, 580bm, 15 x 29 ft, 11-32pdr. Deptford DY 22.10.1858. Sold 23.1.1875 Castle, Charlton.

ICARUS Sloop 950 tons, 167 x 32 ft. Devonport DY 27.7.1885. Sold in 3.1904.

ICARUS Destroyer 1,370 tons, 312 x 32 ft, 4-4.7in, 10-TT. J. Brown 26.11.1936. Sold 29.10.46, BU at Troon.

ICKFORD Seaward defence boat, 'Ford' class. Rowhedge IW 17.6.1954. Sold 4.9.67 at Singapore.

IGNITION (ex-*Jeany*) Fireship 4, 130bm, 69 x 22 ft, 4-12pdr carr. Purchased 5.1804. Wrecked 19.2.1807 off Dieppe.

ILDEFONSO (see SAN ILDEFONSO)

ILEX Destroyer 1,370 tons, 312 x 32 ft, 4-4.7in, 10-TT.J.Brown. 28.1.1937. Sold 1948 at Malta to BU in Sicily.

ILEX A. yacht requis. 1914-15.

ILFRACOMBE (see INSTOW)

ILFRACOMBE Minesweeper, turbine 'Bagnor' class. Hamilton 29.1.1941. Sold 1.1.48. BU Clayton & Davie, Tyne.

ILFRACOMBE Trawler requis. 1917-19.

ILLUSTRIOUS 3rd Rate 74, 1,616bm, 168 x 47 ft. Adams, Bucklers Hard 7.7.1789. Wrecked 14.3.1795 at Avenza.

ILLUSTRIOUS 3rd Rate 74, 1,746bm, 175 x 48½ ft. Randall Rotherhithe 3.9.1803. Gunnery ship 4.1854. BU completed 4.12.1868 at Portsmouth.

ILLUSTRIOUS Battleship 14,900 tons, 390 x 75 ft, 4-12in, 12-6in, 18-12pdr. Chatham DY 17.9.1896. Sold 18.6.1920 Ward, Barrow.

ILLUSTRIOUS A/C carrier 23,000 tons, 673 x 96 ft, 16-4.5in, 36-A/C. Vickers Armstrong, Barrow 5.4.1939. Arrived 3.11.56 Faslane to BU.

ILLUSTRIOUS A/S Cruiser 16,256 tons. Swan Hunter 14.12.1978

ILMINGTON Coastal M/S, 'Ton' class. Camper & Nicholson 8.3.1954. Sold 1967 Argentine navy, renamed FORMOSA.

ILSTON Coastal M/S, 'Ton' class. Camper & Nicholson. Launched 14.10.1954 as BADMINTON. Sold 14.4.70 to BU at Bruges.

IMAUM (ex-E.Indiaman *Liverpool*, Bombay DY 10.11.1826) 3rd Rate 76, 1,776bm, 177 x 48½ ft. Presented 9.3.1836 by the Imaum of Muscat. Harbour service 7.1842. BU 1863 in Jamaica.

IMMORTALITE 5th Rate 42, 1,010bm, 145 x 39 ft. French captured 20.10.1798 by FISGARD off Brest BU 7.1806.

IMMORTALITE 5th Rate 38, 1,157bm. French INFATIGABLE captured 24.9.1806 by a squadron off Rochefort. BU 1.1811.

IMMORTALITE (see DUNIRA)

IMMORTALITE Wood S.frigate, 3,984bm, 251 x 52 ft. Pembroke Dock 25.10.1859. Sold 1883.

IMMORTALITE Armoured cruiser 5,600 tons, 300 x 56 ft, 2-9.2in, 10-6in, 10-3pdr. Chatham DY 7.6.1887. Sold 1.1.1907 S.Bkg Co, Blackwall.

IMOGEN Sloop 18, 399bm, 108 x 29 ft. French privateer DIABLE-a-QUATRE captured 26.10.1800 by THAMES in the Bay of Biscay. Foundered 1.3.1805 in the Atlantic.

IMOGEN Brig-sloop 16, 282bm, 93 x 27 ft. Bailey, Ipswich 11.7.1805. Sold 3.4.1817 Mr Ismay.

IMOGENE (ex-PEARL renamed 23.2.1826) 6th Rate 28, 660bm, 125 x 35 ft, 26-32pdr, 2-pdr. Pembroke Dock 24.6.1831. Burnt 19.9.1840 by accident at Plymouth.

IMOGENE Wood S.corvette, 950bm, 185 x 33 ft. Portsmouth DY. Ordered 1861, cancelled 12.12.1863.

IMOGENE Coastguard vessel 300 tons, 139 x 21 ft, 2-20pdr. White, Cowes 1864. Renamed ARGUS 22.1.1884. Sold 1903.

IMOGENE (ex-*Jacamar*) Iron S. yacht 460 tons, 160 x 24 ft. Purchased 1882. Renamed IMPEY 1919; sold 15.5.19 Ledger Hill.

IMOGEN Destroyer 1,370 tons, 312 x 32 ft, 4-4.7in 10-TT. Hawthorn Leslie 30.10.1936. Sunk 16.7.40 in collision with GLASGOW off Duncansby Head.

L'IMPASSIBLE Stationery A/A ship 2,419 tons, 328 x 39 ft, 2-40mm. French target ship, seized 3.7.1940 at Falmouth. Returned 1947 to the French navy.

IMPERIAL Destroyer 1,370 tons, 312 x 32 ft, 4-4.7in, 10-TT. Hawthorn Leslie 11.12.1936. Bombed 28.5.41 by German A/C north of Crete and sunk next day by HOTSPUR.

IMPERIEUSE 5th Rate 40, 1,040bm, 148½ x 39½ ft. French, captured 11.10.1793 by a squadron off Spezia. Renamed UNITE 3.9.1803. Harbour service 1832. BU 1.1858 at Chatham.

IMPERIEUSE (see AMPHITRITE of 1799)

IMPERIEUSE (see IPHIGENIA of 1804)

IMPERIEUSE Wood S.frigate, 2,358bm, 212 x 50 ft, 10-8in, 1-68pdr, 40-32pdr. Deptford DY 15.9.1852. Sold 3.1867 Castle & Beech.

IMPERIEUSE Armoured cruiser 8,400 tons, 315 x 62 ft, 4-9.2in, 10-6in, 8-6pdr. Portsmouth DY 18.12.1883. Renamed SAPHHIRE II depot ship 2.1905; reverted to IMPERIEUSE 6.09.Sold 24.9.13 Ward, Morecambe.

IMPERIEUSE (see AUDACIOUS of 1869)

IMPERIEUSE Training establishment 1944 comprised the battleships RESOLUTION and REVENGE (ships' names not changed).

IMPETUEUX 3rd Rate 74, 1,878bm, 182 x 47½ ft. French, captured 1.6.1794 at 'The 1st of June' battle. Burnt 24.8.1794 by accident at Portsmouth.

IMPETUEUX (see AMERICA of 1794)

IMPEY (see IMOGENE of 1882)

IMPLACABLE 3rd Rate 74, 1,882bm, 3,223 tons, 181 x 49½ ft. French DUGUAY-TROUIN captured 3.11.1805 at Sir Richard Strachan's action. Training ship 7.1855; lent 1.1912 to Mr Wheatly Cobb for preservation. Scuttled 2.12.1949 off the Owers.

IMPLACABLE Battleship 15,000 tons, 400 x 75 ft, 4-12in, 12-6in, 18-12pdr. Devonport DY 11.3.1899. Sold 8.11.1921 Slough TC; BU in Germany.

IMPLACALBE A/C carrier 26,000 tons, 673 x 96 ft, 16-4.5in, 72-A/C. Fairfield 10.12.1942. Arrived 3.11.55 Ward, Inverkeithing to BU.

IMPREGNABLE 2nd Rate 98, 1,887bm, 178 x 49 ft. Deptford DY 15.4.1789. Wrecked 18.10.1799 near Chichester.

IMPREGNABLE 2nd Rate 98, 2,406bm, 3,880 tons, 197 x 53½ ft. Chatham DY 1.8.1810. Training ship 1862. Renamed KENT 9.11.1888. Renamed CALEDONIA 22.9.91. Sold 10.7.1906 Castle.

IMPREGNABLE Training ships. (see HOWE of 1860, INCONSTANT of 1868, BLACK PRINCE of 1861, CIRCE of 1827, POWERFUL of 1895, ANDROMEDA of 1897, CAROLINE of 1882 and GANGES of 1821.)

IMPULSIVE Destroyer 1,370 tons, 312 x 32 ft, 4-4.7in 10-TT. White 1.3.1937. Sold 22.1.46, BU Young, Sunderland.

INCENDIARY Fireship 8, 397bm, 110½ x 29 ft. Mestears, River Thames 6.11.1778. Wrecked 1780 off the Isle of Wight.

INCENDIARY Fireship 16, 422bm, 109 x 30 ft, 16-18pdr carr. King, Dover 12.8.1782. Captured 29.1.1801 by the French in the Mediterrnean.

INCENDIARY (ex-*Diligence*) Fireship 14, 62bm, 53½ x 17½ ft. Purchased 1804. Sold 4.1812.

INCHARRAN Frigate (RCN), 'River' class. Davie SB 6.6.1944. Sold 1966 Kingston Mariners Association.

L'INCOMPRISE Destroyer 610 tons, 245½ x 26 ft. 2-3.9in, 2-TT. French torpedo boat seized 3.7.1940 at Portsmouth. Commissioned in the

RN 6.7.40. Returned 1946 to the French navy.

INCONSTANT 5th Rate 36, 705bm, 128 x 35½ ft. French PALLAS captured 19.7.1778 by VICTORY. Renamed CONVERT 1778. BU 1791.

INCONSTANT 5th Rate 36, 890bm, 138 x 38½ ft. Barnard, Deptford 28.10.1783. BU 11.1817.

INCONSTANT 5th Rate 46, 1,215bm, 159½ x 42 ft. Sheerness DY, ex-Deptford DY. Ordered 9.6.1825, cancelled 9.3.1832.

INCONSTANT 5th Rate 36, 1,422bm, 160 x 45½ ft, 36-32pdr. Portsmouth DY 10.6.1836. Sold 8.12.1862 Scott, Cork. BU 10.1866 (by Castle?).

INCONSTANT Iron S.frigate, 4,066bm, 5,880 tons, 337 x 50 ft, 10-19in, 6-7in MLR. Pembroke Dock 12.11.1868. Harbour service 1898. Renamed IMPREGNABLE II training ship 6.1906, DEFIANCE IV in 1.22, DEFIANCE II in 12.30. Arrived 4.4.56 in Belgium to BU.

INCONSTANT Light cruiser 3,500 tons, 410 x 39 ft, 2-6in, 6-4in. Beardmore 6.7.1914. Sold 9.6.22 Cashmore, Newport.

INCONSTANT (ex-Turkish MUAVENET purchased 9.1939) Destroyer 1,360 tons, 312 x 33½ ft, 4-4.7in, 8-TT. Vickers Armstrong, Barrow 24.2.41 Returned 9.3.46 to Turkish navy.

INCREASE 12-gun ship, 100/133bm. Captured 1645. Wrecked 1650.

INCREASE Ship, 505bm. In service 1650-54 (perhaps hired).

INDEFATIGABLE 3rd Rate 64, 1,400bm, 160 x 44 ft. Adams, Bucklers Hard 7.1784. Reduced to 38 guns 2.1795. BU 8.1816 at Sheerness.

INDEFATIGABLE A. ship. Purchased 1804. Sold 1805.

INDFATIGABLE 4th Rate 50, 2,084bm, 176 x 53 ft, 50-32pdr. Woolwich DY. Ordered 29.11.1832, cancelled 3.1834.

INDEFATIGABLE 4th Rate 50, 2,044bm, 2,626 tons, 180 x 51½ ft, 28-8in 22-32pdr. Devonport DY 27.7.1848. On loan from 3.1.1865 as training ship. Sold 26.3.1914.

INDEFATIGABLE 2nd class cruiser 3,600 tons, 300 x 44 ft, 2-6in, 6-4.7in 13-6pdr. London & Glasgow Co 12.3.1891. Renamed MELPOMENE 11.1.1910. Sold 7.10.13 Ward, Preston.

INDEFATIGABLE Battlecruiser 19,200 tons, 555 x 80 ft, 8-12in, 20-4in. Devonport DY 28.10.1909. Sunk 31.5.16

at Jutland.

INDEFATIGABLE (see PHAETON of 1883)

INDEFATIGABLE A/C carrier 26,000 tons, 673 x 96 ft, 16-4in, 72-A/C. J.Brown 8.12.1942. Arrived 4.11.56 at Dalmuir to BU.

INDEPENDENCIA Coal hulk. Ex-slaver purchased 1.12.1843. Renamed AT-TENTION 1846. Sold 1847?

INDIAN 44-gun ship, 687bm. Captured 1654. Sold 1659.

INDIAN Sloop 18, 400bm. Bermuda 1805. Sold 24.4.1817.

INDIAN (ex-*Relampago*) Survey schooner. Purchased 24.9.1855. On sale list 7.1856. Sold 1859?

INDIGNANT Gun-brig 12, 182bm, 84 x 22 ft, 10-18pdr carr., 2-12pdr, 1-13in mortar. Boole & Good, Bridport 13.5.1805. BU 6.1811.

INDOMITABLE Battlecruiser 17,250 tons, 560 x 78 ft, 8-12in, 16-4in. Fairfield 16.3.1907. Sold 1.12.21 Stanlee, Dover; arrived 30.8.22 at Dover.

INDOMITABLE A/C carrier 23,000 tons, 673 x 96 ft, 16-4.5in, 36-A/C. Vickers Armstrong, Barrow 26.3.1940. Arrived 30.9.55 at Faslane to BU.

INDOMITABLE Drifter 1915.

INDUS Storeship. Ex-E.Indiaman purchased 1790. Fate unknown.

INDUS 3rd Rate 74, 1,756bm, 177 x 48½ ft. Dudman, Deptford 19.12.1812. Renamed BELLONA 3.11.1818. Harbour service 1840. Completed BU 27.6.1868 at Devonport.

INDUS Iron pad. gunboat (Indian), 303bm. Laird 1838. Listed in 1843.

INDUS 2nd Rate 80, 2,098bm, 3,653 tons, 189 x 51 ft. Portsmouth DY 16.3.1839. Guardship 1860. Sold 11.11.1898.

INDUS Gunvessel (Indian), 522bm. Bombay DY 1851. Fate unknown.

INDUS Training ships. (See DEFEBCE of 1861, TEMERAIRE of 1876, BELLEROPHON of 1865, VALIANT of 1863, GANGES of 1821. TRIUMPH of 1870, FLORA of 1893 and VICTORIOUS of 1895.)

INDUS Sloop (RIN) 1,190 tons, 280 x 35½ ft, 2-4.7in. Hawthorn Leslie 24.8.1934. Sunk 6.4.42 by Japanese A/C at Akyab, Burma.

INDUSTRY Sloop in service in 1765.

INDUSTRY Fire vessel, 70bm, 59½ x 17 ft. Purchased 4.1794. BU 8.1795.

INDUSTRY Gunvessel in service 1806-10.

INDUSTRY Transport, 318bm, 104 x 26 ft, 4-12pdr carr. Warwick, Eling 13.10.1814. Harbour service 1820. BU 1846.

INDUSTRY Iron S.storeship, 638bm, 1,100 tons. Mare, Blackwall 1854 and purchased 19.4.1854. BDV 1901. Sold 10.10.11 Ward, Preston.

INDUSTRY (ex-GLASGOW renamed 1900) Storeship 1,460 tons, 196 x 30 ft. Beardmore 7.6.1901. Sunk 19.10.18 by enemy action.

INDUSTRY (ex-*Tay & Tyne*) Storeship, 180 x 26 ft. Purchased 26.9.1917. Sold 31.10.24 C.A.Beard.

INDUSTRY Drifter requis. 1914-19 and 1939-45.

INFANTA 3rd Rate 74, 1,918bm, 171½ x 51½ ft. Spanish, captured 1762 at Havana. Sold 26.4.1775.

INFANTA DON CARLOS Sloop 16, Spanish, captured 12.1804 by DIAMOND. BU 1811.

INFERNAL Bomb 8, 307bm, 91½ x 28 ft, 8-6pdr, 1-13in & 1-10in mortars. West, Northam 4.7.1757. Sold 26.10.1774.

INFERNAL Fireship 8, 307bm, 97 x 27½ ft. Perry & Hankey, River Thames 6.11.1778 (purchased on stocks). Sold 21.3.1783.

INFERNAL Bomb 6, 374bm, 105 x 28½ ft. Barkworth & Hawkes, North Barton. 26.7.1815. Sold 13.4.1831 Mr Snook.

INFERNAL Wood pad. sloop, 1,059bm, 180 x 36 ft. Woolwich DY 31.5.1843. Renamed ECLAIR 8.1844; ROSAMOND 10.46. Floating factory 1863. BU 1865.

INFLEXIBLE Sloop 18, 180bm, 18-12pdr. St Johns, Lake Champlain 1.10.1776. Fate unknown.

INFLEXIBLE 3rd Rate 64, 1,386bm, 160 x 46 ft. Barnard, Harwich 7.3.1780. Storeship 12.1793; troopship 7.1709 BU 1820 at Halifax NS.

INFLEXIBLE Wood pad. Sloop, 1,122bm, 190 x 36 ft. Pembroke Dock 12.4.1845. Sold 1864 Castle & Beech.

INFLEXIBLE Battleship 11,880 tons, 320 x 75 ft, 4-16in MLR, 8-4in. Portsmouth DY 27.4.1876. Sold 15.9.1903 Ward, Birkenhead & Preston.

INFLEXIBLE Battlecruiser 17,250 tons, 560 x 78 ft, 8-12in, 16-4in. J.Brown 20.6.1907. Sold 1.12.21 Stanlee, Dover.

INGERSOL Corvette (RCN), modified 'Flower' class. Collingwood SY. Cancelled 12.1943.

INGLEFIELD Destroyer leader 1,530 tons, 326 x 34 ft, 5-4.7in, 10-TT. Cammell Laird 15.10.1936. Sunk 25.2.44 by German A/C off Anzio.

INGLESHAM Inshore M/S, 'Ham' class. White 23.4.1952. Sold 9.8.66.

INGLIS Frigate, DE 'Captain' class. Boston N.Yd 2.11.1943. on lend-lease. Returned 3.46 to the USN.

INGONISH Minesweeper, TE 'Bangor' class. N.Vancouver SR Co 30.7.1941. Lent RCN until 2.7.45. Sold 1.1.48, BU Clayton & Davie, Tyne.

INMAN Frigate, DE 'Captain' class. Boston N.Yd 2.11.1943 on lend-lease. Returned 3.46 to the USN.

INSOLENT (see ARROGANTE of 1798)

INSOLENT Wood S.gunboat, 'Albacore' class. Pitcher, Northfleet 26.1.1856. Sold 1.5.1869 at Chefoo.

INSOLENT Iron S.gunboat 265 tons, 87½ x 26 ft, 1-10on MLR. Pembroke Dock 15.3.1881. Gate vessel 1.1918. Foundered 1.7.22 in Portsmouth harbour; wreck sold 18.6.25 Pounds, Portsmouth.

INSPECTOR Sloop 16, 310bm, 97 x 27 ft. Game, Wivenhoe 29.4.1782. Sold 2.1802.

INSPECTOR Sloop 16, 250bm. Purchased 1803. Sold 25.6.1810.

INSPECTOR Survey cutter, 60bm. In service in 1822.

INSTOW (ex-ILFRACOMBE renamed 1918) Minesweeper, later 'Hunt' class. Eltringham 15.4.19. Sold 15.11.20 A.S.Miller, renamed *Tilak*.

INTEGRITY Cutter 6. Purchased in Australia 1805. Listed to 1810.

INTEGRITY Two Drifters WW.I. Tug 1942-46. Tug 1947-65.

INTELLIGENCE Brigantine 4, 75bm. Woolwich DY 11.2.1696. Wrecked 3.2.1700 in Douglas Bay, Isle of Man.

INTELLIGENT Gun-brig 12, 181bm, 84 x 22 ft. Boole & Good, Bridport 26.8.1805. Sold 14.10.1815 but purchaser refused her; made a mooring lighter 8.1816.

INTREPID 3rd Rate 64, 1,300bm, 152 x 44 ft. French SERIEUX captured 3.5.1747 at Cape Finisterre. BU completed 2.8.1765 at Chatham.

INTREPID 3rd Rate 64, 1,374bm, 160 x 44 ft. Woolwich DY 4.12.1770. Harbour service 5.1810. Sold 26.3.1828 Beatson.

INTREPID Sloop 16 (Indian). Bombay 1780. Foundered 10.1800.

INTREPID (ex-PERSEVERANCE renamed 3.1850, ex-*Free Trade*) Wood S.discovery sloop. Purchased 3.1850. Abandoned 15.6.1854 in the Arctic.

INTREPID Wood S.gunvessel, 862bm, 201½ x 30½ ft, 2-68pdr, 4-32pdr. Wigram. Blackwall 13.11.1855. Sold 7.10.1864 Marshall, Plymouth.

INTREPID 2nd class cruiser 3,600 tons, 300 x 44 ft, 2-6in, 6-4.7in, 8-6pdr. London & Glasgow Co 20.6.1891. Minelayer 9.1910. Sunk 23.4.18 as blockship at Zeebrugge.

INTREPID Destroyer 1,370 tons, 312 x 32 ft, 4-4.7in, 10-TT. White 17.12.1936. Sunk 26.9.43 by German A/C in Leros harbour.

INTREPID Assault ship 10,000 tons, 500 x 80 ft 2-40mm, 16-GWS. J.Brown 25.6.1964.

INVENTION Sloop 4, 28bm. Portsmouth 1673. Sold 1683.

INVER Frigate (RCN), 'River' class. Vickers, Montreal 5.12.1942 on lend-lease. Returned 4.3.46 to the USN.

INVERELL Minesweeper (RAN), 'Bathurst' class. Morts Dk 2.5.1942. To RNZN 10.4.52.

INVERMORISTON Coastal M/S, 'Ton' class. Dorset Yt Co. Poole 2.6.1954. Sold Cashmore 2.7.71, BU at Newport.

INVERNESS 6th Rate 22, 354bm, 105 x 28½ ft. 90-9pdr, 2-3pdr. French privateer DUC de CHARTRES captured 18.1.1746 by EDINBURGH off the Lizard. BU 2.1750 at Portsmouth.

INVERNESS Drifter. requis. 1939-40.

INVESTIGATOR (see XENOPHON)

INVESTIGATOR Survey brig 16, 121bm, 76 x 19 ft. Deptford DY 23.4.1811. Police ship 3,1837, BU 10.1857.

INVESTIGATOR Survey sloop (Indian), 450bm. Purchased 1823. Fate unknown.

INVESTIGATOR Discovery vessel, 480bm. Purchased 2.1848. Abandoned circa 1853 in the Arctic.

INVESTIGATOR Wood pad. survey vessel, 149bm. Deptford DY 16.11.1861. Sold 1869 to Lagos local authorities.

INVESTIGATOR Wood pad. survey vessel (Indian) 856 tons, 180 x 26 ft. Bombay DY 1881. Sold circa 1906.

INVESTIGATOR (see RESEARCH of 1888)

INVESTIGATOR (ex-*Consuelo*) Survey vessel 900 tons, 185½ x 29 ft, 1-3pdr. Purchased 12.1903. Renamed SEALARK 29.1.04. Sold 3.9.19 at Melbourne, became mercantile.

INVESTIGATOR Survey vessel (RIM) 1,185 tons, 254 x 33 ft. Vickers

11.6.1907. Sold 1934.

INVESTIGATOR (ex-*Patrick Stewart*) Survey vessel (RIM) 1,572 tons, 226 x 37½ ft. Purchased 1934. Sold 19.6.51 to BU Bombay.

INVESTIGATOR (see TRENT of 1942)

INVETERATE Gun-brig 12,182bm, 84 x 22 ft, 10-18pdr carr. 2-12pdr. Boole & Good, Bridport 30.5.1805. Wrecked 18.2.1807 near St Valery-en Caux.

INVINCIBLE 3rd Rate 74, 1,793bm, 172 x 49 ft. French, captured 3.5.1747 at Cape Finisterre. Wrecked 19.2.1758 near St Helens.

INVINCIBLE 3rd Rate 74, 1,631bm, 168½ x 47½ ft. Wells, Deptford 9.3.1765. Wrecked 16.3.1801 on Harborough Sands, Yarmouth.

INVINCIBLE 3rd Rate 74,1,674bm, 170 x 48½ ft. Woolwich DY 15.3.1808. Coal hulk in 1857. BU 1.1861.

INVINCIBLE (see BLACK PRINCE of 1861)

INVINCIBLE Iron S.ship, 3,774bm, 6,010 tons, 280 x 54 ft. 10-9in. 4-64pdr. Napier 29.5.1869. Renamed EREBUS 4.1904, training ship. Renamed FISGARD II in 1.06. Foundered 17.9.14 off Portland.

INVINCIBLE Battlecruiser 17,250 tons, 550 x 78 ft, 8-12in, 16-4in. Armstrong 13.4.1907. Sunk 31.5.16 at Jutland.

INVINCIBLE A/S cruiser 16,256 tons. Vickers 3.5.1977

IPHIGENIA 5th Rate 32, 681bm, 126 x 35 ft. Betts, Mistleythorn 27.12.1780. Burnt 20.7.1801 by accident at Alexandria.

IPHIGENIA 5th Rate 38, 1,046bm, 147 x 40 ft, 14-32pdr carr., 28-18pdr, 2-9pdr. Spanish MEDEA captured 5.10.1804 by a squadron in the Atlantic. Renamed IMPERIEUSE 1805. Harbour service 5.1818. Sold 10.9.1838. (This ship was captured while at peace with Spain.)

IPHIGENIA 5th Rate 36, 870bm, 137 x 38 ft. Chatham DY 26.4.1808. Lent Marine Society 7.1833-48. BU 5.1851 at Deptford.

IPHIGENIA 2nd class cruiser 3,600 tons, 300 x 44 ft, 2-6in, 6-4.7in, 8-6pdr. London & Glasgow Co 19.11.1891. Minelayer 1910. Sunk 23.4.18 as blockship at Zeebrugge.

IPSWICH 3rd Rate 70, 1,049bm, 150 x 40 ft. Barrett, Harwich 19.4.1694. Large repair Woolwich 1712 as 1,100bm; rebuilt Portsmouth 1730 as 1,142bm; hulked 5.1757 at Gibraltar. BU circa 1764.

IPSWICH Minesweeper, 'Bathurst' class. Evans Deakin 11.8.1941. Lent RAN from 6.42. Sold 1946 Dutch navy as MOROTAI.

IPSWICH Patrol boat (RAN) 211 tons. N. Queensland Co, Cairns 25.9.1982.

IPSWICH Trawler requis. 1914-19.

IRIS 6th Rate 28, 762bm, 137 x 34 ft, 26-12pdr, 6-6pdr. American HANCOCK captured 1777 by RAINBOW. Captured 11.9.1781 by the French in the Chesapeake. Destroyed 18.12.1793 by the RN while in use as a hulk at Toulon.

IRIS 5th 32, 688bm, 126 x 35½ ft. Barnard, Deptford 2.5.1783. Lent Trinity House 10.1803; renamed SOLEBAY 18.11.1809. BU 10.1833 at Devonport.

IRIS 5th Rate 44, 1,020bm. Danish MARIE captured 7.9.1807 at Copenhagen. Sold 31.7.1816. (Was to have been renamed ALARIC.)

IRIS 6th Rate 26, 906bm, 131 x 40½ ft. Pembroke Dock 14.7.1840. Sold 16.10.1869 as cable vessel.

IRIS Despatch vessel (2nd class cruiser) 3,730 tons, 300 x 46 ft, 10-64pdr. Pembroke Dock 12.4.1877. Sold 11.7.1905.

IRIS Sloop,'Acacia' class, Lobnitz 1.6.1915. Sold 26.1.20 C.W.Kellock.

IRIS (see CORIANDER)

IRIS Ferry requis. 1918. Landing ship 1940-46.

IRON DUKE Battleship 6,010 tons, 280 x 54 ft, 10-9in, 4-64pdr. Pembroke Dock 1.3.1870. Sold 15.6.1906 Galbraith, Glasgow.

IRON DUKE Battleship 25,000 tons, 580 x 89½ ft, 10-13.5, 12-6in. Portsmouth DY 12.10.1912. Harbour service 9.32. Sold 2.46, arrived 8.46 Faslane to BU; hulk resold, arrived Port Glasgow 30.11.48.

IROQUOIS M/S sloop, '24' class. Barclay Curle 24.8.1918. Survey ship 1922; handed over 28.6.37 to Messrs Ward in part payment for *Majestic*(CALEDONIA); BU Briton Ferry.

IROQUOIS (ex-ATHABASKAN renamed 1940) Destroyer (RCN) 1,927 tons 355½ x 36½ ft, 6-4.7in 2-4in, 4-TT. Vickers Armstrong, Tyne 23.9.41. Arrived 9.66 Bilbao, Spain to BU.

IROQUOIS Destroyer (RCN) Marine Industries 28.11.1970

IRRAWADDY Wood pad. vessel(Indian), 170bm. Kidderpore DY 1.1827. Fate unknown.

IRAWADDY Iron river gunboat (Indian) 614 tons. Listed 1887 to

1893. Origin and fate unknown.

IRRAWADI Trawler requis. 1915-16.

IRRESISTIBLE 3rd Rate 74, 1,643bm, 168 x 47 ft. Barnard, Harwich 6.12.1782. BU 9.1806.

IRRESISTIBLE (see SWIFTSURE of 1787)

IRRESISTIBLE Screw 2nd Rate 80, 2,589bm, 3,842 tons, 190 x 57 ft. Chatham DY 27.10.1859. Harbour service 9.1868. Sold 1894 at Bermuda.

IRRESISTIBLE Battleship 15,000 tons, 400 x 75 ft, 4-12in, 12-6in, 18-12pdr. Chatham DY 15.12.1898. Sunk 18.3.1915 by torpedo from shore battery, Dardanelles.

IRRESISTIBLE (see ARK ROYAL of 1950)

IRVINE Minesweeper, later 'Hunt' class. Fairfield, 8.12.1917. Sold 21.2.23 J.W.Houston, Montrose.

IRWELL (see SIR BEVIS)

IRWELL (see GOOLE)

ISABELLA Yacht 6, 52bm. Chatham DY 1680. Sold 1683.

ISABELLA Yacht 8, 94bm, 8-3pdr. Greenwich 1683. Rebuilt Deptford 1703 as 105bm. Sold 13.3.1716.

ISABELLA Discovery vessel 1818.

ISHAM Inshore M/S, 'Ham' class. White 13.9.1954. Transferred French navy 22.4.55.

ISINGLASS M/S sloop, '24' class. Greenock & Grangemouth 5.3.1919, not completed. Sold 12.8.20 Moise Mazza, Malta; retained, sold 15.11.22 Ferguson Muir & Co.

ISIS 4th Rate 50, 976bm, 142 x 40 ft. Harwich (Probably launched as COLCHESTER 1744 (QV)).

ISIS 4th Rate 50, 1,013bm, 143 x 40½ ft, 24-24pdr, 24-9pdr, 2-6pdr. French DIAMANT captured 3.5.1747 at Cape Finisterre. Sold 1.7.1766 at Chatham.

ISIS 4th Rate 50, 1,051bm, 146 x 41 ft. Henniker, River Medway 19.11.1774. BU 9.1810.

ISIS 4th Rate 50, 1,190bm, 154½ x 43 ft. Woolwich DY. Ordered 1813; lengthened 1816 to 1,321bm, 164 x 43 ft, 60 guns 22-24pdr, 10-24pdr carr., 24-12pdr, 2-6pdr and launched 5.10.1819. Coal hulk 3.1861. Sold 12.3.1867 C. Heddle at Sierra Leone.

ISIS 2nd class cruiser 5,600 tons, 350 x 54 ft, 5-6in, 6-4.7in (11-6in from 1904). London & Glasgow Co 27.6.1896. Sold 26.2.20 Granton S. Bkg Co.

ISIS Destroyer 1,370 tons, 312 x 32 ft,

4-4.7in, 10-TT. Yarrow 12.11.1936. Sunk 20.7.44 off Normandy, probably mined.

ISIS RNVR tenders, in succession:- ex-FDB.76 renamed 1950-51; ex-MSS.1785 renamed 1951, foundered 1956 off Ostend; ex-PULHAM renamed 31.7.56, reverted to PULHAM 1963. ex-Cradley renamed 1963.

ISKRA Submarine depot ship 560 tons, 128 x 25 ft. Polish training schooner used 1941-45.

ISLE OF WIGHT Yacht 4, 31bm. Portsmouth DY 1676. Rebuilt Portsmouth 1701 as 38bm. Sold 1712.

ISLE OF WIGHT Trawler requis. 1964-19.

ISLIP 22-gun ship. Bailey, Bristol 3.1654. Wrecked 1655 off Inverlochy.

ISTER (ex-BLONDE renamed 1812) 5th Rate 36 (red pine-built), 945bm, 143½ x 38½ ft, 14-32pdr carr., 28-12pdr. Wallis, Blackwall 14.7.1813. Sold 8.3.1819 Beech to BU.

ISTER Wood S.Frigate 36, 2.478bm, 240 x 48ft. Devonport DY. Laid down 8.11.1860, cancelled 12.1864.

ITCHEN Destroyer 550 tons, 225 x 23½ ft, 1-12pdr, 5-6pdr, (4-12 pdr from 1907), 2-TT. Laird 17.3.1903. Sunk 6.7.17 by 'U.99' in the North Sea.

ITCHEN Frigate, 'River' class. Fleming & Ferguson 29.7.1942. Sunk 22.9.43 by U-boat in the N.Atlantic.

ITCHEN Minehunter 757 tons. Richards 30.10.1984

ITCHEN Trawler 1920-26.

ITHURIEL (ex-GABRIEL renamed 1915) Destroyer leader 1,655 tons, 325 x 32 ft, 4-4in, 4-TT. Cammell Laird 8.3.1916. Sold 8.11.21 Slough TC; BU in Germany.

ITHURIEL (ex-Turkish GAYRET purchased 9.1939) Destroyer 1,360 tons, 312 x 33½ ft, 4-4.7in, 8-TT. Vickers Armstrong, Barrow 15.12.40. Sunk 28.11.42 in Bone harbour; raised; sold 25.8.45 and BU 8.46 McLellan, Bo'ness.

IVANHOE (see LAWFORD)

IVANHOE Destroyer 1,370 tons, 312 x 32 ft, 4-4.7 in, 10-TT. Yarrow 11.2.1937. Mined 1.9.40 off the Texel and sunk by HMS KELVIN.

IVANHOE Trawler requis. 1914.

IVESTON Coastal M/S, 'Ton' class. Philip, Dartmouth 1.6.1954.

IVY (see MARIGOLD of 1915).

IVY Sloop, 'Anchusa' class. Blyth SB

31.10.1917. Sold 2.20 Howard, Ipswich, resold 2.6.21 Clan Line.

IVY Corvette, 'Flower' class. Harland & Wolff. Ordered 8.4.1940, cancelled 23.1.41.

IVY Yacht and 3 Drifters. WW.1.

'J' class submarines 1,210 tons (J.7 (ii) 1,260 tons). 270 x 23½ ft, 1-4in, 6-TT.

J.1 Portsmouth DY 11.1915. RAN 1919; Sold 26.2.24. Melbourne Salvage Syndicate; hull scuttled 26.5.26 off Barwon Heads.

J.2 Portsmouth DY 11.15.RAN 1919; fate as J.1 but hull scuttled 1.6.26.

J.3 Pembroke Dock. Cancelled 20.4.15.

J.3 (ex J.7 renamed 4.15) Pembroke Dock 4.12.15. RAN 1919; Sold 1.26 Hill, Melbourne; hull sunk as breakwater at Swan Island, Victoria.

J.4 Pembroke Dock. Cancelled 20.4.15.

J.4 (ex J.8 renamed 4.15) Pembroke Dock 2.2.16. RAN 1919; Sold as J.1, sank at moorings 10.7.24 at Williamstown; raised and scuttled 1972 off Port Phillip.

J.5 Devonport DY 9.9.15. RAN 1919; fate as J.1. but hull scuttled 4.6.26.

J.6 Devonport DY 9.9.15 Sunk 15.10.18 in error by decoy ship CYMRIC off Blyth.

J.7 (ii) Devonport DY 21.2.17. RAN 1919; Sold 11.29 Morris & Watt, Melbourne Hull sunk as breakwater 1930 at Hampton, Victoria.

J.4922 (see JUTLAND).

JACK Sloop 14. Purchased 1780. Captured 21.6.1781 by the French off Cape Breton.

JACKAL Cutter 10. Purchased 4.1778. Sold 17.5.1785.

JACKAL Cutter 14, 187bm, 73 x 25½. Purchased 1779. Handed over to the French at Calais 27.11.1779. by mutineers, became French privateer BOULOGNE and recaptured 1781. Captured 11.4.1782 by by the American Frigate DEANE.

JACKAL Brig 10, 101bm. Purchased vessel in Service in 1792.

JACKAL Gun-brig 12, 186bm, 80 x 23 ft, 2-18pdr, 10-18pdr carr. Perry, Blackwall 1.4.1801. Captured 30.5.1807 by the French after stranding near Calais.

JACKAL Iron Pad. gunvessel, 340bm, 505 tons, 142½ x 23 ft Napier 28.10.1844. Sold 11.1887.

JACKAL (see WOODCOCK of 1885)

JACKAL Destroyer 745 tons, 246 x 25½ ft, 2-4in, 2-12pdr, 2-TT. Hawthorn Leslie 9.9.1911. Sold 28.9.20. J.Smith.

JACKAL Destroyer 1,690 tons, 339½ x 36 ft, 6-4.7in, 10-TT. J.Brown. 25.10.1938. Sunk 12.5.42 by HMS JERVIS after bomb damage on the previous day in the eastern Mediterranean.

JACKDAW Schooner 10, 80bm, 56 x 18 ft. Rowe, Newcastle 19.5.1806. Captured 1.1807 'by a Spanish Rowboat'; recaptured 15.2.1807. Sold 1.11.1816.

JACKDAW Cutter 4, 108bm, 61 x 20½ ft. Chatham DY 4.8.1830. Schooner 3.1833. Wrecked 11.3.1835 in the W.Indies.

JACKDAW Wood S.gunboat, 'Dapper' class. Thompson, Rotherhithe 18.5.1855. cooking depot 1686. Sold 11.1888 C.Wort.

JACKDAW River gunboat 85 tons, 100 x 20 ft, 2-6pdr. Yarrow, Poplar 1898. Transferred 12.1898 W.African Colonial authorities. Sold circa 1912.

JACKDAW Trawler 1914-18.

JACK TAR Sloop 14, 193bm, 14-4pdr. Captured 1794. sold 20.11.1794.

JACKTON Coastal M/S, 'Ton' class. Phillip, Dartmouth 28.2.1955. Renamed TEAL (RAN) 8.62. Become Museum ship at Hobart in 1977.

JAGUAR Destroyer 1,690 tons, 399½ x 36 ft, 6-4.7in, 10-TT. Denny 22.11.1938. Sunk 26.3.42 by 'U.652' north of Sollum.

JAGUAR Frigate 2,300 tons, 330 x 40 ft, 4-4.5in, 2-40mm. Denny 30.7.1957. Sold Bangladesh 6.7.78, renamed ALI HAIDER.

JALOUSE Brig-sloop 18, 384bm, 103 x 27½ ft. French, Captured 13.8.1797 by VESTAL in the North Sea. BU 3.1807.

JALOUSE sloop 18, 425bm, 109 x 29½ ft. Plymouth DY 13.7.1809. Sold 8.3.1819 G.T.Young.

JAMAICA Sloop 14, 113bm, 65 x 21½ ft. Deptford DY 30.9.1710. Wrecked 9.10.1715 on Grand Cayman, W.Indies.

JAMAICA Sloop 14, 273bm, 92 x 26 ft. Deptford DY 17.7.1744. Foundered 17.1.1770 near Jamaica.

JAMAICA Sloop 16. Purchased 1779. Sold 1783.

JAMAICA 6th Rate 26, 520bm, 122 x 31 ft. French PERCENTE captured 21.4.1796 by INTREPID in the W.Indies. Sold 11.8.1814.

JAMAICA 4th Rate 52, 1,487bm, 173 x

44 ft, 16-42pdr carr. 36-24pdr Plymouth DY. Ordered 1.7.1825, Cancelled 5.3.1829.

JAMAICA (see JUNO of 1938)

JAMAICA Cruiser 8,000 tons, 538 x 62 ft, 12-6in, 8-4in. Vickers Armstrong, Barrow 16.11.1940. Arrived 20.12.60 at Dalmuir to BU.

JAMAICA Trawler. Requis, 1914-17.

JAMES Ballinger. Accquired 3.1417, given away in 6.1422.

JAMES 48-gun ship, 660/870bm. Deptford 2.1634. Renamed OLD JAMES 1660. Sold 1682.

JAMES 30-gun ship, 300bm. Royalist EXCHANGE captured 1649 by Parliament at Kinsale. Listed to 1650.

JAMES Hoy, 72bm. Dutch, captured 1665. Recaptured 1673 by the Dutch.

JAMES GALLEY 4th Rate 30, 486bm, 112 x 28 ft, 26-9pdr, 4-3pdr. Deane, Blackwall 1676. Made a 5th Rate 1691. Wrecked 25.11.1694 on Longsand Head.

JAMES & ELIZA Gunvessel 4. Purchased 1796. Gone by 1800.

JAMES BAY Coastal M/S (RCN), 'Ton' class, 370 tons. Yarrow, Canada 12.3.1953. sold 1966 mercantile.

JAMES WATT (ex-AUDACIOUS renamed 18.11.1847 before laying down) screw 2nd Rate 80, 3,083bm, 230 x 55½ ft, 8-10in, 36-8in, 34-32pdr. Pembroke Dock 23.4.1853. Sold 1875 Castle.

JANISSARY Gunvessel 6. In service in 1801.

JANUS 5th Rate 44, 884bm, 140 x 38 ft. Batson, Limehouse 14.5.1778. Storeship 1,1788. Renamed DROMEDARY 3.3.1788. Wrecked 10.8.1800 near Trinidad.

JANUS 5th Rate 32, 704bm, 131 x 36 ft, 6-24pdr carr., 24-12pdr, 6-6pdr. Dutch ARGO captured 12.5.1796 by PHOENIX in the North Sea. Harbour service 1.1798. Sold 21.2.1811.

JANUS Wood pad. sloop 763bm, 180 x 30½ ft; Chatham DY 6.2.1844. Sold 4.1856 Castle, Charlton.

JANUS Wood S.gunboat, 'Clown' class. Pembroke Dock 8.3.1856. coal lighter 12.1869 and renamed YC.6 Sold 1817 at Hong Kong.

JANUS Destroyer 320 tons, 200 x 20 ft, 1-12pdr, 5-6pdr, 2-TT. Palmer12.3.1895. Sold 1914 at Hong Kong to BU.

JANUS Destroyer 1,690 tons, 399½ x 36 ft, 6-4.7in, 10-TT. Swan Hunter 10.11.1938. Sunk 23.1.44 by A/C torpedo off Anzio.

JANUS. Two Trawlers WW.I.

JASEUR Brig-sloop 12. French, captured 1.0.7.1807 by BOMBAY off the Andamans. Gone by 1810.

JASEUR Brig-Sloop 18, 'Cruizer' class, 387bm. Bailey, Ipswich 2.2.1813. Sold 2,1845.

JASEUR Wood S.gunboat, 310bm, 125 x 23 ft, 1-68pdr, 2-24pdr howitzers. Green, Blackwall 7.3.1857. Wrecked 26.2.1859 at Baxo Nuevo, W.Indies.

JASEUR Wood S.gunvessel, 'Philomel' class, Deptford DY 15.5.1862. Sold 12.1874 to the Irish Light Commissioner.

JASEUR Torpedo gunboat 810 tons, 230 x 27 ft, 2-4.7in. 3-4pdr, 3-TT.N.C. & A. (Vickers) 24.9.1892. Sold 11.7.1905.

JASEUR Minesweeper, 'Algerine' class. Redfern, Toronto 19.4.1944. Arrived 26.2.1856 Hughes Bolckow, Blyth to BU.

JESSAMINE Sloop, 'Acacia' class. Swan Hunter 9.9.1915. Sold 21.12.22 T.E.Evans.

JASMINE Corvette, 'Flower' class. Ferguson 14.1.1941. Sold 1948.

JASON Fireship 6, 146bm. Purchased 1673. Sold 5.1674.

JASON 5th Rate 44, 810bm, 131½ x 37½ ft. French, captured 3.5.1747 at Cape Finisterre. Sold 15.3.1763.

JASON 5th Rate 32, 689bm, 130 x 37 ft. Batson, Limehouse 13.6.1763. Sold 10.2.1785.

JASON 3rd Rate 64, 1,452bm, 166 x 45 ft. French, captured 19.4.1782 in the Mona Passage, W.Indies. Renamed ARGONAUT 20.1.1783. BU 2.1831 Chatham.

JASON 5th Rate 38, 384bm, 146 x 39 ft, Dudman, Deptford 3.4.1794. Wrecked 13.10.1798 near Brest.

JASON 5th Rate 36, 1,053bm, 150 x 40 ft, Parsons, Burlesdon 27.1.1800. Wrecked 21.7.1801 in the Bay of St. Malo.

JASON 5th Rate 32 (fir-built), 661bm, 127 x 34 ft. Woolwich DY 21.11.1804. BU 7.1815 at Plymouth.

JASON Gun-brig 12. French Privateer captured 31.12.1813. Renamed?

JASON 5th Rate 46, 1,162bm, Woolwich DY. Ordered 18.7.1817, cancelled 7.2.1831.

JASON Wood S.Corvette, 1, 711bm, 2,431 tons, 225 x 41 ft, 16-8in, 1-7in, 4-40pdr. Devonport DY 10.11.1859. BU 7.1877 at Devonport.

JASON Torpedo gunboat 810 tons, 230 x 27 ft, 2-4.7in, 4-3pdr, 3-TT. N.C. &

A. (Vickers) 14.5.1892. M/S 1909. Sunk 7.4.17 by mine off the west coast of Scotland.

JASON Survey ship 835 tons, 230 x 33½ ft (2-4in 1939). Ailsa 6.10.1937. A/S vessel 1939; M/S 1942. Sold 3.9.46 Wheelock Marden, Renamed JASLOCK. BU 2.50

JASON Tug. 1915, Renamed RIVAL 1937-47, Yacht 1915-19.

JASPER Brig-Sloop 10, 'Cherokee' Class, 237bm. Bailey, Ipswich 27.5.1808. Wrecked 21.1.1817 off Plymouth.

JASPER Brig-sloop 10, 'Cherokee' class, 237bm. Portsmouth DY 26.7.1820. Wrecked 11.10.1828 off Sta. Maura; Wreck sold 1.1831.

JASPER (ex-GPO vessel *Aladdin*) Wood pad. packet, 233bm, 112½ x 21½ ft. Transferred 4.1837. Burnt 15.5.1854 after an explosion off Beachy Head.

JASPER Wood S.gunboat, 'Dapper' class. White 2.4.1855. Grounded in action 24.7.1855 at Taganrog, Sea of Azov.

JASPER Wood S.gunboat, 301bm, 125 x 23 ft, 1-68pdr, 2-24pdr howitzers. Green, Blackwall 16.3.1857. Sold 2.8.1862 to the Emperor of China, renamed AMOY.

JASPER (see GARNET of 1943)

JASPER Trawler 1914-15. Trawler 1935-42.

JASTRZAB (see P.551)

JAVA 5th Rate 32, 850bm. Dutch MARIA REIJGERSBERGEN captured 18.10.1806 by CAROLINE in the Indian Ocean. Foundered 2.1807 off Rodriguez Is, Indian Ocean.

JAVA 5th Rate 38, 1,083bm. French RENOMMEE captured 20.5.1811 by a squadron off Madagascar. Captured 29.12.1812 by the American CONSTITUTION off San Salvador and burnt on the next day.

JAVA 4th Rate 52, 1,460bm, 172 x 44 ft. Plymouth DY 16.11.1815. BU completed 22.11.1862 at Portsmouth.

JAVA Two Tugs requis. WW.1.

JAVELIN (ex-KASHMIR renamed 1937) Destroyer 1,690 tons, 339½ x 36 ft, 6-4.7in, 10-TT. J.Brown 21.12.38. Sold 11.6.49, BU at Troon.

JAVELIN (see KASHMIR)

JAVALIN Trawler 1914-15.

JED Destroyer 550 tons, 222 x 23½ ft, 1-12pdr, 5-6pdr(4-12pdr 1907), 2-TT. Thornycroft, Chiswick 16.2.1904.Sold 29.7.20 J & W Purves, Teignmouth; hull became an embankment at Dartmouth.

JED Frigate, 'River' class. Hill, Bristol 30.7.1942. Arrived 25.7.57 Ward, Milford Haven to BU.

JELLICOE (see ANSON of 1940)

JEMMY Yacht 4, 26bm, 41 x 12½ ft. Pett, Lambeth 1662. BU 1722.

JENNET PYRWIN Ship, Scottish ANDREW BARTON captured 1511. Last mentioned 1514.

JENNET 41-gun ship, 180bm. Portsmouth 1539. Rebuilt 1558 as 200bm. Listed to 1578. (The 1st ship built at Portsmouth.)

JENNET Boom trawler 1939-46.

JERAMIAH Hoy 4, 53bm. Captured 1666. Sold 1667.

JERFALCON ship 120bm. Listed 1550 to 1557.

JERSEY 4th Rate 48, 558bm. Starline, Woodbridge 1654. Captured 18.12.1691 by the French in the W.Indies.

JERSEY 6th Rate 24, 262bm, 94½ x 25½ ft. Deptford 17.1.1694. Renamed MARGATE 21.10.1698. Wrecked 9.12.1707 near Cartagena.

JERSEY 4th Rate 48, 677bm, 132 x 34 ft. Moore & Nye, E. Cowes 24.11.1698. Hulked 8.1731. Sunk 27.5.1763.

JERSEY 4th Rate 60, 1,065bm, 144 x 41½ ft. Plymouth DY 1736. Hospital ship 3.1771. Abandoned 11.1783 at the evacuation of New York.

JERSEY 'Gondola' 7. (Canadian lakes). 52bm, New York 1776. Lost off Valcour Is. 11.10.1776. Saolved by the British 12.10.76 and listed to 1779.

JERSEY Cutter 4, 71bm. White, Cowes 22.3.1860. Sold 8.1873 E.A.S. Mignon.

JERSEY Destroyer 1,690 tons, 339½ x 36 ft, 6-4.7in, 10-TT. White 26.9.1938. Sunk 2.5.41 by mine at the entrance to Malta harbour.

JERSEY Patrol vessel 925 tons. Hall Russell 18.3.1976

JERVIS Destroyer leader 1,695 tons, 339½ x 36 ft, 6-4.7in, 10-TT Hawthorn Leslie 9.9.1939. Sold 3.1.49; BU by Arnott Young, Port Bannatyne.

JESSAMINE (se JASMINE)

JESUS Ballinger Acquired 1416. Rebuilt Bursledon 1436 as LITTLE JESUS.

JESUS 1,000-ton ship. Winchelsea 1416. Given away in 1446.

JESUS of LUBECK Galleon 70, 700bm. Purchased 1544. Captured 1568 by the Spanish while trading.

JESUS & MARY Galley purchased 1409. Sold 1417.

JEWEL 5th Rate 38, 1,135bm, 157 x 40½ ft. French TOPAZE captured 22.1.1809 by a squadron in the W.Indies. Renamed ALCMENE 25.5.1809. BU 2.1816.

JEWEL Minesweeper, 'Algerine' class. Harland & Wolff 20.7.1944. Arrived 7.4.67 Ward, Inverkeithing to BU.

JEWEL Drifter requis. 1940-41.

JHELUM River gunboat (Indian), 499bm. Bombay DY 1851. Fate unknown.

JHELUM (see NARBADA)

JOHN Cog 220 bm Presented 1413. Wrecked 7.10.1414 French Coast.

JOHN BALLINGER. Listed 1417. Sold 1420.

JOHN Vessel captured 1549. Fate unknown.

JOHN 28-gun ship, 275/367bm. Purchased 1646. Wrecked 1652.

JOHN Galliot 4, 81bm. Captured 1666. Sold 1667.

JOHN & ALEXANDER Fireship, 8, 178bm. Purchased 1678. Sold 1686.

JOHN & MARTHA Fire vessel, 18bm. Purchased 1694. Sold 1698.

JOHN & PETER Dogger 6. Purchased 1666. Given away 1666.

JOHN & SARAH Fireship 4, 132bm. Purchased 1666. Sunk 6.1667 as blockship in the Medway.

JOHN BAPTIST 22-gun ship, 400bm. Purchased 1512. Wrecked circa 1534.

JOHN BAPTIST 22-gun ship. Captured 1652; Fireship 1653. Sold 1656.

JOHN OF DUBLIN Fireship captured from the French 1689. Lost 13.1.1690.

JOHN OF GREENWICH 50-ton vessel captured 1523. Listed to 1530.

JOHN EVANGELIST ship purchased 7.1463. Listed to 1484

JOHNSON 10-gun vessel (Canadian lakes). French L'OUTAQUISE captured 1760. Lost 11.1764 on the Lakes.

JOLIETTE Frigate (RCN) 'River' class. Morton 12.11.1943. Sold 3.1.46 Chilian navy as IQUIQUE.

JOLLY 6th Rate 10, 113bm, 67 x 19½ ft. French JOLIE captured 6.1693 at Lagos. Sold 1698.

JOLLY Sloop 6, 168bm. Purchased 13.6.1709. Sold 29.7.1714.

JONQUIERE Frigate (RCN), 'River' class. G.T. Davie 28.10.1943. Sold 8.67.

JONQUIL Sloop, 'Acacia' class. Connell 12.5.1915. Sold 5.20 Portuguese navy

as CARVALHO ARAUJO.

JONQUIL Corvette, 'Flower' class. Fleming & Ferguson 9.7.1940. Sold 5.46 renamed Lemnos.

JOSEPH Fireship 4, 101bm. Purchased 1666. Burnt 1667 by accident.

JOSEPH Fireship 8, 278bm, 99 x 26½ ft. Captured 1692. Sold 1698.

JOSEPH STRAKER (see DIAMOND of 1848)

JOSIAH Storeship 30, 664bm, 131 x 34 t. Purchased 8.1694. Hulk 9.1696. Sunk 26.8.1715 as breakwater, Sheerness.

JOYFUL 6th Rate 10, 106bm, 68 x 18 ft. Captured 1694. Fate unknown.

JUBILANT Destroyer 1,690 tons, 339½ x 36 ft, 6-4.7in 10-TT. Cancelled 1937 (not ordered).

JULIA Brig-sloop 16, 284bm, 93 x 26½ ft, 14-24pdr carr., 2-6pdr. Bailey, Ipswich 4.2.1806. Wrecked 2.10.1817 on Tristan da Cunha.

JULIA Schooner (Canadian lakes), 77bm, 64 x 17 ft. Kingston, Ont. 1814. Fate unknown.

JULIA Wood S.gunboat, 'Albacore' class. Fletcher, Limehouse 27.11.1855. BU 2.1866 Marshall, Plymouth.

JULIA Coastguard vessel, 15bm. Purchased circa 1868. Sold 10.4.1891.

JULIA (ex-yacht Maretanza) Coastguard vessel 310 tons, 120 x 20½ ft, 2-7pdr. Purchased 1.4.1901. Sold 6.11.20 M.S. Hilton.

JULIA Store carrier 1863-71.

JULIAN 6th Rate 14, 104bm, 67 x 19 ft. French, captured 1690. Made a bomb 1694. Sold 3.5.1698.

JULIUS 3rd Rate 74x 1,750bm. Chatham DY. Ordered 1807, cancelled 1812.

JUMNA Iron pad. vessel (Indian). Thames 1832. Fate Unknown. (The 1st iron steam vessel built on the Thames.)

JUMNA (ex-ZEBRA renamed 1846) Brig-sloop 16, 549bm, 110 x 35 ft, 16-32pdr. Bombay DY 7.3.1848. Sold 25.6.1862.

JUMNA Iron S. troopship, 4,173bm, 6,211 tons, 360 x 49 ft, 3-4pdr. Palmer 24.9.1866. Coal hulk 1893 and renamed C.110. Sold 7.1922 A.J. Hellyer as hulk Oceanic.

JUMNA Sloop (RIN) 1,300 tons, 283 x 37½ ft, 6-4in. Denny 16.11.1940. Survey vessel 1957.

JUNEE Minesweeper (RAN), 'Bathurst' class. Poole & Steel, Sydney 16.11.1943. Sold 7.58.

JUNIPER Schooner 10, 150bm, 79 x 22 ft. Bermuda 1808. Sold 3.11.1814.

JUNIPER Trawler 1939.

JUNO 5th Rate 32, 667bm, 128 x 34½ ft. Alexander, Rotherhithe 29.9.1757. Burnt 7.8.1778 to avoid capture at Rhode Island.

JUNO 5th Rate 32, 689bm, 126½ x 35 ft. Batson, Limehouse 30.9.1780. BU 7.1811.

JUNON 5th Rate 36, 1,100bm. French, captured 10.2.1809 by a squadron in the W. Indies. Retaken 13.12.1809 by the French.

JUNON 5th Rate 38. French BELLONE captured 6.12.1810 at Mauritius. BU 2.1817 at Deptford.

JUNO 6th Rate 26, 923bm, 131 x 41 ft, 2-8in, 24-32pdr. Pembroke Dock 1.7.1844. Renamed MARINER police ship 10.1.1878; renamed ATALANTA training ship 22.1.1878. Foundered 12.2.1880 in the Atlantic.

JUNO Wood S.corvette, 1,462bm, 2,216 tons, 200 x 40½ ft, 8-64pdr. Deptford DY 28.11.1867. Sold 12.1887.

JUNO 2nd class cruiser 5,600 tons, 350 x 54 ft, 5-6in, 6-4.7in (11-6in 1904). N.C. & A (Vickers) 16.11.1895. Sold 24.9.1920 Earle, resold Petersen & Albeck.

JUNO (ex-JAMAICA renamed 9.1938) Destroyer 1,690 tons, 339½ x 36 ft, 6-4.7in, 10-TT. Fairfield 8.12.38. Sunk 21.5.41 by German and Italian A/C off Crete.

JUNO Frigate, 'Leander' class. Thornycroft 24.11.1965.

JUPITER 4th Rate 50, 1,044bm, 146 x 41 ft. Randall, Rotherhithe 13.5.1778. Wrecked 10.12.1808 in Vigo Bay.

JUPITER 4th Rate 50, 1,173bm, 150 x 42 ft. Plymouth Dy 22.11.1813. Troopship 11.1837; coal hulk 4.1846. BU completed 28.1.1870 at Devonport.

JUPITER (see FORTH of 1833)

JUPITER Battleship 14,900 tons, 390 x 75 ft, 4-12in 12-6in, 18-12 pdr. Thomson 18.11.1895. Sold 15.1.20 Hughes Bolckow. BU at Dewenthaugh.

JUPITER Destroyer 1,690 tons, 339½ x 36 ft, 6-4.7in, 10-TT. Yarrow 27.10.1938. Torpedoed 27.2.42 by a Japanese destroyer in the Java Sea.

JUPITER Frigate, 'Leander' class. Yarrow 4.9.1967.

JUPITER Minesweeper requis. 1915-20.

JUSTE 2nd Rate 80, 2,144bm, 193½ x 50 ft. French, captured at Ushant 1.6.1794. BU 2.1811.

JUSTITIA Prison ship, 260bm. Merchant, purchased 1777. In service in 1795.

JUSTITIA 3rd Rate 74, 1,758bm. Danish, captured 7.9.1807 at Copenhagen. BU 3.1817. (Was to have been renamed ORFORD.)

JUSTITIA (see ZEALAND)

JUSTITIA (see HINDOSTAN of 1804)

JUTLAND Destroyer 2,380 tons, 355 x 40 ft, 5-4.5in, 8-40mm, 10-TT. Hawthorn Leslie 2.11.1945; not completed. Renamed J.4922 (her contract number) 12.45; target 1947. Arrived 10.57 at Rosyth to BU.

JUTLAND (ex-MALPLAQUET renamed 12.45) Destroyer 2,380 tons. Stephen 20.2.46. Arrived 14.5.65 Hughes Bolckow, Blyth to BU.

'K' class submarines. 1,880 tons, 334 x 26½ ft, 2-4in, 1-3in, 10-TT.

K.1 Portsmouth DY 14.11.1916. Sunk 17.11.17 by HMS BLONDE after collision with K.4 off the coast of Denmark.

K.2 Portsmouth DY 14.10.16. Sold 13.7.26 Cashmore, Newport.

K.3 Vickers 20.5.16. Sold 26.10.21 Barking S.Bkg Co.

K.4 Vickers 15.7.16. Sunk 31.1.18 in collision with K.6 off May Island.

K.5 Portsmouth DY 16.12.16. Sunk 20.1.21 in the Bay of Biscay.

K.6 Devonport DY 31.5.16. Sold 13.7.26 Cashmore, Newport.

K.7 Devonport DY 31.5.16. Sold 9.9.21 Fryer, Sunderland.

K.8 Vickers 10.10.16. Sold 11.10.23 McLellan, Bo'ness.

K.9 Vickers 8.11.16. Sold 23.7.26 Alloa, Charlestown.

K.10 Vickers 27.12.16. Sold 4.11.21 C.A.Beard; foundered in tow 10.1.22.

K.11 Armstrong 16.8.16. Sold 4.11.21 C.A.Beard.

K.12 Armstrong 23.2.17. Sold 23.7.26 Alloa, Charlestown.

K.13 Fairfield 11.11.16. Foundered on trials 29.1.17; salved 3.17; renamed K.22. Sold 16.12.26 Young, Sunderland.

K.14 Fairfield 8.2.17. Sold 1926 Granton S.Bkg Co.

K.15 Scotts 30.10.17. Sold 8.24 Upnor S.Bkg Co.

K.16 Beardmore 5.11.17. Sold 22.8.24

J.Hornby; resold 9.24 Alloa S.Bkg Co, Charlestown.

K.17 Vickers 10.4.17. Sunk 31.1.18 in collision with FEARLESS off May Island.

K.18 Vickers. Launched 9.7.17 as M.1.

K.19 Vickers. Launched 19.10.18 as M.2.

K.20 Armstrong. Launched 19.10.20 as M.3.

K.21 Armstrong. Incomplete hull sold 30.11.21 Armstrong.

K.22 (see K.13).

Modified 'K' class submarines, 2,140 tons, 351½ x 28 ft, 3-4in, 10-TT (all ordered 10.6.18).

K.23 Armstrong. Camcelled 26.11.1918.

K.24 Armstrong. Cancelled 26.11.1918.

K.25 Armstrong. Cancelled 26.11.1918. K.26 Vickers 26.8.19, completed at Chatham 15.9.23. Sold 3.31 Mamo Bros, Malta.

K.27 Vickers. Cancelled 26.11.1918.

K.28 Vickers. Cancelled 26.11.1918.

KAHREN (see Indian TB.2 of 1888)

KALE Destroyer 545 tons, 22 x 23½ ft, 1-12pdr, 5-6pdr (4-12pdr 1907), 2-TT. Hawthorn 8.11.1904. Sunk 27.3.18 by mine in the North Sea.

KALE Frigate, 'River' class. Inglis 24.6.1942. Sold 11.56, BU Cashmore, Newport.

KALGOORLIE Minesweeper, 'Bathurst' class. Broken Hill 7.8.1941. Lent RAN from 4.42. Sold 8.46 Dutch navy.

KAMLOOPS Corvette (RCN), 'Flower' class. Victoria Mcy 7.8.1940. Sold 1946 J.Earl McQueen, Amherstburg.

KAMSACK Corvette (RCN), 'Flower' class. Pt Arthur SY 5.5.1941. Sold 1946.

KANDAHAR Destroyer 1,690 tons, 339½ x 36 ft, 6-4in, 10-TT. Denny 21.3.1939. Mined 19.12.41 off Tripoli and sunk next day by HMS JAGUAR.

KANGAROO Brig-sloop 16 (fir-built), 314bm, 95 x 28 ft. Wells, Rotherhithe 30.9.1795. Sold 2.1802.

KANGAROO Sloop 18, 370bm, 106 x 28 ft. Brindley, Lynn 12.9.1805. Sold 14.12.1815.

KANGAROO Survey brig. Purchased 1818. Wrecked 18.12.1828 in the W.Indies.

KANGAROO (ex-*Las Damas Argentinas*) Schooner tender 3, 84bm, 2-12pdr, 1-2in howitzer. Purchased 1829 in Jamaica. Sold 1.1834.

KANGAROO (ex-DOVE renamed 1850)

Brig 12, 483bm, 105 x 33½ ft, 4-32pdr, 8-32pdr carr. Chatham DY 31.8.1852. Renamed WV.20 on 25.5.1863, coastguard. Sold 10.5.1897 M.Hayhurst.

KANGAROO (see DART of 1860)

KANGAROO Destroyer 380 tons, 215 x 21 ft, 1-12pdr, 5-6pdr, 2-TT. Palmer 8.9.1900. Sold 23.3.20 M.Yates, resold Ward, BU Milford Haven 6.20.

KANGAROO BDV (RAN) 1940-67.

KANIERE (see LOCH ACHRAY)

KAPUNDA Minesweeper (RAN). 'Bathurst' class. Poole & Steel, Sydney 23.6.1942. Sold 6.1.61 to BU in Japan.

KAPUSKASING Minesweeper (RCN), 'Algerine' class. Pt Arthur SY 22.7.1943. Survey vessel 1959. Sunk 3.10.78 as a target.

KARRAKATTA (ex-WIZARD renamed 2.4.1890) Torpedo gunboat 735 tons, 230 x 27 ft, 2-4.7in, 4-3pdr, 3-TT. Armstrong 27.8.1889. Sold 11.1.1905 at Portsmouth.

KASHMIR (see JAVELIN of 1938)

KASHMIR Destroyer 1,690 tons, 339½ x 36 ft, 6-4.7in, 10-TT. Thornycroft 4.4.1939. Sunk 23.5.41 by air attack off Crete.

KATHERINE BARK Vessel in service in 1222.

KATHERINE Ship 200bm. Purchased 1402, BU 1406.

KATHERINE Ship 210bm. Purchased 2.1415. Sold 1425.

KATHERINE BARK Ship, 100bm. Built 1518. Listed to 1525.

KATHERINE BRETON Ballinger captured from French 9.1417. Sold 3.1423

KATHERINE FORTILEZA 700-ton ship. Purchased 1512 from the Genoese. Damaged 1521 in a storm and not listed after.

KATHERINE GALLEY Galley, 80bm. Listed 1512-27.

KATHERINE 36-gun ship. French CATHERINE captured 1653. Sold 1658.

KATHERINE Yacht 8, 94bm. Deptford 1661. Captured 1673 by the Dutch.

KATHERINE 2nd Rate 82, 1,003bm, 153 x 40 ft. Woolwich Dy 26.10.1664. Rebuilt 1702; renamed RAMILLIES 18.12.1706. Rebuilt Portsmouth 1749 as 1,689bm. Wrecked 15.2.1760 on Bolt Head. (Also known as ROYAL KATHERINE from 1696).

KATHERINE Fireship 6, 264bm. Purchased 1672. Expended 1672.

KATHERINE Fireship 6, 180bm. Purchased 1672. Expended 1673.

KATHERINE Yacht 8, 131bm, 8-3pdr. Chatham DY 1674. Rebuilt Deptford 1720 as 166bm and renamed CATHERINE. Sold 14.9.1801.

KATHERINE Storeship 6, 292bm, 97 x 25 ft. Purchased 5.10.1692. Sold 22.5.1701.

KATHIAWAR (ex-HARTLEPOOL renamed 1942) Minesweeper (RIN), turbine 'Bangor' class. Blyth 14.7.1942. Renamed CHITTAGONG (RPN) 1948. Sold 1956.

KATOOMBA (ex-PANDORA renamed 4.1890) 2nd class cruiser 2,575 tons, 265 x 41 ft, 8-4.7in, 8-3pdr. Armstrong 27.8.89. Sold 10.7.1906, BU at Morecambe.

KATOOMBA Minesweeper (RAN), 'Bathurst' class. Poole & Steel 16.4.1941. Sold 2.5.57 to BU in Hong Kong.

KEATS (ex-USS TISDALE) Frigate, DE 'Captain' class. Boston N.Yd 17.7.1943 on lend-lease. Returned 2.46 USN.

KEDLESTON Coastal M/S, 'ton' class. Pickersgill 21.12.1953. Renamed NORTHUMBRIA 1.55; KEDLESTON 1955.

KEITH Destroyer leader 1,400 tons, 312 x 532 ft, 4-4.7in, 8-TT. Vickers Armstrong, Barrow 10.7.1930. Sunk 1.6.40 by air attack at Dunkirk.

KELLETT (ex-UPPINGHAM renamed 1919) Survey ship, 1-3pdr. Simons 31.5.1919. M/S 1939, 2-2pdr. Sold 20.3.45 BU by Young, Sunderland.

KELLINGTON Coastal M/S, 'Ton' class. Pickersgill 12.10.1954.

KELLY Destroyer leader 1,695 tons, 339½ x 36 ft, 6-4.7in, 10-TT. Hawthorn Leslie 25.10.1938. Sunk 23.5.41 by air attack off Crete.

KELOWNA Minesweeper (RCN), TE 'Bangor' class. P. Rupert DD 28.5.1941. Sold 1946 mercantile.

KELVIN Destroyer 1,690 tons, 339½ x 36 ft, 6-4.7in, 10-TT. Fairfield 19.1.1939. Sold 6.4.49, BU at Troon.

KELVIN Trawler requis 1915-17.

KEMERTON Coastal M/S, 'Tons' class. Harland & Wolff 27.11.1953. Renamed KILMORY 1955; KEMERTON 1961. Sold 25.10.71, BU at Poole in 1975.

KEMPENFELT Destroyer leader 1,607 tons, 325 x 32 ft, 4-4in, 4-TT. Cammell Laird 1.5.1915. Sold 9.5.21 Ward, Morecambe.

KEMPENFELT Destroyer leader 1,390 tons, 318 x 33 ft, 4-4.7in, 8-TT.

White 29.10.1931. RCN 8.39. Renamed ASSINIBOINE 18.10.39. Wrecked 10.11.45 on Prince Edward Island. Wreck sold 17.7.52.

KEMPENFELT (ex-VALENTINE) Destroyer leader 1,730 tons, 339½ x 36 ft, 4-4.7in, 4-40mm, 8-TT.J.Brown 8.5.1943. To Jugoslav navy 10.56, renamed KOTOR.

KEMPENFELT (see VALENTINE of 1943)

KEMPTHORNE (ex-USS TRUMPETER) Frigate, DE 'Captain' class. Boston N.Yd 17.7.1943 on lend-lease. Returned 8.45 to the USN.

KEMPTON Paddle M/S, 'Ascot' class. Ferguson 3.6.1916. Sunk 24.6.17 by mine off Dover.

KENDAL Minesweeper, later 'Hunt' class. Fairfield 9.2.1918. Sold 3.10.28 Alloa, Charlestown.

KENILWORTH CASTLE Corvette. 'Castle' class. Smiths DK 17.8.1943. Arrived 20.6.59 Rees, Llanelly to BU.

KENNET Destroyer 550 tons, 222 x 23½ ft, 1-12pdr, 5-6pdr, (4-12 pdr 1907), 2-TT. Thornycroft, Chiswick 4.12.1903. Sold 11.12.19 J.H.Lee.

KENNET Trawler requis. 1915-19. Trawler 1920-46.

KENNINGTON (ex-MERMAID renamed 1735) 6th Rate 24, 429bm, 106 x 30½ ft. Deptford DY 30.6.1736. BU 9.1749 at Plymouth.

KENNINGTON 6th Rate 20, 437bm, 107½ x 30½ ft. Adams, Bucklers Hard 1.5.1756. BU completed 31.1.1774 Sheerness.

KENOGAMI Corvette (RCN), 'Flower' class. Pt Arthur SY 5.9.1940. Sold 1946, BU 1950. at Hamilton, Ont, by steel Co of Canada.

KENORA Minesweeper (RCN), TE 'Bangor' class. PT Arthur SY 20.12.1941. Laid up 1946. Sold 29.11.57 Turkish navy, renamed BANDIRMA.

KENT (see KENTISH)

KENT 3rd Rate 70, 1,040bm, 151 x 40 ft, 26-32pdr, 26-12pdr, 14-4pdr, 4-3pdr. Johnson, Blackwall 1679. Rebuilt Rotherhithe 1699 as 1,064bm; rebuilt 1424 as 1,130bm. BU 1744.

KENT 3rd Rate 70, 1,309bm, 155 x 44½ ft. Deptford 1746. Hulked 1760 in the E.Indies.

KENT 3rd Rate 74, 1,617bm, 168 x 47 ft. Deptford DY 23.3.1762. Sold. 5.8.1784.

KENT 3rd Rate 74, 1,694m, 183 x 50 ft. Perry, Blackwall 17.1.1798. Sheer hulk 1856. BU 1881.

KENT Gunvessel 16 Purchased 1798.

Sold 1801.

KENT Screw 2nd Rate 91, 3,716bm, 252 x 57½ ft. Portsmouth DY. Laid down 13.3.1860, cancelled 12.12.1863.

KENT (see IMPREGNABLE of 1810)

KENT Armoured cruiser 9,800 tons, 440 x 66 ft, 14-6in, 10-12pdr. Portsmouth DY 6.3.1901. Sold 6.20 at Hong Kong.

KENT Cruiser 9,850 tons, 590 x 68 ft, 8-4in. Chatham DY 16.3.1926. Sold 22.1.48, BU at Troon.

KENT GM destroyer 5,600 tons, 505 x 54 ft, 4-45.in, 8-GWS, 20-20 mm. Harland & Wolff 27.9.1961.

KENTISH A.merchant. Purchased 1646. Listed to 1647.

KENTISH 46-gun ship, 601bm. Deptford 1652. Renamed KENT 1660. Wrecked 10.1672 near Cromer.

KENTVILLE Minesweeper (RCN), TE 'Bangor' class. Pt. Arthur SY 17.4.1942. Laid up 1964. Sold 29.11.57 to Turkish navy, renamed BARTIN.

KENYA Cruiser 8,000 tons, 538 x 62 ft, 12-6in, 8-4in. Stephen 18.8.1939. Arrived 29.10.62 Faslane to BU.

KEPPEL Brig 14, 75bm, 14-4pdr. American, captured 1778. Sold 5.8.1783 at New York.

KEPPEL Destroyer leader 1,750 tons, 318 x 32 ft, 5-4.7in, 1-3in, 6-TT. Thornycroft 23.4.1920. Sold 7.45, BU Ward, Barrow.

KEPPEL Frigate 1,180 tons, 300 x 33 ft, 3-40mm, 4-TT. Yarrow 31.8.1954. Arrived Sittingbourne 29.4.79 to BU.

KERTCH Schooner gunboat 2, 94bm. Messrs German, Malta 14.7.1855. Made a yard craft 10.1860, renamed YC.1. In service in 1875.

KESTREL Brigantine, 200bm, ex-yacht. Purchased 5.12.1846. BU 11.1852.

KESTREL Wood S. gunboat, 'Clown' class. Miller, Liverpool 20.5.1856. Sunk in action 6.1859 at Peiho; raised; sold 16.3.1866 Glover & Co, Yokohama; resold Japanese navy.

KESTREL Compos. S.gunvessel 610 tons, 155 x 25 ft, 1-7in, 1-64pdr, 2-20pdr. Chatham DY 29.2.1872. Sold 11.1888.

KESTREL Destroyer 380 tons, 218 x 20 ft, 1-12pdr, 5-6pdr, 2-TT. J. Brown 25.3.1898. Sold 17.3.21 Ward, Rainham.

KESTREL Trawler & Drifter WW.I. Tug requis. 1940-46.

KEW Minesweeper, late 'Hunt' class. Eltringham. Cancelled 1918.

KHARTOUM Destroyer 1,690 tons, 339½ x 36 ft, 6-4in, 10-TT. Swan Hunter 6.2.1939. Beached 23.6.40 Perim harbour after accidental explosion.

KHEDIVE Escort carrier 7,800 tons, Oregon SB Co. Laid down 20.7.1943 for the RN but retained and launched 28.11.43 as USS NEHENTA BAY.

KHEDIVE (ex-Cordova) Escort carrier 11,420 tons, 2-4in, 16-40mm, 24-A/C. Seattle Tacoma 30.1.43, transferred RN 25.8.43 on lend-lease. Returned 26.1.46 to the USN.

KHYBER (ex-HARWICH renamed 10.1941) Minesweeper (RIN), turbine 'Bangor' class. Hamilton 17.2.42. BU 1949.

KIAMA Minesweeper (RAN), 'Bathurst' class. Evans Deakin 3.7.1943. RNZN 5.52.

KIAWO River gunboat. Ex-river steamer purchased 1926, commissioned 25.1.27. Sold 1930.

'Kil' class patrol gunboats. 895 tons, 170 x 30 ft, 1-4in.

KILBEGGAN G.Brown 23.9.1918. Sold 14.2.20 Robinson, Brown & Joplin, renamed Luckner.

KILBERRY G.Brown 2.7.18. Sold as above, renamed Bolam.

KILBIRNIE G.Brown 16.5.19. Sold as above.

KILBRIDE Hall Russell 5.18. Sold as above, renamed Scotsgap.

KILBURN Hall Russell 28.5.18. Sold as above, renamed Tarset.

KILCAVAN Hall Russell 1918. Sold as above.

KILCHATTAN Cook, Welton & Germmell 13.4.18. Sold as above, renamed Benton.

KILCHREEST Smiths Dk 8.6.18. Sold as above, renamed Harrogate.

KILCHRENAN Smiths Dk 15.1.18. Sold as above, renamed Bombardier.

KILCHVAN CW & G 13.7.18. Sold as above, renamed Belsay.

KILCLARE Smiths Dk 14.1.18. Sold as above.

KILCLIEF CW & G. 8.10.18. Sold as above, renamed it Tynehome.

KILCLOGHER CW & G. 24.10.18. Sold as above, renamed Northerner.

KILCOCK Smiths Dk 27.4.18. Sold as above, renamed Spinner.

KILDALKEY Cochrane 13.3.18. Sold as above, same name.

KILDANGAN Cochrane 15.3.18. Sold as above, renamed Bebside.

KILDARE Cochrane 10.4.18. Sold as

above, renamed *Mitford*.

KILDARY Smiths Dk 1.11.17. Sold as above, renamed *Sorcerer*.

KILDAVIN Smiths Dk 13.2.18. Sold as above, renamed *Leaside*.

KILDIMO Smiths Dk 27.4.18. Sold as above, renamed *Southerner*.

KILDONAN Cochrane 11.4.18. Sold 21.11.19 Thornycroft, renamed *Watkin*.

KILDOROUGH Smiths Dk 16.11.17. Sold as 'Kilbeggan', renamed *Wearmouth*.

KILDORRY Smiths Dk 14.2.18. Sold as 'Kilbeggan', renamed *Dempster*.

KILDRESS Cochrane 13.4.18. Sold as 'Kildonan', renamed *Glynarthan*.

KILDWICK Cochrane 27.4.18. Sold as 'Kildonan', renamed *Pengham*.

KILDWICK Cochrane 27.4.18. Sold as 'Kilbeggan', renamed *Empleton*; hired 1940 as INDIRA.

KILFENORA Smiths Dk 14.12.17. Sold as 'Kilbeggan; same name.

KILFINNY Cochrane 10.5.18. Sold as 'Kilbeggan', renamed *Kenrhos*.

KILFREE Cochrane 11.5.18. Sold as 'Kildonan', renamed *Porthminster*.

KILFULLERT Smiths Dk 15.3.18. Sold as 'Kilbeggan', renamed *Wearhome*.

KILGARVAN Smiths Dk 27.5.18. Sold as 'Kilbeggan', renamed *Heather King*.

KILGOBNET Smiths Dk 14.12.17. Sold as 'Kilbeggan', renamed *Maxton*.

KILHAM Smiths Dk 10.6.18. Sold as 'Kilbeggan', renamed *Easterner*.

KILKEEL Smiths Dk 27.3.18. Sold as 'Kilbeggan', renamed *Falconer*.

KILLENA Smiths Dk 9.7.18. Sold as 'Kilbeggan', renamed *Edwin Douglas*.

KILLERIG Smiths Dk 9.7.18. Sold 11.20 as salvage vessel, same name.

KILLINEY Smiths Dk 29.7.18. Sold as 'Kilbeggan', renamed *Thropton*.

KILLOUR Smiths Dk 9.8.18. Sold 1920, renamed *Narworth*.

KILLOWEN Smiths Dk 6.9.18. Sold as 'Kilbeggan', renamed *Curler*.

KILLYBEGS Smiths Dk 7.9.18. Sold as 'Kilbeggan', renamed *Alwinton*.

KILLYGORDON Smiths Dk 10.10.18. Sold as 'Kilbeggan', renamed *Homeford*.

KILMALCOLM Smiths Dk 8.10.18. Sold as 'Kilbeggan', renamed *Nigretia*.

KILMACRENNAN Smiths Dk 5.11.18. Sold as 'Kilbeggan', renamed *Seghill*.

KILMAINE Smiths Dk 5.11.18. Sold as

'Kilbeggan', renamed *Crofter*.

KILMALLOCK Smiths Dk 4.12.18. Sold 14.2.20 L.Gueret, renamed *Mallock*.

KILMANAHAN Smiths Dk 17.12.18. Sold as 'Kilmallock', renamed *Manahan*.

KILMARNOCK Smiths Dk 31.3.19. Sold as 'Kilmallock', same name.

KILMARTIN Smiths Dk 31.3.19. Sold as 'Kilmallock', renamed *Mandrake*.

KILMEAD Smiths Dk 1.5.19. Sold as 'Kilmallock', renamed *Mead*; hired 1940 as MEAD.

KILMELFORD Smiths Dk 14.5.19. Sold as 'Kilmallock', renamed *Melford*.

KILMERSDON Smiths Dk 30.5.19. Sold as 'Kilmallock', renamed *Mersdon*.

KILMINGTON Smiths dk 30.5.19. Sold as 'Kilmallock', renamed *Mington*.

KILMORE Smiths Dk 17.7.19. Sold as 'Kilmallock', renamed *Newtonia*.

KILMUCKRIDGE Smiths Dk 28.7.19. Sold as 'Kilmallock', renamed *Newton Bay*.

KILMUN Smiths Dk 11.10.19. Completed as cable vessel (RFA); sold 16.9.46.

The following 31 vessels were cancelled in 1918:

Two by G.Brown: KILBRACHAN, KILGLASS;

13 by Cochrane: KILGOWAN, KILKEE, KILKENNY, KILKENZIE, KILKERRIN, KILKHAMPTON, KILLADOON, KILLALOO, KILLANE, KILLARNEY, KILLARY, KILLEGAN, KILLEGAR;

ten by C.W & G: KILCOLGAN, KILCONNAN, KILCONNELL, KILCOOLE, KILCORNIE, KILCOT, KILCREGGAN, KILCULLEN, KILCURRIG, KILDALE;

five by Hall Russell: KILBARCHAN, KILBY, KILBANE, KILBRITTAIN, KILCAR;

one by Smiths Dk: KILDPART.

'Kil' class patrol sloops, 795 tons, 176½ x 33 ft, 1-3in, 3-40mm. All built by Pullman Standard Car Co, Chicago on lend-lease.

KILBIRNIE launched 2.5.1943. Returned 12.46 to the USN and sold as 'Haugesund'.

KILBRIDE 15.5.43. Returned 12.46 to the USN.

KILCHATTAN 27.5.43. Returned 12.46, sold as *Stravanger*.

KILCHRENAN 13.6.43. Returned 12.46.

KILDARY 26.6.43. Returned 12.46, sold as *Rio Vouga*.

KILDWICK 10.7.43. Returned 12.46.

KILHAM 2.8.43. Returned 1946, sold as *Sognefjord.*

KILKENZIE 19.8.43. Returned 12.46, sold, same name.

KILHAMPTON 3.9.43. Returned 1946, sold as *Georgios F.*

KILMALCOLM 17.9.43. Returned 12.46, sold as *Rio Agueda.*

KILMARNOCK 1.10.43. Returned 12.46, sold as *Arion.*

KILMARTIN 13.10.43. Returned 12.46, sold as *Marigoula.*

KILMELFORD 23.10.43. Returned 12.46.

KILMINGTON 2.11.43. Returned 12.46, sold as *Athinai.*

KILMORE 9.11.43. Returned 12.46, sold as *Despina.*

KILDARTON Coastal M/S, 'Ton' class. Harland & Wolff 23.5.1955. Sold 28.7.69 to BU.

KILLIECRANKIE RNVR tenders. (See DERRITON)

KILMOREY RNVR tenders. (See KEMERTON and ALFRISTON)

KIMBERLEY Destroyer 1,690 tons, 339½ x 36 ft, 6-4.7in, 10-TT. Thornycroft 1.6.1939. Sold 30.3.49, BU at Troon.

KIMBERLEY 4 Trawlers and a Drifter WW.I.

KINCARDINE (see MARINER of 1944)

KINCARDINE (ex-TAMWORTH CASTLE renamed 1943) Corvette (RCN), 'Castle' class. Smiths Dk 26.1.44. Sold 5.9.46, renamed *Saada.*

KING ALFRED Armoured cruiser 14,100 tons, 500 x 71 ft, 2-9.2in, 16-6in, 12-12pdr. Vickers 28.10.1901. Sold 30.1.20 F.Rijsdijk, BU in Holland.

KING DAVID Storeship. Captured 1653. Sold 1654.

KING EDWARD VII Battleship 16,350 tons, 425 x 78 ft, 4-12in, 4-9.2in, 10-6in , 14-12pdr. Devonport DY 23.7.1903. Sunk 6.1.16 by mine off Cape Wrath.

KING GEORGE Coastguard cutter, 60bm. In 1863. Renamed FLORA 26.5.1883. Wrecked 12.11.1901 near Kingstown.

KING GEORGE V Battleship 22,500 tons. Armstrong. Renamed MONARCH 1910 and launched 30.3.11.

KING GEORGE V (ex-ROYAL GEORGE renamed 1910) Battleship 23,000 tons, 555 x 89 ft, 10-13.5in, 16-4in, Portsmouth DY 9.10.11. Sold 12.26. Alloa S.Bkg Co., arrived Rosyth 1.27 to BU.

KING GEORGE V Battleship 35,000 tons, 700 x 103 ft, 10-14in, 16-5.25in. Vickers Armstrong, Tyne 21.2.1939. Arrived 20.1.58 at Dalmuir and then Troon 25.5.59.

KING OF PRUSSIA Cutter. Purchased 3.1763. Lost 6.2.1765 off Ramsgate.

KINGCUP Corvette, 'Flower' class. Harland & Wolff 31.10.1940. Sold 31.7.46, renamed *Rubis.*

KINGFISH Brig. Listed 3.1807 to 7.1814.

KINGFISHER Ship, 269bm. In service 1664 to 1667.

KINGFISHER 46-gun-ship, 664bm, 136 x 34 ft, 22-18pdr, 20-6pdr, 4-4pdr. Pett, Woodbridge, 1675. Rebuilt Woolwich 1699 as 661bm; hulked 1706. BU 1728 at Sheerness.

KINGFISHER Ketch 4, 61bm. Purchased 1684. Captured 3.1690 by the French.

KINGFISHER Sloop 14, 275bm, 92 x 26½ ft. Darby, Gosport 12.12.1745. Bomb 8 from 9.58 to 3.60. Sold 3.5.1763.

KINGFISHER Sloop 14, 302bm, 97 x 26½ ft. Chatham DY 13.7.1770. Burnt 7.8.1778 to avoid capture at Rhode Island.

KINGFISHER Brig-sloop 18, 369bm, 95 x 30½ ft, 18-6pdr. Rochester 1782 and purchased on stocks. Wrecked 3.12.1798 on Lisbon Bar.

KINGFISHER Sloop 18, 370bm, 106 x 28 ft, 16-32pdr carr., 2-6pdr. King, Dover 10.3.1804. BU 10.1816 at Portsmouth.

KINGFISHER Brig-sloop 10, 'Cherokee' class, 237bm. Woolwich DY 11.3.1823. Sold 16.8.1838 Mr Knowland.

KINGFISHER Brig 12, 446bm, 103 x 32½ ft, 10-32pdr, 2-18pdr. Pembroke Dock 8.4.1845. Laid up 1852; Harbour service 1875. Sold 26.4.1890. W. Tayler.

KINGFISHER Compos. S.sloop 1,130 tons, 170 x 36 ft, 2-7in, 4-64pdr. Sheerness DY 16.12.1879. Renamed LARK 10.11.1892 training ship; renamed CRUIZER 18.5.1893. Sold 1919.

KINGFISHER (see MARTIN of 1850)

KINGFISHER River gunboat. Yarrow, Ordered 1912 and cancelled.

KINGFISHER Patrol vessel 510 tons, 234 x 26½ ft, 1-4in. Fairfield 14.2.1935. Sold 21.4.47, BU Stockton Ship & Salvage Co.

KINGFISHER Patrol boat 187 tons. Dunston 20.9.1974.

KINGFISHER Trawler 1915 and salvage ship 1954-61.

KINGHAM Inshore M/S, 'Ham' class. White 26.1.1955. Transferred French navy 1955.

KINGSALE (see KINSALE)

KINGSFORD Seaward defence boat, 'Ford' class. Rowhedge IW 24.3.1955. Sold 7.4.71, BU at Cairn-ryan 1972.

KINGSMILL Gunvessel 1, 150bm. Listed 1797 to 1801.

KINGSMILL Frigate, DE 'Captain' class. Boston N Yd 13.8.1943 on lend-lease. Returned 7.45 to the USN.

KINGSTON 4th Rate 60, 924bm, 145 x 40 ft, 24-24pdr, 26-9pdr, 10-6pdr. Frame, Hull 13.3.1697. Rebuilt Portsmouth 1719; rebuilt Plymouth 1740 as 1,068bm. Sold 14.1.1762.

KINGSTON (see PRINCE REGENT of 1814)

KINGSTON (see PORTLAND of 1822)

KINGSTON Schooner, 109bm. Slaver *Cortes* captured 4.1858 by FORWARD. Sunk 1861 as a bathing place at Kingston, Jamaica. BU 3.1867.

KINGSTON Destroyer 1,690 tons, 339½ x 36 ft, 6-4.7in, 10-TT. White 9.1.1939 Wrecked 11.4.42 by air attack in dock, Malta; hull used as blockship.

KINGSTON Trawler requis. 1915-19.

KINGUSSIE Minesweeper, later 'Hunt' class. Eltringham. Cancelled 1918.

KINNAIRDS HEAD (see MULL of GALLOWAY)

KINROSS Minesweeper, later 'Hunt' class, Fairfield 4.7.1918. Sunk 16.6.19 by mine in the Aegean.

KINGSALE Ketch 10, 91bm. Irish Royalist, captured 1656 by Parliament. Sold 1663.

KINGSALE 5th Rate 32, 533bm, 117½ 32 ft. Studleigh & Stacey, Kinsale 22.5.1700. Rebuilt Portsmouth 1724 as 607bm. BU 1741.

KINSALE 5th Rate 44, 701bm, 125 x 36 ft. Bird, Rotherhithe 27.11.1741. Ordered to be hulked at Antigua 7.1758. Ordered to be sold 12.1762.

KINSHA (ex-*Pioneer*) River gunboat 616 tons, 180 x 30 f, 6-MG. Purchased 11.1900. Sold 30.4.21 at Shanghai.

KIPLING Destroyer 1,690 tons, 339½ x 36ft, 6-4.7in, 10-TT. Yarrow 19.1.1939. Sunk 11.5.42 by air attack in the eastern Mediterranean.

KIRKLAND LAKE (ex- ST JEROME renamed 3.1944) Frigate (RCN), 'River' class. Morton 27.4.44. Sold 22.9.47 to BU.

KIRKLISTON Coastal M/S, 'Ton' class. Harland & Wolff 18.2.1954. Renamed KILMORY 1955-60.

KISTNA Sloop (RIN) 1,350 tons, 283 x 38½ ft, 6-4in. Yarrow 22.4.1943.

KITCHEN Yacht 8, 101bm, 59 x 19½ ft. Castle, Rotherhithe 1670. Bomb 7.1692. Sold 25.11.1698.

KITCHENER (see VANCOUVER of 1941).

KITCHENER (ex-VANCOUVER renamed 11.41) Corvette (RCN), 'Flower' class. G.T. Davie 18.11.41. Sold 1946, BU 4.49. at Hamilton, Ont.

KITE Cutter 6, 82bm, 56 x 18½ ft. Deptford DY 7.9.1764. Sold 29.10.1771.

KITE Cutter 12, 218bm, 77½ x 27 ft, 12-4pdr. Purchased 4.1778. Rated sloop 4.79 to 1783. to BU 12.1793.

KITE Brig-sloop 16 (fir-built), 365bm, 96 x 30½ ft. Barnard, Deptford 7.1795. Sold 9.1805.

KITE Sloop 16 (fir-built), 284bm, 93 x 26 ft. Warren, Brightlingsea 13.7.1805. Sold 14.12.1815.

KITE (ex-GPO vessel *Aetna*) Wood pad. gunvessel, 300bm, 125 x 23 ft. Transferred. 7.1837. Sold 1864 T. Sargent.

KITE Iron S. gunboat, 'Ant' class. Napier 8.2.1871. Sold 18.5.1920 Hughes Bolckow, became a dredger.

KITE Sloop 1,350 tons, 283 x 38½ ft, 6-4in. Cammell Laird 13.10.1942. Sunk 21.8.44 by 'U 344' in the Greenland Sea.

KITE Trawler and Tug requis. WW1.

KITTIWAKE Patrol vessel 530 tons, 234 x 26½ ft, 1-4in. Thornycroft 30.11.1936. Sold 1946, renamed *Tuch Shing.*

KNARESBOROUGH CASTLE Corvette 'Castle' class. Blyth SB 29.9.1943. Arrived 16.3.56 Smith & Houston, Pt Glasgow to BU.

KNOLE Minesweeper, later 'Hunt' class. Eltringham. Cancelled 1918.

KOKANEE Frigate (RCN), 'River' class. Yarrow, Esquimalt 27.11.1943. Sold 12.45, renamed *Bengal* pilot vessel 1948.

KONKAN (ex-TILBURY renamed 10.1941) Minesweeper (RIN), TE 'Bangor' class. Lobnitz 18.2.42. For disposal 1963.

KOOTENAY (see DECOY of 1932).

KOOTENAY Escort (RCN) 2,365 tons, 4-3in. Burrard 15.6.1954.

KRAIT SSV (RAN) Japanese *Kofuku Maru* Captured 11.12.1941. To N Borneo 2.45. Museum ship Sydney 1964.

KRAKOWIAK (see SILVERTON).

KRISHNA Survey brig (Indian). Listed

1841-60.

KRONPRINCEN 3rd Rate 74. Danish KRONPRINDS FREDERICK captured 7.9.1807 at Copenhagen. Completed 12.1809 as prison ship. Sold 21.11.1814.

KRONPRINCESSEN 3rd Rate 74. Danish KRONPRINDESSE MARIE captured 7.9.1807 at Copenhagen. Sold 15.12.1814.

KUITAN Patrol boat (RCN), 84 x 20 ft, 1-MG. Armstrong, Victoria 25.9.1941. For disposal 1946.

KUJAWIAK (see OAKLEY).

KUKRI (see TRENT of 1942).

KUMAON (ex-MIDDLESBROUGH renamed 10.1941) Minesweeper (RIN), turbine 'Bangor' class. Hamilton 2.5.42. For disposal 1950.

KURNAI (see BATAAN).

'L'class submarines. L.1-8.890 tons, 222 x 23½ ft, 1-4in, 4-TT. L.9-36.890 tons, 228 x 23½ ft, 1-4in, 6-TT (except L9, 15, 17, 19, 20.26, 27 and 33, 1-4in, 4-TT and L14,24 and 25, 4-TT, 14-mines). L.50-74, 960 tons, 230½ x 23½ ft, 2-4in, 6-TT.

L.1 (ex-E.57) Vickers 10.5.1917. Sold. 3.30 Cashmore, Newport, Wrecked at St Just and BU there.

L.2 (ex-E.58) Vickers 6.7.17. Arrived 5.30 Ward, Grays, to BU.

L.3 Vickers 1.9.17. Arrived 29.10.30. Charlestown to BU.

L.4 Vickers 17.11.17. Arrived 24.2.34 Ward, Grays to BU.

L.5 Swan Hunter 26.1.18. BU 1931 Charlestown. (Arrived 20.11.30)

L.6 Beardmore 14.1.18. Arrived 1.35 Cashmore, Newport to BU.

L.7 Cammell Laird 24.4.17. Arrived 26.2.30 Hughes Bolcokow, Blyth to BU.

L.8 Cammell Laird 7.7.17. Sold 7.10.30 Cashmore.

L.9 Denny 29.1.18. Foundered 18.8.23 at Hong Kong; raised 6.9.23. Sold 30.6.67 at Hong Kong.

L.10 Vickers 24.1.18. Torpedoed 30.10.18. by Germany destroyer S.33 off the Texel.

L.11 Vickers 26.2.18. Sold 16.2.32 Young, Sunderland.

L.12 Vickers 16.3.18. Sold 16.2.32 Cashmore, Newport.

L.14 Vickers 10.6.18. Sold 5.34 Cashmore, Newport.

L.15 Fairfield 16.1.18. Sold 2.32 Cashmore, Newport.

L.16 Fairfield 9.4.18. Sold 2.34 Brechin, Granton.

L.17 Vickers 13.5.18. Sold 2.34 Ward, Pembroke Dock.

L.18 Vickers 21.11.18. Sold 10.36 Ward, Pembroke Dock.

L.19 Vickers 4.2.19. Arrived 12.4.37 Ward, Pembroke Dk.

L.20 Vickers 23.9.18. Sold 7.1.35 Cashmore, Newport.

L.21 Vickers 11.10.19. Sold 2.39 Arnott Young; stranded 21.2.39 in tow; arrived 4.39 Dalmuir.

L.22 Vickers 25.10.19. Sold 30.8.35 Cashmore, Newport.

L.23 Vickers 1.7.19, completed Chatham 26.8.24. Foundered in tow 5.46 off Nova Scotia on passage to breakers.

L.24 Vickers 19.2.19. Sunk 10.1.24 in collision with RESOLUTION off Portland.

L.25 Vickers 13.2.19. Arrived 10.35 Cashmore, Newport.

L.26 Vickers 29.5.19, completed Devonport 11.10.26. Sold 1945 in Canada to BU.

L.27 Vickers 14.6.19 BU 1944 in Canada.

L.28-3 all Vickers. cancelled 1919.

L.32 Vickers 23.8.19, not completed. Hull sold 1.3.20 Leith Salvage Co, renamed LS.2 (camel)

L.33 Swan Hunter 29.5.19. Sold 2.32 Ward. Lelant.

L.34 and 35 Pembroke Dock. cancelled 1919.

L.36 Fairfield. Cancelled 1919.

L.37-49 Not ordered.

L.50 Cammell Laird. Laid down 5.17, cancelled 1.4.19.

L.51 Cammell Laird. Cancelled 1919.

L.52 Armstrong 18.12.18. Arrived 9.35 Rees, Llanelly.

L.53 Armstrong 12.8.19, completed Chatham 10.24. Arrived 23.1.39 Ward, Briton Ferry.

L.54 Denny 20.8.19, completed Devonport 9.24. Arrived 2.2.39 Ward, Briton Ferry

L.54 Denny 20.8.19, completed Devonport 9.24. Arrived 2.2.39 Ward, Briton Ferry.

L.55 Fairfield 21.9.18. Sunk 9.6.19 by Russian torpedo boat in the Baltic; salved 1928 and commissioned in the Russian navy.

L.56 Fairfield 29.5.19. Arrived 16.4.38 Ward, Pembroke Dock.

L.57 Fairfield. Laid down 1.18, cancelled 1.4.19.

L.58 Fairfield. Laid down 22.4.18, cancelled 1.4.19.

L.59 Beardmore. Cancelled 1919.

L.60.61. Cammell Laird. Cancelled 1919.

L.62 Fairfield. Laid down 10.10.18, cancelled 30.11.18.

L.63, 64 Scotts. Cancelled 1919.

L.65 Swan Hunter. Laid down 9.18, cancelled 29.6.19.

L.66 Swan Hunter. Cancelled 1919.

L.67, 68 Armstrong. Laid down 11.17 and 12.17 resp. Cancelled 1.4.19 and frames used for Yugoslav HRABRI and NEBOJSA, completed 1927.

L.69 Beardmore 6.12.18, completed Rosyth 3.23. sold 2.39 Arnott Young, Dalmuir.

L.70 Beardmore. Cancelled and hull sold 1.3.20 Leith Salvage Co, renamed LS.3 (Camel)

L.71 Scotts. 17.5.19. Sold 25.3.38 Ward, Milford Haven.

L.72 Scotts. Laid down 12.17, cancelled 1.4.19.

L.73, 74 Denny. Cancelled 1919.

LABUAN (see GOLD COAST)

LABAUN (see LST.3501)

LABUAN Landing craft (RAN) 310 tons. Walker 12.1971

LABURNUM Sloop, 'Acacia' class. Connell 10.6.1915. Drillship 1935. Lost 2.42 at Singapore.

LABURNUM (ex-Japanese minelayer WAKATAKA seized 17.10.47 and renamed 1949) Drillship 1,890 tons.

LABURNUM Drifter requis. 1914-19.

LACEDAEMONIAN Brig 12, 195bm. French privateer LACEDMONIENNE captured 5.1796 by PIQUE and CHARON in the W.Indies. Recaptured 5.1797 by the French in the W.Indies.

LACEDAEMONIAN 5th Rate 38, 1,073bm, 150½ x 40 ft. Portsmouth DY 21.12.1812. BU 11.1822.

LACHINE Minesweeper (RCN), diesel 'Bangor' class. Davie SB 14.6.41. Transferred to RCMP 1950 as *Starnes*.

LACHLAN Frigate (RAN), 'River' class. Morts Dk, Sydney 25.3.1944. RNZN 1948 as survey ship.

LACHUTE Corvette (RCN), modified 'Flower' class. Morton, Quebec 9.6.1944. Sold 1947 Dominican navy, renamed CRISTOBAL COLON.

LADAS Sloop, '24' class. Osbourne Graham, Sunderland 21.9.1918. Sold

1920; repurchased 1920 as mooring vessel. Sold 8.6.36 Metal Industries, Rosyth.

LADAVA Patrol boat (RAN) 100 tons. 11.5.1968. To Papua-New Guinea 9.75

LADY CANNING Paddle sloop (Indian), 527bm. Bombay DY 24.3.1857. Hulked 1870 at Calcutta.

LADY FALKLAND Paddle vessel (Indian). Laird 1854. Foundered in tow 6.5.1854.

LADY LOCH Iron gunboat (Australian) 336 tons, 183 x 24½ ft, 1-6in. Campbell, Melbourne 1886. Listed to 1901.

LADY NELSON Survey brig 6. Purchased 1800. Destroyed 1825 by the natives of Babber Island, Timor.

LADY PREVOST Schooner 12 (Canadian lakes), 230bm. Amherstburg, Lake Erie 13.7.1812. Captured 10.9.1813 by Americans.

LADYBIRD River gunboat 645 tons, 230 x 36 ft, 2-6in, 2-12pdr. Lobnitz 12.4.1916. Sunk 12.5.41 by Italian A/C off Tobruk.

LADYBIRD (ex-*Wusueh*) Base ship 3,400 tons, 295 x 46 ft. Purchased 8.1950. Sold 5.53 China Navig. Co (original owners).

LADYBIRD Tender 213 tons Holmes 27.1.1970

LAE (see LST 3035)

LAE Patrol boat (RAN) 100 tons. Walker 5.10.67 To Papua-New Guinea 9.75

LAERTES (ex-SARPEDON renamed 30.9.1913) Destroyer 982 tons, 260 x 27 ft, 3-4in, 4-TT. Swan Hunter 6.6.13. Sold 1.12.21 Stanlee,, Dover; arrived 8.3.22 after stranding near Newhaven.

LAERTES Minesweeper, 'Algerine' class. Redfern, Toronto 25.3.1944. Arrived 21.4.59 Ward, Barrow to BU.

LAERTES Trawler 1940-42

LAFOREY (ex-FLORIZEL renamed 30.9.1913) Destroyer 995 tons, 260 x 27½ ft, 3-4in, 4-TT. Fairfield 22.8.13. Sunk 23.3.17 by British mine in the Channel.

LAFOREY Destroyer leader 1,935 tons, 354 x 37 ft, 6-4.7in, 8-TT. Yarrow 15.2.1941. Sunk 30.3.44 by 'U.223' north of Sicily.

LAGAN Frigate, 'River' class. Inglis 28.7.1942. Damaged 20.9.43 by torpedo in the Atlantic and not repaired; sold 21.5.46 BU at Troon.

LAGOS Destroyer 2,315 tons, 335 x 40 ft, 4-4.5in, 1-4in, 12-40mm, 8-TT. Cammell Laird 4.8.1944. Arrived 6.67 McLellan, Bo'ness to BU.

LAL Gunboat (RIN) 331 tons, 170 x 22 ft, 2-3in. Iranian SIMORGH captured 1941 by RIN forces. Returned 1946 to Iran.

LALESTON Coastal M/S, 'Ton' class. Harland & Wolff 18.5.1954. BU 4.85

LAMBOURN (see DOVEY)

LAMERTON Destroyer, 'Hunt' class type II. Swan Hunter 14.12.1940. Lent Indian navy 27.4.53 as GOMATI.

LAMPORT (see LANGPORT)

LANARK Paddle M/S, 'Ascot' class, 820 tons. Fleming & Ferguson 18.12.1917. Sold 5.23 Stanlee, Dover.

LANARK Frigate (RCN), 'River' class. Vickers, Montreal 10.12.1943. Arrived 22.5.66 at Spezia to BU.

LANCASTER 2nd Rate 80, 1,198bm, 156 x 42 ft. Wyatt, Bursledon 3.4.1694. Rebuilt Portsmouth 1722 as 1,366bm. BU. 1743

LANCASTER 3rd Rate 66, 1,478bm, 161 x 46 ft. Woolwich DY 1749. BU completed 10.8.1773 at Portsmouth.

LANCASTER (ex-E.Indiaman *Pigot*) 3rd Rate 64, 1,430bm, 173 x 43 ft, 26-24pdr, 26-18pdr, 12-9pdr. Randall, Rotherhithe 29.1.1797; purchased on stocks. Lent W.India Dk Co 11.3.1815. Sold 30.5.1832 Cristall to BU.

LANCASTER 4th Rate 58, 1,476bm, 173 x 44 ft, 26-42pdr carr., 32-24pdr. Plymouth DY 23.8.1823. Sold 17.2.1864 Marshall, Plymouth.

LANCASTER Armoured cruiser 9,800 tons, 440 x 66 ft, 14-16in, 10-12pdr. Armstrong 22.3.1902. Sold 3.3.20 Ward, Birkenhead & Preston

LANCASTER (ex-USS PHILIP) Destroyer 1,090 tons, 309 x 30½ ft, 3-4in, 1-3in, 6-TT. Commissioned in the RN 23.10.1940. Air target 3.45 . Arrived 30.5.47 Hughes Bolckow, Blyth to BU.

LANCASTER Frigate 3000 tons. Yarrow ordered 15.7.1986

LANCASTER CASTLE Corvette, 'Castle' class. Fleming & Ferguson 14.4.1944. Arrived 6.9.60 King, Gateshead to BU.

LANCE (ex-DARING renamed 30.9.1913) Destroyer 997 tons, 260 x 27 ft, 3-4in, 4-TT. Thornycroft 25.2.14. Sold 5.11.21 Granton S.Bkg Co.

LANCE Destroyer 1,920 tons, 254 x 37 ft, 8-4in, 8-TT. 28.11.1940. Sunk 9.4.42 by air attack at Malta; raised and towed to Chatham, found beyond repair; arrived Ward, Grays 6.44 to BU.

LANDGUARD (ex-USS SHOSHONE) Cutter 1,546 tons, 1-5in, 2-3in. To the RN 20.5.1941 on lend-lease. Laid up 1946. Sold 6.10.49 Madrigal Co, Manila.

LANDRAIL Schooner 4, 80bm, 56 x 18 ft, 4-12pdr carr. Sutton, Ringmore 18.6.1806. Sold circa 1816.

LANDRAIL (ex-*Gipsy King*) Wood pad. tug, 36bm. Purchased 24.5.1855 at Constantinople. Sold there, 21.7.1856.

LANDRAIL Wood S. gunvessel, 'Philomel' class. Deptford DY 28.3.1860. Sold 9.1869, renamed *Walrus*.

LANDRAIL Torpedo gunvessel 950 tons, 195 x 28 ft, 1-6in, 3-5in, 3-TT. Devonport DY 19.1.1886. Sunk 4.10.1906 in Lyme Bay in use as a target.

LANDRAIL (ex-HOTSPUR renamed 30.9.1913) Destroyer 983 tons, 260 x 27 ft, 3-4in, 4-TT. Yarrow 7.2.14. Sold 1.12.21 Stanlee, Dover.

LANGPORT (also LAMPORT) 62-gun ship, 794bm. Built at Horsleydown, River Thames 1654. Renamed HENRIETTA 1660. Wrecked 25.12.1689 near Plymouth.

LANTAU (see BEAULIEU).

LANTON Coastal M/S, 'Ton' class. Harland & Wolff 30.7.1954. Sold 14.4.70, BU in Bruges.

LAPWING Cutter 10, 82bm, 48 x 21 ft. White, Broadstairs 21.1.1764. Lost 31.10.1765.

LAPWING 6th Rate 28, 598bm, 120½ x 34 ft. King, Dover 21.9.1785. Harbour service in 1813. BU 5.1828.

LAPWING Packet brig 6, 'Cherokee' class, 228bm. Chatham DY 20.2.1825. Breakwater 6.1845. Sold 22.11.1861 Marshall, Plymouth.

LAPWING Wood S.gunvessel, 675bm, 181½ x 28½ ft, 1-110pdr, 1-68pdr 2-20pdr. White, Cowes 26.1.1856. Sold 1864 Marshall, Plymouth.

LAPWING Wood S.gunvessel, 663bm 774 tons, 170 x 29 ft, 1-7in, 2-40pdr 1-20pdr. Devonport DY 8.11.1867 Sold 15.4.1885 Castle, Charlton.

LAPWING Compos. S.gunvessel 805 tons, 165 x 31 ft, 6-4in, 2-3pdr. Devonport DY 12.4.1889. Sold 10.11.1910 at Bombay.

LAPWING Destroyer 745 tons, 240 x 25½ ft, 2-4in, 2-12pdr, 2-TT. Cammell Laird 29.7.1911. Sold 26.10.21 Barking S.Bkg Co.

LAPWING Sloop 1,350 tons, 283 x 38½ ft, 6-4in, 12-20mm. Scotts 16.7.1943 Sunk 20.3.45 by U-boat off Kola In

196

let.

LAPWING 3 Trawlers & Drifter WW.I.

LARGO BAY (ex-LOCH FIONN renamed 1944) Frigate, 'Bay' class. Pickersgill 3.10.44. Arrived 11.7.58 Ward, Inverkeithing to BU.

LARKE Pinnace, 50bm. In service in 1588.

LARKE 8-gun ship, 86bm. Royalist, captured 1656 by Parliament. Sold 1663.

LARKE 6th Rate 18, 203bm, 76 x 22½ ft. Deane, Blackwall 1675. Sold 3.5.1698.

LARKE 4th Rate 42, 492bm, 115 x 31½ ft. Wells, Rotherhithe 2.1703. Rebuilt Woolwich 1726 as 598bm; hulked 9.1742 at Kingston, Jamaica. Wrecked there 20.10.1744 in a hurricane.

LARKE 5th Rate 44, 710bm, 126 x 36 ft. Golightly, Liverpool 30.6.1744. Sold 4.8.1757 at Woolwich.

LARKE 5th Rate 32, 680bm, 127 x 34½ ft. Bird, Rotherhithe 10.5.1762. Burnt 7.8.1778 to avoid capture at Rhode Island.

LARKE Cutter 16, 198bm, 74½ x 26 ft, 2-12pdr carr., 16-4pdr. Purchased 1779. Sloop from 1781. Sold 16.1.1784.

LARK Sloop 16, 430bm, 108 x 29½ ft. Pitcher, Northfleet 15.2.1794. Foundered 8.8.1809 in the W.Indies.

LARK Survey cutter 2, 109bm, 61 x 21½ ft. Chatham DY 23.6.1830. BU 6.1860 at Devonport.

LARK Wood S.gunboat, 'Dapper' class. Deptford DY 15.3.1855. Sold 18.7.1878 Marshall, Plymouth.

LARK (ex-*Falcon*) Survey schooner, 86bm, 75 x 16½ ft. Purchased 27.9.1877 in the W.Indies. Renamed SPARROWHAWK 4.12.1877. Sold 4.9.1889 in Bermuda.

LARK Survey schooner, 166bm, 1-12pdr. Westacott, Barnstaple 4.12.1880. Sold 12.1887 at Sydney NSW.

LARK (see KINGFISHER of 1879)

LARK (see CRUIZER of 1852)

LARK (ex-HAUGHTY renamed 30.9.1913) Destroyer 968 tons, 260 x 27 ft, 3-4in, 4-TT. Yarrow 26.5.13. Sold 20.1.23, Hayes, Porthcawl.

LARK Sloop 1,350 tons, 283 x 38½ ft, 6-4in, 12-20mm. Scotts 28.8.1943. Torpedoed 17.2.45 by 'U 968' off Kola Inlet and beached at Murmansk; salved by Russians and commissioned as NEPTUN.

LARK Two Trawlers requis. WW.I.

LARKSPUR Sloop 'Acacia' class. Napier & Miller 11.5.1915. Sold 3.22 Ward, Inverkeithing.

LARKSPUR Corvette, 'Flower' class. Fleming & Ferguson 5.9.1940. Lent USN 17.3.42 as FURY. Sold 22.7.46 renamed *Larkslock*.

LARNE 6th Rate 20, 459bm, 115½ x 30 ft, 18-32pdr carr. 2-9pdr. Bottomley, Lynn 8.3.1814. Sold 26.3.1828 Castle Charlton.

LARNE (see LIGHTING of 1829).

LARNE Destroyer 730 tons, 240 x 25 ft, 2-4in, 2-12pdr, 2-TT. Thornycroft, Woolston 23.8.1910. Sold 9.5.21 Ward, Lelant, Cornwall.

LARNE (see GURKHA of 1940).

LARNE Minesweeper, 'Algerine' class. Simons. Laid down 30.1.1942. Contract transferred to Lobnitz. Laid down 25.1.43, launched 2.9.43. Sold 1947 Italian navy as ERITREA.

LARNE Store carrier. Requis. 1918-19.

LASALLE Frigate (RCN), 'River' class. Davie SB 12.11.1943. Sold 13.12.47; hull sunk as breakwater 1948.

LASHAM Inshore M/S, 'Ham' class. Weatherhead, Cockenzie 31.5.1954. Sold Scotroy Ltd in 1981.

LASSOO (ex-MAGIC renamed 15.2.1915) Destroyer 1,010 tons, 260 x 27 ft, 3-4in, 4-TT. Beardmore 24.8.1915. Sunk 13.8.16 by mine in the North Sea.

LASSO Cable ship 1938-59.

LATONA 5th Rate 38, 944bm, 141½ x 39 ft. Graves, Limehouse 13.3.1781. Harbour service 1813. Sold 2.5.1816.

LATONA 5th Rate 46, 1,071bm, 150 x 40 ft. Chatham DY 16.6.1821. Sale list 12.1869. BU completed 20.3.1875 at Chatham.

LATONA 2nd class cruiser 3,400 tons, 300 x 43 ft, 2-6in, 6-4.7in, 8-6pdr. N.C & A (Vickers) 22.5.1890. Minelayer 5.1907, 4-4.7in guns. Sold 22.12.20 at Malta.

LATONA Minelayer 2,650 tons, 410 x 39 ft, 6-4.7in, 160 mines. Thornycroft 20.8.1940. Sunk 25.10.41. by Italian A/C off Libya.

LATROBE Minesweeper (RAN), 'Bathurst' class. Morts DK 19.6.1942. Sold 18.5.56 to BU in Hong Kong.

LAUDERDALE Destroyer, 'Hunt' class type II. Thornycroft 5.8.1941. Lent Greek navy 4.5.46 to 12.11.59 as AIGAION. BU 1960 in Greece.

LAUNCESTON 5th Rate 42, 528bm, 118 x 32 ft. Portsmouth DY 17.10.1711. Renamed PRINCESS LOUISA 1728 and rebuilt as 603bm. Wrecked 29.12.1736 on the Dutch coast.

LAUNCESTON 5th Rate 44, 701bm, 125 x 36 ft. Buxton, Rotherhithe. 29.12.1741. Sold 25.3.1784.

LAUNCESTON Minesweeper 'Bathurst' class. Evans Deakin 30.6.1941. Lent RAN to 1946. Sold 1946 Turkish navy as AYANCIK.

LAUNCESTON Patrol Boat (RAN) 211 tons. N. Queensland Co. 23.1.1982

LAUNCESTON CASTLE Corvette, 'Castle' class. Blyth SB 27.11.1943. Arrived 3.8.59 J.A. White, St Davids to BU.

LAURA Schooner 10, 112bm, 68 x 20 ft, 8-18pdr carr. 2-9pdr. Bermuda 1806. Captured 8.9.1812 by the French privateer DILIGENT off the coast of N. America.

LAUREL 50-gun ship, 489bm. Portsmouth 1651. Wrecked 1657.

LAUREL (ex-privateer BECKFORD) Sloop 12, 104bm, 66 x 19 ft, 12-4pdr. Purchased 7.1759. Sold 31.3.1763.

LAUREL Cutter 10, 58bm, 46 x 17 ft. Purchased 11.1763. Sold 24.9.1771.

LAUREL 6th Rate 28, 602bm, 120 x 34 ft. Raymond, Northam 27.10.1779. Foundered 10.10.1780 in a hurricane in the W. Indies.

LAUREL 6th Rate 28, 600bm. Jacobs, Sandgate. cancelled 10.1783, the builder having failed.

LAUREL 6th Rate 22, 424bm, 107 x 30 ft. French JEAN BART captured 15.4.1795 by a squadron off Rochefort. Sold 1797 in Jamaica.

LAUREL (see DAPHNE of 1796).

LAUREL 6th Rate 22, 526bm, 118½ x 31½ ft. Boole & Good, Bridport 2.6.1806. Captured 12.9.1808 by the French CANONNIERE off Mauritius; recaptured 12.4.1810 as ESPERANCE and renamed LAURESTINUS. Wrecked 22.10.1813 in the W. Indies.

LAUREL 5th Rate 36, 1,104bm. French FIDELLE captured on 17.8.1809 on stocks at Flushing. Wrecked 31.1.1812.

LAUREL 5th Rate 38, 1,088bm, 154½ x 40ft. Parsons, Warsash 31.5.1813. Harbour service 1864. BU 11.1885 Castle.

LAUREL (ex-REDGAUNTLET renamed 30.9.1913) Destoyer 965 tons, 260 x 27 ft, 3-4in, 4-TT. White 6.5.13. Sold 1.11.21 Fryer, Sunderland.

LAUREL Tug 1897-01. Tug 1901-13. Trawler & Drifter WW1. Trawler 1935-48.

LAURESTINUS (see LAUREL of 1806).

LAUZON (see GLACE BAY).

LAUZON (ex-GLACE BAY) Frigate (RCN), 'River' class. G.T. Davie 10.6.1944. Sold 12.2.64.

LAVENDER Sloop, 'Acacia' class. McMillan 12.6.1915. Sunk 5.5.17 by 'UC.75' in the Channel.

LAVENDER Corvette, 'Flower' class Alex Hall 27.11.1940. Sold 9.8.46,

LAVEROCK (ex-HEREWARD renamed 30.9.1913) Destroyer 994 tons, 260 x 27 ft, 3-4in, 4-TT. Yarrow 19.11.13. Sold 9.5.21 Ward Grays.

LAVEROCK Trawler 1939-46.

LAVINIA 5th Rate 48, 1,172bm, 158 x 41½ ft. Jacobs, Milford 6.3.1806. Harbour service 7.1836. Sunk 1868 in collision with SS Cimbria in Plymouth harbour; wreck sold 31.3.1870 A. Dockerill.

LAVINIA (see SEAHORSE of 1830)

LAVINIA Trawler requis. 1915-19. Drifter requis. 1939-41.

LAWFORD (ex-IVANHOE renamed 30.9.1913) Destroyer 1,003 tons, 260 x 27 ft, 3-4in, 4-TT. Fairfield 30.10.13. Sold 24.8.22. Hayes, Porthcawl.

LAWFORD Frigate, DE 'Captain' class. Boston N. Yd 13.8.1943 on lend-lease. Sunk 8.6.44 by air attack off Normandy.

LAWRENCE Fireship 6, 154bm. Purchased 1672. Expended 1673.

LAWRENCE Iron pad. despatch vessel (Indian) 1,154 tons, 212 x 32 ft, 4-4in. Laird 15.6.1886. Renamed OLD LAWRENCE 1918, CANNING 1919. Listed to 1922.

LAWRENCE Sloop (Indian) 1,225 tons, 230 x 34 ft, 4-12pdr. Beardmore 30.7.1919. For disposal 1946.

LAWSON Frigate, DE 'Captain' class. Boston N. Yd 13.8.1943 on lend-lease. Returned 3.46 to the USN.

LEAMINGTON (ex-ALDBOROUGH renamed 1918) Minesweeper, later 'Hunt' class. Ailsa 26.8.18. Sold 19.5.28 Ward, Pembroke Dock.

LEAMINGTON (ex-USS TWIGGS) Destroyer 1,090 tons, 309 x 30½ ft, 3-4in, 1-3in, 6-TT. Commissioned 23.10.1940 in the RN. Lent RCN 12.42 to 12.43; lent Russian navy 16.7.44 to 16.11.50 as ZHGUCHI. Sold 26.7.51, arrived Cashmore Newport 3.12.51.

LEANDER 4th Rate 52, 1,044bm, 146 x 40½ ft. Chatham DY 1.7.1780. Captured 17.8.1798 by the French GENEREUX; recaptured 3.3.1799 by the Russians at Corfu and returned to the RN. Renamed HYGEIA 1813 medical depot. Sold 14.4.1817.

LEANDER 4th Rate 58 (pitch pine-built), 1,572bm, 174 x 45 ft, 26-42pdr carr; 32-24pdr. Wigram & Green, Blackwall 10.11.1813. BU 3.1830.

LEANDER 4th Rate 50, 1, 987bm, 181½ x 51 ft, 10-8in, 40-32pdr. Portsmouth DY 8.3.1848. Undocked 16.2.1861 as screw ship 2,760bm. Sold 1867 Castle & Beech.

LEANDER Steel despatch vessel (2nd class cruiser) 4,300 tons, 300 x 46 ft, 10-6in. Napier 28.10.1882. Depot ship 1904. Sold 1.7.20S. Castle, Plymouth.

LEANDER Cruiser 7,270 tons, 530 x 55 ft, 8-6in, 8-4in. Devonport DY 24.9.1931. Sold 15.12.49, BU Hughes Bolckow.

LEANDER (ex-WEYMOUTH) Frigate, 'Leander' class. Harland & Wolff 28.6.1961.

LEASIDE (see SERENE).

LEASIDE (ex-WALMER CASTLE renamed 1943) Corvette (RCN), 'Castle' class. Smiths DK 10.3.1944. Sold 1946, renamed *Coquitlam*.

LEDA 5th Rate 36, 881bm, 137½ x 38 ft. Randall, Rotherhithe 12.9.1783. Foundered 11.2.1796 off Madeira.

LEDA 5th Rate 38, 1,071bm, 150 x 40½ ft. Chatham DY 18.11.1800. Wrecked 31.1.1808 near Milford Haven.

LEDA 5th Rate 36, 947bm, 145 x 38½ ft. Woolwich DY 9.11.1809. Sold 30.4.1817 Cockshott to BU.

LEDA 5th Rate 46, 1,171bm, 159 x 41 ft. Pembroke Dock 15.4.1828. Police hulk 5.1864. Sold 15.5.1906 Harris, Bristol.

LEDA Torpedo gunboat 810 tons, 230 x 27 ft, 2-4.7in, 4-3pdr, 3-TT. Sheerness DY 13.9.1892. M/S 1909. Sold 14.7.20 Cardiff Marine Stores; BU in Germany.

LEDA Minesweeper 815 tons, 230 x 33½ ft, 2-4in. Devonport DY 8.6.1937. Sunk by 'U.435' 20.9.42 in the Greenland Sea.

LEDBURY Destroyer, 'Hunt' class type II. Thornycroft 27.9.1941. Arrived 5.58 Charlestown to BU at Rosyth.

LEDBURY Minehunter 615 tons. Vosper-Thornycroft 5.12.1979

LEDSHAM Inshore M/S, 'Ham' class. Bolson Poole 30.6.1954. Sold 12.4.71, BU Newhaven.

LEE Sloop 8. On Canadian lakes 1776.

LEE Galley 8. ex-Adder purchased 6.1780. Sold 1784.

LEE 6th Rate 20, 463bm, 115½ x 30ft, 18-32pdr carr; 2-9pdr. Brindley, Frindsbury 24.1.1814. BU 5.1822.

LEE Wood S. gunboat, 301bm, 125 x 23 ft, 1-10in, 2-24pdr howitzers. Pitcher, Northfleet 28.2.1857. Sunk 25.6.1859 in action with the Peiho forts, China.

LEE Wood S. gunvessel, 'Philomel' class. Wigram, Blackwall 25.1.1860. BU 3.1875 at Sheerness.

LEE Destroyer 365 tons, 210 x 20 ft, 1-12pdr, 5-6pdr, 2-TT. Doxford 21.1.1899. Wrecked 5.10.1909 near Blacksod Bay.

LEEDS (ex-USS CONNOR) Destroyer 1,020 tons, 309 x 30½ ft, 2-4in, 4-20mm. Commissioned 13.10.40 in the RN Sold 4.3.47, BU Ward, Grays.

LEEDS Trawler requis, 1918-19.

LEEDS CASTLE Corvette, 'Castle' class. Pickergill 12.10.1943. Arrived 5.5.58 Ward, Grays to BU.

LEEDS CASTLE Patrol Vessel 1427 tons. Hall Russell 22.10.1980

LEGERE 6th Rate 24, 453bm, 116 x 30 ft, 6-18pdr carr., 18-pdr. French, captured 22.6.1796 by APOLLO and DORIS off Scilly. Wrecked 2.2.1801. near Cartagena.

LEGERE Gunvessel 6. French, captured 22.8.1798 by ALCMENE off Alexandria. In service in 1801.

LEGION (ex-VIOLA renamed 30.9.1913) Destroyer 1,072 tons, 260 x 27 ft, 3-4in, 4-TT. Denny 3.2.1914. Sold 9.5.21 Ward, New Holland.

LEGION Destroyer 1,920 tons, 354 x 37 ft, 8-4in, 8-TT. Hawthorn Leslie 26.12.1939. Sunk 26.3.42. by air attack at Malta.

LE HAVRE Frigate (RCN), 'River' class. Victoria BC. Cancelled 12.1943.

LEICESTER 6th Rate 24, 257bm. Purchased 1667. Sunk 7.1667 as blockship in the Thames.

LEICESTER Store carrier requis. 1914-16.

LEIGHTON A.ship 22. Purchased 1798. Listed 1801, gone by 1804.

LEITH A.ship 20. In service in 1782.

LEITH Sloop 990 tons, 250 x 34 ft, 2-4.7in, 1-3in. Devonport DY 9.9.1933. Sold 25.11.46, renamed *Byron*; Danish naval GALATHEA 1949.

LENOX 3rd Rate 70, 1,013bm, 15½ x 40 ft. Deptford 1978. Rebuilt Deptford 1701 as 1,089bm; rebuilt Chatham 1723 as 1,128bm. Sunk 4.1756 as breakwater at Sheerness.

LENOX 3rd Rate 74, 1,579bm, 165½ x 47 ft. Chatham DY 25.2.1758. Sunk 1784 as breakwater. Raised and BU 5.1789 at Plymouth.

LENNOX (ex-PORTIA renamed 30.9.1913) Destroyer 996 tons 260 x 27 ft, Beardmore 17.3.14. Sold 26.10.21 Barking S.Bkg Co.

LENNOX Minesweeper, 'Algerine' class. Simons. Cancelled 3.1942 and contract transferred to Lobnitz, launched 15.10.43. Arrived 1.6.61 Clayton & Davie, Dunston to BU.

LEOCADIA 5th Rate 36, 952bm, 26-12pdr, 10-6pdr. Spanish, captured 1.5.1781 by CANADA. Sold 23.9.1794.

LEOCADIA This name seems to have been borne for a short time by the Spanish prize CLARA, captured 5.10.1804 (qv).

LEOCADIA Brig-sloop 16, 215bm, 85½ x 24½ ft, 14-12pdr carr, 2-6 pdr. Spanish, captured 5.6.1805 by HELENA in the Atlantic. Sold 21.7.1814.

LEONIDAS 5th Rate 36, 1,067bm, 150 x 40 ft. Pelham, Frindsbury 4.9.1807. Powder hulk 1872. Sold 23.11.1894 Castle, Charlton.

LEONIDAS (ex-ROB ROY renamed 30.9.1913) Destroyer 987 tons, 260 x 27 ft, 3-4ln, 4-TT Palmer 30.10.13. Sold 9.5.21 Ward, Hayle; BU 10.22.

LEOPARD 34-gun ship, 516bm, Woolwich 1635. Captured 4.3.1653 by the Dutch.

LEOPARD 54-gun ship, 645bm. Deptford 1659. Hulk 1686. Sunk 7.6.1699 as breakwater at Sheerness.

LEOPARD Fireship 6, 226bm. Purchased 1672. Expended 1673.

LEOPARD 4th Rate 54, 683bm, 131 x 34½ ft. Swallow, Rotherhithe 15.3.1703. Rebuilt Woolwich 1721 as 762bm. BU 1739.

LEOPARD 4th Rate 50, 872bm, 134 x 39 ft. Perry, Blackwall 30.10.1741 BU completed 7.1761.

LEOPARD 4th Rate 50, 1,044bm, 146½ x 41 ft. Portsmouth DY. Laid down 1.1776; frames to Sheerness DY 9.5.1785 and launched 24.4.1790. Troopship 1812. Wrecked 28.6.1814 on Anticosti, St Lawrence River.

LEOPARD Gunvessel 4, 65bm, 66½ x 14½ ft. Dutch hoy purchased 4.1794. DY Craft 1796. Sold 1808.

LEOPARD Wood pad. frigate, 1,406bm, 218 x 37½ ft, 5-110pdr, 1-68pdr, 4-40pdr, 8-32pdr. Deptford DY 5.11.1850. Sold 8.4.1867 Marshall, Plymouth.

LEOPARD Destroyer 385 tons, 210 x 20 ft, 1-12pdr, 5-6pdr, 2-TT. Vickers 20.3.1897. Sold 10.6.1919 J.Jackson.

LEOPARD Destroyer 2,126 tons, 393 x

37½ ft, 5-5.1in, 6-TT. French, seized 3.7.1940 at Portsmouth. Free-French 9.40. Sunk 27.5.43 off Tobruk.

LEOPARD Frigate 2,300 tons, 330 x 40ft, 4-4.5in, 2-40mm. Portsmouth DY 23.5.1955. BU 10.77 at Dartford.

LETHBRIDGE Corvette (RCN), 'Flower' class. Vickers, Montreal 21.11.1940. Sold 1952, renamed *Nicolaas Vinke.*

LETTERSTON Coastal M/S, 'Ton' class. Harland & Wolff 26.10.1954. Sold Belgian interests 9.6.71

LEVANT 6th Rate 28, 595bm, 118½ x 34 ft, Adams, Bucklers Hard 6.7.1758. BU completed 27.9.1780.

LEVANT (ex-VENUS captured 1070) name chosen, not used.

LEVANT 6th Rate 20, 464bm, 116 x 30 ft, 2-32pdr carr. Courtney, Chester 8.12.1813. BU 10.1820.

LEVEN 6th Rate 20, 457bm, 116 x 30 ft, 18-32pdr carr., 2-9pdr. Bailey, Ipswich 23.12.1813. Survey ship 1820; harbour service 1827. BU 7.1848.

LEVEN Wood S.gunboat, 300bm, 126 x 23 ft, 1-10in, 2-24pdr howitzers. Pitcher, Northfleet 7.3.1857. Sold 21.7.1873 at Shanghai.

LEVEN Destroyer 370 tons, 218 x 20ft, 1-12pdr, 5-6pdr, 2-TT. Fairfield 28.6.1898. Sold 14.9.1920 Hayes. Porthcawl.

LEVEN Trawler requis. 1915-19

LEVERET Brig-sloop 18, 'Cruizer' class, 384bm. King, Dover 14.1.1806. Wrecked 10.11.1807 on Galloper Rock.

LEVERET Brig-sloop 10, 'Cherokee' class, 237bm. Perry, Wells & Green, Blackwall 27.2.1808. Sold 18.4.1822 Pittman.

LEVERET Brig-sloop 10, 'Cherokee' class, 232bm. Portsmouth DY 19.2.1825. Sold 7.11.1843.

LEVERET Wood S.gunboat, 'Albacore' class. Pitcher, Northfleet 8.3.1856. BU 10.1867 at Portsmouth.

LEVERTON Coastal M/S, 'Ton' class. Harland & Wolff 2.3.1955. Sold Pounds 13.8.71, BU 1977.

LEVIATHAN (see NORTHUMBERLAND of 1750)

LEVIATHAN 3rd Rate 74, 1,707bm, 172 x 48 ft. Chatham DY 9.10.1790. Convict ship 10.1816; target 10.1846. Sold 7.8.1848 Mr Burns.

LEVIATHAN Armoured cruiser 14,100 tons, 500 x 71 ft, 2-9.2in, 16-6in, 12-12pdr. J.Brown 3.7.1901. Sold 3.3.20 Hughes Bolckow, Blyth.

LEVIATHAN A/C carrier 15,700 tons

694½ x 80 ft. Swan Hunter (ex-Vickers Armstrong, Tyne) 7.6.1945; not completed. Arrived Faslane 27.5.68 to BU.

LEVIS Corvette (RCN), 'Flower' class. G.T. Davie 4.9.1940. Sunk 19.9.41 by U-boat south of Greenland.

LEVIS Frigate (RCN), 'River' class. G.T.Davie 26.11.1943. Sold 13.12.47 to BU; hull sunk as breakwater 1948.

LEWES Paddle M/S, 'Ascot' class. Fleming & Ferguson 12.3.1918. Sold 3.22 Ward, Inverkeithing.

LEWES (ex-USS CONWAY) Destroyer 1,020 tons, 309 x 30½ ft, 2-4in, 5-20mm. Commissioned 23.10.40 in the RN. Air target 1943. scuttled 25.5.46 off the coast of Australia.

LEWISTON Coastal M/S, 'Ton' class. Herd & McKenzie 3.11.1959. BU in 12.85.

LEYDEN 3rd Rate 64, 1,307bm, 156 x 44 ft, 26-24pdr, 26-18pdr, 2-9pdr. Dutch, captured 30.8.1799 in the Texel. Floating battery 1805, 56-24pdr, 10-24pdr carr. Sold 9.2.1815.

LIBERTY (see CHARLES of 1632)

LIBERTY Cutter 14, 187bm, 74½ x 25½ ft, 14-4pdr. Purchased 1779. Sold 2.1816 in Barbados.

LIBERTY Gunvessel 4. Purchased 5.1798. Gone by 1800.

LIBERTY Training brig, 428bm, 447 tons, 101 x 32½ ft. Pembroke Dock 11.6.1850. Sold 11.7.1905.

LIBERTY (ex-ROSALIND renamed 30.9.1913) Destroyer 975 tons, 260 x 27 ft, 3-4in, 4-TT. White 15.9.13. Sold 5.11.21 Granton S.Bkg Co.

LIBERTY Minesweeper, 'Algerine' class. Harland & Wolff 22.8.1944. Sold 29.11.49 Belgian navy as ADRIEN de GERLACHE.

LIBERTY Ferry 1908-13; Store carrier 1915-19; Yacht and 2 Drifters WW.I.

LICHFIELD Fireship 20, 233bm. Royalist PATRICK captured 1658 by Parliament. Renamed HAPPY ENTRANCE 1665. Fate unknown.

LICHFIELD 4th Rate 48, 682bm, 130½ x 34½ ft. Portsmouth 1694. Rebuilt Plymouth 1730 as 754bm. BU 1744.

LICHFIELD PRIZE 5th Rate 36, 397bm, 100x 30½ ft. French, captured 29.7.1703. Sold 24.10.1706 R.Prince.

LICHFIELD 4th Rate 50, 979bm, 140 x 40 ft. Barnard, Harwich 26.6.1746. Wrecked 28.11.1758 on the north coast of Africa.

LICORNE 5th Rate 32, 679bm, 127 x 34½ ft. French, captured 18.6.1778

by AMERICA in the Channel. Sold 22.11.1783.

LICORNE (see UNICORN of 1776)

LIDDESDALE Destroyer, 'Hunt' class, 1,000 tons, 4-4in. Vickers Armstrong. Tyne 19.8.1940. Sold 1.10.48, BU King, Gateshead.

LIFFEY (see ERIDANUS)

LIFFEY 4th Rate 50 (pitch pine-built), 1,240bm, 159 x 42 ft, 20-32pdr carr., 28-24pdr, 2-9pdr. Wigram, Blackwall 25.9.1813. BU 7.1827.

LIFFEY Wood S.frigate, 2,126 bm, 3,915 tons, 235 x 50 ft. Devonport DY 6.5.1856. Store hulk 1877. Sold 4.1903; hulked at Coquimbo.

LIFFEY Destroyer 550 tons, 222 x 23 ft, 1-12pdr, 5-6odr (4-12pdr 1907), 2-TT. Laird 24.9.1904. Sold 23.6.19 Ward, Grays.

LIFFEY Trawler 1916-53.

LIGAERA 6th Rate 22. Spanish DILIGENTIA captured 12.1804 by DIANA and PIQUE in the W.Indies. Sold 1.9.1814.

LIGHTFOOT Destroyer leader 1,607 tons, 325 x 32 ft, 4-4in, 4-TT. White 28.5.1915. Sold 9.5.21 Ward, New Holland.

LIGHTFOOT Minesweeper, 'Algerine' class. Redfern, Toronto 14.11.1942 on lend-lease. Returned USN 1946 and Sold 1947 to the Greek navy as NAVMAKHOS.

LIGHTNING Fireship 8, 270bm, 91 x 25 ft. Taylor. Cuckolds Point 20.3.1691. Captured 24.11.1705 by the French.

LIGHTNING Bomb 8, 275bm, 91 x 26½ ft. 8-14pdr, 2-Mortars. Bird, Rotherhithe 24.10.1740. Capsized 16.6.1746 off Leghorn.

LIGHTNING (see VIPER of 1746)

LIGHTNING (see SYLPH of 1776)

LIGHTNING Fireship 16, 422bm, 109 x 29½ ft. Ayles, Topsham 14.10.1806. Sold 28.8.1816.

LIGHTNING wood pad. gunvessel, 296bm, 126 x 23 ft, 3 guns. Deptford DY 19.9.1823. BU 1872 at Devonport.

LIGHTNING Sloop 18, 463bm, 113½ x 31 ft. Pembroke Dock 2.6.1829. Renamed LARNE 12.9.1832. BU 3.1866 Castle. Charlton.

LIGHTNING (see T.B.1 of 1877)

LIGHTNING Destroyer 320 tons, 200 x 20 ft, 1-12pdr, 5-6pdr, 2-TT. Palmer 10.4.1895. Sunk 30.6.1915 by mine in the North Sea.

LIGHTNING Destroyer 1,920 tons, 354 x 37 ft, 6-4.7in, 8-TT. Hawthorn Leslie 22.4.1940. Sunk 12.3.43. by Italian MTB. north of Algeria.

LILAC Sloop, 'Acacia' class. Greenock & Grangemouth 29.4.1915. Sold 15.12.22 Batson Syndicate.

LILAC Trawler. 1935-47.

LILY 10-gun ship, 110bm. Purchased 1642. Wrecked 9.1653.

LILY Ketch 6, 64bm, 6-4pdr. Deptford 1657. Sold 1667.

LILY Sloop 6. Deptford 1672. Lost 1673.

LILY (see SPENCER of 1795)

LILY (ex-*Swallow*) Brig-sloop 18, 331bm, 108½ x 30ft. Purchased 1804. Sold 11.1811.

LILY Brig 16, 432bm, 101 x 32½ ft, 14-32pdr, 2-18pdr. Pembroke Dock 28.9.1837. Coal hulk 1860, renamed C,29, then C.15 sold 7.4.1908 Castle, Charlton.

LILY Wood S.gunvessel, 702bm, 185 x 28½ ft, 2-68pdr, 2-32pdr. Scott Russell, Millwall 27.2.1861. BU 10.1867 at Sheerness.

LILY Compos. S.sloop 720 tons, 150 x 28½ ft, 1-7in, 2-64pdr. Napier 27.10.1874. Wrecked 16.9.1889 on the coast of Labrador.

LILY Sloop, 'Acacia' class. Barclay Curle 16.6.1915. Renamed VULCAN II depot ship 15.10.23; Renamed ADAMANT II 1930. Sold 25.6.30 Cashmore, Newport.

LILY Drifter requis. 1915-19.

LIMBOURNE Destroyer, 'Hunt' class type III. Stephen 12.5.1942. Scuttled 23.10.43 off the French Channel coast after damage by torpedo from German TB.

LINARIA (ex-USS CLASH) Corvette, modified 'Flower' class. Midland SY 18.11.1942 on lend-lease. Returned 27.7.46 to the USN, renamed *Porto Offuro* 1948.

LINCOLN 4th Rate 48, 676bm, 130½ x 34½ ft. Woolwich 19.2.1695. Foundered 29.1.1703.

LINCOLN (ex-USS YARNALL) Destroyer 1,090 tons, 309 x 30½ ft. 1-4in, 1-3in, 20mm, 3-TT. Commissioned in the RN 10.1940. Lent Norwegian navy 9.41; lent Russian navy as DRUZNI 26.8.44 to 19.8.52. Sold 9.52, BU Charlestown.

LINCOLN Frigate 2.170 tons, 330 x 40 ft, 2-4.5in, 2-40mm. Fairfield 6.4.1959. BU by White, Inverkeithing 4.83.

LINDIFARNE Patrol vessel 925 tons. Hall Russell 1.6.77

LINDSEY (see PASLEY)

LINDSEY Corvette (RCN), modified 'Flower' class. Midland SY 4.6.1943. Sold 1964, renamed *North Shore*.

LING Corvette, 'Flower' class. Harland & Wolff. Ordered 8.4.1940, Cancelled 23.1.41.

LINGANBAR Frigate (RCN), 'River' class. G.T.Davie. Cancelled 12.1943.

LINGFIELD Paddle M/S, 'Ascot' class. Fleming & Ferguson 29.4.1916. Sold 5.23 Stanlee, Dover.

LINNET (ex-Revenue vessel SPEEDWELL renamed 1806) Gun-brig 14, 198bm, 86 x 22 ft, 12-18pdr carr., 2-6pdr. Captured 25.2.1813 by the French GLOIRE near Madeira.

LINNET (ex-GROWLER renamed 1813) Brig 16 (Canadian lakes), 350bm, 16-12pdr. Lake Champlain 1813. Captured 11.9.1814 by Americans on Lake Champlain.

LINNET Survey cutter, 80bm, 56 x 19 ft. Deptford DY 3.1.1817. Sold 7.8.1833 Ledger, Rotherhithe to BU.

LINNET packet brig 8, 36ibm, 95 x 30½ ft, 8-18pdr. White, Cowes 27.7.1835. Coastguard 9.1857; renamed WV.36 on 25.5.1863. Sold 30.10.1866. Marshall, Plymouth.

LINNET Wood S.gunboat, 'Britomart' class. Briggs, Sunderland 7.6.1860. BU 7.1872 at Chatham.

LINNET Compos. S.gunvessel 756 tons, 165 x 29 ft, 2-7in, 3-20pdr. Thames I.W.30.1.1880. Sold 27.4.1904 as salvage vessel *Linnet*.

LINNET (ex-*Napier of Magdala*) Tender 144 tons, 80 x 18 ft. Transferred from War Dept 11.1906. Renamed HASTY 26.12.13. Sold 20.2.32 Reynolds, Torpoint.

LINNET (ex-HAVOCK renamed 30.9.1913) Destroyer 970 tons, 260 x 27 ft, 3-4in, 4-TT. Yarrow 16.8.13. Sold 4.11.21 Rees, Llanelly.

LINNET Minelayer 498 tons, 145 x 27 ft, 1-20mm, 12 mines. Ardrossan DD. 24.2.11.1938. Arrived 11.5.64 Clayton & Davie, Dunston to BU.

LINNET Two trawlers. requis WW.I.

LION 36-gun ship, 120bm. Scottish, Captured 1511. Sold 1513.

LION 50-gun ship. 160bm. Built 1536. Listed to 1559.

LION Ship. Scottish, captured 1549. Later lost off Harwich.

LION (also GOLDEN LION) 40-gun ship. 600bm. Built 1557. Rebuilt 1582 as 500bm, 4-3pdr, 8-18pdr, 14-9pdr, 9-6pdr, 25 small; rebuilt Deptford 1609 as RED LION, 600bm; rebuilt Chatham 1640 as LION, 751bm, 130 x 35½ ft; rebuilt 1658.

Sold 16.12.1698.

LION (also YOUNG LION) Ketch 6, 44bm, Dutch, captured 1665. Sold 1667; repurchased 1668. Sunk 1673 as a foundation at Sheerness.

LION 5th Rate, Circa 300bm, 92½ x 25½ ft. Algerian, Captured 1683. Sold 1683.

LION Hoy 4, 99bm, 54 x 20 ft, 4-4pdr. Purchased 2.1702. Captured 12.1707 by the French; recaptured 1709 and rebuilt Deptford 4.1709 as 108bm. Listed to 1737.

LION 3rd Rate 60, 906bm, 144 x 38 ft. Chatham DY 20.1.1709. Rebuilt Deptford 1738 as 1,068bm. Sold 14.3.1765.

LION Transport, 151bm, 72 x 22½ ft. Adams, Bucklers Hard 3.7.1753. Hulked 1775. Sold 1786.

LION Cutter, 61bm, Purchased 2,1763. Sold 24.9.1771.

LION Discovery vessel in service 1774-1785

LION 3rd Rate 64, 1,378bm, 159 x 45 ft. Portsmouth DY 3.9.1777. Sheer hulk 9.1816. Sold 30.11.1837 at Chatham to BU.

LION Schooner. Purchased circa 1781. Sold 9.6.1785.

LION Gunvessel 4, 74bm, 67 x 15 ft. Dutch hoy, purchased 3.1794. Sold 20.11.1795 in the Channel Islands.

LION Schooner in service 1823. 88bm. Sold 15.5.1826.

LION 2nd Rate 80, 2,580bm, 190 x 57 ft, 12-8in, 68-32pdr. Pembroke Dock 29.7.1847. Undocked Devonport 17.5.1859 as screw ship, 2.611bm, 3,482 tons; training ship 1871. Sold 11.7.1905 at Portsmouth.

LION Battlecruiser 26,350 tons, 660 x 88½ ft, 8-13.5in, 16-4in. Devonport DY 6.8.1910. Sold 31.1.24 Hughes Bolckow, BU at Jarrow and Blyth.

LION Battleship 42,500 tons, 740 x 105 ft, 9-16in, 16-5.25in Vickers Armstrong, Tyne. Laid down 4.7.1939, suspended 10.39, cancelled 1940.

LION (see DEFENCE of 1944)

LIONESS (ex-E.Indiaman *Lioness*) Storeship 26. Purchased 9.1777. Sold 25.6.1783.

LIONESS (ex-PETROLIA renamed 1943) Minesweeper, 'Algerine' class. Redfern, Toronto 15.3.44. Arrived 15.11.56 at Rosyth to BU.

LIONS WHELP Ten 14-gun sloops, all built 1627 and numbered 1 to 10. No 1 sold 1651; No 2 sold 1650; No 3 Lost in 2.1648; No 4 lost 14.8.1636 off Jersey; No 5 wrecked 28.6.1637 on the Dutch coast; No 6 wrecked

off Ushant 11.1628; No 7 blown up 1630 in action with the French; No 8 Hulked in 1645; No 9 wrecked 4.1640; No 10 sold 19.10.1654.

LIONS WHELP Vessel, type unknown, lost at sea 17.5.1591.

LIONS WHELP Ketch 11, 90bm. Purchased 1601. Given away 1625.

LISBURNE Sloop 14. In service 1781. Sold 1.5.1783.

LISMORE Minesweeper, 'Bathurst' class. Morts Dk, Sydney 10.8.1940. Lent RAN to 1946. Sold 7.46 Dutch navy as BATJAN.

LISTON Coastal M/S, 'Ton' class. Harland & Wolff 23.5.1955. Launched as KILDARTON.

LISTOWEL Corvette (RCN), modified 'Flower' class. Kingston SY. Cancelled 12.1943.

LITHGOW Minesweeper (RAN), 'Bathurst' class. Morts Dk 21.12.1940. Sold 8.8.56 to BU in Hong Kong.

LITTLE BELT 6th Rate 20, 460bm, 18-32pdr carr., 2-9pdr. Danish LILLE BELT captured 7.9.1807 at Copenhagen. Captured 16.5.1811 by the American PRESIDENT. (Was to have been renamed ESPION.) Returned by Americans and sold 1811 at Deptford.

LITTLE BELT Sloop 2 (Canadian lakes) Lake Erie 1812. Captured 10.9.1813 by Americans on Lake Erie.

LITTLE CHARITY (see under CHARITY)

LITTLEHAM Inshore M/S, 'Ham' class. Brooke Marine, Lowestoft 4.4.1954. To Indian navy 15.6.55 as BASSEIN.

LITTLE LONDON (see under LONDON)

LITTLE VICTORY (see under VICTORY)

LIVELY 5th Rate 30, 309bm, French, captured 25.7.1689. Recaptured 4.10.1689 by the French.

LIVELY 6th Rate 12, 125bm. Purchased 7.7.1709. Sold 20.10.1712.

LIVELY 6th Rate 20, 279bm, 95 x26ft. Plymouth DY 28.5.1713. BU 10.1738 at Portsmouth.

LIVELY 6th Rate 24, 439bm, 107 x 31 ft. Quallett, Rotherhithe 16.6.1740. Sold 17.7.1750.

LIVELY 6th Rate 20, 438bm, 108 x 30½ ft. Janvrin, Beaulieu 10.8.1756. Captured 10.7.1778 by the French IPHIGENIE; recaptured 29.7.1781 by PERSEVERANCE. Sold 11.3.1784.

LIVELY Sloop 12, 206bm, 73½ x 23½

ft, 12-18pdr carr. Purchased 1779. Handed over 9.12.1782 to the Spanish at Havana, by her American prisoners.

LIVELY 5th Rate 32, 806bm, 135 x 36 ft. Nowlan, Northam 23.10.1794. Wrecked 12.4.1798 on Rota Point near Cadiz.

LIVELY Storeship 16, 111bm, 64 x 20 ft. Parsons, Bursledon 1797. purchased on stocks. Listed in 1802.

LIVELY 5th Rate 38, 10, 076bm, 154 x 40 ft. Woolwich DY 23.7.1804. Wrecked 26.8.1810 Malta.

LIVELY Cutter. Hired 12.8.1805, purchased 27.8.1805. Fate unknown.

LIVELY (see SCAMANDER of 1813)

LIVELY 5th Rate 38, 1,080bm, 150 x 40½ ft. Chatham DY 14.7.1813. Harbour service 1831. Sold 28.4.1862 Marshall.

LIVELY Wood S.gunboat, 'Albacore' class. Smith, Newcastle 23.2.1856. Wrecked 23.12.1863 on the Dutch coast; salved and became mail steamer *Helgolanderin.*

LIVELY Wood pad. despatch vessel, 835bm, 985 tons, 220 x 28 ft, 2-20pdr. Sheerness DY 10.12.1870. Wrecked 7.6.1883 near Stornoway; wreck sold 7.1910.

LIVELY Destroyer 400 tons, 218 x 20 ft, 1-12pdr, 5-6pdr, 2-TT. Laird 14.7.1900. Sold 1.7.20 S.Castle, Plymouth.

LIVELY Destroyer 1,920 tons, 354 x 37 ft, 8-4in, 8-TT. Cammell Laird 28.1.1941. Sunk 11.5.42 by A/C off Sollum.

LIVELY Coastguard vessel 1840-70. Drifter requis. 1915-20.

LIVERPOOL (ex-ENTERPRISE renamed 20.2.1741) 5th Rate 44, 681bm, 125 x 36 ft. Okill, Liverpool 18.7.1741. Sold 14.9.1756 at Woolwich, became privateer (see LOOE)

LIVERPOOL 6th Rate 28, 590bm, 118½ x 34 ft. Gorill & Pownell, Liverpool 10.2.1758. Wrecked 11.2.1778 on Long Is.

LIVERPOOL 4th Rate 50 (pitch pine-built), 1,240bm, 159 x 40 ft, 20-32pdr carr., 28-24pdr, 2-9pdr. Wigram & Green, Blackwall 21.2.1814. Sold 16.4.1822 at Bombay.

LIVERPOOL 4th Rate 58, 1,487bm, 172 x 44 ft, 26-42pdr carr., 32-24pdr. Plymouth DY. Ordered 9.6.1825, cancelled 5.3.1829.

LIVERPOOL Wood S.frigate, 2,656bm, 235 x 50ft, 1-110pdr, 8-8in, 4-70pdr, 18-32pdr, 8-40pdr. Devonport DY 30.10.1860. Sold 26.6.1875 Castle, Charlton.

LIVERPOOL 2nd class cruiser 4,800 tons, 430 x 47 ft, 2-6in, 10-4in. Vickers 30.10.1909. Sold 1921 Stanlee; resold 8.11.21 Slough TC, BU in Germany.

LIVERPOOL Cruiser 9,400 tons, 558 x 62ft, 12-6in, 8-4in. Fairfield 24.3.1937. Arrived 2.7.58 McLellan, Bo'ness.

LIVERPOOL Destroyer 3,150 tons. Cammell Laird 25.9.1980.

LIZARD Ship, 120bm. Listed 1512 to 1522.

LIZARD Fireship 16, 165bm. Royalist, captured 1652 by Parliament. Expended 1666.

LIZARD Sloop 4, 40bm. Deptford 1673. Captured 1674 by the Dutch.

LIZARD 6th Rate 24, 250bm, 94½ x 24½ ft. ft. Chatham DY 1694. Wrecked 31.5.1696 off Toulon.

LIZARD 6th Rate 24, 264bm, 95 x 25 ft. Sheerness DY 1697. Sold 29.7.1714 S.Eyre.

LIZARD Sloop 14, 272bm, 92 x 26 ft. Ewer, Bursledon 22.12.1744. Wrecked 27.2.1748 on the Scilly Isles.

LIZARD 6th Rate 28, 595bm, 119 x 34 ft. Bird, Rotherhithe 7.4.1757. Harbour service in 1795. Sold 22.9.1828.

LIZARD Schooner 18. In service in 1782. Sold 1786 in the E.Indies.

LIZARD Wood pad. vessel, 300bm. Woolwhich DY 7.1.1840. Sunk 24.7.1843 in collision with the French paddle sloop VELOCE

LIZARD Iron pad. gunvessel, 340bm, 142 x 22½ ft, 3 guns. Napier Glasgow 28.11.1844. BU 4.1869 at Chatham.

LIZARD Compos. S.gunvessel 715 tons, 165 x 29 ft, 6-4in. Harland & Wolff 27.11.1886. Sold 1905 at Sydney NSW to BU.

LIZARD Destroyer 745 tons, 240 x 25½ ft, 2-4in, 2-12pdr, 2-TT. Cammell Laird 10.10.1911. Sold 4.11.21 Rees, Llanelly.

LLANDAFF Frigate 2,170 tons, 330 x 40 ft, 2-4.5, 2-40mm. Hawthorn Leslie 30.11.1955. Sold Bangladesh 10.12.76, renamed DOMAR FAROOQ

LLANDUDNO Minesweeper, turbine 'Bangor' class. Hamilton 8.11.1940. Sold 8.5.47, renamed *Borvik.*

LLEWELLYN Wood pad. packet, 650bm, 190 X 26½ ft. Miller & Ravenhill, Blackwall 22.1.1848. Sold 1850 City of Dublin S.P.Co.

LLEWELLYN (ex-PICTON renamed 30.9.1913) Destroyer 996 tons, 260 X 27 ft, 3-4in, 4-TT. Beardmore 30.10.13. Sold 10.3.22 J.Smith.

LLEWELLYN Minesweeper (RCN) 1942-48.

LOBELIA Sloop 'Arabis' class. Simons 7.3.1916. Sold 3.20 Newfoundland Govt. Hulked 1924.

LOBELIA Corvette, 'Flower' class. Alex Hall 15.2.1941. Lent Free-French 2.41 to 4.47; sold 3.5.47, renamed *Thorgeir*.

LOBELIA Trawler 1914-17. 'Loch' class frigates. 1,435 tons, 286 x 38½ ft, 1-4in, 6-20mm. 110 ordered, of which 26 were rearmed as 'Bay' class and 54 were cancelled.

LOCH ACHANALT Robb 23.3.1944. To RNZN 13.9.48 as PUKAKI. BU 1.66 in Hong Kong.

LOCH ACHILTY (see St BRIDES BAY)

LOCH ACHRAY Smiths Dk 7.7.44. To RNZN 28.9.48 as KANIERE. Sold 1966 to BU in Hong Kong.

LOCH AFFRIC Ailsa. Cancelled 1945.

LOCH ALVIE Barclay Curle 14.4.44. Sold st Singapore 18.1.65 to BU.

LOCH ARD Harland & Wolff, Govan 2.8.44. Completed 21.5.45 as TRANSVAAL (SAN).

LOCH ARKAIG Caledon 7.6.45. Arrived 28.1.60 King, Gateshead to BU.

LOCH ARKLET (see START BAY)

LOCH ARNISH (see TREMADOC BAY)

LOCH ASSYNT Swan Hunter 14.12.44. Completed 2.8.45 as DERBY HAVEN. Sold 7.49 Persian navy as BABR.

LOCH AWE Harland & Wolff. Cancelled 1945.

LOCH BADCALL Pickersgill. Cancelled 1945.

LOCH BOISDALE Blyth 5.7.44. Completed 1.12.44 as GOOD HOPE (SAN).

LOCH BRACADALE (see ENARD BAY)

LOCH CAROY Pickersgill. Cancelled 1945.

LOCH CARLOWAY (see BIGBURY BAY)

LOCH CARRON (see GERRANS BAY)

LOCH CLUNIE Ailsa. Cancelled 1945.

LOCH COULSIDE (see PADSTOW BAY)

LOCH CRAGGIE Harland & Wolff 23.5.44. Sold 8.7.63 Dantos Leal; arrived 25.10.63 at Lisbon to BU.

LOCH CREE Swan Hunter 19.6.44.

Completed 8.3.45 as NATAL (SAN).

LOCH CRERAN Smiths Dk. Cancelled 1945.

LOCH DOINE Smiths Dk. Cancelled 1945.

LOCH DUNVEGAN Hill 25.3.44. Arrived 25.8.60 Ward, Briton Ferry to BU.

LOCH EARN Hill. Cancelled 1945.

LOCH ECK Smiths Dk 25.4.44. To RNZN 1.10.48 as HAWEA. Sold 9.65 to BU in Hong Kong.

LOCH EIL Smiths Dk. Launched 15.5.45 as HERNE BAY. (qv)

LOCH ENOCK Harland & Wolff. Cancelled 1945.

LOCH ERICHT Ailsa. Cancelled 1945.

LOCH ERISORT Barclay Curle. Cancelled 1945.

LOCH EYE Harland & Wolff. Cancelled 1945.

LOCH EYNORT Harland & Wolff. Cancelled 1945.

LOCH FADA J.Brown 14.12.43. Sold 21.5.70, BU Faslane.

LOCH FANNICH Smiths Dk. Renamed HOLLESLEY BAY and cancelled 1945.

LOCH FIONN (see LARGO BAY)

LOCH FRISA (see WIDEMOUTH BAY)

LOCH FYNE Burntisland 24.5.44. Sold Cashmore 7.7.70, BU Newport.

LOCH GARASDALE (see WIGTOWN BAY)

LOCH GARVE Hall Russell. Cancelled 1945.

LOCH GLASHAN Smiths Dk. Cancelled 1945.

LOCH GLASS (see LUCE BAY)

LOCH GLENDHU Burntisland 18.10.44. Arrived 14.11.57 Clayton & Davie, Dunston to BU.

LOCH GOIL Harland & Wolff. Cancelled 1945.

LOCH GORM Harland & Wolff 8.6.44. Sold 9.61, renamed *Orion*.

LOCH GRIAM Swan Hunter. Cancelled 1945.

LOCH HARPORT (see BURGHEAD BAY)

LOCH HARRAY Smiths Dk. Cancelled 1945.

LOCH HEILEN (see MORECAMBE BAY)

LOCH HOURNE Harland & Wolff. Cancelled 1945.

LOCH INCHARD Harland & Wolff. Cancelled 1945.

LOCH INSH Robb 10.5.44. To Malaysian navy 2.10.64 as HANG TUAH.

LOCH KATRINE Robb 21.844. To RNZN 1949 as ROTOITI. Left 28.11.66 for Hong Kong to BU.

LOCH KILBIRNIE (see MOUNTS BAY)

LOCH KILLIN Burntisland 29.11.43. Arrived 24.8.60 Cashmore, Newport to BU.

LOCH KILLISPORT Harland & Wolff 6.7.44. Sold 20.20.70, BU at Blyth.

LOCH KEN Smiths Dk. Cancelled 1945.

LOCH KIRBISTER Swan Hunter. Cancelled 1945.

LOCH KIRKAIG Harland & Wolff. Cancelled 1945.

LOCH KISHORN Robb. Cancelled 1945.

LOCH KNOCKIE Pickersgill. Cancelled 1945.

LOCH LARO Harland & Wolff. Cancelled 1945.

LOCH LAXFORD (see CARDIGAN BAY)

LOCH LINFERN Smiths Dk. Cancelled 1945.

LOCH LINNHE Pickersgill. Cancelled 1945.

LOCH LOMOND Caledon 19.6.44. Sold 6.9.68, BU Faslane.

LOCH LUBNAIG (see WHITESAND BAY)

LOCH LURGAIN Harland & Wolff. Cancelled 1945.

LOCH LYDOCH (see ST AUSTELL BAY)

LOCH LYON Swan Hunter. Cancelled 1945.

LOCH MABERRY Hall Russell. Cancelled 1945.

LOCH MADDY (see CARNARVON BAY)

LOCH MINNICK Smith Dk. Cancelled 1945.

LOCH MOCHRUM (see PEGWELL BAY)

LOCH MUICK (ii) (see THURSO BAY)

LOCH MORE Caledon 3.10.44. Arrived 27.8.63 Ward, Inverkeithing to BU.

LOCH MORLICH Swan Hunter 25.1.44. To RNZN 11.4.49 as TUTIRA. Sold 15.12.61.

LOCH NELL Robb. Cancelled 1945.

LOCH ODAIRN Robb. Cancelled 1945.

LOCH OSSAIN Smiths Dk. Cancelled 1945.

LOCH QUOICH Blyth 2.9.44. Arrived 13.11.57 Clayton & Davie, Dunston to BU.

LOCH ROAN (see CAWSAND BAY)

LOCH RONALD Harland & Wolff. Cancelled 1945.

LOCH RUTHVEN Hill 3.6.44. BU 1966 Davies & Cann, Plymouth.

LOCH RYAN Pickersgill. Cancelled 1945.

LOCH SCAMADALE (see DUNDRUM BAY)

LOCH SCAVAIG Hill 9.9.44. Arrived 5.9.59 at Genoa to BU.

LOCH SCRIDAIN Pickersgill. Cancelled 1945.

LOCH SEAFORTH (ex-LOCH MUICK (i)) (see PORLOCK BAY)

LOCH SHEALLAG Harland & Wolff. Cancelled 1945.

LOCH SHIEL Harland & Wolff. Cancelled 1945.

LOCH SHIN Swan Hunter 23.2.44. To RNZN 13.9.48 as TAUPO. Sold 15.12.61.

LOCH SKAIG Smiths Dk. Cancelled 1945.

LOCH SKERROW Hill. Cancelled 1945.

LOCH STEMSTER Harland & Wolff. Cancelled 1945.

LOCH STENNESS Smiths Dk. Cancelled 1945.

LOCH STRIVEN Harland & Wolff. Cancelled 1945.

LOCH SUNART Harland & Wolff. Cancelled 1945.

LOCH SWANNAY (see VERYAN BAY)

LOCH SWIN Harland & Wolff. Cancelled 1945.

LOCH TANNA Blyth. Cancelled 1945.

LOCH TARBERT Ailsa 19.10.44. Arrived 18.9.59 at Genoa to BU.

LOCH TILT Pickersgill. Cancelled 1945.

LOCH TORRIDON Swan Hunter 13.1.45. Completed 19.10.45 as WOODBRIDGE HAVEN, depot ship. BU 8.65 Hughes Bolckow, Blyth.

LOCH TRALAIG Caledon 12.2.45. Arrived 24.8.63 McLellan, Bo'ness to BU.

LOCH TUMMEL Harland & Wolff. Cancelled 1945.

LOCH URIGILL Blyth. Cancelled 1945.

LOCH VANAVIE Harland & Wolff. Cancelled 1945.

LOCH VENNACHAR Blyth. Cancelled 1945.

LOCH VEYATIE Ailsa 14.4.44. Arrived 12.8.65 Arnott Young. Dalmuir to BU.

LOCH WATTEN Blyth. Cancelled 1945.

LOCHINVAR (ex-MALICE renamed 15.2.1915) Destroyer 1,010 tons. 260 x 27 ft, 3-4ins, 4-TT. Beardmore 9.10.15. Sold 25.11.21 Hayes, Porthcawl to BU.

LOCHY Frigate, 'River' class. Hall Russell 30.10.1943. Arrived 29.6.56 at Troon to BU.

LOCKEPORT Minesweeper, TE 'Bangor' class. N.Vancouver SY 22.8.1941. Lent RCN 5.42 to 2.7.45. Sold 1.1.48 BU at Gateshead.

LOCUST Gun-brig 12, 179bm, 80 x 22½ ft, 2-32pdr carr., 10-10 pdr carr. Randall, Rotherhithe 2.4.1801. Sold 11.8.1814.

LOCUST Paddle gunvessel, 248bm, 420 tons, 120 x 23 ft. Woolwich 8.4.1840. Tug 1869. Sold 1895 at Sheerness.

LOCUST Destroyer 385 tons, 210 x 22 ft, 1-12pdr, 5-6pdr, 2-TT. Laird 8.12.1896. Sold 10.6.1919 J.Jackson.

LOCUST River gunboat 585 tons, 2-4in, 1-3.7 howitzer. Yarrow 28.9.1939. RNVR drillship 1951. Sold Cashmore 24.5.68, BU Newport.

LOFOTEN (see LST.3027)

La LOIRE 5th Rate 40, 1,100bm, 153½ x 40 ft, 28-18pdr, 12-9pdr. French, captured 18.10.1798 by ANSON off Ireland. BU 4.1818.

LONDON 40-gun ship, ex-Indiaman. Purchased 1636. Listed in 1653.

LONDON DY 64-gun ship, 1,104bm. Chatham DY 7.1656. Blown up 7.3.1655 by accident at the Nore.

LONDON (see LOYAL LONDON to 1670) 96-gun ship, 1,134bm. Deptford DY 10.6.1666. Partly destroyed by fire 13.6.1667 and rebuilt Deptford 1670 as 1,348bm, 161 x 45 ft; rebuilt Chatham 1706 as 1,685bm; rebuilt Chatham 1721 as 1,711bm. BU completed 10.1747 at Chatham.

LITTLE LONDON Smack, 16bm. Chatham DY 1672. Sold 1697.

LONDON Brigantine 16 (Canadian lakes). Oswego, Lake Ontario 1756. Lost to the French 14.8.1756 on the Lakes.

LONDON (ex-Holden) Busse 6, 80bm, 64 x 16½ ft. Purchased 10.11.1756. Wrecked 29.4.1758 in the Senegal River.

LONDON Busse 6. Purchased 1759. Listed to 1764.

LONDON 2nd Rate 90, 1,894bm, 177 x 49½ ft. Chatham DY 24.5.1766. BU 4.1811.

LONDON (see ROYAL ADELAIDE)

LONDON 2nd Rate 92, 2,598bm, 4,375 tons, 206 x 54½ ft, 10-8in, 82-32pdr. Chatham DY 28.9.1840. Undocked

Devonport 13.5.1858 as screw ship, 2,687bm, 72 guns; harbour storeship 4.1874. Sold 1884 at Zanzibar to BU.

LONDON Battleship 15,000 tons, 400 x 75 ft, 4-12in, 12-6in, 18-12 pdr. Portsmouth DY 21.9.1899. Minelayer 5.18, 3-6in, 1-4in, 240 mines. Sold 4.6.20 Stanlee, resold and BU in Germany.

LONDON Cruiser 9,850 tons, 595 x 66 ft, 8-8in, 8-4in. Portsmouth DY 14.9.1927. Sold 3.1.50 , BU Ward, Barrow.

LONDON GM destroyer 5,600 tons, 505 x 54 ft, 4-4.5in, 2-20mm, 10-GWS. Swan Hunter 7.12.1961. Handed over to Pakistan 24.3.82, renamed BABUR.

LONDON (ex-BLOODHOUND) Frigate 4.200 tons, Yarrow 27.10.1984

LONDON Two 40-gun ships hired between 1650 and 1666.

LONDONDERRY Sloop 990 tons, 250 x 36 ft, 2-4.7in, 1-3in. Devonport DY 16.1.1935. Sold 8.3.48, BU Rees, Llanelly.

LONDONDERRY Frigate 2,150 tons, 360 x 41 ft, 2-4.5in, 1-40mm, 4-GWS. White 20.5.1958.

LONGBOW Destroyer 1,980 tons, 341½ x 38 ft, 6-4in, 6-40mm, 10-TT. Thornycroft. Laid down 11.4.1945, cancelled 10.45.

LONGBRANCH (ex-CANDYTUFT renamed 9.43) Corvette (RCN), modified 'Flower' class. Inglis 28.8.43. Sold 1946, renamed Kent County.

LONGFORD (ex-MINEHEAD renamed 1918) Minesweeper, later 'Hunt' class. Harkess 15.3.19. Sold 18.1.23 Col J. Lithgow.

LONGUEUIL Frigate (RCN), 'River' class. Vickers, Montreal 30.10.1943. Sold 13.1.46 to BU.BU 1948.

LONSDALE Torpedo boat (Australian) 12 tons, 1-TT. Thornycroft 1884. BU in 1913.

LOOE 5th Rate 32, 385bm, 110 x 28 ft. Plymouth 1696. Wrecked 30.4.1697 off Baltimore, Ireland.

LOOE 5th Rate 32, 390bm, 108 x 29 ft. Portsmouth 1697. Wrecked 12.12.1705 in Scatchwell Bay, Isle of Wight.

LOOE 5th Rate 42, 553bm, 120 x 32½ ft. Johnson. Blackwall 7.4.1707. Harbour service 1735. Sunk 1737 as breakwater.

LOOE 5th Rate 44, 685bm, 124½ x 36 ft. Snelgrove, Limehouse 29.12.1741 Foundered 5.2.1744 off Cape Florida, N.America.

LOOE 5th Rate 44, 716bm, 126 x 36½ x

ft. Gorill & Parks, Liverpool 17.8.1745. Sunk 12.1759 as breakwater at Harwich.

LOOE (ex-privateer LIVERPOOL) 5th Rate 30, 681bm, 124 x 36 ft, 20-12pdr, 10-9pdr. Purchased 9.1759. Sold 6.10.1763.

LOOE Minesweeper, TE 'Bangor' class. Hong Kong & Whampoa. Laid down 22.7.1941, renamed LYEMUN 9.41 and captured on stocks 12.41 by the Japanese.

LOOKOUT (ex-DRAGON renamed 30.9.1913) Destroyer 1,002 tons, 260 x 27 ft, 3-4in, 4-TT. Thornycroft 27.4.14. Sold 24.8.22 Hayes, Porthcrawl.

LOOKOUT Destroyer 1,920 tons, 354 x 37 ft, 6-4.7in, 8-TT. Scotts 4.11.1940. Sold 6.1.48, BU Cashmore, Newport.

LOOSESTRIFE Corvette, 'Flower' class. Hall Russell 25.8.1941. Sold 4.10.46, renamed *Kallsevni.*

LORD CLIVE (ex-CLIVE renamed 8.3.1915, ex.M.6 renamed 1915) Monitor 5,920 tons, 320 x 88 ft, 2-12in, 2-6in. Harland & Wolff 10.6.15. Sold 10.10.27 McLellan, Bo'ness.

LORD CLYDE Ironclad battleship, 4,067bm, 7,842 tons, 280 x 59 ft, 24-7in MLR. Pembroke dock 13.10.1864. Sold Castle 11.1885 to BU.

LORD HOWE Cutter, 82bm, 53 x 20 ft. Purchased 2.1763. Sold 20.8.1771.

LORD NELSON Storeship. Purchased 1800. Sold circa 1807.

LORD NELSON Battleship 16,500 tons, 435 x 79½ ft, 4-12in 10-9.2in, 15-12pdr. Palmer 4.9.1906. Sold 4.6.20 Stanlee, resold 8.11.21 Slough TC and BU in Germany.

LORD NELSON Four Cutters hired between 1798 & 1809.

LORD RAGLAN Monitor 1915 (see RAGLAN),

LORD ROBERTS Monitor 1915 (see ROBERTS).

LORD WARDEN Ironclad battleship, 4,080bm, 7,842 tons, 280 x 59 ft, 16-8in, 4-7in MLR. Chatham DY 27.5.1865. (The largest wooden ship built for the RN.) Sold Castle 2.89 to BU.

LORING Frigate, DE 'Captain' class. Boston N. Yd 30.8.1943 on lend-lease. Nominally returned USN 1.47; left Preston 27.3.47 for Greece to BU.

LOSSIE Frigate, 'River' class. Vickers, Montreal 29.4.1943 on lend-lease. Returned 26.1.46 to the USN.

LOTUS Corvette, 'Flower' class. Hill 17.1.1942. Lent Free-French 4.42 to 5.47 as COMMANDANT d'ESTIENNE d'ORVES. Sold 23.10.47 to BU.

LOTUS (see PHLOX).

LOUIS (ex-TALISMAN renamed 30.9.1913) Destroyer 965 tons, 260 x 27 ft, 3-4in, 4-TT. Fairfield 30.12.13. Wrecked 31.10.15 in Suvla Bay and destroyed by Turkish gunfire.

LOUIS Frigate, DE 'Captain' class. Boston N. Yd 13.8.1943 on lend-lease. Returned 3.46 to the USN.

LOUISA Gunvessel 3, 95bm, 66 x 18 ft. Ex-hoy purchased 3.1794. Sold 10.1798.

LOUISA Tender in service 1814. Sold 22.6.1816

LOUISA Cutter. Purchased 1835 at Canton. Foundered 8.1841 on the E. Indies Station.

LOUISA Wood S. gunboat, 'Albacore' class. Fletcher, Limehouse 12.1855. Sold 27.8.1867 Lethbridge to BU.

LOUISBURG Fireship 8. French captured 1746. Recaptured 4.1.1747 by a French privateer in the Channel.

LOUISBURG Corvette (RCN) 'Flower' class. Morton 27.5.1941. Torpedoed 16.2.43 by Italian A/C off Oran.

LOUISBURG Corvette (RCN), modified 'Flower' class. Morton 13.7.1943. Sold 1947 Dominican navy as JUAN ALEJANDRO ACOSTA.

LOVE & FRIENDSHIP Gunvessel 3. Purchased 1796. Listed in 1800.

LOWESTOFFE 5th Rate 28, 357bm, 104½ x 28 ft. Chatham DY 1697. Rebuilt 1723 Portsmouth as 6th Rate 20, 378bm. Sold 12.7.1744.

LOWESTOFFE 6th Rate 24, 512bm, 112 x 32½ ft. Buxton, Deptford 8.7.1742. Sold 2.2.1748.

LOWESTOFFE 6th Rate 28, 594bm, 119 x 34 ft. Graves, Limehouse 17.5.1756. Sunk 16.5.1760 in action with the French in the St. Lawrence.

LOWESTOFFE 5th Rate 32, 717bm, 130½ x 35½ ft. West, Deptford 5.6.1761. Wrecked 11.8.1801 in the West Indies.

LOWESTOFFE PRIZE Brig-sloop 8. Captured 1777 in the W. Indies. Condemned 9.1779 in Jamaica.

LOWESTOFT 5th Rate 38, 870bm, 137 x 38 ft. Woolwich DY. Ordered 9.7.1801, cancelled 26.7.1805.

LOWESTOFT 2nd class cruiser 5,440 tons, 430 x 50 ft, 9-6in. Chatham DY 23.4.1913. Sold 8.1.31 Ward, Milford Haven.

LOWESTOFT Sloop 992 tons, 250 x 34 ft, 2-4.7in, 1-3in. Devonport DY 11.4.1934. Sold 4.10.46, renamed *Miraflores.*

LOWESTOFT Frigate 2,150 tons, 360 x 41 ft, 2-4.5in, 1-40mm, 4-GWS. Stephen 23.6.1960. Sunk 8.6.86 as a target off the Bahamas.

LOYAL (ex-ORLANDO renamed 30.9.1913) Destroyer 995 tons, 260 x 27 ft, 3-4in, 4-TT. Denny 10.11.13. Sold 25.11.21 Hayes, Porthcawl.

LOYAL Destroyer 1,920 tons, 354 x 37 ft, 6-4.7in, 8-TT. Scotts 8.10.1941. Sold 5.8.48, BU Ward, Milford Haven.

LOYALIST Sloop 14, 320bm, 99 x 28 ft, ex-*Restoration* purchased 1780. Captured 30.7.1781 by the French Le GLORIEUX off Cape Henry.

LOYAL LONDON (see LONDON of 1666).

LOYALTY 34-gun ship, 440bm. In service 1650-53.

LOYALTY Store hulk, 400bm. Purchased 11.11.1694 at Cadiz. Foundered 7.4.1701 in the Bay of Bulls.

LOYALTY (see RATTLER of 1942).

LST (1) Tank landing ships (mark 1). Original classification for three ships launched 1942 (see BOXER, BRUIZER and THRUSTER).

LST (2) Tank landing ships 1,625 tons. 115 ships launched between 9.1942 and 7.43 in the USA on lend-lease. 14 lost and the rest returned 1945-1947 to the USN.

LST (3) Tank landing ships 2,256 tons, 330 x 54 ft, 10-20mm (3001 series) or 4-40mm, 6-20mm (3501 series). Nos 3001 Vickers Armstrong, Tyne 15.1.1945. To War Dept 31.10.46 as *Frederick Clover.* Sold 1966 Govt. of Philippine Islands.

3002 VA (Tyne) 29.3.45. To Greek navy 1946 as ÁLIAKMON. Sold 25.4.71.

3003 VA(Tyne) 8.6.45. Renamed ANZIO 1947. Sold 8.2.70, BU in Spain.

3004 VA(Tyne) 30.7.45. Cancelled and sold 1946, renamed *Rio Teja*

3005 VA(Tyne) 1945. BU incomplete 1945.

3006 Harland & Wolff 3.9.44. Renamed TROMSO 1947; renamed *Empire Gannet* 21.9.56 (MOT). Sold at Singapore 1968.

3007 H & W 16.9.44. Lent Greek navy 4.47-2.62 as AXIOS. Sold 24.7.62. BU at Genoa.

3008 H & W 31.10.44. To the RAN 1946. Sold 4.6.50 R.R.Coots, Sydney.

3009 H & W 30.12.44. To War Dept 1946 as *Reginald Kerr.*

3010 H & W 30.9.44. Renamed ATTACKER 1947. To MOT 1954 as *Empire Cymric.* Arrived Faslane 1.10.63 to BU.

3011 H & W 12.2.45. Renamed AVENGER 1947. To RIN 1.3.49, renamed MAGAR 1951.

3012 H & W 12.3.45. Renamed BEN NEVIS 1947. Arrived Faslane 12.3.65 to BU.

3013 H & W 24.4.45. Renamed BEN LOMOND 1947. Arrived 21.3.60 Ward, Grays to BU.

3014 Barclay Curle 11.11.44. To the RAN 7.46. Sold 4.6.50 R.R. Coots, Sydney.

3015 Barclay Curle 16.3.45. Renamed BATTLER 1947; renamed *Empire Puffin* (MOT) 1956. BU at Spezia in 7.66.

3016 Hawthorn Leslie 15.12.44. Renamed DIEPPE 1947. Harbour service 11.64. Sold 25.2.80, BU at Santander.

3017 Hawthorn Leslie 28.11.44. Renamed TARAKAN (RAN) 7.12.48. Sold 12.3.54 E.A.Marr, Sydney.

3018 Hawthorn Leslie 12.6.45. Cancelled 1946, sold as *Rio Minha*

3019 Swan Hunter 4.9.44. Renamed VAAGSO 1947. BU 12.59 at Faslane.

3020 Swan Hunter 31.10.44. Lent Greek navy 1947-2.62 as ALFIOS. Arrived 8.63 at Spezia to BU.

3021 Lithgow 23.10.44. Renamed *Charles McLeod* (War Dept) 1946. BU 7.68 at Spezia.

3022 Lithgow 26.1.45. RAN 1946. Sold 4.6.50 R.R.Coots, Sydney.

3023 Lithgow 13.6.45. Cancelled and completed as mercantile *Rio Tinta*

3024 Smiths Dk 5.10.44. Renamed *Maxwell Brander* (War Dept) 1946. BU. Hong Kong 1969.

3025 Smiths Dk 14.1.45. Renamed BRUIZER 1947. Sold 15.10.54 at Singapore.

3026 Blyth 30.10.44. Rename CHARGER 1947; renamed *Empire Nordic* (MOT) 1956. BU at Bilbao in 10.68.

3027 Blyth 26.1.45. Renamed LOFOTEN 1947. Helicopter support ship 6.64. For sale 1968.

3028 Stephen 16.11.44. Renamed *Snowden Smith* (War Dept) 1946. Arrived 14.1.61 at Spezia to BU, but became mercantile *Elbano Primo* in 1964

3029 Stephen 12.1.45. Renamed CHASER 1947. Sold 1.2.62, arrived 28.3.62 at Spezia to BU.

3030 Hall Russell 12.6.45. Cancelled and completed as *Clupea*

3031 Connell 14.12.44. Renamed SULTAN 1.59. Sold 8.12.70, BU at Valencia

3032 Connell 27.4.1945. Cancelled and completed as *Rio Mondego*.

3033 Pickersgill 11.2.45. Renamed *Empire Shearwater* (MOT) 1956. Sold 16.11.62, BU at Ghent.

3034 Pickersgill 25.8.45. Cancelled and BU at Charlestown in 2.50.

3035 Denny 24.10.44. To the RAN 18.7.46, renamed LAE 7.12.48. Sold 14.11.55 and stranded 3.11.56 on the Queensland coast on passage to Japan to BU.

3036 Ailsa 20.11.44. Renamed PUNCHER 1947. Sold 12.8.60, arrived 4.6.61 at Ghent to BU.

3037 Fairfield 30.1.45. Renamed *Evan Gibb* (War Dept) 1946. Sold 1963 to Italian shipbreakers, BU at Spezia.

3038 Fairfield 14.3.45. Renamed FIGHTER 1947; renamed *Empire Grebe* (MOT) 10.56. Sold at Singapore in 1968.

3039 Fairfield 27.6.45. Cancelled and completed as *Rio Duoro*.

3040 Harland & Wolff (ex-Fairfield) 22.9.45. Cancelled and BU 17.1.49 by Ward, Hayle.

3041 H & W (Govan) 31.10.44. Renamed *Empire Doric* (MOT) 1954. Arrived 13.1.60 at Port Glasgow to BU.

3042 H & W (Govan) 31.1.45. Renamed HUNTER 1947; renamed *Empire Curlew* (MOT) 1956. Arrived 26.8.62 at Spezia to BU.

3043 Scotts 27.4.45. Renamed MESSINA 1947. Sold 9.80, BU at Vigo.

3044 V A (Barrow) 29.7.45. Renamed NARVIK 1947. Sold 1.12.71, BU at Antwerp.

3045 V A (Barrow) 24.10.45. Cancelled and BU 11.45 at Barrow.

3501 Vickers, Montreal 24.8.44. To the RAN 1946; renamed LABUAN 1949. Sold 14.11.55, BU 1956 in Japan.

3502 Vickers, Montreal 31.8.44. Lent Greek navy 5.47 - 2.62 as STRYMON; sold 3.7.62, BU at Spezia.

3503 Vickers, Montreal 12.10.44. Lent Greek navy 1947 as ACHELOOS. Sold Greek interests 26.4.71.

3504 Vickers, Montreal 3.11.44. Renamed PURSUER 1947; renamed *Empire Tern* (MOT) 1956. BU in 1969.

3505 Vickers, Montreal 23.11.44. Renamed RAVAGER 1947. Sold 19.6.61.

3506 Vickers, Montreal 2.12.44. Lent Greek navy 1947 as PINIOS. Sold 28.2.72, BU at Piraeus.

3507 Davie SB 21.10.44. Renamed *Empire Gaelic* (MOT) 1954. Sold 12.8.60, renamed *Rjev*.

3508 Davie SB 30.10.44. Renamed SEARCHER 1947. Arrived 20.6.49 at Milford Haven to BU.

3509 Davie SB 27.11.44. Renamed *Humphrey Gale* (War Dept) 1947. Arrived 10.1.61 at Genoa to BU.

3510 Davie SB 28.11.44. Renamed SLINGER 1947; renamed *Empire Kittiwake* (MOT) 1956. Sold 1968 at Singapore.

3511 Davie SB 29.11.44. Renamed REGGIO 1947. Arrived 12.8.60 Ward, Grsys to BU.

3512 Davie SB 25.4.45. Renamed *Empire Celtic* (MOT) 1956. Arrived 7.9.62 at Spezia to BU.

3513 Davie SB 26.4.45. Renamed SALERNO 1947. Sold 8.6.61 to BU in Italy.

3514 Yarrow, Esquimalt 7.10.44. Renamed SMITER 1947. Sold 3.49 and wrecked 25.4.49 in tow off coast of Portugal.

3515 Yarrow, Esquimalt 16.12.44. Renamed STALKER 1947.

3516 Yarrow, Esquimalt 15.2.45. Renamed STRIKER 1947. Sold 8.2.70, BU Valencia.

3517 Yarrow, Esquimalt 28.4.45. Renamed ST NAZAIRE 1947; renamed *Empire Skua* (MOT) 1956. Arrived 31.1.68 at Spezia to BU.

3518 Vickers, Montreal 6.4.45. Renamed SUVLA 1947. Arrived 8.9.60 Ward, Grays to BU.

3519 Vickers, Montreal 26.4.45. Renamed *Empire Baltic* (MOT) 1956. Arrived 10.7.62 at Spezia to BU.

3520 Vickers, Montreal 2.5.45. Renamed THRUSTER 1947; renamed *Empire Petrel* (MOT) 1956. Sold at Singapore in 1968.

3521 Vickers, Montreal 27.7.45. Scuttled incomplete 2.46 with a cargo of gas shells off Halifax, NS.

3522 Davie SB 9.6.45. Renamed TRACKER 1947. Sold 8.12.70, BU in Spain.

3523 Davie SB 9.7.45. Renamed TROUNCER 1947; renamed *Empire Gull* (MOT) 1956. BU at Santander in 3.80.

3524 Davie SB 25.7.45. Renamed TRUMPETER 1947; renamed *Empire Fulmar* (MOT) 1956. Sold at Singapore in 1968.

3525 Davie SB 29.8.45. Renamed WALCHEREN 1947; renamed *Empire Guil-*

lemot (MOT) 10.56. For sale 1968.

3526 United SY, Montreal 11.8.45. Cancelled 1945 and completed as barge *Mil*.462.

3527-29 all United SY and 3530-31 both Sorel. All cancelled in 8.45.

3532 Marine Ind. Sorel 19.5.45. Renamed ZEEBRUGGE 1947. Sold 16.12.74, BU at Gijon, Spain.

3533 Sorel 1945. Cancelled 1945.

3534 Yarrow, Esquimalt 23.6.45. Renamed *Empire Cedric* (MOT) 1956. Arrived 16.9.60 at Ghent to BU.

3535 Yarrow, Esquimalt 1945. Cancelled and BU 1945.

3536 Vickers, Montreal 1945. Cancelled and BU 1945.

3537 Vickers, Montreal 11.8.45. Cancelled 1945 and completed as barge, *Mil*.463.

3538-3574 Various Canadian builders. All cancelled.

LUCE BAY (ex-LOCH GLASS renamed 1944) Frigate, 'Bay' class. Pickersgill 12.4.45. Renamed DALRYMPLE in 4.47, survey ship and completed 10.2.49 Devonport. Sold 1966 Portuguese navy, renamed ALFONSO de ALBUQUERQUE.

LUCIA Depot ship 5,805 tons, 367½(oa) x 45 ft, 2-3pdr. German mercantile *Spreewald* captured 9.1914 by BERWICK and converted 1916. Sold 4.9.46, renamed *Sinai*.

LUCIFER Fireship 8, 339bm, 98 x 28½ ft. Randall, Rotherhithe 9.10.1778, purchased on stocks. Renamed AVENGER sloop 13.12.1779. Sold 12.6.1783 at New York.

LUCIFER Fireship. Fitted out 11.1783 but not completed. Sold 8.1.1784.

LUCIFER (ex-*Spring*) Bomb 8, 397bm. Purchased 1803. Sold 11.2.1811.

LUCIFER (ex-GPO vessel *Comet*) Wood pad. gunvessel, 387bm, 155 x 22½ ft, 2 guns. Transferred 1837. Renamed WV.41 in 1875 as coastguard watch vessel. Sold 1893.

LUCIFER (ex-ROCKET renamed 30.9.1913) Destroyer 987 tons, 260 x 27 ft, 3-4in, 4-TT. Palmer 29.12.13. Sold 1.12.21 Stanlee, Dover.

LUCIFER (see TRUMPETER)

LUDHAM Inshore M/S, 'Ham' class. Fairlie Yt Co 16.6.1954. Sold Allen, Glasgow 13.3.67.

LUDLOW 5th Rate 32, 382bm, 108 x 28½ ft. Mundy, Woodbridge 12.9.1698. Captured 16.1.1703 by the French ADROIT off Goree.

LUDLOW Paddle M/S, 'Ascot' class. Goole SB 1.5.1916. Sunk 29.12.16 by

mine off the Shipwash.

LUDLOW (ex-USS STOCKTON) Destroyer 1,020 tons, 309 x 30½ ft, 2-4in, 4-20mm. Commissioned in the RN 2.10.40. Beached as RAF target 5.6.45; sold 5.7.45.

LUDLOW CASTLE 5th Rate 42, 531bm, 118 x 32 ft. Sheerness DY 1717. Rebuilt Woolwich 1723 as 595bm; hulked 25.1.1743 at Antigua. Sold 1749.

LUDLOW CASTLE 5th Rate 44, 725bm, 127 x 36½ ft. Taylor, Rotherhithe 31.7.1744. Reduced to a 6th Rate 24 in 1762. BU completed 15.6.1771 at Portsmouth.

LULLINGTON Coastal M/S, 'Ton' class. Harland & Wolff 31.8.1955. Malaysian navy TAHAN 4.66.

LULWORTH (ex-USS CHELAN) Cutter 1,546 tons. Transferred 2.5.1941 on lend-lease. Returned 12.2.46 to the USN.

LUNENBURG Corvette (RCN), 'Flower' class. G.T. Davie 10.7.1941. BU 6.46 Steel Co of Canada, Hamilton.

LUPIN Sloop, 'Arabis' class. Simons 31.5.1916. Sold 22.3.46 Pounds, Portsmouth; foundered 1946, raised and BU at Portchester.

LURCHER Cutter 6, 82bm, 54 x 19½ ft, 6-3pdr. French COMTESSE d'AYEN captured 1761. Sold 1763 in the W.Indies.

LURCHER Cutter 6, 83bm, 50 x 20 ft. Deptford DY 26.9.1763. Sold 1771.

LURCHER Cutter 8. Deptford 1774. Sold 15.12.1778 in the W.Indies.

LURCHER (see PIGMY of 1781)

LURCHER Destroyer 765 tons, 225 x 25½ ft, 2-4in, 2-12pdr, 2-TT. Yarrow 1.6.1912. Sold 9.6.22 Cashmore, Newport.

LUSITANIA (see CHANTICLEER of 1942)

LUTIN Brig-Sloop 16. French, captured 25.7.1793 by PLUTO off Newfoundland. Sold 26.1.1796.

LUTINE 5th Rate 36, 932bm, 144 x 39 ft, 26-12pdr, 10-6pdr. French, handed over 29.8.1793 by Royalists at Toulon and taken away 18.12.93. Wrecked 9.10.1799 off Vlieland, Dutch coast.

LUTINE Sloop 18, 332bm. French, captured 1799. Prison ship 1801. Sold 1802.

LYCHNIS Sloop, 'Anchusa' class. Hamilton 21.8.1917. Renamed CORNWALLIS(RIM) 9.21. BU 1946.

LYDD (ex-LYDNEY renamed 1918) Minesweeper, later 'Hunt' class. Fairfield 4.12.18. Sold 13.3.47 Dohmen & Habets, Leige.

LYDIARD (ex-WAVERLEY renamed 30.9.1913) Destroyer 1,003 tons, 260 x 27 ft, 3-4in, 4-TT. Fairfield 26.2.14. Sold 5.11.21 Granton S. Bkg Co.

LYDIARD Trawler. 1939-46.

LYDNEY (see LYDD)

LYEMUN (see LOOE of 1941)

LYME 52-gun ship, 764bm, 145 x 35 ft. Portsmouth 1654. Renamed MON-TAGU 1660, 3rd Rate 836bm. Re-built Chatham 1675 and Woolwich 1698 as 905bm. Rebuilt Portsmouth 1716 as 920bm. BU 9.1749.

LYME Pink 4, 118bm. Captured 7.1685 from the Duke of Monmouth. Sold 1685.

LYME Dogger, 53bm. Captured 7.1685 with the above ship. Sold 1687.

LYME 5th Rate 32, 384bm, 109 x 29 ft Flint, Plymouth 1695. Reduced 1720 to a 6th Rate, 376bm, 20-6pdr. BU 1.1738 at Deptford.

LYME 6th Rate 24, 446bm, 106½ x 31 ft. Taylor, Rotherhithe 17.5.1740. Foundered 15.9.1747 in the Atlantic.

LYME 6th Rate 28, 587bm, 118 x 34 ft. Deptford DY 10.12.1748. Wrecked 18.10.1760 in the Baltic.

LYME REGIS (see RAJPUTANA)

LYME REGIS (ex-SUNDERLAND re-named 4.1942) Minesweeper, turbine 'Bangor' class. Stephen 19.3.42. Sold 24.8.48, BU Dorkin, Sunderland.

LYNN 5th Rate 32, 380bm, 108 x 28½ ft. Ellis, Shoreham 1696. Sold 16.4.1713 F.Sheldon.

LYNN 5th Rate 42, 553bm, 117 x 32½ ft. Sheerness DY 8.4.1715. BU 10.1732 at Plymouth.

LYNN 5th Rate 44, 688bm, 124 x 36 ft. West, Deptford 7.3.1741. Sold 3.5.1763.

LYNN Minesweeper. requis. 1914-20.

LYNX Sloop 10, 261bm, 88 x 23½ ft. Stanton, Rotherhithe 11.3.1761. Sold 14.2.1777.

LYNX Sloop 16, 324bm, 95 x 28 ft. Randall, Rotherhithe 10.3.1777, pur-chased on stocks. Hospital ship 7.1780. Sold 1.5.1783.

LYNX Sloop 16, 425bm, 108 x 30 ft. Cleveley, Gravesend 14.2.1794. Sold 24.4.1813.

LYNX (see PANDORA 1812)

LYNX Brigantine 3, 'Cherokee' brig class, 231bm. Portsmouth DY 2.9.1833. BU 12.1845.

LYNX Wood S.gunvessel, 477bm, 160 x 25½ft, 2-68pdr. Mare, Blackwall 22.7.1854. Sold 19.5.1862 Marshall, Plymouth.

LYNX Compos. S.gunvessel, 464bm, 584 tons, 155 x 25 ft, 1-7in, 1-64pdr, 2-20pdr. Harland & Wolff 25.4.1868. Sold 12.1888.

LYNX Destroyer 325 tons, 194 x 19 ft, 1-12pdr, 3-6pdr, 3-TT. Laird 24.1.1894. Sold 10.4.1912 Ward, Preston.

LYNX Destroyer 935 tons, 260 x 27 ft, 3-4in, 4-TT. London & Glasgow Co 20.3.1913. Sunk 9.8.15 by mine in the Moray Firth.

LYNX Frigate 2,300 tons, 330 x 40 ft, 4-4.5in, 2-40mm J.Brown 12.1.1955. Handed over to Bangladesh 12.3.82, renamed ABU BAKR.

LYNX Tug & Trawler WW.I. Yacht(RCN) 1940-45.

LYRA Brig-sloop 10, 'Cherokee' class, 240bm. Dudman, Deptford 22.8.1808. Sold 11.7.1818 Pittman to BU.

LYRA Brig-sloop 10, 'Cherokee' class, 235bm. Plymouth DY 1.6.1821. Sold 3.6.1845 Hull Dock Co.

LYRA Wood S.sloop, 488bm, 139 x 28 ft, 9-32pdr. Deptford 26.3.1857. BU 1876 at Portsmouth.

LYRA Destroyer 730 tons, 240 x 25 ft, 2-4in, 2-12pdr, 2-TT. Thornycroft, Woolston 4.10.1910. Sold 9.5.21 Ward, Milford Haven.

LYRA Yacht requis. 1940-46.

LYS 6th Rate 24, 366bm, 106 x 29 ft. French privateer captured 12.1745 by HAMPTON COURT. Sold 13.4.1749.

LYSANDER Brig 4. Listed 1842-44.

LYSANDER (ex-ULYSSES renamed 30.9.1913) Destroyer 976 tons, 260 x 27 ft, 3-4in, 4-TT. Swan Hunter 18.8.13. Sold 9.6.22 Cashmore, New-port.

LYSANDER (ex-HESPELER renamed 6.1943) Minesweeper, 'Algerine' class. Pt Arthur SY 11.11.43. Renam-ed CORNFLOWER 3.50 to 1951. Ar-rived 23.11.57 Hughes Bolckow, Blyth to BU.

LYSANDER Two trawlers requis. in WW.I.

M.1-14. Original designation of 14 mon-itors built in 1915 and given. respec-tively, the following names before completion:

ABERCROMBIE, HAVELOCK, RAG-LAN, ROBERTS, SIR JOHN MOORE, LORD CLIVE, GENERAL CRAUFURD, EARL OF PETER-

BOROUGH, GENERAL WOLFE, PRINCE RUPERT, PRINCE EUGENE, SIR THOMAS PICTON, MARSHAL NEY and MARSHAL SOULT.

'M' class coastal monitors. 540 tons, 170 x 31 ft, (except M.29-33, 535 tons), 1-9.2in, 1-3in, (M.15-22 and M.28); 1-7in, 2-3in (M.23-25); 1-7.5in, 1-3in, 1-12pdr (M.26); 1-4.7in, 2-3in, (M.27); 2-6in, 1-6pdr (M.29-33).

M.15 Gray 28.4.1915. Sunk 11.11,17 by 'UC.38' off Gaza.

M.16 Gray 7.5.15. Sold 29.1.20, renamed *Tiga.*

M.17 Gray 12.5.15. Sold 12.5.20, renamed *Toedjoe.*

M.18 Gray 15.5.15. Sold 29.1.20, renamed *Anam.*

M.19 Raylton Dixon 4.5.15. Sold 12.5.20, renamed *Delapan.*

M.20 Raylton Dixon 11.5.15. Sold 29.1.20, renamed *Lima.*

M.21 Raylton Dixon 27.5.15. Sunk 20.10.18 by mine off Ostend.

M.22 Raylton Dixon 10.6.15. Minelayer 1919. Renamed MEDEA 1.12.25. Sold 12.38 Cashmore; stranded in tow 22.1.39 near Padstow.

M.23 Raylton Dixon 18.6.15. Renamed CLAVERHOUSE 16.12.22, RNVR drillship. Arrived 21.4.59 at Charlestown to BU.

M.24 Raylton Dixon 9.8.15. Sold 29.1.20, renamed *Satoe.* Sunk 29.9.36 as target in the W.Indies.

M.25 Raylton Dixon 24.7.15. Blown up 16.9.19 in the Dvina River to avoid capture, being unable to cross the bar.

M.26 Raylton Dixon 24.8.15. Sold 29.1.20, renamed *Doewa.*

M.27 Raylton Dixon 8.9.15. Blown up 16.9.19 with M.25.

M.28 Raylton Dixon 28.6.15. Sunk 20.1.18 by gunfire from the German GOEBEN off Imbros.

M.29 Harland & Wolff 22.5.15. Minelayer 1919; renamed MEDUSA 1.12.25; depot ship TALBOT 1.9.41; then MEDWAY II in 1943; MEDUSA 21.9.44. Sold 9.9.46., BU 1947 by Dover Industries.

M.30 Harland & Wolff 23.6.15. Sunk 13.5.16 by shore batteries in the Gulf of Smyrna.

M.31 Harland & Wolff 24.6.15. Minelayer 1919; renamed MELPOMENE 1.12.25; MENELAUS 1914. BU 1948 Ress, Llanelly.

M.32 Workman Clark (ex-Harland & Wolff) 22.5.15. Sold 29.1.20, renamed *Ampat.*

M.33 Workman Clark (ex-Harland & Wolff) 22.5.15, renamed MINERVA 1.12.25, hulked 1940m renamed C.23; in service 1987.

'M' class submarines. 1,600 tons, 296oa (M.3-4, 305oa) x 24½ ft, 1-12in, 1-3in, 4-TT.

M.1 (ex-K.18 renamed 1917) Vickers 9.7.17. Sunk 12.11.25 off Start Point, believed to have rammed by SS Vidar.

M.2 (ex-K.19 renamed 1917) Vickers 19.10.18. Fitted at Chatham 4.28 to carry a seaplane (12in gun removed); sunk 26.1.32 off Portland.

M.3 (ex-K.20 renamed 1917) Armstrong 19.10.18. Minelayer 1927 (guns removed). Sold 2.32 Cashmore, arrive Newport 13.4.32 to BU.

M.4 (ex-K.21 renamed 1917) Armstrong. Laid down 1917. Hull sold 30.11.21 to the builder.

'M' class controlled minelayers. 300 tons, 110 x 26½ ft, 1-20mm, 10 mines.

M.I Philip, Dartmouth 6.7.1939. Renamed MINERI in 1942, MINSTREL 1962. Sold in 1967.

M.II Philip 18.8.39. Renamed MINER II in 1942, GOSSAMER 1949. Sunk 18.3.70 off Portland as a target.

M.III Philip 16.11.39. Renamed MINER III in 1942. Sold 2.77, BU at Sittingbourne.

M.IV Philip 6.8.40. Renamed MINER IV in 1942. BU in 5.64.

M.V Philip 2.11.40. Renamed MINER V in 1942; BRITANNIC, cable layer 1960. RAF target 6.6.79.

M.VI Philip 7.2.42. Renamed MINER VI in 1942. Sold mercantile 16.8.88 at Malta.

M.VII(i) Singapore. Ordered 3.10.40. Destroyed on stocks 2.42 at the loss of Singapore.

M.VII(ii) Philip. Laid down as, and launched 29.1.44 as MINER VII. Renamed ETV.VII in 1959, then STEADY, trials vessel. Sold Pounds 3.80 to BU.

M.VIII Philip. Launched 24.3.43 as MINER VIII. Renamed MINDFUL 1.63, tender. Sold D. Arnold 22.2.65, renamed *Rawdhan.*

MACDUFF (See MUNLOCHY)

MACEDONIAN 5th Rate 38, 1,082bm, 154 x 39½ ft. Woolwich DY 2.6.1810. Captured 25.10.1812 by the American UNITED STATES in the Atlantic.

MACHINE Fireship 12, 390bm, 109 x

28 ft. French, captured 15.9.1692. Sunk 9.7.1696 as foundation at Sheerness.

MACKAY (ex-CLAVERHOUSE renamed 1917) Destroyer leaader 1,800 tons, 320 x 32 ft, 5-4.7in, 1-3in, 6-TT. Cammell Laird 21.12.18. Sold 18.2.47; arrived 6.49 Charlestown to BU.

MACKENZIE Escort (RCN) 2,335 tons, 366(oa) x 42 ft, 4-3in. Vickers Montreal 25.5.1961.

MACKEREL Dogger. Captured 1946. Last mentioned 1647.

MACKEREL Schooner 4, 78bm, 56 x 18 ft, 4-12pdr carr. Bermuda 1804. Sold 14.12.1815.

MACKEREL Wood S.gunboat, 'Albacore' class. Pitcher, Northfleet 8.3.1856. BU 7.1862.

MACKEREL Trawler 1942, renamed CORNCRAKE 1942.

MACQUARIE (ex-CULGOA renamed 3.1943) Frigate (RAN), 'River' class. Morts Dk, Sydney 3.3.45. Sold 5.7.62 to BU in Japan.

MADAGASCAR 5th Rate 38, 1,114bm, 154½ x 40½ ft. French NEREIDE captured 26.5.1811 at Tamatave. BU in 5.1819

MADAGASCAR 5th Rate 46, 1,167bm, 159½ x 41 ft. Bombay DY 15.11.1822. Harbour storeship 10.1853. Sold 5.5.1863 at Rio de Janeiro.

MADAGASCAR Wood pad. vessel (Indian). Burnt 9.1841 by accident in the Formosa Channel.

MADANG Patrol boat (RAN) tons. Evans Deakin 10.8.1968. To Papua New Guinea 9.75

MADDISTON Coastal M/S, 'Ton' class. Harland & Wolff 27.1.2956. Sold 20.10.74, BU Sunderland

MADRAS (ex-E.Indiaman *Lascelles*) 4th Rate 56, 1,426bm, 175 x 43ft. Wells, Rotherhithe 4.7.1795. Storeship 1803. Sold 1807 at Malta partly BU.

MADRAS (see MEEANEE)

MADRAS Minesweeper (RIN), 'Bathurst' class. Cockatoo DY 17.2.1942. Sold 1960.

MADRAS Trawler (RIN) 1919 renamed TANJORE 1941-42

MAEANDER 5th Rate 38 (red pine-built), 1,067bm, 150 x 40 ft. Pitcher, Northfleet 13.8.1813. BU 2.1817.

MAEANDER 5th Rate 44, 1,221bm, 159 x 42 ft. Chatham DY 5.5.1840. Coal hulk 11.1859. Ordered to BU 10.1865; wrecked 7.1870 in a gale at Ascension.

MAENAD Destroyer, 'M' class 1,025 tons. Denny 10.8.1915. Sold 22.9.21 G.Cohen; BU in Germany.

MAENAD Minesweeper, 'Algerine' class. Redfern, Toronto 8.6.1944. Arrived 18.12.57 Ward, Grays to BU.

MAESTERLAND Fire vessel 10, 100bm. Dutch, purchased 4.1694. Sold 17.2.1696.

MAGDALA Iron turret ship (Indian), 2,107bm, 3,340 tons, 225 x 45 ft, 4-10in MLR. Thames I.W. 2.3.1870. To RN 31.10.1892; to RIM 19.2.1903. Sold 1904.

MAGDALEN (also MAWDELYN) Ship 120bm. Listed 1522 to 1525

MAGDALEN Store hulk, 290bm. French, captured 1698. Sold 24.8.1699 at Portsmouth.

MAGDALEN Schooner. Purchased 6.1769 in Canada. Sold 23.9.1777 at Quebec.

MAGDALEN Schooner, 90bm. Purchased 1780 in N.America. Fate unknown.

MAGDALEN Drifter WW.I. Trawler 1942-46.

MAGIC (See LASSOO)

MAGIC (ex-MARIGOLD renamed 1915) Destroyer, 'M' class. White 10.9.15. Sold 22.9.21 G.Cohen; BU in Germany.

MAGIC Minesweeper, 'Catherine' class. Savannah Mcy 25.5.43 on lend-lease. Sunk 6.7.44 by human torpedo off Normandy.

MAGICIAN (see MAGICIENNE)

MAGICIENNE 5th Rate 32, 968bm, 144 x 39 ft. French, captured 2.9.1781 by CHATHAM in N.America. Burnt 27.8.1810 to avoid capture by the French after grounding, Mauritius.

MAGICIENNE 5th Rate 36, 949bm, 145 x 38½ ft. List, Fishbourne 8.8.1812. Completed 11.1831 as 6th Rate 24. BU 3.1845 at Portsmouth.

MAGICIENNE Wood pad. frigate, 1,258bm, 210 x 36 ft. Pembroke Dock 2.3.1849. BU 9.1866 Marshall, Plymouth.

MAGICIENNE (see OPAL)

MAGICIENNE 2nd class cruiser 2,950 tons, 265 x 42 ft, 6-6in, 9-6pdr. Fairfield 12.5.1888. Sold 11.7.1905.

MAGICIAN Ferry service vessel 1,050 tons, 206 x 38½ ft Ailsa 27.9.1939. Lent War Dept 1939; RN 1944 and renamed MAGICIAN II. Sold 31.12.51, BU at Faslane.

MAGICIENNE Minesweeper, 'Algerine' class. Redfern 24.6.1944. Arrived 20.3.56 Cashmore, Newport to BU.

MAGNANIME 3rd Rate 74, 1,823bm, 174 x 49½ ft. French, captured 31.1.1748 by NOTTINGHAM and PORTLAND. BU 4.1775.

MAGNANIME 3rd Rate 64, 1,370bm, 159½ x 45 ft. Deptford DY 14.10.1780. Reduced to 5th Rate in 2.1795, 6-42pdr carr, 26-24pdr, 12-12pdr. BU 7.1813 at Sheerness.

MAGNET Brig-sloop 18, 'Cruizer' class, 382bm. Guillaum, Northam 19.10.1807. Lost 11.1.1809 in ice in the Baltic.

MAGNET Brig-sloop 16, 285bm, 90 x 28 ft. French privateer ST JOSEPH captured 12.2.1809 by UNDAUNTED in the Channel. Foundered 9.1812 in the Atlantic.

MAGNET (see SIR SYDNEY SMITH)

MAGNET Packet brig 3, 'Cherokee' class, 237bm. Woolwich DY 13.3.1823. Sold 1847.

MAGNET Gunboat (Canadian lakes). Listed 1830-46.

MAGNET Mortar vessel, 155bm, 70 x 23½ ft, 1-13in mortar. Wigram, Northam 2.5.1855. Renamed MV.15 on 19.10.1855. DY craft 2.57, BU 6.1867.

MAGNET Wood S.gunboat, 'Albacore' class. Briggs, Sunderland 29.1.1856. BU 1874 at Chatham.

MAGNET Tug 1885-1920; 2 Drifters WW.1; BDV 1938-58.

MAGNIFICENT 3rd Rate 74, 1,612bm, 1969 x 47 ft. Deptford DY 20.9.1766. Wrecked 25.3.1804 near Brest.

MAGNIFICENT 3rd Rate 74, 1,732bm, 174 x 48½ ft. Perry, Wells & Green, Blackwall 30.8.1806. Hospital ship 12.1825. Sold 1843 in Jamaica.

MAGNIFICENT Battleship 14,900 tons, 390 x 75 ft, 4-12in, 12-6in, 18-12pdr. Chatham DY 19.12.1894. Storeship 1.1918. Sold 9.5.21 Ward, Inverkeithing.

MAGNIFICENT A/C carrier 15,700 tons, 630 x 80 ft, 19-40mm, 40-A/C. Harland & Wolff 16.11.1944. Lent RCN 4.48 to 1957. Arrived 12.7.65 Faslane to BU.

MAGNIFICENT Two drifters requis. WW.1. Drifter requis.1939-44.

MAGNOLIA Sloop, 'Acacia' class. Scotts 26.6.1915. Sold 2.7.32 Metal Industries; arrived 27.7.32. Charlestown.

MAGNOLIA 2 Trawlers WW.1. Trawler 1935-48.

MAGOG Frigate (RCN), 'River' class. Vickers, Montreal 22.9.1943. Sold 1947 Marine Industries to BU.

MAGPIE Schooner 4, 76bm, 56 x 18 ft. Rowe, Newcastle 17.5.1806. Cap-

tured 19.2.1807 by the French at Perros.

MAGPIE Schooner 5,70bm, 54 x18 ft. McLean, Jamaica 6.1826. Wrecked 27.8.1826 in a squall off Cuba.

MAGPIE Cutter 4, 108bm, 61 x 20½ ft. Sheerness DY 30.9.1830. DY tank vessel 1845, renamed YC.6. In service 1880 and perhaps sold 1908.

MAGPIE Wood S.gunboat, 'Dapper' class.Deptford DY 15.3.1855. Wrecked 8.4.1864 in Galway Bay.

MAGPIE Wood S.gunvessel, 665bm, 774 tons, 170 x 29ft, 1-7in, 2-40pdr, 1-20pdr. Portsmouth DY 12.2.1868. Survey vessel 1878. Sold 9.1885.

MAGPIE Compos. S.Gunboat 805 tons, 165 x 31 ft, 6-4in. Pembroke Dock 15.3.1889. BDV 1902; gunboat 1915; depot ship 10.15.Sold 29.12.21 Duguid & Stewart.

MAGPIE Sloop 1,350 tons, 283 x 38½ ft, 6-4, 12-20mm. Thornycroft 24.3.1943. Arrived 12.7.59 Hughes Bolckow, Blyth.

MAGPIE Tug 1902-23. 2 Trawlers requis.WW.1.

MAGPIE Target vessel purchased 6.1982

MAHONE Minesweeper (RCN), TE 'Bangor' class. N.Vancouver 14.11.1940. Sold 29.3.58 Turkish navy as BEYLERBEY.

MAHONESA 5th Rate 36, 921bm. Spanish, captured 13.10.1796 by TERPISCHORE off Malaga. BU 7.1798.

MAHRATTA (see Indian TB.4 of 1889)

MAHRATTA (ex-MARKSMAN renamed 7.1942) Destroyer 1,920 tons, 354 x 37 ft, 6-4.7in, 8-TT. Scotts 28.7.42. Sunk 25.2.44 by 'U.956' in the Barents Sea.

MAHRATTA (see CHARLOCK)

MAHRATTA M/S requis. 1916-20.

MAIDA 3rd Rate 74, 1,899bm. French JUPITER captured 6.2.1806 at San Domingo. Sold 11.8.1814.

MAIDA Drifter 1940.

MAIDEN CASTE, Corvette Castle class. Fleming & Ferguson 8.6.44. completed as Rescue ship EMPIRE LIFEGUARD. BU 7.55

MAIDSTONE 40-gun ship, 555bm. Mundy, Woodbridge 1654. Renamed MARY ROSE 1660. Captured 12.7.1691 by the French in the Atlantic.

MAIDSTONE 6th Rate 24, 250bm, 94½ x 24½ ft. Chatham DY 11.1693. Sold 29.7.1714.

MAIDSTONE (see ROCHESTER of 1693)

MAIDSTONE 4th Rate 50, 979bm, 140½ x 40½ ft. Wells, Rotherhithe 12.10.1744. Wrecked 27.6.1747 off St. Malo.

MAIDSTONE 6th Rate 28, 593bm, 118½ x 34ft. Seward, Rochester 9.2.1758.BU 7.1794.

MAIDSTONE 5th Rate 32 (fir-built), 796/804bm, 135 x36 ft. Deptford DY 12.12.1795. BU 8.1810 at Chatham.

MAIDSTONE 5th Rate 36, 947bm, 145 x 38½ ft. Deptford DY 18.10.1811. Receiving ship 1832; coal hulk 1839. BU completed 16.6.1865 at Cowes.

MAIDSTONE Depot ship 3,600 tons, 355(oa) x 45 ft. Scotts 29.4.1912. Sold 31.8.29.

MAIDSTONE Depot ship 8,900 tons, 497 x 73 ft, 8-4.5in. J.Brown 21.10.1937. Arrived Inverkeithing 24.5.78 to BU by Ward.

MAJESTIC 3rd Rate 74, 1,623bm, 170½ x 47 ft. Adams & Barnard, Deptford 11.2.1785. Reduced to 4th Rate 58,28-42pdr carr., 28-32pdr, 2-12pdr in 1813. BU 4.1816 after stranding.

MAJESTIC Screw 2nd Rate 80, 2,589bm, 190 x 57 ft, 12-8in, 68-32pdr. Chatham DY 1.12.1853 (12 years on stocks). BU 1868 Marshall, Plymouth.

MAJESTIC (see EDINBURGH of 1882)

MAJESTIC Battleship 14.900 tons, 390 x 75 ft, 4-12in 12-6in, 18-12pdr. Portsmouth DY 31.1.1895. Sunk 27.5.1915 by 'U.21' off Cape Helles.

MAJESTIC A/C carrier 16,000 tons, 630 x 80 ft, 25-40mm, 24-A/C. Vickers Armstrong, Barrow 28.2.1945. Completed 10.55 and renamed MELBOURNE (RAN) 28.10.55. Left Sydney 27.4.85 in tow for Shanghai to BU.

MAJESTIC Tug 1915-19; A/P vessel 1916; 2 Driffers & a Trawler WW.1.

MALABAR (ex-E.Indiaman *Royal Charlotte*) 4th Rate 54, 1,252bm, 161 x 42 ft. Pitcher, Northfleet and purchased 1795. Foundered 10.10.1796 on passage from the W.Indies.

MALABAR (ex-*Cuvera*) 4th Rate 56. 935bm. Purchased 5.1804. Storeship 20 in 1805; renamed COROMANDEL 7.3.1815. Convict ship 10.1827.BU completed 12.1853 at Bermuda.

MALABAR Sloop 20 (Indian). In service in 1810.

MALABAR 3rd Rate 74, 1,715bm, 174½ x 48 ft. Bombay DY 28.12.1818. Coal hulk 10.1848. Renamed MYRTLE 30.10.1883. Sold 11.7.1905 at Portsmouth.

MALABAR Iron S.troopship, 4,713bm, 6.211 tons, 360 x 49 ft, 3-4pdr. Napier 8.12.1866. Base ship 1897. Renamed TERROR 1.5.1901. Sale list 1914. Sold 1.18 R.Tucker in Bermuda.

MALACCA (ex-PENANG renamed 1808) 5th Rate 36, 990bm, 150 x 39 ft. Prince of Wales Island, Penang 1809. BU 3.1816.

MALACCA Wood S.sloop (ex-6th Rate 26), 1034bm, 192 x 34½ ft, 1-10in, 16-32pdr. Moulmein, Burma 9.4.1853 and engined at Chatham 1854. Re-engined 1862 as S.corvette. Sold 6.1869 E. Bates; resold Japanese navy as TSUKUBA. BU in 1906'

MALACCA Minesweeper requis. 1939-42.

MALAGA MERCHANT Fireship 4, 206bm. Purchased 1666. Sold 1667.

MALAYA Battleship 27.500 tons, 600 x 104 ft, 8-15in, 12-6in, 2-3in. Armstrong 18.3.1915. Sold 20.2.48, arrived 12.4.48 at Faslane to BU.

La MALBAI (ex-FORT WILLIAM renamed 11.1941) Corvette (RCN), 'Flower' class. Kingston SY 25.10.41 Sold 1946.

MALCOLM (see VALKYRIE of 1917)

MALCOLM Destroyer leader 1,804 tons, 320 X 32 ft, 5-4.7in, 1-3in, 6-TT. Cammell Laird 29.5.1919. Sold 25.7.45, BU Ward, Barrow.

MALCOLM Frigate 1,180 tons, 300 x 33 ft, 3-40mm, 4-TT. Yarrow 18.10.1955. Sold Ward 13.8.73, BU Inverkeithing.

MALHAM Inshore M/S, 'Ham' class. Fairlie Yt Co 29.8.1958. Sold 10.59 Ghanaian navy.

MALICE (see LOCHINVAR)

MALLAIG Minesweeper, later 'Hunt' class. Fleming & Ferguson 10.10.1918. Sold 25.11.27 Hughes Bolckow, Blyth.

MALLARD Gun-brig 12, 178bm, 80 X 22½ ft, 2-18pdr, 10-18pdr carr. Barnard, Deptford 11.4.1801. Captured 25.12.1804 by the French when aground near Calais.

MALLARD Compos. S-gunboat 455 tons, 125 x 23 ft 2-64pdr, 2-20pdr. Earle, Hull 4.8.1875. Sold 8.1889.

MALLARD Destroyer 310 tons, 210½ x 19½ ft, 1-12pdr, 5-6pdr, 2-TT. Thornycroft 19.11.1896. Sold 10.2.1920 S.Alloa S.Bkg Co.

MALLARD Patrol vessel 510 tons, 234 x 26½ ft, 1-4in. Stephen 26.3.1936. Sold 21.4.47, BU Dorkin, Gateshead.

MALLING CASTLE Corvette, 'Castle' class. Morton. Cancelled 12.1943.

MALLOW Sloop, 'Acacia' class. Barclay Curle 13.7.1915. RAN 7.19; dismantled 7.32. Hull sunk 1.8.35 as target off Sydney.

MALLOW Corvette, 'Flower' class. Harland & Wolff 31.10.1940. Lent Yugoslav navy as NADA 11.1.4446. Sold 28.10.48 Egyptian navy as El SUDAN.

MALMESBURY CASTLE Corvette, 'Castle' class. Morton. Cancelled 12.1943.

La MALOUINE Corvette, 'Flower' class. French, siezed 3.7.40 at Middlesborough. Smiths DK 21.3.40. Arrived 22.5.47 Howells, Gellyswick Bay. Bay, Milford.

MALPEQUE Minesweeper (RCN), TE 'Bangor' class, N.V.Vancouver SY 5.9.1940. Sold 2.59 Marine Industries.

MALPLAQUET (see JUTLAND)

MALTA Schooner 10, 162bm, 80½ x 21½ ft, 10-14pdr. Captured 1800. Renamed GOZO 12.1800. Gone by 1804.

MALTA 2nd Rate 84, 2,265bm, 194½ x 53 ft, French GUILLAUME TELL captured 30.3.1800 by a squadron off Malta. Harbour Service 1831. BU 8.1840.

MALTA (ex-Britannia) Paddle tender. Purchased 1854. Sold 1856.

MALTA A/C carrier circa 45,000 tons, J.Brown. Laid down 12.1944, cancelled 1945.

MALTA Tug. 1875-1921; Trawler requis, 1914-15.

MALVERN Minesweeper, later 'Hunt' class Fleming & Ferguson 19.12.1919. Sold 26.6.28 Alloa S.Bkg Co., BU at Charlestown.

MALWA Minesweeper (RIN). TE 'Bangor' class. Garden Reach, Calcutta 21.6.1944. Renamed PESHAWAR (RPN) 1948. Sold 22.1.59.

MAMBA SSV (RAN) Building Melbourne 1945. Cancelled 8.45.

MAMELUKE Destroyer, 'M' class. J.Brown 14.8.1915. Sold 22.9.21 Cohen; BU in Germany.

MAMELUKE Minesweeper, 'Algerine' class. Redfern, Toronto 19.7.1944. Sold 27.4.50, BU at Thornaby-on-Tees.

MANCHESTER Cruiser 9,400 tons, 558 x 62 ft. 12-6in, 8-4in. Hawthorn Leslie 12.4.1937. Sunk 13.8.42 by Italian MTBs in the Mediterranean

MANCHESTER Destroyer. 3550 tons, Vickers 24.11.1980.

MANDARIN Gun-brig 12, 178bm, Scut-

tled Dutch vessel salved 2.1810 at Amboyna. BU 1812.

MANDARIN BDV 1963

MANDATE Destroyer, 'M' class. Fairfield 24.7.1915. Sold 22.9.21 Cohen, BU in Germany.

MANDATE Minesweeper, 'Algerine' class. Redfern, Toronto 9.8.1944. Arrived 12.57 Rosyth to BU.

MANDRAKE Corvette, modified 'Flower' class. Morton 22.8.1942. Transferred USN 6.4.43 as HASTE. Sold 9.47 renamed Porto Azzura

MANILLA Storeship 14, 406bm. Purchased 11.1780. Lost 1782 in the East Indies.

MANILLA 5th Rate 36, 947bm, 145 x 38½ ft. Woolwich DY 11.9.1809. Wrecked 28.1.1812 in the Texel.

MANILLA 5th Rate 46, 1,215bm, 159½ x 42 ft, Bombay DY. Ordered 5.4.1819, cancelled 21.2.1831.

MANILLA (see ATALANTE of 1860)

MANILLA (ex-Ingeburg) Storeship, 373bm. Taken over 28.2.1870. Sold 14.8.1872 at Yokohama.

MANLY (Gunboat No.37) (ex-Experiment) Gunvessel 12, 157bm, 78 x 21 ft. 2-24pdr, 10-18pdr carr. Purchased 4.1797 at Leith. Sold 10.1802.

MANLY Gun-brig 12, 178bm, 80 x 22½ ft, 10-18pdr carr., 2-12pdr. Dudman, Deptford 7.5.1804. Captured 1.1806. by the Dutch; recaptured 1.1.1809 and renamed BOLD 13.12.13. Sold 11.8.1814.

MANLY Gun-brig 12, 180bm, 84 x 22 ft, 10-18pdr carr., 2-6pdr. Hill, Sandwich 13.7.1812. Sold 12.12.1833.

MANLY Mortar Vessel, 117bm, 65 x 21 ft. 1-13in Mortar. Thompson 16.5.1855. Renamed MV.6 on 19.10.1855. Hulked 7.1866.

MANLY Wood S.Gunboat, 'Albacore' class. Briggs, Sunderland 29.1.1856. BU in 1.1864 at Deptford.

MANLY Destroyer 883 tons, 260 x 25½ ft, 3-4in, 4-TT. Yarrow 12.10.1914. Sold 26.10.21 Barking S.Bkg Co.

MANLY Tug. 1868-1912. Trawler requis. 1939-40.

MANLY Tender 128 tons. Dunston 23.7.1981.

MANNERS Destroyer, 'M' class. Fairfield 15.6.1915. Sold 26.10.21 Barking S.BKg Co.

MANNERS Frigate, DE 'Captain' class. Boston N.Yd 17.12.1943 on lend-lease. Nominally returned 8.11.45 to the USN; sold by the USN 1.47 to BU in Greece.

MANSFIELD Destroyer, 'M' class 1,057 tons. Hawthorn Leslie 3.12.1914. Sold 26.10.21 Barking S.BKg Co.

MANSFIELD (ex-USS EVANS) Destroyer 1,090 tons, 309 x 30½ ft. 1-4in, 1-3in, 4-20mm, 3-TT. Commissioned in the RN 23.10.1940. Lent R.Norwegian Navy 12.40 to 3.42; RCN 9.42 to 6.44 Sold 21.10.44 BU in Canada.

MANSFIELD Trawler. requis 1917-19.

MANTIS River gunboat 645 tons, 230 x 36 ft, 2-6in, 1-3in. Sunderland SB Co 14.9.1915. Sold 20.1.40 at Shanghai.

MANXMAN Minelayer 2,650 tons, 400½ x 40 ft, 6-4.7in, 160 mines. Stephen 5.9.1940. M/S support ship 2.63. Sold Cashmore 1.9.72, BU Newport.

MANXMAN Seaplane carrier 2048 tons. 1916-20.

MAORI Destroyer 1,035 tons, 280 x 27 ft, 2-4in, 2-TT. Denny 24.5.1909. Sunk 7.5.15. by mine in the North Sea.

MAORI Destroyer 1,870 tons, 355½ x 36½ ft, 8-4.7in, 4-TT. Fairfield 29.1937. Sunk 11/12.12.42 by air attack at Malta; salved and scuttled 15.7.45 off Malta.

MARATHON (see DEFENCE of 1815)

MARATHON 2nd class cruiser 2,950 tons, 265 x 42 ft, 6-6in, 9-6pdr. Fairfield 23.8.1888. Sold 11.8.1905 Ward, Preston.

MARAZION Minesweeper. later 'Hunt' class. Fleming & Ferguson 15.4.1919. Sold 3.33 at Hong Kong.

MARENGO 2nd Rate 80, 1,930bm. French, captured 13.2.1806 by LONDON and AMAZON in the Atlantic. Prison ship 9.1809. BU 11.1816.

MARGAREE (see DIANA of 1932)

MARGAREE Escort (RCN) 2,265 tons, 366(oa) x 42 ft, 2-3in. Halifax SY 29.3.1956.

MARGARET Ship purchased in 1413, sold in 5.1421.

MARGARET Ship purchased 7.1461. Listed to 1483.

MARGARET Ship. Captured 1490 from the Scots.

MARGARET 60-ton vessel listed in 1549.

MARGARET Galliot in service 1645-74.

MARGARET Galley built at Pisa, Italy and purchased 1671. Given away 1677.

MARGARET Tender dating from 1785. Wrecked 11.1798.

MARGARET Sloop 20. Purchased 6.1744 in Jamaica. Sold 9.8.1744.

MARGARET Cutter. Captured 12.6.1775 by Americans.

MARGETT (see JERSEY of 1694)

MARGATE Sloop 14, 162bm, 77 x 162bm, 77 x 22½ ft. Deptford 1709. Sold 1712.

MARGATE 6th Rate 24, 438bm, 108 x 31 ft, 22-9pdr, 2-4pdr. French privateer LEOPARD captured 27.10.1746 Sold 7.9.1749.

MARGATE Trawler. Requis. 1914-17.

MARGUERITE Sloop, 'Arabis' class. Dunlop Bremmer 23.11.1915. RAN 1919; dismantled 9.32; Sunk 1.8.35 as target.

MARGUERITE Corvette, 'Flower' class. Hall Russell 8.7.1940. Weather ship Weather Observer 1947. BU 9.61.

MARIA SANDWICH Carrack, 550bm. Captured 1416. Sold 10.9.1424.

MARIA SPAYNE Spanish ship captured 24.8.1417. Listed 1450.

MARIA de LORETO Genoese ship, 800bm. Seized 1512. Released 1514.

MARIA 6-gun vessel, 68bm. Built 1626. Condemned 1644.

MARIA Discovery vessel, 70bm. Exploring Hudsons Bay in 1631.

MARIA SANCTA 50-gun ship, 400bm. Dutch, captured 1665. Burnt 13.6.1667 by the Dutch at Chatham.

MARIA PRIZE Store hulk, 120bm. Algerian, captured 1684. Sold 27.10.1690 at Cadiz.

MARIA Schooner 6 (Canadian lakes). In service 1776.

MARIE Brig 14, 136bm, 71 x 21½ ft. French. MARIE, captured 21.11.1797 by JASON. Renamed HALIFAX 10.1800. Listed to 1802.

MARIA Cutter tender 10. In service 1806-12.

MARIA Gun-brig 14, 172bm. Purchased 1807. Captured 29.9.1808 by the French LANDES off Guadeloupe.

MARIA Brig 16. In service 1812-15.

MARIA Trawler (ex-German) 1941-51.

MARIE Schooner 10, 130bm, 72 x 20 ft, 12-12pdr car., 2-4pdr. French CONSTANCE captured 21.6.1805 by CIRCE. Foundered 16.10.1807 in the W. Indies.

MARIE ANTOINETTE Schooner 10, 187bm, 85½ x 23 ft, 10-4pdr. French CONVENTION NATIONALE captured 9.1793 by a squadron off San Domingo. Taken into a French W. Indian port by mutineers 7.1797.

MARIANA 6th Rate 18, 202bm, 80½ x 24 ft. French MARIANNE captured 27.1.1693 Sold 30.8.1698. (also MARIANA PRIZE)

MARIANA (also MARYANEE) Bomb 4, 82bm. Purchased 4.1694. Sold 13.5.1698.

MARIANNE Storeship. Purchased 1788. Listed to 6.1793.

MARIANNE Gun-brig 12. French, captured 18.3.1799. Sold 9.1801.

MARIANA Schooner 10. Spanish, captured 1805 by SWIFT. Listed 1806.

MARIANNE Receiving ship, 490bm. Ex-slaver purchased 1858. Ordered to BU at Kingston, Jamaica 2.1864. BU 1867.

MARIGOLD 22-gun-ship. Portuguese, captured 1650. Sold 1658.

MARIGOLD Hoy 3, 42bm. Portsmouth DY 1653. BU 1712.

MARIGOLD Fireship 4, 332bm. Purchased 1673. Lost 8.1673 in action.

MARIGOLD 4th Rate 44, 495bm. Algerian, captured 1677. Wrecked 1679.

MARIGOLD (ex-IVY renamed 1915) Sloop, 'Acacia' class. Bow McLachlan 27.5.15. Sold 26.1.20, renamed *Principe de Piamonte.*

MARIGOLD (see MAGIC)

MARIGOLD Corvette, 'Flower' class. Hall Russell 4.9.1940. Sunk 9.12.42 by Italian A/C off Algiers.

MARINER Gun-brig 12, 180bm, 80 x 23 ft, 2-32pdr car., 10-18pdr carr. Pitcher, Northfleet 4.4.1801. Sold 29.9.1814.

MARINER Brig 16, 481bm, 105 x 33½ ft, 4-32pdr, 12-32pdr carr. Pembroke Dock 19.10.1846. Sold 12.6.1865.

MARINER (see JUNO of 1844)

MARINER Compos. S.sloop 970 tons, 167 x 32 ft, 8-5in. Devonport DY 23.6.1884. BDV 1903; salvage vessel 1917. Sold 2.29 Hughes Bolckow, Blyth.

MARINER Minesweeper, 'Algerine' class. Port Arthur SY 9.5.1944. Renamed YAN MYO AUNG 18.4.58, Burmese navy.

MARINER Drifter requis. 1915-19.

MARJORAM Sloop, 'Anchusa' class. Greenock & Grangemouth 26.12.1917. To be renamed PRESIDENT, drillship, 1921 but wrecked 17.1.21 on Flintstone Head on passage to Haulbowline to fit out; wreck sold 8.9.21.

MARJORAM Corvette, 'Flower' class. Harland & Wolff. Ordered 8.4.1940, cancelled 23.1.41.

MARKSMAN Destroyer, 'M' class. Projected 1913, not ordered.

MARKSMAN Destroyer leader 1,604 tons, 325 x 32 ft, 4-4in, 4-TT. Hawthorn Leslie 28.4.1915. Sold 8.11.21

Slough TC, BU in Germany.

MARKSMAN (see MAHRATTA).

MARLBOROUGH (ex-St MICHAEL renamed 18.12.1706 and rebuilt) 2nd Rate 96, 1,579bm reduced to 68 guns 1752. Foundered 29.11.1762 in the Atlantic (see St. MICHAEL of 1669).

MARLBOROUGH 3rd Rate 74, 1,642bm, 169 x 47 ft. Deptford 26.8.1767. Wrecked 4.11.1800 near Belleisle.

MARLBOROUGH 3rd Rate 74, 1,754bm, 175½ x 48½ ft. Barnard, Deptford 22.6.1807. BU 7.1835.

MARLBOROUGH Screw 1st Rate 121 (ex-131), 4,000bm, 6,300 tons, 245 x 61 ft, 1-110pdr. 16-8in, 6-70pdr, 10-40pdr, 88-32pdr. Portsmouth DY 31.7.1855. Training ship 1878. Renamed VERNON II in 3.1904. Sold 10.24 A. Butcher; capsized off Osea Island in tow to shipbreakers. 28.11.1924.

MARLBOROUGH Battleship 25,000 tons, 580 x 89½ ft, 10-13.5in, 12-6in. Devonport DY 24.11.1912. Sold 27.6.32 Metal Industries, Rosyth.

MARLBOROUGH Frigate 3000 tons Swan Hunter. Ordered. 15.7.1986

MARLBOROUGH Trawler requis. 1914-19.

MARLINGFORD Seaward defence boat, 'Ford' class. Yarwood Northwich 17.6.1954. Sold Pounds 8.9.67.

MARLION Pinnace 40bm, French, captured 1545 Listed to 1549.

MARLION (see MORSEBY)

MARLOW Minesweeper, later 'Hunt' class. Harkess, Middlesbro 7.8.1918. Sold 21.4.28 Alloa S.Bkg Co., BU Charlestown.

MAMADUKE (see REVENGE of 1650)

MARMION Destroyer, 'M' class. Swan Hunter 28.5.1915. Sunk 21.10.17 in collision with destroyer TIRADE off Lerwick.

MARMION Minesweeper, 'Algerine' class. Harland & Wolff. Cancelled 4.1943.

MARMION (ex-ORANGEVILLE renamed 1943) Minesweeper, 'Algerine' class. Port Arthur SY 15.6.44. BU 8.59 Clayton & Davie, Dunston.

MARMION Minesweeper requis. 1915-20 & 1939-41; Tug 1900-20.

MARNE Destroyer, 'M' class. J. Brown 29.5.1915. Sold 29.9.21 G.Cohen; BU in Germany.

MARNE Destroyer 1,920 tons, 354 x 37 ft, 6-4.7in, 8-TT. Vickers Armstrong, Tyne 30.10.1940. Sold 26.3.58 Turkish navy, renamed MARSEAL FEVSI

CAKMAK.

MARNE Trawler requis. 1915-19.

MAROON Tender 24 tons, 50 x 12 ft. Transferred from War Dept 1907. Sold 1907 in Jamaica.

MARQUISE de SEIGNELAY Sloop 14, 232bm, 97 x 26 ft. French privateer captured 10.12.1780 by PORTLAND and SOLEBAY. Sold 23.3.1786.

MARS 50-gun ship, 396bm. Dutch, captured 1665. Sold 1667.

MARS 3rd Rate 64, 1,374bm, 160 x 45 ft, 26-24pdr, 28-12pdr, 10-6pdr. French, captured 10.1746 by NOTTINGHAM off Cape Clear. Wrecked 6.1755 near Halifax NS.

MARS 3rd Rate 74, 1,55bm, 165½ x 46½ ft. Woolwich DY 15.3.1759. Harbour service 1778. Sold 17.8.1784.

MARS 5th Rate 32, 703bm, 130½ x 35 ft. Dutch, captured 3.2.1781 in the W. Indies. Sold 25.3.1784.

MARS 3rd Rate 74, 1,842bm, 176 x 49 ft. Deptford DY 25.10.1794. BU 10.1823.

MARS 2nd Rate 80, 2,576bm, 3,482 tons, 190 x 56½ ft, 12-8in, 68-32pdr. Chatham DY 1.7.1848 (nine years on stocks). Undocked 23.11.1855 as screw ship; lent 13.5.1869 as training ship. Sold 10.6.1929 Ward.

MARS Battleship 14,900 tons, 390 x 75 ft, 4-12in, 12-6in, 518-12pdr. Laird 3.3.1896. Sold 9.5.21 Ward, BU Swansea 11.21 and Briton Ferry 8.25.

MARS (ex-ELTHALION renamed 1942) A/C carrier 13,190 tons. Vickers Armstrong, Barrow 20.5.44. Renamed PIONEER 7.44, maintenance carrier. Arrived 9.54 Ward, Inverkeithing to BU.

MARS Cruiser 9,000 tons, Projected 1944, cancelled 3.46.

MARSHAL NEY (ex-M.13) Monitor 6,670 tons, 340 x 90 ft, 2-15in, 8-4in, 2-12pdr. Palmer 17.6.1915. Base ship VIVID 6.22; DRAKE 1.1.34 ALAUNIA II 1947. Arrived 6.10.57 Ward, Milford to BU.

MARSHAL SOULT (ex-M.14) Monitor 6,670 tons, 340 x 90 ft. 2-15in, 8-4in, 2-12pdr. Palmer 24.8.1815. Depot ship 1940. Arrived 8.46 Troon to BU.

MARSOUIN Sloop 16, circa 320bm. French captured 11.3.1795 by BEAULIEU at Guadeloupe. Listed to 1798.

MARSTON MOOR 54-gun ship, 734bm, 139 x 34½ ft. Johnson, Blackwall 1654. Renamed YORK 1660. Wrecked 23.11.1703 on the Ship-wash.

MARTHA & MARY Gunboat. Purchased 5.1797. Fate unknown.

MARTIAL Gun-brig 12, 183bm, 84½ x 22 ft, 10-18pdr carr., 2-9pdr. Ross, Rochester 17.4.1805. Fishery protection 6.1826; hulked 4.1831. Sold 21.1.1836.

MARTIAL Destroyer, 'M' class. Swan Hunter 1.7.1915. Sold 9.5.21 Ward, Briton Ferry; arrived 11.22.

MARTIN Ship. Captured 1651. Sold 1653.

MARTIN Ship 12, 127bm. Portsmouth 1652. Sold 1667.

MARTIN Ketch 10, 103bm. Parker, Southampton 24.12.1694. Captured 30.8.1702 by three French privateers off Jersey.

MARTIN Sloop 14, 289bm, 97 x 26 ft. Randall, Rotherhithe 7.2.1761. Sold 1.7.1784.

MARTIN Sloop 16, 329bm, 101 x 27 ft. Woolwich DY 8.10.1790. Foundered 10.1800 in the North Sea.

MARTIN Sloop 18, 367bm, 106 x 28 ft. Tanner, Dartmouth 1.1.1805. Foundered 1806 in the Atlantic.

MARTIN Sloop 18, 399bm, 100 x 30 ft, 16-24pdr carr., 2-9pdr. Bermuda 5.1809. Wrecked 8.12.1817 on the west coast of Ireland.

MARTIN Sloop 18, 461bm, 108½ x 29 ft. Portsmouth DY 18.5.1821. Foundered 2.1826 off the Cape.

MARTIN Brig 16, 481bm, 105 x 33½ ft, 4-32pdr, 12-pdr carr. Pembroke Dock 19.9.1850. Renamed KINGFISHER 2.5.1890, training brig. Sold 2.10.07 Collins, Dartmouth.

MARTIN (ex-MAYFLOWER renamed 4.1888) Training brig, 508bm, 6-12pdr. Pembroke Dock 20.1.1890. Coal hulk 15.11.1907, renamed C.23.

MARTIN Destroyer 730 tons, 240 x 25 ft, 2-4in, 2-12pdr, 2-TT. Thornycroft, Woolston 15.12.1910. Sold 21.8.20 Agius Bros, Malta.

MARTIN Destroyer 1,920 tons, 354 x 37 ft, 6-4.7in, 8-TT. Vickers Armstrong, Tyne 12.12.1940. Sunk 10.11.42 by 'U.431' north of Algiers.

MARTIN GARCIA ship purchased 7.1470 Listed to 1485

MARTIN Trawler requis. 1914-19.

MARVEL Destroyer, 'M' class. Denny 7.10.1915. Sold 9.5.21 Ward, Hayle.

MARVEL Minesweeper, 'Algerine' class. Redfern, Toronto 30.8.1944. Arrived 7.5.58 Charlestown to BU.

MARY Cinq Ports ship in 1350.

MARY ship 120 bm from 1400. Given

away in 7.1423

MARY Ship. 120 bm from 1413. Lost 5.1426

MARY Ketch (Royalist) in 1648, and captured 1649 by Parliament. Not listed after.

MARY PRIZE 36-gun ship. Captured 1649. Listed 1655.

MARY FLYBOAT 500 ton ship. Captured 1650. Sold 1657.

MARY (see Speaker of 1649)

MARY Yacht 8, 92bm, 67 x 18½ ft, 8-3pdr. Presented by the Dutch 1660. Wrecked 25.3.1675 on the Skerries. (The first Royal Yacht in the RN.)

MARY PRIZE Fireship 4, 106bm. Dutch merchant captured 1666. Lost at sea 1666.

MARY Fireship 4, 111bm. Purchased 1666. Sold 1667.

MARY Fireship 4, 108bm. Purchased 1667. Expended 1667.

MARY Yacht 8, 155bm. Chatham DY 1677. Rebuilt 1727 as 164bm; rebuilt 1761. BU 4.1816.

MARY Ketch 10. Origin unknown. Foundered 19.2.1694 off Gibraltar.

MARY GALLEY 5th Rate 32, 462bm, 177 x 29½ ft. Deane, Rotherhithe 1687. 'Great repair' Deptford 1708 as 536bm; rebuilt Plymouth 1727 as 594bm, 124 x 33½ ft. BU completed 1.6.1743 at Deptford.

MARY Smack 4, 38bm, 43 x 15 ft. Plymouth DY 1702. Rebuilt Plymouth 1728 as 52bm. Lost in Plymouth Sound 3.10.1778.

MARY 3rd Rate 64, 914bm, 145 x 37½ ft. Chatham DY 12.5.1704. Re-built as 1,068bm and renamed PRINCESS MARY 26.7.1728. BU 1.1736

MARY GALLEY 5th Rate 44, 716bm, 126 x 36½ ft. Bird, Rotherhithe 16.6.1744. Sunk 4.1764 as breakwater.

MARY Gunvessel 3, 61bm, 54½ x 16 ft. Purchased 3.1794. Sold 10.1798.

MARY Tender 6. Purchased 1797. Listed in 1805.

MARY Schooner 3 (Canadian lakes). Listed 1812. Captured 1813 by Americans.

MARY Coastguard cutter, 30bm. White, Cowes 1867. Sold 4.4.1905 at Chatham.

MARY 8 vessels hired between 1650 & 1812. Trawler & Drifter WW.I: Tug 1973.

MARY & JOHN Ship 180bm. Purchased 1487. Rebuilt 1512 Listed to 1528.

MARY ANN Bomb 4, 82bm. Purchased 4.1694. Sold 13.5.1698.

MARY ANTRIM 14-gun ship. Irish Royalist captured by Parliament 1649. Renamed TIGER'S WHELP 1649 and lost.

MARY BRETON ship captured from French 1415, recaptured 1421

MARYBOROUGH Minesweeper, 'Bathurst' class. Walker 17.10.1940. Lent RAN 6.41. Sold 9.5.47, renamed *Isobel Queen.*

MARY FORTUNE 80 ton ship. Portsmouth 1497. Rebuilt 1512 and renamed SWALLOW. Listed to 1527.

MARY GEORGE Ship, 240bm. Purchased 1512. Listed 1526.

MARY GLORIA Ship, 300bm. Purchased 1517. Listed 1522.

MARY GRACE. Ship purchased in 12.1468. Listed to 1480

MARY GRACE Hoy, 90bm. Captured 1522. Listed to 1525.

MARY GRACE Storeship, 100bm. Captured 1560. Listed to 1562.

MARY GUILDFORD Ship, 160bm Listed 1524-39.

MARY HAMBORO 70-gun ship, 400bm. Purchased 1544 in Hamburg. Sold 1555.

MARY HAMPTON Carrack captured from Genoese 15.8.1416. Foundered 13.7.1420

MARY IMPERIAL Ship, 100bm. Listed 1513-25.

MARY JAMES Ship, 260bm. Purchased 1512. Listed to 1529.

MARY JAMES Ship, 120bm. Captured 1545. Listed to 1546.

MARY NORWELL Ship, 80bm. Listed 1549.

MARY ODIERNE 70 ton vessel. Captured 1545. Fate unknown.

MARYPORT (see MISTLEY)

MARY PRIZE ship 14, 109bm. Spanish captured 1654. Captured by Dutch 1666.

MARY ROSE 60-gun ship, 500bm. Built Portsmouth 1509. Rebuilt 1536 as 700bm; capsized 20.7.1545 in action with the French off the Isle of Wight. Raised 11.10.1982 for preservation.

MARY ROSE Galleon 39, 600bm, 4-34pdr, 11-18pdr, 10-9pdr, 14-smaller. Built 1556. Rebuilt 1589 as 495bm. Condemned and used as part of a wharf at Chatham in 1618.

MARY ROSE 26-gun ship, 300bm. Deptford 1623. Wrecked 1650 off the Flanders coast.

MARY ROSE 32-gun ship in service 1650-54. (Hired?)

MARY ROSE (see MAIDSTONE of 1654)

MARY ROSE Gun-brig 4. French MARIA ROSE captured 18.3.1799 off Acre. Sold 1801.

MARY ROSE Destroyer, 'M' class. Swan Hunter 8.10.1915. Sunk 17.10.17 by German cruisers in the North Sea.

MARY ROSE Tender. Purchased 1918. Sold 4.22 W. Warren.

MARY ROSE (ex-TORONTO renamed 1943) Minesweeper, 'Algerine' class. Redfern 5.8.43. Arrived 14.11.57 Dorkin, Gateshead to BU.

MARY of ROUEN Ship captured 1626. Listed to 1627.

MARY THOMAS Ship, 100bm. Captured 1545. Listed to 1546.

MARYTON Coastal M/S, 'Ton' class. Montrose SY 3.4.1958. Sold S. BKg. (Q'boro) 28.7.69 to BU.

MARY WILLOUGHBY Ship, 140bm. Listed 1535. Captured 1536 by the Scots; recaptured 1547; rebuilt 1551 as 160bm. Sold 1573.

MASHONA Destroyer 1,870 tons, 355½ x 36½ ft, 8-4.7in, 4-TT. Swan Hunter 3.9.1937. Sunk 28.5.41 by air attack SW of Ireland.

MASON Cutter. Listed 1817. Sold 22.4.1817.

MASTIFF (Gunboat No.35) (ex-Herald) Gunvessel 12, 136bm, 72 x 23 ft, 2-32pdr carr., 10-18pdr carr. Purchased 3.1797 at Leith Wrecked 5.1.1800 in Yarmouth Roads.

MASTIFF Gun-brig 4, 184bm, 84 x 22½ ft, 10-18pdr carr., 2-6pdr. Taylor, Bideford 25.9.1813. Survey vessel 8.1825. BU 5.1.1851.

MASTIFF Mortar vessel, 117bm, 65 x 20½ ft, 1-13in mortar. Mare, Blackwall 5.5.1855. Renamed MV.7 on 19.10.55; coastguard watch vessel renamed WV.37 11.1864. BU 9.1875 at Chatham.

MASTIFF (ex-HOUND renamed 1855) Wood S. gunboat, 'Albacore' class. Briggs, Sunderland 22.2.1856. BU 10.1863 at Deptford.

MASTIFF Iron S. gunboat, 'Ant'class. Armstrong Mitchell 4.4.1871. Renamed SNAPPER 1914. Sold 28.11.31 S. Bkrs Ltd, Thames.

MASTIFF Destroyer, 'M' class. Thornycroft 5.9.1914. Sold 9.5.21. Ward, Briton Ferry.

MASTIFF Trawler 1938-39; Whaler 1941-45; Tug 1966.

MATABELE Destroyer 1,870 tons, 335½ x 36½ ft, 8-4.7in, 4-TT. Scotts 6.10.1937. Sunk 17.1.42 by 'U.454' in the Barents Sea.

MATANE (ex-STORMONT renamed 1942) Frigate (RCN), 'River' class. Vickers, Montreal 29.5.1943. Sold 13.12.47 to BU; hull sunk 1948 as breakwater in Oyster Bay.

MATAPAN Destroyer 2,380 tons, 355 x 40 ft, 5-4.5in, 8-40mm, 10-TT. J.Brown 30.4.1945. Sold H.K.Vickers 18.5.79, BU at Blyth.

MATAPEDIA Corvette (RCN), 'Flower' class. Morton 14.9.1940. Sold 30.8.46. BU 12.50 by Steel Co. of Canada, Hamilton, Ont.

MATCHLESS Destroyer, 'M' class 1,010 tons. Swan Hunter 5.10.1914. Sold 26.10.21 Barking S.Bkg Co.

MATCHLESS Destroyer 1,920 tons, 354 x 37 ft, 6-4.7in, 8-TT. Stephen 4.9.1941. To Turkish navy 16.7.59 as KILICALA PASHA.

MATHIAS 48-gun ship, 588bm. Dutch, captured 1653. Blown up 12.6.1667 by the Dutch at Chatham.

MATILDA 6th Rate 28, 573bm, 120 x 33 ft. French JACOBIN captured 30.10.1794 by a squadron in the W.Indies. Hospital ship by 1805. BU 8.1810.

MATILDA Schooner 10. French privateer MATHILDE captured 3.7.1805 by CAMBRIAN. Listed 1805.

MATTHEW Discovery vessel in 1497 (Cabot).

MATTHEW Ship, 600bm. Purchased 1539. Listed to 1554.

MAURITIUS Cruiser 8,000 tons, 538 x 62 ft, 12-6in, 6-4in. Swan Hunter 19.7.1939. Arrived 27.3.65 Ward, Inverkeithing to BU.

MAVOURNEEN Schooner yacht 160 tons. Purchased 19.7.1900. Sold 7.1912.

MAXTON Coastal M/S, 'Ton' class. Harland & Wolff 24.5.1956.

MAYFLOWER 20-gun ship. Royalist FAME captured 1649 by Parliament. Blown up 1658.

MAYFLOWER 20-gun ship. Purchased 1651. Sold 1658.

MAYFLOWER Fire vessel, 20bm. Purchased 1694. Sold 17.2.1696.

MAYFLOWER Fireship, 109bm. Hired 27.6.1695, purchased 7.1695. Expended 1.8.1695 at Dunkirk.

MAYFLOWER Gunvessel 3, 90bm, 64½ x 19 ft. Purchased 3.1794. Made a DY mud-boat 9.1799.

MAYFLOWER Wood S.gunboat,

'Albacore' class. Pitcher, Northfleet 31.1.1856. BU 8.1867 at Sheerness.

MAYFLOWER (see MARTIN of 1890)

MAYFLOWER Corvette, 'Flower' class. Vickers, Montreal 3.7.1940. BU 1950 at Charlestown.

MAYFLOWER. Drifter requis. 1915-19.

MAYFLY Torpedo boat 225 tons, 2-12pdr, 3-TT. Yarrow 29.1.1907. Renamed TB.11 in 1906. Sunk 7.3.16 by mine in the North Sea.

MAYFLY River gunboat 'Fly' class. Yarrow 1915 in sections. Lent War Dept 1.18. Sold 1.3.23 at Basra.

MAYFORD Seaward defence boat, 'Ford' class. Richards, Lowestoft 30.9.1654. Sold Wessex Power Boats Ltd. 28.8.68.

MAY FRERE Wood pad. despatch vessel (Indian), 450bm, 168 x 20 ft. Bombay DY 1864. Fate unknown.

MAYO Troopship (RIM) 1,125 tons. Built 1896. Listed 1920.

MAZURKA Minesweeper 265 tons, 130 x 26 ft, 1-2pdr. Murdoch & Murray 13.10.1917 for War Dept and transferred. Sold 1.5.20 Crichton Thompson & Co.

MEADOWSWEET Corvette, 'Flower' class. Hill, Bristol 28.3.1942. Sold 31.3.51, renamed *Gerrit W.Vinke*.

MEAFORD Corvette (RCN), modified 'Flower' class. Midland SY. Cancelled 12.1943.

MECKLENBURGH Cutter. Purchased 1.1763. Sold 1.1768.

MECKLENBURGH Gunvessel. Purchased 1768. Sunk 9.1773 as breakwater at Sheerness.

MEDA Survey schooner. 150bm. Westacott, Barnstaple 2.1880 & purchased. Sold W.Australia Govt in 1887.

MEDEA 6th Rate 26. French MEDEE captured 4.4.1744 by DREADNOUGHT. Sold 3.1745, became privateer *Boscawen*.

MEDEA 6th Rate 28, 605bm, 120½ x 33½ ft. Hilhouse, Bristol 28.4.1778. Sold 1795.

MEDEE 5th Rate 36, French, captured 5.8.1800 off Rio by two E. Indiamen. Prison ship 1802. Sold 1805.

MEDEA 5th Rate 32, 658bm, 127 x 34 ft. Woolwich DY. Ordered 1800 and cancelled.

MEDEA Wood pad. sloop, 835bm, 180 x 32 ft, 2-10in, 2-32pdr. Woolwich DY 2.9.1833. Sold 1867.

MEDEA 2nd class cruiser 2,800 tons, 265 x 41 ft, 6-6in, 9-6pdr. Chatham DY 9.6.1888. Sold 2.4.1914.

MEDEA (ex-Greek KRITI purchased 8.1914) Destroyer 1,007 tons, 265 x 27 ft, 3-4in, 4-TT. J.Brown 20.1.15. Sold 9.5.21 Ward, Milford Haven; arrived 10.22.

MEDEA (see M.22)

MEDEA Minesweeper 1942. see CIRCE.

MEDIATOR Sloop 10, 105bm, 61½ x 21 ft, 10-4pdr. Purchased 4.1745. Captured 29.7.1745 by a French privateer off Ostend.

MEDIATOR 5th Rate 44, 879bm, 140 x 37½ ft. Raymond, Northam 30.3.1782. Renamed CAMEL storeship 3.3.1788. BU 12.1810.

MEDIATOR (ex-Indiaman *Ann & Amelia*) 5th Rate 44, 689bm. Purchased 6.1804. Fireship 1809 and expended 11.4.1809 in Basque Roads.

MEDIATOR. Trawler requis. 1914-16; Tug 1944-68.

MEDICINE HAT Minesweeper (RCN), TE 'Bangor' class. Vickers, Montreal 26.6.1941. Sold 29.11.57 Turkish navy as BIGA.

MEDINA (see PORTSMOUTH of 1703)

MEDINA 6th Rate 20, 460bm, 116 x 30½ ft. Adams, Bucklers Hard 13.8.1813. Sold 4.1.1832 Mr Ledger to BU.

MEDINA Wood pad. packet, 889bm, 176x 33 ft. Pembroke Dock 18.3.1840. BU in 3.1864.

MEDINA Iron S.gunboat 363 tons, 110 x 34 ft, 3-64pdr. Palmer 3.8.1876. Sold 1904 at Bermuda.

MEDINA (ex-REDMILL renamed 1915) Destroyer, 'M' class. White 8.3.16. Sold 9.5.21 Ward, Milford Haven.

MEDITERRANEAN Sloop (xebec) 12, circa 200bm, 92½ x 21 ft. 2-6pdr, 10-3pdr. Captured 1756 in the Mediterranean. Listed 1757.

MEDORA (see MEDWAY of 1916)

MEDUSA 4th Rate 50, 910bm, 140½ x 38½ ft. Plymouth DY 23.7.1785. Wrecked 26.11.1798 on the coast of Portugal.

MEDUSA 5th Rate 32, 920bm, 144 x 37½ ft. Pitcher, Northfleet 14.4.1801. BU 11.1816.

MEDUSA 5th Rate 46, 1,063bm, 150 x 40½ ft. Woolwich DY. Ordered 18.7.1817, re-ordered Pembroke DK 7.8.30, cancelled 22.4.1831.

MEDUSA Wood pad. packet, 889bm, 175 x 33 ft. Pembroke Dock 31.10.1838. Sold 17.2.1872 Castle, Charlton.

MEDUSA Iron pad. gunboat (Indian), 432bm. Laird 1839. Wrecked

9.12.1853 on coast of Bengal.

MEDUSA 2nd class cruiser 2,800 tons, 265 x 41 ft, 6-6in, 9-6pdr. Chatham DY 11.8.1888. Harbour service 1910. Sold 1920 Stanlee; resold 21.10.21 J.E.Thomas.

MEDUSA (ex-Greek LESVOS purchased 8.1914) Destroyer 1,007 tons, 265 x 27 ft, 3-4in, 4-TT. J.Brown 27.3.15. Sunk 25.3.16 in collision with destroyer LAVEROCK off the Schleswig coast.

MEDUSA (see M.29)

MEDUSA Yacht 1915-19; M/S 1939 renamed MERCEDES.

MEDWAY 4th Rate 60, 914bm, 145½ x 38 ft. Sheerness DY 20.9.1693. Rebuilt Deptford 1718, hulk 1740; beached 18.11.1748 as sheer hulk at Portsmouth. BU 10.1749 at Portsmouth.

MEDWAY PRIZE 4th Rate 48, 500bm, 117 x 34 ft. French, captured 20.8.1697 by MEDWAY. Hulk 1699. Sunk 1712 as a foundation at Sheerness.

MEDWAY PRIZE 6th Rate 28, 241bm, 92 x 25 ft. French, captured 6.9.1704 by MEDWAY. Sold 1713 in Jamaica.

MEDWAY 4th Rate 60, 1,080bm, 144 x 41½ ft. Bird, Rotherhithe. (Probably re-ordered as the Deptford ship of 1755).

MEDWAY PRIZE 5th Rate 744bm, 128 x 36 ft. French FAVORETTE (?) captured 1.1744 in the E. Indies. Sold 13.2.1749.

MEDWAY 4th Rate 60 x 1,204bm, 149½ x 43 ft. Deptford DY 14.2.1755. Receiving ship 6.1787; renamed ARUNDEL 1802. BU 3.1811.

MEDWAY Storeship (busse) 6, 83bm, 65 x 17 ft, 6-4pdr. Purchased 10.11.1756. Made a DY craft 2.1760. - Sold 17.4.1764.

MEDWAY 3rd Rate 74, 1,768bm, 176 x 49 ft. Pitcher, Northfleet 19.11.1812. Convict ship 10.1847. Sold 2.11.1865 at Bermuda.

MEDWAY Iron S. gunboat 363 tons, 110 x 34 ft, 3-64pdr. Palmer 3.10.1876. Sold 1904 at Bermuda.

MEDWAY (ex-MEDORA renamed 1916, ex-REDWING renamed 1915) Destroyer, 'M' class. White 19.4.1916. Sold 9.5.21 Ward, Milford Haven.

MEDWAY Depot ship 14,650 tons, 545 x 85 ft, 6-4in. Vickers Armstrong, Barrow 19.7.1928. Sunk 30.6.42 by 'U.372' off Alexandra.

MEDWAY II (see M.29)

MEDWAY (see BAGSHOT of 1918)

MEDWAY (ex-MRC.1109 renamed 12.59, ex-LCT.1109) Depot ship 200 tons. Sold at Singapore 1970.

MEEANEE (ex-MADRAS renamed 19.2.1843) 2nd Rate 80, 2,591bm, 190 x 57 ft, 12-8in, 68-32pdr. Bombay DY 11.11.1848. Undocked 31.10.1857 as screw ship, 60 guns; lent War Dept 5.3.1867 as hospital ship. BU 1906.

MEERMIN Brig-sloop 16, 203bm, 74½ x 26 ft, 16-6pdr. Dutch MIERMIN seized 4.3.1796 at Plymouth. Sold 1801.

MEGAERA Fireship 14, 425bm, 109 x 30 ft. Teague, Ipswich 5.1783. Sold 3.4.1817 J. Darkin.

MEGAERA Wood pad. sloop, 717bm, 150 x 32½ ft, 2-9pdr. Sheerness DY 17.8.1837. Wrecked 4.3.1843 coast of Jamaica.

MEGAERA Iron S.frigate, 1,391bm, 207 x 31½ ft. Fairbairn, Millwall 22.5.1849. Troopship 1855. Beached 16.6.1871 on St Pauls Island, Indian Ocean, as unseaworthy.

MELAMPE 5th Rate 36, 747bm, 134½ x 35½ ft. French, captured 2.11.1757 by TARTAR. Beached 1764 at Antigua.

MELAMPUS 5th Rate 36, 947bm, 141 x 39 ft. Hillhouse, Bristol 8.6.1785. Sold 6.1815 to the Dutch navy.

MELAMPUS 5th Rate 46, 1,089bm, 152 x 40½ ft. Pembroke Dock 10.8.1820. Harbour service 1854; lent War Dept 8.86 to 10.91. Sold 3.4.1906 Harris, Bristol.

MELAMPUS 2nd class cruiser 3,400 tons, 300 x 43 ft, 2-6in, 6-4.7in, 8-6pdr. Vickers 2.8.1890. Sold 14.7.1910 Cohen, Felixstowe.

MELAMPUS (ex-Greek CHIOS purchased 8.1914) Destroyer 1,040 tons, 265 x 27 ft, 3-4in, 4-TT. Fairfield 16.12.14. Sold 22.9.21 Cohen; BU in Germany.

MELBOURNE 2nd class cruiser (RAN) 5,440 tons, 430 x 50 ft, 8-6in. Cammell Laird 30.5.1912. Sold 8.12.28 Alloa S.Bkg Co, Rosyth.

MELBOURNE (see MAJESTIC of 1945)

MELBREAK Destroyer, 'Hunt' class type III. Swan Hunter 5.3.1942. Arrived 22.11.56 Ward. Grays to BU.

MELEAGER 5th Rate 32, 682bm, 126 x 35 ft. Graves, Frindsbury 28.2.1785. Wrecked 9.6.1801 in the Gulf of Mexico.

MELEAGER 5th Rate 36, 875bm, 137 x 38 ft. Chatham DY 25.11.1806. Wrecked 30.7.1808 on Bare Bush Cay, Jamaica.

MELITA Compos. S.sloop 970 tons, 167

x 32 ft, 8-5in. Malta DY 20.3.1888. BDV 5.1905; salvage vessel RINGDOVE 12.1915. Sold 9.7.20 Falmouth Docks Board.

MELITA (see RINGDOVE of 1889)

MELITA Minesweeper, 'Algerine' class. Redfern, Toronto 8.12.1942. Arrived 25.2.59. Rees, Llanelly to BU. (Was SATELLITE drillship 4.47 to 1951).

MELPOMENE 5th Rate 38, 1,014bm, 148 x 39 ft. French, captured 10.8.1794 at Calvi. Sold 14.12.1815.

MELPOMENE 5th Rate 38, 1,087bm, 153 x 40 ft. French, captured 30.4.1815 by RIVOLI off Ischia. Sold 7.6.1821.

MELPOMENE Wood S.frigate 2,861bm, 237 x 52 ft (ex-4th Rate, 2,147bm). Pembroke Dock 8.8.1857 (eight years on stocks). Sold 23.1.1875 Castle, Charlton.

MELPOMENE 2nd class cruiser 2,950 tons, 265 x 42 ft, 6-6in, 9-6pdr. Portsmouth DY 20.9.1888. Sold 11.8.1905 Ward, Preston.

MELPOMENE (see INDEFATIGABLE of 1891)

MELPOMENE (ex-Greek SAMOS purchased 8.1914) Destroyer 1,040. tons, 265 x 26½ ft, 3-4in, 4-TT. Fairfield 1.2.15. Sold 9.5.21 Ward, New Holland.

MELPOMENE (see M.31)

La MELPOMENE Destroyer 610 tons, 245 x 26 ft, 2-3.9in, 2-TT. French torpedo boat seized 3.7.1940 at Portsmouth. Free-French 9.40 to 10.42 then RN crew; returned 1946 to the French navy.

MELTON Paddle M/S, 'Ascot class. Hamilton 16.3.1916. Sold 25.11.27 Hughes Bolckow; resold 2.28, renamed *Queen of Thanet.* M/S hired 1939.

MELTON. Tender 128 tons. Dunston 6.3.1981

MELVILLE Brig-sloop 18, 353bm. French NAIADE captured 16.10.1805 by JASON in the W.Indies. Sold 3.11.1808.

MELVILLE (also LORD MELVILLE) Brig 14 (Canadian lakes), 186bm, 73 x 24½ ft. Kingston, Ont. 20.7.1813. Renamed STAR 22.1.1814. Sold 1837.

MELVILLE 3rd Rate 74, 1,768bm 176½ x 49 ft. Bombay DY 17.2.1817. Hospital ship 3.1857. Sold 1873 at Hong Kong.

MELVILLE Minesweeper (RCN), diesel 'Bangor' class. Davie SB 7.6.1941. Transferred RCMP 1950 as *Cygnus.*

MEMNON Paddle sloop (Indian), 1,140bm, 2-64pdr, 4-32pdr. Fletcher,

Limehouse 1841. Wrecked 4.8.1843 near Cape Guardafui.

MENACE Destroyer, 'M' class. Swan Hunter 9.11.1915. Sold 9.5.21 Ward, Grays. BU started 8.2.24.

MENAI 6th Rate 26, 449bm, 108 x 31 ft, 18-32pdr car., 8-12pdr carr., 2-6pdr. Brindley, Frindsbury 5.4.1814. Harbour service 1831; target 1851. BU 4.1853.

MENAI Wood S.corvette, 1,857bm, 225 x 43 ft. Chatham DY. Laid down 5.1.1861, cancelled 16.12.1864. (Frames used for BLANCHE 1865.)

MENAI Tender 128 tons Dunston 15.5.1981.

MENDIP Destroyer, 'Hunt' class type I. Swan Hunter 9.4.1940. Lent Chinese navy 5.48 as LIN FU. Sold 15.11.49 Egyptian navy as IBRAHIM EL AWAL.

MENELAUS 5th Rate 38, 1,077bm, 154 x 40 ft. Plymouth DY 17.4.1810. Quarantine hulk 1832; lent Customs 5.1854. Sold 10.5.1897 J.Read, Portsmouth.

MENELAUS (see M.31)

MENELAUS Kite-baloon ship 4672 tons. Requis, 1915-18.

MENTOR A.ship 16. American, captured 1778. Burnt 8.5.1781 to avoid capture by the Spanish at Pensacola.

MENTOR Sloop 16. American AURORA captured 1781. Wrecked 16.3.1783 near Bermuda.

MENTOR Destroyer, 'M' class 1,053 tons. Hawthorn Leslie 21.8.1914. Sold 9.5.21 Ward, Hayle; arrived 10.22.

MENTOR Tender 128 tons Dunston 7.10.1981

MEON Frigate 'River' class. Inglis 4.8.1943. Arrived 14.5.66 Hughes Bolckow, Blyth to BU.

MEON Tender 128 tons Dunston 13.5.1982

MERCURIUS Brig-sloop 16, 308bm, 94½ x 27½ ft, 16-24pdr. Danish, captured 7.9.1807 at Copenhagen. Sold 23.11.1815. (Was to have been renamed TRANSFER.)

MERCURY Galley 6, 80bm, 1-18pdr, 1-6pdr, 4-smaller. Deptford 1592. Sold 1611.

MERCURY Ship, 300bm. River Thames 16.10.1620. Fate unknown.

MERCURY Ship purchased 31.8.1622. Fate unknown.

MERCURY Advice boat 6, 78bm, 61½ x 16 ft. Portsmouth 3.1694. Captured 19.6.1697 by a French privateer off Ushant.

MERCURY Fireship 8, 217bm, 90 x 24 ft. Purchased 22.6.1739. Foundered 12.1744.

MERCURY Brigantine, 16-6pdr. Purchased 1744. Captured 1745 by the French.

MERCURY 6th Rate 24, 504bm, 113 x 32 ft. Golightly, Liverpool 13.10.1745. BU completed 7.8.1753 at Woolwich.

MERCURY 6th Rate 20, 433bm, 108 x 30 ft. Barnard, Harwich 2.3.1756. Wrecked 24.12.1777 near New York.

MERCURY 6th Rate 28, 594bm, 121 x 34 ft. Mestears, R.Thames 9.12.1779. BU 1.1814 at Woolwich.

MERCURE Sloop 14, 338bm, 103½ x 27½ ft. French Privateer captured 31.8.1798 by PHAETON. Renamed TROMPEUSE 1799. Foundered 17.5.1800 in the channel.

MERCURY Brig 14 (Indian), 185bm. Bombay DY 1806. Coal hulk by 1865.

MERCURY Tender. 50bm. Rotherhithe 1807. BU 10.1835.

MERCURY 5th Rate 46, 1,084bm, 152 x 40½ft. Chatham DY 16.11.1826. Coal hulk 1861. Sold 3.4.1906 Harris, Bristol.

MERCURY Cutter tender, 70bm, 54 x 18 ft. Chatham DY 7.2.1837. Renamed YC.6, yard craft 1866. renamed PLYMOUTH 8.2.1876. Sold 17.5.1904.

MERCURY Despatch vessel (2nd class cruiser) 3,730 tons, 300 x 46 ft, 10-64pdr. Pembroke Dock 17.4.1878. Depot ship 1906.Sold 9.7.19 Forth S.Bkg Co, Bo'ness. (Was to have been renamed COLUMBINE in 1912.)

MERCURY (ex-barque *Illova*) Training ship, 398 gross, 139 x 27 ft. Purchased 1887. Sold 1916 as coal hulk.

MERCURY (see GANNET of 1878)

MERCURY Minesweeper requis. 1915-20; M/S 1939-40.

MEREDITH Cutter 10, 83bm, 54½ x 19½ ft. Purchased 3.1763. Sold 1.7.1784.

MERHONOUR 41-gun ship, 709bm, 4-34pdr, 15-18pdr, 16-9pdr, 4-6pdr, 2-small. Woolwich 1590. Rebuilt Woolwich 1615. Sold 1650.

MERLIN Pinnace 10, 50bm. Built 1579. Listed to 1601.

MERLIN Yacht 14, 129bm Chatham DY 1652. Captured 13.10.1665 by the Dutch.

MERLIN Yacht 8, 109bm. Shish, Rotherhite 1666. Sold 30.8.1698.

MERLIN Sloop 2, 66bm, 59½ x 16 ft. Chatham DY 1699. Sold 1712.

MERLIN Sloop 14, 271bm, 92 x 26 ft. Greville & Whitstone, Limehouse 1744. Sold 1750.

MERLIN Sloop 10. In service 1753.

MERLIN Sloop 10. 224bm Quallett, Rotherhithe 20.3.1756 Captured by French 19.4.57. recaptured 9.57, renamed ZEPHYR. captured by French 23.8.78. Recaptured and burnt 1780.

MERLIN Sloop 10, 304bm, 100 X 26 ft, 10-6pdr. Randall, Rotherhithe 1.7.1757, purchased on stocks. Abandoned and burnt 23.10.1777 in the Delaware.

MERLIN Sloop 18, 340bm, 101 x ft, 18-6pdr, 6-12pdr carr. King, Dover 1780, purchased on stocks. Sold 28.8.1795.

MERLIN Sloop 16, 371bm, 106 x 28 ft. Dudman, Deptford 25.3.1796. BU.1.1803.

MERLIN (ex-*Hercules*) Sloop 16, 395bm, 104 x 30½ ft, 10-32pdr car., 4-24pdr rockets. Purchased 7.1803. Sold 21.1.1836.

MERLIN Wood pad. packet, 889bm, 175 x 33 ft. Pembroke Dock 18.9.1838. Survey vessel 1854; gun-vessel 1856. Sold 18.5.1963 Williams & Co.

MERLIN Compos. S. gunboat, 295bm, 430 tons, 125 x 23 ft, 2-64pdr, 2-20pdr. Pembroke Dock 24.11.1871. Sold 27.2.1891.

MERLIN Sloop 1,070 tons, 185 x 33 ft, 6-4in. Sheerness DY 30.11.1901. Survey vessel 9.06. Sold 3.8.23 at Hong Kong.

MERLIN Tug 1895-1919; Trawler & Yacht WW.1.

MERMAID Galley, 200bm. Captured 1545. Listed to 1563.

MERMAID 24-gun ship, 309bm, 105 x 26 ft. Graves, Limehouse 1651. Rebuilt Woolwich 1689 as 5th Rate 32, 343bm. Rebuilt Chatham 1707 as 421 bm. BU 6.1734.

MERMAID Fireship 8, 174bm, 78 x 23ft. French, captured 8.11.1692. Burnt 25.2.1693 by accident at Plymouth.

MERMAID (see Kennington of 1736)

MERMAID (see RUBY of 1708)

MERMAID 6th Rate 24, 533bm, 115 x 32 ft. Adams, Bucklers Hard 22.5.1749. Wrecked 6.1.1760 in the Bahamas.

MERMAID 6th Rate 28, 613bm, 124 x 33½ ft. Blaydes, Hull 6.5.1761. Chased ashore 8.7.1778 by the

French in Delaware Bay.

MERMAID 5th Rate 32, 693bm, 126 x 35½ ft. Sheerness DY 29.11.1784 (originally LD Woolwich, transferred 3.1782). BU 11.1815.

MERMAID Gunvessel 1. Purchased 1798 in Honduras for local use. Sold 1800.

MERMAID Survey cutter, 84bm, 56 x 18½ ft. Purchased 1817 at Port Jackson. Sold 1823, after grounding 1820.

MERMAID 5th Rate 46, 1,085bm, 152 x 40½ ft. Chatham DY 30.7.1825. Powder hulk 1850; lent War Dept 8.5.1863. BU completed 6.1875 at Dublin.

MERMAID Coastguard vessel, 165bm, 88 x21½ ft. Purchased 1853. Sold 14.8.1890 Tough & Henderson.

MERMAID Destroyer 370 tons, 210 ft, 1-12pdr, 5-6pdr, 2-TT. Hawthorn 22.2.1898. Sold 23.7.1919 Ward, New Holland.

MERMAID Sloop 1,350 tons, 283 x 38½ ft, 6-4in Denny 11.11.1943. To W.German navy 5.5.59 as SCHARNHORST.

MERMAID (see SULLINGTON)

MERMAID Frigate 2300 tons, Ghanaian BLACK STAR purchased from Yarrow in 3.1972. Sold Malaya 4.77, renamed HANG TUAH.

MEROPE Brig-sloop 10, 252bm, 92 x 25½ ft. Chatham DY 25.6.1808. Sold 23.11.1815.

MERRITTONIA (ex-POINTE CLAIRE renamed 3.1944) Corvette (RCN), modified 'Flower' class. Morton 24.6.44. Wrecked 30.11.45 coast of Nova Scotia.

MERRY HAMPTON M/S sloop, '24' class. Blyth SB 19.12.1918. Renamed HERALD 2.23, survey vessel. Scuttled 2.42 at Selatar; raised by the Japanese and commissioned 10.42 as HEIYO. Mined 14.11.44.

MERSEY 6th Rate 26, 451bm, 108½ x 31 ft, 18-32pdr carr., 8-12pdr carr., 2-6pdr. Courtney, Chester 3.1814. Harbour service 1832. BU 7.1852.

MERSEY Wood S.frigate 3,733bm, 300 x 52ft, 28-10in, 12-68pdr. Chatham DY 13.8.1858. Sold 23.1.1875 Castle, Charlton.

MERSEY 2nd class cruiser 4,050 tons, 300 x 46, 2-8in, 10-6in, 3-6pdr. Chatham DY 31.3.1885. Sold 4.4.1905 Issacs.

MERSEY (ex-Brazilian river monitor MADURA purchased 8.8.1914) Gunboat 1,260 tons, 265 x 49 ft, 3-6in, 2-4.7in howitzers. Vickers 1.10.13. Sold 9.5.21 Ward, Morecambe; BU

3.23.

MERSEY Name borne in turn from 1949 by MMS.1075, AMERTON and POLLINGTON as RNVR tenders.

MERSHAM Inshore M/S, 'Ham' class. Harris, Appledore 5.4.1954. Transferred 1955 French navy as M.773.

MESSENGER Dogger 6. Dutch, captured 1672. Sold 1673.

MESSENGER Advice boat 6, 73bm. Plymouth 1694. Foundered 30.11.1701 in the Atlantic.

MESSENGER (ex-Duke of York) Wood pad. vessel, 733bm, 156 x32½ ft. Purchased 20.8.1830. Sold 22.11.1861 Castle.

MESSENGER Mooring vessel 1915-59.

MESSINA (see LST.3043)

MESSINA Tender 128 tons Dunston 5.3.1982

METEOR (Gunboat No.34) (ex-Lady Cathcart) Gunvessel 12, 154bm, 74½ x 22ft, 2-24pdr, 10-18pdr carr. Purchased 3.1797 at Leith. Sold 2.1802.

METEOR (ex-Sarah Ann) Bomb 8, 364bm, 103 x 29ft, 8-24pdr carr., 1-13in mortar. Purchased 10.1803. Sold 28.5.1811.

METEOR (see STAR of 1805)

METEOR Bomb 8, 378bm, 106 x 29 ft, 10-24pdr carr., 2-6pdr, 2-mortars. Pembroke Dock 25.6.1823. Renamed BEACON 1832, survey ship. Sold 8.1846 at Malta.

METEOR Wood pad. Vessel 296bm, 126x 23 ft. Deptford DY 17.2.1824. BU 8.1849 et Woolwich.

METEOR River gunboat (Indian), 149bm. Bombay DY 1839. Fate unknown.

METEOR Wood floating battery, 1,469bm, 172½ x 44 ft, 14-68pdr. Mare, Blackwall 17.4.1855. BU 1861.

METEOR. Destroyer, 'M' class 1,070 tons. Thornycroft 24.7.1914. Sold 9.5.21 Ward, Milford Haven; arrived 10.22.

METEOR Destroyer 1,920 tons, 354 x 37 ft, 6-4.7in, 8-TT. Stephen 3.11.1941. Handed over 29.6.59 to the Turkish navy as PIYALE PASHA.

METEOR Tug 1883-renamed PERSEVERANCE 1914-23.

METEORITE (see U.1407).

MEYNELL Minesweeper, early 'Hunt' class. Henderson 7.2.1917. Sold 4.11.22 Lithgow.

MEYNELL Destroyer, 'Hunt' class type I. Swan Hunter 7.6.1940. Sold 18.10.54 Ecuadorian navy, renamed PRESIDENTE VELASCO IBARRA

8.55.

MICHAEL Ship mentioned in 1350.

MICHAEL Ship captured from the Scots 1488 and listed to 1513.

MICHAEL Destroyer, 'M' class. Thornycroft 19.5.1915. Sold 22.9.21. Cohen; BU in Germany.

MICHAEL Minesweeper, 'Algerine' class. Redfern, Toronto 20.9.1944. Arrived 15.11.56 McLellan, Bo'ness to BU.

MICKLEHAM Inshore M/S, 'Ham' class. Berthon Bt Co 11.3.1954. Sold 5.8.66.

MICMAC Destroyer (RCN) 1,927 tons, 355½ x 37½ ft, 6-4.7in, 2-4in, 4-TT. Halifax SY 18.9.1943. Sold 1964 Marine Salvage Co; resold and arrived 10.64 Faslane to BU.

MIDDLESBROUGH (see KUMAON)

MIDDLESEX Minesweeper (RCN), 'Algerine' class. Pt Arthur SY 27.5.1943. Wrecked 3.12.46 on Bald Island Point near Halifax.

MIDDLETON Destroyer, 'Hunt' class type II. Vickers Armstrong, Tyne 12.5.1941. Hulked 1955; arrived 4.10.57. Hughes Bolckow, Blyth to BU.

MIDDLETON Minehunter 615 tons. Yarrow 27.4.1983.

MIDLAND Corvette (RCN), 'Flower' class. Midland SY 25.6.1941. Sold 1946 Great Lakes Lumber Co.

MIGNONETTE Sloop, 'Arabis' class. Dunlop Bremner 26.1.1916. Sunk 17.3.17 by mine off Galley Head, SW Ireland.

MIGNONETTE Corvette, 'Flower' class. Hall Russell 28.1.1941. Sold 1946, renamed *Alexandrouplis*.

MIGNONETTE Drifter requis. 1915-19.

MIGNONNE 5th Rate 32, 684bm. French, captured 10.8.1794 by the fleet at Calvi. Burnt 31.7.1797 at Puerto Ferrajo as useless.

MIGNONNE Sloop 16, 462bm. French, captured 28.6.1803 by GOLIATH at San Domingo. Damaged by grounding 1804 and beached at Port Royal, Jamaica.

MIGNONNE Brig-sloop 16, 329bm. French PHAETON captured 26.3.1806 by PIQUE in the W.Indies. Renamed MUSETTE 1806. Sold 1.9.1814.

MILAN 5th Rate 38, 1,097bm, 156 x 40 ft. French VILLE de MILAN captured 23.2.1805 by LEANDER and CAMBRIDGE in the Atlantic. BU 12.1815.

MILBROOK Schooner 16, 148bm, 83 x

21½ ft, 16-18pdr carr. Redbridge 1797. Gunvessel 3.1799. Wrecked 25.3.1808 on the Burlings.

MILBROOK Destroyer, 'M' class. Thornycroft 12.7.1915. Sold 22.9.21 Cohen; BU in Germany.

MILBROOK Tender 128 tons Dunston 16.12.1981.

MILDURA (ex-PELORUS renamed 4.1890) 3rd class cruiser 2,575 tons, 265 x 41 ft, 8-4.7in, 8-3pdr. Armstrong 25.11.1889. Sold 3.4.1906 Garnham.

MILDURA Minesweeper (RAN), 'Bathurst' class. Morts Dk, Sydney 15.5.1941. Sold 9.65 Brisbane Metal Co.

MILEHAM Inshore M/S, 'Ham' class. Blackmore, Bideford 1.7.1954. Transferred French navy 1955 as M.783.

MILFOIL Corvette, 'Flower' class. Morton, Quebec 5.8.1942. Transferred USN 31.3.43 as INTENSITY.

MILFORD (see FAGANS)

MILFORD 5th Rate 32, 355bm, 105 x 27½ ft. Woolwich 1689. Captured 11.1693 by the French in the North Sea.

MILFORD 5th Rate 32, 385bm, 108 x 28½ ft. Hubbard, Ipswich 1695. Captured 7.1.1697 by two French privateers in the North Sea.

MILFORD (see SCARBOROUGH of 1694)

MILFORD (see ADVICE of 1712)

MILFORD 6th Rate 28, 589bm, 118 x 34 ft. Chitty, Milford Haven 20.9.1759. Sold 17.5.1785.

MILFORD 3rd Rate 78, 1,919bm, 181½ x 50 ft. Jacobs, Milford Haven 1.4.1809. Harbour service 6.1825. BU 7.1846.

MILFORD Tank Vessel 1816-52

MILFORD Sloop 1,060 tons, 250 x 34 ft, 2-4in. Devonport DY 11.6.1932. Sold 3.6.49, BU Ward, Hayle.

MILFORD Tender 128 tons. Dunston 22.7.1982

MILLTOWN Minesweeper (RCN), TE 'Bangor' class. Pt Arthur SY 22.1.1942. Sold 2.59 Marine Industries.

MILNE Destroyer, 'M' class 1,010 tons. J.Brown 5.10.1914. Sold 22.9.21 Cohen; BU in Germany.

MILNE Destroyer 1,935 tons, 354 x 37 ft, 6-4.7in, 8-TT. Scotts 31.12.1941. To Turkish navy 27.4.59 as ALP ARSLAM.

MIMICO (see MOON of 1943)

MIMICO (ex-BULRUSH renamed 9.1943). Corvette (RCN), modified

'Flower' class. Crown, Sunderland 11.10.43. Sold 1950, renamed *Olympic Victor*.

MIMOSA Sloop, 'Acacia' class. Bow McLachlan 16.7.1915. Sold 18.11.22 S. Wales Salvage Co.

MIMOSA Corvette, 'Flower' class. Hill, Bristol 18.1.1941. Lent Free-French 5.41; sunk 9.6.42 by 'U.124' in the western Atlantic.

MINAS Minesweeper (RCN), TE 'Bangor' class. Burrard 23.1.1941. Arrived 20.8.59 Seattle to BU.

MINDEN 3rd Rate 74, 1,721bm, 171½ x 49 ft. Bombay DY 19.6.1810. Hospital hulk 4.1842. Sold 4.7.1861 at Hong Kong.

MINDFUL Destroyer, 'M' class. Fairfield 24.8.1915. Sold 22.9.21 Cohen; BU in Germany.

MINDFUL (see M.VIII of 1943).

MINDFUL Rescue tug 1943-46.

MINEHEAD (see LONGFORD).

MINER I to VIII (See M.I to VIII).

MINERVA 5th Rate 32, 664bm, 124½ x 35 ft. Quallet, Rotherhithe 17.1.1759. Captured 28.8.1778 by the French CONCORDE; recaptured 4.1.1781 and renamed RECOVERY. Sold 30.12.1784.

MINERVA 5th Rate 38, 941bm, 141 x 39 ft. Woolwich DY 3.6.1780. Renamed PALLAS 1798, troopship. BU 3.1803.

MINERVA Storeship 29. 689bm. Purchased 6.1781. Sold at Bombay. 21.12.1783.

MINERVE 5th Rate 38, 1,102bm, 154½ x 40 ft, 4-36pdr carr., 28-18pdr, 12-8pdr. French, captured 24.6.1795 by LOWESTOFT and DIDO in the Mediterranean. Stranded 3.7.1803 near Cherbourg and captured by the French; recaptured 3.2.1810 as CANONNIERE and renamed CONFIANCE. Listed to 1814.

MINERVE Prison hulk, 246bm, 90 x 24½ ft. French sloop captured 1803. BU 1811.

MINERVA 5th Rate 32 (fir-built), 661bm, 127 x 34 ft. Deptford DY 26.10.1805. BU 2.1815.

MINERVA 5th Rate 46, 1,082bm, 152 x 40½ ft. Portsmouth DY 13.6.1820. Harbour service 1861. Sold 28.2.1895 at Portsmouth.

MINERVA 2nd class cruiser 5,600 tons, 350 x 53 ft, 11-6in, 9-12pdr. Chatham DY 23.9.1895. Sold 5.10.1920 Auten Ltd.

MINERVA (see M.33)

MINERVE Submarine 597 tons, 211 x

20ft, 1-3in, 9-TT. French, seized 3.7.1940 at Plymouth. Free-French crew from 9.40. Wrecked 19.9.45 on Portland Bill.

MINERVA Frigate, 'Leander' class. Vickers Armstrong, Tyne 19.12.1964.

MINERVE (see under MINERVA)

MINGAN (see FORT YORK)

MINION Ship, 180bm. Built 1523. Rebuilt as 300bm. Given away 1549 to Sir T.Seymour.

MINION Ship, circa 600bm. Purchased 1560. Condemned 1570.

MINION Ketch 6, 22bm. Built 1649. Sold 1669.

MINION Destroyer, 'M' class. Thornycroft 11.9.1915. Sold 8.11.21. Slough TC; BU in Germany.

MINION Tug 1940-60.

MINNIKIN Ship listed 1594-95.

MINNOW (see X.54)

MINORCA Storeship 2, 105bm. 63 x 19½ ft, 2-3pdr. Deptford 16.7.1740 captured by the French in 6.1756 at Minorca.

MINORCA Sloop (xebec), 18, 388bm, 97 x 30½ ft, 18-6pdr. Port Mahon, Minorca 27.8.1779. Scuttled 21.8.1781 at Port Mahon to block passage to the harbour.

MINORCA Brig-sloop 16, 248bm, 85 x 26½ ft. French ALERTE captured 18.6.1799 by the fleet in Mediterranean. Sold 5.1802 at Port Mahon.

MINORCA Sloop 18. Port Mahon. Laid down 1799. No trace after; possibly handed over to Spanish navy 1802 with the cession of Minorca.

MINORCA Brig-sloop 18, 'Cruizer' class, 385bm. Brindley, Lynn 6.1805 BU 5.1814.

MINORU M/S sloop, '24' class. Swan Hunter 16.6.1919. Sold 25.2.20 Moise Mazza, Malta.

MINOS Steam vessel (Canadian lakes), 406bm, 153 x 24 ft. Chippawa 6.1840. Sold 1852 Mr Weston.

MINOS Destroyer, 'M' class 883 tons. Yarrow 6.8.1914. Sold 31.8.20 Ward, Hayle.

MINOTAUR 3rd Rate 74, 1,723bm, 172½ x 48 ft. Woolwich DY 6.11.1793. Wrecked 22.12.1810 in the Texel.

MINOTAUR 3rd Rate 74, 1,726bm, 171 x 49 ft. Chatham DY 15.4.1816. Harbour service 11.1842. Renamed HERMES 27.7.1866. BU 1869 at Sheerness.

MINOTAUR (ex-ELEPHANT renamed 1861) Iron screw ship, 6,621bm, 10,690 tons, 400 x 59½ ft, 4-9in,

24-7in, 8-24pdr. Thames IW 12.12.1863. Renamed BOSCAWEN training ship 3.1904, GANGES 21.6.06, GANGES II 25.4.08. Sold 30.1.22, BU at Swansea.

MINOTAUR Armoured cruiser 14,600 tons, 490 x 74½ ft, 4-9.2in, 10-7.5in, 14-12pdr. Devonport DY 6.6.1906. Sold 12.4.20 Ward, Milford Haven.

MINOTAUR (see NEWCASTLE of 1936)

MINOTAUR Cruiser 8,800 tons, 538 x 63 ft, 9-6in, 10-4in, 8-40mm. Harland & Wolff 29.7.1943. Renamed ONTARIO (RCN) 7.44. Sold 6.5.59; resold and arrived 19.11.60 at Osaka, Japan to BU.

MINOTAUR Cruiser. Projected 1945, not ordered.

MINSTREL Sloop 18, 423bm, 108½ x 29½ ft, 16-32pdr carr., 6-18pdr carr. Boole & Goode, Bridport 23.3.1807. Sold 6.3.1817.

MINSTREL Wood S.gunboat, 'Britomart' class. Portsmouth DY 16.2.1865. Coal hulk 1874. Reported sold 1903 but listed to 1906.

MINSTREL Destroyer 730 tons, 246½ x 25 ft, 2-4in, 2-12pdr, 2-TT. Thornycroft 2.2.1911. Lent Japanese navy 6.17 to 1919 as SENDAN. Sold 1.12.21 Stanlee, Dover.

MINSTREL Minesweeper, 'Algerine' class. Redfern, Toronto 5.10.1944. Sold 4.47 Thai navy as PHOSAMPTON.

MINSTREL (see M.I of 1939)

MINTO Troopship (RIM) 960 tons, 206 x 31½ ft. 4-3pdr. Laird 1893. Sold 1925.

MINTO Icebreaker (Canadian) 1,100 tons, 225 x 33 ft, 4-6pdr. Dundee 1899. Sold Russian navy 1915.

MINUET Minesweeper 260 tons, 130 x 26 ft, 1-3pdr. War Dept tug transferred on stocks. Day Summers, Southampton 18.9.1917. Sold 1.5.20 Crichton Thompson.

MINUET Trawler 1941-46.

MINX (Gunboat No.36) (ex-*Tom*) Gunvessel 12, 118bm, 64½ x 21 ft, 2-24pdr, 10-18pdr carr. Purchased 4.1797 at Leith. Sold 1801.

MINX Gun-brig 12, 180bm, 80 x 23 ft, 2-18pdr, 10-18pdr carr. Pitcher, Northfleet 14.4.1801. Captured 2.9.1809 by the Danes off the Scaw.

MINX Schooner 3, 84bm, 60 x 18½ ft. Bermuda 23.12.1829. Sold 6.1833 in Jamaica.

MINX Iron S.gunboat, 303bm, 131 x 22 ft. Miller & Ravenhall, Blackwall 5.9.1846. Tank vessel 1859. Sold 15.12.1899.

MINX Tank vessel 1900-1946.

MIRAMICHI Minesweeper (RCN), TE 'Bangor' class. Burrand, Vancouver 30.5.1941. BU 1949.

MIRAMICHI Coastal M/S, 'Ton' class (RCN), St John DD Co 10.1952. Transferred French navy 9.10.54 as LORIENTAISE.

MIRAMICHI Coastal M/S, 'Ton' class (RCN). Victoria Mcy 12.2.1957.

MIRANDA Wood S.corvette, 1,039bm, 185 x 34½ ft, 10-32pdr,4-20pdr. Sheerness DY 18.3.1851. Sold 2.12.1869 C.Lewis.

MIRANDA Compos. S.sloop 1,130 tons, 170 x 36 ft, 2-7in, 4-64pdr. Devonport DY 30.9.1879. Sold 24.9.1892, Reed, Portsmouth to BU.

MIRANDA Destroyer, 'M' class 883 tons. Yarrow 27.5.1914. Sold 26.10.21 Barking S.Bkg Co.

MIRANDA Yacht requis. 1915-19; Trawler requis. 1916-18.

MISCHIEF Destroyer, 'M' class. Fairfield 12.10.1915. Sold 8.11.21 Slough TC; BU in Germany.

MISTLETOE Schooner 8, 150bm, 79 x 22 ft. Bermuda 1809. Sold circa 1826.

MISTLETOE Wood S.gunboat, 'Albacore' class. Briggs, Sunderland 22.2.1856. BU completed 28.9.1864 at Sheerness.

MISTLETOE Compos. S.gunboat 560 tons, 135 x 26 ft, 2-5in, 2-4in. Laird 7.2.1883. BDV 1903. Sold 14.5.07 S.Bkg Co, London.

MISTLETOE Sloop, 'Anchusa' class. Greenock & Grangemouth Co 17.11.1917. Sold 25.1.21, renamed *Chiapus*.

MISTLETOE Drifter requis. 1914-19; MFV 1939-46.

MISTLEY (ex-MARYPORT renamed 1918) Minesweeper, later 'Hunt' class. Harkess 19.10.1918. Sold 19.5.28 Ward, Pembroke Dock.

MISTRAL Destroyer 1,319 tons, 326 x 33 ft, 4-5.1in, 6-TT. French, seized 3.7.1940 at Portsmouth. Returned 1946 to the French navy.

MISTRAL Drifter 1919-1920

MITCHELL (see HOSTE)

MOA Coal depot. Ex-brig purchased 1.1861. Sold 12.1876.

MOA Trawler (RNZN) 1941-43

MODBURY Destroyer, 'Hunt' class type III. Swan Hunter 13.4.1942. Lent Greek navy 11.42 to 23.9.60 as MIAOULIS; BU 1960 in Greece.

MODERATE 3rd Rate 64, 887bm, 132½

x 39½ ft. French MODERE captured 10.1702. Sold 15.12.1713 J.Williamson.

MODESTE 3rd Rate 64, 1,357 bm, 158½ x 44½ ft, 26-24pdr, 28-12pdr, 10-6pdr. French, captured 18.8.1759 at Lagos. Harbour service 8.1778. BU 8.1800.

MODESTE 5th Rate 36, 940bm, 143½ x 38½ ft. French, captured 17.10.1793 by BEDFORD at Genoa. Floating battery 1804. BU 6.1814.

MODESTE 5th Rate 38, 1,081bm, 152 x 40 ft. French TERPSICHORE captured 3.2.1814 by MAJESTIC in the Atlantic. BU 8.1816.

MODESTE Sloop 18, 562bm, 120 x 33 ft. Woolwich DY 31.10.1837. Sold 3.1866 Castle, Charlton.

MODESTE Wood S corvette, 1,405bm, 1,970 tons, 220 x 37 ft, 14-64pdr. Devonport DY 23.5.1873. Sold 8.1.1888. Castle, Charlton.

MODESTE Sloop 1,350 tons, 283 x 38½ ft, 6-4in. Chatham DY 29.1.1944. Arrived 11.3.61 White, St Davids to BU.

MOHAWK Sloop 6 (Canadian lakes). Oswego 1756. Captured 8.1756 by the French.

MOHAWK Sloop 18 (Canadian lakes). Oswego 1759. Lost 1764.

MOHAWK Sloop 18, 285bm. Purchased 10.1782. Sold in 9.1783

MOHAWK Schooner (Canadian lakes). Kingston, Ontario 14.5.1795. Condemned 1803.

MOHAWK Sloop in service 1798. Fate unknown.

MOHAWK Gun-brig 10, 148bm. Sold 1814. (Perhaps VIPER of 1810).

MOHAWK (see ONTARIO of 1813)

MOHAWK Paddle vessel (Canadian lakes), 174bm, 99 x 19½ ft. Launched 21.2.1843. Sold 13.4.1852 J.F.Parke.

MOHAWK Wood S.gunvessel, 679bm, 181 x 28½ ft. Young & Magnay, Limehouse 11.1.1856. Sold 20.9.1862 to the Emperor of China, renamed PEKIN.

MOHAWK Torpedo cruiser 1,770 tons, 225 x 36 ft, 6-6in, 5-TT. Thomson, Glasgow 6.2.1886. Sold 4.4.1905 Garnham.

MOHAWK Destroyer 865 tons, 270 x 25 ft, 3-12pdr (5-12pdr 1911), 2-TT. White 15.3.1907. Sold 27.5.19 Hughes Bolckow, Blyth.

MOHAWK Destroyer 1,870 tons, 355½ x 36½ ft, 8-4.7in, 4-TT. Thornycroft 5.10.1937. Torpedoed 16.4.41 by the Italian destroyer TARIGO and final-

ly sunk by HMS JANUS.

MOHAWK Frigate 2,300 tons, 350 x 42 ft, 2-4.5in, 2-40mm. Vickers Armstrong, Barrow 5.4.1962. Sold 16.9.82, BU Cairnryan.

MOIRA Schooner 14 (Canadian lakes) Kingston Ont. 1812. Renamed CHARWELL 22.1.1814 and made a brig, 169bm. Powder hulk 1817. Sold 1837.

MONAGHAN (ex-MULLION renamed 1918) Minesweeper, later 'Hunt' class. Harkess 29.5.1919. Sold 15.11.20 A.S.Miller, renamed *Bao Viagem*.

MONARCA (see under MONARCH)

MONARCH 3rd Rate 74, 1,707bm, 175 x 47½ ft. French MONARQUE captured 14.10.1747 at Cape Finisterre. Sold 25.11.1760.

MONARCH 3rd Rate 74, 1,612bm, 168½ x 47 ft. Deptford DY 20.7.1765. BU 3.1813.

MONARCA 3rd Rate 68, 1,911bm, 174½ x 50 ft, 28-24pdr, 30-12pdr, 10-9pdr. Spanish, captured 16.1.1780 at St Vincent. Sold 13.10.1791.

MONARCH 2nd Rate 84, 2,255bm, 194 x 52 ft, 8-8in, 60-32pdr, 16-32pdr carr. Chatham DY (ex-Deptford DY transferred 2.1825) 8.12.1832. Target 1862. BU completed 3.10.1866 White, Cowes.

MONARCH Iron S.ship, 5,103bm, 8,320 tons, 330 x 57½ ft, 4-12in, 3-7in. Chatham DY 25.5.1868. Guardship 1897. Renamed SIMOOM 3.1904, depot ship. Sold 4.4.05 Garnham to BU.

MONARCH Battleship 22,500 tons, 545 x 88½ ft, 10-13.5, 16-4in. Armstrong 30.3.1911. Sunk 20.1.25 as target off Scilly.

MONARCH Cable ship, Tug, 2 Trawlers & Drifter requis. WW.I; Yacht 1941-45.

MONCK 60-gun ship, 684bm, 136 x 34½ ft. Portsmouth DY 1659. Rebuilt Rotherhithe 1702 as 4th Rate 50, 808bm. Wrecked 24.11.1720 in Yarmouth Roads.

MONCK PRIZE 6th Rate 16, 135bm. Captured 9.9.1709 by MONCK at Cape Morrisco. Sold 6.3.1712.

MONCTON Corvette (RCN), 'Flower' class. St John NB 11.8.1941. Sold 1951.

MONDOVI Brig-sloop 16, 211bm, 81½ x 25 ft, 4-12pdr, 12-6pdr. French, captured 13.5.1798 in the Mediterranean. BU 5.1811.

MONGOOSE Gun-brig 12, 140bm. Dutch, captured 1799. Sold 1803.

MONITOR Destroyer, 'M' class. Projected 1913, cancelled.

MONITOR (see MUNSTER)

MONKEY (ex-*Lark*) Cutter 12, 187bm, 73 x 25½ ft, 12-4pdr. Purchased 9.1780. Sold 23.3.1786.

MONKEY Gun-brig 12, 188bm, 80 x 23 ft, 10-18pdr carr., 2-9pdr. Nicholson, Rochester 11.5.1801. Wrecked 25.12.1810 on Belleisle, French coast.

MONKEY Schooner 3, 70bm, 54 x 18 ft. McLean, Jamaica 6.1826. Wrecked 5.1831 on Tampico Bar.

MONKEY (ex-*Courier*) Schooner 6, 68bm, 56 x 18 ft. Purchased 25.10.1831. Sold 8.8.1833 in Jamaica.

MONKEY (ex-*Royal Sovereign*) Wood pad. vessel, 212bm, 106½ x 21 ft, 1-6pdr. From the GPO in 3.1837. Tug 1845. Sold 9.1887 at Chatham.

MONKEY Tank vessel 1896-1942.

MONKSHOOD Corvette, 'Flower' class. Fleming & Ferguson 17.4.1941. Sold 1947, renamed *W.R.Strang.*

MONKTON Coastal M/S, 'Ton' class. Herd & McKenzie, Buckie 30.11.1955. For sale 1985.

MONMOUTH 3rd Rate 66, 856bm, 148½ x 37 ft. Chatham DY 3.1667. Rebuilt Woolwich 1700 as 944bm; rebuilt Deptford 1742 as 3rd Rate 64, 1,225bm. BU completed 28.8.1767 at Chatham.

MONMOUTH Yacht 8, 103bm. Castle, Rotherhithe 1666. Sold 25.11.1698.

MONMOUTH 3rd Rate 64, 1,370bm, 160 x 45 ft. Plymouth DY 18.4.1772. Renamed CAPTIVITY 20.10.1796 prison hulk. BU 1.1818.

MONMOUTH (ex-Indiaman *Belmont* purchased on stocks) 3rd Rate 64, 1,439bm, 173 x 43½ ft. Randall, Rotherhithe 23.4.1796. Sheer hulk 6.1815. BU 5.1834 at Deptford.

MONMOUTH (see HOTSPUR of 1828)

MONMOUTH Armoured cruiser 9,800 tons, 448 x 66 ft, 14-6in, 9-12pdr. London & Glasgow Co 13.11.1901. Sunk 1.11.14 at the battle of Coronel.

MONMOUTH A/C carrier 18,300 tons, 650 x 90 ft, 32-40mm, 50-A/C. Fairfield. Cancelled 10.1945.

MONMOUTH CASTLE Corvette, 'Castle' class. Lewis, Aberdeen. Cancelled 12.1943.

MONNOW Frigate, 'River' class. Hill, Bristol 4.12.1943. Lent RCN to 11.6.45. Sold 1946 Danish navy as HOLGER DANSKE.

MONOWAI Survey ship (RNZN) ex-

Moana Roa. 2938/60 purchased 1973.

MONS Destroyer, 'M' class. J.Brown 1.5.1915. Sold 8.11.21 Slough TC; BU in Germany.

MONS Destroyer 2,380 tons, 355 x 40 ft, 5-4in, 8-40mm, 10-TT. Hawthorn Leslie. Laid down 9.6.1945, cancelled 10.45.

MONS Trawler. requis. 1917-19.

MONSIEUR 5th Rate 36, 818bm, 139 x 36½ ft, 26-12pdr, 10-6pdr. French privateer captured 13.3.1780. Sold 25.9.1783 J.Curry.

MONTAGU (see LYME of 1654)

MONTAGU 4th Rate 60, 1,218bm, 157 x 42 ft. Sheerness DY 15.9.1757. Sunk 8.1774 as breakwater at Sheerness.

MONTAGU 3rd Rate 74, 1,631bm, 169 x 47 ft. Chatham DY 28.8.1779. BU 9.1818.

MONTAGU (ex-MONTAGUE renamed 1901) Battleship 14,000 tons, 405 x 75½ ft, 4-12in, 12-6in, 12-12pdr. Devonport DY 5.3.1901. Wrecked 30.5.06 on Lundy.

MONT BLANC 3rd Rate 74, 1,886bm. French, captured 4.11.1805 in Strachan's action. Powder hulk in 1811. Sold 8.3.1819 J.Ledger to BU.

MONTBRETIA Sloop, 'Anchusa' class. Irvine, Glasgow 3.9.1917. Sold 25.1.21, renamed *Chihuahua.*

MONTBRETIA Corvette, 'Flower' class. Fleming & Ferguson 27.5.1941. Lent R.Norwegian navy 16.9.41. Sunk 18.11.42 by 'U.624' in the N. Atlantic.

MONTEGO BAY Schooner 10. Purchased 1796. Listed to 1800.

MONTFORD Seaward defence boat, 'Ford' class. Pimblott 10.10.1957. Sold Nigerian navy 9.9.66 as IBADAN.

MONTGOMERY (ex-USS WICKES) Destroyer 1,090 tons, 309 x 30½ ft, 1-4in, 1-3in, 4-20mm, 3-TT. Commissioned in the RN 23.10.1940. Lent RCN 1942 to 12.43. Sold 20.3.45, BU Clayton & Davie, Dunston.

MONTREAL 5th Rate 32, 684bm, 125 x 35½ ft. Sheerness DY 15.9.1761. Captured 4.5.1779 by the French BOURGOGNE in the Mediterranean. Destroyed 18.12.1793 by Anglo-Spanish forces at Toulon while serving as a powder hulk.

MONTREAL (see WOLFE of 1813)

MONTREAL Schooner (Canadian lakes). Purchased 18.10.1839. Sold 1848.

MONTREAL Frigate (RCN), 'River' class. Vickers, Montreal 12.6.1943.

BU 1947 Dominion Steel Corp.

MONTROSE (see VALOROUS)

MONTROSE Destroyer leader 1,800 tons, 320 x 32 ft, 5-4.7in, 1-3in, 6-TT. Hawthorn Leslie 10.6.1918. Sold 31.1.46, BU Hughes Bolckow, Blyth.

MONTROSE RNVR Tenders. Name borne in succession from 1949 by: MFV.1077, CHEDISTON, NURTON and DALSWINTON.

MONTSERRAT (ex-HORNBY renamed 9.1943) Frigate, 'Colony' class. Walsh Kaiser, Providence RI 28.8.1943. Returned 6.46 to the USN.

MOOLOCK Patrol boat (RCN), 84 x 20 ft, 1-MG. Star SY 15.10.1941. Sold 1946.

MOON Pinnace 12, 60bm. Built 1549. Lost 1553 off the Gold Coast.

MOON Pinnace 9, 85bm, 4-6pdr, 4-4pdr, 1-1pdr. Deptford 1586. Rebuilt Chatham 1602 as 100bm. Condemned 1626.

MOON Destroyer, 'M' class 1,007 tons. Yarrow 24.4.1915. Sold 9.5.21 Ward, Briton Ferry.

MOON Minesweeper, 'Algerine' class. Harland & Wolff. Ordered 8.1942, cancelled 4.1943.

MOON (ex-MIMICO renamed 1943) Minesweeper, 'Algerine' class. Redfern 2.9.43. Arrived 13.11.57 King, Gateshead.

MOOR 4th Rate 54, 811bm. French MAURE captured 13.12.1710. Sunk 7.3.1716 as breakwater at Plymouth.

MOOR Mooring vessel 1919-42.

MOORHEN Compos. S.gunboat 455 tons, 125 x 23 ft, 2-64pdr, 2-20pdr. Napier 13.9.1875. Sold 11.1888.

MOORHEN (ex-COCKATRICE renamed 1896) Paddle vessel 600 tons. 160 x 25½ ft, 2 guns. Sold 1899 at Malta.

MOORHEN River gunboat 180 tons, 160 x 24½ ft, 2-6pdr. Yarrow, Poplar 13.8.1901. Sold 8.33 at Hong Kong to BU.

MOORHEN Mooring vessel 1943-70.

MOORSOM Destroyer, 'M' class. J.Brown 21.12.1914. Sold 8.11.21 Slough TC; BU in Germany.

MOORSOM Frigate, DE 'Captain' class. Boston N.Yd 24.9.1943 on lend-lease. Returned 10.45 to the USN.

MOOSEJAW Corvette (RCN) 'Flower' class. Collingwood SY 9.4.1941. BU 9.49 Steel Co of Canada, Hamilton Ont.

La MOQUEUSE M/S sloop 630 tons, 256 x 28ft, 2-3.9in. French, seized 3.7.1940 at Falmouth. Free-French from 8.40; returned 1945 to the French navy.

MORAY FIRTH (ex-EMPIRE PITCAIRN renamed 1944) Repair ship 10,100 tons, 431 x 56 ft, 12-20mm. Readhead, S.Shields 17.10.1944. Sold 1947, renamed *Linoria*.

MORDAUNT 4th Rate 48, 567bm, 122 x 32½ ft. Deptford 1681 and purchased 1683. Stranded 21.11.1693 in the W.Indies.

MORDEN Corvette (RCN), 'Flower' class. Pt Arthur SY 5.4.1941. BU 11.56 Steel Co of Canada.

MORECAMBE BAY (ex-LOCH HEILEN) Frigate, 'Bay' class. Pickersgill 1.11.1944. Sold 9.5.61 Portuguese navy as DOM FRANCISCO de ALMEDIA.

MORESBY (ex-MARLION renamed 1914) Destroyer, 'M' class. White 20.11.15. Sold 9.5.21 Ward, Grays. BU 1923.

MORESBY (see SILVIO)

MORESBY Survey ship (RAN) 2,000 tons, 284½ x 42 ft, 2-40mm. Newcastle DY, NSW 7.9.1963.

MORGIANA Brig-sloop 16, 283bm, 96 x 26½ ft, 14-18pdr car., 2-6 pdr. French privateer ACTIF captured 30.11.1800 by THAMES in the Bay of Biscay. BU 8.1811.

MORGIANA Sloop 18, 400bm, 100 x 30 ft. Hill, Bermuda, 12.1811. Sold 27.1.1825 T.Pittman to BU.

MORNE FORTUNEE Schooner 6, 106bm, 65½ x 21 ft, 6-12pdr carr. French privateer MORNE FORTUNE captured 1803 and purchased 1804. Wrecked 6.12.1804 in the W. Indies.

MORNE FORTUNEE Schooner 12, 184bm. French privateer brig REGULUS captured 13.12.1804 by PRINCESS CHARLOTTE in the W. Indies. Foundered 9.1.1809 off Martinique.

MORNE FORTUNEE Brig 14. French privateer MORNE FORTUNE captured 8.1808 by BELETTE.BU 10.1813 in Antigua.

MORNING STAR Ketch 14, 80bm.Dutch, captured 1672. Given away 1674.

MORNING STAR Cutter, 69bm, 48 x 18½ ft. Purchased 1.1763. Sold 4.5.1773.

MORNING STAR Sloop 16. American privateer 191bm, captured 14.1.1781. Sold 19.6.1782 Davis, Rotherhithe.

MORNING STAR Destroyer, 'M' class. Yarrow 26.6.1915. Sold 1.12.21 Stanlee, Dover.

MORNING STAR 2 Trawlers, 4 Drifters

WW.I yacht WW.II.

MORNING STAR Sloop 22 (Indian), 350bm. Bombay DY 1799. Fate unknown.

MORO 3rd Rate 74, 1,880bm, 175 x 49½ ft. Spanish AMERICA captured 13.8.1762. BU completed 18.7.1770 at Portsmouth.

MORPETH CASTLE Corvette, 'Castle' class. Pickersgill 26.11.1943. Arrived 9.8.60 Rees, Llanelly to BU.

MORRIS Destroyer, 'M' class. J. Brown 19.11.1914. Sold 8.11.21 Slough TC; BU in Germany.

MORRIS DANCE Minesweeper 265 tons, 130 x 26 ft, 1-6pdr. War Dept tug transferred 1919. Lytham SB Co 1918. Sold 1.5.20 Crichton Thompson.

MORRIS DANCE Trawler 1940-47.

MORTAR Bomb 12, 260bm, 12-6pdr. Chatham DY 1693. Ran ashore 2.12.1703 on the Dutch coast.

MORTAR Bomb 14, 280bm, 91 x 26½ ft. Perry, Blackwall 26.2.1741. Sold 2.3.1748.

MORTAR Bomb 14, 313bm, 92 x 28 ft. Wells, Rotherhithe 14.3.1759. Sold 2.9.1774.

MORTAR Store carrier 1943-74.

MORTAR vessels (see under MV)

MOSAMBIQUE Schooner 10, 115bm, 67½ x 20 ft, 10-18pdr carr. French privateer MOZAMBIQUE captured 13.3.1804 by EMERALD and DIAMOND. Sold 1810.

MOSELLE sloop 24, 520bm, 120 x 31 ft. French, handed over 18.12.1793 by Royalists at Toulon. Recaptured 7.1.1794 by the French at Toulon' captured 23.5.1794 by AIMABLE off Hyeres. Sold 9.1802.

MOSELLE Brig-sloop 18, 'Cruizer' class. 385bm. King, Dover 10.1804. Sold 14.12.1815.

MOSLEM (ex-Torok) Iron paddle vessel. Purchased 8.1854 at Constantinople. Sold 8.1856.

MUSQUITO Vessel in service in 1777.

MUSQUITO Schooner 6, 71bm, 55½ x 17 ft. French privateer VENUS captured 1793 and purchased 1794. Captured 1799 by the Spanish off Cuba.

MUSQUITO Floating battery 4, 309bm, 80 x 32 ft, 2-68pdr carr., 2-24pdr. Wells, Rotherhithe 1795. Wrecked 5.1795 on the French coast.

MUSQUITO Schooner 12. French, captured 1799. Sold 1802.

MUSQUITO Brig-sloop 18, 'Cruizer' class. 384bm. Preston Yarmouth 4.9.1804. Sold 7.5.1822 T. King.

MUSQUITO Brig-sloop, 'Cherokee' class, 231bm. Portsmouth DY 19.2.1825. Sold 7.11.1843 Greenwood & Clark.

MUSQUITO Brig 16, 549bm, 110 x 35 ft, 16-32pdr. Pembroke Dock 29.7.1851. Sold 9.7.1862 Prussian navy.

MOSQUITO Compos. S.gunboat, 295bm, 430 tons, 125 x 23 ft 2-64pdr, 2-20pdr. Pembroke Dock 9.12.1871. Sold 12.1888.

MOSQUITO Torpedo boat (Australian) 12 tons, 63 x 7½ ft, 1-TT. Thornycroft, Chiswick 16.7.1884. Sold circa 1912.

MOSQUITO Paddle river gunboat 90 tons, 6-3pdr. Yarrow, Poplar 3.5.1890. Sold 19.12.1902 on the Zambesi.

MOSQUITO Destroyer 925 tons, 271 x 28 ft, 1-4in, 3-12pdr, 2-TT. Fairfield 27.1.1910. Sold 31.8.20 Ward, Rainham.

MOSQUITO River gunboat 585 tons, 188 x 33½ ft, 2-4in. Yarrow 14.11.1939. Sunk 1.6.40 by air attack at Dunkirk.

MOTH Coastal destroyer 225 tons, 172 x 18 ft, 2-12pdr, 3-TT. Yarrow, Poplar 15.3.1907. Renamed TB.12 in 1906. Sunk 10.6.15 by mine in the North Sea.

MOTH River gunboat 645 tons, 230 x 36 ft, 2-6in, 1-3in. Sunderland SB Co 9.10.1915. Scuttled 12.12.41 after bomb damage at Hong Kong; salved and commissioned as the Japanese SUMA. Sunk 19.3.45 by mine.

MOTHER SNAKE SSV (RAN) 80 tons. ex-Murchison 316/44 commissioned 30.6.1945. To N.BORNEO Govt. 11.45

MOTI Gunboat (RN) 331 tons, 170 x 22 ft, 2-3in. Iranian KARKAS captured 1941 by RIN forces. Returned 1946 to Iran.

MOUCHERON Brig-sloop 16, 286bm. French, captured 16.2.1801 purchased 1802. Wrecked 9.1807 in the Dardanelles.

MOUNSEY Destroyer, 'M' class. Yarrow 11.9.1915. Sold 8.11.21 Slough TC; BU in Germany.

MOUNSEY Frigate, DE 'Captain' class. Boston N.Yd 24.9.1943 on lend-lease. Returned 2.46 to the USN.

MOUNT EDGCUMBE (see WINCHESTER of 1822)

MOUNTS BAY (ex-LOCH KILBIRNIE) Frigate, 'Bay' class. Pickersgill 8.6.1945. To Portuguese navy 9.5.61 as VASCO da GAMA.

MOURNE Frigate, 'River' class. Smiths Dk 24.9.1942. Sunk 15.6.44 by 'U.767' in the Channel.

MOY Destroyer 550 tons, 222 x 23½ ft, 1-12pdr, 5-6pdr (4-12pdr 1907), 2-TT. Laird 10.11.1904. Sold 27.5.19 T.Oakley.

MOY Trawler 1920-46.

MOYOLA Frigate, 'River' class. Smiths Dk 27.8.1942. To French navy 15.10.44 as TONKINOIS.

MULETTE Sloop 18. French, handed over 18.12.1793 by Royalists at Toulton. For sale in 6.1796.

MULGRAVE 3rd Rate 74, 1,726bm, 176 x 48½ ft. King, Upnor 1.1.1812. Lazaretto 9.1836; powder hulk 9.1844. BU completed 12.1854.

MULGRAVE Minesweeper (RCN), TE 'Bangor' class. Port Arthur 2.5.1942. Mined 8.10.44 in the Channel and not repaired; BU 5.47 Rees, Llanelly.

MULL OF GALLOWAY (ex-KINNAIRDS HEAD renamed 4.1945) Repair ship 10,200 tons, 416 x 57 ft, 11-40mm. N. Vancouver SR Co 26.10.44. BU 1965 at Hamburg.

MULL OF KINTYRE Repair ship 10,200 tons, 416 x 57 ft, 11-40mm. N. Vancouver SR Co. 5.11.1945. Arrived Hong Kong 25.1.70 to BU.

MULL OF OA (ex-TREVOSE HEAD renamed 4.1945) Repair ship 10,200 tons, 416 x 57 ft, 16-20mm. N. Vancouver SR Co 8.11.45. Cancelled 18.8.45, completed as *Turan*.

MULLETT Schooner 5, 78bm, 56 x 18 ft. Bermuda 5.1807. Sold 15.12.1814.

MULLETT Wood S.gunvessel, 'Philomel' class. Lungley, Deptford 13.2.1860. Sold 1872 at Hong Kong.

MULLETT Tug 1855-56; Trawler 1942-46.

MULLION (see MONAGHAN)

MULLION COVE (ex-EMPIRE PENANG renamed 1944) Repair ship 9,730 tons, 425 x 66 ft, 16-20mm. Bartram, Sunderland 10.7.1944. Sold 1948, renamed *Margaret Clunies*.

MUNLOCHY (ex-MACDUFF renamed 1918) Minesweeper, later 'Hunt' class. Fleming & Ferguson 12.6.18. Sold 23.11.22 J.Smith.

MUNSTER Destroyer, 'M' class. Thornycroft 24.11.1915. Sold 15.11.21 Cashmore, Newport.

MURCHISON Frigate (RAN), 'River' class. Evans Deakin, Brisbane 31.10.1944. Sold 9.61 Tolo Mining Co to BU.

MUROS 6th Rate 22, 446bm, 112½ x 30½ ft, 20-pdr carr., 8-12pdr carr., 2-pdr. French privateer ALCIDE captured 8.3.1806 by EGYPTIENNE at Muros. Wrecked 24.3.1808 in the Bay of Honda, Cuba.

MUROS Brig-sloop 14, 252bm, 92 x 25½ ft, 12-24pdr carr., 2-6pdr. Chatham DY 23.10.1809. Sold 18.4.1822 T. Pittman.

MURRAY Destroyer, 'M' class 1,010 tons, Palmer 6.8.14. Sold 9.5.21. Ward, Briton Ferry in 1.23.

MURRAY Frigate 1,180 tons, 300 x 33 ft, 40mm, 4-TT. Stephen 25.2.1955. Sold Arnott Young 14.8.70, BU Dalmuir.

MURRUMBIDGEE Frigate (RAN), 'River' class. Melbourne Harbour Trust. Laid down 28.10.1943, cancelled 12.6.44.

MUSETTE Sloop 22, 312bm, 102 x 27 ft. French privateer captured 21.12.1796 by HAZARD off the Irish coast. Harbour service 1799; floating battery 24 in 1805. Sold 27.8.1806.

MUSETTE (see MIGNONNE of 1806)

MUSK Corvette, 'Flower' class. Morton, Quebec 15.7.1942. Transferred 1942 to the USN as MIGHT. Sold 10.46, renamed *Olympic Explorer*.

MUSKERRY Minesweeper, early 'Hunt' class. Lobnitz 28.11.1916. Sold 22.1.23 Rees, Llanelly.

MUSKET Destroyer 1,980 tons 341½ x 38 ft, 6-4in, 6-40mm, 10-TT. White. Cancelled 5.10.1945 (not laid down).

MUSKETEER Destroyer, 'M' class 900 tons. Yarrow 12.11.1915. Sold 25.11.21 Hayes, Porthcawl.

MUSKETEER Destroyer 1,920 tons, 354 x 37 ft, 6-4.7in, 8-TT. Fairfield 2.12.1941. Sold 3.12.55, BU Young, Sunderland.

MUSQUEDOBET Schooner 10, 225bm, 93 x 24 ft, 8-18pdr carr., 2-6pdr. American privateer LYNX captured 16.3.1813 in the Chesapeake. Sold 13.1.1820 Mr Rundle.

MUSQUITO (see MOSQUITO)

MUSTICO Cutter, 59bm, 49½ x 17 ft. Spanish CATALONIA captured 1800. Harbour service to 1816.

MUTINE Cutter 14, 215bm, 80 x 26 ft, 14-4pdr. French MUTIN captured 2.10.1779. Renamed PIGMY 20.1.1798. Wrecked 8.1805 in St Aubins Bay, Jersey.

MUTINE Brig 12 in service 1795.

MUTINE Brig-sloop 16, 349bm, 104½ x 28 ft, 2-36pdr carr., 14-6pdr. French, captured 29.5.1797 at Santa Cruz Sold 1807.

MUTINE Brig-sloop 18, 'Cruizer' class, 386bm. Chapman, Bideford 15.8.1806. Sold 3.2.1819 G.Young.

MUTINE Brig-sloop 6, 'Cherokee' class, 231bm. Plymouth DY 19.5.1825. Sold 27.5.41, renamed *Aladdin.*

MUTINE Brig 12, 428bm, 112 x 32 ft, 10-32pdr, 2-18pdr. Chatham DY 20.4.1844. Wrecked 21.12.1848 near Venice.

MUTINE Wood S.sloop, 882bm, 173 x 33 ft, 5-40pdr, 12-32pdr. Deptford DY 30.7.1859. Sold 26.2.1870.

MUTINE Compos. S.sloop 1,136 tons, 170 x 36 ft, 2-7in, 4-64pdr. Devonport DY 30.7.1880. BDV 1899; renamed AZOV 3.04. Sold 25.8.21 C.A.Beard, BU at Upnor.

MUTINE Sloop 980 tons, 180 x 33 ft, 6-4in. Laird 1.3.1900. Survey vessel 5.07; RNVR drillship 9.25. Sold 16.8.32. Ward, Briton Ferry.

MUTINE Minesweeper, 'Algerine' class. Harland & Wolff 10.10.1942. Sold 13.12.66, BU at Barrow.

MV.1-22 (see SINBAD and DRAKE of 1834 and BLAZER, GROWLER, HAVOCK, MANLY, MASTIFF, PORPOISE, SURLY, FLAMER, FIRM, HARDY, RAVEN, CAMEL, MAGNET, BEACON, CARRON, GRAPPLER, REDBREAST, ROCKET, PROMPT and PICKLE of 1854 respectively).

MYNGS Destroyer, 'M' class 1,010 tons, Palmer 24.9.1914. Sold 9.5.21 Ward, Rainham.

MYNGS Destroyer leader 1,730 tons, 339½ x 36 ft, 4-4.5in, 2-40mm, 8-TT. Vickers Armstrong, Tyne 31.5.1943. Sold 5.55 Egyptain navy, renamed EL QAHER 8.56.

MYOSOTIS Sloop, 'Arabis' class. Bow McLachlan 4.4.1916. Sold 30.1.23 Fryer, Sunderland.

MYOSOTIS Corvette, 'Flower' class. Lewis 28.1.1941. Sold 2.9.46 renamed *Grunningur.*

MYRMIDON 6th Rate 22, 481bm, 114 x 31 ft. Deptford DY 9.6.1781. Harbour service 1798. BU 4.1811.

MYRMIDON 6th Rate 20, 506bm, 120 x 31 ft. Milford DY 8.6.1813. BU 1.1823 at Portsmouth.

MYRMIDON Iron pad. gunvessel, 374bm, 151 x 23 ft. Ditchburn, Blackwall 2.1845. Sold 1.12.1858 at Fernando Po.

MYRMIDON Wood S.gunvessel, 697bm, 877 tons, 185 x 28½ ft. Chatham DY 5.6.1867; completed 10.67 as survey vessel. Sold 4.1889 at Hong Kong.

MYRMIDON Destroyer 370 tons, 215 x 21 ft, 1-12pdr, 5-6pdr, 2-TT. Palmer 26.5.1900. Sunk 26.3.17 in collision with SS *Hamborn* in the Channel.

MYRMIDON Destroyer 1,920 tons, 354 x 37 ft, 6-4.7in, 8-TT. Fairfield 2.3.1942. Renamed ORKAN 11.42 on loan to Polish navy. Sunk 8.10.43 by 'U.610' south of Iceland.

MYRMIDON Minesweeper, 'Algerine' class. Redfern 21.10.1944. Arrived 2.12.58 Ward, Briton Ferry.

MYRMIDON (see EDDERTON)

MYRTLE Sloop 18, 429bm, 108½ x 30 ft, 16-32pdr carr., 8-18pdr carr., 2-6pdr. Chapman, Bideford 2.10.1807. BU 6.1818.

MYRTLE Packet brig 6, 'Cherokee' class, 231bm. Portsmouth DY 14.9.1825. Wrecked 3.4.1829 off Nova Scotia.

MYRTLE (ex-GPO vessel *Firefly*) Wood pad. packet, 116bm, 97 x 16 ft. Transferred 9.1837. Tug 1866. BU 5.1868 at Sheerness.

MYRTLE (see MALABAR of 1818)

MYRTLE (see MYSTIC)

MYRTLE Sloop, 'Acacia' class. Lobnitz 11.10.1915. Sunk 16.7.1919 by mine in the Gulf of Finland.

MYRTLE Trawler 1939-40. Tug 1973.

MYSTIC (ex-MYRTLE renamed 1915) Destroyer, 'M' class. Denny 20.6.1915. Sold 8.11.21 Slough TC; BU in Germany.

MYSTIC Minesweeper, 'Algerine' class. Redfern 11.11.1944. Arrived 3.5.58 Rees, Llanelly to BU.

N.1 (see NAUTILUS of 1914)

NAAS Minesweeper, later 'Hunt' class. Eltringham. Cancelled 1919.

NABOB (ex-E.Indiaman *Triton*) storeship 26, 637bm, 136½ x 33 ft. Purchased 9.1777. Hospital ship 1780. Sold 10.4.1783.

NABOB (ex-*Edisto*) Escort carrier 11,420 tons, 468½ x 69½ ft, 16-40mm, 24-A/C. Seattle Tacoma Co 9.3.1943 on lend-lease. Torpedoed 22.8.44 by 'U.354' off North Cape and not repaired. Left 9.47 to BU in Holland; resold 1951, renamed *Nabob.*

NADDER Frigate, 'River' class Smiths Dk 15.9.1943. Renamed SHAMSHER (RIN) 1944. RPN 1947. Sold 2.3.59 to BU.

NADUR (see ADUR)

NAIAD 6th Rate 26. French, captured 11.6.1783 by SCEPTRE. Not commissioned. Sold 17.8.1784.

NAIAD 5th Rate 38, 1,020bm, 147 x 40

ft. Hill, Limehouse 27.2.1797. Coal depot 1.1847. Sold 2.2.1866 Pacific SN Co similar service.

NYADEN (also NIJADEN) 5th Rate 36, 909bm, 142 x 38 ft Danish, captured 7.9.1807 at Copenhagen. BU 5.1812.

NAIAD 2nd class cruiser 3,400 tons, 300 x 43 ft, 2-4.7 in 8-6pdr. Vickers 29.11.1890. Minelayer 9.1910. Sold 9.6.22 King, Troon.

NAIAD Cruiser 5,450 tons, 485 x 50½ ft, 10-5.25in. Hawthorn Leslie 3.2.1939. Sunk 11.3.42 by 'U. 565' south of Crete.

NAIAD Frigate, 'Leander' class. Yarrow 4.11.1963.

NAILSEA (ex-NEWQUAY renamed 1918) Minesweeper, later 'Hunt' class. Inglis, Glasgow 7.8.18. Sold 25.11.27 Hughes Bolckow, Blyth.

NAIRANA Seaplane carrier 3,070 tons, 315 x 45½ ft, 4-12pdr, 7-A/C. Denny 1916 and purchased. Sold 1920.

NAIRANA Escort carrier 14,050 tons, 498 x 68 ft, 2-4in, 20-20mm, 15-A/C. J.Brown 20.5.1943; purchased on stocks. Lent Dutch navy 3.46 to 1948. Sold 1948, renamed *Port Victor.*

NAIRANA Trawler requis. 1916-19 and 1939-40.

NAMUR 2nd Rate 90, 1,442bm, 161 x 46 ft. Woolwich DY 28.4.1697. Rebuilt Deptford 1729 as 1,567bm. Wrecked 14.4.1749 in the E.Indies.

NAMUR 2nd Rate 90, 1,814bm, 175 x 49 ft. Chatham DY 3.3.1756. 74-gun 3rd Rate 5.1805; harbour service 9.1807. BU 5.1833 at Chatham.

NAMUR Destroyer 2,380 tons, 355 x 40 ft, 5-4.5in, 8-40mm, 10-TT. Cammell Laird 12.6.1945; not completed. Arrived 2.51 Ward, Barrow to BU.

NAMUR Trawler requis. 1940, renamed PALISADE 1944-46.

NANAIMO Corvette (RCN), 'Flower' class Yarrow, Esquimalt 28.10.1940. For disposal 10.45; sold as *Rene W. Vinke.*

NANCY Schooner (Canadian lakes). Detroit 24.11.1789. Burnt 14.8.1814 by Americans.

NANCY Fireship, 72bm, 55½ x 19 ft. Purchased 4.1794. Sold 12.1801.

NANCY Brig 16, ex-cutter. Purchased 1809. Sold 1813.

NANCY Tug 1973.

NANKIN 4th Rate 50, 2,049bm, 2,540 tons, 185 x 51 ft, 6-8in, 44-32pdr. Woolwich DY 16.3.1850. Hospital hulk 1866. sold 28.2.1885, BU 1905.

NANTWICH 28/48-gun ship, 319/511bm. Bailey, Bristol 13.3.1655.

renamed BREDAH 1960, 4th Rate 48, Wrecked 1666.

NAOMI Frigate (RAN), 'River' class Sydney, NSW. Ordered 12.1942, cancelled 12.6.44.

NAPANEE Corvette (RCN), 'Flower' class. Kingston SY 31.8.1940. BU 6.46 Steel Co of Canada, Hamilton, Ont.

NAPIER Iron river gunboat (Indian), 445bm. Bombay DY 11.9.1844. Listed in 1858.

NAPIER (see TALISMAN)

NAPIER Destroyer, 'M' class. J.Brown 27.11.1916. sold 8.11.21 Slough TC; BU in Germany.

NAPIER Destroyer leader 1,695 tons, 339½ x 36 ft, 6-4.7in, 10-TT. Fairfield 22.5.1940. Arrived 17.1.56 Ward, Briton Ferry to BU.

NERBUDDA Cutter 2, 49bm. Bombay DY 1835. Sold 7.1862.

NERBUDDA (ex-GOSHAWK renamed 1845) Brig-sloop 12, 445bm, 100 x 32½ft, 10-32dr, 2-18pdr. Bombay DY 6.2.1847. Foundered 10.7.1856 off the Cape.

NARBADA Sloop (RIN) 1,300 tons, 283 x 37½ ft, 6-4in Thornycroft 21.11.1942. Renamed JHELUM (RPN) 1948. BU 7.59.

NARBROUGH (see TERMAGANT of 1915)

NARBROUGH Destroyer, 'M' class. J.Brown 2.3.1916. Wrecked 12.1.18 on the Pentland Skerries.

NARBROUGH Frigate, TE 'Captain' class. Bethleham Hingham 27.11.1943 on lend-lease. Returned to the USN in 2.46.

NARCISSUS 6th Rate 20, 429bm, 108 x 30 ft. Plymouth DY 9.5.1781. Wrecked 3.101796 in the Bahamas.

NARCISSUS 5th Rate 32, 894bm, 142 x 38 ft. Deptford DY 12.5.1801. Convict ship 12.1823. Sold 1.1837 Levy.

NARCISSUS 6th Rate 28, 601bm, 115 x 35½ ft. Devonport DY. Ordered 1846, cancelled 1848.

NARCISSUS 4th Rate 50, 1,996bm. Devonport DY. Laid down 11.1849, cancelled 23.3.1857.

NARCISSUS Wood S.frigate, 2,665bm, 3,548 tons, 228 x 51 ft, 10-8in, 1-64pdr, 40-32pdr. Devonport DY 26.10.1859. sold 17.2.1883. Castle to BU.

NARCISSUS Armoured cruiser 5,600 tons, 300 x 56 ft, 2-9.2in, 10-6in. Earle, Hull 15.12.1886. sold 11.9.1906.

NARCISSUS (see NONSUCH of 1915)

NARCISSUS Sloop, 'Acacia' class. Napier & Miller 22.9.1915. sold 6.9.22 A. H. Bond.

NARCISSUS Corvette, 'Flower' class. Lewis 29.3.1941. Sold 4.46, renamed *Este*.

NARVIK (see LST.3044)

NARWHAL Destroyer, 'M' class. Denny 30.12.1915. Back broken in collision 1919; BU 1920 Devonport.

NARWHAL M/L submarine 1,520 tons, 271½ x 25½ ft, 1-4in, 6-TT. 50 mines. Vickers Armstrong, Barrow 29.8.1935. Lost 1.8.40 by unknown cause off Norway.

NARWHAL Submarine 1,605 tons, 241 x 26½ ft, 8-TT. Vickers Armstrong, Barrow 25.10.1957. Scutted 3.8.83 as a bottom target off Falmouth

NASEBY 80-gun ship, 1,230bm, 162 x 42 ft. Woolwich DY 1655. Renamed ROYAL CHARLES 1660. Captured 12.6.1667 by the Dutch at Chatham.

NASSAU Flyboat 4, 180bm. Dutch, captured 1672. Given away 1672.

NASSAU 3rd Rate 80, 1,080bm, 151 x 40 ft. Portsmouth DY 1699. Wrecked 30.10.1706 on the Sussex coast.

NASSAU 3rd Rate 70, 1,104bm, 150½ x 41 ft. Portsmouth DY 9.1.1707. Rebuilt Chatham 1740 as 64-gun 3rd Rate, 1,225bm; sold 4.9.1770.

NASSAU 3rd Rate 64, 1,384bm, 160 x 44½ ft. Hilhouse, Bristol 28.9.1785. 36-gun troopship 1799. Wrecked 14.10.1799 on the Dutch coast.

NASSAU (see HOLSTEIN)

NASSAU Wood S.gunvessel, 695bm, 877 tons, 185 x 28½ ft. Pembroke Dock 20.2.1866; completed 7,1866 as survey ship. Bu 4.1880 at Sheerness.

NASTURTIUM Sloop, 'Arabis' class. McMillan, Dumbarton 21.12.1915. Sunk 27.4.16 by mine near Malta.

NASTURTIUM (ex-French La PAIMPOLAISE seized 3.7.1940 on stocks) Corvette, 'Flower' class. Smiths Dk 4.7.40. sold 1946, renamed *Cania*.

NATAL Armoured cruiser 13,550 tons, 480 x 73½ ft, 6-9.2in, 4-7.5in, 2-12pdr, 28-3pdr. Vickers Maxim, Barrow 30.9.1905. Sunk 31.12.15 by internal explosion in the Cromarty Firth.

NATAL (ex-LOCH CREE renamed 1944) Frigate (SAN), 'Loch' class. Swan Hunter 19.6.44. Survey ship 1957. Sunk 19.9.72 as target off the Cape.

NATAL Trawler requis. 1914-19 and 1939-45.

NATHANIELL Fireship 4, 120bm. Purchased 30.8.1689. Sunk 1692 as a foundation at Sheerness.

NAUTILUS Sloop 16, 316bm, 98 x 27 ft. Hodgson, Hull (ex Deptford DY transferred 4.1761) 24.4.1762. For sale in 10.1780.

NAUTILUS Sloop 16, 346bm, 102 x 28 ft. Crookenden, Itchenor 9.1.1784. Wrecked 2.2.1799 in Filey Bay.

NAUTILUS Brig-sloop 14 (Indian). Built circa 1794. Captured 18.2.1815 by the American PEACOCK in the Sunda Strait.

NAUTILUS Sloop 18, 443bm, 111 x 29½ ft. Jacobs, Milford (Milford DY) 12.4.1804. Wrecked 4.1.1807 in the Mediterranean.

NAUTILUS Brig-sloop 14 (Indian), 185bm. Bombay DY 1806. Wrecked 1834 in the Red Sea.

NAUTILUS Brig-sloop 18, 'Cruizer'class, 384bm. Betts, Mistleythorn 5.8.1807. BU 10.1823.

NAUTILUS Brig-shoop 10, 'Cherokee' class, 233bm. Woolwich DY 11.3.1830. Training ship 1852; hulk 1872. BU completed 17.10.1878 at Devonport.

NAUTILUS Training brig 8, 501 tons, 105 x 33½ ft. Pembroke Dock 20.5.1879. Sold 11.7.1905 Cox, Falmouth.

NAUTILUS Destroyer 975 tons, 267½ x 28 ft, 1-4in, 3-12pdr, 2-TT. Thames IW 30.3.1910. Renamed GRAMPUS 16.12.13. Sold 21.9.20 Ward, Rainham.

NAUTILUS Submarine 1,240 tons, 240 x 26 ft, 1-12pdr, 6-TT. Vickers 16.12.1914. Renamed N.1 in 1918. Sold 9.6.22 Cashmore, Newport.

NAUTILUS Trawler WW.I. Trawler & Drifter WW.II.

NAVARINO Destroyer 2,380 tons, 355 x 40 ft, 5-4.5in, 8-40mm, 10-TT. Cammell Larid 21.9.1945, not completed. Arrived 4.46 Ward, Preston to BU.

NAVY Yacht 2, 67bm. Castle, Rotherhithe 1666. Fate unknown; perhaps rebuilt as the following vessel.

NAVY Yacht 8, 74bm. Portsmouth 1673. Sold 14.4.1698.

NAVY BOARD (ex-cutter HART renamed 1822) Yacht, 80bm, 56 x 19 ft. Reverted to HART 1833, then yard craft.

NAVY TRANSPORT Storeship, 107bm. Deptford 1705. Rebuilt 1730. BU 1742.

NAVY TRANSPORT Storeship, 97bm, 64 x 20 ft. Purchased 12.1752 Sold 13.10.1791.

NEARQUE Sloop 18, 309bm, 94½ x

20½ ft, 14-24pdr carr., 4-9pdr. French, captured 28.3.1806 by NIOBE in the Channel. Sold 21.7.1814.

NEARCHUS Patrol vessel (RIM) 925 tons, 180 x 29 ft, 4-3pdr. Beardmore 15.11.1914. Sold circa 1922.

NEASHAM Inshore M/S, 'Ham' class. White 14.3.1956. To the RAN 1968.

NECKAR 6th Rate 28, French, captured 26.10.1781 by HANNIBAL off the Cape. Foundered 12.1789.

NED ELVIN Brig-sloop 18, 309bm, 98 x 27½ ft, 16-24pdr, 2-6pdr, Danish, captured 7.9.1807 at Copenhagen. Sold 3.11.1814 (Was to have been renamed LEGERE.) Also listed as NID ELVIN.

NEGRESSE Gunvessel 6. French, captured 18.3.1799 by TIGRE off the coast of Syria. Sold 1802.

NEGRO (see NIGER of 1759)

NEGRO Destroyer, 'M' class. Palmer 8.3.1916. Sunk 21.12.16 in collision with destroyer HOSTE in the North Sea.

NEGRO Trawler requis. 1939-45.

NELSON 1st Rate 120, 2,617bm, 205 x 44 ft. Woolwich DY 4.7.1814. Undocked 7.2.1860 as screw ship, 2,736bm, 90 guns; handed over to NSW Govt 2.1867; sold 28.4.1898 as store hulk, later coal hulk. BU 9.1928 at Launceston.

NELSON Iron armoured frigate 7,473 tons, 280 x 60 ft, 4-10in, 8-9in, 6-20pdr, 3-9pdr. Elder 4.11.1876. Training ship 1902. Sold 12.7.10, BU in Holland.

NELSON Battleship 33,500 tons, 660 x 106 t, 9-16in, 12-6in, 6-4.7in. Armstrong, 3.9.1925. Arrived 15.3.49 Ward, Inverkeithing to BU.

NELSON Drifter requis. 1915-19.

NEMESIS 6th Rate 28, 598bm, 121 x 33½ ft. Jolly & Smallshaw, Liverpool 23.1.1780. Sold 9.6.1814. (Was in French hands 9.12.95 to 9.3.96.)

NEMESIS 5th Rate 46, 1,168bm, 159 x 41 ft. Pembroke Dock 19.8.1826. BU completed 4.7.1866 by Marshall Plymouth.

NEMESIS Iron pad. frigate (Indian), 165 x 29 ft, 2-3pdr. Laird 12.1839. For sale in 1852.

NEMESIS Destroyer 740 tons 246½ x 25 ft, 2-4in, 2-12pdr, 2-TT. Hawthorn Leslie 9.8.1910. Lent Japanese navy 6.17 to 1919 as KANRAN; sold 26.11.21 British LEGION Plymouth.

NEMESIS Training ship requis. 1940-45.

NENAMOOK Patrol boat (RCN), 84 x 20 ft, 1-MG. Victoria Bt & Rep Co 10.9.1941. Sold 1946.

NENE Frigate, 'River' class, Smiths DK 9.12.1942. Lent RCN 6.4.44 to 11.6.45. Arrived 8.55 Ward, Briton Ferry to BU.

NEPAL (ex-NORSEMAN renamed 1.1942) Destroyer 1,690 339½ x 36 ft, 6-4.7in, 10-TT Thornycroft 4.12.41. Arrived 16.1.56 Ward, Briton Ferry to BU.

NEPEAN Torpedo beat (Australian) 12 tons, 63 x 7½ ft, 1-TT. Thornycroft, Chiswick 1884, BU in 1913.

NEPEAN Destroyer, 'M' class, Thornycroft 22.1.1916. Sold 15.11.21 Cashmore, Newport; BU 1923.

NEPEAN Frigate (RAN), 'River' class, Sydney, NSW. Ordered 12.1942, cancelled 12.6.44.

NEPETA Corvette, 'Flower' class. Morton, Quebec 28.11.1942. Transferred USN 1943 AS PERT. Sold 10.46 mercantile.

NEPTUNE 2nd Rate 90, 1,377bm, 164 x 45 ft, Deptford DY 17.4.1683. Rebuilt Blackwall 1710 as 1,577bm. rebuilt Woolwich 1730 as 1,573bm. Renamed TORBAY 23.8.1750. Sold 17.8.1784.

NEPTUNE 2nd Rate 90, 1,798bm, 171 x 49 ft. Portsmouth DY 17.7.1757. Sheer hulk 1784. BU 10.1816 at Portsmouth.

NEPTUNE 2nd Rate 98, 2,111bm, 185 x 51 ft, Deptford DY 28.1.1797. BU 10.1818.

NEPTUNE (see ROYAL GEORGE of 1827)

NEPTUNE 1st Rate 120, 2.694bm, 206 x 55½ ft, 6-68pdr, 114-32pdr. Portsmouth DY 27.9.1832. Undocked 7.3.1859 as screw ship, 72 guns, 2,830bm. Sold 1875 Castle Charlton.

NEPTUNE Coastguard cutter, 60bm. Built 1863. Sold 4.4.1905 at Chatham.

NEPTUNE (ex-Brazilian INDEPENDENCIA purchased 3.1878) Battleship 9,310 tons, 300 x 63 ft, 4-12in, 2-9in MLR. Dudgeon, Poplar 10.9.1874. Sold 15.9.1903 Garnham; BU in Germany.

NEPTUNE (ex-FOUDROYANT renamed 1909) Battleship 19,900 tons, 510 x 85 ft, 10-12in, 20-4in. Portsmouth DY 30.9.1909. Sold 1.9.22 Hughes Bolckow, Blyth.

NEPTUNE Cruiser 7,175 tons, 530x 55 ft, 8-6in, 8-4in. Portsmouth DY 31.1.1933. Sunk 19.12.41 by mine off Tripoli.

NEPTUNE Cruiser circa 9,000 tons. Projected 1945. cancelled 3.46 (not ordered).

NEPTUNE 6 vessels hired between 1620 & 1806.2 Tugs WW.I.

NERBUDDA (see NARBADA)

NEREIDE 5th Rate 36, 892bm, 140 x 27½ ft. French, captured 20.12.1797 by PHOEBE off the Scillies. Recaptured 28.8.1810 by the French at Mauritius; again captured 6.12.1810 at Mauritius, laid up there until ordered to be sold 1.3.1816.

NEREIDE 5th Rate 38, 1,165bm, 157½ x 40½ ft. French VENUS captured 18.9.1810 at Reunion, Indian Ocean by BOADICEA, BU 5.1816.

NEREIDE (see NYMPHE of 1812)

NEREIDE Wood S.corvette, 1,857bm, 225 x 43 ft. Woolwich DY. Ordered 1860, cancelled 12.12.1863.

NEREIDE Destroyer 740 tons, 246½ x 25 ft, 2-12pdr, 2-TT.Hawthorn Leslie 6.9.1910. Sold 1.12.21 Stanlee, Dover.

NEREIDE Sloop 1,350 tons, 283 x 38½ ft, 6-4in. Chatham DY 29.1.1944. Arrived 18.5.58 McLellan, Bo'ness to BU.

NEREUS 5th Rate 32. Temple, S.Shields 4.3.1809. BU 2.1817.

NEREUS 5th Rate 46, 1,095bm, 152 x 40 ft. Pembroke Dock 30.7.1821. Storeship, harbour service 1843. Sold 22.1.1879 J.L.Page at Coquimbo for use as hulk.

NEREUS Destroyer, 'M' class. Thornycroft 24.2.1916. Sold 15.11.21 Cashmore, Newport; BU in 7.22.

NERISSA Destroyer, 'M' class 880 tons. Yarrow 2.1916. Sold 15.11.21 Cashmore, Newport.

NERISSA Destroyer 1,690 tons, 339½ x 36 ft, 6-4.7in, 10-TT.J.Brown 7.5.1940. Lent Polish navy 10.40 as PIORUN; returned 9.46, renamed NOBLE. BU 11.55 by Clayton & Davie, Durston.

NERISSA Minesweeper, 'Algerine' class. Redfern 25.11.1944. Arrived 8.60 Rees, Llanelly to BU.

NESS Destroyer 555 tons, 222 x 23 ft, 1-12pdr, 5-6pdr (4-12pdr 1907), 2-TT. White 5.1.1905. Sold 27.5.19 T.R.Sales.

NESS Frigate, 'River' class. Robb, Leith 30.7.1942.Sold 9.56, BU Cashmore, Newport.

NESS Trawler 1920-22.

NESSUS Destroyer, 'M' class. Swan Hunter 24.8.1915. Sunk 8.9.18 in collision with cruiser AMPHITRITE in the North Sea.

NESSUS A.River steamer 150 tons, 1-3pdr. Purchased 1926 at Hong Kong. Sold 1929.

NESTOR 6th Rate 28. French privateer FRANKLIN captured 1781 by RAMILLIES and ULYSSES. Sold 1783.

NESTOR Destroyer, 'M' class. Swan Hunter 22.12.1915. Sunk 31.5.16 in action at Jutland.

NESTOR Destroyer 1,690 tons, 339½ x 36 ft, 6-4.7in, 10-TT. Fairfield 9.7.1940. Bombed 15.6.42 by Italian A/C in the eastern Mediterranean and sank next day.

NETLEY Gun-brig 16, 193bm, 86½ x 21ft. Ex-schooner purchased 4.1798. captured 17.12.1806 by the French in the W.Indies

NETLEY Gun-brig 12, 173bm, 83 x 23½ft, 14-18pdr carr., 2-6pdr. French privateer DETERMINE captured 1807. Wrecked 10.7.1808 in the W.Indies.

NETLEY schooner 12, 140bm, 76 x 21½ ft, 10-12pdr carr., 2-6pdr. American NIMROD captured 1807, purchased 1808. BU 5.1813 in Antigua.

NETLEY (see PRINCE REGENT)

NETLEY Cutter 8, 122bm, 64 x 22½ ft, 4-6pdr carr. Plymouth DY 13.3.1823. Foundered 10.1848 at Spithead; raised. Sold 29.8.1859.

NETLEY Wood S.gunboat, 'Britomart' class. Portsmouth 2.7.1866. Sold 9.1885 to Castle to BU.

NETTLE Wood S.gunboat, 'Cheerful' class. Pembroke Dock 9.2.1856. BU 1867 in Bermuda.

NETTLE (see THUNDERER of 1831)

NETTLE (ex-War Dept vessel Pennah) tender 130 tons, 85 x 20 ft. Transferred 1905. Sold 1934 as tug Topmast 1.

NETTLE (see HYDERABAD)

NETTLE (see ELFIN of 1933)

NETTLHAM Inshore M/S, 'HAM' class. White 19.12.1956. Sold Rye Arc Ltd 27.11.67.

NEW ADVENTURE Transport. Purchased 1799. Listed 1800.

NEWARK 2nd Rate 80, 1,217bm, 157 x 42 ft. Frame, Hull 3.6.1695. Rebuilt Chatham 1717 as 1,283bm; rebuilt Chatham 1747 as 1,521bm. BU 6.1787 at Chatham.

NEWARK (ex-NEWLYN renamed 1918) Minesweeper, later 'HUNT' class. Inglis 19.6.18. Sold 6.28 Alloa, Charlestown.

NEWARK (ex-USS RINGGOLD) Destroyer 1,060 tons, 309 x 30½ ft, 1-4in, 1-3in, 4-20mm, 3-TT. Commissioned 5.12.1940 in the RN. Air target 1.45. Sold 18.2.47, BU McLellan Bo'ness.

NEWASH Schooner 4 (Canadian Lakes), 166bm, 71 x 24½ ft. Chippawa 8.1815.Condemned 3.1832.

NEWBARK ship 200bm, Built 1543, Listed to 1565.

NEWBURY 52-Gun ship, 766bm. Graves, Limehouse 4.1654. Renamed REVENGE 1660. Condemned 1678.

NEWBURY Paddle M/S, 'Ascot' class. Inglis 3.7.1916. Sold 3.22 Ward, Inverkeithing, BU 1923.

NEWCASTLE 50-gun ship, 625bm, 131 x 33 ft. Pett, Ratcliffe 1653. Rebuilt Rotherhithe 1692. Wrecked 27.11.1703 near Chichester.

NEWCASTLE 4th Rate 54, 676bm, 130 x 34 ft. Sheerness DY 24.3.1704. Rebuilt Woolwick 1733 as 759. BU 1746.

NEWCASTLE 4th Rate 50, 1,052bm, 144 x 41 ft. Portsmouth DY 4.12.1750. Foundered 1.1.1761 in a cyclone off Pondicherry.

NEWCASTLE 4th Rate 60 (pitch pine-built), 1,556bm, 176½ x 44 ft. 26-42pdr carr., 32-24pdr. Wigram & Green, Blackwall 10.11.1813. Harbour service 6.1824. Sold 6.1850 J.Brown.

NEWCASTLE Wood S.frigate, 3,035bm, 4,020 tons, 250 x 52 ft, 30-8in. 1-68pdr, 20-32pdr. Deptford DY 16.10.1860. Powder hulk 1889. Sold 1929.

NEWCASTLE 2nd class cruiser 4,800 tons, 430 x 47 ft, 2-6in, 10-4in. Armstrong 25.11.1909. Sold 9.5.21 Ward; arrived Lelant 3.5.23.

NEWCASTLE (ex-MINOTAUR renamed 1936) Cruiser 9,100 tons, 558 x 62 ft, 12-6in, Vickers Armstrong, Tyne 23.1.36. Arrived 19.8.59 Faslane to BU.

NEWCASTLE Destroyer 3,150 tons. Swan Hunter 24.4.1975.

NEWFOUNDLAND Cruiser 8,800 tons, 538 x 62 ft, 9-6in, 8-4in. Swan Hunter 19.12.1941. Sold 2.11.59 Peruvian navy, renamed ALMIRANTE GRAU.

NEW GLASGOW Frigate (RCN), 'River' class . Yarrow, Esquimalt 5.5.1943. sold 1967

NEWHAVEN (see CARNATIC of 1942)

NEWHAVEN Two Trawlers requis WW.I.

NEW LISKEARD Minesweeper (RCN). 'Algerine' class. Port Arthur SY 14.1.1944. Survey ship 1959. Sold 1969.

NEWLYN (see NEWMARK)

NEWMARKET (ex-USS ROBINSON) Destroyer 1,060 tons, 309 x 30½ ft, 1-4in, 1-3in, 4-20mm, 3-TT. Commissioned 26.11.40 in the RN; air target 5.42. sold 9.45, BU Rees. Llanelly.

NEWMARKET Minesweeper requis 1914-17.

NEWPORT 6th Rate 24, 253bm, 94½ x 25 ft. Portsmouth. Captured 7.4.1694 by the French in the Bay of Fundy.

NEWPORT (see ORFORD of 1695)

NEWPORT Wood S.gunvessel, 425bm, 570 tons, 145 x 25½ ft. Pembroke Dock 20.7.1867; completed 4.1868 as survey vessel. Sold 5.1881, renamed *Pandora*

NEWPORT (ex-USS SIGOURNEY) Destroyer 1,060 tons, 309 x 30½ ft, 3-4in, 1-3in, 6-TT. Commissioned 26.11.1940 in the RN; lent R. Norwegian navy 3.41 to 6.42; air target 6.43. Sold 18.2.1947, BU Brechin, Granton.

NEWQUAY (see NAILSEA)

NEWTON Research Vesel 3,940 tons. Scott-Lithgow 25.6.1975

NEW WATERFORD Frigate (RCN), 'River' class Yarrow, Esquimalt 3.7.1943. Sold 16.8.67 to BU.

NEW WESTMINSTER Corvette (RCN), 'Flower' class. Victoria Mcy 14.5.1941. Sold 1947, renamed *Elisa*

NEW ZEALAND Battle ship 16,350 tons, 425 x 78 ft, 4-12in, 4-9.2in, 10-6in, 14-12pdr. Portsmouth DY 4.2.1904. Renamed ZEALANDIA 1.11.11. Sold 8.11.21 Stanlee; BU in Germany.

NEW ZEALAND Battlecruiser 18,800 tons, 555 x 80 ft, 8-12in, 10,-4in. Fairfield 1.7.1911. Sold 10.12.22 A.J.Purves; resold and BU Rosyth.

NEW ZEALAND A/C carrier circa 45,000 tons. Cammell Laird. Cancelled 2.1946.

NEW ZEALAND Trawler requis. 1916-20.

NEZA (see TEST of 1942)

NIAGARA (see ROYAL GEORGE of 1809)

NIAGARA (see PRINCE REGENT)

NIAGARA (ex-USS THATCHER) Destroyer (RCN) 1,060 tons, 309 x 30½ ft, 3-4in, 1-3in, 6-TT. Commissioned 24.9.1940 in the RCN; training ship 2.3.44. BU 12.47.

NICATOR Destroyer, 'M' class. Denny 3.2.1916. Sold 9.5.21 Ward, Milford Haven.

NICATOR Minesweeper, 'Algerine' class. Redfern, Toronto. Laid down 5.10.1944, cancelled 8.11.44.

NICHOLAS Ship in 1398. Given away in 1404

NICHOLAS Ship purchased 1415.

Foundered in the Thames 1419

NICHOLAS Ballinger, 120bm. Presented 3.1417. Sold 11.9.1422

NICHOLAS Vessel captured 1549. Not listed after.

NICHOLAS Fireship. Purchased 1692. Expended 12.7.1694 at Dieppe.

NICHOLAS REEDE (also GREAT NICHOLAS) Ship, 400bm. Purchased 1512. Listed to 1522.

NICODEMUS 6-gun vessel, 105bm. Privateer, captured 1636. Sold 1657.

NIEMEN 5th Rate 38, 1,093bm, 154½ x 40 ft. French, captured 5.4.1809 by AMETHYST and EMERALD in the Bay of Biscay. BU 9.1815.

NIEMEN 6th Rate 28 (fir-built), 502bm, 114 x 31½ ft, 20-32pdr carr., 6-18pdr carr., 2-9pdr. Woolwich DY 23.11.1820. BU completed 1.1828.

NIEUPORT Gunvessel 14. Purchased 4.1795. Listed to 1810.

NIGELLA Sloop, 'Arabis' class. Hamilton 10.12.1915. Sold 29.11.22.

NIGELLA Corvette, 'Flower' class. Philip, Dartmouth 21.9.1940. Sold 1947, renamed Nigelock.

NIGELLA Trawler and drifter requis. WW.I.

NIGER 5th Rate 33, 679bm, 125 x 35 ft. Sheerness DY 25.9.1759. Prison ship 1810. Renamed NEGRO 1813. Sold 29.9.1814.

NIGER 5th Rate 38 (red pine-built), 1,066bm, 150 x 40 ft. Wigram & Green, Blackwall 29.5.1813. BU 1820 Halifax NS.

NIGER Wood S.sloop, 1,013bm, 190 x 35 ft, 2-68pdr, 12-32pdr. Woolwich DY 18.11.1846. Sold 2.12.1769 Castle.

NIGER Compos. paddle vessel, 600 tons, 160 x 25½ ft, 2 guns. Elder 10.3.1880. Renamed COCKATRICE 2.4.1881. Renamed MOORHEN 1896. Sold 1899.

NIGER Torpedo gunboat 810 tons, 230 x 27 ft, 2-4.7in, 4-3pdr, 3-TT. N.C & A(Vickers) 17.12.1892. Minesweeper 1909. Sunk 11.11.14 by 'U.12' off Deal.

NIGER Minesweeper 815 tons, 230 x 33½ ft, 2-4in. White 29.1.1936. Sunk 5.7.42 by mine off Iceland.

NIGER Minesweeper, 'Algerine' class. Redfern, Toronto. Laid down 20.9.1944, cancelled 8.11.44.

NIGER (ex-DISDAIN 11.1944) Minesweeper, 'Algerine' class. Lobnitz 1.5.45. Arrived 2.2.66 at Silloth to BU by Ardmore Steel Co.

NIGERIA Cruiser 8,000 tons, 538 x 62 ft, 12-6in, 8-4in. Vickers Armstrong, Tyne 18.7.1939. Renamed MYSORE (Indian Navy) 29.8.57.

NIGERIA (see HARE of 1944)

NIGERIA Frigate (Nigerian) 1,750 tons, 341 x 37 ft, 2-4in. Wilton-Fijenoord, Holland 9.1965.

NIGHTINGALE Vessel captured 1626. Listed to 1628.

NIGHTINGALE 30-gun ship, 290bm. Horsleydown 1651. Wrecked 16.1.1672 on the Goodwins.

NIGHTINGALE 6th Rate 24, 251bm, 93 x 24½ ft. Chatham DY 16.12.1702. Captured 26.8.1707 by the French; recaptured 12.1707 as ROSSIGNOL, by LUDLOW CASTLE; renamed FOX. Rebuilt Deptford 1727 as 375bm. BU 1.1737 at Deptford.

NIGHTINGALE 6th Rate 24, 253bm, 90 x 25½ ft. Johnson, Blackwall 15.10.1707. Sold 21.6.1716.

NIGHTINGALE 6th Rate 24, 522bm, 114 x 32½ ft. Purchased on stocks 17.6.1746. Bird, Rotherhithe 6.10.1746. Sunk 8.1773 as breakwater at Harwich.

NIGHTINGALE Brig-sloop 16, 248bm, 93 x 26½ ft. King, Dover 29.7.1805. Sold 23.11.1815.

NIGHTINGALE Cutter 6, 122bm. 63½ x 22 ft, 2-6pdr, 4-6pdr carr. Plymouth DY 19.4.1825. Wrecked 17.2.1829 on the Shingles.

NIGHTINGALE (ex-packet Marchioness of Salisbury) Packet brig 8, 208bm. Purchased 1829. Sold 24.11.1842 Greenwood & Clark.

NIGHTINGALE Wood S-gunboat, 'Albacore' class. Mare, Blackwall 22.22.1855. Sold 16.7.1867 W.Lethbridge.

NIGHTINGALE River gunboat 85 tons, 100 x 20 ft, 2-6pdr. Yarrow 1897. Sold 20.11.1919 at Hong Kong.

NIGHTINGALE Mining tender 298 tons, 100 x 24½ ft. Portsmouth DY 30.9.1931. Sold 5.7.57, BU Pollock Brown, Southampton 1958.

NIJADEN (see under NAIAD)

NILAM Gunboat (RIN) 331 tons, 170 x 22 ft. 2-3in. Iranian CHAROGH captured 1941 by RIN forces. Returned 1946.

NILE Cutter 12, 166bm, 12-12pdr carr. Purchased 1806. Sold 18.10.1810 but purchaser refused her; BU 9.1811.

NILE 2nd Rate 92, 2,598bm, 205 x 54 ft. 10-8in, 82-32pdr. Plymouth DY 28.6.1839. Undocked 30.1.1854 as screw ship, 2,622bm. Renamed CONWAY 24.7.1876 as training ship on loan. Stranded 14.4.53 in the Menai strait. Wreck burnt 31.10.56.

NILE Battleship 11,940 tons, 345 x 73 ft. 4-13.5in, 8-6pdr. Pembroke Dock 27.3.1888. Sold 9.7.1912 Ward, Swansea & Briton Ferry.

NILE 4 hired vessels between 1799 and 1804.

NIMBLE Cutter 12, 185bm, 12-4pdr. Purchased 3.1778. Wrecked 11.2.1781 in Mounts Bay.

NIMBLE Cutter 12, 168bm, 10-18pdr carr., 2-3pdr. Jacobs, Folkestone 6.7.1781; purchased on stocks. Grounded and lost 1808 in Stangate Creek, Medway. Wreck for sale 4.1808.

NIMBLE Cutter 10, 144bm, 65½ x 23½ ft, 10-12pdr carr., 2-6pdr. Cowes 14.12.1811. Foundered 6.10.1812 in the North Sea after striking a sunken rock.

NIMBLE Cutter 12, 147bm, 68½ x 23½ ft, 12-12pdr carr. Purchased 1812. Sold 18.4.1816.

NIMBLE Schooner 570bm. McLean, Jamaica 1826. Returned to builder 5.26 as unfit for service.

NIMBLE (ex-Bolivar) Schooner 5, 168bm, 84 x 22 ft. Purchased 1826. Wrecked 4.11.1834 in the Bahama Channel.

NIMBLE Wood S.gunvessel, 'Philomel' class. Pembroke Dock 15.9.1860. Harbour service 1879. Sold 10.7.1906 W.R.Jones.

NIMBLE Tug 1855-56; Ferry 1908-48; Tug 1941-71; Tug 1985.

NIMROD Sloop 18, 395bm. French EOLE captured 22.11.1799 by SOLEBAY in the W.Indies. Sold 21.2.1811.

NIMROD Brig-sloop 18, 'Cruizer' class. 384bm. Bailey, Ipswich 25.5.1812. Foundered 14.1.1827 in Holyhead Bay; wreck sold 1827 Rowland Robert & Co.

NIMROD (ex-6th Rate ANDROMEDA renamed 10.5.1827) Sloop 20, 502bm, 114 x 32 ft. Deptford DY 26.8.1828. Coal hulk 2.1853; renamed C.1 then C.76 Sold 9.7.1907 Hamley & Son.

NIMROD Iron pad. gunboat (Indian), 153bm, 103 x 18 ft. Laird 6.1839 and re-erected 1840 at Basra. Listed in 1859.

NIMROD Wood S.gunvessel, 859bm, 200 x 30½. 2-68pdr, 4-32pdr. Scott Russell 21.4.1856. Sold 2.6.1865 White.

NIMROD Destroyer leader 1,608 tons, 325 x 32 ft. 4-4in, 4-Tt. Denny 12.4.1915. Sold 5.11.26 Alloa, Rosyth.

NIOBE 5th Rate 38, 1,142bm, 156 x 41 ft. French DIANE captured 24.8.1800 by a squadron off Malta. BU 11.1816.

NIOBE 6th Rate 28, 1,051bm, 140 x 42 ft. 2-8in, 26-32pdr. Devonport DY 18.9.1849. Sold 9.7.1862 to the Prussian navy.

NIOBE Wood S.sloop. 1,083bm. 187 x 36 ft. Deptford DY 31.5.1866. Wrecked 21.5.1874 on Miquelon Island.

NIOBE 1st class cruiser 11,000 tons, 435 x 69 ft, 16-6in, 14-12pdr. N.C & A (Vickers) 20.2.1897. RCN from 6.9.1910; depot ship 9.15. BU 1922 in Philadelphia.

NIPIGON Minesweeper (RCN), TE 'Bangor' class. Dufferin 1.10.1940. Sold 29.11.57 Turkish navy as BAFRA.

NIPIGON Escort (RCN) 2,335 tons, 366(oa) x 42 ft, 2-3in. Marine Industries 10.12.1961.

NISUS 5th Rate 38, 1,074bm, 154 x 39½ ft. Plymouth DY 3.4.1810. BU 9.1822.

NISUS (see NOBLE of 1915)

NITH Destroyer 555 tons, 222 x 23 ft, 1-12pdr, 5-6pdr (4-12pdr 1907), 2-TT. White 7.3.1905. Sold 23.6.19 Ward, Preston.

NITH Frigate, 'River' class. Robb 25.9.1942. Sold 11.48 Egyptian navy as DOMIAT.

NITH Trawler 1920, renamed EXCELLENT 1922-54.

NITROCRIS Iron pad. gunboat (Indian), 153bm. Laird 1839 and reerected 1840 at Basra. Fate unknown.

NIZAM Destroyer, 'M' class. Stephen 6.4.1916. Sold 9.5.21 Ward. Rainham.

NIZAM Destroyer 1,690 tons, 339½ x 36 ft, 6-4in, 10-TT. J.Brown 4.7.1940. Arrived 16.11.55 Ward, Grays to BU.

NOBLE (ex-NISUS renamed 1915) Destroyer, 'M' class. Stephen 25.11.1915. Sold 8.11.21 Slough TC.

NOBLE Destroyer 1,690 tons, 339½ x 36 ft, 6-4in, 10-TT. Denny 17.4.1941. To Dutch navy 11.2.42 as VAN GALEN

NOBLE (see NERISSA of 1940)

NOMAD Destroyer, 'M' class. Stephen 7.2.1916. Sunk 31.5.16 at Jutland.

NONPAREIL (see PHILIP & MARY)

NONPAREIL Schooner 14, 210bm, 88 x 24 ft. American, captured 1807 at Montevideo. Damaged 19.12.1812 in a storm in the Tagus and sold there

1813.

NONPAREIL Destroyer, 'M' class. Stephen 16.5.1916. Sold 9.5.21 Ward, Briton Ferry.

NONPAREIL Destroyer 1,690 tons, 339½ x 36 ft, 6-4.7in, 10-TT. Denny 25.6.1941. To Dutch navy 27.5.42, renamed TJERK HIDDES.

NONPAREIL Minesweeper, 'Algerine' class. Redfern, Toronto. Laid down 23.10.1944, cancelled 8.11.44.

NONSUCH (see PHILIP & MARY)

NONSUCH 34-gun ship, 400/500bm. Deptford 1646. Wrecked 1664.

NONSUCH Ketch 8, 47bm. Purchased 1654. Sold 1667.

NONSUCH 4th Rate 42, 359bm. Portsmouth 1668. Captured 4.1.1695 by the French privateer Le FRANCAIS.

NONSUCH Hoy 5, 95bm. Portsmouth 1686. Sold 5.1.1714.

NONSUCH 4th Rate 48, 677bm, 130½ x 34 ft. Deptford 1696. Rebuilt Portsmouth 1717 as 687bm. hulk 1740. BU 1745.

NONSUCH 4th Rate 50, 852bm, 133½ x 39 ft. Quallet, Rotherhithe 29.12.1741. BU 11.1766 at Plymouth.

NONSUCH 3rd Rate 64, 1,373bm, 160 x 44½ ft. Plymouth DY 17.12.1774. Floating Battery 5.1794. BU 6.1802.

NONSUCH (ex-NARCISSUS renamed 1915) Destroyer, 'M' class. Palmer 7.12.1915. Sold 9.5.21 Ward, Milford Haven, arrived 9.22.

NONSUCH Sloop 1,350 tons, 283 x 38½ ft, 6-4in. Chatham DY. Laid down 26.2.1945, cancelled 23.10.45.

NONSUCH (see Z.38)

NOOTKA Destroyer (RCN) 1,927 tons, 355½ x 38 ft, 6-4.7in, 2-4in, 4-TT. Halifax SY 26.4.1944. Arrived 6.10.64 at Faslane to BU.

NOOTKA Trawler (RCN) 1938, renamed NANOOSE 1944-47.

NORANDA Minesweeper (RCN) diesel 'Bangor' class. Davie SB 13.6.1941. Transferred RCMP 1947 as Irvine.

NORFOLK 3rd Rate 80, 1,184bm, 156½ x 41½ ft. Winters, Southampton 28.3.1693. Rebuilt Plymouth 1728 as 1,393bm. Renamed PRINCESS AMELIA 1.11.1755. Harbour service 4.77, transferred customs 11.1788.

NORFOLK 3rd Rate 74, 1,556bm, 165½ x 47 ft. Deptford DY 28.12.1757. BU 12.1774 at Portsmouth.

NORFOLK Cruiser 9,925 tons, 590 x 66 ft, 8-8in, 8-4in. Fairfield 12.12.1928. Sold 3.1.50, arrived 19.2.50 Cashore, Newport to BU.

NORFOLK GM destroyer 5,600 tons, 505 x 54 ft, 4-4.5in 2-20mm, 10-GWS. Swan Hunter 16.11.1967. Sold Chile; left UK 2.82. Renamed PRAT.

NORFOLK Frigate 3000 tons Yarrow 6.1987.

NORGE 3rd Rate 74, 1,960bm. Danish, captured 7.9.1807 at Copenhagen. Sold 3.1816. (Was to have been renamed NONSUCH.)

NORHAM CASTLE (see HUMBERSTONE)

NORMAN Destroyer, 'M' class. Palmer 20.3.1916. Sold 9.5.21 Ward, Milford Haven.

NORMAN Destroyer 1,690 tons, 339½ x 36 ft, 6-4.7in 1-TT. Thornycroft 30.10.1940. Arrived 1.4.58 Cashmore, Newport to BU.

NORMAN Two trawlers in WW.I; Tug 1939-40.

NORSEMAN Destroyer, 'M' class. Doxford 15.8.1916. Sold 9.5.21 Ward, Grays.

NORSEMAN (see NEPAL)

NORSYD Corvette (RCN), modified 'Flower' class. Morton 31.7.1943. Sale list 10.45; sold as Balboa.

NORTH Sloop 18. Purchased 1778. Wrecked at Halifax 12.12.1779.

NORTHAMPTON Iron armoured frigate 7,652 tons, 280 x 60 ft, 4-10in, 8-9in, 6-20pdr, 3-9pdr. Napier 18.11.1876. Training ship 6.1894. Sold 4.4.1905 Ward, Morecambe.

NORTHAMPTON (see SHARPSHOOTER of 1888)

NORTH BAY Corvette (RCN), modified 'Flower' class. Collingwood 27.4.1943. Sold 1946. renamed Kent County II.

NORTHBROOK Troopship (RIM) 5,820 tons, 360 x 52 ft, 6-4.7in, 6-3pdr. J.Brown 6.7.1907. Listed in 1924.

NORTHESK Destroyer, 'M' class. Palmer 5.7.1916. Sold 9.5.21 Ward, Rainham.

NORTH ESK Drifter, requis. 1915-19 and 1939-45.

NORTHOLT Minesweeper, later 'Hunt' class. Eltringham 21.6.1918. BU by Cashmore, Newport 4.28.

NORTHREPPS Minesweeper, later 'Hunt' class. Lobnitz. Cancelled 1919.

NORTH STAR 6th Rate 20, 433bm, 108½ x 30 ft, 16-32pdr carr.,8-18pdr carr., 1-12pr, 2-6pdr. Tanner, Dartmouth 21.4.1810. Sold 6.3.1817 Pittman.

NORTH STAR 6th Rate 28, 501bm, 114 x 32 ft. Woolwich DY 7.12.1824. BU completed 15.3.1860 at Chatham.

NORTH STAR Wood S.corvette, 1,857bm, 225 x 41 ft. Sheerness DY. Laid down 13.7.1860, cancelled 22.5.1865.

NORTH STAR Destroyer, 'M' class. Palmer 9.11.1916. Sunk 23.4.18 by shore batteries at Zeebrugge.

NORTH STAR Yacht 1915-19; Trawler 1914-19.

NORTHUMBERLAND 3rd Rate 70, 1,041bm, 152 x 40½ ft. Bailey, Bristol 1679. Rebuilt Chatham 1701. Wrecked 27.11.1703 on the Goodwins.

NORTHUMBERLAND 3rd Rate 70, 1,105bm, 151 x 41 ft. Deptford 1705. Rebuilt Woolwich 1721 as 1,133bm. BU 11.1739 at Woolwich.

NORTHUMBERLAND 3rd Rate 70, 1300bm, Woolwich DY 7.10.1743. Captured by French CONTENT off Ushant 8.5.1744, renamed L'ATLAS.

NORTHUBERLAND 3rd Rate 70, 1,414bm, 160 x 45 ft. Plymouth DY 1.12.1750 Renamed LEVIATHAN 13.9.1777, storeship. Foundered 27.2.1780 on passage from Jamaica to the UK.

NORTHUMBERLAND 3rd Rate 78, 1,811bm, 179 x 42 ft. French, captured 1.6.1794 at the battle of '1st of June' BU 11.1795.

NORTHUMBERLAND 3rd Rate 74, 1,907bm, 182 x 49 ft. Barnard, Deptford 2.2.1798. Hulk 2.1827. BU 7.1850 at Deptford.

NORTHUMBERLAND Iron armoured frigate (battleship), 6,621bm, 10,780tons, 400 x 59½ ft, 4-9in. 22-8in, 2-7in. Mare, Blackwall 17.4.1866. depot ship 1898; renamed ACHERON 3.1904, training ship. Hulk C.8 in 1909 and C.68 in 1926. Sold 6.27 Ward, resold as hulk *Stedmound*

NORTHUMBERLAND Cruiser 10,000 tons. Devonport DY. Ordered 15.5.1929, cancelled 1.1.30.

NORTHUMBERLAND Frigate (RCN), 'River' class. Victoria BC. Cancelled 12.1943.

NORTHUMBRIA (see HODGESTON and QUAINTON)

NORTHWAY (ex-CUTLASS renamed 8.1943) Dock landing ship 4,270 tons, 454 x 27 ft, 1-3in, 16-20mm. Newport News 18.11.43 on lend-lease. Returned 12.46 to the USN.

NORWICH 28-gun ship, 265bm. Chatham DY 1655. Wrecked 1682.

NORWICH 4th Rate 48, 616bm, 125½ x 34 ft. Portsmouth DY 1691. Wrecked

6.10.1692 in the W. Indies.

NORWICH 4th Rate 48, 618bm, 125½ x 34 ft. Deptford DY 1693. Rebuilt Chatham 1718 as 703bm. Renamed ENTERPRISE 23.5.1744, 5th Rate 44. BU 1771 at Sheerness.

NORWICH 4th Rate 50, 993bm, 140 x 40½ ft. Perry, Blackwall 4.7.1745. Sold 24.5.1768.

NORWICH CASTLE Corvette, 'Castle' class. G. Brown. Cancelled 12.1943.

NOTTINGHAM 4th Rate 60, 924bm, 146 x 38 ft. Deptford 6.1703. Rebuilt Deptford 1719 as 928bm; rebuilt Sheerness 1745 as 1,077bm. Sunk 9.1773 as breakwater at Sheerness.

NOTTINGHAM PRIZE 6th Rate 4, 40bm, 46 x 14½ x ft. Captured 14.4.1704. Sunk 31.7.1706 as breakwater Sheerness.

NOTTINGHAM Gunvessel 3, 67bm, 57 x 16½ ft. Ex-Barge purchased 3.1794. Sold 18.6.1800.

NOTTINGHAM 2nd class cruiser 5,440 tons, 430 x 50 ft, 9-6in. Pembroke Dock 18.4.1913. Sunk 19.8.16 by 'U.52' in the North Sea.

NOTTINGHAM Destroyer 3150 tons. Vosper-Thornycroft 18.2.1980.

NOVA SCOTIA Gun-brig 14, 214bm, 84 x 25 ft, 12-12pdr carr., 2-6dpr. American privateer RAPID captured 17.10.1812 by MAIDSTONE in N.America. Renamed FERRET 1813. Sold 13.1.1820.

NOX Minesweeper, 'Algerine' class. Redfern, Toronto, Cancelled 8.11.1944 (not laid down).

NUBIAN (ex-*Procida*) Coal depot, 2,265 gross, 326 x 36 ft. Purchased 11.2.1901. Renamed C.370 in 1904. Sold 15.7.12 at Simonstown, BU at Morecambe 4.13.

NUBIAN Destroyer 985 tons, 280 x 26½ ft, 3-12pdr (5-12pdr 1911), 2-TT. Thornycroft, Woolston 20.4.1909. Bow wrecked 27.10.16 by torpedo from German destroyer; stern half joined to bow half of wrecked ZULU at Chatham 1917 and new ship renamed ZUBIAN.

NUBIAN Destroyer 1,870 tons, 355½ x 36½ ft, 8-4.7on, 4-TT. Thornycroft 21.12.1937. Sold 11.6.49, BU Ward, Briton Ferry.

NUBIAN Frigate 2,300 tons, 350 x 42 ft, 2-4.5in, 2-40mm. Portsmouth DY 6.9.1960.

NUESTRA SENORA del ROSARIO Galleon 46, 1,000bm. Spanish, captured 1588. BU 1622.

NUGENT Destroyer, 'M' class. Palmer 23.1.1917. Sold 9.5.21 Ward, Hayle.

NUNNEY CASTLE (see BOWMAN-VILLE of 1944)

NURTON Coastal M/S, 'Ton' class. Harland & Wolff 22.10.1956. Renamed MONTROSE 1958; reverted 1961.

NUSA Patrol yacht (RAN) 64 tons. German, captured 13.9.1914 by MELBOURNE in New Ireland. Sold 1921.

NYADEN (see NAIAD)

NYASALAND (ex-HOSTE renamed 1943) Frigate, 'Colony' class. Walsh Kaiser 7.9.1943 on lend-lease. Returned 4.46 to the USN.

NYMPH Sloop 14, 300bm, 96½ x 27 ft. Chatham DY 27.5.1778. Burnt 28.6.1783 by accident at Tortola, W. Indies.

NYMPHE 5th Rate 36, 937bm, 141 x 38 ft. French, captured 10.8.1780 by FLORA off Ushant. Wrecked 18.12.1810 in the Firth of Forth.

NYMPHEN 5th Rate 36. Danish, captured 7.9.1807 at Copenhagen. Sold 11.1.1816. (Was to have been renamed DETERMINEE).

NYMPHE (ex-NEREIDE renamed 1811) 5th Rate 38, 1,087bm, 154 x 40 ft. Parsons, Warsash 12.4.1812. Harbour service 3.1836. Renamed HANDY 7.9.1871. BU completed 3.1875 at Chatham.

NYMPHE Wood S.sloop, 1,084bm, 1,574 tons, 187 x 36 ft. Deptford DY 24.11.1866. Sold 12.1884.

NYMPHE Compos. S.sloop 1,140 tons, 195 x 28 ft, 8-5in. Portsmouth DY 1.5.1888. Renamed WILDFIRE 12.1906, base ship. Renamed GANNET 1916, PEMBROKE 7.17. Sold 10.2.20, BU by Ward, Milford Haven.

NYMPHE Destroyer 740 tons, 246½ x 25 ft, 2-4in, 2-12pdr, 2-TT. Hawthorn Leslie 31.1.1911. Sold 9.5.21 Ward, Hayle.

NYMPHE Sloop 1,350 tons, 283 x 38½ ft, 6-4in. Chatham DY. Laid down 26.2.1945, cancelled 23.10.45.

NYMPHEN (see under NYMPH)

O.1 (see OBERON of 1926)

OAK Ship captured 1652. Lost 31.7.1653 in action with the Dutch

OAK Destroyer 765 tons, 255 x 26ft, 2-4in, 2-12pdr, 2-TT. Yarrow 5.9.1912. Sold 9.5.21 Ward, Hayle; BU in 9.22.

OAK Trawler 1939-46.

OAKHAM CASTLE Corvette, 'Castle' class Inglis 20.7.1944. To Air Ministry 8.57, renamed *Weather Reporter* 4.58.

OAKINGTON Coastal M/S, 'Ton' class. Harland & Wolff. Launched 10.12.1958 as MOSSELBAAI (S.African navy).

OAKLEY Minesweeper, early 'Hunt' class. Lobnitz 10.1.1917. Sold 18.1.23 Alloa, Charlestown.

OAKLEY Destroyer, 'Hunt' class type II. Vickers Armstrong, Tyne 30.10.1940. Renamed KUJAWIAK (Polish navy) 6.41. Mined 16.6.42 off Malta and foundered in tow.

OAKLEY (ex-TICKHAM renamed 6.1941) Destroyer, 'Hunt' class type II. Yarrow 15.1.42. Sold 2.10.58 W.German navy as GNEISENAU.

OAKVILLE Corvette (RCN), 'Flower' class. Pt Arthur SB 21.6.1941. Sold 1946 Venezuelan navy as PATRIA.

OBDURATE Destroyer, 'M' class. Scotts 21.1.1916. Sold 15.11.21 Cashmore, Newport; arrived 5.22.

OBDURATE Destroyer 1,540 tons, 337½ x 35 ft, 4-4in, 8-TT. Denny 19.2.1942. Arrived 30.11.64 Inverkeithing to BU.

OBEDIENT Destroyer, 'M' class. Scotts 16.11.1916. Sold 25.11.21 Hayes, Porthcawl.

OBEDIENT Destroyer 1,540 tons, 338½ x 35 ft, 4-4in, 8-TT. Denny 30.4.1942. Arrived 19.10.62 Hughes Bolckow, Blyth to BU.

OBERON Brig-sloop 16, 283bm, 93 x 26½ ft, 14-24pdr carr, 2-6pdr. Shepherd, Hull 13.8.1805. BU 5.1816.

OBERON Iron pad. sloop, 649bm, 170 x 28 ft. Deptford 2.1.1847. Target 1870; sunk 1874 in mine experiments; raised 1875, sold 16.11.1880 Moss Isaacs.

OBERON (see HAWK of 1888)

OBERON Destroyer, 'M' class. Doxford 29.9.1916. Sold 9.5.21 Ward Rainham.

OBERON (ex-O.1 renamed 1924) Submarine 1,311 tons, 270 x 28 ft, 1-4in, 8-TT. Chatham DY 24.9.1926. BU 8.45 Clayton & Davie, Dunston.

OBERON Submarine 1,610 tons, 241 x 26½ ft, 8-TT. Chatham DY 18.7.1959. Sold Seaforth Group 1987 to refit for resale.

OBSERVER Brig-sloop 12. (Captured?) 1781. Sold 21.10.1784.

OBERVATEUR Brig-sloop 16, 303bm, 90½ x 28 ft, 14-24pdr carr., 2-6pdr. French, captured 9.6.1806 by TARTAR in the W.Indies. Sold 1.9.1814.

OBSERVER Destroyer, 'M' class. Fairfield 1.5.1916. Sold 30.10.21 W. & A.T. Burden.

OBSERVER (see ORIBI)

OCEAN 2nd Rate 90, 1,833bm, 176 x 49½ ft. Chatham DY 21.4.1761. Sold 6.1793.

OCEAN 2nd Rate 98, 2,291bm, 197 x 52ft. Woolwich DY 24.10.1805. Depot ship 1841; coal hulk 1853. BU completed 11.12.1875 at Chatham.

OCEAN Ironclad ship, 4,047bm, 6,832 tons, 273 x 57 ft, 24-7in. Devonport DY 19.3.1863 (laid down 23.8.60 as 2nd Rate 92). Sold 11.5.1882 Castle, Charlton.

OCEAN Battleship 12,950 tons, 390 x 74 ft, 4-12in, 12-6in, 12-12pdr. Devonport DY 5.7.1898. Sunk 18.3.1915 by shore batteries in the Dardanelles.

OCEAN A/C carrier 13,190 tons, 630 x 80 ft, 19-40mm, 48-A/C. Stephen 8.7.1944. Arrived 6.5.62 Faslane to BU.

OCEANWAY (ex-DAGGER renamed 8,1943) Dock landing ship 4,270 tons, 454 x 72 ft, 1-3in, 16-20mm. Newport News 29.12.1943 on lend-lease. Returned USN and transferred Greek navy as OKEANOS.

OCELOT Submarine 1,610 tons, 241 x 26½ ft, 8-TT. Chatham DY 5.5.1962.

OCTAVIA 4th Rate 50, 2,132bm, 180 X 53ft, 10-8in, 40-32pdr Pembroke Dock 18.8.1849. Undocked 11.4.1861 as screw frigate 39 guns. BU 8.1876.

OCTAVIA (ex-ORYX renamed 1915) Destroyer, 'M' class. Doxford 21.6.1916. Sold 5.11.21 Granton S.Bkg Co.

OCTAVIA Minesweeper, 'Algerine' class. Redfern 31.12.1942. Sold 27.4.50, BU Dorkin, Gateshead.

OCTAVIA Trawler requis. 1918-19.

OCKHAM Inshore M/S, 'Ham' class. Ailsa SB 12.5.1959. Sold Mercantile 1.9.67.

ODIHAM Inshore M/S, 'Ham' class. Vosper 21.7.1955. Sold Sutton & Smith in 1980.

ODIN 3rd Rate 74, 1,750bm, 175 x 48 ft. Danish, captured 7.9.1807 at Copenhagan. Harbour service 2.1811. Sold 20.7.1825 Cristall to BU.

ODIN Wood pad. frigate, 1,326bm, 208 x 37 ft, 5-110pdr, 1-68pdr, 4-40pdr, 8-32pdr. Deptford DY 24.7.1846. Sold 1865 Castle & Beech.

ODIN Sloop 1,070 tons, 185 x 33 ft, 6-4in. Sheerness DY 30.11.1901. Sold 12.11.20 at Bombay.

ODIN Submarine 1,475 tons, 260 x 30 ft, 1-4in, 8-TT. Chatham DY

5.5.1928. Sunk 14.6.40 by Italian destroyer STRALE in the Gulf of Taranto.

ODIN Minesweeper, 'Algerine' class. Redfern, Toronto. Cancelled 8.11.1944 (not laid down).

ODIN Submarine 1,610 tons, 241 x 26½ ft, 8-TT. Cammell Laird 4.11.1960.

ODZANI Frigate, 'River' class. Smiths DK 19.5.1943. BU 6.57 Cashmore, Newport.

OFFA (see TRIDENT of 1915)

OFFA Destroyer, 'M' class. Fairfield 7.6.1916. Sold 30.10.21 W. & A.T. Burden.

OFFA Destroyer 1,540 tons, 338½ x 35 ft, 4-4.7in, 1-4in, 4-TT. Fairfield 11.3.1941. To RPN 3.11.49 as TARIQ. BU 10.59 Young, Sunderland.

OFFA Trawler requis. 1915-19.

OGRE (see TURBULENT of 1916)

OISEAU 6th Rate 26. French, captured 23.10.1762 by BRUNE in the Mediterranean. Fate unknown.

OISEAU 5th Rate 32, 783bm, 146½ x 34 ft, 26-9pdr, 6-6pdr. French, captured 31.1.1779 by APOLLO. Sold 19.6.1783.

OISEAU 5th Rate 36, 913bm. French CLEOPATRE captured 18.1.1793. By NYMPHE off the Start. Prison ship in 1810. Sold 18.9.1816.

OJIBWA (ex-ONYX renamed 2.1964) Submarine (RCN) 1,610 tons. 241 x 26½ ft, 8-TT. Chatham DY 29.2.64.

OKANAGAN Submarine (RCN) 1,610 tons, 241 x 26½ ft, 8-TT. Chatham DY 17.9.1966.

OKEHAMPTON Minesweeper, later 'Hunt' class. Lobnitz. Cancelled 1918.

OLIVE BRANCH Fireship 6, 204bm. Purchased 1672. Sold 1674.

OLIVE BRANCH Fireship 6, 200bm. Captured 1673. Sunk 1673.

OLIVE BRANCH Fireship. Purchased 1690. Captured 1690 by the French.

OLIVE BRANCH Fireship, 72bm, 62½ x 20 ft. Purchased 4.1794. Sold 2.1802.

OLYMPIA Schooner 10, 110bm, 68 x 20 ft, 8-18pdr carr., 2-6pdr. Bermuda 1806. Sold 9.2.1815.

OLYMPIA Trawler requis. 1917-19 and 1939-45.

OLYMPUS Submarine 1,475 tons, 260 x 30 ft, 1-4in, 8-TT. Beardmore 11.12.1928. Sunk 8.5.42 by mine off Malta.

OLYMPUS Submarine 1,610 tons, 241 x 26½ ft, 8-TT. Vickers Armstrong,

Barrow 14.6.1961.

OLYMPUS Drifter requis. 1915-20.

OMDURMAN Destroyer 2,380 tons, 355 x 40 ft, 5-4.5in, 8-40mm, 10-TT. Fairfield. Laid down 8.3.1944, cancelled 10.45.

ONONDAGA Sloop 22 (Canadian lakes). Oswego 1759. Lost 1764.

ONONDAGA Schooner 6 (Canadian lakes). Ravens Creek 1790. Wrecked 18.12.1793 at York.

ONONDAGA Submarine (RCN) 1,610 tons, 241 x 26½ ft, 8-TT. Chatham DY 25.9.1965.

ONSLAUGHT Destroyer, 'M' class. Fairfield 4.12.1915. Sold 30.10.21 W. & A.T.Burden.

ONSLAUGHT A.river steamer 102 tons, 1-3pdr. Purchased 1925, commissioned 26.10.25. Sold 1928 at Hong Kong.

ONSLAUGHT (see PATHFINDER)

ONSLAUGHT (ex-PATHFINDER renamed 8.41) Destroyer 1,540 tons, 338½ x 35 ft, 4-4.7in, 4-TT. Fairfield 9.10.1941. To RPN 24.1.50 as TUGHRILL.

ONSLAUGHT Submarine 1,610 tons, 241 x 26½ ft, 8-TT. Chatham DY 24.9.1960.

ONSLOW Destroyer, 'M' class. Fairfield 15.2.1916. Sold 26.10.21 Barking S.Bkg Co.

ONSLOW (see PAKENHAM)

ONSLOW (ex-PAKENHAM renamed 8.1941) Destroyer 1,550 tons, 338½ x 35 ft, 4-4.7in, 4-TT. J.Brown 31.3.41. To RPN 30.9.49, renamed TIPPU SULTAN.

ONSLOW Submarine (RAN) 1,610 tons, 241 x 26½ ft, 8-TT Scotts, Greenock 3.12.1968.

ONTARIO Sloop 12 (Canadian lakes). Oswego 1755. Captured 14.8.1756 by the French at Oswego.

ONTARIO Sloop 16 (Canadian lakes). Carlton Island 10.5.1780. Foundered 1.11.1780.

ONTARIO (ex-MOHAWK renamed 1813) Brig-sloop 18, 'Cruizer' class, 384bm. Chapman, Bideford 26.10.1813. Sold 11.1832.

ONTARIO Wood S.corvette, 1,857bm, 225 x 43 ft. Woolwich DY. Laid down 10.9.1860, cancelled 12.12.1863.

ONTARIO (see MINOTAUR of 1943)

ONYX Brig-sloop 10, 'Cherokee' class, 237bm, Ipswich 8.7.1808. Sold 3.2.1819 T.Pittman to BU.

ONYX Brig-sloop 10, 'Cherokee' class, 236bm. Sheerness DY 24.1.1822.

Sold 1.1837 Cristall to BU.

ONYX Iron pad. packet, 292bm, 139 x 21 ft. Ditchburn & Mare, Blackwall 11.1845. Sold 1854 Jenkins & Churchward.

ONYX Wood S.gunboat, 'Cheerful' class. Young & Magnay, Limehouse 3.4.1856. Made a DY Craft 1869. BU 7.1873 in Jamaica.

ONYX Torpedo gunboat 810 tons, 230 x 27 ft, 2-4.in, 4-3pdr, 3-TT. Laird 7.9.1892. Depot ship 1907. Renamed VULCAN II in 6.19. Sold 1924 King, Garston; resold 9.10.24 L.Basso, Weymouth.

ONYX Minesweeper, 'Algerine' class. Harland & Wolff 27.10.1942. Arrived 5.4.67 Ward, Inverkeithing to BU.

ONYX (see OJIBWA)

ONYX Submarine 1,610 tons, 241 x 26½ ft, 8-TT. Cammell Laird 16.8.1966.

OPAL (ex-MAGICIENNE renamed 12.2.1875) Compos. S.corvette 2,120 tons, 220 x 40ft, 14-64pdr. Doxford 9.3.1875. Sold 11.8.1892.

OPAL Destroyer, 'M' class. Doxford 11.9.1915. Wrecked 21.1.18 in the Orkneys. Wreck sold 18.8.32.

OPHELIA Destroyer, 'M' class. Doxford 13.10.1915. Sold 8.11.21 Slough TC.

OPHELIA Trawler 1940-46.

OPOSSUM Brig-sloop 10, 'Cherokee' class, 237bm. Muddle, Gillingham 8.7.1808. Sold 3.2.1819 G.Bailey.

OPOSSUM Brig-sloop 10, 'Cherokee' class, 236bm. Sheerness DY 11.12.1821. Sold 27.5.1841 Levy, Rochester.

OPOSSUM Wood S.Gunboat, 'Albacore' class. Wigram, Northam 28.2.1856. Hospital hulk 1876; mooring vessel 1891; renamed SIREN 1895. Sold 1896 at Hong Kong.

OPOSSUM Destroyer 320 tons, 200 x 19 ft, 1-12pdr, 5-6pdr, 2-TT. Hawthorn 9.8.1895. Sold 29.7.1920 Ward, Preston.

OPOSSUM Sloop 1,350 tons, 283 x 38½ ft, 6-4in. Denny 30.11.1944. Arrived 26.4.60 Demmelweeck & Reddin, Plymouth to BU.

OPOSSUM Submarine 1,610 tons, 241 x 26½ ft, 8-TT. Cammell Laird 23.5.1963.

OPPORTUNE Destroyer, 'M' class. Doxford 20.11.1915. Sold 7.12.23 King, Garston.

OPPORTUNE Destroyer 1,540 tons, 338½ x 35 ft, 4-4in, 8-TT. Thornycroft 24.1.1942. Arrived 25.11.55 Ward, Milford Haven to BU.

OPPORTUNE Submarine 1,610 tons, 241 x 26½ ft. 8-TT. Scotts 14.2.1964.

ORACLE Destroyer, 'M' class. Doxford 23.12.1915. Sold 30.10.21 W. & A.T.Burden.

ORACLE Submarine 1,610 tons, 241 x 26½ ft, 8-TT. Cammell Laird 26.9.1961.

ORACLE Yacht 1939-44.

ORANGE 5th Rate 32, 251bm. Dutch, captured 1665. Lost 1671.

ORANGE Fireship 6, 194bm. Captured 1672. Burnt 1673 by accident.

ORANGE TREE Hoy. Captured 1652. Sold 1655.

ORANGE TREE Fireship 6, 160bm. Purchased 1672. Burnt 1673 by accident.

ORANGE TREE 5th Rate 30, 280bm. Algerian, captured 1677. Sold 1687.

ORANGEVILLE (see MARMION of 1944)

ORANGEVILLE (ex-HEDINGHAM CASTLE renamed 1943) Corvette (RCN), 'Castle' class. Robb 26.1.44. Sold 5.9.46, renamed *Hsi Lin.*

ORBY M/S sloop, '24' class. Swan Hunter 22.10.1918. Sold 15.11.22 Ferguson Muir.

ORCADIA Destroyer, 'M' class. Fairfield 26.7.1916. Sold 30.10.1921 W. & A.T.Burden, Poole; BU 1923.

ORCADIA Minesweeper, 'Algerine' class. Pt Arthur SY 8.8.1944. Arrived 3.12.58 Ward, Briton Ferry to BU.

ORCHIS Corvette, 'Flower' class. Harland & Wolff 15.10.1940. Damaged 21.8.44 and beached off Coursevilles, Normandy.

ORESTES Brig-sloop 18, 367bm. Dutch MARS captured 3.12.1781. Foundered 5.11.1799 in a hurricane in the Indian ocean.

ORESTES Sloop 16, 280bm. Purchased 8.1803. Wrecked 12.7.1805 off Dunkirk and burnt.

ORESTES Brig-sloop 16, 284bm, 93 x 26½ ft. Bailey, Ipswich 23.10.1805. Sold 6.3.1817 Pittman.

ORESTE Brig-sloop 14, 312bm. French, captured 12.1.1810 by SCORPION off Guadeloupe. Renamed WELLINGTON 18.1810. BU 9.1812 at Portsmouth.

ORESTES Sloop 18, 460bm, 110 x 31 ft, 16-32pdr carr., 2-9pdr. Portsmouth DY 31.5.1824. Coal hulk 11.1852; (also known as 'C.28'). Sold circa 1905.

ORESTES Wood S.corvette, 1,717bm, 225 x 41 ft, 16-8in, 4-40pdr. Sheerness DY 18.8.1860. BU completed 11.1866 at Portsmouth.

ORESTES Destroyer, 'M' class. Doxford 21.3.1916. Sold 30.1.21 W. & A.T.Burden.

ORESTES Minesweeper, 'Algerine' class. Lobnitz 25.11.1942. Arrived 18.3.63 W of Scotland S Bkg Co, Troon.

ORFORD 6th Rate 24, 249bm, 94 x 25 ft. Ellis, Shoreham 29.11.1695. Renamed NEWPORT 3.9.1698. Sold 1714.

ORFORD 3rd Rate 70, 1,051bm, 150½ x 40½ ft. Deptford 1698. Rebuilt Limehouse 1713 as 1,099bm. Wrecked 14.2.1745 in the Gulf of Mexico.

ORFORD PRIZE 5th Rate, 380bm. Captured 7.1703 by ORFORD. Hulked 9.1703.

ORFORD PRIZE 6th Rate 24, 283bm. French, captured 21.10.1708 by ORFORD. Recaptured 27.5.1709 by the French off Lundy.

ORFORD 3rd Rate 70, 1,414bm, 160 x 45 ft. Woolwich DY 1749. Harbour service 3.1777. Sunk as breakwater at Sheerness in 6.1783.

ORFORD 3rd Rate 74. Cancelled 1809.

ORFORD Destroyer, 'M' class. Doxford 19.4.1916. Sold 31.10.21 W. & A.T. Burden.

ORFORD NESS Repair ship 8,580 tons, 439 x 62 ft, 16-20mm. West Coast SB Co, Canada 12.4.1945. Sold 1947, renamed *Rabaul.*

ORIANA Destroyer, 'M' class. Fairfield 23.9.1916. Sold 31.10.21 W. & A.T.Burden.

ORIANA Yacht 1914-17; Tug 1942-46; Tug 1947-48.

ORIBI (ex-OBSERVER renamed 11.1940) Destroyer 1,540 tons, 338½ x 35 ft, 4-4.7in, 1-4in, 4-TT. Fairfield 14.1.41. Transferred 18.6.46 Turkish navy as GAYRET.

ORIFLAMME 4th Rate 50. French, captured 1.4.1761 by ISIS. Fate unknown.

ORILLA Corvette (RCN), 'Flower' class. Collingwood 15.9.1940. BU 1.51 Steel Co of Canada, Hamilton.

ORIOLE Destroyer, 'M' class. Palmer 31.7.1916. Sold 9.5.21 Ward, Grays.

ORIOLE Trawler 1914-19; M/S 1939-45.

ORION 3rd Rate 74, 1,646bm, 170 x 47 ft. Adams & Barnard, Deptford 1.6.1787. BU 7.1814.

ORION Screw 2nd Rate 80, 3,281bm, 238 x 55½ ft, 34-8in, 1-68pdr, 56-32pdr. Chatham DY 6.11.1854. BU 1867 Castle, Charlton.

ORION (ex-Turkish BOORDJI ZAFFER purchased 13.2.1878) Armoured corvette 4,870 tons, 245 x 52 ft, 4-12in MLR, 6-6pdr. Samuda, Poplar 23.1.1879. Renamed ORONTES 12.1909, depot ship. Sold 19.6.13 at Malta.

ORION Armoured cruiser 14,600 tons. Projected 1904 but not ordered.

ORION Battleship 22,500 tons, 545 x 88½ ft, 10-13.5in, 16-4in. Portsmouth DY 20.8.1910. Sold 19.12.22 Cox & Danks, Queenborough.

ORION Cruiser 7,215 tons, 530 x 55 ft, 8-6in, 8-4in. Devonport DY 24.11.1932. Sold 19.7.49, BU at Troon.

ORION Submarine 558 tons, 219 x 22 ft, 1-3in, 9-TT. French, seized 3.7.1940 at Falmouth. Laid up until 5.43 then BU.

ORION Submarine (RAN) 1610 tons. Scott-Lithgow 16.9.1974.

ORION Drifter requis. 1915-19.

ORISSA (ex-CLYDEBANK renamed 1941) Minesweeper (RIN), TE 'Bangor' class. Lobnitz 20.11.41. BU 1949.

ORKAN (see MYRMIDON of 1942)

ORKNEY Frigate (RCN), 'River' class. Yarrow, Esquimalt 18.9.1943. Sold 7.10.47.

ORKNEY Patrol vessel 925 tons. Hall Russell 29.6.1976.

ORLANDO 5th Rate 36, 876bm, 137 x 38 ft. Chatham DY 20.6.1811. Harbour service 10.1819. Sold 3.1824 at Trincomalee.

ORLANDO Wood S.frigate, 3,740bm, 300 x 51 ft, 20-10in, 12-68pdr. Pembroke Dock 12.6.1858. Sold 15.6.1871 Marshall.

ORLANDO Armoured cruiser 5,600 tons, 300 x 56 ft, 2-9in, 10-6in, 10-3pdr. Palmer 3.8.1886. Sold 11.7.1905 Ward, Morecambe.

ORLANDO (se LOYAL)

ORLANDO Trawler 1914-15.

ORMONDE 4th Rate 54, 704bm, 130 x 35 ft. Woolwich DY 18.10.1711. Renamed DRAGON 30.9.1715. BU 1733.

ORMONDE M/S sloop, '24' class. Blyth SB 8.6.1918. Survey vessel 3.24. Sold 6.8.37 Ward, Briton Ferry.

ORMONDE (see EMPIRE SPEARHEAD)

ORMONDE Trawler requis. 1914-19 and 1940-41.

ORNEN Schooner 12, 143bm, 76 x 21½ ft. Danish, captured 7.9.1807 at Copenhagen. Presented 9.1815 to the Clyde Marine Socy. (Was to have been renamed VICTOIRE.)

ORONOQUE Sloop 18. (French privateer?) ORENOQUE captured 1782 at Demerara. Recaptured by the French 3.2.1785 at the loss of Demerara.

OROONOKO Gunvessel 12, 177bm, 80 x 22½ ft, 10-18pdr carr., 2-12pdr. Purchased 1806 in the W.Indies. Sold 1814.

ORONTES (ex-BRILLIANT renamed 1812) 5th Rate 36, (red pine-built), 939bm, 143 x 38½ ft, 14-32pdr carr., 26-18pdr. Brindley, Frindsbury 29.6.1813. BU 4.1817.

ORONTES Iron S.troopship, 2,812bm, 4,857 tons, 300 x 44½ ft, 3-4pdr. Laird 22.11.1862. Lengthened 1876 to 5,600 tons. Sold 3.7.1893 to BU on the Thames.

ORONTES (see SWIFTSURE of 1870)

ORONTES (see ORION of 1879)

OROONOKO (see under ORONOQUE)

ORPHEUS 5th Rate 32, 708bm, 130 x 35 ft. Barnard, Harwich 7.5.1773. Abandoned and burnt 15.8.1778 at Rhode Island.

ORPHEUS 5th Rate 32, 688bm, 126½ x 35 ft. Adams & Barnard, Deptford 3.6.1780. Wrecked 23.1.1807 in the W.Indies.

ORPHEUS 5th Rate 36, 947bm, 145 x 38 ft. Deptford DY 12.8.1809. BU 8.1819.

ORPHEUS 5th Rate 46, 1,215bm, 159½ x 42 ft. Chatham DY. Ordered 1825, cancelled 7.2.1831.

ORPHEUS Wood S.corvette, 1,706bm, 225 x 41 ft, 16-8in, 1-7in, 4-40pdr. Chatham DY 23.6.1860. Wrecked 7.2.1863 on Manukau Bar, New Zealand.

ORPHEUS Destroyer, 'M' class. Doxford 17.6.1916. Sold 1.11.21 Fryer, Sunderland.

ORPHEUS Submarine 1,475 tons, 260 x 30 ft, 1-4in, 8-TT. Beardmore 26.2.1929. Sunk 27.6.40 by Italian destroyer TURBINE between Malta and Alexandria.

ORPHEUS Submarine 1,610 tons, 241 x 26½ ft, 8-TT. Vickers, Armstrong, Barrow 17.11.1959.

ORPHEUS Trawler requis. 1914-19 and 1940-46.

ORQUIJO Sloop 18, 384bm. Spanish, captured 8.2.1805 by PIQUE off Havana. Foundered 10.1805 in the W.Indies.

ORTENZIA Schooner 10. French (ex-Venetian), captured 16.7.1808 by MINSTREL in the Mediterranean.

Sold 1812.

ORWELL Wood S.gunboat, 'Britomart' class. Portsmouth DY 27.12.1866. Sold Customs Board 20.12.1890

ORWELL Destroyer 360 tons, 218x 20 ft, 1-12pdr, 5-6pdr, 2-TT. Laird 29.9.98. Sold 1.7.20 Castle, Plymouth.

ORWELL Destroyer, 1,540 tons, 338½ x 35 ft, 4-4in, 8-TT. Thornycroft 2.4.1942. Arrived 28.6.65 Cashmore, Newport to BU.

ORWELL Minesweeper 890 tons. Richards 7.2.1985

ORYX (see OCTAVIA)

OSBORNE (see VICTORIA & ALBERT of 1843)

OSBORNE Wood paddle yacht 1,856 tons, 250 x 36 ft. Pembroke Dock 19.12.1870. Sold 31.7.1908, BU at Felixstowe.

OSHAWA Minesweeper (RCN), 'Algerine' class. Pt Arthur 6.10.1943. Survey vessel 1958. For disposal 3.65.

OSIRIS Destroyer, 'M' class. Palmer 26.9.1916. Sold 9.5.21 Ward, Rainham.

OSIRIS Submarine 1,475 tons, 260 x 30 ft, 1-4in, 8-TT. Vickers Armstrong, Barrow 19.5.1928. Sold 9.46 at Durban to BU. Finally BU 1952 at Mombasa.

OSIRIS Submarine 1,610 tons, 241 x 26½ ft, 8-TT. Vickers Armstrong, Barrow 29.11.1962.

OSIRIS AMC 1728 tons 1914-19; Trawler 1917-19.

OSPREY Sloop 18, 386bm, 102 x 30 ft. Pitcher, Northfleet 7.10.1797. BU 1.1813.

OSPREY Brig 12, 425bm, 101½ x 32 ft, 10-32pdr, 2-18pdr. Portsmouth DY 2.4.1844. Wrecked 11.3.1846 off Hokianga, New Zealand.

OSPREY Wood S.gunvessel, 682bm, 181 x 28½ ft, 1-110pdr, 1-68pdr, 2-20pdr. Fletcher, Limehouse 22.3.1856. Wrecked 6.1867 on coast of S.Africa.

OSPREY Compos. S.sloop 1,130 tons, 170 x 36 ft, 2-7in, 4-64pdr. Sheerness DY 5.8.1876. Sold 29.4.1890.

OSPREY Destroyer 380 tons, 227 x 22 ft, 1-12pdr, 5-pdr, 2-TT. Fairfield 17.4.1897. Sold 4.11.1919 J.H.Lee.

OSPREY 2 Trawlers & 2 Drifters WW.I.; Whaler 1924-68.

OSSINGTON (see Repton)

OSSORY 2nd Rate 90, 1,307bm, 161 x 44½ ft. Portsmouth DY 1682. Renamed PRINCE 1705, PRINCESS 2.1.1716, PRINCESS ROYAL 1728.

BU 1773.

OSSORY Destroyer, 'M' class. J.Brown 9.10.1916. Sold 8.11.21 Slough TC.

OSSORY Minesweeper, 'Algerine' class. Pt Arthur SY 3.10.1944. Arrived 4.3.59 Troon to BU.

OSTEND Gunvessel 1, 40bm. Purchased 4.1795. Listed in 9.1809.

ESTRIDGE Careening hulk, 811bm. Dutch ship Vogelstruys captured 1653. Sunk 1679 as foundation at Sheerness.

OSTRICH Sloop 14, 280bm, 94 x 26½ ft. Purchased 1777. Sold 9.9.1782.

OSTRICH Destroyer 375 tons, 210 x 21 ft, 1-12pdr, 5-6pdr, 2-TT. Fairfield 22.3.1900. Sold 29.4.20 Barking S.Bkg Co.

OSTRICH Three trawlers requis. in WW.I.

OSWALD Submarine 1,475 tons, 260 x 30 ft, 1-4in, 8-TT. Vickers Armstrong, Barrow 19.6.1928. Rammed 1.8.40 by Italian destroyer VIVALDI south of Calabria.

OSWEGO Sloop 5 (Canadian lakes). Oswego 1755. Captured 14.8.1756 by the French at Oswego.

OSWESTRY CASTLE Corvette, 'Castle' class. Crown, Sunderland. Cancelled 12.1943.

OTAGO (ex-HASTINGS renamed 1957) Frigate (RNZN) 2,150 tons; 360 x 41 ft, 2-4.5in, 4-GWS. Thornycroft 11.12.1958.

OTAMA Submarine (RAN) 1610 tons. Scott-Lithgow 3.12.1975

OTTAWA (see CRUSADER)

OTTAWA (see GRIFFIN of 1935)

OTTAWA Escort (RCN) 2,265 tons, 366(oa) x 42 ft, 4-3in, 2-40mm. Vickers, Montreal 29.4.1953.

OTTER Ketch 4, 83bm, 61 x 18 ft. Deptford 1700. Captured 28.7.1702 by two French frigates on passage to the W.Indies.

OTTER 6th Rate 14, 167bm, 76 x 22½ ft. Smith, Rotherhithe 6.3.1709. Sold 8.1.1713.

OTTER Sloop 8, 91bm, 64½ x 18½ ft. Deptford DY 8.8.1721. Wrecked 13.1.1741 off Aldborough.

OTTER Sloop 14, 247bm, 88½ x 25 ft. Buxton, Rotherhithe 19.8.1742. Sold 16.6.1763.

OTTER Sloop 14, 302bm, 95 x 27 ft. Deptford DY 26.10.1767. Wrecked 25.8.1778 on the coast of Florida.

OTTER Sloop 14. American, captured 1778. Sold at Plymouth 9.10.1783.

OTTER Brig-sloop 14, 202bm, 79 x 25 ft, 8-18pdr carr., 14-pdr. Hills, Sandwich 17.3.1782. Fireship 1800. Sold 16.12.1801.

OTTER Sloop 18, 365bm, 107 x 28 ft, 16-32pdr carr., 2-6pdr. Atkinson Hull 2.3.1805. Harbour service 1814. Sold 6.3.1828 J.Holmes.

OTTER (ex-GPO vessel *Wizard*) Wood pad. packet, 237bm, 120 x 21 ft. Transferred 1837. Gunvessel 1854; tug 1865; coal hulk 1878. Sold 1893.

OTTER S.gunboat (Australian) 220 tons, 1-64pdr. Ramage & Ferguson 19.7.1884, ex-tug purchased on stocks. Sold circa 1906. (Hired 9.39-12.40)

OTTER Destroyer 385 tons, 210 x 20 ft, 1-12pdr, 5-6pdr, 2-TT. N.C & A (Vickers) 23.11.1896. Sold 25.10.1916 at Hong Kong.

OTTER Submarine 1,610 tons, 241 x 26½ ft, 8-TT. Scotts 17.10.1962.

OTTER Tug and Yacht WW.I. Yacht (RCN) 1940-41.

OTTRINGHAM Inshore M/S, 'Ham' class. Ailsa 22.1.1958. To Ghanaian navy 10.59, renamed AFADZATO.

OTUS Submarine 1,475 tons, 260 x 30 ft, 1-4in, 8-TT. Vickers Armstrong, Barrow 31.8.1928. Sold 5.46 R.Scott, Durban; hull scuttled 9.46.

OTUS Submarine 1,610 tons, 241 x 26½ ft, 8-TT. Scotts 17.10.1962.

OTWAY Submarine (RAN) 1,349 tons, 275 x 28 ft, 1-4in, 8-TT. Vickers Armstrong, Barrow 7.10.1926. Transferred to the RN 1931. Sold 24.8.45, BU Ward, Inverkeithing.

OTWAY Submarine (RAN) 1,610 tons, 241 x 26½ ft, 8-TT. Scotts 29.11.1966.

OTWAY AMC 12,077 tons requis. 1941-17.

OUDENARDE Destroyer 2,380 tons, 255 x 40 ft, 5in, 8-40mm, 10-TT. Swan Hunter 11.9.1945, not completed. Target 1947. Arrived 12.57 at Rosyth to BU.

OUDE Minesweeper (RIN), TE 'Bangor' class. Garden Reach, Calcutta 3.3.1942. Renamed DACCA (RPN) 1948. Sold 22.1.59.

OULSTON Coastal M/S. 'Ton' class. Thornycroft 20.7.1954. To Irish Navy 11.70, renamed GRAINNE.

OUNDLE Minesweeper, later 'Hunt' class. Lobnitz. Cancelled 1919.

OURAGAN Destroyer 1,319 tons, 326 x 33 ft, 4-5.1in, 6-TT. French, seized 3.7.1940 at Plymouth. Polish crew 8.40; Free-French 12.40; laid up 1944. Returned 1946 to the French navy.

OUSE Destroyer 550 tons, 222 x 23½ ft,

1-12pdr, 5-6pdr (4-12pdr 1907), 2-TT. Laird 7.1.1905. Sold 22.10.19 J.H.Lee.

OUSE Trawler 1920-41.

OUTARDE Minesweeper (RCN), TE 'Bangor' class. North Vancouver SR 27.1.1941. Sale list 1946.

OUTRAM Iron river gunboat (Indian), 610bm. Bombay DY 1857. Fate unknown.

OUTREMONT Frigate (RCN), 'River' class. Morton 3.7.1943. Arrived 11.4.66 at Spezia to BU.

OVENS Submarine (RAN) 1,610 tons, 241 x 26½ ft, 8-TT. Scotts 4.12.1967.

OVERTON Coastal M/S, 'Ton' class. Camper & Nicholson. Launched 28.1.1956 as KARWAR (Indian) navy.

OVERYSSEL 3rd Rate 64, 1,226bm, 153½ x 48 ft. Dutch, seized 22.10.1795 by POLYPHEMUS AT Queenstown. Hulked 1810 as breakwater at Harwich. Hulk sold 3.1.1822.

OWEN (see THURSO BAY)

OWEN GLENDOWER 5th Rate 36, 951bm, 145½ x 38½ ft. Steemson, Paul near Hull 21.11.1808. Convict ship 10.1842. Sold 1884 F.Danino at Gibraltar.

OWEN SOUND Corvette (RCN), modified 'Flower' class. Collingwood SY 15.6.1943. Sold 2.10.45, renamed *Cadia*

OWL Destroyer 936 tons, 267½ x 27 ft, 3-4in, 2-TT. London & Glasgow Co 7.7.1913. Sold 5.11.21 Granton S. Bkg Co.

OWL Tug 1891-1902; 2 Trawlers requis. WWI.

OWNERS ADVENTURE Bomb, 115bm. Purchased 1694. Sold 3.5.1698.

OWNERS GOODWILL Fire vessel, 25bm. Purchased 1694. Sold 1706.

OWNERS LOVE Fireship 10, 500bm. Purchased 1688. Bilged in ice 28.7.1697 in Hudsons Bay on discovery service.

OXFORD 26-gun ship, 221bm. Deptford 1656. Given to the Governor of Jamaica 1668 and blown up 1669.

OXFORD 4th Rate 54, 677bm, 127 x 34½ ft. Bailey, Bristol 1674. Rebuilt Deptford 1702 as 675bm; rebuilt Portsmouth 1727 as 767bm, 50 guns. BU 10.1758 at Plymouth.

OXFORD CASTLE Corvette, 'Castle' class. Harland & Wolff 11.12.1943. Arrived 6.9.60 Ward, Briton Ferry to BU.

OXLEY Submarine (RAN) 1,354 tons,

275 x 28 ft, 1-4in, 8-TT. Vickers Armstrong, Barrow 29.6.1926. Transferred to the RN 1931. Sunk in error 10.9.39 by HMS/M TRITON off Norway.

OXLEY Submarine (RAN) 1,610 tons, 241 x 26½ ft, 8-TT. Scotts 24.9.1965.

OXLIP Corvette, 'Flower' class. Inglis 28.8.1941. Sold 1946 Irish naval service as MAEVE.

'P' class patrol boats, 613 tons, 230 x 24 ft, 1-4in (2-4in in P.52), 2-TT. Vessels designated 'PC' built as decoy ships, 682 tons, 233 x 25½ ft (except PC.43, 65-68 and 70-74, 694 tons, 233 x 27 ft), 1-4in, 2-12pdr.

P.11 White, Cowes 14.10.1915. Sold 1.12.21 Stanlee.

P.12 White 4.12.15. Sunk 4.11.18 in collision in the Channel.

P.13 Hamilton, Glasgow 7.6.16. Renamed P.75 on 31.7.17; sold 31.7.23 Dover S.Bkg Industries.

P.14 Connell, Scotstoun 4.7.16. Sold 31.7.23 Cashmore.

P.15 Workman Clark, Belfast 24.1.16. Sold 26.11.21 British Legion, Plymouth.

P.16 Workman Clark 23.3.16. Sold with P.15.

P.17 Workman Clark 21.10.15. Sold with P.15.

P.18 Inglis, Glasgow 20.4.16. Sold with P.15.

P.19 Northumberland SB Co. Howden 21.2.16. Sold 24.7.23 British Legion, Richborough.

P.20 Northumberland SB 3.4.16. Sold 5.23 Richardson Westgarth, Saltash.

P.21 Russell, Glasgow 31.3.16. Sold 26.11.21 with P.15.

P.22 Caird, Greenock 22.2.16. Sold 12.2.23 W. G.Keen, Bristol.

P.23 Bartram, Sunderland 5.3.16. Sold 24.7.23 with P.19.

P.24 Harland & Wolff, Govan 24.11.15. Sold 1.12.21 Stanlee, Dover.

P.25 H & W Govan 15.1.16. Sold with P.24.

P.26 Tyne Iron SB Co 22.12.15. Sunk 10.4.17 by mine off Le Havre.

P.27 Eltringham, S. Shields 21.2.15. Sold with P.19.

P.28 Thompson, Sunderland 6.3 16. Sold with P.19.

P.29 Gray, W. Hartlepool 6.12.15. Sold with P.19.

P.30 Gray 5.2.16. Sold with P.19.

P.31 Readhead, S. Shields 5.2.16. Sold 16.12.26 Demellweek & Redding, Plymouth.

P.32 Harkess, Middlesborough 20.1.16. Sold with P.11.

P.33 Napier & Miller 8.6.16. Sold with P.11.

P.34 Barclay Curle 22.3.16. Sold with P.11.

P.35 Caird 29.1.17. Sold 15.1.23 Unity S. Bkg Co, Plymouth.

P.36 Eltringham 25.10.16. Sold 5.23 with P.20.

P.37 Gray 28.10.16. Sold 18.2.24 British Legion, Ramsgate.

P.38 Hamilton 10.2.17. Renamed SPEY 11.2.25. Sold 5.38 Ward, Grays.

P.39 Inglis 1.3.17. Sold 6.9.22 Marple & Gillet.

P.40 White 1916. BU 1938 Ward, Milford Haven.

P.41 Bartram 23.3.17. Sold 6.9.22 Granton S.Bkg Co.

PC.42 Caird 7.6.17. Sold with P.11.

PC.43 Caird 14.8.17. Sold 20.1.23 J. Smith, Poole.

PC.44 Eltringham 25.4.17. Sold 9.4.23 E. Suren.

P.45 Gray 24.1.17. Sold with P.35.

P.46 Harkess 7.2.17. Sold 28.10.25 Cashmore, Newport.

P.47 Readhead 9.7.17. Sold 28.10.25 Alloa, Charlestown.

P.48 Readhead 5.9.17. Sold 5.23 Dover S.Bkg Co.

P.49 Thompson 19.4.17. Sold with P.35.

P.50 Tyne Iron SB 25.11.16. Sold with P.11.

PC.51 Tyne Iron SB 25.11.16. Sold 18.1.23 Alloa; arrived 11.23 Charlestown.

P.52 White 28.9.16. Sold 5.23 Dover S.Bkg Co.

P.53 Barclay Curle 8.2.17. Sold with P.37.

P.54 Barclay Curle 25.4.17. Sold with P.37.

PC.55 Barclay Curle 5.5.17. To RIM 2.22; renamed BALUCHI 5.22. Sold 1935.

PC.56 Barclay Curle 2.6.17.Sold 31.7.23 Dover S.Bkg Co.

P.57 Hamilton 6.8.17.Sold 21.5.20. Egyptian navy, renamed RAQIB.

P.58 Hamilton 9.5.18. Sold with P.11.

P.59 White 2.11.17. Sold 16.6.38 Ward, BU at Milford Haven.

PC.60 Workman Clark 4.6.17. Sold with P.37.

PC.61 Workman Clark 19.6.17. Sold 9.4.23 E.Suren.

PC.62 H & W Govan 7.6.17. Sold with P.11.

PC.63 Connell 2.10.17. Sold 5.23 Cashmore, Newport.

P.64 Inglis 30.8.17. Sold 9.4.23 Cashmore, Newport.

PC.65 Eltringham 5.9.17.Sold 18.1.23 Alloa; arrived 3.23. at Charlestown.

PC.66 Harkess 12.2.18. Sold 31.7.23 Hughes Bolckow, Blyth.

PC.67 White 7.5.17. Sold with P.11.

PC.68 White 29.6.17. Sold with P.11.

PC.69 Workman Clark 11.3.18. to RIM 5.8.21; renamed PATHAN 30.5.22. Sunk 23.6.40 by explosion off Bombay.

PC.70 Workman Clark 12.4.18. Sold 3.9.26 Hughes Bolckow, Blyth.

PC.71 White 18.3.18. Sold 28.10.25 Alloa; wrecked in tow 25.11.25 near S.Shields; wreck resold 29.12.25 North-Eastern Salvage Co.

PC.72 White 8.6.18. Sold 28.10.25 Hayes, Porthcawl.

PC.73 White 1.8.18. Renamed DART 4.25. Sold Ward. 16.6.38, BU Briton Ferry.

PC.74 White 4.10.18. Sold 19.7.48, BU by Hayes. (Operated as decoy ship CHATSGROVE 9.39 to 10.39.)

P.75 (ex-P.13 renamed 31.7.17). Sold 31.7.23 Dover S.Bkg Co.

Submarines, 'U' class. (Numbers missing from the following group were given 'U' names in Jan/Feb 1943 (qv.)

P.32 Vickers Armstrong, Barrow 15.12.1940. Sunk 18.8.41 by mine off Tripoli.

P.33 V.A., Barrow 28.1.41. Presumed mined off Tripoli and formally paid off 20.8.41.

P.34 V.A., Barrow 28.4.41. Sunk 1.4.42 by Italian A/C in Sliema harbour, Malta, raised 7.8.58 and scuttled 22.8.58 off Malta.

P.38 V.A., Barrow 9.7.41. Sunk 25.52.42 by Italian torpedo boats CIRCE and USODIMARE off Tunisia.

P.39 V.A., Barrow 23.8.41. Sunk 26.3.42 by air attack at Malta; raised and beached 6.43; BU 1954.

P.48 V.A., Barrow 15.4.42. Sunk 25.12.42 by Italian corvette ARDENTE in the Gulf of Tunis.

P.222 Submarine, 'S' class. V.A., Barrow 20.9.41. Sunk 12.12.42 by Italian torpedo boat FORTUNALE off Naples.

P.311 (ex-TUTANKHAMEN renamed 1.43, ex-P.311) Submarine, 'T' class. V.A., Barrow 5.3.42. Presumed mined 8.1.43 off Maddalena.

P.411, P.412, P.413 Submarines, 1,520 tons, 271½ x 25½ ft, 1-4in, 6-TT, 50-mines. Scotts. All ordered 13.1.41 and cancelled 9.41.

P.511 (ex-American R.3) Submarine 530 tons, 186 x 18 ft, 1-3in, 4-TT. To the RN 4.11.41 on lend-lease. Nominally returned USN 20.12.44. Foundered at moorings 21.11.47 in Kames Bay; raised and arrived 2.48 at Troon to BU.

P.512 (ex-American R.17) Submarine 530 tons, 186 x 18 ft, 1-3in, 4-TT. To the RN 9.3.42 on lend-lease. Returned 6.9.44 to the USN. BU 11.45.

P.514 (ex-American R.19) Submarine 530 tons, 186 x 18 ft, 1-3in, 4-TT. To the RN 9.3.42 on lend-lease. Rammed in error 21.6.42 by the M/S GEORGIAN in the N. Atlantic.

P.551 (ex-American S.25) Submarine 800 tons, 219 x 20½ ft, 1-4in, 4-TT. To the RN 4.11.41 on lend-lease. Lent Polish navy 11.41 as JASTRZAB; sunk in error 2.5.42 by ST ALBANS and SEAGULL off north Norway.

P.552 (ex-American S.1) Submarine 800 tons, 219 x 20½ ft, 1-4in 4-TT. To the RN 20.4.42 on lend-lease. Nominally returned 16.10.44 to the USN. BU 6.46 at Durban.

P.553 (ex-American S.21) Submarine 800 tons, 219 x 20½ ft, 1-4in, 4-TT. To the RN 14.9.42 on lend-lease. Nominally returned 11.7.44. Sunk 20.3.45 as Asdic target.

P.554 (ex-American S.22) Submarine 800 tons, 219 x 20½ ft, 1-4in, 4-TT. To the RN 19.6.42 on lend-lease. Returned 11.7.44 to the USN.Sold 16.11.45 to BU.

P.555 (ex-American S.24) Submarine 800 tons, 219 x 20½ ft, 1-4in, 4-TT. To the RN 10.8.42 on lend-lease. Nominally returned 1945. Expended 25.8.47 in tests at Portsmouth.

P.556 (ex-American S.29) Submarine 800 tons, 219 x 20½ ft, 1-4in, 4-TT. To the RN 5.6.42 on lend-lease. Nominally returned 26.1.46. Sold to BU and stranded on Porchester beach 1947; refloated 1965. Hulk at Pounds yard 1986.

P.611 (ex-Turkish ORUC REIS commissioned for passage to Turkey) Submarine 683 tons, 193 x 22½ ft, 1-3in, 5-TT. V.A., Barrow 19.7.40. Returned 1942 Turkish navy.

P.612 (ex-Turkish MURAT REIS com-

missioned for passage to Turkey)
Submarine 683 tons, 193 x 22½ ft,
1-3in, 5-TT. V.A, Barrow 20.7.40. Returned 25.5.42 to the Turkish navy.

P.614 (ex-Turkish BURAK REIS requisitioned 1942) Submarine 683
tons, 193 x 22½ ft, 1-3in, 5-TT.
V.A.,Barrow 19.10.40. Returned
12.45 to the Turkish navy.

P.615 (ex-Turkish ULUC ALI REIS requisitioned 1942) Submarine 683
tons, 193 x 22½ ft, 1-3in, 5-TT. V.A.,
Barrow 1.11.40. Sunk 18.4.43 by
'U.23' off W. Africa.

P.711 (see X.2)

P.712 Submarine 620 tons, 197(oa) x 21
ft, 6-TT. Italian PERLA captured
9.7.42. Transferred Greek navy 1.43
as MATROZOS.

P.714 Submarine 629 tons, 197(oa) x 21
ft, 6-TT. Italian BRONZO captured
12.7.43. Transferred French navy
1944 as NARVAL.

PACIFIC Storeship 22, 678bm, 137 x 33
ft. French E.Indianman PACIFIQUE
captured 1777. Sunk 7.1781 as
breakwater at Harwich.

PACIFIC Receiving ship and light vessel, 110bm. Ex-sloop purchased
30.12.1844. BU 1868 at the Cape.

PACKINGTON Coastal M/S, 'Ton'
class. Harland & Wolff. Launched
3.7.1958 as WALVISBAII, S. African
navy.

PACTOLUS 5th Rate 38 (red pine-
built), 1,067bm, 150½ x 40 ft. Barnard, Deptford 14.8.1813. Sold
29.1.1818 Messrs Maund.

PACTOLUS 3rd class cruiser 2,135
tons, 300 x 36½ ft, 8-4in, 8-3pdr.
Armstrong 21.12.1896. Depot ship
9.1912. Sold 25.10.21 Multilocular
S.Bkg Co, Stranraer.

PADSTOW (see PANGBOURNE)

PADSTOW (see ROHILKAND)

PADSTOW BAY (ex-LOCH COULSIDE
renamed 1944) Frigate, 'Bay' class.
Robb 23.8.45. Arrived 11.8.59 at
Spezia to BU.

PAGHAM Inshore M/S, 'Ham' class.
Jones, Buckie 4.10.1955. Sold 1983.

PAKENHAM Gunvessel 1. Purchased
1797. In 1800, not 1805.

PAKENHAM (see ONSLOW)

PAKENHAM (ex-ONSLOW renamed
8.1941) Destroyer 1,550 tons, 338½ x
35 ft, 4-4.7in, 4-TT.Hawthorn Leslie
28.1.41. Badly damaged 16.4.43 by
gunfire of Italian torpedo boats
CASSIOPEA and CIGNO and sunk
by RN forces off Sicily.

PALADIN Destroyer, 'M' class. Scotts
27.3.1916. Sold 9.5.21 Ward, Rainham.

PALADIN Destroyer 1,540 tons, 338½ x
35 ft, 4-4.7in, 4-TT. J.Brown 11.6.41.
Frigate 1956, 1,800 tons, 2-4in. Arrived 25.10.62 Clayton & Davie,
Dunston to BU.

PALADIN Tug requis. 1914-19.

PALINURUS Survey brig (Indian),
192bm. Bombay DY 1823. Listed in
1862.

PALINURUS Survey vessel (RIM) 444
tons, 140 x 24 ft. Cammell Laird
2.3.1907 Listed in 1930.

PALLAS 5th Rate 36, 728bm, 128½ 36
ft. Wells, Deptford 30.8.1757. Run
ashore 24.3.1783 on St Georges Island as unserviceable.

PALLAS 5th Rate 32, 776bm, 135 x 36
ft. Woolwich DY 19.12.1793.
Wrecked 4.4.1798 near Plymouth.

PALLAS (see MINERVA of 1780)

PALLAS (see SHANNON of 1803)

PALLAS 5th Rate 32 (fir-built), 667bm.
Plymouth DY 17.11.1804. Wrecked
18.12.1810 in the Firth of Forth.

PALLAS 5th Rate 36, 951bm, 145½ x
38½ ft. Portsmouth DY 13.4.1816
(ex-Guilaume Northam transferred
10.12.1811). Coal hulk 9.1836; Sold
11.1.1862 Marshall, Plymouth.

PALLAS Armoured corvette, 2,372bm,
3,661 tons, 225 x 50 ft, 6-7in. Woolwich DY 14.3.1865, Sold 20.4.1886.

PALLAS 2nd class cruiser 2,575 tons,
265 x 41 ft, 8-3pdr, Portsmouth DY
30.6.1890. Sold 7.1906 at Bermuda.

PALMA 5th Rate 38, 1,066bm, 154 x 40
ft. French IPHIGENIE captured
16.1.1814 by VENERABLE and
CYANE off Maderia, Renamed
GLOIRE 12.1814 Sold 10.9.1817.

PALM TREE Hoy, 62bm. Captured
1665. Sold 1667.

PALLISER Frigate 1,180 tons, 300 x 33
ft, 3-40mm, 4-TT. Stephen 10.5.1956.
Arrived Neath 16.3.83 to BU by
Deans Marine.

PALUMA Gunboat (Australia) 360 tons,
115 x 26 ft, 1-8in, 1-6in, 1-3pdr.
Armstrong Mitchell 5.1884. Transferred 1931 to Victoria Govt as Rip.
BU in 1957.

PANDORA 6th Rate 24, 520bm, 114½ x
32 ft. Adams & Barnard, Deptford
17.5.1779. Wrecked 28.8.1791 on the
Great Barrier Reef.

PANDORA Gun-brig 14, 231bm, 78 x
27 ft, 14-4pdr. French PANDOUR
captured 31.8.1795 by CAROLINE in
the North Sea. Foundered 6.1797 in
the North Sea.

PANDORA Brig-sloop 18, 'Cruizer'

class, 383bm. Preston, Yarmouth 11.10.1806. Wrecked 13.2.1811 in the Kattegat.

PANDORA Brig-sloop 18, 'Cruiser' class, Woolwich DY. Ordered 6.9.1812, renamed LYNX 24.9.12, cancelled 9.6.1818.

PANDORA Brig-sloop 18, 'Cruiser' class, 383bm, Deptford DY 12.8.1813. Ship-sloop 1825; sale list 4.1827. Sold 13.4.1831.

PANDORA Packet brig 3, 319bm, 90 x 29 ft, 3-32pdr. Woolwich DY 4.7.1833. Coastguard watch vessel 10.1857. Sold 11.1.1862 Marshall, Plymouth.

PANDORA Wood S.gunvessel, 'Philomel' class. Pembroke Dock 7.2.1861. Sold 13.1.1875.

PANDORA (see KATOOMBA)

PANDORA 3rd class cruiser 2,200 tons, 305 x 36½ ft. Portsmouth DY 17.1.1900. Sold 7.10.13 Ward, Morecambe.

PANDORA (ex-*Seti*) Depot ship 4,580 tons, 330 x 43 ft, Purchased 9.11.1914. Renamed DOLPHIN 3.10.24. Sunk 23.12.39 by mine while in tow to Blyth for conversion to blockship.

PANDORA (ex-PYTHON renamed 1928) Submarine 1,475 tons, 260 x 30 ft, 1-4in, 8-TT. Vickers Armstrong, Barrow 22.8.1929. Sunk 1.4.42 by Italian A/C at Malta; raised 9.43 and beached. BU 1957.

PANDOUR Sloop 16, 248bm, 86 x 24 ft, 16-6pdr. French, EUGENIE captured 16.3.1798. Renamed WOLF 1800. BU 3.1802.

PANDOUR 5th Rate 44, 894bm, 134 x 39 ft, Dutch HECTOR captured 28.8.1799 in the Texel. Transferred to the Customs 5.1805 as a store hulk.

PANDOUR (see COSSACK of 1806)

PANGBOURNE (ex-PADSTOW renamed 1918) Minesweeper, later 'Hunt' class. Lobnitz 26.3.1918. Sold 13.3.47.

PAUNCEY (PANSY) Galleon 97, 450bm. Built 1544. Last listed 1557.

PANSY Sloop, 'Arab' class. Hamilton 1.2.1916. Sold 12.1.20 Calcutta Port Commissioners as hulk.

PANSY (see HEARTSEASE)

PANSY Three Drifters requis in WW.I.

PANTALOON Brig 10, 340bm, 92 x 29½ ft. Purchased 5.12.1831. BU 8.1852.

PANTALOON Wood S.sloop, 574bm, 151 x 29 ft, 11-32pdr. Devonport DY 26.9.1860. Sold 18.9.1867 Marshall, Plymouth.

PANTHER 4th Rate, 54, 683bm, 131½ x 34½ ft. Popely, Deptford 3.1703. Rebuilt Woolwich 1716 as 716bm; hulked 1.1743. Sold 26.4.1768.

PANTHER 4th Rate 50, 968bm, 140 x 40 ft. Plymouth DY 24.6.1746. BU 7.1756 at Plymouth.

PANTHER 4th Rate 60, 1,285bm, 154 x 48½ ft. Martin & Henniker, Chatham 22.6.1758. Hospital ship 1791; prison hulk 1807. BU 11.1813.

PANTHER Sloop 14 (Indian), 181bm. Built 1778. Survey vessel in 1802.

PANTHER Destroyer 385 tons, 210½ x 21½ ft, 1-12pdr, 5-6pdr, 2-TT. Laird 21.1.1897. Sold 7.6.1920 J. Kelly.

PANTHER Destroyer 1,540 tons, 338½ x 35 ft, 4-4.7in, 4-TT. Fairfield 28.5.1941. Sunk 9.10.43 by air attack in the Scarpanto Strait.

PANTHER Frigate 2,300 tons. J. Brown Launched 15.3.1957 as BRAHMAPU-TRA (Indian navy).

PANTHER (see GLOUCESTER 1856)

PAPILLON Gun-brig 10, 145bm, 64 x 22½ ft. French, captured 4.9.1803 by VANGUARD in the W.Indies. Foundered 1806 in the Atlantic.

PAPILLON Sloop 16, 345bm, 96 x 29 ft, 14-24pdr carr., 2-6pdr. French, captured 19.12.1809 by ROSAMOND in the W.Indies. Sold 12.10.1815.

PAPUA (ex-HOWETT renamed 1943) Frigate, 'Colony' class. Walsh Kaiser, Providence RI 10.10.43. Returned 13.5.45 to the USN.

PARADOX 14-gun ship, 120bm. Royalist, captured 1649 by Parliament. Sold 1667.

PARAGON (see HENRIETTA MARIA)

PARAGON Destroyer 917 tons, 265 x 26½ ft, 3-4in, 4-TT. Thornycroft 21.2.1913. Sunk 18.3.17 by German destroyer torpedo in the Dover Straits.

PARAGON Drifter requis. in WW.I.

PARAMOUR Pink 6, 89bm, 64 x 18 ft. Deptford 4.1694. Sold 22.8.1706.

PARAPET (ex-LCT.4039 renamed 1956) Tank landing craft 657 tons, 225 x 39 ft. Arrol, Alloa 1945. Sold 1966.

PARIS Battleship 22,189 tons, 541 x 92½ ft. 12-12in, 22-5.5in. French, seized 3.7.1940 at Plymouth. Guardship (Polish crew) 8.40; depot ship completed 7.41. Returned 1945 to the French navy.

PARIS Minelayer 1914. 1774 tons. Requis. 1914-19

PARKER (ex-FROBISHER renamed 1915) Destroyer leader 1,666 tons,

315 x 32 ft, 4-4in, 4-TT. Cammell Laird 19.4.16. Sold 5.11.21 Cashmore, Newport.

PARKES Minesweeper (RAN), 'Bathurst' class. Evans Deakin, Brisbane 30.10.1943. Sold 2.5.57 Hong Kong Rolling Mills to BU.

PARRAMATTA Destroyer (RAN) 700 tons, 246(oa) x 24 ft, 1-4in, 3-12pdr, 3-TT. Fairfield 9.2.1910. Dismantled 10.29 at Sydney; hull later sold G.Rhodes, Cowan, NSW to BU, and foundered 8.12.34 in Hawkesby River,

PARRAMATTA Sloop (RAN) 1,060 tons, 525 x 36 ft, 3-4in. Cockatoo DY 18.6.1939. Sunk 28.11.41 by 'U.559' off Bardia.

PARRAMATTA Frigate (RAN) 2,150 tons, 360 x 41 ft, 2-4.5in, 4-GWS. Cockatoo DY 31.1.1959.

PARRAMATA Trawler requis. in WW.I.

PARRET Frigate, 'River' class. Vickers, Montreal 29.4.1943 on lend-lease. Returned 5.2.46 to the USN.

PARROT Ketch 6,60bm. Chatham DY 1657. Captured 1657 by the French.

PARRSBORO Minesweeper, TE 'Bangor' class. Dufferin 12.7.1941. Sold 1.1.48, BU Hayes, Pembroke Dock.

PARRY SOUND Corvette (RCN), modified 'Flower' class. Midland SB 13.11.1943. Sold 1950, renamed *Olympic Champion*.

PARTHIAN Brig sloop 10, 'Cherokee' class. Barnard, Deptford 13.2.1808. Wrecked 15.5.1828 on the coast of Egypt.

PARTHIAN Wood screw gunvessel, 486bm, 150 x 26 ft. Deptford DY. Ordered 26.3.1846, cancelled 6.1849.

PARTHIAN Wood S.gunboat, 'Albacore' class. Wigram, 8.5.1856. BU completed 14.9.1864.

PARTHIAN Destroyer, 'M' class. Scotts 3.7.1916. Sold 8.11.21 Slough TC; BU in Germany.

PARTHIAN Submarine 1,475 tons, 260 x 30 ft, 1-4in, 8-TT. Chatham DY 22.6.1929. Presumed mined 11.8.43 in the southern Adriatic.

PARTHIAN Trawler requis. 1914-19.

PARTRIDGE Sloop 18, 423bm, 109 x 29½ ft. Avery, Dartmouth 15.7.1809. BU 9.1816.

PARTRIDGE Brig-sloop 10, 'Cherokee' class 235bm. Plymouth DY 22.3.1822. Stranded 28.11.1824 off the Texel.

PARTRIDGE Brig-sloop 10, 'Cherokee' class, 231bm. Pembroke Dock 12.10.1829. Renamed WV.32 on

25.5.1863 as coastguard watch vessel. Sold 2.2.1864 Ransome, Southampton.

PARTRIDGE Wood S.gunboat, 'Albacore' class. Wigram, Northam 29.3.1856. Sold 8.9.1864 Messrs Habgood to BU.

PARTRIDGE Compos. S.gunboat 755 tons, 165 x 30 ft, 6-4in. Devonport DY 10.5.1888. Sold 1909 at Simonstown for Ward, Preston; arrived Preston 6.5.13.

PARTRIDGE Destroyer, 'M' class. Swan Hunter 4.3.1916. Sunk 12.12.17 in action with German destroyers, North Sea.

PARTRIDGE Destroyer 1,540 tons, 338½ x 35 ft, 4-4.7in, 4-TT. Fairfield 5.8.1941. Sunk 18.12.42 by 'U.565' west of Oran.

PARTRIDGE Sloop 1,350 tons, 283 x 38½ ft, 6-4in. Thornycroft. Ordered 9.10.1944, cancelled 10.45.

PARTRIDGE ABV 1461 tons requis. 1914-20.

PASLEY Destroyer, 'M' class. Swan Hunter 15.4.1916. Sold 9.5.21 Ward, Hayle; arrived 9.22.

PASLEY (see ST HELENA)

PASLEY (ex-LINDSAY renamed 1943) Frigate, DE 'Captain' class. Boston N.Yd 30.8.43 on lend-lease. Returned 8.45 to the USN

PATHAN (see Indian TB.3 of 1888)

PATHAN (see PC.69)

PATHFINDER (ex-FASTNET renamed 1903) Scout cruiser 2,940 tons, 370 x 39 ft, 10-12pdr, 8-3pdr. Cammell Laird 16.7.1904. Sunk 5.9.14 by 'U.21' in the North Sea.

PATHFINDER (see ONSLAUGHT)

PATHFINDER (ex-ONSLAUGHT renamed 8.1941) Destroyer 1,540 tons, 338½ x 35 ft, 4-4.7in, 4-TT. Hawthorn Leslie 10.4.41. Damaged 11.2.45 by Japanese A/C at Ramree Island, E. Indies; used for target trials 1947. Arrived 11.48 Howells, Milford Haven to BU.

PATHFINDER Survey vessel (Nigerian), 544 gross, 145 x 27 ft. White, Cowes 23.10.1953.

PATRICIAN Destroyer, 'M' class. 1,004 tons. Thornycroft 5.6.1916. Transferred RCN 9.20. Sold 1929, BU at Esquimalt.

PATRIOT Gunvessel 10. Dutch, captured 1808. Sold 1813.

PATRIOT Destroyer, 'M' class 1,004 tons. Thornycroft 20.4.1916. Transferred RCN 9.20. Sold 1929 Ward, Briton Ferry.

PATROL Scout cruiser 2,940 tons, 370 x 39 ft, 10-12pdr, 8-3pdr. Cammell Laird 13.10.1904. Sold 21.4.20 Machinehandel, Holland.

PATROLLER (ex-*Keeweenaw*) Escort carrier 11,420 tons, 468½ x 36½ ft, 2-4in, 16-40mm, 24-A/C. Seattle Tacoma Co 6.5.1943 on lend-lease. Returned 11.12.46 to the USN.

PATTON (see SARAWAK)

PAUL Carrack. Genoese, captured 25.7.1417. Sold 10.9.1424

PAUL 26-gun ship, 290bm. ex-PAULUS captured 1652. Expended as fireship 12.6.1667 against the Dutch in the Thames.

PAULINA Brig-sloop 16, 287bm, 93 x 26½ ft, 14-24pdr carr., 2-6pdr. Guillaum, Northam 7.12.1805. Sold 30.5.1816.

PAUNCEY (see PANSY 1544)

PAZ Schooner 12, 10-12pdr. Spanish, captured 3.2.1807 at Montevideo. Sold 1814.

PEACE Flyboat 8, 225bm. Captured 1672. Sold 1674.

PEACE Fireship 8, 145bm. Purchased 1678. Sold 1687.

PEACOCK Ship. Captured 1651. Sold 1658.

PEACOCK Brig-sloop 18, 'Cruizer' class, 386bm. Bailey, Ipswich 9.12.1806. Captured 24.2.1831 by the American HORNET and sunk.

PEACOCK Sloop 18, 434bm. American WASP captured 18.10.1812 by POICTIERS in the Atlantic. Foundered 29.8.1814 off the south coast of the USA.

PEACOCK Wood S.gunboat, 'Albacore' class. Pitcher, Northfleet 12.4.1856. BU 3.1869 at Portsmouth.

PEACOCK Compos. S.gunboat 755 tons, 165 x 30 ft, 6-4in. Pembroke Dock 22.6.1888. Sold 15.5.1906 Ellis, Chepstow.

PEACOCK Sloop 1,350 tons, 283 x 38½ ft, 6-4in. Thornycroft 11.12.1943. Arrived 7.5.58 Rosyth to BU.

PEACOCK Patrol vessel 662 tons. Hall Russell 1.12.1982

PEARD (see SEYCHELLES)

PEARL Ship dating from 1625. Captured 14.5.1635 by the French.

PEARL 22-gun ship, 285bm, 103½ x 25 ft. Pett, Ratcliffe 1651. Sunk 6.8.1697 as foundation at Sheerness.

PEARL Sloop 4. Listed 1658. Condemned 1660 in Jamaica.

PEARL Fireship 6, 162bm. Purchased 1673. Lost 1673 in action.

PEARL PRIZE 6th Rate 12, 195bm.

French, captured 1693. Wrecked 17.5.1694 off Goree.

PEARL 4th Rate 42, 559bm, 117 x 33 ft. Burchett, Rotherhithe 5.8.1708. Rebuilt Deptford 1726 as 595bm. Sold 28.6.1744.

PEARL 5th Rate 44, 712bm, 126 x 36 ft. Okill, Liverpool 29.6.1744. Sold 21.6.1759.

PEARL 5th Rate 32, 683bm, 125 x 35½ ft. Chatham DY 27.3.1762. Renamed PROTHEE 19.3.1825, receiving ship. Sold 4.1.1832 Ledger to BU.

PERLEN 5th Rate 38, 1,204bm, 156 x 41½ ft. Danish, captured 7.9.1807 at Copenhagen. Lazaretto 3.1813. Sold 7.1846 J.Brown.(Spelt PEARLEN until 1811, and PERLIN from 1836; was to have been renamed THEBAN 1808.)

PEARL Sloop 20, 558bm, 119 x 33½ ft. Sainty, Wivenhoe 17.3.1828 (to builder's design; cancelled 11.7.25 and resumed 23.2.1826). BU 6.1851.

PEARL (see IMOGENE of 1831)

PEARL Wood S.corvette, 1,469bm, 2,187 tons, 200 x 40½ ft, 20-8in, 1-68pdr. Woolwich DY 13.9.1855. Sold Castle in 8.1884 to BU.

PEARL 2nd class cruiser, 2,575 tons, 265 x 41 ft, 8-47in, 8-3pdr. Pembroke Dock 28.7.1890. Sold 7.1906 at Simonstown; BU Cohen, Felixstowe.

PEARL 2 Trawlers & Drifter WW.1; Trawler 1935-46.

PEARLEN (see under PEARL)

PEDRO Schooner 14. Purchased 1796. Listed to 1803.

PEGASE (see under PEGASUS)

PEGASUS Ship built 1585. Rebuilt 1598. Lost 1599.

PEGASUS Sloop 14, 300bm, 96½ x 27 ft. Chatham DY 27.12.1776. Foundered 10.1777 off Newfoundland.

PEGASUS 6th Rate 28, 594bm, 120½ x 34 ft. Deptford DY 1.6.1779. Sold 28.8.1816.

PEGASE 3rd Rate 74, 1,778bm, 178 x 48 ft. French, captured 21.4.1782 by FOUDROYANT in the Bay of Biscay. Prison ship 1794. BU 12.1815.

PEGASUS 5th Rate 46, 1,063bm, 150 x 40 ft. Ordered 23.7.1817 at Deptford DY, transferred Sheerness 17.2.1825 and re-laid 3.1828. Cancelled 10.1.1831.

PEGASUS (see GREENOCK)

PEGASUS Wood S.sloop, 695bm, 185 x 28½ ft. Woolwich DY Laid down 1.1862, cancelled 12.1863.

PEGASUS Compos. S.sloop 1,130 tons, 170 x 36 ft, 2-7in, 7-64pdr. Devon port DY 13.6.1878. Sold E. Cohen 11.8.1892 to BU.

PEGASUS 3rd class cruiser 2,135 tons, 300 x 36½ ft, 8-4in, 8-3pdr. Palmer 4.3.1897. Sunk 20.9.1914 by the German KONIGSBURG at Zanzibar.

PEGASUS (ex-*Stockholm*) purchased 27.2.1917) Seaplane carrier 3,070 tons, 330 x 43 ft, 4-12pdr, 9-A/C. J.Brown 9.6.17. Sold 22.8.31 Ward, Morecambe.

PEGASUS (see ARK ROYAL of 1914)

PEGASUS Trawler requis. 1917-20.

PEGGY Sloop 8, 141bm, 74½ x 21 ft. Deptford DY 26.7.1749. Listed in 1769.

PEGGY Fireship. Purchased 1804. Expended 2.10.1804 off Boulogne.

PEGGY Drifter requis. 1914-19.

PEGWELL BAY (ex-LOCH MOCHRUM renamed 1944) Frigate, 'Bay' class. Pickersgill 1.9.45. Renamed COOK. survey ship 15.12.47. Sold 2.4.68.

PELARGONIUM Sloop, 'Anchusa' class. Hamilton 18.3.1918. Sold 20.5.21 Clan Line, renamed *Oaxaca*.

PELICAN 18-gun ship (privateer), 100bm. With Drake 1577. Renamed GOLDEN HIND 9.1578. Mentioned in 1662. (Doubtful if ever in the RN).

PELICAN Ship. Captured 1626. Sold 1629.

PELICAN 10-gun ship (Royalist), 100/130bm. In service 1646 to 1648.

PELICAN 38-gun ship, 500bm. Wapping 1650. Burnt 2.1656 by accident at Portsmouth.

PELICAN PRIZE 34-gun ship. Captured 1653. Sold 1655.

PELICAN PRIZE Fireship 8, 200bm. French, captured 7.7.1690 off Dublin. Sunk 26.8.1692 as foundation at Sheerness.

PELICAN (ex-*St George*) Sloop 16, 234bm, 87 x 24½ft. Purchased 28.4.1757. Sold 3.5.1763.

PELICAN Schooner 10, 150bm, 70 x 21½ ft. French privateer captured 1775. Harbour service at Antigua 1776. Renamed EARL OF DENBIGH 1777 Foundered 2.6.1787.

PELICAN 6th Rate 24, 520bm, 114½ x 22 ft. Adams & Barnard, Deptford 24.4.1777. Foundered 2.8.1781 off Jamaica.

PELICAN Brig-sloop 16, 202bm, 85½ x 23½ ft. French privateer FREDERIC captured 8.1781 by EMERALD. Sold 1.5.1783 at Deptford.

PELICAN Brig-sloop 18 (fir-built),

365bm, 96 x 30 ft. Perry, Blackwall 17.6.1795. Sold 1806 in Jamaica.

PELICAN Brig-sloop 16, 328bm, 95½ x 28½ ft, 16-32pdr carr., 2-6pdr. French VOLTIGEUR captured 26.3.1806 by PIQUE in the W.Indies. Sold 16.4.1812 at Deptford.

PELICAN Brig-sloop 18, 'Cruizer' class, 385bm. Davy, Topsham 8.1812. Customs watch vessel 1847; renamed WV.29 on 25.5.1863. Sold 7.6.1865 Fryman, Rye.

PELICAN Wood S.sloop, 952bm, 185 x 33 ft, 5-40pdr, 12-32pdr. Pembroke Dock 19.7.1860. Sold 2.1867 Arthur & Co; renamed *Hawk*; resold Portuguese navy as INFANTA DOM HENRIQUE.

PELICAN Compos. S.sloop 1,130 tons, 170 x 36 ft, 2-7in, 4-64pdr. Devonport DY 26.4.1877. Sold 22.1.1901 Hudsons Bay Co as supply ship. Hulk scuttled 1953.

PELICAN (ex-War Dept vessel *Sir J.Jones*) Tender 100 tons, 77 x 15 ft. Transferred 11.1906. Renamed PETULANT 14.10.16. Sold 23.5.27 B.Zammit, Malta.

PELICAN Destroyer, 'M' class. Beardmore 18.3.1916. Sold 9.5.21 Ward, Briton Ferry. Arrived. Briton Ferry 6.1.23 and Preston 5.24.

PELICAN Sloop 1,200 tons, 276 x 37½ ft, 8-4in. Thornycroft 12.9.1938. Arrived 29.11.58 Ward, Preston.

PELICAN Survey vessel. Cancelled 1967.

PELICAN Two trawlers requis. in WW.I.

PELLEW Destroyer, 'M' class. Beardmore 18.5.1916. Sold 9.5.21 Ward, Briton Ferry; BU 1923.

PELLEW Destroyer 1,710 tons. Cammell Laird. Ordered 4.1942, cancelled and transferred White; renamed CARYSFORT and launched 25.7.44. (qv)

PELLEW Frigate 1,180 tons, 300 x 33 ft, 3-40mm, 4-TT. Swan Hunter 29.9.1954. Sold H.K.Vickers 26.4.71, BU at Fleetwood.

PELORUS Brig-sloop 18, 'Cruizer' class, 385bm. Kidwell, Itchenor 25.6.1808. Sold 10.1841 at Singapore.

PELORUS Wood S.corvette, 1,462bm, 200 x 40 ft, 20-8in, 1-68pdr. Devonport DY 5.2.1857. BU 1869 at Devonport.

PELORUS (see MILDURA)

PELORUS 3rd class cruiser 2,135 tons, 300 x 36½ ft, 8-4in, 8-3pdr. Sheerness DY 15.12.1896. Sold 6.5.1920 Ward, Grays.

PELORUS Minesweeper, 'Algerine' class. Lobnitz 18.6.1943. Renamed PIETERMARITZBURG (S.African navy) 1947.

PELTER Gunvessel 14, 149bm, 75 x 21 ft, Perry, Blackwall 12.5.1794. Sold 10.1802.

PELTER Gun-brig 12, 177bm, 80 x 22½ ft, 10-18pdr carr., 2-12pdr. Dudman, Deptford 25.7.1804. Foundered 12.1809 in the Atlantic.

PELTER Gun-brig 12, 184bm, 84 x 22½ ft, 10-18pdr carr., 2-6pdr. Tucker, Bideford 27.8.1813. Coastguard 1827. Sold 8.8.1862.

PELTER Wood S.gunboat, 218bm, 100 x 22 ft, 1-68pdr, 1-32pdr, 2-24pdr howitzers. Pitcher, Northfleet 26.8.1854. BU completed 1.2.1864 by Tolpult.

PELTER Tank vessel 1867-1905; Tank vessel 1904-46.

PEMBROKE 28-gun ship, 269bm. Woolwich 1655. Sunk 1667 in collision with FAIRFAX off Portland.

PEMBROKE 5th Rate 32, 356bm, 105½ x 27 ft. Deptford 3.3.1690, Captured 12.2.1694 by the French off the Lizard. Wrecked 1694.

PEMBROKE 4th Rate 60, 908bm, 145 x 37½ ft. Snelgrove, Deptford 22.11.1694. Captured 29.12.1709 by the French in the Mediterranean; recaptured 22.3.1711 and foundered.

PEMBROKE 4th Rate 54, 703bm, 130 x 35 ft. Plymouth DY 18.5.1710. BU 8.1726 at Plymouth.

PEMBROKE 4th Rate 60, 956bm, 144 x 39ft. Woolwich DY 27.11.1733. Foundered 1745 in the Medway and raised. Wrecked 13.4.1749 at Fort St David, E.Indies.

PEMBROKE PRIZE Sloop, 196bm, 80 x 23½ ft. Spanish, captured 9.1740. Sold 13.3.1744.

PEMBROKE 4th Rate 60, 1,222bm, 156 x 42 ft. Plymouth DY 2.6.1757. Hulk 7.1776. BU 8.1793 at Halifax NS.

PEMBROKE 3rd Rate 74, 1,758bm, 176 x 48½ ft. Wigram, Wells & Green, Blackwall 27.6.1812. Undocked 3.2.1855 as screw ship; coastguard 1858; base ship Chatham 4.1873; renamed FORTE 1890 receiving hulk. Sold 1905.

PEMBROKE (see DUNCAN of 1859) For ships renamed PEMBROKE, in succession, as nominal base ships at Chatham, see TRENT of 1877, NYMPHE of 1888, ACHILLES of 1863, PRINCE RUPERT of 1915.

PEMBROKE CASTLE (see TILLSONBURG)

PENANG (see MALACCA of 1809)

PENARTH Minesweeper, later 'Hunt' class. Lobnitz 21.5.1918. Sunk 4.2.19 by mine off the East Coast.

PENDENNIS 3rd Rate 70, 1,093bm, 151 x 40 ft. Chatham DY 1679. Wrecked 26.10.1689 on the Kentish Knock.

PENDENNIS 4th Rate 48, 681bm, 130 x 34½ ft. Deptford DY 15.10.1695. Captured 20.10.1705 by the French PROTEE.

PENDENNIS CASTLE Corvette, 'Castle' class. Crown. Cancelled 12.1943.

PENELOPE 6th Rate 24, 524bm, 114½ x 32 ft. Baker, Liverpool 25.6.1778. Captured 10.1780 by her Spanish prisoners.

PENELOPE 5th Rate 32, 721bm, 129 x 36 ft. Barton, Liverpool 27.10.1783. BU 11.1797 at Chatham.

PENELOPE 5th Rate 36, 1,051bm, 150 x 40 ft. Parsons, Bursledon 26.9.1798. Troopship 1813. Wrecked 1.5.1815 in the St. Lawrence.

PENELOPE 5th Rate 46, 1,091bm, 150 x 40½ ft. Chatham DY 13.8.1829 (laid down at Portsmouth and frames transferred to Chatham, relaid 11.1827). Completed 6.1843 as paddle frigate, 1,616bm. Sold 15.7.1864 Castle & Beech to BU.

PENELOPE Armoured corvette, 3,096bm, 4,470 tons, 260 x 50 ft, 8-8in, 3-40pdr. Pembroke Dock 18.6.1867. Coastguard 1869; guardship at the Cape 1891; prison hulk 1897. Sold 12.7.1912 at the Cape. BU at Genoa 1914.

PENELOPE Light cruiser 3,500 tons, 410 x 39 ft, 2-6in, 6-4in. Vickers 25.8.1914. Sold 10.24 Stanlee, Dover.

PENELOPE Tender. Purchased 1918. Sold 4.22 W.Warren.

PENELOPE Cruiser 5,270 tons, 480 x 51 ft, 6-6in, 8-4in. Harland & Wolff 15.10.1935. Sunk 18.2.44 by 'U.410' off Anzio.

PENELOPE Frigate, 'Leander' class. Vickers Armstrong, Tyne 17.8.1962.

PENETANG (ex-ROUYN renamed 1944) Frigate (RCN), 'River' class. Davie SB 6.7.1944. To Norwegian navy 1.56 as DRAUG.

PENGUIN (see DOLPHIN of 1731)

PENGUIN Sloop 8, 35bm, 44 x 14½ ft. Woolwich DY 1772; not completed. BU 1785.

PENGUIN Sloop 16, 336bm, 93 x 29½ ft, 2-18pdr car., 14-9pdr. Dutch KOMEET captured 28.8.1795 by UNICORN off the Irish coast. Sold 27.7.1809.

PENGUIN Brig-sloop 18, 'Cruiser' class. 387bm. Bottomley, Lynn 29.6.1813. Captured 23.3.1815 by the American HORNET off Tristan da Cunha; foundered 24.1.15. (Fought the last action with the USA.)

PENGUIN Packet brig 6, 360bm, 95 x 30½ ft, 6-12pdr. Pembroke Dock 10.4.1838. Coastguard watch vessel 1857; renamed WV.31 on 25.5.1863. Sold 5.6.1871 A.Dockerill.

PENGUIN Wood S.gunvessel, 'Philomel' class. Miller, Liverpool 8.2.1860. Sold 26.2.1870 Lethbridge & Drew to BU.

PENGUIN Compos. S.sloop 1,130 tons, 170 x 36 ft, 2-7in, 4-64pdr. Napier 25.3.1876. Survey ship 1.1890; depot ship at Sydney NSW 1908; to the RAN 18.3.13; sold 1924 Waugh, Sydney and became crane hulk. Burnt 13.12.60.

PENGUIN (see ENCOUNTER of 1902)

PENGUIN (see PLAYTPUS of 1916)

PENGUIN 3 Trawlers requis. in WW.I.

PENLEE POINT (see GIRDLE NESS of 1945)

PENN Destroyer, 'M' class. J. Brown 8.4.1916. Sold 31.10.21 W. & A.T. Burden.

PENN Destroyer 1,540 tons, 338½ x 35 ft, 4-4.7in, 4-TT. Vickers Armstrong, Tyne 12.2.1941. Sold 31.1.50, BU at Troon.

PENNYWORT Corvette, 'Flower' class. Inglis 18.10.1941. Sold 1947; BU 1.49 at Troon.

PENSTON Coastal M/S, 'Ton' class. Cook Welton & Gemmell 9.5.1955. Sold 28.1.70, BU Newhaven.

PENSTEMON Sloop, 'Arabis' class. Workman Clark 5.2.1916. Sold 20.4.20, renamed Lila.

PENSTEMON Corvette, 'Flower' class. Philip 18.1.1941. Sold 1946, renamed Galaxidi.

PENYLAN Destroyer, 'Hunt class. type III. Vickers Armstrong, Barrow 17.3.1942. Sunk 3.12.42 by E-boats in the Channel.

PENZANCE 6th Rate 246bm, 94½ x 25 ft. Ellis, Shoreham 22.4.1695. Ordered to be sold 23.9.1713.

PENZANCE 5th Rate 44, 823bm, 135 x 37½ ft. Chitty & Vernon. Chichester 7.11.1747. Sold 13.5.1766.

PENZANCE Sloop 1,045 tons, 250 x 34 ft, 2-4in. Devonport DY 10.4.1930. Sunk 24.8.40 by 'U.34' south of Greenland.

PEONY Sloop, 'Acacia' class. McMillan, Dumbarton 27.10.1915. Sold 20.8.19, renamed Ardana.

PEONY Corvette, 'Flower' class. Harland & Wolff 4.6.1940. Lent Greek navy 1943 to 9.51 as SAKHTOURIS. Arrived 21.4.52 Clayton & Davie, Dunston to BU.

PERA Wood S.store vessel, 126bm. Purchased 11.1855 at Constantinople. Sold 11.1856 P & O SN Co.

PERDRIX 6th Rate 22, 525bm. French, captured 6.1795 by VANGUARD off Antigua BU 9.1799.

PEREGRINE GALLEY 6th Rate 20, 197bm, 86½ x 23 ft. Sheerness DY 1700. Rebuilt 1733 and 1749 as 229bm; lost 1.1762 in the Atlantic. (Was CAROLINA yacht 1716 and ROYAL CAROLINE 5.1733 to 1749.)

PEREGRINE PRIZE Sloop, 163bm, 76½ x 22½ ft. Spanish, captured 8.1742 Sold. 12.14.1743.

PEREGRINE Destroyer, 'M' class. J. Brown 29.5.1916. Sold 15.11.21 Cashmore, Newport.

PEREGRINE Store carrier requis. 1914-15.

PERIM (ex-PHILLIMORE renamed 1943) Frigate, 'Colony' class. Walsh Kaiser 5.11.1943 on lend-lease. Returned 22.5.46 to the USN. (Was to have been named SIERRA LEONE.)

PERIWINKLE Corvette, 'Flower' class. Harland & Wolff 24.2.1940. Lent USN 15.3.42 to 1945 as RESTLESS. Sold 8.7.46, renamed Perilock.

PERLEN (see PEARL)

PERLIN (see under PEARL)

PERSEUS 6th Rate 20, 432bm, 108 x 30 ft. Randall, Rotherhithe 20.3.1776. Bomb 1799. BU.9.1805 at Sheerness.

PERSEUS 6th Rate 22, 522bm, 118½ x 31½ ft, 22-32pdr carr., 8-18pdr carr., 2-6pdr. Sutton, Ringmore 20.11.1812. Harbour service 5.1818.BU 9.1850 at Deptford.

PERSEUS Wood S.sloop, 955bm, 1,365 tons, 185 x 33 ft, 5-40pdr, 12-32pdr. Pembroke Dock 21.8.1861. Harbour service 1886. Renamed DEFIANCE II in 1904. Sold 26.6.31.

PERSEUS 3rd class cruiser 2,135 tons, 300 x 36½ ft, 8-4in, 8-3pdr. Earle, Hull 15.7.1897. Sold 26.5.1914 Poulson.

PERSEUS Submarine 1,475 tons, 260 x 30 ft, 1-4in, 8-TT. Vickers Armstrong, Barrow 22.5.1929. Sunk 1.12.41 by the Italian S/M ENRICO TOTI off Zante.

PERSEUS (see EDGAR of 1944)

PERSEVERANCE 5th Rate 36, 882bm, 137 x 38½ ft. Randall, Rotherhithe 10.4.1781. Sold 21.5.1823 J. Cristall to BU.

PERSEVERANCE (see INTREPID of 1850)

PERSEVERANCE (ex-Russian *Sobraon* purchased from builder 5.1854) Iron S.troopship, 1,967bm, 273 x 68 ft. Mare, Blackwall 13.7.1854. Wrecked 21.10.1860 in the Cape Verde Islands.

PERSEVERANCE Tug 1875-1911; Tug 1914-23; Tug 1932-60.

PERSIAN Brig-sloop 18, 'Cruizer' class, 390bm. List, Cowes 2.5.1809. Wrecked 16.6.1813 on the Silver Keys.

PERSIAN Brig-sloop 16, 484bm, 105 x 33½ ft, 4-32pdr, 12-32pdr carr. Pembroke Dock 7.10.1839. BU 3.1866 Castle.

PERSIAN (see WALLAROO)

PERSIAN Minesweeper, 'Algerine' class. Redfern 12.2.1943 on lend-lease. Returned 12.46 to the USN.

PERSIMMON M/S sloop, '24' class. Osbourne Graham, Sunderland 4.3.1919. Sold 12.8.20 Moise Mazza but sale cancelled. Sold 13.10.22 Dundas Simpson.

PERSIMMON Landing ship 12,864 tons. 1943-46.

PERSISTENT (see PETARD of 1941)

PERT Brig-sloop 16, 260bm, 84½ x 23 ft, 18-12pdr carr. French privateer BONAPARTE captured 12.11.1804 by CYANE in the W.Indies. Wrecked 16.10.1807 in the W.Indies.

PERT Brig-sloop 18, 239bm, 97 x 24 ft. French SERPENT captured 17.7.1808 by ACASTA off La Guira. BU 10.1813.

PERT Wood S.gunboat, 'Cheerful' class. Young & Magnay, Limehouse 3.4.1856. BU completed 12.3.1864.

PERT Compos. S.gunvesel, 464bm, 155 x 25 ft, 1-7in, 1-64pdr, 2-20pdr. Reid, Glasgow 22.6.1868. Sold 12.1888.

PERT Tank vessel 1896-1907; Tug 1916-62.

PERTH (see AMPHION of 1934)

PERTH GM destroyer (RAN) 3,370 tons, 420 x 47 ft, 2-5in, 2-GWS, 6-TT. Defoe SB, USA 26.9.1963.

PERTH ABS 2060 tons. Requis. 1915-18.

PERUVIAN Brig-sloop 18, 'Cruizer' class. 383bm. Parsons, Warsash 26.4.1808. BU 2.1830.

PESAQUID Frigate (RCN), 'River' class. Victoria BC. Cancelled 8.1943.

PESHAWAR (see MALWA)

PESHAWAR Trawler (RIN) 1942-54.

PESHAWAR Store carrier 1914 requis. 1914-15.

PET Wood S.gunboat, 'Cheerful' class. Pembroke Dock 9.2.1856. Hulked 1865. Sold 12.4.1904 Castle. (Also known as C.17 from 1900.)

PET (ex-War Dept vessel, *Sir Francis Chapman*) Tender 110 tons, 80 x 18 ft. Transferred 11.1906. Sold 13.1.09 at Jamaica.

PETARD Destroyer, 'M' class. Denny 24.3.1916. Sold 9.5.21 Ward; arrived 10.23 at Grays to BU.

PETARD (ex-PERSISTENT renamed 1941) Destroyer 1,540 tons, 338½ x 35 ft, 4-4.7in, 4-TT. Vickers Armstrong, Tyne 27.3.1941. Frigate 1956, 1,800 tons, 2-4in; 5-40mm, 4-TT. BU 1967 McLellan, Bo'ness.

PETER Carrack. Captured from Genoese 25.7.1417. Sold mercantile 10.1424.

PETER POMEGRANATE Ship, 450bm. Built 1510. Rebuilt 1536 as 90-guns, 600bm and renamed PETER. Listed to 1552.

PETER 10-gun vessel, 120bm. Captured 1645. Listed in 1647.

PETER 10-gun vessel. Irish Royalist, captured 1649 by Parliament. Listed to 1652.

PETER 32-gun ship. Captured 1652. Sold 1653.

PETER Flyboat 4, 180bm. Dutch, captured 1665. Sold 1668.

PETERBOROUGH Monitor 1915 (see EARL OF PETERBOROUGH).

PETERBOROUGH Corvette (RCN), modified 'Flower' class. Kingston SY 15.1.1944. Sold Dominican navy 1947 as GERADO JANSEN.

PETERBOROUGH Trawler 1914.

PETEREL (ex-*Duchess of Manchester*) Survey sloop 4, 138bm, 71 x 21½ ft, 4-3pdr. Purchased 4.1777. Sold 28.5.1788.

PETERELL Sloop 16, 365bm, 105 x 28 ft. Wilson, Frindsbury 4.3.1794. Harbour service 1817. Sold 11.7.1827.

PETEREL Schooner 6, 280bm, 95 x 26 ft. Woolwich DY. Ordered 18.7.1829, cancelled 28.2.1831.

PETEREL Packet brig 6, 359bm, 95 x 30½ ft, 6-12pdr. Pembroke Dock 23.5.1838. Sold 11.1.1862 Marshall, Plymouth.

PETEREL Wood S.sloop, 669bm, 913 tons, 160 x 30 ft, 1-40pdr, 6-32pdr, 4-20pdr. Devonport DY 10.11.1860. Coal hulk 12.1885. Sold 1901.

PETEREL Destroyer 370 tons, 215 x 21 ft, 1-12pdr, 5-6pdr, 2-TT. Palmer 30.3.1899. Sold 30.8.1919 TR Sales.

PETEREL River gunboat 310 tons, 177

x 29 ft, 2-3in. Yarrow 18.7.1927. Sunk 8.12.41 by the Japanese cruiser IDZIMO at Shanghai.

PETEREL Patrol vessel 190 tons. Dunston 14.5.1976.

PETERHEAD Minesweeper, TE 'Bangor' class. Blyth 31.10.1940. Sold 1.1.48, BU 5.48 Hayes, Pembroke Dock.

PETERMAN Dogger 6. Captured 1672. Sold 1674.

PETERSFIELD Minesweeper, later 'Hunt' class. Lobnitz 3.3.1919. Wrecked 11.11.31 Tung Yung Island, China coast.

PETERSHAM Inshore M/S, 'Ham' class. M'Lean, Renfrew 12.1.1955. Transferred French navy 1955.

PETROLIA (see LIONESS)

PETROLIA (ex-SHERBORNE CASTLE renamed 1943) Corvette (RCN), 'Castle' class. Harland & Wolff 24.2.44. Sold 1946, renamed *Bharatlaxmi*

PETULANT (see PELICAN of 1906)

PETUNIA Sloop, 'Arabis' class. Workman Clark 3.4.1916. Sold 15.12.22 Batson Syndcate.

PETUNIA Corvette, 'Flower' class. Robb, Leith 19.9.1940. To Chinese navy 1.46 as FU PO. Lost 20.3.47.

PETUNIA Two trawlers requis in WW.I.

PEVENSEY CASTLE Corvette, 'Castle' class. Harland & Wolff 11.1.1944. Transferred Air Ministry 1959. Renamed *Weather Monitor* 12.5.61.

PEYTON Destroyer, 'M' class. Denny 2.5.1916. Sold 9.5.21. Ward, Morecambe.

PEYTON (see TORTOLA)

PHAETON Fireship 8, 263bm, 91½ x 25½ ft. Castle, Deptford 19.3.1961. Burnt 19.5.1692 in action at La Hogue.

PHAETON (ex-*Poole*) Fireship 10, 214bm, 84 x 24½ ft. Purchased 14.9.1739. Sold 22.7.1743.

PHAETON 5th Rate 38, 944bm, 141 x 39 ft. Smallshaw, Liverpool 12.6.1782. Sold 11.7.1827 Freak but retained; sold 26.3.1828 Cristall to BU.

PHAETON 4th Rate 50, 1,942bm, 185 x 49½ ft, 8-8in, 42-32pdr. Deptford DY 25.11.1848. Undocked 12.12.1859 as screw frigate, 2,396bm. BU 1875 at Chatham.

PHAETON Despatch vessel (2nd class cruiser) 4,300 tons, 300 x 46 ft, 10-6in. Napier 27.2.1883. Sold 1913 as training ship *Indefatigable*, renamed 1.1.14. (see CARRICK II).

PHAETON Light cruiser 3,500 tons, 410 x 39 ft, 2-6in, 6-4in. Vickers. 21.10.1914. Sold 16.1.23 King, Troon.

PHAETON (see SYDNEY of 1934)

PHEASANT Sloop 14, 291bm. 106 x 25 ft, 14-6pdr. French FAISAN captured 4.1761 by ALBANY. Foundered 8.1761 in the Channel.

PHEASANT Cutter 12, 149bm, 66 x 24 ft, 12-4pdr. Purchased 3.1778. Capsized 20.6.1781 in the Channel

PHEASANT Sloop 18, 365bm, 106 x 30 ft. Edwards, Shoreham 17.4.1798. Sold 11.7.1827 Ledger to BU.

PHEASANT Sloop 18, 481bm, 116 x 31 ft. Plymouth DY. Ordered 30.1.1829, cancelled 1.11.1832.

PHEASANT Wood S.gunboat, 'Albacore' class. Pitcher, Northfleet 1.5.1856. BU 8.1877 at Sheerness.

PHEASANT Compos. S.gunboat 755 tons, 165x 30 ft, 6-4in. Devonport DY 10.4.1888. Sold 15.5.1906 Cox. Falmouth.

PHEASANT Destroyer, 'M' class. Fairfield 23.10.1916. Sunk 1.3.17 by mine off the Orkneys.

PHEASANT Sloop 1,350 tons, 283 x 38½ ft, 6-4in. Yarrow 21.12.1942. Arrived 15.1.63 Troon to BU.

PHILLIMORE (see PERIM)

PHILIP Ship 130bm Purchased 3.1414. Sold 10.4.1418.

PHILIP & MARY Galleon 44, 550bm. Built 1556. Rebuilt 1584 and renamed NONPAREIL, 600bm, 2-60pdr, 3-34pdr, 7-18pdr, 8-9pdr, 12-6pdr, 24smaller. Rebuilt 1603 as NONSUCH, 619bm. Sold circa 1645.

PHILOCTETES Depot ship 13,980 tons, 507 x 63 ft, 4-4in. Purchased 8.1940 and completed Belfast 6.1.42. Sold 22.1.48. BU Cashmore, Newport. 11.48.

PHILOMEL Brig-sloop 18, 'Cruizer' class, 384bm. Boole, Bridport 11.9.1806. Sold 30.4.1817 Manlove.

PHILOMEL Brig-sloop 10, 'Cherokee' class. Portsmouth DY 28.4.1823. Sold 12.12.1833.

PHILOMEL Brig 8, 360bm, 95 x 30 ft, 8-18pdr. Devonport DY 28.3.1842. Coastguard watch vessel 1857; renamed WV.23 on 25.5.1863. Foundered 1869 in the Swale and sold 2.1870 Hayhurst & Clasper to salve and BU.

PHILOMEL Wood S.gunvessel, 'Philomel' class. White 10.3.1860. Sold 2.6.1865 White, Cowes to BU.

PHILOMEL Wood S.gunvessel, 64bm,

774 tons, 170 x 29 ft. Deptford DY 29.10.1867. Sold 14.4.1886.

PHILOMEL 2nd class cruiser 2,575 tons, 265 x 41 ft, 8-7in, 8-3pdr. Devonport DY 28.8.1890. Base ship at Wellington NZ 3.1921. Sold 17.1.47 Strongman & Co; hulk scuttled 6.8.49 off the east coast of New Zealand.

PHIPPS Schooner 14. Dutch (TWO LYDIAS?) captured 1808. BU 12.1812.

PHLEGETHON Iron paddle gunvessel (Indian), 510bm. Laird 1839. Listed in 1853.

PHLOX Corvette, 'Flower' class. Robb, Leith. 16.1.1942. Renamed LOTUS 4.42. Sold 1947.

PHOEBE 5th Rate 36, 926bm, 143 x 38½ ft. Dudman, Deptford 29.9.1795. Slop ship 10.1826. Sold 27.5.1841 J. Cristall to BU.

PHOEBE 4th Rate 51, 2,044bm, 180 x 52 ft, 10-8in, 1-68pdr, 40-32pdr. Devonport DY 12.4.1854. Undocked 10.4.1860 as screw frigate, 2,96bm. BU 1875 Castle.

PHOEBE 2nd class cruiser 2,575 tons, 265 x 41 ft, 8-4.7in, 8-3pdr. Devonport DY 1.7.1890. Sold 10.7.1906 A.Anderson, Copenhagen.

PHOEBE Destroyer, 'M' class. Fairfield 20.11.1916. Sold 15.11.21 Cashmore, Newport.

PHOEBE Cruiser 5,450 tons, 485 x 50½ ft, 10-5.25in, Fairfield 25.3.1939. Arrived 1.4.56 Hughes Bolckow, Blyth.

PHOEBE Frigate, 'Leander' class. Stephen 8.7,1964.

PHOEBE Two Trawlers requis in WW.I.

PHOENIX 20-gun ship, 60bm. Purchased 1546. Rebuilt 1558 as 70bm. Sold 1573.

PHOENIX 20-gun ship, 246bm. Chatham 27.2.1613. Listed to 1624.

PHOENIX 38-gun ship, 414bm. Woolwich 1847. Wrecked 1664. (In Dutch hands 7.9.52 to 26.11.52.)

PHOENIX Ship, 780bm. Dutch, captured 1665. Sunk 6.1667 as blockship in the Thames.

PHOENIX 5th Rate 42, 368bm, Portsmouth DY 1671. Burnt 12.4.1692 near Malaga to avoid capture by the French.

PHOENIX Bomb 8, 86bm, 55 x 19½ ft. Purchased 1692. Sold 3.5.1698.

PHOENIX Fireship 8, 256bm, 91 x 25½ ft. Dalton & Gardner, Rotherhithe 16.3.1694. Rebuilt Plymouth 1709 as 6th Rate 24, 273bm; rebuilt Woolwich 1727 as 376bm, 106 x 28 ft; hulked 1742. Sold 28.6.1744.

PHOENIX 6th Rate 24, 514bm, 112½ x 32½ ft. Graves, Limehouse 27.7.1743. Hospital hulk 1755. Sold 9.12.1762.

PHOENIX 5th Rate 44, 856bm, 141 x 37 ft. Batson, Limehouse 25.6.1759. Foundered 4.10.1780 in a hurricane off Cuba.

PHOENIX 5th Rate 36, 884bm, 137 x 38½ ft. Parsons, Bursledon 15.7.1783. Wrecked 20.2.1816 near Smyrna.

PHEONIX Wood pad. sloop, 802bm. Chatham DY 25.9.1832 (originally ordered 1.1831 at Woolwich). Converted to screw sloop 1845, 809bm, 174½ x 32ft. Sold 26.1.1864 Castle.

PHOENIX Compos. S.sloop 1,124 tons, 170 x 36 ft, 2-7in, 4-64pdr. Devonport DY 16.9.1879. Wrecked 12.9.1882 on Prince Edward Island.

PHOENIX (see TAURANGA)

PHOENIX Sloop 1,050 tons, 185 x 32½ ft, 6-4in. Devonport DY 25.4.1895. Capsized 18.9.1906 in a typhoon at Hong Kong; raised, sold 7.1.07.

PHOENIX Destroyer 765 tons, 246 x 26 ft, 2-4in, 2-12pdr, 2-TT. Vickers 9.10.1911. Sunk 14.5.18 by the Austrian S/M U.XXVII in the Adriatic.

PHOENIX Submarine 1,457 tons, 260 x 30 ft, 1-4in, 8-TT. Cammell Laird 3.10.1929. Sunk 17.7.40 by the Italian torpedo boat ALBATROS off Sicily.

PHOSPHORUS (ex-Dutch *Haasje*) Fireship 4, 115bm, 4-12pdr carr. Purchased 6.1804. Sold 24.3.1810.

PHOSPHORUS Drifter 1918-19.

PICKLE (see STING of 1800)

PICKLE (see ELCAIR of 1801)

PICKLE Schooner 5, 118bm, 68 x 21 ft. Bermuda 1827. BU 1847 Bermuda.

PICKLE Brig 168bm. Slaver *Eolo* captured 1852 by ORESTES. Listed to 1854.

PICKLE Mortar vessel, 155bm, 70 x 23½ ft, 1-13in mortar Mare, Blackwall 23.5.1855. Renamed MV.22 on 19.10.1855. BU completed 20.10.1865 by Marshall, Plymouth.

PICKLE Wood S.gunboat, 'Albacore' class. Pitcher. Northfleet 3.5.1856. BU completed 12.4.1864.

PICKLE Iron S.gunboat, 'Ant' class. Campbell Johnston, N.Woolwich 15.11.1872. Made a DY lighter 1906.

PICKLE Minesweeper, 'Algerine' class. Harland & Wolff 3.8.1943. To Ceylon navy 6.4.59 as PARAKARAMA. BU 1964.

PICKLE Whaler (ex German) 1914-20.

PICOTEE Corvette, 'Flower' class. Harland & Wolff 19.7.1940. Sunk 12.8.41 by 'U.568' off Iceland.

PICTON (see LLEWELLYN)

PICTON Monitor 1915 (see SIR THOMAS PICTON).

PICTON Coastal M/S, 'Ton' class. Cook, Welton & Gemmell, Selby 20.10.1955. Sold S. Bkg (Queenborough) Ltd 28.7.69.

PICTOU (ex-*Bonne Foi*) Brig-sloop 16, 215bm, 83 x 25 ft. captured 20.4.1813. Captured 14.2.1814 by the American CONSTITUTION.

PICTOU (ex-*Zebra*) Schooner 14, 283bm. Purchased 1814. Sold 13.8.1818 Mr Hughes.

PICTOU Corvette (RCN), 'Flower' class. Davie SB, Lauzon 5.10.1940. Sold 1949, renamed *Olympic Chaser*.

PIEMONTAISE 5th Rate 38, 1,093bm. French, captured 8.3.1808 by ST FIORENZO off Ceylon. BU 1.1813 at Woolwich.

PIEMONTAISE (see PRESIDENT of 1806)

PIERCER Gunvessel 16, 147bm, 75 x 21 ft. King, Dover 6.1794. Sold 30.5.1802.

PIERCER Gun-brig 12, 178bm, 80 x 22½ ft, 10-18pdr carr., 2-12pdr. Ayles, Topsham 29.7.1804. Presented 6.1814 to the Government of Hanover as a guardship.

PIGEON Schooner 4, 85bm. Purchased 1804. Wrecked 11.1805 in the Texel.

PIGEON (ex-*Fanny*) Schooner. Purchased 1805. Lost 1805 (may be above vessel).

PIGEON Schooner 4, 75bm, 56 x 18½ ft, 4-12pdr carr. Custance, Yarmouth 26.4.1806. Wrecked 15.1.1809 near Margate.

PIGEON (see VARIABLE of 1827)

PIGEON (ex-*Brothers*) Wood pad. tender. Purchased 15.8.1854 at Constantinople. Sold there in 7.1856.

PIGEON Wood. S.gunboat, 'Britomart' class. Briggs, Sunderland 7.6.1860. BU 29.9.1876 at Devonport.

PIGEON Compos. S.gunboat 755 tons, 165 x 30 6-4in. Pembroke Dock 5.9.1888. Sold 15.5.1906 V Grech, same name.

PIGEON Destroyer, 'M' class. Hawthorn Leslie 3.3.1916. Sold 9.5.21 Ward, New Holland.

PIGEON Trawler requis. 1914-19.

PIGMY Cutter 12, 181bm, 69½ x 25½ ft. 12-4pdr. King, Dover 2.1781. Captured 22.12.1781 by the French when ashore near Dunkirk; recap-

tured 7.1782 in the Channel and renamed LURCHER 31.5.1783; reverted to PIGMY 7.1783. Wrecked 16.12.1793 on the Motherbank.

PIGMY (see RANGER of 1779)

PIGMY (see MUTINE of 1779)

PIGMY Gun-brig 14, circa 200bm. Purchased 1806. Wrecked 2.3.1807 near Rochefort.

PIGMY (see RANGER of 1806)

PIGMY Schooner 10, 197bm, 83 x 23 ft, 10-12pdr carr. King, Upnor 24.2.1810. Cutter 1819. Sold 21.5.1823 Cristall.

PIGMY (ex-GPO vessel *Sybil*) Wood pad. packet, 227bm, 114½ x 21 ft. Transferred 4.1837. BU 1879 at Portsmouth.

PIGMY Compos.S.gunboat 755 tons, 165 x 30 ft, 6-4in. Sheerness DY 27.7.1888. Sold 4.4.1905 Cox, Falmouth.

PIGMY (ex-*Sir Lothian Nicholson*, War Dept vessel) Tender 100 tons. Transferred 1905. BU 1938.

PIGMY (ex-Polish ISKRA renamed 1940) Depot ship 560 tons, 128 x 35 ft. Reverted to ISKRA 1941.

PIGOT Galley 8, 8-2pdr. Purchased 7.1778 in North America. Captured 28.10.1778 by Americans at Rhode Island.

PIKE Schooner 4, 78bm, 56 x 18 ft, 4-12pdr car. Bermuda 1804. Captured 20.4.1807 by the French privateer MARAT.

PIKE Cutter 10. In service 1809-11.

PIKE Schooner, 14, 251bm, 93 x 24½ ft. 12-12pdr carr., 2-6dpr. American DART captured 1813. Wrecked 5.2.1836 coast of Jamaica.

PIKE (ex-GPO vessel *Spitfire*) Wood pad. packet, 111bm, 89 x 16 ft. Transferred 1837. BU 7.1868.

PIKE Iron S.gunboat, 'Ant' class. Campbell Johnston, N.Woolwich 16.10.1872. BDV 1908. Sold 27.3.20 G.Sharpe.

PILCHARD Schooner 4, 78bm, 56 x 18 ft, 4-12dpr carr. Bermuda 1805. Sold 23.2.1813.

PILFORD (see PITCAIRN)

PILOT Brig-sloop 14, 218b, 78½ x 26 ft, 14-4pdr. French cutter PILOTE captured 2.10.1779 by JUPITER. Sold 5.1799.

PILOT Brig-sloop 18, 'Cruizer' class. 383bm. Guillaum, Northam 6.8.1807. Sold 26.3.1828 Adam Gordon.

PILOT Brig-sloop 16, 485bm, 105 x 33½ ft, 12-32pdr carr., 4-3pdr. Plymouth DY 9.6.1838. Sold 11.1.1862 Marshall, Plymouth.

PILOT Training brig 8, 501 tons, 105 x 33½ x ft. Pembroke Dock 12.11.1879. Sold 2.10.1907 Adrien Merveille, Dunkirk; resold and BU in Holland.

PILOT Tug 1909-60.

PIMPERNEL Corvette, 'Flower' class. Harland & Wolff 16.11.1940. Sold 6.2.48, BU at Portaferry 10.48.

PIMPERNEL Drifter requis. 1915-19.

PINCHER (Gunboat No.39) (ex-*Two Sisters*) Gunvessel 12, 160bm, 74 x 22½ ft, 2-24pdr, 10-18pdr carr. Purchased 3.1797 at Leith. Sold 4.1802.

PINCHER Gun-brig 12, 180bm, 80½ x 22½ ft, 10-18pr carr., 2-12pdr. Graham, Harwich 28.8.1804. Sold 17.5.1816.

PINCHER Schooner 5, 118bm, 69 x 21 ft. Bermuda 1827. Capsized 6.3.1838 off the Owers; raised; sold 31.8.1838.

PINCHER Wood S.gunboat 216bm, 100 x 22 ft, 1-68pdr, 1-32pdr, 2-24pdr howitzers. Pitcher, Northfleet 5.9.1854. BU completed 17.2.1864.

PINCHER Iron S.gunboat 265 tons, 85 x 26 ft, 1-10in. Pembroke Dock 5.5.1879. Sold 11.7.1905 at Portsmouth.

PINCHER Destroyer 975 tons, 267½ x 28 ft, 1-4in, 3-12pdr, 2-TT. Denny 15.3.1910. Wrecked 24.7.18 on the Seven Stones.

PINCHER Minesweeper, 'Algerine' class. Harland & Wolff 19.8.1943. Arrived 7.3.62 Clayton & Davie, Dunston.

PINEHAM Inshore M/S, 'Ham' class. McLean, Renfrew 9.5.1955. Transferred French Navy 10.11.55.

PINK Corvette, 'Flower' class. Robb 16.2.1942. Torpedoed 27.6.44 and not repaired. BU 1947 Rees, Llanelly.

PINNER (see FITZROY)

PINTAIL Patrol vessel 580 tons, 224 x 251½ ft, 1-4in. Denny 18.8.1939. Sunk 10.6.41 by mine off the Humber.

PINTAIL. Trawler 1914-19; Mooring vessel 1963.

PIONEER Gun-brig 12. Listed 1804-07.

PIONEER Cutter 12, 197bm, 83 x 23 ft, 10-12pdr carr., 2-6pdr. King, Upnor 10.3.1810. Schooner 1813; cutter 1819; coastguard 4.1824. Sold 4.9.1849 at Plymouth.

PIONEER (ex-*Eider*) Wood S.discovery vessel, 342bm. Purchased 2.3.1850. Abandoned 1854 in the Arctic; name removed from the list 25.10.1854.

PIONEER Wood S.gunvessel, 868bm, 200 x 30½ ft, 1-110pdr, 1-60pdr, 2-40pdr. Pembroke Dock 19.1.1856. BU 1865 Marshall, Plymouth.

PIONEER Iron pad. gunboat (Australian), 140 x 20 ft, 2-12pdr. Russell, Sydney 1862. Fate unknown.

PIONEER Wood pad. survey vessel, 142bm. Transferred from Colonial Office 1864. Sold 1873 at Fernando Po.

PIONEER Compos. paddle vessel 576 tons, 160 x 25½ ft, 6-20pdr. Blumer, Sunderland 26.10.1874. BU 1888.

PIONEER River gunboat 40 tons, 75 x 12½ ft, 1-3pdr. Yarrow 1892. Transferred BCA government 1.1894.

PIONEER 3rd class cruiser 2,200 tons, 305 x 36½ ft, 8=4in 8-3pdr. Chatham DY 26.6.1899. To the RAN 28.12.12. Sold 1926 at Sydney; hull scuttled 19.2.31 off Sydney.

PIONEER (see MARS of 1944)

PIONEER Yacht and Drifter requis. WW.1.

PIORUN (see NERISSA of 1940)

PIQUE 5th Rate 38, 906bm. French, captured 6.1.1795 by BLANCHE in the W.Indies. Wrecked 29.6.1798 on the French Channel coast while in action with the French SEINE.

PIQUE 5th Rate 36, 1,028bm, 146½ x 39½ ft. French PALLAS captured 6.2.1800 by a squadron on the French coast. Sold 22.7.1819 Freake to BU

PIQUE 5th Rate 46, 1,215bm, 159 x 42 ft. Plymouth DY. Ordered 9.6.1825 cancelled 16.6.1832.

PIQUE 5th Rate 36, 1,633bm, 160 x 49 ft, 36-32pdr. Plymouth DY 21.7.1834. Receiving ship 1872; lent as hospital hulk 30.3.1882. Sold 12.7.1910 Cox, Falmouth.

PIQUE 2nd class cruiser 3,600 tons, 300 x 43½ ft, 2-6in, 6-4.7in, 8-6pdr. Palmer 13.12.1890. Sold 9.5.1911 F.E.Rudge.

PIQUE Destroyer 1,710 tons. Cammell Laird. Ordered 4.1942, cancelled 11.42 and transferred White, renamed CAVALIER. (qv)

PIQUE (ex-CELERITY renamed 1942) Minesweeper, 'Catherine' class. Associated SB, Seattle 26.10.42 on lend-lease. Returned 1946 to the USN and transferred Turkish navy 4.47 as EREGLI.

PIRIE Minesweeper, 'Bathurst' class. Broken Hill 3.12.1941. Lent RAN 10.42. Sold 8.46 Turkish navy as AMASRA.

PIROUETTE Minesweeper 290 tons, 130 x 26 ft, 1-3pdr. ex-War Dept tug transferred on stocks 1917. Rennie Forrest, Wivenhoe 1.11.17. Returned War Dept 1920.

PIROUETTE Trawler 1940-46.

PITCAIRN (ex-PILFORD renamed 1943) Frigate, 'Colony' class. Walsh Kaiser 15.10.43 on lend-lease. Returned 6.46 to the USN.

PITT Cutter, 100bm, 59 x 20½ ft. Purchased 1.1763. Foundered 5.8.1766 in the Atlantic.

PITT Schooner 12. Purchased 1805. Renamed SANDWICH 1807. BU 10.1809. (Listed in 1.1810.)

PITT (see SALSETTE)

PITT 3rd Rate 74, 1.751bm, 176 x 48½ ft. Portsmouth DY 13.4.1816. Coal hulk 1853. BU completed 17.3.1877 at Portsmouth.

PITT Screw 2nd Rate 91, 3,716bm, 252 x 57½ ft. Chatham DY. Ordered 5.3.1860, cancelled 12.12.1863.

PITT (see TRAFALGAR of 1820)

PITTINGTON (see ALDINGTON)

PLACENTIA Sloop 14. Purchased 1779. Wrecked 1782 off Newfoundland.

PLACENTIA Brig-sloop 6, 42bm, 45 x 15 ft. Jeffery & Street, Newfoundland 1790. Wrecked 8.5.1794 Newfoundland.

PLANET River gunboat (Indian), 397bm. Bombay DY 1840. Listed in 1863.

PLANET BDV 1938-58.

PLANTAGENET 3rd Rate 74, 1,777bm, 181 x 47 ft. Woolwich DY 22.10.1801. BU 5.1817.

PLANTAGENET BDV 1939-59.

PLASSY (see PUNJAUB of 1854)

PLASSY Torpedo gunboat (RIM) 735 tons, 230 x 27 ft, 2-4.7in, 3-TT. Armstrong 5.7.1890. Sold 17.5.1904.

PLATYPUS Depot ship (RAN) 3,476 tons, 310 x 44 ft. J. Brown 28.10.1916. Renamed PENGUIN 16.8.29; reverted to PLATYPUS 3.41 Sold 20.2.58 to BU in Japan.

PLATYPUS II (see CERBERUS of 1868)

PLAY PRIZE 5th Rate 30, 367bm, 97½ x 28 ft. French, captured 1689. Sunk 4.8.1697 at Harwich 'to secure the graving place'.

PLESSISVILLE Frigate (RCN), 'River' class. G.T. Davie. Cancelled 1944.

PLOVER 26-gun ship. Dutch MORGEN STAR captured 1652. Sunk 2.1653 in action (or sold 1657).

PLOVER Sloop 18, 422bm, 110 x 30 ft. Betts, Mistleythorn 23.4.1796 Sold 8.3.1819 Young, Limehouse.

PLOVER Brig-sloop 10, 'Cherokee' class, 237bm. Portsmouth DY 30.6.1821. Sold 27.5.1841 Cristall.

PLOVER (ex-*Bentinck*) Survey cutter, 237bm. Purchased 2.1842. Sold 24.11.1854 at San Francisco.

PLOVER Wood S.gunboat, 'Albacore' class. Pitcher, Northfleet 8.9.1855. Sunk 25.6.1859 in action with the Pei Ho forts, China.

PLOVER Wood S.gunvessel, 'Philomel' class. Green, Blackwall, 19.1.1860. Sold 12.9.1865, renamed *Hawk*.

PLOVER Wood S.gunvessel, 663bm, 805 tons, 170 x 29 ft, 1-7in, 2-40pdr. Deptford DY 20.2.1867. Sold Castle 8.1885 to BU

PLOVER Compos. S.gunboat 755 tons, 165 x 30 ft, 6-4in. Pembroke Dock 18.10.1888. BDV 1904. Sold 47.4.27 at Gibraltar.

PLOVER Destroyer, 'M' class. Hawthorn Leslie 19.4.1916. Sold 9.5.21 Ward, Hayle.

PLOVER Minelayer 805 tons, 180 x 37½ ft, 1-12pdr. Denny 8.6.1937. Sold 26.2.69, BU at Inverkeithing.

PLOVER Patrol vessel 662 tons Hall Russell 12.4.1983

PLUCKY Steam tender, 212bm. Purchased 1856. Sold 1858.

PLUCKY Iron S.gunboat, 196bm, 213 tons, 80 x 25 ft, 1-9in. Portsmouth DY 13.7.1870. Renamed BANTERER 6.1915. Sold 1928.

PLUCKY Destroyer, 'M' class. Scotts 21.4.1916. Sold 9.5.21 Ward, Briton Ferry; arrived 5.24 Preston.

PLUCKY Minesweeper, 'Algerine' class. Harland & Wolff 29.9.1943. Arrived 15.3.62 Clayton & Davie, Dunston.

PLUMPER Gunvessel 12, 149bm, 74 x 21 ft. Randall, Rotherhithe 17.5.1794. Sold 1.1802.

PLUMPER Gun-brig 12, 178bm, 81 x 22 ft. Dudman, Deptford 7.9.1804. Captured 16.7.1805 by the French off St Malo.

PLUMPER Gun-brig 12, 177bm, 80 x 22½ ft. Halifax NS 29.12.1807. Wrecked 5.12.1812 in the Bay of Fundy.

PLUMPER Gun-brig 12, 181bm, 84 x 22½ ft. Good, Bridport 9.10.1813. Sold 12.12.1833.

PLUMPER Wood S.sloop, 490bm, 140 x 27½ft. Portsmouth DY 5.4.1848. Sold 2.6.1865 White, Cowes.

PLUMPER Tug 1891-1910.

PLUMPTON Paddle M/S, 'Ascot' class. McMillan 20.3.1916. Sunk 19.10.18.

by mine off Ostend.

PLUTO (ex-*Roman Emperor*) Fireship 8, 272bm, 92 x 26 ft. 14-4pdr. Purchased 21.8.1745. Sold 10.9.1747.

PLUTO (ex-*New Concord*) Fireship 8, 270bm, 86 x 27 ft. Purchased 31.12.1756. Sold 23.12.1762.

PLUTO (see TAMAR of 1758)

PLUTO Fireship 14, 426bm, 109 x 30 ft. Stewart, Sandgate 1.2.1782. Sold 19.7.1817 Warwick.

PLUTO Wood pad. gunvessel, 365bm, 135 x 24 ft. Woolwich DY 28.4.1831. BU 3.1861.

PLUTO Minesweeper, 'Algerine' class. Port Arthur SY 21.10.1944. Sold 13.9. 72, BU Dalmuir.

PLYM Gunvessel ex-hired packet brig. Fitted out 10.1795. Sold 9.1802.

PLYM Frigate, 'River' class. Smiths Dk 4.2.1943. Expended 3.10.52 in atomic tests at Monte Bello Islands.

PLYMOUTH 60-gun ship, 752bm, 140 x 34½ ft. Taylor, Wapping 1653. Rebuilt Blackwall 1705 as 900bm, 64 guns. Foundered 11.8.1705.

PLYMOUTH Sheer hulk, 524bm, 121 x 32 ft. Purchased 19.5.1689. BU 1730.

PLYMOUTH TRANSPORT Storeship, 109bm, 70 x 19 ft. Plymouth DY 1704. Rebuilt Shoreham 1742 as 160bm. Sold 1806.

PLYMOUTH 4th Rate 60, 922bm, 144 x 38 ft. Plymouth DY 25.5.1708. Rebuilt Chatham 1722 as 955bm. BU completed 3.4.1764 at Portsmouth.

PLYMOUTH PRIZE 6th Rate 16, 134bm. Captured 19.7.1709. Captured 21.12.1709 by the French off Scilly.

PLYMOUTH Yacht 6, 88bm, 64½ x 18 ft, 6-2pdr. Plymouth DY 1755. BU 9.1793 at Plymouth.

PLYMOUTH Transport 8 Built 1786. Sold 14.12.1815.

PLYMOUTH Yacht 8, 96bm, 64 x 18½ ft. Plymouth DY 2.11.1796. BU 7.1830.

PLYMOUTH (see ADMIRALTY of 1814)

PLYMOUTH Frigate 2,150 tons, 360 x 41 ft, 2-4.5in, 1-40mm. Devonport DY 20.7.1959.

PLYMOUTH Transport, 64bm, 51½ x 17 ft. Plymouth 1778. Sunk 1815 as breakwater.

POCAHONTAS Sloop 14, 242bm, 91 x 25½ ft. Purchased at New York 2.10.1780. Condemned 26.7.1782 (also listed as PACAHUNTA).

POCHARD Paddle M/S. Ailsa, Troon. Cancelled 1918.

POCHARD Trawler requis. 1918-19.

PODARGUS Brig-sloop 14, 254bm, 92 x 25½ ft, 12-24pdr carr., 2-6pdr. Portsmouth DY 26.5.1808. Sold 7.8.1833 Ledger, Rotherhithe to BU.

POICTIERS 3rd Rate 74, 1,765bm, 176½ x 48½ ft. King, Upnor 9.12.1809. Bu completed 23.3.1857 at Chatham.

POICTIERS Destroyer 2,380 tons, 355 x 40 ft, 5-4.5in, 8-40mm, 10- TT. Hawthorn Leslie 4.1.1946; not completed. BU 4.46 at Sunderland.

POINTE CLAIRE (see MERRITTONIA)

POLACCA Sloop 12, 146bm, 67½ x 22 ft. French, captured 1756. BU 1761.

POLARIS Minesweeper, 'Algerine' class. Port Arthur SY 13.12.1944. Arrived 26.9.56 Ward, Briton Ferry to BU.

POLECAT Brig-sloop 14. Purchased 1782. Captured 1782 by the French in N.America.

POLLINGTON Coastal M/S, 'Ton' class. Camper & Nicholson 10.10.1957. Renamed MERSEY 10.59 to 1975.

POLLUX Radar training ship 2,461 tons, 200 x 50½ ft. French minelayer seized 3.7.40 at Portsmouth. Returned 1946 to the French navy.

POLPERRO (see PONTYPOOL)

POLRUAN Minesweeper, turbine 'Bangor' class. Ailsa 18.7.1940. BU 1950 at Sunderland.

POLSHAM Inshore M/S, 'Ham' class. Morgan Giles 13.10.1958. Sold to the P.L.A. in 2.1967, renamed *Maplin*.

POLYANTHUS Sloop, 'Anchusa' class. Lobnitz 24.9.1917. Sold 20.5.21 Clan Line, renamed *Colima*.

POLYANTHUS Corvette, 'Flower' class. Robb 30.11.1940. Sunk 20.9.43 by U-boat south of Greenland.

POLYPHEMUS 3rd Rate 64, 1,409bm, 160 x 45 ft, Sheerness DY 27.4.1782. Powder hulk 9.1813. BU completed 15.9.1827 at Chatham.

POLYPHEMUS Wood pad. sloop, 801bm, 164 x 33 ft, 5-32pdr. Chatham DY 28.9.1840. Wrecked 29.1.1856 coast of Jutland.

POLYPHEMUS Torpedo ram 2,640 tons, 240 x 40 ft, 2-pdr, 5-TT. Chatham DY 15.6.1881. Sold 7.7.1903 Cohen.

POLYPHEMUS (see SOUTHMAPTON of 1936)

POLYPHEMUS A/C carrier 18,300 tons, 650 x 90 ft. Devonport DY. Cancelled 10.1945.

POMONA Sloop 18, 364bm, 108 x 27½

ft, 18-6pdr. French CHEVERT captured 30.1.1761. Wrecked 8.1776 in a hurricane in the W. Indies.

POMONA 6th Rate 28, 594bm, 120½ x 33 ft. Raymond, Northam 22.9.1778. Renamed AMPHITRITE 14.7.1795. BU 8.1811.

POMONA Trawler requis. 1914-19.

POMONE 5th Rate 44, 1,239bm, 159 x 42 ft, 18-32pdr carr., 26-24pdr, 2-9pdr. French, captured 23.4.1794 by a squadron off Ile Bas. BU 12.1802.

POMONE 5th Rate 38, 1,076bm, 150 x 40 ft. Brindley, Findsbury 17.1.1805. Wrecked 14.10.1811 on the Needles.

POMONE (see ASTREE of 1810)

POMONE Wood S.frigate, 3,027bm, 250 x 52 ft. Chatham DY. Ordered 5.3.1860, cancelled 12.1863.

POMONE 3rd class cruiser 2,135 tons, 300 x 36½ ft, 8-4in, 8-3pdr. Sheerness DY 25.11.1897. Training hulk 1.1910. Sold 25.10.22 J.H.Lee, Dover.

POMPEE 3rd Rate 80, 1,901bm, 182 x 49 ft. French, captured 29.8.1793 at Toulon. BU 1.1817.

PONDICHERRY Transport 10, 697bm, 12-6pdr. Purchased 11.1780. Sold 26.3.1784.

PONIARD Destroyer 1,980 tons, 341½ x 38 ft, 6-40mm, 10-TT. Scotts., Cancelled 1.1945 (not laid down).

PONTEFRACT Paddle M/S, 'Ascot' class. Murdoch & Murray. 2.5.1916. Sold 6.9.22 H.H.Bond.

PONTYPOOL (ex-POLPERRO renamed 1918) Minesweeper, later 'Hunt' class. Lobnitz 25.6.1918. Sold 18.5.22 B.Zammitt.

POOLE 5th Rate 32, 381bm, 108½ x 28 ft. Nye, Cowes 1696. Fireship 1719. Sunk 5.1737 as foundation at Harwich.

POOLE 5th Rate 44, 706bm, 126 x 36 ft. Blaydes, Hull 5.6.1745. BU completed 12.8.1765 at Portsmouth.

POOLE Minesweeper, turbine 'Bangor' class. Stephen 25.6.1941. Sold 1.1.48, BU at Pembroke Dock.

POPHAM (see SOMALILAND)

POPHAM Inshore M/S, 'Ham' class. Vosper 11.1.1955. Sold mercantile 17.2.76.

POPINJAY Gallion. Built 1587. Condemned 1601.

POPPY Sloop, 'Arabis' class. Swan Hunter 9.11.1915. Sold 9.4.23 Rees, Llanelly.

POPPY Corvette, 'Flower' class. Alex Hall 20.11.1941. Sold 1946, renamed *Rami*.

POPPY Drifter 1915 renamed RECLUSE 1918-19.

PORCUPINE Sloop 16, 314bm, 94½ x 28 ft. Purchased on stocks 19.7.1746; Taylor, Rotherhithe 20.9.1746. Sold 31.3.1763.

PORCUPINE 6th Rate 24, 520bm, 114½ x 32 ft. Graves, Deptford 17.12.1777. BU 4.1805.

PORCUPINE Sloop 16, 160bm. Purchased 1777 in Jamaica. Sold 17.1.1788.

PORCUPINE 6th Rate 22, 525bm, 118½ x 31 ft. Owen, Topsham 26.1.1807. Sold 18.4.1816.

PORCUPINE 6th Rate 28, 500bm, 114 x 32 ft, 20-32pdr, 6-18pdr carr., 2-6pdr. Plymouth DY. Ordered 1.6.1819, cancelled 1.11.1832.

PORCUPINE Wood pad. vessel, 382bm, 141 x 24 ft. Deptford DY 17.6.1844. Sold 1883.

PORCUPINE Destroyer 320 tons, 200 x 20 ft, 1-12pdr, 5-6pdr, 2-TT. Palmer 19.9.1895. Sold 29.4.1920 Ward, Rainham.

PORCUPINE Destroyer 1,540 tons, 338½ x 35 ft, 4-4.7in, 4-TT. Vickers Armstrong, Tyne 10.6.1941. Torpedoed 9.12.42 by 'U.602' in the Mediterranean; not repaired; became base ship 1943. Sold 6.5.46, BU 1947 at Plymouth. (stern section at Southampton)

PORCUPINE (ex-BARRACOUTA renamed 1967) Survey ship 1,050 tons. Brooke Marine. Cancelled 1967.

PORGEY Schooner 4, 80bm, 56 x 18 ft, 4-12pdr carr. Bermuda 5.1807. Foundered 1812 in the W.Indies.

PORLOCK (see PRESTATYN)

PORLOCK BAY (ex-LOCH SEAFORTH renamed 1944, ex-LOCH MUICK) Frigate, 'Bay' class. Hill 14.6.1945. To Finnish navy 19.3.62 as MATTI KURKI.

PORPOISE (ex-*Annapolis*) Sloop 16, 285bm. Purchased 1777. Renamed FIREBRAND 23.7.1778 fireship. Burnt and blew up 11.10.1781 off Falmouth.

PORPOISE Storeship 14, 700bm. Purchased 8.1780. Sold 1.1783 at Bombay.

PORPOISE Storeship, 324bm, 96 x 28 ft. Hill, Deptford 16.5.1798; Renamed DILIGENT 5.1.1801. Sold 1802.

PORPOISE Storeship 10, 308bm, 93 x 28 ft, 10-6pdr. Spanish sloop INFANTA AMELIA captured 6.8.1799 by ARGO off Portugal. Wrecked 17.8.1803 on a coral reef off the

NSW coast.

PORPOISE (ex-*Lord Melville*) Storeship 10, 399bm, 100 x 30 ft, 8-18pdr carr., 2-6pdr. Purchased 1804. Sold 16.1.1816.

PORPOISE Mortar vessel, 117bm, 65 x 21 ft, 1-13in mortar. Thompson 26.5.1855. Renamed MV.8 on 19.10.1855; hulked as a bathing place 7.1866. Sold 25.6.1885 Castle.

PORPOISE Wood S.gunboat, 'Albacore' class. Pitcher, Northfleet 7.6.1856. BU completed 22.2.1864.

PORPOISE Torpedo cruiser 1,770 tons, 225 x 36 ft, 6-6in, 8-3pdr. Thomson, Glasgow 7.5.1886. Sold 10.2.1905 at Bombay.

PORPOISE Destroyer 934 tons, 265(oa) x 26½ ft, 3-4in, 2-TT. Thornycroft 21.7.1913. Sold 23.2.20 Thornycroft for resale to Brazilian navy, renamed ALEXANDRINO DEALENCA.

PORPOISE M/L submarine 1,500 tons, 267 x 30 ft, 1-4in, 6-TT, 50 mines. Vickers Armstrong, Barrow 30.8.1932. Sunk 19.1.45 by Japanese A/C in the Malacca Strait.

PORPOISE Submarine 1,605 tons, 241 x 26½ ft, 8-TT. Vickers Armstrong, Barrow 25.4.1956. - Sunk 1985 as A/C target, Mediterranean

PORT ANTONIO Brig 12, 69bm, 59½ x 21 ft. Purchased 1779. Laid up in Jamacia 1784.

PORT ARTHUR Corvette (RCN), 'Flower' class. Pt Arthur SY 18.9.1941. BU 1946.

PORT COLBORNE Frigate (RCN), 'River' class. Yarrow, Esquimalt 21.4.1943. Sold 17.11.47 to BU.

PORT D'ESPAGNE Schooner 14. Presented 1806 by the inhabitants of Trindad. 190bm. Sold in 1811.

PORT HOPE Minesweeper, TE 'Bangor' class (RCN). Dufferin, Toronto 14.12.1941. Sold 2.59 Marine Industries.

PORT MAHON 6th Rate 20, 282bm, 94 x 26½ ft. Deptford 18.10.1711. BU 5.1740 at Plymouth.

PORT MAHON 6th Rate 24, 437bm, 106½ x 30½ ft. Buxton, Deptford 26.8.1740. Sold 29.6.1763.

PORT MAHON Brig-sloop 18, 277bm, 91½ x 25 ft, 18-18pdr. Captured 15.11.1798 on stocks at Port Mahon and launched 1798. Police hulk 1.1817. Sold 8.1837 at Woolwich.

PORT MORANT Armed ship, Spanish captured 1780. Sold 1784 in Jamaica.

PORT ROYAL 18. Dating from 1762. Captured 8.5.1781 by the Spanish at Pensacola.

PORT ROYAL Sloop 14. French privateer COMTESSE de MAUREPAS captured 6.1779 by the privateer COUNTESS of SCARBOROUGH. Listed 1783.

PORT ROYAL Schooner 10. Origin unknown. Captured 5.1769 by the French in the W. Indies. Recaptured 18.10.97 and renamed RECOVERY. Sold 1801.

PORTAGE Minesweeper (RCN), 'Algerine' class. Pt Arthur SY 21.11.1942. BU 1959.

PORTCHESTER CASTLE Corvette, 'Castle' class. Swan Hunter 21.6.1943. Arrived 5.58 at Troon to BU.

PORTCULLIS Pinnace, 20bm. Built 1546. Listed to 1563.

PORTCULLIS (ex-LCT.4044 renamed 1956) Tank landing craft 657 tons, 225 x 39 ft. Arrol, Alloa 1945. Sold Pounds 4.6.70.

PORTIA Brig-sloop 14, 253bm, 92 x 25½ ft, 12-24pdr carr., 2-6pdr. Deptford DY 30.10.1810. Sold 6.3.1817.

PORTIA Wood S.gunvessel, 428bm, 145 x 25½ ft. Deptford DY. Laid down 1861, cancelled 12.12.1863.

PORTIA (see LENNOX of 1914)

PORTIA Destroyer, 'M' class. Scotts 10.8.1916. Sold 9.5.21 Ward, Milford, Haven; arrived 9.22.

PORTIA Fleet Messenger, yacht and Trawler WW.I.

PORTISHAM Inshore M/S, 'Ham' class. Dorset Yt Co 3.11.1955.

PORTLAND 4th Rate 50, 605bm. Taylor, Wapping 1652. Burnt 12.4.1692 to avoid capture by the French.

PORTLAND 4th Rate 48, 636bm, 125½ x 34 ft. Woolwich DY 28.3.1693. Rebuilt Portsmouth 1723 as 772bm. BU 1743.

PORTLAND 4th Rate 50, 976bm, 140 x 40 ft. Snelgrove, Limehouse 11.10.1774. Sold 15.3.1763.

PORTLAND PRIZE 4th Rate 50, 866bm, 134 x 38½ ft, 22-18pdr, 24-9pdr 4-6pdr. French AUGUSTE captured 9.2.1746 by PORTLAND. Sold 17.5.1749.

PORTLAND 4th Rate 50, 1,044bm, 146 x 40½ ft. Sheerness DY 11.4.1770. Storeship 10.1800; prison hulk 1.1802. Sold 19.5.1817 D. List.

PORTLAND Gunvessel. Ex-barge purchased 9.1795. Sold 1.1802.

PORTLAND (ex-KINGSTON renamed 1817) 4th Rate 52, 1,4767bm, 173 x 44½ ft. Plymouth DY 8.5.1822. Sold 19.5.1862 Castle, Charlton.

PORTLAND Minesweeper, TE 'Bagnor' class. Taikoo DY, Hong Kong. Laid down 12.7.1941, renamed TAITAM 9.41 and lost on stocks 12.41. Completed as Japanese M/S 101 in 4.44 Sunk 10.3.45 by American air attack.

PORTLAND BILL Repair ship 8,580 tons, 425 x 57 ft, 16-20mm. Burrard, Vancouver 18.5.1945. sold 1.51 Stag Line, renamed *Zinnia*.

PORTMADOC (see PETERSFIELD)

PORTO sloop 16, 141 bm. French ARLEQUIN captured by SURPRISE 6.6.1780. Renamed HARLEQUIN 1782. Sold 6.1782

PORTREATH (see FITZROY)

PORTSMOUTH 46-gun ship, 422bm. Portsmouth 1649. Captured 7.1689 by the French MARQUIS and blown up.

PORTSMOUTH SHALLOP Sloop 4. French, captured 1655. Captured 7.1655 by Royalists; fate unknown.

PORTSMOUTH Ketch 14, 90bm. Portsmouth 1665. Captured 1673 by the Dutch.

PORTSMOUTH Sloop 6, 43bm. Portsmouth 1667. Captured 1672 by the Dutch.

PORTSMOUTH Yacht 8, 133bm, 70 x 20½ ft, 8-3pdr. Woolwich 1674. Rebuilt Woolwich 1679 as bomb, 143bm. Wrecked 27.11.1703 at the Nore.

PORTSMOUTH 5th Rate 32, 412bm, 106½ x 29½ ft. Portsmouth 13.5.1690 Captured 1.10.1696 by the French.

PORTSMOUTH PRIZE 6th Rate 10, 106bm. French, captured 29.7.1694. Recaptured 28.9.1696 by the French.

PORTSMOUTH Yacht 6, 50bm, 52 x 15 ft, 6-2pdr. Portsmouth DY 9.1.1702. Rebuilt and renamed MEDINA 8.1772, 66bm, 53 x 17 ft. BU 8.1832 at Portsmouth.

PORTSMOUTH 5th Rate 42, 532bm, 118½ x 32 ft. Deptford 1.4.1707. Hospital ship 1720. BU 10.1728 at Deptford.

PORTSMOUTH Storeship 24, 694bm, 125 x 36 ft. Rowcliff, Southampton 12.6.1741. Lost 3.12.1747 near the Longsands.

PORTSMOUTH Yacht 6, 83bm, 59½ x 19 ft, 6-2pdr. Portsmouth DY 30.9.1742. Rebuilt Portsmouth 1794 as 102bm. BU completed 4.9.1869 at Portsmouth.

PORTSMOUTH Transport 4, 114bm, 64 x 24 ft, 4-3pdr. Purchased 6.1747. Sold 25.8.1767.

PORTSMOUTH (ex-*Beckford*) Busse 6, 79bm, 63 x 16½ ft, 6-4pdr. Pur-

chased 10.11.1756. Lost 2.1758 at Senegal.

PORTSMOUTH Transport 4. Bird, Rotherhithe 5.10.1759. Fate Unknown.

PORTSMOUTH (ex-WOOLWICH) Storeship 317bm. 110 x 26 ft. Milford 28.9.1811. Coal hulk 3.1828. BU 8.1834.

PORTSMOUTH Trawler requis, 1915-19.

PORTWAY (ex-SPEAR renamed 8.1943) Dock landing ship 4,270 tons, 454 x 72 ft, 1-3in, 16-20mm. Newport News 11.4.1944 on lend-lease, but retained by the USN.

POSEIDON Submarine 1,475 tons, 260 x 30 ft, 1-4in, 8-TT. Vickers Armstrong, Barrow 21.6.1929. Sunk 9.6.31 in collision with SS *Yuta* off Wei Hai Wei.

POSEIDON Drifter requis. 1914-19 and 1939-45.

POST Brigantine. Listed 1562-66.

POSTBOY Advice boat 6, 73bm. Plymouth 1694. Captured 1.10.1694 by the French off Calais.

POSTBOY Advice boat 4, 77bm, 65½ x 16 ft. Portsmouth 1695. Captured 3.7.1695 by the French FACTEUR de BRISTOL off Plymouth.

POSTBOY Brigantine 4, 76bm. Deptford 1696. Captured 1.6.1702 by the French off Beachy Head.

POSTBOY Trawler requis. 1940-46.

POSTILLION 6th Rate 10, 117bm, 65 x 20 ft. French POSTILLION captured 9.1702 by WORCESTER. Wrecked 7.5.1709 near Ostend.

POSTILLION Sloop 18, 365bm, 97 x 29½ ft, 18-6pdr. French privateer DUC d'AIGUILLON captured 15.4.1757. Sold 3.5.1763.

POSTILLION Schooner 10. Purchased 1776. Sold 1779 in Newfoundland.

POSTILLION Minesweeper, 'Algerine' class. Redfern 18.3.1943 on lend-lease. Returned 12.46 to the USN.

POTENTILLA Corvette, 'Flower' class. Simons, Renfrew 18.12.1941. Lent R. Norwegian navy 16.1.42 to 13.3.44. Sold 13.3.46, BU Dorkin, Gateshead.

POULETTE 6th Rate 28, 480bm. French, handed over by Royalists 18.12.1793 at Toulon. Burnt 20.10.1796 at Ajaccio as unseaworthy.

POULETTE 6th Rate 20, 513bm, 120 x 31 ft. French privateer FOUDROYANT captured 2.1799 by PHOENIX. Sold 2.4.1814.

POULMIC Patrol vessel, 350 tons, 121

x 26½ ft. French, seized 3.7.1940 at Plymouth. Free-French 8.40; lost 6.10.40 off Plymouth.

POUNCER (Gunboat No.38) (ex-*David*) Gunvessel 12, 165bm, 77 x 22 ft, 2-24pdr, 10-18pdr carr. Purchased 3.1797 at Leith. Sold 9.1802.

POUNDMAKER Frigate (RCN), 'River' class. Vickers, Montreal 21.4.1944. Sold 1947 Peruvian navy as FERRE.

POWDERHM Inshore M/S, 'Ham' class. White 27.11.1958. Renamed WATERWITCH 1964, survey vessel. Sold Perch S.Bkr's 1986.

POWERFUL 3rd Rate 74, 1,627bm, 168½ x 47 ft. Perry, Blackwall 3.4.1783. BU 5.1812 at Chatham.

POWERFUL 2nd Rate 84, 2,296bm, 196 X 52½ ft. Chatham DY 21.6.1826. Target 1860. BU completed 29.8.1864.

POWERFUL 1st class cruiser 14,200 tons, 500 x 71 ft, 2-9.2in, 12-6in, 16-12pdr. Vickers 24.7.1895. Renamed IMPREGNABLE 11.1919 training ship. Sold 31.8.29 Hughes Bolckow.

POWERFUL II (see ANDROMEDA of 1897)

POWERFULL III (see CAROLINE of 1882)

POWERFUL A/C carrier 14,000 tons, 630 x 80 ft, 30-40mm, 34-A/C. Harland & Wolff 27.2.1945. Suspended 5.46 to 7.52. Renamed BONAVENTURE (RCN) 17.1.56. 16,000 tons, 8-3in, 7-40mm. 34-A/C. BU 1971 in Taiwan.

POWERFUL Tug 1985.

PREMIER (ex-*Estero*) Escort carrier 11,420 tons, 468½ x 69½ ft, 16-40mm, 24-A/C. Seattle Tacoma Co 22.3.1943 on lend-lease. Returned 12.4.46 to the the USN.

PREMIER Paddle vessel, Trawler & Drifter WW.I.

PRESCOTT Corvette (RCN), 'Flower' class. Kingston SY 7.1.1941. Sold 1946.

PRESIDENT 26-gun ship, 220bm. Purchased 1646. Sold 1656. (Known as OLD PRESIDENT from 1650.)

PRESIDENT 42-gun ship, 462bm, 124 x 30 ft, Deptford 1650. Renamed BONAVENTURE 1660. Rebuilt 1666 as 597bm, 126 x 33 ft. BU 1711.

PRESIDENT 5th Rate 38, 1,148bm, 157½ x 40½ ft. French PRESIDENTE captured 27.9.1806 in the Atlantic. Renamed PIEMONTAISE 1815. BU 12.1815.

PRESIDENT 4th Rate 60, 1,533bm, 173 x 44½ ft. American, captured 15.1.1815 by a squadron off New York. BU 6.1818.

PRESIDENT 4th Rate 52, 1,537bm, 173½ x 45 ft. Portsmouth DY 20.4.1829. RNR drillship 4.1862. Sold 7.7.1903. (OLD PRESIDENT from 25.3.03.)

PRESIDENT Drillships (See GANNET of 1878, BUZZARD of 1887, MARJORAM of 1917 and SAXIFRAGE of 1918).

PRESTATYN (ex-PORLOCK renamed 1918) Minesweeper, later 'Hunt' class. Lobnitz 6.11.18. Sold 1.23 Rees.

PRESTON 40-gun ship, 516bm. Cary, Woodbridge 1653. Renamed ANTÉLOPE 1660. Sold 1693.

PRESTON (see SALISBURY of 1698)

PRESTON 4th Rate 50, 1,044bm, 143½ x 41½ ft. Deptford DY 7.2.1757. Sheer hulk 10.1785. BU 1.1815 at Woolwich.

PRESTON Drifter requis. 1915-19.

PRESTONIAN Frigate (RCN), 'River' class. Davie SB 22.6.1944. To R.Norwegian navy 4.56 as TROLL.

PREVENTION Sloop 4, 46bm. Portsmouth 1672. sold 1683.

PREVOST Schooner 10. Listed 1807-09.

PREVOYANTE 5th Rate 40, 803bm. French, captured 17.5.1795 by THETIS and HUSSAR in the Chesapeake. Storeship 1809. Sold 22.7.1819 Beech to BU.

PRIMROSE Ship, 160bm. Listed from 1523; rebuilt 1538 as 240bm. Listed to 1545.

PRIMROSE Discovery vessel, 240bm. Listed 1551. Sold 1555.

PRIMROSE Ship, 800bm. Purchased 1560. Sold 1578.

PRIMROSE Hoy, 80bm. Built 1590; rebuilt 1612. Condemned 1618.

PRIMROSE 22-gun ship, 287bm. Wapping 1651. Wrecked 1656 on the Seven Stones.

PRIMROSE Brig-sloop 18, 'Cruizer' class, 384bm. Nickells, Fowey 5.8.1807. Wrecked 22.1.1809 on the Manacles.

PRIMROSE Brig-sloop 18, 'Cruizer' class, 383bm. Portsmouth DY 22.1.1810. BU 8.1832.

PRIMROSE Wood s.gunboat, 'Albacore'class. Pitcher, Northfleet 3.5.1856. BU completed 25.5.1864.

PRIMROSE Sloop, 'Acacia' class. Simons 29.6.1915. Sold 9.4.23 Rees, Llanelly.

PRIMROSE Corvette, 'Flower' class. Simons 8.5.1940. Sold 9.8.46, renamed *Norfinn*.

PRIMROSE 2 Drifters & Tug requis. WW.I.

PRIMULA Sloop, 'Arabis' class. Swan Hunter 6.12.1915. Sunk 1.3.16 by 'U.35' in the Mediterranean.

PRIMULA Corvette, 'Flower' class. Simons 22.6.1940. Sold 22.7.46, renamed *Marylock*.

YOUNG PRINCE 4th Rate 38, 375bm. Dutch JONGE PRINS captured 1665. Expended 1666 as a fireship.

PRINCE 1st Rate 100, 1,395bm, 167 x 45½ ft. Chatham DY 1670. Rebuilt 1692 and renamed ROYAL WILLIAM. (qv)

PRINCE (see OSSORY of 1682)

PRINCE (see TRIUMPH of 1698)

PRINCE 2nd Rate 90, 1,871bm, 177½ x 49 ft. Woolwich DY 4.7.1788. Rebuilt Portsmouth 1796 as 2,088bm, 194½ x 49 ft (the ship halved and lengthened). BU 11.1837.

PRINCE Destroyer, 'M' class. Stephen 26.7.1916. Sold 9.5.21 Ward, Hayle.

PRINCE (see RAJAH)

PRINCE Transport 2710 tons hired 1854, Lost 1854

PRINCE ALBERT (see PRINCESS ROYAL of 1853)

PRINCE ALBERT Iron S. turret ship, 2,537bm, 3,687 tons, 240 x 48 ft, 4-9in MLR. Samuda, Poplar 23.5.1864. Sold 16.3.1899 Ward, Preston.

PRINS ALBERT Landing ship 1941-46.

PRINCE ARTHUR Brig-sloop 10, 'Cherokee' class, 239bm. Dudman, Deptford 28.7.1808. Sold 12.1808 to the Emperor of Morocco.

PRINCE AUGUSTUS FREDERICK Cutter 8, 69bm, 56 x 18 ft, 8-4pdr. Listed 1816-21.

PRINCE CONSORT (ex-TRIUMPH renamed 14.2.1862) (qv) Ironclad frigate 4,045bm, 273 x 58½ ft, 11-7in, 24-68pdr. Pembroke Dock 26.6.1862. Sold 3.1882 to Castle to BU.

PRINCE EDWARD 5th Rate 44, 715bm, 126½ x 36ft. Bird, Rotherhithe 2.9.1745. Sold 16.6.1766.

PRINCE EDWARD Brig-sloop 14. Purchased 1780. Captured 1782 by her American prisoners.

PRINCE EDWARD 3rd Rate 62, 1,075bm, 144 x 42 ft. Dutch MARS captured 4.2.1781 in the W.Indies. Harbour service 9.1782. Sold 24.3.1802.

PRINCE EDWARD Netlayer requis. 1915-20

PRINCE EUGENE (ex-M.II renamed 1915) Monitor 5,920 tons, 320 x 88 ft, 2-12in, 2-6in. Harland & Wolff, Govan 14.7.15. Sold 9.5.21 Ward, Preston; arrived 8.23.

PRINCE FREDERICK (see EXPEDITION of 1679)

PRINCE FREDERICK 3rd Rate 64, 1,270bm, 157 x 43 ft. Dutch REVOLUTIE captured 17.8.1796 at the Cape. Hospital ship by 1804. Sold 5.6.1817 G. Bailey.

PRINCE GEORGE (ex-DUKE rebuilt and renamed 3.12.1701) 2nd Rate 90, 1,364bm, 163 x 45 ft. Rebuilt Deptford 1723 as 1,586bm. Burnt 13.4.1758 by accident at sea. (see DUKE of 1682).

PRINCE GEORGE Cutter, 62bm. Purchased 2.1763. Sold 20.9.1771.

PRINCE GEORGE 2nd Rate 90, 1,955bm, 177½ x 50½ ft. Chatham DY 31.8.1772. Sheer hulk 1832.BU 1.1839.

PRINCE GEORGE Battleship 14,900 tons, 390 x 75 ft, 4-12in, 12-6in, 16-12pdr. Portsmouth DY 22.8.1895. Renamed VICTORIOUS II in 1918, harbour service. Sold 29.1.21 Cohen; resold and stranded 30.12.21 off Kamperduin while in tow for Germany to BU.

PRINCE HENRY 5th Rate 44, 819bm, 133 x 37½ ft. Gorrill, Liverpool 12.7.1747 (laid down as CULLODEN, renamed 14.3.1747). BU 1766 at Plymouth.

PRINCE HENRY AMC (RCN) 1939.

PRINCE de NEUCHATEL Schooner 18, 328bm, 110½ x 25½ ft. French privateer (in the service of the USA) captured 28.12.1814 by a squadron in the Atlantic. Capsized in dock and badly damaged 1815; sold 1815.

PRINCE of ORANGE (ex-BREDAH renamed at launch) 3rd Rate 70, 1,128bm, 151 x 41½ ft. Stacey, Deptford 5.9.1734. 4th Rate 60 reduced 8.1748; sheer hulk 1772. Sold 5.1810.

PRINCE REGENT Schooner 8 (Canadian lakes), 187bm, 72 x 21 ft. Toronto 7.1812. Renamed BERESFORD 1813; renamed NETLEY 22.1.1814. Renamed NIAGARA, base ship, BU 1843.

PRINCE REGENT 4th Rate 56 (Canadian lakes), 1,294bm, 161 x 43 ft, 6-68pdr carr., 22-32pdr carr., 32-24pdr. Kingston Ont 15.4.1814. Renamed KINGSTON 9.12.1814. Sold 1.1832.

PRINCE REGENT Yacht, 282bm, 96 x 25½ ft. Portsmouth DY 30.5.1820. To be presented 1836 to the Iman of Muscat.

PRINCE REGENT 1st Rate 120,

2,613bm, 205 x 54½ ft. Chatham DY 12.4.1823 (eight years on stocks). Undocked 27.5.1861 as screw 78 guns, 2,672bm. BU 1873.

PRINCE ROYAL 64-gun ship, 890bm. Woolwich DY 25.9.1610. Rebuilt Woolwich 1641 as 1,187bm. Burnt 13.6.1666 by the Dutch, aground on the Galloper. (Was RESOLUTION 1650-1660).

PRINCE RUPERT (ex-M.10 renamed 1915) Monitor 5,950 tons, 320 x 88 ft, 2-12in, 2-6in. Hamilton 20.5.15. Renamed PEMBROKE 24.4.22, base ship; PRINCE RUPERT 1.9.22. Sold 5.23 Beardmore.

PRINCE RUPERT Frigate (RCN), 'River' class. Yarrow, Esquimalt 3.2.1943. Sold 13.12.47; hull sunk 1948 as breakwater at Comox.

PRINCE OF WALES (ex-HIBERNIA renamed 20.10.1763) 3rd Rate 74, 1,623bm, 170 x 47 ft. Bird & Fisher, Milford 4.6.1765. BU 8.1783 at Plymouth.

PRINCE OF WALES 2nd Rate 90, 2,010bm, 182 x 51 ft. Portsmouth DY 28.6.1794 (10 years on stocks). BU 12.1822 at Portsmouth.

PRINCE OF WALES Transport 38. Purchased 1795. Listed in 1801.

PRINCE OF WALES Sloop 14 (Indian), 248bm. Bombay DY 1805. Fate unknown.

PRINCE OF WALES Screw 1st Rate 121, 3,994bm, 6,201 tons, 252 x 60 ft, 1-110pdr, 16-8in, 6-70pdr, 10-40pdr, 88-32pdr. Portsmouth DY 25.1.1860 (12 years on stocks). Renamed BRITANNIA 3.3.1869 training ship. Hulk 9.09. Sold 13.11.14 Garnham. Resold Hughes Bolckow and arrived 7.16 at Blyth to BU.

PRINCE OF WALES Battleship 15,000 tons, 400 x 75 ft, 4-12in, 12-6in, 18-12pdr. Chatham DY 25.3.1902. Sold 12.4.20 Ward, Milford Haven.

PRINCE OF WALES Battleship 35,000 tons, 700 x 103 ft, 10-14in, 16-5.25in. Cammell Laird 3.5.1939. Sunk 10.12.41 by Japanese air attack east coast of Malaya.

PRINCE WILLIAM Flyboat 4, 253bm. Captured 1665. Captured 1666 by the Dutch.

PRINCE WILLIAM 3rd Rate 64, 1,346bm, 153 x 44 ft, 26-24pdr, 28-12pdr, 10-9pdr. Spanish GUISPUSCOANO captured 1780. Sheer hulk 2.1791. BU 9.1817.

PRINCESSE 4th Rate 54, 602bm. Lydney 1660. BU 1680.

PRINCESS (see OSSORY of 1682)

PRINCESS 3rd Rate 70, 1,709bm, 165 x 50 ft, 28-32pdr, 28-18pdr, 14-9pdr. Spanish PRINCESSA captured 8.4.1740. Hulk 1760. Sold 30.12.1784 at Portsmouth.

PRINCESSA 3rd Rate 70, 1,967bm, 170 x 51 ft, 28-24pdr, 30-18pdr, 12-9pdr. Spanish, captured 16.1.1780 at Cape St Vincent. Sheer hulk 8.1784. BU 12.1809 at Portsmouth.

PRINCESS 6th Rate 28, 677bm. Dutch E.Indiaman *Williamstadt en Boetzlaar* captured 14.9.1795 at the Cape. Floating battery 26 guns 1800. Sold 4.1816 at Liverpool.

PRINCESS Yacht requis. 1939-40.

PRINCESS ALICE Iron pad. packet, 270bm, 140 x 20½ft. 1 gun. Purchased 27.1.1844. BU completed 16.7.1878 at Devonport.

PRINCESS AMELIA (see HUMBER of 1693)

PRINCESS AMELIA (see NORFOLK of 1693)

PRINCESS AMELIA 3rd Rate 80, 1,579bm, 165 x 47½ ft. Woolwich DY 7.3.1757. Sold 11.6.1818 Snook to BU. (Left Navy List 11.1788 on loan to Customs.)

PRINCESS AMELIA 3rd Rate 74, 1,906bm, 182 x 49 ft. Chatham DY. Laid down 1.1.1799, cancelled 3.1800.

PRINCESS ANNE (see DUCHESS of 1679)

PRINCESS AUGUSTA (see AUGUSTA of 1771)

PRINCESS AUGUSTA (ex-Danish PRINCE FREDERICK launched 20.8.1785 for the Prince Royal of Denmark and sent to the UK 1816; commissioned 25.7.1816) Yacht, 218bm. Sold 13.8.1818 Ledger to BU.

PRINCESS CAROLINE (see RANELAGH)

PRINCESS CAROLINE 5th Rate 44, 862bm, 129 x 39 ft. Dutch PRINCESS CAROLINA captured 30.12.1780 by MARLBOROUGH. Receiving ship 8.1791. Sunk 1799 as breakwater Harwich.

PRINCESS CAROLINE (see ROTTERDAM)

PRINCESS CAROLINA (also PRINCESS CAROLINE) 3rd Rate 74, 1,637bm. Danish PRINDSESSE CAROLINA captured 7.9.1807 at Copenhagen. Sold 9.2.1815. (Was to have been BRAGANZA.)

PRINCESS CHARLOTTE 5th Rate 38, 1,029bm, 149 x 39½ ft, 16-32pdr carr., 26-18pdr, 4-9pdr. French JUNON captured 18.6.1799 by the

Fleet in the Mediterranean. Renamed ANDROMACHE 6.1.1812. BU 6.1828 at Deptford.

PRINCESS CHARLOTTE Schooner listed 1805-06.

PRINCESS CHARLOTTE (ex-VITTORIA renamed 1814) 5th Rate 42 (Canadian lakes), 815bm, 121 x 37½ ft, 2-68pdr carr., 14-32pdr carr., 26-24pdr. Kingston Ont 15.4.1814. Renamed BURLINGTON 9.12.1814. Sold 1.1833 and BU.

PRINCESS CHARLOTTE 1st Rate 104, 2,443bm, 198½ x 54 ft. Portsmouth DY 14.9.1825. Receiving ship 1858. Sold 1875 at Hong Kong.

PRINCESS LOUISA (see LAUNCESTON of 1711)

PRINCESS LOUISA (see SWALLOW of 1732)

PRINCESS LOUISA 4th Rate 60, 1,143bm, 148 x 42½ ft. Carter, Limehouse 1744. BU completed 14.12.1766 at Chatham.

PRINCESS MARGARET Minelayer 5,070 tons, 395½(oa) x 54 ft, 2-4in, 2-3in, 400 mines. Denny 24.6.1914; hired 26.12.14, purchased 14.6.19. Sold 30.5.29 Galbraith; resold and arrived 2.7.29 Hughes Bolckow, Blyth to BU.

PRINCESS MARIA 38-gun ship. Captured 1652. Wrecked 1658 on the Goodwins.

PRINCESS MARY Yacht. Built 1688. Sale date unknown but lasted until 1827 as mercantile *Betty Cairns*.

PRINCESS MARY (see MARY of 1704).

PRINCESS MARY Patrol vessel & Trawler requis. WW.I.

PRINCESS OF ORANGE 3rd Rate 74, 1,565bm, 165 x 45 ft. Dutch WASHINGTON captured 30.8.1799 in the Texel. Powder hulk 1812. Sold 18.4.1822 Ledger to BU.

PRINCESS ROYAL (see OSSORY of 1682)

PRINCESS ROYAL Storeship 24, 541bm, 123 x 32 ft. Purchased 21.11.1739. Sold 4.6.1750.

PRINCESS ROYAL 2nd Rate 90, 1,973bm, 177½ x 50½ ft. Portsmouth DY 18.10.1773. 98 guns in 1800; 74 guns 1807. BU 10.1807.

PRINCESS ROYAL (ex-PRINCE ALBERT remaned 26.3.1842) Screw 2nd Rate 91, 3,129bm, 217 x 58 ft. Portsmouth DY 23.6.1853. Sold 1872 Castle, Charlton.

PRINCESS ROYAL Battlecruiser 26,350 tons, 660 x 88½ ft, 8-13.5in, 16-4in. Vickers 29.4.1911. Sold 19.12.22 A.J. Purves; resold and BU Rosyth S. Bkg Co.

PRINCESS ROYAL Trawler and Tug requis WW.I.

PRINCESS SOPHIA FREDERICA 3rd Rate 74, 1,763bm. Danish PRINDSESSE SOPHIE FREDERICA captured 7.9.1807 at Copenhagen. Prison ship circa 1811. BU 9.1816. (Was to have been renamed CAMBRIDGE)

PRIVET Corvette, 'Flower' class. Morton 10.12.1942. Transferred 1942 to the USN as PRUDENT.

PROCRIS Brig-sloop 18, 'Cruizer' class. 384bm. Custance, Yarmouth 27.12.1806. Sold 23.11.1815.

PROCRIS Brig-sloop 10, 'Cherokee' class, 236bm. Chatham DY 21.6.1822. Sold 1.1837.

PROCRIS Wood S.gunboat, 'Albacore' class. Pitcher, Northfleet 13.3.1856. Harbour service 1869. Sold 31.5.1893 T.Hockling, BU at Stonehouse.

PROGRESSO Tank vessel. (Ex-slaver captured and purchased 23.4.1844. BU in 3.1869.

PROHIBITION Sloop 4, 68bm. Sheerness DY 1699. Captured 14.8.1702 by the French off Lands End.

PROJECT Mortar boat, 98bm, 70 x 17½ ft, 1-10in mortar. Woolwich DY 26.3.1806. BU 12.1810.

PROMETHEUS Fireship 18, 432bm, 109½ x 30 ft. Thompson. Southampton 27.3.1807. Harbour service 5.1819. Renamed VETERAN 2.5.1839. BU 8.1852.

PROMETHEUS Wood pad. sloop, 796bm, 164 x 33 ft, 5-32pdr Sheerness DY 21.9.1839. Sold 1863 Castle, Charlton.

PROMETHEUS 3rd class cruiser 2,135 tons, 300 x 36½ ft, 8-4in, 8-3pdr. Earle, Hull 20.10.1898. Sold 28.5.1914 Ward, BU at Preston.

PROMPT PRIZE 3rd Rate 70, 1,391bm, 158 x 45 ft. French PROMPT captured 12.10.1702 at Vigo. Ordered 20.5.1703 to be used as part of a wharf at Chatham.

PROMPTE 6th Rate 20, 509bm, 119 x 31 ft. French, captured 28.5.1793 by PHAETON in the Bay of Biscay. BU 7.1813.

PROMPT 5th Rate 32 (fir-built). Frames made at Chatham DY and sent to Canada early in 1814 for re-erection on the lakes. Ordered 21.7.1814 to sell at Quebec, 'it not being possible to get them to the lakes'.

PROMPT Schooner. Slaver *Josephina* captured 10.1840 and purchased

22.1.1842. Sold 1845.

PROMPT Schooner. Slaver captured 1845 and purchased 17.7.1845. Sold circa 1847.

PROMPT Mortar vessel, 155bm, 70 x 23½ ft, 1-13in mortar. Mare, Blackwall 23.5.1855. Renamed MV.21 on 19.10.1855. BU completed 27.9.1865 Marshall, Plymouth.

PROMPT Wood S.gunboat, 'Albacore' class. Pitcher, Northfleet 21.5.1856. BU completed 6.5.1864.

PROMPT (ex-HUNTSVILLE) renamed 6.1943) Minesweeper, 'Algerine' class. Redfern 30.3.44. Damaged 8.5.45 by mine and not repaired. Sold 16.1.47, BU Rainham, Kent.

PROMPT Tug 1867-1922. Tug (ex-WARDEN) 1958-65.

PROSELYTE (ex-*Stanislaus*) 5th Rate 32, 687bm, 135 x 33½ ft. Purchased 12.1780. Sold 10.2.1785.

PROSELYTE Floating battery 24, 950bm. French frigate handed over by Royalists 28.8.1793 at Toulon. Sunk 11.4.1794 by batteries at Bastia.

PROSELYTE 5th Rate 32, 748bm, 133 x 36 ft. Dutch JASON captured 8.6.1796 from mutinous crew at Greenock. Wrecked 4.9.1801 at St Martin, W. Indies.

PROSELYTE (ex-*Ramillies*) A. ship 24, 404bm. Purchased 6.1804. Bomb 4.1808. Wrecked 1.1809 in the Baltic.

PROSERPINE Sloop? purchased at Port Mahon 1756. Lost to the French 1756.

PROSERPINE (ex-*Maryland Islander*) Fireship 12, 253bm, 91 x 25½ ft. Purchased 3.1.1757. Sold 15.21.1763.

PROSERPINE 6th Rate 28, 596bm, 120½ x 33 ft. Barnard, Harwich 7.7.1777. Wrecked 1.2.1799 near Cuxhaven.

PROSERPINE 5th Rate 36, 852bm, 141 x 38 ft. French BELLONE captured 12.10.1798 by ETHALION off the north coast of Ireland. Hulk 1799. Sold Freake 27.8.1806 to BU.

PROSERPINE 5th Rate 32, 922bm, 144½ x 37½ ft, 10-24pdr carr., 26-18pdr, 4-9pdr. Steemson, Paul near Hull 6.8.1807. Captured 27.2.1809 by two French frigates.

PROSERPINE 5th Rate 46, 1,063bm, 150 x 40 ft. Plymouth DY 1.12.1830. Sold 21.1.1864 R.Ridley.

PROSPERPINE W.S.sloop 1268 bm. Projected 18.12.1866, cancelled 5.67

PROSERPINE 3rd class cruiser 2,135 tons, 300 x 36½ ft, 8-4in, 8-3pdr.

Sheerness DY 5.12.1896. Sold 30.11.1919 at Alexandria; BU 1923 at Genoa.

PROSPERITY Storeship 22, 687bm, 132 x 34½ ft. Purchased 3.1782. Receiving ship 1.1784. BU 10.1796.

PROSPERITY Two drifters requis. 1915-19.

PROSPERO (ex-*Albion*) Bomb 8, 400bm, 107 x 30½ ft, 8-24pdr carr., 1-13in and 1-10in mortars. Purchased 10.1803. Wrecked 18.2.1807 near Dieppe.

PROSPERO Brig-sloop 14, 251bm, 92 x 26½ ft. Woolwich DY 9.11.1809. Sold 30.5.1816.

PROSPERO (ex-GPO vessel *Belfast*) Wood pad. packet, 249bm, 129 x 20½ ft. Transferred 7.8.1837. BU 10.1866 Marshall, Plymouth.

PROSPEROUS Vessel in service in 1598.

PROSPEROUS Hoy, 68bm. Chatham DY 1665. Burnt 6.1667 by the Dutch at Chatham.

PROSPEROUS Fireship 6, 206bm. Purchased 1666. Sold 1667.

PROSPEROUS Pink 120bm. Listed in 1676.

PROSERPOUS Tug 1942-65.

PROTEA (see CROZIER)

PROTEA (see ROCKROSE)

PROTEA Whaler (SAN) requis. 1941-46.

PROTECTOR 5th Rate 44 (Indian). Listed 1749. Foundered 1.1.1761 in a cyclone off Pondicherry.

PROTECTOR Fireship in service in 1758.

PROTECTOR Gun-brig 12, 178bm, 80 x22½ ft. Warren, Brightlingsea 1.2.1805. Survey vessel 4.1817. Sold 30.8.1833 W. Woolcombe to BU.

PROTECTOR Wood S.gunboat, 'Britomart' class. Portsmouth DY. Laid down 1861, cancelled 12.12.1863.

PROTECTOR Cruiser (Australian) 920 tons, 188 x 30 ft, 1-8in, 5-6in. Armstrong 1884. Renamed CERBERUS 1.4.1921 on harbour service; reverted to PROTECTOR 1924. Sold 10.9.24 J.Hill, Melbourne; resold 1931 as *Sidney*. Lost in collision off Gladstone 7.43 on loan U.S. Army.

PROTECTOR Netlayer 2,900 tons, 310 x 53 ft, 2-4in. Yarrow 20.8.1936. Antarctic patrol ship 1955, 3,450 tons. Sold 10.2.70. BU Inverkeithing.

PROTECTOR Support ship (RAN) 20,270 tons. Cockatoo DY cancelled 1974

PROTECTOR Patrol vessel ex-*Seaforth*

Saga purchased 2.1983 sold Pounds 1987

PROTEUS (ex-Indiaman *Talbot*) 6th Rate 26, 675bm, 125 x 34 ft, 20-9pdr, 6-4pdr. Purchased 2.1777. Receiving ship. Sold 1783 in Newfoundland as unfit.

PROTHEE 3rd Rate 64, 1,481bm, 164 x 44½ x ft. French PROTEE captured 24.2.1780. Prison ship in 1799. BU 9.1815.

PROTHEE (see PEARL of 1762)

PROTEUS Submarine 1,475 tons, 260 x 30 ft, 1-4in, 8-TT. Vickers Armstrong, Barrow 23.7.1929. Sold 26.2.46, BU at Troon.

PROTHEE (see under PROTEUS)

PROVIDENCE 30-gun ship, 304bm. Bermondsey 1637. Wrecked 1668.

PROVIDENCE Fireship 6, 150bm. Purchased 1665. Sunk 1666 in action.

PROVIDENCE Fireship 6, 180bm. Purchased 1672. Lost 1673.

PROVINDENCE Fireship 8, 175bm. Purchased 1678. Sold 1686.

PROVIDENCE PRIZE Ketch, 29bm. French, captured 19.4.1691. Re- captured 10.1707 by the French.

PROVIDENCE Sloop 12. American, captured 14.8.1779 at Penobscot. Listed 1780.

PROVIDENCE 5th Rate 32, 514bm, 114 x 32 ft. American captured 12.5.1780 at Charlestown. Sold 11.3.1784.

PROVIDENCE Storeship 16, 462bm, 110 x 30½ ft. Purchased 1782. Sold 25.3.1784.

PROVIDENCE Sloop 12, 420bm, 107 x 29 ft. Purchased 2.1791. Wrecked 16.5.1797 on Formosa.

PROVIDENCE Schooner 14. Purchased 1796. Expended 2.10.1804 as fireship at Boulogne.

PROVIDENCE (ex-QUAIL ordered to be renamed 31.1.1822 but re- naming cancelled 11.4.1822) Cutter tender, 80bm.

PROVIDENCE Coastguard cutter, 40bm. Harvey, Wivenhoe 1866. Sold 17.3.1870 at Liverpool.

PROVIDENCE (ex-FOREST HILL renamed 6.1943) Minesweeper, 'Algerine' class. Redfern 27.10.43. Arrived 17.5.58 Young, Sunderland to BU.

PROVO Schooner listed 1805-07.

PROWSE (see ZANZIBAR)

PRUDENT 3rd Rate 64, 1,367bm, 159 x 44½ ft. Woolwich DY 28.9.1768. Harbour service 7.1779. Sold 11.3.1814.

PRUDENTE 5th Rate 38, 897bm, 136 x

38 ft. French., captured 2.6.1779 by RUBY in the W.Indies. Sold 3.1.1803.

PRUDENT (see DILIGENT of 1806)

PRUDENT Tug 1905-27; Tug 1940, renamed CAUTIOUS 1947

PSYCHE 5th Rate 36, 848bm, 139 x 36 ft. French, captured 14.2.1805 by SAN FIORENZO on the coast of India. Sold 1812.

PSYCHE 5th Rate 32 (fir-built). Frames made at Chatham DY and sent to Canada early in 1814 for re-erection on the lakes. Ordered 21.7.1814 to sell at Quebec 'as not possible to get to the lakes.' (Some of the material may have been used for the following ship).

PSYCHE 4th Rate 56, 769bm, 130 x 36½ ft. Kingston Ont 25.12.1814; not completed. Sold 1837.

PSYCHE Wood pad. despatch vessel, 835bm, 250(oa) x 28 ft. Pembroke Dock 29.3.1862. Wrecked 15.12.1870 near Catania; wreck blown up 2.1871.

PSYCHE Coastguard vessel. Purchased 1.1878. Sold 1884 T.Chalmers, Leith.

PSYCHE (see RINGAROOMA)

PSYCHE 3rd class cruiser 2,135 tons, 300 x 36½ ft. 8-4in, 8-3pdr. Devonport DY 19.7.1898. RAN 1.7.1915. Sold 21.7.22 Waterside Ship Chandlery, Melbourne.

PUCK Schooner gunboat, 1-32pdr. Purchased 1855. Foundered 8.1856 on passage from Balaclava to be handed over to the Turkish navy.

PUCKERIDGE Destroyer, 'Hunt' class type II. White 6.3.1941. Sunk 6.9.43 by 'U.617' off Gibraltar.

PUFFIN Patrol vessel 510 tons, 234 x 26½ ft, 1-4in. Stephen 5.5.1936. Sold 16.1.47, BU Ward, Grays.

PUFFIN Trawler requis. 1914-19.

PUISSANT 3rd Rate 74, 1,794bm. French, handed over 29.8.1793 by Royalists at Toulon. Harbour service 5.1796. Sold 11.7.1816.

PUKAKI (see LOCH ACHANALT)

PUKAKI Patrol boat (RNZN) 105 tons, Brooke Marine 1.3.1974

PULHAM Inshore M/S, 'Ham' class. Saunders Roe, Anglesea 10.1.1956. Sold 10. 8.66, became a yacht

PULTUSK Sloop 16, 200bm. French privateer AUSTERLITZ captured 5.4.1807 by CIRCE in the W.Indies. BU 1810 at Antigua.

PUMA Frigate 2,300 tons, 330 x 40 ft, 4-4.5in, 2-40mm. Scotts 30.6.1954. Arrived Blyth 10.12.76 to BU.

PUMBA Gunboat (Australian) 450 tons, 1-5in. ex-Govt hopper built 1887. Listed 1901.

PUNCHER (ex-*Willapa*) Escort carrier 11,420 tons, 468½ x 69½ ft, 2-4in, 16-40mm, 24-A/C. Seattle Tacoma 8.11.1943 on lend-lease. Returned 16.1.46 to the USN.

PUNCHER (see LST.3036)

PUNCHER Patrol boat 43 tons. Watercraft 1986 and laid-up.

PUNCHESTON Coastal M/S, 'Ton' class. Richards, Lowestoft 20.11.1956. Sold 3.5.72, BU Dartford in 1977.

PUNJAUB (ex-PLASSY) Paddle frigate (Indian), 1,031bm, 10-8in. Bombay DY 21.4.1854. Sold 1863 as barque *Tweed*.

PUNJAB Minesweeper (RIN), 'Bathurst' class. Morts Dk, Sydney 11.10.1941. Sold circa 1949.

PUNJABI Destroyer 1,870 tons, 355½ x 36½ ft, 8-4.7in, 4-TT. Scotts 18.12.1937. Sunk 1.5.42 in collision with battleship KING GEORGE V in the N.Atlantic.

PUNTOONE Sheer hulk, 267bm. For use 1677 at Tangier. Condemned at Cadiz 12.11.1691.

PURSUER (ex-USS ST GEORGE, ex-*Mormacland* (ii)) Escort carrier 11,420 tons, 468½ x 69½ ft, 2-4in, 8-40mm, 18-A/C. Ingalls 18.7.1942 on lend-lease. Returned 12.2.46 to the USN.

PURSUER (see LST. 3504)

PURSUER Patrol boat 43 tons. Watercraft 1986 and laid-up

PUTTENHAM Inshore M/S, 'Ham' class. Thornycroft, Hampton 25.6.1956. Sold 1980.

PYL Brig-sloop 16. Dutch, seized 4.3.1796 at Plymouth. Fireship 1798. Sold 31.8.1801.

PYLADES Sloop 18, 399bm, 90½ x 30½ ft. Dutch privateer HERCULES captured 3.12.1781. BU 3.1790.

PYLADES Sloop 16, 367bm, 105 x 28 ft. Mestears, Rotherhithe 4.1794. Wrecked 26.11.1794 in the Shetlands; salved and sold at Leith; repurchased 1796. Sold 11.1815.

PYLADES Sloop 18, 433bm, 110 x 30½ ft, 16-32pdr carr., 2-9pdr. Woolwich DY 29.6.1824. BU 5.1845.

PYLADES Wood S.corvette 1,278bm, 193 x 38½ ft, 20-8in, 1-68pdr. Sheerness DY 23.11.1854. Sold 23.1.1875 Castle, Charlton.

PYLADES Compos. S.corvette 1,420 tons, 200 x 38 ft, 14-5in. Sheerness DY 5.11.1884. Sold 3.4.1906 Cohen, Felixstowe.

PYLADES Destroyer, 'M' class. Stephen 28.9.1916. Sold 9.5.21 Ward, Hayle. arrived 9.22.

PYLADES Minesweeper, 'Catherine' class. Savannah Mcy 27.6.1943 on lend-lease. Sunk 8.7.44 by torpedo off Normandy.

PYRAMUS 5th Rate 36, 920bm, 141 x 38½ ft. Portsmouth DY 22.1.1810 (originally laid down 4.1806 Greensward, Itchenor; frames sent to Portsmouth 5.08 and relaid 11.08). Receiving ship 1832. BU 11.1879 at Halifax NS.

PYRAMUS 3rd class cruiser 2,135 tons, 300 x 36½ ft, 8-4in, 8-3pdr. Palmer 15.5.1897. Sold 21.4.1920, BU in Holland.

PYRRHUS Minesweeper, 'Algerine' class. Pt Arthur SY 19.5.1945. Arrived 8.9.56 Cashmore, Newport to BU.

PYTCHLEY Minesweeper, early 'Hunt' class. Napier & Miller 24.3.1917. Sold 7.22 Stanlee, Dover.

PYTCHLEY Destroyer, 'Hunt' class type 1. Scotts 13.2.40. Arrived 1.12.56 Rees, Llanelly to BU.

PYTHON (see PANDORA OF 1929)

QUADRA Survey ship (RCN) 5600 tons. Burrard 4.7.1966. Sold 10.82.

QUADRANT Destroyer, 1,705 tons, 339 x 36 ft. 4-4.7in, 8-TT. Hawthorn Leslie 28.2.1942. RAN 10.45; frigate 1954, 2,200 tons, 2-4in, 2-40mm. Sold 7.1.63.

QUADRILLE Minesweeper 260 tons, 130 x 26 ft, 1-3pdr. War Dept tug transferred on stocks; Ferguson 21.9.1917. sold 5.1.20 Crichton Thompson & Co.

QUADRILLE Trawler 1941-46.

QUAIL Schooner 4, 75bm, 56 x 18½ ft, 4-12pr carr. Custance, Yarmouth 26.4.1806. Sold 11.1.1816.

QUAIL Cutter tender, 80bm, 56 x 18½ ft. Deptford DY 31.1.1817. BU completed 10.4.1829. (Was to have been renamed PROVIDENCE 1.1822.)

QUAIL Cutter 4, 108bm, 61 x 20½ ft. Sheerness DY 30.9.1830. Fitted out 2.1859 for the Liberian Govt.

QUAIL Wood S.gunboat, 'Albacore' class. Wigram, Blackwall 2.6.1856. BU 9.1861 at Malta.

QUAIL Destroyer 395 tons, 213½ x 21½ ft, 1-12pr, 5-6pdr, 2-TT. Laird 24.9.1895. Sold 23.7.1919 Ward, New Holland.

QUAIL Destroyer 1,705 tons, 339 x 36 ft, 4-4.7in, 8-TT. Hawthorn Leslie 1.6.1942. Foundered in tow 18.6.44 between Bari and Taranto after being mined 15.11.43 south of Calabria.

QUAIL Two trawlers requis. in WW.I.

QUAINTON Coastal M/S, 'Ton class. Richards, Lowestoft 10.10.1957. Renamed NORTHUMBRIA 4.60 - 72. Sold H.K. Vickers 8.79. BU at Blyth.

QUAKER Ketch 10, 79bm. Purchased 1671. Sold 5.1698.

QUALICUM Minesweeper, TE 'Bagnor' class. Dufferin 3.9.1941. Sold 9.2.49, BU at Charlestown.

QUALITY Destroyer 1,705 tons, 339 x 36 ft, 4-4.7in, 8-TT. Swan Hunter 6.10.1941. RAN 10.45. Sold 10.4.58 to BU in Japan.

QUANGTUNG Iron paddle vessel (Indian), 523bm, 900 tons, 185 x 25 ft, 6-9pdr. Laird 1863. Listed in 1891.

QUANTOCK Destroyer, 'Hunt' class type I. Scotts 22.4.1940. Sold 18.10.54 Ecuadorian navy, renamed PRESIDENTE ALFARO 16.8.55.

QU'APPELLE (see FOXHOUND of 1934)

QU'APPELLE Escort (RCN) 2,335 tons, 366(oa) x 42 ft, 4-3in. Davie SB 2.5.1960.

QUATSINO Minesweeper (RCN), TE 'Bagnor' class. P.Rupert DD Co 9.1.1941. Sold 1949, renamed *Concord*.

QUEBEC 5th Rate 32, 685bm, 125 x 35½ ft. Barnard, Harwich 14.7.1760. Blown up 6.10.1779 in action with the French SURVEILLANTE off Ushant.

QUEBEC Schooner. Purchased 1775. Wrecked Newfoundland 11.9.1775

QUEBEC 5th Rate 32, 700bm, 126½ x 35½ ft. Stares & Parsons, Bursledon 24.5.1781. BU 7.1816.

QUEBEC Corvette (RCN), 'Flower' class. Morton, Quebec 12.11.1941. Renamed VILLE de QUEBEC 1942. Sold 1947.

QUEBEC (see UGANDA)

QUEEN Ship, 250bm. Built 1225. Fate unknown.

QUEEN (see ROYAL CHARLES of 1673)

QUEEN 2nd Rate 98, 1,876bm, 177½ x 49½ ft. Woolwich DY 18.9.1769. Reduced to 74 guns 10.1811. BU 4.1821.

QUEEN (ex-ROYAL FREDERICK renamed 12.4.1839) 1st Rate 110, 3,104bm, 204½ x 60 ft, 10-8in, 100-32pdr. Portsmouth DY 15.5.1839. Undocked 5.4.1859 as screw 86-gun ship, 3,249bm. BU 1871 Castle, Charlton.

QUEEN Paddle sloop (Indian), 766bm. Pitcher, Northfleet 1839. Listed 1860.

QUEEN Battleship 15,000 tons, 400 x 75 ft, 4-12in, 12-6in, 18-12pdr. Devonport DY 8.3.1902. Sold 4.11.20 Ward, Preston; arrived 5.8.21. from Birkenhead.

QUEEN (ex-*St Andrews*) Escort carrier 11,420 tons, 468½ x 69½ ft, 2-4in, 16-40mm, 24-A/C. Seattle Tacoma 2.8.1943 on lend-lease. Returned 31.10.46 to the USN.

QUEEN 5 Vessels hired between 1778 and 1805. Patrol vessel, Tug, Trawler and Drifter requis. in WW.I.

QUEEN CHARLOTTE 1st Rate 100, 2,286bm, 190 x 52½ ft. Chatham DY 15.4.1790. Blown up 17.3.1800 by accident off Leghorn.

QUEEN CHARLOTTE 1st Rate 104, 2,289bm, 190 x 53½ ft. Deptford DY 17.5.1810. Renamed EXCELLENT 31.12.1859 as gunnery training ship. Sold 12.1.1892 J.Read, Portsmouth.

QUEEN CHARLOTTE Sloop 16 (Canadian lakes), 280bm, 16-12pdr carr. Fort Erie 1812 and purchased 1813. Captured 10.9.1813 by Americans on Lake Erie.

QUEEN CHARLOTTE (see BOYNE of 1810)

QUEEN CHARLOTTE Three hired cutters between 1800 and 1814.

QUEEN ELIZABETH Battleship 27,500 tons, 600 x 90½ ft, 8-15in, 16 (later 12)-6in, 2-3in. Portsmouth DY 16.10.1913. Sold 19.3.48, arrived 7.7.48 Arnott Young, Dalmuir to BU.

QUEEN MAB Sloop 18, 490bm. Danish COUREER captured 7.9.1807 at Copenhagen. Renamed COURIER circa 1808. Sold circa 1812.

QUEEN MARY Battlecruiser 26,500 tons, 658 x 89 ft, 8-13.5in, 16-4in. Palmer 20.3.1912. Sunk 31.5.16 at Jutland.

QUEENBOROUGH Yacht 4, 27bm. Chatham DY 1671. Rebuilt Sheerness 1718 as 46bm. Sold 11.7.1777.

QUEENBOROUGH 6th Rate 24, 262bm, 96½ x 25 ft. Sheerness DY 22.12.1694. Rebuilt Portsmouth 1709. Sold 20.8.1719.

QUEENBOROUGH (see FOWEY of 1709)

QUEENBOROUGH 6th Rate 24, 519bm, 113½ x 32½ ft. Sparrow, Rotherhithe 21.1.1747. Foundered

1.1.1761 in a cyclone off Pondicherry.

QUEENBOROUGH Destroyer 1,705 tons, 339 x 36 ft, 4-4.7in, 8-TT. Swan Hunter 6.1.1942. RAN 10.45; frigate 1954, 2,200 tons, 2-4in, 2-40mm. Sold 8.4.75, BU at Hong Kong.

QUENTIN Destroyer 1,705 tons, 339 x 36 ft, 4-4.7in, 8-TT. White 5.11.1941. Sunk 2.12.42 by Italian A/C torpedo north of Algiers.

QUESNEL Corvette (RCN), 'Flower' class. Victoria Mcy 12.11.1940. BU 1946.

QUIBERON Destroyer 1,705 tons, 339 x 36 ft, 4-4.7in, 8-TT. White 31.1.1942. RAN 7.42. Frigate 7.57, 2,200 tons 2-4in, 2-40mm. Sold 15.2.72, BU in Japan.

QUICKMATCH Destroyer 1,705 tons, 339 x 36 ft, 4-4.7 in, 8-TT. White 11.4.1942. RAN 9.42; frigate 9.55. Sold 27.1.72, BU in Japan 7.72.

QUILLIAM Destroyer 1,725 tons, 339 x 36 ft, 4-4.7in, 8-TT. Hawthorn Leslie 29.11.1941. To Dutch navy 11.45 as BANCKERT.

QUINTE Minesweeper (RCN), TE 'Bangor' class. Burrard 8.3.1941. Sale list 8.47; sold Dominion Steel Corp to BU.

QUINTE Coastal M/S (RCN), 'Ton' class. 890 tons. Pt Arthur SY 8.8.1953.

QUITTANCE 25-gun ship, 257bm, 2-18pdr, 6-9pdr, 7-6pdr, 4-4pdr, 6 smaller. Built 1590. Condemned 1618.

QUORN Minesweeper, early 'Hunt' class. Napier & Miller 4.6.1917. Sold 18.9.22 J.Smith.

QUORN Destroyer, 'Hunt' class type I. White 27.3.1940. Sunk 3.8.44 by explosive motor boat off Normandy.

QUORN Minesweeper 615 tons. Ordered 4.6.1985.

'R' class submarines, 420 tons, 163(oa) x 16 ft. 6-TT.

R.1 Chatham DY 25.4.1918. Sold 20.1.23 J.Smith.

R.2 Chatham DY 25.4.18. Sold 21.2.23 E.Suren.

R.3 Chatham DY 8.6.18. sold 21.2.23 E.Suren.

R.4 Chatham DY 8.6.18. Sold 26.5.34 Young, Sunderland.

R.5 and R.6 Both Pembroke Dock (ex-Devonport), laid down 3.18, cancelled 28.8.19.

R.7 Vickers 14.5.18. Sold 21.2.23 E.Suren.

R.8 Vickers 28.6.18. Sold 21.2.23. E.Suren.

R.8 Armstrong 12.8.18. Sold 21.2.23 E.Suren.

R.10 Armstrong 5.10.18. Sold 19.2.29 Cashmore, Newport; arrived 3.30.

R.11 Cammell Laird 16.3.18. Sold 21.2.23 J.Smith.

R.12 Cammell Laird 9.4.18. Sold 21.2.23 J.Smith.

RABY CASTLE Corvette, 'Castle' class. Morton, Quebec. Cancelled 12.1943.

RACEHORSE Bomb 8, 385bm, 96½ x 30 ft. French privateer MARQUIS de VANDREVIL captured 1757 and purchased 28.4.1757. On arctic discovery 1773. Captured 12.1776 by the American ANDREA DORIA; destroyed 15.11.1777 by the RN in Delaware Bay.

RACEHORSE Sloop 16, 183bm, 68 x 20½ ft. Purchased 1777. Captured 14.8.1778 by the French; recaptured 2.11.1780 from the French as SENEGAL. Blew up 22.11.1780.

RACEHORSE Schooner 10, purchased 1778. Wrecked 1.1779 on Beachy Head.

RACEHORSE Sloop 16, 354bm, 102 x 28 ft. Fisher, Liverpool 20.10.1781 (purchased on stocks). BU 5.1799.

RACEHORSE Brig-sloop 18, 'Cruizer' class, 385bm. Hamilton & Breed, Hastings 17.2.1806. Wrecked 14.12.1822 on the Isle of Man.

RACEHORSE Sloop, 18, 438bm, 110 x 31 ft. Plymouth DY 24.5.1830. Coal hulk 1860. Sold 1901.

RACEHORSE Wood S.gunvessel, 695bm, 186 x 28½ ft, 1-110pdr, 2-20pdr, Blackwall 19.3.1860. Wrecked 4.11.1864 near Chefoo, China.

RACEHORSE Destroyer 400 tons, 210 x 21 ft, 1-12pdr, 5-6pdr, 2-TT. Hawthorn 8.11.1900. Sold 23.3.20 M.Yates; resold Ward and BU at Milford Haven 1921.

RACEHORSE Destroyer 1,705 tons, 339 x 36 ft, 4-4.7in, 8-TT. J.Brown 1.6.1942. Sold 8.11.49, arrived 12.49 at Troon to BU.

RACER Cutter 12, 203bm, 75 x 26 ft. Baker, Sandgate 24.4.1810. Stranded 24.5.1810 on the French coast and captured by the French.

RACER Schooner 12, 250bm, 93½ x 25 ft, 12-12pdr carr., 2-6pdr. American privateer INDEPENDENCE captured 9.11.1812. Wrecked 10.10.1814 in the

Gulf of Florida.

RACER Cutter 6, 123bm, 63½ x 22 ft, 2-6pdr, 4-6pdr carr. Pembroke Dock 4.4.1818. Ordered 4.5.1830 to sell at Malta.

RACER Brig-sloop 16, 431bm, 101 x 32½ ft, 14-32pdr carr., 2-12pdr. Portsmouth DY 18.7.1833. Sold 9.1852 Wilson & Co.

RACER Wood S.sloop, 579bm, 151 x 29 ft, 11-32pdr. Deptford DY 4.11.1857. BU 1876 at Portsmouth.

RACER Compos. S.gunvessel 970 tons, 167 x 32 ft, 8-5in. Devonport DY 6.8.1884. Sloop 1885; salvage vessel 1917. Sold 6.11.28 Hughes Bolckow, Blyth.

RACER Drifter requis 1915-19.

RACHEL Fireship 6, 134bm. Purchased 1672. Sunk 1673 in action.

RACKHAM Inshore M/S, 'Ham' class. Saunders Roe 27.4.1956. Sold Pounds 16.7.67.

RACOON Brig-sloop 14. Dating from 1780. Captured 12.9.1782 by two French ships.

RACOON Brig-sloop 16, 317bm, 95 x 28 ft. Randall, Rotherhithe 14.10.1795. BU 4.1806.

RACOON Sloop 18, 426bm, 109 x 29½ ft. Preston, Yarmouth 30.3.1808. Convict ship 1819. Sold 16.8.1838.

RACOON Wood S.corvette, 1,467bm, 200 x 40½ ft, 20-8in, 2-68pdr. Chatham DY 25.4.1857. BU 1877 at Devonport.

RACOON Torpedo cruiser 1,770 tons, 225 x 36 ft, 6-6in, 8-3pdr, 3-TT. Devonport DY 6.5.1887. Sold 4.4.1905 G.Cohen.

RACOON Destroyer 913 tons, 266 x 28 ft, 1-4in, 3-12pdr, 2-TT. Cammell Laird 15.2.1910. Wrecked 9.1.18 on the west coast of Ireland.

RACCOON Yacht (RCN) 1940-42.

RADIANT Destroyer, 'R' class 1,035 tons. Thornycroft 5.11.1916. Sold 21.6.20 Thornycroft for resale to Siam; renamed PHRA RUANG 9.20.

RADIANT Drifter 1916-19; Yacht requis. 1939-45.

RADLEY (see FLINDERS)

RADNOR Minesweeper, later 'Hunt' class. Lobnitz. Cancelled 1918.

RADSTOCK Destroyer, 'R' class. Swan Hunter 3.6.1916. Sold 29.4.27 Ward, Grays.

RAGLAN (ex-LORD RAGLAN renamed 23.6.1915, ex-M.3 renamed 20.6.15, ex-ROBERT E.LEE renamed 1915) Monitor 6,150 tons, 320 x 90 ft, 2-14in, 2-6in, 2-12pdr. Harland & Wolff, Govan 29.4.15. Sunk 20.1.18 by the German GOEBEN off Imbros.

RAIDER Destroyer, 'R' class. Swan Hunter 17.7.1916. Sold 29.4.27 G.Cohen.

RAIDER Destroyer 1,705 tons, 339 x 36 ft, 4-4.7in, 8-TT. Cammell Laird 1.4.1942. To Indian navy 9.9.49 as RANA.

RAIKES Transport. Purchased 9.1780. Captured 6.6.1782 by the French in the E.Indies.

RAIL River gunboat. Yarrow. Ordered 1912, cancelled 1913.

RAILLEUR Sloop 14. French, captured 11.1.1783 by CYCLOPS in N.America. Fate unknown.

RAILLEUR Sloop 20, 261bm, 89½ x 26 ft. French privateer captured 17.11.1797 by BOADICEA. Foundered 17.5.1800 in the Channel.

RAILLEUR (ex *Henry*) Sloop 16, 271bm. Purchased 6.1804. Sold 22.12.1810.

RAINBOW Galleon 26, 384bm, 6--34pdr, 12-18pdr, 7-9pdr, 1-6pdr. Deptford 1586. Rebuilt 1602 and again in 1617, as 548bm, 64 guns. Sunk 1680 as breakwater at Sheerness.

RAINBOW 5th Rate 32, 346bm, 103½ x 27½ ft. French, captured 1697. Sold 20.9.1698.

RAINBOW 5th Rate 44, 831bm, 133½ x 38 ft. Carter, Limehouse 30.5.1747. Troopship 1.1776; harbour service 6.1784. Sold 2.1802.

RAINBOW Brig-sloop 16. French, captured 1806. Sold 1807.

RAINBOW 6th Rate 28, 587bm, 20-32pdr., 6-18pdr carr., 2-6pdr. French IRIS captured 3.1.1809 by AIMABLE in the Texel. Sold 23.5.1815.

RAINBOW 6th Rate 28, 503bm, 114 x 32 ft, 20-32pdr carr., 6-18pdr carr., 2-9pdr. Chatham DY 20.11.1823. Sold 8.11.1838 Messrs Buck.

RAINBOW Wood S.gunboat, 'Albacore' class. Laird 8.3.1856. Survey vessel 1857; training ship 1873. Sold 11.1888 Castle, Charlton.

RAINBOW 2nd class cruiser 3,600 tons, 300 x 43 ft, 2-6in, 2-4.7in, 8-6pdr. Palmer 25.3.1891. RCN from 4.8.1910; depot ship 7.17. Sold 1920 as freighter.

RAINBOW Submarine 1,475 tons, 260 x 30 ft, 1-4in, 8-TT. Chatham DY 14.5.1930. Sunk 1940 by the Italian S/M TOTI off Calabria and formally paid off 19.10.40.

RAINBOW Trawler requis 1915-19.

RAINBOW Submarine (RCN). American ARGONAUT commissioned 2.12.68. Paid off 31.12.74 to BU.

RAISON 6th Rate 26, 472bm, 2-18pdr carr., 2-12pdr., 20-9pdr, 6-6pdr. French, captured with PREVOYANTE 17.5.1795 by THETIS and HUSSAR off the Chesapeake. Sold 5.1802.

RAISONNABLE 3rd Rate 64, 1,327bm, 159 x 44 ft, 26-24pdr, 20-12pdr, 10-6pdr. French, captured 29.5.1758 by DORSETSHIRE and ACHILLES. Lost 3.2.1762 at Martinique.

RAISONNABLE 3rd Rate 64, 1,386bm, 160 x 44½ ft. Chatham DY 10.12.1768. Receiving ship 11.1810. BU 3.1815.

RAJAH (ex-PRINCE renamed 12.1942, ex-*McClure*) Escort carrier 11,420 tons, 468½ x 69½ ft, 2-4in, 16-40mm, 24-A/C. Seattle Tacoma 18.5.43. Returned 13.12.46 to the USN.

RAJAH Trawler requis 1914-18.

RAJPUT (see Indian TB.6 of 1889)

RAJPUTANA (ex-LYME REGIS renamed 1941) Minesweeper (RIN), TE 'Bangor' class. Lobnitz 31.12.1941. BU 1961.

RAJPUTANA AMC requis. 1939-41.

RALEIGH 5th Rate 32, 697bm, 131½ x 34½ ft, 32-12pdr. American, captured 28.9.1778 by EXPERIMENT and UNICORN. Sold 17.7.1783.

RALEIGH Brig-sloop 18, 'Cruizer' class, 383bm. Hurry, Howden Dock 24.12.1806. Target 8.1839. Sold 27.5.1841.

RALEIGH 4th Rate 50, 1,939bm, 180 x 51 ft, 6-8in, 44-32pdr. Chatham DY 8.5.1845. Wrecked 14.4.1857 near Macao.

RALEIGH Wood S.frigate, 3,027bm, 250 x 52 ft. Pembroke Dock. Ordered 5.3.1860, cancelled 12.12.1863.

RALEIGH Iron S.frigate, 3,215bm, 5,200 tons, 280 x 48½ ft, 2-9in, 20-64pdr. Chatham DY 1.3.1873. Sold 11.7.1905 Ward, Morecambe.

RALEIGH Cruiser 9,750 tons, 565 x 65 ft, 7-7.5in, 6-12pdr. Beardmore 28.8.1919. Wrecked 8.8.22 on th coast of Labrador.

RAMBLER Cutter 10. In 1778. Blown up 6.10.1779 in action. (May have been a hired vessel.)

RAMBLER Cutter 10, 139bm, 65½ x 22½ ft. Purchased 4.1778. Sold 24.5.1787.

RAMBLER Brig-sloop 14, 193bm, 75½ x 25½ ft, 14-6pdr. Cutter purchased 12.1796. Sold 18.10.1816.

RAMBLER (ex-RAMBLE renamed 1855) Wood S.gunboat, 'Cheerful'

class. Pembroke Dock 21.2.1856. BU 1.1869 at Haslar.

RAMBLER Compos. S.gunvessel 835 tons, 157 x 29½ ft, 1-7in, 2-64 pdr. Elder, Glasgow 26.1.1880. Survey vessel 1884. Sold 23.1.1907.

RAMBLER Tug 1908-53, Trawler requis. 1915-20.

RAME HEAD Repair ship 8,580 tons, 416 x 57 ft, 16-20mm. N. Vancouver SR 22.11.1944.

RAMILLIES (see KATHERINE of 1664)

RAMILLIES 3rd Rate 74, 1,619bm, 168½ x 47 ft. Chatham DY 15.4.1763. Damaged in a hurricane and burnt 16.9.1782 off the Newfoundland Banks.

RAMILLIES 3rd Rate 74, 1,670bm, 170½ x 48½ ft. Randall, Rotherhithe 12.7.1785. Harbour service 6.1831. BU 2.1850 at Deptford.

RAMILLIES Battleship 14,150 tons, 380 x 75 ft, 4-13.5in, 10-6in, 16-6pdr. Thomson 1.3.1892. Sold 7.10.1913 G.Cohen.

RAMILLIES Battleship 25,750 tons, 580 x 88½ ft, 8-15in, 14-6in. Beardmore 12.9.1916. Harbour service 5.45. Sold 20.2.48, BU at Cairnryan.

RAMILLIES Nuclear S/M Ordered 26.6,1964, Cancelled 15.2.65

RAMILLIES Mine carrier requis. 1914-16

RAMPART (ex-LCT.4037 renamed 1956) Tank landing craft 657 tons, 225 x 39 ft. Arrol, Alloa 1945. To War Dept 1965, renamed *Akyab*.)

RAMPISHAM Inshore M/S, 'Ham' class. Bolson, Poole 1.5.1957. Sold 10.8.66 mercantile.

RAMSEY (see ROSS)

RAMSEY (ex-USS MEADE Destroyer 1,190 tons, 311 x 31 ft, 3-4in, 1-3in, 6-TT. Commissioned in the RN 26.11.1940. Air target 6.43. Sold 18.2.47, arrived 7.47 McLellan, Bo'ness to BU.

RAMSEY ABS 1914-15.

RANEE (ex-*Niantic*) Escort carrier 11,420 tons, 468½ x 69½ ft, 2-4in, 16-40mm, 24-A/C. Seattle Tacoma 2.6.1943 on lend-lease. Returned 21.11.46 to the USN.

RANELAGH 2nd Rate 80, 1,199bm, 158½ x 42 ft. Deptford DY 25.6.1697. Renamed PRINCESS CAROLINE 1728. Rebuilt Woolwich 1731 as 1,353bm. BU completed 28.4.1764 at Chatham.

RANGER 6th Rate 24, 639bm, 123 x 34½ ft, 24-9pdr. French privateer DEUX COURONNES captured 5.5.1747 by GLOUCESTER in the

Channel. Sold 29.5.1749.

RANGER Sloop 8, 142bm, 75 x 20½ ft. Woolwich DY 7.10.1752. Sold 16.1.1783.

RANGER Cutter, 201bm, 80½ x 26 ft. Purchased 1779. Renamed PIGMY 1781 and made a sloop. Sold 21.10.1784.

RANGER Cutter 14, 195bm, 75 x 25½ ft, 14-4pdr. Purchased 2.1787. Captured 28.6.1794 by the French off Brest. Recaptured 14.10.1797 and renamed VENTURER. Sold 2.1803 at Gibraltar.

RANGER Sloop 16, 361bm, 105 x 28 ft. Hill & Mellish, Limehouse 19.3.1794. Captured 17.7.1805 by the French and burnt.

RANGER Brig-sloop, 208bm, 82½ x 24½ ft. Built on the Thames 1797 and later purchased. Fate unknown.

RANGER Cutter 16, 217bm, 80 x 26 ft. Avery, Dartmouth 5.1806 and purchased. Renamed PIGMY 29.5.1806. Lost 6.1814.

RANGER Sloop 18, 428bm, 109 X 29½ ft. Thorn, Fremington 5.9.1807. BU 2.1814.

RANGER 6th Rate 28, 502bm, 113½ x 32 ft, 20-32pdr carr., 6-18pdr carr., 2-9pdr. Portsmouth DY 7.12.1820. Sold 11.1832 J.Jackson.

RANGER Packet brig 8, 363bm, 96 x 30½ ft. Bottomley, Rotherhithe 25.7.1835. Hulk 1860. Sold 1867 at Dublin.

RANGER Wood S.gunvessel, 'Philomel' class. Deptford DY 26.11.1859. Sold 3.11.1869 Moss Isaacs.

RANGER Compos. S.gunvessl 835 tons, 157 x 29½ ft, 1-7in, 2-64pdr. Elder 12.2.1880. Sold 24.9.1892 as salvage vessel (hired 11.14 to 1919 as ammo hulk WW.I. BU 1947)

RANGER Destroyer 320 tons, 200 x 19 ft, 1-12pdr, 5-6pdr, 2-TT. Hawthorn 4.10.1895. Sold 20.5.20 Riddle & Co.

RANGER (see CAESAR of 1944)

RANGER Patrol boat 43 tons, Watercraft 1986 and laid-up

RANPURA Repair ship 18,250 tons, 548 x 71 ft, 20-20mm. Ex-AMC hired 1939, purchased 1943 and converted. Arrived 25.5.61 at Spezia to BU.

RANUNCULUS Corvette, 'Flower' class. Simons 25.6.1941. Lent Free-French 1941-46 as RENONCULE. sold 1947, renamed Southern Lily.

RAPID Gun-brig 12, 178bm, 80 x 22½ ft, 2-18pdr, 10-18pdr carr. Davy, Topsham 20.10.1804. Sunk 18.5.1808 by batteries in the Tagus.

RAPID Schooner 12, 90bm, French, captured 1808. Wrecked 3.1814 on The Saintes, W.Indies.

RAPID Brig-sloop 14, 261bm, 92 x 25½ ft, 12-24pdr carr., 2-6pdr. Davy, Topsham 22.10.1808. Sold 10.12.1814.

RAPID Brig-sloop 10, 'Cherokee' class, 235bm. Portsmouth DY 17.8.1829. Wrecked 12.4.1838 off Crete.

RAPID Brig 8, 319bm, 90 x 29½ ft. Portsmouth DY 3.6.1840. Sold 1.1856 MacDonald & Co at Singapore.

RAPID Wood S.sloop, 672bm, 913 tons, 160 x 30½ ft, 1-40pdr, 6-32pdr, 4-20pdr. Deptford DY 29.11.1860. BU 9.1881 at Malta.

RAPID Compos. S.corvette 1,420 tons, 200 x 38 ft, 2-6in, 10-5in. Devonport DY 21.3.1883. Hulk 1906; coal hulk C.7 in 1912. Renamed HART accommodation ship 1916. Sold 1948 at Gibraltar.

RAPID Destroyer, 'M' class 1,033 tons. Thornycroft 15.7.1916. Sold 20.4.27 G.Cohen.

RAPID Destroyer 1,705 tons, 339 x 36 ft, 4-4.7in, 8-TT. Cammell Laird 16.7.1942. Frigate 1952, 2,300 tons, 2-4in, 2-40mm. Sunk 3.9.81 as target in the Atlantic.

RAPOSO Gun-brig 10, 173bm. Spanish, captured 7.1.1806 by boats of FRANCHISE off Campeche. Destroyed 15.2.1808 to prevent capture near Cartagena.

RATTLE Gun-brig 14. Listed 1802-05.

RATTLER Sloop 16, 342bm, 102 x 28 ft. Wilson, Sandgate 22.3.1783. Sold 6.9.1792.

RATTLER sloop 16, 360bm, 105 x 28 ft. Raymond, Northan 21.3.1795. Sold 12.10.1815.

RATTLER (Gunboat No.41) (ex-Hope) Gunvessel 12, 158bm, 72½ x 22½ ft, 2-24pdr, 10-18pdr carr. Purchased 3.1797 at Leith. Sold 1802.

RATTLER (ex-ARDENT renamed 1842) Wood S.sloop, 888bm, 176½ x 32½ ft. Sheerness DY 12.4.1843. BU completed 26.11.1856 by Fulcher, Woolwich.

RATTLER Wood S.sloop, 950bm, 185 x 33 ft, 5-40pdr, 12-32pdr. Deptford DY 18.3.1862. Wrecked 24.9.1868 on the China Station.

RATTLER Compos. S.gunboat 715 tons, 165 x 29 ft, 6-4in. Armstrong Mitchell 4.8.1886. Harbour service 1910. Renamed DRYAD 9.19 as navigation school ship. Sold 10.24.

RATTLER Minesweeper, 'Algerine' class. Harland & Wolff 9.12.1942. Renamed LOYALTY 6.43. Sunk

22.8.44 by 'U.480' in the Channel.

RATTLER Whaler 1915, renamed PRATTLER 1916-19.

RATTLESNAKE Cutter 10, 185bm, 69½ x 26 ft. Farley, Folkestone 7.6.1777. Made a sloop 1779. (A 14-gun sloop wrecked 2.10.1782 on Trinidad may have been this vessel.)

RATTLESNAKE Sloop 14, 198bm, 84 x 22 ft. Captured 1779. Lost 1781 (in the E.Indies?)

RATTLESNAKE (see CORMORANT of 1781)

RATTLESNAKE Sloop 16, 326bm, 100 x 27 ft. Chatham DY 7.1.1791. Sold 3.11.1814.

RATTLESNAKE (see HERON of 1812)

RATTLESNAKE 6th Rate 28, 503bm, 114 x 32ft, 20-32pdr carr., 6-18pdr carr., 2-9pdr. Chatham DY 26.3.1822. Survey ship 2 guns 1845. BU completed 13.1.1860 at Chatham.

RATTLESNAKE Wood S.corvette, 1,705bm, 2,431 tons, 225 x 41 ft. 16-8in, 1-7in, 4-40pdr. Chatham DY 9.7.1861. BU 3.1882 at Devonport.

RATTLESNAKE Torpedo gunboat 550 tons, 200 x 23ft, 1-4in, 6-3pdr, 4-TT. Laird 11.9.1886. Sold 1910.

RATTLESNAKE Destroyer 946 tons, 270 x 28 ft, 1-4in, 3-12pdr, 2-TT. London & Glasgow Co 14.3.1910. Sold 9.5.21 Ward, Milford Haven.

RATTLESNAKE Minesweeper, 'Algerine' class. Lobnitz 23.2.1943. Sold 11.57. Arrived 10.59 Brunton, Grangemouth to BU.

RATTRAY HEAD Repair ship 8,580 tons, 416 x 57 ft. N. Vancouver SR Co 8.6.1945, not completed. Cancelled 18.8.45, completed as Iran.

RAVAGER (ex-CHARGER renamed 1942). Escort carrier 11,420 tons, 468½ x 69½ ft, 2-4in, 16-40mm, 24-A/C. Seattle Tacoma 16.7.42 on lend-lease. Returned 27.2.46 to the USN.

RAVAGER (see LST.3505)

RAVEN 36-gun ship. Captured 1652. Captured 4.1654 by the Dutch.

RAVEN 6-gun vessel. (French?) ST CORNELIUS captured 1656. Listed to 1659.

RAVEN Sloop 14, 273bm, 31 x 26 ft. Blaydes, Hull 4.7.1745. Sold 31.3.1763.

RAVEN (see VESUVIUS of 1771)

RAVEN (see CERES of 1777)

RAVEN Sloop 14 (fir-built), 365bm, 96 x 30½ ft. Wallis, Blackwall 11.1.1796. Wrecked 3.2.1798 near Cuxhaven.

RAVEN Brig-sloop 18, 390bm, 107½ x 29½ ft. French ARETHUSE captured 10.10.1799 by EXCELLENT off L'Orient. Wrecked 6.7.1804 on the coast of Sicily.

RAVEN Brig-sloop 18, 'Cruiser' class, 384bm. Perry, Blackwall 25.7.1804. Wrecked 29.1.1805 in Cadiz Bay.

RAVEN Brig-sloop 16 (fir-built), 282bm, 96 x 26ft, 14-24pdr carr. 2-6pdr. Warren, Brightlingsea 12.8.1805. Sold 18.9.1816.

RAVEN Survey cutter 4, 108bm, 61 x 20½ ft. Pembroke Dock 21.10.1829. Quarantine ship 1.1848; coastguard 1850. Sold 28.10.1859 at Aldburgh.

RAVEN Mortar vessel, 155bm, 70 x 23½ ft, 1-13in mortar. Green, Blackwall 19.4.1855. Renamed MV.13 on 19.10.1855. Ordered 11.7.1856 to be sold at Constantinople.

RAVEN Wood S.gunboat, 'Albacore' class. Laird 8.3.1856. Sold 13.4.1875 Castle, Charlton.

RAVEN Compos. S-gunboat 465 tons, 125 x 23½ ft, 2-64pdr, 2-20pdr. Samuda, Poplar 18.5.1882. Diving tender 1904. Sold 13.3.25.

RAVEN Seaplane carrier 4,678 tons (ex-German) 1915-17.

RAYLEIGH (see ADVENTURE of 1771)

RAYLEIGH CASTLE (see EMPIRE REST)

READING Minesweeper, later 'Hunt' class. Lobnitz. Cancelled 1919.

READING (ex-USS BAILEY) Destroyer 1,190 tons, 311 x 31ft 3-4in, 1-3in, 6-TT. Commissioned 26.11.1940 in the RN. Air target 10.42. Sold 24.7.45; BU Ward, Inverkeithing.

READY (Gunboat No.42) (ex-Minerva) Gunvessel 12, 152bm, 70 x 22½ ft, 2-24pdr, 10-18pdr carr. Purchased 3.1797 at Leith. Sold 12.1802.

READY Wood S.gunboat, 'Clown' class. Briggs, Sunderland 12.5.1856. BU completed 25.1.1864.

READY Wood S.gunvessel, 462bm, 610 tons, 155 x 25ft, 1-7in, 1-64pdr, 2-20pdr. Chatham DY 24.9.1872. Tank vessel 1894. Renamed DRUDGE 10.1916. Sold 25.2.20 in Bermuda.

READY Destroyer, 'M' class 1,033 tons. Thornycroft 26.8.1916. Sold 13.7.26 King, Garston.

READY Minesweeper, 'Algerine' class. Harland & Wolff 20.3.1943. Sold 4.7.51 Belgian navy as JAN van HAVERBEKE.

REAPER (ex-Winjah) Escort carrier 11,420 tons, 468½ x 69½ ft, 2-4in, 16-40mm, 24-A/C. Seattle Tacoma

22.11.1943 on lend-lease. Returned 20.5.46 to the USN.

REAPER Drifter requis, 1914-19.

REBUFF Gun-brig 12, 180bm, 84 x 22 ft. Richards, Hythe 30.5.1805. Sold 15.12.1814.

RECLAIM (ex-SALVERDANT renamed 1947) Salvage vessel 1,200 tons, 200 x 38 ft. Simons 12.3.48. Sold mercantile 1983.

RECLAIM Drifter requis. 1914-19.

RECOVERY 20-gun ship, 300bm. Captured 1646. Sold 1655.

RECOVERY 26-gun ship. Captured 1652. Sold 1656.

RECOVERY (see MINERVA of 1759)

RECOVERY Sloop 14. American, captured 1782. Sold 1785 in the W.Indies.

RECOVERY (see PORT ROYAL)

RECOVERY Mooring vessel 1907-23. Tug 1902-05. (see ROVER)

RECRUIT Brig-sloop 18, 'Cruiser' class, 383bm. Hills, Sandwich 31.8.1806. Sold 7.8.1822 R.Forbes.

RECRUIT Brig-sloop 10, 'Cherokee' class, 235bm. Portsmouth DY 17.8.1829. Foundered 1832 off Bermuda.

RECRUIT Iron brig 12, 462bm, 114½ x 30½ ft. Ditchburn & Mare, Blackwall 10.6.1846. Sold 28.8.1849 Mr Mare; resold after conversion to screw ship, renamed *Harbinger*. (The only iron-built sailing vessel in the RN.)

RECRUIT (ex-Prussian NIX) Iron pad. gunboat, 540bm, 178(wl) x 26ft, 4-8in, 4-32pdr. Exchanged 12.1.1855 together with SALAMANDER for the 5th Rate THETIS. Sold E.Bates. 23.9.1869.

RECRUIT Destroyer 385 tons, 218 x 20 ft, 1-12pdr, 5-6pdr, 2-TT. Thomson 22.8.1896. Sunk 1.5.1915 by U-boat off the Galloper Light Vessel.

RECRUIT Destroyer, 'R' class. Doxford 9.12.1916. Sunk 9.8.17 by 'UB.16' in the North Sea.

RECRUIT Minesweeper, 'Algerine' class. Harland & Wolff 26.10.1943. BU 9.65 Ward, Burrow.

RECRUIT Drifter requis. 1915-19.

REDBREAST Gun-brig 12, 178bm, 80 x 22½ ft. Preston, Yarmouth 27.4.1805. To Customs 7.1815 as hulk. Sold 4.6.1850 at Liverpool.

REDBREAST Cutter tender 12, 80bm, 56 x 18½ ft. Woolwich DY 18.2.1817. Sold 1850 J. Brown.

REDBREAST Mortar vessel, 155bm, 70 x 23½ ft, 1-13in mortar. Green, Blac-

kwall 5.5.1855. Renamed MV.19 on 19.10.1855. BU completed 27.9.1865 Marshall, Plymouth.

REDBREAST Wood S.gunboat, 'Albacore' class. Laird 11.3.1856. BU completed 24.9.1864.

REDBREAST Compos. S.gunboat 805 tons, 165 x 31 ft, 6-4in. Pembroke Dock 25.4.1889. Sold 1910.

REDBREAST Fleet messenger 1915-17.

REDBRIDGE Schooner 16, 148bm, 80 x 21½ ft. Redbridge 1796 and purchased. Captured 4.8.1803 by the French off Toulon.

REDBRIDGE Schooner 10, 131bm. Purchased 1804. Foundered 1.3.1805 near Jamaica.

REDBRIDGE Schooner 12, 170bm, 81 x 21½ ft. French OISEAU captured 1803 and purchased 1805. Wrecked 4.11.1806 in the W.Indies.

REDBRIDGE Schooner 10, 172bm, 80½ x 22 ft, 8-12pdr carr., 2-6pdr. American ARISTOTLE captured 1807. Sold 1814.

REDCAR Paddle M/S, 'Ascot' class. Ayrshire DY Co 31.7.1916. Sunk 24.6.17 by mine off Dover.

RED DEER Minesweeper (RCN), TE 'Bangor' class. Vickers, Montreal 12.5.1941. Sold 2.59 Marine Industries.

REDGAUNTLET (see LAUREL of 1913)

REDGAUNTLET Destroyer, 'R' class. Denny 23.11.1916. Sold 7.27 King, Garston.

REDGAUNTLET Minesweeper 1916-19; Trawler requis, 1939-43.

RED HART Pink 6. Captured 1653. Sold 1954.

RED LION (see LION of 1557)

REDMILL (see MEDINA of 1916)

REDMILL Frigate, TE 'Captain' class. Bethlehem, Hingham 2.10.1943 on lend-lease. Torpedoed 27.4.45 and not repaired. Sold by the USN 2.47 and BU.

REDOUBT (ex-*Rover*) Floating battery 20, 386bm, 97½ x 30 ft, 20-24pdr carr. Purchased 3.1793. Sold 20.5.1802.

REDOUBT Destroyer, 'R' class. Doxford 28.10.1916. Sold 13.7.26 J. Smith.

REDOUBT Destroyer 1,705 tons, 339 x 36 ft, 4-4.7in, 8-TT. J.Brown 2.5.1942. To Indian navy 4.7.49 as RANJIT.

REDOUBT (ex-LCT.4001 renamed 1956) Tank landing craft 657 tons, 225 x 39 ft. Stockton Co, Thornaby on Tees 27.7.45. Sold 1966 as ferry

Dimitris.

REDOUBTABLE 3rd Rate 74, 1,759 bm, 176½ x 48½ ft. Woolwich DY 26.1.1815. BU 5.1841 at Chatham.

REDOUBTABLE (see REVENGE of 1892)

REDPOLE Brig-sloop 10, 'Cherokee' class, 239bm. Guillaume, Northam 29.7.1808. Sunk 8.1828 in action with pirate CONGRESS of Cape Frio.

REDPOLE Compos. S.gunboat 805 tons, 165 x 31 ft, 6-4in. Pembroke Dock 13.6.1889. Sold 15.5.1906 Cox, Falmouth.

REDPOLE Destroyer 720 tons, 246 x 25 ft, 2-4in, 2-12pdr, 2-TT. White 24.6.1910. Sold 9.5.21 Ward, Milford.

REDPOLE Sloop 1,350 tons, 283 x 38½ ft, 6-4in. Yarrow 25.2.1943. Arrived 20.11.60 St Davids to BU.

REDPOLE Patrol boat ex-*Sea Otter* (RAF) transferred 1985.

REDPOLE Tug 1855-72.

REDSHANK Paddle M/S. Projected 1918. Not ordered.

REDSHANK M/L trawler 1942-57.

REDSTART Minelayer 498 tons, 145 x 27 ft, 1-20mm, 12 mines. Robb 3.5.1938. Scuttled 19.12.41 at Hong Kong.

REDSTART requis. 1915-19.

REDWING Brig-sloop 18, 'Cruizer' class, 383bm. Warren, Brightlingsea 30.8.1806. Foundered 6.1827 off W.Africa. (In 11.1808 fought the last action with Spain.)

REDWING Sloop 18, 481bm, 116 x 31 ft. Plymouth DY. Ordered 30.1.1829. cancelled 1.11.1832.

REDWING (ex-GPO vessel *Richmond*) Wood pad. packet, 139bm, 144 x 15½ ft. Transferred 1.4.1837. Sold 17.1.1849.

REDWING Wood S.gunboat, 'Dapper' class. Pitcher, Northfleet 19.3.1855. Harbour service 1857. Sold 2.12.1878.

REDWING (ex-ESPOIR renamed 3.6.1879) Compos. S.gunboat 461 tons, 125 x 23½ ft, 2-64pdr, 2-20pdr. Pembroke Dock 25.5.1880. Sold 4.4.1905 at Chatham.

REDWING (ex-War Dept vessel *Sir Charles Pasley*) Tender 120 tons, 93 x 18 ft. Transferred 1905. Sold 26.6.1931. (Was to have been renamed REDSTART in 1916.)

REDWING (see MEDWAY of 1916)

REDWING Tender 225 tons, 102 x 25 ft. White 19.10.1933. Sold 16.1.57 Everard & Sons.

REEDHAM Inshore M/S, 'Ham' class. Saunders Roe 19.8.1958. Sold Pounds 8.8.66, became yacht *Marisa*.

REEVES (see COSBY)

REFUGE (see RESOLUTE of 1850)

REGENT (see GRACE DIEU of 1488)

REGENT Brig 14, 350bm, 97 x 29 ft, 10-12pdr carr., 2-9pdr, 2-6pdr. Purchased 1816. On revenue service 1831.

REGENT Submarine 1,475 tons, 260 x 30 ft, 1-4in, 8-TT. Vickers Armstrong. Barrow 11.6.1930. Sunk 16.4.43 by mine in the Taranto Straits.

REGENT Store carrier 19000 tons. 1966.

REGGIO (see LST.3511)

REGINA Corvette (RCN), 'Flower' class. Marine Ind 14.10.1941. Sunk 8.8.44 by mine in the Channel.

REGINA Destroyer (RCN) 4,200 tons. Ordered St.John DD in 1983.

REGINA 3 vessels requis. in WW.I.

REGULUS 5th Rate 44, 889bm, 140 x 38 ft. Raymond, Northam 10.2.1785. Troopship 1793. BU 3.1816.

REGULUS Brig-sloop 14. French privateer captured 13.12.1804 by PRINCESS CHARLOTTE in the W.Indies. Listed in 1806.

REGULUS Submarine 1,475 tons, 260 x 30 ft, 1-4in, 8-TT. Vickers Armstrong. Barrow 11.6.1930. Lost by unknown cause in the Taranto Strait and formally paid off 6.12.40.

REGULUS (ex-LONGBRANCH renamed 1943) Minesweeper, 'Algerine' class. Toronto 18.9.43. Sunk 12.1.45 by mine in the Corfu Channel.

REINDEER Brig-sloop 18, 'Cruizer' class, 385bm. Brent, Rotherhithe 15.8.1804. Captured 28.6.1814 by the American WASP in the Channel and burnt.

REINDEER Packet brig 8, 'Cherokee' class, 230bm. Plymouth DY 29.9.1829. Harbour service 5.1841. Sold in 1847 though listed until 1856.

REINDEER Wood S.sloop, 953bm, 185 x 33 ft, 1-110pdr, 5-64pdr. Chatham DY 29.3.1866 (cancelled 5.1865 and re-started). BU 12.1876 at Chatham.

REINDEER Compos. S.sloop 970 tons, 167 x 32 ft, 8-5in. Devonport DY 14.11.1883. BDV 1904; salvage vessel 1917. Sold 12.7.24 Halifax SY Ltd as salvage vessel.

REINDEER M/S requis. 1914-20. Trawler 1916-19.

RELENTLESS Destroyer, 'M' class 900 tons. Yarrow 15.4.1916. Sold 5.11.26

Cashmore, Newport.

RELENTLESS Destroyer 1,705 tons, 339 x 36 ft, 4-4.7in, 8-TT. J.Brown 15.7.1942. Frigate 1951, 2,300 tons, 2-4in, 2-40mm. Sold Ward 29.4.71, BU Inverkeithing.

RELIANCE Discovery vessel, 394bm, 90 x 30 ft. Purchased 12.1793. Harbour service 1800. Sold 12.10.1815.

RELIANCE Tender 12. In service in 1812-15.

RELIANCE (ex-*Knight Companion*) Repair ship 9,220 tons 469½ x 58 ft. Purchased 14.11.1912. Sold 17.12.19.

RELIANCE Repair ship 14,250 tons, 416 x 57 ft, 1-5in, 10-40mm. Bethlehem, Fairfield. Launched 13.9.1944 as DUTIFUL on lend-lease but retained by the USN as LAERTES.

RELIANCE Two drifters and a trawler requis. WW.I.

RENARD Sloop 18. French, captured 5.1780 by BRUNE in the W.Indies. BU 1784.

RENARD Sloop 18, 347bm, 101 x 28 ft, 16-18pdr carr., 2-6pdr. French privateer captured 14.11.1797 by CERBERUS. Sold 1805.

RENARD Schooner 14, 137bm. French, captured 11.1803 by a squadron in the Mediterranean. Sold 1.1809 and BU.

REYNARD Brig-sloop 10, 'Cherokee' class, 238bm. King, Upnor 15.12.1808. Sold 29.1.1818 Pitman to BU.

REYNARD Brig-sloop 10, 'Cherokee' class, 237bm. Pembroke Dock 26.10.1821. RENARD in 1828; mooring vessel 1841. BU 8.1857.

REYNARD Wood S.sloop, 516bm, 148 x 27½ ft, 8-32pdr. Deptford DY 21.3.1848. Wrecked 31.5.1851 on Pratas Shoal in the China Sea.

RENARD Wood S.sloop, 682bm, 181½ x 28½ ft, 1-110pdr, 1-68pdr, 2-20pdr. Mare, Blackwall 23.4.1856. BU 3.1866 Castle, Charlton.

RENARD Schooner, 120bm, 80 x 17 ft, 1-12pdr. Cuthbert, Sydney NSW 16.1.1873. Sold 1883 at Sydney.

RENARD Torpedo gunboat 810 tons, 230 x 27 ft, 2-4.7in, 4-3pdr, 3-TT. Laird 6.12.1892. Sold 4.4.1905 McLellan Bo'ness.

RENARD Destroyer 918 tons, 266 x 28 ft, 1-4in, 3-12pdr, 2-TT. Cammell Laird 13.11.1909. Sold 31.8.20 Ward, New Holland.

RENARD Yacht (RCN) 1940-47.

RENDLESHAM Inshore M/S, 'Ham' class. Brooke Marine, Lowestoft 13.10.1954. Transferred French navy 1955.

RENEGADE Schooner 4, 94bm. Purchased 7.1823, sold 8.1.1826.

RENFREW Corvette (RCN), modified 'Flower' class. Kingston Ont. Cancelled 12.1943.

RENIRA Schooner tender, 86bm. Ordered 18.5.1847 to be purchased. Sold 1850.

RENNIE Tender, 40bm. Plymouth 18.3.1813 became a tank vessel and BU 6.1863 at Chatham.

RENNINGTON Coastal M/S, 'Ton' class. Richards, Lowestoft 27.11.1958. Sold 1967 Argentine navy, renamed CHACO.

RENOMMEE 5th Rate 38. French, captured 20.7.1796 by ALFRED in the W.Indies. BU 9.1810.

RENOWN Fireship 20. French RENOMMEE captured 12.1651 by NONSUCH. Sold 1654.

RENOWN 5th Rate 30, 669bm, 127 x 35 ft. French RENOMMEE captured 9.1747 by DOVER. BU 5.1771 at Woolwich.

RENOWN 4th Rate 50, 1,050bm, 146 x 40½ ft. Fabian, Northam 4.12.1774. (Named 19.11.74 but stuck on ways.) BU 12.1794.

RENOWN (ex-ROYAL OAK renamed 15.2.1796) 3rd Rate 74, 1,899bm, 182 x 49½ ft. Dudman, Deptford 2.5.1798. Harbour service 1.1814. BU 5.1835.

RENOWN Screw 2nd Rate 91, 3,319bm, 244½ x 55½ ft, 34-8in, 1-68pdr, 56-32pdr. Chatham DY 28.3.1857. Sold 24.3.1870 to the N.German Confederation navy.

RENOWN (see VICTORIA of 1887)

RENOWN (see EMPRESS of INDIA)

RENOWN Battleship 12,350 tons, 380 x 72 ft, 4-10in, 10-6in, 14-12pdr. Pembroke Dock 8.5.1895. Sold 2.4.1914 Hughes Bolckow, Blyth.

RENOWN (see REVENGE of 1915)

RENOWN Battlecruiser 26,500 tons, 750 x 90 ft, 6-15in, 17-4in, 2-3in. Fairfield 4.3.1916. Sold 19.3.48, BU Metal Industries, Faslane, arrived 8.8.48.

RENOWN Nuclear submarine, circa 7,000 tons, 410 x 33 ft, 6-TT, 16-GWS. Cammell Laird 25.2.1967.

RENOWN Drifter and tug requis. in WW.I.

REPTON (ex-WICKLOW renamed 1918) Minesweeper, later 'Hunt' class. Inglis 29.5.19. Sold 10.20 Bombay SN Co, renamed *Rupavati*.

REPTON (ex-OSSINGTON renamed

1956) Coastal M/S 'Ton' class. Harland & Wolff 1.5.57. Sold Pounds in 8.82.

REPUBLICAINE Schooner 18. French, captured 14.10.1795 by MERMAID and ZEBRA in the W.Indies. Sold circa 1802.

REPULSE (also DUE REPULSE) Galleon 50, 622bm. Deptford 1595. Rebuilt 1610 as 764bm. Listed to 1645.

REPULSE 5th Rate 32, 676bm, 122½ x 35 ft. French BELLONE captured 21.2.1759 by VESTAL. Foundered 12.1776 off Bermuda.

REPULSE Cutter 10, 136bm, 64½ x 23 ft. Purchased 1779. Listed to 1781.

REPULSE 3rd Rate 64, 1,387bm, 160 x 44½ ft. Fabian. E.Cowes 28.11.1780. Wrecked 10.3.1800 off Ushant.

REPULSE Cutter 12, 12-4pdr. Purchased 3.1780. Wrecked 3.1782 off Yarmouth.

REPULSE Gunvessel 4, 54bm, 63 x 13½ ft. Hoy purchased 3.1794. BU 4.1795

REPULSE 3rd Rate 74, 1,727bm, 174 x 48½ ft. Barnard, Deptford 22.7.1803. BU 9.1820.

REPULSE Screw 2nd Rate 91, 3,087bm, 230 x 55½ ft. Pembroke Dock 27.9.1855. Renamed VICTOR EMMANUEL 7.1855. Receiving ship 1873. Sold 1899.

REPULSE Ironclad ship, 3,749bm, 6,190 tons, 252 x 58 ft, 12-8in. Woolwich DY 25.4.1868. Sold 2.1889.

REPULSE Battleship 14,150 tons, 380 x 75 ft, 4-13.5in, 10-6in, 16-6pdr. Pembroke Dock 27.2.1892. Sold 11.7.1911 Ward, Morecambe.

REPULSE Battlecruiser 26,500 tons, 750 x 90 ft, 6-15in, 17-4in, 2-3in. J.Brown (ex-Palmer) 8.1.1916. Sunk 10.12.41 by Japanese air attack off the east coast of Malaya.

REPULSE Nuclear submarine, circa 7,000 tons, 410 x 33 ft, 6-TT, 16-GWS. Vickers Armstrong, Barrow 11.11.1967.

REQUIN Gun-brig 12, 165bm, 71 x 24 ft. French, captured 20.2.1795 by THALIA in the Channel. Wrecked 1.1.1801 near Quiberon.

REQUIN Brig 16. In service in 1802.

RESEARCH Tender. Purchased 12.3.1846. BU 6.1859.

RESEARCH (ex-TRENT renamed 9.1862) Ironclad S.Sloop, 1,253bm, 1,741 tons, 195 x 38½ ft, 4-7in. Pembroke Dock 15.8.1863. Sold 1884. (see TRENT)

RESEARCH (ex-INVESTIGATOR renamed 5.11.1887) Paddle survey vessel 520 tons, 155 x 24 ft, 1-6pdr.

Chatham DY 4.12.1888. Sold 29.7.1920 Ward, New Holland.

RESEARCH Survey vessel 757 tons, 142(oa) x 32 ft. Philip, Dartmouth 18.4.1939; not completed. Arrived 20.10.52 Hocking Bros, Plymouth to BU.

RESERVE 42-gun ship, 538bm, 118 x 32½ ft. Pett, Woodbridge 1650. Rebuilt Deptford 1701 as 580bm. Foundered 27.11.1703 off Yarmouth.

RESERVE 4th Rate 54, 675bm, 130 x 34½ ft. Deptford 3.1704. Renamed SUTHERLAND 2.1.1716. Hospital ship 5.1741; condemned at Port Mahon 10.3.1744. Ordered to be BU 15.11.1754.

RESERVE Rescue tug (RAN) 1942-61.

RESISTANCE 5th Rate 44, 895bm, 140 x 38 ft. Graves, Deptford 11.7.1782. Blown up 24.7.1798 in the Banca Strait.

RESISTANCE 5th Rate 36, 963bm, 145 x 38½ ft. Parsons, Bursledon 29.4.1801. Wrecked 31.5.1803 off Cape St Vincent.

RESISTANCE 5th Rate 38, 1,081bm, 154 x 40 ft. Ross, Rochester 10.8.1805. Troopship 1842. BU completed 17.4.1858 at Chatham.

RESISTANCE Armoured frigate, 3,710bm, 6,070 tons, 280 x 54 ft, 6-7in, 10-68pdr, 2-32pdr. Westwood & Baillie, Millwall 11.4.1861. Target 1885. Sold 11.11.1898. Foundered 4.3.99 in Holyhead Bay, raised and BU at Garston in 1900.

RESISTANCE Battleship 25,750 tons. Devonport DY. Ordered 1914, cancelled 26.8.14.

RESOLUE Brig-sloop 10. French, captured 16.8.1795 with three others by the fleet in Alassio Bay Listed to 1802.

RESOLUE 5th Rate 36, 877bm, 140 x 37½ ft. French, captured 13.10.1798 by MELAMPUS off the north of Ireland. Slop-ship 1805. BU 9.1811.

RESOLUTE Gun-brig 12, 181bm, 84 x 22 ft, 10-18pdr carr., 2-12pdr. King, Dover 17.4.1805. Tender 3.1814; diving bell vessel 6.1816; convict hulk 1844. BU 1852 in Bermuda.

RESOLUTE S.Frigate 1235bm Portsmouth DY. Ordered 25.4.1847 transferred Sheerness 8.1.49 cancelled 23.3.1850

RESOLUTE (ex-REFUGE renamed 3.1850, ex-*Ptarmigan*) Discovery vessel, 424bm, 115 x 28½ ft. Purchased 21.2.1850. Abandoned 10.9.1855 in the Arctic; salved by Americans and arrived in the UK 12.12.1856; laid up at Chatham. BU completed 16.8.1879 at Chatham.

RESOLUTE Iron S.storeship, 1,793bm, 283 x 36½ ft. Purchased on stocks 16.1.1855; Laird 19.2.1855. Renamed ADVENTURE 16.2.1857, troopship. BU 1877 at Chatham.

RESOLUTE Coastal M/S (RCN), 'Ton' class 390 tons. Kingston SY 20.6.1953.

RESOLUTE Drifter requis. 1915-19.

RESOLUTION (see PRINCE ROYAL of 1610)

RESOLUTION (see TREDAGH of 1654)

RESOLUTION 3rd Rate 70, 885bm, 148 x 37½ ft. Deane, Harwich 6.12.1667. Rebuilt Chatham 1698. Foundered 27.11.1703 on the Sussex coast.

RESOLUTION 3rd Rate 70, 1,103bm, 151 x 41 ft. Woolwich DY 15.3.1705. Run ashore 21.3.1707 to avoid capture by the French at Ventimiglia.

RESOLUTION 3rd Rate 70, 1,118bm, 150 x 41½ ft. Deptford DY 25.3.1708. Wrecked 10.1.1711 near Barcelona.

RESOLUTION 3rd Rate 74, 1,569bm, 165½ x 47 ft. Bird, Northam 14.12.1758. Wrecked 20.11.1759 at Quiberon.

RESOLUTION 3rd Rate 74, 1,612bm, 168 x 47 ft. Deptford DY 12.4.1770. BU 3.1813 at Portsmouth.

RESOLUTION (see DRAKE of 1770)

RESOLUTION Cutter 14, 200bm, 14-4pdr. Purchased 6.1779. Foundered 6.1797 in the North Sea.

RESOLUTION Battleship 14,150 tons, 380 x 75 ft, 4-13.5in, 10-6in, 16-6pdr. Palmer 28.5.1892. Sold 2.4.1914, BU in Holland.

RESOLUTION Battleship 25,750 tons, 580 x 88½ ft, 8-15in, 14-6in, 2-3in. Palmer 14.1.1915. Harbour service 1945. Sold 5.5.48, BU Metal Industries, Faslane.

RESOLUTION Nuclear submarine, circa 7,000 tons, 410 x 33 ft, 6-TT, 16-GWS. Vickers Armstrong, Barrow 15.9.1966.

RESOURCE 6th Rate 28, 603bm, 120½ x 33½ ft. Randall, Rotherhithe 10.8.1778. Floating battery 22 in 1804. Renamed ENTERPRIZE 17.4.1806, harbour service. Sold 28.8.1816.

RESOURCE Repair ship 12,300 tons, 500 x 83 ft, 4-4in. Vickers Armstrong, Barrow 27.11.1928. BU 2.54 Ward, Inverkeithing.

RESOURCE Mooring vessel 1910-24. Yacht 10.15-11.15

RESOURCE Store carrier 19,000 tons.

1966

RESTIGOUCHE (see COMET of 1931)

RESTIGOUCHE Escort (RCN) 2,365 tons, 366(oa) x 42 ft, 4-3in, 2-40mm. Vickers, Montreal 22.11.1954.

RESTLESS Survey vessel (Canadian) 205 tons. Listed 1906-36.

RESTLESS Destroyer, 'R' class. J.Brown 22.8.1916. Handed over to Messrs Ward 23.11.1936 in part payment for *Majestic* (CALEDONIA); BU at Briton Ferry.

RESTLESS Tug 1902, renamed RESTIVE 1916-37.

RESTORATION 3rd Rate 70, 1,018bm, 150½ x 40 ft. Betts, Harwich 1678. Rebuilt 1702 as 1,045bm. Wrecked 27.11.1703 on the Goodwins.

RESTORATION 3rd Rate 70, 1,106bm, 151 x 41 ft. Deptford DY 1.8.1706. Wrecked 9.11.1711 off Leghorn.

RETALIATION (see HERMIONE of 1782)

RETALICK Frigate, TE 'Captain' class. Bethlehem, Hingham 9.10.1943 on lend-lease. Returned 10.45 to the USN.

RETFORD Minesweeper, later 'Hunt' class. Lobnitz. Cancelled 1919.

RETRIBUTION (see HERMIONE of 1782)

RETRIBUTION (see EDGAR of 1779)

RETRIBUTION (ex-WATT renamed 26.4.1844) Wood pad. frigate 1,641bm, 220 x 40½ ft, 6-8in, 4-32pdr. Chatham DY 2.7.1844. Sold 15.7.1864 Castle & Beech to BU.

RETRIBUTION 2nd class cruiser 3,600 tons, 300 x 44 ft, 2-6in, 6-4.7in. Palmer 6.8.1891. Sold 4.4.1911 F.E.Rudge.

RETRIEVER Destroyer, 'R' class 1,034 tons. Thornycroft 15.1.1917. Sold 26.7.27 Hughes Bolckow, Blyth.

RETRIEVER Drifter and Trawler requis. WW.I. Trawler 1941-46.

REUNION 5th Rate 36, 951bm. French, captured 20.10.1793 by CRESCENT off Cherbourg. Wrecked 7.12.1796 in the Swin.

REVENGE Galleon 46, 580bm. Launched 10.1577. Captured 31.8.1591 by a Spanish squadron off the Azores; foundered 5.9.1591.

REVENGE 42-gun ship, 457bm. Merchant purchased 1650 by Royalists. Deserted to Parliament 1652 and renamed MARMADUKE. Sunk 6.1667 as blockship in the Medway.

REVENGE (see NEWBURY)

REVENGE 3rd Rate 70, 1,065bm, 150 x 40½ ft. Miller, Deptford 1699. Renamed BUCKINGHAM 16.6.1711. Hulk 2.1727. Sunk 5.1745 as a foundation.

REVENGE (see SWIFTSURE of 1673)

REVENGE 6th Rate 28 (Indian), circa 420bm. Bombay DY 22.9.1755. Foundered 19.4.1782 in the Indian Ocean.

REVENGE Brig-sloop 14. In 1778. Captured 1779 by Americans.

REVENGE Cutter 8. Purchased 1796. Listed to 1798.

REVENGE 3rd Rate 74, 1,954bm, 183 x 50 ft. Chatham DY 13.4.1805. BU 10.1849.

REVENGE Screw 2nd Rate 91, 3,322bm, 5,260 tons, 245 x 55½ ft, 34-8in, 1-68pdr, 56-32pdr. Pembroke Dock 16.4.1859. Base ship 8.1872. Renamed EMPRESS 3.1890 training ship. Sold 31.12.23. BU at Appledore.

REVENGE Battleship 14,150 tons, 380 x 75 ft, 4-13.5in, 10-6in, 16-6pdr. Palmer 3.11.1892. Renamed REDOUBTABLE 2.8.1915, 'bombarding ship' 4-12in, 6-6in. Sold 6.11.19 Ward., BU Swansea and Briton Ferry.

REVENGE (ex-RENOWN renamed 22.10.1913) Battleship 25,750 tons, 580 x 88½ ft, 8-15in, 14-6in, 2-3in. Vickers Armstrong, Barrow 29.5.1915. Harbour service 1945. Arrived 5.9.48 Ward, Inverkeithing to BU.

REVENGE Nuclear submarine, circa 7,000 tons, 410 x 33 ft, 6-TT, 16-GWS. Cammell Laird 15.3.1968.

REVOLUTIONAIRE 5th Rate 38, 1,148bm, 157 x 40½ ft. French REVOLUTIONNAIRE captured 21.10.1794 by ARTOIS off Brest. BU 10.1822.

REYNA 3rd Rate 74, 1,849bm, 173 x 48½ ft. Spanish, captured 13.8.1762 at Havana. Sold 13.5.1772.

REYNARD (see RENARD)

RHADAMANTHUS Wood Pad. sloop, 813bm, 175 x 27½ ft. Plymouth DY 16.4.1832. BU completed 8.2.1864 at Sheerness.

RHIN 5th Rate 38, 1,080bm, 152 x 40 ft. French, captured 27.7.1806 by MARS off Rochefort. Quarantine hulk 1838. Sold 26.5.1884 Castle, Charlton.

RHINOCEROS Transport 20, 711bm. Purchased 1781. Sold 1.6.1784.

RHODIAN Brig-sloop 10, 'Cherokee' class, 240bm. Guilaume, Northam 3.1.1809. Wrecked 21.2.1813 and wreck sold 1813 in Jamaica.

RHODODENDRON Sloop, 'Anchusa' class. Irvine 15.10.1917. Sunk 5.5.18

by 'U.70' in the North Sea.

RHODODENDRON Corvette, 'Flower' class. Harland & Wolff 2.9.1940. Sold 17.5.47, renamed *Maj Vinke*.

RHUDDLAN CASTLE Corvette, 'Castle' class. Crown. Cancelled 12.1943.

RHYL Minesweeper, TE 'Bangor' class. Lobnitz 21.6.1940. Sold 28.9.48, BU King, Gateshead.

RHYL Frigate 2,150 tons, 360 x 41 ft, 2-4.5in, 1-40mm. Portsmouth DY 23.4.1959. Left Portsmouth in tow 3.6.85 to BU.

RIBBLE Destroyer 590 tons, 225 x 23½ ft, 1-12pdr (4-12pdr 1907), 5-6pdr, 2-TT. Yarrow 19.3.1904. Sold 29.7.20 Ward, Preston.

RIBBLE Frigate, 'River' class. Simons 23.4.1943. To Dutch navy 25.6.43 as JOHAN MAURITS van NASSAU.

RIBBLE (ex-DUDDON renamed 6.1943) Frigate, 'River' class. Blyth 10.11.43. Lent RCN 24.7.44 to 11.6.45; arrived 9.7.57 Hughes Bolckow, Blyth to BU.

RIBBLE Minehunter 757 tons. Richards 7.5.1985.

RIBBLE Two Trawlers requis in WW.I.

RICHARD 3rd Rate 70, 1,108bm. Woolwich 1658. Renamed ROYAL JAMES 1660. Destroyed 13.6.1667 by the Dutch at Chatham.

RICHARD Fireship 4, 198bm. Purchased 1666. Expended 1666.

RICHARD & JOHN Fireship 10, 160bm. Purchased 1688. Sunk 1692 as foundation at Harwich.

RICHMOND (see WAKEFIELD)

RICHMOND Yacht 8, 64bm. Purchased 1672. Sold 1685.

RICHMOND 6th Rate 24. French E.Indiaman *Dauphin* captured 1.1745. Sold 28.11.1749.

RICHMOND 5th Rate 32, 664bm, 127 x 34 ft. Buxton, Deptford 12.11.1757. Captured 11.9.1781 by the French AIGRETTE off the Chesapeake.

RICHMOND Gun-brig 14, 183bm, 84½ x 22½ ft, 12-18pdr carr., 2-6pdr. Greensward, Itchenor 2.1806. Sold 29.9.1814.

RICHMOND (ex-USS FAIRFAX) Destroyer 1,090 tons, 309 x 30½ ft. 3-4in, 1-3in, 6-TT. Commissioned 5.12.1940 in the RN. Lent RCN 8.43 to 12.43; lent Russian navy 16.7.44 to 24.6.49 as ZHIVUCHI. Sold 12.7.49, BU by Brunton, Grangemouth.

RICHMOND Trawler requis. 1918-19.

RIFLE Destroyer 1,980 tons, 341½ x 38 ft, 6-4in, 6-40mm, 10-TT. Denny. Laid down 30.6.1944, cancelled

27.12.45.

RIFLEMAN Gun-brig 12, 187bm, 80 x 22½ ft. Perry, Blackwall 1804 and purchased 6.1804. Sold 27.7.1809.

RIFLEMAN Brig-sloop 18, 'Cruizer' class, 387bm, King, Upnor 12.8.1809. Sold 21.1.1836.

RIFLEMAN Wood S.gunvessel, 486bm, 150 x 26½ ft. Portsmouth DY 10.8.1846. Sold 18.11.1869 at Hong Kong.

RIFLEMAN Wood S.gunvessel, 462bm, 610 tons, 155 x 25 ft, 1-7in, 1-64pdr, 2-20pdr. Chatham DY 20.11.1872. Sold 26.4.1890.

RIFLEMAN Destroyer 720 tons, 246 x 25 ft, 2-4in, 2-12pdr, 2-TT. White 22.8.1910. Sold 9.5.21 Ward, Briton Ferry. BU in 1923.

RIFLEMAN Minesweeper, 'Algerine' class. Harland & Wolff 25.11.1943. Sold 13.9.72, BU at Fleetwood.

RIGOROUS Destroyer, 'R' class. J.Brown 30.9.1916. Sold 5.11.26 Cashmore, Newport.

RIMOUSKI Corvette (RCN), 'Flower' class. Davie SB 3.10.1940. BU 12.50 Steel Co of Canada.

RINALDO Brig-sloop 10, 'Cherokee' class 237bm. Dudman, Deptford 13.7.1808. Packet brig 2.1824. Sold 6.8.1835.

RINALDO Wood S.sloop, 951bm, 1,365 tons, 185 x 33 ft, 5-40pdr, 12-32pdr. Portsmouth DY 26.3.1860. Sold in 4.1884.

RINALDO Sloop 980 tons, 180 x 33 ft, 6-4in. Laird 29.5.1900. Sold 21.10.21 W.Thomas, Anglesey.

RINALDO Minesweeper, 'Algerine' class. Harland & Wolff 20.3.1943. Arrived 16.8.61 Dorkin, Gateshead to BU.

RINALDO Trawler 1914-21.

RINGAROOMA (ex-PSYCHE renamed 2.4.1890) 2nd class cruiser 2,575 tons, 265 x 41 ft, 8-4.7in, 8-3pdr. Thomson 10.12.1889. Sold 15.5.1906 Forth S.Bkg Co., BU at Bo'ness.

RINGDOVE Brig-sloop 18, 'Cruizer' class, 385bm. Warren, Brightlingsea 16.10.1806. Sold 11.6.1829 at Halifax NS.

RINGDOVE Brig-sloop 16, 429bm, 101 x 32½ ft, 14-32pdr, 2-18pdr. Plymouth DY 6.1833. BU 8.1850.

RINGDOVE Wood S.gunvessel, 674bm, 181 x 28½ ft, 1-110pdr, 1-68pdr, 2-20pdr. White 22.2.1856. Sold 2.6.1865, BU 11.1866 White, Cowes.

RINGDOVE Wood S.gunvessel, 666bm, 774 tons, 170 x 29 ft, 1-7in, 2-40pdr. Portsmouth DY 4.9.1867. Sold

17.5.1882.

RINGDOVE Compos. S.Gunboat 805 tons, 165 x 31 ft, 6-4in. Devonport DY 30.4.1889. Renamed MELITA 7.12.1915 and made a salvage vessel. Sold 22.1.20 Ship Salvage Corp.

RINGDOVE (see MELITA of 1888)

RINGDOVE Minelayer 498 tons, 145 x 27 ft, 1-20mm, 12 mines. Robb 16.6.1938. Sold 8.9.50 Pakistan Govt as pilot vessel.

RINGWOOD Minesweeper, later 'Hunt' class. Lobnitz. Cancelled 1919.

RINGWOOD Netlayer requis. 1941-46.

RIOU Frigate, TE 'Captain' class. Bethlehem, Hingham 23.10.1943. Returned 28.2.46 to the USN.

RIPLEY (ex-USS SHUBRICK) Destroyer 1,190 tons, 311 x 31 ft, 3-4in, 1-3in, 6-TT. Commissioned 26.11.1940 in the RN. Sold 20.3.45; BU Young, Sunderland.

RIPLINGHAM Inshore M/S, 'Ham' class. Brooke Marine, Lowestoft 11.1.1955. To French navy 1955.

RIPON (see under RIPPON)

RIPPLE Wood S.gunboat, 'Albacore' class. Wigram, Blackwall 2.6.1856. BU 4.1865 Marshall, Plymouth.

RIPPLE Tank vessel 1887-1906, Tank vessel 1904-25.

RIPPON 3rd Rate 64, 924bm, 144½ x 38½ ft. Deptford DY 23.8.1712. Rebuilt Woolwich 1735 as 4th Rate 60, 1,021bm. BU 1751.

RIPPON'S PRIZE 6th Rate 28, 396bm, 105½ x 30 ft. Captured 1744. Sold 1747. Was the Spanish CONDE de CHINCAN.

RIPPON 4th Rate 60, 1,229bm, 155½ x 42½ ft. Woolwich DY 20.1.1758. Harbour service 1801. BU 1.1808.

RIPPON 3rd Rate 74, 1,770bm, 176½ x 48 ft. Blake & Scott, Bursledon 8.8.1812. BU 3.1821.

RIPON A/C transport 990 tons, 160 x 30 ft, 1-12pdr, 2-20mm. Pollock, Faversham 15.3.1945. Sold 25.2.59 to BU.

RISING CASTLE (see ARNPRIOR)

RIVAL Destroyer 'M' class 900 tons. Yarrow 14.6.1916. Sold 13.7.26 Cashmore, Newport.

RIVAL Drifter requis. 1915-20 & 1939-40. Tug 1937-47.

RIVER PLATE Destroyer 2,380 tons, 355 x 40 ft. 5-4.5in, 8-40mm, 10-TT. Swan Hunter. Laid down 11.4.1945, cancelled 10.45.

RIVER SNAKE SSV (RAN) 80 tons. Miller Bunning 1944. To N.Borneo Govt in 11.45.

RIVIERE du LOUP Corvette (RCN), modified 'Flower' class Morton, Quebec 2.7.1943. Sold 1947 Dominican navy as JUAN B.MAGGIOLO.

RIVOLI 3rd Rate 74, 1,804bm. French, captured 22.2.1812 by VICTORIOUS in the Mediterranean. BU 1.1819.

Le ROBECQUE Sloop 18, 388bm, 111 x 28 ft, 18-6pdr. French Le ROBECQ captured 1782. Sold 5.6.1783.

ROBERT 12-gun vessel, 133bm. Royalist FORTUNE captured 1642 by Parliament. Captured 1649 by Irish Royalists.

ROBERT Fireship 4, 122bm. Purchased 1666. Sold 1667.

ROBERT Fireship 4, 112bm. Purchased 1672. Sunk 1674 as a foundation at Sheerness.

ROBERT Gunvessel 3, 87bm, 65 x 18½ ft. Purchased 3.1794. Sold 26.12.1799.

ROBERT E.LEE Monitor 1915 (see RAGLAN).

ROBERTS (ex-EARL ROBERTS renamed 22.6.1915, ex-M.4 renamed 19.6.15, ex-STONEWALL JACKSON renamed 31.5.15) Monitor 6,150 tons, 320 x91 ft, 2-14in, 2-6in, 2-12pdr. Swan Hunter 15.4.15. Sold 9.5.21 Ward but retained; handed over 11.9.36 in part payment for *Majestic* (CALEDONIA) arrived 19.9.36 at Preston to BU.

ROBERTS Monitor 7,970 tons, 373(oa) x 90 ft, 2-15in, 8-4in. J.Brown 1.2.1941. Harbour service 1956. Sold 6.65, arrived 3.8.65 Ward, Inverkeithing to BU.

ROBIN River gunboat 85 tons, 108 x 20 ft, 2-6pdr. Yarrow 1897 in sections; re-erected at Hong Kong. Sold 9.1928 at Hong Kong.

ROBIN River gunboat 226 tons, 150 x 27 ft, 1-3.7in howitzer, 1-6pdr. Yarrow 7.3.1934. Scuttled 25.12.41 at Hong Kong.

ROBIN Drifter and trawler requis. in WW.I.

ROB ROY (see LEONIDAS)

ROB ROY Destroyer, 'R' class. Denny 29.8.1916. Sold 13.7.26 King, Garston.

ROBUST 3rd Rate 74, 1,624bm, 168½ x 47 ft. Barnard, Harwich 25.10.1764. Harbour service 1812. BU 1.1817.

ROBUST Screw 2nd Rate 91, 3,716bm, 252 x 58 ft. Devonport DY. Laid down 31.10.1859, suspended 12.3.1861, cancelled 1872.

ROBUST Tug 1907-55. Tug 1974.

ROC A/C transport 990 tons, 160 x 30 ft, 1-12pdr, 2-20mm. Blyth SB 28.3.1945. Sold 1.59 Greek owners; resold R.Duvall, Quebec.

ROCHESTER 4th Rate 48, 607bm, 125½ x 32½ ft. Chatham DY 1693. Rebuilt Deptford 1715 as 719bm. Renamed MAIDSTONE 27.9.1744 as hospital ship. BU 10.1748 at Woolwich.

ROCHESTER PRIZE 6th Rate 18, 200bm, 88 x 22½ ft. French GRACIEUSE captured 18.5.1702 by ROCHESTER. Sold 10.4.1712.

ROCHESTER 4th Rate 50, 1,034bm, 146 x 40 ft. Deptford DY 3.8.1749. Sold 3.4.1770.

ROCHESTER (see HERO of 1759)

ROCHESTER Sloop 1,105 tons, 250 x 34 ft, 2-4in. Chatham DY 16.7.1931. Sold 6.1.51, BU Clayton & Davie.

ROCHESTER DY craft 1833-77. Trawler 1914-19.

ROCHFORT 2nd Rate 80, 2,082bm, 193 x 49½ ft. Jacobs, Milford 6.4.1814. BU completed 20.6.1826 at Chatham.

ROCKCLIFFE Minesweeper (RCN), 'Algerine' class. Pt Arthur SY 19.8.1943. BU 1960.

ROCKET (ex-*Busy*) Fireship 4, 62bm, 52½ x 17 ft. Purchased 1804. Sold 17.6.1807 G.Bailey to BU.

ROCKET Iron paddle tender, 70bm, 90 x 12½ ft. Fairburn, Limehouse 7.1842. BU 6.1850 at Woolwich.

ROCKET Mortar vessel, 156bm, 70 x 23½ ft, 1-13in mortar. Green, Blackwall 5.5.1855. Renamed MV.20 on 19.10.1855. BU completed 27.9.1865 Marshall, Plymouth.

ROCKET Wood S.gunboat, 'Albacore' class. Laird 21.4.1856. BU 10.1864.

ROCKET Compos. S.gunvessel, 464bm, 584 tons, 155 x 25 ft, 1-7in, 1-64pdr, 2-20pdr. London Eng Co, Poplar 8.4.1868. Sold 12.1888.

ROCKET Destroyer 325 tons, 205½ x 19½ ft, 1-12pdr, 5-6pdr, 2-TT. Thompson 14.8.1894. Sold 10.4.1912.

ROCKET (see LUCIFER of 1913)

ROCKET Destroyer, 'R' class. Denny 2.7.1916. Sold 16.12.26 Ward, Inverkeithing.

ROCKET Destroyer 1,705 tons, 339 x 36 ft, 4-4.7in, 8-TT. Scotts 28.10.1942. Frigate 7.51. Arrived 3.67 at Dalmuir to BU.

ROCKHAMPTON Minesweeper (RAN), 'Bathurst' class. Walker, Maryborough 26.6.1941. Sold 6.1.61; BU 5.62 Japan.

ROCKINGHAM (ex-USS SWASEY) Destroyer 1,190 tons, 311 x 31 ft, 1-4in, 1-3in, 4-20mm, 3-TT. Commissioned

26.11.1940 in the RN. Air target 1.44. Sunk 27.9.44 by mine off Aberdeen.

ROCKROSE Corvette, 'Flower' class. Hill, Bristol 26.7.1941. Renamed PROTEA (SAN) 9.47, survey ship.

ROCKSAND M/S Sloop, '24' class. Swan Hunter 10.7.1918. Sold 15.11.22 Ferguson Muir.

ROCKSAND (see EMPIRE ANVIL)

ROCKWOOD Destroyer, 'Hunt' class type III. Vickers Armstrong, Barrow 13.6.1942. Damaged 11.11.43 by air attack in the Aegean and not repaired; sold 2.46, arrived 8.46 King, Gateshead to BU.

RODINGTON Coastal M/S, 'Ton' class. Fleetlands SY 24.2.1955. Sold H.K. Vickers 12.5.72, BU at Fleetwood

RODNEY Cutter 4. In service in 1759.

RODNEY Brig-sloop? 16. In service 1781. Captured 23.1.1782 by the French at Demerara.

RODNEY 3rd Rate 74, 1,754bm, 176½ x 47½ ft. Barnard, Deptford 8.12.1809. Renamed GREENWICH 17.3.1827, 50 guns. Sold 8.9.1836.

RODNEY 2nd Rate 92, 2,598bm, 206 x 54½ ft, 10-8in, 82-32pdr. Pembroke Dock 18.6.1833 (six years on stocks). Undocked Chatham 11.1.1860 as screw ship, 2,770bm, 70 guns. BU in 2.1884.

RODNEY Battleship 10,300 tons, 325 x 68 ft, 4-13.5in, 6-6in, 12-6pdr. Chatham DY 8.10.1884. Sold 11.5.1909 Ward, Morecambe.

RODNEY Battlecruiser 33,600 tons, 810 x 105 ft, 8-15in, 16-5.5in. Fairfield. Ordered 4.1916, suspended 3.17, cancelled 10.18.

RODNEY Battleship 33,900 tons, 660 x 106 ft, 9-16in, 12-6, 8-4in. Cammell Laird 17.12.1925. Arrived 26.3.48 Ward, Inverkeithing to BU.

ROE Ketch 8, 57bm. Page, Wivenhoe 1665. Wrecked 1670.

ROE Dogger 6. Captured 1672. Lost 1673 in action.

ROE Ketch 10, 93bm. Haydon, Limehouse 8.4.1691. Wrecked 12.10.1697 in York River, N.America.

ROEBUCK Flyboat. Purchased 1.1585 from the Dutch. With Raleigh in N.America.

ROEBUCK 10-gun vessel, 90bm. Woolwich 28.3.1636. Lost 1641 in collision.

ROEBUCK 14-gun ship, 110bm. Captured 1646 from Spanish Dunkirkers. Royalist navy 1648. Captured 11.1649 by Parliament at Kinsale;

sold there 1651.

ROEBUCK 34-gun ship. Captured 1653. Hulk 1664. Sold 1668.

ROEBUCK 6th Rate 16, 129bm. Deane, Harwich 1666. Sold 1683.

ROEBUCK Fireship 6, 70bm. Purchased 1688. OLD ROEBUCK 1690. Sunk 1696 as foundation at Portsmouth.

ROEBUCK Fireship 8, 299bm, 96 x 25½ ft. Snelgrove, Wapping 17.4.1690. Foundered 24.2.1701 off Ascension. (With Dampier 1695 as 5th Rate 26 guns.)

ROEBUCK 5th Rate 42, 494bm, 115 x 31½ ft. Portsmouth DY 5.4.1704. Taken to pieces 1725 and rebuilt 1733 at Woolwich as 598bm, 124 x 33½ ft. Sunk 4.1743 as breakwater at Sheerness.

ROEBUCK 5th Rate 44, 708bm, 126 x 36 ft. Rowcliffe, Southampton 21.12.1743. Sold 3.7.1764.

ROEBUCK 5th Rate 44, 886bm, 140 x 38 ft. Chatham DY 28.4.1774. Hospital ship 7.1790; troopship 1799; guardship 1803; floating battery 1805. BU at Sheerness in 7.1811.

ROEBUCK Wood S. gunvessel, 865bm, 200 x 30½ ft, 1-110pdr, 1-60pdr, 4-20pdr. Scott Russell, Millwall 22.3.1856. Sold 1864 Castle, Charlton.

ROEBUCK Destroyer 400 tons, 210 x 21 ft, 1-12pdr, 5-6pdr, 2-TT. Hawthorn 4.1.1901. BU 1919 at Portsmouth.

ROEBUCK Destroyer 1,705 tons, 339 x 36ft, 4-4.7in, 8-TT. Scotts 10.12.1942. (Was 'launched' by a near-miss bomb and submerged 9 months.) Frigate 2.53, 2,300 tons, 2-4in, 2-40mm. Sold Ward 12.6.68. BU Inverkeithing.

ROEBUCK Survey ship 1500 tons Brooke Marine 14.11.1985.

ROEBUCK Minesweeper Requis. WW.1. Balloon Vessel WW.II.

ROGER de COVERLEY Minesweeper 265 tons, 130 x 26ft, 1-3pdr. War Dept tug transferred on stocks; Ferguson 19.7.1917. Renamed COVERLEY 1918. Sold 1.5.20.

ROHILKHAND (ex-PADSTOW renamed 1942) Minesweeper (RIN) turbine 'Bangor' class. Hamilton 29.10.42. Sold 1960.

ROLLA Gun-brig 10, 152bm, 80½ x 21 ft. French, captured 21.2.1806 by a squadron at the Cape. Sold 24.3.1810.

ROLLA Brig-sloop 10, 'Cherokee' class, 238bm. Pitcher, Northfleet 13.2.1808. Sold 18.4.1822 T. Pitman.

ROLLA Brig-sloop 10, 'Cherokee' class, 231bm. Plymouth DY 10.12.1829. BU completed 15.9.1868 Portsmouth.

ROMAN Brig-sloop 18, 333bm. French TEULIE, ex-Venetian, captured 1.6.1808 by UNITE in the Adriatic. Sold 1.9.1814.

ROMAN EMPEROR Fireship 8, 272bm 92 x 26 ft, 8-4pdr. Purchased 16.5.1757. Sold 16.6.1763.

ROMNEY 4th Rate 48, 683bm, 121 x 34½ ft. Johnson, Blackwall 1694. Wrecked 22.10.1707 on the Scilly Isles.

ROMNEY 4th Rate 54, 710bm, 130½ x 35 ft. Deptford DY 2.12.1708. Rebuilt Deptford 1726 as 756bm; reduced to 44 guns 6.1745. Sold 21.7.1757.

ROMNEY 4th Rate 50, 1,046bm, 146 x 40½ ft. Woolwich DY 8.7.1762. Wrecked 19.11.1804 off the Texel.

ROMNEY 4th Rate 58, 1,227bm, 154½ x 43 ft. Pelham, Frindsbury 24.2.1815. Troopship 1820; depot for freed slaves in Jamaica 6.1837. Sold there 12.1845.

ROMNEY Minesweeper, TE 'Bangor' class Lobnitz 3.8.1940. Sold 18.1.50, BU at Granton.

ROMOLA Destroyer, 'R' class. J.Brown 14.5.1916. Sold 13.3.30 King, Troon.

ROMOLA Minesweeper, 'Algerine' class. Pt Arthur SY 19.5.1945. Arrived 19.11.57 Demmelweek & Redding, Plymouth.

ROMULUS 5th Rate 44, 885bm, 140 x 38 ft. Adams, Bucklers Hard 17.12.1777. Captured 19.2.1781 by the French EVEILLE off the Chesapeake.

ROMULUS 5th Rate 36, 879bm, 137 x 38½ ft. Graves, Deptford 21.9.1785. Troopship 7.1799; harbour service 1813 BU 11.1816 in Bermuda.

ROMULUS Trawler requis. 1915-19.

ROO Pinnace 80bm, Built 1545, captured by the French 1547.

ROOK Schooner 4, 80bm, 56 x 18 ft, 4-12pdr carr. Sutton, Ringmore 21.5.1806. Captured 10.1808 by two French privateers in the W.Indies.

ROOKE (see BROKE of 1920)

ROOKE Drifter requis. 1914-16.

RORQUAL M/L submarine 1,520 tons, 271½ ft, 1-4in, 6-TT, 50 mines. Vickers Armstrong, Barrow 21.7.1936. Arrived 17.3.46 Cashmore, Newport to BU.

RORQUAL Submarine 1,605 tons, 241 x 26½ ft, 8-TT. Vickers, Armstrong Barrow 5.12.1956. Arrived Plymouth 5.5.77 to BU by Davies & Cann.

RORQUAL Whaler 1915-20.

ROSA Schooner 12. Listed 1802-03.

ROSA Tender 4, 155bm, 4-3pdr. Hired 27.3.1804 (and later purchased?). Listed 1808-14.

ROSA Trawler 1915-19. Drifter 1939-43.

ROSALIND (see LIBERTY of 1913)

ROSALIND Destroyer, 'R' class 1,037 tons. Thornycroft 14.10.1916. Sold 13.7.26 King, Garston.

ROSALIND Trawler requis. 1915-19. Trawler 1941-58.

ROSAMOND 6th Rate 20, 429bm, 108½ x 30 ft, 18-24pdr carr., 8-18 pdr carr., 2-6pdr. Temple, S.Shields 27.1.1807.Sold 14.12.1815.

ROSAMOND (see INFERNAL of 1843)

ROSAMUND Minesweeper, 'Algerine' class. Pt Arthur SY 20.12.1944. Renamed BLOEMFONTEIN (SAN) 9.47.Sold 3.66.

ROSARIO Hulk, 1,150bm. Spanish galleon Del ROSARIO captured 1588. BU 1622 at Chatham.

ROSARIO Fireship 14, 210bm. Spanish NUESTRA SENORA del ROSARIO captured 24.5.1797 by ROMULUS off Cadiz. Expended 7.7.1800 in Dunkirk Roads.

ROSARIO (see Hardi of 1800)

ROSARIO Brig-sloop 10, 'Cherokee' class, 236bm. Bailey, Ipswich 7.12.1808. Sold 11.1832 Levy, Rochester.

ROSARIO Wood S.sloop, 673bm, 913 tons, 160 x 30 ft, 1-40pdr, 6-32pdr, 4-20pdr. Deptford DY 17.10.1860. Sold Castle 31.1.1884 to BU.

ROSARIO Sloop 980 tons, 180 x 33 ft, 6-4in. Sheerness DY 17.12.1898. Depot ship 1910. Sold 11.11.21 at Hong Kong.

ROSARIO Minesweeper, 'Algerine' class. Harland & Wolff 3.4.1943. To Belgian navy 15.1.53 as De MOOR.

ROSE 'King's ship' in 1222.

ROSE Cinq Ports ship in 1300. Captured 9.1338 by the French.

ROSE Ballinger 30 bm Acquired in 2.1419 Sold 17.2.1425

ROSE Galley, 80bm. Listed 1512-21.

ROSE Pink 6, 55bm. Woolwich 1657. Transferred 1661 to the Irish packet service.

ROSE Fireship 4, 112bm. Algerian, captured 1670. Expended 1671.

ROSE Dogger 6. Dutch, captured 1672 Lost 1673.

ROSE 5th Rate 28, 230bm, 93½ x 24 ft Edgar, Yarmouth 1674. Fireship 1689. Sold 20.9.1698.

ROSE (also SALLY ROSE) 6th Rate 16, 180bm, 64 x 23 ft. Salee pirate, captured 1684. Sold 1696.

ROSE 6th Rate 20, 151bm. Purchased 6.6.1709. Sold 6.3.1712.

ROSE 6th Rate 20, 273bm, 94 x 26 ft. Chatham DY 25.4.1712. Rebuilt Woolwich 1724 as 377bm; hulked 10.1739. Sold 1744.

ROSE 6th Rate 24, 448bm, 106 x 31 ft. Bird, Rotherhithe 14.8.1740. Sold 29.7.1755.

ROSE 6th Rate 24, 449bm, 110 x 30 ft. Blayds, Hull 8.3.1757. Sunk 9.1779 as blockship at Savannah.

ROSE 6th Rate 28, 594bm, 121 x 33½ ft. Stewart & Hall, Sandgate 1.7.1783. Wrecked 28.6.1794 in Jamaica.

ROSE Sloop 18, 367bm, 106 x 28 ft. Hamilton, Hastings 18.5.1805. Sold 30.10.1817 Pitman to BU.

ROSE Cutter listed 1805-06.

ROSE Sloop 18, 398bm, 104½ x 30 ft. Portsmouth DY 1.6.1821. BU 5.1851.

ROSE Survey cutter, 37bm. Purchased 20.5.1857. Stranded 20.7.1864 and wreck sold 9.8.1864.

ROSE Wood S.gunboat, 'Albacore' class. Laird 21.4.1856. BU 8.1868 at Devonport.

ROSE Coastguard yawl, 131bm, 70 x 21 ft. White, Cowes 12.4.1880. Sold 10.7.1906 R.Jones, Rhyl.

ROSE Corvette, 'Flower' class. Simons 22.9.1941. Lent R.Norwegian navy 23.10.41. Sunk 26.10.44 in collision with the frigate MANNERS in the N.Atlantic.

ROSE 2 Hired cutters 1793; 3 Trawlers & 3 Drifters WW.I.

ROSEBAY (ex-SPLENDOR) Corvette, 'Flower' class. Kingston SY 11.2.1943 on lend-lease. Returned 20.3.46 to the USN; sold as *Benmark*.

ROSEBUSH 24-gun ship, 268bm. Captured 1653. Hulk 1664. Sold 1668.

ROSEMARY Sloop, 'Arabis' class. Richardson Duck, Stockton on Tees 22.11.1915. Sold 17.12.47, BU Ward, Milford Haven.

ROSS (ex-RAMSEY renamed 1918) Minesweeper, later 'Hunt' class. Lobnitz 12.6.19. Sold 13.3.47.

ROSSLARE (see CUPAR)

ROSTHERN Corvette (RCN), 'Flower' class. Pt Arthur SY 30.11.1940. BU 6.46 Steel Co of Canada.

ROTA 5th Rate 38, 1,102bm, 153½ x 40 ft. Danish, captured 7.9.1807 at Copenhagen. Sold 11.1.1816. (Was to have been renamed SENSIBLE.)

ROTHER Destroyer 540 tons, 222 x 23½ ft, 1-12pdr, 5-6pdr (4-12pdr 1907), 2-TT. Palmer 5.1.1904. Sold 23.6.19 Ward, Briton Ferry.

ROTHER Frigate, 'River' class. Smiths DK 20.11.1941. Arrived 22.4.55 W of Scotland S Bkg Co, Troon to BU.

ROTHER Trawler 1920-22.

ROTHERHAM Destroyer 1,750 tons, 339 x 36 ft, 4-4.7in, 8-TT. J.Brown 21.3.1942. To Indian navy 29.7.49 as RAJPUT.

ROTHESAY Minesweeper, turbine 'Bangor' class. Hamilton 18.3.1941. BU 4.50 Ward, Milford Haven.

ROTHESAY Frigate 2,150 tons, 360 x 41 ft, 2-4.5in, 1-40mm. Yarrow 9.12.1957.

ROTOITI (see LOCH KATRINE)

ROTOITI Patrol boat (RNZN) 105 tons. Brooke Marine 8.5.1974

ROTTERDAM Hulk, 937bm. Dutch ship captured 1672. BU 1703.

ROTTERDAM 4th Rate 50, 878bm, 134½ x 38½ ft. Dutch, captured 5.1.1781 by WARWICK. Sold 17.7.1806 Beatson. (Was PRINCESS CAROLINE 1799 to 1806.)

ROUYN (see PENETANG)

ROVER Sloop 18, 316bm, 98 x 24 ft American CUMBERLAND captured 1777. Captured 13.9.1780 by the French;

ROVER Sloop in 1780 Wrecked 1781 at Sandyhook

ROVER Sloop 16, 356bm, 104 x 26 ft, 16-24pdr. Pender, Bermuda 1796 and purchased on stocks. Wrecked 23.6.1798 in the Gulf of St Lawrence.

ROVER Brig-sloop 18, 'Cruizer' class, 385bm. Todd, Berwick 13.2.1808. Sold 26.3.1828 Adam Gordon.

ROVER Sloop 18, 481bm, 115 x 31½ ft. Chatham DY. Ordered 30.1.1829 and re-designed as the following ship.

ROVER Sloop 18, 590bm, 113 x 35½ ft, 16-32pdr, 2-9pdr. Chatham DY 17.7.1832. BU 9.1845.

ROVER Brig 16, 560bm, 110 x 35 ft, 16-32pdr. Pembroke Dock 21.6.1853. Sold 9.7.1862 to the Prussian navy.

ROVER Iron S.corvette 3,460 tons, 280 x 43½ ft. 2-7in, 16-64pdr. Thames I.W., Blackwall 12.8.1874. Sold 1893.

ROVER Tug 1908, renamed ROLLICKER 1929, and RECOVERY 1934-1957

ROVER Submarine 1,475 tons, 260 x 30 ft, 1-4in, 8-TT. Vickers Armstrong, Barrow 11.6.1930. Sold 30.7.46 Joubert, Durban to BU.

ROWENA Destroyer, 'R' class. J.Brown 1.7.1916. Handed over 27.1.37 to Ward in part payment for *Majestic* (CALEDONIA); BU Milford Haven.

ROWENA Minesweeper, 'Algerine' class. Lobnitz 5.6.1944. Arrived 23.10.58 Dorkin, Gateshead to BU.

ROWLEY Frigate, TE 'Captain' class. Bethlehem, Hingham 30.10.1943 on lend-lease. Returned 11.45 to th USN.

ROXBOROUGH (ex-USS FOOTE) Destroyer 1,060 tons, 309 x 30½ ft, 1-4in, 1-3in, 4-20mm, 3-TT. Commissioned 23.9.1940 in the RN; lent Russian navy 10.8.44 to 7.2.49 as DOBLESTNI. Sold 5.4.49, BU Clayton & Davie, Dunston.

ROXBURGH Armoured cruiser 10,850 tons, 450 x 68½ ft, 4-7.5in, 6-6in, 2-12pdr, 22-3pdr. London & Glasgow Co 19.1.1904. Sold 1921 Stanlee; resold 8.11.21 Slough TC, BU in Germany.

ROYAL ADELAIDE (ex-LONDON renamed 10.5.1827) 1st Rate 104, 2,446bm, 4,122 tons, 198 x 54 ft. Plymouth DY 28.7.1828 (nine years on stocks). Depot ship 7.1860. Sold 4.4.1905 Laidler, Sunderland; BU at Dunkirk.

ROYAL ADELAIDE Yacht, 50bm, 50 x 15 ft. Sheerness DY 12.1833 and re-erected on Virginia Water 5.1834 for use of the Prince of Wales. (Model of the frigate PIQUE.) BU 1877.

ROYAL ALBERT Screw 1st Rate 121, 3,726bm, 5,517 tons, 233 x 61 ft. Woolwich DY 13.5.1854 (ten years on stocks). Sold 9.1884 Castle.

ROYAL ALFRED Ironclad ship, 4,068bm, 6,707 tons, 273 x 57½ ft, 10-9in, 8-7in. Portsmouth DY 15.10.1864. Sold Castle in 12.1884 to BU.

ROYAL ANNE (see ANDREW of 1670)

ROYAL ANNE (see ROYAL CHARLES of 1673)

ROYAL ANNE GALLEY 5th Rate 42, 511bm, 127 x 21 ft. Woolwich 18.6.1709. Foundered 10.11.1721 off the Lizard.

ROYAL ANNE (see ROYAL GEORGE of 1756)

ROYAL ARTHUR (ex-CENTAUR renamed 1890) 1st class cruiser 7,700 tons, 360 x 61 ft, 1-9.2in, 12-6pdr. Portsmouth DY 26.2.1891. Sold 8.21 G.Cohen, BU in Germany.

ROYAL CAROLINE (see PEREGRINE GALLEY)

ROYAL CAROLINE Sloop 10, 232bm, 90 x 24½ ft. Deptford DY 29.1.1749.

Renamed ROYAL CHARLOTTE 1761. Fate unknown.

ROYAL CHARLES (see NASEBY)

ROYAL CHARLES 1st Rate 100, 1,443bm, Portsmouth DY 1673. Renamed QUEEN 1693 and rebuilt at Woolwich as 1,658bm. Renamed ROYAL GEORGE 9.9.1715 and rebuilt at Woolwich as 1,801bm, 172 x 49½ ft. Renamed ROYAL ANNE 19.1.1756. BU 1767.

ROYAL CHARLOTTE (ex-CHARLOTTE renamed 1749) Yacht 10, 232bm, 90 x 25 ft. BU 7.1820.

ROYAL CHARLOTTE (see ROYAL CAROLINE of 1749)

ROYAL CHARLOTTE Sloop 10 (Canadian lakes). Built on Navy Island 1764. Listed in 1770.

ROYAL CHARLOTTE Transport 14, 520bm, 14-6pdr. French privateer CHARLOTTE captured 1780. Sold 10.4.1783 at Milford.

ROYAL CHARLOTTE Yacht 6, 202bm, 85½ x 23 ft. Woolwich DY 22.11.1824. BU 10.1832.

ROYAL ESCAPE (ex-*Surprise*) Yacht 4, 34bm, 42 x 14½ ft. Purchased 1660. Rebuilt 1714 and 1736 as transport, 74bm. BU 9.1791. (The future King Charles II escaped in *Surprise* after the battle of Worcester.)

ROYAL ESCAPE Storeship, 107bm, 63 x 21 ft. Carter, River Thames 1743. Sold 17.7.1750.

ROYAL ESCAPE Transport, 110bm, 64 x 20 ft. Nowlan, Northam 29.11.1792. To DY service after 1816 and by 1866 renamed YC.4 at Sheerness. BU at Sheerness in 2.1877.

ROYAL EXCHANGE 32-gun ship in service 1594 to 1620.

ROYAL FREDERICK (see QUEEN of 1839)

ROYAL FREDERICK (see FREDERICK WILLIAM)

ROYAL GEORGE (see ROYAL JAMES of 1675)

ROYAL GEORGE (see ROYAL CHARLES of 1673)

ROYAL GEORGE (ex-ROYAL ANNE renamed 19.1.1756) 1st Rate 100, 2,047bm, 178 x 51½ ft. Woolwich DY 18.2.1756. Foundered 29.8.1782 at Spithead.

ROYAL GEORGE Sloop 20 (Canadian lakes). Listed 1776.

ROYAL GEORGE (ex-UMPIRE renamed 9.1782) 1st Rate 100, 2,286bm, 190 x 52½ ft. Chatham DY 15.9.1788. BU 2.1822.

ROYAL GEORGE Sloop 20 (Canadian lakes), 340bm, 97 x 28 ft. Kingston Ont 7.1809. Renamed NIAGARA 22.1.1814. Sold 1837.

ROYAL GEORGE Yacht, 330bm, 103 x 26½ ft. Deptford DY 17.7.1817. Harbour service 1843. BU 9.1905.

ROYAL GEORGE (ex-NEPTUNE renamed 12.2.1822) 1st Rate 120, 2,616bm, 205½ x 54½ ft. Chatham DY 22.9.1827. Undocked 22.6.1853 as screw ship, 102 guns. Sold 23.1.1875 Castle, Charlton.

ROYAL GEORGE (see KING GEORGE V of 1911)

ROYAL JAMES 28-gun ship, 321bm. Royalist ship in 1654. Captured 1654 by Parliament and renamed SORLINGS. Wrecked 17.12.1717.

ROYAL JAMES (see RICHARD of 1658)

ROYAL JAMES 1st Rate 100, 1,426bm. Portsmouth DY 1671. Sunk 28.5.1672 at the battle of Solebay.

ROYAL JAMES 1st Rate 100, 1,486bm, 163 x 45½ ft. Portsmouth DY 1675. Renamed VICTORY 1691. Rebuilt Chatham 1695. Renamed ROYAL GEORGE 27.10.1714; reverted to VICTORY 9.9.1715. Burnt by accident 1721 and taken to pieces 4.1721.

ROYAL KATHERINE (see KATHERINE of 1664)

ROYAL LOUISE 5th Rate 32. Woolwich DY 1732. Fate unknown (renamed?).

ROYAL MOUNT Frigate (RCN), 'River' class. Davie SB 28.4.1944. Renamed BUCKINGHAM 6.44. Arrived 4.66 at Spezia to BU.

ROYAL MOUNT (see ALVINGTON)

ROYAL OAK 2nd Rate 76, 1,021bm. Portsmouth DY 1664. Burnt 13.6.1667 by the Dutch at Chatham.

ROYAL OAK 3rd Rate 70, 1,107bm, 157½ x 40½ ft. Deptford 1674. Rebuilt Chatham 1690 as 1,154bm; rebuilt Woolwich 1713 as 1,108bm; rebuilt Plymouth 1741 as 1,224bm, 64 guns. BU completed 8.4.1764 at Plymouth.

ROYAL OAK 3rd Rate 74, 1,606bm, 168½ x 47 ft. Plymouth DY 13.11.1769. Prison ship 11.1796. Renamed ASSISTANCE 25.10.1805. BU 11.1815.

ROYAL OAK (see RENOWN of 1798)

ROYAL OAK 3rd Rate 74, 1,759bm, 175 x 48 ft. Dudman, Deptford 4.3.1809. Harbour service 12.1825. BU 1850 in Bermuda.

ROYAL OAK Ironclad frigate, 4,056bm, 273 x 58 ft, 11-7in, 24-68pdr. Chatham DY 10.9.1862. Sold 30.9.1885.

ROYAL OAK Battleship 14,150 tons, 380 x 75 ft, 4-13.5in, 10-6in, 16-6pdr. Laird 5.11.1892. Sold 14.1.1914 Ward, Briton Ferry.

ROYAL OAK Battleship 25,750 tons, 580 x 88½ ft, 8-15in, 14-6in, 2-3in. Devonport DY 17.11.1914. Sunk 14.10.39 by 'U.47' at Scapa Flow.

ROYAL PRINCE (see PRINCE ROYAL)

ROYAL SAVAGE (ex-BRAVE SAVAGE) Sloop. Built 1775 at St Jean, Canada. Sunk 10.1775 by American batteries in the Richelieu river; salved by Americans, renamed YANKEE.

ROYAL SOVEREIGN (ex-SOVEREIGN of the SEAS renamed 1660 and rebuilt at Chatham) 100-gun ship, 1,545bm, 168 x 48½ ft. Rebuilt 1685 as 1,683bm. Burnt 29.1.1696 by accident at Chatham while preparing to rebuild. (see SOVEREIGN of 1637)

ROYAL SOVEREIGN 1st Rate 100, 1,883bm, 175 x 50½ ft. Woolwich DY 7.1701. Rebuilt Chatham 1728. BU 4.1768 at Chatham.

ROYAL SOVEREIGN 1st Rate 100, 2,175bm, 184 x 52 ft. Plymouth DY 11.9.1786 (12½ years on stocks). Renamed CAPTAIN 17.5.1825. harbour service. BU 8.1841 at Plymouth.

ROYAL SOVEREIGN Yacht, 278bm, 96 x 26 ft. Deptford DY 5.1804. BU 11.1849 at Pembroke Dock.

ROYAL SOVEREIGN 1st Rate 110. Portsmouth DY. Ordered 12.2.1833, renamed ROYAL FREDERICK 12.4.1839, then FREDERICK WILLIAM. (qv)

ROYAL SOVEREIGN Screw 1st Rate 121, 3,765bm, 240½ x 62 ft, 1-110pdr, 16-8in, 6-70pdr, 10-40pdr, 88-32pdr. Portsmouth DY 25.4.1857. Converted 4.1862 - 8.1864 to ironclad turret ship, 5,080 tons, 5-9in. Sold 5.1885.

ROYAL SOVEREIGN Battleship 14,150 tons, 380 x 75 ft, 4-13.5in, 10-6in, 16-6pdr. Portsmouth DY 26.2.1891. Sold 7.10.1913, BU at Genoa.

ROYAL SOVEREIGN Battleship 25,750 tons, 580 x 88½ ft, 8-15in, 14-6in, 2-3in. Portsmouth DY 29.4.1915. Lent Russian navy 30.5.44 to 9.2.49 as ARCHANGELSK. Sold 5.4.49, BU Inverkeithing.

ROYAL TRANSPORT 6th Rate 18, 220 bm, 90 x 23½ ft. Chatham DY 11.12.1695. Presented 14.3.1698 to the Czar of Muscovy.

ROYAL WILLIAM (ex-PRINCE renamed 1692) 1st Rate 100, 1,568bm, 167½ x 47 ft. Rebuilt Portsmouth 1719 as 1,918bm, 84 guns; guardship circa 1790. BU 8.1813 (see PRINCE of 1670)

ROYAL WILLIAM 1st Rate 120, 2 694bm, 205 x 55½ ft. Pembroke Dock 2.4.1833. Undocked 9.2.1860 as screw ship, 72 guns. Renamed CLARENCE 1885, training ship. Burnt 26.7.1899 by accident in the Mersey.

ROYALIST Schooner 14. Purchased 1797. Listed 1801.

ROYALIST Brig-sloop 18, 'Cruizer' class, 385bm. Hills, Sandwich 10.1.1807. Sold 3.2.1819 W.Harper.

ROYALIST Brig-sloop 10, 'Cherokee' class, 231bm. Portsmouth DY 12.5.1823. Sold 8.11.1838 Mr Lindon.

ROYALIST (ex-*Mary Gordon*) Brig 6, 249bm, 88 x 25½ ft. Purchased 9.7.1841 in China. Lent police as hulk 7.1856. Sold 14.2.1895.

ROYALIST Wood S.sloop, 669bm, 913 tons, 160 x 30 ft, 1-40pdr, 6-32pdr, 4-20pdr. Devonport DY 14.12.1861. BU 9.1875 at Chatham.

ROYALIST Compos. S. corvette 1,420 tons, 200 x 38 ft, 2-6in, 10-5in. Devonport DY 7.3.1883. Harbour service 2.1900. Renamed COLLEEN 1.12.1913. Transferred Irish govt 19.2.23.

ROYALIST Light cruiser 3,500 tons, 410 x 39 ft, 2-6in, 6-4in. Beardmore 14.1.1915. Sold 24.8.22. Cashmore, Newport.

ROYALIST Submarine 1,475 tons, 260 x 30 ft, 1-4in, 8-TT. Beardmore. Laid down 10.6.1929. Cancelled in 7.29.

ROYALIST Cruiser 5,770 tons, 485 x 50½ ft, 8-5.25in, 12-20mm. Scotts 30.5.1942. To RNZN 1956. Sold 11.67, BU at Osaka, Japan.

ROYALIST Gunvessel 4. Purchased 8.1798. Gone by 1800.

RUBIS (see under RUBY)

RUBY 48-gun ship, 556bm, 125½ x 31½ ft. Deptford 15.3.1652. Rebuilt Deptford 1706 as 675bm. Captured 10.10.1707 by the French MARS.

RUBY (also FRENCH RUBY) 3rd Rate 66, 968bm, 139½ x 38 ft. French RUBIS captured 17.9.1666. Hulked 1682 after storm damage. BU 1685.

RUBY PRIZE 4th Rate 44, 420bm, 108 x 31 ft. French, captured 1695. Sold 1698.

RUBY 4th Rate 54, 707bm, 130½ x 35 ft. Deptford DY 25.3.1708. Renamed MERMAID 23.5.1744. Sold 19.5.1748.

RUBY 4th Rate 50, 989bm, 141½ x 40½ ft. Ewer, Bursledon 3.8.1745. BU 5.1765 at Plymouth.

RUBY 3rd Rate 64, 1,369bm, 159½ x 44½ ft. Woolwich DY 26.11.1776. Receiving ship 1813. BU 4.1821 at Bermuda.

RUBY Iron paddle tender, 73bm, 91 x 14 ft. Acreman, Bristol 7.1842. Sold 2.11.1846 Mr Barnard.

RUBY Wood S.gunboat, 215bm, 100 x 22 ft, 1-68pdr, 1-32pdr, 2-24pdr howitzers. Deptford DY 7.10.1854 BU 10.1868.

RUBY Compos. S.corvette 2,120 tons, 220 x 40 ft, 12-64pdr. Earle, Hull 9.8.1876. Renamed C.10 in 12.1904 as coal hulk. Sold 2.21.

RUBY Destroyer 720 tons, 246 x 25 ft, 2-4in, 2-12pdr, 2-TT. White 4.11.1910. Sold 9.5.21 Ward, Grays.

RUBIS Submarine 669 tons, 216 x 23½ ft, 1-3in, 5-TT, 32 mines. French, taken into the RN in 7.40 by her captain (Free-French). Served with the RN until 1945.

RUBY Two Trawlers WW.I. Trawler 1935-46.

RUGBY (ex-FILEY renamed 1918) Minesweeper, later 'Hunt' class. Dunlop, Bremner 6.9.1918. Sold 25.11.27 Hughes Bolckow, Blyth.

RUGBY Trawler. Requis. 1916-19 and 1940-46.

RULER (ex-*St Joseph*) Escort carrier 11,420 tons, 468½ x 69½ ft, 2-4in, 16-40mm, 24-A/C. Seattle Tacoma 21.8.1943 on lend-lease. Returned 29.1.46 to the USN.

RUNCORN Minesweeper, later 'Hunt' class. Lobnitz. Cancelled 1918.

RUNNYMEDE Frigate (RCN), 'River' class. Vickers, Montreal 27.11.1943. BU 1948.

RUPERT 3rd Rate 66, 832bm, 144 x 36½ ft. Deane, Harwich 26.1.1666. Rebuilt 1703 Plymouth as 930bm; rebuilt Sheerness 1740 as 1,060bm. 60 guns. BU 11.1769.

RUPERT'S PRIZE 6th Rate 18, 180bm. French, captured 22.12.1692 by RUPERT. Sold 10.12.1700.

RUPERT'S PRIZE Sloop 6, 142bm, 71 x 21½ ft. Spanish, captured 5.1741 by RUPERT. Sold 6.10.1743.

RUPERT Iron armoured turret ship 5,440 tons, 250 x 53 ft, 2-10in, 2-64pdr. Chatham DY 12.3.1872. Sold 10.7.1907 in Bermuda.

RUPERT Submarine 1,475 tons, 260 x 30 ft, 1-4in, 8-TT. Cammell Laird. Ordered 28.2.1929, cancelled in 7.29.

RUPERT Frigate, TE 'Captain' class.

Bethlehem, Hingham 31.10.1943 on lend-lease. Returned 3.46 to the USN.

RUPERT Trawler requis. 1914-17.

RUSHEN CASTLE Corvette, 'Castle' class. Swan Hunter 15.7.1943. To Air Ministry 26.9.60 as weather ship.

RUSSELL 2nd Rate 80, 1,177bm, 155½ x 41½ ft. Portsmouth DY 3.6.1692. Rebuilt Deptford 1735 as 1,350bm. Sunk 1762 as breakwater at Sheerness.

RUSSELL 3rd Rate 74, 1,642bm, 168½ x 47½ ft. West, Deptford 10.11.1764. Sold 1811 in the E.Indies.

RUSSELL 3rd Rate 74, 1,751bm, 176½ x 48 ft. Deptford DY 22.5.1822 (eight years on stocks). Undocked 2.2.1855 as screw ship. BU 1865.

RUSSELL Battleship 14,000 tons, 405 x 75½ ft, 4-12in, 12-6in, 12-12pdr. Palmer, Jarrow 19.2.1901. Sunk 27.4.16 by mine off Malta.

RUSSELL Frigate 1,180 tons, 300 x 33 ft, 3-40mm, 4-TT. Swan Hunter 10.12.1954. Sold Pounds, arrived Portsmouth 1.7.85.

RUSSELL Trawler 1915-20.

RUTHERFORD Frigate, TE'Captain' class. Bethlehem, Hingham 23.10.1943 on lend-lease. Returned 10.45 to the USN.

RYE 5th Rate 32, 384bm, 109½ x 28½ ft. Sheerness DY 1696. Rebuilt 1717 as 6th Rate 24 guns, 371bm. BU 12.1735. (Breakwater from 1727).

RYE 6th Rate 24, 371bm. Chatham DY 6.10.1727. BU in 12.1735.

RYE 6th Rate 24, 446bm, 106½ x31 ft. Bird, Rotherhithe 1.4.1740. Wrecked 29.11.1744 on the Norfolk coast.

RYE 6th Rate 24, 510bm, 113 x 32½ ft. Carter, Southampton 11.2.1745. Sold 15.3.1763.

RYE Wood S.gunvessel, 428bm, 145 x 25 ft. Pembroke Dock. Ordered 5.3.1860, cancelled 12.12.1863.

RYE Minesweeper, turbine 'Bangor' class. Ailsa, Troon 19.8.1940. Sold 24.8.48, BU at Purfleet.

'S' class submarines. 265 tons, 148½(oa) x 14½ ft, 2-TT. All three built by Scotts, Greenock and all ceded to the Italian navy 25.10.1915.

S.1 Launched 28.2.1914.

S.2 Launched 14.4.15.

S.3 Launched 10.6.15 (not commissioned in the RN).

S.1 (see SWORDFISH of 1916)

SABINE Brig-sloop 18, 338bm, 96 x 28½ ft, 16-24pdr carr., 2-6pdr. French REQUIN captured 28.7.1808 by VOLAGE in the Mediterranean. Sold 29.1.1818 T.Pitman to BU.

SABINE (see SABRINA of 1876)

SABINE Tug 1940-50.

SABLE Destroyer, 'R' class. White 28.6.1916. Sold 8.27 Hughes Bolckow, Blyth.

SABLE (see SALMON of 1916)

SABRE Destroyer, 'S' class. Stephen 23.9.1918. Sold 11.45, BU Brunton, Grangemouth.

SABRE Patrol boat 102 tons Vosper 21.4.1970 Sold 1986.

SABRINA 6th Rate 20, 427bm, 108½ x 30 ft, 16-24pdr carr., 8-18pdr carr., 2-6pdr. Adams, Chapel 1.9.1806. Sold 18.4.1816.

SABRINA Schooner in service 1838.

SABRINA Wood S.sloop, 669bm, 160 x 30 ft, 4-64pdr. Pembroke Dock. Ordered 1860, cancelled 12.12.1863.

SABRINA Iron S.gunboat, 363 tons, 110 x 34 ft, 3-64pdr. Palmer 3.10.1876. Renamed SABINE 1916 diving tender. Renamed VIVID 1920. Sold 7.22 Fryer, Sunderland.

SABRINA Destroyer, 'M' class 900 tons. Yarrow 24.7.1916. Sold 5.11.26 Cashmore, Newport.

SABRINA Yacht requis. 1915-19.

SACKVILLE Corvette (RCN), 'Flower' class. St John DD 15.5.1941. Cable vessel in 1956. Survey vessel in 1966. Paid off in 12.82 for conversion to Museum ship.

SACRETT Ship, 160bm. Captured 1556. Listed to 1559.

SAFARI (ex-P.211) Submarine, 'S' class. Cammell Laird 18.11.1941. Handed over to Cashmore 7.1.46; foundered on passage to Newport 8.1.46.

SAFEGUARD (Gunboat No 43) Gunvessel 12, 172bm, 79 x 22 ft, 2-24pdr, 10-18pdr carr. Purchased 3.1797 at Leith. Sold 9.1802.

SAFEGUARD Gun-brig 12,, 178bm, 80 x 22½ ft, 10-18pdr carr., 2-12 pdr, 1-8in mortar. Davy, Topsham 4.8.1804. Captured 29.6.1811 by the Danes.

SAFEGUARD Coastguard hulk (brig) in service 1849-62.

SAFEGUARD Coastguard vessel 875 tons, 160 x 29 ft, 2-3pdr. Day Summers, Southampton 24.6.1914. Sold 13.2.20, renamed *Safeguarder*.

SAFETY (ex-*Eclair*) Schooner 12,

180bm. Guardship in the W.Indies 1808; prison ship 1810; not listed again until 1841, then receiving hulk at Tortola. BU 1879.

SAGA Submarine, 'S' class. Cammell Laird 14.3.1945. Sold 11.10.48 Portuguese navy as NAUTILLO.

SAGESSE 6th Rate 28, 481bm. French, captured 8.9.1803 by THESEUS in the W.Indies. Sold 7.6.1821.

SAGUENAY Destroyer (RCN) 1,337 tons, 309 x 33 ft, 4-4.7in, 8-TT. Thornycroft 11.7.1930. Damaged and became training ship 8.43. Sold 17.7.48 to BU.

SAGUENAY Escort (RCN) 2,265 tons 366(oa) x 42 ft, 4-3in, 2-40mm. Halifax SY 30.7.1953.

SAHIB (ex-P.212) Submarine, 'S' class. Cammell Laird 19.1.1942. Sunk 24.4.43 by Italian corvette GABBIANO north of Sicily.

SAINFOIN (see SANFOIN)

ST AGATHE Frigate (RCN), 'River' class. Quebec. Cancelled 12.1943.

ST ALBANS 4th Rate 50, 615bm, 128 x 33½ ft. Deptford 1687. Wrecked 8.12.1693 near Kinsale.

ST ALBANS PRIZE 6th Rate 18, 262bm. French, captured 9.10.1691. Sold 13.5.1698.

ST ALBANS 4th Rate 54, 687bm, 131 x 34½ ft. Burchett Rotherhithe 27.8.1706. Rebuilt Plymouth 1718 as 853bm. Wrecked 20.10.1744 near Jamaica.

ST ALBANS 4th Rate 60, 1.207bm, 150 x 43½ ft. West, Deptford 23.12.1747. Sold 14.3.1765.

ST ALBANS 3rd Rate 64, 1,380bm, 159½ x 44½ ft. Perry, Blackwall 12.9.1764. Floating battery 9.1803. BU 6.1814.

ST ALBANS (ex-USS THOMAS) Destroyer 1,060 tons, 309 x 30½ ft, 3-4in, 1-3in, 6-TT. Commissioned 23.9.1940 in the RN. Lent R.Norwegian navy 4.41; lent Russian navy 16.7.44 to 28.2.49 as DOSTOINI. Sold 5.4.49, BU at Charlestown.

ST ANDREW Galleon 50, 900bm, 8-18pdr, 21-9pdr, 7-6pdr, 14 smaller. Spanish, captured 6.1596 at Cadiz. Given away 1604.

ST ANDREW 42-gun ship, 587bm. Deptford 1622. Wrecked 1666. (Known as ANDREW during the Commonwealth.)

ST ANDREW 1st Rate 96, 1,318bm, 159 x 44 ft. Woolwich DY 1670. Renamed ROYAL ANNE 8.7.1703 and rebuilt as 1st Rate 100, 1,722bm, 170 x

48 ft. BU in 5.1727 but listed to 1756.

ST ANGELO (see BULLFROG of 1881)

ST ANGELO (see FIDGET of 1905)

ST ANGELO Base ship 150 tons, 78 x 18 ft. Scott, Bowling 18.3.1935 for use as DY tug. Sunk 30.5.42 by mine off Malta.

ST ANGELO II (see FAREHAM)

ST ANNE Ship, 350bm. French, captured 1626. Sold 1630.

ST ANNE 3rd Rate 64, 1,407bm, 165 x 44 ft, 26-24pdr, 28-18pdr, 10-9pdr. French, captured 25.5.1761 by a squadron in the W.Indies. Sold 21.10.1784.

ST ANNE Tug 1919-22 & requis. (RCN) 1940-43.

SAN ANTONIO Sloop 4, 67bm, 55 x 17 ft. Pirate ship captured 4.1700 from Captain Kidd. Sunk 4.8.1707 as a foundation in Jamaica.

SAN ANTONIO 3rd Rate 64, 1,392bm, 159½ x 44½ ft. Spanish, captured 12.8.1762 at Havana. Sold 28.3.1775.

SAN ANTONIO 3rd Rate 74, 1,700bm. French St ANTOINE captured 12.7.1807 off Cadiz. Prison ship 1809; powder hulk 9.1814. Sold 11.7.1827 and sale cancelled; sold 26.3.1828 J.Ledger to BU.

ST AUSTELL BAY (ex-LOCH LYDOCH renamed 1944) Frigate, 'Bay' class. Harland & Wolff 18.11.1944. Arrived 4.7.59 Charlestown to BU.

ST BONIFACE Minesweeper (RCN), 'Algerine' class. Pt Arthur 5.11.1942. Sold 1946, same name.

ST BONIFACE Rescue tug 1919-25.

ST BRIDES BAY (ex-LOCH ACHILTY renamed 1944) Frigate, 'Bay' class. Harland & Wolff 16.1.45. Arrived 3.9.62 at Faslane to BU.

SAN CARLOS Storeship 22, 676bm, 125 x 35½ ft, 8-18pdr carr., 14-6pdr. Spanish privateer frigate captured 12.12.1779 by SALISBURY in the W.Indies. Sold 5.8.1784.

ST CATHERINES Frigate (RCN), 'River' class. Yarrow, Esquimalt 6.12.1942. Weather ship 1950.

ST CHRISTOPHER (ex-*Mohawk*) (ex-French privateer) Sloop 18. Presented 1807 by the inhabitants of St Kitts. Listed to 1810.

ST CLAIR (ex-USS WILLIAMS) Destroyer (RCN) 1,060 tons, 309 x 30½ ft, 3-4in, 1-3in, 6-TT. Commissioned 24.9.1940 in the RCN. Depot ship 12.43. BU 2.47.

ST CLAUDE Ship, 300bm. Captured

1625. Given away 1632.

ST CLAUDE Rescue tug 1919-25.

ST COLUMBA Wood pad. packet, 720bm, 198½ x 27 ft. Purchased on stocks; Laird 5.7.1847. Sold 1850 City of Dublin SP Co.

ST CROIX (ex-USS McCOOKE) Destroyer (RCN) 1,190 tons, 311 x 31 ft, 3-4in, 1-3in, 6-TT. Commissioned 24.9.1940 in the RCN. Sunk 20.9.43 by 'U.305' south of Iceland.

ST CROIX Frigate (RCN) 2,365 tons, 366(oa) x 42 ft, 4-3in. Marine Ind 15.11.1956.

SAN DAMASO 3rd Rate 74, 1,812bm, 175 x 48 ft. Spanish, captured 17.2.1797 off Trinidad. Prison ship 1800. Sold 30.9.1814.

ST DAVID 4th Rate 54, 646bm. Lydney 1667. Foundered 11.11.1690 in Portsmouth harbour; raised 8.1691 and hulked. Sold 20.8.1713.

ST DAVID Name borne in succession from 1949 by MMS. 1733, BRERETON and CRICHTON as RNVR tenders.

ST DENNIS 38-gun ship, 396bm. Captured 1625. Hulk 1634. Sold 1645.

SAN DOMINGO 3rd Rate 74, 1,820bm. Woolwich DY 3.3.1809. Sold 18.4.1816.

SAN DOMINGO Destroyer 2,380 tons, 355 x 40 ft, 5-4.5in, 8-40mm. 10-TT. Cammell Laird. Laid down 9.12.1944, cancelled 10.45.

SANTA DOROTEA 5th Rate 34, 958bm. Spanish, captured 15.7.1798. by LION in the Mediterranean. BU 6.1814 at Portsmouth.

ST EDOUARD Frigate (RCN), 'River' class. G.T.Davie. Cancelled 12.1943.

ST EUSTATIA 6th Rate 26. Dutch, captured 1781 in the W.Indies. Sold there in 1784.

ST FERMIN Brig, 250bm, 80 x 26 ft. Spanish, captured 8.1.1780. Recaptured 4.1780 by the Spanish off Gibraltar.

ST FIORENZO 5th Rate 38, 1,032bm, 14-32pdr carr., 26-18pdr, 2-9pdr. French MINERVE captured 19.2.1794 (found sunk at San Fiorenzo, Corsica and raised). Harbour service 1812. BU 9.1837.

ST FIORENZO Wood S.frigate, 2,066bm, 188 x 50½ ft. Woolwich DY. Laid down 6.1850, cancelled 4.1856.

ST FLORENTINE 4th Rate 60, 1,109bm, 148 x 41½ ft, 24-24pdr, 26-12pdr, 10-6pdr. French privateer COMPTE de SAINT-FLORENTIN captured 4.4.1759. Sunk 5.1771 as

breakwater at Sheerness.

ST FRANCIS (ex-USS BANCROFT) Destroyer (RCN) 1,190 tons, 311 x 31 ft, 3-4in, 1-3in, 6-TT. Commissioned 24.9.1940 in the RCN. Training ship 1944. Sunk 14.7.45 in collision with SS *Winding Gulf* off Sagonnet Point, RI while on passage to Philadelphia to BU.

SAN GENARO 4th Rate 60. Spanish, captured 13.8.1762 at Havana. Wrecked 1.1763 in the Downs.

ST GEORGE 60-gun ship, 594bm. Burrell, Deptford 1622. Hulked 1687. Sunk 20.10.1697 as blockship to defend Sheerness.

ST GEORGE Ship. Captured 1626. Listed to 1932.

ST GEORGE (ex-CHARLES renamed 1687) 1st Rate 96, 1,129bm, 163 x 42½ ft. Rebuilt Portsmouth 1701 as 1,470bm; rebuilt Portsmouth 1740 as 1,655bm, 166 x 48½ ft. BU 9.1774.

ST GEORGE Discovery ship, 654bm, 132 x 34 ft. Purchased 3.12.1701. Sunk 20.2.1716 as foundation, Chatham.

ST GEORGE 2nd Rate 98, 1,950bm, 177½ x 50 ft. Portsmouth DY 4.10.1785. Wrecked 24.12.1811 on the coast of Jutland.

ST GEORGE (see BRITANNIA of 1762)

ST GEORGE 1st Rate 120, 2,694bm, 205 x 55½ ft. Plymouth DY 27.8.1840 (13 years on stocks). Undocked 19.3.1859 as screw ship, 2,864bm. Sold 1883 Castle, BU 11.1883.

ST GEORGE 1st class cruiser 7,700 tons, 360 x 61 ft, 2-9.2in, 10-6in, 12-6pdr. Earle, Hull 23.6.1892. Depot ship 1909. Sold 1.7.20 S.Castle, Plymouth.

ST GEORGE Yacht requis. 1915-18.

SANTA GERTRUYDA 5th Rate 36. Spanish, captured 7.12.1804 by POLYPHEMUS and LIVELY off Cape St Mary. Receiving ship 11.1807. BU 6.1811.

SAN GIORGIO Repair hulk 9,232 tons, 430 x 69 ft. Italian cruiser found sunk in shallow water at Tobruk and commissioned 3.44 to 1945.

ST HELENA (ex-PASLEY renamed 1943) Frigate, 'Colony' class. Walsh Kaiser 20.10.43 on lend-lease. Returned 23.4.46 to the USN.

SAN ILDEFONSO 3rd Rate 74, 1,752bm. Spanish, captured 21.10.1805 at Trafalgar. Provision depot ILDEFONSO in 1813. BU 7.1816.

ST JACOB Fireship 4, 175bm. Captured

1666. Sold 1667.

ST JACOB Fireship 4, 276bm. Purchased 1667. Expended 1667.

ST JACOB Dogger 6. Captured 1672. Sold 1674.

ST JAMES Ship. Captured 1625. Listed to 1628.

ST JAMES Destroyer 2,325 tons, 335 x 40 ft, 4-4.5in, 1-4in, 12-40mm, 8-TT. Fairfield 7.6.1945. Arrived 19.3.61 Cashmore, Newport to BU.

ST JAMES Rescue tug 1920 renamed ST BREOCK.

ST JEAN d'ACRE Screw 1st Rate 101, 3,199bm, 238 x 55½ ft, 28-8in, 1-68pdr, 72-32pdr. Plymouth DY 23.3.1853. Sold 1.1875 Castle, Charlton, BU 10.75.

ST JOHN PRIZE Advice boat 6, 70bm, 59 x 16½ ft. French, captured 9.1695. Recaptured 5.9.1696 by the French.

ST JOHN Schooner 115bm. Purchased 5.1764 in N.America. Condemned 15.2.1777.

ST JOHN Cutter 14, 90bm. Purchased 1780 in N.America. Listed 1781.

ST JOHN Frigate (RCN), 'River' class. Vickers, Montreal 25.8.1943. Sold 17.11.47 Halifax SY; BU 1948.

SAN JOSEF 1st Rate 114, 2,457bm, 195 x 54 ft. Spanish, captured 14.2.1797 at Cape St Vincent. Gunnery training ship 1837. BU 5.1849 at Devonport.

ST JOSEPH Sloop 8. French, captured 7.1696. Sold 24.8.1699.

ST JOSEPH Hoy, 70bm. Purchased 24.11.1704 at Lisbon. Sold in 4.1710.

SAN JUAN 3rd Rate 74, 1,740bm. Spanish SAN JUAN NEPOMUCENO captured 21.10.1805 at Trafalgar. Listed on harbour service to 1816. Sold 8.1.1818 at Gibraltar. Was BERWICK for a time in 1805).

ST KATHERINE Dogger 6. Captured 1672. Lost 1673.

ST KITTS Destroyer 2,315 tons, 355 x 40 ft, 4-4.5in, 1-4in, 14-40mm, 8-TT. Swan Hunter 4.10.1944. Arrived 19.2.62 Young, Sunderland to BU.

ST KITTS Rescue tug 1919-26.

ST LAMBERT Corvette (RCN), modified 'Flower' class. Morton 6.11.1943. Sold 1946, renamed *Chrysi Hondroulis*.

ST LAURENT (see CYGNET of 1931)

ST LAURENT Escort (RCN) 2,265 tons, 366(oa) x 42 ft, 4-3in, 2-40mm. Vickers Montreal 30.11.1951. Sold Dartmouth Salv. Co 27.9.79. Resold and foundered 12.1.80 in tow to BU.

ST LAWRENCE Schooner purchased at Halifax 5.1764. Blown up by lightning off Cape Breton 26.7.1766.

ST LAWRENCE Schooner 10, 114bm. Purchased 7.67. Sold 6.2.1776.

ST LAWRENCE Schooner. Purchased in N.America 1775. Sold 1783.

ST LAWRENCE Schooner 12, 240bm, 12-12pdr carr., 1-9pdr. American privateer ATLAS captured 13.6.1813 off N.Carolina. Recaptured 26.2.1815 by the American privateer CHASSEUR in the W.Indies.

ST LAWRENCE 1st Rate 112 (Canadian lakes), 2,305bm, 198 x 52½ ft. Kingston Ont 10.9.1814. Sold 1.1832.

ST LAWRENCE (see SHANNON of 1806)

SANTA LEOCADIA Listed 1814 (seems to be LEOCADIA qv).

SAN LEON Brig-sloop 16. Spanish, captured 28.11.1798 by a squadron in the Atlantic. Sold 1800.

ST LEWIS 5th Rate 42, 460bm, 113 x 30½ ft. French SAINT-LOUIS captured 1697. Hulk 1701. Wrecked 1707 in Jamaica.

ST LOE (ST LOOE) Yacht 4, 47bm. Plymouth DY 1700. Sold 2.8.1716.

ST LUCIA Gun-brig 14, 183bm, 85½ x 23 ft, 14-4pdr. French privateer ENFANT PRODIGUE captured 24.6.1803 by EMERALD in the W.Indies. Recaptured 1.1807 by the French in the W.Indies.

ST LUCIA Destroyer 2,380 tons, 355 x40 ft, 5-4.5in, 8-40mm, 10-TT. Stephen. Laid down 19.1.1945, cancelled 10.45.

ST LUCIA Trawler requis. 1918-19.

SANTA MARGARITA 5th Rate 38, 993bm, 145½ x 39 ft, 8-18pdr carr., 26-12pdr, 10-6pdr. Spanish, captured 11.11.1779 on the coast of Portugal; quarantine ship 1817. Sold 8.9.1836.

SANTA MARIA 4th Rate 50, 400bm. Dutch, captured 1665. Burnt 12.6.1667 by the Dutch at Chatham.

ST MARTIN 6th Rate 18, 177bm, 78½ x 23 ft. French, captured 1691. Sunk 24.4.1695 as breakwater at Portsmouth.

ST MARTIN Rescue tug 1919-46.

ST MARY Cog. Cinq Ports vessel in 1299.

ST MARY Ship, 100bm. Purchased 1626. Given away 1628.

ST MARYS (ex-USS DORAN) Destroyer 1,060 tons, 309 x 30½ ft, 3-4in, 1-3in, 6-TT. Commissioned 23.9.1940 in the RN. Sold 20.3.45; arrived 12.45 Rosyth to BU.

ST MATHEW Galleon 50, circa 900bm, 4-60pdr, 4-34pdr, 16-18pdr, 14-9pdr, 4-6pdr, 6 smaller, Spanish SAN MATEO captured 6.1596 at Cadiz. Given away 1604.

ST MICHAEL 2nd Rate 90, 1,080bm, 155 x 41½ ft. Portsmouth DY 1669. Renamed MARLBOROUGH 18.12.1706. (qv)

SAN MIGUEL 3rd Rate 74, 1,925bm, 176 x 49 ft, 28-32pdr, 30-18pdr, 16-9pdr. Spanish, captured 10.9.1782 by the garrison of Gibraltar while she was ashore. Sold 1.12.1791.

SANTA MONICA 5th Rate 32, 956bm, 145 x 38½ ft, 8-18pdr carr., 26-12pdr, 10-6pdr. Spanish, captured 14.9.1779 by PEARL. Wrecked 28.3.1782 off Tortola.

ST NAZAIRE (see LST.3517)

ST NICHOLAS Fireship 4, 108bm, 70½ x 19 ft. Purchased 4.1694. Expended 12.7.1694 at Dieppe.

SAN NICOLAS 3rd Rate 80, 1,942bm, 180 x 49½ ft. Spanish, captured 14.2.1797 at Cape St Vincent. Prison ship 1800. Sold 3.11.1814.

ST PATRICK 4th Rate 48, 621bm. Bailey, Bristol 5.1666. captured 5.2.1667 by the Dutch.

ST PATRICK (ex-SHAMROCK renamed 1.11.1917). Tank vessel 1917-23.

ST PAUL 4th Rate 48, 291bm, Dutch PAULUS captured 1665. Burnt in action 1666.

ST PAUL Fireship 4, 290bm. Dutch, captured 1666. Sold 1667.

ST PAUL 5th Rate 32, 260bm. Algerian, captured 1679. Fireship 1688. Sold 3.5.1698.

ST PETER Dogger 6. Captured 1672. captured 1674 by the Dutch.

ST PHILIPS CASTLE Sloop. Purchased 1780. Sold 10.4.1783.

ST PIERRE Sloop in 1796. Wrecked 12.2.1796 off Port Negro.

ST PIERRE Sloop 18, 371bm. French DILIGENTE captured 2.1809 at Martinique. Sold 1.9.1814.

ST PIERRE Frigate (RCN), 'River' class. Quebec SB Co 1.12.1943. Sold 1947 Peruvian navy as PALACIOS.

SAN RAFAEL 3rd Rate 80, 2,230bm. Spanish, captured 22.7.1805 at Calder's action off Cape Finisterre. Prison ship 1806. Sold 9.1810.

ST ROMUALD Frigate (RCN), 'River' class. G.T.Davie. Cancelled 12.1943.

ST STEPHEN Frigate (RCN), 'River' class. Yarrow, Esquimalt 6.2.1944. Transferred 1958 Dept of Transport as weather ship. Sold Mercantile 1969.

SANTA TERESA 5th Rate 30, 949bm, 144 x 38½ ft. Spanish, captured 6.2.1799 by ARGO off Majorca. Sold 9.1802.

STE THERESE Frigate (RCN), 'River' class. Davie SB 16.10.1943. Sold 12.66.

ST THOMAS (ex-SANDGATE CASTLE renamed 1943) Corvette (RCN), 'Castle' class. Smiths Dk 28.12.43. Sold 1946, renamed Camosum.

ST THOMAS (see SEABEAR)

ST VINCENT Fireship 8, 197bm. French, captured 18.6.1692. Sold 3.5.1698.

ST VINCENT Sloop 14, 276bm, 83 x 24 ft. Spanish SAN VICENTE captured 1780 in the W.Indies. Sold 4.1783 in N.America.

ST VINCENT 1st Rate 120, 2,601bm, 4,672 tons, 205 x 54 ft. Plymouth DY 11.3.1815. Harbour service as flag ship and depot ship from 10.1841; training ship 1.1.1862. Sold 17.5.1906 Castle.

ST VINCENT Battleship 19,250 tons, 500 x 84 ft, 10-12in, 20-4in. Portsmouth DY 10.9.1908. Sold 1.12.21 Stanlee, Dover.

ST VINCENT Trawler requis. 1914-19.

SAN YSIDRO 3rd Rate 72, 1,836bm, 176 x 49 ft. Spanish, captured 14.2.1797 at Cape St Vincent. Prison ship 1797. Sold 3.11.1814.

SAINTES Destroyer 2,325 tons, 355 x 40 ft, 4-4.5in, 1-4in, 14-40mm, 8-TT. Hawthorn Leslie 19.7.1944. Sold 26.6.72, arrived Cairnryan 1.9.72 to BU.

SAKER Pinnace, 50bm. Listed 1545-65.

SALADIN Destroyer, 'S' class. Stephen 17.2.1919. Sold 29.6.47, BU Rees, Llanelly.

SALAMANDER 48-gun ship, 300/450bm. Scots navy, captured 1544. Listed to 1559.

SALAMANDER Bomb 10, 134bm, 64½ x 21½ ft. Chatham DY 1687. Rebuilt Woolwich 1703 as 122bm. Sold 20.8.1713.

SALAMANDER Bomb 10, 265bm. 84 x 27½ ft. Woolwich DY 7.7.1730. Sold 13.3.1743.

SALAMANDER (ex-Pelham) Fireship 8, 304bm, 96 x 27½ ft, 8-6pdr. Purchased 6.9.1745. Sold 23.6.1748.

SALAMANDER (ex-Applewhite & Frere) Fireship 8, 260bm, 89 x 26 ft, 8-6pdr. Purchased 5.1.1757. Sold 30.12.1761.

SALAMANDER (see SHARK of 1776)

SALAMANDER (ex-United) Fire vessel,

78bm, 59½ x 18 ft. Purchased 5.1804. Sold 17.6.1807 J.Cristall to BU.

SALAMANDER Wood pad. sloop, 818bm, 175½ x 32 ft. Sheerness DY 16.5.1832. Sold Castle in 12.1883 to BU.

SALAMANDER Torpedo gunboat 735 tons, 230 x 27 ft, 2-4.7in, 4-3pdr, 3-TT. Chatham DY 31.5.1889. Sold 15.5.1906 Ashdown, London.

SALAMANDER Minesweeper 815 tons, 230 x 33½ ft, 2-4in. White 24.3.1936. Sold 15.12.46. Arrived Blyth 7.5.47 to BU.

SALAMANDER Whaler 1915-19.

SALAMAUA Landing craft (RAN) 310 tons. Walker 1972. To Papua-New Guinea 1975

SALAMINE Brig-sloop 18, 240bm, 93½ x 25 ft. French, captured 18.6.1799 by EMERALD in the Mediterranean. Sold 1802 at Malta.

SALAMIS Wood pad. despatch vessel, 835bm, 929 tons, 220 x 28 ft, 2-9pdr. Chatham DY 19.5.1863. BU 1883 at Sheerness.

SALCOMBE (see SUTTON)

SALDANHA 5th Rate 40, 1,065bm, 147 x 40 ft. Dutch CASTHOR captured 17.8.1796 in Saldanha Bay. Harbour service 2.1798. Sold 1.1806. at Plymouth.

SALDANHA 5th Rate 36, 951bm, 145 x 39 ft. Temple, S.Shields. 8.12.1809. Wrecked 4.12.1811 in Lough Swilly.

SALERNO (see LST.3513)

SALFORD (ex-SHOREHAM renamed 1918) Minesweeper, later 'Hunt' class. Murdoch & Murray 3.4.1919. Sold 10.20 Bombay SN Co, renamed *Vegavati*.

SALISBURY 4th Rate 48, 682bm, 134½ x 34 ft. Herring, Bucklers Hard 18.4.1698. Captured 10.4.1703 by the French ADROIT; recaptured 15.3.1708. Renamed PRESTON 2.1.1716. Rebuilt 1742 as 853bm; hulk at Trincomalee 9.1748. BU there. 11.1749.

SALISBURY 4th Rate 54, 703bm, 130 x 35 ft. Chatham DY 3.7.1707. Rebuilt Portsmouth 1726 as 756bm; hulked 2.1744. Sold 1.5.1749.

SALISBURY 4th Rate 50, 976bm, 140 x 40 ft. Ewer, E.Cowes 29.1.1745. Condemned 24.4.1761 in the E.Indies.

SALISBURY 4th Rate 50, 1,051bm, 146 x 40½ ft. Chatham DY 2.10.1769. Wrecked 13.5.1796 near San Domingo.

SALISBURY 4th Rate 58, 1,199bm, 154½ x 43 ft. Deptford DY 21.6.1814. Sold 1.1837 Beatson to BU.

SALISBURY (ex-USS CLAXTON) Destroyer 1,090 tons, 309 x 30½ ft, 1-4in, 1-3in, 4-20mm, 3-TT. Commissioned 5.12.1940 in the RN. Lent RCN 9.42 to 1944; sold 26.6.44 in Canada.

SALISBURY Frigate 2,170 tons, 330 x 40 ft, 2-4.5in, 2-40mm. Devonport DY 25.6.1953.

SALLY Storeship 14, 398bm. Purchased 4.5.1781. Sold 2.12.1783.

SALLYPORT (ex-LCT.4064 renamed 1956) Tank landing craft 657 tons, 225 x 39 ft. Arrol, Alloa 1945. Sold at Malta 4.66 to Greek interests.

SALLY ROSE see under ROSE

SALMON Destroyer 310 tons, 200 x 19½ ft, 1-12pdr, 5-6pdr, 2-TT. Earle, Hull 15.1.1895. Sold 14.5.1912 Cashmore, Newport.

SALMON Destroyer, 'R' class. Harland & Wolff, Govan 7.10.1916. Renamed SABLE 2.12.33. Handed over to Ward 28.1.37 in part payment for *Majestic* (CALEDONIA); arrived Hayle 3.37 to BU.

SALMON Submarine 670 tons, 193 x 24 ft, 1-3in, 6-TT. Cammell Laird 30.4.1934. Sunk 9.7.40 by mine off Norway.

SALORMAN Cutter 10, 121bm. Danish, captured 10.8.1808 by boats of ED-GAR off Nyborg. Wrecked 22.12.1809 in the Baltic. (Spelt SALOMAN in James.')

SALSETTE (see DORIS)

SALTASH Sloop 14, 200bm, 85½ x 23½ ft. Plymouth DY 7.9.1732. Sold 22.10.1741.

SALTASH Sloop 14, 221bm, 89 x 24 ft. Purchased on stocks; Bird, Rotherhithe 1741. Wrecked 18.4.1742 coast of Portugal.

SALTASH Sloop 14, 248bm, 88 x 25 ft. Quallett, Rotherhithe 30.12.1742. Foundered 24.6.1746 off Beachy Head.

SALTASH Sloop 14, 270bm, 91 x 26 ft. Allin & Quallett, Rotherhithe 19.12.1746. Sold 15.2.1763.

SALTASH Storeship 106bm. Chichester 9.12.1748. Wrecked 26.8.1752.

SALTASH Store lighter, 85bm, 55 x 19 ft. Purchased 1756. BU in 1775.

SALTASH Store lighter, 125bm, 63½ x 22½ ft. Topsham 1809. Sold 12.7.1831.

SALTASH Minesweeper, later 'Hunt' class. Murdoch & Murray 25.7.1918. Sold 13.3.47.

SALTBURN Minesweeper, later 'Hunt' class. Murdoch & Murray 9.10.1918. Sold 23.10.46 Gifford, Bude. Wrecked 12.46 in tow off Hartland Point; salved, BU 1948.

SALVADOR del MUNDO 1st Rate 112, 2,398bm, 191 x 54½ ft, 30-32pdr, 32-24pdr, 32-12pdr, 15-9pdr. Spanish, captured 14.2.1797 at Cape St Vincent. BU 2.1815.

SALVIA Sloop, 'Aubrietia' class. Irvine, Glasgow 16.6.1916. Sunk 20.6.17 by 'U.94' west of Ireland while operating as decoy ship Q.15.

SALVIA Corvette, 'Flower' class. Simons 6.8.1940. Sunk 24.12.41 by 'U.568' west of Alexandria.

SAMARAI Patrol boat (RAN) 100 tons Evans Deakin 14.7.67 To Papua-New Guinea in 9.75.

SAMARANG (see SCIPIO of 1807)

SAMARANG Sloop 18. Portsmouth DY. Ordered 6.9.1815, cancelled 30.9.1820.

SAMARANG 6th Rate 28, 500bm, 113½ x 32 ft. Cochin 1.1.1822. Guardship 5.1847. Sold 10.1883 at Gibraltar.

SAMPHIRE Corvette, 'Flower' class. Smiths DK 14.4.1941. Sunk 30.1.43 by U-boat in the Mediterranean.

SAMPSON 20-gun ship, 300bm. Captured 1643. Given away 1646 in exchange for the 26-gun PRESIDENT.

SAMPSON 32-gun ship. Captured 1652. Lost 18.2.1653 in action with the Dutch.

SAMPSON 32-gun ship. Captured 1652. Sold 1658.

SAMSON Fireship 12, 240bm. Purchased 1678. Expended 14.3.1689.

SAMPSON 3rd Rate 64, 1,380bm, 160 x 44½ ft. Woolwich DY 8.5.1781. Hulk 1802. BU 5.1832 Levy, Rochester.

SAMPSON Wood pad. frigate, 1,299bm, 203 x 37½ ft. Woolwich DY 1.10.1844. Sold 15.7.1864 Castle & Beech.

SAMPSON and SAMSON Tugs 1877-1918, 1940-44., 1918-19. 1953

SAN - (see under SAINT-)

SANDFLY Floating battery 14, 360bm, 80 x 32 ft. Wells, Rotherhithe. 1795. BU 1803.

SANDFLY Wood S.gunboat, 'Albacore' class. Pitcher, Northfleet 1.9.1855. Sold 5.11.1867 W.Lethbridge to BU.

SANDFLY (ex-*Tasmanian Maid*) Paddle gunboat (NZ Govt), 90bm, 2-12pdr. Purchased 6.1863. Sold 1865.

SANDFLY Survey schooner, 120bm, 1-12pdr. Cuthbert, Sydney NSW 5.12.1872. Sold 1883 at Sydney.

SANDFLY Torpedo gunboat 525 tons, 200 x23 ft, 1-4in, 6-3pdr, 4-TT. Devonport DY 30.9.1887. Sold 1905 at Malta.

SANDFLY Coastal destroyer 235 tons, 175 x 17½ ft, 2-12pdr, 3-TT. White 30.10.1906. Renamed TB.4 in 1906. Sold 7.10.20 Ward; ran ashore on passage at Pebble Ridge near Westward Ho.

SANDFLY Destroyer 750 tons, 246 x 26 ft, 2-4in, 2-12pdr, 2-TT. Swan Hunter 26.7.1911. Sold 9.5.21 Ward, Milford Haven.; arrived in 10.22.

SANDGATE CASTLE (see ST THOMAS)

SANDHURST (ex-*Manipur*) Repair ship 11,500 tons, 470 x 58 ft, 4-4in, 2-6pdr. Hired 1914 as dummy battlecruiser INDOMITABLE; purchased 1915, conversion completed 9.16. Arrived 4.46 Arnott Young, Dalmuir to BU.

SANDOWN Paddle M/S, 'Ascot' class. Dunlop Bremner 6.7.1916. Sold 3.22 Ward., BU Inverkeithing 12.23.

SANDOWN Minesweeper requis. 1939-46

SANDPIPER River gunboat 85 tons, 108 x 20 ft, 2-6pdr. Yarrow, Poplar 2.7.1897. Sold 18.10.20 at Hong Kong.

SANDPIPER River gunboat 185 tons, 160 x 30½ ft, 1-3.7in howitzer, 1-6pdr. Thornycroft 6.6.1933. Transferred Chinese navy 2.42 as YING HAO.

SANDPIPER Patrol boat 190 tons. Dunston 20.1.1977

SANDRINGHAM Inshore M/S, 'Ham' class. McLean, Gourock 16.4.57. Sold Pounds 1986 became mercantile.

SANDRINGHAM Trawler 1917-19

SANDWICH 2nd Rate 90, 1,346bm, 161½ x 44½ ft. Betts, Harwich 1679. Rebuilt Chatham 1712 as 1,573bm; hulk 1752. BU completed 24.3.1770 at Chatham.

SANDWICH 2nd Rate 98, 1,869bm, 176 x 49 ft. Chatham DY 14.4.1759. Floating battery 1780; harbour service 10.1790. BU 1810 at Chatham.

SANDWICH (ex-Majority) A.ship 24. Purchased 1780. Captured 24.8.1781 by the French off Charlestown.

SANDWICH Cutter 10, 113bm, 66½ x 20½ ft, 10-12pdr carr. Purchased 1804. Sold 1805 in Jamaica.

SANDWICH (see PITT of 1805)

SANDWICH 3rd Rate 74, 2,039bm, 192 x 49 ft. Milford DY. Laid down 12,1809, cancelled 22.3.1811.

SANDWICH Sloop 1,043 tons, 250 X 34 ft, 2-4in. Hawthorn Leslie 29.9.1928. Sold 8.1.46.

SANFOIN M/S Sloop, '24' class. Greenock & Grangemouth Co 10.6.1918. Sold 15.11.22 Ferguson Muir.

SAINFOIN (see EMPIRE CROSSBOW)

SANGUINE Submarine, 'S' class. Cammell Laird 15.2.1945. Sold Israeli navy 1958, renamed RAHOV 3.59.

SANSOVINO (see EMPIRE CUTLASS)

SANS PAREIL 3rd Rate 80, 2,245bm, 193½ x 51½ ft, 2-42pdr carr., 8-32pdr carr., 30-32pdr, 32-24pdr carr., 22-12pdr. French, captured 1.6.1794 at the battle of the First of June. Sheer hulk 1810. BU 10.1842 at Devonport.

SANS PAREIL Screw 2nd Rate 81, 2,339bm, 200 x 52 ft, 1-10in, 30-8in, 50-32pdr. Devonport DY 18.3.1851. Sold 3.1867 Marshall, Plymouth.

SANS PAREIL Battleship 10,470 tons, 340 x 70 ft, 2-16.25in, 1-10in, 2-6in, 9-6pdr. Thames IW 9.5.1887. Sold 9.4.1907 Ward., Birkenhead & Preston.

SANTA - (see under SAINT-)

SANTON Coastal M/S, 'Ton' class. Fleetlands SY 18.8.1955. Sold 1967 Argentine navy, renamed CHUBUT.

SAPPHIRE 36-gun-ship, 442bm. Ratcliffe 1651. Run ashore 31.3.1671 to avoid capture by the French.

SAPPHIRE 5th Rate 32, 346bm, 106 x 27 ft. Deane, Harwich 1675. Sunk 11.9.1696 by the French in the Bay of Bulls, Newfoundland.

SAPPHIRE 4th Rate 42, 534bm, 118 x 32½ ft. Portsmouth DY 9.1708. Hulked 2.1740. Sold 1.5.1745.

SAPPHIRE 5th Rate 44, 686bm, 124 x 36 ft. Carter, Limehouse 21.2.1741. Reduced to 32 guns 7.1756; hulked by 1780. Sold 11.3.1784.

SAPPHIRE'S PRIZE Sloop 10, 164bm, 78½ x 22 ft. Spanish, captured 5.1745. Wrecked 15.9.1745.

SAPPHIRE Sloop 18, 426bm, 108½ x 30 ft. Brindley, Lynn 11.11.1806. Sold 18.4.1822 Manlove.

SAPPHIRE 6th Rate 28, 604bm, 119 x 34 ft. Portsmouth DY 31.1.1827. Sold 5.11.1864 at Trincomalee.

SAPPHIRE Wood S.corvette, 1,405bm, 1,970 tons, 220 x 37 ft, 14-64pdr. Devonport DY 24.9.1874. Sold 24.9.1892 G. Cohen.

SAPPHIRE 3rd class cruiser 3,000 tons, 360 x 40 ft, 12-4in, 8-3pdr. Palmer 17.3.1904. Sold 9.5.21 Ward, Grays.

SAPPHIRE II (see IMPERIEUSE of 1883)

SAPPHIRE Trawler 1914-18; Yacht 1915-19; Trawler 1935-46.

SAPPHO Brig-sloop 18, 'Cruiser' class, 384bm. Bailey, Ipswich 15.12.1806. BU 1830 at Halifax NS.

SAPPHO Brig-sloop 16, 428bm, 101 x 32½ ft, 14-32pdr, 2-9pdr. Plymouth DY 3.2.1837. Foundered 1859 on the Australian station.

SAPPHO Wood S.sloop, 950bm, 185 x 33 ft. Deptford DY. Laid down 1.5.1861, cancelled 12.12.1863.

SAPPHO (see ECLIPSE of 1867)

SAPPHO Compos. S.sloop, 727bm, 940 tons, 160 x 31½ ft, 2-7in, 2-64pdr. Wigram, Blackwall 20.11.1873 (originally ordered from Oswald & Co, Sunderland). Sold 12.1887 Castle.

SAPPHO 2nd class cruiser 3,400 tons, 300 x 43 ft, 2-6in, 6-4.7in, 8-6pdr. Samuda, Poplar 9.5.1891. Sold 18.3.1921 S.Castle, Plymouth.

SAPPHO Yacht requis 1939-40.

SARABANDE Minesweeper 265 tons, 130 x 26 ft, 1-3pdr. War Dept tug transferred on stocks. Goole SB 16.8.1918. Returned War Dept 1921. BU 10.26 Ward, Preston.

SARACEN Brig-sloop 18 (fir-built), 'Cruiser' class, 384bm. Perry, Wells & Green, Blackwall 25.7.1804. BU 5.1812.

SARACEN Brig-sloop 18, 'Cruiser' class, 387bm. Boole, Bridport 25.7.1812. Sold 18.8.1819 W.Wilkinson.

SARACEN Brig-sloop 10, 'Cherokee' class, 228bm. Plymouth DY 30.1.1831. Survey vessel 2.1854; exchanged 10.9.1862 at Singapore in part payment for *Young Queen*.

SARACEN (ex*Young Queen*) Survey brig, 75bm. Purchased 10.9.1862 and renamed 29.12.1862. Sold 13.3.1870.

SARACEN Destroyer 980 tons, 272 x 26 ft, 2-4in, 2-TT. White 31.3.1908. Sold 22.10.19 Ward, Preston.

SARACEN (ex-P.247) Submarine, 'S' class. Cammell Laird 16.2.1942. Sunk 18.8.43 by the Italian corvette MINERVA off Corsica.

SARAH Fireship 4, 89bm. Purchased 1666. Sold 1667.

SARAH Fireship 6, 143bm. Purchased 1678. Sold 1686.

SARAWAK (ex-PATTON renamed 1943) Frigate, 'Colony' class. Walsh Kaiser 25.10.1943 on lend-lease. Returned 5.46 to the USN.

SARDINE Sloop 16, 300 bm. French, captured 9.3.1796 by EGMONT off Tunis. Sold 1806.

SARDOINE Sloop 14, 255bm, 94½ x 25 ft. 14-4pdr. French, captured 4.1761 in the Bay of Biscay. Sold 26.4.1768.

SARDONYX Destroyer, 'S' class. Stephen 27.5.1919. BU 1945 Ward, Preston, arrived 23.6.45.

SARNIA Minesweeper (RCN), TE 'Bangor' class. Dufferin, Toronto 21.1.1942. Sold 29.3.58 Turkish navy as BUYUKDERE.

SARNIA ABS requis 1914-18.

SARPEDON Brig-sloop 10, 'Cherokee' class, 241bm. Warwick, Eling 1.2.1809. Foundered 1.1.1813.

SARPEDON (see LAERTES)

SARPEDON Destroyer, 'R' class. Hawthorn Leslie 1.6.1916. Sold 13.7.26 Alloa, Charlestown.

SARPENDON Trawler requis 1916-19.

SARPEN Brig-sloop 18, 309bm. Danish, captured 7.9.1807 at Copenhagen. BU 8.1811.

SARTINE 5th Rate 32, 802bm, 132½ x 36 ft. French, captured 25.8.1778 by SEAHORSE and COVENTRY. Wrecked 26.11.1780 off Mangalore, E.Indies.

SASKATCHEWAN (see FORTUNE of 1934)

SASKATCHEWAN Escort (RCN) 2,355 tons, 366(oa) x 42 ft, 4-3in. Victoria 31.1.1961.

SASKATOON Corvette (RCN), 'Flower' class. Vickers, Montreal 7.11.1940. Sold 1947, renamed *Tralosmontes*.

SATELLITE Brig-sloop 16, 289bm, 93 x 26½ ft, 14-24pdr carr., 2-6pdr. Hills, Sandwich 3.1806. Foundered 31.12.1810 in the Channel.

SATELLITE Brig-sloop 18, 'Cruizer' class, 385bm. List, Fishbourne 9.10.1812. Sold 3.1824 in the E.Indies.

SATELLITE Sloop 18, 456bm, 112 x 31 ft, 16-32pdr carr., 2-9pdr. Pembroke Dock 2.10.1826. BU 2.1849.

SATELLITE Paddle gunboat (Indian), 335bm, 2-12pdr. Bombay DY 1840. Listed in 1860.

SATELLITE Wood S.corvette, 1,462bm, 2,187 tons, 200 x 40½ ft, 20-8in, 1-68pdr. Devonport DY 26.9.1855. BU 1879 at Devonport.

SATELLITE Compos. S.corvette 1,420 tons, 200 x 38 ft, 2-6in, 10-5in. Sheerness DY 13.8.1881. RNVR drillship 1904. Sold 21.10.1947 J.G.Potts.

SATELLITE (see MELITA of 1942)

SATELLITE (see Brave of 1943)

SATISFACTION 26-gun ship, 290bm. Captured 1646. Wrecked 19.11.1663 Dutch coast.

SATISFACTION Fireship, 84bm, 64½ x 18 ft. Purchased 4.1794. Sold 5.1802.

SATURN 3rd Rate 74, 1,646bm, 168 x 47½ ft. Raymond, Northam 22.11.1786. Made a 4th Rate 58 in 12.1813; harbour service 9.1825. BU completed 1.2.1868 at Pembroke Dock.

SATURN Destroyer, 'S' class. Stephen. Cancelled 1919.

SATURN Trawler requis. 1916-19 & 1939-45.

SATYR Destroyer, 'R' class. Beardmore 27.12.1916. Sold 16.12.26 Ward, Milford Haven.

SATYR (ex-P.214) Submarine, 'S' class. Scotts 28.9.1942. Lent French navy 2.52 to 8.61 as SAPHIR. BU 4.62 at Charlestown.

SAUDADOES Sloop 10, 83bm. Portsmouth 1669. Rebuilt Deptford 1673 as 180bm, 6th Rate. Captured 23.2.1696 by the French.

SAUDADOES PRIZE 5th Rate 36, 385bm, 103½ x 29 ft. French, captured 9.1692. Sunk 1712 as foundation, Plymouth.

SAUK Schooner 2 (Canadian lakes), 87bm, 58½ x 19 ft. American SOMERS captured 12.8.1814. Listed to 1831.

SAULT STE MARIE (see THE SOO)

SAUMAREZ Destroyer leader 1,673 tons, 315 x 32 ft, 4-4in, 4-TT. Cammell Laird 14.10.1916. Sold 8.1.31 Ward, Briton Ferry.

SAUMAREZ Destroyer leader 1,750 tons, 363 x 36 ft, 4-4.7in, 6-40mm, 8-TT. Hawthorn Leslie 20.11.1942. Sold 8.9.50, BU 10.50 Charlestown. (Had been mined off Corfu 22.10.46).

SAUNDERS Destroyer leader 1,750 tons, 318 x 32 ft. Thornycroft. Cancelled 1.1919.

SAVAGE Sloop 14. Purchased 1748. Wrecked 1748 on the Lizard.

SAVAGE Sloop 8, 144bm, 74 x 21 ft. Woolwich DY 24.3.1750. Wrecked 16.9.1776 at Louisburg, NS.

SAVAGE Sloop 14, 302bm, 97 x 27 ft. Barnard, Ipswich 28.4.1778. Hulked 10.1804. Sold 31.8.1815.

SAVAGE Brig-sloop 16, 284bm, 93 x 26 ft. Adams, Chapel 30.7.1805. Sold 3.2.1819 J.Tibbut.

SAVAGE Brig-sloop 10, 'Cherokee' class, 227bm. Plymouth DY 29.12.1830. Made a DY chain lighter 7.1853. BU 1866.

SAVAGE Wood S.gunboat, 'Albacore' class. Mare, Blackwall 5.5.1856. Renamed YC.3, mooring lighter 1864. BU 9.1888 at Malta.

SAVAGE Destroyer 897 tons, 264 x 28 ft, 1-4in, 3-12pdr, 2-TT. Thornycroft 10.3.1910. Sold 9.5.21 Ward, Portishead.

SAVAGE Destroyer 1,710 tons, 339½ x 36 ft, 4-4.5in, 2-40mm, 8-TT. Hawthorn Leslie 24.9.1942. Arrived 11.4.62 Cashmore, Newport to BU.

SAVANNAH Brig-sloop 14. In 1779. Sunk 16.9.1779 to block the Savannah.

SAWFLY River gunboat, 'Fly' class. Yarrow 1915. Sold 1.3.23 at Basra.

SAWFLY Trawler requis. 1939-45.

SAXIFRAGE Sloop, 'Anchusa' class. Lobnitz 29.1.1918. Renamed PRESIDENT 9.4.21, drillship. For preservation 1986.

SAXIFRAGE Corvette, 'Flower' class. Hill, Bristol 24.10.1941. Sold 8.47 as weather ship *Polarfront I.*

SAXLINGHAM Inshore M/S, 'Ham' class. Berthon Bt Co, Lymington 17.10.1955. Sold Ross & Cromarty Co. Council 24.4.68.

SCAMANDER (ex-LIVELY renamed 1812) 5th Rate 36 (red pine-built), 941bm, 143 x 38½ ft, 14-32pdr carr., 26-18pdr, 2-9pdr. Brindley, Frindsbury 13.7.1813. Sold 22.7.1819 Ledger to BU.

SCARAB River gunboat 645 tons, 230 x 36 ft. 2-6in, 1-3in. Wood Skinner, Newcastle 7.10.1915. Lent Burmese Govt 5.46 to 6.47. BU 5.48 at Singapore.

SCARAB Tender 213 tons. Holmes 26.5.1971.

SCARBOROUGH Ketch 10, 94bm. Frame, Scarborough 2.5.1691. Captured 12.1.1693 by the French.

SCARBOROUGH 5th Rate 32, 374bm, 105 x 29 ft. Woolwich DY 15.2.1694. Captured 18.7.1694 by the French off the North of Ireland; recaptured 15.2.1696 as DUC de CHAULNES and renamed MILFORD. Rebuilt 1705 as 421bm. Wrecked 18.6.1720 at Cape Corrientes.

SCARBOROUGH 5th Rate 32, 391bm, 108 x 28½ ft. Parker, Southampton 1696. Captured 21.10.1710 by the French on the coast of Guinea; recaptured 31.3.1712 and renamed GARLAND. Sold 27.9.1744.

SCARBOROUGH 5th Rate 32, 416bm, 108 x 29½ ft. Sheerness DY 5.1711. Rebuilt Stacey, Deptford 1720 as 6th Rate 20, 378bm. Sold 25.8.1739.

SCARBOROUGH Hospital ship, 501bm, 117 x 31½ ft. Purchased 21.11.1739. Sold 18.12.1744.

SCARBOROUGH 6th Rate 24, 442bm, 106 x 31 ft. Perry, Blackwall 31.5.1740. Sold 13.4.1749.

SCARBOROUGH 6th Rate 22, 433bm, 107½ x 30½ ft. Blaydes, Hull 17.4.1756. Foundered 5.10.1780 in a hurricane in the W.Indies.

SCARBOROUGH 3rd Rate 74, 1,745bm, 176 x 48½ ft. Graham, Harwich 29.3.1812. Sold 8.9.1836.

SCARBOROUGH Sloop 1,045 tons, 250 x 34 ft, 2-4in. Swan Hunter 14.3.1930. Sold 3.6.49, BU by Stockton Ship & Salvage Co.

SCARBOROUGH Frigate 2,150 tons, 360 x 41 ft, 2-4.5in, 2-40mm. Vickers Armstrong, Tyne 4.4.1955. Sold Pakistan 1975 but not taken over. Arrived Blyth 31.8.77 to BU.

SCARBOROUGH CASTLE (see EMPIRE PEACEMAKER)

SCEPTRE 3rd Rate 64, 1,398bm, 160 x 44½ ft. Randall, Rotherhithe 8.6.1781. Wrecked 5.12.1799 in Table Bay.

SCEPTRE 3rd Rate 74, 1,727bm, 171 x 48 ft. Dudman, Deptford 11.12.1802. BU 2.1821.

SCEPTRE Destroyer, 'R' clas. Stephen 18.4.1917. Sold 16.12.26 Ward, Briton Ferry.

SCEPTRE Submarine, 'S' class. Scotts 9.1.1943. BU 9.49 at Gateshead.

SCEPTRE Nuclear S/M 3,800 tons. Vickers 20.11.1976.

SCIMITAR Destroyer, 'S' class. J.Brown 27.2.1918. Arrived 30.6.47 Ward, Briton Ferry to BU.

SCIMITAR Patrol boat 102 tons. Vosper-Thorneycroft 4.12.1969. Sold mercantile 1983.

SCIPIO Fireship 8, 171bm, 71½ x 23 ft. Purchased 28.9.1739. Sold 24.2.1746.

SCIPIO 3rd Rate 64, 1,387bm, 160 x 44½ ft. Barnard, Deptford 22.10.1782. BU 10.1798.

SCIPIO (see BULWARK of 1807)

SCIPIO Sloop 18, 408bm. Dutch PSYCHE, captured 1.9.1807. Renamed SAMARANG 19.4.1808. Sold at Bombay 24.3.1814.

SCIPION 3rd Rate 74, 1,810bm. French, handed over 29.8.1793 by Royalist at Toulon. Burnt 20.11.1793 by accident off Leghorn.

SCIPION 3rd Rate 74, 1,884bm, 183 x 48½ ft. French, captured 4.11.1805 at Strachan's action. BU 1.1819.

SCORCHER Submarine, 'S' class. Cammell Laird 18.12.1944. BU 1962 at Charlestown.

SCORPION Sloop 14, 276bm, 91 x 26½ ft. Wyatt & Major, Beaulieu 8.7.1746. Foundered 9.1762 in the Irish Sea.

SCORPION (see ETNA of 1771 under AETNA)

SCORPION Sloop 16, 342bm, 102 x 27½ ft. Ashman, Shoreham 26.3.1785. Sold 6.12.1802.

SCORPION Gunvessel 4, 70bm, 66½ x 15 ft. Purchased 3.1794. Sold 11.1804.

SCORPION Brig-sloop 18, 'Cruizer' class, 384bm. King. Dover 17.10.1803. Sold 3.2.1819 G.Young.

SCORPION Brig-sloop 10, 'Cherokee' class, 228bm. Plymouth DY 28.7.1832. Survey vessel 1848; lent Thames police 3.3.1858. BU completed 17.10.1874 at Chatham.

SCORPION (ex-Turkish EI TOUSSON purchased 10.1863) Iron turret ship, 1,857bm, 2,751 tons, 220 x 42½ ft, 4-9in. Laird 4.7.1863. Guardship at Bermuda 10.1869. Sold 2.1903 at Bermuda; lost 17.6.03 on passage to Boston.

SCORPION Destroyer 916 tons, 264 x 28 ft, 1-4in, 3-12pdr, 2-TT. Fairfield 19.2.1910. Sold 26.10.21 Barking S.Bkg Co.

SCORPION River gunboat 670 tons, 209(oa) x 34½ ft, 2-4in, 1-3.7in howitzer. White 20.12.1937. Sunk 13.2.42 in action with Japanese destroyers in the Banka Strait.

SCORPION (ex-SENTINEL renamed 1942) Destroyer 1,710 tons, 339½ x 36 ft, 4-4.7in, 2-40mm, 8-TT. Cammell Laird 26.8.42. Sold 1.10.45 Dutch navy as KORTENAER.

SCORPION (ex-TOMAHAWK renamed 9.1943, ex-CENTAUR) Destroyer 1,980 tons, 341½ x 38 ft, 6-4in, 6-40mm, 10-TT. White 15.8.46. Sold 4.6.71. BU at Bo'ness.

SCOTSMAN Destroyer, 'S' class J.Brown 30.3.1918. Handed over to Ward 13.7.37 in part payment for *Majestic* (CALEDONIA); BU at Briton Ferry.

SCOTSMAN Submarine, 'S' class. Scotts 18.8.1944. Arrived 19.11.64 at Troon to BU.

SCOTSMAN Tug 1901-21; Drifter requis. 1915-19.

SCOTSTOUN Repair ship (stern-wheel river stmr) 3300 tons, 132 x 31 ft. Yarrow 1916 in sections and re-erected 10.16 at Abadan. Sold 4.20 at Basra.

SCOTSTOUN AMC 17,046 tons. Requis, 1939-40.

SCOTT Destroyer leader 1,800 tons, 320 x 32 ft, 5-4.7in, 1-3in, 6-TT. Cammell Laird 18.10.1917. Sunk 15.8.18 in the North Sea, probably by 'UC.17'.

SCOTT Survey ship 830 tons, 230 x 33½ ft, 1-3pdr Caledon, Dundee 23.8.1938. Escort 1939-40. Arrived 30.6.65 at Troon to BU.

SCOTT Trawler requis, 1914-15.

SCOURGE Brig-sloop 14, 234bm, 80½ x 27 ft, 16-6pdr. Allin, Dover 26.10.1779, purchased on stocks. Foundered 7.11.1795 off the Dutch coast.

SCOURGE Galley 8. Purchased 1779, listed to 3.1784.

SCOURGE Gunvessel 4, 67bm, 66 x 15 ft. Dutch hoy purchased 4.1794. Renamed CRASH 1798. BU 9.1803.

SCOURGE Sloop 22, 372bm, 103 x 29 ft. French ROBUSTE captured 15.1.1796 by POMONE in the W.indies. Sold 8.1802.

SCOURGE (ex-*Herald*) Sloop 16, 340bm, 107x 27½ ft, 14-32pdr carr., 2-6pdr. Purchased 6.1803. Sold 18.4.1816.

SCOURGE Wood pad. sloop, 1,128bm, 190 x 36 ft. Portsmouth DY 8.11.1844. BU 1865 by Castle, Charlton..

SCOURGE Iron S.gunboat, 'Ant' class. Chatham DY 25.3.1871. Renamed C.79 in 1904 as DY craft. Listed 1930.

SCOURGE Destroyer 922 tons, 267 x 28 ft, 1-4in, 3-12pdr, 2-TT. Hawthorn Leslie 11.2.1910. Sold 9.5.21 Ward, Briton Ferry.

SCOURGE Destroyer 1,710 tons, 339½ x 36 ft, 4-4.7in, 2-40mm, 8-TT. Cammell Laird 8.12.1942. Sold 1.2.46 to the Dutch navy as EVERTSEN.

SCOUT 'Bark' 10, 132bm, 4-6pdr, 6-2pdr. Deptford 1577. Condemned 1604.

SCOUT Sloop 6. Listed 1648. Captured 1649 by Royalists.

SCOUT Advice boat 6, 38bm. Portsmouth 1694. Sold 7.7.1703.

SCOUT Brig-sloop 14, 276bm, 82 x 29 ft, 14-4pdr. Smith, Folkestone 30.7.1780, purchased on stocks. Captured 24.8.1794 by the French CELESTE off Cape Bon.

SCOUT Sloop 18, 406bm, 111 x 29 ft. French VENUS captured 22.10.1800 by FISGARD in the Atlantic. Wrecked 25.3.1801 on the Shingles.

SCOUT Sloop 18, 448bm, 113 x 30 ft, 18-24pdr carr., 2-6pdr. French privateer PREMIER CONSUL captured 5.3.1801 by DRYAD off the coast of Ireland. Foundered 1802 off Newfoundland.

SCOUT Brig-sloop 18, 'Cruizer' class, 382bm. Atkinson, Hull 7.8.1804. Sold 11.7.1827 Ledger to BU.

SCOUT Sloop 18, 488bm, 116 x 31 ft. Chatham DY 15.6.1832. BU 10.1852.

SCOUT Wood S.corvette 1,462bm, 2,187 tons, 200 x 40½ ft, 20-8in, 1-68pdr. Woolwich DY 30.12.1856. BU 1877 at Chatham.

SCOUT Coastguard cutter, 80bm. Built 1861. Sold 2.1870 B.Ackerley.

SCOUT Torpedo cruiser 1,580 tons, 220 x 34 ft, 4-5in, 8-3pdr, 11-TT. Thomson 30.7.1885. Sold 5.7.1904.

SCOUT Destroyer, 'S' class. J.Brown 27.4.1918. Arrived 29.3.46 Ward, Briton Ferry to BU.

SCRUBB Survey schooner, 80bm. Purchased 1815. Sold 19.5.28.

SCRUBB Tender 30bm. Purchased 1823. Sold 10.1.1832 in Jamaica.

SCYLLA Brig-sloop 18, 'Cruizer' class, 385bm. Davy, Topsham 29.6.1809. BU 1.1846.

SCYLLA Wood S.corvette, 1,467bm, 2,187 tons, 200 x 40½ ft, 20-8in, 1-68pdr. Sheerness DY 19.6.1856. Sold Castle 7.11.1882 to BU.

SCYLLA 2nd class cruiser 3,400 tons, 300 x 43 ft, 2-6in, 6-4.7in, 8-6pdr. Samuda, Poplar 17.10.1891. Sold 2.4.1914.

SCYLLA Cruiser 5,450 tons, 485 x 50½ ft, 8-4.5in. Scotts 24.7.1940. Mined 23.6.44 and not repaired. Sold 12.4.50, BU Ward, Barrow.

SCYLLA Frigate, 'Leander' class. Devonport DY. 8.8.1968.

SCYTHE Destroyer, 'S' class. J.Brown 25.5.1918. Sold 28.11.31 Cashmore, Newport.

SCYTHIAN Submarine, 'S' class. Scotts 14.4.1944. Arrived 8.8.60 Charlestown to BU.

SEABEAR Destroyer, 'S' class. J.Brown 6.7.1918. Sold 5.2.31 Ward, Grays.

SEABEAR (ex-ST THOMAS renamed 1943) Minesweeper, 'Algerine' class. Redfern 6.11.1943. Arrived 12.12.58 Ward, Preston to BU.

SEA CLIFF (see GUELPH)

SEA CLIFF Frigate (RCN), 'River' class. Davie SB 8.7.1944. Sold 3.3.46 Chilian nacy as COVADONGA.

SEA DEVIL Submarine, 'S' class. Scotts 30.1.1945. Arrived Newhaven 2.66 to BU.

SEADOG (ex-P.216) Submarine, 'S'

class. Cammell Laird 11.6.1942. Sold 24.12.47, BU 8.48 at Troon.

SEAFIRE Destroyer, 'S' class, J.Brown 10.8.1918. Handed over 14.9.36 to Ward in part payment for *Majestic*; BU at Inverkeithing.

SEAFLOWER Brig-sloop 16, 208bm, 72½ x 26 ft, 16-4pdr. Purchased 4.1782. Captured 28.9.1808 by the French off Bencoolen.

SEAFLOWER Brig-sloop 16. Listed 1809. Sold 1.9.1814.

SEAFLOWER Cutter 4, 116bm, 60 x 21½ ft. Portsmouth DY 20.5.1830. BU completed 8.10.1866 by Castle, Charlton.

SEAFLOWER Training brig 8, 454 tons, 8-6pdr. Pembroke Dock 25.2.1873. Workshop 1.1904. Sold 7.4.08 Castle, Charlton.

SEAFLOWER Trawler, 1909-19; Yacht 1939-46.

SEAFORD 6th Rate 24, 294bm, 98½ x 26 ft. Herring, Bursledon 1695 and purchased 27.12.1695. Captured 5.5.1697 by the French off the Scilly Isles.

SEAFORD 6th Rate 24, 248bm, 93 x 24½ ft. Portsmouth DY 1697. Rebuilt Deptford 1724 as 375bm. BU 6.1740 at Woolwich.

SEAFORD PRIZE 6th Rate 12, 86bm, 62½ x 18 ft. French, captured 4.1708 by SEAFORD. Sold 13.10.1712.

SEAFORD 6th Rate 24, 432bm, 106 x 30½ ft. Stowe & Bartlett, Shoreham 6.4.1741. BU completed 7.8.1754 at Woolwich.

SEAFORD 6th Rate 22, 109 x 30½ ft. Deptford DY 3.9.1754. Sold 16.1.1784.

SEAFORD Minesweeper, TE 'Bangor' class. Taikoo DY, Hong Kong. Laid down 12.7.1941, renamed WAGLAN 9.41 and lost on stocks 12.41. Launched 20.3.43 as Japanese M/S 102. Returned to the RN 1947 and BU 1948 at Uraga.

SEAFORTH Gun-brig 14, 215bm. Purchased 1805. Capsized 2.1806 in a squall in the W.Indies.

SEAFORTH (The French privateer brig DAME ERNOUF, captured 8.2.1805 by CURIEUX in the W.Indies was also reported as renamed SEAFORTH 1806.)

SEAFOX A/C transport 990 tons, 160 x 30 ft. Pollock Faversham 16.5.1946. Store carrier 10.53. Sold 12.58, Renamed *Roubahe Darya*.

SEA GLADIATOR A/C transport 990 tons, 160 x 30 ft. Pollock, Faversham. Cancelled and launched

24.9.1949 as *Goldlynx*.

SEAGULL Brig-sloop 16 (fir-built), 318bm, 105 x 28 ft. Wells, Rotherhithe 7.1795. Foundered 12.1804.

SEAGULL Brig-sloop 16, (285bm?), 93 x 26½ ft. King, Dover 1.7.1806. Captured 19.6.1808 by the Danes and burnt.

SEAGULL Cutter. 1814. (In service 1825). (Revenue vessel?). Renamed ADDER 16.4.1817.

SEAGULL Brig-sloop 16, 343bm, 98½ x 28½ ft, 12-24pdr carr., 4-9pdr. French SYLPHE captured 11.8.1808 by COMET off Martinique. Sold 21.7.1814.

SEAGULL Schooner 6, 279bm, 95 x 26 ft. Chatham DY 21.11.1831. BU 10.1852.

SEAGULL Wood S.gunboat, 'Albacore' class. Pitcher, Northfleet. 4.8.1855. Sold 7.10.1864 Marshall, Plymouth.

SEAGULL Wood S.gunvessel, 663bm, 805 tons, 170 x 29 ft, 1-7in, 2-40pdr. Devonport DY 6.3.1868. Sold 11.1887.

SEAGULL Torpedo gunboat 735 tons, 230 x 27 ft, 2-4.7in, 4-3pdr, 3-TT. Chatham DY 31.5.1889. M/S 1909. Sunk 30.9.18 in collision in the Firth of Clyde.

SEAGULL Minesweeper 815 tons, 230 x 33½ ft, 2-4in. Devonport DY 28.10.1937. Survey ship 1945. Arrived 5.56 Demmelweek & Redding, Plymouth to BU.

SEAHAM Minesweeper, TE 'Bangor' class. Lobnitz 16.6.1941. Sold 11.8.47 Rangoon Port Commissioners, renamed *Chinthe*.

SEAHORSE Ship. Captured 1626. Last mentioned 1635.

SEAHORSE Hoy. Captured 1654. Sold 1655.

SEAHORSE Fire vessel 10, 70bm, 57 x 17 ft. Purchased 4.1694 from the Dutch. Became a water boat. Sunk 12.10.1698 as a foundation at Sheerness.

SEAHORSE 6th Rate 24, 256bm, 94 x 24½ ft. Hayden, Limehouse 27.9.1694. Wrecked 14.3.1704 on the coast of Jamaica.

SEAHORSE 6th Rate 14, 161bm, 76 x 22½ ft. Yeames, Limehouse 4.11.1709. Wrecked 26.12.1711 near Dartmouth.

SEAHORSE 6th Rate 20, 282bm, 94 x 26 ft. Portsmouth DY 13.2.1712. Rebuilt Stacey, Deptford 1727 as 374bm. Sold 28.7.1748.

SEAHORSE 6th Rate 24, 519bm, 114 x

32 ft. Barnard, Harwich 13.9.1748. Sold 30.12.1784.

SEAHORSE 5th Rate 38, 998bm, 146 x 39½ ft. Stalkart, Rotherhithe 11.6.1794. BU 7.1819.

SEAHORSE 5th Rate 46, 1,215bm, 159x 42 ft. Pembroke Dock 21.7.1830. Screw frigate 7.1847; screw mortar vessel 3.1856; 1258bm. Renamed LAVINIA 5.5.1870, coal hulk. Sold 1902.

SEAHORSE Submarine 640 tons, 187 x 23½ ft, 1-3in, 6-TT. Chatham DY 15.11.1932. Sunk 7.1.40 by German minesweepers in the Heligoland Bight.

SEAHORSE Tug, 1880-1920; Yacht & Trawler WW.I.

SEA HURRICANE A/C transport 990 tons, 160 x 30 ft. Pollock, Faversham. Cancelled and launched 18.12.1948 as *Goldhind*.

SEAL Destroyer 385 tons, 218 x 20 ft, 1-12pdr, 5-6pdr, 2-TT. Laird 6.3.1897. Sold 17.3.1921 Ward, Rainham.

SEAL M/L Submarine 1,520 tons, 271½ x 25½ ft, 1-4in, 6-TT, 50 mines. Chatham DY 27.9.1938. Captured in sinking condition 2.5.40 by the Germans in the Kattegat; scuttled 3.5.45, later raised and BU

SEALARK Cutter 4, 80bm, 56 x 18 ft, 4-12pdr carr. Wheaton, Brixham 1.8.1806. Wrecked 18.6.1809 on the east coast.

SEALARK Schooner 10, 178bm, 79 x 22½ ft, 10-12pdr carr. American FLY captured 29.12.1811. Sold 13.1.1820.

SEALARK Brig-sloop 10, 'Cherokee' class, 231bm. Plymouth DY. Laid down 11.1830, cancelled 2.1831.

SEALARK Brig 8, 319bm, 90 x 29½ ft. Portsmouth DY 27.7.1843. Training brig 1875, 311bm. Sold 11.11.1898.

SEALARK (see INVESTIGATOR of 1903)

SEALARK Trawler requis. 1915-18.

SEALION Submarine 670 tons, 193 x 24 ft, 1-3in, 6-TT. Cammell Laird 16.3.1934. Scuttled 3.3.45 as Asdic target off the Isle of Arran.

SEALION Submarine 1,605 tons, 241 x 26½ ft, 8-TT. Cammell Laird 31.12.1959.

SEALION Trawler requis. 1914-19.

SEAMEW Coastguard vessel, 330bm, 376 tons, 143 x 22ft, 1-32pdr. Transferred from Inland Revenue 1857. Sold 3.4.1906 T.Trattles.

SEAMEW River gunboat 262 tons, 160 x 27 ft, 2-3in. Yarrow 16.1.1928. Sold 27.8.47 at Basra.

SEAMEW Trawler 1909-1919.

SEANYMPH Cutter 8. In service in 1782.

SEANYMPH (ex-P.223) Submarine, 'S' class. Cammell Laird 29.7.1942. Arrived 6.48 at Troon to BU.

SEARCHER Brigantine. Built 1562. Sold 1564.

SEARCHER Destroyer, 'S' class. J.Brown 11.9.1918. Sold 25.3.38 Ward, Barrow.

SEARCHER Escort carrier 11,420 tons, 468½ x 69½ ft, 2-4in, 16-40mm, 24-A/C. Seattle Tacoma 20.7.1942 on lend-lease. Returned 29.11.45 to the USN.

SEARCHER (see LST.3508)

SEA RIDER Flyboat 8, 350bm. Captured 1665. Sold 1668.

SEA ROBIN Submarine, 'S' class. Cammell Laird. Cancelled 1945.

SEA ROVER Submarine, 'S' class. Scotts 8.2,1943. Sold 10.49, BU at Faslane from 6.50.

SEASCOUT Submarine, 'S' class. Cammell Laird 24.3.1944. Arrived 14.12.65 at Swansea to BU at Briton Ferry.

SEA SNAKE SSV(RAN) 80 tons. Savage 18.1.1945. To N.Borneo 6.12.45

SEAWOLF Destroyer, 'S' class. J.Brown 2.11.1918. Sold 23.2.31 Cashmore, Newport.

SEAWOLF Submarine 670 tons, 193 x 24 ft, 1-3in, 6-TT. Scotts 28.11.1935. Sold 11.45 Marine Industries, Montreal.

SECURITY Prison ship, 646bm. Purchased 1778. Sold 10.4.1783 at Chatham.

SECURITY Storeship, 142bm, 66 x 22½ ft. Plymouth DY 10.3.1785. Probably on DY service; Listed to 1852.

SECURITY Prison ship, 250bm, 84 x 25 ft. Purchased 1794 at Halifax. NS. Used there and Sold per AO. 28.6.1802.

SECURITY Tug (ex-DILIGENCE) 1914-27; Tug 1947-66.

SEDGEFLY River gunboat, 'Fly' class. Yarrow 9.1916. For disposal 1919 at Basra.

SEDGEFLY Trawler requis. 1939-39.

SEDGEMOOR 4th Rate 50, 633bm, 123 x 34½ ft. Chatham DY 1687. Wrecked 2.1.1689 in St Margarets Bay.

SEFTON M/S sloop, '24' class. Barclay Curle 6.7.1918. Sold 8.22.

SEFTON (see EMPIRE GAUNTLET)

SEFTON Coastal M/S, 'Ton' class.

White, Southampton 15.9.1954. Sold 2.7.68, BU in Belgium.

SEINE 5th Rate 38, 1,146bm, 156½ x 40½ ft, 8-32pdr carr., 28-18pdr, 12-9pdr. French, captured 30.6.1798 by JASON and PIQUE in the Channel. Wrecked 5.6.1803 off the Texel.

SEINE (see AMBUSCADE of 1798)

SEINE 5th Rate 38, 1,074bm, 152 x 40 ft. French CERES captured 6.1.1814 by NIGER and TAGUS off the Cape Verde Islands. BU 5.1823.

SELBY 22-gun ship, 305bm. Taylor, Wapping 1654. Renamed EAGLE 1660. Fireship 1674. Sunk 1694 as foundation at Sheerness.

SELBY Storeship. Purchased 4.1781. Sold 2.12.1783.

SELBY A.Ship 22, 354bm, 100 x 28 ft. Purchased 1798. Sold 12.1801.

SELBY Drifter requis. 1915-17.

SELENE Submarine, 'S' class. Cammell Laird 24.4.1944. Arrived 6.6.61 King, Gateshead to BU.

SELKIRK Minesweeper, later 'Hunt' class. Murdoch & Murray 2.12.1918. Sold Dohmen & Habets 17.5.47; BU at Liege.

SELSEY BILL Repair ship 8,580 tons, 425 x 57 ft. Burrard, Vancouver 11.7.1945. Cancelled 30.8.45; completed as *Waitemata*.

SEMIRAMIS 5th Rate 36, 944bm, 145 x 38½ ft. Deptford DY 25.7.1808. Reduced to 24 guns in 1827. BU 11.1844.

SEMIRAMIS Paddle sloop (Indian). River Thames 1837. Foundered 13.2.1839; raised and renamed CHARGER 1841, coal hulk at Aden.

SEMIRAMIS Iron pad. frigate (Indian), 1,143bm, 189 x 34 ft. Bombay DY 26.2.1842. Hulked 1863.

SEMIRAMIS Trawler requis. 1914-19.

SENATOR Destroyer, 'S' class. Denny 2.4.1918. Handed over 7.9.36 to Ward in part payment for *Majestic*.BU at Jarrow.

SENECA Sloop 18 (Canadian lakes). Oswegatchie 1771. Listed in 1788.

SENEGAL Sloop 14, 292bm, 97 x 26 ft. Bird, Rotherhithe 24.12.1760.

SENEGAL (see RACEHORSE of 1777)

SENESCHAL Submarine, 'S' class. Scotts 23.4.1945. Arrived 23.8.60 Clayton & Davie, Dunston to BU.

SENNEN (ex-USS CHAMPLAIN) Cutter 1,546 tons, 256(oa) x 42 ft, 1-4in, 1-3in. Commissioned 12.5.1941 on lend-lease. Returned 3.46 to the US coastguard.

SENSIBLE 5th Rate 36, 946bm. French,

captured 27.6.1798 by SEAHORSE in the Mediterranean. Wrecked 2.3.1802 near Trincomalee.

SENTINEL (ex-*Friendship*) Gun-brig 12, 194bm, 81 x 24 ft, 10-18pdr carr., 2-9pdr. Purchased 7.1804. Wrecked 10.10.1812 on Rugen Island, Baltic.

SENTINEL (ex-INCHKEITH renamed 1903) Scout cruiser 2,895 tons, 360 x 40 ft, 10-12pdr, 8-3pdr. Vickers 19.4.1904. Sold 18.1.23 Young; arrived Sunderland 20.6.23 after stranding.

SENTINEL (see SCORPION of 1942)

SENTINEL Submarine, 'S' class. Scotts 27.7.1945. Sold 28.2.62 Lynch, Rochester; BU at Gillingham.

SENTINEL Patrol Vessel 934 tons. *Seaforth Warrior* purchased in 2.1983.

SEPOY Wood screw. gunvessel, 483bm, 150 x 26 ft. Portsmouth DY. Ordered 26.3.1846, cancelled 22.5.1849.

SEPOY Wood S.gunboat, 'Albacore' class. Smith, N.Shields 13.2.1856. BU 4.1868.

SEPOY Destroyer, 'S' class. Denny 22.5.1918. Sold 2.7.32 Cashmore, Newport.

SEPOY Minesweeper, 'Catherine' class. Gulf SB, Madisonville 17.1.1943 for the RN, but retained by the USN as DEXTROUS.

SERAPH Destroyer, 'S' class. Denny 8.7.1918. Sold 4.5.34 Ward, Pembroke Dock.

SERAPH (ex-P.219) Submarine, 'S' class. Vickers Armstrong, Barrow 25.10.1941. Arrived 20.12.65 Ward, Briton Ferry to BU.

SERAPIS 5th Rate 44, 886bm, 140 x 38 ft. Randall, Rotherhithe 4.3.1779. Captured 23.9.1779 by the American privateer BONHOMME RICHARD off Flamborough Head; transferred French navy.

SERAPIS 5th Rate 44, 886bm, 140 x 38 ft. Hillhouse, Bristol 7.11.1782. Storeship 20 in 1.1795; floating battery 7.1801; storeship 1803. Sold 17.7.1826 in Jamaica.

SERAPIS Iron S.troopship, 4,173bm, 6,211 tons, 360 x 49 ft, 3-4pdr. Thames SB Co, Blackwall 2.9.1866. Sold 23.11.1894.

SERAPIS Destroyer, 'S' class. Denny 17.9.1918. Sold 25.1.34 Rees, Llanelly.

SERAPIS Destroyer 1,710 tons, 339½ x 36 ft, 4-4.7in, 2-40mm, 8-TT. Scotts 25.3.1943. To Dutch navy 10.45 as PIET HEIN.

SERENE Destroyer, 'S' class. Denny 30.11.1918. Handed over 14.9.36 to Ward in part payment for *Majestic*, BU at Inverkeithing.

SERENE (ex-LEASIDE renamed 1943) Minesweeper, 'Algerine' class. Redfern 18.10.43. Arrived 8.3.59 Rees, Llanelly to BU.

SERENE Drifter requis. 1915-17.

SERINGAPATAM 5th Rate 46, 1,152bm, 157½ x 40½ ft. Bombay DY 5.9.1819. Receiving ship 7.1847; coal hulk 1852. BU 6.1873 at the Cape.

SERPENT 60-ton vessel. Captured 1562. Last mentioned 1563.

SERPENT Bomb 12, 260bm, 86 x 26½ ft, 12-6pdr. Chatham DY 1693. Wrecked 12.2.1694 near Gibraltar.

SERPENT Bomb 4, 140bm, 70 x 23 ft. Chatham DY 1695. Captured 15.10.1703 by a French privateer in the Atlantic.

SERPENT Bomb 12, 275bm, 93 x 26 ft. Snelgrove, Limehouse 15.3.1742. Wrecked 1.9.1748.

SERPENT Bomb 12. Reported built at Sandgate 1771. Not traced.

SERPENT Sloop 16, 322bm, 98 x 27 ft. Jacobs, Sandgate. Laid down 2.1783, cancelled 10.1783, the builder having failed.

SERPENT Sloop 16, 321bm, 100 x 27 ft. Plymouth DY 3.12.1789. Foundered 9.1806 in the W.Indies.

SERPENT Gunvessel 4, 57bm, 65 x 14 ft. Dutch hoy purchased 4.1794. 'Supposed BU in 1796'.

SERPENT Sloop 18, 423bm, 109 x 29½ ft. Sheerness DY. Laid down 1810, cancelled 8.9.1810.

SERPENT Brig-sloop 16, 434bm, 101½ x 32 ft, 14-32pdr, 2-18pdr. Fletcher, Limehouse 14.7.1832. Target 12.1857. BU 7.1861 at Portsmouth.

SERPENT Wood S.gunvessel, 695bm, 877 tons, 185 x 28½ ft, 2-68pdr, 2-32pdr. Mare, Blackwall 23.6.1860. Sold 1875 Castle, Charlton.

SERPENT Torpedo cruiser 1,770 tons, 225 x 36 ft, 6-6in, 8-3pdr, 5-TT. Devonport DY 10.3.1887. Wrecked 10.11.1890 near Corcubion Bay, N.Spain.

SESAME Destroyer, 'S' class. Denny 30.12.1918. Sold 4.5.34. Cashmore, Newport.

SESOSTRIS Paddle sloop (Indian), 876bm. River Thames 1839/40. Transferred 1853 Bengal Govt.

SETTER Destroyer, 'R' class. White 18.8.1916. Sunk 17.5.17 in collision with SYLPH off Harwich.

SETTER Trawler requis. 1916-19;

Whaler 1941-45; Tug 1969.

SEVENOAKS 4th Rate 52, 684bm. Dutch ZEVENWOLDEN captured 1665. Retaken 1666 by the Dutch.

SEVEN SISTERS Gunvessel 4. Hoy, purchased 1794. Sold 18.8.1800.

SEVEN STARS 60-ton vessel. Listed 1549-54.

SEVEN STARS Galley 5, 140bm. Baker, Chatham 1586. Listed to 1603.

SEVEN STARS 14-gun ship, 144bm. Listed 1615-24.

SEVERN 4th Rate 48, 683bm, 131 x 34½ ft. Johnson, Blackwall 1695. Rebuilt Plymouth 1739 as 853bm. Captured 19.10.1746 by the French TERRIBLE; recaptured 14.10.1747 and BU.

SEVERN 4th Rate 50, 1,061bm, 144 x 41 ft. Barnard, Harwich 10.7.1747. Sold 2.1.1759.

SEVERN 5th Rate 44, 904bm, 140 x 38½ ft. Hillhouse, Bristol 29.4.1786. Wrecked 21.12.1804 on the Channel Is.

SEVERN (see TAGUS of 1813)

SEVERN 4th Rate 50 (pitch pine-built), 1,240bm, 159 x 42 ft, 20-32pdr carr., 28-24pdr, 2-9pdr. Wigram & Green, Blackwall 14.6.1813. Sold 20.7.1825 J.Ledger.

SEVERN 5th Rate 46, 1,215bm, 159 x 42 ft. Pembroke Dock. Ordered 9.6.1825, cancelled 7.2.1831.

SEVERN 4th Rate 50, 1,986bm, 180 x 50 ft. Chatham DY 24.1.1856. Undocked 8.2.1860 as screw frigate, 2,767bm. BU 1876.

SEVERN 2nd class cruiser 4,050 tons, 300 x 46 ft, 2-8in, 10-6in. Chatham DY 29.9.1885. Sold 4.4.1905 G.Garnham.

SEVERN (ex-Brazilian SOLIMOES purchased 8.8.1914) River monitor 1,260 tons, 265 x 49 ft, 2-6in, 2-4.7in howitzers. Vickers 19.8.13. Sold 9.5.21 Ward, Preston; arrived 23.3.23.

SEVERN Submarine 1,850 tons, 325 x 28 ft, 1-4in, 8-TT. Vickers Armstrong, Barrow 16.1.1934. Sold 1946 T.Hassanally, Bombay.

SEYCHELLES (ex-PEARD renamed 1943) Frigate, 'Colony' class. Walsh Kaiser 30.10.43 on lend-lease. Returned 6.46 to the USN.

SEYMOUR Destroyer leader 1,673 tons, 315 x 32 ft, 4-4in, 4-TT. Cammell Laird 31.8.1916. Sold 7.1.30 Cashmore, Newport.

SEYMOUR Frigate, TE 'Captain' class. Bethlehem, Hingham 1.11.1943 on lend-lease. Nominally returned to the USN 1.46. BU Ward, Barrow.

SHACKLETON (see SHARPSHOOTER of 1936)

SHAH (ex-BLONDE renamed 1873) Armoured frigate, 4,210bm, 6,250 tons, 334 x 52 ft, 2-9in, 16-7in, 8-64pdr. Portsmouth DY 9.1873. Renamed C.470 coal hulk 12.1904; sold 19.9.19 W.B.Smith. Wrecked 1926 at Bermuda.

SHAH (ex-*Jamaica*) Escort carrier 11,420 tons, 468½ x 69½ ft, 2-4in, 16-40mm, 24-A/C. Seattle Tacoma 21.4.1943 on lend-lease. Returned 6.12.45 to the USN.

SHAKESPEARE Destroyer leader 1,750 tons, 318 x 332 ft, 5-4.7in, 1-3in, 6-TT. Thornycroft 7.7.1917. Handed over 2.9.36 to Ward in part payment for *Majestic*; BU at Jarrow.

SHAKESPEARE (ex-P.221) Submarine, 'S' class. Vickers Armstrong, Barrow 8.12.1941. Sold 14.7.46 Ward, Briton Ferry.

SHALFORD Seaward defence boat, 'Ford' class. Yarrow 21.8.1952. Sold 8.9.67 at Singapore to BU.

SHALIMAR Submarine, 'S' class. Chatham DY 22.4.1943. Arrived 7.50 at Troon to BU.

SHAMROCK Schooner 8, 150bm, 79 x 22 ft. Bermuda 15.9.1808. Wrecked 25.2.1811 on Cape Santa Maria.

SHAMROCK Gun-brig 12, 180bm, 84 x 22 ft. Larking, Lynn 8.8.1812. Harbour service 11.1831; renamed WV.18 on 25.5.1863 coastguard watch vessel. Sold 24.1.1867.

SHAMROCK Wood S.gunboat, 'Albacore' class. Pitcher, Northfleet 13.3.1856. Sold 4.1867 Marshall, Plymouth.

SHAMROCK Destroyer, 'S' class. Doxford 26.8.1918. Handed over 23.11.36 to Ward in part payment for *Majestic*; BU at Milford Haven.

SHAMROCK Tank vessel 1873, ST.PATRICK 1917-23; Trawler WW.I. & II.

SHANNON 6th Rate 28, 587bm, 118½ x 33½ ft. Deptford DY 13.8.1757. BU completed 30.12.1765 at Portsmouth.

SHANNON 5th Rate 32 (fir-built), 796bm, 135 x 36½ ft. Deptford DY 9.2.1796. Sold 5.1802.

SHANNON (ex-PALLAS renamed 11.1802) 5th Rate 36, 881bm. Brindley, Frindsbury 2.9.1803. Ran ashore in a gale 10.12.1803 near La Hogue and burnt to avoid capture.

SHANNON 5th Rate 38, 1,066bm, 150 x 40 ft. Brindley, Frindsbury 5.5.1806. Receiving ship 1832. Renamed ST LAWRENCE 11.3.1844. BU completed 12.11.1859 at Chatham.

SHANNON Schooner 10 (Canadian lakes). Listed 1814.

SHANNON Schooner 2 (Indian), 90bm. Listed 1832.

SHANNON Wood S.frigate, 2,667bm, 235 x 50 ft, 30-8in, 1-68pdr, 20-32pdr. Portsmouth DY 24.11.1855. Sold 31.5.1871 Castle to BU.

SHANNON Iron S.frigate 5,390 tons, 260 x 54 ft, 2-10in, 7-9in, 6-20pdr. Pembroke Dock 11.12.1875. Sold 15.12.1899 King, Garston.

SHANNON Armoured cruiser 14,600 tons, 490 x 75½ ft, 4-9.2in, 10-7.5in, 16-12pdr. Chatham DY 20.9.1906. Sold 12.12.22 McLellan, Bo'ness.

SHARKE Brigantine 8, 58bm, 58 x 15 ft. Deptford 20.4.1691. Sold 25.11.1698 L.Towne.

SHARKE Sloop 14, 66bm. Deptford 1699. Captured 30.3.1703 by the French.

SHARKE Sloop 14, 114bm, 65 x 20½ ft. Deptford DY 20.4.1711. Rebuilt Deptford 1722 as 124bm. Sold 3.8.1732.

SHARK Sloop 14, 201bm, 80 x 24½ ft. Portsmouth DY 7.9.1732. Sold 2.12.1755.

SHARK Sloop 16, 313bm, 96 x 27 ft. Purchased on stocks 11.1775, Randall, Rotherhithe 9.3.1776. Renamed SALAMANDER 23.7.1778, fireship. Sold 14.8.1783.

SHARK 6th Rate 28. Purchased 1780. Foundered in a storm 30.11.1780 N.America.

SHARK Sloop 16, 304bm, 97 x 27 ft. Walton, Hull 25.11.1779. Receiving ship Jamaica by 1805. Foundered 13.1.1818.

SHARK Gunvessel 4, 63bm, 64½ x 14½ ft. Dutch hoy purchased 4.1794. Handed over to the French 11.12.1795 by mutinous crew at La Hogue.

SHARK Destroyer 325 tons, 205 x 19½ ft, 1-12pdr, 5-6pdr, 2-TT. Thompson 22.9.1894. Sold 11.7.1911 Ward, Preston.

SHARK Destroyer 935 tons, 267 x 27 ft, 3-4in, 2-TT. Swan Hunter 30.7.1912. Sunk 31.5.16 at Jutland.

SHARK Destroyer, 'S'class. Swan Hunter 9.14.1918. Sold 5.2.31 Ward, Inverkeithing.

SHARK Submarine 670 tons, 193 x 24 ft, 1-3in, 6-TT. Chatham DY 31.5.1934. Sunk 6.7.40 by German minesweepers off Skudesnes, Norway.

SHARK Destroyer 1,710 tons, 399½ x 36 ft, 4-4in, 2-40mm, 8-TT. Scotts

1.6.1943. Lent R. Norwegian navy 8.3.44 as SVENNER; sunk 6.6.44 by German MTBs off Le Havre.

SHARPSHOOTER Gun-brig 12, 178bm, 80 x 22½ ft. Warren, Brightlingsea 2.2.1805. Sold 17.5.1816.

SHARPSHOOTER Iron S.gunvessel, 503bm, 150½ x 27 ft. Ditchburn & Mare, Blackwall 25.7.1846. Sold 2.12.1869.

SHARPSHOOTER Torpedo gunboat 735 tons, 230 x 27 ft, 2-4.7in, 4-3pdr, 3-TT. Devonport DY 30.11.1888. Renamed NORTHAMPTON 1912, harbour service. Sold 27.3.22, BU by Beard at Upnor.

SHARPSHOOTER Destroyer, 'R' class. Beardmore 27.2.1917. Sold 29.4.27 Ward, Briton Ferry.

SHARPSHOOTER Minesweeper 835 tons, 230 x 33½ ft, 2-4in. Devonport DY 10.12.1936. Renamed SHACKLETON 6.53, survey vessel. Arrived Troon 20.11.65 to BU.

SHAVINGTON Coastal M/S, 'Ton' class. White, Southampton 25.4.1955. For sale 1985.

SHAWINIGAN Corvette (RCN), 'Flower' class. G.T.Davie 16.5.1941. Sunk 25.11.44 by 'U.1228' in the Cabot Strait.

SHEARWATER Brig-sloop 10, 'Cherokee' class, 237bm. Rowe, Newcastle 21.11.1808. Sold 11.1832 Beaton to BU.

SHEARWATER (ex-GPO vessel *Dolphin*) Wood pad. packet, 343bm, 137 x 23 ft. Transferred 1837. Sold at Malta 2.7.1857.

SHEARWATER Wood S.sloop, 669bm, 913 tons, 160 x 30 ft, 4-64pdr. Pembroke Dock 17.10.1861. BU. completed 5.2.1877 at Sheerness

SHEARWATER Sloop 980 tons, 180 x 33 ft, 6-4in. Sheerness DY 10.2.1900. To RCN 1915 as depot ship. Sold 5.22 Western Shipping Co, Canada.

SHEARWATER Patrol vessel 580 tons, 234 x 25½ ft, 1-4in. White 18.4.1939. Sold 21.4.47, BU Stockton Ship & Salvage Co.

SHEDIAC Corvette (RCN), 'Flower' class. Davie SB 29.4.1941. Sold 1951, renamed *Jooske W.Vinke*.

SHEERNESS Smack 2, 18bm. Chatham 1673. Sunk 24.4.1695 as a foundation at Sheerness.

SHEERNESS 5th Rate 32, 359bm, 106 x 27½ ft. Sheerness DY 1691. Rebuilt Deptford 1731 as 6th Rate, 428bm. Sold 5.6.1744.

SHEERNESS 6th Rate 24, 506bm, 112 x 32 ft. Buxton, Rotherhithe 8.10.1743.

Sold 26.7.1768.

SHEERNESS Store lighter, 109bm. Bennett, Faversham 1759. BU 1811.

SHEERNESS 5th Rate 44, 906bm, 141 x 38½ ft. Adams, Bucklers Hard 16.7.1787. Wrecked 7.1.1805 near Trincomalee.

SHEERNESS Tender 4, 148bm, 4-3pdr. Wilson, Sandgate 1788, purchased on stocks 6.8.1788. BU 5.1811.

SHEERNESS Tender 10. Purchased 1791. Sold 1810(?)

SHEERNESS 2 hired Cutters in 1802. Tug 1863-1906.

SHEFFIELD Cruiser 9,100 tons, 558 x 62 ft, 12-6in, 8-4in. Vickers Armstrong, Tyne 23.77.1936. Arrived 9.67 at Faslane to BU.

SHEFFIELD Destroyer 3150 tons. Vickers 10.6.71. Lost 10.5.82 in Falklands operations

SHEFFIELD Frigate 4200 tons. Swan Hunter 26.3.86.

SHELBURNE Schooner 14, 221bm, 94 x 24 ft. American privateer RACER captured 16.3.1813. Sold 10.1817.

SHELDRAKE Brig-sloop 16, 285bm, 93 x 26½ ft. Richards, Hythe 20.3.1806. Sold 6.3.1817.

SHELDRAKE Brig-sloop 10, 'Cherokee' class, 228bm. Pembroke Dock 19.5.1825. Sold 1855 per order dated 3.1853.

SHELDRAKE Wood S.gunboat, 'Albacore' class. Pitcher, Northfleet 1.9.1855. Sold 30.6.1865 at Montevideo.

SHELDRAKE Compos. S.gunboat 455 tons, 125 x 23½ ft, 2-64pdr, 2-20pdr. Napier, Glasgow 3.7.1875. Renamed DRAKE 13.3.1888, drillship. Renamed WV.29 in 1893. DRAKE 1906. Sold 3.4.06 Meyer Issacs.

SHELDRAKE Torpedo gunboat 735 tons, 230 x 27 ft, 2-4.7in, 4-3pdr, 3-TT. Chatham DY 30.3.1889. Sold 9.7.1907 S.Bkg Co, London.

SHELDRAKE Destroyer, 748bm, 240 x 25 ft, 2-4in, 2-12pdr, 2-TT. Denny 18.1.1911. Sold 9.5.21 Ward, Grays.

SHELDRAKE Patrol vessel 530 tons, 234 x 26½ ft, 1-4in. Thornycroft 28.1.1937. Sold 12.8.46, renamed *Tuck Loon.*

SHEPPARTON Minesweeper (RAN), 'Bathhurst' class. Williamstown DY 15.8.1941. BU 1958 in Japan.

SHERATON Coastal M/S, 'Ton' class. White, Southampton 20.7.1955.

SHERBORNE Cutter 10, 86bm, 55 x 19 ft. Woolwich DY 3.12.1763. Sold 1.7.1784.

SHERBORNE (ex-TARBERT renamed 1918) Minesweeper, later 'Hunt' class. Simons 27.6.1918. Sold 19.5.28 Ward, Inverkeithing.

SHERBORNE CASTLE (see PETROLIA)

SHERBROOKE Corvette (RCN), 'Flower' class. Marine Ind 25.10.1940. BU 5.47 Steel Co of Canada.

SHERWOOD (ex-USS RODGERS) Destroyer 1,190 tons, 311 x 31 ft, 3-4in, 1-3in, 6-TT. Commissioned 23.10.1940 in the RN. Air target 8.42; beached 10.43 as rocket target. Listed 1946 as 'destroyed'.

SHETLAND Patrol Vessel 925 tons. Hall Russell 22.11.1976.

SHIEL Frigate, 'River' class. Vickers, Montreal 26.5.1943 on lend-lease. Returned 4.3.46 to the USN.

SHIFNAL Minesweeper, later 'Hunt' class. Lobnitz. Cancelled 1918.

SHIKARI Destroyer, 'S' class. Doxford 14.7.1919; completed Chatham 3.24. Arrived 4.11.45 Cashmore, Newport.

SHINCLIFE Paddle M/S, 'Ascot' class 820 tons. Dundee SB 29.1.1918. Sold 3.22 Ward, Inverkeithing.

SHIPHAM Inshore M/S, 'Ham' class. Brooke Marine 14.7.1955. Sold Pounds 1986.

SHIPPIGAN Minesweeper, TE 'Bangor' class. Dufferin, Toronto 27.9.1941. Sold 1.1.48, BU 6.49 at Charlestown.

SHIPTON Frigate (RCN), 'River' class. Quebec. Cancelled 12.1943.

SHIRLEY galley 6. Purchased 1745. Condemned in 1747.

SHIRLEY Paddle M/S, 'Ascot' class 820 tons. Dunlop Bremner 28.9.1917. Sold 8.4.19 James Dredging Co.

SHISH Smack/Yacht. Built 1670. Fate unknown.

SHOALHAVEN Frigate (RAN), 'River' class. Walker, Maryborough 14.12.1944. Arrived 8.62 in Japan to BU.

SHOALWATER Minesweeper (RAN). 6.1987.

SHOREHAM 5th Rate 32, 359bm, 103 x 28 ft. Ellis, Shoreham 6.1.1694. Rebuilt Woolwich 1720 as 20-gun 6th Rate, 379bm. Sold 5.6.1744.

SHOREHAM PRIZE Sloop 12, 73bm, 57 x 17 ft. French(?), captured 26.8.1709. Sold 11.9.1712.

SHOREHAM PRIZE Sloop. Captured 1746. Lost 1747 at Oporto.

SHOREHAM 6th Rate 24, 514bm, 113 x 32½ ft. Reed, Hull 13.5.1744. Sold 4.4.1758.

SHOREHAM (see SALFORD)

SHOREHAM Sloop 1,105 tons, 250 x 34 ft, 2-4in. Chatham DY 22.11.1930. Sold 4.10.46, renamed *Jorge Fel Joven*.

SHOULTON Coastal M/S, 'Ton' class. Montrose DY 10.9.1954. Sold 2.2.81, BU at Blyth.

SHREWSBURY 2nd Rate 80, 1,257bm, 158 x 42½ ft. Portsmouth DY 6.2.1695. Rebuilt Deptford 1713 as 1,314bm. BU 2.1749 at Portsmouth.

SHREWSBURY 3rd Rate 74, 1,594bm, 166 x 47 ft. Wells, Deptford 23.2.1758. Condemned 1783 and scuttled at Jamaica.

SHREWSBURY Minesweeper, later 'Hunt' class. Napier & Miller 12.2.1918. Sold 25.11.27 Alloa, Charlestown.

SHREWSBURY CASTLE Corvette, 'Castle' class. Swan Hunter 16.8.1943. Renamed TUNSBERG CASTLE 17.4.44 on loan R.Norwegian navy. Sunk 12.12.44 by mine in the Kola Inlet, N.Russia.

SHRIKE Paddle minesweeper. Projected 1918 and cancelled (not ordered).

SHRIVENHAM Inshore M/S, 'Ham' class. Bolson, Poole 28.3.1956. Sold to the P.L.A 21.2.69.

SHROPSHIRE Cruiser 9,830 tons, 595 x 66 ft. 8-8in, 8-4in. Beardmore 5.7.1928. Lent RAN 1.43. Arrived 20.1.55 Arnott Young, Dalmuir and Troon 9.55 to BU.

SIBYL 6th Rate 28, 599bm, 120½ x 33½ ft. Adams, Bucklers Hard 2.1.1779. Renamed GARLAND 14.7.1795. Wrecked 26.7.1798 off Madagascar.

SYBILLE 5th Rate 44, 1,091bm, 154 x 40 ft, 28-18pdr, 16-9pdr. French, captured 17.6.1794 by ROMNEY in the Mediterranean. Harbour service 7.1831. Sold 7.8.1833.

SYBILLE 5th Rate 36, 1,633bm, 160 x 49 ft, 36-32pdr. Pembroke Dock 15.4.1847. BU 1866 at Plymouth.

SYBILLE 2nd class cruiser 3,400 tons, 300 x 43 ft, 2-6in, 6-4.7in, 8-6pdr. Stephenson, Newcastle 27.12.1890. Wrecked 16.1.1901 in Lamberts Bay, S.Africa.

SYBILLE Destroyer, 'M' class 900 tons. Yarrow 5.2.1917. Sold 5.11.26 Cashmore, Newport.

SIBYL (ex-P.217) Submarine, 'S' class. Cammell Laird 29.4.1942. Arrived 3.48 Troon to BU.

SIBYL (see CAVENDISH)

SICKLE (ex-P.224) Submarine, 'S' class. Cammell Laird 27.8.1942.

Sunk 6.44 off Greece, probably mined.

SIDLESHAM Inshore M/S, 'Ham' class. Harris, Appledore 25.3.1955. Sold Pounds 16.7.67; became a club ship.

SIDMOUTH Minesweeper, TE 'Bangor' class. Robb 15.3.1941. Sold 18.1.50, BU at Charlestown.

SIDON Wood pad. frigate, 1,329bm, 211 x 37 ft, 4-56pdr, 4-3pdr. Deptford DY 26.5.1846. Sold 15.7.1864 Castle & Beech.

SIDON Submarine, 'S' class. Cammell Laird 4.9.1944. Sunk 16.6.55 by accidental torpedo explosion at Portland; raised 1955; sunk 6.57 as Asdic target off Portland.

SIERRA LEONE (see PERIM)

SIKH (see Indian TB.5 of 1889)

SIKH Destroyer, 'S' class. Fairfield 7.5.1918. Sold 26.7.27 Granton S. Bkg Co.

SIKH Destroyer 1,870 tons, 355½ x 36½ ft, 8-4in, 4-TT. Stephen 13.12.1937. Sunk 14.9.42 by shore batteries at Tobruk.

SILENE Sloop, 'Anchusa' class 13.3.1918. Sold 29.12.21 Stanlee Dover.

SILVERTON Destroyer, 'Hunt' class type II. White 4.12.1940. Lent Polish navy 5.41 to 9.46 as KRAKOWIAK. Arrived 3.59 Ward, Grays to BU.

SILVIO M/S sloop, '24' class. Barclay Curle 20.4.1918. Renamed MORESBY (RAN) 4.25 as survey ship. Escort 1940. Sold 3.2.47, BU at Newcastle, NSW.

SILVIO (see EMPIRE HALBERD)

SIMCOE Corvette (RCN), modified 'Flower' class. Morton, Quebec. Cancelled 12.1943.

SIMOOM (see TERRIBLE of 1845)

SIMOOM Iron S.frigate, 1,980bm, 2,240 tons, 246 x 41½ ft, 2-6in, 4-56pdr, 14-32pdr. Napier, Govan 24.5.1849. Troopship 1852. Sold 6.1887 Collings, Dartmouth.

SIMOOM (see MONARCH of 1868)

SIMOOM Destroyer, 'R' class. J.Brown 30.10.1916. Sunk 23.1.17 by torpedo from the German 'S.50' in the North Sea.

SIMOOM Destroyer, 'S' class. J.Brown 26.1.1918. Sold 8.1.31 Metal Industries, Charlestown.

SIMOOM (ex-P.225) Submarine, 'S' class. Cammell Laird 12.10.1942. Sunk 19.11.43 by unknown cause off the Dardanelles.

SINBAD DY lighter, 109bm. Pembroke Dock 27.2.1834. Converted to mortar vessel at Deptford 10.1854; renamed MV.2 on 19.10.1855; reverted to SIN-BAD (YC.3) 10.1856. BU completed 10.11.1866 at Woolwich.

SIND Minesweeper (RIN), 'Bathurst' class. Garden Reach, Calcutta. Cancelled 3.1945.

SIND (see BETONY)

SIND (see GODAVERI)

SINGLETON Coastal M/S, 'Ton' class. Montrose SY 23.11.1955. Renamed IBIS (RAN) 9.62.

SIOUX (see VIXEN of 1943)

SIOUX Gate vessel 1940 renamed INDIAN 1944-45.

SIR BEDIVERE Landing Ship 3,270 tons. Hawthorn Leslie 20.7.1966.

SIR BEVIS M/S sloop, '24' class. Barclay Curle 11.5.1918. Renamed IRWELL 9.23, drillship. Renamed EAGLET 1926. BU in 1971.

SIR EDWARD HAWKE Schooner. Built and purchased 1768 in N. America. Sold 11.8.1773.

SIR EDWARD HUGHES 5th Rate 38, 962bm. Ex-E.Indiaman presented 1806. Renamed TORTOISE 28.11.1807 as storeship 22. Coal hulk 11.1824; store hulk 8.1841. Ordered 18.10.1859 to BU at Ascension.

SIR FRANCIS DRAKE (ex-*Asia*) 5th Rate 38, 751bm, 132½ x 35½ ft. Purchased 1805. Sold 13.10.1825.

SIR GALAHAD, Landing Ship 3,270 tons. Stephen 19.4.1966. Lost 24.6.82 in Falklands operations.

SIR GALAHAD Landing ship. Swan Hunter 13.12.1986.

SIR HUGO M/S sloop, '24' class. Greenock & Grangemouth 20.9.1918. Sold 25.6.30 Cashmore, Newport.

SIR HUGO (see EMPIRE LANCE)

SIR JAMES WOLFE Monitor 1915 (see GENERAL WOLFE).

SIR JOHN MOORE (ex-M.5 renamed 1915) Monitor 5,906 tons, 320 x 87 ft, 2-12in, 4-6in, 2-12pdr. Scotts 31.5.1915. Sold 8.11.21 Slough TC, BU in Germany.

SIR ISAAC BROCK 6th Rate 28 (Canadian lakes). Building 1813 at York (Toronto). Destroyed on stocks 27.4.1813.

SIR LANCELOT Landing ship 3,270 tons. Fairfield 25.6.1963.

SIR PERCIVALE Landing ship 3,270 tons. Hawthorn Leslie 4.10.67.

SIR SYDNEY SMITH (ex-*Governor Simcoe*) Brig 10 (Canadian lakes), 72 x 22 ft, 10-18pdr carr. Purchased 1812. Renamed MAGNET 22.1.1814. Burnt 5.8.1814 to avoid capture by Americans.

SIR THOMAS PICTON (ex-PICTON renamed 8.3.1915, ex-M.12) Monitor 5,900 tons, 320 x 87 ft, 2-12in, 2-12pdr. Harland & Wolff 30.9.15. Sold 8.11.21 Slough TC, BU in Germany; arrived 21.12.22 at Bremen.

SIR TRISTRAM Landing ship 3,270 tons. Hawthorn Leslie 12.12.66.

SIR VISTO M/S sloop, '24' class. Osbourne Graham, Sunderland 24.3.1919. Sold 8.20 Moise Mazza.

SIR VISTO (see EMPIRE RAPIER)

SIRDAR Destroyer, 'S' class. Fairfield 6.7.1918. Sold 4.5.34 Cashmore, Newport.

SIRDAR Submarine, 'S' class. Scotts 26.3.1943. Arrived 31.5.65 McLellen, Bo'ness to BU.

SIREN 6th Rate 24, 504bm, 112½ x 32 ft. Snelgrove, Limehouse 3.9.1745. Sold 26.1.1764.

SIREN 6th Rate 28, 603bm, 120½ x 33½ ft. Henniker, Rochester 2.11.1773. Wrecked 10.11.1777 off Rhode Island.

SYREN 6th Rate 24, 514bm, 114 x 32 ft. Baker, Howden Dock, Tyne 29.7.1779. Wrecked 1.1781 Sussex coast.

SYREN 5th Rate 32, 679bm, 126 x 35 ft. Betts, Mistleythorn 24.9.1782. Harbour service 1805. BU 9.1822.

SIRENE Sloop 16, 320bm, 92½ x 26 ft. French, captured 8.1794 by INTREPID and CHICHESTER off San Domingo. Wrecked 8.1796 in the Bay of Honduras.

SIREN 5th Rate 32, 886bm, 142 x 37½ ft. Record, Appledore. Ordered 16.7.1805, cancelled 24.6.1806.

SYEREN 3rd Rate 74, 1,491bm. Danish, captured 7.9.1807 at Copenhagen. Harbour service 1809. Sold 1.9.1814 and retained; resold 23.11.1815.

SIREN Hospital hulk, 298bm, 94 x 27 ft. American SYREN captured 1814. Listed to 1815.

SIREN Brig-sloop 16, 549bm, 110 x 35 ft, 16-32pdr. Woolwich DY 23.4.1841. BU completed 14.12.1868 Portsmouth.

SIREN Steam tender, 145bm, 105 x 17 ft. Laird 21.10.1855. Sold Atwood & Co in 12.1863. (Built for use of Royalty at Bermuda; not in Navy Lists.)

SYREN Training tender, 54bm. Purchased 29.6.1878 and attached to BRITANNIA. Sold 1912.

SIREN (see OPOSSUM of 1856)

SYREN Destroyer 390 tons, 215 x 21 ft, 1-12pdr, 5-6pdr, 2-TT. Palmer

20.12.1900. Sold 14.9.20 Hayes, Porthcawl.

SIRIUS (see BERWICK of 1781)

SIRIUS 5th Rate 36, 1,049bm, 149 x 40 ft. Dudman, Deptford 12.4.1797. Destroyed 24.8.1810 at Mauritius to avoid capture by the French.

SIRIUS 5th Rate 38, 1,090bm, 155 x 40 ft. Tyson & Blake, Bursledon 11.9.1813. Target 7.1860. BU completed 23.9.1862 at Portsmouth. (The last ship built at Bursledon).

SIRIUS Wood S.sloop, 1,268bm, 1,760 tons, 212 x 36 ft, 2-7in, 4-64pdr. Portsmouth DY 24.4.1868. Sold 1885 Castle, Charlton.

SIRIUS 2nd class cruiser 3,600 tons, 300 x 43½ ft, 2-6in, 6-4.7in, 8-6pdr. Armstrong Mitchell 27.10.1890. Sunk 23.4.1918 as blockship at Ostend.

SIRIUS Cruiser 5,450 tons, 485 x 50½ ft, 10-5.25in. Portsmouth DY 18.9.1940. Arrived 15.10.56 Hughes Bolckow, Blyth to BU.

SIRIUS Frigate, 'Leander' class. Portsmouth DY 22.9.1964.

SKATE Destroyer 295 tons, 195 x 20½ft, 1-12pdr, 5-6pdr, 2-TT. N C & A (Vickers) 13.3.1895. Sold 9.4.1907 Cox, Falmouth.

SKATE Destroyer, 'R' class. J.Brown 11.1.1917. Sold 4.3.47, arrived 20.7.47 Cashmore, Newport to BU.

SKEENA Destroyer (RCN) 1,337 tons, 309 x 33 ft, 4-4.7in, 8-TT. Thornycroft 10.10.1930. Wrecked 25.10.44 off Iceland; wreck sold 6.45 locally.

SKEENA Escort (RCN) 2,265 tons, 366(oa) x 42 ft, 4-3in, 2-40mm. Burrard 19.8.1952.

SKILFUL Destroyer, 'R' class. Harland & Wolff, Govan 3.2.1917. Sold 13.7.26 King, Garston.

SKIOLD 3rd Rate 74, 1,747bm, 174½ x 48 ft. Danish, captured 7.9.1807 at Copenhagen. Harbour service 1808. Sold 20.7.1825. J.Ledger to BU.

SKIPJACK Schooner 10, 115bm, 71½ x 19 ft. French privateer CONFIANCE captured 23.8.1808 by BELETTE. BU 1812.

SKIPJACK Schooner 5, 118bm, 60½ x 21 ft. Bermuda 1827. Wrecked 6.1841 in the Cayman Islands.

SKIPJACK Wood S.gunboat, 'Albacore' class. Pitcher, Northfleet 4.8.1855. Cooking depot 1874. BU completed 4.2.1879 at Devonport.

SKIPJACK Torpedo gunboat 735 tons, 230 x 27 ft, 2-4.7in, 4-3pdr, 3-TT. Chatham DY 30.4.1889. M/S 1909. Sold 23.4.1920 Hammond Lane Foundry Co.

SKIPJACK Minesweeper 815 tons, 230 x 33½ ft, 2-4in. J.Brown 18.1.1934. Sunk 1.6.40 by air attack off Dunkirk.

SKIPJACK (ex-SOLEBAY renamed 10.1942) Minesweeper, 'Algerine' class. Redfern, Toronto 7.4.43. Arrived 3.59 Hughes Bolckow, Blyth to BU.

SKIRMISHER Scout cruiser 2,895 tons, 360 x 40 ft, 10-12pdr, 8-3pdr. Vickers 7.2.1905. Sold 3.3.20 Ward, Preston.

SKUA (see WALRUS of 1945)

SKYLARK Brig-sloop 16, 283bm, 93 x 26½ ft. Rowe, Newcastle 2.1806. Burnt 3.5.1812 near Boulogne to avoid capture by the French.

SKYLARK Brig-sloop 10, 'Cherokee' class. Pembroke Dock 6.5.1826. Wrecked 25.4.1845 on Kimmeridge Ledge.

SKYLARK Wood gunboat, 'Dapper' class. Pitcher, Northfleet 3.5.1855. Gunnery tender 1884. Sold 10.7.1906 Garnham.

SKYLARK (ex-War Dept vessel *General Elliot*) Tender 110 tons, 80 x 17 ft. Transferred 1906 and renamed 11.06. Sold 21.10.30 Ward, BU at Grays.

SKYLARK M/L tender 302 tons, 98 x 24½ ft. Portsmouth DY 15.11.1932. Renamed VERNON 9.12.38, VESUVIUS 4.41. Sold 5.7.57. BU 2.58 Pollock Brown, Southampton.

SLADEN Paddle river gunboat (Indian) 270 tons, 161 x 30 ft, 2-12pdr. Listed 1886 to 1921.

SLANEY 6th Rate 20, 460bm, 116 x 30 ft. Brindley, Frindsbury 9.12.1813. Receiving ship 1832. BU 1838 in Bermuda.

SLANEY Wood S.gunboat, 301bm, 125 x 23 ft, 1-10in, 2-24pdr howitzers. Pitcher, Northfleet 17.3.1857. Wrecked 9.5.1870 in a typhoon near Hong Kong.

SLANEY Iron S.gunboat 363 tons, 110 x 34 ft, 3-64pdr. Palmer, Jarrow 28.4.1877. Diving tender 1906. Reported sold 30.8.19 Ward, Grays, but listed to 1921. Arrived Grays 10.10.19 and Rainham 3.1.23 to BU.

SLEUTH Submarine, 'S' class. Cammell Laird 6.7.1944. Arrived 15.9.58 at Charlestown to BU.

SLEUTH Yacht (RAN) 1915-20.

SLIGO Minesweeper, later 'Hunt' class. Napier & Miller 23.3.1918. Sold 4.11.22 Col J.Lithgow.

SLINGER A/C catapult vessel, 875gross. Ex-hopper built Renfrew

1917 and purchased. Sold 16.10.19 M.S.Hilton.

SLINGER (ex-*Chatham*) Escort carrier 11,420 tons, 468½ x 69½ ft, 2-4in, 16-40mm, 24-A/C. Seattle Tacoma 19.9.1942 on lend-lease. Returned 27.2.46 to the USN.

SLINGER (see LST.3510)

SLOTHANY 3rd Rate 60, 772bm. Dutch SLOT van HONINGEN captured 1665. Hulked 1667. Sold 1686.

SLUYS Destroyer 2,315 tons, 555 x 40 ft, 4-4.5in, 8-TT. Cammell Laird 28.2.1945. Handed over 26.1.67 to Iranian navy as ARTIMEZ.

SMETHWICK Minesweeper, later 'Hunt' class. Lobnitz. Cancelled 1918.

SMILAX (ex-USS TACT) Corvette, modified 'Flower' class. Collingwood SY 24.12.1942. Returned 20.3.46 to the USN.

SMITER (ex-*Vermillion*) Escort carrier 11,420 tons, 468½ x 69½ ft, 2-4in, 16-40mm, 24-A/C. Seattle Tacoma 27.9.1943 on lend-lease. Returned 6.4.46 to the USN.

SMITER (see LST.3514)

SMITER Patrol boat 43 tons. Watercraft 1986

SMITHS FALLS Corvette (RCN), modified 'Flower' class. Kingston SY 19.8.1944. Sold 1950, renamed *Olympic Lightning*.

SNAKE Sloop 14. Purchased 6.1777. Captured 13.6.1781 by two American privateers in the Atlantic.

SNAKE Sloop 14. Purchased 1777. Slop ship 1782. Sold 2.4.1783. (Previous vessel recaptured?)

SNAKE Sloop 18, 'Cruizer' class but ship-rigged, 386bm. Adams, Bucklers Hard 18.12.1797. Sold 18.4.1816.

SNAKE Brig-sloop 16, 434bm, 101½ x 32 ft, 14-32pdr, 2-18pdr. Fletcher, Limehouse 3.5.1832. Wrecked 29.8.1847 in the Mozambique Channel.

SNAKE Steam tender (Indian), 40bm. Bombay DY 1838. Harbour service hulk 1863.

SNAKE Wood S.gunvessel, 480bm, 160 x 25½ ft, 2-68pdr. Mare, Blackwall 6.9.1854. Sold 1864 Marshall, Plymouth.

SNAKE Iron S.gunboat, 'Ant' class. Chatham DY 25.3.1871. Completed as DY cable lighter 23.9.1907 and renamed YC.15.

SNAKEFLY River gunboat, 'Fly' class. Yarrow 1916. Sold 1.3.23 at Basra.

SNAKEFLY Trawler requis. 1939-45.

SNAP Brig-sloop 16, 310bm, 92½ x 28½ ft, 16-24pdr carr., 2-6pdr. French PALINURE captured 31.10.1808. BU 6.1811.

SNAP Gun-brig 12, 181bm, 84 x 22½ ft, 10-18pdr carr., 2-6pdr. Russell, Lyme Regis 25.7.1812. Survey vessel 1823; powder hulk 1827. Sold 4.1.1832 Levy, Rochester.

SNAP Steam transport. Slaver *Cacique* captured 1847 and purchased 4.5.1847. Sold 2.1848.

SNAP Wood S.gunboat, 'Dapper' class. Pitcher, Northfleet 3.2.1855. Sold 1868 at Hong Kong; resold Japanese navy as KAKU TEN KAN.

SNAP Iron S.gunboat, 'Ant' class. Campbell Johnstone, N.Woolwich 11.12.1872. Sold 11.5.1909 Deeker, Hull.

SNAPDRAGON Sloop, 'Arabis' class. Ropner, Stockton on Tees 21.12.1915. Sold 4.5.34 Cashmore, Newport.

SNAPDRAGON Corvette, 'Flower' class. Simons 3.9.1940. Sunk 19.12.42 by air attack in the central Mediterranean.

SNAPDRAGON (see ARABIS of 1940)

SNAPPER Cutter. Whitstable 1782 and purchased 1782. Sold 29.9.1817 J.Cristall. (Probably revenue service 1790)

SNAPPER Cutter 4, 78bm, 56 x 18 ft, 4-12pdr carr. Bermuda 1804. Captured 15.7.1811 by the French lugger RAPACE.

SNAPPER Gun-brig 12, 184bm, 84½ x 22½ ft. Hobbs & Hillyer, Redbridge 27.9.1813. Coastguard 5.1824. Sold 1865 Castle per order dated 3.7.61.

SNAPPER Wood S.gunboat, 218bm, 284 tons, 100 x 22 ft, 1-68pdr, 1-32pdr, 2-24pdr howitzers. Pitcher, Northfleet 4.10.1854. Coal hulk 1865. Sold 1906.

SNAPPER Destroyer 310 tons, 200 x 19½ ft, 1-12pdr, 5-6pdr, 2-TT. Earle, Hull 30.1.1895. Sold 14.5.1912 King, Gateshead.

SNAPPER (see MASTIFF of 1871)

SNAPPER II (see HANDY of 1884)

SNAPPER Submarine 670 tons, 193 x 24 ft, 1-3in, 6-TT. Chatham DY 25.10.1934. Sunk 2.41 by unknown cause in the Bay of Biscay.

SNIPE Gun-brig 12, 185bm, 80½ x 23 ft, 2-32pdr carr., 10-18pdr carr. Adams, Bucklers Hard 2.5.1801. Completed 2.1816 as DY mooring lighter. BU 5.1846.

SNIPE Cutter 6, 122bm, 64 x 22 ft, 2-6pdr, 4-6pdr carr. Pembroke Dock

28.6.1828. BU 11.1860 at Devonport.

SNIPE Wood S.gunvessel, 'Philomel' class. Scott Russell, Millwall 5.5.1860. BU at Sheerness in 5.1868.

SNIPE Coastguard vessel, 20bm. Watkins, Blackwall 26.11.1874. Foundered 3.2.1914, raised and sold 16.5.14.

SNIPE River gunboat 85 tons, 108 x 20 ft, 2-6pdr. Yarrow, Poplar 1898. Reported sold 20.11.1919 at Hong Kong, but listed 1921.

SNIPE Sloop 1,350 tons, 283 x 38½ ft, 6-4in. Denny (ex-J.Brown) 20.12.1945. Arrived 23.8.60 Cashmore, Newport to BU.

SNIPE (see ALCASTON)

SNOWBERRY Corvette, 'Flower' class. Davie SB 8.8.1940. Lent RCN to 8.6.45. BU 8.47 Thornaby on Tees.

SNOWDROP Sloop, 'Acacia' class. McMillan 7.10.1915. Sold 15.1.23 Unity S.Bkg Co.

SNOWDROP Corvette, 'Flower' class. Smiths Dk 19.7.1940. Sold 17.5.47, BU 1949 on the Tyne.

SNOWDROP Three drifters requis. in WW.I.

SNOWFLAKE (ex-ZENOBIA renamed 8.1941) Corvette, 'Flower' class. Smiths Dk 22.8.41. To Air Ministry 1947 as *Weather Watcher*.Arrived 5.5.62 at Dublin to BU.

SNOWFLAKE Drifter 1919-1919

SOBERTON Coastal M/S, 'Ton' class. Fleetland SY, Gosport 20.11.1956.

SOBO Depot ship 4,160 tons, 345 x 44 ft. Purchased 10.1914. Sold 12.2.20 W.R.Davies & Co.

SOCIETY Fireship 6, 318bm. Purchased 1673. Expended 1673.

SOCIETY Bomb 8, 102bm. Purchased 4.1694. Sold 3.5.1698.

SOCIETY Hospital ship. Origin unknown. Captured 23.8.1697 by the French.

SOESDYKE Yacht 8, 116bm. Purchased 24.3.1692. Rebuilt Deptford 1702 as 109bm. Sold 13.7.1713.

SOKOTO Depot ship 3,870 tons, 345 x 42 ft. Purchased 10.1914. Sold 9.8.19. mercantile.

SOLEBAY 6th Rate 24, 256bm, 92 x 25 ft. Snelgrove, Deptford 9.1694. Wrecked 25.12.1709 on Boston Rock near Lyme Regis.

SOLEBAY 6th Rate 20, 272bm, 96 x 25 ft. Portsmouth DY 21.8.1711. Fireship 1727; hospital ship 6.1742. Sold 23.6.1748.

SOLEBAY 6th Rate 24, 429bm, 106 x 30½ ft. Plymouth 20.7.1742. In French hands 8.44 to 4.46. Sold 15.3.1763.

SOLEBAY 6th Rate 28, 619bm, 124 x 33½ ft. Airey, Newcastle 9.9.1763. Wrecked 25.1.1782 on Nevis, W.Indies.

SOLEBAY 5th Rate 32, 683bm, 126½ x 35 ft. Adams & Barnard, Deptford 26.3.1785. Wrecked 11.7.1809 coast of Africa.

SOLEBAY (see IRIS of 1783)

SOLEBAY (see SKIPJACK of 1943)

SOLEBAY Destroyer 2,325 tons, 355 x 40 ft, 4-4.5in, 10-40mm, 8-TT. Hawthorn Leslie 22.2.1944. Arrived 11.8.67 at Troon to BU.

SOLENT Storeship 125 tons, 100 x 17½ ft. Transferred from War Dept 1907. Sold 1907 at Hong Kong.

SOLENT Submarine, 'S' class. Cammell Laird 8.6.1944. Arrived 28.8.61 at Troon to BU.

SOLITAIRE 3rd Rate 64, 1,521bm. French, captured. 6.12.1782 by RUBY and POLYPHEMUS. Sold 5.1786.

SOLITAIRE M/S tug 1939-44.

SOLWAY FIRTH (ex-EMPIRE LAGOS renamed 1944) Repair ship 10,000 tons, 431 x 56 ft. Short, Sunderland 31.10.1944. Sold 1946, renamed *Kongsborg*.

SOMALI Destroyer 1,870 tons, 353½ x 36½ ft, 8-4.7in, 4-TT. Swan Hunter 24.8.1937. Torpedoed 20.9.42 by 'U.703' and foundered four days later south of Iceland.

SOMALILAND (ex-POPHAM renamed 1943) Frigate, 'Colony' class. Walsh Kaiser 11.11.43. Returned 31.5.46 to the USN.

SOMERLEYTON (ex-GAMSTON) Coastal M/S, 'Ton' class. Richards IW, Lowestoft 17.9.1855. Renamed HAWK (RAN) 18.7.62. Sold in 1.76.

SOMERS Schooner 10. Listed 1807-12.

SOMERSET 3rd Rate 64, 1,436bm, 160 x 42½ ft. Chatham DY 18.7.1748. Wrecked 12.8.1778 near Cape Cod.

SOMERSETT 3rd Rate 80, 1,263bm, 158 x 42½ ft. Chatham DY 1698. Hulked 1715. BU 7.1740 at Woolwich.

SOMERSET 3rd Rate 80, 1,354bm, 158 x 44½ ft. Woolwich DY 21.10.1731. BU 10.1746 at Chatham.

SOMME Destroyer, 'S' class. Fairfield 10.9.1918. Sold 25.8.32 Ward, Pembroke Dock.

SOMME Destroyer 2,380 tons, 355 x 40 ft, 5-4.5in, 8-40mm, 10-TT. Cammell Laird. Laid down 24.2.1945, cancelled 10.45.

SONNE (see SUN)

SOPHIA (also SPEAKER'S PRIZE) 26-gun ship, 300bm. Captured 1652. Sold 1667.

SOPHIA 12-gun vessel, 145bm. Captured 1685 from the Earl of Argyll by KINGFISHER. Fireship 1688; hoy 1690. BU 1713.

SOPHIE 6th Rate 28, 802bm, 132½ x 34½ ft. French merchant captured 12.9.1782 by WARWICK. Sold 17.8.1784.

SOPHIE Sloop 18, 388bm, 108½ x 29 ft. French privateer PREMIER CONSUL captured 3.1798 by ENDYMION. BU 1809 at Deptford.

SOPHIE Fire vessel, 56bm. Purchased 6.1804. Sold 17.6.1807 T.Graham.

SOPHIE Brig-sloop 18, 'Cruizer' class, 387bm. Pelham, Frindsbury 8.9.1809. Sold 15.8.1825 in the E.Indies.

SOPHIA Discovery vessel, 150bm. Purchased 11.5.1850. Sold 5.5.1853.

SOPHIE (see under SOPHIA)

SORCERESS Destroyer, 'R' class. Swan Hunter 29.8.1916. Sold 29.4.27 Ward, Inverkeithing.

SORCERESS Yacht requis. 1914-15.

SOREL Corvette (RCN), 'Flower' class. Marine Ind 16.11.1940. Sold 16.10.45.

SORLINGS (see ROYAL JAMES of 1654)

SORLINGS 5th Rate 32, 362bm, 102½ x 28½ ft. Barrett, Shoreham 19.3.1694. Captured 20.10.1705 by the French Le JERSEY off the Dogger Bank. Recaptured 2.1711 and sold.

SORLINGS 5th Rate 42, 506bm, 116½ x 40 ft. Sheerness DY 18.2.1706. Wrecked 17.12.1717 on East Friesland.

SORLINGS (ex-*Elizabeth*) Survey vessel, 64bm, 52 x 17 ft. Purchased 1789. DY lighter 1809. To BU 1833.

SOUDAN Iron steam vessel, 250bm, 113 x 22 ft. Laird 7.1840. Wrecked 1844 on the coast of Nigeria.

SOUTHAMPTON 4th Rate 48, 609bm, 122 x 34 ft. Parker & Winter, Southampton 10.6.1693. Rebuilt Deptford 1700 as 636bm; hulked in Jamaica 5.1728. BU 1771.

SOUTHAMPTON 5th Rate 32, 671bm, 124½ x 35 ft. Inwood, Rotherhithe 5.5.1757. Wrecked 27.11.1812 in the Bahamas.

SOUTHAMPTON 4th Rate 60, 1,476bm, 172½ x 44½ ft. Deptford DY 7.11.1820. Lent Hull Committee 18.6.1867 as training ship. Sold 26.6.1912 Hughes Bolckow, Blyth.

SOUTHAMPTON 2nd class cruiser 5,400 tons, 430 x 50 ft, 8-6in. J.Brown 11.5.1912. Sold 13.7.26 Ward, Pembroke Dock.

SOUTHAMPTON (ex-POLYPHEMUS renamed 1936) Cruiser 9,100 tons, 558 x 62 ft, 12-6in, 8-4in. J.Brown 10.3.1936. Bombed 10.1.41 east of Malta and scuttled on the next day.

SOUTHAMPTON Destroyer 3,150 tons. Vosper Thornycroft 29.1.1979.

SOUTHDOWN Minesweeper, early 'Hunt' class. Simons 7.5.1917. Sold 16.12.26 Granton S.Bkg Co.

SOUTHDOWN Destroyer, 'Hunt' class type I. White 5.7.1940. Arrived 1.11.56 Ward, Barrow to BU.

SOUTHLAND (see DIDO)

SOUTHSEA CASTLE 5th Rate 32, 373bm, 106½ x 28 ft. Knowles, Redbridge 1.8.1696. Wrecked 15.9.1697 on Dove Sand.

SOUTHSEA CASTLE 5th Rate 32, 387bm, 108 x 28½ ft. Deptford 1697. Stranded 12.11.1699 on the Isle of Ash, W.Indies.

SOUTHSEA CASTLE 5th Rate 42, 546bm, 119½ x 32½ ft. Swallow, Rotherhithe 18.11.1708. Sold 1744.

SOUTHSEA CASTLE 5th Rate 44, 712bm, 126 x 36 ft. Okill, Liverpool 18.8.1745. Storeship 1.1760, 22-9pdr, 6-2pdr. Lost 8.1762 at Manilla.

SOUTHWOLD (see STOKE)

SOUTHWOLD Destroyer, 'Hunt' class type II. White 29.5.1941. Sunk 24.3.42 by mine off Malta.

SOVERANO 3rd Rate 74, 1,875bm, 175 x 49½ ft. Spanish, captured 8.1762. BU completed 14.8.1770 at Portsmouth.

SOVEREIGN (also TRINITY SOVEREIGN) 800-ton ship. Built 1488. Rebuilt 1510. Listed to 1521.

SOVEREIGN (also SOVEREIGN of the SEAS) 100-gun ship, 1,141bm. Woolwich DY 14.10.1637. Rebuilt 1660 and renamed ROYAL SOVEREIGN.(qv)

SOVEREIGN Nuclear S/M 3,800 tons. Vickers 17.2.1973.

SPANIARD Galleon. Presented 1522 by the king of Spain. Not mentioned after 1523.

SPANIARD Trawler 1939-42.

SPANISH MERCHANT Fireship 8, 250bm. Purchased 1678. Sold 1686.

SPANKER Floating battery 24, circa 500bm, 111½ x 42½ ft, 24-24pdr carr., 2-10in mortars. Barnard, Deptford 14.6.1794. Left navy list 31.8.1810.

SPANKER Wood S.gunboat, 'Albacore'

class. Green, Blackwall 22.3.1856. BU 8.1874 at Chatham.

SPANKER Torpedo gunboat 735 tons, 230 x 27 ft, 2-4.7in, 4-3pdr, 3-TT. Devonport DY 27.2.1889. M/S 1909. Sold 20.3.20 Cornish Salvage Co, Ilfracombe.

SPANKER Minesweeper, 'Algerine' class. Harland & Wolff 20.4.1943. Sold 25.2.53 Belgian navy as De BROUWER.

SPARHAM Inshore M/S, 'Ham' class. Vosper, Gosport 14.10.1954. To French Navy 30.9.55 renamed M.785.

SPARK Submarine, 'S' class. Scotts 28.12.1943. Sold 28.10.49, BU at Faslane. 10.50.

SPARKLER Gun-brig 12, 159bm, 75 x 22 ft, 2-24pdr, 10-18pdr carr. Randall, Rotherhithe 4.1797. Sold 9.1802.

SPARKLER Gun-Brig 12, 178bm, 80½ x 22½ ft, 2-18pdr, 10-18pdr carr. Warren, Brightlingsea 6.8.1804. Wrecked 14.1.1808 on the Dutch coast.

SPARKLER Tug 1940-57.

SPARROW Pink 16, 60bm. Captured 1653. Sold 1659.

SPARROW (ex-*Rattler*) Cutter 12, 123bm, 66½ x 22½ ft, 10-12pdr carr., 2-6pdr. Purchased 1796. BU 1805.

SPARROW Brig-sloop 16, 284bm, 96 x 26 ft. Preston, Yarmouth 29.7.1805. Sold 17.10.1816.

SPARROW Cutter 10, 160bm, 70½ x 24 ft. Pembroke Dock 28.6.1828. Survey ketch 1844. BU 8.1860 at Devonport.

SPARROW Wood S.gunvessel, 'Philomel' class. Scott Russell, Millwall 7.7.1860. BU 1868 Marshall, Plymouth.

SPARROW Compos. S.gunboat 805 tons, 165 x 31 ft, 6-4in, 2-3pdr. Scotts 26.9.1889. To NZ Govt 10.7.1906 as AMOKURA training ship. Sold 2.22 as coal hulk. BU 1955.

SPARROW Sloop 1,350 tons, 283 x 38½ ft, 6-4in. Denny (ex-J.Brown) 18.2.1946. Arrived 26.5.58 Charlestown to BU.

SPARROW Trawler 1909-19.

SPARROWHAWK Brig-sloop 18, 'Cruizer' class, 385bm. Warren, Brightlingsea 20.8.1807. Sold 27.5.1841.

SPARROWHAWK Wood S.gunvessel, 676bm, 181 x 28½ ft, 1-7in, 2-40pdr. Young & Magnay, Limehouse 9.2.1856. Sold 1872 at Esquimalt.

SPARROWHAWK (see LARK of 1877)

SPARROWHAWK Destroyer 360 tons, 210 x 21 ft, 1-12pdr, 5-6pdr, 2-TT. Laird 8.10.1895. Wrecked 17.6.1904 at the mouth of the Yangtse.

SPARROWHAWK Destroyer 935 tons, 260 x 27 ft, 3-4in, 4-TT. Swan Hunter 12.10.1912. Sunk 31.5.16 in collision with BROKE and CONTEST AT Jutland.

SPARROWHAWK Destroyer, 'S' class. Swan Hunter 14.5.1918. Sold 5.2.31 Ward, Grays.

SPARTAN 5th Rate 38, 1,084bm, 154 x 40 ft. Ross, Rochester 16.8.1806. BU 4.1822.

SPARTAN 5th Rate 46, 1,215bm, 159 x 42 ft. Portsmouth DY. Ordered 13.9.1824, cancelled 7.2.1831.

SPARTAN 6th Rate 26, 911bm, 313 x 40½ ft, 2-8in, 24-32pdr Devonport DY 16.8.1841. Sold 19.5.1862 Castle.

SPARTAN Wood S.sloop 1,269bm, 1,755 tons, 212 x 36 ft, 2-7in, 4-64pdr. Deptford DY 14.11.1868. Sold 7.11.1882 Castle.

SPARTAN 2nd class cruiser 3,600 tons, 300 x 43½ ft, 2-6in, 6-4.7in 8-6pdr. Armstrong Mitchell 25.2.1891. Harbour service 1907. Renamed DEFIANCE 8.1921. Sold 26.6.31.

SPARTAN Cruiser 5,770 tons, 485 x 50½ ft, 8-5.25in. Vickers Armstrong, Barrow 27.8.1942. Sunk 29.1.44 by air attack at Anzio.

SPARTAN Nuclear s/m 3,800 tons. Vickers 7.4.1978

SPARTAN Drifter requis. 1914-19.

SPARTIATE 3rd Rate 74, 1,949bm, 182½ x 50 ft. French, captured 1.8.1798 at the Nile. Sheer hulk 8.1842. BU completed 30.5.1857.

SPARTIATE 1st class cruiser 11,000 tons, 435 x 69 ft, 16-6in, 12-12pdr. Pembroke Dock 27.10.1898. Renamed FISGARD 6.1915. Sold 7.32 Ward, Pembroke Dock.

SPEAKER 50-gun ship, 727bm, 142 x 35ft. Woolwich 1649. Renamed MARY 1660, 60 guns. Wrecked 27.11.1703 on the Goodwins.

SPEAKER Gunvessel. Presented by Barbados merchants 10.1756. Listed 1799.

SPEAKER (ex-*Delgada*) Escort carrier 11,420 tons, 468½ x 69½ ft, 2-4in, 16-40mm, 24-A/C. Seattle Tacoma 20.2.1943 on lend-lease. Returned 17.7.46 to the USN.

SPEAR Destroyer, 'S' class. Fairfield 9.11.1918. Sold 13.7.26 Alloa, Charlestown.

SPEAR (see PORTWAY)

SPEAR Destroyer 1,980 tons, 341½ x 38

ft, 6-4in, 6-40mm, 10-TT. Denny. Laid down 29.9.1944, cancelled 27.12.45.

SPEARFISH Submarine 670 tons, 193 x 24 ft, 1-3in, 6-TT. Cammell Laird 21.4.1936. Sunk 1940 by 'U.34' off Norway and formally paid off 5.8.40.

SPEARHEAD Submarine, 'S' class. Cammell Laird 2.10.1944. Sold 8.48 Portugese navy as NEPTUNO.

SPEARMINT M/S sloop, '24' class. Swan Hunter 23.9.1918. Sold 29.11.22 Hallamshire Metal Co.

SPEEDWELL Galley. French, captured 1.1560 in the Forth. BU 1580.

SPEEDWELL (see SWIFTSURE of 1573)

SPEEDWELL (see CHERITON)

SPEEDWELL Fireship 8, 120bm. Purchased 1688. Sunk 1692 as breakwater at Portsmouth.

SPEEDWELL Fireship 8, 259bm, 94 x 25 ft, Gressingham, Rotherhithe 3.4.1690. Rebuilt Limehouse 1702 as 5th Rate 28, 274bm. Wrecked 21.11.1720 on the Dutch coast.

SPEEDWELL PRIZE 6th Rate 20, 155bm, 75½ x 22ft. Captured 4.10.1708 by SPEEDWELL. Sold 1712.

SPEEDWELL Sloop 14, 271bm, 91½ x 26½ ft. Buxton, Deptford 9.11.1744. Sold 13.11.1750.

SPEEDWELL Sloop 8, 142bm, 75½ x 20½ft. Chatham DY 21.10.1752. Renamed SPITFIRE 27.8.1779, fireship. Sold 5.12.1780.

SPEEDWELL Cutter. Origin unknown. Captured 4.4.1761 by the French ACHILLE at Vigo.

SPEEDWELL Sloop 18. Listed in 1775.

SPEEDWELL Cutter 16, 193bm, 75½ x 26 ft, 16-4pdr. Purchased 5.1780. Foundered 18.2.1807 off Dieppe.

SPEEDWELL Schooner 5. Purchased 1815. Sold 1.1834 in Jamaica.

SPEEDWELL Survey cutter, 73bm, 56 x 18 ft. Purchased 12.7.1841. Sold 5.1855 in Canada.

SPEEDWELL Wood S.gunvessel, 'Philomel' class. Deptford 12.2.1861. BU 7.1876 at Chatham.

SPEEDWELL Torpedo gunboat 735 tons, 230 x 27 ft, 2-4.7in, 4-3pdr, 3-TT. Devonport DY 15.3.1889. M/S 1909. Sold 20.3.20 Cornish Salvage Co, Ilfracombe.

SPEEDWELL Minesweeper 815 tons, 230 x 33½ ft, 2-4in Hamilton 21.3.1935. Sold 5.12.46, renamed *Topaz*

SPEEDWELL Vessel hired 1800; Trawl-

er & 3 Drifters WW.1.

SPEEDY Brig-sloop 14, 208bm, 78 x 26 ft. King, Dover 29.6.1782. Captured 2.7.1801 by the French in the Mediterranean. (Also French 6.94 to 3.95.)

SPEEDY Cunvessel (Canadian lakes). Kingston Ontario 1798. Foundered 8.10.1804.

SPEEDY (ex-*George Hibbert*) Brig-sloop 16, 379bm, 101½ x 29½ ft. Purchased 7.1803. Sold 3.1818.

SPEEDY Cutter 6, 123bm, 64 x 22½ ft, 2-6pdr, 4-6pdr carr. Pembroke Dock 28.6.1828. DY mooring lighter 8.1853 and renamed YC.11. BU 1866.

SPEEDY Wood S. gunboat, 'Britomart' class. Lamport, Workington 18.7.1860. Sold Castle in 8.1889 to BU.

SPEEDY Torpedo gunboat 810 tons, 230 x 27 ft, 2-4.7in, 4-3pdr, 3-TT. Thornycroft, Chiswick 18.5.1893. Sunk 3.9.1914 by mine off the Humber.

SPEEDY Destroyer, 'S' class 1,087 tons. Thornycroft 1.6.1918. Sunk 24.9.22 in collision with a tug in the Sea of Marmora.

SPEEDY Minesweeper 875 tons, 230 x 33½ ft, 2-4in. Hamilton 23.11.1938. Sold 5.11.46, renamed *Speedon.*

SPEEDY Jet-foil 117 tons Seattle 9.7.1979. Sold mercantile 1986

SPENCE Sloop 8, 114bm, 64½ x 20 ft. Deptford DY 13.3.1722. BU 3.1730.

SPENCE Sloop 12, 207bm, 87 x 23ft. Deptford DY 24.6.1730. Sold 10.6.1748.

SPENCER (see DILIGENCE of 1795)

SPENCER (ex-Sir Charles Grey) Brig-sloop 16, 200bm, 92½ x 22ft, 14-12pdr carr., 2-4pdr. Purchased 1795. Renamed LILY 1800. Captured 15.7.1804 by the French privateer DAME AMBERT off N.America; recaptured 20.3.05 by RENARD and blew up.

SPENCER 3rd Rate 74, 1,917bm, 181 x 49½ ft. Adams, Bucklers Hard 10.5.1800. BU 4.1822.

SPENSER Destroyer leader 1,750 tons, 318 x 32ft, 5-4.7in, 1-3in, 6-TT. Thornycroft 22.9.1917. Handed over 29.9.36 to Ward in part payment for *Majestic,* BU at Inverkeithing.

SPEY 6th Rate 20, 463bm, 116 x 30 ft, 18-32pdr carr., 2-9pdr. Warwick, Eling 8.1.1814. Sold 18.4.1822.

SPEY Brig-sloop 10, 'Cherokee' class, 231bm. Pembroke Dock 6.10.1827. Packet brig 4 guns,1833. Wrecked 28.11.40 on Racoon Key, W.Indies.

SPEY Wood S.gunboat, 'Albacore' class.

Pitcher, Northfleet 29.3.1856. BU at Deptford in 12.1863.

SPEY Iron S.gunboat 363 tons, 110 x 34ft, 3-64pdr. Palmer 5.10.1876. Sold 1923.

SPEY (see P.38 of 1917)

SPEY Frigate, 'River' class. Smiths Dock 18.12.1941. Sold 11.48 Egyptian navy, renamed RASHEID.

SPEY Minehunter 757 tons Richards 22.5.1985

SPHINX 6th Rate 24, 520bm, 114 x 32½ ft. Allen, Rotherhithe 10.12.1748. Sold 28.8.1770.

SPHINX 6th Rate 20, 431bm, 108 x 30 ft. Portsmouth DY 25.10.1775. BU 1811 at Portsmouth.

SPHYNX Brig-sloop 10, 'Cherokee' class, 238bm. Bombay DY 25.1.1815. Sold 6.8.1835.

SPHYNX Wood pad. sloop, 1,056bm, 180 x 36 ft. Woolwich DY 17.2.1846. BU 1881 at Devonport.

SPHINX Compos. paddle vessel 1,130 tons, 200 x 32 ft, 1-6in, 6-4in. Green, Blackwall 28.11.1882. Sold 27.7.1919 at Calcutta.

SPHINX Minesweeper 875 tons, 230 x 33½ ft, 2-4in. Hamilton 7.2.1939. Foundered 3.2.40 in the Moray Firth after damage by air attack.

SPHINX Drifter requis. 1915-20.

SPIDER Schooner 12, 169bm, 69 X 24 ft, 12-4pdr. French privateer ARAIGNEE captured 9.1782. Sold 1806 at Malta.

SPIDER Brig-sloop 14, 280bm, 92 x 25 ft, 6-18pdr carr., 12-8pdr. Spanish VIGILANTE captured 4.4.1806 by RENOMMEE in the Mediterranean. BU 1815 at Antigua.

SPIDER Schooner 6, 183bm, 80 x 23ft. Chatham DY 23.9.1835. Packet 10.1847. Sold 22.11.1861.

SPIDER Wood S.gunboat, 'Albacore' class. Smith, N.Shields 23.2.1856. Sold 12.5.1870 Castle.

SPIDER Torpedo gunboat 525 tons, 200 x 23 ft, 1-4in, 6-3pdr, 4-TT. Devonport DY 17.10.1887. Sold 5.1903 at Malta; BU Ward, Preston.

SPIDER Coastal destroyer 235 tons, 175 x 17½ ft, 2-12pdr, 3-TT. White 15.12.1906. Renamed TB.5 in 1906. Sold 7.10.20 Ward, Briton Ferry.

SPIDER Trawler 1909-14; Trawler 1915-19; DGV 1941-46.

SPIKE Flyboat, 321bm. Algerian, captured 1679. Exchanged 1680.

SPIKENARD Corvette, 'Flower' class. Davie SB 10.8.1940. Lent RCN from 12.40. Sunk 10.2.42 by 'U.136' in the N.Atlantic.

SPINDRIFT Destroyer, 'S' class. Fairfield 30.12.1918. Sold 7.36 Ward, Inverkeithing.

SPINDRIFT Trawler (ex-GERMAN) 1940, renamed SKILPAD 1951-58.

SPIRAEA Sloop, 'Anchusa' class. Simons 1.11.1917. Sold 6.9.22 Distin Syndicate.

SPIRAEA Corvette, 'Flower' class. Inglis 31.10.1940. Sold 8.45, renamed *Thessaloniki*.

SPIRIT Submarine, 'S' class. Cammell Laird 20.7.1943. Arrived 4.7.50 Ward, Grays to BU.

SPITEFUL Gunvessel 12. Dutch hoy purchased 1794. Listed in 1800.

SPITEFUL (Gunboat No.18) Gunvessel 12, 159bm, 75½ x 22 ft, 2-24pdr, 10-18pdr carr. Barnard, Deptford 24.4.1797. Convict hulk 1818. BU 7.1823.

SPITEFUL Wood pad. sloop, 1,054bm, 180 x 36 ft. Pembroke Dock 24.3.1842. Sold Castle 9.1883.

SPITEFUL Destroyer 365 tons, 215 x 21 ft, 1-12pdr, 5-6pdr, 2-TT. Palmer 11.1.1899. Sold 14.9.1920 Hayes, Porthcawl.

SPITEFUL Submarine, 'S' class. Scotts 5.6.1943. Lent French navy 25.1.52 to 11.58 as SIRENE. Arrived 15.7.63 at Faslane to BU.

SPITFIRE Galley 8. Purchased in N.America, commissioned 25.1.1778. Captured 19.4.1779 by the French SURVEILLANTE at Rhode Island.

SPITFIRE (see SPEEDWELL of 1752)

SPITFIRE Fireship 14, 198bm. Purchased 1780. Fate unknown.

SPITFIRE Fireship 16, 424bm, 110 x 29½ ft. Teague, Ipswich 19.3.1783. Sold 30.7.1825.

SPITFIRE Schooner 4, 61bm, 59½ x 14 ft, 4-3pdr. Purchased 1793. Capsized 2.1794 off San Domingo.

SPITFIRE Schooner, 64bm. French, captured 1798. Gone by 1800.

SPITFIRE Wood pad. vessel, 553bm, 155 x 27½ ft, 2 guns Woolwich DY 26.3.1834. Wrecked 10.9.1842 near Jamaica.

SPITFIRE Wood pad. gunvessel, 432bm, 595 tons, 147 x 25 ft, 5 guns. Lungley, Deptford 26.3.1845. Survey vessel 1851; tug 1862. BU 1888 in Bermuda.

SPITFIRE Destroyer 330 tons, 200 x 19 ft, 1-12pdr, 5-6pdr, 2-TT. Armstrong 7.6.1895. Sold 10.4.1912 Ward, Preston.

SPITFIRE Destroyer 935 tons, 260 x 27

ft, 3-4in, 4-TT. Swan Hunter 23.12.1912. Sold 9.5.21 Ward, Hayle., arrived in 10.22.

SPITFIRE (see CAMBRIAN of 1943)

SPLENDID Ship listed in 1597. Fate unknown.

SPLENDID Destroyer, 'S' class. Swan Hunter 10.7.1918. Sold 8.1.31 Metal Industries, Charlestown.

SPLENDID (ex-P.228) Submarine, 'S' class. Chatham DY 19.1.1942. Scuttled 21.4.43 after damage by German destroyer HERMES off Corsica.

SPENDID Nuclear S/M 3800 tons. Vickers 5.10.1979

SPORTIVE Destroyer, 'S' class. Swan Hunter 19.9.1918. Handed over 25.9.36 to Ward, in part payment for *Majestic*; arrived 25.9.36 at Inverkeithing.

SPORTSMAN (ex-P.229) Submarine, 'S' class. Chatham DY 17.4.1942. Lent French navy 1951 as SIBYLLE. Sunk 24.9.52 off Toulon.

SPRAGGE Fireship 10. Purchased 1673. Lost 1693. (YOUNG SPRAGGE after 1677.)

SPRAGGE Fireship in 1677.

SPRAGGE Destroyer leader 1,750 tons, 318 x 32 ft. Thornycroft. Cancelled 1.1919.

SPRAGGE Frigate, TE 'Captain' class. Bethelehem Hingham 16.10.1943 on lend-lease. Returned 2.46. to the USN.

SPREAD EAGLE Fireship 6, 240bm. Dutch, captured 1666. Lost 6.1666 in action with the Dutch.

SPRIGHTLY Cutter 10. King, Dover 16.8.1777. Capsized 12.1777 off Guernsey.

SPRIGHTLY Cutter 10, 151bm, 66 x 24 ft. King, Dover 4.8.1778. Captured 10.2.1801 by the French in the Mediterranean and scuttled.

SPRIGHTLY (ex-*Lively*) Cutter 14, 120bm, 64 x 22½ ft, 12-12pdr carr., 2-4pdr. Purchased 1805. BU 5.1815.

SPRIGHTLY Cutter 6. Pembroke Dock 3.6.1818. To revenue service 1819.

SPRIGHTLY (ex-GPO vessel *Harlequin*) Wood pad. packet, 234bm, 120 x 21 ft. Transferred 1837. Sold 1889.

SPRIGHTLY Destroyer 400 tons, 218 x 20 ft, 1-12pdr, 5-6pdr, 2-TT. Laird 25.9.1900. Sold 1.7.20 S.Castle, Plymouth.

SPRIGHTLY Submarine, 'S' class. Cammell Laird. Cancelled 1945.

SPRIGHTLY Rescue tug 1942, to RAN 1944-69.

SPRINGBOK Destroyer, 'R' class. Har-

land & Wolff, Govan 9.3.1917. Sold 16.12.26 Granton S.Bkg Co.

SPRINGER Submarine, 'S' class. Cammell Laird 14.5.1945. To Israeli navy 9.10.58 as TANIN.

SPRINGHILL Frigate (RCN), 'River' class. Yarrow, Esquimalt 7.9.1943. Sold 17.11.47 Halifax SY to BU.

SPRITE 30-ton vessel. Captured 1558. Listed 1559.

SPRITE Tug 1896-1906; Tug 1915-60.

SPUR Submarine, 'S' class. Cammell Laird 17.11.1944. Sold 11.48 Portuguese navy, renamed NARVAL.

SPURN POINT Repair ship 8,580 tons, 425 x 57 ft. Burrard 8.6.1945. Sold 10.7.47, renamed *Lakemba*.

SPY Pinnace 9, 49bm, 4-6pdr, 2-4pdr, 3-2pdr. Limehouse 1586. Listed to 1613.

SPY 200-ton vessel. River Thames 18.10.1620. Fate unknown unless she was the ship given as purchased 8.1622 and listed to 1626.

SPY Shallop 6, 40bm. Listed 1644-52.

SPY Sloop 4, 28bm. Deane, Harwich 1666. Sold 1683.

SPY Fireship 8, 253bm, 91½ ft. Taylor, Cuckolds Point 3.4.1690. Burnt 12.1.1693 by accident at Portsmouth.

SPY Brigantine 6, 78bm, 64 x 17 ft. Woolwich DY 15.4.1693. BU 2.1706 at Sheerness.

SPY Sloop 8, 103bm, 62 x 20 ft. Portsmouth DY 9.12.1721. Sold 2.12.1731.

SPY Sloop 14, 201bm, 85½ x 23½ ft. Chatham DY 25.8.1732. Sold 25.4.1745.

SPY Sloop 10, 222bm, 86 x 24½ ft. Inwood, Rotherhithe 3.2.1756. Sold 3.9.1773.

SPY Cutter, 58bm, 47½ x 18 ft. Purchased 1.1763. Sold 4.5.1773.

SPY Sloop 14, 306bm, 96½ x 27 ft. Graves, Limehouse 6.4.1776. Wrecked 16.6.1778 in Newfoundland.

SPY (see ESPION of 1782)

SPY (ex-*Comet*) Sloop 16, 227bm. Purchased 6.1804. Sold 12.1813.

SPY Brigantine 3, 320bm, 90 x 29½ ft, 3-32pdr. Sheerness DY 24.3.1841. Sold 20.1.1862 at Montevideo.

SPY Coastguard cutter, 40bm. Listed from 10.1864. Sold 5.7.1904 at Portsmouth.

SQUIB (ex-*Diligent*) Fireship. Purchased 10.1804. Wrecked 10.1805 near Deal.

SQUIRREL Discovery vessel. With Sir Humphrey Gilbert in 1582. Lost 1583.

SQUIRREL Yacht 4, 37bm. Chatham DY 10.12.1694. Sold 8.7.1714.

SQUIRREL 6th Rate 20, 258bm, 93 x 25 ft. Portsmouth DY 14.6.1703. Captured 21.9.1703 by two French privateers off Hythe, Kent.

SQUIRREL 6th Rate 20, 260bm, 93½ x 24½ ft. Portsmouth DY 28.10.1704. Captured 7.7.1706 by the French; recaptured 15.3.1708 as ECUREUIL and foundered.

SQUIRREL 6th Rate 24, 262bm, 94 x 26 ft. Stacey, Woolwich 29.12.1707. Rebuilt Woolwich 1727 as 377bm. Sold 17.10.1749.

SQUIRREL (see ALDERNEY of 1743)

SQUIRREL 6th Rate 20, 404bm, 107½ x 29 ft. Woolwich DY 23.10.1755. Sold 16.1.1783.

SQUIRREL 6th Rate 24, 563bm, 119 x 32½ ft. Barton, Liverpool 9.5.1785. Sold 6.3.1817 J.Cristall to BU.

SQUIRREL Brig-sloop 12, 428bm, 447 tons, 101½ x 32 ft. Pembroke Dock 8.8.1853. BU completed 11.2.1879 Devonport.

SQUIRREL Coastguard cutter, 40bm. Built 1866. Sold 4.4.1905 at Chatham.

SQUIRREL Coastguard vessel 230 tons, 103 x 21 ft, 2-3pdr. Workman Clark 21.12.1904. Cable vessel 1917. Sold 16.11.21., renamed *Vedra*.

SQUIRREL Minesweeper, 'Algerine' class. Harland & Wolff 20.4.1944. Scuttled 24.7.45 off Puket, Siam after mine damage.

SQUIRREL Fishery protection vessel. Name borne in succession by MFV.1151 (1.11.42), ML.2154 (1956), BURLEY (11.59).

STADTHOUSE Hulk, 440bm. Dutch ship STADHUIS van HAARLEM captured 1667. Sunk 28.10.1690 'to secure the graving place' at Sheerness.

STAFFORD (ex-STAITHES renamed 1918) Minesweeper, later 'Hunt' class. Rennoldson 20.9.18. Sold 26.6.28 Alloa S.Bkg Co.

STAG 5th Rate 32, 707bm, 125 x 36 ft. Stanton, Rotherhithe 4.9.1758. BU 7.1783.

STAG 5th Rate 32, 792bm, 135 x 36 ft. Chatham DY 28.6.1794. Wrecked 6.9.1800 in Vigo Bay.

STAG 5th Rate 36, 947bm, 145 x 38½ ft. Deptford DY 25.7.1812. BU 9.1821.

STAG 5th Rate 46, 1,218bm, 159½ x 42 ft. Pembroke Dock 2.10.1830 BU completed 8.8.1866 Marshall, Plymouth.

STAG Coastguard yawl, 120bm, 65 x 21 ft. Built 1861. Sold 1891.

STAG Destroyer 345 tons, 210 x 20 ft, 1-12pdr, 5-6pdr, 2-TT. Thornycroft 18.11.1899. Sold 17.3.1921 Ward Grays.

STAITHES (see STAFFORD)

STALKER (ex-USS HAMLIN) Escort carrier 11,420 tons, 468½ x 69½ ft, 2-4in, 8-40mm, 18-A/C. Western Pipe & Steel Co 5.3.1942 on lend-lease. Returned 29.12.45 to the USN.

STALKER (see LST.3515)

STALKER Trawler requis. 1915-19.

STALWART Destroyer, 'S' class. Swan Hunter 23.10.1918, RAN 6.19. Sold 4.6.37 at Sydney.

STALWART Repair ship (RAN) 14,500 tons. Cockatoo DY 7.10.1966.

STALWART Trawler 1917-19; Tug 1916-18; Tug 1939-41.

STANDARD 3rd Rate 64, 1,370bm, 159½ x 44½ ft. Deptford DY 8.10.1782. Harbour service 11.1799. BU 17.1816.

STANLEY (ex-USS McCALLA) Destroyer 1,190 tons, 311 x 31 ft, 1-4in, 1-3in, 4-20mm, 3-TT. Commissioned 23.10.40 in the RN. Sunk 19.12.41 by 'U.574' SW of Portugal.

STARR 16-gun ship, 130bm. Purchased 1643. Sold 1652.

STARR Fireship 4, 121bm. Purchased 1667. Expended 1667.

STARR Bomb 8, 117bm. Johnson, Blackwall 1694 and purchased 4.94. Wrecked 29.5.1712 in the W.Indies.

STAR Sloop 14. Purchased 1779. Sold circa 1785.

STAR Brig-sloop 18 (fir-built), 365bm, 96 x 30½ ft. Perry, Blackwall 29.8.1795. Sold 1.1802.

STARR Sloop 18, 371bm, 106 x 28 ft. Tanner, Dartmouth 26.7.1805. Renamed METEOR 1812, bomb. Sold 16.10.1816.

STAR (see MELVILLE of 1813)

STAR Tender, 41bm, 48 x 14 ft. Woolwich DY 1808. Sold 22.9.1828 Levy, Rochester to BU.

STAR Packet brig 8, 358bm, 95 x 30½ ft, 8-18pdr. Woolwich DY 29.4.1835. Coastguard watch vessel 9.1857; renamed WV.11 on 25.5.1863. BU circa 1899.

STAR Wood S.sloop, 695bm, 185 x 28½ ft, 2-pdr, 2-32pdr. Mare, Blackwall 15.12.1860. BU 1877 at Plymouth.

STAR Destroyer 360 tons, 215 x 20½ ft, 1-12pdr, 5-6pdr, 2-TT. Palmer 11.8.1896. Sold 10.6.1919 Ward, New Holland.

STARFISH Destroyer 310 tons, 195 x 20½ ft, 1-12pdr, 5-6pdr, 2-TT. NC & A (Vickers) 26.1.1895. Sold 14.5.1912 Ward, Preston.

STARFISH Destroyer, 'R' class. Hawthorn Leslie 27.9.1916. Sold 21.4.28 Alloa S.Bkg Co., Charlestown.

STARFISH Submarine 640 tons, 187 x 33½ ft, 1-3in, 6-TT. Chatham DY 14.3.1933. Sunk 9.1.40 by the German M/S M.7 in the Heligoland Bight.

STARLING Gun-brig 12, 184bm, 85 x 22 ft. Adams, Bucklers Hard 4.4.1801. Wrecked 18.12.1804 near Calais.

STARLING Gun-brig 12, 181bm, 84½ x 22 ft. Rowe, Newcastle 5.1805. Sold 29.9.1814.

STARLING Cutter 10, 151bm. Chatham DY 3.5.1817. BU 8.1828.

STARLING Schooner 4, 108bm, 61 x 20½ ft. Pembroke Dock 31.10.1829. Survey vessel 1834. Sold 2.1844 in China.

STARLING Wood S.gunboat, 'Dapper' class. Pitcher, Northfleet 1.2.1855. Sold 1.12.1871 at Hong Kong.

STARLING Compos. S.gunboat 465 tons, 125 x 23½ ft, 2-64pdr, 2-20pdr. Samuda, Poplar 19.4.1882. Sold 4.4.1905, renamed *Stella Maris*.

STARLING (ex-War Dept vessel *Miner 17*) Tender. Transferred 1905, renamed 26.11.06. Sold 14.9.23 T.Round, Sunderland.

STARLING Sloop 1,350 tons, 283 x 38½ ft, 6-4in. Fairfield 14.10.1942. Arrived 6.7.65 Lacmots, Queenborough.

STARLING Patrol vessel 690 tons. Hall Russell 7.9.1983

START BAY (ex-LOCH ARKLET renamed 1944) Frigate, 'Bay' class. Harland & Wolff 15.2.45. BU 7.58 Cashmore, Newport.

STARWORT Corvette, 'Flower' class. Inglis 12.2.1941. Sold 8.46, renamed *Southern Broom*.

STATELY 3rd Rate 64, 1,388bm, 160 x 44½ ft. Raymond, Northam 27.12.1784. Troopship 8.1.1799. BU 7.1814.

STATESMAN Submarine, 'S' class. Cammell Laird 14.9.1943. Lent French navy 1952 to 5.11.59 as SULTANE. Sold 3.1.61 Pounds, Portsmouth.

STATICE (ex-USS VIM) Corvette, modified 'Flower' class. Collingwood SY 10.4.1943 on lend-lease. Returned 21.6.46 to the USN.

STATIRA 5th Rate 38, 1,080bm, 154 x 40 ft. Guillaume Northam 7.7.1807. Wrecked 26.2.1815 coast of Cuba.

STATIRA 5th Rate 46, 1,218bm, 159 x 42½ ft. Plymouth DY. Laid down 12.1823, cancelled 31.8.1832.

STAUNCH (Gunboat No.44) Gunvessel 12. Rochester 1.5.1797 and purchased 1797. Sold 1803. in the W.Indies.

STAUNCH Gun-brig 12, 182bm, 80 x 23 ft. Tanner, Dartmouth 21.8.1804. Wrecked 6.1811 off Madagascar.

STAUNCH Wood S.gunboat, 'Albacore' class. Pitcher, Northfleet 31.1.1856. Sold 12.1866 at Hong Kong.

STAUNCH Iron S.gunboat, 200bm, 180 tons, 75 x 25 ft, 1-9in. Armstrong Mitchell 4.12.1867. Sold 1904.

STAUNCH Destroyer 748 tons, 240 x 25 ft, 2-4in, 2-12pdr, 2-TT. Denny 29.10.1910. Sunk 11.11.17 by 'UC.38' off the coast of Palestine.

STAUNCH Trawler 1940-44.

STAVERENS Gun-brig. Origin unknown. Sold 13.6.1811.

STAVOREEN 4th Rate 48, 544bm. Captured 1672. Sold 1682.

STAWELL Frigate (RAN), 'Bathurst' class. Williamstown DY 3.4.1943. To RNZN 5.52. Sold Pacific Scrap Ltd, Auckland in 9.68.

STAYNER Frigate, TE 'Captain class. Bethlehem, Hingham 6.11.1943 on lend-lease. Returned 11.45 to the USN.

STEADFAST Destroyer, 'S' class. Palmer 8.8.1918. Sold 28.7.34 Metal Industries, Charlestown.

STEADFAST Minesweeper, 'Catherine' class. Gulf SB Chickasaw 17.1.1943 on lend-lease. Returned 24.12.46 to the USN; sold Greek navy.

STEADFAST Mooring vessel 1916, STANDFAST 1917-22.

STEADY Storeship 14. Purchased 2.1782. Sold 25.3.1784.

STEADY (Gunboat No.19) Gunvessel 12, 168bm, 76 x 22½ ft, 2-24pdr, 10-18pdr carr. Hill, River Thames 24.4.1797. Sold circa 1802.

STEADY Gun-brig 12, 180bm, 85 x 22 ft. Richards, Hythe 21.7.1804. Sold 9.2.1815.

STEADY Wood S.gunvessel, 'Philomel' class. Miller, Liverpool 8.2.1860. Sold 12.5.1870 W & T.Joliffe.

STEADY (see M.VII of 1944)

STEADY Tug 1855-56; Mooring ves. 1916-40

STEDHAM Inshore M/S, 'Ham' class. Blackmore, Bideford 12.1.1955. To French navy 1955.

STELLARTON Corvette (RCN), modified 'Flower' class. Morton, Quebec 27.4.1944. Sold 1946 Chilian navy as CASMA.

STEPDANCE Minesweeper 265 tons, 130 x 26 ft, 1-6pdr. War Dept tug transferred and commissioned 4.1919. Sold 1.5.20 Crichton Thompson.

STERLET Submarine 670 tons, 193 x 24 ft, 1-3in, 6-TT. Chatham DY 22.9.1937. Sunk 18.4.40 by German trawler in the Skaggerack.

STERLING Gun-brig listed in Rupert Jones' and in James' as wrecked 18.12.1804 near Calais believed to be an error for STARLING (qv) also given by Rupert Jones, as wrecked 18.12.1804 near Calais.

STERLING Destroyer, 'S' class. Palmer 8.10.1918. Sold 25.8.32 Rees, Llanelly.

STETTLER Frigate (RCN), 'River' class. Vickers, Montreal 10.9.1943. Sold H&M Enterprises, Victoria B.C. in 8.67.

STEVENSTONE Destroyer, 'Hunt' class type III. White 23.11.1942. Arrived 2.9.59 Clayton & Davie, Dunston.

STING Cutter 10, 126bm, 73 x 20½ ft. Purchased 1800. Renamed PICKLE 1802. Wrecked 27.7.1808 off Cadiz.

STINGAREE Iron gunboat (Australian) 450 tons, 1-5in. Ex-hopper converted 1887. Listed 1895.

STIRLING CASTLE 3rd Rate 70, 1,059bm, 151 x 40½ ft. Deptford 1679. Rebuilt Chatham 1699 as 1,087bm. Wrecked 27.11.1703 on the Goodwins.

STIRLING CASTLE 3rd Rate 70, 1,122bm, 151 x 41 ft. Chatham DY 21.9.1705. Rebuilt Woolwich 1723 as 1,138bm; hulked 8.1739. BU completed 4.12.1771 at Sheerness.

STIRLING CASTLE 3rd Rate 70, 1,225bm, 151 x 43½ ft. Chatham DY 24.4.1742. Lost 1762 at Havana.

STIRLING CASTLE 3rd Rate 64, 1,374bm, 159 x 44½ ft. Chatham DY 28.6.1775. Wrecked 5.10.1780 in the W.Indies.

STIRLING CASTLE 3rd Rate 74, 1,774bm, 176½ x 48½ ft. Ross, Rochester 31.12.1811. Convict ship 4.1839. BU completed 6.9.1861.

STIRLING CASTLE Paddle vessel 1916.

STOAT (see WEAZEL of 1906)

STOCKHAM Frigate, TE 'Captain' class. Bethlehem, Hingham 31.10.1943 on lend-lease. Returned 2.46 to the USN.

STOIC Submarine, 'S' class. Cammell Laird 9.4.1943. Sold 7.50, BU at Dalmuir.

STOIC Tug 1915-20.

STOKE (ex-SOUTHEWOLD renamed 1918) Minesweeper, late 'Hunt' class. Rennoldson 8.7.1918. Sunk 7.5.41 by air attack at Tobruk.

STONECROP Corvette, 'Flower' class. Smiths Dk 12.5.1941. Sold 17.5.47, renamed *Silver King*.

STONEFLY River gunboat, 'Fly' class. Yarrow 9.1915. Sold 1.3.23 at Basra.

STONEFLY Trawler requis. 1939-45.

STONEHENGE Destroyer, 'S' class. Palmer 19.3.1919. Wrecked 1.11.20 near Smyrna: wreck sold 26.3.21.

STONEHENGE Submarine, 'S' class. Cammell Laird 23.3.1943. Sunk 3.44 by unknown cause off the Nicobar Is.

STONETOWN Frigate (RCN), 'River' class. Vickers, Montreal 28.3.1944. To Dept of Transport 1950 as weather ship. Sold at Vancouver in 1969.

STONEWALL JACKSON Monitor 1915 (see ROBERTS).

STORK 36-gun ship, 397bm. Dutch, captured 1652. Hulk 1653. Sold 1663.

STORK Sloop 10, 233bm, 88½ x 24½ ft. Stowe, Shoreham 8.11.1756. Captured 16.8.1758 by the Spanish in the W.Indies.

STORK Sloop 18, 427bm, 108 x 30 ft. Deptford DY 29.11.1796. Sold 30.5.1816.

STORK Wood S.gunboat, 'Dapper' class. Pitcher, Northfleet 7.4.1855. Coal hulk 1874. Sold 4.1884 to BU.

STORK Compos. S.gunboat 465 tons, 125 x 23½ ft, 2-64pdr, 2-20pdr. Samuda, Poplar 18.5.1882. Survey ship 1887; lent 3.1913 as training ship. BU 1950 by Shaws of Kent, Lower Rainham; hull used as wharf.

STORK Destroyer, 'R' class. Hawthorn Leslie 15.11.1916. Sold 7.10.27 Cashmore, Newport.

STORK Survey vessel (sloop) 1,190 tons, 266 x 37 ft, 103pdr. Denny 21.4.1936. Escort 1939. 4-4.7in. Arrived 6.58 at Troon to BU.

STORK Store carrier requis. 1914-15; Tug 1917-19.

STORM Submarine, 'S' class. Cammell Laird 18.5.1943. BU 11.49 at Troon.

STORMCLOUD Destroyer, 'S' class. Palmer 30.5.1919. Sold 28.7.34 Metal Industries, Charlestown.

STORMCLOUD Minesweeper, 'Algerine' class. Lobnitz 28.12.1943. Arrived 2.8.59 King, Gateshead to BU.

STORMONT Brig-sloop 16, Circa 175bm, 80 x 23½ ft. Purchased 1781. Captured 23.1.1782 by the French at the surrender of Demerara; renamed STORMON to 1786.

STORMONT Sloop. American privateer captured 14.2.1782 by PROTHEE. Sold 1.7.1784.

STORMONT Frigate (RCN), 'River' class. Vickers Montreal 14.7.1943. Sold 1947 mercantile; became yacht *Christina* 1951.

STORMONT (see MATANE)

STORMY PETREL Paddle M/S. Murdoch & Murray. Cancelled 10.1918.

STORNOWAY Minesweeper, TE 'Bangor' class. Robb 10.6.1941. Sold 11.9.46 mercantile.

STOUR Destroyer 570 tons, 220 x 24 ft, 4-12pdr, 2-TT. Laird 3.6.1905 as a speculation; purchased 12.09. Sold 30.8.19 J.Smith.

STOUR Trawler 1920-46 (was PEMBROKE 1922-39)

STRAFFORD 4th Rate 50, 703bm, 130½ x 35 ft. Plymouth DY 16.7.1714. BU 1733.

STRAFFORD 4th Rate 50, 1,067bm, 144 x 41½ ft. Chatham DY 24.7.1735. Sunk 1756 as breakwater Sheerness.

STRAHAN Minesweeper (RAN), 'Bathurst' class. Newcastle DY. NSW 12.7.1943. Sold 6.1.61 to BU in Japan.

STRANRAER (see CLONMEL)

STRATAGEM Submarine, 'S' class. Cammell Laird 21.6.1943. Sunk 22.11.44 by Japanese patrol craft off Malacca.

STRATFORD Minesweeper (RCN), TE 'Bangor' class. Dufferin 14.2.1942. Disposal list 1946.

STRATHADAM Frigate (RCN), 'River' class. Yarrow, Esquimalt 20.3.1944. Sold 1947 mercantile; renamed MISGAV, Israeli navy; renamed GAJABAHU, Ceylon navy.

STRATHROY Corvette (RCN), modified 'Flower' class. Midland SY, Ont 30.8.1944. Sold 1946 Chilian navy, renamed CHIPANO.

STRATTON Coastal M/S, 'Ton' class. Dorset Yt Co 29.7.1957. Renamed KIMBERLEY 1958, S.African navy.

STRENUOUS Gun-brig 12, 180bm, 84 x 22 ft, 10-18pdr carr., 2-12pdr. Row, Newcastle 16.5.1805. Sold 1.9.1814.

STRENUOUS Destroyer, 'S' class. Scotts 9.11.1918. Sold 25.8.32, Metal Ind. Charlestown.

STRENUOUS (see CARRON of 1942)

STRENUOUS (ex-USS VITAL) Minesweeper, 'Catherine' class. Gulf SB, Madisonville 7.9.1942 and transferred 5.43 on lend-lease. Nominally returned 12.46 to the USN. Laid up at Woolston to 4.56 and BU 7.56 in Germany.

STRENUOUS Tug 1912, ren. SANDBOY 1918-47; 2 Trawlers & Drifter WW.I.

STRIKER (ex-USS PRINCE WILLIAM) Escort carrier 11,420 tons, 468½ x 69½ ft, 2-4in, 8-40mm, 18-A/C. Weston Pipe & Steel Co 7.5.1942 on lend-lease. Returned 2.46 to the USN.

STRIKER (see LST.3516)

STRIKER Training boat 34 tons. Fairey Marine 1983.

STROMBOLI Wood pad. sloop, 967bm, 180 x 34½ ft. Portsmouth DY 27.8.1839. Sold 8.1866.

STROMBOLO Fireship 8, 266bm, 91½ x 25½ ft. Johnson, Blackwall 7.3.1691. Rebuilt 1704. Sold 20.8.1713.

STROMBOLO (ex-*Mollineaux*) Fireship 8, 217bm, 88 x 24 ft. Purchased 7.9.1739. Sold 9.2.1743.

STROMBOLO (ex-*Owners Goodwill*) Fireship 8, 268bm, 93 x 26 ft. Purchased 31.12.1756. Sold 26.4.1768.

STROMBOLO (see GRAMPUS of 1746)

STROMBOLI Bomb (Indian), 68bm, Bombay DY 1793. Fate unknown.

STROMBOLO (ex-*Leander*) Bomb 8, 371bm, 100 x 29 ft. Purchased 4.1797. BU 7.1809.

STROMBOLO (see AUTUMN of 1801)

STRONGBOW Destroyer, 'M' class 898 tons. Yarrow 30.9.1916. Sunk 17.10.17 in action with two German cruisers in the North Sea.

STRONGBOW Submarine, 'S' class. Scotts 30.8.1943. BU 4.46 Ward, Preston.

STRONGHOLD Destroyer. 'S' class. Scotts 6.5.1919. Sunk 4.3.42 in action with a Japanese squadron 300 miles south of Java.

STRULE (see GLENARM)

STUART Destroyer leader 1,800 tons, 320 x 32 ft, 5-4.7in, 1-3in, 6-TT. Hawthorn Leslie 22.8.1918. RAN 10.33; fast store carrier 1944. Sold 2.47 T.Carr & Co.

STUART Frigate (RAN) 2,150 tons, 360 x 41 ft, 2-4.5in, 4-GWS. Cockatoo DY 8.4.1961.

STUBBINGTON Coastal M/S, 'Ton' class. Camper & Nicholson 8.8.1956.

STUBBORN (ex-P.238) Submarine, 'S' class. Cammell Laird 11.11.1942.

Sunk 30.4.46 as Asdic target off Malta.

STURDY Destroyer, 'S' class. Scotts 25.6.1919. Wrecked 30.10.40 on Tiree Island, W.Scotland.

STURDY Submarine, 'S' class. Cammell Laird 30.9.1943. Sold 7.57 at Malta; arrived 9.5.58 Clayton & Davie to BU.

STURDY Tug 1912, ren.SWARTHY 1917-61.

STURGEON Destroyer 310 tons, 195 x 20½ ft, 1-2pdr, 5-6pdr, 2-TT. N.C & A(Vickers) 21.7.1894. Sold 14.5.1912 Thames S.Bkg Co.

STURGEON Destroyer, 'R' class. Stephen 11.1.1917. Sold 16.12.26 Plymouth & Devon S.Bkg Co.

STURGEON Submarine 640 tons, 187 x 23½ ft, 1-3in, 6-TT. Chatham DY 8.1.1932. Lent Dutch navy 11.10.43 to 14.9.45 as ZEEHOND. BU 1.46. at Granton.

STYGIAN Submarine, 'S' class. Cammell Laird 30.11.1943. Sold 28.10.49, BU at Ardgour by Metal Ind, in 8.50.

STYX Wood pad. sloop, 1,057bm, 180 x 36 ft. Sheerness DY 26.1.1841. BU 4.1866.

STYX Minesweeper, 'Algerine' class. Collingwood SY. Laid down 18.7.1944, cancelled 8.11.44.

STYX Whaler 1915-19.

SUBSTITUTE Cutter. Purchased 1782. Sold 14.8.1783.

SUBTLE (also RED GALLEY) Galley 31, 200bm. Listed 1544 to 1560.

SUBTLE (see VIGILANT of 1806)

SUBTLE Schooner 12, 125bm. Purchased 1808. Foundered 30.11.1812 off St Barts, W.Indies.

SUBTLE Submarine, 'S' class. Cammell Laird 27.1.1944. BU 7.59 at Charlestown.

SUCCESS 34-gun ship, 450bm. French JULES captured 19.10.1950. Sold 1662. (Known as OLD SUCCESS from 1660.)

SUCCESS (see BRADFORD of 1958)

SUCCESS Fireship 6, 127bm. Purchased 1672. Foundered 1673.

SUCCESS Store hulk, 524bm. Purchased 20.8.1692. Sunk 13.1.1707 as a breakwater at Sheerness.

SUCCESS Sloop 10, 110bm. Purchased 6.1709. Captured 11.4.1710 by the French off Lisbon.

SUCCESS Storeship 24, 546bm, 126½ x 31 ft. Deptford DY 10.9.1709. Hulked 2.1730. Sold 6.12.1748.

SUCCESS 6th Rate 20, 275bm, 94½ x 26 ft. Portsmouth DY 30.4.1712.

Fireship 1739. Sold 22.7.1743.

SUCCESS Sloop 14 (Indian). Bombay DY 1736. Fate unknown.

SUCCESS 6th Rate 24, 436bm, 106 x 30½ ft. Blaydes, Hull 14.8.1740. BU 1779.

SUCCESS Ketch 14 (Indian) Bombay DY 1754. Fate unknown.

SUCCESS 5th Rate 32, 683bm, 126 x 35 ft. Sutton, Liverpool 10.4.1781. Convict ship 1.1814. BU 1820 at Halifax NS.

SUCCESS Gunvessel 3. Ex-barge purchased 9.1797. Sold 1.1802.

SUCCESS 6th Rate 28, 504bm, 114 x 32 ft, 20-32pdr, 6-18pdr carr., 2-6pdr. Pembroke Dock 30.8.1825. Harbour service 1832. BU 6.1849.

SUCCESS Wood S.sloop, 950bm, 185 x 33 ft, 1-110pdr, 5-64pdr. Pembroke Dock. Not laid down; cancelled 12.1863.

SUCCESS Destroyer 385 tons, 210 x 21 ft, 1-12pdr, 5-6pdr, 2-TT. Doxford 21.3.1901. Wrecked 27.12.14 near Fifeness.

SUCCESS Destroyer, 'S' class. Doxford 29.6.1918. RAN 6.19. Sold 4.6.37 at Sydney.

SUCCESS Destroyer 1,710 tons, 339½ x 36 ft, 4-4.7in, 2-40mm, 8-TT. White 3.4.1943. To R.Norwegian navy 8.43 as STORD.

SUCCESS Supply ship (RAN) 17,930 tons (deep) Cockatoo DY 3.3.1984

SUDBURY Corvette (RCN), 'Flower' class. Kingston 31.5.1941. Sold 1949 Badwater Towing Co as tug, same name.

SUFFISANTE Brig-sloop 14, 236bm, 86 x 29 ft. French, captured 31.8.1795 by the fleet in the Texel. Wrecked 15.12.1803 off Queenstown.

SUFFISANTE Brig-sloop 16, 358bm. French VIGILANTE captured 30.6.1803 at San Domingo, renamed 12.03. Sold 6.1807.

SUFFOLK 3rd Rate 70, 1,401bm, 151 x 40 ft. Johnson, Blackwall 1680. Rebuilt Blackwall 1699 as 1,075bm; rebuilt Woolwich 1739 as 1,224bm, 64 guns. BU completed 12.6.1765.

SUFFOLK (also SUFFOLK HAGBOAT) Storeship 30, 477bm, 177 x 30½ ft. Purchased 7.1694. Sold 15.12.1713.

SUFFOLK 3rd Rate 74, 1,616bm, 168 x 47 ft. Randall, Rotherhithe 22.2.1765. BU 2.1803.

SUFFOLK (see SULTAN of 1775)

SUFFOLK Armoured cruiser 9,800 tons, 440 x 66 ft, 14-6in, 10-12pdr. Portsmouth DY 15.1.1903. Sold

1.7.20 S.Castle; BU in Germany 1922.

SUFFOLK Cruiser 9,800 tons, 590 x 68 ft, 8-8in, 8-4in. Portsmouth DY 16.2.1926. Sold 25.3.48, BU Cashmore, Newport.

SUIPPE Sloop 604 tons, 250 x 28½ ft, 4-3.9in. French, seized 3.7.1940 at Falmouth; not commissioned. Sunk 14.4.41 by air attack at Falmouth; raised and BU.

SULHAM Inshore M/S, 'Ham' class. Fairlie Yt Co 24.3.1955. To French navy 1955.

SULINA (ex-*Panscova*) Iron paddle vessel. Purchased 19.8.1854 at Constantinople. Sold 8.1856.

SULLINGTON Coastal M/S, 'Ton' class. Doig, Grimsby 7.4.1954. Renamed MERMAID 4.65, survey vessel. Sold A.K.Vickers 5.9.70, BU at Fleetwood.

SULPHUR Fireship 8. Purchased 7.1778 in N.America. Sold 4.4.1783.

SULPHUR (ex-*Severn*) Bomb 8, 355bm, 97 x 29 ft. Purchased 4.1797. Sold 10.6.1816.

SULPHUR Bomb 10, 375bm, 105½ x 28 ft, 10-24pdr carr., 2-3pdr, 2-mortars. Chatham DY 26.1.1826. Survey vessel 1835 harbour service 1843. BU completed 20.11.1857. (The last bomb vessel in the Navy List.)

SULTAN 3rd Rate 74, 1,614bm, 168½ x 47 ft. Barnard, Harwich 23.12.1775. Prison ship 2.1797. Renamed SUFFOLK 1805. BU 1.1816.

SULTAN 3rd Rate 74, 1,751bm, 175 x 48½ ft. Dudman, Deptford 19.9.1807. Receiving ship 1860 then target. BU completed 28.1.1864.

SULTAN Battleship, 5,234bm, 9,290 tons, 325 x 59 ft, 8-10in, 4-9in. Chatham DY 31.5.1870. Renamed FISGARD IV 1.1.1906; reverted to SULTAN 1932, training hulk. Sold 13.8.46, arrived 8.10.46 at Dalmuir to BU.

SULTAN HISAR Destroyer 1,360 tons. Denny 1941 for the Turkish navy. Commissioned 12.41 in the RN for the passage to Turkey; handed over to Turkey 1942.

SULTAN Schooner 536bm. Purchased 18.3.1768 Sold 11.8.1773

SUMMERSIDE Corvette (RCN), 'Flower' class. Morton 7.5.1941. BU 6.46 Steel Co of Canada.

SONNE Galley 8, 50bm. Listed 1546-62.

SONNE Pinnace 5, 40bm, 1-9pdr, 4-2pdr Chatham 1586. Listed to 1599. (The first RN vessel built at Chatham.)

SUNN 12-gun ship. Captured 1651. Sold 1654.

SUNN PRIZE 6th Rate 24, 214bm, 81 x 24 ft. French, captured 8.1692 by SUNN. Sold 1701. (In French hands 6.93-96.)

SUNN PRIZE 6th Rate 22, 215bm, 83 x 24 ft. French, captured 4.7.1704 by LICHFIELD. Recaptured 18.1.1708 by a French privateer off the Needles.

SUN Tugs Sun II, III, IV, requis WW.I; III, V, VI, VII, VIII, IX, X, XIII in WW.II

SUNDERLAND 4th Rate 60, 915bm, 145 x 38 ft. Winter, Southampton 17.3.1694. Hulked 1715. Sunk 1737 as a foundation at Sheerness.

SUNDERLAND 4th Rate 60, 951bm, 144 x 39ft. Chatham DY 30.4.1724. Rebuilt Portsmouth 1744 as 1,123bm. Foundered 1.1.1761 in a cyclone off Pondicherry.

SUNDERLAND (see LYME REGIS of 1942).

SUNDERLAND Tug requis. 1915-19.

SUNDEW Corvette, 'Flower' class. Lewis 28.5.1941. Lent Free-French 1942-6.47 as ROSELYS. Sold 23.10.47; arrived 5.48 at Troon to BU.

SUNFISH Destroyer 315 tons, 200 x 19 ft, 1-12pdr, 5-6pdr, 2-TT. Hawthorn 23.5.1895. Sold 7.6.1920 J.Kelly.

SUNFISH Submarine 670 tons, 193 x 24ft, 1-3in, 6-TT. Chatham DY 30.9.1936. Lent Russian navy 1944 as B.1; sunk in error 27.7.44 by British aircraft while on passage to North Russia.

SUNFLOWER Sloop, 'Acacia' class. Henderson 28.5.1915. Sold 27.1.21 Rangoon Port Commissioners, renamed *Lanbya*.

SUNFLOWER Corvette, 'Flower' class. Smiths Dk 19.8.1940. BU 8.47 Ward, Hayle.

SUNSTAR M/S sloop, '24' class. Swan Hunter. Cancelled 3.12.1918, sold incomplete 29.11.22 Hallamshire Metal Co.

SUPERB 3rd Rate 64, 1,029bm, 143½ x 40 ft. French SUPERBE captured 29.7.1710 by KENT off the Lizard. BU 1732.

SUPERB 4th Rate 60, 1,068bm, 144 x 41½ ft. Woolwich DY 1736 BU 7.1757 at Sheerness.

SUPERB 3rd Rate 74 1,612bm, 168 x 47 ft. Deptford DY 27.10.1760. Wrecked 5.11.1783 off Tellicherry, India.

SUPERBE 6th Rate 22, 619bm, 120 x 35 ft. French, captured 10.10.1795 by

VANGUARD in the W.Indies. Prison ship at Martinique 1796. Sold 1798.

SUPERB 3rd Rate 74, 1,919bm, 182 x 49 ft. Pitcher, Northfleet 19.3.1798. BU completed 17.4.1826.

SUPERB 2nd Rate 80, 2,583bm, 190 x 57 ft, 12-8in, 68-32pdr. Pembroke Dock 6.9.18.42. BU completed 18.2.1869 at Portsmouth.

SUPERB (see ALEXANDRA)

SUPERB (ex-Turkish HAMIDIYEH purchased 20.2.1878) Battleship 9,310 tons, 332 x 59 ft, 16-10in, 6-4in, 6-6pdr. Thames Iron Works 16.11.1875. Sold 15.5.1906 Garnham.

SUPERB Battleship 18,600 tons, 490 x 82½ ft, 10-12in, 16-4in. Armstrong 7.11.1907. Sold 12.12.22 Stanlee, Dover.

SUPERB Cruiser 8,800 tons, 538 x 64 ft, 9-6in, 10-4in. Swan Hunter 31.8.1943. Arrived 8.8.60 Arnott Young, Dalmuir and Troon to BU.

SUPERB Nuclear s/m 3,800 tons. Vickers 30.11.1974

SUPERB Drifter requis. 1917-18

SUPERIERE Schooner 14, 197bm, 86½ x 23½ ft, 12-18pdr carr., 2-12pdr. French, captured 30.6.1803 off San Domingo. Sold 16.3.1814 Ledger to BU.

SUPERLATIVA Galley 7, 100bm. Deptford 1601. Sold 1629.

SUPPLY Fireship 6, 230bm. Purchased 1672. Expended 1673.

SUPPLY Fireship 9, 130bm. Purchased 1688. Fate unknown.

SUPPLY A.tender 4, 175bm, 79½ x 22½ ft. Bird, River Thames 1759. Sold 17.7.1792.

SUPPLY (ex-*Prince of Wales*) Storeship 26, 512bm. Purchased 10.1777. Burnt 14.6.1779 by accident at St. Kitts.

SUPPLY Storeship 20, 491bm, 115 x 31 ft. Purchased 12.1781. Sold 25.3.1784.

SUPPLY (ex-New Brunswick) Storeship 10 (birch-built), 388bm, 97½ x 20½ ft. Purchased 10.1793. BU 1806 in N.S.W.

SUPPLY Transport, 222bm, 86 x 24½ ft. Pitcher, Northfleet 2.7.1798. BU 10.1834.

SUPPLY Iron S.storeship, 638bm, 1,100 tons. Purchased on stocks 4.1854. Ditchburn & Mare, Blackwall 3.6.1854. BU completed 8.2.1879 at Chatham.

SUPPLY DY craft 1725. Tank vessel 1881-1908; Tank ves 1910-47.

SUPREME Submarine, 'S'class. Cammell Laird 24.2.1944. Sold 7.50, BU at Troon.

SURCOUF Submarine 2,880 tons, 361 x29½ ft, 2-8in, 2-37mm, 10-TT French, seized 3.7.40 at Plymouth. Free-French 8.40; sunk in error 18.2.42 by SS *Thomson Likes* in the Caribbean.

SURF (ex-P.239) Submarine, 'S' class. Cammell Laird 10.12.1942. Sold 28.10.49, BU at Faslane; arrived in 7.50

SURF Yacht requis. 1915-19

SURFACE Submarine, 'S' class. Cammell Laird. Cancelled 1945.

SURGE Submarine, 'S' class. Cammell Laird. Cancelled 1945.

SURGE Drifter 1918 and whaler 1944-45.

SURINAM Sloop 18, 414bm, 20-4pdr. French HUSSARD captured 20.4.1799 at Surinam. Captured 7.1803 by the Dutch at Curacao; recaptured 1.1.1807 and re-added 1808. Listed to 1809.

SURINAM Sloop 16. Dutch PYLADES captured 4.5.1804 at Surinam. Listed to 1808.

SURINAM Sloop 18, 'Cruiser' class, 384bm. Ayles, Topsham 1.1805. Sold 20.7.1825 Ledger to BU.

SURLY Cutter 10, 137bm, 63 x23½ ft. Johnson, Dover 15.11.1806. DY lighter 2.1833. Sold 1.1837.

SURLY Mortar vessel, 117bm, 65 x 21 ft, 1-13in mortar. Wigram, Blackwall 31.3.1855. Renamed MV.9 on 19.10.1855. BU 11.1863.

SURLY Wood S.gunboat, 'Albacore' class. Smith, N.Shields 18.3.1856. Sold 1869 T.Begbie.

SURLY Destroyer 310 tons, 205 x 19 ft, 1-12pdr, 5-6pdr, 2-TT. Thomson 10.11.1894. Sold 23.3.1920 Ward, Milford Haven.

SURPRISE (see under SURPRIZE)

SURPRIZE 6th Rate 24, 508bm, 112½ x 32 ft. Wyatt & Major, Beaulieu 27.1.1745. BU 7.1770.

SURPRIZE 6th Rate 28, 594bm, 120½ x 33½ ft. Woolwich DY 13.4.1774. Sold 17.4.1783.

SURPRIZE Sloop 18.American BUNKER HILL captured 1778 at St Lucia. Sold 1783 at Sheerness.

SURPRIZE Cutter 10, 135bm, 67½ x 29 ft, 10-3pdr. Purchased 2.1780. Sold 30.10.1786.

SURPRIZE Cutter 10, 130bm, 69 x 22½ ft, 10-3pdr. Purchased 10.1786. Sold 2.10.1792 at Sheerness.

SURPRISE 6th Rate 24, 579bm, 24-32pdr carr., 8-18pdr carr., 4-6pdr.

French UNITE captured 20.4.1796 by INCONSTANT in the Mediterranean. Sold 2.1802 at Deptford.

SURPRISE Schooner 10. French merchant *Surprise* captured 1799 by BRAAVE in the E.Indies. Sold 1800.

SURPRISE 5th Rate 38, 1,072bm, 150½ x 40 ft. Milford DY (ex-Jacobs) 25.7.1812. Convict ship 6.1822. Ordered to be sold 2.10.1837.

SURPRISE Schooner 2 (Canadian lakes), 74bm, 57 x 17½ ft, 1-24pdr, 1-24pdr carr. American TIGRESS captured 3.9.1814 on Lake Erie. Listed to 1832.

SURPRISE Wood S.gunvessel, 680bm, 181 x 28½ ft, 1-110pdr, 1-68 pdr, 2-20pdr. Wigram, Blackwall 6.3.1856. BU 11.1866 Marshall, Plymouth.

SURPRISE Despatch vessel, 1,650 tons, 250 x 32½ ft, 4-5in 4-6pdr. Palmer 17.1.1885. Renamed ALACRITY 1913. Sold 1919.

SURPRISE Destroyer, 'M' class 910 tons. Yarrow 25.11.1916. Sunk 23.12.17 by mine in the North Sea.

SURPRISE (see GERRANS BAY)

SURPRISE Yacht 1918-23 and 1939-42.

SURREY Cruiser 10,000 tons, 590 x 66 ft, 8-8in. PortsmouthDY. Cancelled 1.1.1930.

SURVEILLANTE 5th Rate 36, 1,094bm. French, captured 30.11.1803 by a squadron in the W.Indies. BU 8.1814.

SURVEYOR Schooner 6. American, captured 12.6.1813 by boats of NARCISSUS. Gone by 1814.

SUSSEX 46-gun ship, 600bm. Portsmouth DY 1652. Blown up 12.1653 by accident.

SUSSEX 3rd Rate 80, 1,203bm, 157 x 41½ ft. Chatham DY 11.4.1693. Wrecked 19.2.1694 near Gibraltar.

SUSSEX (see Union of 1756)

SUSSEX Cruiser 9,830 tons, 595 x 66 ft, 8-8in, 8-4in. Hawthorn Leslie 22.2.1928. Sold 3.1.50; arrived 23.2.50 Dalmuir and 7.50 Troon.

SUSSEXVALE (ex-VALDORIAN renamed 1944) Frigate (RCN), 'River' class. Davie SB 12.7.1944. Sold Kennedy & Mitsui, Vancouver 12.66 to BU.

SUTHERLAND (see RESERVE of 1704)

SUTHERLAND 4th Rate 50, 874bm, 134 x 38½ ft. Taylor, Rotherhithe 15.10.1741. Sold 5.6.1770.

SUTLEJ 4th Rate 50, 2,066bm, 180 x 51 ft, 28-8in, 22-32pdr. Pembroke Dock 17.4.1855. Undocked 26.3.1860 as screw frigate, 3,066bm. BU 1869 at Portsmouth.

SUTLEJ Armoured cruiser 12,000 tons, 440 x 69½ ft, 2-9.2in, 12-6in, 12-12pdr. J.Brown 18.11.1899. Sold 9.5.21 Ward and laid up at Belfast; arrived 15.8.24 at Preston to BU.

SUTLEJ Sloop (RIN) 1,250 tons, 283 x 37½ ft, 6-4in. Denny 1.10.1940.

SUTTON (ex-SALCOMBE renamed 1918) Minesweeper, later 'Hunt' class. McMillan, Dumbarton 8.5.1918. Sold Dohmen & Habets 7.47 to BU.

SUVLA (see LST.3518)

SVENNER (see SHARK of 1943)

SWAGGERER Brig 16, 300bm. French privateer BONAPARTE captured 1809. BU 1815.

SWALE Destroyer 550 tons, 222 x 23½ ft, 1-12pdr, 5-6pdr (4-12pdr 1907), 2-TT. Palmer 20.3.1905. Sold 23.6.19 Ward, Preston.

SWALE Frigate, 'River' class. Smiths Dk 16.1.1942. Arrived 4.3.55 at Faslane to BU.

SWALLOW (see MARY FORTUNE)

SWALLOW 53-gun ship, 240bm. Built 1544. Rebuilt 1558 as 300bm; rebuilt 1580 as 415bm, 40 guns. Sold 1603.

SWALLOW Discovery vessel, 100bm. With Borrough in the Arctic 1558. Captured 1568 by the Spanish.

SWALLOW Pinnace 8, 2-4pdr, 1-2pdr, 5 smaller. Built 1573. Condemned 1603.

SWALLOW 40-ton vessel. With Sir H. Gilbert in Newfoundland 1583.

SWALLOW 40-gun ship, 478bm. Deptford 1634. Royalist navy from 1648. Sold 1653 in France.

SWALLOW Ketch 6, 56bm. Deptford 1657. To Irish packet service 1661.

SWALLOW (see GAINSBOROUGH of 1653)

SWALLOW KETCH Ketch 6, 54bm. Purchased 1661. Sold 1674.

SWALLOW Sloop 2, 68bm. Deptford 1672. Lost 1673.

SWALLOW PRIZE 6th Rate 18, 119bm, 68 x 20½ ft. French, captured 1693. Recaptured 22.2.1696 by a French privateer off Weymouth.

SWALLOW Sloop 6, 66bm. Chatham DY 30.9.1699. Captured 19.4.1703 by a French privateer off the Maes.

SWALLOW 4th Rate 54, 672bm, 130 x 34½ ft. Deptford 2.1703. Rebuilt Chatham 1719 as 710bm. BU 1728.

SWALLOW PRIZE 5th Rate 32. French, captured 3.1704 by SWALLOW. Wrecked 29.7.1711 off Corsica.

SWALLOW 4th Rate 60, 951bm, 144 x 39 ft. Plymouth DY 6.10.1732. Renamed **PRINCESS LOUISA** 16.1.1737. BU 1742.

SWALLOW see GALGO

SWALLOW Sloop 14, 278bm, 92 x 26½ ft. Bird, Rotherhithe 14.12.1745. Impress service in 1762. Sold 20.6.1769.

SWALLOW Discovery vessel. With Carteret in the Pacific 1766. BU 1769.

SWALLOW Sloop 14, 302bm, 96 x 27 ft. Deptford DY 30.12.1769. Foundered 12.1777 in the Atlantic.

SWALLOW Ketch 14 (Indian). Bombay DY 1770. Lost 1776.

SWALLOW Packet 14 (Indian), 200bm. Bombay DY 2.4.1777. Sold 1780 to the Danish navy; captured 1782 by the RN and reported as renamed SILLY (not traced). Sold 1784 mercantile.

SWALLOW Sloop 14, 226bm, 79½ x 26½ ft. Ladd, Dover 2.4.1779. Driven ashore 26.8.1781 near Long Island by four American privateers.

SWALLOW Sloop 16, 262bm, 78 x 29 ft. Ex-cutter purchased on stocks; Fabian E.Cowes 10.1781. Sold 20.8.1795.

SWALLOW Tender. In service 1793-95.

SWALLOW Brig-sloop 18 (fir-built), 365bm, 96 x 30½ ft. Perry, Blackwall 10.9.1795. Sold 8.1802.

SWALLOW Brig-sloop 18, 'Cruizer' class, 387bm. Tanner, Dartmouth 24.12.1805. BU 11.1815.

SWALLOW Cutter tender, 46bm, 45 x 16ft. Deptford 1811. Lost 1825.

SWALLOW (ex-packet *Marquis of Salisbury*) Brig-sloop 10, 236bm. Purchased 7.1824. Sold 8.9.1836.

SWALLOW (ex-GPO vessel *Ferret*) Wood pad. packet, 133bm. Transferred 1.4.1837. BU 3.1848.

SWALLOW Wood S.sloop, 486bm, 139 x 28 ft, 9-32pdr. Pembroke Dock 12.6.1854. Sold 12.1866.

SWALLOW Wood S.gunvessel, 664bm, 805 tons, 170 x 29ft, 1-7in, 2-40pdr. Portsmouth DY 16.11.1868. Sold 18.10.1882 A.Tobin.

SWALLOW Compos. S.sloop 1,130 tons, 195 x 28 ft 8-5in. Sheerness DY 27.10.1885. Sold 1904 McCausland & Sons.

SWALLOW Destroyer, 'S' class. Scotts 1.8.1918. Handed over 24.9.36 to Ward in part payent for *Majestic*; BU at Inverkeithing.

SWALLOW (see CAPRICE)

SWALLOW Patrol vessel 690 tons, Hall Russell 30.3.1984

SWALLOW Tug 1906; 3 trawlers 1914. One drifter 1915. Note that this name has been borne by 39 naval vessels, one DY craft, two of the Hon.E.I.Co and at least two revenue cutters.)

SWANN Ballinger, 120bm. Acquired in 3.1417. Sold 1.4.1423.

SWANN 25-ton vessel. With Drake in 1572.

SWANN Flyboat, 50bm. With Drake in 1577. Lost 1578.

SWANN 'Frigat', 60bm. Listed 1632-33.

SWANN PRIZE Spanish 'Dunkirker' captured 1636. Sunk 10.1638 off Guernsey.

SWANN 22-gun ship, 200bm. Captured 1652. Sold 1654.

SWANN Flyboat 6, 162bm. Dutch, captured 1665. Sold 1666.

SWANN Smack, 24bm. Deane, Harwich 1666. Captured 1673 by the Dutch.

SWANN Fireship 2, 71bm. Purchased 1667. Expended 1667.

SWANN 5th Rate 32, 246bm, 85 x 26 ft. Dutch, captured 1673. Fireship 10 guns 1688-89. Wrecked 15.6.1692 during an earthquake in Jamaica.

SWANN 6th Rate. Algerian, captured 1684. Sold 1684.

SWANN 6th Rate 24, 249bm, 93½ x 24½ ft. Castle, Deptford 1694. Foundered 17.8.1707.

SWANN 6th Rate 12, 162bm, 78½ x 22ft. Dummer, Rotherhithe 17.9.1709. Sold 8.1.1713.

SWAN Sloop 14, 280bm, 91 x 26½ ft. Hinck, Chester 14.12.1745. Sold 31.3.1763.

SWAN Sloop 14, 302bm, 96½ x 27 ft. Plymouth DY 21.11.1767. Sold 1.9.1814. (Bore the name EXPLOSION 10.1779 to 1783 while in use as a fireship.)

SWAN (see BONETTA of 1781)

SWAN Cutter 10, 90bm, 10-6pdr. Purchased 1788 for Revenue service and transferred RN 1790. Wrecked 26.5.1792 off Shoreham.

SWAN Cutter 10. Purchased 1792 for Revenue service and transferred RN 1795. Captured 1795 by the French.

SWAN Cutter 10, 144bm, 65½ x 23 ft, 10-12pdr carr. Cowes 1.11.1811. Lent 5.1844 to Church Mission Socy. BU completed 7.12.1874 at Sheerness.

SWAN Wood S.gunboat, 'Albacore' class. Smith, N. Shields 12.4.1856. Coal hulk 1869. Sold 1906.

SWAN Destroyer (RAN) 700 tons, 246 x 24 f, 1-4in, 3-12pdr, 3-TT. Cockatoo DY 11.12.1915. Stripped in 9.29;

hulk foundered 2.2.34 in Hawkesbury River.

SWAN Sloop (RAN) 1,060 tons, 250 x 36 ft, 3-4in. Cockatoo DY 28.3.1936. Training ship in 1956. Sold 5.6.64 Hurley & Dewhurst, Sydney.

SWAN Frigate (RAN) 2,150 tons, 360 x 41 ft, 2-4.5in, 5-GWS. Williamstown DY 16.12.1967.

SWANSEA Frigate (RCN), 'River' class. Yarrow, Esquimalt 19.12.1942. Sold Marine Salvage 16.8.67, BU at Savone, Italy.

SWANSTON Coastal M/S, 'Ton' class. Doig, Grimsby 1.7.1954. Renamed GULL (RAN) 19.7.62. Sold in 1.76.

SWASHWAY (ex-SWORD renamed 8.1943) Dock landing ship 4,270 tons, 454 x 72 ft, 1-5in, 12-40mm. Newport News 10.5.44 for the RN but retained by the USN as RUSHMORE.

SWEEPSTAKE (or SWEEPSTAKES) 80-ton ship. Portsmouth 1497. Rebuilt 1511. Listed to 1527.

SWEEPSTAKE Galleon 84, circa 300bm. Built 1535. Listed to 1559.

SWEEPSTAKES 5th Rate 36, 376bm, 109 x 28½ ft. Edgar, Yarmouth 1666. 4th Rate 42 in 1669; 5th Rate 1691. Sold 13.5.1698.

SWEEPSTAKES 5th Rate 32, 416bm, 108½ ft. Stacey, Woolwich 20.9.1708. Captured 16.4.1709 by two French privateers off the Scillies.

SWEEPSTAKES 5th Rate 42, 657bm, 122 x 35 ft. French GLOIRE captured 14.5.1709 by CHESTER. Sold 5.6.1716.

SWEETBRIAR Sloop, 'Anchusa' class. Swan Hunter 5.10.1917. Sold 7.10.27 Cashmore, Newport.

SWEETBRIAR Corvette, 'Flower' class. Smiths DK 26.6.1941. Sold 29.7.46, renamed Star IX.

SWIFT 60-ton ship. Listed 1549-54.

SWIFT 6th Rate 20, 288bm, 87½ x 26½ ft. French, captured 1689. Sunk 24.4.1695 as breakwater at Portsmouth.

SWIFT Brigantine 6, 80bm, 63 x 17 ft. Chatham DY 1695. Foundered 17.8.1696.

SWIFT Advice boat 10, 154bm, 78 x 21½ ft. Moore, Arundel 1697. Wrecked 24.1.1698 in N.Carolina.

SWIFT Sloop 4, 65bm. Portsmouth DY 1699. Captured 18.8.1702 by the French privateer DUC de BOURGOGNE off the Scillies.

SWIFT Sloop 12, 123bm, 73½ x 20 ft. Woolwich 25.10.1704. Sold 20.8.1719.

SWIFT Sloop 12, 93bm, 60½ x 19 ft. Woolwich DY 19.8.1721. Sold 7.7.1741.

SWIFT Sloop 10, 203bm, 85 x 23½ ft. Carter, Limehouse 30.5.1741. Wreck sold 10.1756.

SWIFT Cutter 10, 88bm, 54 x 19½ft. French privateer COMTE de VALENCE captured 1760, purchased 16.1.1761. Captured 30.6.1762 off Ushant by a French privateer.

SWIFT Cutter 6, 54bm, 50 x 17 ft. Purchased 1.1763. Sold 4.5.1773.

SWIFT Sloop 14, 271bm, 91 x 26 ft. Graves, Limehouse 1.3.1763. Lost 3.1770 off the coast of Patagonia.

SWIFT Sloop 8. Purchased 3.1773 at Antigua. Sold 13.5.1784.

SWIFT Sloop 14, 303bm, 97 x 27 ft. Portsmouth DY 9.1.1777. Wrecked and burnt 11.1778 off Cape Henry.

SWIFT Sloop 16. American, captured 1779. Captured 11.8.1782 by the French RESOLUE, renamed RAPIDE. (was American MIDDLETON)

SWIFT Sloop 16, 329bm, 100 x 27 ft. Portsmouth DY 5.10.1793. Foundered 4.1797 in Chinese waters.

SWIFT Schooner, 47bm, 44½ x 16 ft. Purchased 1794. BU 1803.

SWIFT Gunvessel (Canadian lakes). Kingston Ont 1798. Fate unknown.

SWIFT (ex-Pacific) Brig-sloop 16, 327bm. Purchased 6.1804. Sold 3.11.1814.

SWIFT Cutter tender, 80bm, 55½ x 18½ ft. Woolwich DY 15.2.1817. Sold 8.1821.

SWIFT Packet brig 8, 361bm, 95½ x 30½ ft, 8-18pdr. Colson, Deptford 21.11.1835. Mooring vessel 1861 at the Cape and renamed YC.3. Sold 1866.

SWIFT Compos. S.gunvessel 756 tons, 165 x 29 ft, 2-7in, 3-20pdr. Green, Blackwall 29.11.1879. Sale ordered 4.2.1902 at Hong Kong; became mercantile Swift then Hoi Ching.

SWIFT Torpedo boat 125 tons, 153 x 17½ ft, 6-3pdr, 3-TT. White, Cowes 1885 and purchased 1885. Renamed TB.81 in 1887. Sold 22.10.1921 J.E.Thomas.

SWIFT Destroyer 1,825 tons, 345 x 34 ft, 4-4in, 2-TT Cammell Laird 7.12.1907. Rearmed 1917 with 1-6in, 2-4in, 2,170 tons. Sold 9.11.21 Rees, Llanelly.

SWIFT Destroyer 1,710 tons, 339½ x 36 ft, 4-4.7in, 2-40mm, 8-TT. White 15.6.1943. Sunk 24.6.44 by mine off Normandy.

SWIFT Patrol vessel 690 tons. Hall Russell 11.9.1984

SWIFT 5 Hired vessels between 1793 & 1806. Drifter in WW.I.

SWIFT CURRENT Minesweeper (RCN), TE 'Bangor' class. Vickers, Montreal 29.5.1941. Sold 29.3.58 Turkish navy as BOZCAADA.

SWIFTSURE Galleon 41, 360bm, 2-60pdr, 5-18pdr, 12-9pdr, 8-6pdr, 14 smaller. Deptford 1573. Rebuilt 1592 as 416bm. Renamed SPEEDWELL 1607, 40guns. Lost 11.1624 near Flushing.

SWIFTSURE 46-gun ship, 746bm. Deptford 1621. Rebuilt Woolwich 1653 as 898bm. Captured 1.6.1666 by the Dutch.

SWIFTSURE 3rd Rate 70, 978bm, 149 x 38½ ft. Deane, Harwich 8.4.1673. Rebuilt Deptford 1696 as 987bm. Renamed REVENGE 2.1.1716, 3rd Rate 64, 1,104bm. Rebuilt Deptford 1742 as 1,258bm. Sold 24.5.1787.

SWIFTSURE 3rd Rate 70, 426bm, 160 x 45 ft. Deptford DY 25.5.1750. Sold 2.6.1773.

SWIFTSURE 3rd Rate 74, 1,612bm, 169 x 47 ft. Wells, Deptford 4.4.1787. Captured 24.6.1801 by the French in the Mediterranean; recaptured at Trafalgar and renamed IRRESISTI-BLE, prison ship. BU 1.1816 at Chatham.

SWIFTSURE 3rd Rate 74, 1,724bm, 173 x 48 ft. Adams, Bucklers Hard 23.7.1804. Receiving ship 5.1819. Sold 18.10.1845 Barnard.

SWIFTSURE Iron armoured ship, 3,893bm, 6,910 tons, 280 x 55 ft, 10-9in, 4-6pdr. Palmer, Jarrow 15.6.1870. Renamed ORONTES 3.1904 harbour service. Sold 4.7.08 Castle.

SWIFTSURE (ex-Chilian CONSTITUC-ION purchased 3.12.1903) Battleship 11,800 tons, 436 x 71 ft, 4-10in, 14-7.5in, 14-14pdr. Armstrong 12.1.03. Sold 18.6.20 Stanlee, Dover.

SWIFTSURE Cruiser 8,800 tons, 538 x 64 ft, 9-6in, 10-4in. Vickers Armstrong, Tyne 4.2.1943. Arrived 17.10.62 Ward, Inverkeithing to BU.

SWIFTSURE Nuclear S/M 3800 tons. Vickers 7.9.1971.

SWINDON (ex-BANTRY renamed 1918) Minesweeper, later 'Hunt' class. Ardrossan 25.12.18. Sold 1.12.21, renamed *Lady Cecilia*.

SWINGER Gunvessel 14, 147bm, 75½ x 21 ft. Hill, Limehouse 31.5.1794. Sold 10.1802.

SWINGER Gunvessel 6. Purchased 1798 in Honduras for local use. Listed 1799.

SWINGER Gun-brig 12, 178bm, 80 x 22½ ft, 2-18pdr, 10-18pdr carr. Davy, Topsham 9.1804. BU 6.1812.

SWINGER Gun-brig 12, 180bm, 84 x 22 ft, 10-18pdr carr., 2-6pdr. Goode, Bridport 15.5.1813. Mooring lighter 2.1829; BU 3.1877.

SWINGER Wood S.gunboat, 'Dapper' class Pitcher, Northfleet 10.5.1855. BU 9.1864.

SWINGER Compos. S.gunboat, 295bm, 430 tons, 125 x 22½ ft, 2-64pdr, 2-20pdr. Pembroke Dock 7.2.1872. Hulked 1895. Sold 6.1924 Rodgers & Co.

SWORD (see SWASHWAY)

SWORD (ex-CELT renamed 9.1943) Destroyer 1,980 tons. White. Cancelled 5.10.45.

SWORD DANCE Minesweeper 265 tons, 130 x 26 ft, 1-6pdr. Lytham SB 1918 as War Dept tug and transferred 1919. Sunk 24.6.19 by mine.

SWORD DANCE Trawler 1940-42.

SWORDFISH Destroyer 330 tons, 200 x 19 ft, 1-12pdr, 5-6pdr, 2-TT. Armstrong Mitchell 27.2.1895. Sold 11.10.1910 Cashmore, Newport.

SWORDFISH Steam submarine 932 tons, 231½ (oa) x 23 ft, 2-12pdr, 6-TT. Scotts 18.3.1916. Renamed S.1 in 4.16; converted to surface patrol boat and reverted to SWORDFISH 7.17. Sold 7.22 Pounds, Portsmouth. Reported as resold Hayes, Porthcawl in 1923.

SWORDFISH Submarine 640 tons, 187 x 23½ ft, 1-3in, 6-TT. Chatham DY 7.11.1931. Sunk 30 mls S. of I. of Wight, probably mined.

SWORDSMAN Destroyer, 'S' class. Scotts 28.12.1918. To RAN 6.19. Sold 4.6.37 at Sydney.

SYBILLE (see SIBYL)

SYCAMORE Destroyer, 'S' class. Stephen. Cancelled 1919.

SYCAMORE Trawler 1935-46.

SYDENHAM Paddle gunvessel, 596bm, 170 x 27 ft. Purchased 11.1841 at Montreal. Sold 7.1846 at Malta.

SYDNEY Survey brig 6, 139bm, 72 x 21 ft, 6-12pdr carr. Purchased 1813. Sold 27.1.1825 J.Sheldrick.

SYDNEY 2nd class cruiser (RAN) 5,440 tons, 430 x 50 ft, 8-6in. London & Glasgow Co 29.8.1912. BU 4.29 at Cockatoo DY, Sydney.

SYDNEY (ex-PHAETON renamed 9.1935) Cruiser 6,830 tons, 530 x 57 ft, 8-6in, 8-4in. Swan Hunter 22.9.34.

Torpedoed 19.11.41 by the German AMC KORMORAN in the Pacific.

SYDNEY Frigate (RAN) 2100 tons. Todd, Seattle 26.9.1980.

SYDNEY (see TERRIBLE of 1944)

SYLPH (ex-*Lovely Lass*) Sloop 14, 274bm, 85 x 27½ft. Purchased 1776. Renamed LIGHTNING 25.8.1779, fireship. Sold 1.5.1783.

SYLPH (ex-*cutter Active*) Sloop 18, 224bm, 80½ x 26 ft, 18-4pdr. Purchased 5.1780. Captured 3.2.1782 by the French at the loss of Demerara.

SYLPH Sloop 18 (fir-built), 365bm, 96 x 30½ft. Barnard, Deptford 3.9.1795. BU 4.1811.

SYLPH Schooner 8 (Indian). Bombay DY 1806. Captured 1808 by pirates.

SYLPH Brig-sloop 18, 400bm, 100 x 30 ft. Tynes, Bermuda 1812. Wrecked 17.1.1815 on Long Island, N.America.

SYLPH Tender, 114bm, 62 x 21 ft. Woolwich DY 15.6.1821 (not listed until 1832). Lent Customs 15.9.1862 as watch vessel. Sold 7.1888.

SYLPH Destroyer, 'R' class. Harland & Wolff, Govan 15.11.1916. Sold 16.12.26 Cashmore; stranded 28.1.27 at Aberavon and BU.

SYLVIA Cutter 10, 110bm, 68 x 20 ft. Bermuda 1806. Sold 30.5.1816.

SYLVIA Cutter 6, 70bm, 52½ x 18 ft. Portsmouth DY 24.3.1827. Survey vessel 3.1842. Sold 9.1859 at Londonderry.

SYLVIA Wood S.sloop, 695bm, 865 tons, 185 x 28½ ft, 2-68pdr, 2-32pdr. Woolwich DY 20.3.1866. Completed 10.1866 as survey vessel. Sold Cohen 8.1889 to BU.

SYLVIA Destroyer 350 tons, 210 x 21 ft, 1-12pdr, 5-6pdr, 2-TT. Doxford 3.7.1897. Sold 23.7.19 Ward, New Holland.

SYLVIA Minesweeper, 'Algerine' class. Lobnitz 28.2.1944. Sold 16.9.58 at Malta; arrived 24.10.58 King, Gateshead to BU.

SYLVIA Coaster & Trawler requis in WW.I.

SYREN (see SIREN)

SYRINGA Sloop, 'Anchusa' class. Workman Clark 29.9.1917. Sold 31.3.20 Egyptian navy as SOLLUM.

SYRINGA Trawler requis. 1914-19; Trawler 1935-46.

SYRTIS Submarine, 'S' class. Vickers Armstrong, Barrow 4.2.1943. Sunk 28.3.44 by mine off Bodo, Norway.

Torpedo boats, 2nd class. Nos 1-12 (wood built) 12 Tons, 1 spar torpedo. All built by White 1883-88. No 2 sold 1900; Nos 1,3,4,7,8 and 10 sold by 1905; No5 sold 1909; No 6 by 1907; Nos 9, 11 both 1912; No 12 sold 1910.

Nos 38-100 (steel built) 15 tons, 2-TT (except Nos 38-50, 96 and 97, 1-TT). Nos 51-62, 64-73, 76-95, 98-100, all Thornycroft 1878-86;

No 63, Hereschoff Co USA; Nos 74, 75, 96, 97 all Yarrow 1883; Nos 50 working *back* to No 38, all Yarrow 1887-89.

A yard craft 'ex-TB.9' was BU at Devonport in 1919.

No 62 Foundered in tow of BUZZARD in N America 21.10.1890.

Nos 55,58-61,79,81,90,91 and 97 all sold 1902; No 92 condemned 1900;

No 75 sold 1903; Nos 50,52-54,56,57,84 all sold 1904; Nos 66,73,87 sold 1905; Nos 49,69,70,74,76-78,82,94,96 all sold 1906; Nos 39-44,51,65,80,89,99 sold 1907; No 100 sold 1908; No 71 sold 1909; Nos 45-48,95 sold 1912; No 68 transferred to Newfoundland Govt.

Torpedo boats, 1st class.

No 1 (ex-LIGHTNING) 27 tons, 84½ x 11 ft, 1-TT. Thorneycroft 1877. Sold 1910.

Nos 2-12 28 tons, 87 x 11 ft, 1-TT. Thornycroft 1878-79. Nos 4 and 6 sold 1906; Nos 7,10-12 sold 1904; others sold circa 1905.

No 13 28 tons, 87 x 11 ft, 2-TT. Maudslay, Lambeth 1878. Sold 5.97.

No 14 33tons, 88 x 11 ft, 2-TT, Yarrow 1877. Sold circa 1905.

No 15 28 tons, 87 x 11 ft, 2-TT. Hanna Donald, Paisley 1879. Sold circa 1905.

No 16 28 tons, 87 x 11 ft, 2-TT. Lewien, Poole 1878. Not up to Admiralty requirements and not accepted. Sold by builder to Chinese Navy in 8.79.

Nos 17,18, 33 tons, 86 x 11 ft, 2-TT. Yarrow 1877. No 17 sold 1970 at Malta; No 18 sold 1904 at Gibraltar.

No 19 28 tons, 87 x 11 ft, 2-TT, White 1878. Sold 1899.

No 20 28 tons, 87 x 11 ft, 2-TT. Rennie, Greenwich 1880. Sold 1905 at Hong Kong.

Nos 21,22 63 tons, 133 x 12½ ft, 3-TT. Thornycroft 1885. Sold 1907 at Malta.

Nos 23,24 67 tons, 113 x 12½ ft, 2-3pdr, 3-TT. Yarrow 1885-86. Sold 1906/07.

Nos 25-29 60 tons, 127½ x 12½ ft, 4-TT.

Thornycroft 1886. Nos 25-27 sold 2.10.1919 Maden & McKee; No 28 stranded 29.7.98 in Kalk Bay, S.Africa and sunk 12.98 as target; No 29 sold 1.7.1919 at Capetown.

Nos 30-33 64 tons, 125 x 13 ft, 2-3pdr, 5-TT. Yarrow 1886. No 31 sold 1913; No 33 sold 1.8.1919; others sold circa 1905.

Nos 34-38 64 tons, 125 x 14½ ft, 5-TT. White 1886. No 34 sold 2.10.1919 Maden & McKee; others sold 27.11.19 at Hong Kong.

Nos 39,40 40 tons, 100 x 12½ ft, 1-TT, Yarrow 1885 for the Chilian navy and purchased 1888. Sold 2.1905 at Esquimalt.

Nos 41-60 60 tons, 127½ x 12½ ft, 2-3pdr, 4-TT. Thornycroft 1886. Nos 41,45,49,54 all sold 1.8.1919; Nos 42,57 sold 2.10.19 Maden & McKee; Nos 43,44 sold 18.12.19 at Malta; No 47 sold circa 1908; No 48 circa 1915; Nos 50,55 sold 23.2.20 R. Longmate; Nos 51,59 sold circa 1913;

No 53 sold 1913; Nos 52,58 sold 19,12,19 Multilocular S.Bkg Co; No 60 sold 1.7.19 at the Cape; No 46 wrecked in tow 27.12.15 in the Mediterranean, salved an BU 1920; No 56 foundered in tow 17.5.06 off Damietta.

Note: all boats up to TB.79 which survived the year 1906, had a 'O' added to their numbers to avoid confusion with the coastal TBDs which had been renamed TB.1-36 in that year; e.g. the original TB.25 became TB.025.)

Nos 61-79 75 tons, 125 x 13 ft, 2-3pdr, 5-TT. Yarrow 1886. No 61 sold 1909; No 62 sold in 1905.

Nos 63,70 sold 18.12.19 at Malta; No 64 wrecked 21.3.15 in the Aegean;

Nos 65,78 sold 2.10 19 Maden & McKee; Nos 66,68,76 sold 30.6.20 Ward, Hayle; Nos 67,74 sold 27.1.20 Willoughby, Plymouth; No 69 sold circa 1908; No 71 sold 5.7.23 B.Newton; No 72 sold 19.12.19 Ward, Rainham; No 73 sold 6.2.23 L.Basso, Weymouth; No 75 sunk 8.8.1892 in collision with No 77 off the Maidens; No 77 sold 27.3.20 Stanlee, Dover; No 79 sold 19.12.19 Ward Grays.

No 80 105 tons, 135 x 14 ft, 4-3pdr, 5-TT. Yarrow 1887. Sold 22.10.21 J.E.Thomas.

No 81 (ex-SWIFT) 125 tons, 150 x 17½ ft, 6-3pdr, 3-TT. White 1885 and purchased. Sold 22.10.21 J.E.Thomas.

Nos 82-87 85 tons, 130 x 13½ ft, 3-3pdr, 3-TT. Yarrow 1889. Nos 82,85,86 sold 22.10.21 J.E.Thomas; No 83 sold 12.10.19 Brand; No 84 sunk 17.4.06 in collision with ARDENT; No 87 sold 27.3.20 Stanlee, Dover.

Nos 88,89 112 tons, 142 x 14½ ft, 3-3pdr, 3-TT. Yarrow 1894. Both sold 13.10.19 Messrs Brand.

No 90 100 tons, 140 x 14½ ft, 3-3pdr, 3-TT. Yarrow 1895. Capsized 24.4.19 off Gibraltar.

Nos 91-93 130 tons, 140 x 15½ ft, 3-3pdr, 3-TT. Thornycroft 1894.

Nos 91,93 sold 13.10.19 Messrs Brand; No 92 sold 1920 at Gibraltar.

Nos 94-96 As No 91; White 1893. Nos 94,95 sold with No 91; No 96 sunk 1.11.15 in collision with the troopship *Tringa* off Gibraltar.

No 97 As No 91; Laird 16.9.1893. Sold 1920 at Gibraltar.

Nos 98,99 and 107, 108 178 tons, 160 x 17 ft, 3-3pdr, 3-TT. Thornycroft 1901. No 98 sold 30.6.20 Ward, Preston; No 99 sold 29.7.20 Ward, Hayle; No 107 sold 29.7.20 Ward, Morecambe; No 108 sold 29.7.20 Willoughby, Plymouth.

Nos 100-106 (see Nos 1-7 RIM boats)

Nos 109-113 200 tons, 166 x 17½ ft, 3-3pdr, 3-TT.

No 109 Thornycroft 22.7.1902. Sold 27.3.20 Stanlee, Dover.

No 110 Thornycroft 5.9.02. Sold with No 109.

No 111 Thornycroft 31.10.02. Sold 10.2.20 Ward, Grays.

No 112 Thornycroft 15.1.03. Sold with No 111.

No 113 Thornycroft 12.2.03. Sold 19.12.19 Ward, Grays.

Nos 114-117 205 tons, 165 x 17½ ft, 3-3pdr, 3-TT.

No 114 White 8.6.03. Sold 1919 Ward, Grays; moved to Rainham 1920.

No 115 White 19.11.03. Sold 1919 Ward, Rainham.

No 116 White 21.12.03. Sold 22.10.21 J.E.Thomas, Newport.

No 117 White 18.2.04. Sunk 10.6.17 in collision with SS *Kamouraska* in the Channel. Salved? (a DY lighter No 80 'ex-TB.117' was sold 31.3.21 to W.T.Beaumont.)

Indian (RIM) boats, transferred to RN in 1892.

No 1 (BALUCHI) 96 tons, 134½ x 14½ ft, 5-TT. Thornycroft 1888. Renamed No 100 in 1901; sold 1909.

No 2 (KAHREN) 96 tons, 134½ x 14½ ft, 5-TT. Thornycroft 1888. Renamed No 102 in 1901; sold 1909.

No 3 (PATHAN) 96 tons, 134½ x 14½ ft, 5-TT. Thornycroft 1888. Renamed No 103 in 1901; sold 1909.

No 4 (MAHRATTA) 95 tons, 130 x 14½ ft, 5-TT. White 1889. Renamed No 104 in 1901; sold 29.7.20 Willoughby.

No 5 (SIKH) 95 tons, 130 x 14½ ft, 5-TT. White 1889. Renamed No 105 in 1901; sold 27.1.20 Willoughby, Plymouth.

No 6 (RAJPUT) 95 tons, 130 x 14½ ft, 5-TT. White 1889. Renamed No 106 in 1901; sold 11.10.10 Cashmore, Newport.

No 7 (GHURKA) 92 tons, 130½ x 14 ft, 5-TT. M'Arthur, Paisley 1888. Renamed No 101 in 1901; sold 27.3.20 Stanlee, Dover.

No 1 (Tasmanian Govt) 12 tons, 63 x 7½ ft, 1 spar torpedo. Thornycroft 1884. Deleted in 1910.

No 1-4 (New Zealand) 12 tons, 63 x 7½ ft, 1 spar torpedo. Thornycroft 1884. No 1 sold 1900. No 2 BU 1913.

Nos 1-12 (ex-coastal destroyers CRICKET, DRAGONFLY, FIREFLY, SANDFLY, SPIDER, GADFLY, GLOWWORM, GNAT, GRASSHOPPER, GREENFLY, MAYFLY and MOTH respectively renamed 1906 qv).

No 13 256 tons, 182 x 18 ft, 2-12pdr, 3-TT. White 10.7.07. Sunk 26.1.16 in collision in the North Sea.

No 14 as No 13. White 26.9.07. Sold 7.10.20 Philip, Dartmouth for use as pontoon jetty; still such in 1966.

No 15 as No 13. White 19.11.07. Sold 7.10.20 Ward. Arrived Briton Ferry 29.1.21.

No 16 as No 13. White 23.12.07. Sold 7.10.20 Ward. Arrived Briton Ferry 29.1.21.

No 17 251 tons, 180 x 18 ft, 2-12pdr, 3-TT. Denny 21.12.07. Sold 1919 at Gibraltar.

No 18 as No 17. Denny 15.2.08. Sold 1920 at Gibraltar.

No 19 280 tons, 178½ x 20½ ft, 2-12pdr, 3-TT. Thornycroft 7.12.07. Sold 9.5.21 Ward, Grays.

No 20 as No 19. Thornycroft 21.1.08. Sold with No 19.

No 21 308 tons, 185 x 18½ ft, 2-12pdr, 3-TT. Hawthorn 20.12.07. Sold 7.10.20 Maden & McKee then Hayes.

No 22 as No 21. Hawthorn 1.2.08. Sold 7.10.20 Maden & McKee; sold 8.24 Hayes, Porthcawl.

No 22 253 tons, 177½ x 18 ft, 2-12pdr, 3-TT. Yarrow 5.12.07. Sold 9.5.21 Ward, Grays.

No 24 292 tons, 177 x 18 ft, 2-12pdr, 3-TT. Palmer 19.3.08. Wrecked 28.1.17 on Dover breakwater.

No 25 283 tons, 182 x 18 ft, 2-12pdr, 3-TT. White 28.7.08. Sold 9.5.21 Ward, Grays.

No 26 as No 25. White 28.8.08. Sold with No 25. BU at Rainham.

No 27 as No 25. White 29.9.08. Sold 9.5.21 Ward, Rainham.

No 28 as No 25. White 29.10.08. Sold with No 27.

No 29 259 tons, 180 x 18 ft, 2-12pdr, 3-TT. Denny 29.8.08. Sold 28.11.19 at Malta.

No 30 as No 29. Denny 29.9.08. Sold with No 29.

No 31 287 tons, 178½ x 18½ ft, 2-12pdr, 3-TT. Thornycroft 10.10.08. Sold 9.5.21 Ward, Rainham.

No 32 as No 31. Thornycroft 23.11.08. Sold with No 31.

No 33 306 tons, 185 x 18½ ft, 2-12pdr, 3-TT. Hawthorn 22.2.09. Sold 24.8.22 Cashmore, Newport.

No 34 as No 33. Hawthorn 22.2.09. Sold 9.5.21 Ward, Rainham.

No 35 298 tons, 177 x 18 ft, 2-12pdr, 3-TT. Palmer 19.4.09. Sold 24.8.22 Cashmore, Newport.

No 36 as No 35. Palmer 6.5.09. Sold 9.5.21 Ward, Rainham.

TABARD Submarine, 'T' class. Scotts (ex-Vickers, Barrow) 21.11.1945. Sold Cashmore 2.1.74, BU at Newport.

TACITURN Submarine, 'T' class. Vickers Armstrong, Barrow 7.6.1944. Sold Ward 23.7.71, BU Briton Ferry.

TACTICIAN Destroyer, 'S' class. Beardmore 7.8.1918. Sold 2.31 Metal Industries, Charlestown.

TACTICIAN Submarine, 'T' class. Vickers Armstrong, Barrow 29.7.1942. Arrived 6.12.63 Cashmore, Newport to BU.

TACTICIAN Nuclear S/M ordered 10.9.1984.

TADOUSSAC Minesweeper (RCN), TE 'Bangor' class. Dufferin, Toronto 2.8.1941. Sold 18.10.46, renamed *Alexandre*.

TAFF Frigate, 'River' class. Hill, Bristol 11.9.1943. Arrived 6.57 Cashmore, Newport to BU.

TAGUS (ex-SEVERN renamed 1812) 5th Rate 38 (red pine-built), 949bm, 143½ x 38½ ft. List, Fishbourne 14.7.1813. Sold 19.4.1822 Beatson to BU.

TAIN Minesweeper, later 'Hunt' class. Simons. Cancelled 1919.

TAITAM (see PORTLAND of 1941)

TAKU Destroyer 305 tons, 193½ x 20 ft, 6-3pdr, 3-TT. Chinese HAI LUNG captured 17.6.1900 in China. Sold 25.10.16 at Hong Kong.

TAKU Submarine, 'T' class. Cammell Laird 20.5.1939. Sold 11.46, BU Rees, Llanelly.

TALAPUS Patrol boat (RCN), 84 x 20 ft. Armstrong Bros, Victoria 2.7.1941. Sold 1946.

TALAVERA (see WATERLOO 1)

TALAVERA (ex-THUNDERER renamed 23.7.1817) 3rd Rate 74, 1,718bm, 174 x 48½ ft. Woolwich DY 15.10.1818. Burnt 27.9.1840 by accident at Plymouth.

TALAVERA Destroyer 2,380 tons, 355 x 40 ft, 5-4.5in, 8-40mm, 10-TT. J.Brown 27.8.1945; not completed. Arrived 1.46 at Troon to BU.

TALBOT Ship. Listed in 1585.

TALBOT Ketch 10, 94bm, 62 x 19 ft. Taylor, Cuckolds Point 6.4.1691 Wrecked 15.10.1694. (In French hands 6.91 to 11.93.)

TALBOT Sloop 18, 484bm, 113½ x 31 ft, 18-32pdr carr., 8-12pdr carr., 1-12pdr, 2-6pdr. Heath, Teignmouth 22.7.1807. Sold 23.11.1815.

TALBOT 6th Rate 28, 500bm, 114 x 32ft, 20-32pdr, 6-18pdr carr., 2-6pdr. Pembroke Dock 9.10.1824. Powder hulk 2.1855. Sold 5.3.1896 C.P. Ogilvie.

TALBOT 2nd class cruiser 5,600 tons, 350 x 53 ft, 11-6in, 9-12pdr. Devonport DY 25.4.1895. Sold 6.12.1921 Multilocular S.Bkg Co.

TALBOT (see M.29)

TALENT Submarine, 'T' class. Vickers Armstrong, Barrow 17.7.1943. Renamed ZWAARDVISCH 6.12.43 on loan to the Dutch navy. BU 1963.

TALENT Submarine, 'T' class. Vickers Armstrong, Barrow. Ordered 1944, transferred Scotts and cancelled 1945.

TALENT Nuclear S/M 4,200 tons. Vickers LD. 1985.

TALENT (see TASMAN)

TALISMAN (see LOUIS)

TALISMAN (ex-NAPIER renamed 15.2.1915, ex-Turkish) Destroyer 1,098 tons, 300 x 28½ ft, 5-4in, 4-TT. Hawthorn Leslie 15.7.15. Sold 9.5.21 Ward Grays.

TALISMAN Submarine, 'T' class. Cammell Laird 29.1.1940. Sunk 9.42 in the Sicilian Channel by unknown cause.

TALLY-HO (ex-P.317) Submarine, 'T'

class. Vickers Armstrong, Barrow 23.12.1942. Arrived 10.2.67 Ward, Briton Ferry to BU.

TALLY-HO Trawler requis. 1915-19.

TALYBONT Destroyer, 'Hunt' class type III. White 3.2.1943. Arrived 14.2.61, Charlestown to BU.

TAMAR Sloop 16, 343bm, 96½ x 27½ ft. Snook, Saltash 23.1.1758. Renamed PLUTO 23.9.1777, fireship. Captured 30.11.1780 by the French.

TAMAR Store lighter, 126bm, 65 x 21 ft. Cowes 1795 and purchased 1795. BU 1798.

TAMAR 5th Rate 38 (fir-built), 999bm, 146 x 39 ft. Chatham DY 26.3.1796. BU 1.1810 at Chatham.

TAMAR 6th Rate 26, 451bm, 108 x 31 ft. Brindley, Frindsbury 23.3.1814. Coal hulk 3.1831. Sold 3.1837.

TAMAR Iron S.troopship, 2,812bm, 4,650 tons, 320(oa) x 45 ft, 3-6pdr. Samuda, Poplar 5.1.1863. Base ship 1897. Scuttled 12.12.1941 at Hong Kong.

TAMAR (see AIRE)

TAMARISK Sloop, 'Aubrietia' class. Lobnitz 2.6.1916. Sold 17.10.22 Fryer, Sunderland. (Also operated as Q.11.)

TAMARISK (ex-ETTRICK renamed 1941) Corvette, 'Flower' class. Fleming & Ferguson 28.7.41. On loan Greek navy 11.43 to 1952 as TOMPAZIS. Sold 20.3.63. Marine Craft Constructors., BU in Greece.

TAMARISK Trawler 1939-40.

TAMWORTH Minesweeper, 'Bathurst' class. Walker, Maryborough 14.3.1942. Lent RAN to 1946. Sold 1946 Dutch navy.

TAMWORTH CASTLE (see KINCARDINE)

TANAIS 5th Rate 38 (red pine-built), 1,085bm, 150½ x 40½ ft. Ross, Rochester 27.10.1813. Sold Beatson 8.3.1819 to BU.

TANATSIDE Destroyer, 'Hunt' class type III. Yarrow 30.4.1942. Lent Greek navy 9.2.46 to 1.64 as ADRIAS; sold 14.1.64 in Greece to be BU.

TANCRED Destroyer, 'R' class. Beardmore 30.6.1917. sold 17.5.28 Cashmore for Newport; stranded and BU at Port Talbot.

TANCRED Rescue tug 1943, RAN 1943-47.

TANG Schooner 4, 78bm, 56 x 18ft, 4-12pdr carr. Bermuda 9.1807. Foundered 1808 in the Atlantic.

TANGANYIKA Minesweeper, 'Algerine'

class. Lobnitz 12.4.1944. Arrived 2.9.63 Ward, Inverkeithing to BU.

TANTALUS Submarine, 'T' class. Vickers Armstrong, Barrow 24.2.1943. BU 11.50, Ward Milford Haven.

TANTIVY Submarine, 'T' class. Vickers Armstrong, Barrow 6.4.1943. Sunk 1951 as Asdic target, Cromarty Firth.

TAPAGEUR Cutter 14, 14-4pdr. French, captured 4.1779. Wrecked 1780 in the W.Indies.

TAPAGEUSE Brig-sloop 14. French, captured 6.4.1806 by boats of PALLAS off Bordeaux. Fate unknown.

TAPIR Submarine, 'T' class. Vickers Armstrong, Barrow 21.8.1944. Lent Dutch navy 1948-53 as ZEEHOND. Arrived 14.12.66 at Faslane to BU.

TAPTI Survey brig (Indian). Listed 1843-51.

TARA Destroyer, 'S' class. Beardmore 12.10.1918. Sold 17.12.31 Rees, Llanelly.

TARA ABS 1862 tons. Requis. 1914-15.

TARAKAN (see LST.3017)

TARAKAN Landing craft (RAN) Walker 3.1972.

TARANAKI Frigate (RNZN) 2,150 tons, 360 x 41 ft, 2-4.5in, 4-GWS. White 19.8.1959. Sold in 1982.

TARANTELLA Minesweeper 265 tons, 130 x 26½ ft, 1-12pdr, 1-6pdr. War Dept tug transferred on stocks; Hamilton 22.10.1917. Sold 1921 mercantile.

TARANTULA River gunboat 645 tons, 230 x 36 ft, 2-6in, 1-3in. Wood Skinner, Newcastle 8.12.1915. Depot ship 1941. Dismantled 1946 and hull sunk 1.5.46 as target off Ceylon.

TARBAT NESS Repair ship 8,580 tons, 424½ x 57 ft. West Coast SB, Vancouver 29.5.1945. Cancelled 18.8.45 and completed 1.47 as *Lautoka*.

TARBAT NESS Store carrier 15,500 tons. 1967-81.

TARBERT (see SHERBORNE)

TARLETON Brig-sloop 14. Dating from 1782. Captured 1782 by the French.

TARLETON Fireship 14. French, captured 18.12.1793 at Toulon. Listed to 1798. (French records give this as the 1782 vessel recaptured.)

TARLTON Coastal M/S, 'Ton' class. Doig, Grimsby 10.11.1954. Sold 1967 Argentine navy, renamed RIO NEGRO.

TARN Submarine, 'T' class. Vickers Armstrong, Barrow 29.11.1944. To Dutch navy 1945 as TIJGERHAAI.

TARPON Destroyer, 'R' class. J.Brown 10.3.1917. Sold 4.8.27 Cashmore,

Newport.

TARPON Submarine, 'T' class. Scotts 17.10.1939. Sunk 14.4.40 by the German minesweeper M.6 in the North Sea.

TARTAN Advice boat 6, 49bm. French (TARTANE?) captured 1692. Recaptured 17.6.1695 by the French.

TARTAN Trawler Requis. 1915-19 & 1939-45.

TARTAN 5th Rate 32, 420bm, 108 x 30 ft. Woolwich DY 9.1702. Rebuilt Deptford 1733 as 6th Rate, 429bm. BU completed 4.1755 at Deptford.

TARTAR 6th Rate 28, 587bm, 118 x 34 ft. Randall, Rotherhithe 3.4.1756. Wrecked 4.1797 at San Domingo.

TARTAR PRIZE 6th Rate 28, 4-9pdr, 24-6pdr. French privateer. VICTOIRE captured 3.1757 by TARTAR. Wrecked 2.3.1760 Mediterranean.

TARTAR 5th Rate 32, 885bm, 142 x 37½ ft. Brindley, Frindsbury 27.6.1801. Wrecked 18.18.1811 in the Baltic.

TARTAR 5th Rate 36, 949bm, 145 x 38½ ft. Deptford DY 6.4.1814. Receiving ship 3.1830. BU completed 30.9.1859.

TARTAR (ex-Russian WOJN seized on stocks) Wood S.corvette, 1,296bm, 195 x 39 ft, 110pdr, 14-8in, 4-40pdr. Pitcher, Northfleet 17.5.1854. BU 2.1866 Castle, Charlton.

TARTAR Torpedo cruiser 1,770 tons, 225 x 36 ft, 6-6in, 8-3pdr, 3-TT. Thomson 28.10.1886. Sold 3.4.1906 Forrester, Swansea.

TARTAR Destroyer 870 tons, 260 x 26 ft, 3-12pdr, 2-TT. Thornycroft, Woolston 25.6.1907. Sold 9.5.21 Ward, Hayle.

TARTAR Destroyer 1,870 tons, 355½ x 36½ ft, 8-4.7in, 4-TT. Swan Hunter 21.10.1937. Sold 6.1.48, BU Cashmore, Newport.

TARTAR Frigate 2,300 tons, 350 x 42 ft, 2-4.5in, 2-40mm. Devonport DY 19.9.1960. Sold Indonesia 1984, renamed HASANUDDIN.

TARTARUS (ex-*Charles Jackson*) Bomb 8, 344bm, 94½ x 28½ ft. Purchased 4.1797. Wrecked 20.12.1804 on Margate Sands.

TARTARUS Fireship 16, 423bm, 108½ x 30 ft. Davy, Topsham 10.1806. Sloop from 3.1808, 22-24pdr carr., 8-18pdr carr., 2-9pdr. Sold 15.2.1816.

TARTARUS Paddle gunvessel, 523bm, 145 x 28½ ft, 2-9pdr. Pembroke Dock 23.6.1834. BU 11.1860 at Malta.

TARTARUS Wood S.gunvessel, 695bm,

185 x 28½ ft, 2-68pdr, 2-32pdr. Pembroke Dock. Laid down 25.10.1860, cancelled 16.12.1864.

TASMAN Submarine, 'T' class. Vickers Armstrong, Barrow 13.2.1945. Renamed TALENT 4.45. Sold 6.1.70, arrived Troon 28.2.70 to BU.

TASMANIA Destroyer, 'S' class. Beardmore 22.11.1918. To the RAN 6.19. Sold 4.6.37 Penguins Ltd, Sydney.

TATTOO Destroyer, 'S' class. Beardmore 28.12.1918. To the RAN 6.19. Sold 9.1.37 Penguins Ltd, Sydney.

TATTOO Minesweeper, 'Catherine' class. Gulf SB, Chickasaw 27.1.1943. on lend-lease. Returned 1947 to the USN and then to Turkey as CARSAMBA 3.47.

TAUNTON 48-gun ship, 536bm, 120 x 32 ft. Castle, Rotherhithe 1954. Renamed CROWNE 1660. Rebuilt Deptford 1704 as 650bm. Wrecked 29.1.1719 off the Tagus.

TAUPO (see LOCH SHIN)

TAUPO Patrol vessel (RNZN) 105 tons. Brooke Marine 25.7.1975

TAURANGA (ex-PHOENIX renamed 2.4.1890) 2nd class cruiser 2,575 tons. 265 x 41 ft, 8-4.7in, 8-3pdr. Thomson 28.10.89. Sold 10.7.1906 Ward, Preston.

TAURUS Destroyer, 'R' class. Thornycroft 10.3.1917. Sold 18.2.30 Metal Ind, Charlestown.

TAURUS (ex-P.339) Submarine, 'T' class. Vickers Armstrong, Barrow 27.6.1942. Lent Dutch navy 1948 to 12.53 as DOLFIJN. BU 4.60 Clayton & Davie, Dunston.

TAURUS Yacht & Trawler WW.I. Tug 1941-43

TAVISTOCK Sloop 14, 269bm, 91 x 26 ft. Darby, Gosport 22.3.1744. Renamed ALBANY 20.8.1747. Sold 3.5.1763.

TAVISTOCK 4th Rate 50, 1,601bm, 144 x 41 ft. Blaydes Hull 26.8.1747. Hulked 1761. BU completed 24.12.1768 at Woolwich.

TAVY Storeship, 171bm, 71½ x 24 ft. Franks Quarry, Plymouth 1797. Made a DY luggage lighter 7.1862, renamed YC.11. BU in 1.1869 at Devonport.

TAVY Frigate, 'River' class. Hill, Bristol 3.4.1943. Arrived 18.7.55 Cashmore, Newport to BU.

TAY Sloop 18, 460bm, 116 x 30 ft, 18-32pdr carr., 2-9pdr. Adams, Bucklers Hard 26.11.1813. Wrecked 11.11.1816 in the Gulf of Mexico.

TAY Iron S.gunboat 363 tons, 110 x 34 ft, 3-64pdr. Palmer, Jarrow 19.10.1876. Sold 22.10.1920 Stanlee, Dover.

TAY Frigate, 'River' class. Smiths Dk 18.3.1942. Arrived 28.9.56 S.Bkg Ind, Rosyth to BU.

TEAL River gunboat 180 tons, 160 x 24½ ft, 2-6pdr. Yarrow, Poplar 18.5.1901. Sold 10.31 at Shanghai.

TEAL (see JACKTON)

TEAL 2 Trawlers WW.I. Trawler 1940-46.

TEAZER Gunvessel 14, 148bm, 75 x 21 ft. Dudman, Deptford 26.5.1794. Sold 10.1802.

TEAZER Gunvessel 6. Schooner purchased 1798 in Honduras for local use. Fate unknown.

TEAZER Gun-brig 12, 177bm, 80 x 22½ ft, 2-18pdr, 10-18pdr carr. Dudman, Deptford 16.7.1804. Sold 3.8.1815.

TEAZER Wood S.tender, 296bm, 130 x 22 ft, 2 guns. Chatham DY 25.6.1846. BU 1862 Castle, Charlton.

TEAZER Compos. gunvessel, 464bm, 603 tons, 155 x 25 ft, 1-7in, 1-64pdr, 2-20pdr. Laird 28.4.1868. BU 12.1887 at Chatham.

TEAZER Destroyer 320 tons, 200 x 19½ ft, 1-12pdr, 5-6pdr, 2-TT. White 2.2.1895. Sold 9.7.1912 Cox, Falmouth; resold Cashmore, Newport.

TEAZER Destroyer, 'R' class. Thornycroft 31.4.1917. Sold 6.2.31 Cashmore, Newport.

TEAZER Destroyer 1,710 tons, 339½ x 36 ft, 4-4.7in, 2-40mm, 8-TT. Cammell Laird 7.1.1943. Frigate 2.52, 2,200 tons, 2-4in. Arrived 7.8.65 Arnott Young, Dalmuir.

TECUMSETH Schooner 2 (Canadian lakes), 166bm, 70½ x 24½ ft. Moore, Chippewa 8.1815. Condemned 3.1832; foundered circa 1833 at Penetanguishene; raised 1953.

TEDWORTH Minesweeper, early 'Hunt' class. Simons 20.6.1917. Diving tender 8.23. Sold 5.46, BU Ward, Hayle.

TEES 6th Rate 28, 452bm, 108 x 31 ft, 18-32pdr carr., 8-12pdr carr., 2-6pdr. Taylor, Bideford 17.5.1817. Lent 10.1826 as church ship. Sold 28.6.1872 at Liverpool.

TEES Wood S.sloop, 950bm, 185 x 33 ft. Chatham DY. Ordered 5.3.1860, cancelled 12.1863.

TEES Iron S.gunboat 363 tons, 110 x 34 ft. 3-64pdr. Palmer 19.10.1876. Sold 9.7.1907 Harris Bros, Bristol.

TEES Frigate, 'River' class. Hall Russell 20.5.1943. Arrived 16.7.55 Cashmore, Newport to BU.

TEIGNMOUTH Sloop 16 (Indian), 257bm. Bombay DY 1799. Fate unknown.

TEIGNMOUTH (see TRING)

TELEGRAPH Schooner 14, 180bm, 83½ x 22½ ft, 12-12pdr carr., 2-6pdr. American privateer VENGEANCE captured 1813. Wrecked 21.1.1817 on Mount Batten, Plymouth.

TELEMACHUS Destroyer, 'R' class. J.Brown 21.4.1917. Sold 26.7.27 Hughed Bolckow, Blyth.

TELEMACHUS Submarine, 'T' class. Vickers Armstrong, Barrow 19.6.1943. Arrived 28.8.61 Charlestown to BU.

TEME Frigate, 'River' class. Smiths Dk 11.11.1943. Torpedoed 29.3.45. by 'U,246' off Falmouth and not repaired; sold 8.12.45, BU Rees, Llanelly.

TEMERAIRE 3rd Rate 74, 1,685bm, 169 x 48 ft. French, captured 18.8.1759 at Lagos. Sold 6.1784.

TEMERAIRE 2nd Rate 98, 2,121bm, 185 x 51 ft. Chatham DY 11.9.1798. Prison ship 12.1813; receiving ship 6.1820. Sold 16.8.1838 Beatson, Rotherhithe to BU.

TEMERAIRE Iron S.ship 8,540 tons, 285 x 62ft, 4-11in, 4-10in. Chatham DY 9.5.1876. Renamed INDUS II in 4.1904 training ship. Renamed AKBAR 1.15. Sold 26.5.21 Rijsdijk S.Bkg Co.

TEMERAIRE Battleship 18,600 tons, 490 x 82½ ft, 10-12in, 16-4. Devonport DY 24.8.1907. Sold 1.12.21 Stanlee, Dover.

TEMERAIRE Battleship 42,500 tons, 740 x 105 ft, 9-16in, 16-5.25in. Cammell Laird. Laid down 1.6.1939, suspended 10.39, cancelled 1944.

TEMPEST Destroyer, 'R' class. Fairfield 26.1.1917. Handed over 28.1.37 to Ward in part payment for *Majestic*, BU at Briton Ferry.

TEMPEST Submarine, 'T' class. Cammell Laird 10.6.1941. Sunk 13.2.42 by the Italian TB CIRCE in the Gulf of Taranto.

TEMPLAR (ex-P.316) Submarine, 'T' class. Vickers Armstrong Barrow 26.10.1942. Sunk as Asdic target 1950; raised 4.12.58, arrived 17.7.59 at Troon to BU.

TEMPLE 3rd Rate 70, 1,429bm, 160 x 45 ft. Blaydes, Hull 3.11.1758. Foundered 18.12.1762 in the W.Indies.

TENACIOUS Destroyer, 'R' class. Harland & Wolff, Govan 21.5.1917. Sold 26.6.28 Ward, Briton Ferry.

TENACIOUS Destroyer 1,710 tons, 339½ x 36 ft, 4-4.7ins, 2-40mm, 8-TT. Cammell Laird 24.3.1943. Frigate 4.52. Arrived 29.6.65 at Troon to BU.

TENACITY Patrol boat 165 tons, Vosper 18.2.1969 and purchased in 1.72

TENASSERIM Paddle vessel (Indian). Listed 1839-53.

TENASSERIM Iron S.frigate (Indian), 2,570bm, 250 x 35 ft. River Thames 1872. Harbour service 1900-06.

TENBY Minesweeper, turbine 'Bangor' class. Hamilton 10.9.1941. Sold 1.1.48, BU Clayton & Davie, Dunston.

TENBY Frigate 2,150 tons, 360 x 41 ft, 2-4.5in, 2-40mm. Cammell Laird 4.10.1955. Sold Pakistan 1975 but not Taken over. Arrived Briton Ferry 15.9.77 to BU.

TENBY Trawler requis. 1915-19.

TENEDOS 5th Rate 38, 1,083bm, 150 x 40½ ft. Chatham DY 11.4.1812. Convict hulk 4.1843. BU completed 20.3.1875 in Bermuda.

TENEDOS Wood S.sloop, 1,275bm, 1,760 tons, 212 x 36 ft, 2-7in, 4-64pdr. Devonport DY 13.5.1870. Rated corvette from 1875. Sold 11.1887 Pethwick, Plymouth.

TENEDOS Training ships (see TRIUMPH of 1870, DUNCAN of 1859 and GANGES of 1821).

TENEDOS Destroyer, 'S' class. Hawthorn Leslie 21.10.1918. Sunk 5.4.42 by Japanese air attack south of Colombo.

TEREDO Submarine, 'T' class. Vickers Armstrong, Barrow 27.4.1945. Arrived 5.6.65 Ward, Briton Ferry to BU.

TERMAGANT 6th Rate 26, 378bm, 110½ x 28 ft, 4-12pdr carr., 22-6pdr. Hilhouse, Bristol 3.6.1780, purchased on stocks. Reduced to 18-gun sloop 5.1782. Sold 28.8.1795.

TERMAGANT Sloop 18, 427bm, 110 x 30 ft, 18-32pdr carr., 8-12pdr carr., 2-6pdr. Dudman, Deptford 23.4.1796. Sold 3.2.1819 Graham.

TERMAGANT 6th Rate 28, 500bm, 114 x 32 ft. Cochin 15.11.1822. Renamed HERALD 15.5.1824 and made a survey ship. Sold 28.4.1862 Castle, Charlton.

TERMAGANT Brigantine 3, ex-'Cherokee' class, 231bm. Portsmouth DY 26.3.1838. Sold 3.1845.

TERMAGANT Wood S.frigate, 1,560bm, 210 x 40 ft, 1-110pdr, 16-8in, 6-40pdr. Deptford DY 25.9.1847. Sold 3.1867 Castle & Beech to BU.

TERMAGANT (ex-NARBROUGH renamed 15.2.1915, ex-Turkish) Destroyer 1,098 tons, 300 x 28½ ft, 5-4in, 4-TT. Hawthorn Leslie 26.8.15. Sold 9.5.21 Ward; arrived Briton Ferry 25.1.23 to BU.

TERMAGANT Destroyer 1,710 tons, 339½ x 36 ft, 4-4.7in, 2-40mm, 8-T. Denny 22.3.1943. Frigate 1953. Arrived 5.11.65 Arnott Young, Dalmuir to BU.

TERN Paddle M/S. Murdoch & Murray. Cancelled 1918.

TERN River gunboat 262 tons, 160 x 27 ft, 2-3in. Yarrow 29.8.1927. Scuttled 19.12.41 at Hong Kong.

TERNATE Sloop 16 (Indian), 257bm. Bombay DY 1801. Listed in 1830.

TERPSICHORE 6th Rate 24, 467bm, 114 x 31 ft, 24-6pdr. French, captured 28.2.1760 by a squadron off the Isle of Man. Sold 4.11.1766.

TERPSICHORE 5th Rate 32 683bm, 126 x 35 ft, Betts, Mistleythorn 17.12.1785. Receiving ship 1818. BU 11.1830.

TERPSICHORE Sloop 18, 602bm, 115 x 35½ ft, 18-32pdr. Wigram, Blackwall 18.3.1847. Sunk 4.10.1865 in torpedo trials at Chatham; raised and BU 1.1866 Castle & Beech.

TERPSICHORE 2nd class cruiser 3,400 tons, 300 x 43 ft, 2-6in, 6-4.7in, 8-6pdr. Thompson 30.10.1890. Sold 28.5.1914 Ward, Briton Ferry.

TERPSICHORE Destroyer 1,710 tons, 339½ x 36 ft, 4-4.7in, 2-40mm, 8-TT. Denny 17.6.1943. Frigate 11.54. Arrived 17.5.64 at Troon to BU.

TERRA NOVA Escort (RCN) 2,365 tons, 366(oa) x 42 ft, 4-3in, 2-40mm. Victoria Mcy 21.6.1955.

TERRAPIN Submarine, 'T' class. Vickers Armstrong, Barrow 31.8.1943. Damaged by D/Cs 19.5.45 in the Pacific and not repaired; arrived 6.46 at Troon to BU.

TERRIBLE 6th Rate 26, 253bm, 92½ x 25 ft. Ellis, Shoreham 15.6.1694. Captured 20.9.1710 by the Spanish off Cape St Marys.

TERRIBLE Bomb 14, 263bm, 83 x 27½ ft. Stacey, Deptford 4.8.1730. Sold 9.2.1748.

TERRIBLE 3rd Rate 74, 1,590bm, 164 x 47½ ft. French, captured 14.10.1747 off Cape Finisterre. BU completed 16.2.1763 at Chatham.

TERRIBLE 3rd Rate 74, 1,644bm, 169 x 47 ft. Barnard, Harwich 4.9.1762. Burnt 11.9.1781 as unseaworthy after damage in action with the French off the Chesapeake.

TERRIBLE 3rd Rate 74 1,660bm, 170½

x 47½ ft. Wells, Rotherhithe 28.3.1785. Receiving ship 5.1823; coal hulk 4.1829. BU 3.1836 at Deptford.

TERRIBLE (ex-SIMOOM renamed 12.1842) Wood pad. frigate, 1,858bm, 3,189 tons, 226 x 42½ ft, 8-68pdr, 8-56pdr, 3-12pdr. Deptford DY 6.2.1845. Sold 7.7.1879 to BU. (The first 4-Funnelled ship in the RN.)

TERRIBLE 1st class cruiser 14,200 tons, 500 X 71 ft, 2-9.2in, 12-6in, 16-12pdr. Thomson 27.5.1895. Renamed FISGARD III in 8.20, training ship. Sold 7.32 Cashmore.

TERRIBLE A/C carrier 14,000 tons, 630 x 80 ft, 30-40mm, 34-A/C. Devonport DY 30.9.1944. Renamed SYDNEY (RAN) 16.10.48. Fast Transport 3.62, 4-40mm. Left Sydney 23.12.75 for S.Korea to BU.

TERROR Bomb 4, 149bm, 66 x 23½ ft. Davis, Limehouse 11.1.1696. Captured 17.10.1704 by the French at Gibraltar and burnt.

TERROR Bomb 14, 278bm, 92 x 26½ ft. Greville & Whetstone, Limehouse 13.3.1741. Sold 3.12.1754.

TERROR Bomb 8, 301bm, 91½ x 27½ ft. Barnard, Harwich 16.1.1759. Sold 9.8.1774.

TERROR Bomb 8, 307bm, 92 x 28 ft. Randall, Rotherhithe 2.6.1779. Sold 13.8.1812.

TERROR Gunvessel 4, 69bm, 66½ x 15 ft. Dutch hoy purchased 3.1794. Sold 11.1804.

TERROR Bomb 10, 326bm, 102½ x 27½ft. Davy, Topsham 29.6.1813. Discovery vessel 5.1836. Abandoned 1848 in the Arctic.

TERROR Iron S.floating battery, 1,971bm, 1,844 tons, 186 x 48½ ft, 16-68pdr. Palmer, Jarrow 28.4.1856. Base ship at Bermuda 1857. Sold 1902 Walker & Co at Bermuda.

TERROR (see MALABAR of 1866)

TERROR Monitor 8,000 tons, 380 x 88 ft, 2-15in, 8-4in, 2-3in. Harland & Wolff 18.5.1916. Sunk 24.2.41 by Italian A/C off Derna.

TEST Destroyer 570 tons, 220 x 24ft, 4-12pdr, 2-TT. Laird 14.1.1907 as a speculation; purchased 12.09. Sold 30.8.19 Loveridge & Co.

TEST Frigate, 'River' class. Hall Russell 30.5.1942. Lent RIN 5.46 to 4.47 as NEZA. Arrived 25.2.55 at Faslane to BU.

TEST Drifter requis. 1914-19. Trawler 1920-22.

TETCOTT Destroyer, 'Hunt' class type II. White 12.8.1941. Arrived 24.9.56

Ward, Milford Haven to BU.

TETRARCH Destroyer, 'R' class. Harland & Wolff, Govan 20.4.1917. Sold 28.7.34 Metal Ind, Rosyth.

TETRARCH Submarine, 'T' class. Vickers Armstrong, Barrow 14.11.1939. Sunk 2.11.41 by unknown cause in the western Mediterranean.

TEVIOT Destroyer 590 tons, 225 x 23½ ft, 1-12pdr, 5-6pdr (4-12pdr 1907), 2-TT. Yarrow 7.11.1903. Sold 23.6.19 Ward, Morecambe.

TEVIOT Frigate, 'River' class. Hall Russell 12.10.1942. Lent SAN 6.45 to 7.46. Sold 29.3.55, BU Ward, Briton Ferry.

TEVIOT Trawler 1920-23.

TEXEL 3rd Rate 64, 1,317bm. Dutch CERBERUS captured 30.8.1799 in the Texel. Sold 11.6.1818 Beatson to BU.

THAIS Sloop 18, 431bm, 109 x 30 ft. Tanner, Dartmouth 19.8.1806. Sold 13.8.1818. (Also served as fireship.)

THAIS Brig-sloop 10, 'Cherokee' class, 231bm. Pembroke Dock 12.10.1829. Foundered 12.1833 off the west coast of Ireland.

THAIS Tug 1856-69.

THAKENHAM Inshore M/S, 'Ham' class. Fairlie Yt Co 9.9.1957. Sold Pounds in 1977.

THALIA (see UNICORN of 1782)

THALIA 5th Rate 46, 1,082bm, 151½ x 40½ ft. Chatham DY (ex-Portsmouth transferred 5.1827) 1.1830. Harbour service 12.1855. BU completed 25.11.1867 White, Cowes.

THALIA Wood S.corvette, 1,459bm, 2,240 tons, 200 x 40½ ft, 8-64pdr. Woolwich DY 14.7.1869. Troopship 10.1886; powder hulk 1891; base ship commissioned 2.15. Sold 16.9.20 Rose Street Foundry. (The last ship built at Woolwich DY.)

THALIA Yacht 1940-42.

THAMES 5th Rate 32, 656bm, 127 x 34½ ft. Adams, Bucklers Hard 10.4.1758. BU 9.1803. (In French hands as TAMISE 24.10.93 to 7.6.96.)

THAMES 5th Rate 32 (fir-built), 662bm, 127 x 34 ft. Chatham DY 24.10.1805. BU 10.1816.

THAMES Cutter tender, 65bm, 51½ x 17½ ft. Rochester 1805. Made a DY craft 1866 and renamed YC.2. Sold 1872.

THAMES Bomb 6 (Indian), 102bm. Bombay DY 1814. Fate unknown.

THAMES 5th Rate 46, 1,088bm, 151½ x 40½ ft. Chatham DY 21.8.1823. Con-

vict ship 1841. Sunk 6.6.1863 at moorings Bermuda; wreck sold J.Murphy.

THAMES 2nd class cruiser 4,050 tons, 300 x 46 ft, 2-8in, 10-6in. Pembroke Dock 3.12.1885. Depot ship 1903; sold 13.11.20 and renamed *General Botha*, training ship at the Cape; reverted to THAMES 1942 as accommodation ship. Scuttled 13.5.47 in Simons Bay.

THAMES Submarine 1,805 tons, 325 x 28 ft, 1-4in, 8-TT. Vickers Armstrong, Barrow 26.2.1932. Sunk 23.7.40 by mine off Norway.

THAMES Name borne in succession by MMS.1789, ALVERTON and BUTTINGTON as RNVR tenders from 1949.

THAMES store carrier 320 tons. 1880, renamed BEE 1884-1921.

THAMES Tug requis. 1914-18; Tug requis 1940-44.

THANE (ex-*Sunset*) Escort carrier 11,420 tons, 468½ x 69½ ft, 2-4in, 16-40mm, 24-A/C. Seattle Tacoma 15.7.1943 on lend-lease. Torpedoed 15.1.45 by 'U.482' off the Clyde Light vessel and not repaired; nominally returned 5.12.45 to the USN. Arrived Faslane 12.45; BU started 4.47.

THANET Destroyer, 'S' class. Hawthorn Leslie 5.11.1918. Sunk 27.1.42 by a Japanese squadron off Malaya.

THANKERTON Coastal M/S, 'Ton' class. Camper & Nicholson 4.9.1956. Renamed BRINCHANG 5.66, Malaysian navy.

THATCHAM Inshore M/S, 'Ham' class. Jones, Buckie 25.9.1957. Sold Pounds 1986.

THEBAN 5th Rate 36, 954bm, 145 x 48½ ft. Parsons, Warsash 22.12.1809. BU 5.1817.

THEBAN 5th Rate 46, 1,215bm, 159½ x 42 ft. Portsmouth DY. Ordered 13.9.1824, cancelled 7.2.1831.

THEBAN Submarine, 'T' class. Vickers Armstrong, Barrow. Ordered 18.4.1942, cancelled 18.10.44.

THEODOCIA (see VENTURER of 1807)

THE PAS Corvette (RCN), 'Flower' class. Collingwood SY 16.8.1941. BU 6.46.

THERMOPYLAE Submarine, 'T' class. Chatham DY 27.6.1945. Sold 26.5.70, BU at Troon.

THERMOPYLAE Drifter requis, 1915-19 & 1939-46.

THESEUS 3rd Rate 74, 1,660bm, 170x 47½ ft. Perry, Blackwall 25.9.1786. BU 5.1814 at Chatham.

THESEUS 1st class cruiser 7,350 tons, 360 x 60 ft, 2-9.2in, 10-6in, 12-6pdr. Thames I.W.8.9.1892. Sold 8.11.1921 Slough TC; BU in Germany.

THESEUS A/C carrier 13,350 tons, 630 x 80 ft, 19-40mm, 48-A/C. Fairfield 6.7.1944. Arrived 29.5.62 Ward, Inverkeithing to BU.

THE SOO Minesweeper (RCN), 'Algerine' class. Pt Arthur 15.8.1942. Renamed SAULT STE MARIE 1944. Sold 11.59, BU 5.60.

THETFORD MINES Frigate (RCN), 'River' class. Morton, Quebec 30.10.1943. Sold 3.1.46 mercantile.

THETIS Storeship 22, 720bm. Plymouth DY 1717. Fate unknown.

THETIS 5th Rate 44, 720bm, 126½ x 36 ft. Okill, Liverpool 15.4.1747. Hospital ship 7.1757. Sold 9.6.1767.

THETIS 5th Rate 32, 686bm, 126 x 35 ft. Adams, Bucklers Hard 2.11.1773. Wrecked 12.5.1781 off St Lucia, W.Indies.

THETIS 5th Rate 38. 946bm, 141½ x 39 ft. Rotherhithe 23.9.1782. Sold 9.6.1814.

THETIS Schooner 8. Purchased 1796. Listed 1800.

THETIS 6th Rate 24. Dutch, captured 23.4.1796 at Demerara and later scuttled there.

THETIS Gun-brig 10 (Indian), 185bm. Bombay DY 1810. Listed in 1836.

THETIS 5th Rate 46, 1,086bm, 151 x 40½ ft, Pembroke Dock 1.2.1817. Wrecked 5.12.1830 on Cape Frio, Brazil.

THETIS 5th Rate 36, 1,524bm, 164½ x 46½ ft,. 4-8in, 32-32pdr. Devonport DY 21.8.1846. To Prussian navy 12.1.1855 in exchange for two gunboats.

THETIS Wood S.corvette, 1,322bm, 1,860 tons, 220 x 35½ ft, 14-64pdr. Devonport DY 26.10.1871. Sold 11.1887 Pethwick, Plymouth.

THETIS 2nd class cruiser 3,400 tons, 300 x 43 ft, 2-6in, 6-4.7in, 8-6pdr. Thomson 13.12.1890. Minelayer 8.1907. Sunk 23.4.18 as blockship at Zeebrugge.

THETIS Submarine, 'T' class. Cammell Laird 29.6.1938. Foundered 1.6.39 in Liverpool Bay; raised, renamed THUNDERBOLT 4.40. Sunk 13.3.43 by the Italian corvette CICOGNA north of Sicily.

THISBE 6th Rate 28, 596bm, 120½ x 33½ ft. King, Dover 25.11.1783. Sold 9.8.1815.

THISBE 5th Rate 46, 1,083bm, 151½ x 40½ ft. Pembroke Dock 9.9.1824.

Lent 13.8.1863 as church ship at Cardiff. Sold 11.8.1892 W.H.Caple.

THISBE Destroyer, 'R' class. Hawthorn Leslie 8.3.1917. Handed over 31.8.36 in part payment for *Majestic*; BU at Pembroke Dock.

THISBE Minesweeper, 'Algerine' class. Redfern, Toronto 12.4.1943. Arrived 12.57 Charlestown to BU.

THISTLE Schooner 10, 150bm, 79 x 22 ft. Bermuda 27.9.1808. Wrecked 6.3.1811 off New York.

THISTLE Gun-brig 12, 185bm, 84½ x 22½ ft, 10-18pdr carr., 2-6pdr. Ross, Rochester 13.7.1812. BU 7.1823.

THISTLE Wood S.gunboat, 'Dapper' class. Pitcher, Northfleet 3.2.1855. BU. Completed at Deptford 11.11.1863.

THISTLE Compos. S.gunvessel, 465bm, 603 tons, 155 x 25 ft, 1-7in, 1-64pdr, 2-20pdr. Deptford DY 25.1.1868. Sold 11.1888 Read, Portsmouth.

THISTLE 1st class gunboat 710 tons, 180 x 33 ft, 2-4in, 4-12pdr. London & Glasgow Co 22.6.1899. Sold 13.7.1926 Ward, Pembroke Dock.

THISTLE Submarine, 'T' class. Vickers Armstrong, Barrow 25.10.1938. Sunk 10.4.40 by 'U.4' off Skudesnes, Norway.

THISTLE Ferry 1902-21; Yacht 1914-15; 2 Trawlers, 5 Drifters WW.I.

THOMAS Ship mentioned in 1350.

THOMAS 4-gun vessel, 180bn. Built 1420. Sold 1423.

THOMAS 10-gun vessel (Royalist). Captured 1649 by Parliament and renamed LEOPARDS WHELP. Fate unknown.

THOMAS Schooner. Purchased 1796. Listed to 1799.

THOMAS Fireship. Purchased 1808. Expended 1809.

THOMAS & ELIZABETH Fireship 10. Purchased 1688. Expended 24.5.1692 at Cape la Hogue.

THOR Submarine, 'T' class. Portsmouth DY 18.4.1944, not completed. BU 7.46 Rees, Llanelly.

THORLOCK Corvette (RCN), modified 'Flower' class. Midland SY, Ontario 15.5.1944. Sold 1946 Chilian navy as PAPUDO.

THORN Sloop 14, 306bm, 96½ x 27 ft, 14-32pdr carr., 2-6pdr. Betts, Mistleythorn 17.2.1779. Lent 1799 as training ship; sold 28.8.1816. (In French hands 25.8.79 to 20.8.82).

THORN Destroyer 400 tons, 210 x 20½ ft, 1-12pdr, 5-6pdr, 2-TT. Thomson 17.3.1900. BU 1919 at Portsmouth

DY.

THORN Submarine, 'T' class. Cammell Laird 18.3.1941. Sunk 6.8.42 by the Italian TB PEGASO in the Mediterranean.

THORNBROUGH TE 'Captain' class Frigate, Bethlehem, Hingham 13.11.1943 on lend-lease. Nominally returned 30.1.47 to the USN. BU 1947 in Greece.

THORNBURY CASTLE Corvette, 'Castle' class. Fergusson. Cancelled 12.1943.

THORNHAM Inshore M/S, 'Ham' class. Taylor, Shoreham 18.3.1957. BU by G & T. Services Charlton in 5.85.

THOROUGH Submarine, 'T' class. Vickers Armstrong, Barrow 30.10.1943. Arrived 29.6.1961 Clayton & Davie, Dunston to BU.

THRACIAN Brig-sloop 18, 'Cruiser' class, 383bm. Brindley, Frindsbury 15.7.1809. BU completed 6.6.1829.

THRACIAN Destroyer, 'S' class. Hawthorn Leslie 5.3.1920, completed at Sheerness 1.4.22. Bombed by Japanese A/C and beached 24.12.41 at Hong Kong; salved and commissioned 9.42 as Japanese patrol boat No. 101. Returned 4.9.45 to the RN, sold 2.46 at Hong Kong; BU 1947.

THRASHER (ex-*Adamant*) Gun-brig 12, 154bm, 10-18pdr carr., 2-9pdr. Warren, Brightlingsea 1804 and purchased 6.1804. Sold 3.11.1814.

THRASHER Wood S.gunboat, 'Albacore' class. Green. Blackwall 22.3.1856. Sold by order dated 9.5.1883.

THRASHER Destroyer 395 tons, 210 x 21½ ft, 1-12pdr, 5-6pdr, 2-TT. Laird 5.11.1895. Sold 4.11.1919 Fryer.

THRASHER Submarine, 'T' clas. Cammell Laird 28.11.1940. Arrived 9.3.47 Ward, Briton Ferry to BU.

THREAT Submarine, 'T' class. Vickers Armstrong, Barrow. Cancelled 1945, not laid down.

THRUSH (ex-Revenue brig PRINCE OF WALES renamed 12.9.1806) Brig-sloop 18, 307bm. Powder hulk 10.1809 at Port Royal, Jamaica Wrecked 7.1815 and sold.

THRUSH Wood S.gunboat, 'Clown' class. Briggs, Sunderland 12.5.1856. BU completed 14.3.1864.

THRUSH 1st class gunboat 805 tons, 165 x 31 ft, 6-4in, 2-3pdr. Scotts, Greenock 22.6.1889. Coastguard 1906; cable ship 1915; salvage ship 1916. Wrecked 11.4.17 near Glenarm, N.Ireland.

THRUSH 2 Trawlers & 2 Drifters WW.I.

THRUSTER Destroyer, 'R' class. Hawthorn Leslie 10.1.1917. Arrived 16.3.37 Ward, Grays to BU.

THRUSTER Tank landing ship 3,620 tons, 390 x 49 ft, 8-20mm. Harland & Wolff 24.9.1942. To Dutch navy 1945 as PELIKAAN.

THRUSTER (see LST.3520)

THULE (ex-P.325) Submarine, 'T' class. Devonport DY 22.10.1942. Arrived 14.9.62 Ward, Inverkeithing to BU.

THULEN 5th Rate 36. Dutch, seized 8.6.1796 at Plymouth. BU 1811. (Also spelt THOULEN or THOLEN)

THUNDER Bomb 54, 147bm, 65½ x 23½ ft. Snelgrove, Deptford 1695. Captured 21.3.1696 by a French privateer off the Dutch coast.

THUNDER Bomb 6, 254bm, 28 x 27½ ft, 6-9pdr, 1 mortar. Spanish, captured 10.1720. Ordered 27.3.1734 to be BU.

THUNDER Bomb 8, 272bm, 91½ x 26½ ft. Bird, Rotherhithe 30.8.1740. Foundered 20.10.1744 in a hurricane near Jamaica.

THUNDER (ex-Racehorse) Bomb 8, 314bm, 98 x 27 ft. Purchased 7.1771 in India. Captured 17.8.1778 by the French off Rhode Island.

THUNDER Bomb 8, 301bm, 91½ x 28 ft. Heneker, River Medway (Chatham?) 15.3.1759. Sold 2.9.1774.

THUNDER Bomb 8, 305bm, 92 x 28 ft. Randall, Rotherhithe 18.5.1779. Foundered 1.1781 in the Channel.

THUNDER Bomb 8, 230bm. Dutch DUGUSE ERWARTUNG captured 1797. Sold 22.2.1802.

THUNDER (ex-*Dasher*) Bomb 8, 384bm, 111½ x 28 ft. Purchased 10.1803. Sold 30.6.1814.

THUNDER Bomb, 326bm, 102½ x 27½ ft. Brindley, Frindsbury. Ordered 1812 and cancelled.

THUNDER Bomb 12, 372bm, 105 x 29 ft, 10-24pdr carr., 2-6pdr, 2 mortars. Deptford DY 4.8.1829. Survey vessel 6.1.1833. BU 5.1851.

THUNDER Wood ironclad floating battery, 1,469bm, 172½ x 43 ft, 14-68pdr. Mare, Blackwall 17.4.1855. BU 6.1874 at Chatham.

THUNDER Minesweeper (RCN), TE 'Bangor' class. Dufferin 19.3.1941. Sold 1947 Marine Industries.

THUNDER Coastal M/S (RCN), 'Ton' class 370 tons. Vickers, Montreal 17.7.1952. To French navy 1954 as La PAIMPOLAISE.

THUNDER Coastal M/S (RCN), 'Ton' class 390 tons. Port Arthur 27.10.1956.

THUNDERBOLT 5th Rate 32, 530bm, 119 x 32 ft. French, captured 1696. Hulked 1699. BU 1731.

THUNDERBOLT Wood pad. sloop, 1,058bm, 180 x 36 ft. Portsmouth DY 13.1.1842. Wrecked 3.2.1847 on Cape Recife, S.Africa.

THUNDERBOLT Iron S.floating battery, 1,954bm, 186 x 48½ ft, 16-68pdr. Samuda, Poplar 22.4.1856. Became a floating pier-head at Chatham 13.11.1873; rammed by a tug and sunk 3.4.1948; raised and BU 1949 on river bank. (Bore the name DAEDALUS 1916-19 as nominal depot ship for the RN Air Service).

THUNDERBOLT (see THETIS of 1938)

THUNDERBOLT Drifter 1919-20.

THUNDERER 3rd Rate 74, 1,609bm, 166½ x 47 ft. Woolwich DY 19.3.1760. Wrecked 5.10.1780 in the W.Indies.

THUNDERER Ketch 14 (Canadian lakes) Built 1776. Fate unknown.

THUNDERER 3rd Rate 74, 1,690bm, 171 x 47½ ft. Wells, Rotherhithe 13.11.1783. BU 3.1814.

THUNDERER (see TALAVERA of 1818)

THUNDERER 2nd Rate 84, 2,279bm, 196 x 52 ft. Woolwich DY 22.9.1831 (8½ years on stocks). Target 5.1863; renamed COMET 21.4.1869 and NETTLE 9.3.1870. Sold 25.11.1901.

THUNDERER Turret ship, 4,407bm, 9,390 tons, 285 x 62½ ft, 4-12in. Pembroke Dock 25.3.1872. Sold 13.9.1909 Garnham.

THUNDERER Battleship 22,500 tons, 545 x 88½ ft, 10-13.5in, 16-4in. Thames IW 1.2.1911. Sold 12.26 Hughes Bolckow, Blyth.

THUNDERER Battleship 42,500 tons, 740 x 105 ft, 9-16in, 16-5.25in. Fairfield. Laid down 1939, suspended 10.39, cancelled 1944.

THURSO BAY (ex-LOCH MUICK renamed 1944) Frigate, 'Bay' class. Hall Russell 19.10.1945. Completed at Chatham 23.9.49 as OWEN, survey ship. Sold 3.7.70, BU at Blyth.

THYME Corvette, 'Flower' class. Smiths DK 25.7.1941. To Air Ministry 1947 as weather ship *Weather Explorer.*

TIARA Submarine, 'T' class. Portsmouth DY 18.4.1944, not completed. BU 6.47 Dover Industries Ltd.

TIBENHAM Inshore M/S, 'Ham' class. McGruer 10.3.1955. To French navy 1955.

TIBER 5th Rate 38, 1,076bm, 150 x 40 ft. List, Fishbourne 10.11.1813. Sold 1.1820 Durkin, Southampton.

TIBER 5th Rate 46, 1,215bm, 159 x 42 ft. Portsmouth DY. Ordered 9.6.1825 cancelled 7.2.1931.

TICKHAM (see OAKLEY)

TICKLER Brig-sloop 12, circa 250bm, 94 x 25 ft. Purchased 1781. Captured 1783 by the French in the W.Indies.

TICKLER Gunvessel 12, 148bm, 75 x 21 ft. Hill, Limehouse 28.5.1794. Sold 5.1802.

TICKLER Gunvessel 1. Purchased 9.1798 in Honduras for local use. Listed 1800.

TICKLER Gun-brig 12, 178bm, 80½ x 22½ ft, 2-18pdr, 10-18pdr carr. Warren, Brightlingsea 8.8.1804. Captured 4.6.1808 by Danes in the Great Belt.

TICKLER (ex-*Lord Duncan*) Cutter 14, 114bm. Purchased 1808. Sold 28.8.1816.

TICKLER Wood S.gunboat, 'Albacore' class. Pitcher, Northfleet 8.9.1855. BU. Completed at Deptford 21.11.1863.

TICKLER Iron S.gunboat 265 tons, 85 x 26 ft, 1-10in. Pembroke Dock 15.9.1879. DY lighter 1902; renamed AFRIKANDER 26.2.19 as base ship; AFRIKANDER II in 1933. BU 1937 at Simonstown.

TIGER 22-gun ship, 120/200bm, 6-9pdr, 14-6pdr, 2-2pdr. Built 1546. Rebuilt 1570; floating battery 1600. Condemned 1605.

TIGER Discovery vessel, 260bm. In the Arctic 1613.

TIGER 32-gun ship, 457bm, 100 x 29½ ft. Deptford 1647. Rebuilt Deptford 1681 as 448bm; rebuilt Rotherhithe 1701 as 613bm; rebuilt Sheerness 1722 as 712bm. Wrecked 12.1.1743 on Tortuga, W.Indies.

TIGER PRIZE 4th Rate 48, 645bm. Algerian, captured 3.1678 by RUPERT. Sunk 14.2.1696 as a foundation at Sheerness.

TIGER 4th Rate 50, 976bm, 140 x 40 ft. Barnard, Harwich 22.12.1743. Renamed HARWICH 28.11.1743. Wrecked 4.10.1760 on Isle of Pines, Cuba.

TIGER 4th Rate 60, 1,218bm, 151 x 43 ft. Wells & Stanton, Rotherhithe 23.11.1747. Hulk 1760. Sold 12.5.1765 at Bombay.

TIGER 3rd Rate 74, 1,886bm, 169 x 51 ft. Spanish, captured 13.8.1762 at Havana. Sold 10.6.1784.

TIGER (see ARDENT of 1764)

TIGER (see GRAMPUS of 1802)

TIGER Gunvessel 4, 80bm, 68 x 16 ft, 3-32pdr carr., 1-24pdr. Dutch hoy purchased 3.1794. Sold 1798.

TIGRE 3rd Rate 80, 1,887bm, 182 x 48½ ft. French captured 23.6.1795 with two others by the fleet off L'Orient. BU 6.1817.

TIGER Gun-brig 12, 131bm. In service 1808-12. (Perhaps a revenue cutter built Bridport 1805 and transferred.)

TIGER Wood pad. sloop, 1,221bm, 250 x 36 ft, 2-10in, 14-32pdr. Chatham DY 1.12.1849. Rated as frigate 1852. Grounded 12.5.1854 in action near Odessa; became Russian TIGR.

TIGER Destroyer 400 tons, 210 x 21 ft, 1-12pdr, 5-6pdr, 2-TT. Thomson as a speculation 19.5.1900 and purchased. Sunk 2.4.08 in collision with BERWICK off St Catherines.

TIGER Battlecruiser 28,500 tons, 600 x 90½ ft, 8-13.5in, 12-6in. J.Brown 15.12.1913. Sold 2.32 Ward, Inverkeithing

TIGER Cruiser 8,800 tons, 538 x 64 ft, 9-6in, 10-4in. Vickers Armstrong, Tyne. Ordered 3.1942, renamed BELLEROPHON 17.8.42, laid down 8.44, renamed BLAKE 12.44, renamed BELLEROPHON 2.45. Cancelled 3.46.

TIGER (see BLAKE)

TIGER (ex-BELLEROPHON renamed 2.45) Cruiser 9,550 tons, 538 x 64 ft, 9-6in, 10-4in. J.Brown 25.10.45. Arrived Castellon, Spain 28.9.86 to BU.

TIGER BAY patrol boat 81 tons. Argentinian ISLAS MALVINAS captured in Falklands in 6.1982. Sold 1986.

TIGER SNAKE SSV (RAN) 78 tons, Savage 6.1944. to N.Borneo in 11.45.

TIGER WHELP (see MARY ANTRIM)

TIGRE (see TIGER)

TIGRESS Gun-brig 12, 168bm, 76 x 22½ ft, 2-24pdr, 10-18pdr carr. Brindley, Lynn 11.9.1797. Sold 1.1802.

TIGRESS Gun-brig 12, 177bm, 80 x 22½ ft, 2-18pdr, 10-18pdr carr. Dudman, Deptford 1.6.1804. Captured 2.8.1808 by the Danes in the Great Belt.

TIGRESS Gun-brig 12, 219bm, French PIERRE CZAR captured 29.6.1808. Renamed ALGERINE 21.4.14. Sold 29.1.1818.

TIGRESS Destroyer 750 tons, 246 x 26 ft, 2-4in, 2-12pdr, 2-TT. Hawthorn Leslie 20.12.1911. Sold 9.5.21 Ward, Milford Haven; arrived 9.22.

TIGRIS (ex-FORTH renamed 1812) 5th Rate 36, 934bm, 143 x 38½ ft. Pel-

ham, Frindsbury 26.6.1813. Sold 11.6.1818 to BU.

TIGRIS 5th Rate 46, 1,215bm, 159½ x 42 ft. Plymouth DY (from frames made at Bombay). Laid down 6.1822, cancelled 31.8.1832.

TIGRIS Survey brig 10 (Indian), 258bm, 93 x 26 ft, Bombay DY 20.4.1829. Sold 7.1862.

TIGRIS Iron pad. gunboat (Indian), 109bm. Laird 1834 in sections, re-erected 5.1834 at Basra. Lost 21.5.1835 in the Euphrates.

TIGRIS Paddle vessel (Indian) 192 tons, 132 x 18 ft. Bombay DY 1882. Sold 1904, renamed Amarapoora.

TIGRIS Submarine, 'T' class. Chatham DY 31.10.1939. Sunk 10.3.43 by unknown cause in the Gulf of Naples.

TILBURY 4th Rate 54, 691bm, 130 x 34½ ft. Chatham DY 1699. BU 1726.

TILBURY 4th Rate 60, 963bm, 144 x 39 ft. Chatham DY 2.6.1733. Burnt 21.9.1742 by accident off Hispaniola.

TILBURY 4th Rate 58, 1,124bm, 147 x 42 ft. Portsmouth DY 20.7.1745. Foundered 24.9.1757 in a hurricane off Louisburg.

TILBURY (see CHATHAM of 1758)

TILBURY Wood S.gunboat, 'Albacore' class. Pitcher, Northfleet 29.3.1856. BU 12.1865 Marshall, Plymouth.

TILBURY Destroyer, 'S' class. Swan Hunter 13.6.1918. Sold 2.31 Rees, Llanelly.

TILBURY (see KONKAN)

TILFORD Seaward defence boat, 'Ford' class. Vosper 21.11.1956. Sold Pounds 8.9.67.

TILLSONBURG (see FLYING FISH of 1944)

TILLSONBURG (ex-PEMBROKE CASTLE renamed 1943) Corvette (RCN), 'Castle' class. Ferguson 12.2.1944. Sold 5.9.46, renamed Chiu Chin then to Chinese Communist navy.

TIMMINS Corvette (RCN), 'Flower' class. Yarrow, Esquimalt 26.6.1941. Sold 1946, renamed Guayaquil.

TINGIRA (ex-Sobraon) Training ship (RAN) 1,800 tons. Purchased 1912. Sold 3.11.27 W.M.Ford. BU 1940.

TINTAGEL Destroyer, 'S' class. Swan Hunter 9.8.1918. Sold 16.2.32 S.Castle, Plymouth.

TINTAGEL CASTLE Corvette, 'Castle' class. Ailsa 13.12.1943. Arrived 6.58 at Troon to BU.

TINY Wood S.gunboat, 'Cheerful' class. Young & Magnay, Limehouse 8.5.1856. BU completed 28.1.1864.

TIPPERARY (ex-Chilian ALMIRANTE

RIVEROS purchased 8.1914) Destroyer leader 1,737 tons, 320 x 32½ ft, 6-4in, 3-TT. White 5.3.15. Sunk 1.6.16 at Jutland.

TIPPU SULTAN (see ONSLOW of 1941)

TIPTOE Submarine, 'T' class. Vickers Armstrong, Barrow 25.2.1944. Sold Pounds 16.4.71.

TIR (see BANN of 1942)

TIRADE Destroyer, modified 'R' class. Scotts 21.4.1917. Sold 15.11.21 Cashmore, Newport.

TIRADE Trawler 1942-46.

TIRELESS Submarine, 'T' class. Portsmouth DY 19.3.1943. Sold Cashmore 20.9.68, BU Newport.

TIRELESS Nuclear S/M 4000 tons. Vickers 17.3.1984

TISDALE Frigate (RCN), 'River' class. Montreal. Cancelled 1944.

TISIPHONE 6th Rate 20, 425bm, 109 x 30 ft. Ladd, Dover 9.5.1781. Floating battery 16 guns 7.1803. Sold 11.1.1816.

TITANIA Depot ship 5,270 tons, 335 x 46 ft. Clyde SB Co 4.3.1915, purchased 1915. BU by Metal Ind. Faslane in 6.48.

TIVERTON Minesweeper, later 'Hunt' class. Simons 24.9.1918. Sold 12.38 Ward, Grays.

TOBAGO Brig-sloop 14. American TRUMBULL captured 1777 by VENUS. Sold 1783.

TOBAGO Schooner 10, 120bm. Purchased 1805. Captured 18.10.1806 by the French privateer GENERAL ERNOUF; recaptured 24.1.1809 as VENGEUR and sold.

TOBAGO Destroyer, 'S' class 1,085 tons. Thornycroft 15.7.1918. Damaged 12.11.20 by mine and sold 9.2.22 at Malta.

TOBAGO (ex-HONG KONG renamed 1943, ex-HOLMES) Frigate, 'Colony' class. Walsh Kaiser 27.9.43 on lend-lease. Returned 13.5.46 to the USN.

TOBRUK Destroyer (RAN) 2,325 tons, 355 x 40 ft, 4-4.5in, 12-40mm, 10-TT. Cockatoo DY 20.12.1947. Sold 27.1.72 to BU in Japan.

TOBRUK Landing ship (RAN) 3400 tons. Carrington Slip. Newcastle NSW. 1.3.1980

TOKEN Submarine, 'T' class. Portsmouth DY 19.3.1943. Sold Pounds 18.2.70, BU Cairnryan.

TOKEN Drifter 1915-19 and 1939-41.

TOMAHAWK Destroyer, 'S' class 930 tons. Yarrow 16.5.1918. Sold 26.6.28 King, Garston.

TOMAHAWK (see WATERWAY)

TOMAHAWK (see SCORPION of 1946)

TONBRIDGE Minesweeper, later 'Hunt' class. Simons 5.11.1918. Sold 19.5.28 Ward, Briton Ferry.

TONBRIDGE Netlayer requis. 1940-41.

TONBRIDGE CASTLE Corvette, 'Castle' class. Austin, Sunderland. Cancelled 12.1943. (Was to have been transferred to the RCN.)

TONGHAM Inshore M/S, 'Ham' class. Miller, St Monance 30.11.1955. Sold Pounds 1980, resold to Greek interest 1981.

TONNANT 3rd Rate 80, 2,281bm, 194 x 52 ft. French, captured 1.8.1798 at the Nile. BU 3.1821.

TOOWOOMBA Minesweeper, 'Bathurst' class. Walker, Maryborough 26.3.1941. On loan to the RAN from 10.41. Sold Dutch navy 1946 as BOEROE.

TOPAZE 5th Rate 38, 916bm, 144½ x 38 ft. French, handed over 12.1793 by Royalists at Toulon. Sold 1.9.1814.

TOPAZE 5th Rate 38, 1,060bm, 151½ x 40 ft. French ETOILE captured 27.3.1814 by HEBRUS off La Hogue. Receiving ship 2.1823; target 3.1850. BU 12.1851.

TOPAZE Wood S.frigate 51, 2,659bm, 3,915 tons, 235 x 50 ft, 30-8in, 1-68pdr, 20-32pdr. Devonport DY 12.5.1858. Sold Castle 14.2.1884.

TOPAZE 3rd class cruiser 3,000 tons, 360 x 40 ft, 12-4in, 8-3pdr. Laird 23.7.1903. Sold 22.9.21 Cohen, BU in Germany.

TOPAZE and TOPAZ 2 Trawlers WW.I; Trawler 1935-41.

TORBAY 2nd Rate 80, 1,202bm, 156 x 42 ft. Deptford DY 16.12.1693. Rebuilt Woolwich 1719 as 1,296bm. BU completed 1.1.1749 at Portsmouth.

TORBAY (see NEPTUNE of 1683)

TORBAY Destroyer, 'S' class 1,087 tons. Thornycroft 6.3.1919. Renamed CHAMPLAIN (RCN) 1.3.28. Sold 1937.

TORBAY Submarine, 'T' class. Chatham DY 9.4.1940. Sold 19.12.45, BU Ward, Briton Ferry.

TORBAY Nuclear S/M 4000 tons. Vickers 8.3.1985

TORBAY Drifter requis. 1915-19 and 1939-40.

TORCH Fireship 91bm *Fortune* purchased 10.1804. Sold 17.6.1807

TORCH Sloop 18, 557bm. French TORCHE captured 16.8.1805 by GOLIATH and CAMILLA in the Channel.

BU 6.1811. (One Admiralty source gives the vessel BU 1811 as a fireship, ex-*Fortune* purchased.)

TORCH Iron pad. gunvessel, 340bm, 141 x 22½ ft, 1-32pdr. Ditchburn, Blackwall 25.2.1845. Sold 15.5.1856 at Sydney.

TORCH Wood S.gunvessel, 'Philomel' class. Green, Blackwall 24.12.1859. BU 9.1881 at Malta.

TORCH Sloop 690 tos, 180 x 32½ ft, 6-4in. Sheerness DY 28.12.1894. Given to the New Zealand Govt 16.8.17 as training ship and renamed FIREBRAND. Sold 7.20 in New Zealand.

TORCH Destroyer, 'S' class 930 tons. Yarrow 16.3.1918. Sold 7.11.29 King, Garston.

TORCH Torp.Recovery vessel 698 tons (deep) Hall Russell 7.8.1979.

TOREADOR Destroyer, 'S' class 1,087 tons. Thornycroft 7.12.1918. Renamed VANCOUVER (RCN) 1.3.28. Sold 1937, arrived Vancouver 24.4.37 to BU.

TOREADOR Torp. recovery Vessel 680 tons Hall Russell 14.2.1980

TOREADOR Balloon vessel 1942-44.

TORMENTOR Gunvessel. Purchased 1794 in the W.Indies. Fate unknown.

TORMENTOR Destroyer, 'R' class. Stephen 22.5.1917. Sold 7.11.29 King, for Troon; wrecked in tow 13.12.29 on the S.Wales coast.

TORMENTOR Torp. Recovery vessel 680 tons Hall Russell 6.11.1979

TORNADO Destroyer, 'R' class. Stephen 4.8.1917. Sunk 23.12.17 by mine in the North Sea.

TORNADO Minesweeper 1940-46.

TORNADO Torp. Recovery Vessel. 680 tons Hall Russell 24.5.1979

TORONTO Schooner (Canadian lakes). York, Lake Toronto 8.1799. Wrecked and BU 1781 at York.

TORONTO Schooner (Canadian lakes). Listed 1813. Wrecked 2.6.1817 on the lakes.

TORONTO (ex-*sir Charles Adam*) Wood paddle vessel (Canadian lakes). Purchased 7.71838. Sold 1843.

TORONTO (see MARY ROSE of 1943)

TORONTO (ex-GIFFARD renamed 1943) Frigate (RCN), 'River' class. Davie SB 18.9.43. To R.Norwegain navy 4.56.as GARM.

TORONTO Destroyer (RCN) 2100 tons. St John DD ordered 18.8.1983

TORONTO Trawler requis. 1917-19.

TORQUAY Frigate 2,150 tons, 360 x 41 ft, 2-4.5in, 2-40mm. Harland & Wolff 1.7.1954.

TORRENS Destroyer (RAN) 700 tons, 246 x 24 ft, 1-4in, 3-12pdr, 3-TT. Cockatoo DY 28.8.1915. Sunk 24.11.30 as a target off Sydney Heads.

TORRENS Frigate (RAN) 2,150 tons, 360 x 41 ft, 2-4.5in, 4-GWS. Cockatoo DY. 28.9.1968.

TORRENT Destroyer, 'R' class. Swan Hunter 26.11.1916. Sunk 23.12.17 by mine in the North Sea.

TORRENT Torp. Recovery Vessel 680 tons Clelands 29.3.1971

TORRIDE Gunvessel 7. French fireship captured 25.8.1798 by boats of GOLIATH off the Nile. Listed 1802.

TORRID Destroyer. 'R' class. Swan Hunter 10.2.1917. Handed over 27.1.37 to Ward in part payment for *Majestic*, wrecked 16.3.37 in tow for Hayle, near Trefusis Point; BU there 1940.

TORRID Torp. Recovery Vessel 680 tons Clelands 7.9.1971

TORRIDGE Frigate, 'River' class. Blyth 16.8.1943. To French navy 1944 as SURPRISE.

TORRINGTON 62-gun ship, 732bm. Johnson, Blackwall 1654. Renamed DREADNOUGHT 1660. Foundered 16.18.1690 off N.Foreland.

TORRINGTON (see CHARLES GALLEY)

TORRINGTON 5th Rate 44, 711bm, 126 x 36 ft. Rowcliffe, Southampton 15.1.1743. Sold 30.8.1763.

TORRINGTON Frigate, TE 'Captain' class. Bethlehem, Hingham 27.11.1943 on lend-lease. Returned 1946 to the USN

TORTOISE (ex-*Grenville*) Storeship 26. Purchased 1777. Foundered 9.1779 off Newfoundland.

TORTOISE Store lighter, 109bm, 60½ x 20½ ft. Barnard, Deptford 17.7.1780. Lost 11.1787.

TORTOISE (ex-*Russian Eagle*) Storeship 16. Purchased 12.1781. Sold 10.1.1785.

TORTOISE Store lighter, 144bm, 69 x 22 ft. Sibrell, Plymouth 27.4.1789. BU 1.1863 at Plymouth.

TORTOISE (see SIR EDWARD HUGHES)

TORTOISE Tank vessel 1897-1946; Drifter in WW.I.

TORTOLA (ex-PEYTON renamed 1943) Frigate, 'Colony' class. Walsh Kaiser 16.11.43 on lend-lease. Returned 22.5.46 to the USN.

TOTEM Submarine, 'T' class. Devonport DY 28.9.1943. Sold 1964 Israeli navy; renamed DAKAR 10.11.67.

TOTLAND (ex-USS CAYUGA) Cutter 1,546 tons, 256(oa) x 42ft, 1-5in, 3-3in. Commissioned 12.5.1941 in the RN on lend-lease. Returned 5.46 to the USN.

TOTNES Paddle M/S, 'Ascot' class. McMillan 17.5.1916. Sold 3.22 Ward, Inverkeithing.

TOTNES CASTLE (see HUMBERSTONE)

TOURMALINE Compos. S.corvette 2,120 tons, 220 X 40ft, 12-64pdr. Raylton Dixon, Middlesbrough 30.10.1875. Coal hulk 1799; renamed C.115 in 12.04. Sold 11.20 as coal hulk.

TOURMALINE Destroyer, 'S' class 1,087 tons, Thornycroft 12.4.1919. Sold 11.31 Ward, Grays.

TOURMALINE (see CASSANDRA of 1943)

TOURMALINE (ex-USS USAGE) Minesweeper, 'Catherine' class. Gulf SB, Madisonville 4.10.1942 and to the RN 7.6.43 on lend-lease. Returned 1947 to the USN then to Turkish navy as CARDAK.

TOURMALINE Trawler requis. 1915-19; Trawler 1935-41.

TOURTERELLE 6th Rate 28, 581bm, 126 x 32 ft. French, captured 13.3.1795 by LIVELY off Ushant. Sunk 1816 as breakwater in Bermuda.

TOWER Smack 4. Purchased 1668. Sold 1674.

TOWER Tender 6, 145bm, 4-12pdr. Bridport 1809. Lent Thames police 1.1817. Sold 27.1.1825 J.Ledger.

TOWER Destroyer, modified 'R' class. Swan Hunter 5.4.1917. Sold 17.5.28 Cashmore, Newport.

TOWEY 6th Rate 24, 448bm, 108 x 30½ ft. Adams, Bucklers Hard 6.5.1814. BU 11.1822.

TOWY Frigate, 'River' class. Smiths Dk 4.3.1943. Arrived 27.6.56. Smith & Houston, Port Glasgow to BU.

TOWNSVILLE Minesweeper (RAN), 'Bathurst' class. Evans, Deakin, Brisbane 13.5.1941. Sold 8.8.56 Delta Sh. Co.

TOWNSVILLE Patrol boat (RAN) 211 tons, Cairns 16.5.1981.

TOWZER Gunvessel 1. Purchased 1798 in the W.Indies. Listed 1799.

TRACKER (ex-*Mormacmaili*) Escort carrier 11,420 tons, 468½ x 69½ ft, 2-4in, 16-40mm, 24-A/C. Seattle Tacoma 7.3.1942 on lend-lease. Returned 29.11.45 to the USN.

TRACKER (see LST.3522)

TRACOUN Sloop 14. Purchased 1782. Fate unknown.

TRADEWIND Submarine, 'T' class. Chatham DY 11.12.1942. Arrived 14.12.55 at Charlestown to BU.

TRAFALGAR 1st Rate 106, 2,404bm, 196 x 53½ ft. Chatham DY 26.7.1820 (7 years on stocks). Renamed CAMPERDOWN 22.2.1825. Harbour service 1854. Coal hulk 1857. Renamed PITT 29.8.1882. Sold 15.5.1906 Castle.

TRAFALGAR 1st Rate 110, 2,694bm, 205½ x 55½ ft. Woolwich DY 21.6.1841 (11½ years on stocks). Undocked 21.3.1859 as screw ship, 2,900 bm; renamed BOSCAWEN 1873. Sold 10.7.1906 Castle, Thames.

TRAFALGAR Battleship 11,940 tons, 345 x 73 ft, 4-13.5in, 6-4.7in, 8-6pdr. Portsmouth DY 20.9.1887. Sold 9.5.1911 Garnham.

TRAFALGAR Destroyer 2,325 tons, 355 x 40 ft, 4-4.5in, 1-4in, 10-40mm, 8-TT. Swan Hunter 12.1.1944. Sold Arnott Young 8.6.70, BU at Dalmuir.

TRAFALGAR Nuclear S/M 4000 tons. Vickers 1.7.1981

TRAIL Corvette (RCN), 'Flower' class. Burrard 16.10.1940. BU 8.50 Steel Co of Canada, Hamilton.

TRAILER (ex-USS BLOCK ISLAND, ex-*Mormacpenn*) Escort carrier 11,420 tons, 468½ x 69½ ft, 2-4in, 8-40mm, 18-A/C. Ingalls, Pascagoula 22.5.1942, on lend-lease. Renamed HUNTER 11.42. Returned 29.12.45 to the USN.

TRALEE Minesweeper, later 'Hunt' class. Simons 17.12.1918. Sold 2.7.29 Hill, Dover.

TRAMONTANA Bark 21, 150bm, 12-6pdr, 7-4pdr, 2-2pdr. Deptford 1586. BU 1618.

TRANSCONA Minesweeper (RCN), diesel 'Bangor' class. Marine Ind 26.4.1941 To RCMP 1950 as *French*.

TRANSFER Sloop 14. French cutter TEMERAIRE captured 1795 by DIDO in the Mediterranean. BU 1803.

TRANSFER Sloop 12, 181bm, 80 x 23½ ft, 12-6pdr. French privateer QUARTRE FRERES captured 21.11.1797. Sold 1802 at Malta.

TRANSIT Schooner 12, 261bm, 129 x 22½ ft. Bailey, Ipswich 3.3.1809; later shortened to 214bm, 112½ x 22½ ft. Sold 12.10.1815.

TRANSIT Iron S.troopship, 2,587bm, 302½ x 41½ ft. Mare, Blackwall 20.3.1855, purchased on stocks.

Wrecked 10.7.1857 in the Banka Strait.

TRANSIT Drifter requis. 1915-17.

TRANSPORTER (also TRANSPORT LIGHTER) Ketch 7, 92bm. Sheerness 1677. Rebuilt Deptford 1709 as 100bm; sold 8.1.1713 J.Fox.

TRANSVAAL (ex-LOCH ARD renamed 1944) Frigate (SAN), 'Loch' class. Harland & Wolff, Govan 2.8.1944.

TRANSVAAL Trawler requis. 1916-19 & 1939-44.

TRAVE 5th Rate 38, 1,076bm. French, captured 23.10.1813 by AN-DROMACHE in the Atlantic. Sold 7.6.1821.

TRAVELLER Wood pad. vessel (Canadian lakes). Purchased 30.4.1839. Sold 1844 mercantile.

TRAVELLER Wood S.gunboat, 'Albacore' class. Green, Blackwall 13.3.1856. BU completed 28.12.1863 at Portsmouth.

TRAVELLER Submarine, 'T' class. Scotts 27.8.1941. Sunk 1942 by unknown cause in the Gulf of Taranto and formally paid off 12.12.42.

TRAVELLER Tug 1885-1920.

TREDAGH (DROGHEDA) 50-gun ship, 771bm. Ratcliffe 1654. Renamed RESOLUTION 1660. Burnt 25.7.1666 in action with the Dutch.

TREEKRONEN 3rd Rate 74, 1,746bm, 175½ x 48 ft. Danish. captured 7.9.1807 at Copenhagen. Receiving ship 1809. Sold 20.7.1825 Beatson to BU.

TRELAWNEY Storeship 14, 350bm, 106 x 29 ft, 10-9pdr, 4-3pdr. Purchased 2.1743. Sold 19.5.1747.

TREMADOC BAY (ex-LOCH ARNISH renamed 1944) Frigate, 'Bay' class. Harland & Wolff 29.3.1945. Arrived 18.9.59 at Genoa to BU.

TREMATON CASTLE Corvette, 'Castle' class. Morton, Quebec. Cancelled 12.1943.

TREMENDOUS 3rd Rate 74, 1,656bm, 170½ x 48½ ft. Barnard, Deptford 30.10.1784. Rebuilt 1810 as 1,706bm; renamed GRAMPUS 23.5.1845 and reduced to 50 guns. Powder hulk 1856. Sold 10.5.1897 J.Read, Portsmouth.

TRENCHANT Destroyer, modified 'R' class. White 23.12.1916. Sold 15.11.28 to BU.

TRENCHANT Submarine, 'T' class. Chatham DY 24.3.1943. Sold 1.7.63, arrived 23.7.63 at Faslane to BU.

TRENCHANT Nuclear S/M 4200 tons. Vickers 3.11.1986.

TRENT 6th Rate 28 (fir-built), 587bm, 118½ x 34 ft. Woolwich DY 31.10.1757. Sold 21.6.1764 unserviceable.

TRENT 5th Rate 36 (fir-built), 926bm, 142½ x 38 ft. Woolwich DY 24.2.1796. Hospital ship 1803; receiving ship 1818. BU 2.1823 at Haulbowline.

TRENT Wood S.sloop, 950bm, 185 x 33 ft. Pembroke Dock. Laid down 3.9.1861. renamed RESEARCH 9.1862 and launched 15.8.1863 as ironclad sloop. (see RESEARCH)

TRENT Iron S.gunboat 363 tons, 110 x 34 ft, 3-64pdr. Palmer, Jarrow 23.8.1877. Renamed PEMBROKE 9.1905. GANNET 6.17 diving tender. Sold 21.2.23 Dover S.Bkg Co.

TRENT Frigate, 'River' class. Hill, Bristol 10.10.1942. Renamed KUKRI (RIN) 4.46. Renamed INVESTIGATOR, survey vessel 1951.

TRENT Discovery vessel hired 1818; Trawler & Fleet Messenger in WW.I.

TRENTONIAN Corvette (RCN), modified 'Flower' class. Kingston SY 1.9.1943. Sunk 22.2.45 by 'U.1004' off Falmouth.

TREPASSY Brig-sloop 14. Purchased 1779. Captured 28.5.1781 by the American ALLIANCE; Recaptured. Sold 29.4.1784.

TREPASSY Brig, 42bm, 45 x 15 ft. Lester & Stone, Newfoundland 1790. Sold 12.1803 in Newfoundland.

TRESCO 24-gun ship. Royalist MICHAEL captured 1651 by Parliament. Wrecked 1651.

TRESHAM Inshore M/S, 'Ham' class. Morgan Giles, Teignmouth 11.5.1954. Sold 1966 Reardon Smith Nautical College, Cardiff, renamed Margherita II.

TRESPASSER (ex-P.312) Submarine, 'T' class. Vickers Armstrong. Barrow 29.5.1942. Arrived 26.9.61 at Gateshead to BU.

TREVOSE HEAD (see MULL of OA)

TRIAD Submarine, 'T' class. Vickers Armstrong, Barrow 5.5.1939. Sunk 20.10.40 by unknown cause off Libya.

TRIAD Yacht 1915-33.

TRYALL Pink. Listed 1645-47.

TRYALL Hoy. Origin unknown. Sold 13.5.1713 at Plymouth to E.Bailing.

TRYALL Sloop 14, 113bm, 64½ x 20½ ft. Deptford DY 30.9.1710. Rebuilt Deptford 1719 as 142bm. BU 10.1731.

TRYALL Sloop 14, 201bm, 84 x 23½ ft. Stacey, Deptford 6.9.1732. Scuttled

4.10.1741 in the South Seas as unserviceable.

TRYALL Sloop 14, 272bm, 91½ x 26 ft. Deptford DY 17.7.1744. BU 1.1776.

TRIAL Cutter 12. Listed 1781-94.

TRIAL Cutter 12, 123bm, 65 x 21½ ft, 4-12pdr carr., 8-3pdr. Dunsterville, Plymouth 9.9.1790. Sold 1814.

TRIAL Gunvessel 6. Listed 1805-11.

TRIAL Coal hulk. Listed 1843. Sold 3.2.1848.

TRIBUNE 5th Rate 36, 916bm, 8-32pdr carr., 26-12pdr, 8-6pdr. French, captured 8.6.1796 by UNICORN off Ireland. Wrecked 16.11.1797 on Thrum Shoal, Halifax NS.

TRIBUNE 5th Rate 36, 884bm, 137 x 38½ ft. Parsons, Bursledon 5.7.1803. 6th Rate 24 from 1832. Wrecked 28.11.1839 near Tarragona.

TRIBUNE Wood S.corvette, 1,570bm, 192 x 43 ft, 1-10in, 30-32pdr. Sheerness DY 21.1.1853. Sold 8.1866 Marshall, Plymouth.

TRIBUNE 2nd class cruiser 3,400 tons, 300 x 43 ft, 2-6in, 6-4.7in, 8-6pdr. Thomson 24.2.1891. Sold 9.5.1911 Cashmore, Newport.

TRIBUNE Destroyer, 'S' class. White 28.3.1918. Sold 17.12.31 Cashmore, Newport.

TRIBUNE Submarine, 'T' class. Scotts 8.12.1938. BU 11.47 by Ward, Milford Haven.

TRIBUNE Trawler requis. 1915-19.

TRYDENT 4th Rate 58, 762bm, 129½ x 36½ ft. French TRIDENT captured 1695. Sunk 3.7.1702 as a breakwater at Harwich.

TRYDENT 3rd Rate 64, 1,258bm, 151 x 44 ft. French TRIDENT captured 14.10.1747 at Finisterre. Sold 15.3.1763.

TRIDENT 3rd Rate 64, 1,366bm, 159 x 44½ ft. Plymouth DY 20.4.1768. Sold 3.7.1816 at Malta.

TRIDENT Iron pad. sloop, 850bm, 180 x 31½ ft. Ditchburn & Mare, Blackwall 16.12.1845. BU 1.1866 Castle.

TRIDENT (ex-OFFA renamed 15.2.1915, ex-Turkish) Destroyer 1,098 tons, 300 x 28½ ft, 5-4in, 4-TT. Hawthorn Leslie 20.11.15. Sold 9.5.21 Ward, Grays.

TRIDENT Submarine, 'T' class. Cammell Laird 7.12.1938. Arrived 17.2.46 Cashmore, Newport to BU.

TRIDENT Drifter requis. 1915-19.

TRILLIUM Corvette, 'Flower' class. Vickers, Montreal 26.6.1940. Lent RCN to 27.6.45. Sold 17.5.47, renamed *Olympic Runner*.

TRIMMER Brig-sloop 14, 275bm, 84 x 24½ ft, 14-6pdr. (American?) cutter ANTI-BRITON captured 1782 by STAG. Sold 6.1801.

TRINCOMALEE Sloop 16, 315bm. Ex-prize purchased 1799. Blown up 12.10.1799 in action with the French privateer IPHIGENIE in the Strait of Bab el Mandib.

TRINCOMALE sloop 16, 320bm. French privateer GLOIRE captured 23.3.1801 by ALBATROSS in the Indian Ocean. Recaptured 1803 by the French; recaptured 25.9.1806 by CULLODEN in the E.Indies and readded as EMILIEN. Sold circa 1808.

TRINCOMALEE 5th Rate 46, 1,066bm, 1,447 tons, 150½ x 40 ft. Bombay DY 12.10.1817 26-gun 6th Rate 9.1847; RNR drillship 1.1861; sold 19.5.1897 J.Read; resold as training ship *Foudroyant*. (The oldest RN ship still afloat.)

TRINCOMALEE Destroyer 2,380 tons, 355 x 40 ft, 5-4.5in, 8-40mm, 10-TT.J.Brown 8.1.1946, not completed. Arrived 2.46 at Troon to BU.

TRINCULO Brig-sloop 18, 'Cruizer' class, 389bm. Tyson & Blake, Bursledon 15.7.1809. BU 7.1841.

TRINCULO Wood S.gunboat, 'Britomart' class. Banks, Plymouth 15.9.1860. Wrecked 5.9.1870 after collision with SS *Moratin* off Gibraltar.

TRINCULO Mooring vessel 1915, ren. MOLLUSC 1916-22. Tug 1873-1902.

TRING (ex-TEIGNMOUTH renamed 1918) Minesweeper, later 'Hunt' class. Simons 23.8.1918. Sold 7.10.27 Alloa, BU Charlestown.

TRINIDAD Schooner 10. Listed 1805-09.

TRINIDAD Destroyer, 'S' class. White 8.4.1918. Sold 16.2.32 Ward, Grays.

TRINIDAD Cruiser 8,000 tons, 538 x 62 ft, 12-6in, 8-4in. Devonport 21.3.1940. Bombed 30.4.42 by German A/C in the Barents Sea and scuttled 15.5.42.

TRINITY ship 120bm, purchased 1413, sold 1418.

TRINITY ROYAL Ship, 540bm. Built 1398, rebuilt 1416. Abandoned 1429.

TRINITY HENRY Ship, 80bm. Listed 1519-25.

TRINITY HENRY 64-gun ship, 250bm. Listed 1530. Sold 1566.

TRINITY Ship, 80bm. Captured 1545. Not Listed after.

TRINITY Coastal M/S (RCN), 'Ton' class, 370 tons. G.T. Davie 31.7.1953.

To Turkish navy 1958.

TRIOMPHANT Destroyer 2,569 tons, 411 x 39 ft, 5-5.5in, 9-TT. French, seized 3.7.40 at Plymouth. Free-French 8.40. French navy 1945.

TRISTRAM Destroyer, modified 'R' class. White 24.2.1917. Sold 9.5.21 Ward, Briton Ferry. Demolition started 29.8.24.

TRYTON 5th Rate 42, 661bm, 128 x 34½ ft. French TRITON captured 10.1702 at Vigo. Sold 4.10.1709 at Woolwich.

TRYTON PRIZE 6th Rate 28, 274bm, 75 x 26½ FT. French privateer ROY-AL captured 3.3.1705 by TRYTON. Sold 26.11.1713.

TRYTON Sloop in commission 1741. No details.

TRYTON 6th Rate 24, 501bm, 113 x 32 ft. Heather, Bursledon 17.8.1745. Burnt 28.4.1758 to avoid capture by the French in the E.Indies.

TRITON 6th Rate 28, 620bm, 124 x 33½ ft. Adams, Bucklers Hard 1.10.1771 (Bucklers Hard records say 1773). BU 1.1796.

TRITON 5th Rate 32 (fir-built), 856bm, 142 x 36 ft. Barnard, Deptford 5.9.1796. Harbour service 1800. Hulked 1817, BU 1820 in Newfoundland.

TRITON Iron pad. sloop, 654bm, 170 x 28 ft. Ditchburn & Mare, Blackwall 24.10.1846. Sold 1872 Moss Isaacs.

TRITON Paddle survey vessel 410 tons. Samuda, Poplar 4.3.1882. Harbour service 1914; lent 24.6.19 to Gravesend Sea School. BU 10.1961 at Bruges.

TRITON Submarine, 'T' class. Vickers Armstrong, Barrow 5.10.1937. Sunk 18.12.40 by the Italian TB CLIO in the southern Adriatic.

TRITON Tug 1918 : Trawler requis 1939-40

TRIUMPH Galleon 68, 741bm. Built 1561. Rebuilt 1596 as 928bm, 4-60pdr, 3-34pdr, 17-18pdr, 8-9pdr, 36 small. Sold 1618.

TRIUMPH 44-gun ship, 898bm. Durell, Deptford 1623. BU 1687.

TRIUMPH 2nd Rate 90, 1,482bm, 160 x 46 ft. Chatham DY 1698. Renamed PRINCE 27.8.1714. Rebuilt Chatham 1750 as 1,677bm, 168½ x 48 ft. BU 1775 at Plymouth.

TRIUMPH Sloop 18. Spanish TRIUNFO captured 23.11.1739 at Puerto Bello. Foundered 1.1740 in the W.Indies.

TRIUMPH 3rd Rate 74, 1,825bm, 171½ x 50 ft. Woolwich DY 3.3.1764. Harbour service 10.1813. BU 6.1850 at Pembroke Dock.

TRIUMPH Screw 2nd Rate 91, 3,715bm, 252 x 57½ ft. Pembroke Dock. Renamed PRINCE CONSORT 14.2.1862 and launched 26.6.1862 as armoured frigate, 4,045bm. (qv)

TRIUMPH Iron armoured ship, 3,893bm, 6,640 tons, 280 x 55 ft, 10-9in, 4-64pdr. Palmer 27.9.1870. Renamed TENEDOS 4.1904, depot ship, then training ship. Renamed INDUS IV in 1912, ALGIERS 1.15. Sold 7.1.21 Fryer, Sunderland.

TRIUMPH (ex-Chilian LIBERTAD purchased 3.12.1903) Battleship 11,985 tons, 436 x 71 ft, 4-10in, 14-7.5in, 14-14pdr. Vickers 15.1.1903. Sunk 25.5.15 by 'U.21' off Gallipoli.

TRIUMPH Submarine, 'T' class. Vickers Armstrong, Barrow 16.2.1938. Sunk 14.1.42 by unknown cause in the Aegean.

TRIUMPH A/C carrier 13,350 tons, 630 x 80 ft, 19-40mm, 48-A/C. Hawthorn Leslie 2.10.1944. Repair ship 12.64, 4-40mm guns. Left Chatham 9.12.81 to BU in Spain.

TRIUMPH Nuclear Submarine 4200 tons. Vickers, laid down 1985

TRIUMPH Two Drifters requis. in WW.1.

TROIS RIVIERES Minesweeper (RCN), diesel 'Bangor' class. Marine Ind 30.6.1941. To RCMP 1950 as *MacBrien.*

TROJAN Destroyer, 'S' class. White 20.7.1918. Handed over 24.9.36 to Ward in part payment for *Majestic*; BU at Inverkeithing.

TROJAN Trawler requis 1914-19.

TROLLOPE Frigate, TE 'Captain' class. Bethlehem, Hingham 20.11.1943, on lend-lease. Damaged by torpedo 6.7.44 and not repaired; nominally returned 1.47 to the USN. Arrived 7.51 at Troon to BU.

TROMP 4th Rate 60, 1,040bm, 144 x 41 ft. Dutch, captured 17.8.1796 at the Cape. Harbour service 1799. Sold 9.8.1815.

TROMPEUSE Brig-sloop 16, 342bm. French, captured 12.1.1794 by SPHINX off Cape Clear. Wrecked 15.7.1796 near Kinsale.

TROMPEUSE Sloop 18, 338bm. French privateer MERCURE captured 5.1797 by MELAMPUS in the Bay of Biscay. Foundered 17.5.1800 in the Channel.

TROMPEUSE Sloop 18, 380bm, 101 x 30 ft. French, captured 4.3.1800 BU 3.1811.

TROMSO (see LST.3006)

TROON (see ELGIN)

TROOPER Submarine, 'T' class. Scotts 5.3.1942. Sunk 17.10.43 in the Aegean, probably mined.

TROOPER Trawler 1915-20.

TROUBRIDGE Destroyer 1,730 tons, 339½ x 36 FT, 4-4.7in, 2-40mm, 8-TT. J.Brown 23.9.1942. Frigate 1957, 2,240 tons, 2-4in, 2-3in, 2-40mm. Sold Cashmore 27.2.70, BU at Newport.

TROUNCER (ex-*Perdito*) Escort carrier 11,420 tons, 468½ x 69½ ft, 2-4in, 8-40mm, 18-A/C. Seattle Tacoma 16.6.1943 on lend-lease. Returned 3.3.46 to the USN.

TROUNCER (see LST.3523)

TRUANT Destroyer, 'S' class. White 18.9.1918. Sold 28.11.31 Rees, Llanelly.

TRUANT Submarine, 'T' class. Vickers Armstrong, Barrow 5.5.1939. Sold 19.12.45; wrecked in tow to Briton Ferry 12.46.

TRUCULENT Destroyer, 'M' class. 900 tons. Yarrow 24.3.1917. Sold 29.4.27 Cashmore, Newport.

TRUCULENT (ex-P.315) Submarine, 'T' class. Vickers Armstrong, Barrow 12.9.1942. Sunk 12.1.50 in collision with *Dvina* off the Nore; raised and sold 8.5.50, BU Ward, Grays.

TRUE BRITON Cutter 10, 190bm. Purchased 3.1778. Captured 9.8.1780 by the French. (Recaptured? a cutter was sold 9.6.1785.)

TRUELOVE 14-gun ship, 100b. Royalist KATHERINE captured 1647 by Parliament. Fireship 1668. Lost 1673.

TRUELOVE Ship 20, 259bm. Purchased 1650. Fate unknown.

TRUELOVE Bomb 4, 65bm. Purchased 4.1694. Sold 24.5.1698.

TRUELOVE Hoy, 76bm, 66½ x 17½ ft. Portsmouth DY 11.1707. Re-built Portsmouth 1720 as 58bm. Listed as OLD TRUELOVE to 1823.

TRUELOVE Minesweeper, 'Algerine' class. Redfern, Toronto 8.7.1943. Arrived 23.11.57 Hughes Bolckow, Blyth.

TRUMP Submarine, 'T' class. Vickers Armstrong, Barrow 25.3.1944. Sold Cashmore 23.7.71, BU Newport.

TRUMPET Fire vessel. Dutch hoy purchased 4.1694. Sunk 24.4.1695 as a foundation at Portsmouth.

TRUMPETER (ex-LUCIFER renamed 1942, ex-*Bastian*) Escort carrier 11,420 tons, 468½ x 69½ ft, 2-4in, 8-40mm, 18-A/C. Seattle Tacoma 15.12.42 on lend-lease. Returned 6.4.46 to the USN.

TRUMPETER (see LST.3524)

TRUMPETER Patrol boat 43 tons. Watercraft 1986 and laid-up.

TRUMPETER Trawler requis. 1914-19

TRUNCHEON Submarine, 'T' class. Devonport DY 22.2.1944. To Israeli navy 1968, renamed DOLPHIN.

TRURO Minesweeper, later 'Hunt' class. Simons 16.4.1919. Sold 19.5.28 Ward, Milford Haven.

TRURO Minesweeper (RCN), diesel 'Bangor' class. Davie SB 5.6.1942. To RCMP 1950 as *Herchmer*.

TRUSTY 4th Rate 50, 1,088bm, 150½ x 40½ ft. Hilhouse, Bristol 9.10.1782. Troopship 8.1799; prison ship 5.1809. BU 4.1815.

TRUSTY Armoured wood S.floating battery, 1,539bm, 173½ x 45 ft, 14-68pdr. Green, Blackwall 18.4.1855. BU 1864 by Castle.

TRUSTY Destroyer, 'S' class. White 6.11.1918. Handed over 25.9.36 to Ward in part payment for *Majestic*, BU at Inverkeithing.

TRUSTY Submarine, 'T' class. Vickers Armstrong, Barrow 14.3.1941. Sold 1.47; BU by Ward, Milford Haven.

TRUSTY Tug 1866, ren. TRUSTFUL 1917-20.

TRYALL (see TRIAL)

TRYDENT (see TRIDENT)

TRYPHON Destroyer, 'S' class 930 tons. Yarrow 22.6.1918. Sold 27.9.20 Agius Bros, Malta after stranding 4.5.19.

TRYPHON Tug 1947-59.

TRYRIGHT Galley. Probably French, captured 1.1560 in the Forth. Listed to 1579.

TRYTON (see TRITON)

TSINGTAU Repair ship 1,970 tons, 279 x 44 ft. German, seized 1945. BU 1950 Clayton & Davie, Dunston.

TUBEROSE Sloop, 'Anchusa' class. Swan Hunter 16.11.1917. Sold 15.1.23 Unity S.Bkg Co.

TUDOR (ex-P.326) Submarine, 'T' class. Devonport Dy 23.9.1942. Sold 1.7.63, arrived 23.7.63 at Faslane to BU.

TUI Survey ship (RNZN) 1380 tons. American CHARLES H.DAVIS purchased in 8.1970

TULIP 32-gun ship Captured 1652. Sold 1657.

TULIP Sloop 2, 22bm. Deptford 1672. Lost 1673.

TULIP Dogger 6. Dutch, captured 1672. Sold 1674.

TULIP Sloop, 'Aubrietia' class. Richardson Duck, Stockton on Tees

15.7.1916. Sank in tow of DAFFO-DIL after being torpedoed 30.4.17 by 'U.62' in the Atlantic. (Operated as decoy ship Q.12.)

TULIP Corvette, 'Flower' class. Smiths DK 4.9.1940. Sold 5.47, renamed *Olympic Conqueror*.

TULIP Drifter requis. 1915-18

TUMULT Destroyer, 'S' class 930 tons. Yarrow 17.9.1918. Sold 3.10.28 Alloa S.Bkg, Charlestown.

TUMULT Destroyer 1,710 tons, 339½ x 36 ft, 4-4.7in, 2-40mm, 8-TT. J.Brown 9.11.1942. Frigate 10.54. Arrived 25.10.65 Arnott Young, Dalmuir to BU.

TUNA Torpedo boat (RCN) 130 tons, 153 x 15 ft, 1-3pdr, 2-TT. Purchased (1915?). Sold 1920.

TUNA Submarine, 'T' class. Scotts 10.5.1940. Sold 19.12.45, arrived 24.6.46 Ward, Briton Ferry to BU.

TUNA Storeship requis. 1940-41.

TUNSBERG CASTLE (see SHREWSBURY CASTLE).

TURBULENT Gun-brig 12, 181bm, 84½ x 22 ft. Tanner, Dartmouth 17.7.1805. Captured 10.6.1808 by the Danes in Malmo Bay.

TURBULENT (ex-OGRE renamed 15.2.1915, ex-Turkish) Destroyer 1,098 tons, 300 x 28½ ft, 5-4in, 4-TT. Hawthorn Leslie 5.1.16. Sunk 1.6.16 at Jutland.

TURBULENT Destroyer, 'S' class. Hawthorn Leslie 29.5.1919. Handed over 25.8.36 to Ward in part payment for *Majestic*; BU at Inverkeithing.

TURBULENT Submarine, 'T' class. Vickers Armstrong Barrow 12.5.1941. Sunk circa 23.3.43 by an Italian MTB off Sardinia.

TURBULENT Nuclear s/m Vickers 1.12.1982

TURPIN Submarine, 'T' class. Chatham DY 5.8.1944. Sold Israeli navy 1965, renamed LEVIATHAN.

TURQUOISE Compos. S.corvette, 2,120 tons, 220 x 40 ft, 12-64pdr. Earle, Hull 22.4.1876. Sold 24.9.1892 Pounds, Hartlepool.

TURQUOISE Destroyer, 'S' class 930 tons. Yarrow 9.11.1918. Sold 1.32, BU at Charlestown.

TURQUOISE Fleet messenger 1915; Trawler 1935-46.

TUSCAN Brig-sloop 16, 334bm. French , ex-Italian RONCO captured 2.5.1808 by UNITE in the Gulf of Venice. Sold 29.1.1818 T.Pitman to BU.

TUSCAN Destroyer, 'S' class 930 tons.

Yarrow 1.3.1919. Sold 25.8.32 Metal Ind, Charlestown.

TUSCAN Destroyer 1,710 tons, 339½x 36 ft, 4-4.7in, 2-40mm, 8-TT. Swan Hunter 28.5.1942. Frigate 8.53. Arrived 26.5.66 McLellan, Bo'ness to BU.

TUTANKHAMEN (see P.311)

TUTBURY CASTLE Corvette, 'Castle' class. Morton, Quebec. Cancelled 12.1943.

TUTIRA (see LOCH MORLICH)

TWEED 5th Rate 32, 661bm, 128½ x 34 ft. Blaydes, Hull 20.4.1759. Sold 1776.

TWEED (see GLENMORE)

TWEED Sloop 18, 431bm, 109 x 30 ft. Iremonger, Littlehampton 10.1.1807. Wrecked 5.11.1813 in Shoal Bay, Newfoundland.

TWEED 6th Rate 28, 500bm, 113½ x 32 ft, 20-32pdr carr., 6-18pdr carr., 2-9pdr. Portsmouth DY 14.4.1823. Sold 1852 Willson & Co.

TWEED Wood S.frigate 3,027bm, 250 x 52 ft. Pembroke Dock. Laid down 3.7.1860, cancelled 16.12.1864.

TWEED Iron S.gunboat 363 tons, 110 x 34 ft, 3-64pdr. Palmer 23.8.1877. Sold 21.11.1905 at Hong Kong.

TWEED Frigate, 'River' class. Inglis 24.11.1942. Sunk 7.1.44 by 'U.305' SW of Ireland.

TWEED Escort requis. 1916-19.

TWO LIONS 48-gun ship, 552bm, 115½ x 33½ ft. Captured 1682. Sold 1687.

TYLER Frigate, TE 'Captain' class. Bethlehem, Hingham 20.11.1943 on lend-lease. Returned 11.45 to the USN.

TYNE 6th Rate 24, 446bm, 108½ x 30½ ft, 18-32pdr carr., 8-12pdr carr., 2-6pdr. Davy, Topsham 20.4.1814. Sold 27.1.1825 T.Pitman to BU.

TYNE 6th Rate 28, 600bm, 125 x 33 ft. Woolwich DY 30.11.1826. Storeship 1848. Sold 17.2.1862 Castle & Beech to BU.

TYNE (see ACTIVE of 1845)

TYNE (ex-*Mariotis*) Iron S.storeship 3,560 tons, 320 x 34 ft, 2-24pdr. Armstrong 19.1.1878 and purchased 8.3.1878. Foundered 15.11.1920 in a gale off Sheerness while on sale list.

TYNE Depot ship 10,850 tons, 585 x 66 ft, 8-4in. Scotts 28.2.1940. Sold H.K.Vickers 25.7.72, BU at Barrow.

TYNEDALE Destroyer, 'Hunt' class type I. Stephen 5.6.1940. Sunk 12.12.43 by 'U.593' off Bougie.

TYRANT Destroyer, 'M' class 900 tons. Yarrow 19.5.1917. Arrived 15.1.39

Cashmore, Newport to BU.

TYRANT Yacht requis. 1940-46.

TYRIAN Brig-sloop 10, 'Cherokee' class, 239bm. Guillaume, Northam 16.12.1808. Sold 22.7.1819.

TYRIAN Brig-sloop 10, 'Cherokee' class, 233bm. Woolwich DY 16.9.1826. Quarantine hulk 1847; coastguard depot ship 1866. Sold 11.8.1892.

TYRIAN Wood S.gunboat, 'Britomart' class. Courtenay, Newhaven 7.9.1861. Tug in Jamaica 1883, sold there 1891.

TYRIAN Destroyer, 'S' class 930 tons. Yarrow 2.7.1919. Arrived 26.3.30 Charlestown to BU. by Metal Industries.

TYRIAN Destroyer 1,710 tons, 339½ x 36 ft, 4-4.7in, 2-40mm, 8-TT. Swan Hunter 27.7.1942. Frigate 5.53. Arrived 4.3.65 at Troon to BU.

TYRIAN Tug 1904-18.

TYRONE Gunvessel 2. Listed 1798-1800.

U-boats (ex-German).

U.190 Surrendered to The RCN 11.5.45 in Newfoundland and commissioned 14.5.45. Sunk 21.10.47 on A/S exercises.

U.889 Surrendered to the RCN 13.5.45 at Shelburne. Transferred 12.1.46 to the USN.

U.1407 Commissioned in the RN 25.9.45. Renamed METEORITE 6.47. BU 9.49 Ward, Barrow.

Of the many others which surrendered, the following were used for trials purposes:

U.249; U.712 listed to 1948; **U.776; U.875; U.953** listed to 1948; **U.1023; U.1105; U.1108** listed to 1948; **U.1171** listed to 1948; **U.2326** transferred French navy 1945; **U.2348** listed to 1948; **U.2518** transferred French navy 1948; **U.3017** arrived 30.10.49 Cashmore, Newport to BU.

UGANDA Cruiser 8,800 tons, 538 x 62 ft, 9-6in, 8-4in. Vickers Armstrong, Tyne 7.8.1941. Renamed QUEBEC (RCN) 14.1.52. Arrived 6.2.61 at Osaka, Japan to BU.

ULEX Submarine, 'V' class Vickers Armstrong, Barrow. Cancelled 2.1944; not laid down.

ULLESWATER Destroyer, 'M' class 923 tons. Yarrow 4.8.1917. Sunk 15.8.18 by U-boat in the North Sea.

ULLSWATER (ex-P.31 renamed 2.1943) Submarine, 'U' class. Vickers Armstrong, Barrow 27.11.40. Renamed UPROAR 4.43. Sold 13.2.46. BU Ward, Inverkeithing.

ULLSWATER Whaler 1939-42.

ULSTER Destroyer, modified 'R' class. Beardmore 10.10.1917. Sold 21.4.28 Ward, Pembroke Dock.

ULSTER Destroyer 1,710 tons, 339½ x 36 ft, 4-4.7in, 2-40mm, 8-TT. Swan Hunter 9.11.1942. Frigate 1953. Sold Ward 4.8.80, BU Inverkeithing

ULTIMATUM (ex-P.34) Submarine 'U' class. Vickers Armstrong, Barrow 11.2.1941. Sold 23.12.49, BU Smith & Houston.

ULTOR (ex-P.53) Submarine, 'U' class. Vickers Armstrong, Barrow 12.10.1942. Arrived 22.1.46 Ward, Briton Ferry to BU.

ULYSSES 5th Rate 44, 887 bm, 140 x 38 ft. Fisher, Liverpool 14.7.1779. Troop ship 6.1790.Sold 11.1.1816.

ULYSSES (see LYSANDER of 1913)

ULYSSES Destroyer, modified 'R' class. Doxford 24.3.1917. Sunk 29.10.19 in collision with SS *Ellerie* in the Firth of Clyde.

ULYSSES Destroyer 1,710 tons, 339½ x 36 ft, 4-4.7in, 2-40mm, 8-TT. Cammell Laird 22.4.1943. Frigate 1953. Sold Davies & Cann 29.10.79. BU at Plymouth.

UMBRA (ex-P.35) Submarine, 'U' class. Vickers Armstrong, Barrow 15.3.1941. Sold 9.7.46, BU Hughes Bolckow, Blyth.

UMPIRE (see ROYAL GEORGE of 1788)

UMPIRE Destroyer, modified 'R' class. Doxford 9.6.1917. Sold 7.1.30 Metal Ind, Charlestown.

UMPIRE Submarine, 'U' class. Chatham DY 30.12.1940. Accidentally rammed and sunk 19.7.41 by a trawler in the North Sea.

UNA Sloop (RAN) 1,438 tons, 210 x 31 ft, 3-4in, 2-12pdr. German KOMET captured 11.10.1914 by the yacht NUSA on the north coast of New Britain. Sold 1921, renamed *Akuna*.

UNA Submarine, 'U' class. Chatham DY 10.6.1941. Sold 11.4.49, BU Rees, Llanelly.

UNBEATEN Submarine, 'U' class. Vickers Armstrong, Barrow 9.7.1940. Bombed in error 11.11.42 by British A/C in the Bay of Biscay.

UNBENDING (ex-P.37) Submarine, 'U' class. Vickers Armstrong, Barrow 12.5.1941. Sold 23.12.49. BU 1950 Dorkin, Gateshead.

UNBRIDLED Submarine, 'V' class. Vickers Armstrong, Tyne. Cancelled 20.11.1943; not laid down.

UNBROKEN (ex-P.42) Submarine, 'U' class. Vickers Armstrong, Barrow 4.11.1941. Lent Russian navy 1944-49 as B.2. Arrived 9.5.50 King, Gateshead to BU.

UNDAUNTED 6th Rate 28. French storeship BIEN VENUE captured 17.3.1794 by a squadron at Martinique. Sold 24.7.1795.

UNDAUNTED (see ARETHUSE under ARETHUSA)

UNDAUNTED Gunvessel. Dutch, captured 13.8.1799 by boats of PYLADES on the Dutch coast. Sold 1800.

UNDAUNTED 5th Rate 38, 1,086bm, 155 x 40 ft. Woolwich DY (ex-Graham, Harwich) 17.10.1807. Target 1856. BU completed 12.1860.

UNDAUNTED Wood S.frigate, 3.039bm, 4,020 tons, 250 x 52 ft. Chatham DY 1.1.1861. Sold 7.11.1882 Castle.

UNDAUNTED Armoured cruiser 5,600 tons, 300 x 56 ft, 2-9.2in, 10-6in, 10-3pdr. Palmer 25.11.1886. Sold 9.4.1907 Harris, Bristol.

UNDAUNTED Light cruiser 3,500 tons, 410 x 39 ft, 2-6in, 6-4in. Fairfield 28.4.1914. Sold 9.4.23 Cashmore, Newport.

UNDAUNTED Submarine, 'U' class. Vickers Armstrong, Barrow 20.8.1940. Sunk 13.5.41 by unknown cause off Libya.

UNDAUNTED Destroyer 1,710 tons, 339½ x 36 ft, 4-4.7in, 2-40mm, 8-TT. Cammell Laird 19.7.1943. Frigate 1954. Sunk 11.78 as a target in the Atlantic.

UNDINE Iron pad. packet, 284bm. Purchased 13.2.1847. Sold 5.2.1854 Jenkins & Churchward, Dover.

UNDINE Wood S.gunvessel, 428bm, 145 x 25½ ft. Deptford DY. Laid down 31.12.1861, cancelled 12.12.1863.

UNDINE (ex-*Morna*) Schooner 280 tons, 114 x 23 ft. Purchased 15.3.1881. Sold 4.1888 Millar, Sydney, NSW.

UNDINE (see HAWK of 1888)

UNDINE (see WILDFIRE of 1888)

UNDINE Destroyer, modified 'R' class. Fairfield 22.3.1917. Sold 4.28 Ward; wrecked off Horse Fort, Portsmouth and wreck sold 27.8.28 Middlesbrough Salvage Co.

UNDINE Submarine, 'U' class. Vickers Armstrong, Barrow 5.10.1937. Sunk 7.1.40 by German minesweepers off Heligoland.

UNDINE Destroyer 1,710 tons, 339½ x 36 ft, 4-4.7in, 2-40mm, 8-TT. Thornycroft 1.6.1943. Frigate 1954. Arrived 15.11.65 Cashmore Newport to BU.

UNGAVA Minesweeper (RCN), TE 'Bangor' class. N. Vancouver SR Co 9.10.1940. Sold circa 1947 T.Harris, Barber, NJ.

UNGAVA Coastal M/S, 'Ton' class 390 tons. Davie SB 20.5.1953. Sold Turkish navy 1958.

UNICORN 36-gun ship, circa 240bm. Scots, captured 1544. Sold 1555.

UNICORN 56-gun ship, 700bm. Woolwich 2.1634.Sold 27.1.1687.

UNICORN (also LITTLE UNICORN) 18-gun ship, 185bm Dutch EENHOORN captured 1665. Expended as a fireship 2.6.1666.

UNICORN Fireship 6, 180bm. Purchased 1666. Sunk 6.1667 at Chatham to block entrance to the DY.

UNICORN 6th Rate 28, 581bm, 118 x 33½ ft. Plymouth DY 7.12.1748. BU completed 9.12.1771 at Sheerness.

UNICORN 6th Rate 20, 433bm, 108 x 30 ft. Randall, Rotherhithe 23.3,1776. Captured 4.9.1780 by the French ANDROMAQUE in the W.Indies; recaptured 20.4.1781 as LICORNE. BU 8.1787 at Deptford.

UNICORN 5th Rate 36, 881bm, 137 x 38½ ft. Calhoun, Bursledon 7.11.1782. Renamed THALIA 15.8.1783. BU 7.1814.

UNICORN 5th Rate 32, 791bm, 135 x 36 ft. Chatham DY 12.7.1794. BU 3.1815 at Deptford

UNICORN 5th Rate 46, 1,084bm, 151½ x 40½ ft. Chatham DY 30.3.1824. Powder hulk 1860; RNR drillship 11.1873 at Dundee. (Bore the name UNICORN II 2.39 then CRESSY 20.11.41 to 14.7.59.) Handed over to Unicorn Preservation Society 29.9.1968.

UNICORN A/C maintenance carrier 14,750 tons, 564 x 90 ft, 8-4.5in 35-A/C. Harland & Wolff 20.11.1941. Arrived 15.6.59 at Dalmuir to BU.; Hulk to Troon in 3.60.

UNICORN Submarine 2,160 tons. Cammell Laird, ordered 3.1.1986.

UNICORN Trawler requis. 1915-20

UNION 5th Rate. Origin unknown (perhaps a hired vessel). Burnt 1695 to avoid capture by the French.

UNION (see ALBEMARLE of 1680)

UNION 2nd Rate 90, 1,781bm, 171 x 48½ ft. Chatham DY 25.9.1756. Hospital ship by 1799. Renamed SUSSEX 6.2.1802 BU 10.1816. at Cha ham.

UNION Gunvessel 3, 81bm, 59½ x 18 ft. Ex-barge purchased 3.1794. Listed to 1798.

UNION Cutter. In 1806. BU 6.1810.

UNION 2nd Rate 98, 2,149bm, 186 x 52 ft. Plymouth DY 16.9.1811. BU 3.1833.

UNION Schooner 3, 85bm, 60 x 19 ft. Purchased 1823. Wrecked 17.5.1828 in the W.Indies.

UNION Submarine, 'U' class. Vickers Armstrong, Barrow 1.10.1940. Sunk 22.7.41 by Italian patrol boat in the central Mediterranean.

UNION Drifter requis. 1915-19.

UNIQUE Schooner 10, 120bm, 74 x 21 ft. French, captured 1803. Captured 23.2.1806 by a French privateer in the W.Indies.

UNIQUE Gun-brig 12, 183bm. French privateer DUQUESNE captured 23.9.1807 by BLONDE in the W.Indies. Burnt 31.5.1809 by the French at Guadeloupe.

UNIQUE Submarine, 'U' class. Vickers Armstrong, Barrow 6.6.1940. Sunk 24.10.42 by unknown cause west of Gibraltar.

UNISON (ex-P.43) Submarine, 'U' class. Vickers Armstrong, Barrow 5.11.1941. Lent Russian navy 1944-49 as B.3. Arrived 19.5.50 Stockton on Tees to BU.

UNISON Drifter requis. 1915-19 & 1940-43.

UNITE (see UNITY)

UNITED (ex-P.44) Submarine, 'U' class. Vickers Armstrong, Barrow 18.12.1941. Arrived 12.2.46 Troon to BU.

UNITY 32-gun ship. Dutch EEN-DRACHT captured 2.1665. Recaptured 12.6.1667 by the Dutch at Chatham.

UNITY Flyboat 4, 172bm. Dutch, captured 1672. Given away 1672.

UNITY Fireship 6, 120bm. Purchased 1688. Rebuilt Portsmouth 1707 as hoy, 130bm, 67 x 21½ ft. sold 27.10.1773.

UNITY II Hoy 4, 79bm, 59 x 18 ft. Chatham DY 19.8.1693. Sold 8.1.1713.

UNITY III Hoy 4 (as UNITY II). Chatham DY 1693. Sold 8.1.1713.

UNITY Hoy, 80bm, 60 x 18½ ft. Plymouth DY 1728. Sold 20.12.1788.

UNITY Store vessel, 142bm, 66 x 22½ ft. Hooper, Torpoint 1788. BU 1878 as YC.13.

UNITE 5th Rate 38, 893bm, 142½ x

37½ ft. French, captured 12.4.1796 by REVOLUTIONNAIRE off the French coast. Sold 5.1802.

UNITE (see IMPERIEUSE of 1793)

UNITY Destroyer 954 tons, 265 x 26½ ft, 3-4in, 2-TT. Thornycroft 19.9.1913. Sold 25.10.22 Rees, Llanelly.

UNITY Submarine, 'U' class. Vickers Armstong, Barrow 16.2.1938. Sunk 29.4.40 in collision with SS *Atle Jarl* off the Tyne.

UNITY Three drifters requis WW.I.

UNIVERSAL (ex-P.57) Submarine, 'U' class. Vickers Armstrong, Tyne 10.11.1942. Sold 2.46 for Cashmore; BU 2.46 Ward, Milford Haven.

UNRIVALLED (ex-P.45) Submarine, 'U' class. Vickers Armstrong, Barrow 16.2.1942. Arrived 22.1.46 Ward, Briton Ferry to BU.

UNRUFFLED (ex-P.46) Submarine, 'U' class. Vickers Armstrong, Barrow 19.12.1941. BU 1.46. by W.of Scotland S.Bkg. Co, Troon.

UNRULY (ex-P.49) Submarine, 'U' class. Vickers Armstrong, Barrow 28.7.1942. Arrived 2.46 Ward, Inverkeithing to BU.

UNSEEN (ex-P.51) Submarine, 'U' class. Vickers Armstrong, Barrow 16.4.1942. Arrived 11.5.49. Ward, Hayle.

UNSEEN Submarine 2160 tons. Cammell Laird, ordered 1986.

UNSHAKEN (ex-P.54) Submarine, 'U' class. Armstrong, Barrow 17.2.1942. BU 3.46 by W.of Scotland S.Bkg Co, Troon.

UNSPARING (ex-P.55) Submarine, 'U' class. Vickers Armstrong, Tyne 28.7.1942. Sold 14.2.46, BU Inverkeithing.

UNSWERVING Submarine, 'U' class. Vickers Armstrong, Tyne 19.7.1943. Arrived 10.7.49 Cashmore, Newport to BU

UNTAMED (Ex-P.58) Submarine, 'U' class. Vickers Armstrong, Tyne 8.12.1942. Foundered 30.5.43; raised 5.7.43 and renamed VITALITY. Sold 13.2.46, arrived 3.46 at Troon to BU.

UNTIRING Submarine, 'U' class. Vickers Armstrong, Tyne 20.1.1943. Lent Greek navy 7.45 to 1952 as XIFIAS. Sunk 25.7.57 as Asdic target off Start Point.

UPAS Submarine, 'V' class. Vickers Armstrong, Barrow. Laid down 10.18.1943, cancelled 2.44.

UPHOLDER Submarine, 'U' class. Vickers Armstrong, Barrow 8.7.1940. Sunk 14.4.42 by the Italian TB

PEGASO off Tripoli.

UPHOLDER Submarine 2160 tons. Vickers 2.12.1986

UPPINGHAM (see KELLETT)

UPRIGHT Submarine, 'U' class. Vickers Armstrong, Barrow 21.4.40. Sold 19.12.45; arrived Troon 3.46.

UPROAR (see ULLSWATER of 1940)

UPSHOT Submarine, 'V' class. Vickers Armstrong, Barrow 24.2.1944. Arrived 22.11.49 Ward, Preston to BU.

UPSTART (ex-P.66) Submarine, 'U' class. Vickers Armstrong, Barrow 24.11.1942. Lent Greek navy 9.8.43 to 1952 as AMFITRITE. Sunk 29.7.57 as Asdic target off the Isle of Wight.

UPTON Coastal M/S, 'Ton' class. Thornycroft 15.3.1956.

UPWARD Submarine, 'V' class. Vickers Armstrong, Tyne. Cancelled 20.11.1943; not laid down.

URANIE 5th Rate 38, 1,100bm, 154½ x 40 ft, 16-32pdr carr., 28-12pdr, 2-9pdr. French TARTU captured 5.1.1797 by POLYPHEMUS off Ireland. Sold 10.1807. (Spelt TARTU in French lists but TORTUE in James'.)

URANIA Destroyer 1,710 tons, 339½ x 36 ft, 4-4.7in, 2-40mm, 8-TT. Vickers Armstrong, Barrow 19.5.1943. Frigate 1954. Sold 16.12.70, BU at Faslane.

URANIA Two trawlers requis. in WW.I.

URCHIN Gunvessel, 154bm. Purchased 1797. Foundered 12.10.1800 in tow of HECTOR in Tetuan Bay.

URCHIN Destroyer, modified 'R' class. Palmer 7.6.1917. Sold 7.1.30 Metal Ind, Charlestown.

URCHIN Submarine, 'U' class. Vickers Armstrong, Barrow 30.9.1940. Lent Polish navy 11.41 to 1946 as SOKOL; renamed P.97 in 1946. BU 1949.

URCHIN Destroyer 1,710 tons, 339½ x 36 ft, 4-4.7in, 2-40mm, 8-TT. Vickers Armstrong, Barrow 8.3.1954. Arrived 6.8.67 at Troon to BU.

URE Destroyer 550 tons, 222 x 23½ ft, 1-12pdr, 5-6pdr (4-12pdr in 1907), 2-TT. Palmer 25.10.1903. Sold 27.5.19 TR Sales.

URE Trawler 1920-22.

UREDD (ex-P.41) Submarine, 'U' class. Vickers Armstrong, Barrow 24.8.1941. Renamed on loan R.Norwegian navy 12.41. Sunk circa 24.2.43 by unknown cause off Bodo, Norway.

URGE Submarine, 'U' class. Vickers Armstrong, Barrow 19.8.1940. Sunk 6.5.42 by the Italian TB PEGASO in

the eastern Mediterranean.

URGENT Gun-brig 12, 178bm, 80 x 22½ ft. Bass, Lympstone 2.11.1804. Sold 31.7.1816.

URGENT (ex-GPO vessel Collonsay) Wood pad. packet, 561bm, 170½ x 26 ft. Transferred 27.7.1837. Sold 12.1850 H.Hall.

URGENT (ex-Assaye purchased on stocks) Iron S.troopship, 1,981bm, 2,801 tons, 723 x 38 ft, 2-pdr. Mare, Blackwall 2.4.1855. Depot ship 1876. Sold 6.1903 Butler & Co.

URGENT Tank vessel 1910-60.

URSA Destroyer, modified 'R' class. Palmer 23.7.1817. Sold 13.7.26 J.Smith.

URSA Destroyer 1.710 tons, 339½ x 36ft, 4-4in, 2-40mm 8-TT. Thornycroft 22.7.1943. Frigate 1954. BU 1967 Cashmore, Newport, arrived 25.9.67

URSULA Destroyer, modified 'R' class. Scotts 2.8.1917. Sold 19.11.29 Cashmore, Newport.

URSULA Submarine, 'U' class. Vickers Armstrong, Barrow 16.2.1938. Lent Russian navy 1944-49 as B.4. Sold 5.50, BU Brechin, Granton.

URSULA Submarine 2160 tons Cammell Laird, ordered 3.1.1986.

URSULA Drifter requis 1915-19.

URTICA Submarine, 'V' class. Vickers Armstrong, Barrow 23.3.1944. BU 3.50 Ward, Milford Haven.

USK Destroyer 590 tons, 225 x 23½ ft, 1-12pdr, 5-6pdr (4-12pdr 1907), 2-TT. Yarrow 25.7.1903. Sold 29.7.20 Ward, Morecambe.

USK Submarine, 'U' class. Vickers Armstrong, Barrow 7.6.1940. Sunk 3.5.41 off Cape Bon, Tunisia; probably mined.

USK Frigate, 'River' class. Smiths Dk 3.4.1943. Sold 1948 Egyptian navy.

USURPER (ex-P.56) Submarine, 'U' class. Vickers Armstrong, Tyne 24.9.1942. Sunk 10.43 by German patrol vessel 'UJ.2208' in the Gulf of Genoa.

UTHER Submarine, 'U' class. Vickers Armstrong, Tyne 6.4.1943. Sold 2.50; arrived 20.2.50 Ward, Hayle to BU.

UTILE 6th Rate 24, 279bm, 89½ x 26½ ft, 14-24pdr, 2-6pdr. French. captured 9.6.1796 by SOUTHAMPTON in the Mediterranean. Sold 7.6.1798.

UTILE Brig-sloop 16. French captured 1.4.1799 by BOADICEA in the Channel. Foundered 11.1801 in the Mediterranean.

UTILE (ex-Volunteer) Sloop 16, 340bm.

Purchased 6.1804. Sold 30.6.1814.

UTMOST Submarine, 'U' class. Vickers Armstrong, Barrow 20.4.1940. Sunk 24.11.42 by the Italian GROPPO west of Sicily.

UTOPIA Submarine, 'V' class. Vickers Armstrong, Barrow. Cancelled 2.1944; not laid down.

UTRECHT 3rd Rate 64, 1,331bm. Dutch, captured 30.8.1799 in the Texel. Hulk by 1810. Sold 23.3.1815.

1912/13 'V' class submarines 364 tons, 147½(oa) x 16 ft, 2-TT.

V.1 Vickers 23.7.1914. Sold 29.11.21 J.Kelly. (Believed resold Ward, Rainham.)

V.2 Vickers 17.2.15. Sold 29.11.21. J.Kelly. (Believed resold Ward, Rainham.)

V.3 Vickers 1.4.15. Sold 8.10.20 J.W.Towers.

V.4 Vickers 25.11.15. Sold 8.10.20 J.W.Towers.

VAAGSO (see LST.3019)

VAGABOND Submarine, 'V' class. Vickers Armstrong, Tyne 19.9.1944. Arrived 26.1.50 Cashmore, Newport to BU.

VALDORIAN (see SUSSEXVALE)

VALENTINE 'Barge', 100bm. Built 1418. sold 1.3.1424.

VALENTINE Destroyer leader, 'V/W' class. Cammell Laird 24.3.1917. Escort 4.40; beached 15.5.40 at the mouth of the Schelde after air attack. BU 1953.

VALENTINE (see KEMPENFELT of 1943)

VALENTINE (ex-KEMPENFELT renamed 1942) Destroyer 1,710 tons, 339½ x36 ft, 4-4. 7in, 2-40mm, 8-TT. J.Brown 2.9.43. To the RCN 28.2.44 as ALGONQUIN. BU at Halifax, NS, in 1952.

VALERIAN Sloop, 'Arabis' class. Rennoldson 21.2.1916. Foundered 22.10.26 in a hurricane off Bermuda.

VALEUR 6th Rate 24, 321bm, 101 x 27½ ft, French, captured 5.5.1705 by WORCESTER. Fireship 3.1716. Ordered 14.3.1718 to be BU at Deptford.

VALEUR 6th Rate 28, 524bm, 115½ x 32½ ft, French, captured 18.10.1759 by LIVELY. Sold 26.1.1764.

VALHALLA Destroyer leader, 'V/W' class 1,339 tons. Cammell Laird 22.5.1917. Sold 17.12.31 Cashmore,

Newport.

VALHALLA Yacht requis. 1916-19.

VALIANT 3rd Rate 74, 1,799 bm, 171½ x 49½ ft. Chatham DY 10.8.1759. harbour service 11.1799. BU 4.1826 at Sheerness.

VALIANT 3rd Rate 74, 1,718bm, 174 x 48½ ft. Perry, Wells & Green, Blackwall 24.1.1807. BU 11.1823 at Portsmouth.

VALIANT 3rd Rate 76, 1,925bm, 182 x 50 ft, 4-68pdr carr., 26-32pdr, 12-32pdr carr., 28-24pdr, 6-12pdr. Plymouth DY. Ordered 9.6.1825, cancelled 11.1832.

VALIANT Iron armoured ship, 4,063bm, 6,710 tons, 280 X 56½ ft, 2-8in, 16-7in. Westwood Baillie, Poplar 14.10.1863. Harbour service 1888; depot ship 1897; renamed INDUS IV in 1904; depot ship; VALIANT (OLD) 1916; VALIANT III in 1919; oil hulk 1924. Arrived 9.12.56 at Zeebrugge to BU.

VALIANT Battleship 27,500 tons, 600 x 90½ ft, 8-15in, 14-6in. Fairfield 4.11.1914. Sold 19.3.48, arrived 16.8.48 at Cairnryan to BU. Hulk to Troon in 3.50.

VALIANT Yacht requis. 1914-19.

VALIANT Nuclear submarine 3,500 tons, 285 x 33 ft, 6-TT. Vickers Armstrong, Barrow 3.12.1963.

VALKYRIE (ex-MALCOLM renamed 1916) Destroyer leader, 'V/W' class 1,325 tons. Denny 13.3.1917. Handed over 24.8.36 to Ward in part payment for Majestic; BU at Inverkeithing.

VALKYRIE Drifter requis 1915-19.

VALLEYFIELD Frigate (RCN), 'River' class. Morton 7.7.1943. Sunk 7.5.44 off Cape Race, probably by 'U.548'.

VALOROUS Sloop 18, 422bm, 109½ x 29½ ft. Blunt, Hull 11.1804. Army depot 1810. Sold 7.5.1817.

VALOROUS 6th Rate 20, 514bm, 122 x 31 ft. Pembroke Dock 10.2.1816. BU completed 13.8.1829 at Chatham.

VALOROUS Wood pad. frigate, 1,257bm, 2,300 tons, 210 x 26 ft. Pembroke Dock 30.4.1851. Sold 27.2.1891 Marshall, Plymouth. (The last paddle frigate built.)

VALOROUS (ex-MONTROSE renamed 1916) Destroyer leader, 'V/W' class 1,325 tons. Denny 8.5.1917. Escort 6.39; sold 4.3.47, BU Stockton Shipping & Salvage, Thornaby.

VALOROUS Drifter requis. 1915-19

VAMPIRE Destroyer leader, 'V/W' class 1,316 tons. White 21.5.1917. RAN 10.33. Sunk 9.4.42 by Japanese

A/C in the Bay of Bengal.

VAMPIRE Submarine, 'V' class. Vickers Armstrong, Barrow 20.7.1943. Arrived 5.3.50 King, Gateshead to BU.

VAMPIRE Destroyer (RAN) 2,616 tons, 366 x 43 ft, 6-4.5in, 8-40mm, 5-TT. Cockatoo DY 27.10.1956.

VANCOUVER Destroyer, 'V/W' class. Beardmore 28.12.1917. Renamed VIMY 1.4.28. Escort 5.42. BU 12.47 by Metal Ind, Rosyth

VANCOUVER (see TOREADOR)

VANCOUVER (see KITCHENER)

VANCOUVER (ex-KITCHENER renamed 11.1941) Corvette (RCN), 'Flower' class. Yarrow, Esquimalt 26.8.41. Sold 1946.

VANCOUVER Survey ship (RCN) 5600 tons. Burrard 29.6.65. Sold 10.82 mercantile.

VANCOUVER Destroyer (RCN) 4200 tons. St John DD, ordered 1986.

VANDAL (ex-P.64) Submarine, 'U' class. Vickers Armstrong, Barrow 23.11.1942. Wrecked 24.2.43 in the Firth of Clyde.

VANESSA Destroyer, 'V/W' class. Beardmore 16.3.1918. Escort 6.42. Sold 4.3.47; arrived 5.9.48 Charlestown to BU. by Metal Ind.

VANESSA Yacht requis. 1914-19.

VANGUARD Galleon 31, 450bm, 108 x 32 ft, 4-32pdr, 14-18pdr, 11-9pdr, 2-6pdr. Woolwich 1586. Rebuilt Chatham 1615 as 650bm, 40 guns; rebuilt Woolwich 1631 as 731bm, 56 guns. Sunk 12.6.1667 as a blockship at Rochester to bar the upper Medway to the Dutch.

VANGUARD 2nd Rate 90, 1,357bm, 126 x 45 ft. Portsmouth DY 1678. Overset 26.11.1703 in the Medway; raised 1704; rebuilt Chatham 1710 as 1,551bm. Rebuilt as 1,625bm and renamed DUKE 26.7.1728. BU 8.1769 at Plymouth.

VANGUARD 3rd Rate 70, 1,419bm, 160 x 45 ft. Ewer, E.Cowes 16.4.1748. Sold 13.4.1774.

VANGUARD Gunvessel 4. Spanish, captured 1780. Sold 1783.

VANGUARD 3rd Rate 74, 1,644bm, 168 x 47 ft. Deptford DY 6.3.1787. Prison ship 12.1812; powder hulk 9.1814. BU 9.1821 at Portsmouth.

VANGUARD 3rd Rate 78, 2,609bm, 190 x 57 ft. Pembroke Dock 25.8.1835. Renamed AJAX 20.10.1867. BU 6.1875 at Chatham.

VANGUARD Battleship, 3,774bm, 6,010 tons, 280 x 54 ft, 10-9in, 4-6in. Laird 3.1.1870. Sunk 1.9.1875 in collision with IRON DUKE off the Wicklow coast.

VANGUARD Battleship 19,250 tons, 490 x 84 ft, 10-12in, 20-4in. Vickers 22.2.1909. Sunk 9.7.17 by internal explosion at Scapa; raised and BU 1927 on Tyne.

VANGUARD Battleship 42,500 tons, 760 x 107½ ft, 8-15in, 16-5.25in, 71-40mm. J.Brown 30.11.1944. Arrived 9.8.60 at Faslane to BU.

VANGUARD Nuclear S/M. Vickers Ordered 1986

VANGUARD 3 Drifters requis. WW.I.

VANITY Ship in service 1650-54, probably hired.

VANITY Destroyer, 'V/W' class. Beardmore 3.5.1918. Escort 7.40. Sold 4.3.47; BU Brunton, Grangemouth.

VANNEAU Gun-brig 6, 120bm. French, captured 6.6.1793 by COLOSSUS in the Bay of Biscay. Wrecked 21.10.1796 near Porto Ferrajo, Italy.

VANOC Destroyer, 'V/W' class. J.Brown 14.6.1917. Escort 11.43. Sold 26.7.45; stranded at Penrhyn and BU Ward, in situ.

VANQUISHER Destroyer, 'V/W' class. J.Brown 18.8.1917. Escort 4.43. Sold 4.3.47, arrived 12.48 Charlestown to BU.

VANSITTART Destroyer, modified 'W' class. Beardmore 17.4.1919. Escort 6.42. Sold 25.2.46, arrived 5.5.46 Cashmore, Newport to BU.

VANSITTART Cutter 1821 hired 1821-27.

VANTAGE Destroyer, modified 'W' class. Beardmore. Laid down 16.9.1918, renamed VIMY 1918, cancelled 9.19.

VANTAGE Submarine, 'V' class. Vickers Armstrong, Tyne. Cancelled 23.1.1944.

VANTROMP 4th Rate 1796 (see TROMP).

VANTRUMP Flyboat 8, 312bm. Dutch, captured 1665. Sold 1667.

VARANGIAN Submarine, 'U' class. Vickers Armstrong, Tyne 4.3.1943. Sold 6.49, BU King, Gateshead.

VARIABLE (ex-*Redbridge*) Sloop/schooner 12, 210bm. Purchased 1808. 'Name removed from Navy List 23.11.1814'.

VARIABLE (ex-*Edward*) Schooner 14, 324bm, 104½ x 27½ ft, 12-24pdr carr., 2-6pdr. Purchased 1814. BU 2.1817.

VARIABLE Brig-sloop 10, 'Cherokee' class, 231bm. Pembroke Dock 6.10.1827. Renamed PIGEON 1829, packet brig, 6. Ordered to be sold

27.7.1847.

VARIANCE Submarine, 'V' class. Vickers Armstrong, Barrow 22.5.1944. To R.Norwegian navy 8.44 as UTSIRA.

VARNE Submarine, 'U' class. Vickers Armstrong, Barrow 22.1.1943. To R.Norwegian navy 28.3.43 as ULA.

VARNE Submarine, 'V' class. Vickers Armstrong, Tyne 24.2.1944. BU 9.58

VASHON Destroyer, modified 'W' class. Beardmore. Cancelled 12.1918.

VAUGHAN Sloop 14 Purchased 1781. Sold 17.7.1783.

VAUTOUR Brig-sloop 16, 336bm,. French, captured 8.1809 on stocks at Flushing; Taken to Chatham and completed 15.9.1810. Foundered 8.1813.

VECTIS Destroyer, 'V/W' class. White 4.9.1917. Handed over 25.8.36 to Ward, in part payment for *Majestic;* BU at Inverkeithing.

VEGA Coal Hulk, 304bm. Slaver brig. captured 1860 by LYRA and purchased 2.4.1860. Sold 23.2.1863.

VEGA Destroyer, 'V/W' class. Doxford 1.9.1917. Escort 10.39. Sold 4.3.47; arrived 26.3.48 Clayton & Davie, Dunston to BU.

VEGREVILLE Minesweeper, TE 'Bangor' class. Vickers, Montreal 7.8.1941. BU 5.47 Ward, Hayle.

VEHEMENT Destroyer, 'V/W' class. Denny 6.7.1917. Sunk 1.8.18 by mine in the North Sea.

VEHEMENT Submarine, 'V' class. Vickers Armstrong, Tyne. Cancelled 23.1.1944.

VELDT Submarine, 'V' class. Vickers Armstrong, Barrow 19.7.1943. Lent Greek navy 1944 to 10.12.57 as PIPINOS. Arrived 23.2.58 Clayton & Davie, Dunston to BU.

VELOX (ex-PYTHON purchased 7.6.1902) Destroyer 420 tons, 210 x 21 ft, 1-12pdr, 5-6pdr, 2-TT. Hawthorn 11.2.02 as a speculation. Sunk 25.10.15 by mine near the Nab.

VELOX Destroyer, 'V/W' class. Doxford 17.11.1917. Escort 4.42. Sold 18.2.47; arrived 11.47 Charlestown.

VENDETTA Destroyer, 'V/W' class. Fairfield 3.9.1917. RAN 10.33. Scuttled 2.7.48 off Sydney Heads.

VENDETTA Destroyer (RAN) 2,616 tons, 366 x 43 ft, 6-4.5in, 8-40mm, 5-TT. Williamstown DY 3.5.1954.

VENERABLE 3rd Rate 74, 1,669bm, 170½ x 47½ ft. Perry, Blackwall 19.4.1784. Wrecked 24.11.1804 off Torbay.

VENERABLE 3rd Rate 74, 1,716bm, 174 x 48 ft. Pitcher, Northfleet 12.4.1808. Harbour service 10.1825. BU 10.1838 at Plymouth.

VENERABLE Battleship 15,000 tons, 400 x 75 ft, 4-12in, 12-6in, 18-12pdr. Chatham DY 2.11.1899. Sold 4.6.1920 Stanlee, resold and BU in Germany.

VENERABLE A/C carrier 13,190 tons, 630 x 80 ft, 19-40mm, 48-A/C. Cammell Laird 30.12.1943. Sold Dutch navy 1.4.48; renamed KAREL DOORMAN 5.48.

VENETIA Destroyer, 'V/W' class. Fairfield 29.10.1917. Sunk 19.10.40 by mine in the Thames estuary.

VENETIA Trawler and yacht WW.I. Yacht (RCN) 1942-46

VENGEANCE 6th Rate 28, 533bm, 117 x 32½ ft, 24-9pdr, 4-4pdr. French, captured 2.1758 by HUSSAR. Sunk 10.1766 as breakwater at Plymouth.

VENGEANCE 3rd Rate 74, 1,627bm, 166 x 46 ft. Randall, Rotherhithe 25.6.1774. Prison ship 1.1808. BU 1.1816 at Portsmouth.

VENGEANCE Tender. Dutch hoy purchased 21.11.1793. Sold 11.1804.

VENGEANCE 4th Rate 50, 1,370bm, 160 x 41½ ft. French, captured 20.8.1800 by SEINE in the Mona Passage. Damaged by stranding 1801 and BU.

VENGEANCE 2nd Rate 84, 2,284bm, 196½ x 52 ft, 2-68pdr carr., 28-32pdr, 14-32pdr carr., 40-24pdr. Pembroke Dock 27.7.1824. Receiving ship 1861. Sold 10.5.1897.

VENGEANCE Battleship 12,950 tons, 390 x 74 ft, 4-12in, 12-6in, 12-12pdr. Vickers 25.7.1899. Sold 1.12.1921 Stanlee, Dover. Arrived 9.1.23 to BU.

VENGEANCE A/C carrier 13,190 tons, 630 x 80 ft, 19-40mm, 48-A/C. Swan Hunter 23.2.1944. To Brazilian navy 13.12.56, renamed MINAS GERAIS.

VENGEFUL Destroyer, modified 'W' class. Beardmore. Cancelled 12.1918.

VENGEFUL Submarine, 'V' class. Vickers Armstrong, Barrow 20.7.1944. Lent Greek navy 1945-57 as DELFIN. Arrived 22.3.58 King, Gateshead to BU.

VENGEUR 3rd Rate 74, 1,765bm, 176½ x 48 ft. Graham, Harwich 19.6.1810. Receiving ship 2.1824. BU 8.1843.

VENOM Gun-brig 8, 128bm, 65½ x 23 ft 4-18pdr carr., 4-6pdr. French GENIE captured 31.5.1796 by a squadron in the Mediterranean. Listed to 1799.

VENOM Destroyer, modified 'V' class. J.Brown 21.12.1918. Renamed VENOMOUS 24.4.1919. Escort 8.42. Sold 4.3.47, arrived 7.47 at Charlestown to BU.

VENOM Submarine, 'V' class. Vickers Armstrong, Tyne. Cancelled 23.1.1944.

VENOMOUS (see VENOM of 1918)

VENTNOR (see CROZIER)

VENTURE Training schooner (RCN) 250 tons, 126½ x 27½ ft, 2-3pdr. Meteghan NS 6.1937. Sold 1946.

VENTURE Trawler requis. 1914-19 and 1939-41.

VENTURER (see RANGER of 1787)

VENTURER Schooner 10, 126bm, 72 x 20½ ft. French privateer NOUVELLE ENTERPRISE captured 27.12.1807 by NIMROD in the W.Indies. Renamed THEODOCIA 1812. Sold 15.12.1814.

VENTURER Submarine, 'V' class. Vickers Armstrong, Barrow 4.5.1943. Sold 1946 R.Norwegian navy as UTSTEIN.

VENTURER Name borne in succession as RNVR tenders by MMS.1761, BUTTINGTON and HODGESTON.

VENTUROUS Destroyer, 'V/W' class. Denny 21.9.1917. Handed over 25.8.36 to Ward in part payment for *Majestic*; BU at Inverkeithing.

VENUS 5th Rate 36, 722bm, 128½ x 36 ft. Okill, Liverpool 11.3.1758. Reduced to 32 guns 3.1792. Renamed HEROINE 1809. Harbour service 1817. Sold 22.9.1828.

VENUS 5th Rate 36, 942bm. Danish, captured 7.9.1807 at Copenhagen. Harbour service 1809. Sold 9.8.1815. (Was to have been renamed LEVANT in 1809.)

VENUS 5th Rate 46, 1,069bm, 153½ x 40 ft. Deptford DY 10.8.1820. Lent Marine Socy 1848-62 as training ship. Sold 7.10.1864 Castle, Charlton.

VENUS 2nd class cruiser 5,600 tons, 350 x 54 ft, 5-6in, 6-4.7in (11.6in from 1904). Fairfield 5.9.1895. Sold 22.9.21 Cohen, BU in Germany.

VENUS Destroyer 1,710 tons, 339½ x 36 ft, 4-4.7in, 4-40mm, 8-TT. Fairfield 23.2.1943. Frigate 1952, 2,240 tons, 2-4in, 2-3in, 2-40mm. Sold Ward 6.11.72, BU at Briton Ferry.

VENUS 4 hired cutters between 1793 & 1806. Drifter WW.I.

VERBENA Sloop, 'Arabis' class. Blyth DD 9.11.1915. Sold 13.10.33 Rees, Llanelly.

VERBENA Corvette, 'Flower' class.

Smiths Dk 1.10.1940. Sold 17.5.47 Wheelock Marden.

VERBENA Trawler requis. 1915-19

VERDUN Destroyer, 'V/W' class. Hawthorn Leslie 21.8.1917. Escort 7.40. Arrived Ward, Inverkeithing 3.3.46

VERDUN Minesweeper 1916-22.

VERDUN OF CANADA (see DUNVER)

VERITY Destroyer, modified 'W' class. J.Brown 19.3.1919. Escort 10.43. Sold 4.3.47, arrived 14.9.47 Cashmore, Newport to BU.

VERITY Drifter requis. 1915-18.

VERNON A.ship 14. Listed 1781-82.

VERNON 4th Rate 50, 2,080bm, 2,388 tons, 176 x 52½ ft, 50-32pdr. Woolwich DY 1.5.1832. Torpedo school ship 1876. Renamed ACTAEON 14.1.1886. Sold 14.9.1923.

For the various ships renamed VERNON as torpedo school ships, see DONEGAL of 1858, MARLBOROUGH of 1855, WARRIOR of 1860, and SKYLARK of 1932.

VERONICA Sloop, 'Acacia' class. Dunlop Bremner 27.5.1915. Sold 22.2.35 Cashmore, Newport.

VERONICA Corvette, 'Flower' class. Smiths Dk 17.10.1940. Lent USN 21.3.42 to 1945 as TEMPTRESS. Sold 1946, renamed *Verolock*.

VERSATILE Destroyer, 'V/W' class. Hawthorn Leslie 31.10.1917. Escort 10.43. Sold 7.5.47, BU Brechin, Granton., arrived 10.9.48.

VERTU (see VIRTUE)

VERULAM Destroyer, 'V/W' class. Hawthorn Leslie 3.10.1917. Sunk 4.9.19 by mine in the Gulf of Finland.

VERULAM Destroyer 1,710 tons, 339½ X 36 ft, 4-4.7in, 2-40mm, 8-TT. Fairfield 22.4.1943. Frigate 1952. Sold Cashmore 1.9.72, BU Newport.

VERVAIN (ex-BROOM renamed 1.1941) Corvette, 'Flower' class. Harland & Wolff 12.3.41. Sunk 20.2.45 by 'U.1208' south of Ireland.

VERVE Submarine, 'V' class. Vickers Armstrong, Tyne. Cancelled 23.1.1944.

VERWOOD (see CROZIER)

VERYAN BAY (ex-LOCH SWANNAY renamed 1944) Frigate, 'Bay' class. Hill, Bristol 11.11.44. Arrived 1.7.59 at Charlestown to BU.

VESPER Destroyer, 'V/W' class. Stephen 15.12.1917. Escort 5.43. Sold 4.3.47, BU Ward, Inverkeithing; arrived 14.3.49.

VESPER Trawler requis. 1914-19.

VESTA Schooner 10, 111bm, 63 x 20½

ft, 10-18pdr carr. Bermuda 1806. Sold 11.1.1816.

VESTAL 5th Rate 32, 659bm, 124½ 35 ft. Barnard & Turner, Harwich 17.6.1757. BU 1775.

VESTAL 6th Rate 20, 429bm, 108 x 30 ft. Plymouth DY 23.5.1777. Foundered 10.1777 off Newfoundland.

VESTAL 6th Rate 28, 601bm, 120 x 34 ft. Batson, Limehouse 24.12.1779. Troopship 3.1800; lent Trinity House 10.1803. Sold 2.1816 at Barbados.

VESTAL Brig 10 (Indian), 159bm. Bombay DY 1809. Fate unknown.

VESTAL 6th Rate 26, 913bm, 130 x 40½ ft, 24-32pdr, 2-12pdr. Sheerness DY 6.4.1833. BU completed 17.2.1862 by Castle & Beech.

VESTAL Wood S.sloop, 1,081bm, 1,574 tons, 187 x 36 ft, 9-64pdr. Pembroke Dock 16.11.1865. Sold 12.1884 Castle.

VESTAL Sloop 980 tons, 180 x 33 ft, 6-4in, 4-3pdr. Sheerness DY 10.2.1900. Sold 21.10.21 Thomas, Anglesey.

VESTAL Minesweeper, 'Algerine' class. Harland & Wolff 19.6.1943. Sunk 26.7.45 by Japanese A/C off Puket, Siam.

VESUVIUS Fireship 8, 248bm, 92 x 25 ft. Taylor, Cuckolds Point 30.3.1691. Expended 19.11.1693 at St Malo.

VESUVIUS Fireship 8, 269bm, 92 x 25½ ft. Barrett, Shoreham 4.12.1693; purchased on stocks. Stranded 26.11.1703 at Spithead; refloated 12.03 and condemned 7.9.1705.

VESUVIUS (ex-*Worcester*) Fireship 16, 200bm, 83 x 24 ft. Purchased 12.9.1739. BU 10.1742 at Deptford.

VESUVIUS (ex-*King of Portugal*) Fireship 8, 299bm, 91½ x 28 ft, 8-4pdr. Purchased 17.11.1756. Sloop 12.56. Sold 3.5.1763.

VESUVIUS Fireship 8, 8-4pdr. Randall, Rotherhithe 15.5.1771. Re- named RAVEN 10.8.1771, sloop. Sold 19.7.1780 at New York.

VESUVIUS Bomb 8, 299bm, 91½ x 27½ ft. Perry, Blackwall 3.7.1776. Sold 3.8.1812.

VESUVE Gunvessel 3, 160bm, 74 x 22½ ft, 3-18pdr. French, captured 3.7.1795 by MELAMPUS off St Malo. Sold 12.1802.

VESUVIUS Bomb 8, 298bm(?). Purchased 4.1797. Sold 13.8.1812.

VESUVIUS Bomb 8, 326bm, 102½ x 27½ ft. Davy, Topsham 1.5.1813. Sold 22.7.1819.

VESUVIUS Bomb 8, 372bm, 105 x 29ft, 10-24pdr carr., 2-6pdr, 2 mortars.

Ordered 1823 at Deptford DY; transferred Chatham DY 8.1828, laid down 8.1830, cancelled 10.1.1831.

VESUVIUS Wood pad. sloop, 970bm, 180 x 34½ ft, 4 guns. Sheerness DY 11.7.1839. Sold White 6.1865 to BU at Cowes.

VESUVIUS Iron S.torpedo vessel 244 tons, 90 x 22 ft, 4-TT. Pembroke Dock 24.3.1874. Sold 14.9.1923 Cashmore; foundered in tow to Newport.

VESUVIUS Torpedo-discharge lighter. Purchased 1933. Renamed TL.1 in 1940.

VESUVIUS (see SKYLARK of 1932)

VETCH Corvette, 'Flower' class. Smiths DK 27.5.1941. Sold 8.45, re- named *Patrai*.

VETERAN 3rd Rate 64, 1,397bm, 160½ x 45 ft. Fabian, E.Cowes 14.8.1787. Prison ship 1799. BU 6.1816.

VETERAN (see PROMETHEUS of 1807)

VETERAN Destroyer, modified 'W' class. J.Brown 26.4.1919. Escort 1941. Sunk 26.9.42 by 'U.404' in the N.Atlantic.

VETERAN Tug 1915, ren. ANCIENT 1918-54; Drifter 1915-19.

VETO Submarine, 'V'class. Vickers Armstrong, Barrow. Cancelled 23.1.1944.

VICEROY Destroyer, 'V/W' class. 1,325 tons. Thornycroft 17.11.1917. Escort 12.40. Sold 17.5.47, arrived Brechin, Granton 10.9.48 to BU.

VICTOIRE (see under VICTORY)

VICTOR Brig-sloop 10. Purchased 1777. Foundered 5.10.1780 in a hurricane in the W.Indies.

VICTOR Sloop 14. American, captured 1779. Listed to 1782.

VICTOR Sloop 18, 385bm, 101 x 31 ft. Brindley, Lynn 19.3.1798. Paid off 5.9.1808 to sell in the E.Indies.

VICTOR Brig-sloop 18, 425bm, 16-32pdr carr., 2-6pdr taken out of previous ship. French IENA (spelt JENA in British lists), captured 8.10.1808 by MODESTE in the Bay of Bengal. Recaptured 2.11.1809 by the French BELLONE in the same area; again captured 2.12.1810 at Mauritius and Sold.

VICTOR Brig-sloop 18, 'Cruizer' class, 382bm. Bombay DY 29.1.1814. Foundered 8.1842 in the Atlantic.

VICTOR Wood. S.gunvessel, 859bm, 201½x 30½ ft, 1-110pdr, 1-60pdr, 4-20pdr. Blackwall 24.11.1855. Sold 11.1863, renamed *Scylla*, then Confederate RAPPAHANNOCK.

VICTOR Destroyer 954 tons, 260 x 26½ ft, 3-4in, 2-TT. Thornycroft 28.11.1913. Sold 20.1.23. King, Garston.

VICTOR 2 Trawlers WW.I.; Tug requis. 1939-45

VICTOR EMANUEL (see REPULSE of 1855)

VICTORIA Wood pad. sloop (Indian), 705bm, 5 guns. Bombay DY 10.1839. Sold circa 1864.

VICTORIA Wood S.sloop (Australian), 580bm, 13-32pdr. Young & Magnay, Limehouse 7.1855. Survey vessel 1864. Sold 8.1894 W.Marr, Williamstown; BU 8.1895.

VICTORIA (see WINDSOR CASTLE of 1858)

VICTORIA Screw 1st Rate 121, 4,127bm, 6,959 tons, 260 x 60 ft, 32-8in, 1-68pdr, 88-32pdr. Portsmouth DY 12.11.1859. Sold 5.1893 to BU.

VICTORIA Coastguard yawl, 131bm, 70 x 21 ft. Built 1864. Sold 4.4.1905 at Chatham.

VICTORIA S.gunvessel (Australian) 530 tons, 140 x 27 ft, 1-10in, 2-13pdr. Armstrong Mitchell 6.1883. Sold 1896, became mercantile *Victoria*

VICTORIA (ex-RENOWN renamed 18.3.1887) Battleship 10,470 tons, 340 x 70 ft, 2-16.25in, 1-10in, 12-6in, 12-6pdr. Armstrong Mitchell 9.4.1887. Sunk 22.6.1893 in collision with CAMPERDOWN off Tripoli.

VICTORIA Trawler, Drifter, Ferry & Decoy ship WW.I. Trawler in WW.II.

VICTORIA & ALBERT Wood pad. yacht, 1,034bm, 225(oa) x 33(oa) ft. Pembroke Dock 26.4.1843. Renamed OSBORNE 22.12.1854. BU 1868 at Portsmouth.

VICTORIA & ALBERT (ex-WINDSOR CASTLE renamed 12.1854) Wood pad. yacht, 2,345bm, 2,470 tons, 329(oa) x 69(oa) ft. Pembroke Dock 16.1.1855. BU 1904 at Portsmouth.

VICTORIA & ALBERT S.yacht 4,700 tons, 380 x 40 ft. Pembroke Dock 9.5.1899. Accommodation ship 1939. Arrived Faslane 6.12.54 to BU.

VICTORIAVILLE Frigate (RCN), 'River' class. G.T.Davie 23.6.1944. Renamed GRANBY 1966 as diving tender.

VICTORIEUSE (see under VICTORIOUS)

VICTORIOUS 3rd Rate 74, 1,683bm, 170½ x 47 ft. Perry, Blackwall 27.4.1785. BU 8.1803 at Lisbon.

VICTORIEUSE Brig-sloop 12, 350bm,

103 x 27½ ft, 2-36pdr carr., 12-12pdr. French, captured 31.8.1795 by the fleet off the Texel. BU 7.1805.

VICTORIOUS 3rd Rate 74, 1,724bm, 173 x 47½ ft. Adams, Bucklers Hard 20.10.1808. Receiving ship 5.1826. BU in 1.1862 Portsmouth.

VICTORIOUS Battleship 14,900 tons, 390 x 75 ft, 4-12in, 12-6in, 16-12pdr. Chatham DY 19.10.1895. Repair ship 3.1916; renamed INDUS II in 1920. Sold 19.12.22 A.J.Purves; resold 4.23 Stanlee, Dover.

VICTORIOUS II (see PRINCE GEORGE of 1895)

VICTORIOUS A/C carrier 23,000 tons, 673 x 96 ft, 16-4.5in, 36-A/C. Vickers Armstrong, Tyne 14.9.1939. Rebuilt 1958 as 30,530 tons, 12-3in, 6-40mm, 54-A/C. Sold S.Bkg. Ind. 20.6.69, BU at Faslane.

VICTORY (ex-*Great Christopher*) 42-gun ship, 565bm. Purchased 1560. Rebuilt 1586, 12-18pdr, 18-9pdr, 9-6pdr, 20 smaller guns. BU 1608.

VICTORY 42-gun ship, 541bm. Deptford 1620. Rebuilt Chatham 1666 as 2nd Rate 82, 1,020bm. BU 1691 at Woolwich.

VICTORY PRIZE Ship. Captured and Listed 1663-67.

LITTLE VICTORY 5th Rate 28, 175bm. Chatham DY 1665. Expended 8.5.1671 as a fireship.

FRENCH VICTORY 5th Rate 38, 394bm. French VICTOIRE captured 5.4.1666. Captured 1672 by the Dutch.

VICTORY (see ROYAL JAMES of 1675)

VICTORY 1st Rate 100, 1,921bm, 174½ x 50½ ft. Portsmouth DY 23.2.1737 (technically a rebuild from frames of previous ship (see ROYAL JAMES) restarted 6.3.1726). Wrecked 5.10.1744 on the Casquets.

VICTORY Schooner 8 (Canadian lakes). Navy Island, Canada 1764. Burnt (by the French?) 1768.

VICTORY 1st Rate 100, 2,142bm, 186 x 52 ft. Chatham DY 7.5.1765. Rebuilt 1801 as 2,164bm; harbour service 1824. Dry-docked at Portsmouth 1.1922.

VICTOIRE Lugger 14. Purchased 1795. Listed to 1800.

VICTOIRE (VICTORIE in some lists) Fire vessel, 73bm, 63 x 16½ ft, 2-4pdr. French privateer schooner captured 28.12.1797 by TERMAGANT off Spurn Point. Sold 16.12.1801.

VICTORY Tug 1904-34; Trawler & Drifter WW.I.

VIDAL Survey ship 1,940 tons, 297 x 40 ft, 4-3pdr. Chatham DY 31.7.1951. BU at Bruges in 6.76.

VIDETTE Destroyer, 'V/W' class. Stephen 28.2.1918. Escort 1.43; sold 4.3.47, BU Brunton, Grangemouth.

VIDETTE Sloop hired 1800, Trawler WW.I. & II.

VIGILANTE 4th Rate 58, 1,318bm, 154 x 43½ ft, 24-24pdr, 24-12pdr, 10-6pdr. French VIGILANT captured 5.1745 by SUPERB off Cape Breton. Sold 11.12.1759.

VIGILANT Schooner 8 (Canadian lakes). Oswego Lake Ontario 1755. Captured 14.8.1756 by the French at Oswego.

VIGILANT 3rd Rate 64, 1,347bm, 159½ x 44½ ft. Adams, Bucklers Hard 6.10.1774. Prison ship in 1799. Sank 1.1806 in Portsmouth harbour, raised 4.06; BU 4.1816.

VIGILANT (ex-*Empress of Russia*) A.ship 20, 14-24pdr, 6-6pdr. Purchased 1777 in N.America. Burnt as unfit 1780 at Beaufort, S.Carolina.

VIGILANTE Cutter 4. French ALERTE captured 8.1793. Burnt 18.12.1793 at the evacuation of Toulon.

VIGILANT Schooner 4, 61bm. Purchased 1803. Sold 1808.

VIGILANT Schooner 8, 102bm, French IMPERIAL captured 24.5.1806 by CYGNET off Dominica. Renamed SUBTLE 20.11.06; wrecked 26.10.1807 off Bermuda.

VIGILANT Cutter 12, 161bm, 67½ x 21½ ft. Deptford DY 18.4.1821. Sold 11.1832 W.Clarke.

VIGILANT Wood S.frigate, 1,536bm, 210 x 40 ft. Portsmouth DY. Ordered 26.3.1846, cancelled 22.5.1849.

VIGILANT Wood S.gunvessel, 680bm, 181 x 28½ ft, 1-110pdr, 1-68pdr, 2-20pdr. Mare, Blackwall 20.3.1856. Ordered 25.2.1869 to be sold at Bombay.

VIGILANT Wood pad. despatch vessel, 835bm, 1,000 tons, 2-20pdr. Devonport DY 17.2.1871. Sold 10.1886 at Hong Kong.

VIGILANT Destroyer 400 tons, 210 x 21 ft, 1-12pdr, 5-6pdr, 2-TT. J.Brown 16.8.1900; built as a speculation and purchased 31.3.1900. Sold 10.2.20 S.Alloa S.Bkg Co.

VIGILANT Destroyer 1,710 tons, 339½ x 36 ft, 4-4.7in, 2-40mm, 8-TT. Swan Hunter 18.10.1943. Frigate 1952. Arrived 4.6.65 S.Bkg Ind, Faslane to BU.

VIGILANT Patrol boat 3.1975, renamed MEAVY 7.86.

VIGILANT Tug 1900-19; Tug 14-19;2 Trawlers & Drifter WW.I.; Patrol vessel. (RAN) & 2 Tugs WW.II.

VIGO (see DARTMOUTH of 1693)

VIGO 3rd Rate 74, 1,787bm, 177 x 48 ft. Ross, Rochester 21.2.1810. Receiving ship 1827. BU 8.1865 Marshall, Plymouth.

VIGO (see AGINCOURT of 1817)

VIGO Destroyer, modified 'W' class. J.Brown. Cancelled 12.1918.

VIGO Destroyer 2,315 tons, 355 x 40 ft, 4-4.5in, 1-4in, 14-40mm, 8-TT. Fairfield 27.9.1945. Arrived 6.12.64 Faslane to BU.

VIGOROUS Destroyer, modified 'W' class. J.Brown. Laid down 1918, renamed WISTFUL 6.18, cancelled 12.18.

VIGOROUS Submarine, 'V' class. Vickers Armstrong, Barrow 15.10.1943. Sold 23.12.49, BU Stockton on Tees.

VIKING Destroyer 1,090 tons, 280 x 27½ ft, 2-4in, 2-TT. Palmer 14.9.1909. Sold 12.12.19 Ward, Briton Ferry. (The only 6-funnelled vessel in the RN.)

VIKING Training ketch (RNZN). Listed 1937-45.

VIKING Submarine, 'V' class. Vickers Armstrong, Barrow 5.5.1943. To R.Norwegian navy 1946 as UTVAER.

VIKING Drifter requis. 1915-19; Tug 1940-41.

VILLE de PARIS 1st Rate 104, 2,347bm, 187 x 53½ ft. French, captured 12.4.1782 by the fleet in the W.Indies. Foundered 9.9.1782 in a gale off Newfoundland.

VILLE de PARIS 1st Rate 110, 2,351bm, 190 x 53 ft. Chatham DY 17.7.1795. Harbour service 1825. BU 6.1845 at Pembroke Dock.

VILLE de QUEBEC (see QUEBEC of 1941)

VILLE de QUEBEC Destroyer (RCN) 4200 tons. St.John D.D.Co, ordered 1986.

VIMIERA Brig-sloop 16, 304bm, 91 x 28 ft, 14-24pdr carr., 2-6pdr. French PYLADE captured 21.10.1808 by POMPEE. Sold 1.9.1814.

VIMIERA Destroyer, 'V/W' class. Swan Hunter 22.6.1917. Escort 1.40. Sunk 9.1.42 by mine in the Thames estuary.

VIMIERA (see DANAE of 1945)

VIMY (see VANTAGE of 1918)

VIMY (see VANCOUVER of 1917)

VIMY Trawler (RCN) 1917-20.

VINCEJO Brig-sloop 16, 277bm. Spanish, captured 19.3.1799 by CORMO-

RANT in the Mediterranean. Captured 20.5.1804 by the French in Quiberon Bay.

VINDEX (ex-*Viking*) Seaplane carrier 2,950 tons, 350½ x 42 ft, 4-12pdr, 1-6pdr, 7-A/C. Hired 15.3.1915, purchased 9.15. Sold 12.2.20 Isle of Man SP Co.

VINDEX Escort carrier 13,455 tons, 499½ x 68½ ft, 2-4in, 15-A/C. Swan Hunter 4.5.1943. Sold 2.10.47, renamed *Port Vindex*.

VINDICTIVE Galley 8. Purchased in N.America. 1779, listed to 1784.

VINDICTIVE 6th Rate 28, 506bm, 112 x 32 ft. Dutch BELLONA captured 17.8.1796 at Saldanha Bay. BU 1816 at Sheerness (Left navy list in 7.1810.)

VINDICTIVE 3rd Rate 74, 1,758bm, 176 x 48½ft. Portsmouth DY 23.11.1813. Reduced to 50 guns 10.1832. Storeship 1862 at Fernando Po then at Jellah Coffee; returned to Fernando Po for sale 1871 and foundered there; sold as wreck 24.11.1871.

VINDICTIVE 2nd class cruiser 5,750 tons, 320 x 54 ft, 4-6in, 6-4.7in (10-6in from 1904). Chatham DY 9.12.1897. Sunk 10.5.18 as blockship at Ostend; raised 8.20 and BU.

VINDICTIVE (ex-CAVENDISH renamed 1918) Cruiser A/C carrier 9,750 tons, 565 x 58 ft, 4-7.5in, 4-3in, 4-3in, 4-12pdr, 6-A/C. Harland & Wolff 17.1.18. Cruiser 1925, 7-7.5in; training ship 1937; repair ship 1940. Sold 2.46, BU Hughes Bolckow, Blyth.

VINEYARD Submarine, 'V' class. Vickers Armstrong, Barrow 8.5.1944. Lent French navy 1944 to 11.47 as DORIS; arrived 6.50 Charlestown to BU.

VIOLA (see LEGION)

VIOLA Sloop, 'Aubrietia' class. Ropner, Stockton on Tees 14.7.1916. Sold 17.10.22 Fryer, Sunderland. (Served as decoy ship Q.14.)

VIOLA Two trawlers and drifter requis. WW.I.

VIOLENT Destroyer, 'V/W' class. Swan Hunter 1.9.1917. Handed over 8.3.37 to Ward in part payment for *Majestic*; BU at Inverkeithing.

VIOLET Ship, 220bm. In the Armada fleet 1588, perhaps a hired vessel.

VIOLET 44-gun ship, 400bm. Captured 1652. BU 1672.

VIOLET Lugger, 82bm, 60½ x 18½ ft, 10-12pdr carr. Transferred from Customs 1806. BU 6.1812.

VIOLET Tender. Purchased 20.6.1835 on stocks at Scheveningen. Sold 24.11.1842.

VIOLET Iron pad. packet, 292bm. Ditchburn & Mare, Blackwall 1.12.1845. Sold 1854 Jenkins & Churchward.

VIOLET Wood S.gunboat, 'Albacore' class. Ditchburn & Mare, Blackwall 9.1.1856. Sold 7.10.1864 Marshall.

VIOLET Destroyer 350 tons, 210 x 21 ft, 1-12pdr, 2-TT. Doxford 3.5.1897. Sold 7.6.1920 J.Houston, Montrose.

VIOLET Corvette, 'Flower' class. Simons 30.12.1940. Sold 17.5.47 mercantile.

VIOLET 5 Drifters & a Tug requis. WW.I.

VIPER Sloop 14, 270bm, 91 x 26 ft. Durrell, Poole 11.6.1746. Renamed LIGHTNING 29.7.1755, fireship, 8-4pdr. Sold 30.12.1762.

VIPER Sloop 10, 228bm, 88½ x 24½ ft. West, Deptford 31.3.1756. Captured 1762 by the French.

VIPER Cutter 12. Dating from 1762. Wrecked 11.10.1780 in the Gulf of St Lawrence.

VIPER (see GREYHOUND of 1780)

VIPER Cutter 10, 149bm, 10-3pdr. Purchased in N.America and commissioned 17.7.1777. Foundered 15.12.1779 off Newfoundland (was to have been sold in 2.80)..

VIPER Galley 8. Purchased 1779, listed to 1785.

VIPERE Cutter 4. French privateer captured 1793. Wrecked 12.1793 in Hieres Bay.

VIPERE Brig-sloop 16, 290bm, 95½ x 26½ ft, 2-pdr carr., 16-6pdr. French privateer captured 23.1.1794 by FLORA in the Channel. Foundered 2.1.1797 off the mouth of the Shannon.

VIPER Gunvessel 4, 69bm, 65½ x 45 ft. Dutch hoy, purchased 1794. BU 1801 at Portsmouth.

VIPER Cutter 14, 14-4pdr. Purchased 1.1797. Sold 10.1809.

VIPER (ex-*Niger*) Cutter 8, 104bm, 63 x 20½ ft. White, Cowes 1809 and purchased 1809. Sold 11.8.1814.

VIPER Gun-brig 10, 148bm. Purchased 1810. Perhaps renamed MOHAWK 1810. (Not listed 1811)

VIPER Schooner 6, 183bm, 80 x 23 ft. Pembroke Dock 12.5.1831. BU 5.1851.

VIPER Wood S.gunvessel, 477bm, 160 x 25½ ft, 2-68pdr. Green Blackwall 22.7.1854. Sold 19.5.1862 Marshall.

VIPER Iron armoured gunvessel, 737bm, 1,230 tons, 160 x 32½ ft, 2-7in, 2-20pdr. Dudgeon, Limehouse 21.12.1865. Harbour service 1890; tank vessel 1901. Sold 1908 at Bermuda.

VIPER Destroyer 440 tons, 210 x 21 ft, 1-12pdr, 5-6pdr, 2-TT. Hawthorn 6.9.1899. Wrecked 3.8.1901 on Bushon Island near Alderney. (The first turbine destroyer.)

VIRAGO Gun-brig 12, 181bm, 84½ x 22 ft. Tanner, Dartmouth 23.9.1805. Sold 30.5.1816.

VIRAGO Wood pad. sloop, 1,059bm, 180 x 36 ft. Chatham DY 25.7.1842. BU 1876 at Chatham.

VIRAGO Destroyer 395 tons, 210½ x 21½ ft, 1-12pdr, 5-6pdr, 2-TT. Laird 19.11.1895. Sold 10.10.1919 at Hong Kong; BU in China.

VIRAGO Destroyer 1,710 tons, 339½ x 36 ft, 4-4.7in, 2-40mm, 8-TT. Swan Hunter 4.2.1943. Frigate 1952. Arrived 6.65 at Faslane to BU.

VIRGIN Fireship 4, 148bm. Purchased 1666. Expended 1667.

VIRGIN PRIZE 5th Rate 32, 322bm, 95 x 28 ft. French, captured 1690. Sold 20.9.1698.

VIRGIN sloop 12. Origin unknown. Sold in 1764. (Was in French hands as VIERGE 5.1760 to 9.1760.)

VIRGINIA 6th Rate 28, (802bm?), 132½ x 34½ ft, 28-9pdr. American, captured 30.3.1778 when aground in the Chesapeake. BU 12.1782.

VIRGINIA Schooner 4. Purchased 1796. Gone by 1800.

VIRGINIE 5th Rate 38, 1,066bm, 151½ X 40 ft. French, captured 23.4.1796 by INDEFATIGABLE in the Atlantic. Receiving ship in 1817. Sold 11.7.1827 to BU.

VIRGINIA Brig-sloop. Sold 11.1811.(Was the French transport VIRGINIE captured 14.3.1808.)

VIRGINIA Coal hulk, 195bm. Ex-barque purchased 22.1.1862. BU 3.1866 at Bermuda.

VIRGINIA Yacht requis. 1939-45.

VIRILE Submarine, 'V' class. Vickers Armstrong, Barrow. Laid down 2.11.1943, cancelled 23.1.1944.

VIRTUE (spelt VERTU in some lists) 5th Rate 40, 1,073bm. French VERTU captured 30.11.1803 at San Domingo. BU 12.1810.

VIRTUE Submarine, 'V' class. Vickers Armstrong, Barrow 28.11.1943. Arrived 19.5.46 at Cochin, India to BU.

VIRULENT Destroyer, modified 'W' class. J.Brown. Cancelled 12.1918.

VIRULENT Submarine, 'V' class. Vickers Armstrong, Tyne 23.5.1944. Lent Greek navy 29.5.46 to 3.10.58 as ARGONAFTIS. Left Malta 11.58 for Tyne, broke adrift and stranded N.coast of Spain; sold there in 1961.

VISCOUNT Destroyer, 'V/W' class 1,325 tons. Thornycroft 29.12.1917. Escort 12.41; sold 20.3.45, BU 5.45 Clayton & Davie, Dunston.

VISIGOTH Submarine, 'V' class. Vickers Armstrong, Barrow 30.11.1943. Sold 3.49, arrived 20.2.50 Ward, Hayle.

VISITANT Submarine, 'V' class. Vickers Armstrong, Barrow. Cancelled 23.1.1944, not laid down.

VITALITY (see UNTAMED)

VITALITY Trawler requis. 1915-17.

VITTORIA (see PRINCESS CHARLOTTE of 1814)

VITTORIA Destroyer, 'V/W' class. Swan Hunter 29.10.1917. Torpedoed 1.9.19 by Russian MTB in the Baltic.

VIVACIOUS Destroyer, 'V/W' class. Yarrow 3.11.1917. Escort 12.42. Sold 4.3.47, arrived 10.48 Charlestown to BU.

VIVID Wood pad. packet, 352bm, 350 tons, 150 x 22 ft, 2 guns. Chatham DY 7.2.1848. Sold 1894.

VIVID (ex-Capercailzie) Iron S.yacht 550 tons, 192 x 24 ft, 1 gun. Purchased 26.9.1891. Base ship at Devonport from 1.1892. Sold 20.11.1912. After sale was wrecked off Colonsay in 7.13.

VIVID Nominal base ships (see CUCKOO of 1873, SABRINA of 1876, CAMBRIAN of 1893, MARSHAL NEY).

VIVID Submarine, 'V' class. Vickers Armstrong, Tyne 15.9.1943. Arrived 10.50 at Faslane to BU.

VIVIEN Destroyer, 'V/W' class. Yarrow 16.2.1918. Escort 10.39; sold 18.2.47, arrived 11.47 Charlestown to BU.

EL VIVO Sloop 14, 216bm, 81 x 26 ft, 14-18pdr. Spanish, captured 30.9.1800 by FISGARD on the coast of Spain. Sold 7.9.1801.

VIXEN Gun-brig 14, 186bm, 80½ x 23 ft. Adams, Bucklers Hard 9.1.1801. Sold 28.3.1815.

VIXEN Wood pad. sloop, 1,054bm, 180 x 36 ft, 1-110pdr, 1-10in, 4-32pdr. Pembroke Dock 4.2.1841. Sold 12.11.1862 Castle, Charlton.

VIXEN Armoured composite gunboat, 754bm, 1,230 tons, 160 x 32 ft, 2-7in, 2-20pdr. Lungley, Deptford 18.11.1865. Ordered 11.10.1895 to be BU in Bermuda. (The first twin-screw and the first composite vessel in the RN.)

VIXEN Destroyer 400 tons, 210 x 20 ft, 1-12pdr, 5-6pdr, 2-TT. Vickers Maxim 29.3.1.1900. Sold 17.3.1921 Ward Grays.

VIXEN Destroyer 1,710 tons, 339½ x 36 ft, 4-4.7in, 2-40mm, 8-TT. White 14.9.1943. Renamed SIOUX (RCN) 5.3.44. Frigate 11.59, 2-4.7in, 4-TT. Arrived 28.8.65 at Spezia to BU.

VLIETER 5th Rate 40, 1,357bm, 156 x 45 ft. Dutch MARS captured 30.8.1799 in the Texel. Floating battery 7.1801; sheer hulk in 1809. BU 4.1817.

VOLADOR Brig-sloop 16, 273bm. (Spanish?) captured 1807. Wrecked 23.10.1808 in the Gulf of Coro, W.Indies.

VOLAGE 6th Rate 22, 523bm, 119 x 31½ ft. French privateer captured 23.1.1798 by MELAMPUS off SW Ireland. BU 8.1804.

VOLAGE 6th Rate 22, 530bm, 118 x 31½ ft. Chapman, Bideford 23.3.1807. Sold 29.1.1818.

VOLAGE 6th Rate 28, 516bm, 111 x 32 ft. Portsmouth DY 19.2.1825. Survey ship 4.1847; lent War Dept 19.10.64 as powder hulk. BU completed 12.12.1874 at Chatham.

VOLAGE Iron S.corvette, 2,322bm, 3,080 tons, 270 x 42 ft, 6-7in, 6-6.3in. TIW, Blackwall 27.2.1869. Sold 17.5.1904 Cohen, London to BU. Was ordered as CERBERUS and renamed 2.5.67.

VOLAGE Destroyer, modified 'W' class. J.Brown. Cancelled 12.1918.

VOLAGE Destroyer 1,710 tons, 339½ x 36 ft, 4-4.7in, 2-40mm, 8-TT. White 15.12.1943. Frigate 1952. Sold Pounds, Portsmouth 28.10.72.

VOLANTE Schooner. Origin unknown. Captured 1775 by Americans.

VOLANTE Trawler requis. 1914-19.

VOLATILE Submarine, 'V' class. Vickers Armstrong, Tyne 20.6.1944. Lent Greek navy 5.46 to 10.58 as TRIANA; arrived 23.12.58 Clayton & Davie, Dunston to BU.

VOLATILE Tug 1919 (see VOLCANO)

VOLATILLIA Galley 7, 100bm. Deptford 1602. Sold 1629.

VOLCANO Fireship 8, 247bm, 89 x 25½ ft, 8-32pdr carr. Purchased 1778, commissioned 31.7.1778. Sold 7.5.1781.

VOLCANO Bomb 8. Purchased 1780, sold 8.1.1784.

VOLCANO (ex-*Cornwall*) Bomb 8, 368bm, 100 x 29 ft. Purchased 3.1797. Sold 22.12.1810.

VOLCANO (see HERON of 1804)

VOLCANO Bomb 8, 372bm, 105 x 29 ft. Plymouth DY. Ordered 18.5.1819, cancelled 10.1.1831.

VOLCANO Wood pad. sloop, 720bm, 150½ x 33 ft, 2-9pdr. Portsmouth DY 29.6.1836. Floating factory 1862. BU at Portsmouth in 11.1894.

VOLCANO Destroyer, modified 'W' class. J.Brown. Cancelled 12.1918.

VOLCANO. Tug 1899, ren. VOLATILE 1919-57.

VOLPE Gunvessel 1. Said to have been captured 1808 and lost 1809. (Vessel not traced.)

VOLTIGEUR Sloop 18, 408bm, 115 x 28½ ft. French privateer AUDACIEUX captured 4.1798 by MAGNANIME. Sold 8.1802.

VOLUNTEER (ex-*Harmony*) Gunvessel 12, 135bm, 2-18pdr, 10-18pdr carr. Purchased 6.1804. Sold 6.1812.

VOLONTAIRE 5th Rate 38, 1,084bm, 152 x 40 ft. French, captured 4.3.1806 at the Cape. BU 2.1816.

VOLUNTEER Destroyer, modified 'W' class. Denny 17.4.1919. Escort 1943. Sold 4.3.47, arrived 12.47 at Granton to BU. by Brechin.

VOLUNTEER Mooring vessel 1916, ren. VOLENS 1918-47.

VORACIOUS Submarine, 'V' class. Vickers Armstrong, Tyne 11.11.1943. Arrived 19.5.46 at Cochin, India to BU.

VORSECHTERKITE A.transport, 167bm, 77½ x 24 ft. Dutch, captured 1800. Sold 1802.

VORTEX Submarine, 'V' class. Vickers Armstrong, Barrow 19.8.1944. Lent French navy 1944-47 as MORSE; lent Danish navy 1947 to 16.1.58 as SAELEN. Arrived 8.58 at Faslane to BU.

VORTIGERN Destroyer, 'V/W' class. White 15.10.1917. Sunk 15.3.42 by German MTB torpedo off Cromer.

VOTARY Destroyer, modified 'W' class. Denny. Laid down 18.6.1918, cancelled 12.18.

VOTARY Submarine, 'V' class. Vickers Armstrong, Tyne 21.8.1944. To R.Norwegian navy 7.46 as UTHAUG.

VOX Submarine 'U' class. Vickers Armstrong, Barrow 23.1.1943. Lent French navy 5.43 to 7.46 as CURIE; renamed P.67 in 7.46. Arrived 2.5.49 Ward, Milford Haven.

VOX Submarine, 'V' class. Vickers Armstrong, Barrow 28.9.1943. Arrived 19.5.46 at Cochin, India to BU.

VOYAGER Destroyer, 'V/W' class. Stephen 8.5.1918. RAN from 10.33. Grounded 23.9.42 south coast of Timor after Japanese air attack and destroyed by her crew.

VOYAGER Destroyer (RAN) 2,616 tons, 366 x 43 ft, 6-4.5in, 8-40mm, 5-TT. Cockatoo DY 1.3.1952. Sunk 11.2.64 in collision with MELBOURNE off Jervis Bay.

VRYHEID 3rd Rate 72, 1,562bm, 167½ x 46 ft. Dutch VRIJHEID captured 11.10.1797 at Camperdown. Prison ship 1799. Sold 6.1811.

VULCAN Fireship 8, 273bm, 91 x 25½ ft. Shish, Rotherhithe 21.2.1691. Sunk 10.8.1709 as breakwater at Sheerness.

VULCAN (ex-*Hunter*) Fireship 8, 253bm, 89 x 26 ft, 8-6pdr. Purchased 7.9.1739. Hulked 10.1743 in Jamaica.

VULCAN (ex-*Mary*) Fireship 8, 225bm, 87 x 24½ ft, 8-6pdr. Purchased 21.8.1745. Sold 9.11.1749.

VULCAN Fireship, ex-American Merchantman 1777. Sunk in action 10.10.1781 at Yorktown.

VULCAN Fireship 14, 425bm, 109 x 29½ ft. Edwards, Shoreham 12.9.1783. Destroyed to avoid capture 18.12.1793 at the evacuation of Toulon.

VULCAN (ex-*Hector*) Bomb 10, 320bm. Purchased 1796. Sold in Madagascar in 5.1802.

VULCAN Iron S. frigate, 1,747bm, 220 x 41 ft. Ditchburn & Mare, Blackwall 27.1.1849. Troopship 1851, 1,764bm. Sold 1.2.1867 as barque *Jorawur*.

VULCAN Depot ship cruiser 6,620 tons, 350 x 58 ft, 8-4.7in, 12-3pdr. Portsmouth DY 13.6.1889. Renamed DEFIANCE III on 17.2.1931. Arrived 12.55 in Belgium to BU.

VULCAN II (see ONYX of 1892)

VULCAN II (see LILY of 1915)

VULCAN Tug 1914-23: Trawler 1936-47.

VULPINE Submarine, 'V' class. Vickers Armstrong, Tyne 28.12.1943. Lent R.Danish navy 9.47-58 as STOREN. Arrived 29.4.59 at Faslane to BU.

VULTURE Ketch 6. Royalist, captured 1648 by Parliament. Fate unknown.

VULTURE 10-gun vessel, 88bm. Privateer, captured 1656. Sold 1663.

VULTURE Sloop 4, 68bm. Deptford 1673. Sold 1686.

VULTURE Fireship 8, 270bm, 93 x 25 ft. Deptford 18.4.1690. Captured 10.12.1708 by the French in the Atlantic.

VULTURE (see PEMBROKE PRIZE of 1740)

VULTURE Sloop 14, 267bm, 91½ x 26 ft. Graves, Limehouse 4.5.1744. Sold 30.1.1761.

VULTURE Sloop 14, 269bm, 91½ x 26 ft. Davis, Northam 14.1.1763. BU 8.1771.

VULTURE Sloop 14, 304bm, 97 x 27 ft. Wells, Deptford 18.3.1776. Sold 8.1802.

VULTURE (ex-*Warrior*) Sloop 16, 391bm, 105 x 30 ft. Purchased 6.1803. Sold 30.9.1814.

VULTURE Wood pad. frigate, 1,191bm, 190 x 37½ ft. Pembroke Dock 21.9.1843. Sold 1866 Castle, Charlton.

VULTURE Wood S.gunvessel, 664bm, 805 tons, 170 x 29 ft, 1-7in, 2-40pdr. Sheerness DY 69.11.1869. Sold 9.1885 Castle, Charlton.

VULTURE Destroyer 380 tons, 218 x 20 ft, 1-12pdr, 2-TT. Thomson 22.3.1898. Sold 27.5.1919 Hayes, Porthcawl.

VULTURE Trawler requis. 1914-18.

W.1 Submarine 340 tons, 171½ x 15½ ft, 2-TT. Armstrong 19.11.1914. To Italian navy 23.8.16.

W.2 Submarine 340 tons, 150 x 17 ft, 2-TT. Armstrong 15.2.15. To Italian navy 23.8.16.

W.3 Submarine 340 tons, 150 x 17 ft, 2-TT. Armstrong 28.7.15. To Italian navy 23.8.16.

W.4 Submarine 340 tons, 150 x 17 ft, 2-TT. Armstrong 11.9.15. To Italian navy 7.8.16; lost 4.8.17.

WAAKZAAMHEID 6th Rate 24, 504bm, 114½ x 31½ ft. Dutch, captured 24.10.1798 by SIRIUS off the Texel. Sold 9.1802.

WAGER 6th Rate 24, 559bm, 123 x 32 ft. Purchased 21.11.1739. Wrecked 14.5.1741 south coast of Chile.

WAGER 6th Rate 24, 511bm, 112½ x 32½ ft. Quallett, Rotherhithe 2.6.1744. Sold 11.11.1763.

WAGER Destroyer, modified 'W' class. Denny. Laid down 2.8.1918, cancelled 12.18.

WAGER Destroyer 1,710 tons, 339½ x 36 ft, 4-4.7in, 2-40mm, 8-TT. J.Brown 1.11.1943. To Yugoslav navy 10.56, renamed PULA.

WAGGA Minesweeper (RAN), 'Bathurst' class. Morts Dk 25.7.1942.

Sold 3.62.

WAGLAN (see SEAFORD 1941)

WAGTAIL Schooner 4, 76bm, 56½ x 18½ ft, 4-12pdr carr. Lovewell, Yarmouth 12.4.1806. Wrecked 13.2.1807 in the Azores.

WAIKATO Frigate (RNZN), 'Leander' class. Harland & Wolff 18.2.1965.

WAIKATO Trawler (RNZN), 1945-46.

WAKATAKA (see LABURNUM of 1949)

WAKE Destroyer, modified 'W' class. Denny. Laid down 14.10.1918, cancelled 12.18.

WAKEFIELD 26-gun ship, 232bm, 90 x 24½ ft. Portsmouth 1655. Renamed RICHMOND 1660. Fireship 1688-89. Sold 30.8.1698.

WAKEFUL Destroyer, 'V/W' class. J.Brown 6.10.1917. Sunk 29.5.40 by German MTB off Dunkirk.

WAKEFUL (see ZEBRA of 1944)

WAKEFUL (ex-ZEBRA renamed 1.1943) Destroyer 1,710 tons, 339½ x 36 ft, 4-4.7in, 2-40 mm, 8-TT. Fairfield 30.6.43. Frigate 1953. Sold Ward 10.6.71, BU at Inverkeithing.

WAKEFUL Tender, ex-tug Dan (492/65) commissioned in 4.1974.

WALCHERN (see LST.3525)

WALDEGRAVE Destroyer, modified 'W' class. Denny. Cancelled 12.1918, not laid down.

WALDEGRAVE Frigate, TE 'Captain' class. Bethlehem, Hingham 4.12.1943 on lend-lease. Returned 12.45 to the USN.

WALDEMAAR 3rd Rate 80. Danish, captured 7.9.1807 at Copenhagen. Prison ship in 1812. BU 8.1816. (Was to have been renamed YARMOUTH 1808.)

WALKER Destroyer, 'V/W' class. Denny 29.11.1917. Escort 5.43. Sold 15.3.46, BU at Troon.

WALKERTON Coastal M/S, 'Ton' class. Thornycroft 21.11.1956.

WALLACE (ex-Lyons) Iron paddle vessel, 128bm, 112½ x 20 ft. Purchased 7.1855. Sold 1869 Pollock & Brown.

WALLACE Destroyer leader 1,750 tons, 318 x 32 ft, 5-4.7in, 1-3in, 6-TT. Thornycroft 26.10.1918. Escort 9.39. Sold 20.3.45, BU Clayton & Davie, Dunston.

WALLACE Trawler requis. 1918-19.

WALLACEBURG Minesweeper (RCN), 'Algerine' class. Pt Arthur SY 17.12.1942. To Belgian navy 31.7.59 as GEORGES LECOINTE.

WALLAROO (ex-PERSIAN renamed 2.4.1890) 2nd class cruiser 2,575 tons, 265 x 41 ft, 8-4.7in, 8-3pdr. Armstrong 5.2.1890. Harbour service 1906. Renamed WALLINGTON 5.3.19; sold 27.2.20 G.Sharpe.

WALLAROO Minesweeper (RAN), 'Bathurst' class. Poole & Steele 18.2.1942. Sunk 11.6.43 in collision with SS Gilbert Costin off Fremantle.

WALLFLOWER Sloop, 'Arabis' class. Irvine SB Co 8.11.1915. Sold 28.8.31 Ward, Inverkeithing.

WALLFLOWER Corvette, 'Flower' class. Smiths DK 14.11.1940. Sold 29.7.46, renamed Asbjorn Larsen.

WALLINGTON (ex-yacht ST GEORGE renamed 10.1918) Base ship 871 tons tm. In service in 12.18. to 3.19.

WALLINGTON (see WALLAROO of 1890)

WALMER (see WEM)

WALMER CASTLE (see LEASIDE)

WALNEY (ex-USS SEBAGO) Cutter 1,546 tons, 250(oa) x 42 ft, 2-5in, 2-6pdr. Commissioned in the RN 12.5.1941 on lend-lease. Sunk 8.11.42 by gunfire from shore batteries and French destroyers at Oran.

WALPOLE Destroyer, 'V/W' class. Doxford 12.2.1918. Mined 6.1.45 in the North Sea and not repaired; sold 8.2.45, BU Ward, Grays:

WALPOLE Trawler requis. 1915-19.

WALRUS Destroyer, 'V/W' class. Fairfield 27.12.1917. Stranded 12.2.38 in Filey Bay; refloated 29.3.38, BU 10.38.

WALRUS A/C transport 990 tons, 160 x 30 ft. Blyth DD Co 28.5.1945. Renamed SKUA 1953. Sold 28.2.62, became mercantile 12.62.

WALRUS Submarine 1,605 tons, 214 x 26½ ft, 8-TT. Scotts 22.9.1959. Sold Seaforth Group 1987 to refit for resale.

WALTON Destroyer, modified 'W' class. Denny. Cancelled 12.1918; not laid down.

WANDERER 6th Rate 20, 431bm, 109½ x 30 ft, 16-32pdr carr., 6-12pdr carr., 2-6pdr. Betts, Mistleythorn 29.9.1806. Sold 6.3.1817.

WANDERER Brig-sloop 16, 428bm, 100½ x 32½ ft, 14-32pdr, 2-9pdr. Chatham DY 10.7.1835. BU 3.1850 at Chatham.

WANDERER Wood S.gunvessel, 675bm, 181 x 28½ ft, 1-110pdr, 1-68pdr, 2-20pdr. Green, Blackwall 22.11.1855. Arrived 31.8.1866 Castle, Charlton to BU.

WANDERER Compos. S.sloop 925 tons, 157 x 32 ft, 2-5in. Raylton Dixon,

Middlesbrough 8.2.1883. Training brig 1894. Sold 2.1907 Ward to BU. at Preston.

WANDERER Destroyer, modified 'W' class. Fairfield 1.5.1919. Escort 4.43. Sold 1.46, BU Hughes Bolckow, Blyth.

WANDERER Paddle ferry 1917, ren. WARDEN 1918-21.

WARBURTON Frigate (RAN), 'River' class. Evans Deakin. Ordered 2.6.1942, cancelled 12.6.44.

WARKWORTH CASTLE Corvette, 'Castle' class. Fleming & Ferguson. Cancelled 12.1943.

WARMINGHAM Inshore M/S, 'Ham' class. Thornycroft, Hampton 23.4.1954. Sold Pounds in 1983.

WARNING Signal station vessel, 97bm, 70½ x 18 ft. Danish gun-brig STEECE captured 1807. Sold 15.12.1814.

WARRAMUNGA Destroyer (RAN) 1,927 tons, 355½ x 36½ ft, 6-4.7in, 2-4in, 4-TT. Cockatoo DY 7.2.1942. Sold 15.2.63 to BU in Japan.

WARREGO Destroyer (RAN) 700 tons, 246(oa) x 24 ft, 1-4in, 3-12pdr, 3-TT. Fairfield 4.4.1911 in sections; re-erected Sydney, launched 4.11. Dismantled 9.29 at Cockatoo DY; hull sank 22.7.31 at Cockatoo wharf, later blown up.

WARREGO Sloop (RAN) 1,060 tons, 250 x 36 ft, 3-4in. Cockatoo DY 10.2.1940. BU 1966 Rozelle Bay, Sydney.

WARREN Destroyer, modified 'W' class. Chatham DY (ex-Fairfield). Cancelled 9.1919.

WARREN HASTINGS Troopship (RIM) 3, 910 tons. N.C & A (Vickers) 18.4.1893. Wrecked 14.1.97 on Reunion Island.

WARRINGTON 30-gun ship, 200bm. Purchased or hired 14.7.1692. Captured 1693 by the French.

WARRIOR 3rd Rate 74, 1,642bm, 169 x 47½ ft. Portsmouth DY 18.10.1781. Receiving ship 1818; convict ship 2.1840. BU completed 12.1857 at Woolwich.

WARRIOR Iron armoured ship, 6,109bm, 9,210 tons, 380 x 58½ ft, 11-110pdr, 26-68pdr. T.I.W, Blackwall 29.12.1860. Depot ship 7.1902; renamed VERNON III in 3.04; hulk WARRIOR 1923. Renamed C.77 in 1945. Reverted to WARRIOR and handed over for preservation in 1979.

WARRIOR Armoured cruiser 13,550 tons, 480 x 73½ ft, 6-9in, 4-7.5in,

24-3pdr. Pembroke Dock 25.11.1905. Disabled 31.5.16 at Jutland and foundered next day.

WARRIOR (ex-BRAVE renamed 1942) A/C carrier 13,350 tons, 630 x 80 ft, 19-40mm, 48-A/C. Harland & Wolff 20.5.44. Lent RCN 1.46 to 2.48. To Argentine navy 7.58, renamed IN-DEPENDENCIA 11.58.

WARRIOR Trawler, tug and yacht W.W.I; yacht WW.II

WARRNAMBOOL Minesweeper (RAN), 'Bathurst' class. Morts Dk, Sydney 8.5.1941. Sunk 13.9.47 by mine off Cockburn Reef, Queensland.

WARRNAMBOOL Patrol vessel (RAN) 211 tons. Cairns 25.10.1980

WARSPITE (also WARSPIGHT) Galleon, 648bm, 2-60pdr, 2-34pdr, 13-18pdr, 10-9pdr, 2-6pdr. Built 1596. Harbour service 1635. Sold 1649.

WARSPITE 3rd Rate 70, 898bm, 142 x 38 ft. Johnson & Castle, Blackwall 8.6.1666. Rebuilt Rotherhithe 1702 as 952bm. Renamed EDINBURGH 2.1.1716. Rebuilt Chatham 1721 as 1,119 bm. Rebuilt Chatham 1744 as 1,286bm, 64 guns. BU 12.1771 Plymouth.

WARSPITE 3rd Rate 74, 1,580bm, 166 x 47 ft. West, Deptford 8.4.1758. Harbour service 1778. Renamed AR-UNDEL in 3.1800, BU 11.1801.

WARSPITE 3rd Rate 76, 1,890bm, 180 x 49ft. Chatham DY 16.11.1807. Reduced to 50 guns 1840; lent Marine Socy 27.3.1862 as training ship. Burnt 3.1.1876 by accident at Woolwich; wreck sold 2.2.1876 McArthur & Co.

Warspite (see WATERLOO of 1833)

WARSPITE Armoured cruiser 8,400 tons, 315 x 62 ft, 4-9.2in, 6-6in. Chatham DY 29.1.1884. Sold 4.4.1905 Ward, Preston; arrived Mersey 3.10.05, then Preston.

WARSPITE Battleship 27,500 tons, 600 x 90½ ft, 8-15in, 14-6in. Devonport DY 26.11.1913. Sold 12.7.46 and wrecked 23.4.47 in tow to breakers; wreck resold R.H.Bennett, Bristol.

Warspite (see HERMIONE of 1893)

WARSPITE Nuclear submarine 3,500 tons, 285 x 33 ft, 6-TT. Vickers Armstrong, Barrow 25.9.1965.

WARSASH (see ALFRISTON and BOULSTON)

WARWICK 22-gun ship, 186bm. Privateer captured 1643. BU 1660. (OLD WARWICK from 1650.)

WARWICK 4th Rate 48, 909bm, 130½ x 34½ ft. Deptford 1696. Rebuilt

Rotherhithe 1710 as 721bm. BU 1726.

WARWICK 4th Rate 60, 951bm, 144 x 39 ft. Plymouth DY 25.10.1733. Captured 11.3.1756 by the French L'ATLANTE; recaptured 24.1.1761 by MINERVA and BU.

WARWICK 4th Rate 50, 1,073bm, 151 x 40 ft. Portsmouth DY 28.2.1767. Receiving ship 9.1783. Sold 24.3.1802.

WARWICK Destroyer, 'V/W' class. Hawthorn Leslie 28.12.1917. Escort 5.43. Sunk 20.2.44 by 'U.413' off north Cornwall.

WARWICK (see also CONSTANT WARWICK)

WASAGA Minesweeper (RCN), TE 'Bangor' class. Burrard 12.12.1940. Sold 1946 Marine Industries.

WASKESIU Frigate (RCN), 'River' class. Yarrow, Esquimalt 6.12.1942. Sold 1947, renamed *Hooghly*.

WASP Sloop 8, 140bm, 73½ x 21 ft. Portsmouth DY 4.7.1749. Sold 4.1.1781.

WASP Brig-sloop 16, 207bm, 73½ x 26 ft. Folkestone 1780, purchased 1782. Fireship 4.1798, 8-18pdr. Expended 7.7.1800 in Dunkirk Roads.

WASP (see ESPION of 1782)

WASP Gunvessel 4, 63bm 64½ x 14½ ft. Dutch hoy purchased 3.1794. Sold 22.11.1801.

WASP (see GUEPE)

WASP Brig-sloop 18, 'Cruizer' class, 387bm. Davy, Topsham 9.7.1812. BU 9.1847.

WASP Wood S.sloop, 973bm, 186½ x 34 ft, 2-68pdr, 12-32pdr. Deptford DY 28.5.1850. Sold 2.12.1869 Marshall.

WASP Compos. S.gunboat 465 tons, 125 x 23½ ft, 2-64pdr, 2-20pdr. Barrow SB (Vickers) 5.10.1880. Wrecked 9.1884 on Tory Island. Wreck sold 11.1910 Cornish Salv Co.

WASP Torpedo boat (Australia) 12 tons, 63 x 8 ft, 1-TT. Thornycroft, Chiswick 1884. Sold circa 1906. (Listed in 'Brassey', not traced).

WASP Compos S.gunboat 715 tons, 165 x 29 ft, 6-4in. Armstrong Mitchell 13.9.1886. Foundered circa 10.10.1887 after leaving Singapore.

WASPERTON Coastal M/S, 'Ton' class. White, Southampton 28.2.1956. Sold Pounds 1986

WASSANAER 3rd Rate 64, 1,270bm, 169 x 42½ ft. Dutch, captured 11.10.1797 at Camperdown. Powder hulk in 1804. Sold 13.8.1818 J.Ledger to BU.

WATCHFUL (ex-*Jane*) Gunvessel 12, 169bm, 76 x 23 ft, 10-18pdr carr., 2-9pdr. Purchased 6.1804. Tender 3.1811. Sold 3.11.1814.

WATCHFUL Wood S.gunboat, 'Clown' class. Smith, N.Shields 4.6.1856. Sold 1.2.1871 at Hong Kong.

WATCHFUL Compos S.gunboat 560 tons, 135 x 26 ft, 2-5in, 2-4in. Laird 13.2.1883. BDV 1903. Sold 14.5.07.

WATCHFUL Coastguard vessel 612 tons, 154(oa) x 25 ft, 2-3pdr. Hall Russell 26.4.1911. Sold 15.5.20 Newfoundland Govt.

WATCHFUL Name borne in succession as fishery protection vessels by: ex-MFV 1080 renamed 1.11.1948 to 1956. ex-ML.2840 renamed 1956 to 1959. ex-BROOMLEY renamed 1959 to 1965.

WATCHMAN Destroyer, 'V/W' class. J.Brown 2.12.1917. Escort 1941. BU 7.45 Ward, Inverkeithing.

WATERFLY River gunboat, 'Fly' class. Yarrow 1915. Sold 17.2.23 Anglo Persian Oil Co, at Basra.

WATERFLY Trawler. requis. 1939-42.

WATERHEN Destroyer, 'V/W' class. Palmer 26.3.1918. To RAN 10.33. Sank 30.6.41 off Sollum after air attack on previous day.

WATERHEN Sloop 1,350 tons, 283 x 38½ ft, 6-4in. Denny. Cancelled 2.11.1945.

WATERHEN Destroyer (RAN) 2,616 tons, 366 x 43 ft, 6-4.5in, 6-40mm, 10-TT. Williamstown DY. Cancelled 1954.

WATERHOUND 32-gun ship. Captured 1652. Sold 1656.

WATERLOO (ex-TALAVERA renamed 23.7.1817) 3rd Rate 80, 2,056bm, 192 x 50 ft. Portsmouth DY 16.10.1818. Renamed BELLEROPHON 5.10.1824. Harbour service 1848. Sold 12.1.92 J. Read.

WATERLOO 1st Rate 120, 2,694bm, 218 x 55 ft. Chatham DY 10.6.1833. Undocked 12.11.1859 as screw ship. Renamed CONQUEROR 27.2.1862. 2,845bm. Renamed WARSPITE 11.8.1876, training ship (Marine Society). Burnt 20.1.1918 in the Thames.

WATERLOO Destroyer 2,380 tons, 355 x 40 ft, 5-4.5in, 8-40mm, 10-TT. Fairfield. Laid down 14.6.1945, cancelled 10.45.

WATERWAY (ex-TOMAHAWK renamed 8.1943) Dock landing ship 4,270 tons, 454 x 72 ft, 1-3in, 16-20mm. Newport News 24.5.1944 for the RN but retained by the USN as SHADWELL.

WATERWITCH Brig-sloop 10, 319bm, 90½ x 29½ ft, 8-18pdr carr., 2-6pdr. Ex-yacht purchased 15.11.1834. Sold 22.11.1861 Castle, Charlton.

WATERWITCH Iron hydraulic gunboat, 777bm, 1,205 tons, 162 x 32 ft, 2-7in, 2-20pdr. T.I.W, Blackwall 28.6.1866. Sold 26.4.1890 Castle, Charlton.

WATERWITCH (ex-*Lancashire Witch*) Iron S.survey vessel, 620 tons, 160 x - ft. Purchased 17.3.1893. Rammed and sunk 1.9.1912 while at anchor at Singapore.

WATERWITCH (ex-Turkish *Rechid Pasha*) Despatch vessel 400 tons, 165(oa) x 26 ft. Purchased 1915 on completion by Fairfield. Sold 1921 Turkish Govt.

WATERWITCH Minesweeper, 'Algerine' class. Lobnitz 22.4.1943. Sold G.Deckers 9.10.70.

WATERWITCH (see POWDERHAM)

WATSON Destroyer, modified 'W' class. Devonport DY (ex-Fairfield). Cancelled 9.1919.

WATT (see RETRIBUTION of 1844)

WAVE Wood S.gunboat, 'Albacore' class. Wigram, Northam 25.6.1956. Coal hulk 1869. Renamed CLINKER 30.12.1882. Sold 1890.

WAVE (ex-*Edeline*) Wood S.tender 308 tons, 134 x - ft. Purchased 27.11.1882. Sold 1907.

WAVE (ex-Turkish *Buyak Ada* purchased 1914) Despatch vessel 400 tons, 201 x 28 ft. Rennie Forrest, Wivenhoe 7.2.1914. Ranamed WAYWARD 8.19. Foundered in tow 11.11.22 off the coast of Anatolia.

WAVE Destroyer, modified 'W' class. Fairfield. Cancelled 12.1918.

WAVE Minesweeper, 'Algerine' class. Lobnitz 18.8.1944. Arrived 4.4.62 King, Gateshead to BU.

WAVE Tug 1939 ren WAVELET 1947-58.

WAVENEY Destroyer 550 tons, 220 x 23½ ft, 1-12pdr, 5-6pdr (4-12pdr 1907), 2-TT. Hawthorn 16.4.1903. Sold 10.2.20 Ward, Grays.

WAVENEY Frigate, 'River' class. Smiths DK 30.4.1942. Arrived 12.57 at Troon to BU.

WAVENEY Minehunter 757 tons Richards 8.9.1983.

WAVENEY Drifter 1915-16; Trawler 1920-22.

WAVERLEY (see LYDIARD)

WAVERLEY Minesweeper requis. 1915-20 & 1939-40.

WAYFARER Destroyer, modified 'W' class. Cancelled 12.1918; not ordered.

WAYLAND (ex-ANTONIA renamed 1942) Repair ship 18,750 tons, 528 x 65 ft, 4-4in. Purchased 1940, conversion completed 17.8.42. Sold 1.48, arrived Cairnryan 4.48 and Troon 4.49 to BU.

WAYWARD (see WAVE of 1914)

WEAR Destroyer 550 tons, 222 x 23½ ft, 1-12pdr, 5-6pdr (4-12pdr 1907), 2-TT. Palmer 21.1.1905. Sold 4.11.19 Ward, Grays.

WEAR Frigate, 'River' class. Smiths DK. 1.6.1942. Arrived 29.10.57 Young, Sunderland to BU.

WEAR Drifter requis. 1914-19; Trawler 1920-22.

WEAZLE Sloop 10, 128bm, 72 x 20 ft. Dummer, Blackwall 1704. Sold 20.11.1712.

WEAZLE Sloop 8, 102bm, 61½ x 20 ft. Woolwich DY 7.11.1721. Sold 30.11.1732.

WEAZLE Sloop 16, 308bm, 94½ x 27½ ft. Purchased on stocks 22.4.1745; Taylor & Randall, 22.5.1745. Captured 13.1.1779 by the French BOUDEUSE in the W.Indies.

WEAZLE Brig-sloop 14, 202bm, 79 x 25½ ft. Hills, Sandwich 18.4.1783. Wrecked 12.1.1799 in Barnstaple Bay.

WEAZLE Brig-sloop 16, 214bm, 77 x 26 ft, 12-10pdr carr., 4-6pdr. King, Dover 1799 and purchased 3.1799. Wrecked 1.3.1804 near Gibraltar.

WEAZLE Brig-sloop 18, 'Cruizer' class, 388bm. Owen, Topsham 2.3.1805. Sold 23.11.1815.

WEAZLE Schooner 10, 141bm. Purchased 1808. Listed in 1811.

WEAZLE Brig-sloop 10, 'Cherokee' class, 237bm. Chatham DY 26.3.1822. Sold 30.4.1844 W.Beech to BU.

WEAZEL Wood S.gunboat, 'Dapper' class. Pitcher, Northfleet 19.3.1855. Sold 18.11.1869 at Hong Kong.

WEAZEL Iron S.gunboat, 'Ant' class. Laird 4.9.1873. Renamed C.118, oil fuel lighter 1904.

WEAZEL (ex-War Dept vessel *Sir W. Green*) Tender 110 tons, 80 x 17 ft. Transferred 1906, renamed 26.11.06. Renamed STOAT 1.12.18. Sold 14.9.23.

WEAZEL Destroyer, modified 'W' class. Fairfield. Cancelled 12.1918.

WEAZEL Trawler 1939-40; Tug 1943-46; Tug 1947-68.

WEDGEPORT Minesweeper, TE

'Bangor' class. Dufferin, Toronto 2.8.1941. Sold 11.9.46.

WELCOME Pink 8, 100bm. Listed 1644. Captured 1647 by the French.

WELCOME 36-gun ship, 400bm. Captured 1652. Expended 1673 as a fireship.

WELCOME 36-gun ship, 367bm. Captured 1652. Sunk 6.1667 to block the Medway.

WELCOME Destroyer, modified 'W' class. Hawthorn Leslie. Laid down 9.4.1918, cancelled 12.18.

WELCOME Minesweeper, 'Algerine' class. Lobnitz 14.11.1944. Arrived 3.5.62 Dunston to BU. by Dorkin.

WELFARE King's ship mentioned in 1350.

WELFARE Destroyer, modified 'W' class. Hawthorn Leslie. Laid down 22.6.1918, cancelled 12.18.

WELFARE Minesweeper, 'Algerine' class. Redfern 15.7.1943. BU 11.57 Ward, Grays.

WELFARE Drifter requis. 1915-19.

WELLAND Destroyer 590 tons, 225 x 23½ ft, 1-12pdr, 5-6pdr (4-12pdr 1907), 2-TT. Yarrow 14.4.1904. Sold 30.6.20 Ward, Preston.

WELLAND Drifter requis. 1915-19.

WELLESLEY 3rd Rate 74, 1,746bm, 176 x 48½ ft. Bombay DY 24.2.1815. Guardship 1854. Renamed CORNWALL 18.6.1868 training ship. Sunk 24.9.1940 by air attack in the Thames.

WELLESLEY (see CORNWALL of 1812)

WELLESLEY No 2 (see BOSCAWEN of 1844)

WELLESLEY Destroyer, modified 'W' class. Hawthorn Leslie. Laid down 30.8.1918, cancelled 12.18.

WELLINGTON (see ORESTE of 1810)

WELLINGTON (see HERO of 1816)

WELLINGTON Sloop 990 tons, 250 x 36 ft, 2-4.7in, 1-3in. Devonport DY 29.5.1934. Sold 6.2.47 as H/Q ship for the Hon Co of Master Mariners.

WELLINGTON see BACCHANTE

WELLS Cutter 10, 84bm, 48 x 21 ft. Folkestone 6.1764. Sold 24.11.1780.

WELLS (ex-USS TILLMAN) Destroyer 1,090 tons, 309 x 30½ ft, 1-4in, 1-3in, 3-TT. Commissioned 5.12.1940 in the RN. Sold 24.7.45, BU at Troon.

WELSHMAN Minelayer 2,650 tons, 400½ x 40 ft, 6-4.7in, 160mines. Hawthorn Leslie 4.9.1940. Sunk 1.2.43 by 'U.617' off Crete.

WELSHMAN Tug 1901-47.

WEM (ex-WALMER renamed 1918) Minesweeper, later 'Hunt' class. Simons 12.9.19. Sold 22.4.21. The Cutch SN Co.

WEMBDON Minesweeper, later 'Hunt' class. Simons. Cancelled 1919.

WENNINGTON Coastal M/S, 'Ton' class. Doig, Grimsby 6.4.1955. Renamed CUDDALORE, Indian navy 1955.

WENSLEYDALE Destroyer, 'Hunt' class type III. Yarrow 20.6.1942. Damaged in collision 11.44 and not repaired. Sold 15.2.46, arrived 2.47 Hughes Bolckow, Blyth to BU.

WENTWORTH Frigate (RCN), 'River' class. Yarrow, Esquimalt 6.3.1943. Sold 17.11.47 Halifax SY; BU 1948 Dominion Steel Corp.

WEREWOLF Destroyer, modified 'W' class. White 17.7.1919, not completed. Cancelled 9.19 and BU.

WESER 5th Rate 44, 1,081bm. French, captured 21.10.1813 by a squadron off Ushant. Sold 17.9.1817 to BU.

WESER (ex-Prussian SALAMANDER) Iron pad. gunboat, 590bm, 178(wl) x 26 ft, 4-8in. Taken 12.1.1855 with RECRUIT in exchange for the frigate THETIS. Harbour service 1866; sold 29.10.1873 at Malta.

WESSEX Destroyer, 'V/W' class. Hawthorn Leslie 12.3.1918. Sunk 24.5.40 by air attack off Calais.

WESSEX (see ZENITH of 1944)

WESSEX (ex-ZENITH renamed 1.43) Destroyer 1,710 tons, 339½ x 36 ft, 4-4.7in, 5-40mm, 8-TT. Fairfield 2.9.1943. Renamed JAN VAN RIEBEECK 29.3.50 S.African navy. Sunk 25.3.80 as target off Capetown.

WESSEX (see DERG and ERNE)

WESTBURY Frigate (RCN), 'River' class. Montreal. Cancelled 12.1943.

WESTCOTT Destroyer, 'V/W' class. Denny 14.2.1918. Escort 7.43. Sold 8.1.46 to BU. by W.of Scotland S.Bkg Co.

WESTERGATE 34-gun ship, 274bm. Captured 1653. Lost 1664 in the West Indies.

WESTERNLAND (ex-Regina) Repair ship 16,479 tons gross, 575 x 68 ft. Purchased 1.1943. Sold 7.47, BU Hughes Bolckow, Blyth.

WESTMINSTER Destroyer, 'V/W' class. Scotts 24.2.1918. Escort 12.39 Sold 4.3.47, BU 8.48 Metal Industries.

WESTMOUNT Minesweeper (RCN). TE 'Bangor' class. Dufferin 14.3.1942. To Turkish navy 29.3.58 as BORNOVA.

WESTON (ex-WESTON SUPER MARE

renamed 1932) Sloop 1,060 tons, 250 x 34 ft, 2-4in. Devonport DY 23.7.32. Sold 22.5.47, BU Howells, Gelleswick Bay.

WESTPHAL Destroyer, modified 'W' class. White (ex-Hawthorn Leslie). Cancelled 12.1918.

WESTWARD HO Destroyer, modified 'W' class. White (ex-Hawthorn Leslie). Cancelled 12.1918.

WETASKIWIN (see BANFF)

WETHERBY Paddle M/S, 'Ascot' class. 820 tons. Murdoch & Murry 2.3.1918. Sold 10.6.24 Alloa S.Bkg Co., Charlestown.

WEWAK Landing craft (RAN) 810 tons. Walker 5.1972.

WEXFORD 14-gun ship, 150bm. Royalist FLEETWOOD captured 1655 by Parliament. Renamed DOLPHIN 1660. Expended 1665 as a fireship.

WEXFORD Minesweeper, later 'Hunt' class. Simons 10.10.1919. Sold 1.12.21 Stanlee; resold mercantile; served in WW.II as DOOMBA.

WEXHAM Inshore M/S, 'Ham' class. Taylor, Shoreham 3.4.1954. Transferred French navy 1955.

WEYBOURNE Minesweeper, later 'Hunt' class. Inglis 21.2.1919. Sold 4.10.28 Ward, Pembroke Dock.

WEYBURN Corvette (RCN), 'Flower' class. Port Arthur SY 26.7.1941. Sunk 22.2.43 by mine off Gibraltar.

WEYMOUTH 14-gun ship, 230bm. Royalist CAVENDISH captured 1645 by Parliament. Sold 1662.

WEYMOUTH 4th Rate 48, 673bm, 132½ x 34½ ft. Portsmouth DY 1693. Rebuilt Woolwich 1718 as 715bm. BU completed 6.1.1732.

WEYMOUTH 4th Rate 60, 1,061bm, 144 x 41½ ft. Plymouth DY 31.3.1736. Wrecked 16.2.1745 at Antigua.

WEYMOUTH 4th Rate 60, 1,198bm, 150 x 43 ft. Plymouth DY 1752. BU completed 12.2.1772 at Chatham.

WEYMOUTH (ex-E.Indiaman *Earl Mansfield* purchased on stocks) 4th Rate 56, 1,434bm, 175½ x 43 ft. Wells, Rotherhithe 30.9.1795. Storeship 26 guns 1798. Wrecked 21.1.1800 on Lisbon Bar.

WEYMOUTH (ex-Indiaman *Wellesley*) 5th Rate 36, 826bm, 136 x 37 ft. Purchased 1804. Storeship 16 guns 1811; convict ship 10.1828. Sold 10.3.1865 at Bermuda.

WEYMOUTH Wood S.corvette, 1,857bm, 225 x 43 ft. Sheerness DY. Laid down 10.1860, cancelled 12.12.1863.

WEYMOUTH 2nd class cruiser 5,250 tons, 430 x 48½ ft, 8-6in. Armstrong 18.11.1910. Sold 2.10.28 Hughes Bolckow, Blyth.

WEYMOUTH (see LEANDER of 1961)

WEYMOUTH Trawler requis. 1915-19.

WHADDON Destroyer, 'Hunt' class type I. Stephen 16.7.1940. Arrived 5.4.1959 at Faslane. to BU by S.BKg. Industries.

WHARTON Survey ship 1565 tons. Ordered Chatham DY 20.6.1949 and cancelled 19.9.51

WHEATLAND Destroyer, 'Hunt' class type II. Yarrow 7.6.1941. Hulk 1955. Arrived 20.9.57 McLellan, Bo'ness.

WHEELER Destroyer, modified 'W' class. Scotts. Laid down 7.1918, cancelled 12.18.

WHELP (see LIONS WHELP sloops of 1627).

WHELP Destroyer, modified 'W' class. Pembroke Dock (ex-Scotts). Cancelled 9.1919.

WHELP Destroyer 1,710 tons, 339½ x 36 ft, 4-4.7in, 6-40mm, 8-TT. Hawthorn Leslie 3.6.1943. Renamed SIMON van der STEL (SAN) 23.2.53.

WHIMBREL Sloop 1,300 tons, 283 x 37½ ft, 6-4in. Yarrow 25.8.1942. Sold 11.49 Egyptian navy, renamed El MALEK FAROUK.

WHIMBREL (ex-NSC.1012,ex-LCT) Repair craft 200 tons, 171 x 39 ft. Renamed 1954. Sold Pounds in 6.81, resold mercantile.

WHIMBREL Store carrier requis. 1914-15.

WHIP Destroyer, modified 'W' class. Scotts. Cancelled 12.1918.

WHIPPET Destroyer, modified 'W' class. Scotts. Cancelled 12.1918.

WHIPPET Whaler requis. 1941-41.

WHIPPINGHAM Inshore M/S, 'Ham' class. Taylor, Chertsey 28.8.1954. Transferred French navy 1955.

WHIPPINGHAM Paddle M/S requis. 1942-45.

WHIPSTER Brigantine 4, 64bm. Deptford 1672. Sold 1683.

WHIRLWIND Destroyer, 'V/W' class. Swan Hunter 15.12.1917. Sunk 5.7.40 by 'U.34' southwest of Ireland.

WHIRLWIND Destroyer 1,710 tons, 339½ x 36 ft, 4-4.7in, 5-40mm, 8-TT. Hawthorn Leslie 30.8.1943. Frigate 1953. Foundered Cardigan Bay 29.10.74 in use as a target.

WHITAKER Destroyer, modified 'W' class. Denny. Cancelled 12.1918.

WHITAKER Frigate. TE 'Captain' class. Bethlehem, Higham 12.12.1943 on lend-lease. Damaged 1.11.44 by

'U.483' off Malin Head and not repaired; nominally returned 3.45 to the USN. BU 1948 at Whitchurch.

WHITBY Storeship 14, 434bm, 108 x 30 ft, 14-6pdr. Purchased 12.1780. Sold 27.10.1785.

WHITBY Corvette (RCN), modified 'Flower' class. Midland SY 18.9.1943. Sold 30.8.46, renamed *Bengo*.

WHITBY Frigate 2,150 tons, 360 x 41 ft, 2-4.5in, 2-40mm. Cammell Laird 2.7.1954. Sold 30.10.78, BU at Queenborough.

WHITE BEAR 40-gun ship, 729bm, 3-60pdr, 11-34pdr, 7-18pdr, 10-9pdr, 9 smaller. Built 1563. Rebuilt 1599 as 732bm. Sold 1629.

WHITE BEAR Destroyer, modified 'W' class. Fairfield. Cancelled 12.1918.

WHITE BEAR Yacht 1939-47.

WHITEHALL Destroyer, modified 'W' class. Swan Hunter 11.9.1919, completed Chatham 7.24. Escort 8.42. BU Ward, Barrow, arrived 25.7.45.

WHITEHAVEN A.ship 14, Origin unknown. Burnt 9.1747 by accident off the coast of Ireland (probably a hired vessel).

WHITEHAVEN Minesweeper, turbine 'Bangor' class. Philip, Dartmouth 29.5.1941. Arrived 18.8.48 Ward, Briton Ferry.

WHITEHEAD Destroyer, modified 'W' class. Swan Hunter. Cancelled 12.1918.

WHITEHEAD Trials vessel 2900 tons. Scotts 5.5.1970

WHITEHEAD Store carrier 1914-17

WHITE ROSE Flyboat 6, 180bm. Captured 1666. Sold 1667.

WHITESAND BAY (ex-LOCH LUBNAIG renamed 1944) Frigate, 'Bay' class. Harland & Wolff 16.12.44. Arrived 13.2.56 S.Bkg Ind, Charlestown to BU.

WHITING 6-gun vessel, 45bm. Captured 6.1711. Sold 10.4.1712 P.Ford.

WHITING Schooner 4, 78bm, 56 x 18 ft, 4-12pdr carr. Bermuda 1805. Captured 22.8.1812 by the French privateer le DILIGENT in N.America.

WHITING Schooner 12, 225bm, 98 x 24 ft, 12-12pdr carr. American ARROW captured 1812. Wrecked 21.9.1816 in Padstow harbour.

WHITING Wood S.gunboat, 'Albacore' class. Wigram, Northam 9.1.1856. BU 12.1881.

WHITING Torpedo gunboat 735 tons, 230 x 27 ft, 2-4.7in, 4-3pdr. Armstrong Mitchell 24.7.1889. Renamed BOOMERANG 2.4.1890. Sold

11.7.1905 at Portsmouth.

WHITING Destroyer 360 tons, 215 x 21 ft, 1-12pdr, 5-6pdr, 2-TT. Palmer 26.8.1896. Sold 27.11.1919 at Hong Kong; BU in China

WHITING Trawler 1942-46.

WHITLEY Destroyer, 'V/W' class. Doxford 13.4.1918. Escort 10.38. Beached 19.5.40 near Nieuport after air attack.

WHITSHED Destroyer, modified 'W' class. Swan Hunter 31.1.1919. Sold 18.2.47, arrived 4.48 King. Gateshead to BU.

WHITTON Coastal M/S, 'Ton' class. Fleetlands SY. Launched 30.1.1956 as CANNANORE Indian navy.

WHYALLA (ex-GLENELG renamed 3.1941) Minesweeper, 'Bathurst' class. Broken Hill Pty, Whyalla 12.5.1941. Lent RAN from 1.42. Sold 9.5.47 as pilot vessel *Rip*.

WHYALLA Patrol boat (RAN) 211 tons. Cairns 22.5.1982

WICKLOW (see REPTON)

WIDEMOUTH Bay (ex-LOCH FRISA renamed 1944) Frigate, 'Bay' class. Harland & Wolff 19.10.44. Arrived 23.11.57 Hughes Bolckow, Blyth to BU.

WIDGEON Schooner 4, 80bm, 56 x 18 ft, 4-12pdr carr. Wheaton, Brixham 19.6.1806. Wrecked 20.4.1808 Scottish coast.

WIDGEON Wood pad. packet, 164bm, 200 tons, 108 x 18 ft. Chatham DY 12.9.1837. Sold in 3.1884.

WIDGEON Compos. S.gunboat 805 tons, 165 x 31 ft, 6-4in, 2-3pdr. Pembroke Dock 9.8.1889. Sold 15.5.1906 Castle, Charlton.

WIDGEON River gunboat 195 tons, 2-6pdr. Yarrow 16.4.1904. Sold 10.31 at Shanghai.

WIDGEON Patrol vessel 530 tons, 234 x 26½ ft, 1-4in. Yarrow 2.2.1938. Sold 21.4.47, arrived 25.9.47 King, Gateshead to BU.

WIDNES (ex WITHERNSEA renamed 1918) Minesweeper, later 'Hunt' class. Napier & Miller 28.6.18. Beached 20.5.41 in Suda Bay after air attack; salved by Germans, became patrol vessel 12.V4 then UJ.2109; sunk 17.10.43 by RN destroyers in the Dodecanese.

WIGMORE CASTLE Corvette, 'Castle' class. Midland SY. Cancelled 12.1943.

WIGTOWN BAY (ex-LOCH GARASDALE renamed 1944) Frigate, 'Bay' class. Harland & Wolff 26.4.45. Arrived 4.59 at Faslane to BU.

WILBERFORCE Iron S.survey vessel, 459bm, 138 x 27 ft. Laird 10.1840; purchased on stocks. BU 6.1850 in W.Africa.

WILD 6th Rate 12, 97bm. French, captured 1692. Recaptured 18.6.1694 by the French.

WILD BOAR Flyboat 6, 172bm. Captured 1665. Sold 1667.

WILD BOAR Brig-sloop 10, 'Cherokee' class, 238bm. Pelham, Frindsbury 9.7.1808. Wrecked 15.2.1810 on the Runnelstone, Scilly.

WILDFIRE (ex-*John*) Fire vessel, 64bm, 61 x 16½ ft. Purchased 1804. Sold 17.6.1807 Freake to BU.

WILDFIRE (ex-GPO vessel *Watersprite*) Wood pad, packet, 186bm, 116½ x 18½ ft. Transferred 1.1838. Sold W. Walker in 12.1888.

WILDFIRE (ex-*Hiawatha*) S.yacht tender 453 tons, 162 x 22 ft. Purchased 26.1.1888. Base ship Sheerness 4.1889. Renamed UNDINE 1.1907. Sold 9.7.12 Ward, Preston.

WILDFIRE (see NYMPHE of 1888)

WILDFIRE (see CORNWALLIS of 1813)

WILD GOOSE Sloop 1,300 tons, 283 x 37½ ft, 6-4in. Yarrow 14.10.1942. Arrived 27.2.56 McLellan, Bo'ness to BU.

WILDMAN Fireship 12. Captured 1652. Sold 1658.

WILD SWAN Compos. S.sloop 1,130 tons, 170 x 36 ft, 2-7in, 4-64pdr. Napier 28.1.1876. Renamed CLYDE 1.5.1904. (see CLYDE)

WILD SWAN Destroyer, modified 'W' class. Swan Hunter 17.5.1919. Damaged by air attack and sunk 17.6.42 in collision with a Spanish trawler, Bay of Biscay.

WILHELMINA 5th Rate 32, 827bm, 133 x 37½ ft.Dutch FURIE captured 24.10.1798 by SIRIUS off the Texel. Sold 1813 at Penang.

WILK Submarine 965 tons, 246 x 18 ft, 1-3.9in, 6-TT, 38 mines. Polish, served in the RN (Polish crew) 1939 to 6.42 then laid up. Returned 3.51 to Polish navy.

WILKIESTON Coastal M/S, 'Ton' class. Cook Welton & Gemmell 26.6.1956. Sold White, St David in 9.76 to BU.

WILLIAM Dogger 8. Dutch, captured 1672. sold 1674.

WILLIAM Ketch 10. Origin unknown. Foundered 19.2.1694 off Gibraltar.

WILLIAM Gunvessel 3, 80bm, 59 x 18 ft, 3-12pdr. Purchased 3.1794. Sold 11.1801.

WILLIAM Storeship 22, 374bm, 99½ x 29 ft. Purchased 4.1798. Wrecked 11.11.1807 in the Gut of Canso.

WILLIAM Storeship 12. Listed 1808. BU 8.1810 at Woolwich (above ship salved?).

WILLIAM & ELIZABETH Fire vessel. Purchased 1695. Expended 1.8.1695 at Dunkirk.

WILLIAM & MARY Fire vessel. Purchased 1694. Expended 12.9.1694 at Dunkirk.

WILLIAM & MARY Yacht 10, 172bm, 76½ x 22½ ft. Chatham DY 9.1694. Sold 14.9.1801 to B.U.

WILLIAM & MARY Yacht 8, 199bm, 85 x 23 ft. Deptford DY 14.11.1807. BU 4.1849.

WILLIAMSON Sloop 10. French IROQUOISE captured 1760. Lost 1761.

WILLIAMSTOWN Frigate (RAN), 'River' class. Cancelled 1944.

WILLOUGHBY Destroyer, modified 'W' class. Swan Hunter. Cancelled 12.1918.

WILLOWHERB (ex-USS VITALITY) Corvette, modified 'Flower' class. Midland SY 24.3.1943 on lend-lease. Returned 11.6.46 to the USN.

WILTON Destroyer, 'Hunt' class type II. Yarrow 17.10.1941. Arrived 30.11.59 at Faslane to BU.

WILTON Minehunter 615 tons, Vosper-Thorneycroft 18.1.1972.

WIMMERA Frigate (RAN), 'River' class. Sydney NSW. Ordered 12.1942, cancelled 12.6.44.

WINCHELSEY 5th Rate 32, 364bm, 103½ x 38½ ft. Wyatt, Redbridge 13.8.1694. Captured 6.6.1706 by four French privateers off Hastings.

WINCHELSEY 5th Rate 26, 422bm, 105½ x 30½ ft. Johnson, Blackwall 9.9.1706. Foundered 29.8.1707 in a hurricane in the Leeward Islands.

WINCHELSEY 5th Rate 32, 414bm, 108 x 30 ft. Purchased 2.1708. Reduced to 6th Rate in 5.1716. BU 12.1735. (In French hands 8.2.09 to 2.3.09.)

WINCHELSEA 6th Rate 24, 441bm, 106 x 31 ft. Carter, Limehouse 3.5.1740. BU 8.1761 at Portsmouth. (In French hands 10.10.58 to 27.10.58.)

WINCHELSEA 5th Rate 32, 679bm, 125 x 35 ft. Sheerness DY 31.5.1764. Rebuilt 1782; prison ship 1805. Sold 3.11.1814.

WINCHELSEA Cutter. Purchased 1.1763. Sunk 4.1774 as breakwater at Sheerness.

WINCHELSEA Destroyer, 'V/W' class.

White 15.12.1917. Escort 4.42. Sold 20.3.45, BU Inverkeithing by Metal Ind.

WINCHESTER 4th Rate 60, 933bm, 146½ x 38 ft. Wyatt, Bursledon 11.4.1693. Foundered 24.9.1695 off Cape Florida.

WINCHESTER 4th Rate 48, 673bm, 130 x 34½ ft. Wells, Rotherhithe 17.3.1698. Rebuilt Plymouth 1717 as 711bm; hulked 2.1774. BU completed 5.7.1781 at Chatham.

WINCHESTER 4th Rate 50, 987bm, 140½ x 40½ ft. Bird, Rotherhithe 5.1744. Sold 20.6.1769.

WINCHESTER Cutter 8, 69bm, 47 x 20 ft, 4-carr., 8-3pdr. Purchased 1763. Fate unknown.

WINCHESTER 4th Rate 52, 1,487bm, 173 x 44½ ft, 16-42pdr carr., 36-24pdr. Woolwich DY 21.6.1822. Renamed CONWAY 11.1861, training ship. MOUNT EDGCOMBE 1.9.76. Sold 8.4.21.

WINCHESTER (see CONWAY of 1832)

WINCHESTER Destroyer, 'V/W' class. White 1.2.1918. Escort 5.40. Sold 5.3.46, BU Ward, Inverkeithing.

WINCHESTER Drifter requis. 1915-19.

WINDFLOWER Sloop, 'Anchusa' class. Workman Clark 12.4.1918. Sold 7.10.27 Cashmore, Newport.

WINDFLOWER Corvette, 'Flower' class. Davie SB 4.7.1940. On loan RCN from 10.40. Sunk 7.12.41 in collision with SS *Zypenberg* in the N.Atlantic.

WINDRUSH Frigate, 'River' class. Robb, Leith 18.6.1943. To French navy 2.44 as La DECOUVERTE.

WINDSOR 4th Rate 60, 912bm, 146½ x 38 ft. Snelgrove, Deptford 31.10.1695. Rebuilt Deptford 1729 as 951bm; rebuilt Woolwich 1745 as 1,201bm. BU 6.1777.

WINDSOR Destroyer, 'V/W' class. Scotts 21.6.1918. Sold 4.3.47, arrived 5.49 Charlestown to BU.

WINDSOR Trawler requis. 1916-19.

WINDSOR CASTLE 2nd Rate 90, 1,462bm. Woolwich DY 1678. Wrecked 28.4.1693 near Deal.

WINDSOR CASTLE (see DUCHESS of 1679)

WINDSOR CASTLE 2nd Rate 98, 1,874bm, 177½ x 50 ft. Deptford DY 3.5.1790. Reduced to 74 guns 6.1814. BU 5.1839 at Pembroke Dock.

WINDSOR CASTLE 1st Rate 120, 3,700bm, 241 x 60ft. Prmbroke Dock 14.9.1852. Renamed DUKE OF WELLINGTON 1.10.1852, screw ship. (see DUKE OF WELLING-

TON)

WINDSOR CASTLE (see VICTORIA & ALBERT of 1855)

WINDSOR CASTLE (ex-VICTORIA renamed 6.1.1855) 1st Rate 116, 3,101bm, 3204 x 60 ft. Pembroke Dock 26.8.1858 (14 years on stocks). Converted on stocks to screw ship 100 guns; 97 guns 1862, 30-8in, 1-110pdr, 4-70pdr, 6-40pdr, 56-32pdr. Renamed CAMBRIDGE 1869, gunnery ship. Sold 24.6.1908 Cox, Falmouth.

WINDSOR CASTLE A.Merchant (ex-Russian) seized 1918-19.

WINNIPEG Minesweeper (RCN), 'Algerine' class. Pt Arthur 19.9.1942. Sold 7.8.59 Belgian navy as A.F.DUFOUR.

WINSBY 50-gun ship, 608bm. Edgar, Yarmouth 1654. Renamed HAPPY RETURN 1660. Captured 4.11.1691 by the French. Became HEUREUX RETOUR to 1709.

WINTER Destroyer, modified 'W' class. Swan Hunter. Cancelled 12.1918.

WINTRINGHAM Inshore M/S, 'Ham' class. White 24.5.1955. To the RAN 1967, renamed SEAL.

WISHART Destroyer, modified 'W' class 1,350 tons. Thornycroft 18.6.1919. Sold 20.3.45, BU Ward, Inverkeithing.

WISTARIA Sloop, 'Arabis' class. Irvine, Glasgow 7.12.1915. Sold 18.1.31 Ward, Inverkeithing.

WISTARIA Trawler requis. 1915-19; Trawler 1939-46.

WISTFUL (see VIGOROUS of 1918)

WISTON Coastal M/S, 'Ton' class. Wivenhoe SY 3.6.1958. Sold H.K.Vickers 9.8.82 to BU Blyth.

WITCH Destroyer, modified 'W' class 1,350 tons. Thornycroft 11.11.1919. Sold 12.7.46, BU by Brechin at Granton.

WITHERINGTON Destroyer, modified 'W' class. White 16.1.1919. Sold 20.3.47 for Metal Industries; wrecked 29.4.47 in tow to Charlestown.

WITHERNSEA (see WIDNES)

WITHERNSEA Trawler 1939-46.

WIVENHOE Ketch 8, 83bm. Page, Wivenhoe 1666. Fireship 1673. Sold 1683.

WIVENHOE Drifter requis. 1915-19.

WIVERN (ex-Turkish EI MONASSIR purchased 10.1863, ex-Confederate ship) Iron coast defence ship, 1,899bm, 2,751 tons, 224 x 42½ ft, 4-9in. Laird 29.8.1863. Harbour service 1898. Sold 5.1922 at Hong Kong.

WIVERN Destroyer, modified 'W' class. White 16.4.1919. Sold 18.2.47, arrived 10.48 at Rosyth to BU by Metal Industries.

WYVERN Tug requis. 1915-18.

WIZARD Brig-sloop 16, 283bm, 96½ x 26 ft. Sutton, Ringmore 11.1805. Sold 17.10.1816.

WIZARD Brig-sloop 10, 'Cherokee' class, 231bm. Pembroke Dock 24.5.1830. Wrecked 8.2.1859 at Berehaven.

WIZARD Wood S.gunboat, 'Britomart' class. Smith, Newcastle 3.8.1860. BU 1879 at Malta.

WIZARD (see KARRAKATTA)

WIZARD Destroyer 320 tons, 200 x 19½ ft. 1-12pdr, 5-6pdr, 2-TT. White 26.2.1895. Sold 20.5.1920 Ward, Milford Haven.

WIZARD Destroyer, 1,710 tons, 339½ x 36 ft, 4-4.7in, 5-40mm, 8-TT. Vickers Armstrong, Barrow 29.9.1943. Frigate 1954. Arrived 7.3.67 Ward, Inverkeithing to BU.

WOLDINGHAM Inshore M/S, 'Ham' class. White 30.11.1955. Sold founds 29.9.66; became a yacht.

WOOLF 16-gun ship, 120bm. Spanish LOBO captured 1656. Sold 1663.

WOOLF Fireship 8, 253bm, 93 x 25 ft. Castle, Deptford 18.4.1690. Expended 23.5.1692 at Cherbourg.

WOOLF Sloop 2, 65bm. Portsmouth 1699. Sold 10.4.1712. (In French hands 24.6.04 to 1708 and 19.6.08 to 21.6.08.)

WOLF Sloop 14, 244bm, 87 x 25 ft. Stacey, Deptford 20.11.1731. Wrecked 2.3.1741 on the coast of Florida.

WOLF Sloop 14, 246bm, 89 x 25 ft. West, Deptford 27.2.1742. Wrecked 31.12.1748 on the coast of Ireland (In French hands 14.11.45 to 1747.)

WOLF Sloop 10, 141bm, 75½ x 20½ ft. Chatham DY 24.5.1754. Sold 15.8.1781.

WOLF A.ship 8. Origin unknown. Wrecked 7.1780 off Newfoundland.

WOLF Gunvessel 4, 68bm, 61½ x 15½ ft, 3-32pdr, 1-24pdr. Dutch hoy purchased 3.1794. BU 8.1803.

WOLF (see PANDOUR of 1798)

WOLF Cutter tender, 81bm, 55 x 19 ft, 6-6pdr, 2-3pdr. White, Cowes 1801. BU 1829 at Portsmouth. (Also on revenue service.)

WOLF Brig-sloop 16 (fir-built), 367bm, 106 x 28 ft, 16-32pdr carr., 2-6pdr. Tanner, Dartsmouth 4.6.1804.

Wrecked 5.9.1806 in the Bahamas.

WOLF (see DILIGENT of 1806)

WOLF Brig-sloop 14, 253bm, 92 x 25½ft. Woolwich DY 16.9.1814. Sold 27.1.1825 T.S.Benson.

WOLF Sloop 18, 454bm, 113½ x 31 ft. Portsmouth DY 1.12.1826. Hulk 5.1848; coal hulk 7.1859. BU completed 5.8.1878 at Devonport.

WOLF Wood S.gunboat, 'Albacore' class. Mare, Blackwall 5.7.1856. BU completed 8.7.1864.

WOLF Destroyer 385 tons, 218 x 20 ft, 1-12pdr, 5-6pdr, 2-TT. Laird 2.6.1897. Sold 1.7.1921 S.Castle, Plymouth.

WOLF Yacht (RCN) 1940-46.

WOLFE Sloop 20 (Canadian lakes), 426bm, 102 x 30½ ft. Kingston Ont 5.5.1813. Renamed MONTREAL 22.1.1814. Sold 1.1832.

WOLFE 1st Rate 104 (Canadian lakes), 2,152bm, 191½ x 50½ ft. Kingston Ont. Laid down 1814, cancelled 1831; hull destroyed on stocks 31.7.1832 by storm.

WOLFE Monitor 1915 (see GENERAL WOLFE).

WOLFE (ex-*Montcalm*) AMC, 16,420 tons gross, 550 x 70 ft, 7-6in, 2-12pdr. Commissioned 21.11.39, purchased and converted to depot ship 5.42, 19,557 tons, 4-4in. Arrived 8.11.52 at Faslane to BU.

WOLFHOUND Destroyer, 'V/W' class. Fairfield 14.3.1918. Escort 4.40. Sold 18.2.48, BU at Granton.

WOLLONDILLY Frigate (RAN), 'River' class. Sydney NSW. Ordered 12.1942, cancelled 12.6.44.

WOLLONGONG Minesweeper, 'Bathurst' class. Cockatoo DY 5.7.1941. Lent RAN from 10.41. Sold 1946 Dutch navy as BANDA.

WOLLONGONG Patrol boat (RAN) 211 tons. Cairns 17.8.1981.

WOLSEY Destroyer, 'V/W' class 1,325 tons. Thornycroft 16.3.1918. Escort 12.39. Sold 4.3.47, BU Young, Sunderland.

WOLVERINE (ex-*Rattler*) Gun-brig 12, 286bm, 98 x 27½ ft, 6-24pdr carr., 2-18pdr, 5-12pdr carr. Purchased 3.1798. Sunk 24.3.1804 in action with the French privateer BLONDE in the western Atlantic.

WOLVERINE Brig-sloop 18, 'Cruizer' class, 387bm. Owen, Topsham 1.3.1805. Sold 15.2.1816.

WOLVERINE Brig-sloop 16, 428bm, 101 x 32½ ft, 14-32pdr, 2-9pdr. Chatham DY 13.10.1836. Wrecked 11.8.1855 on Courtown Bank.

WOLVERENE Wood S.corvette, 1,703bm, 2,431 tons, 225 x 41 ft, 16-8in, 1-7in, 4-40pdr. Woolwich DY 29.8.1863. To Australia 1881 as training ship. Sold 24.8.23 as sheer hulk.

WOLVERINE Destroyer 914 tons, 266 x 28 ft, 1-4in, 3-12pdr, 2-TT. Cammell Laird 15.1.1910. Sunk 12.12.17 in collision with sloop ROSEMARY off Donegal.

WOLVERINE Destroyer, modified 'W' class. White 17.7.1919. Sold 28.1.46, BU at Troon.

WOLVERTON Coastal M/S, 'Ton' class. Montrose SY 22.10.1956. Sold 1986 at Hong Kong.

WOODBRIDGE HAVEN (see LOCH TORRIDON)

WOODCOCK Cutter 4, 76bm, 56 x 18½ ft, 4-12pdr carr. Crane, Yarmouth 11.4.1806. Wrecked 13.2.1807 in the Azores.

WOODCOCK Wood S.gunboat, 'Clown' class. Smith, N.Shields 6.6.1856. Sold 1871 at Hong Kong.

WOODCOCK Fishery protection vessel 750 tons, 148 x 26 ft. Purchased 4.1885. Renamed JACKAL 1.5.86. Sold 10.7.06.

WOODCOCK River gunboat 150 tons, 148½ x 24 ft, 2-6pdr. Thornycroft 1897 in sections; re-launched in China 8.4.1898. Sold 1927 at Hong Kong.

WOODCOCK Sloop 1,300 tons, 283 x 37½ ft, 6-4in. Fairfield 26.11.1942. Arrived 28.11.55 S.Bkg Ind, Rosyth to BU.

WOODLARK Gun-brig 12, 182bm, 80½ x 23 ft, 10-18pdr carr, 2-18pdr. Menzies, Leith 1.1805, Wrecked 13.11.1805 near Calais.

WOODLARK Brig-sloop 16, 'Cherokee' class, 237bm. Rowe, Newcastle 17.11.1808. Sold 29.1.1818.

WOODLARK Survey tender (laid down as revenue cutter), 81bm, 55½ x 18½ ft, 2-6pdr. Deptford DY 31.7.1821. Sold 23.9.1863.

WOODLARK Wood S.gunvessel., 663bm, 805 tons, 170 x 29 ft, 1-7in, 2-40pdr. Chatham DY 9.3.1871. Sold 9.3.1887 at Bombay.

WOODLARK River gunboat 150 tons, 148½ x 24 ft, 2-6pdr. Thornycroft, Chiswick 1897 in sections. Sold 7.1928 at Hong Kong.

WOODLARK (see YAXHAM)

WOODPECKER Destroyer, modified 'W' class. Projected 1918, not ordered.

WOODPECKER Sloop, 1,300 tons, 283 x 37½ ft, 6-4in. Denny 29.6.1942.

Torpedoed 20.2.44 by U-boat in the N.Atlantic and foundered seven days later.

WOODRUFF Corvette, 'Flower' class. Simons 28.2.1941. Sold 1947, renamed *Southern Lupin.*

WOODSTOCK Corvette (RCN), 'Flower' class. Collingwood SY 10.12.1941. Sold 1.3.48, renamed *Olympic Winner.*

WOOLASTON Coastal M/S, 'Ton' class. Herd & McKenzie 6.3.1958. Sold Liguria Maritime 14.11.80, BU at Sittingbourne.

WOOLF (see under WOLF)

WOOLSTON Destroyer, 'V/W' class 1,325 tons. Thornycroft 27.4.1918. Escort 10.39. Sold 18.2.47, BU Brunton, Grangemouth.

WOOLVESEY CASTLE (see HUNTSVILLE)

WOOLWICH Sloop 4, 57bm. Woolwich 1673. Wrecked 1675.

WOOLWICH 4th Rate 54, 741bm, 138½ x 35½ ft. Woolwich DY 1675. Rebuilt Woolwich 1702 as 761bm, 50 guns; rebuilt Deptford 1741 as 866bm. BU 6.1747 at Chatham.

WOOLWICH TRANSPORT Hoy 4, 45bm, 48½ x 15 ft. Woolwich DY 17.10.1705; rebuilt Woolwich 1726 as 65bm. Sold 25.8.1767.

WOOLWICH 5th Rate 44, 825bm, 133½ x 38 ft. Darley & Janvrin, Beaulieu 7.3.1749. Sold 30.12.1762.

WOOLWICH Storeship. Woolwich DY 11.2.1755. Listed 1760. (May be above WOOLWICH TRANSPORT rebuilt and renamed.)

WOOLWICH 5th Rate 44, 907bm, 140 x 38½ ft. Calhoun & Newland, Bursledon 15.12.1785. Storeship by 1794. Wrecked 6.11.1813 in the W.Indies.

WOOLWICH (ex-*Marianne*) Tender 6, 169bm, 6-3pdr. Purchased 30.1.1788. Sold 3.11.1808.

WOOLWICH (see PORTSMOUTH of 1811)

WOOLWICH Store lighter, 114bm, 63½ x 20½ ft. Woolwich DY 1815. Renamed PORT ROYAL 1818. Fate unknown.

WOOLWICH Depot ship 3,380 tons, 320 x 40 ft. 2-4in. London & Glasgow Co 5.9.1912. Sold 13.7.26 Ward, Hayle.

WOOLWICH Depot ship 8,750 tons, 575 x 64 ft, 4-4in. Fairfield 20.9.1934. Arrived 10.62 Arnott Young, Dalmuir.

WORCESTER 48-gun ship, 662bm, 141½ x 33½ ft. Woolwich 1651. Renamed DUNKIRK 1660. (see DUN-

KIRK)

WORCESTER 4th Rate 48, 684bm, 132 x 35 ft. Winter, Southampton 31.5.1698. Rebuilt Deptford 1714 as 719bm. BU 1733.

WORCESTER PRIZE 6th Rate 14, 140bm, 73 x 21 ft. French, captured 1.1705 by WORCESTER. Recaptured 6.10.1708 by the French off Lands End. (Was also in French hands 27.5.08 to 14.6.08.)

WORCESTER 4th Rate 60, 1,061bm, 144 x 41½ ft. Portsmouth DY 20.12.1735. BU completed 5.9.1765 at Plymouth.

WORCESTER 3rd Rate 64, 1,380bm, 159 x 44½ ft. Portsmouth DY 17.10.1769. Hulk 1.1788. BU 12.1816 at Deptford.

WORCESTER 4th Rate 52, 1,468bm, 172 x 44 ft, 4-8in, 30-32pdr, 16-32pdr carr., 2-12pdr. Deptford DY 10.10.1843 (23 years on stocks). Lent 1862 as training ship. BU 8.1885 Castle, Charlton.

WORCESTER (see FREDERICK WILLIAM)

WORCESTER Destroyer, modified 'W' class. White 24.10.1919. Mined 23.12.43 in the North Sea and not repaired; accommodation ship 5.44. Renamed YEOMAN 6.45. Sold 17.9.46, BU Ward, Grays 2.47.

WORTHING Minesweeper, turbine 'Bangor' class. Philip 22.8.1941. Sold 7.7.48; BU by Stockton Shipping & Salvage, Thornaby.

WOTTON Coastal M/S, 'Ton' class. Philip 24.4.1956. To Sea Cadets 1986.

WRANGLER (Gunboat No 40) (ex-*Fortune*) Gunvessel 12, 138bm, 72½ x 30 ft, 2-24pdr, 10-18pdr carr. Purchased 3.1797 at Leith. Sold 12.1802.

WRANGLER Gun-brig 12, 177bm, 80 x 22½ ft, 10-18pdr carr., 2-12pdr. Dudman, Deptford 28.5.1805. Sold 14.12.1815.

WRANGLER Wood S.gunvessel, 477bm, 160 x 25½ ft, 2-68pdr. Green, Blackwall 19.6.1854. BU 5.1866 Castle, Charlton.

WRANGLER Compos. S.gunboat 465 tons, 125 x 23½ ft, 2-64pdr, 2-20pdr. Barrow SB (Vickers) 5.10.1880. Coastguard 1891; BDV 1903. Sold 2.12.19, BU at Dover.

WRANGLER Destroyer, modified 'W' class. White. Laid down 3.2.1919. cancelled 9.19.

WRANGLER Destroyer 1,710 tons, 339½ x 36 ft, 4-4.7in, 5-40mm, 8-TT.

Vickers Armstrong, Barrow 30.12.43. Renamed VRYSTAAT (SAN) 29.11.56. Sunk 1976 as a target off S.Africa.

WRENN 12-gun vessel. Captured 1653. Sold 29.9.1657.

WRENN Pink 10, 103bm, 64 x 19 ft. Stigant, Redbridge 21.3.1694. Captured 28.3.1697 by the French off Rye.

WREN Destroyer, modified 'W' class. Yarrow 11.11.1919. Sunk 27.7.40 by air attack off Aldeburgh.

WREN Sloop 1,300 tons, 283 x 37½ ft. 6-4in. Denny 11.8.1942. Arrived 2.2.56 S.Bkg Ind, Rosyth to BU.

WREN Trawler requis. 1914-19.

WRENTHAM Inshore M/S Ham class. ex-EDGELEY renamed 11.53. Dorset Yt. Co. 8.2.1955. Sold 10.8.66.

WRESTLER Destroyer, 'V/W' class. Swan Hunter 25.2.1918. Escort 4.43; mined 6.6.44 and not repaired. Sold 20.7.44. BU Cashmore, Newport.

WRESTLER Two tugs requis. in WW.I.

WRYNECK Destroyer, 'V/W' class. Palmer 13.5.1918. Escort 10.40. Sunk 27.4.41 by air attack south of Morea.

WRYNECK Sloop 1,350 tons, 283 x 38½ ft, 6-4in. Denny. Cancelled 2.11.1945.

WULASTOCK Frigate (RCN), 'River' class. Victoria BC. Cancelled 12.1943.

WYE 6th Rate 24, 447bm, 108 x 31 ft. Hobbs, Redbridge 17.8.1814. Convict ship 1828. Ordered 10.1852 to be BU.

WYE (ex-*Hecla* renamed 6.6.1855) Iron S.storeship, 700bm. Transferred from Treasury Dept 24.5.1855. Sold 3.7.1866.

WYE Iron S.storeship 1,370 tons. Osbourne Graham, Sunderland 1873 and purchased 17.12.1873. Sold 3.4.1906 Adrienne Merveille, Dunkirk to BU.

WYE Destroyer, modified 'W' class. Yarrow. Laid down 1.1918, cancelled 9.19.

WYE Frigate, 'River' class. Robb, Leith 16.8.1943. Arrived 22.2.55 at Troon to BU.

X.1 Submarine 2,780 tons, 350 x 30 ft, 4-5.2in, 6-TT. Chatham DY 16.6.1923. Arrived 12.36 Ward, Pembroke Dock to BU.

X.2 Submarine 880 tons, 231(oa) x 22½

ft, 8-TT. Italian GALILEO GALILEI captured 19.6.1940 by the trawler MOONSTONE in the Red Sea. Renamed P.711 in 8.42. BU 1946 at Port Said.

'X.51' class 35 tons, 50 x 6½ ft, 2-explosive charges. All Built Vickers Armstrong, Barrow.

X.51 launched 1.10.54, renamed STICKLEBACK 12.54. Sold 15.7.58 Swedish navy as SPIGGER. Returned from Sweden and became museum ship at Doxford in 1977.

X.52-54 launched 30.12.54, 1.3.55 and 5.5.55 resp. and renamed SHRIMP, SPRAT & MINNOW 12.54. BU 1965 Rosyth DY. (X.53 & 54 Faslane 1966)

XENOPHON A.ship 22, 334bm, 100½ x 28½ ft. Purchased 1798. Renamed INVESTIGATOR 1801, survey vessel. BU 11.1810.

'X' class 'midget' S/Ms, 27 tons, 2 explosive charges, all built 1943-44. X.3-4 Varley Marine, X.5-10 VA, Barrow, X.20-21 Broadbent, Huddersfield, X.22-23 Markham, Chesterfield, X.24-25 Marshall, Gainsborough, XT.1-6 VA, Barrow, (The following, ordered in 5.43 were cancelled 12.43: XT.7-11 Broadbent, XT.12 and XT.13 Markham, XT.14-18 Marshall.) X.3, X.4 BU 1945, X.5-10 all lost 9.43/10.43 in attacks on the German TIRPITZ in Alten Fiord. X.20, 21 listed to 10.45, X.22 lost 7.2.44 in collision with SYRTIS in Pentland Firth, X.23 listed to 7.45, X.24 preserved at Gosport, X.25, XT.1 & 2 all listed to 10.45 and XT.3-6 to 6.45.

'XE' class 'midget' S/Ms, 30 tons, explosive charges, all built 1944-45. XE.1-6 VA, Barrow, XE.7-8 Broadbent, XE.9-10 Marshall, XE.11-12 Markham. XE.1-6 BU 1945 in Australia, XE.7 BY 1952, XE.8-9 sunk 1954 as bottom targets (the former being raised 5.73 for preservation), XE.10 cancelled 6.45, XE.11 lost 6.3.45 in collision, raised and BU 5.45, XE.12 BU 12.53 by Metal Industries.

YARMOUTH 50-gun ship, 608bm. Edgar, Yarmouth 1653. BU 1680.

YARMOUTH 3rd Rate 70, 1,058bm, 151 x 40 ft. Barrett, Harwich 7.1.1695. Rebuilt 1709 as 1,110bm; hulked 11.1740. Sold 11.9.1769.

YARMOUTH 3rd Rate 64, 1,359bm, 160

x 44 ft. Deptford DY 28.12.1748. 60 guns 4.1781; receiving ship 12.1783. BU 4.1811 at Plymouth.

YARMOUTH Store lighter, 106bm, 61 x 20 ft. Yarmouth 1798. Rebuilt Yarmouth 1810; coastguard 4.1828. Sold in 8.1835.

YARMOUTH 2nd class cruiser 5,250 tons, 430 x 48½ ft, 8-6in. London & Glasgow Co 12.4.1911. Sold 2.7.29 Alloa S.Bkg Co, Rosyth.

YARMOUTH Frigate 2,150 tons, 360 x 41 ft, 2-4.5in, 1-40mm. J.Brown 23.3.1959.

YARMOUTH Trawler requis. 1914-19.

YARNTON Coastal M/S, 'Ton' class. Pickersgill 26.3.1956. Sold Pounds 1986.

YARRA Destroyer (RAN) 700 tons, 246(oa) x 24 ft, 1-4in, 3-12pdr, 3-TT. Denny 8.4.1910. Dismantled 10.29 at Cockatoo DY; hulk sunk 22.8.32 as a target.

YARRA Sloop (RAN) 1,060 tons, 250 x 36 ft, 3-4in. Cockatoo DY 28.3.1935. Sunk 4.3.42 by a Japanese squadron 300 mls south of Java.

YARRA Frigate (RAN) 2,150 tons, 360 x 41 ft, 2-4.5in, 4-GWS. Williamstown DY 30.9.1958.

YAXHAM Inshore M/S, 'Ham' class. White 21.1.1958. Renamed WOODLARK 1964, survey vessel. Target 1986.

YEALMPTON Minesweeper, later 'Hunt' class. Simons. Cancelled 1919.

YEOMAN Destroyer, modified 'W' class. Yarrow. Cancelled 3.1919.

YEOMAN (see WORCESTER of 1919)

YEOVIL Minesweeper, later 'Hunt' class. Napier & Miller 27.8.1918. Sold 4.10.28 Ward, Pembroke Dock.

YORK (see MARSTON MOOR)

YORK 4th Rate 60, 987bm, 146 x 39 ft. Plymouth DY 4.1706. Sunk 4.2.1751 as breakwater at Sheerness.

YORK 4th Rate 60, 1,203bm, 150 x 43 ft. Plymouth DY 10.11.1753. BU completed 6.1772.

YORK (ex-*Betsy*) Brig-sloop 12, 65 x 22 ft. Purchased 29.3.1777 in N.America. Captured 7.1779 by a French squadron at Grenada, W.Indies. (Also in French hands 10.7.78 to 23.8.78.)

YORK Storeship 14, 664bm, 14-6pdr. Purchased 3.1779. Sold 1781 in the E.Indies.

YORK (ex-E.Indiaman *Royal Admiral* purchased on stocks) 3rd Rate 64, 1,433bm, 174 x 43 ft, 26-24pdr,

26-18pdr, 12-12pdr. Barnard, Deptford 24.3.1796. Foundered 1.1804 in the North Sea.

YORK 3rd Rate 74, 1,743bm, 175 x 47½ ft. Brent, Rotherhithe 7.7.1807. Convict ship 11.1819. BU 3.1854 at Portsmouth.

YORK Cruiser 8,250 tons, 540 x 57 ft, 6-8in, 4-4in. Palmer 17.7.1928. Hit by Italian explosive motor boat 21.3.41 and beached to avoid sinking, Suda Bay; further damaged by air attack and abandoned 22.5.41. Hulk arrived 2.52 at Bari to BU.

YORK Destroyer 3,550 tons. Swan Hunter 21.6.1982.

YORK ABS requis. 1915-19.

YORK CASTLE (see EMPIRE COMFORT)

YOUNG HEBE Schooner, 45bm. Purchased 1843 in China. Sold 7.1.1847 at Hong Kong.

YOUNG HOBLIN Flyboat, 172bm. Captured 1665. Sold 1666.

YOUNG KING Hoy, 102bm. Captured 1665. Sold 1666.

YOUNG LADY Fire vessel, 63bm, 63 x 15 ft. Purchased 1694. Sold 2.1695 or 1696.

YOUNG LION 10-gun vessel, 44bm. Captured 1665. Sunk 1673 as a foundation at Sheerness.

YOUNG PRINCE (see PRINCE)

YOUNG SHISH Smack, 24bm. Deptford 1673. Listed to 1688.

YOUNG SPRAG 6th Rate 10, 79bm. Purchased 1673. Fireship 1677; sunk 1693 as a foundation at Portsmouth. (This vessel may be SPRAGGE of 1673qv .)

YPRES Destroyer 2,610 tons. Fairfield. Ordered 1944, renamed DISDAIN 3.45, renamed DELIGHT 6.46, launched 21.12.50. (see DELIGHT)

YPRES Trawler (RCN) 1917-40.

YUKON Escort (RCN) 2,335 tons, 366(oa) x 42 ft, 4-3in. Burrard 27.7.1961.

Z.4 Destroyer 2,232 tons, 374 x 37 ft. German seized Oslofjord 5.45. Arrived Inverkeithing 1.11.48 to BU.

Z.5 Tender 264 tons, 193 x 20 ft, 2-3in. Dutch torpedo boat commissioned 1940 in the RN. Renamed BLADE 5.43. Arrived 10.45 at Troon to BU.

Z.6 Torpedo boat 264 tons, 193 x 20 ft, 2-3in, 4-TT. Dutch, taken into the RN 1940 but not commissioned. Ar-

rived 2.43 at McLellan, Bo'ness to BU.

Z.7 Torpedo boat, as Z.6. Hulked 10.43. BU 1946 Rees, Llanelly.

Z.8 Tender, as Z.6. Commissioned 1940 in the RN. Hulked 1942. Arrived 22.8.44 Cashmore, Newport to BU.

Z.10 Destroyer 2,270 tons, 350 x 37 ft. German, seized at Flensburg 5.45. Arrived 17.1.49 Young, Sunderland to BU.

Z.30 Destroyer 2,603 tons, 393 x 39 ft. German, seized in Oslofjord 5.45 Arrived 9.48 at Troon to BU.

Z.38 Destroyer 2,603 tons, 400 x 39 ft. German, seized at Flensburg 5.45 renamed NONSUCH 11.46. BU 5.50 by W.of Scotland S.Bkg. Co., Troon.

ZAMBESI Destroyer 1,710 tons, 339½ x 36 ft, 4-4.5in, 5-40mm, 8-TT. Cammell Laird 21.11.1943. Arrived 12.2.59 Ward, Briton Ferry to BU.

ZANZIBAR (ex-PROWSE renamed 1943) Frigate, 'Colony' class. Walsh Kaiser 21.11.43 on lend-lease. Returned 31.5.46 to the USN.

ZEALAND 4th Rate 42, 402bm. Dutch WAPEN van ZEELAND captured 1665. Sold 1667.

ZEALAND Flyboat 8, 420bm. Dutch, captured 1667. Sold 1668.

ZEALAND 3rd Rate 64. Dutch, seized 19.1.1796 at Plymouth. Harbour service 5.1803. Renamed JUSTITIA by A.O. dated 19.8.1812. Sold. 2.11.1830 to BU.

ZEALANDIA (see NEW ZEALAND of 1904)

ZEALOUS 3rd Rate 74, 1,607bm, 168½ x 47 ft. Barnard, Deptford. 25.6.1785. BU 12.1816.

ZEALOUS Ironclad, 3,176bm, 6,096 tons, 20-7in. Pembroke Dock 7.3.1864. Sold 9.1886 Castle, Charlton.

ZEALOUS Destroyer, modified 'W' class. Yarrow. Cancelled 3.1919.

ZEALOUS Destroyer 1,710 tons, 339½ x 36 ft, 4-4.5in, 5-40mm, 8-TT. Cammell Laird 28.2.1944. To Israeli navy 15.7.55 as ELATH.

ZEALOUS Tank Vessel 1913 renamed ZEST 1918, ZEAL 1945-49.

ZEBRA Sloop 14, 306bm, 97 x 27 ft. Barnard, Ipswich 8.4.1777. Wrecked 10.1778 in north Scotland.

ZEBRA Sloop 18, 314bm, 98 x 27½ ft. Clevely, Gravesend 31.8.1780. Bomb 1800. Sold 13.8.1812.

ZEBRA Brig-sloop 18, 'Cruiser' class, 385bm. Bombay DY 18.11.1815. Wrecked 2.12.1840 in the Levant.

ZEBRA (see JUMNA of 1848)

ZEBRA Wood S.sloop, 951bm, 185 x 33 ft, 5-40pdr, 12-32pdr. Deptford DY 13.11.1860. Sold 20.8.1873 in the Far East.

ZEBRA Destroyer 340 tons, 200 x 20 ft, 1-12pdr, 5-6pdr, 2-TT. Thames Iron Works 3.12.1895. Sold 30.7.1914.

ZEBRA Destroyer, modified 'W' class. Yarrow. Cancelled 3.1919.

ZEBRA (see WAKEFUL of 1943)

ZEBRA (ex-WAKEFUL renamed 1.1943) Destroyer 1,710 tons, 339½ x 36 ft, 4-4.5in, 5-40mm, 8-TT. Denny 8.3.44. Arrived 12.2.59 Cashmore, Newport to BU.

ZEEBRUGGE (see LST.3532)

ZENITH (see WESSEX of 1943)

ZENITH (ex-WESSEX renamed 1.1943) Destroyer 1,710 tons, 339½ x 36 ft, 4-4.5in, 5-40mm, 8-TT. Denny 6.6.44. Sold 5.55 Egyptian navy. Handed over 8.56 as EI FATEH.

ZENITH Drifter cancelled 1919.

ZENOBIA Schooner 10, 112bm, 68 x 20 ft. Bermuda 1806. Wrecked 10.1806 on the coast of Florida.

ZENOBIA Brig-sloop 18, 'Cruizer' class, 385bm. Brindley, Lynn 7.10.1807. Sold 8.1835 to BU.

ZENOBIA (ex-*Kilkenny* purchased on stocks) Wood pad. sloop (Indian), 684bm. Waterford 1839. Hulked 1850.

ZENOBIA Steam frigate (Indian), 1,003bm. Bombay DY 1.5.51. To Bombay Marine 1863.

ZENOBIA (see SNOWFLAKE)

ZEPHYR (see MARTIN of 1756)

ZEPHYR Sloop 14, 187bm, 75½ x 24 ft, 14-4pdr. Purchased on stocks 10.3.1779; Adams & Barnard, Deptford 31.5.1779. Renamed NAVY TRANSPORT 1782 and DISPATCH 1.1783. Sold 3.12.1798.

ZEPHYR Fireship 10, 244bm, 82 x 27 ft, 10-4pdr. King Dover 1795 and purchased 2.1795. Sold 21.7.1808.

ZEPHYR Brig-sloop 16, 253bm, 92 x 26 ft. Portsmouth DY 28.4.1809. Sold 29.1.1818. T.Pitman to BU.

ZEPHYR Packet brig 6, 'Cherokee' class, 228bm. Pembroke Dock 1.11.1823. Sold 8.9.1836.

ZEPHYR (ex-GPO vessel *Dragon*) Wood pad. packet, 237bm, 116 x 21 ft, 3 guns. Transferred 1.4.37. Sold Marshall 6.1865, BU at Plymouth.

ZEPHYR Compos. S.gunboat 438 tons, 125 x 22½ ft, 2-64pdr, 2-20pdr. Chatham DY 11.2.1873. Sold 2.1889 G.Cohen became salvage vessel &

BU 6.1929 at Briton Ferry.

ZEPHYR Destroyer 310 tons, 200 x 19 ft, 1-12pdr, 5-pdr, 2-TT. Hanna Donald, Paisley 10.5.1895. Sold 10.2.1920 Ward Rainham.

ZEPHYR Destroyer 1,710 tons, 339½ x 36 ft, 4-4.5in, 5-40mm, 8-TT. Vickers Armstrong, Tyne 15.7.1943. Arrived 2.7.58 Clayton & Davie, Dunston to BU.

ZEST Destroyer 1,710 tons, 339½ x 36 ft, 4-4.5in, 5-40mm, 8-TT. Thornycroft 14.10.1943. Frigate 1956. Sold Arnott Young 24.7.70, BU at Dalmuir.

ZEST Tank vessel (see ZEALOUS)

ZETLAND Minesweeper, early 'Hunt' class. Murdoch & Murray, Glasgow 1917. Sold 18.1.23. North-East Salvage Co, W.Hartlepool.

ZETLAND Destroyer, 'Hunt' class type II. Yarrow 7.3.1942. To R. Norwegian navy 2.9.54 as TROMSO.

ZETLAND Trawler requis. 1917-19.

ZINGARELLA Store carrier 190 tons gross, 115 x 21½ ft. Italian aux. ketch captured 30.12.1940 by destroyers at Bardia. Sold 1945.

ZINNIA Sloop, 'Acacia' class. Swan Hunter 12.8.1915. Sold 19.4.20 Belgian navy, retained name.

ZINNIA Corvette, 'Flower' class. Smiths DK 28.11.1940. Sunk 23.8.41 by 'U.564' west of Portugal.

ZODIAC Destroyer, modified 'W' class. Yarrow. Cancelled 12.1918.

ZODIAC Destroyer 1,710 tons, 339½ x 36 ft, 4-4.5in, 5-40mm, 8-TT. Thornycroft 11.3.1944. To Israeli navy 15.7.55 as YAFFA. Sunk 1973 as target.

ZODIAC Drifter and trawler requis. in WW.I.

ZUBIAN (ex-fore part ZULU plus aft part NUBIAN renamed 7.6.1917) Destroyer 1,050 tons, 288 x 27 ft, 2-4in, 2-TT. Completed Chatham DY 1917. Sold 9.12.19 Fryer, Sunderland. (see NUBIAN and ZULU)

ZULU Destroyer 1,027 tons, 280 x 27 ft, 2-4in, 2-TT. Hawthorn Leslie 16.9.1909. Disabled 8.11.16 by mine in the Dover Straits; stern wrecked; rebuilt with part NUBIAN at Chatham 1917, renamed ZUBIAN. (qv)

ZULU Destroyer 1,870 tons, 355½ x 36½ ft, 8-4.7in, 4-TT. Stephen 23.9.1937. Foundered in tow after air attack 14.9.42 off Tobruk.

ZULU Frigate 2,300 tons, 350 x 42 ft, 2-4.5in, 8-GWS. Stephen 3.7.1962. Sold Indonesia in 1984, renamed MARTHA KRISTINA TIYAHAHU.

Military